```
796.357    MacFarlane,
Mac        Paul.

           Daguerreotypes
           of great stars
           of baseball
```

Clark Public Library
303 Westfield Ave.
Clark, NJ 07066

DAGUERREOTYPES
OF GREAT STARS OF BASEBALL

PUBLISHER

C. C. JOHNSON SPINK

EDITOR

PAUL MAC FARLANE

PUBLISHED BY

The Sporting News

1212 N. LINDBERGH BLVD. • ST. LOUIS, MO. 63166

Copyright 1981 by THE SPORTING NEWS Publishing Co.
a Times Mirror company

ISBN 0-89204-066-1

PROLOGUE

by

Paul Mac Farlane

This revised edition of DAGUERREOTYPES is a complete departure from its early predecessors. Records carried in the smaller-sized editions prior to 1968 represented the top players, the not-so-great and many of the more obscure performers who played major league baseball. There were no guidelines used in the selections.

This book is a first of its kind in the history of the game. The editor pared the all-time list of those no longer active as major league players to an All-Star group which is supreme in categories which lend themselves to accurate rating.

The standards were chosen to weed out the merely good player and include the genuine standout whose feats will stand—or have stood—the test of time. Fielding statistics were ignored because defensive brilliance, nearly all baseball men concede, is a matter of subjective judgment. In short, the figures fail to tell the story of fielding ability, nor do they allow for improved equipment and better playing surfaces which exist today.

Every player in DAGUERREOTYPES meets at least one of the following criteria:

Batting—A lifetime average of .300, with a minimum of ten years in the majors; 2,000 major league games; 2,000 hits; 200 homers.

Pitching—175 victories; 4,000 innings; 2,000 strikeouts.

In addition, all Hall of Fame members are in the book.

Names of the selected stars are in the back of the book, and behind each name are the categories in which the player qualified.

The playing records in this book are constantly researched, checked and rechecked. We believe this latest edition of DAGUERREOTYPES is the most accurate compilation of statistics on all-time stars ever published. Clifford Kachline, historian of the Hall of Fame, collaborated in the new research of most of the Hall of Famers. The first book of this latest series required nearly four years of research. This edition contains the lifetime records of 432 former greats of the game, players, umpires, managers and executives.

TABLE OF CONTENTS

Among the 432 records and personality sketches in this book are 27 Hall of Famers who would not have been eligible for inclusion as players were it not for their membership in the Cooperstown shrine, including nine former Black Baseball greats added to the Hall. Also included are 24 men who were honored for their contributions to the game as builders of the National Pastime or for abilities primarily as managers or umpires.

A 32-page picture section is inserted following Page 192.

Major league records of all players in DAGUERREOTYPES are based on performances in the following leagues:

> National League—1876 through 1980.
>
> American Association—1882 through 1891.
>
> Union Association—1884.
>
> Players League—1890.
>
> American League—1901 through 1980.

Federal League records of 1914-15, although carried in the players' year-by-year performances, are not included in the players' major league career totals. This league was not recognized at that time by THE SPORTING NEWS, the commissioner, Kenesaw M. Landis, or the American and National leagues as a major league.

COVER—Babe Ruth—The player who spanned both eras as first a record-setting pitcher and then the greatest slugger in the game's history. He changed the entire pattern of baseball and was the top drawing card of all time. The Bambino's booming bat restored the fans' faith in baseball after the sordid events of the 1919 Black Sox Series cast a pallor over the game.

COVER ARTIST—JACK HAVEY.

Ty Cobb, rated by many as game's top player sliding hard into New York's Jimmy Austin at third, in 1910.

*Denotes led league.   •Denotes tied for league lead.   †In 1887, bases on balls counted as hits.

HENRY LOUIS (HANK) AARON

Born February 5, 1934, at Mobile, Ala.
Height, 6.00. Weight, 190.
Threw and batted righthanded.
Brother of Tommie Aaron, former infielder-outfielder with Milwaukee-Atlanta Braves franchise and manager in the Braves' organization.

Established following major league records: most games, lifetime (3.298), 1976; most at-bats, lifetime (12,364), 1976; most home runs, lifetime (755), 1976; most plate appearances, lifetime (13,940), 1976; most years, 100 or more runs scored (15), 1970; most years leading league, total bases (8), 1969; most years, 300 or more total bases (15), 1971; most years, 150 or more games (14), 1970 (since broken by Brooks Robinson, 1974, with 15); most consecutive years, 20 or more home runs (20), 1974; most extra-base hits, lifetime (3,085), 1976; most consecutive years, 100 or more extra bases on long hits (19), 1973; most years, 30 or more home runs (15), 1973; most consecutive years, 20 or more home runs (20), 1974; most total bases, lifetime (6,856), 1976; most runs batted in, lifetime (2,297), 1976; most consecutive seasons, 100 or more games (22), 1976; most long hits, lifetime (1,477), 1976; most seasons, 100 or more games (22), 1975.
    Tied major league record for most consecutive years, 100 or more runs scored (13), 1967.
    Established following National League records: most seasons hitting home runs in each league park (9), 1966; most seasons, 100 or more runs batted in (11), 1971; most seasons, 40 or more home runs (8), 1973; most runs scored, lifetime (2,107), 1974; most home runs, bases full, lifetime (16), 1974 (since passed by Willie McCovey, with 18).
    Tied following National League records: most years, leading league in runs batted in (4), 1966; most bases on balls, game, since 1900 (5), July 11, 1972 (15 innings).
    One of five players in major league history to hit 30 home runs and steal 30 bases in the same season (44 home runs and 31 stolen bases in 1963).
    Hit three home runs in a game, June 21, 1959.
    Tied World Series record, one or more hits in each game, 1957.
    Led National League outfielders in double plays with 6 in 1960, 5 in 1964 and 5 in 1966.
    Led National League in slugging percentage with .636 in 1959, .586 in 1963, .573 in 1967 and .669 in 1971; led in total bases with 340 in 1956; 369 in 1957; 400 in 1959; 334 in 1960; 358 in 1961; 370 in 1963; 344 in 1967; 332 in 1969.
    Named outfielder on THE SPORTING NEWS All-Star Major League Teams, 1956-58-59.
    Named outfielder on THE SPORTING NEWS National League All-Star Teams, 1963-65-67-69-70-71.
    Most Valuable Player in National League, 1957.
    Named National League Player of the Year by THE SPORTING NEWS, 1956 and 1963.
    Named outfielder on THE SPORTING NEWS National League All-Star fielding team, 1958-59-60.
    Vice-President, director of player personnel, Atlanta Braves, 1977 to date.

Year	Club	League	Pos.	G.	AB.	R.	H.	2B.	3B.	HR.	RBI.	B.A.	PO.	A.	E.	F.A.
1952	Eau Claire	North.	SS	87	345	79	116	19	4	9	61	.336	137	265	35	.920
1953	Jacksonville	Sally	2B	137	574	*115	*208	*36	14	22	*125	*.362	*330	*310	*36	.947
1954	Milwaukee (a)	Nat.	OF	122	468	58	131	27	6	13	69	.280	223	5	7	.970
1955	Milwaukee	Nat.	OF-2B	153	602	105	189	•37	9	27	106	.314	340	93	15	.967
1956	Milwaukee	Nat.	OF	153	609	106	*200	*34	14	26	92	*.328	316	17	•13	.962
1957	Milwaukee	Nat.	OF	151	615	*118	198	27	6	*44	*132	.322	346	9	6	.983
1958	Milwaukee	Nat.	OF	153	601	109	196	34	4	30	95	.326	305	12	5	.984
1959	Milwaukee	Nat.	OF-3B	154	629	116	*223	46	7	39	123	*.355	263	22	5	.983
1960	Milwaukee	Nat.	OF-2B	153	590	102	172	20	11	40	*126	.292	321	13	6	.982
1961	Milwaukee	Nat.	OF-3B	*155	603	115	197	*39	10	34	120	.327	379	15	7	.983
1962	Milwaukee	Nat.	OF-1B	156	592	127	191	28	6	45	128	.323	341	11	7	.981
1963	Milwaukee	Nat.	OF	161	631	*121	201	29	4	*44	*130	.319	267	10	6	.979
1964	Milwaukee	Nat.	OF-2B	145	570	103	187	30	2	24	95	.328	284	28	6	.981
1965	Milwaukee	Nat.	OF	150	570	109	181	*40	1	32	89	.318	298	9	4	.987
1966	Atlanta	Nat.	OF-2B	158	603	117	168	23	1	*44	▲127	.279	315	12	4	.988
1967	Atlanta	Nat.	OF-2B	155	600	•113	184	37	3	*39	109	.307	322	12	7	.979
1968	Atlanta	Nat.	OF-1B	160	606	84	174	33	4	29	86	.287	418	20	5	.989
1969	Atlanta	Nat.	OF-1B	147	547	100	164	30	3	44	97	.300	299	13	5	.984
1970	Atlanta	Nat.	OF-1B	150	516	103	154	26	1	38	118	.298	319	10	7	.979
1971	Atlanta	Nat.	1B-OF	139	495	95	162	22	3	47	118	.327	733	40	5	.994
1972	Atlanta	Nat.	1B-OF	129	449	75	119	10	0	34	77	.265	996	70	17	.984
1973	Atlanta	Nat.	OF	120	392	84	118	12	1	40	96	.301	206	5	5	.977
1974	Atlanta (b)	Nat.	OF	112	340	47	91	16	0	20	69	.268	142	3	2	.986
1975	Milwaukee	Amer.	DH-OF	137	465	45	109	16	2	12	60	.234	2	0	0	1.000
1976	Milwaukee	Amer.	DH-OF	85	271	22	62	8	0	10	35	.229	1	0	0	1.000
American League Totals				222	736	67	171	24	2	22	95	.232	3	0	0	1.000
National League Totals				3076	11628	2107	3600	600	96	733	2202	310	7433	429	144	.982
Major League Totals				3298	12364	2174	3771	624	98	755	2297	.305	7436	429	144	.982

aFractured right ankle September 5, 1954; out for rest of season.
bTraded to Milwaukee Brewers for outfielder Dave May (plus pitcher Roger Alexander), November 2, 1974.

WORLD SERIES RECORD

Year	Club	League	Pos.	G.	AB.	R.	H.	2B.	3B.	HR.	RBI.	B.A.	PO.	A.	E.	F.A.
1957—Milwaukee		Nat.	OF	7	28	5	11	0	1	3	7	.393	11	0	0	1.000
1958—Milwaukee		Nat.	OF	7	27	3	9	2	0	0	2	.333	14	0	0	1.000
World Series Totals				14	55	8	20	2	1	3	9	.364	25	0	0	1.000

CHARLES BENJAMIN (BABE) ADAMS

Born May 18, 1882, at Tipton, Ind.
Died July 28, 1968, at Silver Spring, Md.
Height, 5.11½. Weight, 180.
Threw right and batted lefthanded.
Married Blanche Wright, March 2, 1909.

Holds major league record for fewest bases on balls, 250 or more innings, season (18), 1920; tied with Stanley Coveleski (Cleveland Indians, 1920), Harry Brecheen (St. Louis Cardinals, 1946), Lou Burdette (Milwaukee Braves, 1957), Bob Gibson (St. Louis Cardinals, 1967) and Mickey Lolich (Detroit Tigers, 1968) for most games won in seven-game World Series (3), 1909.
Manager, Johnstown (Middle Atlantic), start of 1927 season.

Year	Club	League	G.	IP.	W.	L.	Pct.	H.	R.	ER.	SO.	BB.	ERA.
1905—Parsons		Missouri Valley						(No averages)					
1906—Parsons		Missouri Valley						(No averages)					
1906—St. Louis		Nat.	1	4	0	1	.000	9	8	....	0	2	......
1906—Denver		Western	18	167	8	10	.444	....	....	....	....	....	......
1907—Denver		Western	38	....	....	....	....	....	....	....	....	....	......
1907—Pittsburgh		Nat.	4	22	0	2	.000	40	25	....	11	3	......
1908—Louisville		Amer. Assn.	41	312	22	12	.647	262	94	....	118	40	......
1909—Pittsburgh		Nat.	25	130	12	3	.800	88	25	....	65	23	......
1910—Pittsburgh		Nat.	34	245	18	9	.667	217	95	....	101	60	......
1911—Pittsburgh		Nat.	40	293	22	12	.647	253	97	....	133	42	......
1912—Pittsburgh		Nat.	28	170	11	8	.579	169	73	55	63	35	2.91
1913—Pittsburgh		Nat.	43	314	21	10	.677	271	94	75	144	49	2.15
1914—Pittsburgh		Nat.	40	283	13	16	.448	253	97	81	91	39	2.58
1915—Pittsburgh		Nat.	40	245	14	14	.500	229	90	78	62	34	2.87
1916—Pittsburgh		Nat.	16	72	2	9	.182	91	51	46	22	12	5.75
1917—St. Joseph-Hutchinson		Western	35	308	20	13	.606	244	....	60	197	34	1.75
1918—Kansas City		Amer. Assn.	19	167	14	3	.824	122	45	31	79	29	1.67
1918—Pittsburgh		Nat.	3	23	1	1	.500	15	4	3	6	4	1.17
1919—Pittsburgh		Nat.	34	263	17	10	.630	213	66	58	92	23	1.98
1920—Pittsburgh		Nat.	35	263	17	13	.567	240	83	63	84	18	2.16
1921—Pittsburgh		Nat.	25	160	14	5	.737	155	57	47	55	18	2.64
1922—Pittsburgh		Nat.	27	171	8	11	.421	191	77	68	39	15	3.58
1923—Pittsburgh		Nat.	26	159	13	7	.650	196	83	78	38	25	4.42
1924—Pittsburgh		Nat.	9	40	3	1	.750	31	9	5	5	3	1.13
1925—Pittsburgh		Nat.	33	101	6	5	.545	129	67	61	18	17	5.44
1926—Pittsburgh		Nat.	19	37	2	3	.400	51	32	25	7	8	6.08
1927—Johnstown		Mid Atlantic	2	18	2	0	1.000	17	....	....	11	....	......
1927—Springfield		West. Assn	7	53	4	1	.800	40	13	8	29	11	1.36
Major League Totals			482	2995	194	140	.581	2841	1133	....	1036	430	......

WORLD SERIES RECORD

Year	Club	League	G.	IP.	W.	L.	Pct.	H.	R.	ER.	SO.	BB.	ERA.
1909—Pittsburgh		National	3	27	3	0	1.000	18	5	4	11	6	1.33
1925—Pittsburgh		National	1	1	0	0	.000	2	0	0	0	0	0.00
World Series Totals			4	28	3	0	1.000	20	5	4	11	6	1.29

JOSEPH WILBUR ADCOCK

Born October 30, 1927, at Coushatta, La.
Height, 6.04. Weight, 231.
Threw and batted righthanded.
Married Joan James, November 16, 1956.

Hit four home runs and double in one game against the Brooklyn Dodgers, at Brooklyn, July 31, 1954—breaking the following major league records; most extra bases on long hits, game (13); most total bases, game (18). Tied the following major league records; most long hits, game (5) and most home runs in one game (4).

Tied with Adrian C. Anson, Ralph Kiner, Don Mueller, Stan Musial, Ty Cobb and Tony Lazzeri for most home runs in two consecutive games (5), one on July 30 and four, July 31, 1954; tied with Ty Cobb for major league record for most total bases, two consecutive games (25), with seven on July 30 and 18 on July 31, 1954; tied with Al Schoendienst and Ed Delahanty for most long hits in two consecutive games (7), two on July 30 and five on July 31, 1954; set National League record when he hit nine home runs on the road against one club (Brooklyn), 1954; also tied National League record held by Hank Sauer (Chicago, 1954) by hitting 13 home runs against one club, season, (Brooklyn), 1956. Led N.L. first basemen in double plays, 1960.

Manager, Cleveland Indians, 1967; manager, Seattle, Pacific Coast League, 1968.

Year	Club	League	Pos.	G.	AB.	R.	H.	2B.	3B.	HR.	RBI.	B.A.	PO.	A.	E.	F.A.
1947	Columbia	Sally	1B	73	280	35	74	11	5	7	43	.264	731	37	8	.990
1948	Columbia	Sally	1B	117	434	58	121	25	2	6	64	.279	1100	*89	14	*.988
1949	Tulsa	Tex.	1B	149	598	95	178	41	7	19	116	.298	1332	77	7	*.995
1950	Cincinnati	Nat.	OF-1B	102	372	46	109	16	1	8	55	.293	346	17	8	.978
1951	Cincinnati	Nat.	OF	113	395	40	96	16	4	10	47	.243	221	8	4	.983
1952	Cincinnati(a)(b)	Nat.	OF-1B	117	378	43	105	22	4	13	52	.278	306	8	3	.991
1953	Milwaukee	Nat.	1B	157	590	71	168	33	6	18	80	.285	1389	96	13	.991
1954	Milwaukee	Nat.	1B	133	500	73	154	27	5	23	87	.308	1229	67	6	.995
1955	Milwaukee(c)	Nat.	1B	84	288	40	76	14	0	15	45	.264	725	44	8	.990
1956	Milwaukee	Nat.	1B	137	454	76	132	23	1	38	103	.291	1086	75	6	*.995
1957	Milwaukee(d)	Nat.	1B	65	209	31	60	13	2	12	38	.287	477	30	2	.996
1958	Milwaukee	Nat.	1B-OF	105	320	40	88	15	1	19	54	.275	564	37	7	.988
1959	Milwaukee	Nat.	1B-OF	115	404	53	118	19	2	25	76	.292	807	81	7	.992
1960	Milwaukee	Nat.	1B	138	514	55	153	21	4	25	91	.298	*1229	104	9	•.993
1961	Milwaukee	Nat.	1B	152	562	77	160	20	0	35	108	.285	*1471	102	11	.993
1962	Milwaukee(e)	Nat.	1B	121	391	48	97	12	1	29	78	.248	907	57	3	*.997
1963	Cleveland(f)	Amer.	1B	97	283	28	71	7	1	13	49	.251	608	36	3	.995
1964	Los Angeles	Amer.	1B	118	366	39	98	13	0	21	64	.268	959	54	7	.993
1965	California	Amer.	1B	122	349	30	84	14	0	14	47	.241	789	45	3	.996
1966	California	Amer.	1B	83	231	33	63	10	3	18	48	.273	565	39	2	.997
American League Totals				420	1229	130	316	44	4	66	208	.256	2921	174	15	.995
National League Totals				1539	5377	693	1516	251	31	270	914	.282	10757	726	87	.992
Major League Totals				1959	6606	823	1832	295	35	336	1122	.277	13678	900	102	.993

aTransferred to Boston Braves as part of four-club deal; trade started with Boston Braves sending first baseman Earl Torgeson to the Philadelphia Phillies for pitcher Russ Meyer and cash. The Braves then traded Meyer to the Brooklyn Dodgers for infielders Rocky Bridges and Jim Pendleton; Bridges and cash were sent to the Cincinnati Reds for Adcock, February 16, 1953.

bBoston franchise transferred to Milwaukee, March 18, 1953.

cSuffered fracture of right forearm when hit by pitched ball by Jim Hearn of New York Giants, July 31, 1955; out of game remainder of season.

dFractured right leg sliding into second base in game with Philadelphia Phillies, June 23, 1957; returned to lineup, September 5, 1957.

eTraded to Cleveland Indians with pitcher Jack Curtis for pitcher Frank Funk, outfielder Don Dillard and player to be named later, November 27, 1962; outfielder Ty Cline assigned to Braves March 18, 1963, to complete deal.

fTraded to Los Angeles Angels with pitcher Barry Latman for outfielder Leon Wagner. Latman and Wagner changed clubs December 2, and Adcock completed deal on December 6, 1963.

WORLD SERIES RECORD

Year	Club	League	Pos.	G.	AB.	R.	H.	2B.	3B.	HR.	RBI.	B.A.	PO.	A.	E.	F.A.
1957	Milwaukee	Nat.	1B-PH	5	15	1	3	0	0	0	2	.200	38	2	1	.976
1958	Milwaukee	Nat.	1B-PH	4	13	1	4	0	0	0	0	.308	23	2	0	1.000
World Series Totals				9	28	2	7	0	0	2	.250	61	4	1	.985	

GROVER CLEVELAND (PETE) ALEXANDER

Born February 26, 1887, at St. Paul, Neb.

Died November 4, 1950, at St. Paul, Neb.

Height, 6.01. Weight, 185.

Threw and batted righthanded.

Married Amy Arrants, May 31, 1918.

Led league in complete games, 1911-14-15-16-17 and 1920; shutouts, 1911-13-15-16-17 and 1919, and tied in 1911 and 1921. Hold modern National League records for complete games, 436; shutouts, season—16—1916; total shutouts, 90; tied with Christy Mathewson in games won, 373. Set major league record for most one-hit games, season—4 (June 5 and 26, July 5, September 29, 1915); pitched four consecutive shutouts, September 7, 13, 17 and 21, 1911; won two games in a day twice, September 23, 1916, and September 3, 1917.

Named to Hall of Fame, 1938.

Year Club	League	G.	IP.	W.	L.	Pct.	H.	R.	ER.	SO.	BB.	ERA.
1909–Galesburg	Ill.-Mo.	24	219	15	8	.652	124	49	....	198	42	.....
1910–Syracuse	N.Y. State	*43	245	*29	14	.674	215	....	....	204	67	.....
1911–Philadelphia	Nat.	48	*366	*28	13	.683	285	133	....	227	129	.....
1912–Philadelphia	Nat.	46	●310	19	17	.528	289	133	97	*195	105	2.81
1913–Philadelphia	Nat.	47	306	22	8	.733	288	106	96	159	75	2.82
1914–Philadelphia	Nat.	46	*355	●27	15	.643	*327	133	94	*214	76	2.38
1915–Philadelphia	Nat.	49	*376	*31	10	*.756	253	86	51	*241	64	*1.22
1916–Philadelphia	Nat.	48	*390	*33	12	.733	*323	90	67	*167	50	*1.55
1917–Philadelphia(a)	Nat.	45	*387	*30	13	.698	*336	107	79	*200	56	*1.83
1918–Chicago(b)	Nat.	3	26	2	1	.667	19	7	5	15	3	1.73
1919–Chicago	Nat.	30	235	16	11	.593	180	51	45	121	38	*1.72
1920–Chicago	Nat.	46	*363	*27	14	.659	*335	96	77	*173	69	*1.91
1921–Chicago	Nat.	31	252	15	13	.536	286	110	95	77	33	3.39
1922–Chicago	Nat.	33	246	16	13	.552	283	111	99	48	34	3.62
1923–Chicago	Nat.	39	305	22	12	.647	308	128	108	72	30	3.19
1924–Chicago	Nat.	21	169	12	5	.706	183	82	57	33	25	3.03
1925–Chicago	Nat.	32	236	15	11	.577	270	106	89	63	29	3.39
1926–Chicago(c)-St. Louis	Nat.	30	200	12	10	.545	191	83	68	47	31	3.06
1927–St. Louis	Nat.	37	268	21	10	.677	261	94	75	48	38	2.52
1928–St. Louis	Nat.	34	244	16	9	.640	262	106	91	59	37	3.36
1929–St. Louis(d)	Nat.	22	132	9	8	.529	149	65	57	33	23	3.89
1930–Philadelphia	Nat.	9	22	0	3	.000	40	24	22	6	6	9.00
1930–Dallas	Texas	5	24	1	2	.333	35	23	22	4	11	8.25
Major League Totals		696	5188	373	208	.642	4868	1851	†1372	2198	951	†2.56

†Does not include 1911 season when earned runs were not compiled.
aTraded with catcher William Killefer to Chicago Cubs for pitcher Mike Prendergast, catcher Pickles Dillhoefer and $60,000, November 11, 1917.
bIn Military Service most of season.
cWaived to St. Louis Cardinals, June 22, 1926.
dTraded to Philadelphia Phillies with catcher Harry McCurdy for outfielder Homer Peel and pitcher Bob McGraw, December 11, 1929.

WORLD SERIES RECORD

Year Club	League	G.	IP.	W.	L.	Pct.	H.	R.	ER.	SO.	BB.	ERA.
1915–Philadelphia	National	2	17⅔	1	1	.500	14	3	3	10	4	1.53
1926–St. Louis	National	3	20⅓	2	0	1.000	12	4	3	17	4	1.33
1928–St. Louis	National	2	5	0	1	.000	10	11	11	2	4	19.80
World Series Totals		7	43	3	2	.600	36	18	17	29	12	3.56

ETHAN NATHAN ALLEN

Born January 1, 1904, at Cincinnati, O.

Height, 6.01. Weight, 180.

Threw and batted righthanded.

Married Doris Wetzel, October 16, 1928.

Year Club League	Pos.	G.	AB.	R.	H.	2B.	3B.	HR.	RBI.	B.A.	PO.	A.	E.	F.A.
1926–Cincinnati Nat.	OF	18	13	3	4	1	0	0	0	.308	9	0	0	.000
1927–Cincinnati Nat.	OF	111	359	54	106	26	4	2	20	.295	250	6	3	.988
1928–Cincinnati Nat.	OF	129	485	55	148	30	7	1	62	.305	348	12	7	.981
1929–Cincinnati Nat.	OF	143	538	69	157	27	11	6	64	.292	393	12	5	*.988
1930–Cinn.(a)-N. Y. Nat.	OF	97	284	58	83	10	2	10	38	.292	153	6	3	.981
1931–New York Nat.	OF	94	298	58	98	18	2	5	43	.329	151	2	4	.975
1932–New York(b) Nat.	OF	54	103	13	18	6	2	1	7	.175	44	1	2	.957
1933–St. Louis(c) Nat.	OF	91	261	25	63	7	3	0	36	.241	179	8	3	●.984
1934–Philadelphia Nat.	OF	145	581	87	192	●42	4	10	85	.330	337	19	8	.978
1935–Philadelphia Nat.	OF	●156	645	90	198	46	1	8	63	.307	412	*26	9	*.980
1936–Phil.(d)-Chi.(e) Nat.	OF	121	498	68	141	27	7	4	48	.295	273	3	8	.972
1937–St. Louis Amer.	OF	103	320	39	101	18	0	1	31	.316	186	8	4	.980
1938–St. Louis Amer.	OF	19	33	4	10	3	1	0	4	.303	11	0	0	1.000
National League Totals		1159	4065	580	1214	234	43	47	466	.299	2549	95	52	.981
American League Totals		122	353	43	111	21	1	1	35	.314	197	8	4	.981
Major League Totals		1281	4418	623	1325	255	44	48	501	.300	2746	103	56	.981

aTraded with pitcher Peter Donohue to New York Giants for infielder Clifford Crawford, May 27, 1930.
bTraded with pitchers Bill Walker and Jim Mooney and catcher Bob O'Farrell to St. Louis Cardinals for catcher Gus Mancuso and pitcher Ray Starr, October 10, 1932.
cSold to Philadelphia Phillies, January, 1934.
dTraded with pitcher Curt Davis to Chicago Cubs for outfielder Chuck Klein and pitcher Fabian Kowalik, May 21, 1936.
eSold to St. Louis Browns, December 2, 1936.

RICHARD ANTHONY (DICK) ALLEN

Born March 8, 1942, at Wampum, Pa.
Height, 5.11. Weight, 187.
Threw and batted righthanded.
Brother of Hank Allen, former utilityman with Washington Senators,
Milwaukee Brewers and Chicago White Sox, and Ron Allen, former first baseman
with Philadelphia Phillies and St. Louis Cardinals.

Tied major league records for most games, rookie season (162), 1964; and by making 200 or more hits in rookie season (201), 1964.
Established National League record for most total bases, rookie season (352), 1964.
Tied National League record for most walks, game (5), August 16, 1968.
Hit three home runs in a game, September 29, 1968.
Led National League in total bases with 352 in 1964; led third basemen in double plays with 29 in 1965; led in slugging percentage with .632 in 1966.
Led American League in slugging percentage with .603 in 1972 and .563 in 1974.
Named American League Most Valuable Player in 1972.
Named National League Rookie of the Year, 1964, by Baseball Writers' Association and National League Rookie Player of the Year by THE SPORTING NEWS, 1964.
Named first baseman on THE SPORTING NEWS American League All-Star Team, 1972 and 1974.
Named THE SPORTING NEWS American League Player of the Year, 1972.
Received reported $60,000 bonus to sign with Philadelphia Phillies, 1960.

Year	Club	League	Pos.	G.	AB.	R.	H.	2B.	3B.	HR.	RBI.	B.A.	PO.	A.	E.	F.A.
1960	Elmira	NYP	SS	88	320	56	90	19	10	8	42	.281	141	173	*48	.867
1961	Magic Valley	Pion.	2B	117	460	101	146	17	8	21	94	.317	*258	*298	*27	.953
1962	Williamsport	East.	OF-2B	132	511	97	168	*32	10	20	109	.329	255	59	17	.949
1963	Arkansas	Int.	OF	145	544	93	157	19	*12	*33	*97	.289	246	8	*11	.958
1963	Philadelphia	Nat.	OF-3B	10	24	6	7	2	1	0	2	.292	10	0	2	.833
1964	Philadelphia	Nat.	3B	162	632	*125	201	38	●13	29	91	.318	154	325	*41	.921
1965	Philadelphia	Nat.	3B-SS	161	619	93	187	31	14	20	85	.302	130	305	26	.944
1966	Philadelphia	Nat.	3B-OF	141	524	112	166	25	10	40	110	.317	146	182	14	.959
1967	Philadelphia	Nat.	*3B-2B-SS	122	463	89	142	31	10	23	77	.307	95	249	*35	.908
1968	Philadelphia	Nat.	OF-3B	152	521	87	137	17	9	33	90	.263	215	20	12	.951
1969	Philadelphia (a)	Nat.	1B	118	438	79	126	23	3	32	89	.288	1024	54	16	.985
1970	St. Louis (b)	Nat.	1B-3B-OF	122	459	88	128	17	5	34	101	.279	708	109	18	.978
1971	Los Angeles (c)	Nat.	3B-OF-1B	155	549	82	162	24	1	23	90	.295	382	151	21	.962
1972	Chicago	Amer.	1B-3B	148	506	90	156	28	5	*37	*113	.308	1235	69	7	.995
1973	Chicago	Amer.	1B-2B	72	250	39	79	20	3	16	41	.316	601	46	4	.994
1974	Chicago (d-e)	Amer.	*1B-2B	128	462	84	139	23	1	*32	88	.301	998	50	*16	.985
1975	Philadelphia	Nat.	1B	119	416	54	97	21	3	12	62	.233	900	70	*18	.982
1976	Philadelphia (f)	Nat.	1B	85	298	52	80	16	1	15	49	.268	671	44	8	.989
1977	Oakland	Amer.	1B	54	171	19	41	4	0	5	31	.240	389	37	7	.984
	American League Totals			402	1389	232	415	75	9	90	273	.299	3223	202	34	.990
	National League Totals			1347	4943	867	1433	245	70	261	846	.290	4435	1509	211	.966
	Major League Totals			1749	6332	1099	1848	320	79	351	1119	.292	7658	1711	245	.975

aTraded with infielder Octavio (Cookie) Rojas and pitcher Jerry Johnson for catcher Tim McCarver, pitcher Joe Hoerner, outfielder Curt Flood and outfielder Byron Browne to St. Louis Cardinals, October 7, 1969. Flood refused to report and the Cardinals sent first baseman Guillermo Montanez and a player to be named later to Philadelphia to complete the deal, April 8, 1970. Pitcher James Robert Browning was sent "as the player to be named later" from the Cardinals to Philadelphia, August 30, 1970.
bTraded to Los Angeles Dodgers for infielder Ted Sizemore and catcher Bob Stinson, October 5, 1970.
cTraded to Chicago White Sox for pitcher Tommy John and infielder Steve Huntz, December 2, 1971.
dTraded to Atlanta Braves for $5,000 and a player to be named later, December 3, 1974; Braves sent catcher Jim Essian to White Sox, May 15, 1975, to complete deal.
eTraded with catcher Johnny Oates by Atlanta Braves to Philadelphia Phillies for catcher Jim Essian, outfielder Barry Bonnell, a player to be named later and an estimated $150,000, May 7, 1975; deal was completed with a cash payment.
fSigned as free agent with Oakland A's, March 16, 1977.

WILLIAM ROBERT (BOB) ALLISON

Born July 11, 1934, at Raytown, Mo.
Height, 6.04. Weight, 212.
Threw and batted righthanded.
Attended University of Kansas, Lawrence, Kan.

Tied following major league records: Most two-base hits inning (2), July 1, 1964 (fourth inning) and most strikeouts, game, nine innings (5), September 2, 1965.

Hit three home runs in game, May 17, 1963.

Named American League Rookie Player of the Year by THE SPORTING NEWS, 1959 and American League Rookie of the Year by Baseball Writers' Association, 1959.

Year	Club	League	Pos.	G.	AB.	R.	H.	2B.	3B.	HR.	RBI.	B.A.	PO.	A.	E.	F.A.
1955—Hagerstown		Pied.	OF	122	446	55	114	15	2	5	49	.256	★289	★24	12	.963
1956—Charlotte		Sally	OF	122	344	47	80	10	6	12	55	.233	240	20	11	.959
1957—Chattanooga		South.	OF	125	395	56	97	14	●11	2	38	.246	239	8	7	.972
1958—Chattanooga		South.	OF	150	525	84	161	28	9	9	93	.307	372	13	★18	.955
1958—Washington		Amer.	OF	11	35	1	7	1	0	0	0	.200	24	0	0	1.000
1959—Washington		Amer.	OF	150	570	83	149	18	★9	30	85	.261	333	8	9	.974
1960—Washington		Amer.	OF-1B	144	501	79	126	30	3	15	69	.251	311	13	11	.967
1961—Minnesota		Amer.	OF-1B	159	556	83	136	21	3	29	105	.245	417	18	10	.978
1962—Minnesota		Amer.	OF	149	519	102	138	24	8	29	102	.266	287	10	7	.977
1963—Minnesota		Amer.	OF	148	527	★99	143	25	4	35	91	.271	326	11	10	.971
1964—Minnesota		Amer.	1B-OF	149	492	90	141	27	4	32	86	.287	829	58	12	.987
1965—Minnesota		Amer.	OF-1B	135	438	71	102	14	5	23	78	.233	247	12	7	.974
1966—Minnesota		Amer.	OF	70	168	34	37	6	1	8	19	.220	86	3	3	.967
1967—Minnesota		Amer.	OF	153	496	73	128	21	6	24	75	.258	220	6	5	.978
1968—Minnesota		Amer.	OF-1B	145	469	63	116	16	8	22	52	.247	316	16	8	.976
1969—Minnesota		Amer.	OF-1B	81	189	18	43	8	2	8	27	.228	96	3	0	1.000
1970—Minnesota†		Amer.	OF-1B	47	72	15	15	5	0	1	7	.208	54	4	2	.967
Major League Totals				1541	5032	811	1281	216	53	256	796	.255	3546	162	84	.978

†Voluntarily retired list, October 19, 1970.

WORLD SERIES RECORD

Year	Club	League	Pos.	G.	AB.	R.	H.	2B.	3B.	HR.	RBI.	B.A.	PO.	A.	E.	F.A.
1965—Minnesota		Amer.	OF	5	16	3	2	1	0	1	2	.125	11	0	0	1.000

FELIPE ROJAS ALOU

Born May 12, 1935, at Haina, Dominican Republic.

Height, 6.01. Weight, 195.

Threw and batted righthanded.

Brother of Jesus and Mateo, major league outfielders.

Named as first baseman on THE SPORTING NEWS National League All-Star Team, 1966.

Coach, Montreal Expos, 1980 to date.

Year	Club	League	Pos.	G.	AB.	R.	H.	2B.	3B.	HR.	RBI.	B.A.	PO.	A.	E.	F.A.
1956—Lake Charles		Evang.	OF	5	9	1	2	0	0	0	1	.222	6	1	0	1.000
1956—Cocoa		Fla.St.	OF-3B	119	445	111	169	15	6	21	99	★.380	199	60	23	.918
1957—Minneapolis		A.A.	OF	24	57	7	12	2	0	0	3	.211	32	1	1	.971
1957—Springfield		East.	OF-3B	106	359	45	110	14	3	12	71	.306	215	26	9	.964
1958—Phoenix		P.C.	OF	55	216	61	69	16	2	13	42	.319	150	3	3	.981
1958—San Francisco		Nat.	OF	75	182	21	46	9	2	4	16	.253	126	2	2	.985
1959—San Francisco		Nat.	OF	95	247	38	68	13	2	10	33	.275	111	0	3	.974
1960—San Francisco		Nat.	OF	106	322	48	85	17	3	8	44	.264	156	5	7	.958
1961—San Francisco		Nat.	OF	132	415	59	120	19	0	18	52	.289	196	10	2	.990
1962—San Francisco		Nat.	OF	154	561	96	177	30	3	25	98	.316	262	7	8	.971
1963—San Fran.(a)		Nat.	OF	157	565	75	159	31	9	20	82	.281	279	9	4	.986
1964—Milwaukee		Nat.	OF-1B	121	415	60	105	26	3	9	51	.253	329	12	5	.986
1965—Milwaukee		Nat.	OF-1-3-SS	143	555	80	165	29	2	23	78	.297	626	43	6	.991
1966—Atlanta		Nat.	1-OF-3-SS	154	★666	★122	★218	32	6	31	74	.327	935	64	13	.987
1967—Atlanta		Nat.	1B-OF	140	574	76	157	26	3	15	43	.274	864	34	9	.990
1968—Atlanta		Nat.	OF	160	★662	72	●210	37	5	11	57	.317	379	8	8	.980
1969—Atlanta (b)		Nat.	OF	123	476	54	134	13	1	5	32	.282	260	4	3	.989
1970—Oakland		Amer.	OF-1B	154	575	70	156	25	3	8	55	.271	290	11	7	.977
1971—Oak.(c)-N.Y.		Amer.	OF-1B	133	469	52	135	21	6	8	69	.288	513	23	4	.993
1972—New York		Amer.	1B-OF	120	324	33	90	18	1	6	37	.278	669	54	7	.990
1973—New York (d)		Amer.	1B-OF	93	230	25	66	12	0	4	27	.236	512	31	7	.987
1973—Montreal (e)		Nat.	OF-1B	19	48	4	10	1	0	1	4	.208	30	3	0	1.000
1974—Milwaukee		Amer.	OF	1	3	0	0	0	0	0	0	.000	0	0	1	.000
National League Totals				1579	5688	805	1654	283	39	180	664	.291	4553	203	70	.985
American League Totals				501	1651	180	447	76	10	26	188	.271	1984	119	26	.988
Major League Totals				2080	7339	985	2101	359	49	206	852	.286	6537	322	96	.986

aTraded to Milwaukee Braves with pitcher Billy Hoeft, catcher Ed Bailey and infielder Ernie Bowman for pitchers Bob Hendley and Bob Shaw and catcher Del Crandall, December 3, 1963.
bTraded to Oakland Athletics for pitcher Jim Nash, December 3, 1969.
cTraded to New York Yankees for pitchers Rob Gardner and Ron Klimkowski, April 9, 1971.
dReleased on waivers to Montreal Expos, September 6, 1973.
eSold to Milwaukee Brewers, December 7, 1973.

WORLD SERIES RECORD

Year	Club	League	Pos.	G.	AB.	R.	H.	2B.	3B.	HR.	RBI.	B.A.	PO.	A.	E.	F.A.
1962	San Francisco	Nat.	OF	7	26	2	7	1	1	0	1	.269	8	0	1	.889

MATEO ROJAS (MATTY) ALOU

Born December 22, 1938, at Haina, Dominican Republic.
Height, 5.09. Weight, 160.
Threw and batted lefthanded.
Brother of Felipe and Jesus, former major league outfielders.

Established major league record for most at-bats, season, 698, in 1969.
Named outfielder on THE SPORTING NEWS National League All-Star Team, 1969.

Year	Club	League	Pos.	G.	AB.	R.	H.	2B.	3B.	HR.	RBI.	B.A.	PO.	A.	E.	F.A.
1957	Michigan City	Midwest	OF	124	481	79	119	15	1	6	46	.247	271	20	10	.967
1958	St. Cloud	North.	OF	121	448	92	144	13	5	4	52	.321	261	11	10	.965
1959	Springfield	East.	OF	121	489	93	141	30	7	11	57	.288	319	*23	13	.963
1960	Tacoma	P.C.	OF	150	*627	97	192	39	8	14	73	.306	*408	●20	●13	.971
1960	San Francisco	Nat.	OF	4	3	1	1	0	0	0	0	.333	1	0	0	1.000
1961	San Francisco	Nat.	OF	81	200	38	62	7	2	6	24	.310	85	2	2	.978
1962	San Francisco	Nat.	OF	78	195	28	57	8	1	3	14	.292	80	3	2	.976
1963	San Francisco	Nat.	OF	63	76	4	11	1	0	0	2	.145	19	1	1	.952
1963	Tacoma	P.C.	OF	25	83	6	26	2	1	2	10	.313	48	0	1	.980
1964	San Francisco	Nat.	OF	110	250	28	66	4	2	1	16	.264	120	2	3	.976
1965	San Fran.(a)	Nat.	OF-P	117	324	37	75	12	2	2	18	.231	139	6	2	.986
1966	Pittsburgh	Nat.	OF	141	535	86	183	18	9	2	27	*.342	264	11	8	.972
1967	Pittsburgh	Nat.	OF-1B	139	550	87	186	21	7	2	28	.338	252	9	3	.989
1968	Pittsburgh	Nat.	OF	146	558	59	185	28	4	0	52	.332	298	8	5	.984
1969	Pittsburgh	Nat.	OF	162	*698	105	*231	*41	6	1	48	.331	327	10	8	.977
1970	Pittsburgh (b)	Nat.	OF	155	*677	97	201	21	8	1	47	.297	297	15	8	.975
1971	St. Louis	Nat.	OF-1B	149	609	85	192	28	6	7	74	.315	710	35	9	.988
1972	St. Louis (c)	Nat.	1B-OF	108	404	46	127	17	2	3	31	.314	587	44	7	.989
1972	Oakland (d)	Amer.	OF-1B	32	121	11	34	5	0	1	16	.281	57	3	0	1.000
1973	New York (e)	Amer.	OF-1B	123	497	59	147	22	1	2	28	.296	522	26	12	.979
1973	St. Louis (f)	Nat.	1B-OF	11	11	1	3	0	0	0	1	.273	3	1	0	1.000
1974	San Diego	Nat.	OF-1B	48	81	8	16	3	0	0	3	.198	33	0	1	.971
	National League Totals			1512	5171	710	1596	209	49	28	383	.309	3215	147	59	.983
	American League Totals			155	618	70	181	27	1	3	44	.293	579	29	12	.981
	Major League Totals			1667	5789	780	1777	236	50	31	427	.307	3794	176	71	.982

aTraded to Pittsburgh Pirates for pitcher Joe Gibbon and infielder Ossie Virgil, December 1, 1965.
  bTraded with pitcher George Brunet to St. Louis Cardinals for pitcher Nelson Briles and outfielder Vic Davalillo, January 29, 1971.
  cTraded to Oakland A's for outfielder Bill Voss and pitcher Steve Easton, August 27, 1972.
  dTraded to New York Yankees for pitcher Rob Gardner (plus third baseman Rich McKinney), November 24, 1972.
  eTraded to St. Louis Cardinals, September 6, 1973.
  fSold to San Diego Padres, October 25, 1973.

WORLD SERIES RECORD

Year	Club	League	Pos.	G.	AB.	R.	H.	2B.	3B.	HR.	RBI.	B.A.	PO.	A.	E.	F.A.
1962	San Francisco	Nat.	OF	6	12	2	4	1	0	0	1	.333	3	0	0	1.000
1972	Oakland	Amer.	OF	7	24	0	1	0	0	0	0	.042	11	1	1	.923
	World Series Totals			13	36	2	5	1	0	0	1	.139	14	1	1	.938

PITCHING RECORD

Year	Club	League	G.	IP.	W.	L.	Pct.	H.	R.	ER.	SO.	BB.	ERA.
1965	San Francisco	National	1	2	0	0	.000	3	0	0	3	1	0.00

DID YOU KNOW—
That Matty, Felipe and Jesus Alou batted in same inning, September 10, 1963?

LEON KESSLING (RED) AMES

Born August 2, 1884, at Warren, O.
Died October 8, 1936, at Warren, O.
Height, 5.10½. Weight, 185.
Threw and batted righthanded.
Married Rena Brainard, January 17, 1905.

Pitched five-innings, 5-0 no-hitter against St. Louis in major league debut, September 14, 1903 (second game). Pitched nine-inning, no-hit, no-run game against Brooklyn in opening game of 1909 season, April 15, but New York lost in 13 innings, 3-0.
Manager, Daytona, Florida State League, 1923.

Year Club	League	G.	IP.	W.	L.	Pct.	H.	R.	ER.	SO.	BB.	ERA.
1903–Ilion	N.Y. State	27	229	12	12	.500	200	106	....	221	77	......
1903–New York	National	2	14	2	0	1.000	5	2	....	14	8	......
1904–New York	National	16	115	4	6	.400	94	44	....	93	38	......
1905–New York	National	34	263	22	8	.733	220	113	....	198	105	......
1906–New York	National	31	203	12	10	.545	166	79	....	156	93	......
1907–New York	National	39	233	10	12	.455	184	93	....	146	108	......
1908–New York	National	18	114	7	4	.636	96	33	....	81	27	......
1909–New York	National	34	244	15	10	.600	217	109	....	160	81	......
1910–New York	National	33	190	12	11	.522	161	78	....	94	63	......
1911–New York	National	34	205	11	10	.524	170	80	....	118	54	......
1912–New York	National	33	179	11	5	.688	194	82	49	83	35	2.46
1913–N.Y.(a-)-Cin.	National	39	227	13	14	.481	220	93	70	110	78	2.78
1914–Cincinnati	National	47	297	15	*23	.395	274	125	87	128	94	2.64
1915–Cin.(b)-St. Louis	National	32	181	11	7	.611	175	74	65	74	56	3.23
1916–St. Louis	National	45	228	11	16	.407	225	100	67	98	57	2.64
1917–St. Louis	National	43	209	15	10	.600	189	75	63	62	57	2.71
1918–St. Louis	National	27	207	9	14	.391	192	75	53	68	52	2.30
1919–St. Louis(c)-Phila.	National	26	86	3	7	.300	114	56	49	23	28	5.13
1920–Kansas City	Amer. Assn.	39	249	16	17	.485	296	149	120	73	50	4.34
1921–Kansas City	Amer. Assn.	36	256	17	15	.531	321	174	147	79	78	5.17
1922–Kansas City	Amer. Assn.	8	18	2	0	1.000	24	9	....	2	2	......
1923–Daytona	Fla. State	7	45	2	3	.400	55	31	....	17	8	......
Major League Totals		533	3195	183	167	.523	2896	1311	....	1706	1034	......

aTraded to Cincinnati Reds with third baseman Heine Groh and outfielder Josh Devore and $20,000 for pitcher Art Fromme and infielder Eddie Grant, May 22, 1913.
bSold to St. Louis Cardinals, July 24, 1915.
cReleased to Philadelphia Phillies on waivers, September 5, 1919; returned to Cardinals, October, 1919–then released, April 8, 1920.

WORLD SERIES RECORD

Year Club	League	G.	IP.	W.	L.	Pct.	H.	R.	ER.	SO.	BB.	ERA.
1905–New York	National	1	1	0	0	.000	1	0	0	1	1	0.00
1911–New York	National	2	8	0	1	.000	6	5	2	6	1	2.25
1912–New York	National	1	2	0	0	.000	3	1	1	0	1	4.50
World Series Totals		4	11	0	1	.000	10	6	3	7	3	2.45

ADRIAN CONSTANTINE (CAP) ANSON

Born April 17, 1852, at Marshalltown, Ia.
Died April 14, 1922, at Chicago, Ill.
Height, 6.01. Weight, 220.
Threw and batted righthanded.
Married Virginia M. Fiegel, 1876.

Holds league record of hitting .300 or better for 20 years; tied with Ty Cobb, Mel Ott and Stan Musial most years with one N. L. club–22 (surpassed by Brooks Robinson, 23 years one club, Baltimore, A. L.).
Manager, Chicago Nationals, 1879-1897; manager, New York Giants, June 11 to July 6, 1898.
Named to Hall of Fame, 1939.

Year-Club	League	Pos.	G.	AB.	R.	H.	2B.	3B.	HR.	S.B.	B.A.	PO.	A.	E.	F.A.
1870–Marshalltown	Ind.	....	....	....	....	....	....	....	....	....	....	....	....	....	....
1871–Rockford	N.As'n	C-2-3	25	122	30	43	....	....	....	....	.352	56	67	....	....
1872–Ath. of Phila.	N.As'n	3B	45	231	60	88	....	....	....	....	.381	86	82	33	.836
1873–Ath. of Phila.	N.As'n	C-1-O	51	....	52	103	....	....	....	....	....	440	28	....	....
1874–Ath. of Phila.	N.As'n	1-OF	55	267	51	98	....	....	....	....	.367	285	95	....	....
1875–Ath. of Phila.	N.As'n	1-C-3-O	69	330	83	105	....	....	....	....	.318	273	14	32	.900
1876–Chicago	Nat.	3B	66	321	63	110	13	6	2	....	.343	137	147	50	.850
1877–Chicago	Nat.	3B-C	47	200	36	67	★20	1	0	....	.335	137	93	35	.871
1878–Chicago	Nat.	2B-OF	59	256	54	86	12	2	0	....	.336	80	31	21	.841
1879–Chicago	Nat.	1B	49	221	41	90	22	1	0	....	★.407	602	8	16	.974
1880–Chicago	Nat.	INF	84	346	52	117	22	1	1	....	.338	811	15	19	.978
1881–Chicago	Nat.	1-C-SS	84	343	66	★137	25	7	1	....	★.399	892	43	24	.975
1882–Chicago	Nat.	1B-C	82	348	69	126	30	8	1	....	.362	810	27	45	.949
1883–Chicago	Nat.	1-C-P	98	413	69	127	33	6	0	....	.308	1031	41	40	.964
1884–Chicago	Nat.	1-C-S-P	111	471	108	★159	32	5	19	....	.338	1203	39	58	.955
1885–Chicago	Nat.	1B-C	112	464	100	144	★35	6	7	....	.310★	1253	39	★57	.958
1886–Chicago	Nat.	1B	125	504	117	★187	34	11	10	29	.371	1188	★66	★48	.963
1887–Chicago†	Nat.	1B	122	532	107	224	33	13	7	27	★.421	1232	★70	36	.973
1888–Chicago	Nat.	1B	134	515	101	177	17	13	10	28	★.344	1314	65	20	★.986
1889–Chicago	Nat.	1B	134	518	99	177	30	6	7	27	.342★	1409	★79	27	★.982
1890–Chicago	Nat.	1B	★139	504	102	157	17	4	6	29	.312	1345	★49	31	.978
1891–Chicago	Nat.	1B	136	537	82	158	25	9	8	21	.294	1406	77	28	.981
1892–Chicago	Nat.	1B	147	561	62	154	23	9	1	15	.275	1491	61	★46	.971
1893–Chicago	Nat.	1B	101	381	70	123	25	3	0	13	.323	998	42	20	.981
1894–Chicago	Nat.	1B	83	347	87	137	26	6	5	17	.395	748	45	9	.989
1895–Chicago	Nat.	1B	122	476	88	161	23	6	2	16	.338	1172	67	14	.989
1896–Chicago	Nat.	1B	106	403	72	135	17	3	2	28	.335	886	53	17	.982
1897–Chicago	Nat.	1B	112	423	66	128	16	3	3	16	.303	940	23	13	.987
National League Totals			2253	9084	1712	3081	530	129	92	266	.339	21085	1180	674	.971

†Bases on balls counted as hits in 1887.

WORLD SERIES RECORD

Year-Club	League	Pos.	G.	AB.	R.	H.	SB.	B.A.	PO.	A.	E.	F.A.
1885–Chicago	Nat.	1B	7	26	8	11	0	.423	60	3	10	.863
1886–Chicago	Nat.	1B	6	20	3	5	1	.250	51	2	2	.964
World Series Totals			13	46	11	16	1	.348	111	5	12	.906

LUIS ERNESTO APARICIO

Born April 29, 1934, at Maracaibo, Venezuela.
Height, 5.08. Weight, 155.
Threw and batted righthanded.

Established major league records for most consecutive years leading league in stolen bases (9), 1964; most years leading league in chances accepted, shortstop (7), 1968; most double plays by shortstop (1,553), 1973; most games, shortstop (2,581), 1973; most assists, shortstop, league (8,016), 1973.
    Tied major league records for most consecutive years leading league in fielding average, shortstop (8), 1966; most years leading league in assists, shortstop (7), 1968.
    Established American League records for most years leading league in games played by shortstop (5), 1960; most putouts, shortstop, league (4,548), 1973; most chances accepted, shortstop, league (12,564), 1973.
    Led American League in stolen bases with 21 in 1956, 28 in 1957, 29 in 1958, 56 in 1959, 51 in 1960, 53 in 1961, 31 in 1962, 40 in 1963 and 57 in 1964.
    Led American League shortstops in double plays, 1960, 1968 (tie).
    Named American League Rookie of the Year by the Baseball Writers' Association and THE SPORTING NEWS, 1956.
    Named shortstop on THE SPORTING NEWS American League All-Star Team, 1963-66-68-70-72.
    Named shortstop on THE SPORTING NEWS American League All-Star fielding team, 1958-59-60-61-62-64-66-68-70.

Year-Club	League	Pos.	G.	AB.	R.	H.	2B.	3B.	HR.	RBI.	B.A.	PO.	A.	E.	F.A.
1954–Waterloo	I.I.I.	SS	94	390	85	110	18	4	4	47	.282	220	275	31	.941
1955–Memphis	South.	SS	150	564	92	154	24	3	6	51	.273	★314	★433	●44	.944
1956–Chicago	Amer.	SS	152	533	69	142	19	6	3	56	.266	★250	★474	★35	.954
1957–Chicago	Amer.	SS	143	575	82	148	22	6	3	41	.257	246	★449	20	.972
1958–Chicago	Amer.	SS	145	557	76	148	20	9	2	40	.266	★289	★463	21	.973
1959–Chicago	Amer.	SS	152	612	98	157	18	5	6	51	.257	★282	★460	23	★.970
1960–Chicago	Amer.	SS	153	600	86	166	20	7	2	61	.277	305	★551	18	★.979
1961–Chicago	Amer.	SS	156	625	90	170	24	4	6	45	.272	264	★487	30	★.962
1962–Chicago (a)	Amer.	SS	153	581	72	140	23	5	7	40	.241	280	452	20	★.973
1963–Baltimore	Amer.	SS	146	601	73	150	18	8	5	45	.250	275	403	12	★.983

Year	Club	League	Pos.	G.	AB.	R.	H.	2B.	3B.	HR.	RBI.	B.A.	PO.	A.	E.	F.A.
1964	–Baltimore	Amer.	SS	146	578	93	154	20	3	10	37	.266	260	437	15	*.979
1965	–Baltimore	Amer.	SS	144	564	67	127	20	10	8	40	.225	238	439	20	*.971
1966	–Baltimore	Amer.	SS	151	*659	97	182	25	8	6	41	.276	*303	441	17	*.978
1967	–Baltimore (b)	Amer.	SS	134	546	55	127	22	5	4	31	.233	221	333	25	.957
1968	–Chicago	Amer.	SS	155	622	55	164	24	4	4	36	.264	269	*535	19	.977
1969	–Chicago	Amer.	SS	156	599	77	168	24	5	5	51	.280	248	563	20	.976
1970	–Chicago (c)	Amer.	SS	146	552	86	173	29	3	5	43	.313	251	483	18	.976
1971	–Boston	Amer.	SS	125	491	56	114	23	0	4	45	.232	194	338	16	.971
1972	–Boston	Amer.	SS	110	436	47	112	26	3	3	39	.257	183	304	16	.968
1973	–Boston	Amer.	SS	132	499	56	135	17	1	0	49	.271	190	404	21	.966
Major League Totals				2599	10230	1335	2677	394	92	83	791	.262	4548	8016	366	.971

aTraded to Baltimore Orioles with outfielder-third baseman Al Smith for pitcher Hoyt Wilhelm, third baseman Pete Ward, shortstop Ron Hansen and outfielder Dave Nicholson, January 14, 1963.

bTraded with outfielder Russ Snyder and outfielder-first baseman John Matias to Chicago White Sox for infielder Don Buford and pitchers Bruce Howard and Roger Nelson, November 29, 1967.

cTraded to Boston Red Sox for second baseman Mike Andrews and shortstop Luis Alvarado, December 1, 1970.

WORLD SERIES RECORD

Year	Club	League	Pos.	G.	AB.	R.	H.	2B.	3B.	HR.	RBI.	B.A.	PO.	A.	E.	F.A.
1959	–Chicago	Amer.	SS	6	26	1	8	1	0	0	0	.308	10	16	2	.929
1966	–Baltimore	Amer.	SS	4	16	0	4	1	0	0	2	.250	9	8	0	1.000
World Series Totals				10	42	1	12	2	0	0	2	.286	19	24	2	.956

LUCIUS BENJAMIN (LUKE) APPLING

Born April 2, 1907, at High Point, N. C.

Height, 5.11. Weight, 200.

Threw and batted righthanded.

Married Fay Nell Dodd, February 13, 1932.

Led league shortstops in assists, seven seasons, to set major league mark; held A.L. record for most putouts by a shortstop, lifetime (4,348), passed by Luis Aparicio with 4,548; also held A. L. mark for most assists by a shortstop (7,218), exceeded by Aparicio (8,016); A. L. standard for most chances accepted by shortstop (11,566), topped by Aparicio (12,564); holds American League record, highest batting average, season, 100 or more games, shortstop (.388), 1936. Led A.L. shortstops in double plays, 1936, 1937, 1946.

Named as shortstop on THE SPORTING NEWS' All-Star Major League Teams, 1936-40-43.

Manager, Memphis, Southern Association, 1951-52-53; manager, Richmond, International League, 1955; manager, Memphis, Southern Association, 1959; coach, Detroit Tigers, 1960 until August 8, when he traded jobs with Jo Jo White of Cleveland Indians; coach, Cleveland Indians, through 1961; manager, Indianapolis, American Association, 1962; coach, Baltimore Orioles, 1963; coach, Kansas City Athletics, 1964 to 1967; manager, Kansas City Athletics, August 20 to October 1, 1967; scout, Oakland Athletics, 1968-69; coach, Chicago White Sox, 1970-71.

Named to Hall of Fame, 1964.

Year	Club	League	Pos.	G.	AB.	R.	H.	2B.	3B.	HR.	RBI.	B.A.	PO.	A.	E.	F.A.
1930	–Atlanta	South.	SS	104	374	63	122	19	17	5	75	.326	224	302	*42	.926
1930	–Chicago	Amer.	SS	6	26	2	8	2	0	0	2	.308	12	17	4	.879
1931	–Chicago	Amer.	SS-2B	96	297	36	69	13	4	1	28	.232	151	233	43	.899
1932	–Chicago	Amer.	INF	139	489	66	134	20	10	3	63	.274	270	419	49	.934
1933	–Chicago	Amer.	SS	151	612	90	197	36	10	6	85	.322	314	*534	*55	.939
1934	–Chicago	Amer.	SS-2B	118	452	75	137	28	6	2	61	.303	264	357	35	.947
1935	–Chicago	Amer.	SS	153	525	94	161	28	6	1	71	.307	*335	*556	*39	.958
1936	–Chicago	Amer.	SS	138	526	111	204	31	7	6	128	*.388	320	471	41	.951
1937	–Chicago	Amer.	SS	154	574	98	182	42	8	4	77	.317	280	*541	*49	.944
1938	–Chicago(a)	Amer.	SS	81	294	41	89	14	0	0	44	.303	149	258	20	.953
1939	–Chicago	Amer.	SS	148	516	82	162	16	6	0	56	.314	289	*461	*39	.951
1940	–Chicago	Amer.	SS	150	566	96	197	27	13	0	79	.348	307	436	37	.953
1941	–Chicago	Amer.	SS	154	592	93	186	26	8	1	57	.314	294	*473	42	.948
1942	–Chicago	Amer.	SS	142	543	78	142	26	4	3	53	.262	269	418	38	.948
1943	–Chicago	Amer.	SS	•155	585	63	192	33	2	3	80	*.328	300	*500	36	.957
1944–							(In Military Service)									
1945	–Chicago(b)	Amer.	SS	18	57	12	21	2	1	1	10	.368	37	56	7	.930
1946	–Chicago	Amer.	SS	149	582	59	180	27	5	1	55	.309	252	*505	*39	.951
1947	–Chicago	Amer.	SS-3B	139	503	67	154	29	0	8	49	.306	233	423	35	.949
1948	–Chicago	Amer.	3B-SS	139	497	63	156	16	2	0	47	.314	217	373	35	.944
1949	–Chicago	Amer.	SS	142	492	82	148	21	5	5	58	.301	253	450	26	.964
1950	–Chicago	Amer.	INF	50	128	11	30	3	4	0	13	.234	128	62	3	.984
Major League Totals				2422	8856	1319	2749	440	102	45	1116	.310	4674	7543	672	.948

aFractured leg sliding into base in exhibition game against Chicago Cubs, March 27, 1938.

bIn Military Service part of season.

DON RICHARD (RICHIE) ASHBURN

Born March 19, 1927, at Tilden, Neb.
Height, 5.10. Weight, 175.
Threw right and batted lefthanded.
Married Herberta Cox, November 6, 1949.

Led National League in stolen bases (32), 1948.
Hit safely in 23 consecutive games, May 9 through June 5, 1949, tied National League record for rookie season, set by Joseph Rapp, Philadelphia Phillies, 1921.
Holds major league record for most years 400 or more putouts, season, by outfielder (9), 1949 through 1954 and 1956-57-58; tied major league record for most years leading outfielders in putouts (9), 1958; holds major league mark for most years 500 or more putouts by outfielder, season (4), 1949-51-56-57.
Tied National League record for most years leading league in one-base hits (4), (181) 1951, (169) 1953, (152) 1957, (176) 1958.
Ashburn had not missed a game for the Phils since June 6, 1950, and had a consecutive game string of 731, up to the opening of the 1955 season; because of a sore knee suffered in spring training and a muddy field in Philadelphia, Manager Mayo Smith of the Phils decided not to risk further injury to Ashburn's knee. This snapped Richie's string just 91 games short of the National League record then held by Gus Suhr and now held by Billy Williams, Chicago Cubs, 1,117 consecutive games.
Named by THE SPORTING NEWS as Rookie of the Year, 1948.

Year	Club	League	Pos.	G.	AB.	R.	H.	2B.	3B.	HR.	RBI.	B.A.	PO.	A.	E.	F.A.
1945	Utica	East.	OF-C	106	356	63	111	17	6	1	42	.312	189	19	7	.967
1946	Utica	East.					(In Military Service)									
1947	Utica	East.	OF	137	536	*128	*194	21	12	3	52	.362	242	14	6	.977
1948	Philadelphia(a)	Nat.	OF	117	463	78	154	17	4	2	40	.333	344	14	7	.981
1949	Philadelphia	Nat.	OF	154	*662	84	188	18	11	1	37	.284	*514	13	11	.980
1950	Philadelphia	Nat.	OF	151	594	84	180	25	*14	2	41	.303	*405	8	5	.988
1951	Philadelphia	Nat.	OF	154	643	92	*221	31	5	4	63	.344	*538	15	7	.988
1952	Philadelphia	Nat.	OF	*154	613	93	173	31	6	1	42	.282	*428	*23	9	.980
1953	Philadelphia	Nat.	OF	156	622	110	*205	25	9	2	57	.330	*496	*18	5	.990
1954	Philadelphia	Nat.	OF	153	559	111	175	16	8	1	41	.313	*483	12	8	.984
1955	Philadelphia	Nat.	OF	140	533	91	180	32	9	3	42	*.338	387	10	7	.983
1956	Philadelphia	Nat.	OF	154	628	94	190	26	8	3	50	.303	*503	11	9	.983
1957	Philadelphia	Nat.	OF	•156	626	93	186	26	8	0	33	.297	*502	*18	7	.987
1958	Philadelphia	Nat.	OF	152	615	98	*215	24	*13	2	33	*.350	*495	8	8	.984
1959	Philadelphia(b)	Nat.	OF	153	564	86	150	16	2	1	20	.266	359	4	11	.971
1960	Chicago	Nat.	OF	151	547	99	159	16	5	0	40	.291	317	11	8	.976
1961	Chicago(c)	Nat.	OF	109	307	49	79	7	4	0	19	.257	131	4	3	.978
1962	New York	Nat.	OF	135	389	60	119	7	3	7	28	.306	187	9	5	.975
Major League Totals				2189	8365	1322	2574	317	109	29	586	.308	6089	178	110	.983

aFractured finger sliding into second base, August 28, 1948; out for rest of season.
bTraded to Chicago Cubs for pitcher John Buzhardt, infielder Al Dark and third baseman Jim Woods, January 11, 1960.
cSold to New York Mets, December 8, 1961.

WORLD SERIES RECORD

Year	Club	League	Pos.	G.	AB.	R.	H.	2B.	3B.	HR.	RBI.	B.A.	PO.	A.	E.	F.A.
1950	Philadelphia	Nat.	OF	4	17	0	3	1	0	0	1	.176	9	0	0	1.000

HOWARD EARL (ROCK) AVERILL

Born May 21, 1902, Snohomish, Wash.
Height, 5.09½. Weight, 172.
Threw right and batted lefthanded.
Married Gladys Loette Hyatt, May 15, 1922.

Hit home run off Earl Whitehill, Detroit lefthander, in first plate appearance in majors, April 16, 1929; hit four home runs and had 11 RBIs in doubleheader vs. Washington at Cleveland, September 17, 1930, hitting three successive homers in first game and just missing fourth in row when his long drive was barely foul; hit for cycle, August 17, 1933.
Son, Earl Douglas Averill, Cleveland Indians, 1956-58; Chicago Cubs, 1959-60; Chicago White Sox, 1960; Los Angeles Angels, 1961, Philadelphia Phillies, 1963.

Selected by Baseball Writers' Association of America as outfielder on THE SPORTING NEWS All-Star Major League Teams, 1931-32-34-36.
Named to Hall of Fame, 1975.

Year	Club	League	Pos.	G.	AB.	R.	H.	2B.	3B.	HR.	RBI.	B.A.	PO.	A.	E.	F.A.
1926	San Francisco	P. C.	OF	188	679	131	236	49	6	23	119	.348	364	17	14	.965
1927	San Francisco	P. C.	OF	183	754	134	244	47	6	20	116	.324	451	★45	19	.963
1928	San Francisco	P. C.	OF	189	763	★178	270	53	11	36	173	.354	462	25	18	.964
1929	Cleveland(a)	Amer.	OF	152	596	110	198	43	13	18	96	.332	★383	14	14	.966
1930	Cleveland	Amer.	OF	139	534	102	181	33	8	19	119	.339	345	11	★19	.949
1931	Cleveland	Amer.	OF	155	★627	140	209	36	10	32	143	.333	398	9	10	.976
1932	Cleveland	Amer.	OF	153	631	116	198	37	14	32	124	.314	412	12	16	.964
1933	Cleveland	Amer.	OF	151	599	83	180	39	16	17	92	.301	390	8	12	.971
1934	Cleveland	Amer.	OF	●154	598	128	187	48	6	31	113	.313	★410	12	13	.970
1935	Cleveland	Amer.	OF	140	563	109	162	34	13	19	79	.288	371	6	7	.982
1936	Cleveland	Amer.	OF	152	614	136	★232	39	●15	28	126	.378	369	11	12	.969
1937	Cleveland	Amer.	OF	156	609	121	182	33	11	21	92	.299	362	11	9	.976
1938	Cleveland	Amer.	OF	134	482	101	159	27	15	14	93	.330	331	14	9	.975
1939	Clev.(b)-Detroit	Amer.	OF	111	364	66	96	28	6	11	65	.264	169	3	4	.977
1940	Detroit	Amer.	OF	64	118	10	33	4	1	2	20	.280	23	2	1	.962
1941	Boston	Nat.	OF	8	17	2	2	0	0	0	2	.118	5	2	0	1.000
1941	Seattle	P. C.	OF	78	223	24	55	9	0	1	17	.247	147	10	3	.981
American League Totals				1661	6335	1222	2017	401	128	238	1162	.318	3963	113	126	.970
National League Totals				8	17	2	2	0	0	0	2	.118	5	2	0	1.000
Major League Totals				1669	6352	1224	2019	401	128	238	1164	.318	3968	115	126	.970

aPurchased for reported price of $50,000.
bTraded to Detroit Tigers for pitcher Harry Eisenstat and cash, June 14, 1939.

WORLD SERIES RECORD

Year	Club	League	Pos.	G.	AB.	R.	H.	2B.	3B.	HR.	RBI.	B.A.	PO.	A.	E.	F.A.
1940	Detroit	Amer.	PH	3	3	0	0	0	0	0	0	.000	0	0	0	.000

JOHN FRANKLIN (HOME RUN) BAKER

Born March 13, 1886, at Trappe, Md.
Died June 28, 1963, at Trappe, Md.
Height, 5.11. Weight, 173.
Threw right and batted lefthanded.
Married Margaret Mitchell, January 16, 1922.

In World Series, Baker scored six runs in five-game Series, 1910; made nine hits in five-game Series of 1910 and 1913; hit home runs to win games, October 16 and 17, 1911 and October 7, 1913; accepted 25 chances in four games at third base, 1914, ten putouts and 15 assists.
Manager, Easton, Eastern Shore League, 1924-25; president of Easton club in 1941.
Named to Hall of Fame, 1955.

Year	Club	League	Pos.	G.	AB.	R.	H.	2B.	3B.	HR.	RBI.	B.A.	PO.	A.	E.	F.A.
1907	Baltimore	East.	3B	5	15	0	2	0	0	0	....	.133	9	5	2	.875
1908	Reading	Tri-State	3B	119	451	65	135	11	12	6	....	.299	★174	246	27	.940
1908	Philadelphia	Amer.	3B	9	30	5	9	3	0	0	4	.300	12	18	0	1.000
1909	Philadelphia	Amer.	3B	148	541	73	165	27	★19	4	89	.305	★209	★277	★42	.920
1910	Philadelphia	Amer.	3B	146	561	83	159	25	15	2	73	.283	★207	313	45	.920
1911	Philadelphia	Amer.	3B	148	592	96	198	40	14	★11	115	.334	217	274	30	★.942
1912	Philadelphia	Amer.	3B	149	577	116	200	40	21	●10	★133	.347	217	321	34	.941
1913	Philadelphia	Amer.	3B	149	564	116	190	34	9	★12	★126	.337	★233	279	★45	.919
1914	Philadelphia	Amer.	3B	150	570	84	182	23	10	★9	97	.319	★221	292	24	.955
1915	Philadelphia (a)	Amer.			(Refused to report; played with Upland, Pa.)											
1916	New York	Amer.	3B	100	360	46	97	23	2	10	52	.269	133	210	22	★.940
1917	New York	Amer.	3B	146	553	57	156	24	2	6	70	.282	★202	★317	28	★.949
1918	New York	Amer.	3B	126	504	65	154	24	5	6	68	.306	★175	282	13	★.972
1919	New York	Amer.	3B	●141	567	70	166	22	1	10	78	.293	★176	286	22	.955
1920	New York	Amer.			(Voluntarily retired; played with Upland, Pa.)											
1921	New York	Amer.	3B	94	330	46	97	16	2	9	71	.294	84	173	11	.959
1922	New York	Amer.	3B	69	234	30	65	12	3	7	36	.278	68	108	7	.962
1924	Easton	Ea. Shore	3B	43	92	14	27	1	1	5	....	.293	25	43	4	.944
Major League Totals				1575	5983	887	1838	313	103	96	1012	.307	2154	3150	323	.942

aSold to New York Yankees for $35,000, February 15, 1916.

WORLD SERIES RECORD

Year	Club	League	Pos.	G.	AB.	R.	H.	2B.	3B.	HR.	RBI.	B.A.	PO.	A.	E.	F.A.
1910–Philadelphia		Amer.	3B	5	22	6	9	3	0	0	4	.409	9	11	3	.869
1911–Philadelphia		Amer.	3B	6	24	7	9	2	0	2	5	.375	10	10	2	.909
1913–Philadelphia		Amer.	3B	5	20	2	9	0	0	1	7	.450	6	6	1	.923
1914–Philadelphia		Amer.	3B	4	16	0	4	2	0	0	2	.250	10	15	0	1.000
1921–New York		Amer.	3B-PH	4	8	0	2	0	0	0	0	.250	2	3	0	1.000
1922–New York		Amer.	PH	1	1	0	0	0	0	0	0	.000	0	0	0	.000
World Series Totals				25	91	15	33	7	0	3	18	.363	37	45	6	.932

DAVID JAMES (BEAUTY) BANCROFT

Born April 20, 1892, at Sioux City, Ia.
Died October 9, 1972, at Superior, Wis.
Height, 5.09½. Weight, 160.
Threw right and batted left and righthanded.
Married Edna H. Gisin, November 22, 1910.

Had six singles in six times at bat against Philadelphia, June 28, 1920.
Led N.L. shortstops in double plays, 1922.
Manager, Boston Braves, 1924 through 1927; coach, New York Giants, 1930-31-32; manager, Minneapolis, American Association, 1933; manager, Sioux City, Western League, 1936; manager, St. Cloud, Northern League, 1947.
Named to Hall of Fame, 1971.

Year	Club	League	Pos.	G.	AB.	R.	H.	2B.	3B.	HR.	RBI.	B.A.	PO.	A.	E.	F.A.
1909–Duluth-Sup		Wis.-Min.	SS	111	367	43	77	4	1	1	....	.210	*230	*359	54	.916
1910–Superior		Wis.-Min.	SS	•127	438	55	117	16	1	1	....	.267	*323	350	59	.919
1911–Superior		Wis.-Min.	SS	122	524	73	143	....	....	....	....	.273	....	....	....	....
1912–Portland		P. C.	SS-2B	166	565	68	120	29	8	0	....	.213	390	512	52	.945
1913–Portland		N. W.	SS-2B	133	483	79	118	19	9	2	....	.244	325	418	46	.942
1914–Portland		P. C.	SS-2B	177	668	99	185	35	14	2	....	.277	*453	585	59	.946
1915–Philadelphia		Nat.	SS	153	563	85	143	18	2	7	33	.254	336	492	64	.928
1916–Philadelphia		Nat.	SS	142	477	53	101	10	0	3	27	.212	326	510	*60	.933
1917–Philadelphia		Nat.	SS	127	478	56	116	22	5	4	38	.243	274	439	49	.936
1918–Philadelphia		Nat.	SS	125	499	69	132	19	4	0	18	.265	*371	457	*64	.928
1919–Philadelphia		Nat.	SS	92	335	45	91	13	7	0	29	.272	242	306	28	.951
1920–Phila. (a)-N.Y.		Nat.	SS	150	613	102	183	36	9	0	36	.299	*362	*598	45	*.955
1921–New York		Nat.	SS	153	606	121	193	26	15	6	67	.318	*396	*546	39	.960
1922–New York		Nat.	SS	•156	651	117	209	41	5	4	60	.321	*405	*579	*62	.941
1923–New York (b)		Nat.	SS-3B	107	444	80	135	33	3	1	31	.304	246	381	43	.936
1924–Boston		Nat.	SS	79	319	49	89	11	1	2	21	.279	186	259	18	.961
1925–Boston		Nat.	SS	128	479	75	153	29	8	2	49	.319	300	459	44	*.945
1926–Boston		Nat.	SS	127	453	70	141	18	6	1	44	.311	287	398	33	.956
1927–Boston (c)		Nat.	SS	111	375	44	91	13	4	1	31	.243	275	329	39	.939
1928–Brooklyn		Nat.	SS	149	515	47	127	19	5	0	51	.247	350	484	46	.948
1929–Brooklyn (d)		Nat.	SS	104	358	35	99	11	3	1	44	.277	224	309	25	.955
1930–New York		Nat.	SS-PH	10	17	0	1	1	0	0	0	.059	13	15	1	.966
1936–Sioux City		West.	SS	1	4	1	1	0	0	0	0	.250	1	1	0	1.000
Major League Totals				1913	7182	1048	2004	320	77	32	579	.279	4623	6561	660	.944

aTraded to New York Giants for shortstop Art Fletcher and pitcher Wilbur Hubbell, June 8, 1920.
bTraded with outfielders Casey Stengel and Bill Cunningham to Boston Braves for pitcher Joe Oeschger and outfielder William Southworth, November, 1923.
cUnconditionally released, October 17, 1927; signed with Brooklyn Dodgers.
dReleased by Brooklyn Dodgers following 1929 season and signed by New York Giants as player-coach.

WORLD SERIES RECORD

Year	Club	League	Pos.	G.	AB.	R.	H.	2B.	3B.	HR.	RBI.	B.A.	PO.	A.	E.	F.A.
1915–Philadelphia		Nat.	SS	5	17	2	5	0	0	0	1	.294	13	10	1	.958
1921–New York		Nat.	SS	8	33	3	5	1	0	0	3	.152	16	17	1	.971
1922–New York		Nat.	SS	5	19	4	4	0	0	2	2	.211	9	17	1	.963
1923–New York		Nat.	SS	6	24	1	2	0	0	0	1	.083	11	24	0	1.000
World Series Totals				24	93	10	16	1	0	2	7	.172	49	68	3	.975

DID YOU KNOW—

That there are two players nicknamed Piano Legs in this book? Also a Cupid, Sadie, Biddie and the player above?

ERNEST BANKS

Born January 31, 1931, at Dallas, Tex.
Height, 6.01. Weight, 186.
Threw and batted righthanded.

Established following major league records: most consecutive games played from start of major league career (424), September 17, 1953, through August 10, 1956; most home runs by shortstop, season (47), 1958.
Tied following major league records: most home runs with bases full, season (5), May 11 and 29, July 17 (first game), August 2 and September 19, 1955; most games by first baseman, 162-game season (162), 1965; most sacrifice flies, game (3), June 2, 1961; most putouts by first baseman, nine-inning game (22), May 9, 1963; most three-base hits, game (3), June 11, 1966.
Established National League record for most seasons leading in games played (6), 1960.
Hit three home runs in a game, August 4, 1955; September 14, 1957; May 29, 1962, and June 9, 1963.
Named Outstanding National League Player by THE SPORTING NEWS, 1958-59.
Named Most Valuable Player, National League, 1958-59.
Named shortstop on THE SPORTING NEWS All-Star Major League Teams, 1955-58-59-60.
Named shortstop on THE SPORTING NEWS National League All-Star fielding team, 1960.
Player-coach, Chicago Cubs, 1967 through 1969; coach, Chicago Cubs, 1972-73; Cub organization instructor, batting and infield, 1974 to date.
Named to Hall of Fame, 1977.

Year	Club	League	Pos.	G.	AB.	R.	H.	2B.	3B.	HR.	RBI.	B.A.	PO.	A.	E.	F.A.
1953	Chicago	Nat.	SS	10	35	3	11	1	1	2	6	.314	19	33	1	.981
1954	Chicago	Nat.	SS	•154	593	70	163	19	7	19	79	.275	312	475	34	.959
1955	Chicago	Nat.	SS	•154	596	98	176	29	9	44	117	.295	290	482	22	*.972
1956	Chicago	Nat.	SS	139	538	82	160	25	8	28	85	.297	279	357	25	.962
1957	Chicago	Nat.	SS-3B	•156	594	113	169	34	6	43	102	.285	241	348	14	.977
1958	Chicago	Nat.	SS	*154	*617	119	193	23	11	*47	*129	.313	292	468	•32	.960
1959	Chicago	Nat.	SS	•155	589	97	179	25	6	45	*143	.304	271	*519	12	*.985
1960	Chicago	Nat.	SS	*156	597	94	162	32	7	*41	117	.271	*283	*488	18	*.977
1961	Chicago	Nat.	SS-OF-1B	138	511	75	142	22	4	29	80	.278	273	370	21	.968
1962	Chicago	Nat.	*1B-3B	154	610	87	164	20	6	37	104	.269	*1462	*107	11	.993
1963	Chicago	Nat.	1B	130	432	41	98	20	1	18	64	.227	1178	78	9	.993
1964	Chicago	Nat.	1B	157	591	67	156	29	6	23	95	.264	*1565	*132	.10	.994
1965	Chicago	Nat.	1B	163	612	79	162	25	3	28	106	.265	*1682	93	15	.992
1966	Chicago	Nat.	1B-3B	141	511	52	139	23	7	15	75	.272	1183	92	13	.990
1967	Chicago	Nat.	1B	151	573	68	158	26	4	23	95	.276	*1383	*91	10	.993
1968	Chicago	Nat.	1B	150	552	71	136	27	0	32	83	.246	1379	88	6	.996
1969	Chicago	Nat.	1B	155	565	60	143	19	2	23	106	.253	*1419	87	4	*.997
1970	Chicago	Nat.	1B	72	222	25	56	6	2	12	44	.252	528	35	4	.993
1971	Chicago	Nat.	1B	39	83	4	16	2	0	3	6	.193	167	12	0	1.000
Major League Totals				2528	9421	1305	2583	407	90	512	1636	.274	14206	4355	261	.986

EDWARD GRANT (COUSIN EGBERT) BARROW

(Former manager and later known as the Yankee Empire Builder.)

Born May 10, 1868, near Springfield, Ill.
Died December 15, 1953, at Port Chester, N. Y.

The name of Ed Barrow was synonymous with the success of the New York Yankees for a quarter of a century. During his tenure as front-office boss, the Bombers became the scourge of both leagues, winning 14 American League pennants and ten World Series, five of them without the loss of a game.
An acquaintanceship he made in Pittsburgh with Harry Stevens, the caterer and scorecard man, helped Barrow get into baseball. The two formed a partnership and had the scoreboard and pop concessions at the Pirates' old Exposition Park, among other places. In 1894 Barrow took his first fling in baseball when he and Stevens backed the Wheeling (W. Va.) club of the Interstate League. Ed was manager as well as business manager.
When the Atlantic League was organized in December, 1895, Barrow acquired the Paterson (N. J.) franchise. One of the players he signed for his club was Honus Wagner, whom he later sold to Louisville (N.L.). Barrow was elected president of the Atlantic League in 1897 and headed the circuit three years.
In 1900 he bought a quarter interest in the Toronto club and became manager. After leading the team to a

pennant in '02, he moved up to Detroit as pilot the next year. He also managed the Tigers part of '04 before resigning following a dispute with Frank J. Navin, then business manager and minority stockholder.

Barrow piloted Indianapolis and Montreal in 1905 and Toronto again in '06. Out of the game the next three years, he returned in December, 1910, as president of the Eastern League, which he subsequently renamed the International. He retained that position until 1918, when he became manager of the Boston Red Sox. Ed immediately led the club to another pennant. That same season he began the conversion of Babe Ruth, then an ace Red Sox pitcher, into an outfielder. In January, 1920, Red Sox Owner Harry Frazee sold Ruth to the Yankees for $125,000, and at the close of the '20 season Barrow left Boston to become business manager of the Yankees, succeeding Harry Sparrow, who had died.

In 1921, Barrow's first year with the club, the Yankees won their initial pennant, repeating in 1922-23. Later with the help of a farm system built by Barrow and his assistant, George Weiss, the Yankees developed into the most consistent pennant-winning organization in major league history. During Barrow's long reign as front-office chief, the Yankees had only three managers—Miller Huggins, Bob Shawkey for one year, 1930, and Joe McCarthy.

When Col. Jake Ruppert, owner of the club, died in 1939, Barrow became president. He continued in this position until January, 1945, when the Ruppert estate sold the club to Larry MacPhail, Dan Topping and Del Webb. Barrow then became chairman of the board, but relinquished the title two years later.

Barrow was named to the Hall of Fame as a manager-executive by the Committee on Veterans on September 28, 1953, less than three months before his death.

RICHARD (ROWDY) BARTELL

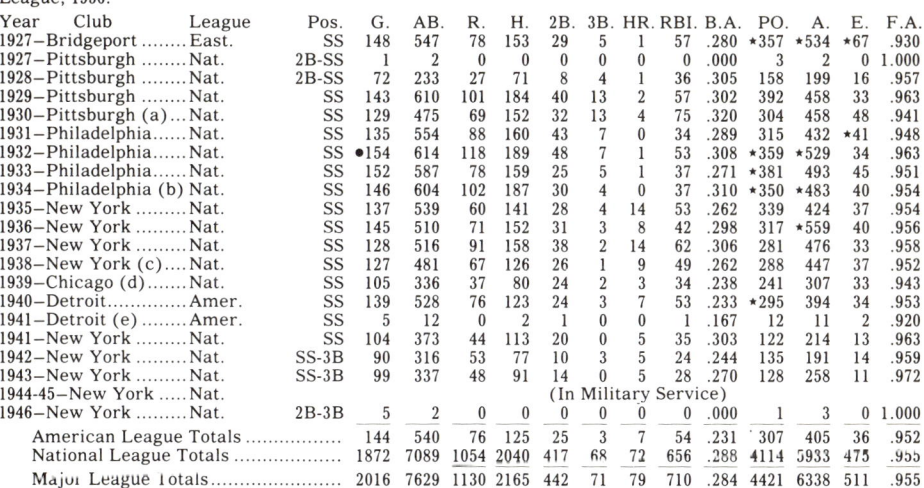

Born November 22, 1907, at Chicago, Ill.
Height, 5.09. Weight, 160.
Threw and batted righthanded.
Married Olive Loretta Jensen, October 24, 1928.

Equaled major league record for most two-base hits, game (4), April 25, 1933. Did not have a single fielding chance in ten-inning game, July 3, 1935.

Manager, Sacramento, Pacific Coast League, 1947; Kansas City, American Association, 1948; coach, Detroit Tigers, 1949-50-51-52; coach, Cincinnati Reds, 1954-55; manager, Montgomery-Knoxville, Sally League, 1956.

Year	Club	League	Pos.	G.	AB.	R.	H.	2B.	3B.	HR.	RBI.	B.A.	PO.	A.	E.	F.A.
1927	Bridgeport	East.	SS	148	547	78	153	29	5	1	57	.280	*357	*534	*67	.930
1927	Pittsburgh	Nat.	2B-SS	1	2	0	0	0	0	0	0	.000	3	2	0	1.000
1928	Pittsburgh	Nat.	2B-SS	72	233	27	71	8	4	1	36	.305	158	199	16	.957
1929	Pittsburgh	Nat.	SS	143	610	101	184	40	13	2	57	.302	392	458	33	.963
1930	Pittsburgh (a)	Nat.	SS	129	475	69	152	32	13	4	75	.320	304	458	48	.941
1931	Philadelphia	Nat.	SS	135	554	88	160	43	7	0	34	.289	315	432	*41	.948
1932	Philadelphia	Nat.	SS	•154	614	118	189	48	7	1	53	.308	*359	*529	34	.963
1933	Philadelphia	Nat.	SS	152	587	78	159	25	5	1	37	.271	*381	493	45	.951
1934	Philadelphia (b)	Nat.	SS	146	604	102	187	30	4	0	37	.310	*350	*483	40	.954
1935	New York	Nat.	SS	137	539	60	141	28	4	14	53	.262	339	424	37	.954
1936	New York	Nat.	SS	145	510	71	152	31	3	8	42	.298	317	*559	40	.956
1937	New York	Nat.	SS	128	516	91	158	38	2	14	62	.306	281	476	33	.958
1938	New York (c)	Nat.	SS	127	481	67	126	26	1	9	49	.262	288	447	37	.952
1939	Chicago (d)	Nat.	SS	105	336	37	80	24	2	3	34	.238	241	307	33	.943
1940	Detroit	Amer.	SS	139	528	76	123	24	3	7	53	.233	*295	394	34	.953
1941	Detroit (e)	Amer.	SS	5	12	0	2	1	0	0	1	.167	12	11	2	.920
1941	New York	Nat.	SS	104	373	44	113	20	0	5	35	.303	122	214	13	.963
1942	New York	Nat.	SS-3B	90	316	53	77	10	3	5	24	.244	135	191	14	.959
1943	New York	Nat.	SS-3B	99	337	48	91	14	0	5	28	.270	128	258	11	.972
1944-45	New York	Nat.						(In Military Service)								
1946	New York	Nat.	2B-3B	5	2	0	0	0	0	0	0	.000	1	3	0	1.000
American League Totals				144	540	76	125	25	3	7	54	.231	307	405	36	.952
National League Totals				1872	7089	1054	2040	417	68	72	656	.288	4114	5933	475	.955
Major League Totals				2016	7629	1130	2165	442	71	79	710	.284	4421	6338	511	.955

aTraded to Philadelphia Phillies for shortstop Thomas J. Thevenow and pitcher Claude B. Willoughby, November 6, 1930.

bTraded to New York Giants for pitcher John Pezzulo, shortstop John Ryan, third baseman John Vergez, outfielder George Watkins and cash, November 1, 1934.

cTraded with outfielder Henry Leiber and catcher Gus Mancuso to Chicago Cubs for outfielder Frank Demaree, shortstop Bill Jurges and catcher James O'Dea, December 6, 1938.

dTraded to Detroit for shortstop Bill Rogell, December 6, 1939.

eReleased by Detroit, May 11, 1941, and signed by New York Giants, May 15, 1941.

WORLD SERIES RECORD

Year	Club	League	Pos.	G.	AB.	R.	H.	2B.	3B.	HR.	RBI.	B.A.	PO.	A.	E.	F.A.
1936	New York	Nat.	SS	6	21	5	8	3	0	1	3	.381	8	13	1	.954
1937	New York	Nat.	SS	5	21	3	5	1	0	0	1	.238	13	11	3	.889
1940	Detroit	Amer.	SS	7	26	2	7	2	0	0	3	.269	12	12	1	.960
World Series Totals				18	68	10	20	6	0	1	7	.294	33	36	5	.932

CLARENCE HOWETH (GINGER) BEAUMONT

Born July 23, 1876, at Rochester, Wis.
Died April 10, 1956, at Burlington, Wis.
Height, 5.08. Weight, 190.
Threw right and batted lefthanded.
Married Norma Olive Vaughn, November 4, 1901.

Made six hits, all singles, and scored six runs in six times at bat, July 22, 1899.
First player to bat in modern World Series, being Pittsburgh's opening batsman in Boston, October 1, 1903, flying out to center fielder Charles S. Stahl.

Year	Club	League	Pos.	G.	AB.	R.	H.	2B.	3B.	HR.	SB.	B.A.	PO.	A.	E.	F.A.
1898	Milwaukee	West.	OF	24	96	24	34	....	....	....	11	.354	43	3	6	.885
1899	Pittsburgh	Nat.	OF	104	425	87	149	15	7	3	32	.351	227	24	20	.926
1900	Pittsburgh	Nat.	OF	138	566	107	160	14	9	5	19	.283	270	9	15	.949
1901	Pittsburgh	Nat.	OF	132	555	118	182	14	6	8	32	.328	289	7	19	.939
1902	Pittsburgh	Nat.	OF	131	544	101	*194	21	6	0	33 *	.357	260	15	8	.972
1903	Pittsburgh	Nat.	OF	•141	*613	*137	*209	30	6	7	23	.341	258	15	15	.948
1904	Pittsburgh	Nat.	OF	153	*615	97	*185	12	12	3	28	.301	287	14	10	.968
1905	Pittsburgh	Nat.	OF	97	384	60	126	12	8	3	21	.328	200	12	6	.972
1906	Pittsburgh(a)	Nat.	OF	78	310	48	82	9	3	2	1	.265	148	6	9	.944
1907	Boston	Nat.	OF	149	580	67	*187	19	14	4	25	.322	296	30	13	.962
1908	Boston	Nat.	OF	121	476	66	127	20	6	2	13	.267	259	17	10	.965
1909	Boston(b)	Nat.	OF	111	407	35	107	11	4	0	12	.263	234	15	8	.969
1910	Chicago	Nat.	OF	56	172	30	46	5	1	2	4	.267	107	5	5	.957
1911	St. Paul	A. A.	OF	74	233	35	58	5	5	2	8	.249	117	10	5	.962
Major League Totals				1411	5647	953	1754	182	82	39	243	.311	2835	169	138	.956

aTraded with second baseman Claude Ritchey to Boston Braves for infielder Ed Abbaticchio, December, 1906.
bTraded to Chicago Cubs for pitcher Fred Liese, February, 1910.

WORLD SERIES RECORD

Year	Club	League	Pos.	G.	AB.	R.	H.	2B.	3B.	HR.	SB.	B.A.	PO.	A.	E.	F.A.
1903	Pittsburgh	Nat.	OF	8	34	6	9	0	1	0	2	.265	22	0	0	1.000
1910	Chicago	Nat.	PH	3	2	1	0	0	0	0	0	.000	0	0	0	.000
World Series Totals				11	36	7	9	0	1	0	2	.250	22	0	0	1.000

JACOB PETER (JAKE) BECKLEY

Born August 4, 1867, at Hannibal, Mo.
Died June 25, 1918, at Kansas City, Mo.
Height, 6.01. Weight, 180.
Threw and batted lefthanded.

Holds major league record for most games played at first base—2,368; played 2,247 games at first base in National League, also tops for N. L.; record holder for most putouts at first base in majors—23,696—and has top mark for N. L. first sackers with 22,438, also a major league record for putouts by first baseman in a league; led N. L. in putouts in six seasons—tied for major league record for first basemen; accepted 25,000 chances at first for another big league mark and had 23,687 chances in the National—tops for a single league.
Hit three homers in a game, September 26, 1897, first game.
Manager, Kansas City, American Association, 1908-09; manager, Bartlesville, Western Association, 1910; umpire, Federal League, 1913.
Named to Hall of Fame, 1971.

Year	Club	League	Pos.	G.	AB.	R.	H.	2B.	3B.	HR.	SB.	B.A.	PO.	A.	E.	F.A.
1886	Leavenworth	West.	1B	....	305	65	104	....	....	....	....	.341	147	171	54	.855
1887	Leav.-Lincoln	West.	1B	....	526	....	211	....	....	....	....	.401	957	29	47	.955
1888	St. Louis	W. A.	1B	34	145	23	41	....	....	....	17	.283	342	6	7	.980
1888	Pittsburgh	Nat.	1B	71	283	35	97	16	3	1	20	.343	744	19	16	.979
1889	Pittsburgh	Nat.	1B	123	522	92	157	22	10	9	11	.301	1236	53	24	•.982
1890	Pittsburgh	Play	1B	121	517	109	168	•41	20	9	19	.325	1258	55	27	.980
1891	Pittsburgh	Nat.	1B	129	535	91	156	20	*20	4	17	.292	1220	84	23	.983
1892	Pittsburgh	Nat.	1B	152	603	102	151	21	19	10	40	.250	*1524	*127	32	.981
1893	Pittsburgh	Nat.	1B	131	497	108	161	23	19	5	24	.324	1360	*96	22	.985

Year−Club	League	Pos.	G.	AB.	R.	H.	2B.	3B.	HR.	SB.	B.A.	PO.	A.	E.	F.A.
1894−Pittsburgh	Nat.	1B	132	534	122	184	32	19	7	20	.345	★1236	★82	31	.977
1895−Pittsburgh	Nat.	1B	131	536	105	174	30	20	5	19	.325	★1375	57	31	.979
1896−Pitts.-N.Y.	Nat.	1B	99	395	79	106	15	10	9	19	.268	941	51	16	.984
1897−N.Y.-Cinn.	Nat.	1B	114	437	84	142	19	11	8	22	.325	994	58	23	.979
1898−Cincinnati	Nat.	1B	116	458	86	137	17	13	3	7	.299	1172	54	18	★.986
1899−Cincinnati	Nat.	1B	135	519	87	173	23	18	3	18	.333	1294	71	18	★.987
1900−Cincinnati	Nat.	1B	138	559	99	192	26	9	2	22	.343	★1388	92	31	.979
1901−Cincinnati	Nat.	1B	140	590	80	177	●39	13	3	6	.300	1353	69	★32	.978
1902−Cincinnati	Nat.	1B	129	532	82	176	21	7	5	16	.331	★1275	69	★23	.983
1903−Cincinnati	Nat.	1B	119	459	85	150	29	10	2	23	.327	1127	78	30	.976
1904−St. Louis	Nat.	1B	142	551	72	179	22	9	1	17	.325	★1526	64	20	.988
1905−St. Louis	Nat.	1B	134	514	48	147	20	10	1	12	.286	1442	69	28	.982
1906−St. Louis	Nat.	1B	85	320	29	79	16	6	0	3	.247	928	43	13	.987
1907−St. Louis	Nat.	1B	32	115	6	24	3	0	0	0	.209	303	13	4	.988
1907−Kansas City	A. A.	1B	100	378	65	138	10	4	1	12	.365	1118	52	18	.985
1908−Kansas City	A. A.	1B	136	496	66	134	19	5	1	13	.270	1432	87	15	.990
1909−Kansas City	A. A.	1B	113	428	41	120	16	3	1	12	.280	1186	57	21	.983
1910−Bartlesville	W. A.	1B	70	249	21	64	15	0	0	13	.257	561	26	3	.995
1910−Topeka	West.	1B	63	233	19	60	11	0	1	1	.258	565	35	13	.979
1911−Hannibal	C. A.	1B	98	355	50	100	7	4	0	22	.282	917	45	10	.990
National League Totals			2252	8959	1492	2762	414	226	78	316	.308	22438	1249	435	.982
Players' League Totals			121	517	109	168	41	20	9	19	.325	1258	55	27	.980
Major League Totals			2373	9476	1601	2930	455	246	87	335	.309	23696	1304	462	.982

DAVID RUSSELL (GUS) BELL

Born November 15, 1928, at Louisville, Ky.
Height, 6.02. Weight, 196.
Threw right and batted lefthanded.
Married Joyce Sutherland, December 4, 1949.
Father of Buddy Bell, major league infielder.

Hit three consecutive home runs in a game, July 21, 1955 and May 29, 1956; hit for cycle, June 4, 1951.
Tied National League record for most consecutive years leading in fielding (2), 1958-59.
Scout, Cleveland Indians, 1966-69.

Year−Club	League	Pos.	G.	AB.	R.	H.	2B.	3B.	HR.	RBI.	B.A.	PO.	A.	E.	F.A.
1947−Keokuk	C. A.	OF	23	95	11	24	3	3	1	17	.253	24	6	0	1.000
1947−Leesburg	Fla. St.	OF	53	194	22	46	7	2	1	23	.237	122	5	5	.962
1948−Keokuk	C. A.	OF	128	502	86	160	27	★20	6	98	★.319	196	★19	10	.956
1949−Albany	East.	OF	134	535	100	★174	27	13	12	85	.325	283	14	14	.955
1950−Indianapolis	A. A.	OF	38	165	33	66	10	6	5	21	.400	73	8	2	.976
1950−Pittsburgh	Nat.	OF	111	422	62	119	22	11	8	53	.282	203	10	5	.977
1951−Pittsburgh	Nat.	OF	149	600	80	167	27	●12	16	89	.278	267	18	4	.986
1952−Hollywood	P. C.	OF	17	64	12	19	3	1	2	13	.297	31	4	1	.972
1952−Pittsburgh(a)	Nat.	OF	131	468	53	117	21	5	16	59	.250	202	8	6	.972
1953−Cincinnati	Nat.	OF	151	610	102	183	37	5	30	105	.300	447	16	★11	.977
1954−Cincinnati	Nat.	OF	153	619	104	185	38	7	17	101	.299	406	12	6	.986
1955−Cincinnati	Nat.	OF	●154	610	88	188	30	6	27	104	.308	364	4	5	.987
1956−Cincinnati	Nat.	OF	150	603	82	176	31	4	29	84	.292	330	12	5	.986
1957−Cincinnati	Nat.	OF	121	510	65	140	20	2	10	61	.292	311	7	4	.988
1958−Cincinnati	Nat.	OF	112	385	42	97	16	2	10	46	.252	235	7	1	★.995
1959−Cincinnati	Nat.	OF	148	580	59	170	27	2	19	115	.293	269	15	1	★.996
1960−Cincinnati	Nat.	OF	143	515	65	135	19	5	12	62	.262	239	13	3	.988
1961−Cincinnati(b)	Nat.	OF	103	235	27	60	10	1	3	33	.255	112	1	1	.991
1962−N.Y.(c)-Milw	Nat.	OF	109	315	36	76	13	3	6	30	.241	115	10	2	.984
1963−Milwaukee	Nat.	PH	23	3	0	1	0	0	0	0	.333	0	0	0	.000
1964−Milwaukee	Nat.	PH	3	3	0	0	0	0	0	0	.000	0	0	0	.000
Major League Totals			1741	6478	865	1823	311	66	206	942	.281	3500	133	54	.985

aTraded to Cincinnati Reds for catcher Joe Rossi and outfielders Cal Abrams and Gail Henley, October 15, 1952.
bSelected by New York Mets, October 10, 1961.
cSent to Milwaukee Braves, May 21, 1962.

WORLD SERIES RECORD

Year−Club	League	Pos.	G.	AB.	R.	H.	2B.	3B.	HR.	RBI.	B.A.	PO.	A.	E.	F.A.
1961−Cincinnati	Nat.	PH	3	3	0	0	0	0	0	0	.000	0	0	0	0

JAMES THOMAS (COOL PAPA) BELL

Born May 17, 1903, at Starkville, Miss.
Height, 6.00. Weight, 143.
Threw left and batted right and lefthanded.
Married Clarabelle Bell, September 8, 1928.
Named to Hall of Fame, 1974.

Cool Papa Bell is rated by most observers of both the white and Negro major leagues as the fastest base runner ever to wear a professional baseball uniform. He was such a student of pitching and on-base moves that situations became patent to him. A prime, documented example occurred when he played, at 45 years of age, in an exhibition game in California against major leaguers on an all-star type club, common in those days of post-season and winter barnstorming. The date: October 24, 1948, at Los Angeles, Calif.

To set the stage, Bell had been managing a second Kansas City Monarchs team, on which the Monarchs placed their young talent for Bell to develop. His pitcher for a while was Satchel Paige, who was nursing an ailing arm after chilling it in a cool breeze while playing Caribbean ball. After the season was over, Paige, who then had joined Cleveland, told Bell he'd help him make some money, on a percentage basis, from the sale of young players. But Paige was going out to the West Coast to pick up some fresh money by barnstorming and he asked Bell to come along, bring some of his best young players and play center field whenever he (Satch) pitched.

Bell begged off, protesting that he was out of playing condition, 45 years old, and working out only while he was coaching the kids and playing occasional league and World Series ball when needed by the Monarchs. That meant nothing to Satch, so Bell reluctantly agreed.

Paige headed westward first to line up some games and firm up the ones he already had scheduled. On meeting teammate Bob Lemon, Cleveland's pitching star, Satch told him, "I've got an old man, older than I am, I'm going to bring out to play against you and he's going to make a damn fool out of you." Lemon vowed no one would do that to him.

Bell, three years older than Paige, arrived in Los Angeles before the game. He had no throwing warmup at all. Cool Papa had to go into the outfield to scamper around and loosen up his aching bones. He told Satch to bat him low in the lineup because he was going to leave the game the minute Satch did. Bell batted eighth.

Facing Lemon the first time, Bell punched a low strike into right center for two bases following two brushback pitches. But the second time he faced Lemon, Bell lined out a single. With Paige up and Bell on first, they worked a sacrifice.

Paige dropped the ball down perfectly and the third baseman, pitcher, first baseman and catcher all converged plateward. Bell had watched Lemon on television and at Sportsman's Park in St. Louis many times and concentrated on his man-on-base motion, as all good base stealers do. He noticed that Lemon, once he had checked the base runner with a hard look, never looked back again. On the bunt, Bell saw the look and, when Lemon turned plateward, he took off for second which he made without a throw on him. But his trained eye noticed that third base was uncovered because the third baseman had failed to retreat after the bunt, and he kept on running.

Roy Partee, Red Sox and Browns catcher, was handling Lemon. He saw Bell heading for third unmolested and ran toward the bag trying to head him off. Bell peeked at Partee waving the ball and saw past him to the plate, which also was uncovered. So Bell coolly rounded third, eluded Partee easily and flew across home plate without a play being made on him the whole trip around the bases. Partee also had tried to call time out as Bell passed him and headed for home, but the umpire said there was no way he could do it with the ball in play.

Lemon was fit to be tied, but old Cool Papa had done it, aching muscles and all.

This incident bears out the mark of a true professional—one who has all his wits about him while in the heat of competition. This is the residue of years of practice, study and performance. When blessed with blinding speed, a consistently high batting average in Negro competition and a trigger-quick brain, all the elements for stardom were present. Then when you add the high level of morality he maintained and his constant care of his body by a sensible intake of food and abstinence from drinking, you can understand better how James (Cool Papa) Bell remained the scourge of catchers, pitchers and infielders throughout most of his 29 years as a professional player.

Bell is most proud of the fact his center field-expertise was recognized by the former master of the middle garden, Oscar Charleston, Oscar, playing center field for the Indianapolis ABCs at the time, saw the handwriting on the wall one day while both were out in center field in practice. Bell was pitching for San Juan at the time and played little in the outfield. Charleston had fungoes hit out there. Whoever got the ball first would catch it. Bell was there, catching it and in the act of throwing the ball back to the infield by the time Oscar arrived at the spot. This was the first time Bell had a chance to show he also could rank with the best center fielders of the time.

Cool Papa was born in Mississippi and played sandlot and semi-pro ball there, always competing with and against adults, never against youngsters his own age. He was a pitcher then, primarily, with a good curve and a devilish knuckler. Only his sister could hold his knuckler. He also played in the outfield and was rated a top versatile athlete. Four of his brothers had gone to St. Louis and played on the Compton Hills, a strong local semi-pro club, and they urged James to join them. At age 15, Bell went to St. Louis and then there were five Bells in action. The catchers refused to call for his knuckler because they were getting split fingers trying to corral it. Bell could make the knuckler break three ways, but they liked it no ways.

On May 3, 1922, at 16, Bell signed his first professional contract with the St. Louis Stars of the National League's Western Division. He signed at the urging of his older brother Lewis. James didn't have any wish to play professional ball, but his brother wanted him to sign so that he could say proudly he had a brother who played major league professional baseball.

Bell starred for the St. Louis club for 10 seasons, the first two of which were spent as a part-time pitcher. That first season, 1922, on a trip to Chicago to play the Giants, Bell discovered his reputation for speed had preceded him. When the Stars arrived, Rube Foster, organizer of the Negro professional leagues when "league" ball was revived in 1920 and owner-manager of the Chicago Giants, challenged Bell to race the fastest man in the league up to that time, his own Jimmy Lyons. Bell won handily and Foster purchased for Bell the best pair of spikes made then, a $21.50 (Spalding) kangaroo beauty.

In his first season of pro ball, Bell picked up the nickname of Cool Papa. "I had become 17 just 14 days after signing my contract and the players said I looked cool out there, so they called me Cool. The manager, Bob Gatewood, said that was not enough and added Papa. That's how I became Cool Papa."

It should be noted here that Cool Papa had a brother, Fred, two years older, who was an outstanding pitcher. He played about seven years and had the most fabulous throwing arm anyone ever saw. He could, in the opinion of Cool Papa, who is more straight-laced honest than a flock of angels, pitch faster what Satchel Paige at his best. Fred, six foot and rangy, pitched for Oscar Charleston on the Harrisburg (Pa.) Giants.

As the Depression dried up Negro league cash sources, the Pittsburgh Crawfords persuaded Bell to play for them in the Negro Eastern League, the other division. Cool Papa starred for them and then joined the Pittsburgh Homestead Grays, where he saw the younger Josh Gibson and Buck Leonard grow in stature.

As Leonard said, "Cool Papa was a veteran by that time, 1933, but he still could fly, still could run those bases like no one else and catch balls all over the outfield. He had a touch of arthritis by then and would get all tuckered out after a doubleheader, but he would recover fast and fly some more."

Then Leonard added, "Cool Papa also was our resident doctor—with all sorts of remedies for aches, pains, coughs and colds and even injuries. He was so doggoned talented, he even could shave while the bus was moving."

Bell was rated a solid .350 hitter and even gave away some of his percentage points to assure younger blacks the chance to be batting champions and thus rate a better shot at the white major leagues. That also included Bell giving up some batting championships of his own.

Cool Papa did some scouting after his playing and managing days were over, but his total reward (for Ernie Banks) was a basket of fruit. He became an employee of the City of St. Louis, working in City Hall until his retirement.

He still looks sharp—tall, lean, proud and vibrant. His proudest possession is his Hall of Fame ring.

"We just felt it wasn't the right time when we played," Cool Papa said on his visit to THE SPORTING NEWS, in 1979. "They said they'd sign a colored player when they found one good enough, and we kept on beating them regularly, out-hitting them and out-stealing them, but they signed nobody. That's why we knew it wasn't the right time yet. We knew it was coming, but we didn't know when. It was too late for me, but thank God I've lived for the day when I made the Hall of Fame. And that's a pure gift from white big league baseball and I appreciate it. And I thank Ted Williams for starting it all with his kind words the day he, too, entered the Hall of Fame."

CHARLES ALBERT (CHIEF) BENDER

Born May 5, 1884, at Brainerd, Minn.
Died May 22, 1954, at Philadelphia, Pa.
Height, 6.02. Weight, 185.
Threw and batted righthanded.
Married Marie Clements, October 3, 1904.

Pitched 4-0 no-hitter against Cleveland May 12, 1910, at Philadelphia; also pitched 3-0 no-hit game against Bridgeport, August 19, 1920.

Manager, Richmond, Virginia League, 1919; New Haven, Eastern League, 1920-21; Reading, International League, 1922; coach, Chicago White Sox, 1925-26; manager, Johnstown, Middle Atlantic League, second half of 1927 season; coached at U.S. Naval Academy, 1928 and then signed to manage Richmond of the Virginia League after close of school semester. Virginia League was to disband and plans to enter the club in the Piedmont League failed; coach, New York Giants, 1931; manager, Wilmington, Inter-State League, 1940; manager, Newport News, Virginia League, 1941; scout, Philadelphia Athletics, 1945; manager, Savannah, Sally League, 1946; scout, Philadelphia Athletics, 1947 through 1950; coach, Philadelphia Athletics, 1951-53.

Named to Hall of Fame, 1953.

Year	Club	League	G.	IP.	W.	L.	Pct.	H.	R.	ER.	SO.	BB.	ERA.
1903	Philadelphia	Amer.	36	270	17	15	.531	233	116	....	122	67	......
1904	Philadelphia	Amer.	29	205	10	11	.476	174	66	....	148	59	......
1905	Philadelphia	Amer.	35	230	18	11	.621	199	105	....	142	83	......
1906	Philadelphia	Amer.	36	240	15	10	.600	211	96	....	159	48	......
1907	Philadelphia	Amer.	33	222	16	8	.667	183	72	....	125	31	......
1908	Philadelphia	Amer.	18	139	8	9	.471	121	48	....	85	21	......
1909	Philadephia	Amer.	34	250	18	8	.692	196	68	....	162	45	......
1910	Philadelphia	Amer.	30	250	23	5	*.821	182	63	....	155	47	......
1911	Philadelphia	Amer.	31	216	17	5	*.773	198	66	....	114	58	......
1912	Philadelphia	Amer.	27	171	13	8	.619	169	63	....	90	33	......
1913	Philadelphia	Amer.	48	238	21	10	.667	208	78	58	135	59	2.19
1914	Philadelphia	Amer.	28	179	17	3	*.850	159	49	45	107	55	2.26
1915	Baltimore	Federal	26	179	4	16	.200	198	101	85	90	38	4.27
1916	Philadelphia	Nat.	27	123	7	7	.500	137	71	51	43	34	3.73
1917	Philadelphia	Nat.	20	113	8	2	.800	84	24	21	43	26	1.67
1918	—					(Voluntarily retired—worked in shipyards)							
1919	Richmond	Va.	34	*280	*29	2	*.935	209	53	....	*195	22	......
1920	New Haven	East.	*47	*324	*25	12	.676	256	104	70	252	71	1.94
1921	New Haven	East.	36	196	13	7	.650	168	70	42	131	59	1.93
1922	Reading	Inter.	30	183	8	13	.381	172	76	49	88	33	2.42
1923	Baltimore	Inter.	18	93	6	3	.667	109	65	52	44	30	5.03
1924	New Haven	East.	12	91	6	4	.600	94	38	31	55	18	3.07

Year	Club	League	G.	IP.	W.	L.	Pct.	H.	R.	ER.	SO.	BB.	ERA.
1925–Chicago		Amer.	1	1	0	0	.000	1	2	2	0	1	18.00
1927–Johnstown		Mid. Atlantic	18	108	7	3	.700	74	18	16	39	13	1.33
American League Totals			386	2611	193	103	.652	2234	982	....	1544	607	......
National League Totals			47	236	15	9	.625	221	95	72	86	60	2.75
Major League Totals			433	2847	208	112	.650	2455	987	....	1630	667	......

WORLD SERIES TOTALS

Year	Club	League	G.	IP.	W.	L.	Pct.	H.	R.	ER.	SO.	BB.	ERA.
1905–Philadelphia		Amer.	2	17	1	1	.500	9	2	2	13	6	1.06
1910–Philadelphia		Amer.	2	18⅔	1	1	.500	12	5	4	14	4	1.93
1911–Philadelphia		Amer.	3	26	2	1	.667	16	6	3	20	8	1.04
1913–Philadelphia		Amer.	2	18	2	0	1.000	19	9	8	9	1	4.00
1914–Philadelphia		Amer.	1	5⅓	0	1	.000	8	6	6	3	2	10.13
World Series Totals			10	85	6	4	.600	64	28	23	59	21	2.44

WALTER ANTONE (WALLY) BERGER

Born October 10, 1905, at Chicago, Ill.

Height, 6.03. Weight, 205.

Threw and batted righthanded.

Married Martha Subzhak, April 19, 1942.

Holds the following Boston Braves records: Most home runs, season (38), 1930 (rookie season); most extra bases on long hits (169), 1930, and most runs batted in, season (130), 1935.
Named as outfielder on THE SPORTING NEWS All-Star Major League Team, 1933.
Manager, Manchester, New England League, 1949.

Year	Club	League	Pos.	G.	AB.	R.	H.	2B.	3B.	HR.	RBI.	B.A.	PO.	A.	E.	F.A.
1927–Pocatello		Ut.-Ida.	OF	92	361	73	139	21	8	24	.....	•.385	★223	16	7	.972
1927–Los Angeles		Pac. C'st	OF	14	63	7	23	2	0	3	.....	.365	21	3	1	.960
1928–Los Angeles		Pac. C'st	OF	138	535	94	175	34	7	20	94	.327	310	12	12	.964
1929–Los Angeles		Pac. C'st	OF	199	744	170	249	41	5	40	166	.335	449	16	13	.973
1930–Boston		Nat.	OF	151	555	98	172	27	14	38	119	.310	307	10	11	.966
1931–Boston		Nat.	OF	•156	617	94	199	44	8	19	84	.323	457	16	11	.977
1932–Boston		Nat.	1B-OF	145	602	90	185	34	6	17	73	.307	498	14	3	★.994
1933–Boston		Nat.	OF	137	528	84	165	37	8	27	106	.313	382	6	9	.977
1934–Boston		Nat.	OF	150	615	92	183	35	8	34	121	.298	385	9	9	.978
1935–Boston		Nat.	OF	150	589	91	174	39	4	★34	★130	.295	★458	8	★17	.965
1936–Boston		Nat.	OF	138	534	88	154	23	3	25	91	.288	384	10	14	.966
1937–Boston(a)-N.Y.		Nat.	OF	89	312	54	89	20	3	17	65	.285	158	5	4	.976
1938–N.Y.(b)-Cin.		Nat.	OF	115	439	79	131	23	4	16	60	.298	221	7	7	.970
1939–Cincinnati		Nat.	OF	97	329	36	85	15	1	14	44	.258	158	6	5	.970
1940–Cin.(c)-Phila.		Nat.	OF	22	43	3	13	2	0	1	5	.302	18	0	1	.947
1940–Indianapolis		A. Assn.	PH	41	155	27	38	8	1	5	19	.245	104	1	3	.972
1941–Los Angeles		P. C.	1B-OF	59	141	19	34	7	0	8	18	.241	68	4	4	.947
Major League Totals				1350	5163	809	1550	299	59	242	898	.300	3426	91	91	.975

aTraded to New York Giants for pitcher Frank Gabler and $35,000, June 15, 1937.
bTraded to Cincinnati Reds for second baseman Alex Kampouris, June 6, 1938.
cUnconditionally released by Cincinnati Reds, 1940; signed with Philadelphia Phillies.

WORLD SERIES RECORD

Year	Club	League	Pos.	G.	AB.	R.	H.	2B.	3B.	HR.	RBI.	B.A.	PO.	A.	E.	F.A.
1937–New York		Nat.	OF	3	3	0	0	0	0	0	0	.000	0	0	0	.000
1939–Cincinnati		Nat.	OF	4	15	0	0	0	0	0	1	.000	8	0	0	1.000
World Series Totals				7	18	0	0	0	0	0	1	.000	8	0	0	1.000

LAWRENCE PETER (YOGI) BERRA

Born May 12, 1925, at St. Louis, Mo.

Height, 5.08. Weight, 191.

Threw right and batted lefthanded.

Married Carmen Short, January 26, 1949.

Tied American League record for most home runs by catcher, season (30), 1952 and 1956.
Holds major league record for most consecutive chances accepted by catcher without an error (950), July

28, 1957 through May 10, 1959; also holds major league mark for catchers by playing 148 consecutive games without an error, July 28, 1957 through May 10, 1959.

American League record holder for most putouts by catcher in a league, lifetime (8,696); also holds league mark for most chances accepted, lifetime (9,493).

Tied major league record for making unassisted double play as catcher in game against St. Louis Browns, June 15, 1947; accomplished feat second time against Kansas City Athletics, August 17, 1962.

Led American League catchers in double plays, 1949-50-51-52-54-56–tying major league record.

Holds following World Series records: Most Series played (14); most games (75); most times on winning team (10); most at-bats (259); most hits (71); most one-base hits (49); most Series played by catchers (12); most games caught (63); most putouts by catcher (457); most Series, one or more runs batted in (11).

Tied for the following World Series records: First player to hit pinch home run in World Series, October 2, 1947; hit home run with bases loaded, second inning, October 5, 1956–which also gave him a tie for most runs batted in, inning (4); made one or more hits in a game, seven-game Series, 1955; hit by pitcher twice in a game, October 2, 1953; most two-base hits, total Series (10).

Named Most Valuable Player, American League, 1951-54-55.

Named as catcher on THE SPORTING NEWS All-Star Major League Teams, 1950-52-54-56.

Manager, New York Yankees, 1964; player-coach, New York Mets, 1965; coach only, 1966-71; manager, 1972-75; coach, New York Yankees, 1976 to date.

Named to Hall of Fame, 1972.

Year	Club	League	Pos.	G.	AB.	R.	H.	2B.	3B.	HR.	RBI.	B.A.	PO.	A.	E.	F.A.
1943	Norfolk	Pied.	C	111	376	52	95	17	8	7	56	.253	★480	75	★16	.972
1944-45	Kansas City	A. A.						(In Military Service)								
1946	Newark	Int.	C-OF	77	277	41	87	14	1	15	59	.314	344	45	11	.973
1946	New York	Amer.	C	7	22	3	8	1	0	2	4	.364	28	6	0	1.000
1947	New York	Amer.	C-OF	83	293	41	82	15	3	11	54	.280	307	18	9	.973
1948	New York	Amer.	C-OF	125	469	70	143	24	10	14	98	.305	390	40	9	.979
1949	New York	Amer.	C	116	415	59	115	20	2	20	91	.277	544	60	7	.989
1950	New York	Amer.	C	151	597	116	192	30	6	28	124	.322	★777	●64	13	.985
1951	New York	Amer.	C	141	547	92	161	19	4	27	88	.294	★693	★82	●13	.984
1952	New York	Amer.	C	142	534	97	146	17	1	30	98	.273	★700	★73	6	.992
1953	New York	Amer.	C	137	503	80	149	23	5	27	108	.296	566	64	9	.986
1954	New York	Amer.	★C-3B	151	584	88	179	28	6	22	125	.307	★718	64	8	.990
1955	New York	Amer.	C	147	541	84	147	20	3	27	108	.272	★721	54	★13	.984
1956	New York	Amer.	★C-OF	140	521	93	155	29	2	30	105	.298	★733	57	★11	.986
1957	New York	Amer.	★C-OF	134	482	74	121	14	2	24	82	.251	★707	61	4	★.995
1958	New York	Amer.	★C-OF-1B	122	433	60	115	17	3	22	90	.266	558	44	2	.997
1959	New York	Amer.	★C-OF	131	472	64	134	25	1	19	69	.284	★706	62	4	★.995
1960	New York	Amer.	C-OF	120	359	46	99	14	1	15	62	.276	312	24	5	.985
1961	New York	Amer.	OF-C	119	395	62	107	11	0	22	61	.271	237	15	2	.992
1962	New York	Amer.	C-OF	86	232	25	52	8	0	10	35	.224	238	17	6	.977
1963	New York	Amer.	C	64	147	20	43	6	0	8	28	.293	244	13	3	.988
1964	New York(a)	Amer.					(Did not play–served as manager.)									
1965	New York	Nat.	C	4	9	1	2	0	0	0	0	.222	15	1	1	.941
American League Totals				2116	7546	1174	2148	321	49	358	1430	.285	9179	818	124	.988
National League Totals				4	9	1	2	0	0	0	0	.222	15	1	1	.941
Major League Totals				2120	7555	1175	2150	321	49	358	1430	.285	9194	819	125	.988

aReleased by New York Yankees, October 16, 1964.

WORLD SERIES RECORD

Year	Club	League	Pos.	G.	AB.	R.	H.	2B.	3B.	HR.	RBI.	B.A.	PO.	A.	E.	F.A.
1947	New York	Amer.	C-OF	6	19	2	3	0	0	1	2	.158	21	2	2	.920
1949	New York	Amer.	C	4	16	2	1	0	0	1	1	.063	37	3	0	1.000
1950	New York	Amer.	C	4	15	2	3	0	0	1	2	.200	30	1	0	1.000
1951	New York	Amer.	C	6	23	4	6	1	0	0	0	.261	27	3	1	.968
1952	New York	Amer.	C	7	28	2	6	1	0	2	3	.214	59	7	1	.985
1953	New York	Amer.	C	6	21	3	9	1	0	1	4	.429	36	3	0	1.000
1955	New York	Amer.	C	7	24	5	10	1	0	1	2	.417	40	4	0	1.000
1956	New York	Amer.	C	7	25	5	9	2	0	3	10	.360	50	3	0	1.000
1957	New York	Amer.	C	7	25	5	8	1	0	1	2	.320	44	2	1	.979
1958	New York	Amer.	C	7	27	3	6	3	0	0	2	.222	60	6	0	1.000
1960	New York	Amer.	C-OF-PH	7	22	6	7	0	0	1	8	.318	18	1	0	1.000
1961	New York	Amer.	OF	4	11	2	3	0	0	1	3	.273	11	0	1	.917
1962	New York	Amer.	C	2	2	0	0	0	0	0	0	.000	6	1	0	1.000
1963	New York	Amer.	PH	1	1	0	0	0	0	0	0	.000	0	0	0	.000
World Series Totals				75	259	41	71	10	0	12	39	.274	439	36	6	.988

FRANCIS RAYMOND (RAY) BLADES

Born August 6, 1896, at Mt. Vernon, Ill.

Died May 18, 1979, at Lincoln, Ill.

Height, 5.07½. Weight, 180.

Threw and batted righthanded.

Married Golda Marie Bennett, October 29, 1924.

Had seven putouts, right field, October 5, 1930, World Series game (St. Louis N. L., vs. Philadelphia A. L.). Manager, Columbus, American Association, 1933 through '35; manager, Rochester, International, 1936 through 1938; manager, St. Louis Cardinals, 1939 through June 8, 1940; manager, New Orleans, Southern Association, 1941 and second half in 1943; coach, Cincinnati Reds, 1942; manager, St. Paul, American Association, 1944 through 1946; coach, Brooklyn Dodgers, 1947-48; coach, St. Louis Cardinals, 1951; coach-scout, Chicago Cubs, 1953, and coach only 1954 through 1956.

Year	Club	League	Pos.	G.	AB.	R.	H.	2B.	3B.	HR.	RBI.	B.A.	PO.	A.	E.	F.A.
1920	Memphis	So.	1B-SS-OF	140	435	50	110	15	7	0	....	.253	276	272	60	.901
1921	Houston	Tex.	*2B-SS	158	515	98	143	25	11	9	69	.278	417	420	*78	.916
1922	Houston	Tex.	*2B-SS	118	409	82	135	19	*20	9	57	.330	311	286	*53	.924
1922	St. Louis	Nat.	INF-OF	37	130	27	39	2	4	3	21	.300	61	6	5	.931
1923	St. Louis	Nat.	3B-OF	98	317	48	78	21	5	5	44	.246	194	11	7	.967
1924	St. Louis	Nat.	3B-OF	131	456	86	142	21	13	11	68	.311	256	6	12	.956
1925	St. Louis	Nat.	OF	122	462	112	158	37	8	12	57	.342	266	13	6	.979
1926	St. Louis	Nat.	OF	107	416	81	127	17	12	8	43	.305	229	10	5	.980
1927	St. Louis	Nat.	OF	61	180	33	57	8	5	2	29	.317	64	0	6	.914
1928	St. Louis	Nat.	OF	51	85	9	20	7	1	1	19	.235	34	1	1	.972
1929	Houston	Tex.	OF	24	69	8	19	6	1	0	14	.275	21	1	0	1.000
1929	Rochester	Int.	OF	31	48	8	7	1	2	0	2	.146	15	1	2	.889
1930	St. Louis	Nat.	OF	45	101	26	40	6	2	4	25	.396	66	1	3	.957
1931	St. Louis	Nat.	OF	35	67	10	19	4	0	1	5	.284	26	1	4	.871
1932	St. Louis	Nat.	OF	80	201	35	46	10	1	3	29	.229	117	2	3	.975
1933	Columbus	A. A.	OF	62	149	35	43	9	2	3	20	.289	85	4	4	.957
1934	Columbus	A. A.	OF	63	140	18	37	6	1	0	20	.264	79	3	3	.965
Major League Totals				767	2415	467	726	133	51	50	340	.301	1313	51	52	.963

WORLD SERIES RECORD

Year	Club	League	Pos.	G.	AB.	R.	H.	2B.	3B.	HR.	RBI.	B.A.	PO.	A.	E.	F.A.
1928	St. Louis	Nat.	PH	1	1	0	0	0	0	0	0	.000	0	0	0	.000
1930	St. Louis	Nat.	OF-PH	5	9	2	1	0	0	0	0	.111	10	0	0	1.000
1931	St. Louis	Nat.	PH	2	2	0	0	0	0	0	0	.000	0	0	0	.000
World Series Totals				8	12	2	1	0	0	0	0	.083	10	0	0	1.000

THOMAS HENRY BOND

Born April 2, 1856, at New York, N. Y.
Died January 24, 1941, at Boston, Mass.
Height, 5.7½. Weight, 165.
Threw and batted righthanded.
Married Louise G. Siebert, December 18, 1879.

Umpire, New England League, 1882-83.

Year	Club	League	G.	H.	R.	W.	L.	Pct.	ShO.
1876	Hartford	National	45	357	164	32	13	.711	6
1877	Boston	National	●49	460	221	*31	17	*.646	●4
1878	Boston	National	*59	571	239	*40	19	*.678	*9
1879	Boston	National	62	554	216	42	19	.689	*12
1880	Boston	National	56	541	282	26	29	.473	3
1881	Boston	National	3	40	17	0	3	.000	0
1882	Worcester	National	2	10	10	0	1	.000	0
1884	Boston	Union Assoc.	23	185	120	12	9	.571	0
1884	Indianapolis	Amer. Assoc.	5	62	51	0	5	.000	0
National League Totals			276	2533	1149	171	101	.629	34
Union Assoc. Total			23	185	120	12	9	.571	0
American Assoc. Totals			5	62	51	0	5	.000	0
Major League Totals			304	2780	1320	183	115	.614	34

JAMES LEROY (SUNNY JIM) BOTTOMLEY

Born April 23, 1900, at Oglesby, Ill.
Died December 11, 1959, at St. Louis, Mo.
Height, 6.00. Weight, 175.
Threw and batted lefthanded.
Married Betty Browner, February 4, 1933.

Set major league single-game record of 12 runs batted in with six hits, September 16, 1924, against the

Brooklyn Dodgers; also made six hits in six times at bat, August 5, 1931; hit seven home runs in five consecutive games, July 5, 6, 6, 8, 9, 1929; lost batting championship in closest batting race in the National League, 1931, when he finished with a mark of .3482 for a third-place finish, while Chick Hafey topped the league with a .3489 mark and Bill Terry finished second with .3486; had seven unassisted double plays at first base, 1924. Led N. L. first basemen in double plays, 1925, 1927.

Named Most Valuable Player, National League, 1928. Named as first baseman on THE SPORTING NEWS All-Star Major League Team, 1925.

Manager, St. Louis Browns, July 22, 1937, to end of season; manager, Syracuse, International League, 1938; scout, Chicago Cubs, 1957, until named manager, Pulaski, Appalachian League, that season.

Named to Hall of Fame, 1974.

Year	Club	League	Pos.	G.	AB.	R.	H.	2B.	3B.	HR.	RBI.	B.A.	PO.	A.	E.	F.A.
1920	Sioux City	West.	1B	6	14	0	1	0	0	0	0	.071	35	1	0	1.000
1920	Mitchell	S. Dak.	1B	•97	378	69	118	....	....	7	....	.312	•1110	37	15	*.987
1921	Houston	Tex.	1B-2B	130	459	50	104	16	5	4	62	.227	1114	59	•27	.978
1922	Syracuse	Int.	1B	119	460	78	160	29	15	14	94	.348	1245	61	10	.992
1922	St. Louis	Nat.	1B	37	151	29	49	8	5	5	35	.325	346	12	5	.986
1923	St. Louis	Nat.	1B	134	523	79	194	34	14	8	94	.371	1264	43	18	.986
1924	St. Louis	Nat.	1B	137	528	87	167	31	12	14	111	.316	1297	48	*24	.982
1925	St. Louis	Nat.	1B	•153	619	92	*227	*44	12	21	128	.367	*1466	74	*21	.987
1926	St. Louis	Nat.	1B	154	603	98	180	*40	14	19	*120	.299	1607	54	*19	.989
1927	St. Louis	Nat.	1B	152	574	95	174	31	15	19	124	.303	*1656	70	20	.989
1928	St. Louis	Nat.	1B	149	576	123	187	42	*20	•31	*136	.325	1454	52	•20	.987
1929	St. Louis	Nat.	1B	146	560	108	176	31	12	29	137	.314	1347	75	13	.991
1930	St. Louis	Nat.	1B	131	487	92	148	33	7	15	97	.304	1164	41	12	.990
1931	St. Louis	Nat.	1B	108	382	73	133	34	5	9	75	.348	897	43	12	.987
1932	St. Louis (a)	Nat.	1B	91	311	45	92	16	3	11	48	.296	662	41	10	.986
1933	Cincinnati	Nat.	1B	145	549	57	137	23	9	13	83	.250	1511	72	15	.991
1934	Cincinnati	Nat.	1B	142	556	72	158	31	11	11	78	.284	1303	77	15	.989
1935	Cincinnati (b)	Nat.	1B	107	399	44	103	21	1	1	49	.258	934	53	8	.992
1936	St. Louis	Amer.	1B	140	544	72	162	39	11	12	95	.298	1250	47	10	.992
1937	St. Louis (c)	Amer.	1B	65	109	11	26	7	0	1	12	.239	179	12	1	.995
1938	Syracuse	Int.	1B	7	14	0	1	0	0	0	0	.071	31	0	1	.969
	American League Totals			205	653	83	188	46	11	13	107	.288	1429	59	11	.993
	National League Totals			1786	6818	1094	2125	419	140	206	1315	.312	16908	755	212	.988
	Major League Totals			1991	7471	1177	2313	465	151	219	1422	.310	18337	814	223	.988

aTraded to Cincinnati Reds for pitcher Owen Carroll and outfielder Estel Crabtree, December 17, 1932.
bTraded to St. Louis Browns for infielder John Burnett, March 21, 1936.
cUnconditionally released by St. Louis Browns, November 19, 1937.

WORLD SERIES RECORD

Year	Club	League	Pos.	G.	AB.	R.	H.	2B.	3B.	HR.	RBI.	B.A.	PO.	A.	E.	F.A.
1926	St. Louis	National	1B	7	29	4	10	3	0	0	5	.345	79	1	0	1.000
1928	St. Louis	National	1B	4	14	1	3	0	1	1	3	.214	36	2	0	1.000
1930	St. Louis	National	1B	6	22	1	1	1	0	0	0	.045	58	2	0	1.000
1931	St. Louis	National	1B	7	25	2	4	1	0	0	2	.160	61	2	1	.984
	World Series Totals			24	90	8	18	5	1	1	10	.200	234	7	1	.996

LOUIS BOUDREAU

Born July 17, 1917, at Harvey, Ill.
Height, 5:11. Weight, 193.
Threw and batted righthanded.
Married Dela Elizabeth DeRuiter, June 5, 1938.

Led A. L. shortstops in fielding eight seasons, for a tie of major league record; led A. L. shortstops in putouts four seasons, tying league mark; held major league record for most double plays by shortstop, season (134), 1944; led A. L. shortstops in double plays five seasons, 1940-43-44-47-48; had 4 doubles, one home run in 5 times at bat, July 14, 1944, first game.

Named Most Valuable American League Player, 1948.
Named Major League Player of the Year by THE SPORTING NEWS, 1948.
Named as shortstop on THE SPORTING NEWS All-Star Major League Teams, 1947-48.
Tied World Series mark for highest fielding percentage by shortstop (1.000), 1948.
Manager, Cleveland Indians, 1942 through 1950; manager, Boston Red Sox, 1952 through 1954; manager, Kansas City Athletics, 1955 through 1957; manager, Chicago Cubs, May 5, 1960, and released October 4, same season.

As leader of Indians in first playoff in A. L. history, 1948, he had 4-for-4, including two home runs, in the 8-3 victory over the Boston Red Sox.

As World Series manager, he led Indians to victory, with bat and glove, over Boston Braves, four games to two, in 1948.

Named to Hall of Fame, 1970.

Year–Club	League	Pos.	G.	AB.	R.	H.	2B.	3B.	HR.	RBI.	B.A.	PO.	A.	E.	F.A.
1938–Cedar Rapids	I.I.I.	3B	60	231	56	67	13	4	3	29	.290	74	128	14	.935
1938–Cleveland	Amer.	3B	1	1	0	0	0	0	0	0	.000	0	0	0	.000
1939–Buffalo	Int.	SS	115	481	88	159	32	7	17	57	.331	234	371	38	.941
1939–Cleveland	Amer.	SS	53	225	42	58	15	4	0	19	.258	103	184	14	.953
1940–Cleveland	Amer.	SS	155	627	97	185	46	10	9	101	.295	277	*454	24	*.968
1941–Cleveland	Amer.	SS	148	579	95	149	*45	8	10	56	.257	*296	444	26	*.966
1942–Cleveland	Amer.	SS	147	506	57	143	18	10	2	58	.283	281	426	26	*.965
1943–Cleveland	Amer.	*SS-C	152	539	69	154	32	7	3	67	.286	*331	489	25	*.970
1944–Cleveland	Amer.	*SS-C	150	584	91	191	*45	5	3	67	*.327	*340	*517	19	*.978
1945–Cleveland	Amer.	SS	97	345	50	106	24	1	3	48	.307	217	289	9	.983
1946–Cleveland	Amer.	SS	140	515	51	151	30	6	6	62	.293	*315	405	22	*.970
1947–Cleveland	Amer.	SS	150	538	79	165	*45	3	4	67	.307	305	475	14	*.982
1948–Cleveland	Amer.	*SS-C	152	560	116	199	34	6	18	106	.355	297	483	20	*.975
1949–Cleveland	Amer.	INF	134	475	53	135	20	3	4	60	.284	253	353	12	.981
1950–Cleveland(a)	Amer.	INF	81	260	23	70	13	2	1	29	.269	156	176	4	.988
1951–Boston	Amer.	INF	82	273	37	73	18	1	5	47	.267	94	181	15	.948
1952–Boston	Amer.	SS-3B	4	2	1	0	0	0	0	2	.000	0	1	0	1.000
Major League Totals			1646	6029	861	1779	385	66	68	789	.295	3265	4877	230	.973

aUnconditionally released by Cleveland Indians, November 22, 1950; signed with Boston Red Sox, November 27, 1950.

WORLD SERIES RECORD

Year–Club	League	Pos.	G.	AB.	R.	H.	2B.	3B.	HR.	RBI.	B.A.	PO.	A.	E.	F.A.
1948–Cleveland	Amer.	SS	6	22	1	6	4	0	0	0	.273	11	14	0	1.000

KENTON LLOYD BOYER

Born May 20, 1931, at Liberty, Mo.

Height, 6.02. Weight, 208.

Threw and batted righthanded.

Brother of Cletis and Cloyd, former major leaguers
and Len and Ron, former minor leaguers.

Tied major league mark for most years leading third basemen in double plays (5), 1962; tied National League mark for most consecutive games, no putouts, by third baseman (8), August 4 through 11, 1963; tied National League record for most games played by third baseman, season (162), 1964.

Led National League third basemen in double plays with 37 in 1956, 41 in 1958, 32 in 1959, 37 in 1960 and 34 in 1962.

Hit home run with bases full in World Series, October 11, 1964, sixth inning–tying Series record for most runs batted in, inning, 4.

Named as third baseman on THE SPORTING NEWS All-Star Major League Team, 1956, and on THE SPORTING NEWS National League All-Star Team, 1961-62-63-64.

Named Major League Player of the Year by THE SPORTING NEWS, 1964.

Named Most Valuable Player in National League, 1964.

Received Rawlings Gold Glove award as outstanding National League fielder at third base, 1958-59-60-61-63.

Signed as minor league instructor, St. Louis Cardinals, in November of 1969, but later signed to manage St. Louis farm team, Arkansas, Texas League, 1970; coach, St. Louis Cardinals, 1971-72; retained as minor league instructor, then became non-playing manager, Sarasota, Gulf Coast League, 1973; Manager, Tulsa, American Association, 1974-76; manager, Rochester, International League, 1977; manager, St. Louis Cardinals, 1978 to June 8, 1980.

Year–Club	League	Pos.	G.	AB.	R.	H.	2B.	3B.	HR.	RBI.	B.A.	PO.	A.	E.	F.A.
1949–Lebanon	N. Atl.	P	16	33	10	15	1	1	3	9	.455	4	10	5	.737
1950–Hamilton	Pony	3-P-O	80	240	41	82	17	6	9	61	.342	55	89	10	.935
1951–Omaha	West.	3B	151	565	87	173	28	7	14	90	.306	*154	231	●33	.921
1952-53–Houston	Tex.					(In Military Service)									
1954–Houston	Tex.	3B	159	634	116	202	42	7	21	116	.319	145	333	*39	.925
1955–St. Louis	Nat.	3B-SS	147	530	78	140	27	2	18	62	.264	155	295	21	.955
1956–St. Louis	Nat.	3B	150	595	91	182	30	2	26	98	.306	130	*309	18	.961
1957–St. Louis	Nat.	*OF-3B	142	544	79	144	18	3	19	62	.265	316	95	14	*.966
1958–St. Louis	Nat.	*3-OF-S	150	570	101	175	21	9	23	90	.307	*168	350	20	.963
1959–St. Louis	Nat.	3B-SS	149	563	86	174	18	5	28	94	.309	143	310	22	.954
1960–St. Louis	Nat.	3B	151	552	95	168	26	10	32	97	.304	140	300	19	.959
1961–St. Louis	Nat.	3B	153	589	109	194	26	11	24	95	.329	117	*346	24	.951
1962–St. Louis	Nat.	3B	160	611	92	178	27	5	24	98	.291	158	318	22	.956
1963–St. Louis	Nat.	3B	159	617	86	176	28	2	24	111	.285	129	293	*34	.925
1964–St. Louis	Nat.	3B	162	628	100	185	30	10	24	*119	.295	131	337	24	.951
1965–St. Louis (a)	Nat.	3B	144	535	71	139	18	2	13	75	.260	113	250	12	*.968
1966–New York	Nat.	3B-1B	136	496	62	132	28	2	14	61	.266	125	294	21	.952
1967–New York (b)	Nat.	3B-1B	56	166	17	39	7	2	3	13	.235	79	87	6	.965
1967–Chicago	Amer.	3B-1B	57	180	17	47	5	1	4	21	.261	154	79	5	.979

Year	Club	League	Pos.	G.	AB.	R.	H.	2B.	3B.	HR.	RBI.	B.A.	PO.	A.	E.	F.A.
1968–Chicago (c)		Amer.	3B-1B	10	24	0	3	0	0	0	0	.125	12	8	1	.952
1968–Los Angeles		Nat.	3B-1B	83	221	20	60	7	2	6	41	.271	279	64	10	.972
1969–Los Angeles		Nat.	1B	25	34	0	7	2	0	0	4	.206	31	2	1	.971
National League Totals				1967	7251	1087	2093	313	67	278	1120	.289	2214	3650	268	.956
American League Totals				67	204	17	50	5	1	4	21	.245	166	87	6	.977
Major League Totals				2034	7455	1104	2143	318	68	282	1141	.287	2380	3737	274	.957

aTraded to New York Mets for third baseman Charlie Smith and pitcher Al Jackson, October 20, 1965.

bTraded to Chicago White Sox for cash and infielder Billy Southworth (transferred from Evansville to Williamsport), July 22. As part of deal White Sox obtained infielder Santos Alomar from New York Mets, August 15, 1967, and White Sox sent catcher J. C. Martin to Mets, November 27, 1967.

cReleased by Chicago White Sox, May 2, 1968; signed by Los Angeles Dodgers, May 10, 1968.

WORLD SERIES RECORD

Year	Club	League	Pos.	G.	AB.	R.	H.	2B.	3B.	HR.	RBI.	B.A.	PO.	A.	E.	F.A.
1964–St. Louis		National	3B	7	27	5	6	1	0	2	6	.222	9	16	1	.962

PITCHING RECORD

Year	Club	League	G.	IP.	W.	L.	Pct.	H.	R.	ER.	SO.	BB.	ERA.
1949–Lebanon		N. Atl.	12	71	5	1	.833	57	35	27	32	34	3.42
1950–Hamilton		Pony	21	121	6	8	.429	117	76	59	43	71	4.39

ROGER PHILLIP (DUKE) BRESNAHAN

Born June 11, 1879, at Toledo, O.
Died December 4, 1944, at Toledo, O.
Height, 5.08. Weight, 180.
Threw and batted righthanded.

In first major league game, August 27, 1897, pitched and won over St. Louis, 3-0, allowing six hits, one a double, one base on balls and one strikeout.

Manager, St. Louis Cardinals, 1909 through 1912; manager, Chicago Cubs, 1915; manager and owner, Toledo, American Association, 1916 through 1923; coach, New York Giants, 1925 through 1928; coach, Detroit Tigers, 1930-31.

Named to Hall of Fame, 1945.

Year	Club	League	Pos.	G.	AB.	R.	H.	2B.	3B.	HR.	SB.	B.A.	PO.	A.	E.	F.A.
1897–Washington		Nat.	P	7	18	2	6	0	0	0	0	.333	2	8	0	1.000
1898–Toledo		Int.-State	P	4	12	0	5	3	0	0	0	.417	1	3	1	.800
1899–Minneapolis		West.	P-C	3	1	0	1	0	1	0	0	1.000	1	5	1	.857
1900–Chicago		Nat.	C	1	2	0	0	0	0	0	0	.000	0	0	0	.000
1901–Baltimore(a)		Amer.	P-C	86	293	40	77	9	9	1	10	.263	193	69	20	.929
1902–Baltimore(b)		Amer.	C-3-O	66	234	31	64	9	6	4	11	.274	141	72	20	.914
1902–New York		Nat.	C-INF	50	178	16	52	13	3	1	6	.292	113	25	8	.945
1903–New York		Nat.	OF	111	406	87	142	30	8	4	34	.350	150	14	6	.965
1904–New York		Nat.	OF	107	402	81	114	21	8	5	13	.284	151	14	8	.954
1905–New York		Nat.	C	95	331	58	100	18	3	0	11	.302	492	114	19	.970
1906–New York		Nat.	C-OF	124	405	69	114	22	4	0	25	.281	478	131	17	.973
1907–New York		Nat.	C	104	328	57	83	9	7	4	15	.253	483	94	8	.986
1908–New York(c)		Nat.	C	139	449	70	127	25	3	1	14	.283	*657	140	12	.985
1909–St. Louis		Nat.	C	69	234	27	57	4	1	0	11	.244	211	78	12	.960
1910–St. Louis		Nat.	C	78	234	35	65	15	3	0	13	.278	295	100	16	.961
1911–St. Louis		Nat.	C	78	227	22	63	17	8	3	4	.278	325	102	14	.968
1912–St. Louis		Nat.	C	48	108	8	36	7	2	1	4	.333	138	49	5	.974
1913–Chicago(d)		Nat.	C	69	162	20	37	5	2	0	7	.228	194	67	10	.963
1914–Chicago		Nat.	C	101	248	42	69	10	4	0	14	.278	365	113	11	.978
1915–Chicago		Nat.	C	77	221	19	45	8	1	1	19	.204	345	95	8	.982
1916–Toledo		A. A.	C	44	120	19	29	6	1	2	4	.242	95	13	0	1.000
1917–Toledo		A. A.	C	40	80	10	22	5	0	0	1	.275	67	20	3	.967
1918–Toledo		A. A.	C	19	52	4	12	2	0	1	0	.231	24	1	1	.962
National League Totals				1258	3953	613	1110	204	57	21	190	.281	4399	1144	154	.973
American League Totals				152	527	71	141	18	15	5	21	.268	334	141	40	.922
Major League Totals				1410	4480	684	1251	222	72	26	211	.279	4733	1285	194	.969

aJumped to American League.

bJumped with John McGraw, catcher Frank Bowerman and pitchers Joe McGinnity and John Cronin to New York Giants, July 6, 1902.

cTraded to St. Louis Cardinals for pitcher Bugs Raymond, outfielder John Murray and catcher George Schlei, December, 1908, Cardinals getting Schlei from Cincinnati for pitchers Art Fromme and Eddie Karger.

dPurchased by Chicago Cubs, June 8, 1913, after prolonged contract squabble with St. Louis club, which had attempted to release him in October, 1912, without asking waivers.

PITCHING RECORD

Year	Club	League	G.	W.	L.	Pct.	SO.	BB.	H.
1897—Washington		National	7	4	0	1.000	12	8	52
1898—Toledo		Inter-State	4	2	2	.500	11	8	40
1899—Minneapolis		Western	3	0	2	.000	5	8	....
1901—Baltimore		American	1	0	0	.000	4	0	10
1910—St. Louis		National	1	0	0	.000	0	1	6
American League Totals			1	0	0	.000	4	0	10
National League Totals			8	4	0	1.000	12	8	58
Major League Totals			9	4	0	1.000	16	8	68

WORLD SERIES RECORD

Year	Club	League	Pos.	G.	AB.	R.	H.	2B.	3B.	HR.	SB.	B.A.	PO.	A.	E.	F.A.
1905—New York		Nat.	C	5	16	3	5	2	0	0	1	.313	27	7	0	1.000

RAYMOND BLOOM (RUBE) BRESSLER

Born October 10, 1894, at Brookville, Pa.
Died November 7, 1966, at Mt. Washington, O.
Height, 6.00. Weight, 190.
Threw left and batted righthanded.
Married Helen F. Kopf, April 14, 1923.

Manager, Springfield, Middle Atlantic, 1934.

Year	Club	League	Pos.	G.	AB.	R.	H.	2B.	3B.	HR.	SB.	B.A.	PO.	A.	E.	F.A.
1913—Harrisburg		Tri-St.	P-OF	43	100	12	29	....	....	....	1	.290	7	67	4	.949
1914—Philadelphia		Amer.	P	26	51	6	11	1	1	0	0	.216	6	26	2	.941
1915—Philadelphia		Amer.	P	33	55	9	8	0	1	1	0	.145	7	56	7	.900
1916—Philadelphia		Amer.	P	4	5	1	1	0	1	0	0	.200	1	3	0	1.000
1916—Newark		Int.	P	2	2	0	0	0	0	0	0	.000	0	0	0	.000
1916—New Haven		East.	P-OF	89	297	25	69	....	....	....	3	.232	117	61	9	.952
1917—Atlanta		South.	P	61	127	21	38	6	1	6	0	.277	34	78	9	.927
1917—Cincinnati		Nat.	P	3	5	0	1	0	0	0	0	.200	1	1	0	1.000
1918—Cincinnati		Nat.	P-OF	23	62	10	17	5	0	0	0	.274	8	51	1	.983
1919—Cincinnati		Nat.	P-OF	61	165	22	34	3	4	2	0	.206	107	19	5	.962
1920—Cincinnati		Nat.	P-OF-1B	21	30	4	8	1	0	0	1	.267	25	7	4	.889
1921—Cincinnati		Nat.	OF	109	323	41	99	18	6	1	5	.306	155	6	8	.953
1922—Cincinnati		Nat.	OF-1B	52	53	7	14	0	2	0	1	.264	17	0	1	.944
1923—Cincinnati		Nat.	OF-1B	54	119	25	33	3	1	0	3	.277	227	9	4	.983
1924—Cincinnati		Nat.	OF-1B	115	383	41	133	14	13	4	9	.347	561	35	9	.969
1925—Cincinnati		Nat.	OF-1B	97	319	43	111	17	6	4	9	.348	602	23	12	.981
1926—Cincinnati		Nat.	OF-1B	86	297	58	106	15	9	1	3	.357	177	5	5	.973
1927—Cincinnati (a)		Nat.	OF	124	467	43	136	14	8	3	4	.291	261	15	8	.972
1928—Brooklyn		Nat.	OF	145	501	78	148	29	13	4	2	.295	254	7	4	*.985
1929—Brooklyn		Nat.	OF	136	456	72	145	22	8	9	4	.318	263	7	13	.954
1930—Brooklyn		Nat.	OF	109	335	53	100	12	8	3	4	.299	200	5	1	.995
1931—Brooklyn (b)		Nat.	OF	67	153	22	43	4	5	0	0	.281	54	1	1	.982
1932—Phil.(c)-St.L		Nat.	OF	37	102	9	22	6	1	0	0	.216	51	4	0	1.000
1934—Springfield		Mid. Atl.	PH	4	4	1	1	0	0	0	0	.250	0	0	0	.000
American League Totals				63	111	16	20	1	3	1	0	.180	14	85	9	.917
National League Totals				1239	3770	528	1150	163	84	31	47	.305	2953	195	76	.976
Major League Totals				1302	3881	544	1170	164	87	32	47	.301	2967	280	85	.974

aSold to Brooklyn Dodgers, March 13, 1928.
bReleased unconditionally and signed by Philadelphia Phillies, March, 1932.
cUnconditionally released and signed by St. Louis Cardinals, July, 1932.

PITCHING RECORD

Year	Club	League	G.	IP.	W.	L.	Pct.	H.	R.	ER.	SO.	BB.	ERA.
1913—Harrisburg		Tri-St.	34	....	15	13	.536	....	....	....	....	....	....
1914—Philadelphia		Amer.	29	148	10	4	.714	112	37	29	96	56	1.76
1915—Philadelphia		Amer.	32	178	4	17	.190	183	133	103	69	118	5.20
1916—Philadelphia		Amer.	4	15	0	3	.000	16	11	11	8	14	6.60
1916—Newark		Int.	2	....	0	2	.000	....	....	....	....	....	....
1916—New Haven		East.	20	158	7	9	.438	....	....	....	22	24	....
1917—Atlanta		South.	46	326	25	15	.625	225	122	....	133	92	....
1917—Cincinnati		Nat.	2	9	0	0	.000	15	11	6	2	5	6.00
1918—Cincinnati		Nat.	17	128	8	5	.615	124	48	35	37	39	2.46
1919—Cincinnati		Nat.	13	42	2	4	.333	37	19	16	13	8	3.43
1920—Cincinnati		Nat.	10	20	2	0	1.000	24	8	4	4	2	1.80
American League Totals			65	341	14	24	.368	311	181	143	173	178	3.57
National League Totals			42	199	12	9	.571	200	86	61	56	54	2.76
Major League Totals			107	540	26	33	.441	511	267	204	229	242	3.40

THOMAS DAVIS BRIDGES

Born December 28, 1906, at Gordonsville, Tenn.
Died April 19, 1968, at Nashville, Tenn.
Height, 5.11. Weight, 160.
Threw and batted righthanded.
Married Carolyn Jellicorse, March 21, 1930.

Pitched perfect game until two were out in ninth when pinch-hitter Dave Harris singled for only Washington hit, August 5, 1932. Won game, 13-0.
Coach-scout, Cincinnati Reds, 1951; scout, Detroit Tigers, 1958 through 1960.

Year	Club	League	G.	IP.	W.	L.	Pct.	H.	R.	ER.	SO.	BB.	ERA.
1929	Wheeling	Mid.-Atlantic	21	129	10	3	.769	92	51	45	106	65	3.13
1930	Evansville	I. I. I.	20	140	7	8	.467	102	66	46	*189	85	2.96
1930	Detroit	American	8	38	3	2	.600	28	18	17	17	23	4.03
1931	Detroit	American	35	173	8	16	.333	182	120	96	105	108	4.99
1932	Detroit	American	34	201	14	12	.538	174	95	75	108	119	3.36
1933	Detroit	American	33	233	14	12	.538	192	102	80	120	110	3.09
1934	Detroit	American	36	275	22	11	.667	249	117	112	151	104	3.67
1935	Detroit	American	36	274	21	10	.677	277	129	107	*163	113	3.51
1936	Detroit	American	39	295	*23	11	.676	289	141	118	*175	115	3.60
1937	Detroit	American	34	245	15	12	.556	267	129	111	138	91	4.08
1938	Detroit	American	25	151	13	9	.591	171	83	77	101	58	4.59
1939	Detroit	American	29	198	17	7	.708	186	87	77	129	61	3.50
1940	Detroit	American	29	198	12	9	.571	171	89	74	133	88	3.36
1941	Detroit	American	25	148	9	12	.429	128	66	56	90	70	3.41
1942	Detroit	American	23	174	9	7	.563	164	66	53	97	61	2.74
1943	Detroit	American	25	192	12	7	.632	159	57	51	124	61	2.39
1944	Detroit	American					(In Military Service)						
1945	Detroit	American	4	11	1	0	1.000	14	6	4	6	2	3.27
1946	Detroit	American	9	21	1	1	.560	24	16	14	17	8	6.00
1947	Portland	Pacific Coast	13	104	7	3	.700	84	29	19	73	31	*1.64
1948	Portland	Pacific Coast	29	195	15	11	.577	173	72	62	123	75	2.86
1949	Portland	Pacific Coast	28	184	11	11	.500	179	80	78	110	75	3.82
1950	San Fran.-Seattle	Pacific Coast	11	24	0	0	.000	18	16	14	11	23	5.25
	Major League Totals		424	2827	194	138	.584	2675	1321	1122	1674	1192	3.57

WORLD SERIES RECORD

Year	Club	League	G.	IP.	W.	L.	Pct.	H.	R.	ER.	SO.	BB.	ERA.
1934	Detroit	American	3	17⅓	1	1	.500	21	9	7	12	1	3.63
1935	Detroit	American	2	18	2	0	1.000	18	6	5	9	4	2.50
1940	Detroit	American	1	9	1	0	1.000	10	4	3	5	1	3.00
1945	Detroit	American	1	1⅔	0	0	.000	3	3	3	1	3	16.20
	World Series Totals		7	46	4	1	.800	52	22	18	27	9	3.52

LOUIS CLARK BROCK

Born June 18, 1939, at El Dorado, Ark.
Height, 5.11½. Weight, 172.
Threw and batted lefthanded.
Cousin of Dale Brock, outfielder in St. Louis Cardinals' organization.

Established major league records for most consecutive years, 50 or more stolen bases (12), 1965 through 1976; most seasons, 50 or more stolen bases, lifetime (12); most season leading majors, stolen bases (6); most times caught stealing, lifetime (307).
 Established modern major league record for most stolen bases, season (118), 1974; and most stolen bases, lifetime (938).
 Established National League record for fewest times grounded into double play, season, 150 or more games (2), 1965 and 1969.
 Tied National League record for most consecutive seasons, 600 or more at bats (11), 1964 through 1974.
 Major League stolen bases: 1961 (0), 1962 (16), 1963 (24), 1964 (43), 1965 (63), 1966 (74), 1967 (52), 1968 (62), 1969 (53), 1970 (51), 1971 (64), 1972 (63), 1973 (70), 1974 (118), 1975 (56), 1976 (56), 1977 (35), 1978 (17), 1979 (21). Total—938.

— 31 —

Led National League outfielders in double plays with 7 in 1963.
Led National League in stolen bases with 74 in 1966, 52 in 1967, 62 in 1968, 53 in 1969, 64 in 1971, 63 in 1972, 70 in 1973 and 118 in 1974.
One of three players in major league history to steal 50 or more bases and hit 20 or more home runs in the same season (52 stolen bases and 21 home runs in 1967).
Established World Series records for highest batting average, total Series (.391), 20 or more games; most hits, two consecutive Series (25), 1967 and 1968; most long hits, two consecutive games, one Series (5), October 6 and 7, 1968; most stolen bases, seven-game Series (7), 1967 and 1968.
Tied World Series records for most times reached first base safely, game (batting 1.000) (5), October 4, 1967; most hits, game (4), and most one-base hits, game (4), October 4, 1967; most stolen bases game (3), October 12, 1967, and October 5, 1968; most stolen bases, inning (2), October 12, 1967, (fifth inning); most runs, seven-game Series (8), 1967; most hits, seven-game Series (13), 1968; most stolen bases, total Series (14); most times reached first base, seven-game Series (13), 1968; one or more hits, each game of seven-game Series, 1968; most two-base hits, game, batting in three runs (1), October 6, 1968.
Named National League and Major League Player of the Year by THE SPORTING NEWS, 1974.
Named as outfielder on THE SPORTING NEWS National League All-Star Team, 1974.
Named National League Comeback Player of the Year by THE SPORTING NEWS, 1979.
Received reported $30,000 bonus to sign with Chicago Cubs, 1961.

Year	Club	League	Pos.	G.	AB.	R.	H.	2B.	3B.	HR.	RBI.	B.A.	PO.	A.	E.	F.A.
1961	St. Cloud	North.	OF	•128	501	★117	★181	★33	6	14	82	★.361	★277	14	14	.954
1961	Chicago	Nat.	OF	4	11	1	1	0	0	0	0	.091	6	0	2	.750
1962	Chicago	Nat.	OF	123	434	73	114	24	7	9	35	.263	243	7	9	.965
1963	Chicago	Nat.	OF	148	547	79	141	19	11	9	37	.258	269	17	8	.973
1964	Chi.(a)-St. Louis	Nat.	OF	155	634	111	200	30	11	14	58	.315	266	15	★14	.953
1965	St. Louis	Nat.	OF	155	631	107	182	35	8	16	69	.288	272	11	★12	.959
1966	St. Louis	Nat.	OF	156	643	94	183	24	12	15	46	.285	269	9	★19	.936
1967	St. Louis	Nat.	OF	159	★689	•113	206	32	12	21	76	.299	272	12	★13	.956
1968	St. Louis	Nat.	OF	159	660	92	184	★46	★14	6	51	.279	269	9	•14	.952
1969	St. Louis	Nat.	OF	157	655	97	195	33	10	12	47	.298	255	7	14	.949
1970	St. Louis	Nat.	OF	155	664	114	202	29	5	13	57	.304	247	9	10	.962
1971	St. Louis	Nat.	OF	157	640	★126	200	37	7	7	61	.313	262	7	14	.951
1972	St. Louis	Nat.	OF	153	621	81	193	26	8	3	42	.311	253	6	★13	.952
1973	St. Louis	Nat.	OF	160	650	110	193	29	8	7	63	.297	310	3	•12	.963
1974	St. Louis	Nat.	OF	153	635	105	194	25	7	3	48	.306	283	8	10	.967
1975	St. Louis	Nat.	OF	136	528	78	163	27	6	3	47	.309	247	5	9	.966
1976	St. Louis	Nat.	OF	133	498	73	150	24	5	4	67	.301	221	6	4	.983
1977	St. Louis	Nat.	OF	141	489	69	133	22	6	2	46	.272	184	2	9	.954
1978	St. Louis	Nat.	OF	92	298	31	66	9	0	0	12	.221	114	2	3	.975
1979	St. Louis	Nat.	OF	120	405	56	123	15	4	5	38	.304	152	7	7	.958
Major League Totals				2616	10332	1610	3023	486	141	149	900	.293	4394	142	196	.959

aTraded to St. Louis Cardinals with pitchers Jack Spring and Paul Toth for pitchers Ernie Broglio and Bobby Shantz and outfielder Doug Clemens, June 15, 1964.

WORLD SERIES RECORD

Year	Club	League	Pos.	G.	AB.	R.	H.	2B.	3B.	HR.	RBI.	B.A.	PO.	A.	E.	F.A.
1964	St. Louis	Nat.	OF	7	30	2	9	2	0	1	5	.300	8	1	1	.900
1967	St. Louis	Nat.	OF	7	29	8	12	2	1	1	3	.414	13	0	0	1.000
1968	St. Louis	Nat.	OF	7	28	6	13	3	1	2	5	.464	13	0	1	.929
World Series Totals				21	87	16	34	7	2	4	13	.391	34	1	2	.946

WALTER SCOTT (STEVE) BRODIE

Born September 11, 1868, at Warrenton, Va.
Died October 29, 1933, at Baltimore, Md.
Threw righthanded and batted lefthanded.
Married Caroline Amanda Henry, 1890.

Had six hits in game (three singles, two doubles, one triple) in six times at bat, July 9, 1894.

Year	Club	League	Pos.	G.	AB.	R.	H.	2B.	3B.	HR.	SB.	B.A.	PO.	A.	E.	F.A.
1888	Wheeling	Tri-St.	OF	....	....	....	....	....	....	....	....	....	....	....	....	....
1889	Hamilton	Int.	OF	111	487	87	141	....	....	....	50	.302	200	26	19	.922
1890	Boston	Nat.	OF	132	514	78	152	18	9	0	29	.295	225	19	12	.953
1891	Boston	Nat.	OF	134	519	83	138	17	6	2	23	.266	259	22	15	.943
1892	St. Louis	Nat.	2B-OF	154	600	86	154	9	8	3	28	.256	290	22	17	.948
1893	St. L.-Balt.	Nat.	OF	132	549	89	188	20	11	2	52	.342	275	26	16	.950
1894	Baltimore	Nat.	OF	129	574	132	212	22	12	2	50	.369	311	11	19	.944
1895	Baltimore	Nat.	OF	130	528	84	193	26	11	2	36	.365	301	20	11	.961
1896	Baltimore	Nat.	OF	132	516	90	152	19	10	2	30	.294	★321	20	10	.972
1897	Pittsburgh	Nat.	OF	100	372	47	111	10	11	2	17	.298	216	11	4	★.983
1898	Pitts.-Baltimore	Nat.	OF	65	255	28	71	10	2	0	4	.278	164	9	7	.961
1899	Baltimore	Nat.	OF	138	533	80	165	29	1	3	20	.309	309	18	7	★.979
1900	Chicago	Amer.	OF	64	229	41	60	6	3	0	8	.262	117	8	11	.919

Year	Club	League	Pos.	G.	AB.	R.	H.	2B.	3B.	HR.	SB.	B.A.	PO.	A.	E.	F.A.
1901	Baltimore	Amer.	OF	84	309	41	96	5	6	2	10	.311	182	4	9	.954
1902	New York	Nat.	OF	109	417	35	117	8	2	3	12	.281	222	20	11	.957
1903	Balt.-Montreal	East.	OF	103	389	34	97	12	1	0	15	.255	230	12	14	.945
1904	Binghamton	N.Y.	OF	50	177	21	20	....	....	....	12	.163	77	7	5	.943
1905	Providence	East.	OF	134	500	45	135	12	3	0	18	.270	236	18	13	.951
1906	Prov.-Newark	East.	OF	112	387	41	110	14	4	0	10	.284	220	16	11	.955
1907	Birmingham	South.	OF	5	17	2	2	0	0	0	0	.117	11	2	0	1.000
1907	Roanoke	Va.	OF	72	238	26	74	....	....	....	20	.311	130	8	1	.993
1908	Ports.-Norfolk	N.Y.	OF	51	177	18	40	....	....	....	6	.226	101	7	1	.991
1909	Wilmington	E. Car.	OF	80	262	31	67	....	....	....	....	.255	190	8	2	.990
1910	Newark	East.	OF	11	28	2	6	0	0	0	0	.214	....	....	....	....
American League Totals				84	309	41	96	5	6	2	10	.311	182	4	9	.954
National League Totals				1355	5377	832	1653	188	83	21	301	.307	2893	198	129	.960
Major League Totals				1439	5686	873	1749	193	89	23	311	.308	3075	202	138	.960

DENNIS (DAN) BROUTHERS

Born May 8, 1858, at Sylvan Lake, N. Y.
Died August 3, 1932, at East Orange, N. J.
Height, 6.02. Weight, 200.
Threw and batted lefthanded.

Had six hits in game (four singles, two doubles) in six times at bat, July 19, 1883.
Scout, New York Giants, 1907.
Named to Hall of Fame, 1945.

Year	Club	League	Pos.	G.	AB.	R.	H.	2B.	3B.	HR.	SB.	B.A.	PO.	A.	E.	F.A.
1879	Troy	Nat.	P-1B	39	168	17	46	13	1	4	....	.274	406	6	33	.926
1880	Troy	Nat.	1B	3	13	0	2	0	0	0	....	.154	25	0	3	.893
1881	Buffalo	Nat.	1B-OF	65	270	60	86	15	7	*8	....	.319	377	18	33	.923
1882	Buffalo	Nat.	1B	84	351	71	*129	25	11	6	....	*.368	882	19	24	.974
1883	Buffalo	Nat.	P-1-3	97	420	83	*156	39	*17	2	....	*.371	1030	34	44	.960
1884	Buffalo	Nat.	1B-3B	90	381	80	124	22	16	14	....	.325	908	29	35	.964
1885	Buffalo(a)	Nat.	1B	98	407	87	146	27	13	7	....	.359	996	25	26	.975
1886	Detroit	Nat.	1B	121	489	139	181	*41	16	10	21	.370	1256	27	42	.968
1887	Detroit†	Nat.	1B	122	570	*153	*239	*35	20	13	34	.419	1189	35	38	.970
1888	Detroit(b)	Nat.	1B	129	522	*118	160	35	13	10	34	.306	1345	48	*42	.970
1889	Boston(c)	Nat.	1B	126	485	105	181	25	8	6	22	*.373	1243	58	35	.974
1890	Boston(d)	Players	1B	123	464	116	160	32	9	1	26	.345	1193	66	*52	.960
1891	Boston	A. A.	1B	123	458	111	*160	26	20	5	33	*.349	1239	33	24	.981
1892	Brooklyn	Nat.	1B	152	588	121	*197	*33	*20	3	36	●.335	1485	99	37	.977
1893	Brooklyn(e)	Nat.	1B	75	267	53	93	21	11	2	8	.348	729	42	14	.982
1894	Baltimore	Nat.	1B	123	528	137	182	33	25	9	40	.345	1180	65	31	.976
1895	Balt.(f)-L'ville.	Nat.	1B	29	121	15	35	9	2	2	1	.289	255	14	10	.964
1896	Philadelphia	Nat.	1B	57	218	41	72	15	3	1	8	.330	570	23	10	.983
1896	Springfield	East.	1B	51	205	42	82	....	....	....	9	.400	513	13	12	.977
1897	Springfield	East.	1B	126	501	112	*208	44	13	14	21	*.415	1239	44	22	.983
1898	Spring.-Toronto	East.	1B	50	189	42	63	10	2	4	2	.333	511	19	13	.976
1899	Spring.-Roch.	East.	1B	45	170	27	40	5	4	3	2	.235	421	26	13	.972
1904	New York	Nat.	1B	2	5	0	0	0	0	0	0	.000	6	0	0	1.000
1904	Poughkeepsie	Hudson River	1B	....	424	....	158	....	....	....	....	.373	1129	31	31	.974
1905	Poughkeepsie	Hudson River	1B	....	308	....	91	....	....	....	....	.295	810	29	31	.967
American Association Totals				123	458	111	160	26	20	5	33	.349	1239	33	24	.981
National League Totals				1412	5803	1280	2029	388	183	97	204	.350	13882	542	457	.969
Players League Totals				123	464	116	160	32	9	1	26	.345	1193	66	52	.960
Major League Totals				1658	6725	1507	2349	446	212	103	263	.349	16314	641	533	.970

†Bases on balls counted as hits in 1887.
aSold to Detroit with utilityman Hardie Richardson, third baseman Jim White and shortstop Charlie Rowe for 1886 season.
bDisbanding of Detroit team caused players to be distributed throughout circuit. Brouthers awarded to Boston, 1888.
cJumped to Players League (Brotherhood), 1890.
dSigned with Boston (A. A.) after disbanding of Brotherhood.
eTraded to Baltimore with outfielder Willie Keeler for third baseman Billy Shindle and outfielder George Treadway, January, 1894.
fSold to Louisville for $700, May 9, 1895.

DID YOU KNOW—
That Lou Brock's first career steal came against the Cardinals, April 13, 1962?

MORDECAI PETER CENTENNIAL (MINER) BROWN

Born October 19, 1876, at Nyesville, Ind.
Died February 14, 1948, at Terre Haute, Ind.
Height, 5.10. Weight, 175.
Threw right and batted both ways.
Married Sarah Bingham, December 16, 1903.

Won four consecutive shutouts, June 13, June 25, July 2 (first game), July 4 (morning game), 1908. Manager, St. Louis Feds, 1914; manager, Terre Haute, Three-I League, 1919; manager, Indianapolis, American Association, September, 1919; again manager, Terre Haute, 1920.
Named to Hall of Fame, 1949.

Year Club	League	G.	IP.	W.	L.	Pct.	H.	R.	ER.	SO.	BB.	ERA.
1901–Terre Haute	I.I.I.	31	....	*23	8	*.742	198	....	....	138	41	......
1902–Omaha	Western	•43	352	27	15	.643	309	....	....	140	82	......
1903–St. Louis (a)	National	26	201	9	13	.409	231	105	....	83	59	......
1904–Chicago	National	26	212	15	10	.600	155	74	....	81	50	......
1905–Chicago	National	30	249	18	12	.600	219	89	....	89	44	......
1906–Chicago	National	36	278	26	6	.813	198	56	....	143	61	......
1907–Chicago	National	34	233	20	6	.769	180	51	....	107	40	......
1908–Chicago	National	44	312	29	9	.763	214	64	....	123	49	......
1909–Chicago	National	*50	*343	*27	9	.750	246	78	....	172	53	......
1910–Chicago	National	46	295	25	14	.641	256	95	....	143	64	......
1911–Chicago	National	*53	270	21	11	.656	267	110	....	129	55	......
1912–Chicago (b)	National	15	89	5	6	.455	92	35	26	34	20	2.63
1913–Cincinnati (c)	National	39	167	11	12	.478	174	79	56	41	44	3.02
1914–St.L. (d)–Brooklyn	Federal	35	233	14	11	.560	233	106	80	118	61	3.09
1915–Chicago (e)	Federal	35	238	17	8	.680	190	75	56	97	65	2.12
1916–Chicago	National	12	48	2	3	.400	52	27	21	21	9	3.94
1917–Columbus	Am. Assoc.	30	185	10	12	.455	167	70	57	61	51	2.77
1918–Columbus	Am. Assoc.	12	50	3	2	.600	49	18	15	13	9	2.70
1919–Terre Haute	I.I.I.	33	175	16	6	.727	161	69	56	72	20	2.88
1919–Indianapolis	Am. Assoc.	6	34	0	3	.000	39	....	....	9	11	......
1920–Terre Haute	I.I.I.	13	80	4	6	.400	74	31	23	42	13	2.59
Federal League Totals		70	471	31	19	.620	423	181	136	215	126	2.60
National League Totals		411	2697	208	111	.652	2284	863	....	1166	548	......
Major League Totals		411	2697	208	111	.652	2284	863	....	1166	548	......

aTraded to Chicago with catcher Jack O'Neill for pitcher Jack Taylor.
bReleased to Louisville, October, 1912, and traded to Cincinnati for pitcher Grover Lowdermilk, January, 1913.
cReleased by Cincinnati, January, 1914, and signed as manager of St. Louis Feds.
dReleased as St. Louis Feds manager, July, 1914, but remained as player until released to Brooklyn in August, 1914.
eAssigned to Chicago Cubs in peace agreement, January, 1916.

WORLD SERIES RECORD

Year Club	League	G.	IP.	W.	L.	Pct.	H.	R.	ER.	SO.	BB.	ERA.
1906–Chicago	National	3	19⅔	1	2	.333	14	9	7	12	4	3.20
1907–Chicago	National	1	9	1	0	1.000	7	0	0	4	1	0.00
1908–Chicago	National	2	11	2	0	1.000	6	1	0	5	1	0.00
1910–Chicago	National	3	18	1	2	.333	23	16	11	14	7	5.50
World Series Totals		9	57⅔	5	4	.556	50	26	18	35	13	2.81

LOUIS RODGERS (PETE) BROWNING

Born July 17, 1861, at Louisville, Ky.
Died September 10, 1905, at Louisville, Ky.
Height, 6.02. Weight, 200.
Threw and batted righthanded.

Year Club	League	Pos.	G.	AB.	R.	H.	2B.	3B.	HR.	SB.	B.A.	PO.	A.	E.	F.A.
1882–Louisville	A.A.	INF	69	288	64	110	*19	3	5	......	*.382	192	185	68	.847
1883–Louisville	A.A.	INF	84	360	95	121	14	11	4	......	.336	134	96	50	.821

Year	Club	League	Pos.	G.	AB.	R.	H.	2B.	3B.	HR.	SB.	B.A.	PO.	A.	E.	F.A.
1884—Louisville		A.A.	P-1B-3B	105	454	101	155	34	8	4	.....	.341	382	86	51	.902
1885—Louisville		A.A.	OF	113	479	98	*176	32	10	9	.....	*.367	214	21	28	.894
1886—Louisville		A.A.	OF	112	469	88	159	29	7	3	32	.339	153	14	37	.819
1887—Louisville		A.A.	OF	134	596	133	281	36	18	4	121	.471	291	22	43	.879
1888—Louisville		A.A.	OF	99	384	59	120	23	8	3	39	.313	169	17	20	.903
1889—Louisville		A.A.	OF	83	324	39	82	18	4	2	23	.253	157	14	18	.903
1890—Cleveland		Players	OF	118	488	114	191	•41	7	5	33	*.391	245	18	27	.907
1891—Pitts.-Cin.		Nat.	OF	101	398	62	129	22	5	3	15	.324	206	12	19	.920
1892—Louis.-Cin.		Nat.	OF	102	387	58	113	15	5	3	8	.292	197	15	20	.914
1893—Louisville		Nat.	OF	57	214	37	79	9	3	1	10	.369	114	4	15	.887
1894—St. Louis-Brook.		Nat.	OF	3	9	2	3	0	0	0	0	.333	3	0	0	1.000
American Association Totals				799	3354	677	1204	205	69	34	.....	.359	1692	455	315	.872
National League Totals				263	1008	159	324	46	13	7	33	.321	520	31	54	.911
Players League Totals				118	488	114	191	41	7	5	33	.391	245	18	27	.907
Major League Totals				1180	4850	950	1719	292	89	46	.....	.354	2457	504	396	.882

Bases on balls counted as hits in 1887.

CHARLES G. BUFFINTON

Born June 14, 1861, at Fall River, Mass.
Died September 23, 1907, at Fall River, Mass.
Threw and batted righthanded.
Married Alice Thornley, September 15, 1884.

Year	Club	League	G.	W.	L.	Pct.	H.	R.	CG.	ShO.
1882—Boston		National	5	2	3	.400	55	34	4	1
1883—Boston		National	37	24	13	.649	310	169	32	•5
1884—Boston		National	65	47	16	.746	496	228	60	8
1885—Boston		National	50	22	27	.449	423	237	45	6
1886—Boston		National	18	8	10	.444	196	132	18	0
1887—Philadelphia		National	39	21	17	.553	471	233	34	1
1888—Philadelphia		National	45	28	17	.622	321	134	45	6
1889—Philadelphia		National	43	26	17	.605	393	200	39	2
1890—Philadelphia		Players	34	19	14	.576	340	219	30	0
1891—Boston		American Assn.	41	28	9	*.757	266	140	33	4
1892—Baltimore		National	13	5	3	.385	130		10	0
National League Totals			315	183	128	.588	2795	1367	287	29
Players League Totals			34	19	14	.576	340	219	30	0
American Association Totals			41	28	9	.757	266	140	33	4
Major League Totals			390	230	151	.604	3401	1726	350	33

MORGAN G. BULKELEY

(First President of National League.)
Born December 26, 1837, at East Haddam, Conn.
Died November 6, 1922, at Hartford, Conn.

    In the first year of its organization, the National League needed a man of prominence and firmness to handle the executive affairs of the circuit, and its members prevailed upon Morgan Bulkeley to accept the office, although he announced at that time his probable inability to continue as head of the organization after one year of service.
    Bulkeley's father was the first president of the Aetna Life Insurance Co. In 1872, Bulkeley organized the United States Bank of Hartford, serving as its president until 1879. That year he was chosen as the head of the Aetna Life Insurance Co. and, subsequently, as the head of its two affiliated concerns. He became a director of other Hartford institutions. Bulkeley served on the Hartford City Council in 1875, on the Board of Aldermen in 1876, and was mayor from 1880 to 1888. While mayor he gave his salary to the city's poor fund.
    Bulkeley was chosen Governor of the state of Connecticut in 1888 and served in that office until 1893. He

was elected United States Senator in 1905 for the six-year term. He was a delegate to the Republican National Convention, 1888 to 1896. During the drive for the sale of Liberty Bonds, Bulkeley was instrumental in obtaining more than 30 percent of Hartford's quota. Yale University conferred upon him the degree of Master of Arts in 1889, and in 1917 Trinity College honored him with the LLD degree. He was a member of the G.A.R., being former department commander; Massachusetts Commandery of the Loyal Legion, Society of the Cincinnati Sons of the American Revolution, Society of Mayflower Descendants, Society of Colonial Wars and Society of the War of 1812. Bulkeley was former president of the Sons of the American Revolution and former marshal of the Baronial Order of Runnymede. For more than 30 years, he was a member of the National Trotting Association, and his fondness for horses lasted all his life.

He was named to Hall of Fame in 1937 for service to baseball apart from playing the game.

JAMES PAUL DAVID BUNNING

Born October 23, 1931, at Southgate, Ky.
Height, 6.03. Weight, 203.
Threw and batted righthanded.
Married Mary Theis, January 26, 1952.

Tied major league record by striking out three batters on nine pitched balls, August 2, 1959, ninth inning.
Pitched 6-0 perfect-game victory against New York Mets, June 21, 1964, and 3-0 no-hit victory against Boston Red Sox, July 20, 1958.
Named as pitcher on THE SPORTING NEWS All-Star Major League Team, 1957; named as pitcher on the National League All-Star Team by THE SPORTING NEWS, 1964.
Manager, Reading, Eastern League, 1972; manager, Eugene, Pacific Coast League, 1973; minor league instructor and manager, Philadelphia Phillies system, 1974-75; manager, Oklahoma City (American Association), 1976.

Year – Club	League	G.	IP.	W.	L.	Pct.	H.	R.	ER.	SO.	BB.	ERA.
1950 – Richmond	Ohio-Ind.	17	123	7	8	.467	120	69	44	83	68	3.22
1951 – Davenport	I.I.I.	22	150	8	10	.444	110	61	48	103	105	2.88
1952 – Williamsport	Eastern	20	129	5	9	.357	113	62	50	85	63	3.49
1953 – Buffalo	International	3	5	0	0	.000	6	1	1	4	0	1.80
1953 – Little Rock	Southern	34	158	5	12	.294	151	98	80	124	66	4.56
1954 – Little Rock	Southern	35	193	13	11	.542	182	107	92	140	91	4.29
1955 – Buffalo	International	20	129	8	5	.615	106	59	54	105	81	3.77
1955 – Detroit	American	15	51	3	5	.375	59	38	36	37	32	6.35
1956 – Charleston	Amer. Assoc.	22	163	9	11	.450	142	70	64	144	56	3.53
1956 – Detroit	American	15	53	5	1	.833	55	24	22	34	28	3.74
1957 – Detroit	American	45	*267	•20	8	.714	214	91	80	182	72	2.70
1958 – Detroit	American	35	220	14	12	.538	188	96	86	177	79	3.52
1959 – Detroit	American	40	250	17	13	.567	220	111	108	*201	75	3.89
1960 – Detroit	American	36	252	11	14	.440	217	92	78	*201	64	2.79
1961 – Detroit	American	38	268	17	11	.607	232	113	95	194	71	3.19
1962 – Detroit	American	41	258	19	10	.655	*262	112	103	184	74	3.59
1963 – Detroit (a)	American	39	248	12	13	.480	245	•119	107	196	69	3.88
1964 – Philadelphia	National	41	284	19	8	.704	248	99	83	219	46	2.63
1965 – Philadelphia	National	39	291	19	9	.679	253	92	84	268	62	2.60
1966 – Philadelphia	National	43	314	19	14	.576	260	91	84	252	55	2.41
1967 – Philadelphia (b)	National	40	*302	17	15	.531	241	94	77	*253	73	2.29
1968 – Pittsburgh	National	27	160	4	14	.222	168	75	69	95	48	3.88
1969 – Pitts.(c)-Los Angeles (d)	National	34	212	13	10	.565	212	97	87	157	59	3.69
1970 – Philadelphia	National	34	219	10	15	.400	233	111	100	147	56	4.11
1971 – Philadelphia	National	29	110	5	12	.294	126	72	67	58	37	5.48
American League Totals		304	1867	118	87	.576	1692	796	715	1406	564	3.45
National League Totals		287	1892	106	97	.522	1741	731	651	1449	436	3.10
Major League Totals		591	3759	224	184	.549	3433	1527	1366	2855	1000	3.27

aTraded to Philadelphia Phillies with catcher Gus Triandos for pitcher Jack Hamilton and outfielder Don Demeter, December 4, 1963.
bTraded to Pittsburgh Pirates for infielder Don Money and pitchers Woodie Fryman, Harold Clem and Bill Laxton, December 15, 1967.
cTraded for cash and outfielder Ron Mitchell and infielder Chuck Goggin, to Los Angeles Dodgers, August 16, 1969.
dSigned as free agent by Philadelphia Phillies, October 29, 1969.

DID YOU KNOW –
That Jim Bunning had more than 100 wins and a no-hitter in each major league?

SELVA LEWIS (LOU) BURDETTE, JR.

Born November 22, 1926, at Nitro, W. Va.
Height, 6.02. Weight, 201.
Threw and batted righthanded.
Married Mary Ann Shelton, June 30, 1949.

Pitched 1-0 no-hit victory against Philadelphia Phillies, August 18, 1960.
Led National League in shutouts with 6 in 1956 and tied for lead with 4 in 1959; tied for lead in complete games with 18 in 1960; hit two homers, one single, August 13, 1957, and two homers, July 10, 1958.
Established World Series record for most shutouts pitched in seven-game Series (2), 1957; tied Series record for most games won, Series (3), 1957; tied Series mark for most complete games pitched, Series (3), 1957; tied for Series record, most home runs allowed, Series (5), 1958; tied record for most games lost in a World Series (2), 1958.
Scout, southeastern area, Central Scouting Bureau, 1968; coach, Atlanta Braves, 1972-73.

Year — Club	League	G.	IP.	W.	L.	Pct.	H.	R.	ER.	SO.	BB.	ERA.
1947—Norfolk	Pied.	6	27	1	1	.500	23	18	13	10	20	4.33
1947—Amsterdam	Can.-Am.	24	150	9	10	.474	125	66	47	79	80	2.82
1948—Quincy	I. I. I.	31	214	•16	11	.593	164	73	48	185	72	2.02
1949—Kansas City	A. A.	36	118	6	7	.462	147	76	69	51	47	5.26
1950—Kansas City	A. A.	27	139	7	7	.500	150	79	74	77	52	4.79
1950—New York	American	2	1	0	0	.000	3	1	1	0	0	9.00
1951—San Francisco(a)	P. C.	30	210	14	12	.538	202	88	75	118	78	3.21
1951—Boston	National	3	4	0	0	.000	6	4	3	1	5	6.75
1952—Boston	National	45	137	6	11	.353	138	58	55	47	47	3.61
1953—Milwaukee	National	46	175	15	5	.750	177	73	63	58	56	3.24
1954—Milwaukee	National	38	238	15	14	.517	224	87	73	79	62	2.76
1955—Milwaukee	National	42	230	13	8	.619	253	114	103	70	73	4.03
1956—Milwaukee	National	39	256	19	10	.655	234	92	77	110	52	*2.71
1957—Milwaukee	National	37	257	17	9	.654	260	117	106	78	59	3.71
1958—Milwaukee	National	40	275	20	10	•.667	279	102	89	113	50	2.91
1959—Milwaukee	National	41	290	•21	15	.583	*312	*144	*131	105	38	4.07
1960—Milwaukee	National	45	276	19	13	.594	•277	116	103	83	35	3.36
1961—Milwaukee	National	40	*272	18	11	.621	*295	*131	*121	92	33	4.00
1962—Milwaukee	National	37	144	10	9	.526	172	85	78	59	23	4.88
1963—Milwaukee(b)-St. L.	National	36	183	9	13	.409	177	90	75	73	40	3.69
1964—St. Louis(c)-Chicago	National	36	141	10	9	.526	162	77	73	43	22	4.66
1965—Chicago(d)-Phila.(e)	National	26	91	3	5	.375	121	67	55	28	21	5.44
1966—California	American	54	80	7	2	.778	80	32	30	27	12	3.38
1967—California	American	19	18	1	0	1.000	16	10	10	8	0	5.00
1967—Seattle	P. C.	13	19	0	0	.000	18	12	9	8	4	4.26
National League Totals		551	2969	195	142	.579	3087	1357	1205	1039	616	3.65
American League Totals		75	99	8	2	.800	99	43	41	35	12	3.73
Major League Totals		626	3068	203	144	.585	3186	1400	1246	1074	628	3.66

aRecalled by New York Yankees and sent to Boston Braves with $50,000 for pitcher Johnny Sain, August 29, 1951.
bTraded to St. Louis Cardinals for pitcher Bob Sadowski and catcher-outfielder Gene Oliver, June 15, 1963.
cTraded to Chicago Cubs for pitcher Glen Hobbie, June 2, 1964.
dSold to Philadelphia Phillies May 30, 1965.
eReleased by Philadelphia Phillies, October 13, 1965, and signed by California Angels, December 15, 1965.

WORLD SERIES RECORD

Year — Club	League	G.	IP.	W.	L.	Pct.	H.	R.	ER.	SO.	BB.	ERA.
1957—Milwaukee	Nat.	3	27	3	0	1.000	21	2	2	13	4	0.67
1958—Milwaukee	Nat.	3	22⅓	1	2	.333	22	17	14	12	4	5.64
World Series Totals		6	49⅓	4	2	.667	43	19	16	25	8	2.92

JESSE CAIL (CRAB) BURKETT

Born February 12, 1870, at Wheeling, W. Va.
Died May 27, 1953, at Worcester, Mass.
Height, 5.08. Weight, 155.
Threw and batted lefthanded.

Tied with Ty Cobb and Rogers Hornsby for most years hitting .400 or over—3.

Owner and manager, Worcester, New England League, 1906-13; manager, Lawrence and Hartford, Eastern League, 1916; scout, New York Nationals and coach, Holy Cross College, 1920; coach, New York Nationals, 1921; manager, Worcester, Eastern League, 1923-24; manager, Lewiston, New England League, 1928; Lewiston, Northeastern League, 1929; manager, Lowell, New England League, 1933; was coach, Assumption College two times, for one 26-0 victory in 1928 and the other for two years, 1931-32, with aid of Rube Marquard in 1931.

Named to Hall of Fame, 1946.

Year Club League	Pos.	G.	AB.	R.	H.	2B.	3B.	HR.	SB.	B.A.	PO.	A.	E.	F.A.
1888–Scranton............Cent.	2B	35	115	25	26	2	1	0	.....	.226	29	229	13	.952
1889–Worcester.........Atl. A.	2B	49	175	31	49	8	1	3	16	.280	16	200	17	.927
1890–New York(a) ....Nat.	OF-P	101	401	67	124	22	12	4	14	.309	108	23	28	.824
1891–Lincoln.............W. A.	OF	93	395	78	138	15	11	3	.....	.349	165	16	28	.866
1891–Cleveland............Nat.	OF	40	166	30	45	7	4	0	2	.271	50	3	5	.914
1892–Cleveland..........Nat.	OF	145	605	117	168	15	14	3	36	.278	282	18	28	.915
1893–Cleveland..........Nat.	OF	124	480	144	179	23	15	6	39	.373	240	18	*42	.860
1894–Cleveland..........Nat.	OF-P	124	518	134	185	25	15	8	32	.357	242	18	24	.915
1895–Cleveland..........Nat.	OF	132	555	149	*235	21	15	5	47	*.423	274	18	35	.893
1896–Cleveland..........Nat.	OF	•133	*585	*159	*240	26	16	6	32	*.410	271	15	23	.926
1897–Cleveland..........Nat.	OF	128	519	128	199	28	8	2	27	.383	220	14	14	.944
1898–Cleveland(b).....Nat.	OF	148	624	115	*215	18	9	0	20	.345	266	18	10	.966
1899–St. Louis ....Nat.	OF	138	567	115	228	17	10	7	22	.402	300	20	25	.928
1900–St. Louis ....Nat	OF	•142	560	88	202	14	12	7	31	.361	*345	16	23	.940
1901–St. Louis ....Nat.	OF	•142	*597	*139	*228	21	17	10	27	*.382	305	17	21	.939
1902–St. Louis(c) ......Amer.	SS-3-O	137	549	99	168	29	9	5	22	.306	296	17	*26	.923
1903–St. Louis ....Amer.	OF-P	133	514	74	152	20	7	3	16	.296	231	10	15	.941
1904–St. Louis(d) ......Amer.	OF	147	576	72	157	15	9	2	12	.273	258	26	15	.950
1905–Boston ....Amer.	OF	149	573	78	147	13	13	4	13	.257	276	11	*22	.929
1906–Worcester.........N. Eng.	OF	98	363	59	125	21	7	1	.....	*.344	137	6	6	.960
1907–Worcester.........N. Eng.	OF	52	195	23	66	8	1	1	9	.338	80	7	7	.926
1908–Worcester.........N. Eng.	OF	97	375	49	110	11	5	1	8	.293	165	9	16	.916
1909–Worcester.........N. Eng.	OF	75	218	30	71	10	1	1	6	.326	99	4	9	.920
1910–Worcester.........N. Eng.	OF	38	72	3	24	3	0	0	1	.333	15	1	2	.889
1911–Worcester.........N. Eng.	OF	76	243	42	83	8	1	1	1	.342	80	10	11	.891
1912–Worcester.........N. Eng.	OF	28	60	6	21	4	0	0	1	.350	17	0	0	1.000
1913–Worcester.........N. Eng.	OF	19	42	4	10	3	0	0	0	.238	18	1	4	.826
1916–Low.-Law.-Hart. East.	OF	24	38	5	8	.....	.....	.....	0	.211	8	0	1	.889
American League Totals		566	2212	323	624	77	38	14	63	.282	1061	64	78	.935
National League Totals		1497	6177	1385	2248	237	147	58	329	.364	2903	198	278	.918
Major League Totals		2063	8389	1708	2872	314	185	72	392	.342	3964	262	356	.922

aSold to Cleveland in 1891 and farmed to Lincoln until mid-August.
bTransferred with pick of Cleveland players to St. Louis by Frank De Hass Robison, owner of both clubs, 1899.
cJumped to American League.
dTraded to Boston Red Sox for outfielder George Stone, January 1905.

PITCHING RECORD

Year Club League	G.	CG.	IP.	W.	L.	Pct.	ShO.	H.	SO.	BB.
1890–New York ....National.............	21	6	116	1	11	.083	0	130	81	91
1894–Cleveland..................National.............	1	0	4	0	0	.000	0	6	0	1
1902–St. Louis ....American	1	0	1	0	1	.000	0	4	2	1
National League Totals	22	6	120	1	11	.083	0	136	81	92
American League Totals	1	0	1	0	1	.000	0	4	2	1
Major League Totals	23	6	121	1	12	.077	0	140	83	93

GEORGE HENRY (TIOGA) BURNS

Born January 31, 1893, at Niles, O.

Died January 7, 1978, at Kirkland, Wash.

Height, 6.01. Weight, 185.

Threw and batted righthanded.

Married Marion R. Harris, April, 1919.

Made unassisted triple play against Cleveland Indians, September 14, 1923; had six hits in six at-bats (two singles, three doubles, one triple), June 19, 1924, first game.

Named Most Valuable American League player, 1926.

Manager, Seattle, Pacific Coast League, 1932-33-34; manager, Portland, Pacific Coast League, 1934-35.

Year Club League	Pos.	G.	AB.	R.	H.	2B.	3B.	HR.	RBI.	B.A.	PO.	A.	E.	F.A.
1913–Burl.-Ottumwa..C.A.	1B	37	142	26	48	.....	.....	.....	.....	.338	405	17	9	.979
1913–Sioux City ....West.	1B	92	355	54	107	20	6	2	.....	.301	854	61	23	.975
1914–Detroit..............Amer.	1B	137	478	55	139	22	5	5	57	.291	*1576	79	*30	.982

Year	Club	League	Pos.	G.	AB.	R.	H.	2B.	3B.	HR.	RBI.	B.A.	PO.	A.	E.	F.A.
1915–Detroit		Amer.	1B	105	392	49	99	18	3	5	56	.253	1155	57	17	.986
1916–Detroit		Amer.	1B	135	479	60	137	22	6	4	73	.286	1355	54	22	.985
1917–Detroit(a)		Amer.	1B	119	407	42	92	14	10	1	42	.226	1127	57	12	.990
1918–Philadelphia		Amer.	1B	•130	505	61	*178	22	9	6	•74	.352	*1384	*104	*26	.983
1919–Philadelphia		Amer.	1B	126	470	63	139	29	9	8	53	.296	971	75	24	.978
1920–Phila.(b)-Cleve.		Amer.	1B	66	116	8	29	7	1	1	20	.250	97	11	4	.964
1921–Cleveland(c)		Amer.	1B	84	244	52	88	21	4	0	48	.361	534	41	6	.990
1922–Boston		Amer.	1B	147	558	71	171	32	5	12	73	.306	1412	94	*20	.987
1923–Boston(d)		Amer.	1B	146	551	91	181	47	5	7	82	.328	1485	92	*16	.990
1924–Cleveland		Amer.	1B	129	462	64	143	37	5	4	68	.310	1227	110	18	.987
1925–Cleveland		Amer.	1B	127	488	69	164	41	4	6	79	.336	1195	82	14	.989
1926–Cleveland		Amer.	1B	151	603	97	•216	*64	3	4	114	.358	1499	99	19	.988
1927–Cleveland		Amer.	1B	140	549	84	175	51	2	3	78	.319	1362	102	15	.990
1928–Cleve.(e)-N.Y.		Amer.	1B	86	213	30	54	12	1	5	30	.254	477	38	8	.985
1929–N.Y.(f)-Phila.		Amer.	1B	38	58	5	13	5	0	1	11	.224	99	5	0	1.000
1930–Missions		P.C.	1B	200	767	106	268	58	4	22	131	.349	*1896	*154	24	.988
1931–Missions-L.A.		P.C.	1B	178	696	131	226	52	4	18	129	.325	1575	*120	16	*.991
1932–Seattle		P.C.	1B	172	687	125	243	53	7	11	*140	.354	1629	117	22	.988
1933–Seattle		P.C.	1B	169	643	116	217	32	5	27	128	.337	1515	85	16	.990
1934–Seat.-Portland		P.C.	1B	118	394	45	115	10	1	2	54	.292	914	57	16	.984
Major League Totals				1866	6573	901	2018	444	72	72	958	.307	16955	1100	251	.986

aTraded to Philadelphia Athletics for outfielder Frank Bodie, March 8, 1918.
bSold to Cleveland Indians, May 29, 1920.
cTraded to Boston Red Sox with outfielders Elmer J. Smith and Joseph Harris for first baseman John McInnis, December 24, 1921.
dTraded to Cleveland Indians with catcher Alfred J. Walters and infielder Wilson Fewster for pitcher J. A. Boone, catcher Steve O'Neill, outfielder Joe Donnelly and infielder William Wambsganss, January 7, 1924.
eUnconditionally released by Cleveland Indians, September, 1928; subsequently signed with New York Yankees.
fUnconditionally released by New York Yankees and signed by Philadelphia Athletics, June, 1929.

WORLD SERIES RECORD

Year	Club	League	Pos.	G.	AB.	R.	H.	2B.	3B.	HR.	RBI.	B.A.	PO.	A.	E.	F.A.
1920–Cleveland		Amer.	1B	5	10	1	3	1	0	0	3	.300	38	1	1	.975
1929–Philadelphia		Amer.	PH	1	2	0	0	0	0	0	0	.000	0	0	0	.000
World Series Totals				6	12	1	3	1	0	0	3	.250	38	1	1	.975

GEORGE JOSEPH BURNS

Born November 24, 1889, at St. Johnsville, N. Y.
Died August 15, 1966, at Gloversville, N. Y.
Height, 5.07. Weight, 170.
Threw and batted righthanded.
Married Mary Baker, October 7, 1914.

Manager, Williamsport, NYP League, 1927-28; Hanover, Blue Ridge League, 1928; Springfield, Eastern League, 1929; San Antonio, Texas League, 1930; coach, New York Giants, 1931.

Year	Club	League	Pos.	G.	AB.	R.	H.	2B.	3B.	HR.	SB.	B.A.	PO.	A.	E.	F.A.
1909–Utica		N.Y. St.	C-O	74	198	19	51	....	....	....	5	.251	257	58	10	.969
1910–Utica		N.Y. St.	C-O	113	348	37	84	....	....	....	26	.241	419	107	24	.956
1911–Utica(a)		N.Y. St.	C-O	129	477	77	138	....	....	....	40	.289	270	35	9	.971
1911–New York		Nat.	OF	6	17	2	1	0	0	0	0	.059	7	0	0	1.000
1912–New York		Nat.	OF	29	51	11	15	4	0	0	7	.294	24	3	0	1.000
1913–New York		Nat.	OF	150	605	81	173	37	4	2	40	.286	321	22	13	.963
1914–New York		Nat.	OF	154	561	*100	170	35	10	3	*62	.303	326	19	18	.950
1915–New York		Nat.	OF	155	*622	83	169	27	14	3	27	.272	278	13	12	.960
1916–New York		Nat.	OF	155	*623	*105	174	24	8	5	37	.279	289	19	12	.963
1917–New York		Nat.	OF	152	597	*103	180	25	13	5	40	.302	325	16	9	.974
1918–New York		Nat.	OF	119	465	80	135	22	6	4	40	.290	292	10	11	.965
1919–New York		Nat.	OF	139	534	*86	162	30	9	2	*40	.303	290	15	3	*.990
1920–New York		Nat.	OF	154	631	*115	181	35	9	6	22	.287	336	11	5	.983
1921–New York(b)		Nat.	OF	149	605	111	181	28	9	4	19	.299	360	16	11	.972
1922–Cincinnati		Nat.	OF	•156	631	104	180	20	10	1	30	.285	386	20	10	.976
1923–Cincinnati		Nat.	OF	•154	614	99	168	27	13	3	12	.274	327	11	14	.960
1924–Cincinnati(c)		Nat.	OF	93	336	43	86	19	2	2	3	.256	168	13	7	.963
1925–Philadelphia		Nat.	OF	88	349	65	102	29	1	1	4	.292	189	9	2	.990
1926–Newark		Int.	OF	163	644	129	194	*49	5	7	38	.301	375	13	5	.987
1927–Williamsport		NYP	OF	120	403	54	119	28	4	3	18	.295	245	9	5	.981
1928–Williamsport		NYP	OF	95	321	64	105	23	5	1	16	.327	225	6	4	.983
1928–Hanover		Bl. Ridge	OF	18	65	15	23	6	0	0	6	.354	34	6	0	1.000

Year	Club	League	Pos.	G.	AB.	R.	H.	2B.	3B.	HR.	SB.	B.A.	PO.	A.	E.	F.A.
1929–Springfield		Eastern	OF	110	379	68	114	26	7	1	8	.301	193	8	4	.980
1930–San Antonio		Texas	OF	23	61	7	12	5	0	0	5	.197	21	1	0	1.000
Major League Totals				1853	7241	1188	2077	363	108	41	383	.287	3918	197	128	.969

aSold to New York Giants for $14,000, August, 1911.
bTraded with catcher Mike Gonzalez and $100,000 to Cincinnati Reds for third baseman Heine Groh, December, 1921.
cClaimed on waivers by Philadelphia Phillies, April, 1925.

WORLD SERIES RECORD

Year	Club	League	Pos.	G.	AB.	R.	H.	2B.	3B.	HR.	SB.	B.A.	PO.	A.	E.	F.A.
1913–New York		Nat.	OF	5	19	2	3	2	0	0	1	.158	14	0	1	.933
1917–New York		Nat.	OF	6	22	3	5	0	0	0	1	.227	10	0	0	1.000
1921–New York		Nat.	OF	8	33	2	11	4	1	0	1	.333	9	0	0	1.000
World Series Totals				19	74	7	19	6	1	0	3	.257	33	0	1	.971

THOMAS P. (OYSTER) BURNS

Born September 6, 1862, at Philadelphia, Pa.
Died November 16, 1928, at Brooklyn, N.Y.
Height, 5.09. Weight, 187.
Threw and batted righthanded.

Hit three doubles and a home run in a game, June 30, 1887.
Manager, Hartford, Atlantic League, 1897.

Year	Club	League	Pos.	G.	AB.	R.	H.	2B.	3B.	HR.	SB.	B.A.	PO.	A.	E.	F.A.
1883–Harrisburg		Int.-St.	OF-IF-P	....	....	....	....	....	....	....	....	.220	....	....	....	....
1884–Wilmington		East.	SS-P	55	249	....	84	....	....	....	....	.337	44	175	35	.862
1884–Wilmington		Union Assn.	SS	2	7	0	1	0	1	0	0	.143	1	6	2	.778
1884–Baltimore		A.A.	IF-OF-P	36	135	35	41	2	6	6	....	.304	....	....	....	....
1885–Baltimore		A.A.	OF-IF-P	76	319	49	73	11	6	5	....	.229	....	....	....	....
1885–Newark		East.	3B-P	12	45	2	8	0	0	0	....	.178	(13 PO-A)		1	.929
1886–Newark		East.	3B	82	262	74	79	25	4	9	20	.302	93	106	17	*.921
1887–Baltimore		A.A.	SS-3B	140	611	120	245	33	20	10	57	.401	....	....	....	....
1888–Balt.-Brooklyn		A.A.	SS-OF	129	528	95	158	27	13	6	48	.299	....	....	....	....
1889–Brooklyn		A.A.	OF	132	499	104	157	19	11	5	37	.315	134	23	16	.908
1890–Brooklyn		Nat.	OF	119	472	102	134	22	13	•13	21	.284	137	23	10	.941
1891–Brooklyn		Nat.	OF	122	465	75	131	23	14	4	23	.282	177	16	23	.894
1892–Brooklyn		Nat.	OF	139	545	94	168	25	18	4	35	.308	155	14	10	.944
1893–Brooklyn		Nat.	OF	107	397	67	111	31	10	6	21	.280	155	19	14	.926
1894–Brooklyn		Nat.	OF	126	513	107	184	30	14	5	29	.359	212	16	14	.942
1895–Brook.-N.Y.		Nat.	OF	50	187	28	48	5	5	1	5	.257	85	8	9	.912
1896–Newark		Atl.	OF-1B-P	111	426	118	168	39	15	10	51	.394	300	28	17	.951
1897–Hartford		Atl.	OF	128	478	82	159	35	8	1	32	.333	168	12	15	.923
American Association Totals				513	2092	403	674	92	56	32	142	.322	....	....	....	....
National League Totals				663	2579	473	776	136	74	33	134	.301	921	96	80	.927
Union Association Totals				2	7	0	1	0	1	0	0	.143	1	6	2	.778
Major League Totals				1178	4678	876	1451	228	131	65	276	.310	....	....	....	....

Pitching record shows no wins, no losses in 1884 with Baltimore; seven wins, four losses in 1885. With Harrisburg in 1883, record was 8-3–.727.

WORLD SERIES RECORD

Year	Club	League	Pos.	G.	AB.	R.	H.	2B.	3B.	HR.	SB.	B.A.	PO.	A.	E.	F.A.
1889–Brooklyn		A.A.	OF	9	35	8	8	4	1	0	0	.229	7	0	2	.778

GUY T. BUSH

Born August 23, 1903, at Aberdeen, Miss.
Height, 6.00. Weight, 175.
Threw and batted righthanded.
Married Delores Rosing, 1938.

Pitched two one-hitters August 9, 1931, and September 13, 1931, second game.

Year	Club	League	G.	IP.	W.	L.	Pct.	H.	R.	ER.	SO.	BB.	ERA.
1923	Greenville (a)	Cotton St.					(No Averages Issued)						
1923	Chicago	National	1	1	0	0	.000	1	0	0	2	0	0.00
1924	Chicago	National	16	81	2	5	.286	91	51	36	36	24	4.00
1924	Wichita Falls	Texas	18	99	9	3	.750	112	61	46	44	31	4.18
1925	Chicago	National	42	182	6	13	.316	213	102	87	76	52	4.30
1926	Chicago	National	35	157	13	9	.591	149	58	50	32	42	2.87
1927	Chicago	National	36	193	10	10	.500	177	76	65	62	79	3.03
1928	Chicago	National	42	204	15	6	.714	229	104	87	61	86	3.84
1929	Chicago	National	50	271	18	7	.720	277	135	110	82	107	3.65
1930	Chicago	National	46	225	15	10	.600	291	174	*155	75	86	6.20
1931	Chicago	National	39	180	16	8	.667	190	104	90	54	66	4.50
1932	Chicago	National	40	239	19	11	.633	262	106	85	73	70	3.20
1933	Chicago	National	41	264	20	12	.625	261	95	79	84	68	2.69
1934	Chicago (b)	National	40	209	18	10	.643	213	96	89	75	54	3.83
1935	Pittsburgh	National	41	204	11	11	.500	237	115	98	42	40	4.32
1936	Pitts.(c)-Boston	National	31	125	5	8	.385	147	66	57	38	31	4.10
1937	Boston (d)	National	32	181	8	15	.348	201	77	71	56	48	3.53
1938	St. Louis	National	6	6	0	1	.000	6	3	3	1	3	4.50
1938	Los Angeles	Pacific Coast	26	108	8	5	.615	121	62	47	44	16	3.92
1939-43							(Voluntarily Retired)						
1944	Chattanooga	Southern Assn.	10	69	5	3	.625	82	34	24	19	18	3.13
1945	Cincinnati	National	4	4	0	0	.000	5	4	4	1	3	9.00
	Major League Totals		542	2726	176	136	.564	2850	1366	1166	850	859	3.97

WORLD SERIES RECORD

Year	Club	League	G.	IP.	W.	L.	Pct.	H.	R.	ER.	SO.	BB.	ERA.
1929	Chicago	Nat.	2	11	1	0	1.000	12	3	1	4	2	0.82
1932	Chicago	Nat.	2	5⅔	0	1	.000	5	9	9	2	6	14.29
	World Series Totals		4	16⅔	1	1	.500	17	12	10	6	8	5.29

aLeague disbanded. Sold to Chicago Cubs.
bTraded to Pittsburgh Pirates, November 22, 1934, with outfielder Babe Herman and pitcher James Weaver for infielder Fred Lindstrom and pitcher Larry French.
cReleased by Pittsburgh Pirates, July 20, 1936. Signed with Boston Braves, July 23, 1936.
dSold to St. Louis Cardinals, February 2, 1938.

LESLIE AMBROSE (BULLET JOE) BUSH

Born November 27, 1892, at Brainerd, Minn.
Died November 1, 1974, at Fort Lauderdale, Fla.
Height, 5.11. Weight, 175.
Threw and batted righthanded.
Married Alice Marie Wray, November 6, 1937.

Pitched 5-0, no-hit victory vs. Cleveland Indians, August 26, 1916; had three one-hitters, May 28, 1918, August 1, 1921, August 27, 1925.
Manager, Allentown, Eastern League, 1930-31.

Year	Club	League	G.	IP.	W.	L.	Pct.	H.	R.	ER.	SO.	BB.	ERA.
1912	Missoula	Union	54	....	29	12	.709	....	....	....	....	....	......
1912	Philadelphia	American	1	8	0	0	.000	14	10	....	3	4	......
1913	Philadelphia	American	39	202	14	6	.700	193	97	80	78	65	3.56
1914	Philadelphia	American	38	206	16	12	.571	184	84	70	100	81	3.00
1915	Philadelphia	American	25	146	6	14	.300	137	86	67	89	89	4.13
1916	Philadelphia	American	40	287	15	24	.387	222	109	82	157	130	2.57
1917	Philadelphia(a)	American	37	233	11	17	.393	207	101	64	121	111	2.47
1918	Boston	American	36	273	15	15	.500	241	88	64	125	91	2.11
1919	Boston	American	3	9	0	0	.000	11	5	5	3	4	5.00
1920	Boston	American	35	244	15	15	.500	287	138	115	88	94	4.24
1921	Boston(b)	American	37	254	16	9	.640	244	111	99	96	93	3.51
1922	New York	American	39	255	26	7	*.788	240	109	94	92	85	3.32
1923	New York	American	37	276	19	15	.559	263	115	105	125	117	3.42
1924	New York(c)	American	39	252	17	16	.515	262	117	100	80	*109	3.57
1925	St. Louis(d)	American	33	209	14	14	.500	239	129	118	63	91	5.08
1926	Washington(e)	American	12	71	1	8	.111	83	54	53	27	35	6.72
1926	Pittsburgh	National	19	111	6	6	.500	97	45	37	38	35	3.00
1927	Pitts.(f)-N.Y.	National	8	19	2	3	.400	32	24	20	7	10	9.47
1927	Toledo	Amer. Assn.	6	51	4	2	.667	45	20	15	20	17	2.65
1928	Philadelphia	American	11	35	2	1	.667	39	21	20	15	18	5.14
1929	Portland	Pac. Coast		(Played in 27 games in outfield–did not pitch)									
1929	Newark	Int'national	7	42	3	3	.500	45	25	23	15	21	4.93

Year	Club	League	G.	IP.	W.	L.	Pct.	H.	R.	ER.	SO.	BB.	ERA.
1930–Allentown		Eastern	3	8	0	0	.000	15	5	3	3	5	3.38
1931–Allentown		Eastern	3	8	1	0	1.000	4	1	....	3	4	......
American League Totals			462	2960	187	173	.519	2866	1374	1136	1271	1217	3.45
National League Totals			27	130	8	9	.471	129	69	57	45	45	3.95
Major League Totals			489	3090	195	182	.517	2995	1443	1193	1316	1262	3.47

aTraded to Boston Red Sox with outfielder Amos Strunk and catcher Walter Schang for pitcher Vean Gregg, outfielder Merlin Kopp, catcher Chet Thomas and $60,000, December 20, 1917.

bTraded to New York Yankees with pitcher Sam Jones and shortstop Everett Scott for pitchers Jack Quinn, Warren Collins and Bill Piercy and shortstop Roger Peckinpaugh, December 20, 1921.

cTraded to St. Louis Browns with pitchers Milt Gaston and Joe Giard for pitcher Urban Shocker, December 17, 1924.

dTraded to Washington Senators with outfielder Johnny Tobin for pitchers Tom Zachary and Win Ballou, February, 1926.

eUnconditionally released by Washington Senators, June 24, 1926; signed with Pittsburgh Pirates, June 30, 1926.

fUnconditionally released by Pittsburgh Pirates, June, 1927; subsequently signed with New York Giants.

WORLD SERIES RECORD

Year	Club	League	G.	IP.	W.	L.	Pct.	H.	R.	ER.	SO.	BB.	ERA.
1913–Philadelphia		American	1	9	1	0	1.000	5	2	1	3	4	1.00
1914–Philadelphia		American	1	11	0	1	.000	9	5	4	4	4	3.27
1918–Boston		American	2	9	0	1	.000	7	3	3	0	3	3.00
1922–New York		American	2	15	0	2	.000	21	8	8	6	5	4.80
1923–New York		American	3	16⅔	1	1	.500	7	2	2	5	4	1.08
World Series Totals			9	60⅔	2	5	.286	49	20	18	18	20	2.67

JOHN WESLEY CALLISON

Born March 12, 1939, at Qualls, Okla.
Height, 5.10. Weight, 180.
Threw right and batted lefthanded.

Tied major league record for highest fielding percentage by outfielder, season, 100 or more games (1,000), 1968.

Hit three home runs in a game, September 27, 1964, and June 6, 1965 (second game).

Year	Club	League	Pos.	G.	AB.	R.	H.	2B.	3B.	HR.	RBI.	B.A.	PO.	A.	E.	F.A.
1957–Bakersfield		Calif.	OF	86	350	83	119	18	6	17	61	.340	176	8	9	.953
1958–Indianapolis		A.A.	OF	•154	545	92	154	23	9	•29	93	.283	331	11	•14	.961
1958–Chicago		Amer.	OF	18	64	10	19	4	2	1	12	.297	39	2	1	.976
1959–Chicago		Amer.	OF	49	104	12	18	3	0	3	12	.173	54	3	1	.983
1959–Indianapolis (a)		A.A.	OF	79	311	51	93	16	9	10	46	.299	193	3	3	.985
1960–Philadelphia		Nat.	OF	99	288	36	75	11	5	9	30	.260	176	7	2	.989
1961–Philadelphia		Nat.	OF	138	455	74	121	20	11	9	47	.266	227	10	8	.967
1962–Philadelphia		Nat.	OF	157	603	107	181	26	•10	23	83	.300	327	•24	7	.980
1963–Philadelphia		Nat.	OF	157	626	96	178	36	11	26	78	.284	298	•26	2	.994
1964–Philadelphia		Nat.	OF	162	654	101	179	30	10	31	104	.274	319	•19	4	.988
1965–Philadelphia		Nat.	OF	160	619	93	162	25	•16	32	101	.262	313	•21	6	.982
1966–Philadelphia		Nat.	OF	155	612	93	169	•40	7	11	55	.276	275	12	3	.990
1967–Philadelphia		Nat.	OF	149	556	62	145	30	5	14	64	.261	286	12	7	.977
1968–Philadelphia		Nat.	OF	121	398	46	97	18	4	14	40	.244	187	10	0	★1.000
1969–Philadelphia (b)		Nat.	OF	134	495	66	131	29	5	16	64	.265	273	12	3	.990
1970–Chicago		Nat.	OF	147	477	65	126	23	2	19	68	.264	244	8	7	.973
1971–Chicago (c)		Nat.	OF	103	290	27	61	12	1	8	38	.210	158	3	3	.982
1972–New York		Amer.	OF	92	275	28	71	10	0	9	34	.258	127	4	1	.992
1973–New York		Amer.	OF	45	136	10	24	4	0	1	10	.176	46	2	0	.960
American League Totals				204	579	60	132	21	2	14	68	.228	266	11	5	.982
National League Totals				1682	6073	866	1625	300	87	212	772	.268	3083	164	52	.984
Major League Totals				1886	6652	926	1757	321	89	226	840	.264	3349	175	57	.984

aRecalled by Chicago White Sox; traded to Philadelphia Phillies for third baseman Gene Freese, December 8, 1959.

bTraded to Chicago Cubs for pitcher Dick Selma and outfielder Oscar Gamble, November 17, 1969.

cSold to New York Yankees, January 20, 1972, for pitcher Jack Aker.

DID YOU KNOW—
That Johnny Callison's three-run, ninth-inning HR won the 1964 All-Star Game?

ADOLPH LOUIS (DOLPH) CAMILLI

Born April 23, 1908, at San Francisco, Calif.
Height, 5.10½. Weight, 185.
Threw and batted lefthanded.
Married Ruth Wallace, October 26, 1931.

Manager, Oakland, Pacific Coast League, 1944 and until June 12, 1945, when he resigned to sign as player with Boston Red Sox; manager, Spokane, Western International League, August 3, 1948, to close of season; coach, Sacramento, Pacific Coast League, June 24, 1949, to close of season; manager, Dayton, Central League, 1950; manager, Magic Valley, Pioneer League, 1953; coach, Sacramento, Pacific Coast League, 1951 and 1954-55; scout, New York Yankees, 1960 through 1967; scout, Oakland Athletics, 1968; scout, California Angels, 1969-71.
Named Most Valuable Player, National League, 1941.
Named as first baseman on THE SPORTING NEWS All-Star Major League team, 1941.

Year	Club	League	Pos.	G.	AB.	R.	H.	2B.	3B.	HR.	RBI.	B.A.	PO.	A.	E.	F.A.
1926	Logan	Utah-Ida.	1B	68	267	51	83	20	7	10	....	.311	....	....	....	......
1926	San Francisco	P. C.	1B	81	298	37	93	25	2	7	41	.312	777	50	25	.971
1927	San Francisco	P. C.	1B	81	254	22	62	18	0	2	31	.244	690	43	11	.985
1927	Logan	Utah-Ida.	1B	47	164	35	51	10	7	5	....	.311	398	24	7	.984
1928	Salt Lake	Utah-Ida.	1B	*117	387	99	129	21	11	20	....	.333	1097	*69	11	*.991
1929	Sacramento	P. C.	1B	117	446	72	132	25	6	12	74	.296	1203	69	12	.991
1930	Sacramento	P. C.	1B	166	619	94	170	44	4	17	118	.275	1615	98	20	.988
1931	Sacramento	P. C.	1B	185	714	120	210	42	9	16	100	.294*1762		117	22	.988
1932	Sacramento	P. C.	1B	187	727	141	224	*56	9	17	107	.308	1830	*147	18	●.991
1933	Sacramento	P. C.	1B	159	622	133	182	52	9	20	116	.293	1494	107	12	.993
1933	Chicago	Nat.	1B	16	58	8	13	2	1	2	7	.224	163	14	1	.994
1934	Chicago(a)-Phil	Nat.	1B	134	498	69	133	28	3	16	87	.267	1176	79	*18	.986
1935	Philadelphia	Nat.	1B	●156	602	88	157	23	5	25	83	.261*1442		96	●20	.987
1936	Philadelphia	Nat.	1B	151	530	106	167	29	13	28	102	.315*1446		79	18	.988
1937	Philadelphia(b)	Nat.	1B	131	475	101	161	23	7	27	80	.339	1256	99	8	*.994
1938	Brooklyn	Nat.	1B	146	509	106	128	25	11	24	100	.251	1356	95	8	.995
1939	Brooklyn	Nat.	1B	*157	565	105	164	30	12	26	104	.290	1515	*129	17	.990
1940	Brooklyn	Nat.	1B	142	512	92	147	29	13	23	96	.287	1299	79	11	.992
1941	Brooklyn	Nat.	1B	149	529	92	151	29	6	*34	*120	.285	1379	98	16	.989
1942	Brooklyn	Nat.	1B	150	524	89	132	23	7	26	109	.252	1334	85	12	.992
1943	Brooklyn(c) (d)	Nat.	1B	95	353	56	87	15	6	6	43	.246	853	60	7	.992
1944	Oakland	P. C.	1B	113	357	78	103	16	4	14	60	.289	917	69	10	.990
1945	Oakland	P. C.	1B	11	17	4	6	3	0	1	4	.353	7	4	0	1.000
1945	Boston	Amer.	1B	63	198	24	42	5	2	2	19	.212	505	44	5	.991
American League Totals				63	198	24	42	5	2	2	19	.212	505	44	5	.991
National League Totals				1427	5155	912	1440	256	84	237	931	.279	13219	913	136	.990
Major League Totals				1490	5353	936	1482	261	86	239	950	.277	13724	957	141	.990

aTraded to Philadelphia Phillies for first baseman Frank O. Hurst, June 11, 1934.
bTraded to Brooklyn Dodgers for outfielder Edwin W. Morgan and $50,000, March 6, 1938.
cTraded to New York Giants with pitcher John Allen for pitchers Bill Lohrman and Bill Sayles and infielder Joe Orengo, July 31, 1943.
dDid not report to Giants; sent to Oakland, Pacific Coast League, in deal for infielder Bill Rigney, December, 1943.

WORLD SERIES RECORD

Year	Club	League	Pos.	G.	AB.	R.	H.	2B.	3B.	HR.	RBI.	B.A.	PO.	A.	E.	F.A.
1941	Brooklyn	Nat.	1B	5	18	1	3	1	0	0	1	.167	45	5	0	1.000

ROY CAMPANELLA

Born November 19, 1921, at Philadelphia, Pa.
Height, 5.09½. Weight, 205.
Threw and batted righthanded.
Married Roxie Doles, May 8, 1964.

Established major league records for most home runs, season, catcher (41), 1953, and most runs batted in, season, catcher (142), 1953; held following National League records: most consecutive years, 100 or more games, catcher (9), 1957; most years leading catchers in chances accepted (6), 1956; most no-hit games caught (3), 1956; tied National League record for most years leading catchers in putouts (6), 1956; hit three home runs in a game, August 26, 1950; led National League catchers in double plays with 12 in 1948 and tied lead with 12 in 1951; established World Series records for most chances accepted, 5-game Series, catcher (56), 1953, and most men caught stealing, inning (2), October 2, 1952, first inning.

Named Outstanding Player in the National League by THE SPORTING NEWS, 1953.
Named Most Valuable Player, National League, 1951-53-55.
Named as catcher on THE SPORTING NEWS All-Star Major League Teams, 1949-51-53-55.
Named to Hall of Fame, 1969.

Year	Club	League	Pos.	G.	AB.	R.	H.	2B.	3B.	HR.	RBI.	B.A.	PO.	A.	E.	F.A.
1946	Nashua	New Eng.	C	113	396	75	115	19	8	13	96	.290	*687	*64	*15	.980
1947	Montreal	Int.	C	135	440	64	120	25	3	13	75	.273	*642	*83	9	*.988
1948	St. Paul	A.A.	C-OF	35	123	31	40	5	2	13	39	.325	147	19	6	.965
1948	Brooklyn	Nat.	C	83	279	32	72	11	3	9	45	.258	413	45	9	.981
1949	Brooklyn	Nat.	C	130	436	65	125	22	2	22	82	.287	*684	55	11	*.985
1950	Brooklyn	Nat.	C	126	437	70	123	19	3	31	89	.281	*683	54	11	.985
1951	Brooklyn	Nat.	C	143	505	90	164	33	1	33	108	.325	*722	*72	*11	.986
1952	Brooklyn	Nat.	C	128	468	73	126	18	1	22	97	.269	662	55	4	*.994
1953	Brooklyn	Nat.	C	144	519	103	162	26	3	41	*142	.312	*807	57	10	*.989
1954	Brooklyn	Nat.	C	111	397	43	82	14	3	19	51	.207	600	58	7	.989
1955	Brooklyn	Nat.	C	123	446	81	142	20	1	32	107	.318	*672	54	6	.992
1956	Brooklyn	Nat.	C	124	388	39	85	6	1	20	73	.219	*659	49	11	.985
1957	Brooklyn (a)	Nat	C	103	330	31	80	9	0	13	62	.242	618	51	5	*.993
Major League Totals				1215	4205	627	1161	178	18	242	856	.276	6520	550	85	.988

aIncurred injuries in automobile accident, January 28, 1958, which ended his playing career.

WORLD SERIES RECORD

Year	Club	League	Pos.	G.	AB.	R.	H.	2B.	3B.	HR.	RBI.	B.A.	PO.	A.	E.	F.A.
1949	Brooklyn	Nat.	C	5	15	2	4	1	0	1	2	.267	32	2	0	1.000
1952	Brooklyn	Nat.	C	7	28	0	6	0	0	1	1	.214	39	5	0	1.000
1953	Brooklyn	Nat.	C	6	22	6	6	0	0	1	2	.273	47	9	0	1.000
1955	Brooklyn	Nat	C	7	27	4	7	3	0	2	4	.259	42	3	1	.978
1956	Brooklyn	Nat.	C	7	22	2	4	1	0	0	3	.182	49	3	0	1.000
World Series Totals				32	114	14	27	5	0	4	12	.237	209	22	1	.996

MAX GEORGE (SCOOPS) CAREY

Born January 11, 1890, at Terre Haute, Ind.

Died May 30, 1976, at Miami Beach, Fla.

Height, 5.11½. Weight, 170.

Threw right and batted both ways.

Married Aurelia Behrens, January 22, 1913.

Held modern National League record for most stolen bases, lifetime (738); holds major league record for most years leading league in stolen bases (10)–1913 (61), 1915 (36), 1916 (63), 1917 (46), 1918 (58), 1920 (52), 1922 (51), 1923 (51), 1924 (49), and 1925 (46); tied with Urban Hodapp (1928) and Sherman Lollar (1955) for major league record for most times two singles, one inning, one game—two in first inning and two in eighth, June 22, 1925; tied for major league record for most years leading league outfielders in putouts and most chances accepted (9)–1912-13-16-17-18-21-22-23-24; holds modern National League record for most assists by outfielder, lifetime (339); scored 20 runs in 15 consecutive games when with Pittsburgh Pirates, August 23 to September 6, second game, 1924; negotiated 51 successful steals in 53 attempts in 1922; stole 50 or more bases six seasons, 1913, 1916, 1918, 1920, 1922, 1923.

Selected as outfielder on THE SPORTING NEWS All-Star Major League Team, 1925.

Coach, Pittsburgh Pirates, 1930; manager, Brooklyn Dodgers, 1932-33; manager, Miami, Florida East Coast League, 1940; scout, Baltimore, American League, 1955; manager, Cordele, Georgia-Florida League; non-playing manager, Louisville, American Association, July 21, 1956.

Named to Hall of Fame, 1961.

Year	Club	League	Pos.	G.	AB.	R.	H.	2B.	3B.	HR.	RBI.	B.A.	PO.	A.	E.	F.A.
1909	South Bend	Cent.	OF	48	158	5	25	2	0	0	.....	.158	129	92	24	.902
1910	South Bend	Cent.	OF	96	327	39	96	15	8	2	.....	.293	192	56	15	.943
1910	Pittsburgh	Nat.	OF	2	6	2	3	0	1	0	2	.500	10	1	0	1.000
1911	Pittsburgh	Nat.	OF	122	427	77	110	15	10	5	41	.258	304	11	8	.975
1912	Pittsburgh	Nat.	OF	150	587	114	177	23	8	5	61	.302	*369	19	13	*.968
1913	Pittsburgh	Nat.	OF	154	*620	•99	172	23	10	5	53	.277	*363	*28	16	.961
1914	Pittsburgh	Nat.	OF	•156	*593	76	144	25	*17	1	32	.243	318	23	12	.966
1915	Pittsburgh	Nat.	OF	140	564	76	143	26	5	3	28	.254	307	21	6	.982
1916	Pittsburgh	Nat.	OF	154	599	90	158	23	11	7	42	.264	*419	*32	8	.983
1917	Pittsburgh	Nat.	OF	155	588	82	174	21	12	1	53	.296	*440	28	10	.979
1918	Pittsburgh	Nat.	OF	126	468	70	128	14	6	3	44	.274	*359	*25	*17	.958
1919	Pittsburgh	Nat.	OF	66	244	41	75	10	2	0	9	.307	173	5	10	.947
1920	Pittsburgh	Nat.	OF	130	485	74	140	18	4	1	35	.289	345	10	12	.967
1921	Pittsburgh	Nat.	OF	140	521	85	161	34	4	7	56	.309	*431	15	*20	.957

Year	Club	League	Pos.	G.	AB.	R.	H.	2B.	3B.	HR.	RBI.	B.A.	PO.	A.	E.	F.A.
1922–Pittsburgh		Nat.	OF	155	629	140	207	28	12	10	70	.329	★449	22	15	.969
1923–Pittsburgh		Nat.	OF	153	610	120	188	32	●19	6	63	.308	★450	★28	19	.962
1924–Pittsburgh		Nat.	OF	149	599	113	178	30	9	7	55	.297	★428	16	●16	.965
1925–Pittsburgh		Nat.	OF	133	542	109	186	39	13	5	44	.343	363	20	★20	.950
1926–Pitts.(a)-Brook.		Nat.	OF	113	424	64	98	17	6	0	35	.231	295	8	19	.941
1927–Brooklyn		Nat.	OF	144	538	70	143	30	10	1	54	.266	331	19	11	.970
1928–Brooklyn		Nat.	OF	108	296	41	73	11	0	2	19	.247	202	8	3	.986
1929–Brooklyn		Nat.	OF	19	23	2	7	0	0	0	1	.304	7	0	0	1.000
Major League Totals				2469	9363	1545	2665	419	159	69	797	.285	6363	339	235	.966

Also played shortstop in 1909.
aReleased to Brooklyn Dodgers on waivers, July, 1926.

WORLD SERIES RECORD

Year	Club	League	Pos.	G.	AB.	R.	H.	2B.	3B.	HR.	RBI.	B.A.	PO.	A.	E.	F.A.
1925–Pittsburgh		Nat.	OF	7	24	6	11	4	0	0	2	.458	14	0	1	.933

ALEXANDER JOY CARTWRIGHT

(Pitcher and Organizer.)
Born April 17, 1820, at New York, N. Y.
Died July 12, 1892, at Honolulu, T. H.
Height, 6.02. Weight, 210.

Organized first baseball club, the Knickerbocker Ball Club of New York, 1845. Served as Secretary and vice-president. Umpired first match game of baseball ever played. New York vs. Knickerbockers, June 19, 1846. Also played infield, outfield and catcher (then called "behind"). Four years after he organized the Knickerbockers, Cartwright left New York and set out on horseback and later afoot for California. He taught the game to frontiersmen and Indians along the way. After reaching California, he and his brother, Alfred, whom he met there, intended to sail back to New York—by way of China—but Alexander took sick near the Sandwich Islands (Hawaii) and was put ashore. He prospered there and set up baseball leagues while he made a financial bonanza out of the Islands.
Named to Hall of Fame in 1938 for service apart from playing the game.

Year	Club	G.	†O.	R.
1845–Knickerbockers of New York City		10	19	30
1846–Knickerbockers of New York City		40	137	161
1847–Knickerbockers of New York City		45	131	161
1848–Knickerbockers of New York City		26	67	96
Totals		121	354	448

†Outs means number of times put out.

ROBERT LEE (PARISIAN BOB) CARUTHERS

Born January 5, 1864, at Memphis, Tenn.
Died August 5, 1911, at Peoria, Ill.
Height, 5.10. Weight, 150.
Threw right and batted lefthanded.

Had been tied with Lefty Grove for highest lifetime percentage for pitchers winning 200 or more games—.682 (Later broken by Whitey Ford, who leads with .690 on his 236-106 record.)
Umpire, Western League, 1905-06; Three-I League, 1910-11.

Year	Club	League	G.	IP.	W.	L.	Pct.	H.	R.	BB.	SO.	ShO.	C.G.
1883–Grand Rapids		Northwestern	35	....	15	16	.484	....	....	....	....	....	27
1884–Minneapolis		Northwestern	12	76	7	2	.778	78	51	15	47	0	6
1884–St. Louis		Amer. Assn.	53	482	★40	13	★.755	416	196	79	195	6	53
1885–St. Louis		Amer. Assn.	44	390	30	14	.682	323	163	81	173	2	43
1886–St. Louis		Amer. Assn.	39	399	29	9	★.763	392	182	62	50	2	39
1887–St. Louis†		Amer. Assn.	44	393	29	15	.659	341	180	80	110	4	44
1888–Brooklyn		Amer. Assn.	55	442	★40	12	★.769	326	206	104	109	★7	45
1889–Brooklyn		Amer. Assn.											

Year	Club	League	G.	IP	W.	L.	Pct.	H.	R.	BB.	SO.	ShO.	C.G.
1890–Brooklyn		National	37	304	23	11	.676	294	159	89	62	2	30
1891–Brooklyn		National	41	311	17	17	.500	336	201	101	69	2	29
1892–St. Louis		National	16	102	2	8	.200	125	77	32	23	0	10
1893–Chicago		National	1				(Played outfield)						
1894–Grand Rapids		Western					(No pitching record)						
1895–Jackson		West. Assn.					(No pitching record)						
1896–Burlington		West. Assn.					(No pitching record)						
American Association Totals			247	2122	175	65	.729	1972	961	356	701	21	230
National League Totals			95	717	42	36	.538	755	437	235	162	4	69
Major League Totals			342	2839	217	101	.682	2727	1398	591	863	25	299

BATTING RECORD

Year	Club	League	Pos.	G.	AB.	R.	H.	2B.	3B.	HR.	SB.	B.A.
1883–Grand Rapids		Northwestern	OF-P	50	227	51	63	...	...	...	...	.288
1884–Minneapolis		Northwestern	OF-P	....	....	....	....	....	....	....	....	....
1884–St. Louis		Amer. Assn.	OF-P	23	84	15	22	2	0	2	....	.262
1885–St. Louis		Amer. Assn.	OF-P	60	217	38	45	9	2	1	....	.207
1886–St. Louis		Amer. Assn.	OF-P	86	313	91	107	22	12	3	24	.342
1887–St. Louis†		Amer. Assn.	OF-P	98	425	94	195	23	9	7	59	.459
1888–Brooklyn		Amer. Assn.	OF-P	94	335	59	77	11	4	4	33	.230
1889–Brooklyn		Amer. Assn.	OF-P	57	171	45	46	8	3	2	15	.269
1890–Brooklyn		National	OF-P	71	238	46	63	6	3	1	13	.265
1891–Brooklyn		National	OF-P	47	165	25	48	5	3	2	5	.291
1892–St. Louis		National	OF-P	142	508	75	141	16	7	3	21	.277
1893–Chicago-Cincinnati		National	OF	14	52	15	14	2	0	1	3	.269
1894–Grand Rapids		Western	OF	132	544	166	181	...	...	...	...	.333
1895–Jackson		West. Assn.	OF	92	371	100	119	...	...	...	...	.319
1896–Burlington		West. Assn.	OF	52	....	45	....	....	....	...	23	.291
American Association Totals				418	1545	342	492	75	30	19	131	.318
National League Totals				274	963	161	266	29	13	7	42	.276
Major League Totals				692	2508	503	758	104	43	26	173	.302

†Bases on balls counted as hits in 1887.

NORMAN DALTON CASH

Born November 10, 1934, at Justiceburg, Tex.
Height, 5.11½. Weight, 190.
Threw and batted lefthanded.
Married Myrta Harper, January 24, 1954.

Tied major league records by having no putouts or chances at first base, June 27, 1963.
Tied World Series records for most hits, inning (2), and most at-bats, inning (2), third inning, October 9, 1968.
Named first baseman on The Sporting News American League All-Star Team, 1961 and 1971.
Named American League Comeback Player of the Year by The Sporting News, 1965 and 1971.

Year	Club	League	Pos.	G.	AB.	R.	H.	2B.	3B.	HR.	RBI.	B.A.	PO.	A.	E.	F.A.
1955–Waterloo		I.I.I.	OF	92	315	54	100	13	5	17	64	.290	173	6	7	.962
1956–Waterloo		I.I.I.	OF	115	419	81	140	20	3	23	96	.334	201	6	6	.972
1957–Chicago		Amer.					(In Military Service)									
1958–Chicago		Amer.	OF	13	8	2	0	0	0	0	0	.250	2	0	0	1.000
1958–Indianapolis		A.A.	OF-1B	29	81	10	20	6	0	1	10	.247	40	3	2	.956
1959–Chicago (a-b)		Amer.	1B	58	104	16	25	0	1	4	16	.240	231	4	4	.984
1960–Detroit		Amer.	1B-OF	121	353	64	101	16	3	18	63	.286	743	59	7	.991
1961–Detroit		Amer.	1B	159	535	119	*193	22	8	41	132	*.361	*1231	127	11	.992
1962–Detroit		Amer.	1B-OF	148	507	94	123	16	2	39	89	.243	1091	116	10	.992
1963–Detroit		Amer.	1B	147	493	67	133	19	1	26	79	.270	1161	99	7	.994
1964–Detroit		Amer.	1B	144	479	63	123	15	5	23	83	.257	1105	92	4	*.997
1965–Detroit		Amer.	1B	142	467	79	124	23	1	30	82	.266	1091	●97	9	.992
1966–Detroit		Amer.	1B	160	603	98	168	18	3	32	93	.279	1271	*114	*17	.988
1967–Detroit		Amer.	1B	152	488	64	118	16	5	22	72	.242	1135	*112	6	*.995
1968–Detroit		Amer.	1B	127	411	50	108	15	1	25	63	.263	924	88	8	.992
1969–Detroit		Amer.	1B	142	483	81	135	15	4	22	74	.280	1016	96	7	.994
1970–Detroit		Amer.	1B	130	370	58	96	18	2	15	53	.259	868	70	10	.989
1971–Detroit		Amer.	1B	135	452	72	128	10	3	32	91	.283	1020	75	9	.992
1972–Detroit		Amer.	1B	137	440	51	114	16	0	22	61	.259	1060	70	8	.993
1973–Detroit		Amer.	1B	121	363	51	95	19	0	19	40	.262	856	64	8	.991
1974–Detroit		Amer.	1B	53	149	17	34	3	2	7	12	.228	368	24	6	.985
Major League Totals				2089	6705	1046	1820	241	41	377	1103	.271	15173	1317	131	.992

aTraded to Cleveland Indians with catcher John Romano and third baseman-outfielder Bubba Phillips for pitchers Don Ferrarese and Jake Striker, catcher Dick Brown and outfielder Minnie Minoso, December 6, 1959.
bTraded by Cleveland Indians to Detroit Tigers for third baseman Steve Demeter, April 12, 1960.

WORLD SERIES RECORD

Year	Club	League	Pos.	G.	AB.	R.	H.	2B.	3B.	HR.	RBI.	B.A.	PO.	A.	E.	F.A.
1959	Chicago	Amer.	PH	4	4	0	0	0	0	0	0	.000	0	0	0	.000
1968	Detroit	Amer.	1B	7	26	5	10	0	0	1	5	.385	58	7	2	.970
World Series Totals				11	30	5	10	0	0	1	5	.333	58	7	2	.970

PHILIP JOSEPH CAVARRETTA

Born July 19, 1916, at Chicago, Ill.
Height, 5.11½. Weight, 175.
Threw and batted lefthanded.
Married Lorayne Clares, November 9, 1936.

Had six assists as first baseman, April 21, 1945. Led N. L. first basemen in double plays, 1935.
Named Most Valuable Player, National League, by Baseball Writers' Association, 1945. Named as first baseman for THE SPORTING NEWS' All-Star Major League Team, 1945.
Manager, Chicago Cubs, 1951-52-53; manager, Buffalo, International League, 1956-57-58; manager, Lancaster, Eastern League, 1960; coach, Detroit Tigers, 1961-62-63; scout, Detroit Tigers, 1964; manager, Salinas, California League, 1965; manager, Reno, California League, 1966-67; manager, Waterbury, Eastern League, 1968; manager, Birmingham, Southern League, 1970-72; minor league batting instructor, New York Mets, 1973 to date.

Year	Club	League	Pos.	G.	AB.	R.	H.	2B.	3B.	HR.	RBI.	B.A.	PO.	A.	E.	F.A.
1934	Peoria	Central	1B	23	98	22	31	7	3	3	.....	.316	149	10	2	.988
1934	Reading	N.Y.P.	1B	85	341	65	105	33	5	4	49	.308	727	52	18	.977
1934	Chicago	Nat.	1B	7	21	5	8	0	1	1	6	.381	53	5	0	1.000
1935	Chicago	Nat.	1B	146	589	85	162	28	12	8	82	.275	1347	98	•20	.986
1936	Chicago	Nat.	1B-OF	124	458	55	125	18	1	9	56	.273	980	71	14	.987
1937	Chicago	Nat.	1B-OF	106	329	43	94	18	7	5	56	.286	454	40	10	.980
1938	Chicago	Nat.	1B	92	268	29	64	11	4	1	28	.239	277	21	4	.987
1939	Chicago	Nat.	1B	22	55	4	15	3	1	0	0	.273	106	6	1	.991
1940	Chicago	Nat.	1B-OF	65	193	34	54	11	4	2	22	.280	524	30	5	.991
1941	Chicago	Nat.	1B-OF	107	346	46	99	18	4	6	40	.286	463	15	5	.990
1942	Chicago	Nat.	1B-OF	136	482	59	130	28	4	3	54	.270	744	49	7	.991
1943	Chicago	Nat.	1B-OF	143	530	93	154	27	9	8	73	.291	1305	67	★18	★.987
1944	Chicago	Nat.	1B-OF	152	614	106	•197	35	15	5	82	.321	1363	78	13	.991
1945	Chicago	Nat.	1B-OF	132	498	94	177	34	10	6	97	★.355	1172	78	9	.993
1946	Chicago	Nat.	1B-OF	139	510	89	150	28	10	8	78	.294	646	47	11	.984
1947	Chicago	Nat.	1B-OF	127	459	56	144	22	5	2	63	.314	420	24	8	.982
1948	Chicago	Nat.	1B-OF	111	334	41	93	16	5	3	40	.278	446	32	3	.994
1949	Chicago	Nat.	1B-OF	105	360	46	106	22	4	8	49	.294	712	67	5	.994
1950	Chicago	Nat.	1B-OF	82	256	49	70	11	1	10	31	.273	609	47	9	.986
1951	Chicago	Nat.	1B-OF	89	206	24	64	7	1	6	28	.311	444	42	3	.994
1952	Chicago	Nat.	1B	41	63	7	15	1	1	1	8	.238	98	10	1	.991
1953	Chicago	Nat.	PH	27	21	3	6	3	0	0	3	.286	0	0	0	.000
1954	Chicago	Am.	1-O-PH	71	158	21	50	6	0	3	24	.316	269	17	3	.990
1955	Chicago	Am.	1B-PH	6	4	1	0	0	0	0	0	.000	3	0	0	1.000
1956	Buffalo	Int.	1B	57	69	10	18	2	0	1	10	.261	58	4	0	1.000
American League Totals				77	162	22	50	6	0	3	24	.309	272	17	3	.990
National League Totals				1953	6592	968	1927	341	99	92	896	.292	12163	827	146	.989
Major League Totals				2030	6754	990	1977	347	99	95	920	.293	12435	844	149	.989

WORLD SERIES RECORD

Year	Club	League	Pos.	G.	AB.	R.	H.	2B.	3B.	HR.	RBI.	B.A.	PO.	A.	E.	F.A.
1935	Chicago	Nat.	1B	6	24	1	3	0	0	0	0	.125	58	3	1	.984
1938	Chicago	Nat.	OF	4	13	1	6	1	0	0	0	.462	4	1	0	1.000
1945	Chicago	Nat.	1B	7	26	7	11	2	0	1	5	.423	71	3	0	1.000
World Series Totals				17	63	9	20	3	0	1	5	.317	133	7	1	.993

DID YOU KNOW—

That Phil Cavarretta was fired as manager of the Cubs during the 1954 training camp?

ORLANDO MANUEL CEPEDA

Born September 17, 1937, at Ponce, Puerto Rico.
Height, 6.02. Weight, 215.
Threw and batted righthanded.

Tied major league record for most doubles, game (4), August 8, 1973.
Hit three home runs in a game, July 26, 1970 (first game).
Named National League Rookie Player of the Year by THE SPORTING NEWS, 1958 and National League Rookie of the Year by Baseball Writers' Association, 1958.
Named First Baseman on THE SPORTING NEWS All-Star Major League Team, 1959.
Named First Baseman on THE SPORTING NEWS National League All-Star Team, 1961-62-67.
Named National League Most Valuable Player, 1967.
Named National League Player of the Year by THE SPORTING NEWS, 1967.
Batting instructor, White Sox organization, 1980 to date.

Year	Club	League	Pos.	G.	AB.	R.	H.	2B.	3B.	HR.	RBI.	B.A.	PO.	A.	E.	F.A.
1955	Salem	Appal.	3B	26	93	12	23	6	1	1	16	.247	33	49	16	.837
1955	Kokomo	M.-O.V.	3B	92	374	83	147	23	2	21	91	★.393	93	158	27	.903
1956	St. Cloud	North.	1B-3B	●125	499	100	★177	33	9	★26	★112	★.355	.958	106	26	.976
1957	Minneapolis	A.A.	1B-3B-OF	151	563	91	174	31	3	25	108	.309	1162	103	18	.986
1958	San Francisco	Nat.	1B	148	603	88	188	★38	4	25	96	.312	★1322	97	●16	.989
1959	San Francisco	Nat.	1B-OF-3B	151	605	92	192	35	4	27	105	.317	995	74	22	.980
1960	San Francisco	Nat.	OF-1B	151	569	81	169	36	3	24	96	.297	681	37	13	.982
1961	San Francisco	Nat.	1B-OF	152	585	105	182	28	4	★46	★142	.311	774	51	5	.994
1962	San Francisco	Nat.	1B-OF	162	625	105	191	26	1	35	114	.306	1356	88	14	.990
1963	San Francisco	Nat.	★1B-OF	156	579	100	183	33	4	34	97	.316	1262	83	★21	.985
1964	San Francisco	Nat.	★1B-OF	142	529	75	161	27	2	31	97	.304	1211	80	★18	.986
1965	San Francisco	Nat.	1B-OF	33	34	1	6	1	0	1	5	.176	28	2	0	1.000
1966	S.F.(a)-St. Louis	Nat.	1B-OF	142	501	70	151	26	0	20	73	.301	1171	63	15	.988
1967	St. Louis	Nat.	1B	151	563	91	183	37	0	25	★111	.325	1304	90	10	.993
1968	St. Louis (b)	Nat.	1B	157	600	71	149	26	2	16	73	.248	1362	90	17	.988
1969	Atlanta	Nat.	1B	154	573	74	147	28	2	22	88	.257	1318	101	9	.994
1970	Atlanta	Nat.	1B	148	567	87	173	33	0	34	111	.305	1288	112	12	.992
1971	Atlanta	Nat.	1B	71	250	31	69	10	1	14	44	.276	586	49	5	.992
1972	Atlanta (c)	Nat.	1B	28	84	6	25	3	0	4	9	.298	171	13	0	1.000
1972	Oakland (d)	Amer.	PH	3	3	0	0	0	0	0	0	.000	0	0	0	.000
1973	Boston (e)	Amer.	DH	142	550	51	159	25	0	20	86	.289	0	0	0	.000
1974	Yucatan (f)	Mex.	1B	28	80	7	17	1	0	4	17	.213	19	1	0	1.000
1974	Kansas City	Amer.	DH	33	107	3	23	5	0	1	18	.215	0	0	0	.000
	National League Totals			1946	7267	1077	2169	387	27	358	1261	.298	14829	1030	177	.989
	American League Totals			178	660	54	182	30	0	21	104	.276	0	0	0	.000
	Major League Totals			2124	7927	1131	2351	417	27	379	1365	.297	14829	1030	177	.989

aTraded to St. Louis Cardinals for pitcher Ray Sadecki, May 8, 1966.
bTraded to Atlanta Braves for catcher-first baseman Joe Torre, March 17, 1969.
cTraded for cash and pitcher Dennis McLain to Oakland A's, June 29, 1972.
dSigned by Boston Red Sox as free agent, January 19, 1973.
eSigned as free agent by Yucatan (Mexican League), June 15, 1974.
fSigned as free agent by Kansas City Royals, August 6, 1974.

WORLD SERIES RECORD

Year	Club	League	Pos.	G.	AB.	R.	H.	2B.	3B.	HR.	RBI.	B.A.	PO.	A.	E.	F.A.
1962	San Francisco	Nat.	1B	5	19	1	3	1	0	0	2	.158	39	4	0	1.000
1967	St. Louis	Nat.	1B	7	29	1	3	2	0	0	1	.103	52	4	0	1.000
1968	St. Louis	Nat.	1B	7	28	2	7	0	0	2	6	.250	47	4	0	1.000
	World Series Totals			19	76	4	13	3	0	2	9	.171	138	12	0	1.000

HENRY CHADWICK

(Originator of the system of scoring and compiler of first rule book.)

Henry Chadwick, "Father of Baseball," was born on October 5, 1824, in Jessamine Cottage, St. Thomas, Exeter, England. He died on April 20, 1908, in Brooklyn, N. Y. He was the son of James Chadwick, editor of the Western Times, Exeter, and a brother of Sir Edwin Chadwick.

The "Dean of Baseball Writers," as he subsequently became known, came to the United States when a boy of 13. Six years later, he did his first newspaper work, contributing to the Long Island Star, and when he was 32, he became a reporter on the New York Times. In 1858, when he was 34 years old, he joined the editorial staff of the New York Clipper, a famous amusement-sports weekly of the time, and remained with that publication until 1888. He did his first baseball writing in 1858. In 1864, he wrote baseball for the old New York Herald, remaining a contributor to that paper for several years, and then transferred to the New York Sun.

As early as 1860, Chadwick's name is found in Beadle's "Dime Baseball Player." He also was editor of Haney's Baseball Book of Reference, 1866 to 1870; DeWitt's Baseball Guide, 1869 to 1880; Our Boys' Baseball Guide, 1877 to 1878; "The Art of Batting and Base Running," which was printed in the early eighties; "The American Boy's Book of Sports," and books on how to play cricket, handball, football, chess and many other sports and other works, mostly on baseball. Chadwick was a member of the editorial staff of the Brooklyn Eagle more than 45 years chiefly as a baseball writer and also occasionally covering other sports events. He contributed to Outing Magazine and for years articles from his pen appeared in THE SPORTING NEWS and Sporting Life. Chadwick became editor of the Spalding Official Baseball Guide in 1881 and held the position until his death. He frequently wrote for the New York World, the New York Evening Telegram and other eastern dailies, contributing specialized articles for which he had a reputation from coast to coast, especially for those which had to do largely with statistical and itemized detail. He was editor of the first weekly newspaper devoted exclusively to baseball, the "Ball Players' Chronicle," published from June, 1867 to July, 1869. He also edited the first fans' paper, a weekly known as "The Metropolitan, a Journal of the Polo Grounders," published between 1882 to 1884.

Chadwick became connected with the National Baseball Association in 1858, and up to the last year of its existence—1870—he was conspicuous as chairman of its committee on rules and author of many changes in the rules from which developed the game of today.

He was named to Hall of Fame in 1938 for service to baseball apart from playing the game.

FRANK LEROY (HUSK) CHANCE

Born September 9, 1877, at Fresno, Calif.
Died September 15, 1924, at Los Angeles, Calif.
Height, 6.00. Weight, 190.
Threw and batted righthanded.
Married Priscilla Pancake, October 8, 1901.

Succeeded Frank Selee as manager, Chicago Cubs, midseason, 1905; named manager New York Americans, January 8, 1913, and resigned September 15, 1914; out of game, 1915. Owner and manager, Los Angeles, Pacific Coast League, 1916-17; manager, Boston Red Sox, 1923.
Named to Hall of Fame, 1946.

Year Club	League	Pos.	G.	AB.	R.	H.	2B.	3B.	HR.	SB.	B.A.	PO.	A.	E.	F.A.
1898—Chicago	Nat.	C-OF	42	146	32	42	2	3	1	5	.288	85	20	8	.929
1899—Chicago	Nat.	C	57	190	36	55	6	2	1	11	.289	165	66	12	.951
1900—Chicago	Nat.	C	48	151	26	46	8	4	0	9	.305	160	64	17	.929
1901—Chicago	Nat.	C	63	228	37	66	11	4	0	30	.289	63	7	5	.933
1902—Chicago	Nat.	C-1B-O	67	236	40	67	8	4	1	28	.284	503	45	15	.978
1903—Chicago	Nat.	1B	123	441	83	144	24	10	2	*67	.327	1204	68	*36	.972
1904—Chicago	Nat.	1B	124	451	89	140	16	10	6	42	.310	1205	106	13	•.990
1905—Chicago	Nat.	1B	115	392	92	124	16	12	2	38	.316	1165	75	13	.990
1906—Chicago	Nat.	1B	136	474	•103	151	24	10	3	*57	.319	1376	82	16	.989
1907—Chicago	Nat.	1B	109	382	58	112	19	2	1	35	.293	1129	80	10	*.992
1908—Chicago	Nat.	1B	126	452	65	123	27	4	2	27	.272	1291	86	15	.989
1909—Chicago	Nat.	1B	92	324	53	88	16	4	0	29	.272	901	40	6	.994
1910—Chicago	Nat.	1B	87	295	54	88	12	8	0	16	.298	773	38	3	.996
1911—Chicago	Nat.	1B	29	88	23	21	6	3	1	9	.239	289	11	3	.990
1912—Chicago(a)	Nat.	1B	2	5	2	1	0	0	0	1	.200	22	0	0	1.000
1913—New York	Amer.	1B	11	24	3	5	0	0	0	1	.208	88	4	0	1.000
1914—New York	Amer.	1B	1	0	0	0	0	0	0	0	.000	1	0	0	1.000
American League Totals			12	24	3	5	0	0	0	1	.208	89	4	0	1.000
National League Totals			1220	4255	793	1268	195	80	20	404	.298	10331	788	172	.985
Major League Totals			1232	4279	796	1273	195	80	20	405	.297	10420	792	172	.985

aReleased by Chicago Cubs, September 28, 1912, and signed by New York Americans, January 8, 1913.

WORLD SERIES RECORD

Year Club	League	Pos.	G.	AB.	R.	H.	2B.	3B.	HR.	SB.	B.A.	PO.	A.	E.	F.A.
1906—Chicago	Nat.	1B	6	21	3	5	1	0	0	2	.238	60	2	0	1.000
1907—Chicago	Nat.	1B	4	14	3	3	1	0	0	3	.214	44	1	0	1.000
1908—Chicago	Nat.	1B	5	19	4	8	0	0	0	5	.421	66	0	3	.957
1910—Chicago	Nat.	1B	5	17	1	6	1	0	0	0	.353	51	4	0	1.000
World Series Totals			20	71	11	22	3	1	0	10	.310	221	7	3	.987

WILLIAM BENJAMIN CHAPMAN

Born December 25, 1908, at Nashville, Tenn.
Height, 6.00. Weight, 190.
Threw and batted righthanded.
Married Ola Sanford, October 7, 1935.

Hit three home runs in a game, July 9, 1932 (second game); tied modern major league record for most three-base hits in a game (3), July 3, 1939; led South Atlantic League in stolen bases (30), 1928, and American League base stealers (61) 1931, (38) 1932, (27) 1933; (35) tied in 1937. Led A.L. outfielders in double plays, 1935, 1938.

Manager, Richmond, Piedmont League, 1942 and 1944; manager, Philadelphia Phillies, 1946-47 through July 16, 1948; manager Gadsden, Southeastern League, 1949; manager, Danville, Carolina League, 1950; manager, Tampa, Florida-International League, 1951; coach, Cincinnati Reds, 1952; manager, Tampa, Florida-International League, 1953; manager Toronto, International League, August 1 through close of season, 1953.

Year Club	League	Pos.	G.	AB.	R.	H.	2B.	3B.	HR.	RBI.	B.A.	PO.	A.	E.	F.A.
1928—Asheville	Sally	SS	147	545	105	183	32	17	7	98	.336	★316	★508	★67	.925
1929—St. Paul	A. A.	3B	168	660	★162	222	43	17	31	137	.336	163	307	★43	.916
1930—New York	Amer.	2-★3B	138	513	74	162	31	10	10	81	.316	232	295	★42	.926
1931—New York	Amer.	2-OF	149	600	120	189	28	11	17	122	.315	325	47	14	.964
1932—New York	Amer.	OF	151	581	101	174	41	15	10	107	.299	303	13	17	.949
1933—New York	Amer.	OF	147	565	112	176	36	4	9	98	.312	288	★24	8	.975
1934—New York	Amer.	OF	149	588	82	181	21	★13	5	86	.308	368	12	13	.967
1935—New York	Amer.	OF	140	553	118	160	38	8	8	74	.289	372	★25	15	.964
1936—N.Y.(a)-Wash.	Amer.	OF	133	540	110	170	50	10	5	81	.315	377	13	16	.961
1937—Wash.(b)-Boston	Amer.	OF	148	553	99	164	30	12	7	69	.297	349	10	8	.978
1938—Boston(c)	Amer.	OF-3	127	480	92	163	40	8	6	80	.340	267	16	10	.966
1939—Cleveland	Amer.	OF	149	545	101	158	31	9	6	82	.290	356	12	11	.971
1940—Cleveland(d)	Amer.	OF	143	548	82	157	40	6	4	50	.286	307	10	12	.964
1941—Wash.(e)-Chi.	Amer.	OF	85	200	35	71	15	1	3	29	.237	176	9	1	.995
1942—Richmond(f)	Pied.	IF-O-P	118	373	48	121	27	4	3	69	.324	137	161	29	.911
1943—Richmond	Pied.						(Ineligible)								
1944—Richmond(g)	Pied.	P-3B	57	165	31	50	10	2	2	38	.303	34	62	8	.923
1944—Brooklyn	Nat.	P-PH	20	38	11	14	4	0	0	11	.368	3	6	1	.900
1945—Brook.(h)-Phil	Nat.	PH-O-3	37	73	6	19	2	0	0	7	.260	17	21	4	.905
1946—Philadelphia	Nat.	P	1	1	1	0	0	0	0	0	.000	0	0	0	.000
1949—Gadsden	So'east	P-PH	11	12	1	3	1	0	0	2	.250	....	....	....	....
American League Totals			1659	6366	1126	1925	401	107	90	959	.302	3720	486	167	.962
National League Totals			58	112	18	33	6	0	0	18	.295	20	27	5	.900
Major League Totals			1717	6478	1144	1958	407	107	90	977	.302	3740	513	172	.961

aTraded to Washington Senators for outfielder Alvin (Jake) Powell, June 14, 1936.
bTraded to Boston Red Sox with pitcher Louis (Bobo) Newsom for outfielder Mel Almada, catcher Rick Ferrell and pitcher Wesley Ferrell, June 10, 1937.
cTraded to Cleveland Indians for pitcher Dennis Galehouse and infielder Tom Irwin, December 15, 1938.
dTraded to Washington Senators for pitcher Joe Krakauskas, December 24, 1940.
eUnconditionally released by Washington Senators, May 26, 1941, and signed by Chicago White Sox, May 29, 1941.
fSuspended one year for assault on umpire I. H. Case, September 16, 1942.
gSold to Brooklyn Dodgers, August 1, 1944.
hTraded to Philadelphia Phillies for catcher John Peacock, September 16, 1945.

WORLD SERIES RECORD

Year Club	League	Pos.	G.	AB.	R.	H.	2B.	3B.	HR.	RBI.	B.A.	PO.	A.	E.	F.A.
1932—New York	Amer.	OF	4	17	1	5	2	0	0	6	.294	6	1	0	1.000

PITCHING RECORD

Year Club	League	G.	IP.	W.	L.	Pct.	H	R.	ER.	SO.	BB.	ERA.
1942—Richmond	Pied.	16	95	6	3	.667	77	24	18	56	34	1.71
1943—Richmond	Pied.					(Ineligible)						
1944—Richmond	Pied.	21	163	13	6	.684	127	46	40	147	63	2.21
1944—Brooklyn	Nat.	11	79	5	3	.625	75	36	30	37	33	3.42
1945—Brooklyn-Philadelphia	Nat.	13	61	3	3	.500	71	41	39	27	38	5.75
1946—Philadelphia	Nat.	1	1	0	0	.000	1	0	0	1	0	.000
1949—Gadsden	So'east	9	22	0	1	.000	22	17	....	19	14	.....
Major League Totals		25	141	8	6	.571	147	77	69	65	71	4.40

DID YOU KNOW—
That Ben Chapman beat Cleveland by scoring on a triple steal June 14, 1932?

OSCAR CHARLESTON

Born October 14, 1896, at Indianapolis, Ind.
Died, October 5, 1954, at Philadelphia, Pa.
Height, 5:11½. Weight, 190
Threw and batted lefthanded.

Oscar Charleston is credited in Negro circles with writing the book on how to play center field and he was the model for base runners who find themselves blocked from a base by a fielder who's holding the ball. He was a fielding stylist and a "mean" base runner, but Charleston also was a tremendous hitter, and for distance, too.

Called the "Hoosier Comet" by his fans, Oscar became a student of the inside game and later was a manager. But he was a poor manager because, like most stars, he demanded his players all play as well as he did. A player playing as best he could did not satisfy Oscar.

He was a record-setting speedster as a youngster and blossomed into one of the Negro League's most popular players. He drew kids around him like Babe Ruth did. He was lauded, in particular, for his great sense in locating a ball while on the dead run, always coming under it in position to catch it and throw.

After a tour of duty in the army (he was stationed in the Philippines), Charleston joined the Indianapolis ABCs in 1915. By the time he left them to seek greener pastures, he was the game's highest-paid player and the unquestioned "big man" of Negro baseball. He became the No. 1 power of the league when it came to a combination of perfect defense and awesome offense. Called a gazelle in center in his prime, he eventually slowed up so much that first base became his base of operations, both as a player and a manager. A powerful man physically, his body was heavily muscled on top in the power areas but slim ankles supported his frame. His legs weakened, but his bat never lost its destructive power, to the day he quit.

But he never lost his fire as a base runner, either, and never lost his trace of meanness. As Buck Leonard recalled, "I remember in 1934, on July 4, the Homestead Grays were playing a game at Greenlee Field in Pittsburgh. Charleston came home and 'undressed' our Grays' catcher, Tex Burnett. Tex was out of action for a long time as a result. Charleston said later that all he was trying to do was get home safe. He was 39 years old at the time, but just as mean as ever."

An insight into the "mean" part of the game was given by Cool Papa Bell. "Charleston would run over men he knew he could whip. We had other strong players in the league, but they didn't fight each other. They just picked on men they thought they could take easily.

"I remember," Bell said, "back in 1933, Charleston grabbed Josh Gibson to 'test him out.' Gibson was young, but big and strong, and he stretched Charleston's neck around but good, Charleston said, 'I give up. Turn me loose.' And he never bothered Gibson again. But Gibson, always a fun-loving man, never seemed to have that kind of a mean streak in him. I guess with his talent, too, he didn't have to prove anything to anyone."

As a stylist in center field, Charleston also had his light moments. Sometimes, while playing the small parks that dotted the East and Central U.S. at the time, Oscar would put on a show for the fans with his center field antics. He had absolute knowledge of the position of a fly ball, whether over his head or either side of him. When a good straight fly would come out to him, he'd turn a flip and catch the ball or sometimes just walk after the ball and catch it. To give the fans a special treat, he'd even make tumbling catches. A master at the art of clowning—and a good clown is only a good professional who wants to clown—he never gave a batter a free ride. Everyone was an out—period.

Note what 84-year-old Dave Malarcher, one of the Negro leagues' greatest third basemen and smartest managers, had to say about Charleston as a center fielder:

"I was young and had just joined the Indianapolis ABCs. I was a third basemen, but they put me at second base because Bingo DeMoss had left the club. But he returned and they put me out in right field, with Oscar in center.

"Some people asked me, 'Why are you playing so close to the right field foul line?' What they didn't know was Charleston played ALL THREE fields and I made sure of the balls down the line and all foul ones, too.

"Oh, that man could play the outfield! There was no one like him for all-round greatness. He and John Henry Lloyd," said Gentleman Dave, "were the two greatest ballplayers I ever saw, black or white."

The line on Charleston as a hitter runs like this:

If there was no one on base, the pitcher would throw every bit of junk he had in his repertoire and hope for better results. Oscar always was itching to hit, and slow stuff was a pitcher's only way to get an even break against him. With men on base and fast balls necessary to keep the runners honest, Charleston would power the ball every time he connected. It didn't do any good to throw curves at him; he'd murder them. He hit long, hard and often. In his later years as a manager and pinch-hitter, he often would pass up at-bat opportunities when no one was on base. He said he could get aroused only when there were runners to be driven home.

The test of his greatness is that Charleston's name is one of the first mentioned when you think in terms of an all-time Negro league team—just Charleston, not by position, just Charleston.

Because Oscar was a great hitter and fielder, had a fine arm and was a clutch batter to boot, he is ranked as one of Negro baseball's premier players of any era. Also tabbed the Greyhound of the Garden, Charleston was often compared with Tris Speaker in center field skills . . . both could field, hit, throw and run in levels far above the ordinary major leaguer.

In Negro ball, there were only two center fielders mentioned at any time—Charleston and later Bell. All others couldn't draw a vote on their own clubs.

Oscar also played with the Harrisburg Giants, the Pittsburgh Crawfords and Homestead Grays in the Smoky City area and the Hillsdales of Philadelphia, among others. He turned into the game's resident slugger when the chips were down and the elder statesman in player and club councils.

A credit to all of baseball, Charleston was selected to take his place in the Hall of Fame in 1976 when the Special Committee on Negro Leagues named him to join his fellow Black players in that other world of major league professional baseball.

JOHN DWIGHT (HAPPY JACK) CHESBRO

Born June 5, 1874, at North Adams, Mass.
Died November 6, 1931, at Conway, Mass.
Height, 5.09. Weight, 180.
Threw and batted righthanded.
Married Mabel Shuttleworth, 1896.

Only pitcher to lead both major leagues in won and lost percentage—Pittsburgh, 1902, .824; New York, 1904, .774. Holds American League record for most victories, season, 41; won 14 consecutive games, May 14, through July 4, first game, 1904; pitched 41 consecutive scoreless innings, June 26 (last eight innings) through July 16 (first six innings).
Named to Hall of Fame, 1946.

Year Club	League	G.	IP.	W.	L.	Pct.	ShO.	H.	R.	SO.	BB.
1895–Albany-Johnstown	N.Y.L.	19	156	7	10	.412	....	206	....	85	56
1895–Springfield	Eastern	7	33	3	0	1.000	....	34	....	8	23
1896–Roanoke	Virginia	20	156	7	11	.389	....	162	....	56	62
1897–Richmond	Atlantic	38	283	16	18	.471	....	281	....	89	58
1898–Richmond	Atlantic	40	351	23	15	.605	....	296	....	135	80
1899–Richmond	Atlantic	21	192	17	4	.810	....	165	....	67	51
1899–Pittsburgh	National	19	141	6	10	.375	0	158	98	27	61
1900–Pittsburgh	National	32	213	14	12	.538	3	213	125	58	75
1901–Pittsburgh	National	36	289	21	9	*.700	•6	245	101	123	49
1902–Pittsburgh(a)	National	35	286	*28	6	*.824	•8	240	81	137	64
1903–New York	American	40	325	21	15	.583	1	289	137	147	65
1904–New York	American	*55	*454	*41	13	*759	6	337	128	240	87
1905–New York	American	41	302	19	13	.594	3	265	121	172	72
1906–New York	American	*49	326	24	16	.600	4	313	142	150	67
1907–New York	American	30	206	10	10	.500	1	194	85	78	52
1908–New York	American	45	289	14	20	.412	3	271	133	124	67
1909–New York(b)-Boston	American	10	55	0	4	.000	0	77	51	20	15
American League Totals		270	1957	129	91	.586	18	1746	797	931	425
National League Totals		122	929	69	37	.651	17	856	405	345	249
Major League Totals		392	2886	198	128	.607	35	2602	1202	1276	674

aJumped to New York A.L. for 1903 season.
bReleased to Boston, August, 1909.

CLARENCE ALGERNON (CUPID) CHILDS

Born August 14, 1868, at Calvert County, Md.
Died November 8, 1912, at Baltimore, Md.
Height, 5.08. Weight, 186.
Threw right and batted lefthanded.

Had nine putouts and nine assists as second baseman, June 1, 1890, and six putouts and 10 assists as second baseman, September 18, 1894, first game.

Year Club	League	Pos.	G.	AB.	R.	H.	2B.	3B.	HR.	SB.	B.A.	PO.	A.	E.	F.A.
1886–Petersburg	Virginia	2B	(No averages available)												
1887–Shamokin	Cen. Pa.	2B	(No averages available)												
1888–Philadelphia	Nat.	2B	2	4	0	0	0	0	0	0	.000	2	4	1	.857
1888–Kalamazoo	Tri-St.	2B	53	216	....	61	....	....	....	19	.283	....	....	....	.904
1889–Syracuse	Int.	2B	105	425	79	145	....	....	....	53	.341	322	356	47	.935
1890–Syracuse	A.A.	2B	136	494	109	170	32	14	2	59	.344	374	360	61	.923
1891–Cleveland	Nat.	2B	141	549	119	162	20	11	2	41	.295	373	456	*74	.918
1892–Cleveland	Nat.	2B	144	552	*135	185	15	12	3	31	•.335	358	440	46	*.946
1893–Cleveland	Nat.	2B	122	481	143	160	16	12	3	27	.332	342	425	60	.916
1894–Cleveland	Nat.	2B	117	476	144	174	19	11	3	20	.365	308	380	56	.924
1895–Cleveland	Nat.	2B	120	461	97	144	15	4	4	26	.312	335	394	55	.930
1896–Cleveland	Nat.	2B	132	502	109	175	22	10	1	21	.348	*369	*496	•57	.938
1897–Cleveland	Nat.	2B	114	443	105	149	15	10	1	25	.336	322	386	42	.944
1898–Cleveland	Nat.	2B	109	422	91	122	12	2	1	5	.289	271	375	49	.915
1899–St. Louis	Nat.	2B	125	465	73	124	12	10	1	9	.266	324	348	46	.936
1900–Chicago	Nat.	2B	138	538	70	131	13	6	0	18	.243	*334	*425	*49	.939
1901–Chicago	Nat.	2B	63	237	23	61	9	0	0	3	.257	151	192	20	.945

Year	Club	League	Pos.	G.	AB.	R.	H.	2B.	3B.	HR.	SB.	B.A.	PO.	A.	E.	F.A.
1901	Toledo	W.A.	2B	71	287	....	71	17	0	0	14	.247	163	224	26	.937
1902	Jersey City	East.	2B	33	138	29	40	....	....	....	....	.290	88	103	16	.923
1902	Syracuse	N.Y.	2B	74	285	59	102	....	....	....	14	.357	231	225	27	.944
1903	Montgomery	South.	2B	108	331	12	38	....	....	....	5	.314	279	313	*47	.925
1904	Scranton	N.Y.	2B	41	155	12	38	....	....	....	1	.245	50	52	26	.874
	American Association Totals			136	494	109	170	32	14	2	59	.344	374	360	61	.923
	National League Totals			1327	5130	1109	1587	168	88	19	226	.309	3489	4321	555	.934
	Major League Totals			1463	5624	1218	1757	200	102	21	285	.312	3863	4681	616	.933

EDWARD V. (KNUCKLES) CICOTTE

Born June 19, 1884, at Detroit, Mich.
Died May 5, 1969, at Detroit, Mich.
Height, 5.07. Weight, 160.
Threw and batted righthanded.
Married Rose Ellen Freer, May 16, 1905.

Pitched 11-0, no-hit victory over St. Louis, April 14, 1917; had three one-hitters, May 19, 1914, July 26, 1916, July 17, 1917, first game.

Year	Club	League	G.	IP.	W.	L.	Pct.	H.	R.	ER.	SO.	BB.	ERA.
1905	Augusta	South Atlantic	32	....	15	9	.625	153	65	....	182	71	......
1905	Detroit	American	3	19	1	1	.500	25	8	....	2	5	......
1906	Indianapolis	Amer. Assn.	10	72	1	4	.200	65	40	....	33	17	......
1906	Des Moines	Western	27	....	18	9	.667	....	....	....	....	....	......
1907	Lincoln	Western	39	....	23	10	.697	....	....	....	....	....	......
1908	Boston	American	38	208	11	12	.478	193	73	....	93	57	......
1909	Boston	American	27	160	13	5	.722	117	58	....	82	56	......
1910	Boston	American	36	250	15	11	.577	213	94	....	104	86	......
1911	Boston	American	35	220	11	15	.423	236	118	....	106	73	......
1912	Boston (a)-Chicago	American	29	197	10	10	.500	217	97	....	90	52	......
1913	Chicago	American	42	267	18	12	.600	222	77	48	119	68	1.62
1914	Chicago	American	45	269	13	16	.448	220	96	61	122	72	2.04
1915	Chicago	American	39	223	13	12	.520	216	89	75	106	48	3.03
1916	Chicago	American	44	187	15	7	*.682	138	56	37	91	70	1.78
1917	Chicago	American	49	*345	*28	12	.700	246	76	59	150	70	*1.54
1918	Chicago	American	38	265	12	•19	.387	275	98	78	104	40	2.65
1919	Chicago	American	40	*307	*29	7	*.806	256	77	62	110	49	1.82
1920	Chicago	American	37	303	21	10	.677	316	128	110	87	74	3.27
	Major League Totals		502	3220	210	149	.585	2890	1145	....	1366	820	......

aSold to Chicago White Sox, July 10, 1912.

WORLD SERIES RECORD

Year	Club	League	G.	IP.	W.	L.	Pct.	H.	R.	ER.	SO.	BB.	ERA.
1917	Chicago	American	3	23	1	1	.500	23	6	5	13	2	1.96
1919	Chicago	American	3	21⅔	1	2	.333	19	9	7	7	5	2.91
	World Series Totals		6	44⅔	2	3	.400	42	15	12	20	7	2.42

FRED CLIFFORD CLARKE

Born October 3, 1872 in Madison County (Winterset), Ia.
Died August 14, 1960, at Winfield, Kan.
Height, 5.10. Weight, 165.
Threw right and batted lefthanded.
Married Annette B. Gray, July 5, 1898.

Had five hits in five at-bats (four singles, one triple) in first major league game, June 30, 1894; had 10 putouts, left field, April 25, 1911.
Manager, Louisville N. L., 1897-98-99; manager, Pittsburgh N. L., 1900-15; coach, part of 1925; vice-president and assistant manager, 1926.
Named to Hall of Fame, 1945.

Year	Club	League	Pos.	G.	AB.	R.	H.	2B.	3B.	HR.	SB.	B.A.	PO.	A.	E.	F.A.
1892	Hastings	Neb. St.	OF	(No Records Available)												
1893	St. Joseph	W. Ass'n	OF	(No Records Available)												
1893	Montgomery	South.	OF	32	120	21	35	5	5	0	1	.292	72	9	5	.942
1894	Savannah	South.	OF	54	219	60	68	11	2	2	20	.311	100	14	9	.927
1894	Louisville	Nat.	OF	76	316	55	87	10	5	7	24	.275	166	14	23	.887
1895	Louisville	Nat.	OF	132	556	94	197	23	4	3	36	.354	338	25	*41	.899
1896	Louisville	Nat.	OF	131	517	93	169	13	18	9	32	.327	276	17	*31	.904
1897	Louisville	Nat.	OF	129	525	122	213	28	15	6	60	.406	283	23	24	.927
1898	Louisville	Nat.	OF	147	598	115	190	24	11	2	*66	.318	346	22	14	.963
1899	Louisville(a)	Nat.	OF	147	601	124	209	21	11	5	47	.348	324	21	13	.964
1900	Pittsburgh	Nat.	OF	103	398	85	112	14	12	3	18	.281	263	9	16	.944
1901	Pittsburgh	Nat.	OF	128	525	118	166	26	14	6	22	.316	283	14	10	.967
1902	Pittsburgh	Nat.	OF	114	461	104	148	27	14	2	34	.321	217	12	9	.962
1903	Pittsburgh	Nat.	OF	102	427	88	150	•32	15	5	21	.351	168	10	7	.962
1904	Pittsburgh	Nat.	OF	70	278	51	85	7	11	0	11	.306	135	4	3	.979
1905	Pittsburgh	Nat.	OF	137	525	95	157	18	15	2	24	.299	270	16	7	.976
1906	Pittsburgh	Nat.	OF	110	417	69	129	14	•13	1	18	.309	209	15	6	.974
1907	Pittsburgh	Nat.	OF	144	501	97	145	18	13	2	37	.289	298	15	4	*.987
1908	Pittsburgh	Nat.	OF	151	551	83	146	18	15	2	24	.265	*346	15	10	.973
1909	Pittsburgh	Nat.	OF	152	550	97	158	16	11	3	31	.287	*362	17	5	*.987
1910	Pittsburgh	Nat.	OF	118	429	57	113	23	9	2	12	.263	284	10	10	.967
1911	Pittsburgh	Nat.	OF	101	392	73	127	25	13	5	10	.324	216	8	7	.970
1913	Pittsburgh	Nat.	OF	9	13	0	1	1	0	0	0	.077	2	0	0	1.000
1914	Pittsburgh	Nat.	PH	2	2	0	0	0	0	0	0	.000	0	0	0	.000
1915	Pittsburgh	Nat.	OF	1	2	0	1	0	0	0	0	.500	0	0	0	.000
Major League Totals				2204	8584	1620	2703	358	219	65	527	.315	4786	267	240	.955

aTransferred with 14 other players to Pittsburgh when Louisville dropped out of the National League.

WORLD SERIES RECORD

Year	Club	League	Pos.	G.	AB.	R.	H.	2B.	3B.	HR.	SB.	B.A.	PO.	A.	E.	F.A.
1903	Pittsburgh	Nat.	OF	8	34	3	9	2	1	0	1	.265	17	0	1	.944
1909	Pittsburgh	Nat.	OF	7	19	7	4	0	2	3	.211	20	0	1	.952	
World Series Totals				15	53	10	13	2	1	2	4	.245	37	0	2	.949

JOHN GIBSON CLARKSON

Born July 1, 1861, at Cambridge, Mass.
Died February 4, 1909, at Cambridge, Mass.
Height, 5.10. Weight, 160.
Threw and batted righthanded.
Married Ella Barr, March, 1886.

Pitched 4-0 no-hit game against Providence, July 27, 1885; won 12 consecutive games, June 1 through June 24, 1885. Month of June 1885, won 14 games, lost 1.
Named to Hall of Fame, 1963.

Year	Club	League	G.	IP.	W.	L.	Pct.	SO.	BB.	H.	CG.	ShO.
1882	Worcester	National	3	24	1	2	.333	4	2	51	2	0
1883	Saginaw(a)	Northwestern	23	....	....	....	....	....	....	....	....	....
1884	Saginaw	Northwestern	42	357	31	8	.795	399	45	329	46	10
1884	Chicago	National	14	109	10	3	.769	101	30	96	12	0
1885	Chicago	National	*70	*622	*53	16	.768	*318	99	502	*68	*10
1886	Chicago	National	53	469	35	17	.673	340	86	400	51	3
1887	Chicago(b)	National	•60	*496	*38	21	.644	*233	87	620	*55	2
1888	Boston	National	53	*485	33	20	.623	228	119	436	*53	3
1889	Boston	National	*72	*629	*49	19	*.721	292	204	572	*69	*8
1890	Boston	National	44	383	26	18	.591	132	141	369	44	2
1891	Boston	National	52	465	34	18	.654	135	155	444	48	3
1892	Boston(c)-Cleveland	National	42	386	24	16	.600	136	125	354	42	5
1893	Cleveland	National	34	296	16	18	.471	61	100	359	31	0
1894	Cleveland	National	22	150	8	8	.500	33	44	181	13	1
Major League Totals			519	4514	327	176	.650	2013	1192	4384	488	37

aPlayed 30 games in the outfield and had 84 hits, batting .295, in 1883. He participated in 14 games in the outfield in 1884, batting an overall .302, with 14 doubles, seven triples and four home runs. Seven times he struck out 15 or more batters in a game. Over five successive games, June 30, July 4, p.m. game, July 8, July 10 and July 14, he fanned 19, 16, 8, 16 and 14 batters. The Saginaw club was suspended after Clarkson's victory of August 13 and he was called up immediately by Chicago.
bSold to Boston for $10,000 in winter of 1887-88.
cReleased by Boston in midseason of 1892, due to arm trouble and signed with Cleveland.

ROBERTO WALKER CLEMENTE

Born August 18, 1934, at Carolina, Puerto Rico.
Died December 31, 1972, at San Juan, Puerto Rico.
Height, 5.11. Weight, 185.
Threw and batted righthanded.
Married Vera Cristina Zabala, November 14, 1964.

Holds National League record for most years leading league, assists, outfielder (5), 1967.
Tied National League record for most triples, game (3), September 8, 1958.
Hit three home runs in game, May 15, 1967, and August 13, 1969.
Tied World Series record by hitting safely in every game, seven-game Series, 1960 and 1971.
Named outfielder on THE SPORTING NEWS National League All-Star Teams, 1961-64-66-67-72.
Named outfielder on THE SPORTING NEWS National League All-Star fielding teams, 1961-62-63-64-65-66-67-68-69-70-71-72.
Named National League Most Valuable Player, 1966.
Named National League Player of the Year by THE SPORTING NEWS, 1966.
Named to Hall of Fame, 1973.

Year	Club	League	Pos.	G.	AB.	R.	H.	2B.	3B.	HR.	RBI.	B.A.	PO.	A.	E.	F.A.
1954	Montreal (a)	Int.	OF-3B	87	148	27	38	5	3	2	12	.257	81	1	1	.988
1955	Pittsburgh	Nat.	OF	124	474	48	121	23	11	5	47	.255	253	18	6	.978
1956	Pittsburgh	Nat.	•OF-2B-3B	147	543	66	169	30	7	7	60	.311	275	20	•15	.952
1957	Pittsburgh	Nat.	OF	111	451	42	114	17	7	4	30	.253	272	9	6	.979
1958	Pittsburgh	Nat.	OF	140	519	69	150	24	10	6	50	.289	312	★22	6	.982
1959	Pittsburgh	Nat.	OF	105	432	60	128	17	7	4	50	.296	229	10	★13	.948
1960	Pittsburgh	Nat.	OF	144	570	89	179	22	6	16	94	.314	246	★19	8	.971
1961	Pittsburgh	Nat.	OF	146	572	100	201	30	10	23	89 ★	.351	256	★27	9	.969
1962	Pittsburgh	Nat.	OF	144	538	95	168	28	9	10	74	.312	269	19	8	.973
1963	Pittsburgh	Nat.	OF	152	600	77	192	23	8	17	76	.320	239	11	11	.958
1964	Pittsburgh	Nat.	OF	155	622	95	•211	40	7	12	87 ★	.339	289	13	10	.968
1965	Pittsburgh	Nat.	OF	152	589	91	194	21	14	10	65 ★	.329	288	16	10	.968
1966	Pittsburgh	Nat.	OF	154	638	105	202	31	11	29	119 ★	.317	318	★17	12	.965
1967	Pittsburgh	Nat.	OF	147	585	103	★209	26	10	23	110 ★	.357	273	★17	9	.970
1968	Pittsburgh	Nat.	OF	132	502	74	146	18	12	18	57	.291	297	9	5	.984
1969	Pittsburgh	Nat.	OF	138	507	87	175	20	★12	19	91	.345	226	14	5	.980
1970	Pittsburgh	Nat.	OF	108	412	65	145	22	10	14	60	.352	189	12	7	.966
1971	Pittsburgh	Nat.	OF	132	522	82	178	29	8	13	86	.341	267	11	2	.993
1972	Pittsburgh (b)	Nat.	OF	102	378	68	118	19	7	10	60	.312	199	5	0	1.000
Major League Totals				2433	9454	1416	3000	440	166	240	1305	.317	4697	269	142	.972

aDrafted by Pittsburgh Pirates from Brooklyn Dodgers' organization, November 22, 1954.
bDied on plane loaded with food, clothing and medical supplies which crashed after takeoff on mercy mission to aid quake victims in Nicaragua.

WORLD SERIES RECORD

Year	Club	League	Pos.	G.	AB.	R.	H.	2B.	3B.	HR.	RBI.	B.A.	PO.	A.	E.	F.A.
1960	Pittsburgh	Nat.	OF	7	29	1	9	0	0	0	3	.310	19	0	0	1.000
1971	Pittsburgh	Nat.	OF	7	29	3	12	2	1	2	4	.414	15	0	0	1.000
World Series Totals				14	58	4	21	2	1	2	7	.362	34	0	0	1.000

TYRUS RAYMOND (GEORGIA PEACH) COBB

Born, December 18, 1886, at Narrows, Banks County, Ga.
Died at Atlanta, Ga., July 17, 1961.
Height, 6.00¾. Weight, 175.
Threw right and batted lefthanded.
Married Mrs. Frances Cass, September 24, 1949.

Was tied for major league record for most years playing with one club (22), since exceeded by Brooks Robinson; holds major league record for most games played, league (3,033); played 100 or more games 19 years—a tie for American League mark; has lifetime batting average of .366, highest total recorded by any player in major league ball; led American League in batting 11 seasons for another record; made 4,190 hits during career in majors for major league standard; led in hits eight seasons—a major league record; holds American League record for most triples (298); tied for American League record for most years, 20 or more three-base hits (4); set major league record for most years 200 hits, nine (since passed by Pete Rose with 10).
Set American League record for most stolen bases, season (96), 1915; stole 893 bases during major

league career, leading American League six times, (49) 1907, (76) 1909, (83) 1911, (96) 1915, (68) 1916, (55) 1917. Made six hits in six trips to the plate, May 5, 1925, tied major league record by making five or more hits in a game, season (four times), May 7, July 7 (second game), July 12 and July 17, 1922; hit three home runs in a game, May 5, 1925. Led A.L. outfielders in double plays, 1924 (tie).
 Named Most Valuable Player, American League (Chalmers Award), 1911.
 Manager, Detroit Tigers, 1921-26.
 Named to Hall of Fame, 1936.

Year	Club	League	Pos.	G.	AB.	R.	H.	2B.	3B.	HR.	RBI.	B.A.	PO.	A.	E.	F.A.
1904–Augusta		Sally	OF	37	135	14	32	6	0	1	....	.237	62	9	4	.946
1904–Ann.-Shef.(a)		Tn.-Ala.	OF-P	32	128	22	40	4	8	0	....	.313	46	2	5	.906
1905–Augusta		Sally	OF	103	411	60	134	13	4	1	....	*.326	149	15	13	.927
1905–Detroit		Amer.	OF	41	150	19	36	6	0	1	12	.240	85	6	4	.958
1906–Detroit†		Amer.	OF	98	358	45	113	13	7	1	41	.316	209	14	9	.961
1907–Detroit		Amer.	OF	150	605	97	*212	29	15	5	*116	*.350	238	30	11	.961
1908–Detroit		Amer.	OF	150	581	88	*188	*36	*20	4	*101	*.324	212	*23	14	.944
1909–Detroit		Amer.	OF	156	573	*116	*216	33	10	*9	*115	*.377	222	24	14	.946
1910–Detroit†		Amer.	OF	140	508	*106	194	35	13	8	88	.382	300	18	14	.958
1911–Detroit		Amer.	OF	146	591	*147	*248	*47	*24	8	*144	*.420	*376	24	18	.957
1912–Detroit		Amer.	OF	140	553	119	*227	30	23	7	90	*.410	324	21	22	.940
1913–Detroit		Amer.	OF	122	428	70	167	18	16	4	65	*.390	262	22	16	.947
1914–Detroit		Amer.	OF	97	345	69	127	22	11	2	57	*.368	177	8	10	.949
1915–Detroit		Amer.	OF	156	563	*144	*208	31	13	3	95	*.369	328	22	18	.951
1916–Detroit		Amer.	OF-1B	145	542	*113	201	31	10	5	67	.371	335	18	17	.954
1917–Detroit		Amer.	OF	152	*588	107	*225	*44	*24	6	108	*.383	373	27	11	.973
1918–Detroit		Amer.	OF-INF	111	421	83	161	19	*14	3	64	*.382	359	26	9	.977
1919–Detroit		Amer.	OF	124	497	92	•191	36	13	1	69	*.384	272	19	8	.973
1920–Detroit		Amer.	OF	112	428	86	143	28	8	2	63	.334	246	8	9	.966
1921–Detroit		Amer.	OF	128	507	124	197	37	16	12	101	.389	301	27	10	.970
1922–Detroit		Amer.	OF	137	526	99	211	42	16	4	99	.401	330	14	7	.980
1923–Detroit		Amer.	OF	145	556	103	189	40	7	6	88	.340	362	14	12	.969
1924–Detroit		Amer.	OF	•155	625	115	211	38	10	4	79	.338	417	12	6	•.986
1925–Detroit		Amer.	OF-P	121	415	97	157	31	12	12	102	.378	267	10	15	.949
1926–Detroit (b)		Amer.	OF	79	233	48	79	18	5	4	62	.339	109	4	6	.950
1927–Philadelphia		Amer.	OF	133	490	104	175	32	7	5	94	.357	243	9	8	.969
1928–Philadelphia		Amer.	OF	95	353	54	114	27	4	1	40	.323	154	7	6	.964
Major League Totals				3033	11436	2245	4190	723	298	117	1960	.366	6501	407	274	.962

aLeague not in Organized Ball.
bReleased by Detroit Tigers November 2, 1926, and signed as player with Philadelphia Athletics, February, 1927.
†Other housekeeping changes have been made in Ty Cobb's record, but two changes based on research of the 1906 and 1910 seasons bear explanation.
 In 1906, for an unaccountable reason, his first two games of the season, April 22 and 23, never were entered on Cobb's official sheet in the A.L. office. Cobb went 0-for-3 on the 22nd and 1-for-5 on the 23rd, thus giving him eight extra at-bats and one additional hit, a single, on the 23rd.
 In 1910, Cobb and Larry Lajoie were running neck-and-neck for the batting title. Cobb was well ahead of Lajoie going into the last day of the season and sat out the final game, content to let his mark stand at .383 (194-for-506). To explain further, the Lajoie games, a doubleheader in St. Louis October 9, became suspect because Lajoie's hits were a leadoff triple and seven subsequent bunt safeties.
 Red Corriden, rookie third baseman of the Browns, was told by Jack O'Connor, his manager, to play deep on Lajoie because Larry's vicious line drives pulled to left were too tough for a youngster to handle. Lajoie's smash past Corriden in the first inning, too fast for even the left fielder to block, went for a stand-up triple and convinced the rookie that his manager was correct. Corriden played deep and Lajoie took advantage of it. His second time up, he pushed a bunt that the shortstop, Bobby Wallace, fielded too late. The rest of the day, Lajoie mixed up his approach to befuddle Corriden. He would drop a bunt, or fake a swing and drop the bunt.
 A rhubarb was raised, and there were charges of a frameup by the Browns to throw the batting title to Lajoie. It was no secret that even though Cobb was universally respected, he was also hated by teammates and rivals alike.
 Lajoie was never a part of any maneuvering, but nonetheless his 8-for-8 day had raised his batting average to .384 (227-for-591), one point above the idle Cobb. The St. Louis doubleheader ended the 1910 season, and Lajoie was hailed as A.L. batting champion. Even eight of Cobb's teammates sent wires of congratulations.
 Ban Johnson, founder and president of the American League, was furious when he learned the details of Lajoie's eight-hit day and the alleged bribe. After summoning all the principals to his office in Chicago, he ousted O'Connor, the St. Louis manager, from baseball, but absolved Corriden and Lajoie of blame.
 Johnson then ordered a check of Cobb's official batting average. On October 16, he announced to the press that a discrepancy had been found in Cobb's record on a re-check and that Cobb's final official average, authenticated by the American League, was .385 (196-for-509), one point above Lajoie. Thus, Cobb was declared the official A.L. batting champion.
 It was found that the A.L. statistician who entered the performance figures onto the players' official sheets had inadvertently entered the Detroit club's figures of the second game of September 24 as the second game of September 25, when only one game was played by the Tigers. Apparently finding the second game of September 24 missing, the line was repeated as a September 24 game at the tail end of the month's day-by-day player sheets. These incorrect additions were added to the player sheets of everyone who participated for Detroit that day.
 Cobb had picked up two hits in three at-bats in the second game on September 24, and thus his sheet showed two 2-for-3s instead of one. Plainly seen on the official A.L. sheets are the crossouts of the extra September 24 game stats on every Detroit player in the original game—EXCEPT Cobb's extra 2-for-3.
 Johnson directed after the season had closed that the two extra hits be added to Cobb's official record. He never announced what discrepancy was found in Cobb's record, closing the book on all discussion. However, research for the 1981 edition of Daguerreotypes has resulted in revisions of both Cobb's and Lajoie's records.
 The extra 2-for-3 entry of September 24 has been removed from Cobb's totals, and two at-bats (one each found for May 26 and August 10) have been added. His average thus is .382 (194-for-508). An additional at-bat was found for Lajoie as well, on May 13. Nap's corrected average is .383 (227-for-592).

WORLD SERIES RECORD

Year	Club	League	Pos.	G.	AB.	R.	H.	2B.	3B.	HR.	RBI.	B.A.	PO.	A.	E.	F.A.
1907—Detroit		Amer.	OF	5	20	1	4	0	1	0	0	.200	9	0	0	1.000
1908—Detroit		Amer.	OF	5	19	3	7	1	0	0	4	.368	3	0	2	.600
1909—Detroit		Amer.	OF	7	26	3	6	3	0	0	6	.231	8	0	1	.889
World Series Totals				17	65	7	17	4	1	0	10	.262	20	0	3	.870

GORDON STANLEY (MICKEY) COCHRANE

Born April 6, 1903, at Bridgewater, Mass.
Died June 28, 1962, at Lake Forest, Ill.
Height, 5.10½. Weight, 180.
Threw right and batted lefthanded.
Married Mary Greene Bohr, March 25, 1924.

Caught 100 or more games 11 successive seasons. Led A. L. catchers in double plays, 1930, 1932. Won pennants first two years as manager at Detroit, 1934-35; hit three home runs, one game, May 21, 1925.
Manager, Detroit Tigers, 1934, until August 6, 1938; coach and later general manager, Philadelphia Athletics, 1950; scout, New York Yankees, 1955; scout, Detroit Tigers, 1960 until named vice-president of club, 1961-62.
Named Most Valuable Player in A. L., 1928, 1934.
Named to Hall of Fame, 1947.

Year	Club	League	Pos.	G.	AB.	R.	H.	2B.	3B.	HR.	RBI.	B.A.	PO.	A.	E.	F.A.
1923—Dover(a)		East. Sh.	C	65	245	56	79	12	6	5	.....	.322	222	70	*13	.957
1924—Portland		P. C.	C	99	300	43	100	8	5	7	56	.333	278	49	14	.959
1925—Philadelphia		Amer.	C	134	420	69	139	21	5	6	55	.331	419	79	8	*.984
1926—Philadelphia		Amer.	C	120	370	50	101	8	9	8	47	.273	*502	90	*15	.975
1927—Philadelphia		Amer.	C	126	432	80	146	20	6	12	80	.338	*559	85	9	.986
1928—Philadelphia		Amer.	C	131	468	92	137	26	12	10	57	.293	*645	71	*25	.966
1929—Philadelphia		Amer.	C	135	514	113	170	37	8	7	95	.331	*659	77	13	*.983
1930—Philadelphia		Amer.	C	130	487	110	174	42	5	10	85	.357	*654	*69	5	*.993
1931—Philadelphia		Amer.	C	122	459	87	160	31	6	17	89	.349	560	63	9	.986
1932—Philadelphia		Amer.	C	139	518	118	152	35	4	23	112	.293	*652	*94	5	*.993
1933—Philadelphia(b)		Amer.	C	130	429	104	138	30	4	15	60	.322	476	67	6	.989
1934—Detroit		Amer.	C	129	437	74	140	32	1	2	76	.320	517	69	7	.988
1935—Detroit		Amer.	C	115	411	93	131	33	3	5	47	.319	504	50	6	.989
1936—Detroit		Amer.	C	44	126	24	34	8	0	2	17	.270	159	13	3	.983
1937—Detroit(c)		Amer.	C	27	98	27	30	10	1	2	12	.306	103	13	0	1.000
Major League Totals				1482	5169	1041	1652	333	64	119	832	.320	6409	840	111	.985

aPlayed under name of Frank King.
bSold to Detroit Tigers for $100,000 and catcher John Pasek, December, 1933.
cSuffered fractured skull when hit by pitched ball by pitcher Irving (Bump) Hadley of New York, May 25, 1937, ending career as active player.

WORLD SERIES RECORD

Year	Club	League	Pos.	G.	AB.	R.	H.	2B.	3B.	HR.	RBI.	B.A.	PO.	A.	E.	F.A.
1929—Philadelphia		Amer.	C	5	15	5	6	1	0	0	.400	59	2	0	1.000
1930—Philadelphia		Amer.	C	6	18	5	4	1	0	2	4	.222	39	1	1	.976
1931—Philadelphia		Amer.	C	7	25	2	4	0	0	0	1	.160	40	4	1	.978
1934—Detroit		Amer.	C	7	28	2	6	1	0	0	1	.214	36	5	0	1.000
1935—Detroit		Amer.	C	6	24	3	7	1	0	0	1	.292	32	3	1	.972
World Series Totals				31	110	17	27	4	0	2	7	.245	206	15	3	.987

ROCCO DOMENICO (ROCKY) COLAVITO

Born August 10, 1933, at New York, N. Y.
Height, 6.03. Weight, 198.
Threw and batted righthanded.
Married Carmen Perrotti, October 30, 1955.

Established American League record for most consecutive errorless games (234), September 6, 1964, through June 15, 1966.

Tied following major league records: Fewest errors, season, 150 or more games, outfielder (0), 1965, and highest fielding percentage by outfielder, season, 150 or more games (1.000), 1965.

Tied major league record for most consecutive home runs in a game (4), June 10, 1959; also tied major league mark for most home runs in a game (4), June 10, 1959; tied American League standard for most total bases in a game (16), June 10, 1959; tied A. L. mark for most home runs in a doubleheader (4), hitting one in first game and three in nightcap, August 27, 1961.

Hit three home runs in game, August 27, 1961 (second game) and July 5, 1962.

Set. A. L. record for most years leading outfielders in games played (5).

Named as outfielder on THE SPORTING NEWS American League All-Star Team, 1961.

Scout, New York Yankees, 1969; coach, Cleveland Indians, October 4, 1972-73, and 1975 through 1978.

Year	Club	League	Pos.	G.	AB.	R.	H.	2B.	3B.	HR.	RBI.	B.A.	PO.	A.	E.	F.A.
1951	Daytona Beach	Fl. St.	OF-P	•140	506	98	139	35	3	•23	111	.275	*303	19	•20	.942
1952	Cedar Rapids	I. I. I.	OF	32	94	14	16	1	1	8	21	.170	49	4	1	.981
1952	Spartanburg	Tri.-St.	OF	66	226	42	57	14	1	11	55	.252	100	4	1	.990
1953	Reading	East.	OF	146	528	89	143	21	6	*28	*121	.271	263	12	5	.982
1954	Indianapolis	A. A.	OF	149	528	94	143	30	3	*38	116	.271	271	16	7	.976
1955	Indianapolis	A. A.	OF	150	555	92	149	30	3	30	104	.268	314	*23	10	.971
1955	Cleveland	Amer.	OF	5	9	3	4	2	0	0	0	.444	7	1	0	1.000
1956	San Diego	P. C.	OF	35	133	31	49	10	1	12	32	.368	50	3	3	.946
1956	Cleveland	Amer.	OF	101	322	55	89	11	4	21	65	.276	177	6	6	.968
1957	Cleveland	Amer.	OF	134	461	66	116	26	0	25	84	.252	268	12	•11	.962
1958	Cleveland	Amer.	O-1B-P	143	489	80	148	26	3	41	113	.303	327	15	9	.974
1959	Cleveland(a)	Amer.	OF	154	588	90	151	24	0	•42	111	.257	319	7	5	.985
1960	Detroit	Amer.	OF	145	555	67	138	18	1	35	87	.249	271	11	7	.976
1961	Detroit	Amer.	OF	•163	583	129	169	30	2	45	140	.290	329	*16	9	.975
1962	Detroit	Amer.	OF	161	601	90	164	30	2	37	112	.273	359	10	3	.992
1963	Detroit(b)	Amer.	OF	160	597	91	162	29	2	22	91	.271	319	10	4	.988
1964	Kansas City(c)	Amer.	OF	160	588	89	161	31	2	34	102	.274	275	10	8	.973
1965	Cleveland	Amer.	OF	•162	592	92	170	25	2	26	*108	.287	265	9	0	1.000
1966	Cleveland	Amer.	OF	151	533	68	127	13	0	30	72	.238	261	10	5	.982
1967	Clev.(d)-Chi.(e)	Amer.	OF	123	381	30	88	13	1	8	50	.231	158	4	5	.970
1968	Los Angeles(f)	Nat.	OF	40	113	8	23	3	0	3	11	.204	45	2	0	1.000
1968	New York	Amer.	OF-P	39	91	13	20	2	2	5	13	.220	27	1	2	.933
	American League Totals			1801	6390	963	1707	280	21	371	1148	.267	3362	122	74	.979
	National League Totals			40	113	8	23	3	0	3	11	.204	45	2	0	1.000
	Major League Totals			1841	6503	971	1730	283	21	374	1159	.266	3407	124	74	.979

aTraded to Detroit Tigers for outfielder Harvey Kuenn, April 17, 1960.

bTraded to Kansas City Athletics with pitcher Bob Anderson and reported $50,000 for pitchers Ed Rakow and Dave Wickersham and second baseman Jerry Lumpe, November 18, 1963.

cTraded to Chicago White Sox for outfielders Jim Landis and Mike Hershberger and a pitcher to be named later, January 20, 1965, as part of three-way deal which saw White Sox immediately send Colavito and catcher Camilo Carreon to Cleveland Indians for pitcher Tommy John, catcher John Romano and outfielder Tommie Agee; White Sox assigned pitcher Fred Talbot to Athletics, February 10, 1965, to complete deal.

dTraded to Chicago White Sox for outfielder Jim King and player to be named later, July 29, 1967. Infielder Marv Staehle assigned to Portland to complete deal, July 29, 1967.

eSold to Los Angeles Dodgers, March 26, 1968.

fReleased by Los Angeles Dodgers, July 11, 1968; signed by New York Yankees, July 15, 1968.

PITCHING RECORD

Year	Club	League	G.	IP.	W.	L.	Pct.	H.	R.	ER.	SO.	BB.	ERA.
1951	Daytona Beach	Fla. St.	1	4	0	0	.000	1	1	1	3	3	2.52
1958	Cleveland	Amer.	1	3	0	0	.000	0	0	0	1	3	0.00
1968	New York	Amer.	1	3	1	0	1.000	1	0	0	1	2	0.00
	Major League Totals		2	6	1	0	1.000	1	0	0	2	5	0.00

EDWARD TROWBRIDGE (COCKY) COLLINS

Born May 2, 1887, at Millerton, N. Y.

Died March 25, 1951, at Boston, Mass.

Height, 5.09. Weight, 175.

Threw right and batted lefthanded.

Married Emily Jane Mann Hall, February 13, 1945.

Holds record for longest service in American League as active player, 25 years; holds A. L. record for stolen bases in a game (6), made twice, September 11 and 22 (first game), 1912; stole 67 bases in 1909; 81 in 1910 and 63 in 1912; holds with Lou Brock all-time World Series record for most stolen bases—14; had 743 stolen bases in A. L.; led A. L. four times in stolen bases, 1910 (81), 1919 (33), 1923 (49), 1924 (42).

Holds major league record for second basemen in following categories: most years (21), most games (2,651), most putouts (6,527), most assists (7,629), most chances accepted (14,156) and leading league in fielding average, nine times.

Named Most Valuable Player in American League, 1914.

Manager, Chicago A. L. club, 1925-26; named coach, Philadelphia A. L. club, June 1931-32; released by Philadelphia to become vice-president, treasurer and business manager, Boston A. L. club, 1933.

Named to Hall of Fame, 1939.

Year	Club	League	Pos.	G.	AB.	R.	H.	2B.	3B.	HR.	RBI.	B.A.	PO.	A.	E.	F.A.
1906	Philadelphia(a)	Amer.	3B	6	17	1	4	0	0	0	0	.235	8	12	2	.909
1907	Philadelphia	Amer.	SS	14	20	0	5	0	0	0	3	.250	11	10	3	.875
1907	Newark	East.	2B-SS	4	16	6	7	0	0	0	....	.438	5	12	4	.810
1908	Philadelphia	Amer.	2B-SS	102	330	39	90	18	7	1	37	.273	190	189	24	.940
1909	Philadelphia	Amer.	2B	153	571	104	198	30	10	3	69	.346	*373	*406	27	*.967
1910	Philadelphia	Amer.	2B	153	581	81	188	16	15	3	80	.322	*402	*451	25	*.972
1911	Philadelphia	Amer.	2B	132	493	92	180	22	13	3	71	.365	*348	349	24	.967
1912	Philadelphia	Amer.	2B	153	543	*137	189	25	11	0	66	.348	*387	426	38	.955
1913	Philadelphia	Amer.	2B	148	534	*125	184	23	13	3	75	.345	314	*449	28	.965
1914	Philadelphia(b)	Amer.	2B	152	526	*122	181	23	14	2	81	.344	354	387	23	*.970
1915	Chicago	Amer.	2B	155	521	118	173	22	10	4	78	.332	344	*487	22	*.974
1916	Chicago	Amer.	2B	155	545	87	168	14	17	0	56	.308	346	415	19	*.976
1917	Chicago	Amer.	2B	156	564	91	163	18	12	0	67	.289	*353	388	24	.969
1918	Chicago(c)	Amer.	2B	97	330	51	91	8	2	2	32	.276	231	285	14	.974
1919	Chicago	Amer.	2B	140	518	87	165	19	7	4	73	.319	*347	401	20	.974
1920	Chicago	Amer.	2B	153	600	113	220	37	13	3	75	.369	*449	471	23	*.976
1921	Chicago	Amer.	2B	139	526	79	177	20	10	2	58	.337	376	458	28	*.968
1922	Chicago	Amer.	2B	154	598	92	194	20	12	1	69	.324	406	451	21	*.976
1923	Chicago	Amer.	2B	145	505	89	182	22	5	5	67	.360	347	430	20	.975
1924	Chicago	Amer.	2B	152	556	108	194	27	7	6	86	.349	396	446	20	*.977
1925	Chicago	Amer.	2B	118	425	80	147	26	3	3	80	.346	290	346	20	.970
1926	Chicago(d)	Amer.	2B	106	375	66	129	32	4	1	62	.344	228	307	15	.973
1927	Philadelphia	Amer.	2B	95	226	50	76	12	1	1	15	.338	124	150	10	.965
1928	Philadelphia	Amer.	SS	36	33	3	10	3	0	0	7	.303	0	1	0	1.000
1929	Philadelphia	Amer.	PH	9	7	0	0	0	0	0	0	.000	0	0	0	.000
1930	Philadelphia	Amer.	PH	3	2	1	1	0	0	0	0	.500	0	0	0	.000
Major League Totals				2826	9946	1816	3309	437	186	47	1307	.333	6624	7715	450	.970

aPlayed under name of Edward Sullivan.
bSold to Chicago White Sox for $50,000, December 8, 1914.
cIn Military Service most of season.
dReleased by Chicago White Sox, November 11, 1926; signed with Philadelphia Athletics, December 23, 1926.

WORLD SERIES RECORD

Year	Club	League	Pos.	G.	AB.	R.	H.	2B.	3B.	HR.	RBI.	B.A.	PO.	A.	E.	F.A.
1910	Philadelphia	Amer.	2B	5	21	5	9	4	0	0	3	.429	17	17	1	.971
1911	Philadelphia	Amer.	2B	6	21	4	6	1	0	0	0	.286	12	22	4	.895
1913	Philadelphia	Amer.	2B	5	19	5	8	0	2	0	3	.421	16	18	1	.971
1914	Philadelphia	Amer.	2B	4	14	0	3	0	0	0	1	.214	9	12	0	1.000
1917	Chicago	Amer.	2B	6	22	4	9	1	0	0	2	.409	11	22	0	1.000
1919	Chicago	Amer.	2B	8	31	2	7	1	0	0	1	.226	21	31	2	.963
World Series Totals				34	128	20	42	7	2	0	10	.328	86	122	8	.963

JAMES JOSEPH (JIMMY) COLLINS

Born January 16, 1873, at Niagara Falls, N. Y.
Died March 6, 1943, at Buffalo, N. Y.
Height, 5.07½. Weight, 160.
Threw and batted righthanded.
Married Sarah Edwina Murphy, July 4, 1907.

Holds National League record for most chances accepted, exclusive of errors, third base, season, 601, 1899.
Manager, Boston A. L., 1901 to 1906; manager, Minneapolis, American Association, 1909; manager, Providence, Eastern League, 1910-11.
Named to Hall of Fame, 1945.

Year	Club	League	Pos.	G.	AB.	R.	H.	2B.	3B.	HR.	SB.	B.A.	PO.	A.	E.	F.A.
1893	Buffalo	East.	SS-OF	76	297	49	85	13	2	2	10	.286	131	249	65	.854
1894	Buffalo	East.	OF	125	562	126	*198	51	13	8	18	.352	299	*34	21	.940
1895	Bos.(a)-L'ville	Nat.	3B	104	410	75	114	15	8	7	14	.278	128	185	30	.913
1896	Boston	Nat.	3B	83	303	52	91	7	6	1	10	.300	135	208	32	.915
1897	Boston	Nat.	3B	133	529	102	183	25	11	6	16	.346	*213	*303	38	.931
1898	Boston	Nat.	3B	152	600	106	202	34	4	*14	10	.337	*246	333	40	.935
1899	Boston	Nat.	3B	151	597	98	164	26	13	4	16	.275	225	376	30	.952
1900	Boston	Nat.	3B	•142	*585	104	175	20	6	6	20	.299	*252	*323	47	.924
1901	Boston(b)	Amer.	3B	138	563	109	185	42	16	5	18	.329	210	•323	50	.914
1902	Boston	Amer.	3B	105	425	71	138	21	10	6	11	.325	138	247	20	*.951
1903	Boston	Amer.	3B	130	541	87	160	34	17	5	22	.296	172	258	26	.943
1904	Boston	Amer.	3B	156	633	85	168	32	13	3	19	.265	*191	320	30	.945
1905	Boston	Amer.	3B	131	508	66	140	25	5	4	18	.276	164	268	36	.923
1906	Boston	Amer.	3B	37	142	17	39	9	4	1	1	.275	43	70	11	.911

Year	Club	League	Pos.	G.	AB.	R.	H.	2B.	3B.	HR.	SB.	B.A.	PO.	A.	E.	F.A.
1907	Bos.(c)-Phila.	Amer.	3B	141	523	51	146	29	1	0	8	.279	143	257	47	.895
1908	Philadelphia	Amer.	3B	115	433	34	94	14	3	0	5	.217	116	216	26	.928
1909	Minneapolis	A. A.	3B	153	556	61	152	21	3	2	13	.273	170	342	45	.919
1910	Providence	East.	3B	121	438	35	98	11	4	1	12	.224	148	255	30	.931
1911	Providence	East.	3B	8	23	3	4	0	0	0	0	.174	6	15	2	.913
American League Totals				953	3768	520	1070	206	69	24	102	.284	1178	1959	246	.927
National League Totals				765	3024	537	929	127	48	38	86	.307	1199	1728	217	.931
Major League Totals				1718	6792	1057	1999	333	117	62	188	.294	2377	3687	463	.929

aLoaned to Louisville, subject to recall, May 17, 1895.
bJumped to American League.
cTraded to Philadelphia for infielder Jack Knight, June 7, 1907.

WORLD SERIES RECORD

Year	Club	League	Pos.	G.	AB.	R.	H.	2B.	3B.	HR.	SB.	B.A.	PO.	A.	E.	F.A.
1903	Boston	Amer.	3B	8	36	5	9	1	2	0	3	.250	7	23	2	.938

EARLE BRYAN COMBS

Born May 14, 1899, at Pebworth, Ky.
Died July 21, 1976, at Richmond, Ky.
Height, 6.00. Weight, 185.
Threw right and batted lefthanded.
Married Ruth McCollum, October 16, 1922.

Tied American League record for most three-base hits in game (3), September 22, 1927.
Tied record most runs, World Series game (4), October 2, 1932. Accepted most chances for outfielder, World Series (4 games, 1927), 16. Most putouts for outfielder, one Series (4 games, 1927), 16.
Coach, New York Yankees, 1935 through 1944; St. Louis Browns, 1947; Boston Red Sox, 1948 through 1952; Philadelphia Phillies, 1954.
Named to Hall of Fame, 1970.

Year	Club	League	Pos.	G.	AB.	R.	H.	2B.	3B.	HR.	RBI.	B.A.	PO.	A.	E.	F.A.
1922	Louisville	A.A.	OF	130	485	86	167	21	•18	4	55	.344	282	12	17	.945
1923	Louisville	A.A.	OF	166	634	127	•241	46	15	14	145	.380	373	13	18	.955
1924	New York	Amer.	OF	24	35	10	14	5	0	0	2	.400	12	0	0	1.000
1925	New York	Amer.	OF	150	593	117	203	36	13	3	61	.342	370	12	9	.977
1926	New York	Amer.	OF	145	606	113	181	31	12	8	56	.299	375	8	12	.970
1927	New York	Amer.	OF	152	•648	137	•231	36	•23	6	64	.356	•411	6	14	.968
1928	New York	Amer.	OF	149	626	118	194	33	•21	7	56	.310	•424	11	9	.980
1929	New York	Amer.	OF	142	586	119	202	33	15	3	65	.345	358	10	13	.966
1930	New York	Amer.	OF	137	532	129	183	30	•22	7	82	.344	275	5	9	.969
1931	New York	Amer.	OF	138	563	120	179	31	13	5	58	.318	335	5	9	.974
1932	New York	Amer.	OF	144	591	143	190	32	10	9	65	.321	343	6	12	.967
1933	New York	Amer.	OF	122	417	86	125	22	16	5	60	.300	227	3	6	.975
1934	New York (a)	Amer.	OF	63	251	47	80	13	5	2	25	.319	145	1	1	.993
1935	New York	Amer.	OF	89	298	47	84	7	4	3	35	.282	143	2	1	.993
Major League Totals				1455	5746	1186	1866	309	154	58	629	.325	3418	69	95	.973

aFractured skull and sustained other injuries crashing into wall at St. Louis, July 24, 1934.

WORLD SERIES RECORD

Year	Club	League	Pos.	G.	AB.	R.	H.	2B.	3B.	HR.	RBI.	B.A.	PO.	A.	E.	F.A.
1926	New York	Amer.	OF	7	28	3	10	2	0	0	2	.357	17	0	0	1.000
1927	New York	Amer.	OF	4	16	6	5	0	0	0	2	.313	16	0	0	1.000
1928	New York	Amer.	OF	1	0	0	0	0	0	0	1	.000	0	0	0	.000
1932	New York	Amer.	OF	4	16	8	6	1	0	1	4	.375	10	0	0	1.000
World Series Totals				16	60	17	21	3	0	1	9	.350	43	0	0	1.000

CHARLES ALBERT (OLD ROMAN) COMISKEY

Born August 15, 1859, at Chicago, Ill.
Died October 26, 1931, at Eagle River, Wis.
Height, 6.00. Weight, 180.
Threw and batted righthanded.
Married Nan Kelly, 1892.

Revolutionized style of first base play by playing off the sack and making pitcher come to bag to take throws.

Manager, St. Louis Browns, American Association, 1883, 1885 to 1889; Chicago, Players League, 1890; St. Louis Browns, 1891; Cincinnati, 1892-93-94; owner-manager, St. Paul, Western League, 1895 to 1899; owner and manager, Chicago A. L., 1900; president, Chicago A. L., 1901 to time of death.

Named to Hall of Fame in 1939 for exceptional ability among players whose active careers ended prior to 1900, and also as a builder of baseball.

Year	Club	League	Pos.	G.	AB.	R.	H.	2B.	3B.	HR.	SB.	B.A.	PO.	A.	E.	F.A.
1877	Elgin	Ind.														
1878	Dubuque	Ind.	P-1B	21								.282				.883
1879	Dubuque	N.W.	P-1B	45								.235				.824
1880	Dubuque	Ind.														
1881	Dubuque	Ind.														
1882	St. Louis	A.A.	P-1B	78	327	58	80	9	7	1		.245	859	18	29	.968
1883	St. Louis	A.A.	1B-OF	96	404	76	120	17	9	2		.297	(1088 PO-A)	43		.962
1884	St. Louis	A.A.	1B	108	461	86	111	17	6	2		.241	(1205 PO-A)	36		.971
1885	St. Louis	A.A.	1B	83	342	66	89	13	7	2		.260	(973 PO-A)	27		.973
1886	St. Louis	A.A.	1B	131	577	94	150	17	8	3	47	.260	1152	44	29	.976
1887	St. Louis	A.A.	1B	125	563	136	207	22	6	4	122	.368	1137	49	29	.976
1888	St. Louis	A.A.	1B	137	576	101	156	20	5	5	77	.271	1279	44	42	.969
1889	St. Louis (a)	A.A.	1B	137	586	105	169	24	10	3	71	.288	1223	39	35	.973
1890	Chicago	Players	1B	88	375	53	93	11	3	0	35	.248	883	45	32	.967
1891	St. Louis (b)	A.A.	1B	130	532	82	141	16	2	3	39	.265	1431	60	27	.982
1892	Cincinnati	Nat.	1B	140	554	60	124	14	5	4	28	.224	1460	71	25	.984
1893	Cincinnati	Nat.	1B	62	253	38	58	11	1	0	12	.229	671	21	14	.980
1894	Cincinnati	Nat.	1B	59	230	26	61	8	0	0	9	.265	558	26	16	.973
1895	St. Paul	West.	1B	17	67	15	23				3	.343	134	5	4	.972
American Association Totals				1025	4368	804	1223	155	60	25	356	.280	(10601 PO-A)	297		.973
National League Totals				261	1037	124	243	33	6	4	49	.234	2689	118	55	.981
Players League Totals				88	375	53	93	11	3	0	35	.248	883	45	32	.967
Major League Totals				1374	5780	981	1559	199	69	29	440	.270	(14336 PO-A)	884		.974

aJumped to Players League.
bSigned with Cincinnati after consolidation of National League and American Association.

WORLD SERIES RECORD

Year	Club	League	Pos.	G.	AB.	R.	H.	2B.	3B.	HR.	SB.	B.A.	PO.	A.	E.	F.A.
1885	St. Louis	A.A.	1B	7	24	6	6	0	0	0	0	.250	62	3	6	.915
1886	St. Louis	A.A.	1B	6	23	1	6	0	0	0	0	.261	45	2	4	.922
1887	St. Louis	A.A.	1B	15	62	8	20	2	0	0	4	.323	150	6	3	.981
1888	St. Louis	A.A.	1B	10	41	6	11	1	1	0	5	.268	90	5	3	.969
World Series Totals				38	150	21	43	3	1	0	9	.287	347	16	16	.958

JOHN BERTRAND (JOCKO) CONLAN

Born, December 6, 1899, at Chicago, Ill.
Height, 5.07½. Weight, 160.
Threw and batted lefthanded.
Married Ruth Anderson, January 12, 1926.

Jocko Conlan was a fiesty son of the sod who took no extra lip from anyone. He took the brunt of legitimate beefs but one cuss word and the offender was gone. He was a master psychologist in the charged-up world of the baseball diamond, knowing when to cajole, when to rebuff and when to ignore. He knew the rules as well as any umpire but he also used the feel of the rules as they applied to plays and players. He was a vocal defender of the umpires' integrity and he lived that integrity to the hilt all the years of his career. Doubtless his years as a player gave him an insight that few others could match, but it never affected the correctness or proper application of the rules and decisions therefrom. There is no mold from which can be made another Jocko.

Umpire, New York-Pennsylvania League, 1936-37; American Association, 1938-39-40; National League, 1941-64.
World Series umpire, 1945-50-54-57-61.
All-Star Game umpire, 1943-47-50-53-58-62 (second game).
Named to Hall of Fame, 1974.

RECORD AS PLAYER

Year	Club	League	Pos.	G.	AB.	R.	H.	2B.	3B.	HR.	RBI.	B.A.	PO.	A.	E.	F.A.
1920	Wichita	West.	OF	117	430	50	106	15	5	4		.247	209	14	19	.921
1921							(Out of game)									
1922	Wichita	West.	OF	10	40	5	11	1	1	1		.275	22	1	0	1.000
1923	Wichita	West.	OF	167	656	135	204	37	7	18		.311	*465	28	16	.969
1924	Rochester	Int.	OF	165	*666	135	*214	44	15	12	64	.321	*420	•24	13	.972
1925	Rochester	Int.	OF	143	544	95	168	36	10	6	69	.309	328	*25	15	.959
1926	Rochester	Int.	OF	123	497	98	142	29	8	3	49	.286	277	19	•17	.946
1927	Newark	Int.	OF	157	626	119	201	33	11	4	75	.321	373	15	10	.975
1928	Newark	Int.	OF	154	609	104	183	27	9	7	58	.300	382	23	12	.971

Year	Club	League	Pos.	G.	AB.	R.	H.	2B.	3B.	HR.	RBI.	B.A.	PO.	A.	E.	F.A.
1929—Newark		Int.	OF	160	613	116	186	34	13	10	62	.303	287	13	10	.968
1930—Toledo		A.A.	OF	69	279	46	81	13	2	2	....	.290	141	9	7	.955
1931—Montreal		Int.	OF	149	594	77	178	28	6	2	43	.300	257	12	9	.968
1932—Montreal		Int.	OF	112	353	50	100	22	5	2	31	.283	149	14	4	.976
1933—							(Out of game)									
1934—Chicago		Amer.	OF	63	225	35	56	11	3	0	16	.249	122	5	6	.955
1935—Chicago		Amer.	OF	65	140	20	40	7	1	0	15	.286	71	3	3	.961
Major League Totals				128	365	55	96	18	4	0	31	.263	193	8	9	.957

THOMAS HENRY CONNOLLY

(American League arbiter and umpire supervisor for 53 years.)
Born December 31, 1870, at Manchester, England.
Died April 28, 1961, at Natick, Mass.
Height, 5.07. Weight, 170.

A pioneer member of the American League umpire staff, Tommy Connolly spent 60 years in Organized Ball's umpiring profession. He served the A. L. for 53 seasons, the last 23 as chief of staff, before retiring on January 14, 1954 at the age of 83.

Born in England, he came to the United States with his family at the age of 13. He mastered the baseball rules as a youth and turned to umpiring. While working school and sandlot games around Natick, Mass., he was spotted by Tim Hurst, National League arbiter, who recommended him to the New England League in 1894. Four years later, Connolly advanced to the National League. He called them in that loop from 1898 through 1900.

In 1901, President Ban Johnson expanded the American League to major status and hired Connolly as an umpire on the recommendation of Connie Mack, manager of the new Philadelphia club. Tommy fitted perfectly into Johnson's policy that the arbiters were boss of the game and should be respected as representatives of the league.

Connolly had the distinction of umpiring the first game in the A. L.'s initial season as a major. On opening day, April 24, 1901, he called the Cleveland-Chicago game at the old White Sox park. The three other games scheduled for that day were rained out. Tommy handled the game alone and continued to call 'em by himself until 1907. He also umpired the first games played at the old New York Highlander's field, Comiskey Park in Chicago, Shibe Park (now Connie Mack Stadium) in Philadelphia, Fenway Park in Boston and Yankee Stadium in New York. He and Hank O'Day of the National League were the umpires in charge of the first modern World Series in 1903. Tommy was on duty in eight World Series.

Connolly quit the active ranks in June, 1931, and became chief of staff for the American League. He retained this job until his retirement in January, 1954. For many years he was a member of O. B.'s Rules Committee and in this capacity was responsible for numerous changes in the playing code. On May 27, 1953, he was awarded a gold lifetime pass—a memento usually reserved for players with 20 years of service—by both majors.

He and Bill Klem were named to the Hall of Fame in September, 1953, by the Committee on Veterans as the first umpires to be so recognized.

ROGER CONNOR

Born July 1, 1857, at Waterbury, Conn.
Died January 4, 1931, at Waterbury, Conn.
Height, 6.02. Weight, 210.
Threw and batted lefthanded.

Hit three home runs in game against Indianapolis, May 9, 1888; made six hits in six times at bat (three singles, two doubles, one triple) against New York, June 1, 1985.

Manager, St. Louis, National League, part of 1896; manager and owner, Springfield, Connecticut Lecgue, 1902.

Named to Hall of Fame, 1976.

Year	Club	League	Pos.	G.	AB.	R.	H.	2B.	3B.	HR.	SB.	B.A.	PO.	A.	E.	F.A.
1880—Troy		Nat.	3B	83	340	53	113	17	10	3	....	.332	116	159	60	.821
1881—Troy		Nat.	1B	84	361	54	104	17	6	2	....	.288	826	40	44	.952
1882—Troy		Nat.	1-3B-O	79	339	63	111	22	*17	4	....	.327	474	24	34	.936
1883—New York		Nat.	1B	96	401	80	145	28	14	1	....	.362	941	39	44	.957
1884—New York		Nat.	2-3B-O	112	462	93	146	27	4	4	....	.316	284	212	82	.858
1885—New York		Nat.	1B	110	455	102	*169	23	●15	1	....	*.371	1178	42	31	.975

Year	Club	League	Pos.	G.	AB.	R.	H.	2B.	3B.	HR.	SB.	B.A.	PO.	A.	E.	F.A.
1886	New York	Nat.	1B	118	485	105	172	30	*19	7	17	.355	1164	65	34	.973
1887	New York	Nat.	1B	127	546	113	209	26	22	17	43	.383	1325	44	30	.979
1888	New York	Nat.	1B	134	481	98	140	15	●17	14	27	.291	1337	43	26	.982
1889	New York	Nat.	1B	131	496	117	157	32	●17	13	21	.317	1265	32	30	.977
1890	New York	Players	1B	123	484	134	180	25	15	14	23	.372	1332	80	18	.987
1891	New York	Nat.	1B	129	477	110	140	27	12	7	32	.293	1380	52	27	.981
1892	Philadelphia	Nat.	1B	153	558	122	159	31	11	11	20	.285	1461	60	23	*.985
1893	New York	Nat.	1B	●135	490	111	158	25	8	11	29	.322*	1419	81	*40	.974
1894	N.Y.-St. Louis	Nat.	1B-OF	121	462	93	145	34	26	8	15	.313	1084	81	28	.977
1895	St. Louis	Nat.	1B	104	402	78	131	28	7	6	8	.326	957	63	17	.984
1896	St. Louis	Nat.	1B	126	485	68	137	19	6	8	14	.282	1223	*86	17	●.987
1897	St. Louis	Nat.	1B	22	83	13	19	3	1	1	3	.229	237	11	4	.984
1987	Fall River	N. Eng.	1B	47	171	32	49	....	....	....	9	.287	473	31	9	.982
1898	Waterbury	Conn.	1B	95	....	....	....	....	....	....	....	.319	*890	....	....	*.980
1899	Waterbury	Conn.	1B	92	347	79	136	28	2	5	18	*.392	....	....	....	*.982
1900	Waterbury	Conn.	1B	83	286	54	82	9	3	2	20	.287	851	32	15	.983
1901	Water.-N. Hav.	Conn.	1B	107	411	58	123	....	....	....	....	.299	....	....	....	....
1902	Springfield	Conn.	1B	62	224	25	58	7	1	1	15	.259	642	27	15	.978
1903	Springfield	Conn.	1B	75	279	28	76	12	3	0	12	.272	789	28	21	.975
	National League Totals			1864	7323	1473	2355	404	212	118	229	.322	16671	1134	571	.969
	Players League Totals			123	484	134	180	25	15	14	23	.372	1332	80	18	.987
	Major League Totals			1987	7807	1607	2535	429	227	132	252	.325	18003	1214	589	.970

WORLD SERIES RECORD

Year	Club	League	Pos.	G.	AB.	R.	H.	HR.	B.A.	PO.	A.	E.	F.A.
1888	New York	National	1B	7	23	7	6	0	.261	77	1	2	.975
1889	New York	National	1B	9	36	9	12	0	.333	86	3	2	.978
	World Series Totals			16	59	16	18	0	.305	163	4	4	.977

ARLIE WILBUR COOPER

Born February 24, 1892, at Bearsville, W. Va.
Died August 7, 1973, at Van Nuys, Calif.
Height, 5.11½. Weight, 165.
Threw left and batted righthanded.
Married Edith Warden, July 15, 1916.

Led National League in complete games 1919 and 1922.
Manager, McKeesport in Penn State Association in 1935; manager, Jeannette, Evangeline League, 1936; manager, Greensburg, Penn State Association, 1937.

Year	Club	League	G.	IP.	W.	L.	Pct.	H.	R.	ER.	SO.	BB.	ERA.
1911	Marion	Ohio State	34	....	17	11	.607	....	....	....	....	....	....
1912	Columbus	Amer. Assn.	31	219	16	9	.640	184	95	....	117	107	....
1912	Pittsburgh	National	6	38	3	0	1.000	32	7	7	30	15	1.67
1913	Pittsburgh	National	30	93	5	3	.625	98	52	34	39	45	3.29
1914	Pittsburgh	National	40	267	16	15	.516	246	99	63	102	79	2.12
1915	Pittsburgh	National	38	186	5	16	.238	180	92	68	71	52	3.29
1916	Pittsburgh	National	42	246	12	11	.522	189	72	51	111	74	1.87
1917	Pittsburgh	National	40	298	17	11	.607	276	96	78	99	54	2.36
1918	Pittsburgh	National	38	273	11	14	.576	219	86	64	117	65	2.11
1919	Pittsburgh	National	35	287	19	13	.594	229	97	*85	106	74	2.66
1920	Pittsburgh	National	44	327	24	15	.615	307	113	87	114	52	2.39
1921	Pittsburgh	National	38	▲327	●22	14	.611	*341	146	*118	134	80	3.25
1922	Pittsburgh	National	41	295	23	14	.622	330	130	104	129	61	3.18
1923	Pittsburgh	National	39	295	17	*19	.472	331	136	117	77	71	3.57
1924	Pittsburgh(a)	National	38	269	20	14	.588	296	116	98	62	40	3.28
1925	Chicago	National	32	212	12	14	.462	249	115	101	41	61	4.29
1926	Chicago(b)	National	8	55	2	1	.667	65	32	27	18	21	4.42
1926	Detroit	American	8	14	0	4	.000	27	18	17	2	9	10.93
1926	Toledo	Amer. Assn	9	55	2	5	.286	75	38	26	25	9	4.45
1927	Oakland	Pac. Coast	36	231	15	12	.556	238	99	86	65	51	3.35
1928	Oakland	Pac. Coast	27	212	10	16	.385	261	113	82	45	45	3.48
1929	Shreveport	Texas	30	232	17	9	.654	260	131	110	55	56	4.23
1930	Shreve.-San Ant.	Texas	24	104	3	11	.214	133	86	73	38	44	6.30
	American League Totals		8	14	0	4	.000	27	18	17	2	9	10.93
	National League Totals		509	3468	216	174	.554	3388	1388	1102	1250	844	2.86
	Major League Totals		517	3482	216	178	.548	3415	1406	1119	1252	853	2.89

aTraded with first baseman Charlie Grimm and infielder Walter Maranville to Chicago Cubs for first baseman Al Niehaus, infielder George Grantham and pitcher Vic Aldridge, October, 1924.
bSold to Detroit Tigers, May, 1926.

THOMAS W. CORCORAN

Born January 4, 1869, at New Haven, Conn.
Died June 24, 1960, at Plainfield, Conn.
Threw and batted righthanded.
Married Daisy Sykes, 1898.

Established major league record for assists by a shortstop in a nine-inning game (14), August 7, 1903, vs. St. Louis.

Manager, Uniontown, Pennsylvania-Ohio-Maryland League, 1907; manager, New Bedford, New England League, 1908; umpire, Connecticut League, 1912; New York State League, 1913-14; Federal League, 1915; International League, 1919.

Year	Club	League	Pos.	G.	AB.	R.	H.	2B.	3B.	HR.	S.B.	B.A.	PO.	A.	E.	F.A.
1887	Lynn	N. Eng.	3-2B	97	.....	82	.....	....	....	....	40	.295	(See note below)			
1888	Wilkes-Barre	Cent.	SS	104	442	71	107	....	....	....	44	.242	196	272	69	.871
1889	New Haven	Atl.	SS	65	241	31	56	....	....	....	19	.232	126	241	57	.886
1890	Pittsburgh	Play.	SS	123	505	80	121	14	13	2	42	.240	214	442	75	.897
1891	Athletics	A. A.	SS	129	498	82	126	12	16	7	35	.253	*286	418	66	*.914
1892	Brooklyn	Nat.	SS	151	615	77	146	12	6	1	47	.237	291	494	63	.926
1893	Brooklyn	Nat.	SS	115	437	59	123	10	11	2	18	.281	218	437	70	.903
1894	Brooklyn	Nat.	SS	129	573	124	173	22	18	5	33	.302	282	446	69	.913
1895	Brooklyn	Nat.	SS	128	541	84	150	16	10	2	23	.277	305	496	60	.930
1896	Brooklyn	Nat.	SS	132	527	64	158	14	7	3	18	.300	321	*477	68	.921
1897	Cincinnati	Nat.	SS-2B	108	444	76	128	27	4	3	16	.288	289	354	43	.937
1898	Cincinnati	Nat.	SS	153	620	80	151	29	14	2	22	.244	349	*564	68	.931
1899	Cincinnati	Nat.	SS	135	531	94	148	13	7	0	30	.279	281	422	54	.929
1900	Cincinnati	Nat.	SS	128	523	66	127	17	9	1	30	.243	270	440	56	.927
1901	Cincinnati	Nat.	SS	30	114	13	21	4	2	0	7	.184	72	106	15	.922
1902	Cincinnati	Nat.	SS	137	537	54	135	20	4	0	23	.251	288	422	55	.928
1903	Cincinnati	Nat.	SS	115	459	61	113	18	7	2	12	.246	283	367	38	.943
1904	Cincinnati	Nat.	SS	150	578	55	133	17	9	2	19	.230	353	471	56	*.936
1905	Cincinnati	Nat.	SS	151	605	70	150	21	10	2	28	.248	344	*531	44	*.952
1906	Cincinnati	Nat.	SS	117	430	29	89	13	1	1	8	.207	263	379	40	.941
1907	New York	Nat.	SS	62	226	21	60	9	2	0	9	.265	108	183	19	.939
1907	Uniontown	P-O-M	SS	34	122	15	40	....	....	....	0	.328	69	104	6	.966
1908	New Bedford	N. Eng.	SS	50	180	13	44	6	0	0	6	.244	111	135	13	.950
	American Association Totals			129	498	82	126	12	16	7	35	.253	286	418	66	.941
	National League Totals			1941	7760	1027	2005	262	122	26	343	.258	4297	6589	818	.930
	Players League Totals			123	505	80	121	14	13	2	42	.240	214	442	75	.897
	Major League Totals			2193	8763	1189	2252	288	151	35	420	.257	4797	7449	959	.927

In 1887, 85 games at third base with .834 fielding average and 10 games at second base with .800 fielding average.

STANLEY COVELESKI

Born July 13, 1890, at Shamokin, Pa.
Height, 5.09½. Weight, 178.
Threw and batted righthanded.
Married Frances Shivetts, January, 1922.
Brother of Frank, pitcher with outlaw Union League (1907); John, former minor league third baseman and outfielder, and Harry, pitcher with Philadelphia and Cincinnati, National League, and Detroit, American League (1908-1918).

Pitched most shutouts, 1917 and 1923. Won 13 straight games in 1925. Named to Hall of Fame, 1969.

Year	Club	League	G.	IP.	W.	L.	Pct.	H.	R.	ER.	SO.	BB.	ERA.
1908	Shamokin	Atlantic	12	....	6	2	.750	....	....	....	....	....	......
1909	Lancaster	Tri-State	43	272	*23	11	.676	225	84	....	78	68	......
1910	Lancaster	Tri-State	30	....	15	8	.652	....	....	....	....	....	......
1911	Lancaster	Tri-State	36	272	15	•19	.441	288	120	....	154	65	......
1912	Atlantic City	Tri-State	39	....	20	13	.606	....	....	....	....	....	......
1912	Philadelphia	Amer.	5	21	2	1	.667	18	9	....	9	4	......
1913	Spokane	N. W.	48	316	17	*20	.459	300	140	....	197	95	......
1914	Spokane	N. W.	43	314	20	15	.571	269	109	....	*214	99	......
1915	Portland	P. C.	•64	293	17	17	.500	279	123	87	171	82	2.67

Year	Club	League	G.	IP	W.	L.	Pct.	H.	R.	ER.	SO.	BB.	ERA
1916	Cleveland	Amer.	45	232	15	12	.556	247	100	88	76	58	3.41
1917	Cleveland	Amer.	45	297	19	14	.576	202	78	60	133	94	1.81
1918	Cleveland	Amer.	38	311	22	13	.629	261	90	63	87	76	1.82
1919	Cleveland	Amer.	43	286	24	12	.657	*286	99	83	118	60	2.52
1920	Cleveland	Amer.	41	315	24	14	.632	284	110	87	*133	65	2.49
1921	Cleveland	Amer.	43	316	23	13	.639	341	137	118	99	84	3.36
1922	Cleveland	Amer.	35	277	17	14	.548	292	120	102	98	64	3.31
1923	Cleveland	Amer.	33	228	13	14	.481	251	98	70	54	42	*2.76
1924	Cleveland (a)	Amer.	37	240	15	16	.484	286	140	108	58	73	4.05
1925	Washington	Amer.	32	241	20	5	*.800	230	86	76	58	73	*2.84
1926	Washington	Amer.	36	245	14	11	.560	272	122	85	50	81	3.12
1927	Washington (b)	Amer.	5	14	2	1	.667	13	7	5	3	8	3.21
1928	New York	Amer.	12	58	5	1	.833	72	41	37	5	20	5.74
Major League Totals			450	3081	215	141	.604	3055	1237	982	981	802	2.88

aTraded to Washington for pitcher Byron Speece and outfielder Carr Smith, December 12, 1924.
bUnconditionally released by Washington, June 12, 1927; signed by New York Yankees, December, 1927.

WORLD SERIES RECORD

Year	Club	League	G.	IP	W.	L.	Pct.	H.	R.	ER.	SO.	BB.	ERA
1920	Cleveland	Amer.	3	27	3	0	1.000	15	2	2	8	2	0.67
1925	Washington	Amer.	2	14⅓	0	2	.000	16	7	6	3	5	3.77
World Series Totals			5	41⅓	3	2	.600	31	9	8	11	7	1.74

ROGER MAXWELL (DOC and FLIT) CRAMER

Born July 22, 1906, at Beach Haven, N. J.
Height, 6.02. Weight, 185.
Threw right and batted lefthanded.
Married Helen Letts, December 25, 1927.

Made six hits, in six consecutive times at bat, June 20, 1932 and July 13, 1935 (first game), to tie major league record held by Edward J. Delahanty, Cleveland P. L., Philadelphia N. L., and James L. Bottomley, St. Louis N. L.; holds major league record for most years leading league in at-bats with seven; hit for cycle, June 10, 1934. Led A. L., outfielders in double plays, 1936 (tie).
Named as outfielder on THE SPORTING NEWS All-Star Major League Team in 1935.
World Series records—Tied record for most times at bat, game (6), October 8, 1945 and most times at bat, inning (2) (sixth inning), October 7, 1945.
Coach, Detroit Tigers, 1948; coach, Seattle, Pacific Coast League, 1950; coach, Chicago White Sox, 1951 through 1953.

Year	Club	League	Pos.	G.	AB.	R.	H.	2B.	3B.	HR.	RBI.	B.A.	PO.	A.	E.	F.A.
1929	Martinsburg	B. R.	IN-P	104	366	75	148	31	13	5		*.404	153	126	17	.943
1929	Philadelphia	Amer.	OF	2	6	0	0	0	0	0	0	.000	6	0	0	1.000
1930	Philadelphia	Amer.	OF	30	82	12	19	1	1	0	6	.232	37	1	3	.927
1930	Portland	P. C.	OF	74	300	53	104	24	3	5	46	.347	141	11	3	.961
1931	Philadelphia	Amer.	OF	65	223	37	58	8	2	2	20	.260	133	5	3	.979
1932	Philadelphia	Amer.	OF	92	384	73	129	27	6	3	46	.336	233	7	6	.976
1933	Philadelphia	Amer.	OF	152	*661	109	195	27	8	8	75	.295	387	13	12	.971
1934	Philadelphia	Amer.	OF	153	*649	99	202	29	9	6	46	.311	385	12	6	.985
1935	Philadelphia (a)	Amer.	OF	149	*644	96	214	37	4	3	70	.332	429	6	11	.975
1936	Boston	Amer.	OF	154	643	99	188	31	7	0	41	.292	*443	20	12	.975
1937	Boston	Amer.	OF	133	560	90	171	22	11	0	51	.305	365	12	12	.969
1938	Boston	Amer.	OF-P	148	*658	116	198	36	8	0	71	.301	*417	15	6	.984
1939	Boston	Amer.	OF	137	589	110	183	30	6	0	56	.311	356	12	6	.984
1940	Boston (b)	Amer	OF	150	*661	94	•200	27	12	0	51	.303	333	11	11	.969
1941	Washington (c)	Amer.	OF	154	*660	93	180	25	8	2	66	.273	369	9	6	.984
1942	Detroit	Amer.	OF	151	*630	71	166	26	4	0	43	.263	352	15	7	.981
1943	Detroit	Amer.	OF	140	606	79	182	18	4	1	43	.300	346	9	4	.989
1944	Detroit	Amer.	OF	143	578	69	169	20	9	2	42	.292	337	13	7	.980
1945	Detroit	Amer.	OF	141	541	62	149	22	8	6	58	.275	314	7	3	*.991
1946	Detroit	Amer.	OF	68	204	26	60	8	2	1	26	.294	89	2	0	1.000
1947	Detroit	Amer.	OF	73	157	21	42	2	2	0	30	.268	79	3	3	.965
1948	Detroit (d)	Amer.	OF	4	4	1	0	0	0	0	1	.000	2	0	0	1.000
1949	Buffalo	Int.	OF	65	135	22	37	7	0	3	27	.274	44	2	2	.958
1950	Seattle	P. C.	PH	2	2	0	0	0	0	0	0	.000	0	0	0	.000
Major League Totals				2239	9140	1357	2705	396	109	37	842	.296	5412	172	118	.979

WORLD SERIES RECORD

Year	Club	League	Pos.	G.	AB.	R.	H.	2B.	3B.	HR.	RBI.	B.A.	PO.	A.	E.	F.A.
1931	Philadelphia	Amer.	PH	2	2	0	1	0	0	0	2	.500	0	0	0	.000
1945	Detroit	Amer.	OF	7	29	7	11	0	0	0	4	.379	21	0	0	1.000
World Series Totals				9	31	7	12	0	0	0	6	.387	21	0	0	1.000

aTraded to Boston Red Sox with infielder Donald McNair for pitcher Henry Johnson, infielder Al Niemiec and cash, January 4, 1936.
bTraded to Washington Senators for outfielder Gerald Walker, December 12, 1940.
cTraded to Detroit Tigers with infielder James Bloodworth for outfielder Bruce Campbell and shortstop Frank Croucher, December 12, 1941.
dUnconditionally released by Detroit Tigers, November 11, 1948.

PITCHING RECORD

Year	Club	League	G.	IP.	W.	L.	Pct.	H.	R.	ER.	SO.	BB.	ERA.
1929	Martinsburg	B. Ridge	11	44	2	2	.500	43	27	....	35	23	.....
1938	Boston	Amer.	1	4	0	0	.000	3	2	2	1	3	4.50

SAMUEL EARL (WAHOO SAM) CRAWFORD

Born April 18, 1880, at Wahoo, Neb.
Died June 15, 1968, at Hollywood, Calif.
Height, 6.00. Weight, 190.
Threw and batted lefthanded.
Married Mary Blazer, July 9, 1943.

Holds major league record, most three-base hits, lifetime—312 (National League four years—62 and American League, 15 years—250); holds major league record, most years, 20 or more three-base hits (5); tied major league record most consecutive years leading league in three-base hits (3); tied A.L. record, most three-base hits, season (26), 1914; led American League in runs batted in, 1910, 1914 and 1915. Played 472 consecutive games, April 10, 1913, through April 17, 1916.
Umpire, Pacific Coast, 1935-36-37-38.
Named to Hall of Fame, 1957.

Year	Club	League	Pos.	G.	AB.	R.	H.	2B.	3B.	HR.	SB.	B.A.	PO.	A.	E.	F.A.
1899	Chatham	Canadian	OF	43	173	34	64	...	...	0	7	.370	(110 PO-A)		13	.894
1899	Col.-Gr. Rapids	Western	OF	60	261	46	87	...	...	5	3	.333	112	9	8	.938
1899	Cincinnati	Nat.	OF	31	127	25	39	2	8	0	3	.307	60	9	3	.958
1900	Cincinnati	Nat.	OF	96	385	67	104	14	15	6	15	.270	230	16	12	.953
1901	Cincinnati	Nat.	OF	124	523	89	175	22	16	*16	12	.335	.208	20	20	.919
1902	Cincinnati (a)	Nat.	OF	•140	555	94	185	16	*23	3	15	.333	204	•25	18	.927
1903	Detroit	Amer.	OF	137	545	93	181	23	*25	4	23	.332	225	16	9	.964
1904	Detroit	Amer.	OF	150	571	46	141	21	17	2	20	.247	230	17	8	.969
1905	Detroit	Amer.	1B-OF	154	575	73	171	40	10	6	22	.297	630	59	13	*.981
1906	Detroit	Amer.	1B-OF	145	563	65	166	23	16	2	24	.295	458	36	5	.990
1907	Detroit	Amer.	OF	144	582	*102	188	34	17	4	18	.323	311	22	12	.965
1908	Detroit	Amer.	1B-OF	152	*591	102	184	33	16	*7	15	.311	428	22	14	.970
1909	Detroit	Amer.	1B-OF	156	589	83	185	*35	14	6	30	.314	486	17	17	.967
1910	Detroit	Amer.	OF	154	588	83	170	26	*19	5	20	.289	223	10	9	.963
1911	Detroit	Amer.	OF	146	574	109	217	36	14	7	37	.378	181	15	5	.975
1912	Detroit	Amer.	OF	149	581	81	189	30	21	4	41	.325	169	16	3	.984
1913	Detroit	Amer.	OF	153	*610	78	193	32	*23	9	13	.316	357	21	14	.964
1914	Detroit	Amer.	1B-OF	157	582	74	183	22	*26	8	25	.314	193	18	5	.977
1915	Detroit	Amer.	OF	156	612	81	183	31	*19	4	24	.299	219	8	6	.974
1916	Detroit	Amer.	OF	100	322	41	92	11	13	0	10	.286	85	6	2	.978
1917	Detroit	Amer.	OF	61	104	6	18	4	0	2	0	.173	158	2	2	.988
1918	Los Angeles	P.C.	1B-OF	96	356	38	104	14	7	1	8	.292				
1919	Los Angeles	P.C.	OF	173	664	103	*239	41	18	14	14	.360	289	10	4	.987
1920	Los Angeles	P.C.	OF	187	719	99	239	46	*21	12	3	.332	284	30	7	.978
1921	Los Angeles	P.C.	OF	175	626	92	199	40	10	9	10	.318	323	21	8	.977
American League Totals				2114	7989	1117	2461	401	250	70	322	.308	4353	286	124	.974
National League Totals				391	1590	275	503	54	62	25	45	.316	702	70	53	.936
Major League Totals				2505	9579	1392	2964	455	312	95	367	.309	5055	356	177	.968

aJumped from Cincinnati to Detroit.

WORLD SERIES RECORD

Year	Club	League	Pos.	G.	AB.	R.	H.	2B.	3B.	HR.	SB.	B.A.	PO.	A.	E.	F.A.
1907	Detroit	Amer.	OF	5	21	1	5	1	0	0	0	.238	7	2	0	1.000
1908	Detroit	Amer.	OF	5	21	2	5	1	0	0	0	.238	16	0	0	1.000
1909	Detroit	Amer.	OF	7	28	4	7	3	0	1	1	.250	17	1	2	.900
World Series Totals				17	70	7	17	5	0	1	1	.243	40	3	2	.956

DID YOU KNOW—
That Sam Crawford had 17 straight big league seasons of ten or more triples?

JOSEPH EDWARD CRONIN

Born October 12, 1906, at San Francisco, Calif.
Height, 6.00. Weight, 187.
Threw and batted righthanded.
Married Mildred Robertson, September 27, 1934.

Established league record with five home runs as pinch-hitter in 1943, four coming with two mates aboard (two in successive appearances—seventh inning of first game and eighth inning of second game, June 17), and other with one aboard.
Selected Most Valuable Player, American League, 1930. Named by Baseball Writers' Association of America as shortstop for THE SPORTING NEWS All-Star Major League Teams, 1930-31-32-33-34-38 and 1939.
Manager of Washington Senators, 1933-34; manager, Boston Red Sox, 1935 through 1947; vice-president, treasurer and general manager, Red Sox, 1948 to January 31, 1959, when he was named president of American League; in 1973, he became chairman of the board, relinquishing the presidency to Lee MacPhail.
Named to Hall of Fame, 1956.

Year	Club	League	Pos.	G.	AB.	R.	H.	2B.	3B.	HR.	RBI.	B.A.	PO.	A.	E.	F.A.
1925	Johnstown	Mid.-Atl.	2B-SS	99	352	64	110	18	11	3	....	.313	....	....	....	....
1926	Pittsburgh	Nat.	2B-SS	38	83	9	22	2	2	0	11	.265	55	82	3	.979
1926	New Haven	East.	SS	66	244	61	78	11	8	2	....	.320	136	222	27	.930
1927	Pittsburgh	Nat.	SS	12	22	2	5	1	0	0	3	.227	12	10	4	.846
1928	Kansas City	A.A.	SS	74	241	34	59	10	6	2	32	.245	87	146	14	.943
1928	Washington	Amer.	SS	63	227	23	55	10	4	0	25	.242	133	190	16	.953
1929	Washington	Amer.	SS	145	494	72	139	29	8	8	60	.281	285	•459	*62	.923
1930	Washington	Amer.	SS	•154	587	127	203	42	9	13	126	.346	*336	*509	35	.960
1931	Washington	Amer.	SS	*156	611	103	187	44	13	12	126	.306	*323	488	43	.950
1932	Washington	Amer.	SS	143	557	95	177	43	*18	6	116	.318	*306	*448	32	*.959
1933	Washington	Amer.	SS	152	602	89	186	*45	11	5	118	.309	297	528	34	*.960
1934	Washington (a)	Amer.	SS	127	504	68	143	30	9	7	101	.284	246	486	38	.951
1935	Boston	Amer.	1B-SS	144	556	70	164	37	14	9	95	.295	277	435	37	.951
1936	Boston	Amer.	SS-3B	81	295	36	83	22	4	2	43	.281	133	229	26	.933
1937	Boston	Amer.	SS	148	570	102	175	40	4	18	110	.307	300	414	31	.958
1938	Boston	Amer.	SS	143	530	98	172	*51	5	17	94	.325	304	449	36	.954
1939	Boston	Amer.	SS	143	520	97	160	33	3	19	107	.308	306	437	32	.959
1940	Boston	Amer.	SS-3B	149	548	104	156	35	6	24	111	.285	253	445	*38	.948
1941	Boston	Amer.	1-SS-3-OF	143	518	98	161	38	8	16	95	.311	247	362	*27	.958
1942	Boston	Amer.	1B-SS-3B	45	79	7	24	3	0	4	24	.304	47	28	6	.926
1943	Boston	Amer.	3B	59	77	8	24	4	0	5	29	.312	12	18	1	.968
1944	Boston	Amer.	1B	76	191	24	46	7	0	5	28	.241	428	27	9	.981
1945	Boston (b)	Amer.	3B	3	8	1	3	0	0	0	1	.375	2	8	0	1.000
	American League Totals			2074	7474	1222	2258	513	116	170	1409	.302	4235	5960	503	.953
	National League Totals			50	105	11	27	3	2	0	14	.257	67	92	7	.958
	Major League Totals			2124	7579	1233	2285	516	118	170	1423	.301	4302	6052	510	.953

aTraded to Boston Red Sox for shortstop Lyn Lary and $250,000, October, 1934.
bSuffered fractured right leg, April 19, 1945, and out of action remainder of season.

WORLD SERIES RECORD

Year	Club	League	Pos.	G.	AB.	R.	H.	2B.	3B.	HR.	RBI.	B.A.	PO.	A.	E.	F.A.
1933	Washington	Amer.	SS	5	22	1	7	0	0	0	2	.318	7	15	1	.957

LAFAYETTE NAPOLEON (LAVE) CROSS

Born May 12, 1867, at Milwaukee, Wis.
Died September 6, 1927, at Philadelphia, Pa.
Height, 5.08½. Weight, 165.
Threw and batted righthanded.

Played 447 consecutive games, April 23, 1902, through May 8, 1905.
Had 15 assists in 12-inning game, August 5, 1897, vs. New York, at second base.

Year	Club	League	Pos.	G.	AB.	R.	H.	2B.	3B.	HR.	SB.	B.A.	PO.	A.	E.	F.A.
1887	Louisville	A.A.	C	54	214	27	70	9	3	0	15	.327	(PO-A 307)		24	.927
1888	Louisville	A.A.	C	47	183	21	39	4	0	0	9	.213	(PO-A 271)		21	.928

Year	Club	League	Pos.	G.	AB.	R.	H.	2B.	3B.	HR.	SB.	B.A.	PO.	A.	E.	F.A.
1889–Philadelphia	A. A.		C	55	199	25	45	7	2	0	10	.226	278	102	19	.952
1890–Philadelphia	Players		C	60	244	42	73	9	8	3	5	.299	184	68	24	.913
1891–Philadelphia	A. A.		3-OF-C	106	387	64	115	19	13	4	14	.297	287	102	22	.946
1892–Philadelphia	Nat.		C-O-3B	134	530	85	139	14	10	4	17	.262	292	180	26	.948
1893–Philadelphia	Nat.		C-3B	94	414	85	125	16	6	4	15	.302	190	151	18	.950
1894–Philadelphia	Nat.		3B	120	543	128	211	32	12	5	28	.389	177	240	40	.912
1895–Philadelphia	Nat.		3B	124	535	95	148	24	8	2	19	.277	184	297	36	.930
1896–Philadelphia	Nat.		3B-SS	106	409	62	107	22	4	0	10	.262	173	266	27	.942
1897–Philadelphia	Nat.		2B-3B	88	345	37	90	17	4	3	11	.261	136	212	26	.930
1898–St. Louis	Nat.		2B	151	601	71	192	26	7	3	14	.319	213	349	33	.945
1899–St. Louis-Cleve.	Nat.		3B	141	561	77	164	19	5	5	16	.292	222	364	26	.958
1900–St. Louis-Brook.	Nat.		3B	133	519	79	152	15	6	4	21	.293	184	317	31	.941
1901–Philadelphia	Amer.		3B	100	420	82	139	31	11	2	21	.331	144	239	32	.923
1902–Philadelphia	Amer.		3B	137	558	90	189	37	8	0	26	.339	*197	309	28	*.947
1903–Philadelphia	Amer.		3B	137	554	61	162	23	5	2	13	.292	157	216	18	.954
1904–Philadelphia	Amer.		3B	155	611	80	177	29	9	2	13	.290	173	246	31	.931
1905–Philadelphia	Amer.		3B	146	583	68	155	26	5	0	8	.266	161	249	32	.928
1906–Washington	Amer.		3B	130	494	55	130	14	6	1	19	.263	157	242	20	*.952
1907–Washington	Amer.		3B	41	161	13	32	8	0	0	3	.199	38	98	3	.978
1907–New Orleans	South.		3B	86	337	40	90	....	....	....	11	.267	99	178	3	.989
1908–New Orleans	South.		3B	15	55	4	14	....	....	....	1	.254	24	27	3	.944
1909–Charlotte	Car. Assn.		2B	50	187	20	59	....	....	....	....	.315	111	142	5	.981
1910–Charlotte	Car. Assn.		3B	109	396	43	117	....	....	....	....	.295	139	225	18	.953
1911–Charlotte	Car. Assn.		3B	79	295	32	95	....	....	....	....	.322	147	219	25	.936
1912–Haverhill	New Eng.		3B	126	452	53	132	20	1	1	14	.292	113	220	14	.960
American Association Totals				262	983	137	269	39	18	4	48	.274	565	204	86	.940
Players League Totals				60	244	42	73	9	8	3	5	.299	184	68	24	.913
American League Totals				846	3381	449	984	168	44	7	103	.291	1027	1599	164	.941
National League Totals				1091	4457	719	1328	185	62	30	151	.298	1771	2376	263	.940
Major League Totals				2259	9065	1347	2654	401	132	44	307	.293	3547	4247	537	.936

WORLD SERIES RECORD

Year	Club	League	Pos.	G.	AB.	R.	H.	2B.	3B.	HR.	RBI.	B.A.	PO.	A.	E.	F.A.
1905–Philadelphia	Amer.		3B	5	19	0	2	0	0	0	0	.105	6	7	2	.867

MIGUEL ANGEL (MIKE) CUELLAR

Born May 8, 1937, at Santa Clara, Cuba.

Height, 5.11. Weight, 175.

Threw and batted lefthanded.

Tied major league record for most strikeouts, inning (4), 4th inning, May 29, 1970.
Named lefthanded pitcher on THE SPORTING NEWS American League All-Star Team, 1969 and 1974.
Co-winner with Denny McLain for the American League Cy Young Memorial Award, 1969.

Year	Club	League	G.	IP.	W.	L.	Pct.	H.	R.	ER.	SO.	BB.	ERA.
1957–Havana	International		44	155	8	7	.533	122	53	42	74	54	2.44
1958–Havana	International		40	221	13	12	.520	204	75	68	98	70	2.77
1959–Cincinnati	National		2	4	0	0	.000	7	8	7	5	4	15.75
1959–Havana	International		29	212	10	11	.476	184	82	66	111	57	2.80
1960–Havana-Jersey City	International		33	148	6	9	.400	146	75	58	74	48	3.53
1961–Jersey City-Syracuse	International		28	102	4	10	.286	116	64	53	65	32	4.68
1961–Indianapolis	American Assoc.		5	16	0	1	.000	18	7	7	8	4	3.94
1962–Monterrey	Mexican		37	155	11	6	.647	173	74	62	*134	60	3.60
1963–Knoxville	Sally		8	39	1	1	.500	33	15	11	39	20	2.54
1963–Jacksonville	International		24	126	6	7	.462	116	56	53	85	47	3.79
1964–Jacksonville	International		10	76	6	1	.857	57	17	15	64	16	1.78
1964–St. Louis	National		32	72	5	5	.500	80	43	36	56	33	4.50
1965–Jacksonville (a)	International		15	97	9	1	.900	74	32	27	91	35	2.51
1965–Houston	National		25	56	1	4	.200	55	24	22	46	21	3.54
1966–Houston	National		38	227	12	10	.545	193	79	56	175	52	2.22
1967–Houston	National		36	246	16	11	.593	233	99	83	203	63	3.04
1968–Houston (b)	National		28	171	8	11	.421	152	60	52	133	45	2.74
1969–Baltimore	American		39	291	23	11	.676	213	94	77	182	79	2.38
1970–Baltimore	American		40	298	●24	8	*.750	273	126	●115	190	69	3.47
1971–Baltimore	American		38	292	20	9	.690	250	111	100	124	78	3.08
1972–Baltimore	American		35	248	18	12	.600	197	78	71	132	71	2.58
1973–Baltimore	American		38	267	18	13	.581	265	120	97	140	84	3.27
1974–Baltimore	American		38	269	22	10	*.688	253	106	93	106	86	3.11
1975–Baltimore	American		36	256	14	12	.538	229	112	104	105	84	3.66

Year	Club	League	G.	IP.	W.	L.	Pct.	H.	R.	ER.	SO.	BB.	ERA.
1976—Baltimore		American	26	107	4	13	.235	129	63	59	32	50	4.96
1977—California (c)		American	2	3	0	1	.000	9	7	7	3	3	21.00
American League Totals			292	2031	143	89	.616	1818	817	723	1014	604	3.20
National League Totals			161	776	42	41	.506	720	313	256	618	218	2.97
Major League Totals			453	2807	185	130	.587	2538	1130	979	1632	822	3.14

aRecalled by St. Louis Cardinals and traded with pitcher Ron Taylor to Houston Astros for pitchers Hal Woodeshick and Chuck Taylor, June 15, 1965.

bTraded with infielder Elijah (Tom) Johnson to Baltimore Orioles for outfielder-catcher Curt Blefary, December 4, 1968.

cSigned as free agent by California Angels, January 18, 1977.

WORLD SERIES RECORD

Year	Club	League	G.	IP.	W.	L.	Pct.	H.	R.	ER.	SO.	BB.	ERA.
1969—Baltimore		American	2	16	1	0	1.000	13	2	2	13	4	1.13
1970—Baltimore		American	2	11⅓	1	0	1.000	10	7	4	5	2	3.18
1971—Baltimore		American	2	14	0	2	.000	11	7	6	10	6	3.86
World Series Totals			6	41⅓	2	2	.500	34	16	12	28	12	2.61

WILLIAM ARTHUR (CANDY) CUMMINGS

Born October 17, 1848, at Ware, Mass.
Died May 17, 1924, at Toledo, O.
Height, 5.09. Weight, 120.
Threw and batted righthanded.

Credited with inventing curve ball and claim endorsed by Henry Chadwick, who called him outstanding pitcher of 1871. President of first minor league, International Association, 1877.
Named to Hall of Fame, 1939.

Year	Club	League	G.	W.	L.	Pct.	ERA.	Sh.O.
1866—Hercules of Fulton, N. Y.		Ind.	....	....	....	....	....	....
1866—Excelsior Jrs. of Brooklyn		Ind.	6	....	....	....	....	....
1867—Excelsior Jrs. of Brooklyn		Ind.	15	....	....	....	....	....
1868—Star of Brooklyn		Ind.	11	....	....	....	....	....
1869—Star of Brooklyn		Ind.	22	....	....	....	....	....
1870—Star of Brooklyn		Ind.	26	....	....	....	....	....
1871—Star of Brooklyn		Ind.	....	....	....	....	....	3
1872—Mutuals of New York		Nat. Assn.	53	34	19	.642	....	1
1873—Baltimore		Nat. Assn.	43	29	14	.674	....	3
1874—Philadelphia		Nat. Assn.	54	28	26	.519	....	6
1875—Hartford		Nat. Assn.	52	34	11	.756	1.73	5
1876—Hartford		Nat.	24	16	8	.667	1.66	1
1877—Live Oaks of Lynn		I. Assn.	8	1	7	.125	....	0
1877—Cincinnati		Nat.	19	5	14	.263	....	
1878—Forest City of Cleveland		Ind.	(No record available)					5
Major League Totals			43	21	22	.488	....	5

HAZEN SHIRLEY (KIKI) CUYLER

Born August 30, 1899, at Harrisville, Mich.
Died February 11, 1950, at Ann Arbor, Mich.
Height, 5.11. Weight, 185.
Threw and batted righthanded.
Married Bertha Kelly, January 8, 1919.

Made ten hits in succession to equal league record, September 18, 19 and 21, 1925. Collected six hits in six consecutive times at bat, August 9, 1924, first game (six at-bats, two singles, three doubles and one triple) vs. Philadelphia. Led league in stolen bases, 1926-28-29 and 1930. Named by Baseball Writers' Association of America for THE SPORTING NEWS All-Star Major League Team, 1925.
Manager, Chattanooga, Southern Association, 1939-40 and until August 6, 1941; Atlanta, Southern Association, 1945 through 1948; coach, Chicago Cubs, August 7, 1941 through 1943; Boston Red Sox, 1949.

Named to Hall of Fame, 1968.

Year	Club	League	Pos.	G.	AB.	R.	H.	2B.	3B.	HR.	RBI.	B.A.	PO.	A.	E.	F.A.
1920	Bay City	Mich.-Ont.	OF	69	240	24	62	8	3	1	26	.258	108	10	7	.944
1921	Bay City	Mich.-Ont.	OF	116	417	79	132	18	16	8	82	.317	*271	20	13	.957
1921	Pittsburgh	Nat.	OF	1	3	0	0	0	0	0	0	.000	1	0	0	1.000
1922	Charleston	Sally	OF	131	489	84	151	29	15	12	46	.309	274	13	12	.960
1922	Pittsburgh	Nat.	PR	1	0	0	0	0	0	0	0	.000	0	0	0	.000
1923	Nashville	Southern	OF	149	574	114	195	39	17	9	108	.340	*383	*35	•12	.972
1923	Pittsburgh	Nat.	OF	11	40	4	10	1	1	0	2	.250	26	1	2	.931
1924	Pittsburgh	Nat.	OF	117	466	94	165	27	16	9	85	.354	246	19	•16	.943
1925	Pittsburgh	Nat.	OF	•153	617	*144	220	43	*26	18	102	.357	362	21	13	.967
1926	Pittsburgh	Nat.	OF	*157	614	*113	197	31	15	8	92	.321	405	19	14	.968
1927	Pittsburgh(a)	Nat.	OF	85	285	60	88	13	7	3	31	.309	195	6	4	.980
1928	Chicago	Nat.	OF	133	499	92	142	25	9	17	79	.285	257	18	5	.982
1929	Chicago	Nat.	OF	139	509	111	183	29	7	15	102	.360	288	15	8	.974
1930	Chicago	Nat.	OF	•156	642	155	228	50	17	13	134	.355	377	21	8	.980
1931	Chicago	Nat.	OF	154	613	110	202	37	12	9	88	.330	347	11	11	.970
1932	Chicago	Nat.	OF	110	446	58	130	19	9	10	77	.291	239	7	8	.969
1933	Chicago	Nat.	OF	70	262	37	83	13	3	5	35	.317	130	2	3	.978
1934	Chicago	Nat.	OF	142	559	80	189	•42	8	6	69	.338	319	15	10	.971
1935	Chi.(b)-Cinc	Nat.	OF	107	380	58	98	13	4	6	40	.258	221	10	4	.983
1936	Cincinnati	Nat.	OF	144	567	96	185	29	11	7	74	.326	322	9	9	.974
1937	Cincinnati(c)	Nat.	OF	117	406	48	110	12	4	0	32	.271	174	8	5	.973
1938	Brooklyn	Nat.	OF	82	253	45	69	10	8	2	23	.273	125	9	1	.993
1939	Chattanooga	Southern	OF	58	159	19	43	7	3	0	18	.270	105	5	2	.982
1940	Chattanooga	Southern	PH	1	1	1	1	0	0	0	0	1.000	0	0	0	.000
Major League Totals				1879	7161	1305	2299	394	157	128	1065	.321	4034	191	121	.972

aTraded to Chicago Cubs for infielder Earl Adams and outfielder Floyd Scott, November 28, 1927.
bReleased by Chicago Cubs, July 3, 1935, and signed by Cincinnati, July 5, 1935.
cUnconditionally released by Cincinnati, October, 1937, and signed with Brooklyn, February, 1938.

WORLD SERIES RECORD

Year	Club	League	Pos.	G.	AB.	R.	H.	2B.	3B.	HR.	RBI.	B.A.	PO.	A.	E.	F.A.
1925	Pittsburgh	Nat.	OF	7	26	3	7	3	0	1	6	.269	12	0	1	.923
1929	Chicago	Nat.	OF	5	20	4	6	1	0	0	4	.300	8	0	1	.889
1932	Chicago	Nat.	OF	4	18	2	5	1	1	1	2	.278	5	0	0	1.000
World Series Totals				16	64	9	18	5	1	2	12	.281	25	0	2	.926

WILLIAM FREDERICK (BAD BILL) DAHLEN

Born January 5, 1871, at Fort Plain, N. Y.

Died December 5, 1950, at Brooklyn, N. Y.

Height, 5.08. Weight, 170.

Threw and batted righthanded.

Married Jeannette Hoglund, December 22, 1903.

Hit safely in 42 consecutive games, June 20 to August 6, 1894 (74 hits, 16 doubles, 7 triples and 4 home runs); failing to hit in game of August 7, he followed with a streak of 28 consecutive games, thus hitting safely in 70 out of 71; holds National League record for most assists by a shortstop in his major league career (7,414); hit three triples in a game on two occasions, May 3, 1896 and June 6, 1898; had eight putouts and eight assists on June 15, 1900, vs. Boston.

Manager, Brooklyn Dodgers, 1910 through 1913.

Year	Club	League	Pos.	G.	AB.	R.	H.	2B.	3B.	HR.	SB.	B.A.	PO.	A.	E.	F.A.
1890	Cobleskill	N.Y. St.	2B	85	400	88	137	....	....	....	20	.343	353	284	58	.917
1891	Chicago	Nat.	INF-OF	135	551	113	145	20	13	9	29	.263	212	258	63	.882
1892	Chicago	Nat.	SS-3B	143	587	116	173	19	5	5	60	.295	295	430	58	.926
1893	Chicago	Nat.	SS-OF	115	463	113	144	28	16	5	43	.311	256	303	66	.894
1894	Chicago	Nat.	SS-3B	121	508	150	184	30	14	15	49	.362	286	384	75	.899
1895	Chicago	Nat.	SS	131	509	107	139	19	9	6	44	.273	290	*533	*84	.907
1896	Chicago	Nat.	SS	125	476	137	172	24	18	9	60	.361	315	463	75	.912
1897	Chicago	Nat.	SS	75	277	67	82	17	8	6	16	.296	215	297	39	.929
1898	Chicago	Nat.	SS	141	524	96	152	34	9	1	25	.290	369	410	78	.909
1899	Brooklyn	Nat.	SS	122	428	88	118	20	9	4	29	.276	257	373	42	.938
1900	Brooklyn	Nat.	SS	134	485	87	126	15	12	1	31	.260	317	*515	51	•.942
1901	Brooklyn	Nat.	SS	130	513	69	134	17	10	4	23	.261	306	446	51	.936
1902	Brooklyn	Nat.	SS	136	520	68	139	26	7	2	29	.267	271	438	67	.914
1903	Brooklyn	Nat.	SS	138	474	71	124	17	9	2	47	.262	296	*477	42	*.948
1904	New York	Nat.	SS	145	523	70	140	26	2	2	47	.268	316	*494	51	.930
1905	New York	Nat.	SS	148	520	67	126	20	4	7	37	.242	313	501	45	.948
1906	New York	Nat.	SS	143	471	63	113	18	3	1	16	.240	287	454	49	.938
1907	New York	Nat.	SS	143	464	40	96	20	1	0	11	.207	292	436	45	.941
1908	Boston	Nat.	SS	144	524	50	125	23	2	3	10	.239	291	553	43	.952
1909	Boston	Nat.	SS	57	197	22	46	6	1	2	4	.234	101	184	29	.908

Year	Club	League	Pos.	G.	AB.	R.	H.	2B.	3B.	HR.	SB.	B.A.	PO.	A.	E.	F.A.
1910—Brooklyn		Nat.	PH	3	2	0	0	0	0	0	0	.000	0	0	0	.000
1911—Brooklyn		Nat.	SS	1	3	0	0	0	0	0	0	.000	2	5	0	1.000
1913—Brooklyn		Nat.	3B	1	0	0	0	0	0	0	0	.000	0	0	0	.000
Major League Totals				2431	9019	1594	2478	403	166	83	587	.275	5287	7944	1063	.926

WORLD SERIES RECORD

Year	Club	League	Pos.	G.	AB.	R.	H.	2B.	3B.	HR.	SB.	B.A.	PO.	A.	E.	F.A.
1905—New York		Nat.	SS	5	15	1	0	0	0	0	2	.000	10	19	0	1.000

ALVIN RALPH DARK

Born January 7, 1922, at Comanche, Okla.
Height, 5.11½. Weight, 175.
Threw and batted righthanded.

Had 11 assists at shortstop July 29, 1958, vs. Milwaukee, N. L.
Tied World Series record for most one-base hits in a 4-game Series (7), 1954.
Named as shortstop on THE SPORTING NEWS All-Star Major League Team, 1954.
Named N.L. Rookie of the Year (BBWAA), 1948.
Manager, San Francisco Giants, 1961 through 1964; coach; Chicago Cubs, 1965; manager, Kansas City Athletics, 1966-67; manager, Cleveland Indians, 1968 through July 29, 1971; manager, Oakland A's, 1974-75; coach, Chicago Cubs, January 5, 1977, to May 29, 1977; manager, San Diego Padres, May 30, 1977 to March 21, 1978.

Year	Club	League	Pos.	G.	AB.	R.	H.	2B.	3B.	HR.	RBI.	B.A.	PO.	A.	E.	F.A.
1946—Boston		Nat.	SS-OF	15	13	0	3	3	0	0	1	.231	6	14	2	.909
1947—Milwaukee		A. A.	SS	149	*614	*121	186	*49	7	10	66	.303	*290	*454	*46	.942
1948—Boston		Nat.	SS	137	543	85	175	39	6	3	48	.322	253	393	25	.963
1949—Boston(a)		Nat.	SS-3B	130	529	74	146	23	5	3	53	.276	233	395	26	.960
1950—New York		Nat.	SS	154	587	79	164	36	5	16	67	.279	286	465	30	.962
1951—New York		Nat.	SS	156	646	114	196	*41	7	14	69	.303	*295	*465	*45	.944
1952—New York		Nat.	SS	151	589	92	177	29	3	14	73	.301	*324	423	27	.965
1953—New York		Nat:	IF-O-P	155	*647	126	194	41	6	23	88	.300	325	433	24	.969
1954—New York		Nat.	SS	•154	*644	98	189	26	6	20	70	.293	289	487	*36	.956
1955—New York		Nat.	SS	115	475	77	134	20	3	9	45	.282	213	324	21	.962
1956—N.Y.(b)-St.L.		Nat.	SS	148	619	73	170	26	7	6	54	.275	267	424	29	.960
1957—St. Louis		Nat.	*SS-3B	140	583	80	169	25	8	4	64	.290	*276	421	25	.965
1958—St.L.(c)-Chicago		Nat.	3B-SS	132	528	61	156	16	4	4	48	.295	121	260	21	.948
1959—Chicago(d)		Nat.	INF	136	477	60	126	22	9	6	45	.264	138	260	21	.950
1960—Phila.(e)-Mil.(f)		Nat.	INF-OF	105	339	45	90	11	3	4	32	.265	146	90	10	.959
Major League Totals				1828	7219	1064	2089	358	72	126	757	.289	3174	4854	342	.959

aTraded to New York Giants with second baseman Eddie Stanky for pitcher Sam Webb, third baseman Sid Gordon, shortstop John (Buddy) Kerr and outfielder Willard Marshall, December 14, 1949.
bTraded to St. Louis Cardinals with pitcher Don Liddle, catcher Ray Katt and outfielder-first baseman Whitey Lockman for pitchers Gordon Jones and Dick Littlefield, catcher Bill Sarni, second baseman Al Schoendienst and outfielder Jack Brandt. All players but Jones exchanged clubs June 14, 1956—Jones being assigned to Giants October 1, 1956.
cTraded to Chicago Cubs for pitcher Jim Brosnan, May 20, 1958.
dTraded to Philadelphia Phillies with pitcher John Buzhardt and third baseman Jim Woods, for outfielder Richie Ashburn, January 11, 1960.
eTraded to Milwaukee Braves for third baseman Joe Morgan and cash, June 23, 1960.
fTraded to San Francisco Giants for infielder Andre Rodgers, October 31, 1960.

WORLD SERIES RECORD

Year	Club	League	Pos.	G.	AB.	R.	H.	2B.	3B.	HR.	RBI.	B.A.	PO.	A.	E.	F.A.
1948—Boston		Nat.	SS	6	24	2	4	1	0	0	0	.167	7	12	3	.864
1951—New York		Nat.	SS	6	24	5	10	3	0	1	4	.417	10	16	0	1.000
1954—New York		Nat.	SS	4	17	2	7	0	0	0	0	.412	7	12	1	.950
World Series Totals				16	65	9	21	4	0	1	4	.323	24	40	4	.941

PITCHING RECORD

Year	Club	League	G.	IP.	W.	L.	Pct.	H.	R.	ER.	SO.	BB.	ERA.
1953—New York		Nat.	1	1	0	0	.000	1	2	2	0	1	18.00

DID YOU KNOW—

That Al Dark was a star halfback at Louisiana State and Southwest La. Institute?

JACOB ELLSWORTH (JAKE) DAUBERT

Born May 14, 1885, at Lewellyn, Pa.
Died October 9, 1924, at Cincinnati, O.
Height, 5.10. Weight, 160.
Threw and batted lefthanded.
Married Gertrude Viola Acaley, September 5, 1903.

Named Most Valuable Player, National League, 1913 (Chalmers Award).
Brother of Harry Daubert, Pittsburgh Pirates 1915.
Led N.L. first basemen in double plays, 1922.

Year	Club	League	Pos.	G.	AB.	R.	H.	2B.	3B.	HR.	RBI.	B.A.	PO.	A.	E.	F.A.
1907	Kane	Int.St.	1B	42	157	18	47	....	....	....	....	.299	433	26	7	.985
1907	Marion	O.-P.	1B	71	265	26	75	....	....	....	....	.283	709	40	8	.989
1908	Nashville	South.	1B	138	473	49	124	12	11	6	....	.262	1331	17	15	.989
1909	Toledo	A. A.	1B	35	129	16	24	6	0	0	....	.186	371	23	7	.983
1909	Memphis	South.	1B	81	283	35	89	11	2	0	....	.314	806	58	4	.995
1910	Brooklyn	Nat.	1B	144	552	67	146	15	15	8	52	.264	1418	72	16	.989
1911	Brooklyn	Nat.	1B	149	573	89	176	17	8	5	46	.307	1485	88	18	.989
1912	Brooklyn	Nat.	1B	145	559	81	172	19	16	3	73	.308	1373	76	10	*.993
1913	Brooklyn	Nat.	1B	139	508	76	178	17	7	2	46	*.350	1279	80	13	.991
1914	Brooklyn	Nat.	1B	126	474	89	156	17	7	6	44	*.329	1097	48	8	.993
1915	Brooklyn	Nat.	1B	150	544	62	164	21	8	2	42	.301	1441	*102	11	.993
1916	Brooklyn	Nat.	1B	127	478	75	151	16	7	3	35	.316	1195	66	9	*.993
1917	Brooklyn	Nat.	1B	125	468	59	122	4	4	2	30	.261	1188	82	12	.991
1918	Brooklyn(a)	Nat.	1B	108	396	50	122	12	*15	2	47	.308	1069	63	10	.991
1919	Cincinnati	Nat.	1B	•140	537	79	148	10	12	2	42	.276	1437	80	17	.989
1920	Cincinnati	Nat.	1B	142	553	97	168	28	13	4	48	.304	1358	63	15	.990
1921	Cincinnati	Nat.	1B	136	516	69	158	18	12	2	64	.306	1290	78	10	.993
1922	Cincinnati	Nat.	1B	•156	610	114	205	15	*22	12	66	.336	*1652	79	11	•.994
1923	Cincinnati	Nat.	1B	125	500	63	146	27	10	2	54	.292	1224	77	9	.993
1924	Cincinnati	Nat.	1B	102	405	47	114	14	9	1	31	.281	1128	74	12	.990
Major League Totals				2014	7673	1117	2326	250	165	56	720	.303	19634	1128	181	.991

aTraded to Cincinnati Reds for outfielder Thomas Griffith, March, 1919.

WORLD SERIES RECORD

Year	Club	League	Pos.	G.	AB.	R.	H.	2B.	3B.	HR.	RBI.	B.A.	PO.	A.	E.	F.A.
1916	Brooklyn	Nat.	1B	4	17	1	3	0	1	0	0	.176	40	3	0	1.000
1919	Cincinnati	Nat.	1B	8	29	4	7	0	1	0	1	.241	81	5	2	.977
World Series Totals				12	46	5	10	0	2	0	1	.217	121	8	2	.985

GEORGE AUGUST (HOOKS) DAUSS

Born September 22, 1889, at Indianapolis, Ind.
Died July 27, 1963, at St. Louis, Mo.
Height, 5.10. Weight, 160.
Threw and batted righthanded.
Married Ollie Speake, 1915.

Leading Detroit hurler for lifetime wins in Tiger uniform (222).

Year	Club	League	G.	IP.	W.	L.	Pct.	H.	R.	ER.	SO.	BB.	ERA.
1909	Duluth	Minn.-Wis.	33	....	19	10	.655	....	....	....	....	....	......
1910	Duluth	Minn.-Wis.	18	....	7	7	.500	....	....	....	....	....	......
1911	St. Paul	Amer. Assn.	3	....	1	1	.500	....	6	....	6	3	......
1912	St. Paul	Amer. Assn.	•51	271	12	19	.387	277	154	....	156	120	......
1912	Detroit	American	2	17	1	1	.500	11	7	....	7	9	......
1913	Detroit	American	31	226	13	12	.520	186	101	67	107	82	2.67
1914	Detroit	American	45	302	18	15	.545	286	126	*96	150	87	2.86
1915	Detroit	American	46	310	24	13	.649	261	115	86	132	115	2.50
1916	Detroit	American	39	239	19	12	.613	220	102	85	95	90	3.20
1917	Detroit	American	38	270	17	14	.548	243	105	73	102	87	2.43
1918	Detroit	American	33	250	12	16	.429	243	105	•83	73	58	2.99
1919	Detroit	American	34	256	21	9	.700	262	*125	101	73	63	3.55

Year	Club	League	G.	IP.	W.	L.	Pct.	H.	R.	ER.	SO.	BB.	ERA.
1920	Detroit	American	38	270	13	21	.382	308	*158	107	82	84	3.57
1921	Detroit	American	32	233	10	15	.400	275	141	112	68	81	4.33
1922	Detroit	American	39	219	13	13	.500	251	123	102	78	59	4.19
1923	Detroit	American	50	316	21	13	.618	331	140	127	105	78	3.62
1924	Detroit	American	40	131	12	11	.522	155	78	67	44	40	4.60
1925	Detroit	American	35	228	16	11	.593	238	110	80	58	85	3.16
1926	Detroit	American	34	124	12	6	.667	135	63	58	27	49	4.21
Major League Totals			536	3391	222	182	.550	3405	1599	1244	1201	1067	3.32

GEORGE STACEY DAVIS

Born August 23, 1870, at Cohoes, N.Y.
Died October 17, 1940, at Philadelphia, Pa.
Height, 5.09. Weight, 180.
Threw right and batted right and lefthanded.
Married Jane Holden.

Had six hits in six times at bat, August 15, 1895; hit three triples in game, April 23, 1894; hit two doubles, a triple and a home run in a game, May 18, 1906.

Manager, New York Giants, 1895 and 1900-01; manager, Des Moines, Western League, 1910; scout, New York Yankees, 1915; scout, St. Louis Browns, 1917.

Year	Club	League	Pos.	G.	AB.	R.	H.	2B.	3B.	HR.	SB.	B.A.	PO.	A.	E.	F.A.
1889	Albany, N.Y.															
1890	Cleveland	Nat.	OF	134	526	98	139	22	12	6	22	.264	282	*35	18	.946
1891	Cleveland	Nat.	OF-3B-P	136	571	115	167	34	11	3	43	.292	292	71	30	.924
1892	Cleveland	Nat.	INF-OF	143	595	96	151	22	14	4	36	.254	192	226	36	.921
1893	New York (a)	Nat.	3B	133	533	112	199	23	26	10	54	.373	191	307	58	.896
1894	New York	Nat.	3B	124	492	124	170	28	20	9	37	.346	154	251	40	.910
1895	New York	Nat.	3B	110	433	106	143	32	11	5	45	.330	121	162	33	.896
1896	New York	Nat.	3B-SS	124	495	98	155	22	10	3	49	.313	224	312	41	.929
1897	New York	Nat.	SS	131	525	114	188	34	11	9	64	.358	*346	436	57	.932
1898	New York	Nat.	SS	121	484	80	148	21	5	1	22	.306	351	420	57	.931
1899	New York	Nat.	SS	111	413	69	144	25	4	1	38	.349	313	421	39	*.950
1900	New York	Nat.	SS	113	425	70	138	20	4	3	32	.325	276	455	45	.942
1901	New York	Nat.	SS-3B	130	495	69	153	21	6	7	26	.309	325	442	44	.946
1902	Chicago	Amer.	SS	132	480	77	143	27	7	3	33	.298	289	421	40	.947
1903	New York (b)	Nat.	SS	4	15	2	4	0	0	0	0	.267	11	10	3	.875
1904	Chicago	Amer.	SS	152	558	74	143	25	14	1	32	.256	351	*518	59	.936
1905	Chicago	Amer.	SS	151	550	74	153	28	3	1	31	.278	330	475	42	*.948
1906	Chicago	Amer.	SS	133	484	63	134	25	6	0	27	.277	236	475	42	.944
1907	Chicago	Amer.	SS	132	466	59	111	18	2	1	15	.238	223	485	38	.949
1908	Chicago	Amer.	2B-SS	128	419	41	91	14	1	0	22	.217	242	379	32	.951
1909	Chicago	Amer.	1B	28	68	5	9	1	0	0	4	.132	189	15	3	.986
1910	Des Moines	West.	2B-SS	32	99	14	19	0	0	0	4	.192	64	60	10	.925
American League Totals				856	3025	393	784	138	33	6	164	.259	1860	2794	260	.947
National League Totals				1514	6002	1153	1899	304	134	61	468	.316	3078	3548	501	.930
Major League Totals				2370	9027	1546	2683	442	167	67	632	.297	4938	6342	761	.937

aTraded to New York for catcher Buck Ewing, March, 1893.

bJumped Chicago American League club and played in game for New York Nationals against Pittsburgh, June 26, 1903, in defiance of peace treaty between American and National leagues; President Charles Comiskey of Chicago secured an injunction in New York courts to prevent Davis from playing with the New Yorkers on July 3, 1903, and on July 15, the courts issued an injunction against Davis playing with any club but Chicago; Davis played his last game for the New York club on July 1 and reported to Chicago for the 1904 season.

Pitching Record: Saw brief service as pitcher in 1891, no wins or losses.

WORLD SERIES RECORD

Year	Club	League	Pos.	G.	AB.	R.	H.	2B.	3B.	HR.	SB.	B.A.	PO.	A.	E.	F.A.
1906	Chicago	Amer.	SS	3	13	4	4	3	0	0	1	.308	7	14	2	.913

DID YOU KNOW—

That George Dauss claimed he was the most unknown pitching leader in history? He ranks as the Detroit Tigers' all-time top game winner, leading George Mullin's 209 victories.

HERMAN THOMAS (TOMMY) DAVIS, JR.

Born March 21, 1939, at Brooklyn, N.Y.
Height, 6.02. Weight, 200.
Threw and batted righthanded.

Tied major league record for most clubs, lifetime (10), since 1900.
Tied World Series records for most three-base hits, game (2), October 3, 1963; most three-base hits, four-game Series (2), 1963; most putouts, game, by left fielder (6), October 3, 1963—and in same game most putouts by outfielder, inning (3), seventh inning.
Named outfielder on THE SPORTING NEWS National League All-Star Team, 1962-63.
Named designated hitter on THE SPORTING NEWS American League All-Star Team, 1974.

Year—Club	League	Pos.	G.	AB.	R.	H.	2B.	3B.	HR.	RBI.	B.A.	PO.	A.	E.	F.A.
1956—Hornell	Pony	OF	43	154	14	50	5	1	0	26	.325	49	7	4	.933
1957—Kokomo	Midw.	OF-3B	127	*518	*115	*185	23	6	17	104	*.357	179	32	19	.917
1958—Victoria	Texas	OF-1B	122	461	74	140	21	10	13	66	.304	261	17	7	.975
1958—Montreal	Int.	OF-2B-3B	14	26	3	8	0	1	1	7	.308	6	0	1	.857
1959—Spokane	P.C.	OF	*153	*612	90	*211	32	9	18	78	*.345	*414	15	•10	.977
1959—Los Angeles	Nat.	PH	1	1	0	0	0	0	0	0	.000	0	0	0	.000
1960—Los Angeles	Nat.	OF-3B	110	352	43	97	18	1	11	44	.276	153	17	4	.977
1961—Los Angeles	Nat.	OF-3B	132	460	60	128	13	2	15	58	.278	173	91	17	.940
1962—Los Angeles	Nat.	OF-3B	163	665	120	*230	27	9	27	*153	*.346	269	60	20	.943
1963—Los Angeles	Nat.	OF-3B	146	556	69	181	19	3	16	88	*.326	204	67	15	.948
1964—Los Angeles	Nat.	OF	152	592	70	163	20	5	14	86	.275	264	9	5	.982
1965—Los Angeles	Nat.	OF	17	60	3	15	1	1	0	9	.250	21	1	0	1.000
1966—Los Angeles (a)	Nat.	OF-3B	100	313	27	98	11	1	3	27	.313	99	9	3	.973
1967—New York (b)	Nat.	OF-1B	154	577	72	174	32	0	16	73	.302	236	7	7	.972
1968—Chicago (c)	Amer.	OF-1B	132	456	30	122	5	3	8	50	.268	211	9	8	.965
1969—Seattle (d)	Amer.	OF-1B	123	454	52	123	29	1	6	80	.271	183	3	7	.964
1969—Houston	Nat.	OF	24	79	2	19	3	0	1	9	.241	27	1	0	1.000
1970—Hou.(e)-Chi.(f)	Nat.	OF	68	255	28	71	14	2	5	38	.278	86	4	5	.947
1970—Oakland (g)	Amer.	OF-1B	66	200	17	58	9	1	1	27	.290	110	4	4	.966
1971—Oakland	Amer.	1-OF-2-3	79	219	26	71	8	1	3	42	.324	275	37	5	.984
1972—Chicago (h-i)	Nat.	1B-OF	15	26	3	7	1	0	0	6	.269	31	1	1	.970
1972—Baltimore	Amer.	OF-1B	26	82	9	21	3	0	0	6	.256	51	4	0	1.000
1973—Baltimore	Amer.	1B	137	552	53	169	20	3	7	89	.306	32	2	1	.971
1974—Baltimore	Amer.	DH	158	626	67	181	20	1	11	84	.289	0	0	0	.000
1975—Baltimore	Amer.	DH	116	460	43	130	14	1	6	57	.283	0	0	0	.000
1976—Calif.(j)-K.C.(k)	Amer.	DH-1B	80	238	17	63	5	0	3	26	.265	4	0	0	1.000
American League Totals			917	3287	314	938	113	11	45	461	.285	866	59	25	.974
National League Totals			1082	3936	497	1183	159	24	108	591	.301	1563	267	77	.960
Major League Totals			1999	7223	811	2121	272	35	153	1052	.294	2429	326	102	.964

aTraded with outfielder-infielder Derrell Griffith to New York Mets for second baseman Ron Hunt and outfielder-infielder Jim Hickman, November 29, 1966.
bTraded with pitchers Jack Fisher and Billy Wynne to Chicago White Sox for outfielder Tommie Agee and infielder Al Weiss, December 15, 1967.
cSelected by Seattle Pilots from Chicago White Sox in expansion draft, October 15, 1968.
dTraded to Houston Astros for outfielders Hilario Valdespino and Dan Walton, August 31, 1969.
eSold to Oakland Athletics, June 22, 1970.
fSold to Chicago Cubs, September 16, 1970.
gSigned by Oakland Athletics, March 29, 1971.
hSigned by Chicago Cubs, July 6, 1972.
iTraded to Baltimore Orioles for catcher Ellie Hendricks, August 18, 1972.
jSigned by California Angels, June 2, 1976.
kSold to Kansas City Royals, September 20, 1976.

WORLD SERIES RECORD

Year—Club	League	Pos.	G.	AB.	R.	H.	2B.	3B.	HR.	RBI.	B.A.	PO.	A.	E.	F.A.
1963—Los Angeles	Nat.	OF	4	15	0	6	0	2	0	2	.400	6	0	0	1.000
1966—Los Angeles	Nat.	OF	4	8	0	2	0	0	0	0	.250	3	0	0	1.000
World Series Totals			8	23	0	8	0	2	0	2	.348	9	0	0	1.000

DID YOU KNOW—

That Tommy Davis ranks as the first great designated hitter in history and set the pattern and production figures for DHers to come?

VIRGIL LAWRENCE (SPUD) DAVIS

Born December 20, 1904, at Birmingham, Ala.
Height, 6.01. Weight, 220.
Threw and batted righthanded.
Married Helen Ball, April 30, 1928.

Made unassisted double play, first game, Philadelphia vs. Cincinnati, July 24, 1928. Led N. L. catchers in double plays, 1932.
Coach, Pittsburgh Pirates, 1941-42-43-46; scout, Pirates, 1947-48-49; coach, Chicago Cubs, 1950-51-52-53.

Year	Club	League	Pos.	G.	AB.	R.	H.	2B.	3B.	HR.	RBI.	B.A.	PO.	A.	E.	F.A.
1926	Gulfport	Ct. St.	C-PH	27	90	10	32	8	5	2	.....	.356	26	6	3	.914
1927	Reading	Int.	C-PH	137	383	50	118	17	3	11	70	.308	271	86	12	.967
1928	St.L. (a)-Phila.	Nat.	C	69	168	17	47	2	0	3	19	.280	155	46	6	.971
1929	Philadelphia	Nat.	C	98	263	31	90	18	0	7	48	.342	198	47	10	.961
1930	Philadelphia	Nat.	C	106	329	41	103	16	1	14	65	.313	307	50	5	.986
1931	Philadelphia	Nat.	C	120	393	30	128	32	1	4	51	.326	420	*78	3	.994
1932	Philadelphia	Nat.	C	125	402	44	135	23	5	14	70	.336	408	54	6	.987
1933	Philadelphia (b)	Nat.	C	141	495	51	173	28	3	9	65	.349	395	69	8	.983
1934	St. Louis	Nat.	C	107	347	45	104	22	4	9	65	.300	459	42	6	.988
1935	St. Louis	Nat.	C-1B	102	315	28	100	24	2	1	60	.317	335	34	3	.992
1936	St. Louis (c)	Nat.	C-3B	112	363	24	99	26	2	4	59	.273	390	59	7	.985
1937	Cincinnati	Nat.	C	76	209	19	56	10	1	3	33	.268	300	40	7	.980
1938	Cin. (d)-Phila.	Nat.	C	82	251	14	59	8	0	2	24	.235	260	34	7	.977
1939	Philadelphia (e)	Nat.	C	87	202	10	62	8	1	0	23	.307	260	40	0	1.000
1940	Pittsburgh	Nat.	C	99	285	23	93	14	1	5	39	.326	288	61	12	.967
1941	Pittsburgh (f)	Nat.	C	57	107	3	27	4	1	0	6	.252	97	16	0	1.000
1944	Pittsburgh	Nat.	C	54	93	6	28	7	0	2	14	.301	76	10	3	.966
1945	Pittsburgh	Nat.	C	23	33	2	8	2	0	0	6	.242	26	4	1	.968
Major League Totals				1458	4255	388	1312	244	22	77	647	.308	4374	684	84	.984

aTraded with outfielder Homer Peel to Philadelphia Phillies for catcher James Wilson, May 11, 1928.
bTraded with infielder Eddie Delker to St. Louis Cardinals for catcher James Wilson, November 15, 1933.
cSold to Cincinnati, December 2, 1936.
dTraded with pitcher Albert W. Hollingsworth and $55,000 to Philadelphia Phillies for pitcher William H. Walters, June 13, 1938.
eSold to Pittsburgh, October 27, 1939.
fReleased as active player, October 2, 1941; restored to active list, April, 1944.

WORLD SERIES RECORD

Year	Club	League	Pos.	G.	AB.	R.	H.	2B.	3B.	HR.	RBI.	B.A.	PO.	A.	E.	F.A.
1934	St. Louis	Nat.	PH	2	2	0	2	0	0	0	1	1.000	0	0	0	.000

JAY HANNA (DIZZY) DEAN

Born January 16, 1911, at Lucas, Ark.
Died July 17, 1974, at Reno, Nev.
Height, 6.03. Weight, 202.
Threw and batted righthanded.
Married Patricia Nash, June 10, 1931.

Brother of Paul Dean, major league pitcher.
Struck out 17 Chicago Cubs in first game of doubleheader, July 30, 1933.
Named to Hall of Fame, 1953.

Year	Club	League	G.	IP.	W.	L.	Pct.	H.	R.	ER.	SO.	BB.	ERA.
1930	St. Joseph	Western	32	217	17	8	.680	204	118	89	134	77	3.69
1930	Houston	Texas	14	85	8	2	.800	62	31	27	95	49	2.86
1930	St. Louis	National	1	9	1	0	1.000	3	1	1	5	3	1.00
1931	Houston	Texas	41	304	*26	10	.722	210	71	52	*303	90	*1.57
1932	St. Louis	National	46	*286	18	15	.545	280	122	105	*191	102	3.30
1933	St. Louis	National	*48	293	20	18	.526	279	113	99	*199	64	3.04
1934	St. Louis	National	50	312	*30	7	*.811	288	110	92	*195	75	2.65
1935	St. Louis	National	50	*324	*28	12	.700	*326	128	112	*182	82	3.11
1936	St. Louis	National	●51	*315	24	13	.649	310	128	111	195	53	3.17

Year	Club	League	G.	IP.	W.	L.	Pct.	H.	R.	ER.	SO.	BB.	ERA.
1937—St. Louis (a)		National	27	197	13	10	.565	200	76	59	120	33	2.70
1938—Chicago		National	13	75	7	1	.875	63	20	15	22	8	1.80
1939—Chicago		National	19	96	6	4	.600	98	40	36	27	17	3.38
1940—Chicago		National	10	54	3	3	.500	68	35	31	18	20	5.17
1940—Tulsa		Texas	21	142	8	8	.500	149	69	50	51	19	3.17
1941—Chicago (b)		National	1	1	0	0	.000	3	3	2	1	0	18.00
1947—St. Louis (c) (d)		American	1	4	0	0	.000	3	0	0	0	1	0.00
American League Totals			1	4	0	0	.000	3	0	0	0	1	0.00
National League Totals			316	1962	150	83	.644	1918	776	663	1155	457	3.04
Major League Totals			317	1966	150	83	.644	1921	776	663	1155	458	3.04

aTraded to Chicago Cubs for pitchers Curt Davis and Clyde Shoun, outfielder Tuck Stainback and $185,000, April 16, 1938.
bReleased as player and signed as coach with Chicago Cubs, May 14, 1941; retired as coach to accept baseball broadcasting job in St. Louis, July 12, 1941.
cSigned by St. Louis Browns to pitch final game as gate attraction.
dMade promotional appearances with Sioux Falls and Denver in Western League and Fargo-Moorhead in Northern in 1941; with Clovis in West Texas-New Mexico in 1949.

WORLD SERIES RECORD

Year	Club	League	G.	IP.	W.	L.	Pct.	H.	R.	ER.	SO.	BB.	ERA.
1934—St. Louis		National	3	26	2	1	.667	20	6	5	17	5	1.73
1938—Chicago		National	2	8⅓	0	1	.000	8	6	6	2	1	6.48
World Series Totals			5	34⅓	2	2	.500	28	12	11	19	6	2.88

EDWARD JAMES (BIG ED) DELAHANTY

Born October 31, 1867, at Cleveland, O.
Died July 2, 1903, at Fort Erie, Ont.
(Fell off railroad bridge over Niagara River. Body recovered at foot of falls.)
Height, 5.10. Weight, 170.
Threw and batted righthanded.

One of five brothers, all of whom were major league players: Frank G. (New York and Cleveland, A. L.); James C. (Chicago, New York, Boston, Cincinnati in N. L., and St. Louis, Washington, Detroit in A. L.); Joseph N. (St. Louis N. L.), and Thomas S. (Philadelphia, Cleveland, Pittsburgh, Louisville in N. L.).
Only player in major league history to lead both leagues in hitting—National, 1899; American, 1902. Twice made six hits in six times at bat, June 2, 1890, and June 16, 1894. Made ten hits in succession, July 13 (two games), 14, 1897. Hit four home runs and single, July 13, 1896. Tied record most two-base hits, game, four, May 3, 1899.
Named to Hall of Fame in 1945.

Year	Club	League	Pos.	G.	AB.	R.	H.	2B.	3B.	HR.	SB.	B.A.	PO.	A.	E.	F.A.
1887—Mansfield		Ohio St.	2-1B	73	366	90	130	20	7	5		.355	212	184	47	.894
1888—Wheeling		Tri. St.	2-1B	21	98	20	40	9	4	5	15	.408	64	59	18	.872
1888—Philadelphia		Nat.	2B	74	290	40	66	11	1	1	38	.228	157	173	47	.875
1889—Philadelphia(a)		Nat.	2B-OF	54	246	37	72	13	3	0	19	.293	116	61	17	.912
1890—Cleveland(b)		Play.	2-S-O	115	513	106	152	24	15	3	24	.296	244	300	92	.855
1891—Philadelphia		Nat.	1B-OF	128	545	92	136	19	9	5	27	.250	463	34	34	.936
1892—Philadelphia		Nat.	OF	120	470	78	147	*33	19	6	35	.313	254	29	23	.925
1893—Philadelphia		Nat.	OF	132	*588	145	218	31	20	*19	36	.371	312	32	19	.948
1894—Philadelphia		Nat.	OF	114	497	149	199	36	16	4	29	.400	224	21	16	.939
1895—Philadelphia		Nat.	OF	116	481	148	192	*47	8	11	46	.399	230	29	15	.915
1896—Philadelphia		Nat.	1B-OF	122	505	131	199	*42	14	†13	37	.394	482	27	23	.957
1897—Philadelphia		Nat.	OF	129	530	110	200	37	15	4	28	.377	262	22	10	.966
1898—Philadelphia		Nat.	OF	142	547	114	183	37	11	3	62	.335	300	20	12	.964
1899—Philadelphia		Nat.	OF	145	573	133	*234	*56	9	9	38	*.408	285	20	9	.971
1900—Philadelphia		Nat.	1B	130	542	82	173	32	10	1	14	.319	1293	69	25	.982
1901—Philadelphia(c)		Nat.	1B-OF	138	538	106	192	38	16	8	28	.357	723	24	21	.973
1902—Washington		Amer.	1B-OF	123	474	103	178	41	15	10	14	*.376	251	12	9	.967
1903—Washington		Amer.	OF	43	154	22	52	11	1	1	3	.338	74	6	3	.964
American League Totals				166	628	125	230	52	16	11	17	.366	325	18	12	.966
National League Totals				1544	6352	1365	2211	432	151	84	437	.348	5101	561	271	.954
Players League Totals				115	513	106	152	24	15	3	24	.296	244	300	92	.855
Major League Totals				1825	7493	1596	2593	508	182	98	478	.346	5670	879	375	.946

aJumped to Players League (Brotherhood), 1890.
bReturned to Philadelphia N. L. after disbanding of Brotherhood in 1890.
cJumped to American League, 1902.

EUGENE NAPOLEON DeMONTREVILLE

Born March 26, 1874, at St. Paul, Minn.
Died February 18, 1935, at Memphis, Tenn.
Threw and batted righthanded.
Married Anna D. Kelley, August 29, 1900.

Manager, Worcester, Montreal, Eastern League, 1903; manager, New Orleans, Southern League, 1910.

Year — Club	League	Pos.	G.	AB.	R.	H.	2B.	3B.	HR.	SB.	B.A.	PO.	A.	E.	F.A.
1894—Buf.-Bing.-Scr.	Eastern	SS	36	146	31	45	....	....	....	4	.308	68	117	21	.898
1894—Pittsburgh	National	SS	2	8	0	2	0	0	0	0	.250	1	7	1	.875
1895—Toronto	Eastern	SS	112	456	92	144	....	....	....	40	.315	238	393	76	.892
1895—Washington	National	SS	12	44	7	10	1	2	1	2	.227	34	39	5	.936
1896—Washington	National	SS	130	523	93	183	21	6	0	29	.349	300	475	92	.892
1897—Washington	National	2B-SS	132	563	92	197	24	6	3	33	.349	342	457	89	.900
1898—Baltimore	National	2B-SS	151	567	95	185	19	1	0	56	.325	372	490	51	.944
1899—Balti.-Chicago	National	2B	143	550	83	154	20	7	1	45	.280	374	503	66	.930
1900—Brooklyn	National	2B	63	232	32	58	10	0	0	20	.250	129	131	12	.956
1901—Boston	National	2B-3B	140	570	83	174	14	5	5	23	.305	291	392	39	*.946
1902—Boston	National	2B-SS	123	483	50	130	18	5	0	27	.269	272	281	42	.929
1903—Washington	American	2B	11	40	0	12	2	0	0	0	.300	29	26	3	.948
1903—Wor.-Mont.	Eastern	2B	45	117	20	45	....	....	....	2	.254	82	130	16	.930
1904—St. Louis	American	2B	4	9	0	1	0	0	0	0	.111	4	5	0	1.000
1904—Indianapolis	A. A.	SS	20	70	10	21	1	0	0	1	.300	21	43	15	.810
1905—Toledo	A. A.	2B	152	589	93	171	*49	4	1	36	.290	376	500	46	.950
1906—Toledo	A. A.	SS-OF	133	524	67	148	29	5	3	33	.282	197	261	43	.914
1907—Birmingham	Sou. Lg.	SS	107	400	65	105	....	....	....	19	.262	190	346	35	.938
1908—Birmingham	Sou. Lg.	SS	69	239	28	53	....	....	....	26	.212	132	203	24	.933
1909—New Orleans	So. L.	2B-SS	109	375	33	86	....	....	....	20	.229	298	305	21	.966
1910—New Orleans	So. L.	2B-SS	107	339	29	64	....	....	....	11	.188	227	325	32	.945
National League Totals			896	3540	535	1093	127	32	10	235	.309	2115	2775	397	.925
American League Totals			15	49	0	13	2	0	0	0	.265	33	31	3	.955
Major League Totals			911	3589	535	1106	129	32	10	235	.308	2148	2806	400	.925

PAUL M. (DUKE AND OOM PAUL) DERRINGER

Born October 17, 1907, at Springfield, Ky.
Height, 6.04. Weight, 217.
Threw and batted righthanded.
Married Mary Jane Stein, September 3, 1944.

Led National League in complete games pitched, 1938; pitched one-hit games against St. Louis Cardinals, May 6, 1940, and Chicago Cubs, July 6, 1940.
Named by Baseball Writers' Association of America for THE SPORTING NEWS All-Star Major League Team, 1940.

Year — Club	League	G.	IP.	W.	L.	Pct.	H.	R.	ER.	SO.	BB.	ERA.
1927—Danville	I.I.I.	26	172	10	8	.556	160	84	64	46	75	3.35
1928—Danville	I.I.I.	33	243	15	11	.577	248	109	99	92	80	3.67
1929—Rochester	Int.	41	244	17	12	.586	259	120	106	94	96	3.91
1930—Rochester	Int.	44	*289	*23	11	.676	*310	147	125	164	72	3.89
1931—St. Louis	Nat.	35	212	18	8	*.692	225	88	79	134	65	3.35
1932—St. Louis	Nat.	39	233	11	14	.440	296	*133	105	78	67	4.06
1933—St. Louis(a)-Cincinnati	Nat.	36	248	7	*27	.206	264	117	91	89	60	3.30
1934—Cincinnati	Nat.	47	261	15	21	.417	297	129	104	122	59	3.59
1935—Cincinnati	Nat.	45	277	22	13	.629	295	132	108	120	49	3.51
1936—Cincinnati	Nat.	•51	282	19	19	.500	*331	*147	*126	121	42	4.02
1937—Cincinnati	Nat.	43	223	10	14	.417	240	112	100	94	55	4.04
1938—Cincinnati	Nat.	41	*307	21	14	.600	*315	110	100	132	40	2.93
1939—Cincinnati	Nat.	38	301	25	7	*.781	*321	115	98	128	35	2.93
1940—Cincinnati	Nat.	37	297	20	12	.625	280	110	101	115	48	3.06
1941—Cincinnati	Nat.	29	228	12	14	.462	233	91	84	76	54	3.32
1942—Cincinnati(b)	Nat.	29	209	10	11	.476	203	83	71	68	49	3.06

Year Club	League	G.	IP.	W.	L.	Pct.	H.	R.	ER.	SO.	BB.	ERA.
1943—Chicago	Nat.	32	174	10	14	.417	184	90	69	75	39	3.57
1944—Chicago	Nat.	42	180	7	13	.350	205	96	83	69	39	4.15
1945—Chicago	Nat.	35	214	16	11	.593	223	99	82	86	51	3.45
1946—Indianapolis	A.A.	32	180	9	11	.450	185	74	53	84	55	2.65
Major League Totals		579	3646	223	212	.513	3912	1652	1401	1507	761	3.46

aTraded to Cincinnati Reds with infielder Earl Adams and pitcher Allen Stout for shortstop Leo Durocher and pitchers Frank Henry and John Ogden, May 7, 1933.
bSold to Chicago Cubs, January 7, 1943.

WORLD SERIES RECORD

Year Club	League	G.	IP.	W.	L.	Pct.	H.	R.	ER.	SO.	BB.	ERA.
1931—St. Louis	Nat.	3	12⅔	0	2	.000	14	10	6	14	7	4.26
1939—Cincinnati	Nat.	2	15⅓	0	1	.000	9	4	4	9	3	2.35
1940—Cincinnati	Nat.	3	19½	2	1	.667	17	8	6	6	10	2.79
1945—Chicago	Nat.	3	5⅓	0	0	.000	5	4	4	1	7	6.75
World Series Totals		11	52⅔	2	4	.333	45	26	20	30	27	3.42

WILLIAM MALCOLM DICKEY

Born June 6, 1907, at Bastrop, La.
Height, 6.01½. Weight, 185.
Threw right and batted lefthanded.
Married Violet Ann Arnold, October 5, 1932.

Tied major league record for most home runs with bases filled, two consecutive games—2, second game, New York vs. Chicago A. L., August 3 and August 4, 1937. Equaled major league record for most assists, by catcher, inning—3, sixth inning, May 13, 1929. Did not have passed ball, 125 games, 1931. Caught 100 or more games 13 consecutive seasons to set major league record; also holds record for seasons catching 100 or more games—13. Hit three home runs in game, July 26, 1939. Made unassisted double play, first game, St. Louis vs. New York, June 8, 1941, to tie record.
Tied World Series records—Six times at bat, game, October 2, 1932. Two times at bat, inning—2 (seventh inning, October 2, 1932, and ninth inning, October 6, 1936). Most base hits, game—4 (October 5, 1938).
Named by Baseball Writers' Association of America for THE SPORTING NEWS All-Star Major League Teams, 1932-33-36-38-39 and 1941.
Manager, New York Yankees, May 24, 1946, to September 12, 1946; Little Rock, Southern Association, 1947; coach, Yankees, 1949 through 1957; scout, Yankees, January 19, 1959, signed as coach, January 15, 1960; released in July, 1960.
Named to Hall of Fame, 1954.

Year Club	League	Pos.	G.	AB.	R.	H.	2B.	3B.	HR.	RBI.	B.A.	PO.	A.	E.	F.A.
1925—Little Rock	South.	C	3	10	1	3	0	0	0		.300	8	2	0	1.000
1926—Muskogee	W.A.	C	61	212	27	60	6	2	7		.283	300	58	13	.965
1926—Little Rock	South.	C	21	46	6	18	1	5	0	8	.391	36	4	2	.952
1927—Jackson	Cot. St.	C	101	364	46	108	31	3	3		.297	*457	*84	9	*.984
1928—Little Rock	South.	C	60	203	22	61	12	6	4	32	.300	151	52	8	.962
1928—Buffalo	Int.	C	3	8	0	1	0	1	0	0	.125	12	4	2	.889
1928—New York	Amer.	C	10	15	1	3	1	1	0	2	.200	6	2	0	1.000
1929—New York	Amer.	C	130	447	60	145	30	6	10	65	.324	476	*95	12	.979
1930—New York	Amer.	C	109	366	55	124	25	7	5	65	.339	418	51	*11	.977
1931—New York	Amer.	C	130	477	65	156	17	10	6	78	.327	*670	78	3	*.996
1932—New York	Amer.	C	108	423	66	131	20	4	15	84	.310	639	53	9	.987
1933—New York	Amer.	C	130	478	58	152	24	8	14	97	.318	*721	82	6	.993
1934—New York	Amer.	C	104	395	56	127	24	4	12	72	.322	527	49	8	.986
1935—New York	Amer.	C	120	448	54	125	26	6	14	81	.279	*536	63	3	*.995
1936—New York	Amer.	C	112	423	99	153	26	8	22	107	.362	499	61	14	.976
1937—New York	Amer.	C	140	530	87	176	35	2	29	133	.332	*692	†80	7	*.991
1938—New York	Amer.	C	132	454	84	142	27	4	27	115	.313	*518	*74	8	*.987
1939—New York	Amer.	C	128	480	98	145	23	3	24	105	.302	*571	57	7	*.989
1940—New York	Amer.	C	106	372	45	92	11	1	9	54	.247	425	55	3	†.994
1941—New York	Amer.	C	109	348	35	99	15	5	7	71	.284	422	45	3	*.994
1942—New York	Amer.	C	82	268	28	79	13	1	2	37	.295	322	44	9	.976
1943—New York	Amer.	C	85	242	29	85	18	2	4	33	.351	322	37	2	.994
1944-45—New York	Amer.	C	(In Military Service)												
1946—New York	Amer.	C	54	134	10	35	8	0	2	10	.261	201	29	3	.987
1947—Little Rock	South.	C	8	12	2	4	2	0	1	2	.333	13	2	0	1.000
Major League Totals			1789	6300	930	1969	343	72	202	1209	.313	7965	954	108	.988

WORLD SERIES RECORD

Year Club	League	Pos.	G.	AB.	R.	H.	2B.	3B.	HR.	RBI.	B.A.	PO.	A.	E.	F.A.
1932—New York	Amer.	C	4	16	2	7	0	0	0	4	.438	25	1	0	1.000
1936—New York	Amer.	C	6	25	5	3	0	0	1	5	.120	38	4	1	.977

Year	Club	League	Pos.	G.	AB.	R.	H.	2B.	3B.	HR.	RBI.	B.A.	PO.	A.	E.	F.A.
1937—New York		Amer.	C	5	19	3	4	0	1	0	3	.211	26	1	0	1.000
1938—New York		Amer.	C	4	15	2	6	0	0	1	2	.400	31	5	0	1.000
1939—New York		Amer.	C	4	15	2	4	0	0	2	5	.267	27	2	0	1.000
1941—New York		Amer.	C	5	18	3	3	1	0	0	1	.167	24	2	0	1.000
1942—New York		Amer.	C	5	19	1	5	0	0	0	0	.263	25	1	1	.963
1943—New York		Amer.	C	5	18	1	5	0	0	1	4	.278	28	3	0	1.000
World Series Totals				38	145	19	37	1	1	5	24	.255	224	19	2	.992

MARTIN DIHIGO

Born May 24, 1905, at Matanzas, Cuba.
Died May 20, 1971, at Cienfuegos, Cuba.
Height, 6.03. Weight, 225.
Threw and batted righthanded.

Possessor of one of the finest arms in baseball, Martin Dihigo was unquestionably the best all-round baseball performer in the history of the Negro leagues. He was a top pitcher, with a blazing fast ball, and a standout at every position on the diamond.

He is the first Cuban to enter the Hall of Fame and was the first to pitch a no-hitter in the history of the Mexican League. He's also the first to be a member of the Cuban, Mexican and American Halls of Fame. Noted for his warm, friendly attitude, he was among the best-liked players by his teammates and rivals.

As Buck Leonard said, "Dihigo was the best all-round baseball player I have ever seen. He could run, hit, throw, think, pitch and manage. He both knew the game and could play it. I was in the game for 23 years and I never saw anyone better than he was. And that includes not only the United States but also Puerto Rico, Venezuela, Colombia, Cuba and Mexico. When I heard of Dihigo's passing, I was really saddened for I had lost a dear friend."

Dihigo was the hero of the islands, and was a player-manager in the winter leagues. He brought Leonard down there to play for his Marianao team. Buck told of one special time when Dihigo invited him to his home on an off-day. He lived in Matanzas, Cuba, not far from Havana. In Leonard's honor, Martin cooked a big pig.

"They dug a hole in the ground and heated rocks on the bottom with a wood fire. They put a spit through the pig, put a cover over it and then shoveled dirt over the whole thing. They left it in the ground a long while, until it was time to eat. Then they dug up the pig and you never tasted anything so delicious. Martin was a supreme host. I guess you couldn't match him at that, either."

As a Cuban teenager, Dihigo played against the winter travelers from the American Negro leagues. Two in particular, Oscar Charleston and John Henry Lloyd, took Martin under their wings and taught him the tricks of the trade. Both Oscar and John Henry were amazed at Dihigo's versatility and they encouraged him to follow his talents. At 18, then a Cuban phenom, Dihigo headed for the States and a pro career.

He joined the New York Cubans and later starred for the Philadelphia Hilldales and the Derby (Pa.) Daisies. He spent two years with the Homestead Grays as an outfielder almost exclusively. A big player, 6-3 and 225 pounds, he could belt the long ball consistently and was a smart player. He was fast on the bases and had one of the greatest arms of any player. It was good enough to be an outstanding pitcher, a fast-baller, but he was sufficiently maneuverable to be capable of playing any infield or outfield position.

As Cool Papa Bell put it, "Dihigo was the greatest all-round player we ever had. Now, a super star at his position, say an Oscar Charleston in center field or a Judy Johnson at third or a Buck Leonard at first or a John Henry Lloyd at short, no one was their equal and neither was Dihigo, but no one else could play so many positions and as well as he could. He was a great player at all of them; therefore, he was a great addition to your ball club. His disposition was even-tempered and he never caused any trouble. He was a manager when he played back home, and he made no enemies there, either."

So respected was Dihigo and so admired both as a player and as a man, he became the favorite of President Batista of Cuba, who continually praised Dihigo for his all-round excellence and the contribution he made to Cuban sports. The people of Mexico also adopted him as their native hero because of his fan-pleasing play, his popular switching of positions in a game to demonstrate the multiplicity of his talents, and his personal warmth and regard for the fans. His charm and persuasive ability lured many of the stars of the Negro professional leagues to the islands to play for the teams he managed. For the most part, aside from occasional government problems, tours to the Caribbean area on a Dihigo junket were pure fun for the players.

Dihigo was a hero to Minnie Minoso, Cuba's contribution to the American League as a longtime star of the Chicago White Sox. As Minoso, also from Matanzas, said:

"Dihigo used to let me carry his shoes and glove and that's how I got into the ball park down there when I was a kid. He was a big man, all muscle with not an ounce of fat on him. He helped me by teaching me how to play properly. When I played a few years in the Negro leagues, with the New York Cubans, Dihigo was past his prime and just a manager then, so I never really competed against him as a player. But it is difficult to explain what a great hero he was in Cuba. Everywhere he went, he was recognized and mobbed for autographs. I'd have to say he was most responsible for me getting to the major leagues. He was a big man, but he was big in all ways, as a player, as a manager, as a teacher, as a man."

Leonard said that Dihigo could hit "a long ball, a real long one." He added, "He had a picture swing, effortless and smooth, and he had a great batting eye. He was fast for so big a man and they all had to play him honest. What a lineup we had when he was pitching down there in the Caribbean. We had nine hitters in the lineup and he used to bat anywhere from second spot to fifth. That little old ball took one hell of a beating that day. And he was such a great fellow to have around the club, never a dull moment. As I said, he could do anything."

Minoso disagreed on this. He said he never heard Dihigo sing.

In his declining years (Dihigo died four days short of his 66th birthday), he spent much time working with youth teams and encouraging the young to play baseball. At the time of his death, the Cuban government was utilizing his talents as the nation's Minister of Sports.

U.S. sports representatives who visited Cuba during the 1977 lifting of travel barriers saw baseball diamonds all over the island, excellent lighted stadiums with good seating capacities, games in progress at all hours and the whole nation seemingly involved. And the visitors estimated there was an immense lode of untapped talent.

The hand of Martin Dihigo fashioned a great deal of this program. It would be fitting that more Cubans make the major leagues, a tribute from him to the United States he loved next to his native land, and a nation which gave him the highest honor a ballplayer can attain—the Hall of Fame.

Dihigo was named to the Hall of Fame in 1977.

JOSEPH PAUL (YANKEE CLIPPER) DI MAGGIO

Born November 25, 1914, at Martinez, Calif.

Height, 6.02. Weight, 193.

Threw and batted righthanded.

Brother, Dominic with Boston Red Sox, 1940 to spring of 1953, brother, Vincent with Boston Braves, 1937-38; made two home runs, fifth inning, June 24, 1936; Cincinnati Reds, 1939-40; Pittsburgh Pirates, 1940 through 1944; Philadelphia Phillies, 1945-46 and New York Giants, 1946.

Hit safely in 61 consecutive games with San Francisco, Pacific Coast League, 1933; made 206 hits in his first season with New York Yankees (1936); equaled modern major and American League record for most three-base hits, game (3), first game, August 27, 1938; made two home runs, fifth inning, June 24, 1936; hit three home runs in a game, second game, June 13, 1937, May 23, 1948 and September 10, 1950; first player to hit three home runs in a game at Griffith Stadium, Washington, D. C. September 10, 1950; hit for cycle, July 9, 1937 and May 20, 1948; batted safely in 56 consecutive games before being stopped by pitchers Al Smith and Jim Bagby of Cleveland in a night game, July 17, 1941, for a major league record. Streak began on May 15.

World Series record—Co-holder, most times at bat, game (6), October 6, 1936; most times at bat, inning (2), ninth inning, October 6, 1936 and sixth inning, October 6, 1937; most hits, inning (2), ninth inning, October 6, 1936; most putouts, inning (3), ninth inning, October 2, 1936 and sixth inning, October 7, 1937; holds record for most putouts, one Series, five games (20), 1942.

Led A.L. outfielders in double plays, 1941 (tie).

Named Most Valuable Player, American League, 1939, 1941 and 1947. Named by Baseball Writers' Association of America for THE SPORTING NEWS All-Star Major League Team, 1937-38-39-40-41-42-47-48. Topped the poll from 1937 to 1941, being unanimous choice in 1939 and 1941. Named by THE SPORTING NEWS as the No. 1 Major League Player of the Year, 1939.

Executive vice-president-coach, Oakland Athletics, 1968, 1969; Board of Directors, Baltimore Orioles, 1980.

Named to Hall of Fame, 1955.

Year	Club	League	Pos.	G.	AB.	R.	H.	2B.	3B.	HR.	RBI.	B.A.	PO.	A.	E.	F.A.
1932	San Francisco	P. C.	*SS	3	9	2	2	1	1	0	2	.222	4	7	1	.917
1933	San Francisco	P. C.	OF	187	762	129	259	45	13	28	*169	.340	407	*32	17	.963
1934	San Francisco	P. C.	OF	101	375	58	128	18	6	12	69	.341	236	11	8	.969
1935	San Francisco	P. C.	OF	172	679	*173	270	48	*18	34	*154	.398	430	*32	21	.957
1936	New York	Amer.	OF	138	637	132	206	44	*15	29	125	.323	339	*22	8	.978
1937	New York	Amer.	OF	151	621	*151	215	35	15	*46	167	.346	*413	21	*17	.962
1938	New York	Amer.	OF	145	599	129	194	32	13	32	140	.324	366	20	15	.963
1939	New York	Amer.	OF	120	462	108	176	32	6	30	126	*.381	328	13	5	.986
1940	New York	Amer.	OF	132	508	93	179	28	9	31	133	*.352	359	5	8	.978
1941	New York	Amer.	OF	139	541	122	193	43	11	30	*125	.357	385	16	9	.978
1942	New York	Amer.	OF	154	610	123	186	29	13	21	114	.305	409	10	8	.981
1943-44-45	New York							(In Military Service)								
1946	New York	Amer.	OF	132	503	81	146	20	8	25	95	.290	314	15	6	.982
1947	New York	Amer.	OF	141	534	97	168	31	10	20	97	.315	316	2	1	*.997
1948	New York	Amer.	OF	153	594	110	190	26	11	*39	*155	.320	441	8	13	.972
1949	New York	Amer.	OF	76	272	58	94	14	6	14	67	.346	195	1	3	.985
1950	New York	Amer.	OF	139	525	114	158	33	10	32	122	.301	376	9	9	.977
1951	New York	Amer.	OF	116	415	72	109	22	4	12	71	.263	288	11	3	.990
Major League Totals				1736	6821	1390	2214	389	131	361	1537	.325	4529	153	105	.978

*Played without contract.

WORLD SERIES RECORD

Year	Club	League	Pos.	G.	AB.	R.	H.	2B.	3B.	HR.	RBI.	B.A.	PO.	A.	E.	F.A.
1936	New York	Amer.	OF	6	26	3	9	3	0	0	3	.346	18	0	1	.947
1937	New York	Amer.	OF	5	22	2	6	0	0	1	4	.273	18	0	0	1.000
1938	New York	Amer.	OF	4	15	4	4	0	0	1	2	.267	10	0	0	1.000
1939	New York	Amer.	OF	4	16	3	5	0	0	1	3	.313	11	0	0	1.000
1941	New York	Amer.	OF	5	19	1	5	0	0	0	1	.263	19	0	0	1.000
1942	New York	Amer.	OF	5	21	3	7	0	0	0	3	.333	20	0	0	1.000
1947	New York	Amer.	OF	7	26	4	6	0	0	2	5	.231	22	0	0	1.000
1949	New York	Amer.	OF	5	18	2	2	0	0	1	2	.111	7	0	0	1.000
1950	New York	Amer.	OF	4	13	2	4	1	0	1	2	.308	8	0	0	1.000
1951	New York	Amer.	OF	6	23	3	6	2	0	1	5	.261	17	0	0	1.000
World Series Totals				51	199	27	54	6	0	8	30	.271	150	0	1	.993

LAWRENCE EUGENE DOBY

Born December 13, 1924, at Camden, S. C.
Height, 6.01. Weight, 180.
Threw right and batted lefthanded.
Married Helen F. Curvy, August 10, 1946.

Hit three home runs in a game, August 2, 1950; hit for cycle, June 4, 1952.
Named by Baseball Writers' Association of America as center fielder on THE SPORTING NEWS All-Star Major League Team, 1950.
Scout, Montreal Expos, 1969; Montreal minor league instructor, 1970; coach, Expos, 1971-73; coach, Cleveland Indians, 1974; coach, Montreal, 1976; coach, Chicago White Sox, 1977 to June 30, 1978, when he became manager until October 19, 1978; became White Sox batting instructor, January 15, 1979, to date.

Year	Club	League	Pos.	G.	AB.	R.	H.	2B.	3B.	HR.	RBI.	B.A.	PO.	A.	E.	F.A.
1947	Cleveland	Amer.	INF	29	32	3	5	1	0	0	2	.156	11	4	0	1.000
1948	Cleveland	Amer.	OF	121	439	83	132	23	9	14	66	.301	287	12	*14	.955
1949	Cleveland	Amer.	OF	147	547	106	153	25	3	24	85	.280	355	7	9	.976
1950	Cleveland	Amer.	OF	142	503	110	164	25	5	25	102	.326	367	2	5	.987
1951	Cleveland	Amer.	OF	134	447	84	132	27	5	20	69	.295	321	12	8	.977
1952	Cleveland	Amer.	OF	140	519	*104	143	26	8	*32	104	.276	398	11	6	.986
1953	Cleveland	Amer.	OF	149	513	92	135	18	5	29	102	.263	354	10	6	.984
1954	Cleveland	Amer.	OF	153	577	94	157	18	4	*32	*126	.272	411	14	2	.995
1955	Cleveland(a)	Amer.	OF	131	491	91	143	17	5	26	75	.291	313	6	2	.994
1956	Chicago	Amer.	OF	140	504	89	135	22	3	24	102	.268	371	4	5	.985
1957	Chicago(b)	Amer.	OF	119	416	57	120	27	2	14	79	.288	255	3	4	.985
1958	Cleveland(d)	Amer.	OF	89	247	41	70	10	1	13	45	.283	141	5	0	1.000
1959	Det.(e)-Chicago	Amer.	OF	39	113	6	26	4	2	0	13	.230	43	2	2	.957
1960	San Diego	PCL	OF	9	27	2	6	0	1	0	3	.222	7	0	0	1.000
Major League Totals				1533	5348	960	1515	243	52	253	970	.283	3627	92	63	.983

aTraded to Chicago White Sox for shortstop Alfonso (Chico) Carrasquel and outfielder Jim Busby, October 25, 1955.
bTraded to Baltimore Orioles with pitcher Jack Harshman and first baseman Jim Marshall for pitcher Ray Moore, first baseman-outfielder Tito Francona and infielder-outfielder Billy Goodman, December 3, 1957.
cTraded to Cleveland Indians with pitcher Don Ferrarese for pitcher Bud Daley and outfielders Dick Williams and Gene Woodling, April 1, 1958.
dTraded to Detroit Tigers for outfielder Tito Francona, March 3, 1959.
eReleased to Chicago White Sox, May 13, 1959.

WORLD SERIES RECORD

Year	Club	League	Pos.	G.	AB.	R.	H.	2B.	3B.	HR.	RBI.	B.A.	PO.	A.	E.	F.A.
1948	Cleveland	Amer.	OF	6	22	1	7	1	0	1	2	.318	11	0	1	.917
1954	Cleveland	Amer.	OF	4	16	0	2	0	0	0	0	.125	7	0	0	1.000
World Series Totals				10	38	1	9	1	0	1	2	.237	18	0	1	.947

ROBERT PERSHING (BOBBY) DOERR

Born April 7, 1918, at Los Angeles, Calif.
Height, 5.11. Weight, 185.
Threw and batted righthanded.
Married Monica Terpin, October 24, 1938.

Set A. L. record for second basemen when he handled 414 chances (177 putouts, 227 assists) without an error, June 24 to September 19, 1948 (since passed by Rich Dauer, Baltimore, 1978, 425 chances); led A. L. second basemen in double plays, 1938-40-43-46-47; hit for cycle, May 17, 1944 and May 13, 1947.
World Series records—Set World Series record for assists by second baseman in 7-game Series (31) in 1946; tied for most assists nine-inning game, 8, 1946.
Named Most Valuable Player, American League, by THE SPORTING NEWS, 1944. Named as second baseman for THE SPORTING NEWS All-Star Major League Team, 1944.
Scout, Boston Red Sox, 1957-66; coach, Red Sox, October 17, 1966 to November 17, 1969; minor league instructor and coach, Toronto Blue Jays organization, October 12, 1976, to date.

Year	Club	League	Pos.	G.	AB.	R.	H.	2B.	3B.	HR.	RBI.	B.A.	PO.	A.	E.	F.A.
1934	Hollywood	P. C.	2B	67	201	12	52	6	0	0	11	.259	135	164	14	.955
1935	Hollywood	P. C.	2B	172	647	87	205	22	8	4	74	.317	444	466	38	.960

Year	Club	League	Pos.	G.	AB.	R.	H.	2B.	3B.	HR.	RBI.	B.A.	PO.	A.	E.	F.A.
1936—San Diego		P. C.	2B	175	695	100	*238	37	12	2	77	.342	399	*504	33	.965
1937—Boston		Amer.	2B	55	147	22	33	5	1	2	14	.224	94	124	6	.973
1938—Boston		Amer.	2B	145	509	70	147	26	7	5	80	.289	372	420	26	.968
1939—Boston		Amer.	2B	127	525	75	167	28	2	12	73	.318	336	431	19	.976
1940—Boston		Amer.	2B	151	595	87	173	37	10	22	105	.291	*401	480	21	●.977
1941—Boston		Amer.	2B	132	500	74	141	28	4	16	93	.282	290	389	20	.971
1942—Boston		Amer.	2B	144	545	71	158	35	5	15	102	.290	376	453	21	*.975
1943—Boston		Amer.	2B	●155	604	78	163	32	3	16	75	.270	*415	●490	9	*.990
1944—Boston		Amer.	2B	125	468	95	152	30	10	15	81	.325	341	363	17	.976
1945—Boston		Amer.					(In Military Service)									
1946—Boston		Amer.	2B	151	583	95	158	34	9	18	116	.271	*420	*483	13	*.986
1947—Boston		Amer.	2B	146	561	79	145	23	10	17	95	.258	376	●466	16	.981
1948—Boston		Amer.	2B	140	527	94	150	23	6	27	111	.285	366	430	6	●.993
1949—Boston		Amer.	2B	139	541	91	167	30	9	18	109	.309	395	439	17	.980
1950—Boston		Amer.	2B	149	586	103	172	29	●11	27	120	.294	*443	431	11	*.988
1951—Boston		Amer.	2B	106	402	60	116	21	2	13	73	.289	303	311	12	.981
Major League Totals				1865	7093	1094	2042	381	89	223	1247	.288	4928	5710	214	.980

WORLD SERIES RECORD

Year	Club	League	Pos.	G.	AB.	R.	H.	2B.	3B.	HR.	RBI.	B.A.	PO.	A.	E.	F.A.
1946—Boston		Amer.	2B	6	22	1	9	1	0	1	3	.409	18	31	0	1.000

MICHAEL J. (TURKEY MIKE) DONLIN

Born Erie, Pa., May 30, 1878.
Died September 24, 1933, at Hollywood, Calif.
Height, 5.09. Weight, 170.
Threw and batted lefthanded.
Married Mabel Hite, stage star, April 10, 1906.

Had six hits, (two singles, two doubles and two triples) in six times at bat June 24, 1901.

Year	Club	League	Pos.	G.	AB.	R.	H.	2B.	3B.	HR.	SB.	B.A.	PO.	A.	E.	F.A.
1899—Santa Cruz		Calif.	OF	29	117	33	47	12	4	1	9	.402	31	42	6	.924
1899—St. Louis		Nat.	OF	67	267	49	88	10	5	6	20	.330	97	9	13	.891
1900—St. Louis (a)		Nat.	1B	77	275	40	90	7	6	10	12	.327	208	4	12	.946
1901—Baltimore (b)		Am.	1B-OF	122	481	108	164	22	14	5	32	.341	617	44	28	.959
1902—Cincinnati (c)		Nat.	OF	33	143	30	42	4	5	0	9	.294	59	.5	8	.889
1903—Cincinnati		Nat.	OF	124	496	110	174	25	18	7	26	.351	209	15	25	.900
1904—Cin. (d)-N. Y.		Nat.	OF	96	368	59	121	18	10	3	22	.329	131	9	18	.886
1905—New York		Nat.	OF	150	606	*124	216	31	16	7	33	.356	250	17	19	.934
1906—New York		Nat.	OF	30	121	15	38	5	1	1	9	.314	39	0	3	.929
1907—New York							(Out of Game)									
1908—New York		Nat.	OF	155	593	71	198	26	13	6	30	.334	239	21	6	.977
1909—New York							(Out of Game)									
1910—New York							(Out of Game)									
1911—N.Y. (e)-Bos. (f)		Nat.	OF	59	234	36	74	16	1	3	9	.316	118	8	12	.913
1912—Pittsburgh (g)		Nat.	OF	77	244	27	77	9	8	2	8	.316	102	8	2	.982
1913—Jersey City		Nat.	OF	36	136	17	37	2	5	1	0	.272	84	7	2	.978
1914—New York		Nat.	OF	35	31	1	5	1	1	1	0	.161	0	0	0	.000
American League Totals				122	481	108	164	22	14	5	32	.341	617	44	28	.959
National League Totals				903	3378	562	1123	152	84	46	178	.332	1452	96	118	.929
Major League Totals				1025	3859	670	1287	174	98	51	210	.334	2069	140	146	.938

aJumped to Baltimore.
bJumped to Cincinnati.
cIn jail six months for assault.
dSold to New York, N. L., July, 1904.
eSold to Boston, N. L., August, 1911.
fTraded to Pittsburgh for outfielder Vince Campbell, February, 1912.
gClaimed by Philadelphia Phillies on waivers, December, 1912, but would not report.

WORLD SERIES RECORD

Year	Club	League	Pos.	G.	AB.	R.	H.	2B.	3B.	HR.	SB.	B.A.	PO.	A.	E.	F.A.
1905—New York		Nat.	OF	5	19	4	6	1	0	0	2	.316	18	1	2	.905

DID YOU KNOW—
That Mike Donlin quit the game twice to go on tour with his actress wife?

PATRICK JOSEPH (PATSY) DONOVAN

Born March 16, 1865, at Lawrence, Mass.
Died December 25, 1953, at Lawrence, Mass.
Height, 5.11½. Weight, 175.
Threw and batted lefthanded.
Married Terese Mahoney, November 10, 1910.

Manager, Pittsburgh, National League, 1897-99; St. Louis Cardinals, 1901-02-03; Washington Senators, 1904; Brooklyn Dodgers, 1906-07-08; Boston Red Sox, 1910-11; Buffalo, International, 1915-16-17; Syracuse, International, 1918; Newark, International, 1919; Jersey City, International, 1921; Springfield, Eastern, 1923; Jersey City, International, 1924-25-26; Providence, Eastern, 1927; Attleboro, New England, 1928.

Year	Club	League	Pos.	G.	AB.	R.	H.	2B.	3B.	HR.	SB.	B.A.	PO.	A.	E.	F.A.
1886	Lawrence	N. Eng.	OF	66	281	45	82	8	1	0	....	.292	101	9	14	.887
1887	Lawrence-Salem	N. Eng.	OF	88	....	120	....	....	....	....	54 *.398	....	....	....	.821
1888	London	Int.	OF	103	460	115	165	25	10	1	80 *.359	224	15	28	.895
1889	London	Int.	OF	53	224	45	60	8	1	1	27	.268	120	21	12	.922
1890	Boston-Brooklyn	Nat.	OF	58	244	34	62	6	1	0	19	.254	110	9	8	.937
1891	Louisv'le-Wash.	A.A.	OF	115	475	79	143	9	3	2	31	.301	199	17	19	.919
1892	Wash'gton-Pitts.	Nat.	OF	128	543	108	159	18	7	4	59	.293	171	28	29	.873
1893	Pittsburgh	Nat.	OF	110	465	110	154	6	7	2	49	.331	173	14	14	.930
1894	Pittsburgh	Nat.	OF	133	575	146	176	21	9	4	31	.306	267	24	21	.933
1895	Pittsburgh	Nat.	OF	126	522	124	165	18	6	1	36	.316	189	13	10	.953
1896	Pittsburgh	Nat.	OF	129	569	110	180	21	5	3	50	.316	222	*30	14	.947
1897	Pittsburgh	Nat.	OF	120	475	83	155	17	6	0	39	.326	185	16	11	.948
1898	Pittsburgh	Nat.	OF	147	610	112	184	17	8	0	43	.302	239	21	16	.942
1899	Pittsburgh	Nat.	OF	123	537	82	159	10	6	1	24	.296	187	12	11	.948
1900	St. Louis	Nat.	OF	127	509	78	165	12	1	0	44	.324	181	12	8	.960
1901	St. Louis	Nat.	OF	129	524	91	154	23	6	1	24	.294	216	17	5	.979
1902	St. Louis	Nat.	OF	126	502	68	155	12	4	0	41	.309	178	22	9	.962
1903	St. Louis	Nat.	OF	105	410	63	134	15	3	0	25	.327	142	16	8	.952
1904	Washington	Amer.	OF	125	434	32	104	6	0	0	16	.240	215	15	9	.962
1905	—					(Out of Organized Ball)										
1906	Brooklyn	Nat.	OF	7	21	1	5	0	0	0	0	.238	9	0	0	1.000
1907	Brooklyn	Nat.	OF	1	1	0	0	0	0	0	0	.000	4	0	0	1.000
	American League Totals			125	434	32	104	6	0	0	16	.240	215	15	9	.962
	American Association Totals			115	475	79	143	9	3	2	31	.301	199	17	19	.919
	National League Totals			1569	6507	1210	2007	196	69	16	484	.308	2473	234	163	.943
	Major League Totals			1809	7416	1321	2254	211	72	18	531	.304	2887	266	191	.943

WORLD SERIES RECORD

Year	Club	League	Pos.	G.	AB.	R.	H.	2B.	3B.	HR.	SB.	B.A.	PO.	A.	E.	F.A.
1890	Brooklyn	Nat.	OF	5	18	5	8	1	0	0	1	.444	3	2	0	1.000

WILLIAM E. (WILD BILL) DONOVAN

Born October 13, 1876, at Lawrence, Mass.
Died December 9, 1923, in train wreck near Forsyth, N. Y.
Height, 5.11. Weight, 190.
Threw and batted righthanded.
Married Nellie Stearns, March 4, 1905.

Manager, Providence, International League, 1913-14; New York Yankees, 1915-16-17; Jersey City, International, 1919-20; Philadelphia Phillies, 1921 until July of that season; New Haven, Eastern, 1922-23.

Year	Club	League	G.	IP.	W.	L.	Pct.	H.	R.	SO.	BB.	CG.	ShO.
1898	Washington	National	17	93	1	6	.143	99	77	33	59	6	0
1899	Brooklyn	National	5	25	1	2	.333	34	24	11	13	2	0
1900	Brooklyn	National	5	26	1	2	.333	32	18	10	14	3	0
1901	Brooklyn	National	•45	353	*25	15	.625	320	152	226	151	36	2
1902	Brooklyn	National	35	298	17	15	.531	250	122	166	108	30	4
1903	Detroit	American	36	307	17	16	.515	247	104	183	95	34	4
1904	Detroit	American	35	304	17	16	.515	242	114	116	91	30	3
1905	Detroit	American	34	282	19	14	.576	241	118	144	104	27	5
1906	Detroit	American	25	212	9	15	.375	219	92	85	73	22	0
1907	Detroit	American	32	270	25	4	*.862	220	88	133	83	27	3

Year	Club	League	G.	IP.	W.	L.	Pct.	H.	R.	SO.	BB.	CG.	ShO.
1908–Detroit		American	29	243	18	7	.720	210	78	141	53	25	6
1909–Detroit		American	21	140	8	7	.533	121	50	76	60	13	4
1910–Detroit		American	26	209	18	7	.720	184	74	107	61	20	3
1911–Detroit		American	20	168	10	9	.526	160	83	81	64	15	1
1912–Detroit		American	3	10	1	1	.500	5	2	6	2	0	0
1912–Providence		International					(Less than ten games)						
1913–Providence		International	9	41	3	2	.600	49	25	20	20	....	....
1914–Providence		International	8	31	0	1	.000	41	23	18	12	....	....
1915–New York		American	9	34	0	3	.000	35	18	17	10	0	0
1916–New York		American	1	1	0	0	.000	1	0	0	1	0	0
1917–New York		American					(Did not pitch)						
1918–Detroit		American	2	6	1	0	1.000	5	1	1	1	0	0
1919–Jersey City		International					(Did not pitch)						
1920–Jersey City		International	1	2	0	0	.000	3	1	2	2	0	0
1921–Philadelphia		National					(Did not pitch)						
1922–New Haven		Eastern	1	4	1	0	1.000	1	0	1	4	....	....
1923–New Haven		Eastern	5	17	1	0	1.000	21	11	3	10	....	....
American League Totals			273	2186	143	99	.591	1893	822	1090	697	213	29
National League Totals			107	795	45	40	.529	747	393	446	340	77	6
Major League Totals			380	2981	188	139	.575	2640	1215	1536	1037	290	35

WORLD SERIES RECORD

Year	Club	League	G.	IP.	W.	L.	Pct.	H.	R.	SO.	BB.	CG.	ShO.
1907–Detroit		American	2	21	0	1	.000	17	9	16	5	2	0
1908–Detroit		American	2	17	0	2	.000	17	8	10	4	2	0
1909–Detroit		American	2	12	1	1	.500	7	4	7	8	1	0
World Series Totals			6	50	1	4	.200	41	21	33	17	5	0

JOHN JOSEPH (JACK) DOYLE

Born October 25, 1869, at Killorglin, Co. Kerry, Ireland.
Died December 31, 1958, at Holyoke, Mass.
Height, 5.09. Weight, 174.
Threw and batted righthanded.

Credited with making the first hit by pinch-hitter in baseball for Cleveland, at Brooklyn, June 7, 1892, when he singled.
Had six hits, (four singles, two doubles) in six times at bat September 3, 1897.
Manager, Milwaukee, American Association, 1907; umpire, Eastern League, 1910; umpire, National League, 1911; umpire, New England League, 1911; scout, Cleveland Indians, 1913; umpire, American Association, 1915; umpire, Pacific Coast League, 1916; umpire, Three-I League, 1919; scout, Chicago Cubs, 1920-1958.

Year	Club	League	Pos.	G.	AB.	R.	H.	2B.	3B.	HR.	SB.	B.A.	PO.	A.	E.	F.A.
1888–Lynn		N. Eng.	C	12	48	12	16	4	0	1	8	.333	78	27	21	.838
1889–Canton		Tri-St.	C	80	368	89	103	....	....	....	81	.280	327	81	26	.940
1889–Columbus		A. A.	C	11	31	6	11	1	1	0	2	.355	33	17	5	.909
1890–Columbus		A. A.	C-SS	76	290	48	79	16	8	2	29	.272	201	140	36	.905
1891–Cleveland		Nat.	C-3-OF	64	247	43	65	13	4	0	23	.263	167	77	37	.868
1892–Cleve.-N.Y.		Nat.	C-3-OF	108	449	97	133	24	3	5	70	.296	247	129	49	.885
1893–New York		Nat.	C-OF	80	307	55	100	17	6	1	49	.326	242	68	16	.951
1894–New York		Nat.	1B	105	425	94	157	29	8	3	48	.369	987	60	*33	.969
1895–New York		Nat.	1B	78	316	52	100	20	3	1	33	.316	591	34	21	.967
1896–Baltimore		Nat.	1B	118	487	115	168	27	4	1	71	.345	1157	43	*33	.973
1897–Baltimore		Nat.	1B	114	463	93	165	27	3	1	62	.356	1102	75	25	.979
1898–Wash.-N.Y.		Nat.	1B-OF	121	472	68	138	19	4	3	20	.292	590	35	20	.969
1899–New York		Nat.	1B	117	454	57	140	14	7	3	41	.308	1129	69	31	.975
1900–New York		Nat.	1B	130	504	69	138	23	1	0	45	.274	1281	*95	*43	.970
1901–Chicago		Nat.	1B	73	278	19	67	10	2	0	11	.241	687	62	17	.978
1902–Washington		Amer.	2B	78	315	50	75	15	2	0	7	.238	144	193	25	.931
1902–New York		Nat.	1B	50	190	25	57	12	2	0	10	.300	506	30	9	.984
1903–Brooklyn		Nat.	1B	139	524	84	164	27	6	0	34	.313	*1418	83	29	.981
1904–Brook.-Phila.		Nat.	1B	72	258	22	57	11	3	1	5	.221	667	59	15	.980
1905–New York		Amer.	1B	1	3	0	0	0	0	0	0	.000	10	0	2	.833
American Association Totals				87	321	54	90	17	9	2	31	.280	234	157	41	.905
American League Totals				79	318	50	75	15	2	1	7	.236	154	193	27	.928
National League Totals				1369	5374	893	1649	273	56	20	522	.307	10771	928	378	.969
Major League Totals				1535	6013	997	1814	305	67	23	560	.302	11159	1278	446	.965

DONALD SCOTT (BIG D) DRYSDALE

Born July 23, 1936, at Van Nuys, Calif.
Height, 6.06. Weight, 208.
Threw and batted righthanded.

Established major league records for most consecutive shutout games won (6), May 14 through June 4, 1968, and most consecutive shutout innings (58), May 14 through June 8, 1968.
Tied following National League records: Most home runs by pitcher, season (7), 1958 and 1965; most shutout games won month (5), May, 1968.
Tied following World Series records: most games lost, Series (2), 1966; most home runs allowed, inning (2), first inning, October 5, 1966; most home runs allowed, total Series (8), 1956, 1965 and 1966.
Received Cy Young Award as outstanding major league pitcher, 1962.
Named Major League Pitcher of the Year by THE SPORTING NEWS, 1962.
Named as pitcher on THE SPORTING NEWS All-Star National League Team, 1962.

Year	Club	League	G.	IP.	W.	L.	Pct.	H.	R.	ER.	SO.	BB.	ERA.
1954	Bakersfield	Calif.	15	112	8	5	.615	97	54	43	73	58	3.45
1955	Montreal	Int.	28	173	11	11	.500	163	78	64	80	68	3.33
1956	Brooklyn	Nat.	25	99	5	5	.500	95	35	29	55	31	2.64
1957	Brooklyn	Nat.	34	221	17	9	.654	197	76	66	148	61	2.69
1958	Los Angeles	Nat.	44	212	12	13	.480	214	107	98	131	72	4.16
1959	Los Angeles	Nat.	44	271	17	13	.567	237	113	104	*242	93	3.45
1960	Los Angeles	Nat.	41	269	15	14	.517	214	93	85	*246	72	2.84
1961	Los Angeles	Nat.	40	244	13	10	.565	236	111	100	182	83	3.69
1962	Los Angeles	Nat.	43	*314	*25	9	.735	272	122	99	*232	78	2.84
1963	Los Angeles	Nat.	42	315	19	17	.528	*287	114	92	251	57	2.63
1964	Los Angeles	Nat.	40	*321	18	16	.529	242	91	78	237	68	2.19
1965	Los Angeles	Nat.	44	308	23	12	.657	*270	113	95	210	66	2.78
1966	Los Angeles	Nat.	40	274	13	16	.448	279	114	104	177	45	3.42
1967	Los Angeles	Nat.	38	282	13	16	.448	269	101	86	196	60	2.74
1968	Los Angeles	Nat.	31	239	14	12	.538	201	68	57	155	56	2.15
1969	Los Angeles	Nat.	12	63	5	4	.556	71	34	31	24	13	4.43
Major League Totals			518	3432	209	166	.557	3084	1292	1124	2486	855	2.95

WORLD SERIES RECORD

Year	Club	League	G.	IP.	W.	L.	Pct.	H.	R.	ER.	SO.	BB.	ERA.
1956	Brooklyn	Nat.	1	2	0	0	.000	2	2	2	1	1	9.00
1959	Los Angeles	Nat.	1	7	1	0	1.000	11	1	1	5	4	1.29
1963	Los Angeles	Nat.	1	9	1	0	1.000	3	0	0	9	1	0.00
1965	Los Angeles	Nat.	2	11⅔	1	1	.500	12	9	5	15	3	3.86
1966	Los Angeles	Nat.	2	10	0	2	.000	8	5	5	6	3	4.50
World Series Totals			7	39⅔	3	3	.500	36	17	13	36	12	2.95

HUGH DUFFY

Born November 26, 1866, at River Point, R. I.
Died October 19, 1954, at Allston, Mass.
Height, 5.07. Weight, 168.
Threw and batted righthanded.
Married Nora Moore, October 16, 1895.

Compiled all-time highest major league season batting average, .438, in 1894.
Manager, Milwaukee A. L., 1901; manager, Milwaukee W. L., 1902-03; manager, Philadelphia N. L., 1904-05-06; owner and manager, Providence, Eastern League, 1907-08-09; manager, Chicago A. L., 1910-11; manager, Milwaukee, American Association, 1912; president-manager, Portland, New England League, 1913-14-15-16; scout, Boston N. L., 1917-18-19; manager, Toronto, International League, 1920; manager, Boston A. L., 1921-22; scout, Boston A. L., 1924 to time of death, 1954.
Named to Hall of Fame, 1945.

Year	Club	League	Pos.	G.	AB.	R.	H.	2B.	3B.	HR.	SB.	B.A.	PO.	A.	E.	F.A.
1886	Hartford	East.	OF	7	18	3	5	1	0	0	1	.278	16	16	3	.914
1887	Springfield	East.	OF	17	80	20	28	4	2	1	17	.350				
1887	Salem-Lowell	N. Eng.	OF	78	325	103	139	24	8	16	16	.428				.831
1888	Chicago	Nat.	OF	71	298	60	84	11	4	7	13	.282	103	19	12	.910
1889	Chicago (a)	Nat.	OF	•136	*584	144	182	21	7	12	52	.312	184	19	24	.894

Year Club League	Pos.	G.	AB.	R.	H.	2B.	3B.	HR.	SB.	B.A.	PO.	A.	E.	F.A.
1890–Chicago (b)........Play.	OF	137	591	*161	194	33	14	7	79	.328	261	33	22	.930
1891–Boston (c) ....A. A.	OF	121	511	124	174	23	10	10	83	.341	154	23	13	.932
1892–Boston ....Nat.	OF	146	609	125	184	25	13	5	61	.302	259	21	23	.924
1893–Boston ....Nat.	OF	131	537	*149	203	23	7	6	50	*.378	313	13	14	*.959
1894–Boston ....Nat.	OF	124	539	160	*236	*50	13	•18	49	*.438	313	23	28	.923
1895–Boston ....Nat.	OF	131	540	113	190	25	6	8	42	.352	327	21	20	.946
1896–Boston ....Nat.	OF	131	533	93	161	17	8	5	45	.302	250	17	12	.957
1897–Boston ....Nat.	OF	134	554	131	189	23	10	8	45	.341	263	12	12	.958
1898–Boston ....Nat.	OF	151	561	97	179	12	3	8	32	.319	328	14	19	.947
1899–Boston ....Nat.	OF	147	588	102	164	25	8	5	18	.279	343	9	13	.964
1900–Boston ....Nat.	OF	50	181	28	54	5	4	2	12	.298	107	5	6	.949
1901–Milwaukee.......Amer.	OF	78	286	41	88	14	8	2	13	.308	143	5	4	.974
1902–Milwaukee.......West.	OF	140	505	79	147	25	6	2	37	.291	302	12	11	.966
1903–Milwaukee.......West.	OF	71	257	45	77	8	1	0	30	.300	157	6	13	.926
1904–Philadelphia.....Nat.	OF	18	46	10	13	1	1	0	3	.283	16	0	3	.842
1905–Philadelphia.....Nat.	OF	15	40	7	12	2	1	0	0	.300	17	1	2	.900
1906–Philadelphia.....Nat.	PH	1	1	0	0	0	0	0	0	.000	0	0	0	.000
1907–Providence ......East.	OF	35	73	9	22	1	0	0	5	.301	38	1	0	1.000
1908–Providence ......East.	OF	37	57	10	19	5	2	1	5	.333	18	0	0	1.000
American Association Totals...........		121	511	124	174	23	10	10	83	.340	154	23	13	.931
American League Totals		78	286	41	88	14	8	2	13	.308	143	5	4	.947
National League Totals		1386	5611	1219	1851	240	85	84	422	.330	2823	174	188	.941
Players League Totals		137	591	161	194	33	14	7	79	.328	261	33	22	.930
Major League Totals.......................		1722	6999	1545	2307	310	117	103	597	.330	3381	235	227	.941

aJumped to Players League (Brotherhood), 1890.
bSigned with Boston A. A. after disbanding of Brotherhood, 1891.
cAwarded to Boston N. L. following consolidation of National League and American Association, 1892.

JAMES JOSEPH DYKES

Born November 10, 1896, at Philadelphia, Pa.
Died June 15, 1976, at Philadelphia, Pa.
Height, 5.09. Weight, 192.
Threw and batted righthanded.
Married Mary McMonagle, October 13, 1920.

Shares American League record with Nelson Fox, Chicago, A. L., 1952, for most chances accepted by second baseman in game, 17 (9 putouts, 8 assists), Philadelphia, A. L., August 28, 1921.
World Series–Made two hits in seventh inning, October 12, 1929 (Chicago N. L., vs. Philadelphia A. L.).
Manager, Chicago White Sox, 1934 until May 25, 1946; manager, Hollywood, Pacific Coast League, 1946 until August 28, 1948; coach, Philadelphia Athletics, 1949 until named manager, May 26, 1950; manager, 1951-52-53; manager, Baltimore Orioles, 1954; coach, Cincinnati Reds, 1955 until named manager, August 14, 1958; coach, Pittsburgh Pirates, 1959 until named manager, Detroit Tigers, May 3, 1959-60; swapped managerial jobs with Joe Gordon, shifting to manager of Cleveland Indians, August 3, 1960-61; coach of Milwaukee Braves, 1962; coach, Kansas CIty Athletics, 1963-64.

Year Club League	Pos.	G.	AB.	R.	H.	2B.	3B.	HR.	RBI.	B.A.	PO.	A.	E.	F.A.
1917–Gettysburg........B. R.	2B	79	286	52	62	11	2	4	.....	.217	189	173	17	.955
1918–Philadelphia (a) Amer.	2B	59	186	13	35	3	3	0	18	.188	139	189	21	.940
1919–Philadelphia......Amer.	2B	17	49	4	9	1	0	0	0	.184	28	58	5	.945
1919–Atlanta ....South.	2B	110	390	58	96	28	5	2	.....	.246	337	264	30	.952
1920–Philadelphia......Amer.	2-3B	142	546	81	140	25	4	8	35	.256	353	458	45	.947
1921–Philadelphia......Amer.	2B	155	613	88	168	32	13	16	77	.274	*434	*522	*46	.954
1922–Philadelphia......Amer.	3B	145	501	66	138	23	7	12	68	.275	*186	*295	*28	.945
1923–Philadelphia......Amer.	2B-SS	124	416	50	105	28	1	4	43	.252	283	363	25	.963
1924–Philadelphia......Amer.	2B-3B	110	410	68	128	26	6	3	50	.312	249	318	26	.956
1925–Philadelphia......Amer.	2B-3B	122	465	93	150	32	11	5	55	.323	225	302	21	.962
1926–Philadelphia......Amer.	2B-3B	124	429	54	123	32	5	1	44	.287	195	324	20	.963
1927–Philadelphia......Amer.	1B-3B	121	417	61	135	33	6	3	60	.324	839	101	14	.985
1928–Philadelphia......Amer.	2-3B-SS	85	242	39	67	11	0	5	30	.277	130	164	8	.974
1929–Philadelphia......Amer.	2-3B-SS	119	401	76	131	34	6	13	79	.327	203	273	33	.935
1930–Philadelphia......Amer.	3B	125	435	69	131	28	4	6	73	.301	124	191	13	.960
1931–Philadelphia......Amer.	SS-3B	101	355	48	97	28	2	3	46	.273	136	188	15	.956
1932–Philadelphia (b) Amer.	*3-2B-SS	153	558	71	148	29	5	7	90	.265	158	282	11	*.976
1933–Chicago ....Amer.	3B	151	554	49	144	22	6	1	68	.260	132	*296	21	.953
1934–Chicago ....Amer.	1-2B-3B	127	456	52	122	17	4	7	82	.268	383	252	27	.959
1935–Chicago ....Amer.	1B-3B	117	403	45	116	24	2	4	61	.288	290	185	15	.969
1936–Chicago ....Amer.	3B	127	435	62	116	16	3	7	60	.267	108	140	18	.951
1937–Chicago ....Amer.	1-3B	30	85	10	26	5	0	1	23	.306	152	27	1	.994
1938–Chicago ....Amer.	2-3B-SS	26	89	9	27	4	2	2	13	.303	75	72	9	.942
1939–Chicago ....Amer.	3B	2	1	0	0	0	0	0	0	.000	2	0	1	.667
Major League Totals.......................		2282	8046	1108	2256	453	90	108	1075	.280	4824	5100	423	.959

aIn Military Service after close of 1918 season.
bSold with outfielders Al Simmons and George Haas to Chicago White Sox for $150,000, September 28, 1932.

WORLD SERIES RECORD

Year	Club	League	Pos.	G.	AB.	R.	H.	2B.	3B.	HR.	RBI.	B.A.	PO.	A.	E.	F.A.
1929–Philadelphia		Amer.	3B	5	19	2	8	1	0	0	4	.421	3	5	2	.800
1930–Philadelphia		Amer.	3B	6	18	2	4	3	0	1	5	.222	8	6	1	.933
1931–Philadelphia		Amer.	3B	7	22	2	5	0	0	0	2	.227	4	12	0	1.000
World Series Totals				18	59	6	17	4	0	1	11	.288	15	23	3	.927

ROBERT IRVING ELLIOTT

Born November 26, 1916, at San Francisco, Calif.
Died May 4, 1966, at San Diego, Calif.
Height, 6.00. Weight, 195.
Threw and batted righthanded.
Married Iva Reah Skipper, March 12, 1938.

Tied World Series mark for most putouts by third baseman, game (4), October 11, 1948.
Named Most Valuable National League Player, 1947.
Named as third baseman on THE SPORTING NEWS All-Star Major League Teams, 1944-48.
Manager, San Diego, Pacific Coast League, 1955-56-57; manager, Sacramento, Pacific Coast League, 1959; manager, Kansas City Athletics, 1960; coach, Los Angeles Angels, 1961.

Year	Club	League	Pos.	G.	AB.	R.	H.	2B.	3B.	HR.	RBI.	B.A.	PO.	A.	E.	F.A.
1936–Savannah		Sally	OF-3B	144	566	80	165	19	5	12	84	.292	219	37	30	.895
1937–Savannah		Sally	*OF-3B	139	565	92	165	21	16	9	88	.292	310	39	10	*.972
1938–Knoxville		South.	OF	11	43	7	10	2	1	0	3	.233	17	2	0	1.000
1938–Savannah		Sally	OF	132	532	97	173	30	11	12	93	.325	247	21	*19	.934
1939–Louisville		A. A.	OF	14	53	5	14	0	2	0	4	.264	18	1	0	1.000
1939–Toronto		Int.	OF	115	427	59	140	27	8	7	51	.328	200	11	2	*.991
1939–Pittsburgh		Nat.	OF	32	129	18	43	10	3	3	19	.333	88	1	2	.978
1940–Pittsburgh		Nat.	OF	148	551	88	161	34	11	5	64	.292	302	12	7	.978
1941–Pittsburgh		Nat.	OF	141	527	74	144	24	10	3	76	.273	281	9	9	.970
1942–Pittsburgh		Nat.	*3B-OF	143	560	75	166	26	7	9	89	.296	*176	*286	*36	.928
1943–Pittsburgh		Nat.	*3-SS-2	156	581	82	183	30	12	7	101	.315	150	*296	*25	.947
1944–Pittsburgh		Nat.	*3B-SS	143	538	85	160	28	16	10	108	.297	169	*285	*27	.944
1945–Pittsburgh		Nat.	3B-OF	144	541	80	157	36	6	8	108	.290	219	185	23	.946
1946–Pittsburgh(a)		Nat.	OF-3B	140	486	50	128	25	3	5	68	.263	232	90	7	.979
1947–Boston		Nat.	3B	150	555	93	176	35	5	22	113	.317	129	302	20	*.956
1948–Boston		Nat.	3B	151	540	99	153	24	5	23	100	.283	*146	298	26	.945
1949–Boston		Nat.	3B	139	482	77	135	29	5	17	76	.280	141	300	17	.963
1950–Boston		Nat.	3B	142	531	94	162	28	5	24	107	.305	141	256	20	.952
1951–Boston(b)		Nat.	3B	136	480	73	137	29	2	15	70	.285	138	242	●24	.941
1952–New York(c)		Nat.	OF-3B	98	272	33	62	6	2	10	35	.228	102	31	4	.971
1953–St.L(d)-Chi.(e)		Am.	3B-OF	115	368	43	94	19	2	9	61	.255	105	197	14	.956
1954–San Diego		P.C.	3-2B-OF	81	203	28	52	6	1	12	39	.256	41	131	11	.940
American League Totals				115	368	43	94	19	2	9	61	.255	105	197	14	.956
National League Totals				1863	6773	1021	1967	364	92	161	1134	.290	2414	2593	247	.953
Major League Totals				1978	7141	1064	2061	383	94	170	1195	.289	2519	2790	261	.953

aTraded to Boston Braves with catcher Hank Camelli for pitcher Elmer Singleton, second baseman Billy Herman, shortstop Bill Wietelmann and outfielder Stan Wentzel, September 30, 1946.
bTraded to New York Giants for pitcher Sheldon Jones and reported $50,000, April 8, 1952.
cUnconditionally released by New York Giants, October 1, 1952; signed with St. Louis Browns, March 25, 1953.
dTraded to Chicago White Sox with pitcher Virgil Trucks for pitcher Lou Kretlow, catcher Darrell Johnson and estimated $75,000, June 13, 1953.
eUnconditionally released by Chicago White Sox, December 18, 1953.

WORLD SERIES RECORD

Year	Club	League	Pos.	G.	AD.	R.	H.	2B.	3B.	HR	RBI.	B.A.	PO.	A.	E.	F.A.
1948–Boston		Amer.	3B	6	21	4	7	0	0	2	5	.333	11	14	3	.893

DELMER ENNIS

Born June 8, 1925, at Philadelphia, Pa.
Height, 6.00. Weight, 200.
Threw and batted righthanded.
Married Lenore Claar, February 1, 1947.

Hit three home runs in a game, July 23, 1955.
Named Rookie of the Year by THE SPORTING NEWS, 1946.

Year	Club	League	Pos.	G.	AB.	R.	H.	2B.	3B.	HR.	RBI.	B.A.	PO.	A.	E.	F.A.
1943	Trenton	Int.-St.	OF	•140	570	104	197	37	16	18	93	.346	201	★24	10	.957
1944-45	Philadelphia	Nat.					(In Military Service)									
1946	Philadelphia	Nat.	OF	141	540	70	169	30	6	17	73	.313	332	16	9	.975
1947	Philadelphia	Nat.	OF	139	541	71	149	25	6	12	81	.275	320	12	7	.979
1948	Philadelphia	Nat.	OF	152	589	86	171	40	4	30	95	.290	297	15	★14	.957
1949	Philadelphia	Nat.	OF	154	610	92	184	39	11	25	110	.302	359	•16	★13	.966
1950	Philadelphia	Nat.	OF	153	595	92	185	34	8	31	★126	.311	279	10	9	.970
1951	Philadelphia	Nat.	OF	144	332	76	142	20	5	15	73	.267	268	14	9	.969
1952	Philadelphia	Nat.	OF	151	592	90	171	30	10	20	107	.289	277	11	9	.970
1953	Philadelphia	Nat.	OF	152	578	79	165	22	3	29	125	.285	184	14	6	.980
1954	Philadelphia	Nat.	★OF-1B	145	556	73	145	23	2	25	119	.261	311	9	★15	.955
1955	Philadelphia	Nat.	OF	146	564	82	167	24	7	29	120	.296	298	9	4	.987
1956	Philadelphia(a)	Nat.	OF	153	630	80	164	23	3	26	95	.260	269	8	11	.962
1957	St. Louis	Nat.	OF	136	490	61	140	24	3	24	105	.286	180	3	11	.943
1958	St. Louis(b)	Nat.	OF	106	329	22	86	18	1	3	47	.261	122	11	1	.993
1959	Cincinnati(c)	Nat.	OF	5	12	1	4	0	0	0	1	.333	5	0	0	1.000
1959	Chicago	Amer.	OF	26	96	10	21	6	0	2	7	.219	23	2	3	.909
American League Totals				26	96	10	21	6	0	2	7	.219	23	2	3	.909
National League Totals				1877	7158	975	2042	352	69	286	1277	.285	3601	148	118	.969
Major League Totals				1903	7254	985	2063	358	69	288	1284	.284	3624	150	121	.969

aTraded to St. Louis Cardinals for infielder Bobby Morgan and outfielder Eldon (Rip) Repulski, November 19, 1956.
bTraded to Cincinnati Reds with pitcher Bobby Mabe and shortstop Eddie Kasko for pitcher Alex Kellner, first baseman George Crowe and shortstop Alex Grammas, October 3, 1958.
cStarted season with Cincinnati; traded to Chicago White Sox for pitcher Don Rudolph and outfielder Lou Skizas, May 2, 1959.

WORLD SERIES RECORD

Year	Club	League	Pos.	G.	AB.	R.	H.	2B.	3B.	HR.	RBI.	B.A.	PO.	A.	E.	F.A.
1950	Philadelphia	Nat.	OF	4	14	1	2	1	0	0	0	.143	9	0	0	1.000

WILLIAM GEORGE (BILLY) EVANS

Born February 10, 1884, at Chicago, Ill.
Died January 23, 1956, at Miami, Fla.
Height, 5.11½. Weight, 205.
Married Hazel Baldwin, September 28, 1907.

Attended Cornell University three years (1903). Reporter, Youngstown (O.) Vindicator (1904). Umpire, Ohio-Pennsylvania League, 1905; umpire, American League, 1906-27.
Vice-president/general manager, Cleveland Indians, 1928-35; supervisor, farm clubs, Boston Red Sox, 1936-41; general manager, Cleveland Rams football team, 1941-42; president of Southern League, 1942-46; general manager, Detroit Tigers, 1946-51.
Evans wrote classic books on umpiring, models today on their advice on position, decorum and rules interpretations. He was a master of the rule book and began a series of interpretations of tricky plays for THE SPORTING NEWS which evolved into the book, "KNOTTY PROBLEMS," an unquestioned leader in the field of rules applications on tricky plays and odd situations on the field. Billy was a fearless man when he knew he was right, having taken on Ty Cobb in a fight that lasted anywhere from a "brief encounter" to an hour-long, no-holds-barred, back-alley type of fight. Each version agrees on the outcome—a bloody draw, and deep, respected friends thereafter.
Evans, Bill Klem and Bill McGowan are considered the three greatest ball-and-strike umpires in the history of the game.
Evans was named to the Hall of Fame, 1973.

JOHN JOSEPH (CRAB) EVERS

Born July 21, 1881, at Troy, N. Y.
Died March 28, 1947, at Albany, N. Y.
Height, 5.09. Weight, 140.
Threw right and batted lefthanded.
Married Helen C. Fitzgibbons, January 12, 1909.

Stole home 21 times in N. L.; had total of 324 stolen bases, lifetime, in National League.
Manager, Chicago N. L., 1913; coach, New York N. L., 1920; manager, Chicago N. L., 1921; coach, Chicago A. L., 1922-23; manager, Chicago A. L., 1924; assistant manager, Boston N. L., 1929 through 1932; scout, Boston N. L., 1933-34; manager, Albany, International League, 1935; vice-president and general manager, Albany, Eastern League, 1939.
Named Most Valuable Player in National League, 1914.
Named to Hall of Fame, 1946.

Year	Club	League	Pos.	G.	AB.	R.	H.	2B.	3B.	HR.	RBI.	B.A.	PO.	A.	E.	F.A.
1902	Troy	N.Y.S.	SS-2B	84	333	50	95	7	6	10	.....	.285	238	285	65	.889
1902	Chicago	Nat.	SS-2B	25	89	7	20	0	0	0	.....	.225	38	58	1	.990
1903	Chicago	Nat.	2B	123	464	70	136	27	7	0	.....	.293	245	306	17	.937
1904	Chicago	Nat.	2B	152	532	49	141	14	7	0	.....	.265	*381	*518	*54	.943
1905	Chicago	Nat.	2B	99	340	44	94	11	2	1	.....	.276	249	290	36	.937
1906	Chicago	Nat.	2B	154	533	65	136	17	6	1	.....	.255	*344	441	●44	.947
1907	Chicago	Nat.	2B	151	508	66	127	18	4	2	55	.250	346	*500	32	.964
1908	Chicago	Nat.	2B	123	416	83	125	19	6	0	35	.300	237	361	25	.960
1909	Chicago	Nat.	2B	126	463	88	122	19	6	1	20	.263	262	354	38	.942
1910	Chicago	Nat.	2B	125	433	87	114	11	7	0	25	.263	282	347	33	.950
1911	Chicago	Nat.	2B	44	155	29	35	4	3	0	9	.226	66	90	4	.975
1912	Chicago	Nat.	2B	143	478	73	163	23	11	1	56	.341	319	439	32	.959
1913	Chicago(a)	Nat.	2B	136	446	81	127	20	5	3	48	.285	303	426	30	.960
1914	Boston	Nat.	2B	139	491	81	137	20	3	1	33	.279	301	397	17	*.976
1915	Boston	Nat.	2B	83	278	38	73	4	1	0	23	.263	170	209	16	.959
1916	Boston	Nat.	2B	71	241	33	52	4	1	0	15	.216	98	175	14	.951
1917	Bos.(b)-Phila.	...Nat.	2B	80	266	25	57	5	1	1	11	.214	114	210	9	.973
1922	Chicago	Amer.	2B	1	3	0	0	0	0	0	1	.000	3	3	0	1.000
1929	Boston	Nat.	2B	1	0	0	0	0	0	0	0	.000	0	0	1	.000
Major League Totals				1776	6136	919	1659	216	70	12	....	.270	3758	5124	423	.955

aReleased by Chicago Cubs, December 12, 1913, and signed by Boston Braves, February, 1914.
bReleased to Philadelphia Phillies, July 12, 1917.

WORLD SERIES RECORD

Year	Club	League	Pos.	G.	AB.	R.	H.	2B.	3B.	HR.	RBI.	B.A.	PO.	A.	E.	F.A.
1906	Chicago	Nat.	2B	6	20	2	3	1	0	0	1	.150	12	20	1	.970
1907	Chicago	Nat.	2B	5	20	2	7	2	0	0	1	.350	9	12	3	.875
1908	Chicago	Nat.	2B	5	20	5	7	1	0	0	2	.350	5	21	1	.963
1914	Boston	Nat.	2B	4	16	2	7	0	0	0	2	.438	8	16	1	.960
World Series Totals				20	76	11	24	4	0	0	6	.316	34	69	6	.946

WILLIAM BUCKINGHAM (BUCK) EWING

Born October 27, 1859, at Cincinnati, O.
Died October 20, 1906, at Cincinnati, O.
Height, 5.10. Weight, 188.
Threw and batted righthanded.
Married Anna Lawson McCaig, December 13, 1889.

Manager, New York, Players' League, 1890; Cincinnati, 1895-1896-1897-1898-1899; New York Giants, part of 1900.
Named to Hall of Fame, 1939.

Year	Club	League	Pos.	G.	AB.	R.	H.	2B.	3B.	HR.	SB.	B.A.	PO.	A.	E.	F.A.
1878	Mohawk Browns	Ind.		.....	.....	.....	.....	.....	.....	.....	.....	.....	.....	.....	.....	.....
1879	Mohawk Browns	Ind.		.....	.....	.....	.....	.....	.....	.....	.....	.....	.....	.....	.....	.....
1880	Cin. Buckeyes	Ind.		.....	.....	.....	.....	.....	.....	.....	.....	.....	.....	.....	.....	.....
1880	Rochester	N. Assn.	C-OF	13	.....	.....	.....	.....	.....	.....	.....	.148	.....	.....	.....	.931
1880	Troy	Nat.	C-OF	13	46	1	8	1	0	0	.....	.174	45	5	13	.794
1881	Troy	Nat	C-3-S-O	65	267	38	65	13	6	0	.....	.243	211	89	28	.915
1882	Troy(a)	Nat.	C-3-1-2-O	72	318	65	87	16	11	2	.....	.274	69	108	22	.889
1883	New York	Nat.	C-2-3-OF	85	369	88	113	9	13	*10	.....	.306	262	92	31	.919
1884	New York	Nat.	C-SS-OF	88	374	87	104	13	*18	3	.....	.278	431	125	41	.931
1885	New York	Nat.	C-1-3-S-O	81	342	81	104	14	11	6	.....	.304	354	*106	41	.918
1886	New York	Nat.	C-OF	70	275	59	85	10	8	4	18	.309	297	95	33	.922
1887	New York	Nat.	2B-3B	76	348	81	127	17	13	6	36	.365	159	46	46	.856
1888	New York	Nat.	C-3B	103	415	83	127	17	15	5	53	.306	480	143	35	.947
1889	New York(b)	...Nat.	C	96	407	91	133	23	14	3	34	.327	*524	*149	45	.937
1890	New York	Play.	C	83	349	99	122	20	15	7	39	.350	372	123	23	.956
1891	New York	Nat.	C-2B	14	49	8	17	1	1	0	3	.347	30	33	10	.863
1892	New York(c)	...Nat.	C-1B	97	394	58	126	12	15	8	53	.320	855	96	30	.969
1893	Cleveland	Nat.	OF	114	477	116	177	27	17	6	53	.371	197	10	18	.920
1894	Cleveland(d)	Nat.	OF	53	212	32	54	12	4	2	19	.255	91	7	8	.925
1895	Cincinnati	Nat.	1B	103	439	90	139	23	13	3	34	.317	948	83	24	.977

Year Club	League	Pos.	G.	AB.	R.	H.	2B.	3B.	HR.	SB.	B.A.	PO.	A.	E.	F.A.
1896—Cincinnati	Nat.	1B	67	266	41	75	9	5	1	47	.282	669	49	14	.981
1897—Cincinnati	Nat.	1B	1	1	0	0	0	0	0	0	.000	3	0	1	.750
National League Totals			1198	4999	1019	1541	217	164	59	....	.308	5581	1349	440	.940
Players League Totals			83	349	99	122	20	15	7	39	.350	372	123	23	.956
Major League Totals			1281	5348	1118	1663	237	179	66	....	.311	5953	1472	463	.941

aTroy disbanded.
bJumped to Players League.
cTraded to Cleveland for shortstop George Davis, March, 1893.
dReleased by Cleveland and signed to manage Cincinnati, December, 1894.

WORLD SERIES RECORD

Year Club	League	Pos.	G.	AB.	R.	H.	2B.	3B.	HR.	SB.	B.A.	PO.	A.	E.	F.A.
1888—New York	Nat.	C	7	26	5	9	0	2	1	5	.346	46	10	6	.903
1889—New York	Nat.	C	8	36	5	9	4	0	0	2	.250	36	13	4	.925
World Series Totals			15	62	10	18	4	2	1	7	.290	82	23	10	.913

URBAN CLARENCE (RED) FABER

Born September 6, 1888, at Cascade, Ia.
Died September 25, 1976, at Chicago, Ill.
Height, 6.01. Weight, 195.
Threw right and batted both ways.
Married Frances Knudtzon, April 12, 1947.

In 1917 World Series, pitched most innings in a six-game Series—27; pitched perfect game, August 18, 1910, against Davenport; pitched for Chicago White Sox 20 seasons. Coach, White Sox, May 25, 1946, through 1948. Named to Hall of Fame, 1964.

Year Club	League	G.	IP.	W.	L.	Pct.	H.	R.	ER.	SO.	BB.	ERA.
1909—Dubuque	I.I.I.	15	114	7	6	.538	93	58	....	92	50	.....
1910—Dubuque	I.I.I.	44	334	18	19	.486	239	119	....	200	98	.....
1911—Minneapolis	Amer. Assn.	2	6	0	0	.000	10	....	....	1	1	.....
1911—Pueblo	Western	29	180	12	8	.600	191	....	....	99	39	.....
1912—Des Moines	Western	43	304	21	14	.600	293	142	....	190	69	.....
1913—Des Moines	Western	50	*373	20	17	.541	*328	157	103	*265	103	2.49
1914—Chicago	American	40	181	10	9	.526	154	77	54	88	64	2.69
1915—Chicago	American	•50	300	24	14	.632	264	118	85	182	99	2.55
1916—Chicago	American	35	205	17	9	.654	167	67	46	87	61	2.02
1917—Chicago	American	41	248	16	13	.552	222	92	53	84	85	1.92
1918—Chicago	American	11	81	4	1	.800	70	23	11	26	23	1.22
1919—Chicago	American	25	162	11	9	.550	185	92	69	45	45	3.83
1920—Chicago	American	40	319	23	13	.639	332	136	106	108	88	2.99
1921—Chicago	American	43	331	25	15	.625	293	107	91	124	87	*2.47
1922—Chicago	American	43	*353	21	17	.553	334	128	110	148	83	*2.80
1923—Chicago	American	32	234	14	11	.560	233	114	88	91	62	3.41
1924—Chicago	American	21	161	9	11	.450	173	78	69	47	58	3.86
1925—Chicago	American	34	238	12	11	.522	266	117	100	71	59	3.78
1926—Chicago	American	27	185	15	8	.652	203	84	73	65	57	3.55
1927—Chicago	American	18	111	4	7	.364	131	64	56	39	41	4.54
1928—Chicago	American	27	201	13	9	.591	223	98	84	43	68	3.76
1929—Chicago	American	31	234	13	13	.500	241	119	101	68	61	3.88
1930—Chicago	American	29	169	8	13	.381	188	101	79	62	49	4.21
1931—Chicago	American	44	184	10	14	.417	210	96	78	49	57	3.82
1932—Chicago	American	42	106	2	11	.154	123	61	44	26	38	3.74
1933—Chicago	American	36	86	3	4	.429	92	41	33	18	28	3.45
Major League Totals		669	4089	254	212	.545	4104	1813	1430	1471	1213	3.15

WORLD SERIES RECORD

Year Club	League	G.	IP.	W.	L.	Pct.	H.	R.	ER.	SO.	BB.	ERA.
1917—Chicago	American	4	27	3	1	.750	21	7	7	9	3	2.33

DID YOU KNOW—

That Red Faber was one of the last legal spitballers in the majors? He, along with 16 others, were allowed to continue to throw the wet one after pitch was outlawed in 1920.

RONALD RAY (RON) FAIRLY

Born July 12, 1938, at Macon, Ga.
Height, 5.10. Weight, 178.
Threw and batted lefthanded.

Tied World Series record for one or more hits each game, seven-game Series, 1965.

Year	Club	League	Pos.	G.	AB.	R.	H.	2B.	3B.	HR.	RBI.	B.A.	PO.	A.	E.	F.A.
1958	Des Moines	West.	OF	51	172	32	51	7	0	13	41	.297	128	7	3	.978
1958	St. Paul	A.A.	OF	18	57	8	17	2	1	1	8	.298	57	1	1	.983
1958	Los Angeles	Nat.	OF	15	53	6	15	1	0	2	8	.283	33	0	1	.971
1959	Los Angeles	Nat.	OF	118	244	27	58	12	1	4	23	.238	97	8	4	.963
1960	Los Angeles	Nat.	OF	14	37	6	4	0	3	1	3	.108	15	1	0	1.000
1960	Spokane	P.C.	OF	147	505	98	153	34	4	27	100	.303	299	•20	8	.976
1961	Los Angeles	Nat.	OF-1B	111	245	42	79	15	2	10	48	.322	242	18	3	.989
1962	Los Angeles	Nat.	1B-OF	147	460	80	128	15	7	14	71	.278	1007	45	11	.990
1963	Los Angeles	Nat.	★1B-OF	152	490	62	133	21	0	12	77	.271	946	48	7	★.993
1964	Los Angeles	Nat.	1B	150	454	62	116	19	5	10	74	.256	1081	82	15	.987
1965	Los Angeles	Nat.	OF-1B	158	555	73	152	28	1	9	70	.274	361	13	6	.984
1966	Los Angeles	Nat.	OF-1B	117	351	53	101	20	0	14	61	.288	264	14	4	.986
1967	Los Angeles	Nat.	OF-1B	153	486	45	107	19	0	10	55	.220	727	55	11	.986
1968	Los Angeles	Nat.	OF-1B	141	441	32	103	15	1	4	43	.234	406	26	3	.993
1969	L.A.(a)-Montreal	Nat.	1B-OF	100	317	38	87	16	6	12	47	.274	543	46	7	.988
1970	Montreal	Nat.	1B-OF	119	385	54	111	19	0	15	61	.288	945	90	5	.995
1971	Montreal	Nat.	1B-OF	146	447	58	115	23	0	13	71	.257	1116	104	10	.992
1972	Montreal	Nat.	OF-1B	140	446	51	124	15	1	17	68	.278	646	46	6	.991
1973	Montreal	Nat.	OF-1B	142	413	70	123	13	1	17	49	.298	202	5	5	.976
1974	Montreal (b)	Nat.	1B-OF	101	282	35	69	9	1	12	43	.245	603	43	7	.989
1975	St. Louis	Nat.	1B-OF	107	229	32	69	13	2	7	37	.301	383	33	8	.981
1976	St. Louis (c)	Nat.	1B	73	110	13	29	4	0	0	21	.264	174	21	1	.995
1976	Oakland (d)	Amer.		15	46	9	11	1	0	3	10	.239	121	10	0	1.000
1977	Toronto (e)	Amer.	1B-OF	132	458	60	128	24	2	19	64	.279	375	34	7	.983
1978	California	Amer.	1B-DH	91	235	23	51	5	0	10	40	.217	482	31	1	.998
	National League Totals			2204	6445	839	1723	277	31	183	930	.267	9791	698	114	.989
	American League Totals			238	739	92	190	30	2	32	114	.257	978	75	8	.992
	Major League Totals			2442	7184	931	1913	307	33	215	1044	.266	10769	773	122	.989

Received reported $60,000 bonus to sign with Los Angeles Dodgers, 1958.
 aTraded with infielder Paul Popovich to Montreal Expos for infielder Maury Wills and outfielder Manny Mota, June 11, 1969.
 bTraded to St. Louis Cardinals for second baseman Rudy Kinard and outfielder-first baseman Ed Kurpiel, December 6, 1974.
 cSold to Oakland A's, September 14, 1976.
 dTraded to Toronto Blue Jays for infielder Mike Weathers and cash estimated at $30,000, February 24, 1977.
 eTraded to California Angels for catcher Pat Kelly and first baseman Butch Alberts, December 8, 1977.

WORLD SERIES RECORD

Year	Club	League	Pos.	G.	AB.	R.	H.	2B.	3B.	HR.	RBI.	B.A.	PO.	A.	E.	F.A.
1959	Los Angeles	Nat.	OF	6	3	0	0	0	0	0	0	.000	0	0	0	.000
1963	Los Angeles	Nat.	OF	4	1	0	0	0	0	0	0	.000	3	0	0	1.000
1965	Los Angeles	Nat.	OF	7	29	7	11	3	0	2	6	.379	8	0	0	1.000
1966	Los Angeles	Nat.	OF-1B	3	7	0	1	0	0	0	0	.143	5	0	1	.833
	World Series Totals			20	40	7	12	3	0	2	6	.300	16	0	1	.941

BIBB AUGUST (JOCKEY) FALK

Born January 27, 1899, at Austin, Tex,.
Height, 6.00. Weight, 180.
Threw and batted lefthanded.

Manager, Toledo, American Association, 1932; coach, Cleveland Indians, 1933; coach, Boston Red Sox, 1934-39.

Year	Club	League	Pos.	G.	AB.	R.	H.	2B.	3B.	HR.	RBI.	B.A.	PO.	A.	E.	F.A.
1920—Chicago		Amer.	OF	7	17	1	5	1	1	0	2	.294	5	0	0	1.000
1921—Chicago		Amer.	OF	152	585	62	167	31	11	5	82	.285	288	9	13	.958
1922—Chicago		Amer.	OF	131	483	58	144	27	1	12	79	.298	253	10	10	.963
1923—Chicago		Amer.	OF	87	274	44	84	18	6	5	38	.307	148	6	8	.951
1924—Chicago		Amer.	OF	138	526	77	185	37	8	6	99	.352	292	26	10	.970
1925—Chicago		Amer.	OF	154	602	80	181	35	9	4	99	.301	306	18	14	.959
1926—Chicago		Amer.	OF	155	566	86	195	43	4	8	108	.345	338	16	3	*.992
1927—Chicago		Amer.	OF	145	535	76	175	35	6	9	83	.327	372	22	9	.978
1928—Chicago (a)		Amer.	OF	98	286	42	83	18	4	1	37	.290	164	9	5	.972
1929—Cleveland		Amer.	OF	126	430	66	133	30	7	13	94	.309	219	15	14	.944
1930—Cleveland		Amer.	OF	82	191	34	62	12	1	4	36	.325	84	4	3	.967
1931—Cleveland		Amer.	OF	79	161	30	49	13	1	2	28	.304	55	1	3	.949
1932—Toledo		A.A.	OF	79	246	42	79	11	5	5	46	.321	140	4	6	.960
Major League Totals				1354	4656	656	1463	300	59	69	785	.314	2524	136	92	.967

aTraded to Cleveland Indians for catcher Martin Autry, February 28, 1929.

ROBERT WILLIAM ANDREW FELLER

Born November 3, 1918, at Van Meter, Ia.
Height, 6.00. Weight, 185.
Threw and batted righthanded.
Married Virginia Winther, January 16, 1943.

Held American League record for most no-hit games pitched, league—3. Feller pitched his first no-hitter against the Chicago White Sox, April 16, 1940, for the first opening day no-hit game in the history of the American League. He walked five and fanned eight. His second no-hitter came against the New York Yankees, April 30, 1946, allowing five bases on balls and striking out 11; scores of the first two no-hitters were identical, 1 to 0. The third and record-setting no-hit game was against the Detroit Tigers, July 1, 1951 (first game), 2-1; Bob allowed three walks and whiffed five (Nolan Ryan holds present record with four no-hitters).

Pitched twelve one-hit games during major league career. April 20, 1938 vs. St. Louis Browns, Billy Sullivan's bunt single in the sixth only hit; May 25, 1939 vs. Boston Red Sox, Bobby Doerr singled in second; June 27, 1939 vs. Detroit Tigers, Earl Averill singled in sixth; July 12, 1940 vs. Philadelphia Athletics, Dick Siebert singled in eighth; September 26, 1941 vs. St. Louis Browns, Rick Ferrell singled in fifth; September 19, 1945 vs. Detroit Tigers, Jimmy Outlaw singled in fifth; July 31, 1946 vs. Boston Red Sox, Bobby Doerr singled in second; August 8, 1946 vs. Chicago White Sox, Frank Hayes singled second inning; April 22, 1947 vs. St. Louis Browns, Al Zarilla singled seventh inning; May 2, 1947 vs. Boston Red Sox, Johnny Pesky singled first inning; April 23, 1952 vs. St. Louis Browns, Bobby Young tripled in first inning; May 1, 1955 vs. Boston Red Sox, Sammy White singled in seventh inning.

Lost April 23, 1952 one-hitter to St. Louis Browns in duel with Bob Cain who also tossed one-hitter, which set an American League record for lowest number of hits by both teams in a game (2). Lone run of game was scored when Bobby Young led off with a triple and Marty Marion followed with a hard smash to Al Rosen at third, who fumbled the ball.

Held American League record for most strikeouts, nine-inning game—18—(first game) vs. Detroit Tigers, October 2, 1938 (exceeded by Nolan Ryan with 19); also fanned 17 (first game) vs. Philadelphia Athletics, September 13, 1936, and struck out 16 (first game) vs. Boston Red Sox, August 25, 1937; established modern major league record for most bases on balls, season (208), 1938.

Scout, Cleveland Indians, 1958.

Named by Baseball Writers' Association of America for The Sporting News All-Star Major League Teams, 1939-40-41-46-47.

Named by The Sporting News as the No. 1 Major League Player of the Year, 1940.

Named by The Sporting News as Top Pitcher in the American League, 1951.

Named to Hall of Fame, 1962.

Year	Club	League	G.	IP.	W.	L.	Pct.	H.	R.	ER.	SO.	BB.	ERA.
1936—Cleveland		Amer.	14	62	5	3	.625	52	29	23	76	47	3.34
1937—Cleveland		Amer.	26	149	9	7	.563	116	68	56	150	106	3.38
1938—Cleveland		Amer.	39	278	17	11	.607	225	136	126	*240	*208	4.08
1939—Cleveland		Amer.	39	*297	*24	9	.727	227	105	94	*246	*142	2.85
1940—Cleveland		Amer.	*43	*320	*27	11	.711	245	102	93	*261	118	*2.62
1941—Cleveland		Amer.	*44	*343	*25	13	.658	*284	129	120	*260	*194	3.15
1942-43-44—Cleveland		Amer.					(In Military Service)						
1945—Cleveland		Amer.	9	72	5	3	.625	50	21	20	59	35	2.50
1946—Cleveland		Amer.	*48	*371	●26	15	.634	*277	101	90	*348	*153	2.18
1947—Cleveland		Amer.	42	*299	*20	11	.645	230	97	89	*196	127	2.68
1948—Cleveland		Amer.	44	280	19	15	.559	*255	123	111	*164	116	3.57
1949—Cleveland		Amer.	36	211	15	14	.517	198	104	88	108	84	3.75
1950—Cleveland		Amer.	35	247	16	11	.593	230	105	94	119	103	3.43
1951—Cleveland		Amer.	33	250	*22	8	*.733	239	105	97	111	95	3.49
1952—Cleveland		Amer.	30	192	9	13	.409	219	●124	101	81	83	4.73
1953—Cleveland		Amer.	25	176	10	7	.588	168	78	70	60	60	3.58
1954—Cleveland		Amer.	19	140	13	3	.813	127	53	48	59	39	3.09
1955—Cleveland		Amer.	25	83	4	4	.500	71	43	32	25	31	3.47
1956—Cleveland		Amer.	19	58	0	4	.000	63	34	32	18	23	4.97
Major League Totals			570	3828	266	162	.621	3271	1557	1384	2581	1764	3.25

WORLD SERIES RECORD

Year Club	League	G.	IP.	W.	L.	Pct.	H.	R.	ER.	SO.	BB.	ERA.
1948—Cleveland	Amer.	2	14⅓	0	2	.000	10	8	8	7	5	5.02

WESLEY CHEEK FERRELL

Born February 2, 1908, at Greensboro, N. C.
Height, 6.02. Weight, 195.
Threw and batted righthanded.
Married Lois Johnston, September 1, 1940.

Brother, Rick Ferrell, St. Louis Browns, 1929-1933; Boston Red Sox, 1933-1937; Washington Senators, 1937-41; St. Louis Browns, 1941-43; Washington Senators, 1944-47; coach, Washington Senators, 1948-49; coach, Detroit Tigers, 1950-53; scout, 1954-58; general manager, 1960-61; vice-president, 1962-75; consultant, 1976-79.

Holds major league record for most home runs, season, by a pitcher (9), 1931; holds major league record for pitchers for most times hitting two home runs in a game (5)—accomplishing the feat once in 1931, twice in 1934 and once each in 1935-36; pitched no-hit game against St. Louis Browns, winning, 9-0, April 29, 1931; only pitcher in modern history of game to win 20 or more games in his first four full seasons in the majors; won 13 straight games in 1930.

Manager, Leaksville, Bi-State League, 1941; manager, Lynchburg, Virginia League, 1942; manager, Greensboro, Carolina League, 1945; manager, Lynchburg, Piedmont League, 1946; manager, Marion, Western Carolina League, 1948; manager, Greensboro, Carolina League, 1949; manager, Tampa, Florida-International League, 1949; manager, Rock Hill, Western Carolinas League, 1963; manager, Shelby, Western Carolinas League, 1965.

Year Club	League	G.	IP.	W.	L.	Pct.	H.	R.	ER.	SO.	BB.	ERA.
1927—Cleveland	Amer.	1	1	0	0	.000	3	3	3	0	2	27.00
1928—Terre Haute	I.I.I.	33	240	•20	8	.714	218	81	73	122	46	2.74
1928—Cleveland	Amer.	2	16	0	2	.000	15	5	4	4	5	2.25
1929—Cleveland	Amer.	43	243	21	10	.677	256	112	97	100	109	3.59
1930—Cleveland	Amer.	43	297	25	13	.658	299	141	109	143	106	3.30
1931—Cleveland	Amer.	40	276	22	12	.647	276	134	115	123	*130	3.75
1932—Cleveland	Amer.	38	288	23	13	.639	299	141	117	105	104	3.66
1933—Cleveland(a)	Amer.	28	201	11	12	.478	225	108	94	41	70	4.21
1934—Boston	Amer.	26	181	14	5	.737	205	87	73	67	49	3.63
1935—Boston	Amer.	41	*322	*25	14	.641	*336	•149	126	110	108	3.52
1936—Boston	Amer.	39	*301	20	15	.571	*330	160	140	106	119	4.19
1937—Boston(b)-Washington	Amer.	37	*281	14	19	.424	*325	*177	*153	123	122	4.90
1938—Washington-New York	Amer.	28	179	15	10	.600	245	144	125	43	86	6.28
1939—New York	Amer.	3	19	1	2	.333	14	10	10	6	17	4.74
1940—Brooklyn	Nat.	1	4	0	0	.000	4	3	3	4	4	6.75
1941—Boston	Nat.	4	14	2	1	.667	13	8	8	10	9	5.14
1941—Leaksville	Bi-State	7	42	3	1	.750	56	31	....	26	9	......
1942—Lynchburg	Va.	....	....	....	....	....	....	....	....	....	....	......
1946—Lynchburg	Pied.	2	7	0	2	.000	2	2	2	6	1	2.57
1948—Marion	W. Carol.	3	8	1	1	.500	13	5	2	9	1	2.25
1949—Tampa	Fla. Int.	1	⅓	0	0	.000	0	0	0	0	0	0.00
American League Totals		369	2605	191	127	.601	2828	1371	1166	971	1027	4.03
National League Totals		5	18	2	1	.667	17	11	11	14	13	5.50
Major League Totals		374	2623	193	128	.601	2845	1382	1177	985	1040	4.04

aTraded to Boston Red Sox with outfielder Dick Porter for pitcher Bob Weiland, outfielder Bob Seeds and $25,000, May 25, 1934.

bTraded to Washington Senators with catcher Rick Ferrell and outfielder Melo Almada for pitcher Louis (Buck) Newsom and outfielder Ben Chapman, June 10, 1937.

WORLD SERIES RECORD

Year Club	League	G.	IP.	W.	L.	Pct.	H.	R.	ER.	SO.	BB.	ERA.
1933—New York	National	1	7	0	1	.000	9	4	4	2	0	5.14
1936—New York	National	2	11⅔	0	2	.000	13	7	7	6	2	5.40
1941—Brooklyn	National	1	7	0	0	.000	4	0	0	1	3	0.00
World Series Totals		4	25⅔	0	3	.000	26	11	11	9	5	3.86

DID YOU KNOW—
That Wes Ferrell out-homered his brother, Rick 38 to 28, during their major league careers, although Rick had over 4,800 more at-bats?

FREDERICK LANDIS FITZSIMMONS

Born July 28, 1901, at Mishawaka, Ind.
Died November 18, 1979, at Yucca Valley, Calif.
Height, 5.11. Weight, 205.
Threw and batted righthanded.
Married Helen Borger, January 1, 1925.

Voted by the fans as Veteran of the Year for 1940, in contest conducted by THE SPORTING NEWS. Coach, Brooklyn Dodgers, 1942; manager, Philadelphia Phillies, 1943-44-45; coach, Boston Braves, 1948; coach, New York Giants, 1949 through 1955, although assigned as manager of a Giants' farm club for part of 1953 season; manager, Binghamton, Eastern, 1956; coach, Chicago Cubs, 1957-58-59; coach, Kansas City Athletics, 1960; coach, Salt Lake City, Pacific Coast, 1961; coach, Chicago Cubs, 1966.

Year	Club	League	G.	IP.	W.	L.	Pct.	H.	R.	ER.	SO.	BB.	ERA.
1920	Muskegon	Central	12	100	3	9	.250	114	59	....	38	30	......
1921	Muskegon	Central	34	251	14	13	.519	244	118	89	126	81	3.19
1922	Muskegon	Central	36	245	16	11	.593	250	110	91	138	74	3.34
1922	Indianapolis	Am. Assoc.	7	48	3	4	.429	48	21	17	16	20	3.19
1923	Indianapolis	Am. Assoc.	33	173	9	4	.692	185	104	87	58	49	4.53
1924	Indianapolis	Am. Assoc.	39	279	14	17	.452	313	170	141	100	74	4.55
1925	Indianapolis	Am. Assoc.	27	184	14	6	.700	189	91	77	55	50	3.77
1925	New York	National	10	75	6	3	.667	70	25	22	17	18	2.64
1926	New York	National	37	219	14	10	.583	224	90	70	48	58	2.88
1927	New York	National	42	245	17	10	.630	260	127	101	78	67	3.71
1928	New York	National	40	261	20	9	.690	264	119	107	67	65	3.69
1929	New York	National	37	222	15	11	.577	242	122	101	55	66	4.09
1930	New York	National	41	224	19	7	*.731	230	125	106	76	59	4.26
1931	New York	National	35	254	18	11	.621	242	111	86	78	62	3.05
1932	New York	National	35	238	11	11	.500	287	132	*117	65	83	4.42
1933	New York	National	36	252	16	11	.593	243	106	81	65	72	2.89
1934	New York	National	38	263	18	14	.563	266	114	89	73	51	3.05
1935	New York	National	18	94	4	8	.333	104	43	42	23	22	4.02
1936	New York	National	28	141	10	7	.588	147	58	52	35	39	3.32
1937	N.Y.(a)-Brooklyn	National	19	118	6	10	.375	119	61	57	42	40	4.35
1938	Brooklyn	National	27	203	11	8	.579	205	83	68	38	43	3.01
1939	Brooklyn	National	27	151	7	9	.438	178	79	65	44	28	3.87
1940	Brooklyn	National	20	134	16	2	*.889	120	43	42	35	25	2.82
1941	Brooklyn	National	13	83	6	1	.857	78	33	19	19	26	2.06
1942	Brooklyn	National	1	3	0	0	.000	6	5	5	0	1	15.00
1943	Brooklyn(b)	National	9	45	3	4	.429	50	29	27	12	21	5.40
Major League Totals			513	3225	217	146	.598	3335	1505	1257	870	846	3.51

aTraded to Brooklyn for pitcher Thomas Baker, June 11, 1937.
bReleased by Brooklyn Dodgers, July 28, 1943, to become manager of Philadelphia Phillies.

WORLD SERIES RECORD

Year	Club	League	G.	IP.	W.	L.	Pct.	H.	R.	ER.	SO.	BB.	ERA.
1933	New York	National	1	7	0	1	.000	9	4	4	2	0	5.14
1936	New York	National	2	11⅔	0	2	.000	13	7	7	6	2	5.40
1941	Brooklyn	National	1	7	0	0	.000	4	0	0	1	3	0.00
World Series Totals			4	25⅔	0	3	.000	26	11	11	9	5	3.86

ELMER HARRISON FLICK

Born January 11, 1876, at Bedford, O.
Died January 9, 1971, at Bedford, O.
Height, 5.08½. Weight, 160.
Threw right and batted lefthanded.
Married Rose Ella Gates, January 3, 1901.

Hit three triples, July 6, 1902; tied with Sam Crawford and Zolio Versalles for major league record for consecutive years leading in three-base hits, three.
Named to Hall of Fame, 1963.

Year	Club	League	Pos.	G.	AB.	R.	H.	2B.	3B.	HR.	SB.	B.A.	PO.	A.	E.	F.A.
1896–Youngstown		Int. St.	OF	31	130	34	57					.438				.826
1897–Dayton		Int. St.	OF	126	474	135	183					.386	197	25	19	.921
1898–Philadelphia		Nat.	OF	133	447	84	142	16	14	7	29	.318	242	25	13	.954
1899–Philadelphia		Nat.	OF	125	486	101	167	21	14	2	31	.344	234	21	14	.948
1900–Philadelphia		Nat.	OF	138	547	106	207	33	16	11	37	.378	237	19	23	.918
1901–Philadelphia		Nat.	OF	138	542	111	182	31	17	8	26	.336	275	22	12	.961
1902–Phil.(a)-Cleve		Amer.	OF	121	464	83	137	22	12	2	24	.295	171	16	13	.935
1903–Cleveland		Amer.	OF	*142	529	84	158	22	16	2	27	.299	216	14	11	.954
1904–Cleveland		Amer.	OF	149	575	95	174	31	18	5	•42	.303	231	18	10	.961
1905–Cleveland		Amer.	OF	131	500	72	154	29	*19	4	35	*.308	177	18	13	.938
1906–Cleveland		Amer.	OF	*157	*624	*98	194	33	*22	1	•39	.311	248	13	5	.981
1907–Cleveland		Amer.	OF	147	549	80	166	17	*18	3	41	.302	219	22	11	.956
1908–Cleveland		Amer.	OF	9	35	4	8	1	1	0	0	.229	10	1	0	1.000
1909–Cleveland		Amer.	OF	66	235	28	60	10	2	0	9	.255	87	4	4	.958
1910–Cleveland		Amer.	OF	24	68	5	18	2	1	1	2	.265	21	0	1	.955
1911–Toledo		A. A.	OF	84	313	63	102	13	7	3	10	.326	165	10	9	.951
1912–Toledo		A. A.	OF	115	382	60	100	16	5	2	28	.262	177	9	13	.935
American League Totals				946	3579	549	1069	167	109	18	218	.299	1380	106	68	.956
National League Totals				534	2022	402	698	101	61	28	123	.345	988	87	62	.945
Major League Totals				1480	5601	951	1767	268	170	46	341	.315	2368	193	130	.952

aSold to Cleveland Indians, May 16, 1902.

LEWIS ALBERT FONSECA

Born January 21, 1900, at Oakland, Calif.
Height, 5.10½. Weight, 175.
Threw and batted righthanded.
Married Sigrun Magnusson, December 2, 1950.

Named Most Valuable Player in American League, 1929; hit two home runs and two triples as Cleveland defeated Chicago White Sox, 11-1, May 29, 1929.
Led A. L. first basemen in double plays, 1929.
Manager, Chicago White Sox, 1932 until released, May 8, 1934; appointed director of motion picture promotion for American League in 1939, and now director for both major leagues.
Served as batting instructor for various major league clubs.

Year	Club	League	Pos.	G.	AB.	R.	H.	2B.	3B.	HR.	RBI.	B.A.	PO.	A.	E.	F.A.
1920–San Francisco		P. C.		(Reported for Spring Training, then joined an independent club.)												
1921–Cincinnati		Nat.	1B-2B-OF	82	297	38	82	10	3	1	41	.276	307	155	14	.971
1922–Cincinnati		Nat.	2B	81	291	55	105	20	3	4	45	.361	197	251	14	.970
1923–Cincinnati		Nat.	1B-2B	65	237	33	66	11	4	3	28	.278	123	169	13	.957
1924–Cincinnati(a)		Nat.	1B-2B	20	57	5	13	2	1	0	9	.228	93	43	5	.965
1925–Philadelphia(b)		Nat.	1B-2B	126	467	78	149	30	5	7	60	.319	648	245	20	.978
1926–Newark(c)		Int.	1B-2B	147	543	127	207	40	11	21	126	.381	335	439	17	*.979
1927–Cleveland		Amer.	1B-2B	112	428	60	133	20	7	2	40	.311	347	305	16	.976
1928–Cleveland		Amer.	1B-2B	75	263	38	86	19	4	3	36	.327	552	73	2	.995
1929–Cleveland		Amer.	1B	148	566	97	209	44	15	6	103	*.369	1486	*107	6	.995
1930–Cleveland		Amer.	1B	40	129	20	36	9	2	0	17	.279	274	24	6	.980
1931–Clev.-Chi.(d)		Amer.	1-2B-OF	147	573	86	179	35	6	3	85	.312	518	68	9	.985
1932–Chicago(e)		Amer.	OF	18	37	0	5	1	0	0	6	.135	14	2	0	1.000
1933–Chicago		Amer.	1B	23	59	8	12	2	0	2	15	.203	138	12	0	1.000
American League Totals				563	2055	309	660	130	34	16	302	.321	3329	591	42	.989
National League Totals				374	1349	209	415	73	16	15	183	.308	1368	863	66	.971
Major League Totals				937	3404	518	1075	203	50	31	485	.316	4697	1454	108	.983

aInjured and out most of 1924 season, then was sold to Philadelphia Phillies for waiver price, March 30, 1925.
bHeld out against salary cut and was sold to Newark for $7,500, February, 1926.
cSold to Cleveland Indians for reported $50,000 in players and cash, September 4, 1926.
dTraded to Chicago White Sox for infielder Willie Kamm, May 17, 1931.
ePitched one inning (three batters) without decision.

DID YOU KNOW—

That Lou Fonseca pioneered the use of motion pictures in baseball?

EDWARD CHARLES (WHITEY) FORD

Born October 21, 1928, at New York, N. Y.
Height, 5.10. Weight, 181.
Threw and batted lefthanded.
Married Joan Foran, April 14, 1951.

Tied major league record for most consecutive one-hit games (2), September 2 and 7, 1955.
Set the following World Series records; most Series played by pitcher (11); most games pitched, total Series (22); most putouts, total Series (11); most putouts by pitcher, four-game Series (3); most games started (22); most opening games started (8); most games won, total Series (10); most games lost, total Series (8); most innings pitched, total Series (146); most bases on balls, total Series (34); most strikeouts, total Series (94); most consecutive scoreless innings pitched, total Series (33).
Named as Pitcher on THE SPORTING NEWS All-Star Major League Teams, 1955-56.
Named as Pitcher on THE SPORTING NEWS American League All-Star Teams, 1961-63.
Named American League Pitcher of the Year by THE SPORTING NEWS, 1955-61-63.
Won Cy Young Memorial Award, 1961.
Scout and minor league pitching coach, New York Yankees, May 30, 1967, through end of season; coach, New York Yankees, 1968.
Named to Hall of Fame, 1974.

Year Club	League	G.	IP.	W.	L.	Pct.	H.	R.	ER.	SO.	BB.	ERA.
1947—Butler	Mid. Atl.	24	157	13	4	.765	151	86	67	114	58	3.84
1948—Norfolk	Pied.	30	216	16	8	.667	182	83	62	171	113	2.58
1949—Binghamton	East.	26	168	16	5	.762	118	38	30	151	54	•1.61
1950—Kansas City	A. A.	12	95	6	3	.667	81	39	34	80	48	3.22
1950—New York	Amer.	20	112	9	1	.900	87	39	35	59	52	2.81
1951-52—New York	Amer.					(In Military Service)						
1953—New York	Amer.	32	207	18	6	.750	187	77	69	110	110	3.00
1954—New York	Amer.	34	211	16	8	.667	170	72	66	125	101	2.82
1955—New York	Amer.	39	254	•18	7	.720	188	83	74	137	113	2.62
1956—New York	Amer.	31	226	19	6	•.760	187	70	62	141	84	•2.47
1957—New York	Amer.	24	129	11	5	.688	114	46	37	84	53	2.58
1958—New York	Amer.	30	219	14	7	.667	174	62	49	145	62	•2.01
1959—New York	Amer.	35	204	16	10	.615	194	82	69	114	89	3.04
1960—New York	Amer.	33	193	12	9	.571	168	76	66	85	65	3.08
1961—New York	Amer.	39	•283	•25	4	•.862	242	108	101	209	92	3.21
1962—New York	Amer.	38	258	17	8	.680	243	90	83	160	69	2.90
1963—New York	Amer.	38	•269	•24	7	•.774	240	94	82	189	56	2.74
1964—New York	Amer.	39	245	17	6	.739	212	67	58	172	57	2.13
1965—New York	Amer.	37	244	16	13	.552	241	97	88	162	50	3.25
1966—New York(a)	Amer.	22	73	2	5	.286	79	33	20	43	24	2.47
1967—New York	Amer.	7	44	2	4	.333	40	11	8	21	9	1.64
Major League Totals		498	3171	236	106	.690	2766	1107	967	1956	1086	2.74

aUnderwent operation for circulatory blockage in left shoulder; on disabled list from August 22 through end of season.

WORLD SERIES RECORD

Year Club	League	G.	IP.	W.	L.	Pct.	H.	R.	ER.	SO.	BB.	ERA.
1950—New York	Amer.	1	8⅔	1	0	1.000	7	2	0	7	1	0.00
1953—New York	Amer.	2	8	0	1	.000	9	4	4	7	2	4.50
1955—New York	Amer.	2	17	2	0	1.000	13	6	4	10	8	2.12
1956—New York	Amer.	2	12	1	1	.500	14	8	7	8	2	5.25
1957—New York	Amer.	2	16	1	1	.500	11	2	2	7	5	1.13
1958—New York	Amer.	3	15⅓	0	1	.000	19	8	7	16	5	4.11
1960—New York	Amer.	2	18	2	0	1.000	11	0	0	8	2	0.00
1961—New York	Amer.	2	14	2	0	1.000	6	0	0	7	1	0.00
1962—New York	Amer.	3	19⅔	1	1	.500	24	9	9	12	4	4.12
1963—New York	Amer.	2	12	0	2	.000	10	7	6	8	3	4.50
1964—New York	Amer.	1	5⅓	0	1	.000	8	5	5	4	1	8.44
World Series Totals		22	146	10	8	.556	132	51	44	94	34	2.71

DID YOU KNOW—

That Whitey Ford's feat of pitching 33⅔ consecutive scoreless innings in World Series play broke all-time slugger Babe Ruth's record of 29⅔ innings set in 1916 and 1918? Yankees' lefty also holds Series records for most games started (22), most opening games started (8) and most total wins (10).

ROBERT ROY (FATTY) FOTHERGILL

Born August 16, 1899, at Massillon, O.
Died March 20, 1938, at Detroit, Mich.
Height, 5.10½. Weight, 225.
Threw and batted righthanded.

Year	Club	League	Pos.	G.	AB.	R.	H.	2B.	3B.	HR.	RBI.	B.A.	PO.	A.	E.	F.A.
1920	Bloomington	I.I.I.	OF	136	542	88	*180	21	*15	10	116	.332	312	28	8	.977
1921	Rochester	Int.	OF	143	582	114	197	34	●23	12	....	.338	283	19	16	.950
1922	Rochester	Int.	OF	101	397	76	152	35	12	4	79	*.383	174	10	8	.958
1922	Detroit	Amer.	OF	42	152	20	49	12	4	0	29	.322	50	2	3	.945
1923	Detroit	Amer.	OF	101	241	34	76	18	2	1	49	.315	121	4	3	.977
1924	Detroit	Amer.	OF	54	166	28	50	8	3	0	15	.301	89	2	3	.968
1925	Detroit	Amer.	OF	71	204	38	72	14	0	2	28	.353	113	5	2	.983
1926	Detroit	Amer.	OF	110	387	63	142	31	7	3	73	.367	245	3	10	.961
1927	Detroit	Amer.	OF	143	527	93	189	38	9	9	114	.359	315	3	13	.961
1928	Detroit	Amer.	OF	111	347	49	110	28	10	3	63	.317	179	6	8	.959
1929	Detroit	Amer.	OF	115	277	42	98	24	9	6	62	.354	116	2	4	.967
1930	Det.(a)-Chicago	Amer.	OF	107	278	24	77	18	3	2	38	.280	106	3	10	.913
1931	Chicago	Amer.	OF	108	312	25	88	9	4	3	56	.282	169	2	5	.972
1932	Chicago (b)	Amer.	OF	116	346	36	102	24	1	7	50	.295	136	4	7	.952
1933	Boston	Amer.	OF	28	32	1	11	1	0	0	5	.344	4	0	0	1.000
1933	Minneapolis	A.A.	OF	30	96	19	33	6	1	2	14	.344	34	3	1	.974
Major League Totals				1106	3269	453	1064	225	52	36	582	.325	1643	36	68	.961

aSold to Chicago White Sox on waivers, July 18, 1930.
bTraded with outfielders Robert Seeds, Urban J. Hodapp and Gregory Mulleavy to Boston Red Sox for pitcher Edward Durham and infielder Harold Rhyne, December 15, 1932.

JACQUES FRANK (JACK) FOURNIER

Born September 28, 1892, at Au Sable, Mich.
Died September 5, 1973, at Tacoma, Wash.
Height, 6.00. Weight, 190.
Threw right and batted lefthanded.
Married Helen L. Cummings, 1913.

Hit three consecutive home runs, July 3, 1926.
Manager, Johnstown, Middle Atlantic League, 1937; Toledo, American Association, 1943; coach, University of California at Los Angeles, 1934-35; scout, St. Louis Browns, 1938 through 1942, 1944 through 1947; Chicago Cubs, 1950 through 1957; Detroit Tigers, 1960; Cincinnati Reds, 1961-62.

Year	Club	League	Pos.	G.	AB.	R.	H.	2B.	3B.	HR.	SB.	B.A.	PO.	A.	E.	F.A.
1908	Aberdeen-Seat.	N.W.	1B	34	114	5	26	4	1	1	5	.228	166	44	9	.951
1909	Portland	P.C.	1B	17	28	2	7	2	1	0	2	.250	33	9	3	.933
1909	Portland	N.W.	1B	101	345	39	73	7	4	3	17	.212	374	78	28	.942
1910	Sacramento	P.C.	1B	14	27	4	7	4	0	0	2	.259	53	10	4	.940
1911	Moose Jaw	W. Can.	1B	109	395	*106	*149	*28	*19	5	33	.377	261	121	40	.906
1912	Chicago	Amer.	1B	35	73	5	14	5	2	0	1	.192	154	16	2	.988
1912	Montreal	Int.	1B	60	217	39	67	12	8	3	13	.309	551	18	12	.979
1913	Chicago	Amer.	1B-OF	68	171	20	40	8	5	1	9	.234	306	23	5	.985
1914	Chicago	Amer.	1B	109	379	44	118	14	9	6	10	.311	1025	78	25	.978
1915	Chicago	Amer.	1B-OF	126	422	86	136	20	18	5	21	.322	784	51	17	.980
1916	Chicago	Amer.	1B	105	313	36	75	13	9	3	19	.240	855	49	20	.978
1917	Chicago	Amer.	PH	1	1	0	0	0	0	0	0	.000	0	0	0	.000
1917	Los Angeles	P.C.	1B	144	512	76	156	29	6	7	38	.305	1431	88	17	.989
1918	Los Angeles	P.C.	1B	*104	400	52	130	●26	*13	4	37	.325	....	....	....	....
1918	New York	Amer.	1B	27	100	9	35	6	1	0	7	.350	274	13	10	*.995
1919	Los Angeles	P.C.	1B	169	638	108	209	*19	10	44	.328	1731	114	*25	.983
1920	St. Louis	Nat.	1B	141	530	77	162	33	14	3	26	.306	1373	88	*25	.983
1921	St. Louis	Nat.	1B	149	574	103	197	27	9	16	20	.343	1416	73	19	.987
1922	St. Louis (a)	Nat.	1B	128	404	64	119	23	9	10	6	.295	902	60	18	.979
1923	Brooklyn	Nat.	1B	133	515	91	181	30	13	22	11	.351	1281	82	*21	.985
1924	Brooklyn	Nat.	1B	*154	563	93	188	25	4	*27	7	.334	1388	*99	22	.985

Year Club	League	Pos.	G.	AB.	R.	H.	2B.	3B.	HR.	SB.	B.A.	PO.	A.	E.	F.A.
1925—Brooklyn	Nat.	1B	145	545	99	191	21	16	22	4	.350	1317	82	15	.989
1926—Brooklyn (b)	Nat.	1B	87	243	39	69	9	2	11	0	.284	548	28	8	.986
1927—Boston	Nat.	1B	122	374	55	106	18	2	10	4	.283	901	63	11	.989
1928—Newark	Int.	1B	148	504	87	145	26	8	22	16	.288	1177	79	17	.987
American League Totals			471	1459	200	418	66	44	15	67	.286	3398	230	76	.979
National League Totals			1059	3748	621	1213	186	69	121	78	.324	9126	575	139	.986
Major League Totals			1530	5207	821	1631	252	113	136	145	.313	12524	805	215	.984

aTraded to Brooklyn Dodgers for outfielder Henry (Hi) Myers and first baseman Ray Schmandt, February 15, 1923.
bSold to Boston Braves, November 5, 1926.

JACOB NELSON (NELLIE) FOX

Born December 25, 1927, at St. Thomas, Pa.
Died December 1, 1975, at Baltimore, Md.
Height, 5.09. Weight, 160.
Threw right and batted lefthanded.
Married Joanne A. Statler, June 30, 1947.

Holds major league record for most years leading league in fewest strikeouts (11)—leading in the following years: (11) 1951, (14) 1952, (12) 1954, (15) 1955, (14) 1956, (13) 1957, (11) 1958, (13) 1959, (13) 1960, (12) 1961, and (12) 1962.
Holds major league mark for most consecutive years leading in singles (7)—hitting (167) 1954, (157) 1955, (158) 1956, (155) 1957, (160) 1958, (149) 1959 and (139) 1960; also led in singles (141) 1952, giving him major league record for most years leading in one-base hits (8).
Appeared at bat 600 or more times for 12th season for major league mark, 1962, and set another major league high as all 12 were in succession.
Major league record holder for most consecutive games played at second base (798), August 7, 1955 through September 3, 1960; tops for most years leading second basemen in chances accepted (9), 1952 through 1960; also holds major league standard for most years leading second basemen in games played (8), 1952 through 1959; holds major league record for most years leading league second sackers in putouts (10), 1952 through 1961, and all were in succession.
Most years leading A.L. second basemen in double plays (5) 1954-56-57-58-60—tied for A.L. record.
Named Most Valuable Player, American League, 1959.
Named Outstanding American League Player by The Sporting News, 1959.
Named as second baseman on The Sporting News All-Star Major League Teams, 1955-56-58-59.
Received Rawlings Gold Glove award as outstanding major league fielding second baseman, 1957; named for Gold Glove award as outstanding American League fielding second baseman, 1958-59-60.
Player-coach, Houston Astros, 1965; coach, 1966 through 1967; coach, Washington Senators, 1968 through 1971; coach, Texas Rangers, 1972.

Year Club	League	Pos.	G.	AB.	R.	H.	2B.	3B.	HR.	RBI.	B.A.	PO.	A.	E.	F.A.
1944—Lancaster	Int.St.	1-OF	24	77	11	25	6	0	0	12	.325	123	10	6	.957
1944—Jamestown	Pony	OF	56	230	40	70	11	0	0	18	.304	114	5	3	.975
1945—Lancaster	Int.-St.	2B	•140	•573	•128	•180	19	•19	1	68	.314	•426	•400	24	•.972
1946—Philadelphia	Amer.					(In Military Service)									
1947—Lancaster	Int.-St.	2B	55	228	42	64	8	4	1	22	.281	178	165	9	.974
1947—Philadelphia	Amer.	2B	7	3	2	0	0	0	0	0	.000	1	0	0	1.000
1948—Lincoln	West.	2B	136	•576	97	•179	28	14	5	67	.311	•354	•361	28	.962
1948—Philadelphia	Amer.	2B	3	13	0	2	0	0	0	0	.154	13	6	1	.950
1949—Philadelphia(a)	Amer.	2B	88	247	42	63	6	2	0	21	.255	191	196	7	.982
1950—Chicago	Amer.	2B	130	457	45	113	12	7	0	30	.247	340	344	18	.974
1951—Chicago	Amer.	2B	147	604	93	189	32	12	4	55	.313	413	449	17	.981
1952—Chicago	Amer.	2B	152	•648	76	•192	25	10	0	39	.296	•406	•433	13	•.985
1953—Chicago	Amer.	2B	154	624	92	178	31	8	3	72	.285	•451	426	15	.983
1954—Chicago	Amer.	2B	•155	631	111	•201	24	8	2	47	.319	•400	392	9	.989
1955—Chicago	Amer.	2B	•154	•636	100	198	28	7	6	59	.311	•399	•483	•24	.974
1956—Chicago	Amer.	2B	154	•649	109	192	20	10	4	52	.296	•478	•396	12	•.986
1957—Chicago	Amer.	2B	•155	619	110	•196	27	8	6	61	.317	•453	•453	13	.986
1958—Chicago	Amer.	2B	•155	623	82	•187	21	6	0	49	.300	•444	399	13	•.985
1959—Chicago	Amer.	2B	•156	•624	84	191	34	6	2	70	.306	•364	•453	10	•.988
1960—Chicago	Amer.	2B	150	•605	85	175	24	•10	2	59	.289	•412	•447	15	.985
1961—Chicago	Amer.	2B	159	606	67	152	11	5	2	51	.251	•413	407	15	.982
1962—Chicago	Amer.	2B	157	621	79	166	27	7	2	54	.267	376	428	•8	•.990
1963—Chicago(b)	Amer.	2B	137	539	54	140	19	2	2	42	.260	305	342	8	•.928
1964—Houston(c)	Nat.	2B	133	442	45	117	12	6	0	28	.265	231	317	13	.977
1965—Houston	Nat.	3-1-2B	21	41	3	11	2	0	0	1	.268	12	14	0	1.000
American League Totals			2213	8749	1231	2535	341	106	35	761	.290	5859	6054	196	.984
National League Totals			154	483	48	128	14	6	0	29	.265	243	331	13	.978
Major League Totals			2367	9232	1279	2663	355	112	35	790	.288	6102	6385	209	.984

aTraded to Chicago White Sox for catcher Joe Tipton, October 19, 1949.
bTraded to Houston Colt .45's for pitcher Jim Golden, outfielder Danny Murphy and cash, December 10, 1963.
cReleased as player and signed as coach by Houston Colts, October 9, 1964; reactivated as player, May 13, 1965.

WORLD SERIES RECORD

Year	Club	League	Pos.	G.	AB.	R.	H.	2B.	3B.	HR.	RBI.	B.A.	PO.	A.	E.	F.A.
1959	Chicago	Amer.	2B	6	24	4	9	3	0	0	0	.375	14	23	0	1.000

JAMES EMORY (JIMMIE) FOXX

Born October 22, 1907, at Sudlersville, Md.
Died July 21, 1967, at Miami, Fla.
Height, 5.11½. Weight, 190.
Threw and batted righthanded.
Married Dorothy Anderson Yard, June 18, 1943.

Tied major league record with most home runs, consecutive times at bat—4 (June 7—last time up and June 8—second, fourth and fifth innings, 1933). Hit three home runs in game—June 8, 1933 (successive), and July 10, 1932 (18 innings). Equaled American League record with four home runs in doubleheader (2—first game, 2—second game, July 2, 1933). Led league in bases on balls, 1934; tied for leadership in 1938. Tied major league record by hitting home run with bases loaded in two successive games, May 20 and 21, 1940. Hit 500th home run of career, September 24, 1940. Holds record for most consecutive years, 30 or more home runs—12—1929 to 1940.

Manager, Portsmouth, Piedmont League, August 25, 1944, to end of season; manager, St. Petersburg, Florida International League, 1947; manager, Bridgeport, Colonial League, August, 1949; coach, Minneapolis, American Association, 1958. Named Most Valuable Player in American League, 1932-33-38.

Named to Hall of Fame, 1951.

Year	Club	League	Pos.	G.	AB.	R.	H.	2B.	3B.	HR.	RBI.	B.A.	PO.	A.	E.	F.A.
1924	Easton	East.Sh.	C	76	260	33	77	11	2	10	....	.296	379	*73	•16	.966
1925	Philadelphia	Amer.	C	10	9	2	6	1	0	0	0	.667	0	0	0	.000
1925	Providence	Int.	C	41	101	12	33	6	3	1	15	.327	75	9	4	.955
1926	Philadelphia	Amer.	C	26	32	8	10	2	1	0	5	.313	19	5	0	1.000
1927	Philadelphia	Amer.	1B	61	130	23	42	6	5	3	20	.323	263	15	7	.975
1928	Philadelphia	Amer.	1B-3B-C	118	400	85	131	29	10	13	79	.328	416	155	17	.971
1929	Philadelphia	Amer.	1B	149	517	123	183	23	9	33	117	.354	1226	74	6	.995
1930	Philadelphia	Amer.	1B	153	562	127	188	33	13	37	156	.335	*1362	79	14	.990
1931	Philadelphia	Amer.	1B-3B	139	515	93	150	32	10	30	120	.291	988	104	15	*.986
1932	Philadelphia	Amer.	1B-3B	154	585	*151	213	33	9	*58	*169	.364	1338	97	11	*.992
1933	Philadelphia	Amer.	1B	149	573	125	204	37	9	*48	*163	.356	1402	*93	15	.990
1934	Philadelphia	Amer.	1B	150	539	120	180	28	6	44	130	.334	1378	85	10	.993
1935	Philadelphia(a)	Amer.	1B-3B-C	147	535	118	185	33	7	•36	115	.346	1226	93	4	*.997
1936	Boston	Amer.	1B-OF	•155	585	130	198	32	8	41	143	.338	1253	76	13	.990
1937	Boston	Amer.	1B	150	569	111	162	24	6	36	127	.285	1287	*106	8	*.994
1938	Boston	Amer.	1B	149	565	139	197	33	9	50	*175	*.349	1282	116	*19	.987
1939	Boston	Amer.	1B	124	467	130	168	31	10	*35	105	.360	1101	91	10	.992
1940	Boston	Amer.	1B-3B-C	144	515	106	153	30	4	36	119	.297	1023	100	10	.991
1941	Boston	Amer.	1B-3B-C	135	487	87	146	27	8	19	105	.300	1162	*118	14	*.989
1942	Boston(b)	Amer.	1B	30	100	18	27	4	0	5	14	.270	231	34	1	.996
1942	Chicago	Nat.	1B-C	70	205	25	42	8	0	3	19	.205	491	24	9	.983
1943	Chicago	Nat.						(Did not play)								
1944	Chicago(c)	Nat.	PH-1B	15	20	0	1	1	0	0	2	.050	9	6	0	1.000
1944	Portsmouth(d)	Pied.	PH-1B	5	2	0	0	0	0	0	0	.000	0	1	0	1.000
1945	Philadelphia	Nat.	1B-3B	89	224	30	60	11	1	7	38	.268	304	54	8	.978
1946	—						(Out of Organized Ball)									
1947	St. Petersburg	Fla. Int.	PH	6	6	0	1	....	....	....	....	.167	....	....	....	....
	American League Totals			2143	7685	1696	2543	438	124	524	1862	.331	16957	1441	173	.991
	National League Totals			174	449	55	103	20	1	10	59	.229	804	84	17	.981
	Major League Totals			2317	8134	1751	2646	458	125	534	1921	.325	17761	1525	190	.990

aTraded with pitcher John Marcum to Boston Red Sox for pitcher Gordon Rhodes, catcher George Savino and $150,000, December 10, 1935.
bReleased on waivers to Chicago Cubs, June 1, 1942.
cReleased as player and signed as coach, July 6, 1944; released to Portsmouth as manager, August 25, 1944.
dReleased by Portsmouth, December, 1944, and signed by Philadelphia Phillies, February 10, 1945.

PITCHING RECORD

Year	Club	League	G.	IP.	W.	L.	Pct.	H.	R.	ER.	SO.	BB.	ERA.
1939	Boston	Amer.	1	1	0	0	.000	0	0	0	0	0	0.00
1945	Philadelphia	Nat.	9	23	1	0	1.000	13	4	4	10	14	1.57
	Major League Totals		10	24	1	0	1.000	13	4	4	10	14	1.50

WORLD SERIES RECORD

Year	Club	League	Pos.	G.	AB.	R.	H.	2B.	3B.	HR.	RBI.	B.A.	PO.	A.	E.	F.A.
1929–Philadelphia		Amer.	1B	5	20	5	7	1	0	2	5	.350	38	1	0	1.000
1930–Philadelphia		Amer.	1B	6	21	3	7	2	1	1	3	.333	53	3	0	1.000
1931–Philadelphia		Amer.	1B	7	23	3	8	0	0	1	3	.348	69	2	1	.986
World Series Totals				18	64	11	22	3	1	4	11	.344	160	6	1	.994

CHARLES CARROLTON (CHIC) FRASER

Born March 17, 1871, at Chicago, Ill.
Died May 8, 1940, at Wendell, Ida.
Height, 5.10½. Weight, 190.
Threw and batted righthanded.
Married Mina Gray, 1897.

Pitched no-hit game against Chicago Cubs, winning, 10-0, September 18, 1903.
Manager, Decatur, Three-I League, 1912; manager, Pittsfield, Northeastern League, 1913; scout, Pittsburgh Pirates, 1913 to 1930, inclusive; manager, Peoria, Three-I League, 1931; scout, Brooklyn Dodgers, 1932 to 1938, inclusive; scout, New York Yankees, 1939.

Year	Club	League	G.	IP.	W.	L.	Pct.	H.	R.	SO.	BB.	CG.	ShO.
1894–Minneapolis		Western					(No averages issued)						
1895–Minneapolis		Western	48	....	....	....	....	474	366	....	....	....	....
1896–Louisville		National	42	344	13	25	.342	390	270	91	154	35	0
1897–Louisville		National	36	296	15	17	.469	340	213	74	141	32	0
1898–Louis (a)-Cleve (b)		National	32	241	9	22	.290	284	198	77	111	26	1
1899–Philadelphia		National	35	269	21	13	.618	276	140	76	96	29	4
1900–Philadelphia		National	31	237	16	10	.615	255	121	57	94	23	1
1901–Philadelphia (c)		American	39	329	20	15	.571	338	212	115	★127	35	2
1902–Philadelphia		National	27	224	12	13	.480	232	117	92	71	24	3
1903–Philadelphia		National	31	250	12	17	.414	259	160	104	97	26	1
1904–Philadelphia (d)		National	41	302	14	24	.368	297	164	127	100	31	3
1905–Boston (e)		National	39	334	15	22	.405	320	174	130	★149	35	2
1906–Cincinnati (f)		National	31	236	10	20	.333	225	92	58	80	25	2
1907–Chicago		National	22	138	8	5	.615	112	51	41	46	9	2
1908–Chicago		National	26	163	11	9	.550	141	71	66	61	12	4
1909–Chicago		National	1	3	0	0	.000	2	1	1	4	0	0
1909-10–New Orleans		Southern					(Voluntarily retired)						
1911–New Orleans		Southern	11	....	4	6	.400	....	....	....	....	....	....
1912–Decatur		I.I.I.	15	98	6	6	.500	82	44	68	52	....	....
American League Totals			39	329	20	15	.571	338	212	115	127	35	2
National League Totals			394	3037	156	197	.442	3133	1772	994	1204	307	23
Major League Totals			433	3366	176	212	.454	3471	1984	1109	1331	342	25

aReleased and signed by Cleveland Spiders, September, 1898.
bReleased and signed by Philadelphia Phillies.
cJumped to Philadelphia Athletics in 1901 but returned to Philadelphia Phillies in 1902.
dReleased and signed by Boston Braves, 1905.
eTraded to Cincinnati Reds for shortstop Al Bridwell, March, 1906.
fTraded to Chicago Cubs for pitcher Charles Harper, October, 1906.

WILLIAM ASHLEY FREEHAN

Born November 29, 1941, at Detroit, Mich.
Height, 6.03. Weight, 208.
Threw and batted righthanded.

Established major league records for highest fielding average, catcher, lifetime (.9933), 1976; and putouts, catcher, lifetime (9,941), 1976; and most chances accepted, catcher, lifetime (10,662), 1976.
Established following American League records: most putouts, game, nine innings, catcher (19), June 15, 1965; most putouts, catcher, season (971), 1968; and most chances accepted, catcher, season (1,044), 1968.
Hit three home runs in a game, August 9, 1971.
Named catcher on THE SPORTING NEWS American League All-Star fielding teams, 1965-66-67-68-69.

Named catcher on THE SPORTING NEWS American League All-Star Teams, 1967-68-69-71.
Received reported $100,000 bonus to sign with Detroit Tigers, 1961.

Year	Club	League	Pos.	G.	AB.	R.	H.	2B.	3B.	HR.	RBI.	B.A.	PO.	A.	E.	F.A.
1961–Duluth-Superior		North.	C	30	99	22	34	5	1	7	26	.343	166	22	6	.969
1961–Knoxville		Sally	C	47	159	29	46	6	3	4	29	.289	260	18	6	.979
1961–Detroit		Amer.	C	4	10	1	4	0	0	0	4	.400	14	4	0	1.000
1962–Denver		A.A.	*C-1B	113	392	47	111	22	2	9	58	.283	684	55	11	*.985
1963–Detroit		Amer.	C-1B	100	300	37	73	12	2	9	36	.243	554	38	3	.995
1964–Detroit		Amer.	C-1B	144	520	69	156	14	8	18	80	.300	930	61	7	.993
1965–Detroit		Amer.	C	130	431	45	101	15	0	10	43	.234	*865	57	4	.996
1966–Detroit		Amer.	*C-1B	136	492	47	115	22	0	12	46	.234	*942	60	4	*.996
1967–Detroit		Amer.	*C-1B	155	517	66	146	23	1	20	74	.282	*1027	68	8	.993
1968–Detroit		Amer.	*C-1B-OF	155	540	73	142	24	2	25	84	.263	*1133	83	7	.994
1969–Detroit		Amer.	*C-1B	143	489	61	128	16	3	16	49	.262	*959	56	10	.990
1970–Detroit		Amer.	C	117	395	44	95	17	3	16	52	.241	742	42	2	*.997
1971–Detroit		Amer.	*C-OF	148	516	57	143	26	4	21	71	.277	*912	50	4	.996
1972–Detroit		Amer.	C-1B	111	374	51	98	18	2	10	56	.262	654	60	8	.989
1973–Detroit		Amer.	*C-1B	110	380	33	89	10	1	6	29	.234	638	53	3	*.996
1974–Detroit		Amer.	1B-C	130	445	58	132	17	5	18	60	.297	902	81	9	.991
1975–Detroit		Amer.	*C-1B	120	427	42	105	17	3	14	47	.246	635	66	6	*.992
1976–Detroit		Amer.	C-1B-DH	71	237	22	64	10	1	5	27	.270	328	34	6	.984
Major League Totals				1774	6073	706	1591	241	35	200	758	.262	11235	813	81	.993

WORLD SERIES RECORD

Year	Club	League	Pos.	G.	AB.	R.	H.	2B.	3B.	HR.	RBI.	B.A.	PO.	A.	E.	F.A.
1968–Detroit		Amer.	C	7	24	0	2	1	0	0	2	.083	45	6	2	.962

LAWRENCE HERBERT (LARRY) FRENCH

Born November 1, 1908, at Visalia, Calif.
Height, 6.01. Weight, 194.
Threw left and batted right and lefthanded.
Married Thelma Olmstead, June 2, 1928.

Last game he pitched in National League was a one-hit shutout in which he faced 27 men, winning, 6-0, over Philadelphia Phillies, September 23, 1942.

Year	Club	League	G.	IP.	W.	L.	Pct.	H.	R.	ER.	SO.	BB.	ERA.
1926–Portland		Pac. Coast	7	17	1	0	1.000	20	13	11	7	0	5.82
1926–Ogden		Utah-Idaho	22	134	8	7	.533	151	89	88	78	65	5.91
1927–Portland		Pac. Coast	44	181	11	12	.478	191	114	96	71	98	4.77
1928–Portland		Pac. Coast	43	251	11	17	.393	274	138	113	105	128	4.05
1929–Pittsburgh		National	30	123	7	5	.583	130	78	67	49	62	4.90
1930–Pittsburgh		National	42	275	17	•18	.486	325	163	133	90	89	4.35
1931–Pittsburgh		National	39	276	15	13	.536	*301	127	100	73	70	3.26
1932–Pittsburgh		National	*47	274	18	16	.529	*301	127	92	72	62	3.02
1933–Pittsburgh		National	47	291	18	13	.581	*290	106	88	88	55	2.72
1934–Pittsburgh (a)		National	49	264	12	18	.400	299	135	105	103	59	3.58
1935–Chicago		National	42	246	17	10	.630	279	94	81	90	44	2.96
1936–Chicago		National	43	252	18	9	.667	262	103	95	104	54	3.39
1937–Chicago		National	42	208	16	10	.615	229	106	92	100	65	3.98
1938–Chicago		National	43	201	10	19	.345	210	95	85	83	62	3.81
1939–Chicago		National	36	194	15	8	.652	205	80	71	98	50	3.29
1940–Chicago		National	40	246	14	14	.500	240	93	90	107	64	3.29
1941–Chicago (b)-Brooklyn		National	32	154	5	14	.263	177	94	77	68	47	4.50
1942–Brooklyn (c)		National	38	148	15	4	*.789	127	39	30	62	36	1.82
Major League Totals			570	3152	197	171	.535	3375	1440	1206	1187	819	3.44

aTraded with third baseman Fred Lindstrom to Chicago Cubs for pitchers Guy Bush and James D. Weaver and outfielder Floyd C. Herman, November 22, 1934.
bWaived to Brooklyn, August 20, 1941.
cEnlisted in U.S. Navy, January 8, 1943, and retired from game following discharge.

WORLD SERIES RECORD

Year	Club	League	G.	IP.	W.	L.	Pct.	H.	R.	ER.	SO.	BB.	ERA.
1935–Chicago		National	2	10⅔	0	2	.000	15	5	4	8	2	3.38
1938–Chicago		National	3	3⅓	0	0	.000	1	1	1	2	1	2.70
1941–Brooklyn		National	2	1	0	0	.000	0	0	0	0	0	.000
World Series Totals			7	15	0	2	.000	16	6	5	10	3	3.00

FORD FRICK

(Third Commissioner of Baseball)
Born December 19, 1894, at Wawaka, Ind.
Died April 8, 1978, at Bronxville, N.Y.

Named to Hall of Fame, 1970.

Born on a small farm outside Wawaka, Ind., Ford Frick retained his quiet, reserved Hoosier background his entire life. After graduating from his home state's De Pauw University in 1915, he traveled to Walsenburg, Colo., where he played first base for a semi-pro team. He remained to teach English in the high school there. From that position, he moved to an assistant professorship at Colorado College in Colorado Springs. While there, he did some sports writing for the local Gazette. By the end of the 1917 school term, he quit teaching to become a full-time reporter for the Gazette. In World War I, he did rehabilitation work with the War Department in Colorado, New Mexico and Wyoming.

Later returning to newspaper work, he did a masterful job in covering the disastrous Pueblo flood, which inundated the city and swept away hundreds of lives and millions of dollars in property. Frick found a pilot with a two-seater plane and covered the flood on-scene from the low-flying craft. He also took graphic pictures of the devastation which earned him national recognition. Arthur Brisbane, editor of the New York American, saw Frick's work and offered him a post on the sports staff, which Ford accepted.

Frick preferred the simple life and quickly settled in Bronxville, N. Y., a suburb in Westchester County, where he lived all through his active career. He covered spring training of the New York teams and even ghosted for Babe Ruth, writing a syndicated column and also a work entitled "Babe Ruth's Own Book of Baseball." Frick was an oddity in the press box, using all his fingers when he typed, whereas most of the writers used the one-, two- and three-fingered pick and peck method.

In the summer of 1934, Frick surprised his sportswriter friends by leaving the newspaper beat to become director of the National League Service Bureau, the league's publicity outlet. He didn't have to wait long for a promotion. In October of the same year, John Heydler, president of the National League, retired and a month later, Frick became N. L. president.

His chief problem as National League head was the advent of the Negro into major league ball. Jackie Robinson, the first of the modern Negroes in the majors, entered midst a storm of protest caused by racist sympathizers who feared the demise of their white refuge. Frick warned the rabble-rousers that if they persisted they would be barred from baseball . . . "even if there are so many of them that it would mean the dissolution of the National League."

After Commissioner Happy Chandler resigned under fire early in 1951, Frick became the popular choice to succeed. He was elected on September 20, 1951, and took office on October 8. He served through December 14, 1965, when he himself retired.

During his 15-year span, franchises were shifted and new ones created. The game expanded from coast-to-coast, TV became a dominant financial force in the game's policies and outcome on the field, according to the size of the market in which a club played, and the never-ending battle with Congress and the courts continued. Frick above all was a solid administrator and the financial health of the National League and the majors during his reign attest to his acumen. He felt his role was to tie in the wishes of one owner with the wishes of another, so that both could work together for the common purpose and, in a larger sense, channel all the drives of all the owners into one direction—the betterment of the game.

ROBERT BARTMESS FRIEND

Born November 24, 1930, at Lafayette, Ind.
Height, 6.00. Weight, 198.
Threw and batted righthanded.
Married Patricia Koval, September 30, 1957.

First pitcher in major league history to top league in earned-run average pitching for a last-place team, 1955.

Named as pitcher on THE SPORTING NEWS All-Star Major League Team, 1958.

Year	Club	League	G.	IP.	W.	L.	Pct.	H.	R.	ER.	SO.	BB.	ERA.
1950	Waco	Big State	29	190	12	9	.571	173	95	65	107	91	3.08
1950	Indianapolis	Amer. Assn.	11	56	2	4	.333	75	41	34	34	16	5.46
1951	Pittsburgh	National	34	150	6	10	.375	173	94	71	41	68	4.26
1952	Pittsburgh	National	35	185	7	17	.292	186	96	86	75	84	4.18
1953	Pittsburgh	National	32	171	8	11	.421	193	103	93	66	57	4.89
1954	Pittsburgh	National	35	170	7	12	.368	204	106	96	73	58	5.08
1955	Pittsburgh	National	44	200	14	9	.609	178	80	63	98	52	*2.84

Year	Club	League	G.	IP	W.	L.	Pct.	H.	R.	ER.	SO.	BB.	ERA.
1956	Pittsburgh	National	49	*314	17	17	.500	310	137	121	166	85	3.47
1957	Pittsburgh	National	40	*277	14	18	.438	*273	121	104	143	68	3.38
1958	Pittsburgh	National	38	274	●22	14	.611	*299	*120	*112	135	61	3.68
1959	Pittsburgh	National	35	235	8	*19	.296	267	129	105	104	52	4.02
1960	Pittsburgh	National	38	276	18	12	.600	266	97	92	183	45	3.00
1961	Pittsburgh	National	41	236	14	●19	.424	271	119	101	108	45	3.85
1962	Pittsburgh	National	39	262	18	14	.563	280	99	89	144	53	3.06
1963	Pittsburgh	National	39	269	17	16	.515	236	87	70	144	44	2.34
1964	Pittsburgh	National	35	240	13	18	.419	253	98	89	128	50	3.34
1965	Pittsburgh (a)	National	34	222	8	12	.400	221	89	80	74	47	3.24
1966	New York (b)	American	12	45	1	4	.200	61	25	24	22	9	4.80
1966	New York	National	22	86	5	8	.385	101	52	42	30	16	4.40
	American League Totals		12	45	1	4	.200	61	25	24	22	9	4.80
	National League Totals		590	3567	196	226	.464	3711	1627	1414	1712	885	3.57
	Major League Totals		602	3612	197	230	.461	3772	1652	1438	1734	894	3.58

aTraded to New York Yankees for pitcher Pete Mikkelsen and cash, December 10, 1965.
bReleased to New York Mets, June 15, 1966.

WORLD SERIES RECORD

Year	Club	League	G.	IP	W.	L.	Pct.	H.	R.	ER.	SO.	BB.	ERA.
1960	Pittsburgh	National	3	6	0	2	.000	13	10	9	7	3	13.50

FRANK FRANCIS (FORDHAM FLASH) FRISCH

Born September 9, 1898, at New York, N. Y.
Died March 12, 1973, at Wilmington, Del.
Height, 5.10. Weight, 185.
Threw right and batted right and lefthanded.
Married Ada E. Lucy, November 4, 1922.

Holds major league record, most chances accepted, season, second base, 1,037, in 1927; most assists, season, second base, 641, 1927; led National League in stolen bases, 1921, 1927 and 1931. Led N. L. second baseman in double plays, 1927, 1928.
Manager, St. Louis Cardinals, July 24, 1933, to September 10, 1938; Pittsburgh, 1940 through 1946; Chicago Cubs, June 10, 1949, until July 21, 1951.
Named Most Valuable Player, National League, 1931.
Named to Hall of Fame, 1947.

Year	Club	League	Pos.	G.	AB.	R.	H.	2B.	3B.	HR.	RBI.	B.A.	PO.	A.	E.	F.A.
1919	New York	Nat.	2B-3B	54	190	21	43	3	2	2	22	.226	100	130	6	.975
1920	New York	Nat.	3B	110	440	57	123	10	10	4	77	.280	104	251	12	.967
1921	New York	Nat.	2B-3B	153	618	121	211	31	17	8	100	.341	226	418	33	.951
1922	New York	Nat.	2B-3B	132	514	101	168	16	13	5	51	.327	228	405	22	.966
1923	New York	Nat.	*2B-3B	151	641	116	*223	32	10	12	111	.348	327	493	22	*.974
1924	New York	Nat.	2B	145	603	●121	198	33	15	7	69	.328	*391	537	27	.972
1925	New York	Nat.	2B-3B-SS	120	502	89	166	26	6	11	48	.331	215	393	37	.943
1926	New York (a)	Nat.	2B	135	535	75	171	29	4	5	44	.314	261	471	19	.975
1927	St. Louis	Nat.	2B	153	617	112	208	31	11	10	78	.337	396	*641	22	*.979
1928	St. Louis	Nat.	2B	141	547	107	164	29	9	10	86	.300	383	474	21	●.976
1929	St. Louis	Nat.	2B-3B	138	527	93	176	40	12	5	74	.334	304	407	22	.970
1930	St. Louis	Nat.	2B-3B	133	540	121	187	46	9	10	114	.346	315	493	27	.968
1931	St. Louis	Nat.	2B	131	518	96	161	24	4	4	82	.311	290	424	19	.974
1932	St. Louis	Nat.	2B-3B	115	486	59	142	26	2	3	60	.292	252	309	14	.976
1933	St. Louis	Nat.	●2B-SS	147	585	74	177	32	6	4	66	.303	395	413	18	●.978
1934	St. Louis	Nat.	2B-3B	140	550	74	168	30	6	3	75	.305	325	388	20	.973
1935	St. Louis	Nat.	2B	103	354	52	104	16	2	1	55	.294	193	252	8	.982
1936	St. Louis	Nat.	2B-3B	93	303	40	83	10	0	1	26	.274	159	192	14	.962
1937	St. Louis	Nat.	2B	17	32	3	7	2	0	0	4	.219	12	14	0	1.000
	Major League Totals			2311	9112	1532	2880	466	138	105	1242	.316	4876	7105	363	.971

aTraded with pitcher Jimmy Ring to St. Louis Cardinals for second baseman Rogers Hornsby, December 20, 1926.

WORLD SERIES RECORD

Year	Club	League	Pos.	G.	AB.	R.	H.	2B.	3B.	HR.	RBI.	B.A.	PO.	A.	E.	F.A.
1921	New York	Nat.	3B	8	30	5	9	0	1	0	1	.300	13	24	2	.949
1922	New York	Nat.	2B	5	17	3	8	1	0	0	2	.471	10	20	1	.968
1923	New York	Nat.	3B	6	25	2	10	0	1	0	0	.400	17	18	1	.972
1924	New York	Nat.	2B-3B	7	30	1	10	4	1	0	0	.333	17	25	0	1.000
1928	St. Louis	Nat.	2B	4	13	1	3	0	0	0	1	.231	8	13	0	1.000
1930	St. Louis	Nat.	2B	6	24	0	5	2	0	0	0	.208	13	14	3	.900
1931	St. Louis	Nat.	2B	7	27	2	7	2	0	0	1	.259	23	19	0	1.000
1934	St. Louis	Nat.	2B	7	31	2	6	1	0	0	4	.194	16	26	2	.955
	World Series Totals			50	197	16	58	10	3	0	10	.294	117	159	9	.968

JAMES F. (PUD and GENTLE JAMES) GALVIN

Born December 25, 1856, at St. Louis, Mo.
Died March 7, 1902, at Pittsburgh, Pa.
Threw and batted righthanded.
Married Bridget Griffin, February 20, 1878,
at Immaculate Conception Church, St. Louis, Mo.

Pitched no-hit games against Worcester, August 20, 1880, and Detroit, August 4, 1884, his previous game against Detroit being a one-hitter. On an independent team pitching for St. Louis, Galvin hurled no-hitters against Philadelphia, July 4, 1876, and Detroit, August 17, 1876, and also for N. L. Buffalo in an exhibition against Philadelphia, October 11, 1881.
Named to Hall of Fame, 1965.

Year	Club	League	G.	IP.	W.	L.	Pct.	H.	R.	SO.	BB.	CG.	ShO.
1875	St. Louis	National Assn.	9	....	4	2	.667	....	....	....	....	....	....
1876	St. Louis Red Stockings						(Independent ball)						
1877	Allegheny	Int. Assn.	19	....	....	....	96	....	....	....	....	....	4
1878	Buffalo	Int. Assn.	38	....	....	....	....	....	....	....	....	....	....
1879	Buffalo	National	66	592	37	27	.578	573	299	129	28	65	6
1880	Buffalo	National	58	462	20	37	.351	534	276	123	32	46	5
1881	Buffalo	National	56	470	29	24	.547	531	248	127	47	48	5
1882	Buffalo	National	52	437	28	22	.560	472	256	153	40	48	3
1883	Buffalo	National	76	*656	46	29	.613	644	363	293	48	72	●5
1884	Buffalo	National	72	636	46	22	.676	525	254	373	55	71	★12
1885	Buffalo	National	33	287	13	19	.406	347	204	89	37	31	3
1885	Allegheny	American Assn.	11	89	3	7	.300	103	64	28	9	9	0
1886	Allegheny (a)	American Assn.	50	443	29	21	.580	461	228	77	85	49	2
1887	Pittsburgh	National	49	440	28	21	.571	571	259	81	70	47	3
1888	Pittsburgh	National	50	436	23	25	.479	437	191	113	58	49	6
1889	Pittsburgh	National	41	347	23	16	.590	397	226	69	79	38	4
1890	Pittsburgh	Players	26	216	12	13	.480	280	192	33	44	23	1
1891	Pittsburgh	National	33	260	14	13	.519	275	145	47	60	25	2
1892	Pitt. (b)-St. L.	National	24	188	10	13	.435	184	98	51	52	20	0
1894	Buffalo	Eastern	2	....	0	2	.000	....	....	....	....	....	......
	National League Totals		610	5211	317	268	.542	5490	2819	1648	606	560	54
	American Association Totals		61	532	32	28	.533	564	292	105	94	58	2
	Players League Totals		26	216	12	13	.480	280	192	33	44	23	1
	Major League Totals		697	5959	361	309	.539	6334	3303	1786	744	641	57

aPittsburgh withdrew from American Association and joined National League in 1887.
bReleased by Pittsburgh and signed with St. Louis, June, 1892.

HENRY LOUIS (LOU or IRON HORSE) GEHRIG

Born June 19, 1903, at New York, N. Y.
Died June 2, 1941, at Riverdale, N. Y.
Height, 6.01. Weight, 212.
Threw and batted lefthanded.
Married Eleanor Twitchell, September 29, 1933.

Established major league record by playing 2,130 consecutive games, June 1, 1925, to April 30, 1939, inclusive; set American League record for most runs batted in, season, 184, in 1931; tied record with four home runs (consecutive), game, June 3, 1932; holds major league record for most home runs with bases filled, lifetime, 23. Named Most Valuable Player, American League, 1927 and 1936, by the Baseball Writers Association of America; and in 1931, 1934 and 1936 by THE SPORTING NEWS.
Led A. L. first basemen in double plays, 1938.
Stole home 15 times in his career, with 102 stolen bases overall total.
Named to THE SPORTING NEWS All-Star Major League Teams, 1927-28-31-34-36-37.
Named to Hall of Fame, 1939.

Year	Club	League	Pos.	G.	AB.	R.	H.	2B.	3B.	HR.	RBI.	B.A.	PO.	A.	E.	F.A.
1921	Hartford*	East.	1B	12	46	5	12	1	2	0	....	.261	130	4	2	.985
1922—							(Not in Organized Ball)									
1923	New York	Amer.	1B-PH	13	26	6	11	4	1	9	.423	53	3	4	.933	
1923	Hartford	East.	1B	59	227	54	69	13	8	24	....	.304	623	23	6	.991
1924	New York	Amer.	PH-1-O	10	12	2	6	1	0	0	5	.500	10	1	0	1.000
1924	Hartford	East.	1B	134	504	111	186	40	13	37	....	.369	1391	66	●23	.984

— 104 —

Year	Club	League	Pos.	G.	AB.	R.	H.	2B.	3B.	HR.	RBI.	B.A.	PO.	A.	E.	F.A.
1925—New York		Amer.	1B-OF	126	437	73	129	23	10	20	68	.295	1126	53	13	.989
1926—New York		Amer.	1B	155	572	135	179	47	★20	16	107	.313	1565	73	15	.991
1927—New York		Amer.	1B	★155	584	149	218	★52	18	47	★175	.373	★1662	88	15	.992
1928—New York		Amer.	1B	154	562	139	210	●47	13	27	●142	.374	★1488	79	★18	.989
1929—New York		Amer.	1B	154	553	127	166	33	9	35	126	.300	1458	82	9	.994
1930—New York		Amer.	1B-OF	●154	581	143	220	42	17	41	★174	.379	1298	★89	15	★.989
1931—New York		Amer.	1B-OF	155	619	★163	★211	31	15	●46	★184	.341	1352	58	13	.991
1932—New York		Amer.	1B	★156	596	138	208	42	9	34	151	.349	1293	75	18	.987
1933—New York		Amer.	1B	152	593	★138	198	41	12	32	139	.334	1290	64	9	.993
1934—New York		Amer.	1B-SS	●154	579	128	210	40	6	★49	★165	★.363	1284	80	8	.994
1935—New York		Amer.	1B	149	535	★125	176	26	10	30	119	.329	1337	82	15	.990
1936—New York		Amer.	1B	●155	579	★167	205	37	7	★49	152	.354	1377	82	9	.994
1937—New York		Amer.	1B	★157	569	138	200	37	9	37	159	.351	1370	74	★16	.989
1938—New York		Amer.	1B	●157	576	115	170	32	6	29	114	.295	1483	100	14	.991
1939—New York		Amer.	1B	8	28	2	4	0	0	0	1	.143	64	4	2	.971
Major League Totals				2164	8001	1888	2721	535	162	493	1990	.340	19511	1087	193	.991

*Played under name of Lewis with Hartford in 1921.

WORLD SERIES RECORD

Year	Club	League	Pos.	G.	AB.	R.	H.	2B.	3B.	HR.	RBI.	B.A.	PO.	A.	E.	F.A.
1926—New York		Amer.	1B	7	23	1	8	2	0	0	3	.348	78	1	0	1.000
1927—New York		Amer.	1B	4	13	2	4	2	2	0	4	.308	41	3	0	1.000
1928—New York		Amer.	1B	4	11	5	6	1	0	4	9	.545	33	0	0	1.000
1932—New York		Amer.	1B	4	17	9	9	1	0	3	8	.529	37	2	1	.975
1936—New York		Amer.	1B	6	24	5	7	1	0	2	7	.292	45	2	0	1.000
1937—New York		Amer.	1B	5	17	4	5	1	1	1	3	.294	50	1	0	1.000
1938—New York		Amer.	1B	4	14	4	4	0	0	0	0	.286	25	3	0	1.000
World Series Totals				34	119	30	43	8	3	10	34	.361	309	12	1	.997

CHARLES LEONARD (MECHANICAL MAN) GEHRINGER

Born May 11, 1903, at Fowlerville, Mich.
Height, 5.11½. Weight, 185.
Threw right and batted lefthanded.
Married Josephine Stillen, June 18, 1949.

Named Most Valuable Player, American League, 1937. Named to THE SPORTING NEWS All-Star Major League Teams, 1933-34-37-38. Led American League in stolen bases, 1929.
Led A. L. second basemen in double plays, 1927, 1932 (tie), 1933, 1936.
Coach, Detroit Tigers, 1942. Vice-president and general manager, Detroit, August 10, 1951, to October, 1953; vice-president of club until 1959.
Named to Hall of Fame, 1949.

Year	Club	League	Pos.	G.	AB.	R.	H.	2B.	3B.	HR.	RBI.	B.A.	PO.	A.	E.	F.A.
1924—London		Mich.-Ont.	2B	112	401	60	117	19	18	3	60	.292	309	335	23	.966
1924—Detroit		Amer.	2B	5	13	2	6	0	0	0	1	.462	12	17	1	.966
1925—Toronto		Int.	2B	155	633	128	206	38	9	25	108	.325	403	471	31	★.966
1925—Detroit		Amer.	2B	8	18	3	3	0	0	0	0	.167	8	20	0	1.000
1926—Detroit		Amer.	2B	123	459	62	127	19	17	1	48	.277	255	323	16	.973
1927—Detroit		Amer.	2B	133	508	110	161	29	11	4	61	.317	304	★438	27	.965
1928—Detroit		Amer.	2B	154	603	108	193	29	16	6	74	.320	377	★507	35	.962
1929—Detroit		Amer.	2B	●155	634	★131	●215	●45	★19	13	106	.339	★404	501	23	★.975
1930—Detroit		Amer.	2B	●154	610	144	201	47	15	16	98	.330	399	501	19	●.979
1931—Detroit		Amer.	2B	101	383	67	119	24	5	4	53	.311	224	236	10	.979
1932—Detroit		Amer.	2B	152	618	112	184	44	11	19	107	.298	★396	495	30	.967
1933—Detroit		Amer.	2B	●155	628	103	204	42	6	12	105	.325	358	★542	17	.981
1934—Detroit		Amer.	2B	●154	601	★134	★214	50	7	11	127	.356	★516	17	●.981	
1935—Detroit		Amer.	2B	150	610	123	201	32	8	19	108	.330	349	★489	13	★.985
1936—Detroit		Amer.	2B	154	641	144	227	★60	12	15	116	.354	397	★524	★25	★.974
1937—Detroit		Amer.	2B	144	564	133	209	40	1	14	96	★.371	331	485	12	★.986
1938—Detroit		Amer.	2B	152	568	133	174	32	5	20	107	.306	★393	★455	21	.976
1939—Detroit		Amer.	2B	118	406	86	132	29	6	16	86	.325	245	312	13	★.977
1940—Detroit		Amer.	2B	139	515	108	161	33	3	10	81	.313	276	374	19	.972
1941—Detroit		Amer.	2B	127	436	65	96	19	4	3	46	.220	279	324	11	★.982
1942—Detroit		Amer.	2B	45	45	6	12	0	0	1	7	.267	7	9	0	1.000
Major League Totals				2323	8860	1774	2839	574	146	184	1427	.320	5369	7068	309	.976

WORLD SERIES RECORD

Year	Club	League	Pos.	G.	AB.	R.	H.	2B.	3B.	HR.	RBI.	B.A.	PO.	A.	E.	F.A.
1934—Detroit		Amer.	2B	7	29	5	11	1	0	1	2	.379	19	26	3	.938
1935—Detroit		Amer.	2B	6	24	4	9	3	0	0	4	.375	14	25	0	1.000
1940—Detroit		Amer.	2B	7	28	3	6	0	0	1	1	.214	18	20	0	1.000
World Series Totals				20	81	12	26	4	0	1	7	.321	51	71	3	.976

JOSHUA (JOSH) GIBSON

Born December 21, 1911, at Buena Vista, Ga.
Died, January 20, 1947, at Pittsburgh, Pa.
Height, 6.01. Weight, 215.
Batted and threw righthanded.

With Josh Gibson, the question is: Where do you start?
This man hit longer home runs in major league parks than the top sluggers of the A.L. or N.L. could. He hit a home run up the side of a mountain behind a small-town park. He was the man white ballplayers on barnstorming would call the most powerful hitter they ever saw.
Some say he was the best catcher, too, with a powerful arm and great sense in handling pitchers. But there are those who say he was weak on pop-ups and couldn't hit a side-arm curve. Some say he ran fast and others say he wasn't too fast.
But no one disagrees when Gibson and a bat are the subject. Tall, chesty, good legs, powerful and supple arms, big hands to wrap around a bat and the sweetest swing in the world. He had all these attributes. Add to this a great love for baseball, an insatiable urge to bat and a God-given talent to combine eye, mind and muscle in one powerful swing and you have Josh Gibson at the plate.
Walter Johnson, the respected fireballer of the Washington Senators and considered the top righthander in the white game by most, said it all:
"There is a catcher that any big league club would like to buy for $200,000. His name is Gibson. He can do everything. He hits the ball a mile, he catches so easily he might as well be in a rocking chair, throws like a bullet. Bill Dickey isn't as good a catcher. Too bad this Gibson is a colored fellow."
Long hits? Listen to Buck Leonard, Josh's partner as the "Thunder Twins," the name given to Gibson and Leonard, who batted 3-4 in the Homestead Grays' lineup:
"I saw so many long shots hit by Josh that they got sort of commonplace after a few years. But there were two that were so different I'll never forget them. In Welch, W. Va., Josh hit a ball out of the park in dead center field and it landed on the side of a mountain. We could see the boys looking for the ball on the mountain from our dugout inside the park.
"He also hit one in Monessen, Pa., that went so far the mayor of the town had it measured. The length was determined to be 575 feet from home plate and they used one of those long tape measures."
Then Leonard had second thoughts and recalled, "There was another one, in a major league park, when we played in the old Polo Grounds, the Giants' park. He connected with one that shot into the upper deck corner in deep left-center. The night watchman brought the ball back. He said, 'They never got any balls that high and far from the plate.' "
The way Gibson broke into professional ball was unique. In 1930, the first-string catcher of the Homestead Grays broke his finger. Gibson at the time was playing for the Pittsburgh Crawfords, then a semi-pro outfit, and was a spectator at this game. Judy Johnson, manager of the Grays, was told there was a catcher in the stands who could catch and hit, too. Johnson stopped the game so Gibson could change clothes.
The Grays visited St. Louis to play the Stars and took Gibson along without a contract. Now hear Cool Papa Bell tell it:
"We had lights in St. Louis and it was a treat for the visiting players to hit balls into the air and see if they could catch them. Gibson came out and tried to catch some pop flies. We were going to sign him because he hit the longest home run ever hit in the Stars' park, but the Grays heard about our plans and they signed Gibson quick."
Cum Posey, owner of the Grays and one of the Negro executives most respected by the white press, hovered over his new charge like a doting father. Johnson, also a member of the Hall of Fame for his third base wizardry, brought Josh along slowly. Gibson did fill-in catching as a late-inning sub, worked batting practice and caught pop flies until they came out of his ears.
But Josh's bat was so powerful the Grays had to make room for him in the lineup. He became the home-run threat the fans loved to watch. That he was no Biz Mackey as a catcher or a Bruce Petway, either, no one ever argued. Bell, both a teammate and opponent of Gibson at varied times in his career, rates Mackey among the greatest catchers, white or black, and gives Mackey credit for making a glove master out of Roy Campanella, who became a Hall of Famer, but by the regular voting procedure.
Bell rates Gibson as a "good" catcher, with a strong arm, and a good handler of pitchers, but said he was poor on pop-ups. Buck Leonard had an unwritten rule that he'd take every pop-up, fair or foul, he could reach. But it was wood, not leather, that put Gibson in the Hall of Fame in 1972.
Gibson was a fun-loving, warm person who liked people and who drew people to him, but he didn't have the charisma of a Satchel Paige, who electrified a town before he even arrived. Like all sluggers, fans "hoped" Josh would connect for them, but they just "knew" Satch would mow 'em down.
Josh had a nose for the dollar and skipped to the Crawfords for four seasons and then hopped back to the Grays in 1937. He played Mexican League and Caribbean ball to pick up extra pesos, but he always came back in time to lead the Grays' drive, which resulted in nine straight Negro National League pennants. The last one was in 1945.
In 1942, he suffered severe headaches and had blacked out a few times. Medical examinations determined the presence of a brain tumor, but Gibson was afraid of the results of such an operation and refused to submit to the knife. After banging up his knees as a result of so many plate collisions, when runners came high and hard with spikes flashing, he slowed down as a runner. From one of the team's fastest base runners, he became a lumbering giant his last few seasons. On the evening of January 20, 1947, Josh came home and predicted his own demise, telling his mother that he was going to have a stroke. One version, by Robert W. Peterson in "Only The Ball Was White," tells of a fun and laughing night as Gibson lay in his bed. He asked for all his trophies to be assembled at his bedside. Once this was accomplished, he laughed, sat up in bed, then fell over dead.
Thus was snuffed out a life, at 35, which hardly had fulfilled its role.

ROBERT GIBSON

Born November 9, 1935, at Omaha, Neb.
Height, 6.01. Weight, 193.
Threw and batted righthanded.

Established following major league records: lowest earned-run average, season, 300 or more innings (1.12), 1968; most seasons, 200 or more strikeouts (9), 1972; most consecutive games, starting pitcher, 303, August 31, 1965 through May 31, 1975.
Tied major league record for most strikeouts, inning (4), June 7, 1966 (fourth inning); struck out three batters on nine pitched balls, May 12, 1969 (seventh inning).
Established National League records for lowest earned-run average, season, 200 or more innings (1.12), 1968; most strikeouts, lifetime, righthanded pitcher (3,117), 1975, and most clubs shut out (won or tied), season, 8 in 1968 (all clubs except Los Angeles).
Tied National League record for most shutout games won or tied, one month (5), June, 1968.
Pitched 11-0 no-hit victory against Pittsburgh Pirates, August 14, 1971.
Established following World Series records: most consecutive games won, total Series (7); most consecutive complete games won, total Series (7); most consecutive complete games, total Series (8); most strikeouts, game (17), October 2, 1968; most strikeouts, Series (35), 1968; most games, 10 or more strikeouts, total Series (5).
Tied following World Series records: most games won, seven-game Series (3), 1967; most games won, no losses, seven-game Series (3), 1967; most complete games, seven-game Series (3), 1967 and 1968; most innings, one or more strikeouts, game (9), October 2, 1968.
Named National League Most Valuable Player, 1968.
Won National League Cy Young Memorial Award, 1968-70.
Named as pitcher on THE SPORTING NEWS National League All-Star Team, 1968-70.
Named THE SPORTING NEWS National League Pitcher of the Year, 1968-70.
Named pitcher on THE SPORTING NEWS National League All-Star fielding teams, 1965-66-67-68-69-70-71-72-73.
Named to Hall of Fame in 1981.

Year	Club	League	G.	IP.	W.	L.	Pct.	H.	R.	ER.	SO.	BB.	ERA.
1957	Omaha	Amer. Assoc.	10	42	2	1	.667	46	26	20	25	27	4.29
1957	Columbus	Sally	8	43	4	3	.571	36	26	18	24	34	3.77
1958	Omaha	Amer. Assoc.	13	87	3	4	.429	79	45	32	47	39	3.31
1958	Rochester	International	20	103	5	5	.500	88	35	28	75	54	2.45
1959	Omaha	Amer. Assoc.	24	135	9	9	.500	128	59	46	98	70	3.07
1959	St. Louis	National	13	76	3	5	.375	77	35	28	48	39	3.32
1960	St. Louis	National	27	87	3	6	.333	97	61	54	69	48	5.59
1960	Rochester	International	6	41	2	3	.400	33	15	13	36	17	2.85
1961	St. Louis	National	35	211	13	12	.520	186	91	76	166	★119	3.24
1962	St. Louis	National	32	234	15	13	.536	174	84	74	208	95	2.85
1963	St. Louis	National	36	255	18	9	.667	224	110	96	204	96	3.39
1964	St. Louis	National	40	287	19	12	.613	250	106	96	245	86	3.01
1965	St. Louis	National	38	299	20	12	.625	243	110	102	270	103	3.07
1966	St. Louis	National	35	280	21	12	.636	210	90	76	225	78	2.44
1967	St. Louis (a)	National	24	175	13	7	.650	151	62	58	147	40	2.98
1968	St. Louis	National	34	305	22	9	.710	198	49	38	★268	62	★1.12
1969	St. Louis	National	35	314	20	13	.606	251	84	76	269	95	2.18
1970	St. Louis	National	34	294	●23	7	.767	262	111	102	274	88	3.12
1971	St. Louis	National	31	246	16	13	.552	215	96	83	185	76	3.04
1972	St. Louis	National	34	278	19	11	.633	226	83	76	208	88	2.46
1973	St. Louis	National	25	195	12	10	.545	159	71	60	142	57	2.77
1974	St. Louis	National	33	240	11	13	.458	236	111	102	129	104	3.83
1975	St. Louis	National	22	109	3	10	.231	120	66	61	60	62	5.04
Major League Totals			528	3885	251	174	.591	3279	1420	1258	3117	1336	2.91

aSuffered broken leg when hit by line drive, July 15.

WORLD SERIES RECORD

Year	Club	League	G.	IP.	W.	L.	Pct.	H.	R.	ER.	SO.	BB.	ERA.
1964	St. Louis	National	3	27	2	1	.667	23	11	9	31	8	3.00
1967	St. Louis	National	3	27	3	0	1.000	14	3	3	26	5	1.00
1968	St. Louis	National	3	27	2	1	.667	18	5	5	35	4	1.67
World Series Totals			9	81	7	2	.778	55	19	17	92	17	1.89

DID YOU KNOW—
That from Bob Gibson you have to go back to Carl Hubbell to find an N.L. Meal Ticket to compare with the Cardinal fireballer?

WARREN CRANDALL GILES

Born May 28, 1896, at Tiskilwa, Ill.
Died February 7, 1979, at Cincinnati, O.

Smoke seemed to be a part of Warren Giles' life throughout his long sports career. He was a steadfast rules man, and ignited fires as a fearless football official on the college level. As a club boss at Cincinnati, he ranted and raved and sent sulphuric telegrams to league headquarters in defense of his men on the field and against the men in blue on the field. As a league head, he directed every fiber of his being against the American League, firing up the NL pride in the All-Star and World Series engagements. Once the AL had a seemingly insurmountable spread over the older league, but when Warren ignited the NL pride, the advantage swung so sharply toward his league that the American League now is far behind in All-Star Game victories. His fires made NL pride burn brightly ever since.

He also was baseball's barbecue king. tops in the smoky outdoor art.

But the most smoke was raised when he was president of the National League and ran its umpires with an iron hand. Where once he castigated these men while a club head, as league president he was their unbridled champion. He canned a few and eased out a few more, but all others knew that when they did their job on the field, Giles would back them up all the way. Warren made spot rulings on play situations as easily and as often as he had made successful decisions along the minor league trail that led to the majors.

Giles was a protege of Branch Rickey, plantation boss of the most widespread farm system in the game's history. Giles' talents in organization and fiscal control caught Rickey's eye. When the St. Louis Cardinals continued contract rights to Taylor Douthit only through Giles' honesty, the Mahatma was convinced his farm organization could use those solid talents in the front office.

Giles was born on May 28, 1896, in Tiskilwa, Ill., but played all his sports around Moline, where he was raised. A participant in all sports for Moline High School, Warren later transferred to Staunton (Va.) Military Academy, where he played football, basketball and baseball. Short finances caused his early dropout from Washington and Lee U. He enlisted in April, 1917, in officer's school and came out of WW I a 1st lieutenant.

After returning home, his advice to the committee that ran the local Moline club of the Three-I League earned him the club presidency. He saw in THE SPORTING NEWS that Earle Mack, son of the legendary Connie Mack, had been fired as a minor league manager and Giles promptly hired him. With help from the Athletics, he did well. Moving to the business manager's job at St. Joseph, Mo., he picked up help from Rickey in the form of a fine outfielder, Douthit. But a St. Louis clerical error gave the St. Joseph club title to Douthit. However, Giles brought the error to Rickey's attention and told him, "Douthit is still yours."

In thanks, Rickey gave Giles the job as chief executive of Syracuse, the Redbirds' top farm. Giles considered it the real start of his baseball climb. His minor days ended in 1936, when he was given the job of getting the Cincinnati Reds out of debt, which then was $700,000, a huge figure at that time.

Giles made the Reds a club to be reckoned with on the field, a financially solid franchise and an organization with a productive farm system. He was GM from 1937 through 1947, when he became president of the Reds. His club won quick pennants in both 1939 and 1940. A strong candidate for the commissioner's post, he and Ford Frick, head of the National League, were deadlocked in the voting blocs in 1951, but Giles graciously bowed out, giving Frick the opportunity to assume the game's top position. Giles was named almost immediately to succeed Frick as NL president. He served the league well from 1952 through 1969.

Though the league climbed to the top of efficiency, surpassing the American League in new parks, income, attendance and performance, during Giles' reign as prexy, seldom did a month or week or day go by that controversy was not the way of life. Umpires were at the root of most of the smoke, but Giles added his own with beanball rulings, spitter edicts and balk interpretations—none of which was a pleasant matter for the pitchers or the umpires. Don Drysdale and his "brushbacks" of Willie Mays, Orlando Cepeda, Ed Mathews, Johnny Logan, etc., made Giles' life a bed of nails. His attempts to make the umpires cops on the scene as to beanball intentions backfired on him (Drysdale again), but Giles was man enough to backtrack when he saw a need for adjustment.

This was Giles' strength, the executive ability to take charge when he felt it necessary and the integrity to bow to a change of his previous stand whenever the need arose. Giles' pride, his integrity and his courage to stand up and be counted were his hallmark. The strength of the National League merely reflects the personal strength of Warren Giles. He was named to the Hall of Fame in 1979.

JOHN WESLEY (PEBBLY JACK) GLASSCOCK

Born July 22, 1860, at Wheeling, W. Va.
Died February 24, 1947, at Wheeling, W. Va.
Height, 5.10. Weight, 170.
Threw and batted righthanded.
Married Rodah Rose Deubal.

Made six singles in six trips to the plate, September 27, 1890.

Manager, Indianapolis, National League, from August 22 to end of season, 1889; Fort Wayne, Inter-State League, 1899-1900; Sioux City, Western, 1900.

Year Club	League	Pos.	G.	AB.	R.	H.	2B.	3B.	HR.	SB.	B.A.	PO.	A.	E.	F.A.
1879—Cleveland	Nat.	2B-3B	80	325	31	68	13	3	0	.....	.209	233	238	43	.916
1880—Cleveland	Nat.	SS	76	291	36	72	9	4	0	.....	.247	107	249	43	.892
1881—Cleveland	Nat.	SS	84	330	49	86	8	6	0	.....	.261	*105	*274	37	*.911
1882—Cleveland	Nat.	SS	82	350	65	100	26	9	4	.....	.286	109	*307	44	.904
1883—Cleveland	Nat.	SS	93	372	64	108	17	3	0	.....	.290	126	304	38	*.919
1884—Cleveland	Nat.	SS	72	281	45	70	6	3	1	.....	.249	118	267	46	.893
1884—Cincinnati	Union	SS	34	155	42	60	11	5	2	.....	.387	.....	.....	.....	.....
1885—St. Louis	Nat.	SS	111	446	66	125	18	3	1	.....	.280	156	*397	50	*.917
1886—St. Louis	Nat.	SS	121	486	96	158	28	8	3	38	.325	156	*392	57	*.906
1887—Indianapolis	Nat.	SS	121	524	91	183	18	7	0	62	.349	211	*493	*73	.906
1888—Indianapolis	Nat.	SS	112	442	63	119	18	2	1	48	.269	201	334	59	*.901
1889—Indianapolis	Nat.	SS	134	582	128	*209	*39	2	6	57	.359	*246	*478	67	*.915
1890—New York	Nat.	SS	124	512	91	•172	33	10	1	54	*.336	275	421	69	.910
1891—New York	Nat.	SS	95	369	42	90	12	7	0	30	.244	158	278	50	.897
1892—St. Louis	Nat.	SS	139	564	84	154	28	3	3	27	.273	281	475	67	.919
1893—St. L.-Pitts.	Nat.	SS	114	457	81	159	12	11	2	39	.348	245	429	47	.935
1894—Pittsburgh	Nat.	SS	86	332	47	94	9	8	1	20	.283	195	300	35	.934
1895—Lou.-Wash.	Nat.	SS	43	178	29	52	4	1	1	5	.292	84	155	26	.902
1895—Wheeling	I.-St.						(No Records Available)								
1896—St. Paul	West.	1B	135	610	*172	*263	*38	3	5	.....	*.431	*1221	*93	19	.986
1897—St. Paul	West.	1B	132	563	137	195	32	7	4	56	.346	1235	59	30	.977
1898—St. Paul	West.	1B	120	475	70	125	15	3	0	27	.263	1115	54	36	.970
1899—Fort Wayne	I.-St.	1B	137	551	96	179	26	5	6	41	.325	1325	60	22	.984
1900—Fort Wayne	I.-St.	1B	13	46	5	12	0	0	0	2	.261	122	4	1	.992
1900—Sioux City	West.	1B	65	247	30	63	.....	.....	.....	17	.255	662	25	12	.983
National League Totals			1687	6841	1108	2019	298	90	24	380	.295	3006	5791	851	.912
Union Association Totals			34	155	42	60	11	5	2	.....	.387	.....	.....	.....	.....
Major League Totals			1721	6996	1150	2079	309	95	26	380	.297	.....	.....	.....	.....

VERNON (LEFTY) GOMEZ

Born November 26, 1910, at Rodeo, Calif.

Height, 6.02. Weight, 178.

Threw and batted lefthanded.

Married June O'Dea, musical comedy star, February 26, 1933.

Holds World Series record for most victories without defeat, total Series—6 (1932—1, 1936—2, 1937—2 and 1938—1), and most bases on balls received, inning—2 (sixth inning, October 6, 1937).
Led league in shutouts, 1937, and tied in 1934 and 1938; complete games, 1934.
Manager, Binghamton, Eastern League, June 26, 1946, to September 30, 1947.
Named to Hall of Fame, 1972.

Year Club	League	G.	IP.	W.	L.	Pct.	H.	R.	ER.	SO.	BB.	ERA.
1928—Salt Lake	Utah-Idaho	*39	194	12	*14	.462	206	109	75	*172	61	3.48
1929—San Francisco (a)	Pacific Coast	41	267	18	11	.621	277	140	102	159	108	*3.44
1930—New York	American	15	60	2	5	.286	66	41	37	22	28	5.55
1930—St. Paul	Amer. Assn.	17	86	8	4	.667	83	46	39	57	37	4.08
1931—New York	American	40	243	21	9	.700	206	88	72	150	85	2.63
1932—New York	American	31	265	24	7	.774	266	140	124	176	105	4.21
1933—New York	American	35	235	16	10	.615	218	108	83	*163	106	3.18
1934—New York	American	38	*282	*26	5	*.839	223	86	73	*158	96	*2.33
1935—New York	American	34	246	12	15	.444	223	104	87	138	86	3.18
1936—New York	American	31	189	13	7	.650	184	104	92	105	122	4.38
1937—New York	American	34	278	*21	11	.656	233	88	72	*194	93	*2.33
1938—New York	American	32	239	18	12	.600	239	110	89	129	93	3.35
1939—New York	American	26	198	12	8	.600	173	80	75	102	84	3.41
1940—New York	American	9	27	3	3	.500	37	20	20	14	18	6.67
1941—New York	American	23	156	15	5	*.750	151	76	65	76	103	3.75
1942—New York (b)	American	13	80	6	4	.600	67	42	38	41	65	4.28
1943—Washington	American	1	5	0	1	.000	4	4	3	0	5	5.40
1946—Binghamton	Eastern	1	3	0	0	.000	5	3	3	1	0	9.00
1947—Binghamton	Eastern	1	1	0	0	.000	1	0	0	0	1	0.00
Major League Totals		368	2503	189	102	.649	2290	1091	930	1468	1095	3.34

aSold to New York Yankees for $35,000.

bSold to Boston Braves, January 25, 1943; released by Braves, May 19, 1943, and signed with Washington, May 24, 1943.

WORLD SERIES RECORD

Year	Club	League	G.	IP.	W.	L.	Pct.	H.	R.	ER.	SO.	BB.	ERA.
1932—New York		American	1	9	1	0	1.000	9	2	1	8	1	1.00
1936—New York		American	2	15⅓	2	0	1.000	14	8	8	9	11	4.70
1937—New York		American	2	18	2	0	1.000	16	3	3	8	2	1.50
1938—New York		American	1	7	1	0	1.000	9	3	3	5	1	3.86
1939—New York		American	1	1	0	0	.000	3	1	1	1	0	9.00
World Series Totals			7	50⅓	6	0	1.000	51	17	16	31	15	2.86

WILLIAM DALE GOODMAN

Born March 22, 1926, at Concord, N.C.
Height, 5.11½. Weight, 160.
Threw right and batted lefthanded.
Married Margaret Evelyn Little, October 25, 1947.

Player-manager, Durham, Carolina League, 1963-64; scout, Houston Astros, 1965; released as scout to manage Houston farm at Cocoa, Florida State League, April 30, 1965; scout, Boston Red Sox, 1966; instructor, Kansas City farm organization, 1967; coach, Atlanta Braves, 1968-70; minor league instructor, Atlanta Braves system, 1976, coach at Richmond, International League.

Year	Club	League	Pos.	G.	AB.	R.	H.	2B.	3B.	HR.	RBI.	B.A.	PO.	A.	E.	F.A.
1944—Atlanta		South.	OF	137	*554	*122	186	22	•13	2	64	.336	258	19	12	.958
1945—Atlanta		South.					(In Military Service)									
1946—Atlanta		South.	OF-1B	86	332	65	129	14	3	1	46	.389	228	10	11	.956
1947—Boston		Amer.	OF	12	11	1	2	0	0	0	1	.182	2	0	0	1.000
1947—Louisville		A.A.	SS-OF	94	329	55	112	18	8	2	49	.340	155	130	15	.950
1948—Boston		Amer.	INF	127	445	65	138	27	2	1	66	.310	1101	73	9	.992
1949—Boston		Amer.	1B	122	443	54	132	23	3	0	56	.298	1069	79	9	*.992
1950—Boston		Amer.	INF-OF	110	424	91	150	25	3	4	68	*.354	344	89	9	.890
1951—Boston		Amer.	INF-OF	141	546	92	162	34	4	0	50	.297	742	170	14	.985
1952—Boston		Amer.	INF-OF	138	513	79	157	27	3	4	56	.306	475	367	20	.977
1953—Boston		Amer.	2B-1B	128	514	73	161	33	5	2	41	.313	418	319	21	.972
1954—Boston		Amer.	INF-OF	127	489	71	148	25	4	1	36	.303	393	248	14	.979
1955—Boston		Amer.	2-1-OF	149	599	100	176	31	2	0	52	.294	395	378	24	.970
1956—Boston		Amer.	2B	105	399	61	117	22	8	2	38	.293	215	266	•17	.966
1957—Bos.(a)-Balt.(b)		Amer.	INF-OF	91	279	37	82	11	3	3	33	.294	134	110	11	.957
1958—Chicago		Amer.	INF	116	425	41	127	15	5	0	40	.299	89	210	13	.958
1959—Chicago		Amer.	3B-2B	104	268	21	67	14	1	1	28	.250	61	140	10	.953
1960—Chicago		Amer.	3B-2B	30	77	5	18	4	0	0	6	.234	26	52	1	.987
1961—Chicago(c)		Amer.	INF	41	51	4	13	4	0	1	10	.255	11	14	1	.962
1962—Houston		Nat.	2B-3B	82	161	12	41	4	1	0	10	.255	67	9	8	.905
1963—Durham		Caro.	1B-2B	71	175	29	62	12	0	6	37	.354	258	55	6	.981
1964—Durham		Caro.	2B-3B	43	80	13	26	6	0	1	22	.325	36	63	4	.961
American League Totals				1541	5483	795	1650	295	43	19	581	.301	5475	2515	173	.979
National League Totals				82	161	12	41	4	1	0	10	.255	67	9	8	.905
Major League Totals				1623	5644	807	1691	299	44	19	591	.300	5542	2524	181	.978

aTraded to Baltimore Orioles for pitcher Mike Fornieles, June 14, 1957.
bTraded to Chicago White Sox with pitcher Ray Moore and first baseman-outfielder Tito Francona for pitchers Jack Harshman and Russ Heman, first baseman Jim Marshall and outfielder Larry Doby, December 3, 1957.
cUnconditionally released by Chicago White Sox, May 9, 1962; signed with Houston Colts, May 14, 1962.

WORLD SERIES RECORD

Year	Club	League	Pos.	G.	AB.	R.	H.	2B.	3B.	HR.	RBI.	B.A.	PO.	A.	E.	F.A.
1959—Chicago		Amer.	3B	5	13	1	3	0	0	0	1	.231	1	2	0	1.000

JOSEPH LOWELL GORDON

Born February 18, 1915, at Los Angeles, Calif.
Died April 14, 1978, at Sacramento, Calif.
Height, 5.10. Weight, 175.
Threw and batted righthanded.
Married Dorothy Crum, June 4, 1938.

Tied for American League record for most assists by second baseman in a game (11), September 15, 1939; hit for cycle, September 8, 1940.

Holds World Series record for most putouts by a second baseman in a five-game Series (20), 1943; also holds mark for most assists by second baseman in five-game Series (23), 1944; most chances accepted by second baseman in five-game Series (43), 1943; tied for record for most double plays by a second baseman in a five-game Series (5), 1941, and for most DPs in six-game Series (7), 1948; record holder for most double plays started by second sacker in five-game Series (4), 1941; tied Series mark for second basemen with eight assists in a game, October 5, 1943 and by having three assists in eighth inning, October 11, 1943; tied mark for most double plays started by a second baseman in a game (2), October 2, 1941.

Named as second baseman on THE SPORTING NEWS All-Star Major League Teams, 1939-40-41-42-47.

Named Most Valuable Player in American League, 1942.

Player-manager, Sacramento, Pacific Coast League, 1951-52; scout, Detroit Tigers, 1953-54-55; coach, Detroit, 1956 until June 28, 1956; manager, San Francisco, Pacific Coast League, July 9, 1956-57; manager, Cleveland Indians, June 27, 1958-59 until swapped managerial jobs with Jimmie Dykes of Detroit Tigers, August 3, 1960; manager, Kansas City Athletics, October 5, 1960 until released on June 6, 1961; scout, batting instructor, Los Angeles Angels, October 6, 1961 through 1968; manager, Kansas City Royals, 1969, American League; special assignment scout, Kansas City, 1970-71.

Year	Club	League	Pos.	G.	AB.	R.	H.	2B.	3B.	HR.	RBI.	B.A.	PO.	A.	E.	F.A.
1936	Oakland	P. C.	SS	143	533	73	160	33	4	6	56	.300	217	390	42	.935
1937	Newark	Int.	2B	151	635	109	178	33	6	26	89	.280	383	481	47	.948
1938	New York	Amer.	2B	127	458	83	117	24	7	25	97	.255	290	450	*31	.960
1939	New York	Amer.	2B	151	567	92	161	32	5	28	111	.284	*370	*461	28	.967
1940	New York	Amer.	2B	•155	616	112	173	32	10	30	103	.281	374	*505	23	.975
1941	New York	Amer.	*2B-1B	*156	588	104	162	26	7	24	87	.276	556	414	*36	.964
1942	New York	Amer.	2B	147	538	88	173	29	4	18	103	.322	354	442	*28	.966
1943	New York	Amer.	2B	152	543	82	135	28	5	17	69	.249	407	•490	•29	.969
1944-45	New York	Amer.					(In Military Service)									
1946	New York(a)	Amer.	2B	112	376	35	79	15	0	11	47	.210	281	346	17	.974
1947	Cleveland	Amer.	2B	155	562	89	153	27	6	29	93	.272	341	•466	18	.978
1948	Cleveland	Amer.	2B-SS	144	550	96	154	21	4	32	124	.280	332	439	23	.971
1949	Cleveland	Amer.	2B	148	541	74	136	18	3	20	84	.251	297	430	15	.980
1950	Cleveland	Amer.	2B	119	368	59	87	12	1	19	57	.236	224	283	16	.969
1951	Sacramento	P.C.	2B-SS	148	485	97	145	24	3	*43	*136	.299	349	390	24	.969
1952	Sacramento	P.C.	2B-1B	122	370	39	91	18	0	16	46	.246	301	285	17	.972
1953-54-55-56							(Did not play)									
1957	San Francisco	P.C.	2B	1	3	0	2	0	0	0	0	.667	1	1	0	1.000
Major League Totals				1566	5707	914	1530	264	52	253	975	.268	3826	4726	264	.970

aTraded to Cleveland Indians with infielder Eddie Bockman for pitcher Allie Reynolds, October 19, 1946.

WORLD SERIES RECORD

Year	Club	League	Pos.	G.	AB.	R.	H.	2B.	3B.	HR.	RBI.	B.A.	PO.	A.	E.	F.A.
1938	New York	Amer.	2B	4	15	3	6	2	0	1	6	.400	12	12	2	.923
1939	New York	Amer.	2B	4	14	1	2	0	0	0	1	.143	7	12	0	1.000
1941	New York	Amer.	2B	5	14	2	7	1	1	1	5	.500	6	19	1	.962
1942	New York	Amer.	2B	5	21	1	2	1	0	0	0	.095	11	12	0	1.000
1943	New York	Amer.	2B	5	17	2	4	1	0	1	2	.235	20	23	0	1.000
1948	Cleveland	Amer.	2B	6	22	3	4	0	0	1	2	.182	15	13	1	.966
World Series Totals				29	103	12	25	5	1	4	16	.243	71	91	4	.976

SIDNEY GORDON

Born August 13, 1918, at Brooklyn, N. Y.
Died June 17, 1975, at New York City, N. Y.
Height, 5.10. Weight, 180.
Threw and batted righthanded.
Married Mary Goldberg, August 31, 1940.

Tied major league record by hitting two home runs in one inning, second inning of second game, July 31, 1949.

Year	Club	League	Pos.	G.	AB.	R.	H.	2B.	3B.	HR.	RBI.	B.A.	PO.	A.	E.	F.A.
1938	Milford	E. Shore	3B	112	412	104	*145	18	*9	25	83	*.352	*136	*210	29	.923
1939	Clinton	I.I.I.	3B-2B	121	459	89	150	14	*24	8	83	.327	193	234	28	.938
1939	Jersey City	Int.	3B	3	9	1	2	0	0	0	0	.222	3	2	0	1.000
1940	Jersey City	Int.	3B	136	501	76	131	21	7	5	39	.261	143	255	27	.936
1941	Jersey City	Int.	INF-OF	150	523	69	159	15	6	7	76	.304	256	339	31	.950
1941	New York	Nat.	OF	9	31	4	8	1	1	0	4	.258	18	0	0	1.000
1942	Jersey City	Int.	O-IN-P	145	517	68	155	17	5	10	85	.300	293	62	9	.975
1942	New York	Nat.	3B	6	19	4	6	0	1	0	2	.316	9	12	0	.913
1943	New York	Nat.	INF-OF	131	474	50	119	9	11	9	63	.251	551	148	17	.976
1944-45	New York	Nat.					(In Military Service)									
1946	New York	Nat.	*OF-3B	135	450	64	132	15	4	5	45	.293	215	62	5	*.982
1947	New York	Nat.	OF-3B	130	437	57	119	19	8	13	57	.272	254	13	12	.957
1948	New York	Nat.	*3B-OF	142	521	100	156	26	4	30	107	.299	166	223	19	*.953

Year	Club	League	Pos.	G.	AB.	R.	H.	2B.	3B.	HR.	RBI.	B.A.	PO.	A.	E.	F.A.
1949—New York(a)		Nat.	3-O-1B	141	489	87	139	26	2	26	90	.284	151	206	14	.962
1950—Boston		Nat.	OF-3B	134	481	78	146	33	4	27	103	.304	283	32	4	.987
1951—Boston		Nat.	OF-3B	150	550	96	158	28	1	29	109	.287	300	75	9	.977
1952—Boston		Nat.	*OF-3B	144	522	69	151	22	2	25	75	.289	266	13	1	*.996
1953—Milwaukee(b)		Nat.	OF	140	464	67	127	22	4	19	75	.274	245	10	6	.977
1954—Pittsburgh		Nat.	OF-3B	131	363	38	111	12	0	12	49	.306	149	80	11	.954
1955—Pitt.(c)-N. York		Nat.	3B-OF	82	191	21	43	7	1	7	26	.225	69	82	1	.993
1956—Miami		Int.	3B-PH	55	140	23	33	8	0	4	23	.236	28	69	8	.924
Major League Totals				1475	4992	735	1415	220	43	202	805	.283	2676	956	101	.973

aTraded to Boston Braves with pitcher Sam Webb, shortstop John (Buddy) Kerr and outfielder Willard Marshall for second baseman Eddie Stanky and shortstop Alvin Dark, December 14, 1949.

bTraded to Pittsburgh Pirates with pitcher Max Surkont, plus outfielder Sam Jethroe from the Braves' farm at Toledo, American Association, pitchers Larry Lassalle and Curtis Raydon of Jacksonville, Sally League, and pitcher Fred Waters of Lincoln, Western League, and estimated $75,000 for third baseman Danny O'Connell, December 26, 1953.

cSold to New York Giants, May 23, 1955.

GEORGE F. (PIANO LEGS) GORE

Born May 3, 1857, at Saccarappa, Me.
Died September 16, 1933, at Utica, N. Y.
Height, 6.00. Weight, 180.
Threw right and batted lefthanded.

Made five consecutive extra-base hits in a game (2 triples and 3 doubles), July 9, 1885; made six hits in six trips to the plate, May 7, 1880; stole seven bases in a game, June 25, 1881.

Year	Club	League	Pos.	G.	AB.	R.	H.	2B.	3B.	HR.	SB.	B.A.	PO.	A.	E.	F.A.
1878—New Bedford				(Independent club—no record available)												
1879—Chicago		Nat.	OF	60	253	43	68	17	5	0	....	.269	91	9	15	.870
1880—Chicago		Nat.	OF-1B	75	312	69	114	21	2	2	....	*.365	119	16	20	.871
1881—Chicago		Nat.	O-1-SS	73	309	*86	92	20	8	1	....	.298	146	21	24	.874
1882—Chicago		Nat.	OF	84	367	*99	117	14	7	3	....	.319	153	23	33	.842
1883—Chicago		Nat.	OF	91	392	105	131	27	9	1	....	.334	196	27	34	.868
1884—Chicago		Nat.	OF	101	417	103	132	18	5	5	....	.317	184	25	32	.867
1885—Chicago		Nat.	OF	109	441	115	138	19	12	4	....	.313	204	17	29	.884
1886—Chicago		Nat.	OF	118	444	150	135	19	13	6	23	.304	184	20	29	.876
1887—New York		Nat.	OF	111	500	95	174	16	5	1	39	.348	221	20	30	.889
1888—New York		Nat.	OF	64	254	37	56	5	4	2	11	.220	88	4	18	.836
1889—New York		Nat.	OF	119	488	131	149	21	7	7	36	.305	239	21	*41	.864
1890—New York		Play.	OF	93	400	131	134	25	9	9	30	.335	150	12	20	.890
1891—New York		Nat.	OF	130	526	104	150	24	7	2	28	.285	231	16	28	.898
1892—N.Y.-St.L.		Nat.	OF	73	263	56	63	11	3	0	25	.240	136	9	14	.912
1893—				(Out of Organized Ball)												
1894—Binghamton		East.	OF	48	191	46	61	17	1	1	5	.319	99	10	5	.959
Players League Totals				93	400	131	134	25	9	9	30	.335	150	12	20	.890
National League Totals				1208	4966	1193	1519	232	87	34	162	.306	2192	228	347	.868
Major League Totals				1301	5366	1324	1653	257	96	43	192	.308	2342	240	367	.876

WORLD SERIES RECORD

Year	Club	League	Pos.	G.	AB.	R.	H.	2B.	3B.	HR.	SB.	B.A.	PO.	A.	E.	F.A.
1882—Chicago		Nat.	OF	2	8	1	1	0	0	0	0	.125	1	0	0	1.000
1885—Chicago		Nat.	OF	1	3	1	0	0	0	0	0	.000	0	1	1	.500
1886—Chicago		Nat.	OF	6	23	4	4	0	0	0	0	.174	6	1	3	.700
1888—New York		Nat.	OF	3	11	5	5	1	0	0	2	.455	3	2	2	.714
1889—New York		Nat.	OF	5	21	5	7	3	0	0	2	.333	6	1	2	.778
World Series Totals				17	66	16	17	4	0	0	4	.258	16	5	8	.724

LEON ALLEN (GOOSE) GOSLIN

Born October 16, 1900, at Salem, N. J.
Died May 15, 1971, at Bridgeton, N. J.
Height, 5.11. Weight, 180.
Threw right and batted lefthanded.
Married Marian Wallace, December 10, 1940.

Hit three home runs in a game three times: June 19, 1925, August 19, 1930, and June 23, 1932.
Led A. L. outfielders in double plays, 1926, 1933 (tie).
Set World Series record, most consecutive hits, one Series, 6, Washington AL, October 6 (1 hit), October 7 (4) and October 8 (1) in 1924 (tied by Thurman Munson, 1976).
Manager, Trenton, Inter-State League, 1939-41.
Named to Hall of Fame, 1968.

Year	Club	League	Pos.	G.	AB.	R.	H.	2B.	3B.	HR.	RBI.	B.A.	PO.	A.	E.	F.A.
1920	Columbia	Sally	OF-P	90	319	52	101	18	8	4	65	.317	134	32	9	.949
1921	Columbia	Sally	OF	142	549	*124	*214	38	13	16	*131	*.390	321	20	15	.958
1921	Washington	Amer.	OF	14	50	8	13	1	1	1	6	.260	30	1	0	1.000
1922	Washington	Amer.	OF	101	358	44	116	19	7	3	53	.324	197	8	15	.932
1923	Washington	Amer.	OF	150	600	86	180	29	•18	9	99	.300	310	26	15	.957
1924	Washington	Amer.	OF	154	579	100	199	30	17	12	*129	.344	369	12	*16	.960
1925	Washington	Amer.	OF	150	601	116	201	34	*20	18	113	.334	385	•24	12	.971
1926	Washington	Amer.	OF	147	568	105	201	26	15	17	108	.354	373	•25	•15	.964
1927	Washington	Amer.	OF	148	581	96	194	37	15	13	120	.334	356	8	17	.955
1928	Washington	Amer.	OF	135	456	80	173	36	10	17	102	*.379	266	14	11	.962
1929	Washington	Amer.	OF	145	553	82	159	28	7	18	91	.288	299	7	10	.968
1930	Wash.(a)-St.L.	Amer.	OF	148	584	115	180	36	12	37	138	.308	309	15	12	.964
1931	St. Louis	Amer.	OF	151	591	114	194	42	10	24	105	.328	319	14	14	.960
1932	St. Louis(b)	Amer.	OF	150	572	88	171	28	9	17	104	.299	330	*16	18	.951
1933	Washington(c)	Amer.	OF	132	549	97	163	35	10	10	64	.297	261	17	10	.965
1934	Detroit	Amer.	OF	151	614	106	187	38	7	13	100	.305	290	15	15	.953
1935	Detroit	Amer.	OF	147	590	88	172	34	6	9	109	.292	326	6	12	.965
1936	Detroit	Amer.	OF	147	572	122	180	33	8	24	125	.315	266	11	13	.955
1937	Detroit(d)	Amer.	OF	79	181	30	43	11	1	4	35	.238	81	2	4	.954
1938	Washington	Amer.	OF	38	57	6	9	3	0	2	8	.158	25	0	0	1.000
1939	Trenton	Int.-St.	OF	99	349	65	113	12	5	3	58	.324	120	9	2	.985
1940	Trenton	Int.-St.	OF	49	128	24	32	4	2	1	16	.250	50	0	2	.962
Major League Totals				2287	8656	1483	2735	500	173	248	1609	.316	4792	221	209	.960

aTraded to St. Louis Browns for pitcher Alvin Crowder and outfielder Henry Manush, June 14, 1930.
bTraded to Washington Senators with pitcher Walter Stewart and outfielder Fred Schulte for pitcher Lloyd Brown, outfielders Carl Reynolds and Sam West and $20,000, December 14, 1932.
cTraded to Detroit Tigers for outfielder Jonathan Stone, December 14, 1933.
dUnconditionally released by Detroit Tigers, May, 1938; subsequently signed with Washington Senators.

WORLD SERIES RECORD

Year	Club	League	Pos.	G.	AB.	R.	H.	2B.	3B.	HR.	RBI.	B.A.	PO.	A.	E.	F.A.
1924	Washington	Amer.	OF	7	32	4	11	1	0	3	7	.344	15	1	0	1.000
1925	Washington	Amer.	OF	7	26	6	8	1	0	3	6	.308	15	0	0	1.000
1933	Washington	Amer.	OF	5	20	2	5	1	0	1	1	.250	8	1	0	1.000
1934	Detroit	Amer.	OF	7	29	2	7	1	0	0	2	.241	20	1	2	.913
1935	Detroit	Amer.	OF	6	22	2	6	1	0	0	3	.273	12	0	1	.923
World Series Totals				32	129	16	37	5	0	7	19	.287	70	3	3	.961

GEORGE FARLEY (BOOTS) GRANTHAM

Born May 20, 1900, at Galena, Kan.
Died March 16, 1954, at Kingman, Ariz.
Height, 5.10. Weight, 155.
Threw right and batted lefthanded.
Married Ruby Gates, April 26, 1926.

Batted .300 or more for eight successive seasons in National League, 1924-1931.

Year	Club	League	Pos.	G.	AB.	R.	H.	2B.	3B.	HR.	RBI.	B.A.	PO.	A.	E.	F.A.
1920	Tacoma	P. Int.	3B	58	169	19	38	9	1	6	.....	.225	63	46	10	.916
1921	Tacoma	P. Int.	3B-2B	46	153	28	55	10	6	4	.....	.359	77	78	12	.928
1921	Portland	P. C.	2B-3B	77	269	32	82	15	2	1	.....	.305	120	217	40	.894
1922	Omaha	West.	3B	157	601	160	216	47	13	22	.....	.359	*162	281	*57	.886
1922	Chicago	Nat.	3B	7	23	3	4	1	0	3	.174	5	4	0	1.000
1923	Chicago	Nat.	2B	152	570	81	160	36	8	8	70	.281	*374	*518	*55	.942
1924	Chicago(a)	Nat.	2B	127	469	85	148	19	6	12	60	.316	273	426	*44	.941
1925	Pittsburgh	Nat.	1B	114	359	74	117	24	6	8	52	.326	925	44	11	.989
1926	Pittsburgh	Nat.	1B	141	449	66	143	27	13	8	70	.318	1203	66	13	.990
1927	Pittsburgh	Nat.	1B-2B	151	531	96	162	33	11	8	66	.305	375	35	.963
1928	Pittsburgh	Nat.	1B	124	440	93	142	24	9	10	85	.323	1117	71	17	.986
1929	Pittsburgh	Nat.	1-2-OF	110	349	85	107	23	10	12	90	.307	301	244	17	.970
1930	Pittsburgh	Nat.	2B	146	552	120	179	34	14	18	99	.324	324	488	*36	.958
1931	Pittsburgh(b)	Nat.	1B-2B	127	465	91	142	26	6	10	46	.305	856	169	35	.967
1932	Cincinnati	Nat.	1B-2B	126	493	81	144	29	6	6	39	.292	373	352	28	.963
1933	Cincinnati(c)	Nat.	1B-2B	87	260	32	53	14	3	4	28	.204	274	196	19	.961
1934	New York	Nat.	1B-3B	32	29	5	7	2	0	1	4	.241	17	2	0	1.000

Year	Club	League	Pos.	G.	AB.	R.	H.	2B.	3B.	HR.	RBI.	B.A.	PO.	A.	E.	F.A.
1934–Nashville		Sou. Assn.	1B	46	162	29	52	8	2	4	29	.321	427	17	5	.989
1935–Seattle		P. C.	1B	47	168	30	48	9	1	1	13	.286	359	19	8	.979
Major League Totals				1444	4989	912	1508	292	93	105	712	.302	6568	2955	310	.968

aTraded to Pittsburgh Pirates with pitcher Vic Aldridge and first baseman Al Niehaus for pitcher Wilbur Cooper, first baseman Charlie Grimm and infielder Walter Maranville, October 27, 1924.

bSold to Cincinnati Reds, February 4, 1932.

cTraded to New York Giants for pitcher Glenn Spencer, November 15, 1933.

WORLD SERIES RECORD

Year	Club	League	Pos.	G.	AB.	R.	H.	2B.	3B.	HR.	RBI.	B.A.	PO.	A.	E.	F.A.
1925–Pittsburgh		Nat.	1B-PH	5	15	0	2	0	0	0	0	.133	42	6	0	1.000
1927–Pittsburgh		Nat.	2B	3	11	0	4	1	0	0	0	.364	6	7	1	.929
World Series Totals				8	26	0	6	1	0	0	0	.231	48	13	1	.984

HENRY BENJAMIN (HANK) GREENBERG

Born January 1, 1911, at New York, N.Y.

Height, 6.03½. Weight, 215.

Threw and batted righthanded.

Married Caral Gimbel, February 18, 1946.

Tied major and American League record for most home runs (58) by righthanded batsman, season, 1938. Set major league record for most times two or more home runs, game, season—11 (1938—May 25, June 24, July 9-26-27-29, August 10, September 11-17-23-27).

World Series record—Co-holder, most hits in game (4), October 6, 1934.

Named by Baseball Writers' Association of America as first baseman for THE SPORTING NEWS All-Star Major League Team, 1935, and left fielder, 1940. Selected as Most Valuable Player, American League, 1935 and 1940.

General manager, Cleveland Indians, 1948-57; vice-president, Chicago White Sox, 1959-63.

Named to Hall of Fame, 1956.

Year	Club	League	Pos.	G.	AB.	R.	H.	2B.	3B.	HR.	RBI.	B.A.	PO.	A.	E.	F.A.
1930–Hartford		East.	1B	17	56	10	12	1	2	2	6	.214	157	13	2	.988
1930–Raleigh		Pied.	1B	122	452	88	142	26	14	19	93	.314	1052	*78	23	.980
1930–Detroit		Amer.	1B	1	1	0	0	0	0	0	0	.000	0	0	0	.000
1931–Evansville		I.I.I.	1B	•126	487	88	155	*41	10	15	85	.318	*1248	*84	*25	.982
1931–Beaumont		Texas	PH	3	2	0	0	0	0	0	0	.000	0	0	0	.000
1932–Beaumont		Texas	1B	154	600	*123	174	31	11	*39	131	.290	1437	103	17	.989
1933–Detroit		Amer.	1B	117	449	59	135	33	3	12	87	.301	1133	63	14	.988
1934–Detroit		Amer.	1B	153	593	118	201	*63	7	26	139	.339	1454	84	16	.990
1935–Detroit		Amer.	1B	152	619	121	203	46	16	*36	*170	.328	1437	*99	13	.992
1936–Detroit		Amer.	1B	12	46	10	16	6	2	1	16	.348	119	9	1	.992
1937–Detroit		Amer.	1B	154	594	137	200	49	14	40	*183	.337	*1477	102	13	.992
1938–Detroit		Amer.	1B	155	556	*144	175	23	4	*58	146	.315	*1484	*120	14	.991
1939–Detroit		Amer.	1B	138	500	112	156	42	7	33	112	.312	1205	75	9	•.993
1940–Detroit		Amer.	OF	148	573	129	195	*50	8	*41	*150	.340	298	14	*15	.954
1941–Detroit		Amer.	OF	19	67	12	18	5	1	2	12	.269	32	0	3	.914
1942-43-44–Detroit		Amer.					(In Military Service)									
1945–Detroit		Amer.	OF	78	270	47	84	20	2	13	60	.311	129	3	0	1.000
1946–Detroit (a)		Amer.	1B	142	523	91	145	29	5	*44	*127	.277	1272	93	•15	.989
1947–Pittsburgh (b)		Nat.	1B	125	402	71	100	13	2	25	74	.249	983	79	9	.992
American League Totals				1269	4791	980	1528	366	69	306	1202	.319	10040	662	113	.990
National League Totals				125	402	71	100	13	2	25	74	.249	983	79	9	.992
Major League Totals				1394	5193	1051	1628	379	71	331	1276	.313	11023	741	122	.990

aSold to Pittsburgh Pirates for undisclosed sum, January 8, 1947.

bReleased unconditionally by Pittsburgh Pirates, September 29, 1947, and joined Cleveland Indians' front office, March 27, 1948.

WORLD SERIES RECORD

Year	Club	League	Pos.	G.	AB.	R.	H.	2B.	3B.	HR.	RBI.	B.A.	PO.	A.	E.	F.A.
1934–Detroit		Amer.	1B	7	28	4	9	2	1	1	7	.321	60	4	1	.985
1935–Detroit		Amer.	1B	2	6	1	1	0	0	1	2	.167	17	2	3	.864
1940–Detroit		Amer.	OF	7	28	5	10	2	1	1	6	.357	12	0	0	1.000
1945–Detroit		Amer.	OF	7	23	7	7	3	0	2	7	.304	8	1	0	1.000
World Series Totals				23	85	17	27	7	2	5	22	.318	97	7	4	.963

DID YOU KNOW—

That Hank Greenberg became first N.L. player to earn $100,000 contract in 1947?

MICHAEL JOSEPH GRIFFIN

Born March 20, 1865, at Utica, N.Y.
Died April 10, 1908, at Utica, N.Y.
Height, 5.08. Weight, 173.
Threw right and batted lefthanded.
Married Margaret Barney, June 20, 1900.

Finished 1898 season as Brooklyn manager, succeeding Bill Barnie.

Year	Club	League	Pos.	G.	AB.	R.	H.	2B.	3B.	HR.	SB.	B.A.	PO.	A.	E.	F.A.
1885	Utica	N.Y. St.	OF	75	287	52	80	...	...	...	...	.279	114	18	16	.892
1886	Utica	Int.	OF	96	406	86	116	...	...	...	...	.286	196	7	17	.923
1887	Baltimore	A.A.	OF	136	581	142	214	32	12	4	98	.368	256	14	20	.931
1888	Baltimore	A.A.	OF	137	540	94	141	24	9	0	53	.261	282	28	19	.942
1889	Baltimore	A.A.	OF-SS	137	533	152	149	24	13	5	43	.280	279	86	45	.890
1890	Philadelphia	Play.	OF	115	492	127	143	28	5	6	30	.291	281	41	12	.961
1891	Brooklyn	Nat.	OF	133	517	106	141	*36	9	3	75	.273	243	25	16	.944
1892	Brooklyn	Nat.	OF	129	459	103	127	18	11	2	64	.277	260	26	9	*.969
1893	Brooklyn	Nat.	OF	93	348	84	106	22	8	6	47	.305	220	24	10	.961
1894	Brooklyn	Nat.	OF	106	405	123	148	29	5	5	48	.365	298	13	12	*.963
1895	Brooklyn	Nat.	OF	132	522	139	175	35	8	4	27	.335	*361	20	11	*.972
1896	Brooklyn	Nat.	OF	122	492	102	155	28	10	4	27	.315	315	7	13	.961
1897	Brooklyn	Nat.	OF	134	530	137	170	23	11	1	23	.321	•352	13	17	.955
1898	Brooklyn (a)	Nat.	OF	134	544	92	161	17	5	1	14	.296	319	19	7	.980
American Association Totals				410	1654	388	504	80	34	9	194	.312	817	128	84	.918
National League Totals				983	3817	886	1183	208	67	26	325	.310	2368	147	95	.964
Players League Totals				115	492	127	143	28	5	6	30	.291	281	41	12	.961
Major League Totals				1508	5963	1401	1830	316	106	41	549	.307	3466	316	191	.952

aSold to St. Louis, National League, after season, but refused to report and retired instead.

CLARK CALVIN (OLD FOX) GRIFFITH

Born November 20, 1869, at Nevada, Mo.
Died October 27, 1955, at Washington, D. C.
Height, 5.08. Weight, 175.
Threw and batted righthanded.
Married Addie Ann Robertson, December 12, 1900.

Manager, Chicago White Sox, 1901-02; New York Highlanders, 1903-04-05-06-07-08; Cincinnati, 1909-10-11; Washington Americans, 1912-13-14-15-16-17-18-19-20; president, 1920 until time of death.
Named to Hall of Fame, 1946.

Year	Club	League	G.	IP.	W.	L.	Pct.	ShO.	H.	SO.	BB.
1888	Bloomington	Cent.-Int. St.	14	....	10	4	.714	....	90	123	16
1888	Milwaukee	Western	23	....	12	10	.545	....	176	130	50
1889	Milwaukee	Western	31	....	18	13	.581	....	281	159	91
1890	Milwaukee	Western	34	....	27	7	.794	....	268	169	92
1891	St. Louis-Boston	Amer. Assn.	24	225	17	7	.708	0	219	65	69
1892	Tacoma	P. N. W.	24	....	13	7	.650	....	153	114	55
1893	Oakland	Pacific Coast	48	....	30	18	.625	....	455	151	119
1893	Chicago	National	3	22	1	1	.500	0	....	....	....
1894	Chicago	National	32	274	21	11	.656	0	302	67	79
1895	Chicago	National	39	352	25	13	.658	0	423	83	88
1896	Chicago	National	35	319	22	13	.629	0	348	68	69
1897	Chicago	National	46	344	21	19	.525	1	414	105	86
1898	Chicago	National	37	316	26	10	.722	4	261	99	63
1899	Chicago	National	39	319	22	13	.629	0	312	71	67
1900	Chicago(a)	National	27	249	14	13	.519	•4	215	61	51
1901	Chicago	American	32	257	24	7	*.774	•5	209	54	34
1902	Chicago(b)	American	25	216	15	9	.625	3	239	46	37
1903	New York	American	24	214	14	10	.583	2	194	61	35
1904	New York	American	12	92	7	5	.583	1	86	30	17
1905	New York	American	16	100	9	6	.600	2	89	48	16
1906	New York	American	17	61	2	2	.500	0	31	16	14
1907	New York	American	4	6	0	0	.000	-0	17	5	4
1909	Cincinnati	National	1	1	0	1	.000	0	11	3	2

Year	Club	League	G.	IP.	W.	L.	Pct.	ShO.	H.	SO.	BB.
1910–Cincinnati		National			(One game as pinch-hitter)						
1912–Washington		American	1	1	0	0	.000	0	1	0	0
1913–Washington		American	1	1	0	0	.000	0	0	....	....
1914–Washington		American	1	1	0	0	.000	0	1	1	0
American League Totals			133	949	71	39	.645	13	867	261	157
National League Totals			259	2196	152	94	.618	9	2286	636	574
American Association Totals			24	225	17	7	.708	0	219	65	69
Major League Totals			416	3370	240	140	.632	22	3372	962	800

aJumped to American League to manage Chicago White Sox, 1901.
bTransferred to New York at request of League President Ban Johnson, 1902.

BURLEIGH ARLAND (OLD STUBBLEBEARD) GRIMES

Born August 18, 1893, at Emerald, Wis.
Height, 5.10. Weight, 195.
Threw and batted righthanded.
Married Zerita Brickell, September 30, 1966.

Won 13 straight games for the New York Giants in 1927—and lost 13 consecutive decisions with the Pittsburgh Pirates, 1917.
Manager, Bloomington, Three–I League, 1935; Louisville, American Association, 1936; Brooklyn Dodgers, 1937-38; Montreal, International League, 1939; Grand Rapids, Michigan State League, 1940 until suspended on July 7, 1940, for one year; Toronto, International League, 1942-43-44; Rochester, International League, 1945-46; Toronto, International League, 1947; scout, New York Yankees, 1947-52; manager, Toronto, 1952-53; coach, Kansas City Athletics, 1955; scout, Kansas City, 1956-57; scout, Baltimore Orioles, 1960 through 1971.
Named to Hall of Fame, 1964.

Year	Club	League	G.	IP.	W.	L.	Pct.	H.	R.	ER.	SO.	BB.	ERA.
1912–Eau Claire		Minn.-Wis.			(League disbanded July 1)								
1913–Ottumwa		Cent. Assn.	9	70	6	2	.750	46	22	....	67	22	....
1913–Chattanooga		Southern	17	112	6	7	.462	110	58	....	33	50	....
1914–Chat.-Birm.		Southern	4	10	0	2	.000	14	7	....	5	11	....
1914–Richmond		Virginia	39	296	23	13	.639	260	113	....	190	77	....
1915–Birmingham		Southern	41	296	17	13	.567	227	96	....	158	101	....
1916–Birmingham		Southern	40	276	20	11	.645	214	80	....	119	86	....
1916–Pittsburgh		National	6	46	2	3	.400	40	19	12	20	10	2.35
1917–Pittsburgh(a)		National	37	194	3	16	.158	186	101	76	72	70	3.53
1918–Brooklyn		National	*40	270	19	9	.679	210	94	64	113	76	2.13
1919–Brooklyn		National	25	181	10	11	.476	179	97	70	82	60	3.48
1920–Brooklyn		National	40	304	23	11	*.676	271	101	75	131	67	2.22
1921–Brooklyn		National	37	302	•22	13	.629	313	120	95	*136	76	2.83
1922–Brooklyn		National	35	256	17	14	.548	318	157	*135	99	84	4.75
1923–Brooklyn		National	39	*327	21	18	.538	*356	*165	130	119	100	3.58
1924–Brooklyn		National	38	*311	22	13	.629	*351	*161	*132	135	91	3.82
1925–Brooklyn		National	33	247	12	*19	.387	305	164	*138	73	102	5.03
1926–Brooklyn(b)		National	30	225	12	13	.480	238	114	93	64	88	3.72
1927–New York(c)		National	39	260	19	8	.704	274	116	102	102	87	3.53
1928–Pittsburgh		National	*48	*331	•25	14	.641	311	*146	110	97	77	2.99
1929–Pittsburgh(d)		National	33	233	17	7	.708	245	108	81	62	70	3.13
1930–Bos.(e)-St.L.		National	33	201	16	11	.593	246	119	91	73	65	4.07
1931–St. Louis(f)		National	29	212	17	9	.654	240	97	86	67	59	3.65
1932–Chicago		National	30	141	6	11	.353	174	89	75	36	50	4.79
1933–Chi.(g)-St.L.		National	21	84	3	7	.300	86	42	35	16	37	3.75
1934–St.L.(h)-Pitt.(j)		National	12	35	3	3	.500	41	27	25	10	12	6.43
1934–New York(i)		American	10	18	1	2	.333	22	11	11	5	14	5.50
1935–Bloomington		I.I.I.	21	119	10	5	.667	113	44	....	54	32	.....
American League Totals			10	18	1	2	.333	22	11	11	5	14	5.50
National League Totals			605	4160	269	210	.562	4384	2037	1625	1507	1281	3.52
Major League Totals			615	4178	270	212	.560	4406	2048	1636	1512	1295	3.52

aTraded to Brooklyn Dodgers with shortstop Charles Ward and pitcher Al Mamaux for second baseman George Cutshaw, outfielder Charles (Casey) Stengel and $20,000, January 8, 1918.
bTraded to New York Giants in three-cornered deal which sent second baseman Fresco Thompson and pitcher Jack Scott from the Giants to the Philadelphia Phillies; outfielder George Harper to the Giants from the Phils and catcher Walter (Butch) Henline from the Phils to the Dodgers, January 9, 1927.
cTraded to Pittsburgh Pirates for pitcher Vic Aldridge, February 11, 1928.
dTraded to Boston Braves for pitcher Percy L. Jones and cash, April 9, 1930.
eTraded to St. Louis Cardinals for pitchers Bill Sherdel and Fred Frankhouse, June 16, 1930.
fTraded to Chicago Cubs for pitcher Arthur Teachout and outfielder Lewis (Hack) Wilson, December, 1931.
gReleased to St. Louis Cardinals on waivers, August 4, 1933.

hReleased to New York Yankees, May, 1934.
iUnconditionally released by New York Yankees, August, 1934, and signed by Pittsburgh Pirates.
jUnconditionally released by Pittsburgh Pirates, September, 1934.

WORLD SERIES RECORD

Year	Club	League	G.	IP.	W.	L.	Pct.	H.	R.	ER.	SO.	BB.	ERA.
1920	Brooklyn	National	3	19⅓	1	2	.333	23	10	9	4	9	4.19
1930	St. Louis	National	2	17	0	2	.000	10	7	7	13	6	3.71
1931	St. Louis	National	2	17⅔	2	0	1.000	9	4	4	11	9	2.04
1932	Chicago	National	2	2⅔	0	0	.000	7	7	7	0	2	23.63
	World Series Totals		9	56⅔	3	4	.429	49	28	27	28	26	4.05

CHARLES JOHN (JOLLY CHOLLY) GRIMM

Born August 28, 1898, at St. Louis, Mo.
Height, 5.11½. Weight, 173.
Threw and batted lefthanded.
Married Lillian Lyle, September 29, 1922.

Led N.L. first basemen in double plays, 1924, 1932.

Manager, Chicago Cubs, August, 1932; released, July 1938; coach, Chicago Cubs, January, 1941; released June 23, 1941; manager, Milwaukee, American Association, June 23, 1941-42-43; vice-president and manager, January, 1944; manager, Chicago Cubs, May 7, 1944-45-46-47-48-49; manager, Dallas, Texas League, January 13, 1950; released, November 11, 1950; Milwaukee, American Association, 1951, and until named manager of Boston Braves, May 31, 1952; Milwaukee Braves, 1953 through June 17, 1956; vice-president, Chicago Cubs, 1957-58-59; manager, Chicago Cubs, 1960 until May 4; coach, Cubs, 1961; vice-president, Cubs, 1961 to date.

Year	Club	League	Pos.	G.	AB.	R.	H.	2B.	3B.	HR.	RBI.	B.A.	PO.	A.	E.	F.A.
1916	Philadelphia	Am.	OF-PH	12	22	0	2	0	0	0	0	.091	7	0	1	.875
1917	Durham	N.C.	O-P-1	29	101	8	25	1	2	2	....	.248	50	14	4	.941
1918	St. Louis	Nat.	1-3-O	50	141	11	31	7	0	0	16	.220	385	14	12	.971
1918	Little Rock	South.	1B	56	205	25	61	3	6	1	....	.298	586	22	5	.992
1919	Little Rock	South.	1B	131	494	61	141	21	10	3	....	.285	•1436	69	11	*.993
1919	Pittsburgh	Nat.	1B	14	44	6	14	1	3	0	7	.318	118	2	4	.968
1920	Pittsburgh	Nat.	1B	148	533	38	121	13	7	2	54	.227	1496	95	8	*.995
1921	Pittsburgh	Nat.	1B	151	562	62	154	21	17	7	71	.274	1517	67	9	.994
1922	Pittsburgh	Nat.	1B	154	593	64	173	28	13	0	76	.292	1478	68	10	•.994
1923	Pittsburgh	Nat.	1B	152	563	78	194	29	13	7	99	.345	1453	81	8	*.995
1924	Pittsburgh(a)	Nat.	1B	151	542	53	156	25	12	2	63	.288	*1596	72	8	*.995
1925	Chicago	Nat.	1B	141	519	73	159	29	5	10	76	.306	1317	73	15	.989
1926	Chicago	Nat.	1B	147	524	58	145	30	6	8	82	.277	1416	68	18	.988
1927	Chicago	Nat.	1B	147	543	68	169	29	6	2	74	.311	1437	99	15	.990
1928	Chicago	Nat.	1B	147	547	67	161	25	5	5	62	.294	1458	70	10	•.993
1929	Chicago	Nat.	1B	120	463	66	138	28	3	10	91	.298	1228	74	10	.992
1930	Chicago	Nat.	1B	114	429	58	124	27	2	6	66	.289	1040	68	6	*.995
1931	Chicago	Nat.	1B	146	531	65	176	33	11	4	66	.331	1357	79	10	*.993
1932	Chicago	Nat.	1B	149	570	66	175	42	2	7	80	.307	1429	123	11	•.993
1933	Chicago	Nat.	1B	107	384	38	95	15	2	3	37	.247	979	84	4	*.996
1934	Chicago	Nat.	1B	75	267	24	79	8	1	5	47	.296	683	43	4	.995
1935	Chicago	Nat.	1B	2	8	0	0	0	0	0	0	.000	27	1	0	1.000
1936	Chicago	Nat.	1B	39	132	13	33	4	0	1	16	.250	297	33	0	1.000
1941	Milwaukee	A.A.	PH	1	1	0	1	0	0	0	0	1.000	0	0	0	.000
	National League Totals			2154	7895	908	2297	394	108	79	1083	.291	20711	1214	162	.993
	American League Totals			12	22	0	2	0	0	0	0	.091	7	0	1	.875
	Major League Totals			2166	7917	908	2299	394	108	79	1083	.290	20718	1214	163	.993

aTraded to Chicago Cubs with shortstop Walter Maranville and pitcher Wilbur Cooper for second baseman George Grantham, pitcher Vic Aldridge and first baseman Albert Niehaus, October 27, 1924.

WORLD SERIES RECORD

Year	Club	League	Pos.	G.	AB.	R.	H.	2B.	3B.	HR.	RBI.	B.A.	PO.	A.	E.	F.A.
1929	Chicago	Nat.	1B	5	18	2	7	0	0	1	4	.389	40	1	0	1.000
1932	Chicago	Nat.	1B	4	15	2	5	2	0	0	1	.333	28	3	0	1.000
	World Series Totals			9	33	4	12	2	0	1	5	.364	68	4	0	1.000

DID YOU KNOW—

That Jolly Cholly Grimm worked hard on the field, but got most of his fame because he was an accomplished lefthanded banjo player?

RICHARD MORROW GROAT

Born November 4, 1930, at Swissvale, Pa.
Height, 6.00. Weight, 170.
Threw and batted righthanded.
Married Barbara Womble, November 11, 1955.

Tied National League record for most seasons leading league in double plays by shortstop (5), with 127 in 1958, 97 in 1959, 117 in 1961, 126 in 1962 and 91 in 1964. Made six hits in six trips to the plate (three singles, three doubles), May 13, 1960.
Named Most Valuable National League Player, 1960. Named as shortstop on the National League All-Star Team by THE SPORTING NEWS, 1963-64.
Played pro basketball with Fort Wayne Pistons, 1952-53.

Year	Club	League	Pos.	G.	AB.	R.	H.	2B.	3B.	HR.	RBI.	B.A.	PO.	A.	E.	F.A.
1952	Pittsburgh	Nat.	SS	95	384	38	109	6	1	1	29	.284	229	272	25	.952
1953-54	Pittsburgh	Nat.					(In Military Service)									
1955	Pittsburgh	Nat.	SS	151	521	45	139	28	2	4	51	.267	*330	450	*32	.961
1956	Pittsburgh	Nat.	*SS-3B	142	520	40	142	19	3	0	37	.273	288	424	*34	.954
1957	Pittsburgh	Nat.	SS-3B	125	501	58	158	30	5	7	54	.315	226	385	21	.967
1958	Pittsburgh	Nat.	SS	151	584	67	175	36	9	3	66	.300	*307	461	20	.975
1959	Pittsburgh	Nat.	SS	147	593	74	163	22	7	5	51	.275	*301	473	*29	.964
1960	Pittsburgh	Nat.	SS	138	573	85	186	26	4	2	50	*.325	237	443	24	.966
1961	Pittsburgh	Nat.	*SS-3B	148	596	71	164	25	6	6	55	.275	237	474	*32	.957
1962	Pittsburgh(a)	Nat.	SS	161	678	76	199	34	3	2	61	.294	*314	*521	*38	.956
1963	St. Louis	Nat.	SS	158	631	85	201	*43	11	6	73	.319	257	448	26	.964
1964	St. Louis	Nat.	SS	161	636	70	186	35	6	1	70	.292	249	*499	*40	.949
1965	St. Louis(b)	Nat.	SS-3B	153	587	55	149	26	5	0	52	.254	242	455	27	.963
1966	Philadelphia	Nat.	SS-3-1B	155	584	58	152	21	4	2	53	.260	278	491	20	.975
1967	Phil.(c)-S.F.	Nat.	SS-2B	44	96	7	15	1	1	0	5	.156	31	68	8	.925
Major League Totals				1929	7484	829	2138	352	67	39	707	.286	3526	5864	374	.962

aTraded to St. Louis Cardinals with pitcher Diomedes Olivo for pitcher Don Cardwell and shortstop Julio Gotay, November 19, 1962.
bTraded with first baseman Bill White and catcher Bob Uecker to Philadelphia Phillies for pitcher Art Mahaffey, outfielder Alex Johnson and catcher Pat Corrales, October 27, 1965.
cSold to San Francisco Giants, June 22, 1967.

WORLD SERIES RECORD

Year	Club	League	Pos.	G.	AB.	R.	H.	2B.	3B.	HR.	RBI.	B.A.	PO.	A.	E.	F.A.
1960	Pittsburgh	Nat.	SS	7	28	3	6	2	0	0	2	.214	12	12	2	.923
1964	St. Louis	Nat.	SS	7	26	3	5	1	1	0	1	.192	11	16	2	.931
World Series Totals				14	54	6	11	3	1	0	3	.204	23	28	4	.927

ROBERT MOSES (LEFTY) GROVE

Born March 6, 1900, at Lonaconing, Md.
Died May 22, 1975, at Norwalk, O.
Height, 6.03. Weight, 204.
Threw and batted lefthanded.
Married Ethel Gardner, January 30, 1921.

Won 16 consecutive games in season to equal American League record (June 8 to August 19, 1931); registered 14 straight victories, 1928.
Three-strikeout innings on nine pitched balls, twice, August 23, 1928, vs. Cleveland, second inning; September 27, 1928, vs. Chicago, seventh inning.
THE SPORTING NEWS All-Star Major League Teams, 1928-29-30-31-32.
Named A.L. Most Valuable Player, BBWAA, 1931.
Named to Hall of Fame, 1947.

Year	Club	League	G.	IP.	W.	L.	Pct.	H.	R.	ER.	SO.	BB.	ERA.
1920	Martinsburg	Blue Ridge	6	59	3	3	.500	30	16	....	60	24	......
1920	Baltimore	International	19	123	12	2	.857	120	69	52	88	71	3.80
1921	Baltimore	International	47	313	25	10	.714	237	131	89	*254	*179	2.56
1922	Baltimore	International	41	209	18	8	.692	146	90	65	*205	*152	2.80
1923	Baltimore	International	*52	303	27	10	.730	223	128	105	*330	*186	3.12

Year	Club	League	G.	IP.	W.	L.	Pct.	H.	R.	ER.	SO.	BB.	ERA.
1924	Baltimore	International	47	236	*27	6	*.813	196	95	79	*231	108	3.01
1925	Philadelphia	American	45	197	10	12	.455	207	120	104	*116	*131	4.75
1926	Philadelphia	American	45	258	13	13	.500	227	97	72	*194	101	*2.51
1927	Philadelphia	American	51	262	20	13	.606	251	116	93	*174	79	3.19
1928	Philadelphia	American	39	262	●24	8	.750	228	93	75	*183	64	2.58
1929	Philadelphia	American	42	275	20	6	*.769	278	104	86	*170	81	*2.81
1930	Philadelphia	American	*50	291	*28	5	*.848	273	101	82	*209	60	*2.54
1931	Philadelphia	American	41	289	*31	4	*.886	249	84	66	*175	62	*2.06
1932	Philadelphia	American	44	292	25	10	.714	269	101	92	188	79	*2.84
1933	Philadelphia(a)	American	45	275	●24	8	*.750	280	113	98	114	83	3.21
1934	Boston	American	22	109	8	8	.500	149	84	79	43	32	6.52
1935	Boston	American	35	273	20	12	.625	269	105	82	121	65	*2.70
1936	Boston	American	35	253	17	12	.586	237	90	79	130	65	*2.81
1937	Boston	American	32	262	17	9	.654	269	101	88	153	83	3.02
1938	Boston	American	24	164	14	4	.778	169	65	56	99	52	*3.07
1939	Boston	American	23	191	15	4	*.789	180	63	54	81	58	*2.54
1940	Boston	American	22	153	7	6	.538	159	73	68	62	50	4.00
1941	Boston	American	21	134	7	7	.500	155	84	65	54	42	4.37
Major League Totals			616	3940	300	141	.680	3849	1594	1339	2266	1187	3.06

aTraded to Boston with second baseman Max Bishop and pitcher George Walberg for infielder Harold Warstler, pitcher Bob Kline and $125,000, December 12, 1933.

WORLD SERIES RECORD

Year	Club	League	G.	IP.	W.	L.	Pct.	H.	R.	ER.	SO.	BB.	ERA.
1929	Philadelphia	American	2	6⅓	0	0	.000	3	0	0	10	1	0.00
1930	Philadelphia	American	3	19	2	1	.667	15	5	3	10	3	1.42
1931	Philadelphia	American	3	26	2	1	.667	28	7	7	16	2	2.42
World Series Totals			8	51⅓	4	2	.667	46	12	10	36	6	1.75

STANLEY CAMFIELD (STANISLAUS) HACK

Born December 6, 1909, at Sacramento, Calif.
Died December 15, 1979, at Dixon, Ill.
Height, 6.00. Weight, 175.
Threw right and batted lefthanded.
Married Glennyce Mary Graf, November 30, 1957.

Led N.L. third basemen in double plays, 1937, 1938 (tie), 1940.
Named by Baseball Writers' Association as third baseman for THE SPORTING NEWS All-Star Major League Teams, 1940-41-42.
World Series records—Tied record for most one-base hits, Series (four games)—7—(1938); and tied record for most hits, game—4—October 8, 1945.
Manager, Des Moines, Western League, 1948-49; manager, Springfield, International League, 1950; manager, Los Angeles, Pacific Coast League, 1951-52-53; manager, Chicago Cubs, 1954-55-56; coach, St. Louis Cardinals, 1957-58; manager, Denver, American Association, 1959; manager, Salt Lake City, Pacific Coast League, 1965; manager, Dallas-Fort Worth, Texas League, 1966; released May 28, 1966.

Year	Club	League	Pos.	G.	AB.	R.	H.	2B.	3B.	HR.	RBI.	B.A.	PO.	A.	E.	F.A.
1931	Sacramento	P. C.	3B	164	660	128	232	36	13	2	37	.352	167	354	32	.942
1932	Chicago	Nat.	3B	72	178	32	42	5	6	2	19	.236	36	90	12	.913
1933	Albany	Int.	3B	137	515	102	154	28	8	6	64	.299	▲171	272	17	.963
1933	Chicago	Nat.	3B	20	60	10	21	3	1	1	2	.350	19	40	1	.983
1934	Chicago	Nat.	3B	111	402	54	116	16	6	1	21	.289	102	198	16	.949
1935	Chicago	Nat.	3B-1B	124	427	75	133	23	9	4	64	.311	87	237	20	.942
1936	Chicago	Nat.	3B-1B	149	561	102	167	27	4	6	78	.298	225	210	17	.962
1937	Chicago	Nat.	*3B-1B	154	582	106	173	27	6	2	63	.297	*151	*247	13	.968
1938	Chicago	Nat.	3B	●152	609	109	195	34	11	4	67	.320	*178	300	23	.954
1939	Chicago	Nat.	3B	156	641	112	191	28	6	8	56	.298	*177	278	21	.956
1940	Chicago	Nat.	3B-1B	149	603	101	*191	38	6	7	40	.317	*182	*304	23	.955
1941	Chicago	Nat.	3B-1B	151	586	111	*186	33	5	7	45	.317	139	295	21	.954
1942	Chicago	Nat.	3B	140	553	91	166	36	3	6	39	.300	154	261	15	*.965
1943	Chicago	Nat.	3B	144	533	78	154	24	4	3	35	.289	149	264	17	.960
1944	Chicago(a)	Nat.	3B-1B	98	383	65	108	16	1	3	32	.282	226	174	19	.955
1945	Chicago	Nat.	*3B-1B	150	597	110	193	29	7	2	43	.323	*233	314	14	*.975
1946	Chicago	Nat.	3B	92	323	55	92	13	4	0	26	.285	102	168	9	.968
1947	Chicago	Nat.	3B	76	240	28	65	11	2	0	12	.271	64	136	8	.962
Major League Totals				1938	7278	1239	2193	363	81	57	642	.301	2224	3516	249	.958

aDid not join club until mid-June, 1944.

WORLD SERIES RECORD

Year	Club	League	Pos.	G.	AB.	R.	H.	2B.	3B.	HR.	RBI.	B.A.	PO.	A.	E.	F.A.
1932–Chicago	....	Nat.	PR	1	0	0	0	0	0	0	0	.000	0	0	0	.000
1935–Chicago	....	Nat.	3B-SS	6	22	2	5	1	1	0	0	.227	6	10	0	1.000
1938–Chicago	....	Nat.	3B	4	17	3	8	1	0	0	1	.471	4	4	0	1.000
1945–Chicago	....	Nat.	3B	7	30	1	11	3	0	0	4	.367	12	13	3	.893
World Series Totals.........................				18	69	6	24	5	1	0	5	.348	22	27	3	.942

CHARLES JAMES (CHICK) HAFEY

Born February 12, 1904, at Berkeley, Calif.
Died July 2, 1973, at Calistoga, Calif.
Height, 6.01. Weight, 185.
Threw and batted righthanded.
Married Bernice Stigliano, December 1, 1922.

Tied National League record for most consecutive hits (10), July 6-8-9, 1929.
Had eight hits in doubleheader, July 28, 1928, 21 innings; two singles, four doubles, two home runs, for 18 total bases.
World Series record–Set record for most doubles (5) and tied record for most long hits (5) in six-game Series, 1930 (long hits total since broken by Reggie Jackson, 1977, with six).
Named to Hall of Fame, 1971.

Year	Club	League	Pos.	G.	AB.	R.	H.	2B.	3B.	HR.	RBI.	B.A.	PO.	A.	E.	F.A.
1923–Fort Smith	....	W. Assn.	OF	141	573	83	163	42	14	16	.....	.284	280	30	16	.951
1924–Houston	....	Tex.	OF	126	481	82	173	39	*20	9	90	.360	358	18	11	.972
1924–St. Louis	....	Nat.	OF	24	91	10	23	5	2	2	22	.253	48	3	4	.927
1925–Syracuse	....	Int.	OF	21	84	17	24	3	3	2	8	.286	49	3	1	.981
1925–St. Louis	....	Nat.	OF	93	358	36	108	25	2	5	57	.302	180	9	9	.955
1926–St. Louis	....	Nat.	OF	78	225	30	61	19	2	4	38	.271	106	6	3	.974
1927–St. Louis	....	Nat.	OF	103	346	62	114	26	5	18	63	.329	179	19	4	.980
1928–St. Louis	....	Nat.	OF	138	520	101	175	46	6	27	111	.337	287	13	11	.965
1929–St. Louis	....	Nat.	OF	134	517	101	175	47	9	29	125	.338	278	8	10	.966
1930–St. Louis	....	Nat.	OF	120	446	108	150	39	12	26	107	.336	189	11	5	.976
1931–St. Louis (a)	.....	Nat.	OF	122	450	94	157	35	8	16	95	*.349	226	4	4	.983
1932–Cincinnati	....	Nat.	OF	83	253	34	87	19	3	2	36	.344	131	5	5	.965
1933–Cincinnati	....	Nat.	OF	144	568	77	172	34	6	7	62	.303	364	16	5	.987
1934–Cincinnati	....	Nat.	OF	140	535	75	157	29	6	18	67	.293	380	7	13	.968
1935–Cincinnati	....	Nat.	OF	15	59	10	20	6	1	1	9	.339	31	0	3	.912
1936–Cincinnati	....	Nat.	OF						(Voluntarily Retired)							
1937–Cincinnati	....	Nat.	OF	89	257	39	67	11	5	9	41	.261	128	5	4	.971
Major League Totals.....................				1283	4625	777	1466	341	67	164	833	.317	2527	106	80	.971

aTraded to Cincinnati Reds for infielder Harvey Hendrick and pitcher Benny Frey and cash, April 11, 1932.

WORLD SERIES RECORD

Year	Club	League	Pos.	G.	AB.	R.	H.	2B.	3B.	HR.	RBI.	B.A.	PO.	A.	E.	F.A.
1926–St. Louis	....	Nat.	OF	7	27	2	5	2	0	0	0	.185	21	1	0	1.000
1928–St. Louis	....	Nat.	OF	4	15	0	3	0	0	0	0	.200	8	0	1	.889
1930–St. Louis	....	Nat.	OF	6	22	2	6	5	0	0	2	.273	9	0	0	1.000
1931–St. Louis	....	Nat.	OF	6	24	1	4	0	0	0	0	.167	8	0	1	.889
World Series Totals.........................				23	88	5	18	7	0	0	2	.205	46	1	2	.959

JESSE JOSEPH (POP) HAINES

Born Clayton, O., July 22, 1893.
Died August 5, 1978, at Dayton, O.
Height, 6.00. Weight, 180.
Threw and batted righthanded.
Married Carrie Marie Weidner, September 29, 1915.

Pitched no-hit, no-run game against Boston, 5-0, July 17, 1924; coach, Brooklyn Dodgers, 1938.
Named to Hall of Fame, 1970.

Year	Club	League	G.	IP.	W.	L.	Pct.	H.	R.	ER.	SO.	BB.	ERA.
1913	Dayton	Central	(Pitched one game, last day of season vs. Evansville)										
1914	Saginaw	S. Mich.	33	258	17	14	.548	221	94	....	159	52	.....
1914	Fort Wayne	Central	(No records available)										
1915	Saginaw	S. Mich.	(League disbanded July 1—no records available)										
1916	Springfield	Central	41	310	23	12	.657	247	78	58	143	84	1.68
1917	Springfield	Central	35	275	19	10	.655	204	67	....	129	88	.....
1918	Topeka-Hutch'on	Western	16	132	12	4	.750	93	....	....	71	28	.....
1918	Cincinnati	National	1	5	0	0	.000	5	1	1	2	1	1.80
1919	Tulsa	Western	14	101	5	9	.357	87	47	....	40	47	.....
1919	Kansas City	Amer. Assn.	28	213	21	5	.808	199	54	50	66	52	2.11
1920	St. Louis	National	*47	302	13	20	.394	303	136	100	120	80	2.98
1921	St. Louis	National	37	244	18	12	.600	261	112	95	84	56	3.50
1922	St. Louis	National	29	183	11	9	.550	207	103	78	62	45	3.84
1923	St. Louis	National	37	266	20	13	.606	283	125	92	73	75	3.11
1924	St. Louis	National	35	223	8	19	.296	275	129	109	69	66	4.40
1925	St. Louis	National	29	207	13	14	.481	234	116	105	63	52	4.57
1926	St. Louis	National	33	183	13	4	.765	186	76	66	46	48	3.25
1927	St. Louis	National	38	301	24	10	.706	273	114	91	89	77	2.72
1928	St. Louis	National	33	240	20	8	.714	238	98	85	77	72	3.19
1929	St. Louis	National	28	180	13	10	.565	230	123	114	59	73	5.70
1930	St. Louis	National	29	182	13	8	.619	215	107	87	68	54	4.30
1931	St. Louis	National	19	122	12	3	.800	134	48	41	27	28	3.02
1932	St. Louis	National	20	85	3	5	.375	116	51	45	27	16	4.76
1933	St. Louis	National	32	115	9	6	.600	113	46	32	37	37	2.50
1934	St. Louis	National	37	90	4	4	.500	86	42	35	17	19	3.50
1935	St. Louis	National	30	115	6	5	.545	110	49	46	24	28	3.60
1936	St. Louis	National	25	99	7	5	.583	110	44	43	19	21	3.91
1937	St. Louis	National	16	66	3	3	.500	81	36	33	18	23	4.50
Major League Totals			555	3208	210	158	.571	3460	1556	1298	981	871	3.64

WORLD SERIES RECORD

Year	Club	League	G.	IP.	W.	L.	Pct.	H.	R.	ER.	SO.	BB.	ERA.
1926	St. Louis	National	3	16⅔	2	0	1.000	13	2	2	5	9	1.08
1928	St. Louis	National	1	6	0	1	.000	6	6	3	3	3	4.50
1930	St. Louis	National	1	9	1	0	1.000	4	1	1	2	4	1.00
1934	St. Louis	National	1	⅔	0	0	.000	1	0	0	2	0	0.00
World Series Totals			6	32⅓	3	1	.750	24	9	6	12	16	1.67

SAMUEL DOUGLAS HALE

Born September 10, 1896, at Glenrose, Tex.
Height, 5.08½. Weight, 160.
Threw and batted righthanded.
Married Alma C. Richerson, September 26, 1917.

Led A.L. third basemen in double plays, 1927.
Manager, Midland, West Texas-New Mexico League, 1940; Wichita Falls and Pampa, West Texas-New Mexico League, 1941.

Year	Club	League	Pos.	G.	AB.	R.	H.	2B.	3B.	HR.	SB.	B.A.	PO.	A.	E.	F.A.
1917	San Antonio	Texas	OF	....	58	8	12	....	....	....	1	.206	....	....	....	......
1917	Muskogee	West. Assn.														
1918	San Antonio	Texas	3B	81	275	24	76	....	....	....	17	.276	69	187	32	.889
1919	San Antonio	Texas	3B	135	410	56	142	25	7	10	12	.302	137	262	30	.930
1920	Detroit	Amer.	3B OF	76	116	13	34	3	3	1	2	.293	14	32	5	.002
1921	Detroit	Amer.	PR-PH	9	2	2	0	0	0	0	0	.000	....	....	....	......
1921	Portland	P.C.	3B	136	530	80	181	39	9	9	14	.342	147	259	35	921
1922	Portland	P.C.	3B	152	525	91	188	39	6	10	18	.358	130	261	21	.949
1923	Philadelphia	Amer.	3B	115	434	68	125	22	8	3	8	.288	85	222	8	.914
1924	Philadelphia	Amer.	3B	80	261	41	83	14	2	2	3	.318	39	108	8	.948
1925	Philadelphia	Amer.	2B-3B	110	391	62	135	20	11	8	7	.345	98	173	24	.918
1926	Philadelphia	Amer.	3B	111	327	49	92	22	9	4	1	.281	82	152	13	.947
1927	Philadelphia	Amer.	3B	131	501	77	157	24	8	5	11	.313	152	247	16	.961
1928	Philadelphia	Amer.	3B	88	314	38	97	20	9	4	2	.309	86	189	20	.932
1929	Philadelphia(a)	Amer.	3B	101	379	51	105	14	3	1	6	.277	90	171	12	.956
1930	St. Louis	Amer.	3B	62	190	21	52	8	1	2	1	.274	46	80	7	.947
1930	Portland	P.C.	3B	36	140	19	41	10	3	1	4	.293	24	68	2	.979
1931	Portland	P.C.	3B	133	555	95	179	35	5	2	7	.323	121	176	17	.946
1932	Indianapolis	A.A.	3B	104	421	56	128	28	1	1	4	.304	84	216	21	.935
1933	Tulsa	Texas	3B	147	524	63	142	24	12	3	12	.271	113	267	30	.927
1934	Tul. & Ok. C.	Tex.	3B-2B	141	532	75	135	26	8	4	9	.254	188	283	35	.931
Major League Totals				883	2915	422	880	157	54	30	41	.302	692	1374	133	.935

aTraded to St. Louis Browns for catcher Wally Schang, December, 1929.

WILLIAM ROBERT (SLIDING BILLY) HAMILTON

Born February 16, 1866, at Newark, N. J.
Died December 16, 1940, at Worcester, Mass.
Height, 5.06. Weight, 165.
Threw right and batted lefthanded.

Holds major league record for scoring most runs in season, 196, in 1894. Held National League record for most stolen bases in season, 115, in 1891 (since broken by Lou Brock, 118 in 1974). Held major league career stolen base record with 937 (since broken by Brock with 938).
Manager, Haverhill, New England League, 1902-03-04; Harrisburg, Tri-State League, 1905; Haverhill, New England League and Harrisburg, Tri-State League, 1906; Haverhill, New England League, 1907-08; Lynn, New England League, 1909-10; Fall River, New England League, 1913; Springfield, Eastern League, 1914. Part owner and manager, Worcester, Eastern League, 1916. Served as scout for Boston, American League, 1911-12.
Named to Hall of Fame, 1961.

Year Club	League	Pos.	G.	AB.	R.	H.	2B.	3B.	HR.	SB.	B.A.	PO.	A.	E.	F.A.
1888—Worcester	N. Eng.	OF	61	247	76	87	...	...	...	70	.352	....	....	5	.904
1888—Kansas City	A. A.	OF	35	128	17	32	4	4	0	23	.250	41	1	2	.943
1889—Kansas City	A. A.	OF	137	532	145	160	15	*15	3	*117	.301	233	19	34	.902
1890—Philadelphia	Nat.	OF	123	496	131	161	10	9	2	*102	.325	232	23	34	.881
1891—Philadelphia	Nat.	OF	133	529	*142	*179	21	6	2	*115	*.338	281	22	26	.921
1892—Philadelphia	Nat.	OF	136	539	131	178	18	7	3	56	.330	292	29	22	.936
1893—Philadelphia	Nat.	OF	82	349	111	138	21	7	5	41	.395	229	8	15	.940
1894—Philadelphia	Nat.	OF	131	559	*196	223	22	14	4	*99	.399	*363	16	15	.962
1895—Philadelphia	Nat.	OF	121	517	*166	203	19	6	5	*95	.393	310	12	29	.917
1896—Boston	Nat.	OF	131	523	153	190	26	8	2	93	.363	278	8	19	.938
1897—Boston	Nat.	OF	125	506	*153	174	17	6	3	70	.344	299	9	15	.954
1898—Boston	Nat.	OF	109	417	111	153	16	4	3	59	.367	193	8	23	.897
1899—Boston	Nat.	OF	81	294	62	90	6	1	1	19	.306	163	10	6	.966
1900—Boston	Nat.	OF	135	524	103	174	19	5	1	29	.332	325	13	19	.947
1901—Boston	Nat.	OF	99	349	70	102	11	2	3	19	.292	234	7	20	.923
1902—Haverhill	N. Eng.	OF	66	243	67	82	23	2	2	26	.337	127	10	5	.964
1903—Haverhill	N. Eng.	OF	37	132	37	60	15	2	4	27	.446	67	4	3	.960
1904—Haverhill	N. Eng.	OF	113	408	*113	*168	32	8	0	*74	*.412	*242	7	11	.958
1905—Harrisburg	Tri-St.					(No Record Available)									
1906—Haverhill	N.Eng.	OF	14	51	1	10	1	0	0	...	.196	26	2	3	.903
1906—Harrisburg	Tri.-St.	OF	43	155	33	43	5	1	0	16	.278	82	4	6	.935
1907—Haverhill	N. Eng.	OF	91	324	50	108	16	4	0	29	*.333	161	6	2	*.988
1908—Haverhill	N. Eng.	OF	85	300	63	87	19	0	1	39	.290	164	11	13	.931
1909—Lynn	N. Eng.	OF	109	376	61	125	17	2	0	23	*.332	195	6	14	.935
1910—Lynn	N. Eng.	OF	41	112	14	28	1	2	0	5	.250	45	3	1	.980
American Association Totals			172	660	162	192	19	19	3	140	.291	274	20	36	.891
National League Totals			1406	5602	1529	1965	206	75	34	797	.351	3199	165	243	.933
Major League Totals			1578	6262	1690	2157	225	94	37	937	.344	3473	185	279	.929

MELVIN LE ROY HARDER

Born October 15, 1909, at Beemer, Neb.
Height, 6.01. Weight, 210.
Threw and batted righthanded.
Married Hazel Claire Schmidt, December 27, 1932.

Tied for league leadership in shutouts (6), 1934.
Player-coach, Cleveland Indians, 1947; made coach, 1948-1963; coach, New York Mets, 1964; coach, Chicago Cubs, 1965-66; coach, Cincinnati Reds, 1967-68; coach, Kansas City Royals, 1969.

Year Club	League	G.	IP.	W.	L.	Pct.	H.	R.	ER.	SO.	BB.	ERA.
1927—Omaha	West.	11	87	4	7	.364	106	65	....	40	33	......
1927—Dubuque	Miss. Val.	22	....	13	6	.684	....	....	....	....	....	......
1928—Cleveland	Amer.	23	49	0	2	.000	64	42	36	15	32	6.61
1929—Cleveland	Amer.	11	18	1	0	1.000	24	15	11	4	5	5.50
1929—New Orleans	South.	16	72	7	2	.778	65	31	20	32	24	2.50
1930—Cleveland	Amer.	36	175	11	10	.524	205	108	82	44	68	4.22
1931—Cleveland	Amer.	40	194	13	14	.481	229	119	94	63	72	4.36
1932—Cleveland	Amer.	39	255	15	13	.536	277	125	106	90	68	3.74

Year	Club	League	G.	IP.	W.	L.	Pct.	H.	R.	ER.	SO.	BB.	ERA.
1933	Cleveland	Amer.	43	253	15	17	.469	254	113	83	81	67	2.95
1934	Cleveland	Amer.	44	255	20	12	.625	246	97	74	91	81	2.61
1935	Cleveland	Amer.	42	287	22	11	.667	313	120	105	95	53	3.29
1936	Cleveland	Amer.	36	225	15	15	.500	294	155	129	84	71	5.16
1937	Cleveland	Amer.	38	234	15	12	.556	269	127	111	95	86	4.27
1938	Cleveland	Amer.	38	240	17	10	.630	257	115	102	102	62	3.83
1939	Cleveland	Amer.	29	208	15	9	.625	213	89	81	67	64	3.50
1940	Cleveland	Amer.	31	186	12	11	.522	200	96	84	76	59	4.06
1941	Cleveland(a)	Amer.	15	69	5	4	.556	76	43	40	21	37	5.22
1942	Cleveland	Amer.	29	199	13	14	.481	179	83	76	74	82	3.44
1943	Cleveland	Amer.	19	135	8	7	.533	126	57	46	40	61	3.07
1944	Cleveland	Amer.	30	196	12	10	.545	211	95	81	64	69	3.72
1945	Cleveland	Amer.	11	76	3	7	.300	93	37	31	16	23	3.67
1946	Cleveland	Amer.	13	92	5	4	.556	85	37	35	21	31	3.42
1947	Cleveland	Amer.	15	80	6	4	.600	91	41	40	17	27	4.50
Major League Totals			582	3426	223	186	.545	3706	1714	1447	1160	1118	3.80

aGiven unconditional release, September 9, 1941. Had pitching arm operated on, September 30, 1941. Re-signed, March 24, 1942.

EUGENE FRANKLIN (BUBBLES) HARGRAVE

Born July 15, 1892, at New Haven, Ind.
Died February 23, 1969, at Cincinnati, O.
Height, 5.10½. Weight, 168.
Threw and batted righthanded.
Married Hester Wolf, May 20, 1918.

Led N.L. catchers in double plays, 1923 (tie).
Manager, St. Paul, American Association, 1929; manager, Cedar Rapids, Western League, 1934.

Year	Club	League	Pos.	G.	AB.	R.	H.	2B.	3B.	HR.	RBI.	B.A.	PO.	A.	E.	F.A.
1911	Terre Haute	Central	C	91	235	20	67	12	7	0	....	.285	263	57	14	.958
1912	Terre Haute	Central	C	92	271	25	79	10	3	1	....	.292	365	96	•18	.962
1913	Terre Haute	Central	C	126	444	77	137	32	7	5	....	.309	599	179	20	.975
1913	Chicago	National	C	3	3	0	1	0	0	0	1	.333	3	1	0	1.000
1914	Chicago	National	C	23	36	3	8	2	0	0	2	.222	34	6	3	.930
1915	Chicago	National	C	15	19	2	3	0	1	0	1	.158	13	7	0	1.000
1916	Kansas City	Am. Assn.	C	105	243	22	77	15	6	0	....	.317	328	99	12	.973
1917	Kansas City	Am. Assn.	C	86	231	23	51	10	3	2	....	.221	235	54	10	.967
1918	Memphis	Southern	C	64	209	22	47	12	0	0	....	.225	204	70	8	.973
1918	St. Paul	Am. Assn.	C	23	83	10	25	3	4	0	....	.301	68	15	1	.988
1919	St. Paul	Am. Assn.	C	146	511	71	155	35	5	11	....	.303	*612	145	17	.978
1920	St. Paul(a)	Am. Assn.	C	142	496	115	166	36	12	22	109	.335	489	121	10	*.984
1921	Cincinnati	National	C	93	263	28	76	17	8	1	38	.289	270	50	9	.973
1922	Cincinnati	National	C	98	320	49	101	22	10	7	57	.316	261	60	6	.982
1923	Cincinnati	National	C	118	378	54	126	23	9	10	78	.333	404	90	6	.988
1924	Cincinnati	National	C	98	312	42	94	19	10	3	33	.301	322	80	7	.983
1925	Cincinnati	National	C	87	273	28	82	13	6	2	33	.300	283	42	7	.979
1926	Cincinnati	National	C	105	326	42	115	22	8	6	62	*.353	276	50	4	.988
1927	Cincinnati	National	C	102	305	36	94	18	3	0	35	.308	261	57	4	.988
1928	Cincinnati	National	C	65	190	19	56	12	3	0	23	.295	181	37	2	.991
1929	St. Paul	Am. Assn.	C	104	317	57	117	20	3	9	85	*.369	333	77	10	.976
1930	New York(b)	American	C	45	108	11	30	7	0	0	12	.278	112	13	1	.992
1931	Minneapolis	Am. Assn.	C	117	361	67	110	19	2	12	63	.305	333	58	5	*.987
1932	Buffalo	Int'tional	C	83	239	43	89	21	3	10	60	.372	256	41	2	.993
1933							(Out of Organized Ball.)									
1934	Cedar Rapids	Western	C	32	71	9	18	2	0	2	14	.254	102	8	4	.965
American League Totals				45	108	11	30	7	0	0	12	.278	112	13	1	.992
National League Totals				807	2425	303	756	148	58	29	363	.312	2308	480	48	.983
Major League Totals				852	2533	314	786	155	58	29	375	.310	2420	493	49	.983

aSold to Cincinnati Reds for $10,000.
bUnconditionally released by New York Yankees, October 24, 1930.

DID YOU KNOW—

That 870 of Billy Hamilton's stolen bases were purloined while the pitcher could fake a runner back to first base without completing the throw?

GEORGE WASHINGTON HARPER

Born June 24, 1892, at Arlington, Ky.
Died August 18, 1978, at Magnolia, Ark.
Height, 5.08. Weight, 165.
Threw right and batted lefthanded.
Married Johnnie Warmack, December 5, 1913.

Hit three home runs, September 20, first game, 1928.
Manager, El Dorado, East Dixie League, 1934-35.

Year	Club	League	Pos.	G.	AB.	R.	H.	2B.	3B.	HR.	RBI.	B.A.	PO.	A.	E.	F.A.
1913	Paris	Tex.-Ok.	OF	125	446	71	138	....	....	....	....	.309	237	114	3	*.992
1914	Paris	Tex.-Ok.	OF	116	413	62	127	22	6	3	....	.308	235	*89	16	.953
1915	Fort Worth	Tex.	OF	•156	542	89	162	30	14	2	....	.299	*337	•26	13	.965
1916	Detroit	Amer.	OF	44	56	4	9	1	0	0	4	.161	15	0	1	.938
1917	Detroit	Amer.	OF	47	117	6	24	3	0	0	10	.205	48	2	1	.980
1917	Columbus	A. A.	OF	26	58	9	20	1	0	3	....	.345	24	1	5	.833
1918	Detroit	Amer.	OF	69	227	19	55	5	2	0	18	.243	125	5	6	.956
1919	'Frisco-Seattle	P. C.	OF	70	264	33	71	7	1	2	....	.269	126	7	5	.964
1920	Oklahoma City	West.	OF	79	302	55	92	17	6	4	....	.305	218	13	3	.987
1921	Oklahoma City	West.	OF	168	606	130	238	50	11	19	....	.393	*486	29	9	.983
1922	Cincinnati	Nat.	OF	128	430	67	146	22	8	2	68	.340	220	15	11	.955
1923	Cincinnati	Nat.	OF	61	125	14	32	4	2	3	16	.256	56	3	2	.967
1924	Cin.(a)-Phila.	Nat.	OF	137	485	75	141	29	6	16	58	.291	270	16	4	*.986
1925	Philadelphia	Nat.	OF	132	495	86	173	35	7	18	97	.349	319	16	10	.971
1926	Philadelphia(b)	Nat.	OF	56	194	32	61	6	5	7	38	.314	111	2	7	.941
1927	New York	Nat.	OF	145	483	85	160	19	6	16	87	.331	299	13	8	.975
1928	N.Y.(c)-St.L.(d)	Nat.	OF	118	329	52	96	9	2	19	65	.292	196	17	4	.982
1929	Boston	Nat.	OF	136	457	65	133	25	5	10	68	.291	266	7	8	.972
1930	Los Angeles	P. C.	OF	160	546	104	168	40	1	8	97	.308	305	15	14	.958
1931	L.A.-Oakland	P. C.	OF	100	220	31	59	10	1	3	33	.268	138	7	6	.960
1932	Shreve.-Tyler	Tex.	OF	44	142	20	39	7	1	2	21	.275	75	8	2	.976
1933							(Voluntarily Retired)									
1934	El Dorado	E. Dixie	OF	122	403	70	128	26	4	4	64	.318	216	15	13	.947
1935	El Dorado	E. Dixie	OF	135	497	83	171	44	8	3	78	.344	257	11	9	.968
1936	Jackson	Cot. St.	OF	91	424	58	127	22	6	2	62	.300	130	8	8	.945
1936	Augusta	Sou. Atl.	OF	27	91	17	26	7	1	0	21	.286	38	4	2	.955
	American League Totals			160	400	29	88	9	2	0	32	.220	188	7	8	.961
	National League Totals			913	2998	476	942	149	41	91	497	.314	1737	89	54	.971
	Major League Totals			1073	3398	505	1030	158	43	91	529	.303	1925	96	62	.970

aTraded to Philadelphia Phillies for outfielder William Curtis Walker, July, 1924.
bSold to New York Giants, January 7, 1927.
cTraded to St. Louis Cardinals for catcher Robert O'Farrell, May 10, 1928.
dSold to Boston Braves with infielder Walter Maranville, December 8, 1928.

WORLD SERIES RECORD

Year	Club	League	Pos.	G.	AB.	R.	H.	2B.	3B.	HR.	RBI.	B.A.	PO.	A.	E.	F.A.
1928	St. Louis	Nat.	OF	3	9	1	1	0	0	0	0	.111	5	0	0	1.000

WILLIAM HARRIDGE

Born October 16, 1883, at Chicago, Ill.
Died April 9, 1971, at Evanston, Ill.

William Harridge was a tall, dignified, efficient, truthful and sensitive person throughout his adult life, a conservative who felt the winds of change and was sufficiently perceptive to follow them intelligently.
 The American League reached its zenith under his presidency and the distinguished gentleman set the tone—firm guidance, thoughtful decisions, top-to-bottom loyalty, inborn pride, fierce honesty and aggressive penalties whenever warranted.
 Will (which he preferred over William), a native of Chicago's South Side and born on October 16, 1883, was whisked into Organized Baseball; he did not choose the career. From the job of office boy in the Wabash Railroad, he attended evening classes and rose to the position of transportation head in the office. The

American League, under Ban Johnson at the time, arranged all transportation of its umpires through the Wabash. Harridge did such an excellent job of error-free booking that he came to the personal attention of Johnson.

In December, 1911, Will's Wabash boss told him, "You have just worked your last day for this railroad." Will thought he was canned. But he was told to report to the American League office and begin work as Ban Johnson's private secretary.

As a result of Ban's later battles with Commissioner Kenesaw M. Landis and the AL owners as well, he was set down early in 1927. He actually resigned on October 17, when Ernest Barnard of Cleveland was named AL president and Harridge was voted in as the league secretary. Barnard died suddenly on March 27, 1931, and Will was made acting president. Two months later, on May 27, he was officially named the president, having been championed by Charles Comiskey of Chicago and Phil Ball of St. Louis. Harridge stepped down on December 3, 1958, when he became chairman of the board, a post he held until his death on April 9, 1971.

Harridge's mettle was tried early—just one year after taking over, Carl Reynolds of the Washington Senators slid hard into catcher Bill Dickey of the Yankees in a home-plate collision on July 4, 1932. Dickey leaped to his feet and delivered a haymaker that broke Reynolds' jaw. Observers wondered if the neophyte would stand up to the Yankees, then the dominant club in the league, if not all baseball.

They didn't have to wonder long. Harridge fined Dickey $1,000 and suspended him for a month in the midst of a pennant race. The Yankees' owner, Jake Ruppert, was furious, but Will held his ground. "He didn't talk to me for a year," Harridge said, "but the next year he softened up and became one of my best friends."

Will continued Johnson's high regard and proper respect for his umpires. American League umpires felt his ire when they came up short but Harridge defended them to the hilt when they were attacked by others.

He fined and suspended the belligerent George Moriarty and hired the humiliated NL umpire Scotty Robb. He fined and suspended the league's chief arbiter baiter, Jimmy Dykes, the pixie skipper of the White Sox, a total of 37 times.

The business-as-usual sign typified the AL—the Yankees ruled the roost most of his reign and other clubs played catch-up with second place the usual reward. But many important things eventuated during Will's tenure—formation of a public relations department and a film bureau, the All-Star Game, night baseball, re-entry of the Negro to the majors, televising of games, expansion of the majors and formation of the players' association.

Thus Harridge spanned from pre-Landis days to the middle of every problem of today. He personally sold the All-Star Game to the owners for a one-shot Chicago World's Fair feature and did his utmost to see that it continued; he resisted night ball in its early stages because he feared a drop in field performance, particularly batting, but when the lights proved to be excellent substitutes for sunlight, no one was more vehement in proclaiming the boost of family attendance which the lights gave to the game.

Will saw the burgeoning sports world in need of fresh appeals to potential ticket buyers and to assuage that need, he formed the public relations and baseball film departments to service his league fans and organizations. He tried to slow down expansion when he saw the original setup of franchises in danger of becoming watered down from a paucity of top-level performers to staff them, but he changed his stance completely when logistics, finances and public clamor screamed the need.

Harridge disliked shenanigans on the field, from Bill Veeck's midget to showboating players and managers, because he knew that rigid discipline on the field, monitored by competent, backed-up umpires, assured the fans of clean games and good family entertainment, a climate which mirrored his deep pride in the American League.

Contrary to his sober look and dignified mien, he was a sublime host at his annual Christmas party for the entire Chicago sporting scene—players, writers, club personnel, league members, whoever was around. They stopped counting guests when 400 passed through the portal.

Will enjoyed the complete backing of the league owners, having had his contract extended by five- and ten-year leaps, and his snow-white hair was the sign of law and order wherever baseball people met. His pride and joy was the All-Star Game and the AL enjoyed a pronounced winning margin over the NL during his presidency. He considered the 1941 All-Star Game at Detroit won by Ted Williams' winning homer off Claude Passeau the top one, having done everything short of kissing the stringbean when they embraced in the clubhouse. "I would have kissed him, too," said Will, in unusual exuberance, "if there hadn't been so many people around."

Harridge had a great perception of the rules of the game, knew when to step in and when to let the owners run their own show. Turmoil found no place in the American League scene. As was said at his passing, "Any enemy of Will Harridge was an enemy of good, clean baseball and sound organization."

Harridge was named to the Hall of Fame in 1972.

JOSEPH (MOON) HARRIS

Born May 20, 1891, At Coulters, Pa.
Died December 10, 1959, at PlumBorough, Pa.
Height, 5.09. Weight, 170.
Threw and batted righthanded.
Married Pearl Hepner, February 24, 1921.

Year	Club	League	Pos.	G.	AB.	R.	H.	2B.	3B.	HR.	RBI.	B.A.	PO.	A.	E.	F.A.
1912	McKeesport	Ohio-Pa.					(No Averages Issued)									
1913	Bay City	S. Mich.	1B	96	331	48	109	26	14	2	....	.329	551	41	5	*.992
1914	New York	Amer.	1B-OF	2	1	0	0	0	0	0	0	.000	10	1	0	1.000
1914	Bay City	S. Mich.	1B	139	510	135	*197	39	*22	10	....	*.386	1024	82	24	.979
1915	Chattanooga	South.	1B	155	531	60	137	28	15	2	....	.258	*1567	92	20	.988
1916	Chattanooga	South.	1B	141	501	73	155	20	14	*9	....	.309	867	85	19	.980
1917	Cleveland	Amer.	1B	112	369	40	112	22	4	0	59	.304	1019	86	16	.986
1918	Cleveland	Amer.					(In Military Service)									

Year	Club	League	Pos.	G.	AB.	R.	H.	2B.	3B.	HR.	RBI.	B.A.	PO.	A.	E.	F.A.
1919—Cleveland		Amer.	1B	62	184	30	69	16	1	1	47	.375	451	38	6	.988
1920-21—Cleveland(a)		Amer.			(Ineligible—Played Outlaw Ball)											
1922—Boston		Amer.	1B-OF	119	408	53	129	30	9	6	54	.316	359	29	13	.968
1923—Boston		Amer.	OF	142	483	82	162	28	11	13	76	.335	289	13	10	.968
1924—Boston		Amer.	1B	133	491	82	148	36	9	3	77	.301	1288	103	10	.993
1925—Boston(b)-Wash.		Amer.	1B-OF	108	319	64	100	21	10	13	61	.313	506	42	6	.989
1926—Washington(c)		Amer.	1B-OF	92	257	43	79	13	9	5	55	.307	354	20	3	.992
1927—Pittsburgh		Nat.	1B	129	411	57	134	27	9	5	73	.326	1056	78	11	.990
1928—Pitts.(d)-Brook.		Nat.	1B-OF	71	112	10	30	8	2	1	10	.268	21	2	1	.958
1929—Sacramento		P. C.	OF	54	190	37	65	16	1	6	42	.342	73	6	0	1.000
1930—Toronto		Int.	1B-OF	114	345	52	115	21	8	11	82	.333	657	41	6	.991
1931—Buffalo-Toronto		Int.	1B	74	222	32	69	12	5	4	38	.311	444	39	6	.988
American League Totals				770	2512	394	799	166	53	41	429	.318	4276	331	64	.986
National League Totals				200	523	67	164	35	11	6	83	.314	1077	80	12	.985
Major League Totals				970	3035	461	963	201	64	47	512	.317	5353	411	76	.987

aTraded to Boston Red Sox with first baseman George Burns and outfielder Earl Smith for first baseman John (Stuffy) McInnis, December, 1921.
bTraded to Washington Senators for pitcher Paul Zahniser and outfielder Roy Carlyle, April 26, 1925.
cReleased to Pittsburgh Pirates on waivers, February 4, 1927.
dTraded to Brooklyn Dodgers with catcher Johnny Gooch for catcher Charles Hargreaves, June 8, 1928.

WORLD SERIES RECORD

Year	Club	League	Pos.	G.	AB.	R.	H.	2B.	3B.	HR.	RBI.	B.A.	PO.	A.	E.	F.A.
1925—Washington		Amer.	OF	7	25	5	11	2	0	3	6	.440	10	1	0	1.000
1927—Pittsburgh		Nat.	1B	4	15	0	3	0	0	0	1	.200	35	2	0	1.000
World Series Totals				11	40	5	14	2	0	3	7	.350	45	3	0	1.000

STANLEY RAYMOND (BUCKY) HARRIS

Born November 8, 1896, at Port Jervis, N.Y.

Died November 8, 1977, at Bethesda, Md.

Height, 5.09½. Weight, 156.

Threw and batted righthanded.

Married Marie Desmond, 1949.

Holds major league record for most putouts (154-game season), by second baseman (479), 1922.
World Series records: holds record for most putouts by second baseman in seven-game Series (26), 1924; holds record for most chances accepted in seven-game Series by second baseman (54), 1924; holds record for second basemen for most double plays in a seven-game series (8), 1924; holds second base record for most putouts in a nine-inning game (8), October 8, 1924 (tied by Dave Lopes, Los Angeles Dodgers, 1974); tied record for most assists, nine-inning game, by a second baseman (8), October 7, 1924; tied record for most chances accepted by second baseman in a game (13), October 11, 1925.
Named Major League Manager of the Year by THE SPORTING NEWS, 1947.
Manager, Washington Senators, 1924-28; manager, Detroit Tigers, 1929-33; manager, Boston Red Sox, 1934; manager, Washington, 1935-42; manager, Philadelphia Phillies, 1943; manager, Buffalo, International League, 1944-45; manager, New York Yankees, 1947-48; manager, San Diego, Pacific Coast League, 1949; manager, Washington, 1950-54; manager, Detroit, 1955; also general manager, Buffalo, 1945-46; assistant to general manager, Boston Red Sox, 1956-60; scout, Chicago White Sox, 1962; scout, Washington, 1963-71.
Named to Hall of Fame, 1975.

Year	Club	League	Pos.	G.	AB.	R.	H.	2B.	3B.	HR.	RBI.	B.A.	PO.	A.	E.	F.A.
1916—Muskegon		Central	3B	55	169	8	28	....	....	....	....	.166	82	91	21	.892
1917—Norfolk (a)		Virginia	SS	15	50	4	6	0	0	0	2	.120	40	34	14	.841
1917—Reading		N.Y.S.	2B	75	280	44	70	....	....	....	....	.250	153	214	26	.934
1918—Buffalo		Int.	2B-SS	85	320	51	77	11	7	0	....	.241	216	273	34	.935
1919—Buffalo		Int.	2B	120	447	68	126	18	8	2	....	.282	281	366	41	.940
1919—Washington		Amer.	2B	8	28	0	6	1	0	0	4	.214	21	27	4	.923
1920—Washington		Amer.	2B	137	506	76	152	26	6	1	68	.300	345	401	33	.958
1921—Washington		Amer.	2B	154	584	82	169	22	8	0	54	.289	407	481	38	.959
1922—Washington		Amer.	2B	154	602	95	162	24	8	2	40	.269	*479	483	30	.970
1923—Washington		Amer.	2B	145	532	60	150	21	13	2	70	.282	*418	449	*35	.961
1924—Washington		Amer.	2B	143	544	88	146	28	9	1	58	.268	393	386	26	.968
1925—Washington		Amer.	2B	144	551	91	158	30	3	1	66	.287	402	429	26	.970
1926—Washington		Amer.	2B	141	537	94	152	39	9	1	63	.283	*356	427	30	.963
1927—Washington		Amer.	2B	128	475	98	127	20	3	1	55	.267	*316	413	21	*.972
1928—Washington (b)		Amer.	2B	99	358	34	73	11	5	0	28	.204	251	326	18	.970
1929—Detroit		Amer.	2B-SS	7	11	3	1	0	0	0	0	.091	5	13	2	.900
1930—Detroit		Amer.					(Did not play)									
1931—Detroit		Amer.	2B	4	8	1	1	0	0	0	.125	5	6	0	1.000	
Major League Totals				1264	4736	722	1297	223	64	9	506	.274	3398	3841	263	.965

aLeague disbanded in May.
bTraded to Detroit for infielder Jack Warner, October, 1928, and appointed manager of Tigers.

WORLD SERIES RECORD

Year	Club	League	Pos.	G.	AB.	R.	H.	2B.	3B.	HR.	RBI.	B.A.	PO.	A.	E.	F.A.
1924–Washington		Amer.	2B	7	33	5	11	0	0	2	7	.333	26	28	2	.694
1925–Washington		Amer.	2B	7	23	2	2	0	0	0	0	.087	24	18	0	1.000
World Series Totals				14	56	7	13	0	0	2	7	.232	50	46	2	.980

CHARLES LEO (GABBY) HARTNETT

Born December 20, 1900, at Woonsocket, R. I.
Died December 20, 1972, at Park Ridge, Ill.
Height, 6.01. Weight, 218.
Threw and batted righthanded.
Married Martha Henrietta Marshall, January 28, 1929.

Caught 100 or more games per season for 12 years, for a National League record.
Set major league record for catchers, most double plays, season, 6 (1925 (tie), 1927, 1930 (tie), 1931 1934, 1935).
World Series performances–Had five assists, four-game Series, 1932.
Named Most Valuable Player, National League, 1935.
Named by Baseball Writers' Association of America as catcher for THE SPORTING NEWS All-Star Major League Teams, 1927 and 1937.
Manager, Chicago Cubs, July 20, 1938, to November 13, 1940; player-coach, New York Giants, 1941; manager, Indianapolis, 1942; manager, Jersey City, 1943; manager, Buffalo, 1946; coach, Kansas City Athletics, February 4, 1965; and became scout and joined public relations staff, April 12, 1966.
Named to Hall of Fame, 1955.

Year	Club	League	Pos.	G.	AB.	R.	H.	2B.	3B.	HR.	RBI.	B.A.	PO.	A.	E.	F.A.
1921–Worcester		East.	C	100	345	38	91	21	7	3	.....	.264	447	104	19	.967
1922–Chicago		Nat.	C	31	72	4	14	1	1	0	4	.194	79	29	2	.982
1923–Chicago		Nat.	C-1B	85	231	28	62	12	2	8	39	.268	413	39	5	.989
1924–Chicago		Nat.	C	111	354	56	106	17	7	16	67	.299	369	97	*18	.963
1925–Chicago		Nat.	C	117	398	61	115	28	3	24	67	.289	*409	*114	*23	.958
1926–Chicago		Nat.	C	93	284	35	78	25	3	8	41	.275	307	86	9	.978
1927–Chicago		Nat.	C	127	449	56	132	32	5	10	80	.294	*479	*99	*16	.973
1928–Chicago		Nat.	C	120	388	61	117	26	9	14	57	.302	455	•103	6	*.989
1929–Chicago(a)		Nat.	PH-C	25	22	2	6	2	1	1	9	.273	4	0	0	1.000
1930–Chicago		Nat.	C	141	508	84	172	31	3	37	122	.339	*646	*68	8	*.989
1931–Chicago		Nat.	C	116	380	53	107	32	1	8	70	.282	444	68	10	.981
1932–Chicago		Nat.	C	121	406	52	110	25	3	12	52	.271	484	75	10	.982
1933–Chicago		Nat.	C	140	490	55	135	21	4	16	88	.276	550	77	7	.989
1934–Chicago		Nat.	C	130	438	58	131	21	1	22	90	.299	*605	*86	3	*.996
1935–Chicago		Nat.	C	116	413	67	142	32	6	13	91	.344	477	*77	9	*.984
1936–Chicago		Nat.	C	121	424	49	130	25	6	7	64	.307	504	75	5	*.991
1937–Chicago		Nat.	C	110	356	47	126	21	6	12	82	.354	436	65	2	*.996
1938–Chicago		Nat.	C	88	299	40	82	19	1	10	59	.274	358	40	2	.995
1939–Chicago		Nat.	C	97	306	36	85	18	2	12	59	.278	336	47	3	.992
1940–Chicago(b)		Nat.	C	37	64	3	17	3	0	1	12	.266	69	9	4	.951
1941–New York		Nat.	C	64	150	20	45	5	0	5	26	.300	138	15	1	.994
1942–Indianapolis		A. A.	C	72	186	17	41	12	2	4	24	.220	190	36	7	.970
1943–Jersey City		Int.	C	16	16	0	4	1	0	0	5	.250	9	4	1	.929
1944–Jersey City		Int.	C	31	11	1	2	1	0	0	6	.182	0	0	0	.000
Major League Totals				1990	6432	867	1912	396	64	236	1179	.297	7562	1269	143	.984

aHad sore arm and was used as pinch-hitter.
bUnconditionally released by Chicago Cubs, November 13, 1940, signed as player-coach, New York Giants, December 2, 1940.

WORLD SERIES RECORD

Year	Club	League	Pos.	G.	AB.	R.	H.	2B.	3B.	HR.	RBI.	B.A.	PO.	A.	E.	F.A.
1929–Chicago		Nat.	PH	3	3	0	0	0	0	0	0	.000	0	0	0	.000
1932–Chicago		Nat.	C	4	16	2	5	2	0	1	1	.313	31	5	1	.973
1935–Chicago		Nat.	C	6	24	1	7	0	0	1	2	.292	33	6	0	1.000
1938–Chicago		Nat.	C	3	11	0	1	0	1	0	0	.091	14	3	0	1.000
World Series Totals				16	54	3	13	2	1	2	3	.241	78	14	1	.989

DID YOU KNOW–

That Gabby Hartnett, bawled out by Judge Landis for having picture taken with Al Capone, told Landis, "Judge, if you want me to refuse, YOU tell him!"?

GUY JACKSON HECKER

Born April 3, 1856, at Youngsville, Pa.
Died December 3, 1938, at Wooster, O.
Threw and batted righthanded.

Outstanding performances—Pitched 3-1 no-hit game against Allegheny, September 19, 1882; led American Association pitchers with 368 strikeouts, 1884; made six hits in seven plate appearances, including three home runs and scoring seven runs in game against Baltimore, August 15, 1886, while pitching a four-hitter; played entire game (8 innings) at first base without a fielding chance, October 9, 1887, against Cincinnati.

Umpire, American Association, in 1889 following release by Louisville; manager, Pittsburgh, National League, 1890; manager, Fort Wayne, Western League, 1892; manager, Oil City, Oil and Iron League, 1895.

PITCHING RECORD

Year Club	League	G.	CG.	ShO.	W.	L.	Pct.	H.	R.	BB.	SO.
1882—Louisville	American Assn.	13	10	0	6	6	.500	81	49	6	35
1883—Louisville	American Assn.	55	....	3	28	25	.528	507	271	74	180
1884—Louisville	American Assn.	*76	....	6	*52	20	.722	525	232	59	*368
1885—Louisville	American Assn.	54	48	2	30	24	.556	473	264	89	209
1886—Louisville	American Assn.	52	45	2	27	23	.540	394	263	....	....
1887—Louisville	American Assn.	33	31	2	19	12	.613	376	211	51	57
1888—Louisville	American Assn.	28	25	0	8	17	.320	255	154	42	55
1889—Louisville	American Assn.	17	14	0	5	11	.313	224	148	49	37
1890—Pittsburgh	National	14	11	0	2	12	.143	....	....	....	....
American Association Totals		328	....	15	175	138	.559	2835	1592	....	....
National League Totals		14	11	0	2	12	.143	....	....	....	....
Major League Totals		342	....	15	177	150	.541	....	....	....	....

BATTING RECORD

Year Club	League	Pos.	G.	AB.	R.	H.	2B.	3B.	HR.	SB.	B.A.
1882—Louisville	American Assn.	1B-P	78	349	64	97	14	4	3	....	.278
1883—Louisville	American Assn.	1B-P	81	334	59	90	7	6	1	....	.269
1884—Louisville	American Assn.	P-1B	79	321	53	95	15	8	4	....	.296
1885—Louisville	American Assn.	P-1B	72	299	45	82	9	2	2	....	.274
1886—Louisville	American Assn.	P-1B	84	345	76	118	13	5	4	24	.342
1887—Louisville	American Assn.	1B-P	91	409	83	153	22	6	4	49	.374
1888—Louisville	American Assn.	1B-P	55	208	31	53	8	2	0	23	.255
1889—Louisville	American Assn.	1B-P	82	329	42	91	16	5	1	16	.277
1890—Pittsburgh	National League	1B-P	86	340	43	77	12	7	0	13	.226
American Association Totals			622	2594	453	779	104	38	19	112	.300
National League Totals			86	340	43	77	12	7	0	13	.226
Major League Totals			708	2934	496	856	116	45	19	125	.292

HARRY EDWIN HEILMANN

Born August 3, 1894, at San Francisco, Calif.
Died July 9, 1951, at Detroit, Mich.
Height, 6.01. Weight, 200.
Threw and batted righthanded.
Married Harriett Maynes, October 5, 1920.

Had ten consecutive hits, June 16, 17, 18, 19, 1922; holds major league record for most home runs, season, against one club, on road with 10 vs. Philadelphia, 1922.
Led outfielders in assists (27), 1924. Had 4 at first base.
Coach, Cincinnati Reds, 1932.
Named to Hall of Fame, 1952.

Year Club	League	Pos.	G.	AB.	R.	H.	2B.	3B.	HR.	RBI.	B.A.	PO.	A.	E.	F.A.
1913—Portland	N. W.	OF-1B	122	417	55	127	26	2	11	....	.305	748	67	20	.976
1914—Detroit	Amer.	OF-1B	66	182	25	41	8	1	2	22	.225	200	17	10	.956
1915—San Francisco	P. C.	1B	98	371	57	135	23	4	12	....	.364	1019	72	*25	.978
1916—Detroit	Amer.	OF-1B	136	451	57	127	30	11	2	76	.282	426	27	9	.981
1917—Detroit	Amer.	OF-1B	150	556	57	156	22	11	5	84	.281	466	40	13	.975

Year	Club	League	Pos.	G.	AB.	R.	H.	2B.	3B.	HR.	RBI.	B.A.	PO.	A.	E.	F.A.
1918–Detroit		Amer.	OF	79	286	34	79	10	6	5	44	.276	427	25	8	.983
1919–Detroit		Amer.	1B	140	537	74	172	30	15	8	95	.320	1402	78	*31	.979
1920–Detroit		Amer.	OF-*1B	145	543	66	168	28	5	9	90	.309	1234	86	*19	*.986
1921–Detroit		Amer.	OF	149	602	114	*237	43	14	19	139	*.394	257	13	11	.961
1922–Detroit		Amer.	OF	118	455	92	162	27	10	21	92	.356	175	6	10	.948
1923–Detroit		Amer.	OF	144	524	121	211	44	11	18	115	*.403	272	15	12	.960
1924–Detroit		Amer.	*OF-1B	153	570	107	197	•45	16	10	114	.346	263	*31	9	.970
1925–Detroit		Amer.	OF	150	573	97	225	40	11	13	134	*.393	278	9	9	.970
1926–Detroit		Amer.	OF	141	502	90	184	41	8	9	103	.367	228	18	7	.972
1927–Detroit		Amer.	OF	141	505	106	201	50	9	14	120	*.398	218	11	8	.966
1928–Detroit		Amer.	OF-1B	151	558	83	183	38	10	14	107	.328	449	34	9	.982
1929–Detroit(a)		Amer.	OF	125	453	86	156	41	7	15	120	.344	193	8	7	.966
1930–Cincinnati		Nat.	OF-1B	142	459	79	153	43	6	19	91	.333	457	30	19	.962
1931–Cincinnati		Nat.						Out of game all season								
1932–Cincinnati		Nat.	1B	15	31	3	8	2	0	0	6	.258	44	2	1	.979
American League Totals				1988	7297	1209	2499	497	145	164	1455	.343	6488	418	172	.976
National League Totals				157	490	82	161	45	6	19	97	.329	501	32	20	.964
Major League Totals				2145	7787	1291	2660	542	151	183	1552	.342	6989	450	192	.975

aReleased on waivers to Cincinnati, October 29, 1929.

HARVEY HENDRICK

Born November 9, 1897, at Mason, Tenn.
Died October 29, 1941, at Covington, Tenn.
Height, 6.02. Weight, 190.
Threw right and batted lefthanded.

Led N.L. first basemen in double plays, 1931.

Year	Club	League	Pos.	G.	AB.	R.	H.	2B.	3B.	HR.	RBI.	B.A.	PO.	A.	E.	F.A.
1920–Memphis		South. As.		....	....	....	....	....	....	....	....	....	....	....	....	....
1921–Chattanooga		South. As.	OF	141	570	87	156	27	10	6	50	.274	294	15	22	.934
1922–Galveston (a)		Texas	OF	134	559	95	174	33	11	16	69	.311	255	22	13	.955
1923–New York		Amer.	OF	37	66	9	18	3	1	3	12	.273	16	2	1	.947
1924–New York (b)		Amer.	OF	40	76	7	20	0	0	1	11	.263	38	1	1	.975
1925–Cleveland		Amer.	1B-PH-PR	25	28	2	8	1	2	0	9	.286	26	2	0	1.000
1925–Providence		Inter.	1B	114	434	68	138	10	13	8	74	.318	1092	68	20	.983
1926–New Orleans		South. As.	1B	151	624	137	*231	40	24	11	86	.371	1617	99	21	.988
1927–Brooklyn		Nat.	1B-OF	128	458	55	142	18	11	4	50	.310	556	37	10	.983
1928–Brooklyn		Nat.	3B-OF	126	425	83	135	15	10	11	59	.318	110	202	26	.923
1929–Brooklyn		Nat.	1B-OF	110	384	69	136	25	6	14	82	.354	455	36	9	.982
1930–Brooklyn		Nat.	OF	68	167	29	43	10	1	5	28	.257	68	4	4	.975
1931–Brook-Cin (c)		Nat.	1B-PH	138	531	74	167	32	9	3	75	.315	1348	67	18	.987
1932–St. Louis-Cin		Nat.	1B-3B	122	470	64	138	32	3	5	45	.294	930	77	18	.982
1933–Chicago		Nat.	1-3B-OF	69	189	30	55	13	3	4	23	.291	344	25	8	.979
1934–Philadelphia		Nat.	OF	59	116	12	34	8	0	0	19	.293	24	1	1	.962
American League Totals				102	170	18	46	4	3	4	32	.271	80	5	2	.977
National League Totals				820	2740	416	850	153	43	44	381	.310	3835	449	94	.978
Major League Totals				992	2910	434	896	157	46	48	413	.308	3915	454	96	.978

aTraded to New York by parent Red Sox for catcher Al Devormer, December, 1922.
bPicked up on waivers by Cleveland, October, 1924.
cThis and all subsequent trades were waiver pickups for nominal sums.

WORLD SERIES RECORD

Year	Club	League	Pos.	G.	AB.	R.	H.	2B.	3B.	HR.	RBI.	B.A.	PO.	A.	E.	F.A.
1923–New York		Amer.	PH	1	1	0	0	0	0	0	0	.000	0	0	0	.000

FLOYD CAVES (BABE) HERMAN

Born June 26, 1903, at Buffalo, N. Y.
Height, 6.04. Weight, 190.
Threw and batted lefthanded.
Married Anna Merriken, November 9, 1923.

Hit three home runs in game, July 20, 1933; hit first home run ever hit by a major league player under the

lights, at Cincinnati against Brooklyn, July 10, 1935. Led N. L. outfielders in double plays, 1932 (tie).
Scout, Pittsburgh Pirates, 1946-47-48-49-50; coach, Pittsburgh Pirates, 1951; coach, Seattle, 1952; scout, New York Yankees, 1953-54; scout, Phillies, 1955-56-57-58-59; scout, New York Mets, 1961; scout, Yankees, 1962-63; scout, San Francisco Giants, 1964.

Year	Club	League	Pos.	G.	AB.	R.	H.	2B.	3B.	HR.	RBI.	B.A.	PO.	A.	E.	F.A.
1921	Edmonton	W. Can.	OF	107	409	53	135	24	*18	7	....	.330	677	41	25	.966
1922	Reading	Int.	1B-OF	8	31	3	8	0	0	0	....	.258	78	2	3	.964
1922	Omaha	West.	1B-OF	92	310	55	129	34	7	9	....	.416	481	34	17	.968
1923	Atl.-Mem.	South.	1B	145	551	69	187	36	10	13	100	.339	1278	76	*29	.979
1924	San Antonio	Tex.	1B	21	86	13	30	6	0	2	21	.349	153	9	1	.994
1924	Little Rock	South.	1B	69	239	32	76	14	3	4	40	.318	570	44	21	.967
1925	Seattle	P. C.	1B	167	651	115	206	52	13	15	131	.316	1456	99	26	.984
1926	Brooklyn	Nat.	OF-1B	137	496	64	158	35	11	11	81	.319	974	64	17	.984
1927	Brooklyn	Nat.	OF	130	412	65	112	26	9	14	73	.272	968	68	*21	.980
1928	Brooklyn	Nat.	OF	134	486	64	165	37	6	12	91	.340	225	12	*16	.937
1929	Brooklyn	Nat.	OF	146	569	105	217	42	13	21	113	.381	244	10	*16	.941
1930	Brooklyn	Nat.	OF	153	614	143	241	48	11	35	130	.393	260	10	6	.978
1931	Brooklyn(a)	Nat.	OF	151	610	93	191	43	16	18	97	.313	287	24	13	.960
1932	Cincinnati(b)	Nat.	OF	148	577	87	188	38	*19	16	87	.326	392	18	13	.969
1933	Chicago	Nat.	OF	137	508	77	147	36	12	16	93	.289	252	12	12	.957
1934	Chicago(c)	Nat.	OF	125	467	65	142	34	5	14	84	.304	192	7	6	.971
1935	Pitts.(d)-Cin.	Nat.	OF-1B	118	430	52	136	31	6	10	65	.316	319	15	9	.974
1936	Cincinnati(e)	Nat.	OF-1B	119	380	59	106	25	2	13	71	.279	175	3	6	.967
1937	Detroit	Amer.	OF	17	20	2	6	3	0	0	3	.300	5	0	0	1.000
1937	Toledo	A. A.	OF	85	336	76	117	37	4	12	79	.348	141	3	1	.993
1938	Jersey City	Int.	OF	145	527	89	171	40	5	18	93	.324	188	10	9	.957
1939	Hollywood	P. C.	1B-OF	90	350	69	111	36	5	13	71	.317	748	45	13	.984
1940	Hollywood	P. C.	1B-OF	148	469	62	144	45	7	9	80	.307	460	33	17	.967
1941	Hollywood	P. C.	1B-OF	110	272	41	94	16	1	11	63	.346	572	53	4	.994
1942	Hollywood	P. C.	1B-OF	85	149	18	48	5	0	5	42	.322	247	32	3	.989
1943	Hollywood	P. C.	OF	81	147	15	52	8	1	4	22	.354	24	2	1	.963
1944	Hollywood	P. C.	OF	78	107	8	37	8	1	0	23	.346	79	7	3	.966
1945	Brooklyn	Nat.	OF	37	34	6	9	1	0	1	9	.265	0	0	0	.000
American League Totals				17	20	2	6	3	0	0	3	.300	5	0	0	1.000
National League Totals				1535	5583	880	1812	396	110	181	994	.325	4288	243	135	.971
Major League Totals				1552	5603	882	1818	399	110	181	997	.324	4293	243	135	.971

aTraded with catcher Ernie Lombardi and third baseman Walter Gilbert to Cincinnati Reds for third baseman Joe Stripp, second baseman Tony Cuccinello and catcher Clyde Sukeforth, March 14, 1932.
bTraded to Chicago Cubs for pitcher Robert E. Smith, catcher Rollie Hemsley, outfielders John F. Moore and Lance Richbourg and cash, November 30, 1932.
cTraded with pitchers Guy Bush and Jim Weaver to Pittsburgh Pirates for pitcher Larry French and third baseman Fred Lindstrom, November 22, 1934.
dSold to Cincinnati Reds, June 21, 1935.
eReleased to Detroit Tigers on waivers, April 1, 1937.

WILLIAM JENNINGS HERMAN

Born July 7, 1909, at New Albany, Ind.
Height, 5.11. Weight, 195.
Threw and batted righthanded.
Married Frances Ann Antonucci, May 23, 1961.

Tied National League record for most years leading league second basemen in putouts (7); holds major league record for most putouts at second base in a doubleheader (16), June 28, 1933; holds major league record of accepting 900 or more chances as a second baseman in five seasons, (1932-33-35-36-38); tied National League record by making 11 putouts at second base in a game, June 28, 1933 (first game).
Named as second baseman on THE SPORTING NEWS All-Star Major League Team, 1943.
Manager, Pittsburgh Pirates, 1947; manager, Minneapolis, American Association, 1948; manager, Richmond, Piedmont League, 1951; coach, Brooklyn Dodgers, 1952-57; coach, Milwaukee Braves, 1958-59; coach, Boston Red Sox, 1960 until named manager, October 15, 1964; released as manager, October 3, 1966; coach, California Angels, 1967; manager, Bradenton, Gulf Coast Rookie League, 1968; manager, Tri-City, Northwest League, 1969; scout, Oakland Athletics, American League, 1968 through 1974; coach, San Diego, National League, 1978 to date.
Named to Hall of Fame, 1975.

Year	Club	League	Pos.	G.	AB.	R.	H.	2B.	3B.	HR.	RBI.	B.A.	PO.	A.	E.	F.A.
1928	Vicksburg	Cot.St.	INF	106	364	63	121	12	15	4	....	.332	237	322	24	.959
1928	Louisville	A. A.	2B	4	15	3	5	1	1	0	4	.333	9	14	0	1.000
1929	Dayton	Cent.	2B	138	529	96	174	36	7	13	79	.329	*390	*432	*39	.955
1929	Louisville	A. A.	2B	24	93	17	30	3	4	1	13	.323	72	85	7	.957
1930	Louisville	A. A.	2B	143	617	108	188	40	7	8	86	.305	354	495	*40	.955
1931	Louisville	A. A.	2B	118	486	100	170	24	3	7	59	.350	352	375	28	.963
1931	Chicago	Nat.	2B	25	98	14	32	7	0	0	16	.327	76	79	10	.939

Year	Club	League	Pos.	G.	AB.	R.	H.	2B.	3B.	HR.	RBI.	B.A.	PO.	A.	E.	F.A.
1932–Chicago		Nat.	2B	•154	656	102	206	42	7	1	51	.314	401	*527	*38	.961
1933–Chicago		Nat.	2B	153	619	82	173	35	2	0	44	.279	*466	512	*45	.956
1934–Chicago		Nat.	2B	113	456	79	138	21	6	3	42	.303	278	385	17	.975
1935–Chicago		Nat.	2B	154	666	113	*227	*57	6	7	83	.341	*416	*520	35	*.964
1936–Chicago		Nat.	2B	153	632	101	211	57	7	5	93	.334	*457	492	24	*.975
1937–Chicago		Nat.	2B	138	564	106	189	35	11	8	65	.335	384	458	*41	.954
1938–Chicago		Nat.	2B	•152	624	86	173	34	7	1	56	.277	*404	517	18	*.981
1939–Chicago		Nat.	2B	156	623	111	191	34	*18	7	70	.307	*377	*485	*29	.967
1940–Chicago		Nat.	2B	135	558	77	163	24	4	5	57	.292	*366	448	22	.974
1941–Chi.(a)-Brook		Nat.	2B	144	572	81	163	30	5	3	41	.285	330	374	26	.964
1942–Brooklyn		Nat.	*2B-1B	*155	571	76	146	34	2	2	65	.256	*457	404	23	.973
1943–Brooklyn		Nat.	2B-3B	153	585	76	193	41	2	2	100	.330	345	390	21	.972
1944-45–Brooklyn		Nat.					(In Military Service)									
1946–Brk.(b)-Bos.(c)		Nat.	INF	122	436	56	130	31	5	3	50	.298	352	207	16	.972
1947–Pittsburgh		Nat.	2B-1B	15	47	3	10	4	0	0	6	.213	20	15	0	1.000
1948–Minneapolis		A. A.	2B-1B	10	31	9	14	4	0	2	9	.452	18	11	3	.906
1949–							(Out of Organized Ball)									
1950–Oakland		P. C.	INF	71	202	32	62	8	0	4	29	.307	62	81	4	.973
Major League Totals				1922	7707	1163	2345	486	82	47	839	.304	5084	5823	365	.968

aTraded to Brooklyn Dodgers for infielder John Hudson, outfielder Charley Gilbert and cash, May 6, 1941.
bTraded to Boston Braves for catcher Stewart Hofferth, June 15, 1946.
cTraded to Pittsburgh Pirates with infielder William Wietelmann, pitcher Elmer Singleton and outfielder Stan Wentzel for outfielder Bob Elliott and catcher Hank Camelli, September 30, 1946.

WORLD SERIES RECORD

Year	Club	League	Pos.	G.	AB.	R.	H.	2B.	3B.	HR.	RBI.	B.A.	PO.	A.	E.	F.A.
1932–Chicago		Nat.	2B	4	18	5	4	1	0	0	1	.222	5	12	1	.944
1935–Chicago		Nat.	2B	6	24	3	8	2	1	1	6	.333	15	19	1	.971
1938–Chicago		Nat.	2B	4	16	1	3	0	0	0	0	.188	5	14	2	.905
1941–Brooklyn		Nat.	2B	4	8	0	1	0	0	0	0	.125	4	13	0	1.000
World Series Totals				18	66	9	16	3	1	1	7	.242	29	58	4	.956

CHARLES TAYLOR (PIANO LEGS) HICKMAN

Born March 4, 1876, at Dunkirk, N.Y.
Died April 19, 1934, at Morgantown, W. Va.
Height, 5.11½. Weight, 215.
Threw and batted righthanded.

Made eight hits (three singles, three doubles, two home runs) in ten times at bat in doubleheader on September 7, 1905. As a pitcher, Hickman was 9-2 for Boston, 3-5 for New York and 0-1 for Cleveland. Scout, Cleveland Indians, 1912-14.

Year	Club	League	Pos.	G.	AB.	R.	H.	2B.	3B.	HR.	SB.	B.A.	PO.	A.	E.	F.A.
1896–Newcastle		I.-St.	3B	8	27	4	9	....	....	....	....	.333	0	22	4	.846
1897–Newcastle		I.-St.	3B	26	45	10	15	....	....	....	....	.333	8	17	2	.926
1897–Boston		Nat.	P	2	4	1	2	0	0	0	....	.500	1	1	0	1.000
1898–Boston		Nat.	P	17	58	4	15	2	0	0	....	.259	....	....	....	....
1899–Boston		Nat.	P	18	63	15	25	2	7	0	1	.397	29	11	5	.889
1900–New York		Nat.	3B	125	473	66	148	18	15	9	11	.313	181	283	*91	.836
1901–New York		Nat.	3-S-O-P	101	401	43	115	20	6	4	6	.287	127	113	34	.876
1902–Bos.-Cleveland		Amer.	1-O-P	130	535	73	*194	36	12	11	10	.363	1140	49	47	.962
1903–Cleveland		Amer.	1B	130	518	67	171	31	12	12	15	.330	1300	81	26	.975
1904–Clev.-Detroit		Amer.	1B	126	479	52	135	21	15	6	12	.282	783	43	26	.969
1905–Detroit-Wash.		Amer.	1-2B-O	147	573	69	159	38	12	4	6	.277	378	300	49	.933
1906–Washington		Amer.	1B-OF	120	451	53	128	26	4	9	9	.284	297	21	11	.967
1907–Wash.-Chicago		Amer.	1-2-P	81	221	21	61	11	4	1	4	.276	314	20	14	.960
1908–Cleveland		Amer.	1B-OF	65	197	16	46	6	1	2	2	.234	248	20	12	.957
1909–Toledo		A.A.	OF-1B	167	644	70	183	*49	7	5	21	.284	346	35	14	.964
1910–Toledo		A.A.	OF-1B	167	598	64	190	25	*15	4	12	.317	300	24	22	.936
1911–Toledo-Milw.		A.A.	OF-1B	88	307	36	106	23	6	1	11	.345	117	8	14	.899
National League Totals				263	999	129	305	43	28	13	18	.305	....	....	....	....
American League Totals				799	2974	351	894	169	60	45	58	.301	....	....	....	....
Major League Totals				1062	3973	480	1199	212	88	58	76	.302	....	....	....	....

PITCHING RECORD

Year	Club	League	G.	CG.	W.	L.	Pct.	ShO.	SO.	BB.
1897–Boston		National	2	0	0	0	.000	0	....	....
1898–Boston		National	17	3	2	2	.500	1	....	....
1899–Boston		National	18	5	7	0	1.000	2	13	41
1901–New York		National	8	7	3	5	.375	0	....	....

Year	Club	League	G.	GC.	W.	L.	Pct.	ShO.	SO.	BB.
1902—Cleveland		American	1	1	0	1	.000	0	....	....
1907—Washington		American	1	0	0	0	.000	0	....	....
American League Totals			2	1	0	1	.000	0	....	....
National League Totals			45	15	12	7	.632	3	....	....
Major League Totals			47	16	12	8	.600	3	....	....

PAUL A. HINES

Born March 1, 1852, at Washington, D.C.
Died July 10, 1935, at Hyattsville, Md.
Threw and batted righthanded.

Made six singles in six times at bat in 10-inning game, August 26, 1879.

Year	Club	League	Pos.	G.	AB.	R.	H.	2B.	3B.	HR.	SB.	B.A.	PO.	A.	E.	F.A.
1876—Chicago		Nat.	OF	64	306	62	101	21	3	2	....	.330	159	8	15	.917
1877—Chicago		Nat.	2B-OF	48	202	25	51	12	6	0	....	.252	91	39	32	.803
1878—Providence		Nat.	OF	60	248	40	87	12	4	*4	....	.351	104	20	24	.838
1879—Providence		Nat.	OF	84	406	81	*145	23	8	2	....	.357	145	24	26	.866
1880—Providence		Nat.	1-2B-O	82	356	61	109	19	2	2	....	.306	145	16	13	.925
1881—Providence		Nat.	2B-OF	79	356	64	101	27	5	2	....	.283	176	14	22	.896
1882—Providence		Nat.	1B-OF	84	379	73	117	28	10	4	....	.308	151	16	27	.860
1883—Providence		Nat.	1B-OF	97	442	93	132	11	4	4	....	.298	168	21	18	.913
1884—Providence		Nat.	P-1-O	112	480	92	146	*34	8	3	....	.304	202	20	26	.895
1885—Providence		Nat.	INF-OF	98	411	63	111	19	4	1	....	.270	199	18	34	.864
1886—Washington(a)		Nat.	3B-OF	121	487	80	152	25	7	9	21	.312	200	52	35	.878
1887—Washington		Nat.	OF	123	526	83	195	32	5	9	46	.370	180	14	25	.885
1888—Indianapolis		Nat.	OF	132	513	84	144	25	3	4	31	.280	255	13	26	.911
1889—Indianapolis		Nat.	1B	121	486	77	148	29	1	0	34	.304	1090	57	43	.964
1890—Pittsburgh-Bos		Nat.	OF-1B	100	393	51	93	11	3	1	14	.237	320	20	25	.932
1891—Washington		Am. Assn.	OF	51	199	25	52	6	5	0	5	.261	77	7	14	.857
National League Totals				1405	5991	1029	1832	328	73	47	....	.306	3585	352	391	.910
American League Totals				51	199	25	52	6	5	0	5	.261	77	7	14	.857
Major League Totals				1456	6190	1054	1884	334	78	47	....	.304	3662	359	405	.909

aBeaned by Grasshopper Jim Whitney and became deaf as a result. Used acoustic cane as hearing aid. One of most gracious players in the game.

GILBERT RAY HODGES

Born April 4, 1924, at Princeton, Ind.
Died April 2, 1972, at West Palm Beach, Fla.
Height, 6.01½. Weight, 211.
Threw and batted righthanded.
Married Joan Lombardi, December 26, 1948.

Tied major league record by hitting four home runs in a game, August 31, 1950; tied major league mark by facing pitcher three times in an inning, eighth inning, August 8, 1954.
Held National League record for most home runs with bases filled, lifetime (14), since passed by Hank Aaron with 16 and Willie McCovey with 18.
Led National League first basemen in double plays, 1949-50-51-58.
World Series Records—Holds record for most double plays by a first baseman in World Series (11), 1955; holds record for most double plays started by first baseman (3), 1953, 1956 (tied) and 1959. Holds career marks for first basemen of most games played (38), most putouts (326), most chances accepted (350) and most double plays (31).
Named to THE SPORTING NEWS All-Star Fielding Team as first baseman, 1957-58-59.
Manager, Washington Senators, May 22, 1963 through 1967; manager, New York Mets, 1968 to time of death during spring training, 1972.

Year	Club	League	Pos.	G.	AB.	R.	H.	2B.	3B.	HR.	RBI.	B.A.	PO.	A.	E.	F.A.
1943—Brooklyn		Nat.	3B	1	2	0	0	0	0	0	0	.000	1	2	2	.600
1943-44-45—Brooklyn		Nat.					(In Military Service)									

Year	Club	League	Pos.	G.	AB.	R.	H.	2B.	3B.	HR.	RBI.	B.A.	PO.	A.	E.	F.A.
1946	Newport News	Pied.	C	129	406	65	113	27	7	8	64	.278	*731	*90	14	*.983
1947	Brooklyn	Nat.	C	28	77	9	12	3	1	1	7	.156	79	12	4	.958
1948	Brooklyn	Nat.	1B-C	134	481	48	120	18	5	11	70	.249	990	72	17	.984
1949	Brooklyn	Nat.	1B	156	596	94	170	23	4	23	115	.285	*1336	80	7	*.995
1950	Brooklyn	Nat.	1B	153	561	98	159	26	2	32	113	.283	1273	100	8	*.994
1951	Brooklyn	Nat.	1B	•158	582	118	156	25	3	40	103	.268	1365	*126	12	.992
1952	Brooklyn	Nat.	1B	153	508	87	129	27	1	32	102	.254	1322	*116	11	.992
1953	Brooklyn	Nat.	1B-OF	141	520	101	157	22	7	31	122	.302	1062	101	9	.992
1954	Brooklyn	Nat.	1B	•154	579	106	176	23	5	42	130	.304	*1381	*132	7	.995
1955	Brooklyn	Nat.	1B-OF	150	546	75	158	24	5	27	102	.289	1291	106	14	.990
1956	Brooklyn	Nat.	1-O-C	153	550	86	146	29	4	32	87	.265	1234	103	12	.991
1957	Brooklyn	Nat.	1-3-2B	150	579	94	173	28	7	27	98	.299	*1319	117	14	*.990
1958	Los Angeles	Nat.	1-3-O-C	141	475	68	123	15	1	22	64	.259	932	103	9	.991
1959	Los Angeles	Nat.	*1B-3B	124	413	57	114	19	2	25	80	.276	896	74	8	*.992
1960	Los Angeles	Nat.	1B-3B	101	197	22	39	8	1	8	30	.198	411	44	5	.989
1961	Los Angeles(a)	Nat.	1B	109	215	25	52	4	0	8	31	.242	454	37	1	*.998
1962	New York	Nat.	1B	54	127	15	32	1	0	9	17	.252	315	32	5	.986
1963	New York(b)	Nat.	1B	11	22	2	5	0	0	0	3	.227	61	8	0	1.000
Major League Totals				2071	7030	1105	1921	295	48	370	1274	.273	15722	1365	145	.992

aSelected by New York Mets in National League expansion draft, October 10, 1961.
bTraded to Washington Senators for outfielder Jimmy Piersall, May 22, 1963.

WORLD SERIES RECORD

Year	Club	League	Pos.	G.	AB.	R.	H.	2B.	3B.	HR.	RBI.	B.A.	PO.	A.	E.	F.A.
1947	Brooklyn	Nat.	PH	1	1	0	0	0	0	0	0	.000	0	0	0	.000
1949	Brooklyn	Nat.	1B	5	17	2	4	0	0	1	4	.235	38	3	0	1.000
1952	Brooklyn	Nat.	1B	7	21	1	0	0	0	0	1	.000	60	5	1	.985
1953	Brooklyn	Nat.	1B	6	22	3	8	0	0	1	1	.364	47	4	1	.981
1955	Brooklyn	Nat.	1B	7	24	2	7	0	0	1	5	.292	74	4	0	1.000
1956	Brooklyn	Nat.	1B	7	23	5	7	2	0	1	8	.304	54	5	0	1.000
1959	Los Angeles	Nat.	1B	6	23	2	9	0	1	1	2	.391	53	3	0	1.000
World Series Totals				39	131	15	35	2	1	5	21	.267	326	24	2	.994

JAMES WEAR (BUG) HOLLIDAY

Born February 8, 1867, at St. Louis, Mo.
Died February 15, 1910, at Cincinnati, O.
Height, 5.10. Weight, 160.
Threw and batted righthanded.
Married May Rich, August, 1899.

Pitching Record: Saw brief service as pitcher in 1892, no wins or loses.

In World Series, 1885, Holiday appeared in one game, October 17, as an amateur, two years before he entered professional ball. He was 18 years, eight months and nine days old at the time.

Year	Club	League	Pos.	G.	AB.	R.	H.	2B.	3B.	HR.	SB.	B.A.	PO.	A.	E.	F.A.
1887	Topeka	West.	OF	'98	509	160	215	36	17	15	....	.422	111	17	22	.853
1888	Des Moines	W. A.	OF	114	473	101	•147	...	...	...	65	.311	150	24	22	*.879
1889	Cincinnati	A. A.	OF	135	562	107	193	28	7	•19	51	.343	232	27	22	.922
1890	Cincinnati	Nat.	OF	131	518	93	140	14	15	2	50	.270	253	20	15	.948
1891	Cincinnati	Nat.	OF	110	440	75	140	19	8	8	28	.318	184	10	10	.951
1892	Cincinnati	Nat.	P-OF	149	600	114	172	23	15	*13	39	.287	266	26	22	.930
1893	Cincinnati	Nat.	OF	122	475	106	158	23	11	5	25	.333	266	12	15	.949
1894	Cincinnati	Nat.	OF	122	519	125	199	24	8	13	39	.383	247	26	25	.916
1895	Cincinnati	Nat.	OF	31	126	25	38	9	2	0	6	.302	60	3	3	.955
1896	Cincinnati	Nat.	OF	22	75	15	26	4	0	1	....	.347	33	1	3	.919
1897	Cincinnati	Nat.	OF	53	189	49	62	9	4	2	4	.328	67	4	5	.934
1898	Cincinnati	Nat.	OF	26	100	24	24	2	1	0	6	.240	61	1	2	.969
American Association Totals				135	562	107	193	28	7	19	51	.343	232	27	22	.922
National League Totals				766	3042	626	959	127	64	43	198	.315	1437	103	100	.939
Major League Totals				901	3604	733	1152	155	71	62	249	.320	1669	130	122	.936

WORLD SERIES RECORD

Year	Club	League	Pos.	G.	AB.	R.	H.	2B.	3B.	HR.	SB.	B.A.	PO.	A.	E.	F.A.
1885	Chicago	National	OF	1	4	0	0	0	0	0	0	.000	1	0	1	.500
World Series Totals				1	4	0	0	0	0	0	0	.000	1	0	1	.500

THOMAS FRANCIS HOLMES

Born March 29, 1918, at Brooklyn, N. Y.
Height, 5.10. Weight, 180.
Threw and batted lefthanded.
Married Lillian Helen Pettersen, January 5, 1941.

Held modern National League record by hitting in 37 consecutive games, June 6 (first game) to (second game) July 8, 1945 (since passed by Pete Rose with 44).
Led N.L. outfielders in double plays, 1944, 1946.
Named Most Valuable Player, National League, by THE SPORTING NEWS, 1945.
Named as outfielder for THE SPORTING NEWS All-Star Major League Team, 1945.
Player-manager, Hartford, Eastern League, 1951, until made player-manager, Boston Braves, June 19, 1951; released as manager, June 1, 1952, and signed as player with Brooklyn Dodgers, June 17, 1952; manager, Toledo, American Association, 1953; released on May 14, 1953, and became Brooklyn scout; player-manager, Elmira, Eastern League, 1954; manager, Fort Worth, Texas League, 1955; manager, Portland, Pacific Coast League, 1956, until released, July 11, 1956; signed as manager, Montreal, International League, June 29, 1957; scout, Los Angeles Dodgers, 1958.

Year	Club	League	Pos.	G.	AB.	R.	H.	2B.	3B.	HR.	RBI.	B.A.	PO.	A.	E.	F.A.
1937	Norfolk	Piedmont	OF	137	547	107	175	31	8	25	111	.320	282	11	11	.964
1938	Binghamton	Eastern	OF	135	543	110	*200	*41	9	6	62	*.368	279	14	11	.964
1939	Kansas City	A. A.	OF	7	20	2	3	0	0	0	1	.150	5	0	1	.833
1939	Newark	Int.	OF	107	386	73	131	23	10	4	55	.339	131	8	2	.986
1940	Newark	Int.	OF	162	*665	*126	*211	33	7	7	60	.317	360	15	6	.984
1941	Newark	Int.	OF	•154	*630	105	*190	17	7	9	59	.302	*332	8	4	*.988
1942	Boston	Nat.	OF	141	558	56	155	24	4	4	41	.278	373	16	4	.990
1943	Boston	Nat.	OF	152	*629	75	170	33	10	5	41	.270	408	18	3	.993
1944	Boston	Nat.	OF	155	631	93	195	42	6	13	73	.309	426	14	4	.991
1945	Boston	Nat.	OF	154	636	125	*224	*47	6	*28	117	.352	334	13	6	.983
1946	Boston	Nat.	OF	149	568	80	176	35	6	6	79	.310	294	17	4	.987
1947	Boston	Nat.	OF	150	618	90	*191	33	3	9	53	.309	336	12	4	.989
1948	Boston	Nat.	OF	139	585	85	190	35	7	6	61	.325	283	8	5	.983
1949	Boston	Nat.	OF	117	380	47	101	20	4	8	59	.266	210	10	3	.987
1950	Boston	Nat.	OF	105	322	44	96	20	1	9	51	.298	151	6	0	1.000
1951	Hartford	Eastern	OF	41	113	24	36	7	2	5	29	.319	33	4	1	.974
1951	Boston	Nat.	OF	27	29	1	5	2	0	0	5	.172	2	0	0	1.000
1952	Brooklyn	Nat.	OF	31	36	2	4	1	0	1	1	.111	6	1	0	1.000
1954	Elmira	Eastern	OF	24	19	3	7	1	0	0	5	.368	0	0	0	.000
Major League Totals				1320	4992	698	1507	292	47	88	581	.302	2823	115	33	.989

WORLD SERIES RECORD

Year	Club	League	Pos.	G.	AB.	R.	H.	2B.	3B.	HR.	RBI.	B.A.	PO.	A.	E.	F.A.
1948	Boston	Nat.	OF	6	26	3	5	0	0	0	1	.192	10	2	0	1.000
1952	Brooklyn	Nat.	OF	3	1	0	0	0	0	0	0	.000	2	0	0	1.000
World Series Totals				9	27	3	5	0	0	0	1	.185	12	2	0	1.000

HARRY BARTHOLOMEW HOOPER

Born August 24, 1887, at Santa Clara County (on Elephant Head Homestead), Calif.
Died December 18, 1974, at Santa Cruz, Calif.
Height, 5.10. Weight, 168.
Threw right and batted lefthanded.
Married Esther Henchy, November 26, 1912.

Led A.L. outfielders in double plays, 1922, 1924 (tie). Stole 375 bases in his major league career.
Baseball coach, Princeton University, 1931, 1932.
Named to Hall of Fame, 1971.

Year	Club	League	Pos.	G.	AB.	R.	H.	2B.	3B.	HR.	RBI.	B.A.	PO.	A.	E.	F.A.
1907	Oak.-Sacra'to	Calif. St.	OF	36	139	26	43	4	4	1	....	.309	....	....	....	.....
1908	Sacramento	Calif. St.	OF	77	294	47	101	....	....	....	....	.344	116	17	4	.971
1909	Boston	Amer.	OF	81	255	29	72	3	4	0	16	.282	124	14	7	.952
1910	Boston	Amer.	OF	155	584	81	156	9	10	2	33	.267	241	•30	*18	.938
1911	Boston	Amer.	OF	130	524	93	163	20	6	4	43	.311	181	27	10	.954

Year	Club	League	Pos.	G.	AB.	R.	H.	2B.	3B.	HR.	RBI.	B.A.	PO.	A.	E.	F.A.
1912—Boston		Amer.	OF	147	590	98	143	20	12	2	46	.242	220	22	9	.964
1913—Boston		Amer.	OF	148	585	100	169	29	12	4	40	.289	248	25	9	.968
1914—Boston		Amer.	OF	141	530	85	137	23	15	1	44	.258	231	23	7	.973
1915—Boston		Amer.	OF	149	566	90	133	20	13	2	48	.235	255	23	8	.972
1916—Boston		Amer.	OF	151	575	75	156	20	11	1	33	.271	266	19	10	.966
1917—Boston		Amer.	OF	151	559	89	143	21	11	3	43	.256	245	20	8	.971
1918—Boston		Amer.	OF	126	474	81	137	26	13	1	46	.289	221	16	9	.963
1919—Boston		Amer.	OF	128	491	76	131	25	6	3	48	.267	262	19	6	.979
1920—Boston(a)		Amer.	OF	139	536	91	167	30	17	7	53	.312	263	22	11	.963
1921—Chicago		Amer.	OF	108	419	74	137	26	5	8	58	.327	182	12	5	.975
1922—Chicago		Amer.	OF	152	602	111	183	35	8	11	80	.304	288	19	12	.962
1923—Chicago		Amer.	OF	145	576	87	166	32	4	10	65	.288	272	15	12	.960
1924—Chicago		Amer.	OF	130	476	107	156	27	8	10	62	.328	251	22	4	•.986
1925—Chicago		Amer.	OF	127	442	62	117	23	5	6	55	.265	231	16	6	.976
1926—						(Out of Organized Ball)										
1927—Missions		P. C.	OF	78	218	35	62	9	0	1	19	.284	113	11	3	.976
Major League Totals				2308	8784	1429	2466	389	160	75	813	.281	3981	344	151	.966

aTraded to Chicago White Sox for first baseman John (Shano) Collins and outfielder Harry (Nemo) Leibold, March 4, 1921.

WORLD SERIES RECORD

Year	Club	League	Pos.	G.	AB.	R.	H.	2B.	3B.	HR.	RBI.	B.A.	PO.	A.	E.	F.A.
1912—Boston		Amer.	OF	8	31	3	9	2	1	0	2	.290	16	3	0	1.000
1915—Boston		Amer.	OF	5	20	4	7	0	0	2	3	.350	8	0	1	.889
1916—Boston		Amer.	OF	5	21	6	7	1	1	0	1	.333	8	2	0	1.000
1918—Boston		Amer.	OF	6	20	0	4	0	0	0	0	.200	11	0	0	1.000
World Series Totals				24	92	13	27	3	2	2	6	.293	43	5	1	.980

ROGERS (RAJAH) HORNSBY

Born April 27, 1896, at Winters, Tex.
Died January 5, 1963, at Chicago, Ill.
Height, 5.11½. Weight, 200.
Threw and batted righthanded.
Married Margorie Bernice Frederick, January 27, 1957.

Hit safely in 33 consecutive games, August 13 through September 19, 1922; hit three consecutive home runs, April 24, 1931, vs. Pittsburgh. Led N. L. second basemen in double plays, 1922, 1929.

Manager, St. Louis Cardinals, June 1, 1925 through 1926; manager, Boston Braves, May 23, 1928, to end of season; manager, Chicago Cubs, September 23, 1930, to August 2, 1932; manager, St. Louis Browns, July 27, 1933 through July 20, 1937; coach, Baltimore, International League, 1938; manager, Chattanooga, Southern Association, July, 1938, to end of season; manager, Baltimore, International League, 1939; manager, Oklahoma City, Texas League, June 9, 1940, to June 23, 1941; manager and general manager, Fort Worth, Texas League, November, 1941, until league suspended, February, 1943; manager, Beaumont, Texas League, 1950; manager, Seattle, Pacific Coast League, 1951; manager, St. Louis Browns, 1952, through June 9, 1952; manager, Cincinnati Reds, August 1, 1952, to September 17, 1953; coach, Chicago Cubs, 1958-59; scout, New York Mets, 1961; coach, New York Mets, 1962.

Named Most Valuable Player, National League, 1925 and 1929.
Named to Hall of Fame, 1942.

Year	Club	League	Pos.	G.	AB.	R.	H.	2B.	3B.	HR.	RBI.	B.A.	PO.	A.	E.	F.A.
1914—Hugo-Denison		Tex.-Ok	SS	113	393	47	91	12	3	3	....	.232	208	285	45	.916
1915—Denison		W. A.	SS	119	429	75	119	26	2	4	....	.277	267	354	58	.915
1915—St. Louis		Nat.	SS	18	57	5	14	2	0	0	4	.246	48	46	8	.922
1916—St. Louis		Nat.	INF	139	495	63	155	17	15	6	60	.313	325	315	45	.934
1917—St. Louis		Nat.	SS	145	523	86	171	24	*17	8	70	.327	268	527	52	.939
1918—St. Louis		Nat.	SS-OF	115	416	51	117	19	11	5	59	.281	211	434	46	.933
1919—St. Louis		Nat.	INF	138	512	68	163	15	9	8	68	.318	185	367	34	.942
1920—St. Louis		Nat.	2B	149	589	96	*218	*44	20	9	•94	*.370	*343	*524	*34	.962
1921—St. Louis		Nat.	INF-OF	*154	592	*131	*235	*44	•18	21	*126	*.397	305	477	25	.969
1922—St. Louis		Nat.	2B	154	623	*141	*250	*46	14	*42	*152	*.401	*398	473	30	*.967
1923—St. Louis		Nat.	2B	107	424	89	163	32	10	17	83	*.384	192	283	19	.962
1924—St. Louis		Nat.	2B	143	536	*121	*227	*43	14	25	94	*.424	301	517	30	.965
1925—St. Louis		Nat.	2B	138	504	133	203	41	10	*39	*143	*.403	287	416	34	.954
1926—St. Louis(a)		Nat.	2B	134	527	96	167	34	5	11	93	.317	245	433	27	.962
1927—New York(b)		Nat.	2B	•155	568	•133	205	32	9	26	125	.361	299	582	25	.972
1928—Boston(c)		Nat.	2B	140	486	99	188	42	7	21	94	*.387	295	450	21	.973
1929—Chicago		Nat.	2B	*156	602	*156	229	47	8	39	149	.380	286	*547	23	.973
1930—Chicago		Nat.	2B	42	104	15	32	5	1	2	18	.308	44	76	11	.916
1931—Chicago		Nat.	2B-3B	100	357	64	118	37	1	16	90	.331	128	255	22	.946
1932—Chicago(d)		Nat.	3B-OF	19	58	10	13	2	0	1	7	.224	17	10	4	.871

Year	Club	League	Pos.	G.	AB.	R.	H.	2B.	3B.	HR.	RBI.	B.A.	PO.	A.	E.	F.A.
1933–St. Louis		Nat.	2B	46	83	9	27	6	0	2	21	.325	24	35	2	.967
1933–St. Louis		Amer.	PH	11	9	2	3	1	0	1	2	.333	0	0	0	.000
1934–St. Louis		Amer.	3B-OF	24	23	2	7	2	0	1	11	.304	2	3	0	1.000
1935–St. Louis		Amer	INF	10	24	1	5	3	0	0	3	.208	38	5	0	1.000
1936–St. Louis		Amer.	1B	2	5	1	2	0	0	0	2	.400	10	0	0	1.000
1937–St. Louis		Amer.	2B	20	56	7	18	3	0	1	11	.321	30	41	4	.947
1938–Baltimore		Int.	2-1B-OF	16	27	2	2	0	0	0	0	.074	22	2	0	1.000
1939–Chattanooga		South.	2B	3	3	1	2	0	0	1	2	.667	0	0	0	.000
1940–Oklahoma City		Tex.	PH	1	1	0	1	0	0	0	0	1.000	0	0	0	.000
1942–Ft. Worth		Tex.	2B	1	4	0	1	0	0	0	2	.250	2	2	0	1.000
	National League Totals			2192	8056	1566	2895	532	169	298	1550	.359	4201	6767	492	.957
	American League Totals			67	117	13	35	9	0	3	29	.299	80	49	4	.970
	Major League Totals			2259	8173	1579	2930	541	169	301	1579	.358	4281	6816	496	.957

aTraded to New York Giants for infielder Frank Frisch and pitcher Jimmy Ring, December 20, 1926.
bTraded to Boston Braves for outfielder Jimmy Welsh and catcher Francis Hogan, January 10, 1928.
cTraded to Chicago Cubs for infielder Fred Maguire, catcher Doc Leggett, pitchers Percy Jones, Harry Seibold and Bruce Cunningham and $200,000, November 7, 1928.
dSigned with St. Louis Cardinals, October 24, 1932.

WORLD SERIES RECORD

Year	Club	League	Pos.	G.	AB.	R.	H.	2B.	3B.	HR.	RBI.	B.A.	PO.	A.	E.	F.A.
1926–St. Louis		Nat.	2B	7	28	2	7	1	0	0	4	.250	15	21	0	1.000
1929–Chicago		Nat.	2B	5	21	4	5	1	1	0	1	.238	9	11	1	.952
	World Series Totals			12	49	6	12	2	1	0	5	.245	24	32	1	.982

FRANK OLIVER HOWARD

Born August 8, 1936, at Columbus, O.
Height, 6.07. Weight, 250.
Threw and batted righthanded.

Established following major league records: Most home runs, six consecutive games (10), May 12 through May 18, 1968; most home runs, five consecutive games (8), May 12 through May 17, 1968.
Tied American League record for most home runs, four consecutive games (7), May 12 through May 16, 1968.
Tied American League record for most consecutive games, hitting homer each game (6), 1968.
Named Minor League Player of the Year by THE SPORTING NEWS, 1959.
Named National League Rookie of the Year by the Baseball Writers' Association and THE SPORTING NEWS, 1960.
Named outfielder on THE SPORTING NEWS American League All-Star Team, 1968-69-70.
Manager-instructor, Milwaukee Brewers minor league organization, 1976; coach, Milwaukee, 1977 to 1980. Manager, San Diego Padres, 1981 to date.

Year	Club	League	Pos.	G.	AB.	R.	H.	2B.	3B.	HR.	RBI.	B.A.	PO.	A.	E.	F.A.
1958–Green Bay		I.I.I.	OF-P	●129	487	★104	162	34	2	★37	★119	.333	186	6	8	.960
1958–Los Angeles		Nat.	OF	8	29	3	7	1	0	1	2	.241	12	1	0	1.000
1959–Victoria		Tex.	OF-3B	63	261	59	93	13	0	27	79	.356	99	16	5	.958
1959–Spokane		P.C.	OF-1B	76	295	43	94	19	2	16	47	.319	243	16	6	.977
1959–Los Angeles		Nat.	OF	9	21	2	3	0	1	1	6	.143	10	0	0	1.000
1960–Spokane		P.C.	1B	26	97	17	36	11	0	4	24	.371	233	19	8	.969
1960–Los Angeles		Nat.	OF-1B	117	448	54	120	15	2	23	77	.268	196	11	4	.981
1961–Los Angeles		Nat.	OF-1B	92	267	36	79	10	2	15	45	.296	122	10	8	.943
1962–Los Angeles		Nat.	OF	141	493	80	146	25	6	31	119	.296	187	19	6	.972
1963–Los Angeles		Nat.	OF	123	417	58	114	16	1	28	64	.273	190	4	8	.960
1964–Los Angeles(a)		Nat.	OF	134	433	60	98	13	2	24	69	.226	183	2	4	.979
1965–Washington		Amer.	OF	149	516	53	149	22	6	21	84	.289	204	5	4	.981
1966–Washington		Amer.	OF	146	493	52	137	19	4	18	71	.278	216	5	4	.982
1967–Washington		Amer.	OF-1B	149	519	71	133	20	2	36	89	.256	225	6	3	.987
1968–Washington		Amer.	OF-1B	158	598	79	164	28	3	★44	106	.274	576	52	19	.971
1969–Washington		Amer.	OF-1B	161	592	111	175	17	2	48	111	.296	602	34	14	.978
1970–Washington		Amer.	OF-1B	161	566	90	160	15	1	★44	★126	.283	601	31	11	.983
1971–Washington		Amer.	OF-1B	153	549	60	153	25	2	26	83	.279	555	65	5	.992
1972–Tex.(b)-Det.		Amer.	1B-OF	109	320	29	78	10	0	10	38	.244	521	32	13	.977
1973–Detroit		Amer.	1B	85	227	26	58	9	1	12	29	.256	12	0	1	.923
	American League Totals			1271	4380	571	1207	165	21	259	737	.276	3512	230	74	.981
	National League Totals			624	2108	293	567	80	14	123	382	.269	900	47	30	.969
	Major League Totals			1895	6488	864	1774	245	35	382	1119	.273	4412	277	104	.978

aTraded to Washington Senators with pitchers Phil Ortega and Pete Richert and infielder Ken McMullen (plus first baseman Dick Nen) for pitcher Claude Osteen, infielder John Kennedy and cash estimated at $100,000, December 4, 1964.
bSold to Detroit Tigers, August 31, 1972.

WORLD SERIES RECORD

Year	Club	League	Pos.	G.	AB.	R.	H.	2B.	3B.	HR.	RBI.	B.A.	PO.	A.	E.	F.A.
1963	Los Angeles	Nat.	OF	3	10	2	3	1	0	1	1	.300	4	0	0	1.000

WILLIAM ELLSWORTH (DUMMY) HOY

Born May 23, 1862, at Houcktown, O.
Died December 15, 1961, at Cincinnati, O.
Height, 5;05. Weight, 155.
Threw right and batted lefthanded.
Married Anna Maria Lowrey, October 26, 1898.
Was a deaf mute, and graduated with highest honors and was valedictorian of his class, School for Deaf at Columbus, O., in 1879.

Threw out three base-runners at home plate, June 19, 1889.

Year	Club	League	Pos.	G.	AB.	R.	H.	2B.	3B.	HR.	SB.	B.A.	PO.	A.	E.	F.A.
1886	Oshkosh	N. W.	OF	71	232	69	76	...	...	...	...	.219	102	13	21	.846
1887	Oshkosh	N. W.	OF	116	532	108	195	...	...	...	67	.367	227	19	31	.888
1888	Washington	Nat.	OF	136	503	77	138	9	9	2	*82	.274	296	26	37	.897
1889	Washington	Nat.	OF	127	507	98	143	10	6	0	36	.282	255	29	35	.890
1890	Buffalo	Play.	OF	122	494	107	148	16	7	0	36	.299	284	26	28	.917
1891	St. Louis	A. A.	OF	130	522	131	155	14	6	5	57	.296	229	22	24	.913
1892	Washington	Nat.	OF	149	583	107	163	20	8	3	60	.280	267	17	40	.877
1893	Washington	Nat.	OF	130	532	105	138	15	6	0	51	.259	282	26	37	.893
1894	Cincinnati	Nat.	OF	128	506	118	158	19	12	5	30	.312	322	37	41	.895
1895	Cincinnati	Nat.	OF	107	427	92	117	20	12	3	50	.274	233	13	35	.875
1896	Cincinnati	Nat.	OF	121	449	120	133	24	6	4	53	.296	307	14	17	.950
1897	Cincinnati	Nat.	OF	128	493	88	144	20	6	3	40	.292	•352	11	24	.938
1898	Louisville	Nat.	OF	148	579	102	184	15	16	5	37	.318	340	*27	18	.953
1899	Louisville	Nat.	OF	•155	*643	113	197	16	12	5	31	.306	333	18	24	.936
1900	Chicago	Amer.	OF	137	547	115	139	...	...	...	32	.254	*337	*45	9	*.977
1901	Chicago	Amer.	OF	131	536	113	157	22	10	4	30	.293	281	16	13	.958
1902	Cincinnati	Nat.	OF	72	279	48	82	16	2	2	12	.294	151	4	11	.934
1903	Los Angeles	P. C.	OF	211	806	156	210	...	...	...	46	.261	413	26	23	.950
	American Association Totals			130	522	131	155	14	6	5	57	.288	229	22	24	.913
	American League Totals			131	536	113	157	22	10	4	30	.293	281	16	13	.958
	National League Totals			1401	5501	1068	1597	184	95	32	482	.290	3138	222	319	.913
	Players League Totals			122	494	107	148	16	7	0	36	.299	284	26	28	.917
	Major League Totals			1784	7053	1419	2057	236	118	41	605	.292	3932	286	384	.917

WAITE CHARLES (SCHOOLBOY) HOYT

Born September 9, 1899, at Brooklyn, N.Y.
Height, 5.11½. Weight, 185.
Threw and batted righthanded.
Married Ellen Burbank, May 12, 1933.

Tied with Dick Rudolph, William James, Charles Ruffing and Sandy Koufax for most games won in four-game World Series (2), 1928; tied with Christy Mathewson for lowest earned-run average in World Series as a starter, three games (0.00), 1921.
Named to Hall of Fame, 1969.

Year	Club	League	G.	IP.	W.	L.	Pct.	H.	R.	ER.	SO.	BB.	ERA.
1916	Mt. Carmel	Pa. State	6	....	5	1	.833	....	....	....	....	....	......
1916	Hartford-Lynn	Eastern	10	71	4	5	.444	....	....	....	22	24	......
1917	Memphis	Southern	17	103	3	9	.250	96	48	....	41	25	......
1917	Montreal	International	28	215	7	17	.292	206	....	60	65	78	2.51
1918	Nashville	Southern	19	137	5	10	.333	103	....	....	51	35	......
1918	New York	National	1	1	0	0	.000	0	0	0	2	0	0.00
1918	Newark	International	5	43	2	2	.400	33	17	10	25	9	2.09

Year	Club	League	G.	IP.	W.	L.	Pct.	H.	R.	ER.	SO.	BB.	ERA.
1919	Boston	American	13	105	4	6	.400	99	42	38	28	22	3.26
1920	Boston(a)	American	22	121	6	6	.500	123	72	59	45	47	4.39
1921	New York	American	44	282	19	13	.594	301	121	97	102	81	3.10
1922	New York	American	37	265	19	12	.613	271	114	101	95	76	3.43
1923	New York	American	37	239	17	9	.654	227	97	80	60	66	3.01
1924	New York	American	46	247	18	13	.581	295	117	104	71	76	3.79
1925	New York	American	46	243	11	14	.440	283	124	108	86	78	4.00
1926	New York	American	40	218	16	12	.571	224	112	93	79	62	3.84
1927	New York	American	36	256	•22	7	*.759	242	90	75	86	54	2.64
1928	New York	American	42	273	23	7	.767	279	118	102	67	60	3.36
1929	New York	American	30	202	10	9	.526	219	115	95	57	69	4.23
1930	N.Y.(b)-Detroit	American	34	183	11	10	.524	240	116	96	35	56	4.72
1931	Detroit(c)-Phila.(d)	American	32	203	13	13	.500	254	130	112	40	69	4.97
1932	Brooklyn(e)-N.Y.(f)	National	26	124	6	10	.375	141	70	60	36	37	4.35
1933	Pittsburgh	National	36	117	5	7	.417	118	45	38	44	19	2.92
1934	Pittsburgh	National	48	191	15	6	.714	184	75	62	105	43	2.92
1935	Pittsburgh	National	39	164	7	11	.389	187	72	62	63	27	3.40
1936	Pittsburgh	National	22	117	7	5	.583	115	44	35	37	20	2.69
1937	Pittsburgh(g)-Brooklyn	National	38	195	8	9	.471	211	97	74	65	36	3.42
1938	Brooklyn	National	6	16	0	3	.000	24	9	9	3	5	5.06
American League Totals			459	2837	189	131	.591	3057	1368	1160	851	816	3.68
National League Totals			216	925	48	51	.485	980	412	340	355	187	3.31
Major League Totals			675	3762	237	182	.566	4037	1780	1500	1206	1003	3.59

aTraded to New York Yankees with pitcher Harry Harper, catcher Walter Schang and third baseman Mike McNally for pitcher Herbert Thormahlen, catcher Herold (Muddy) Ruel, second baseman Derrill Pratt and outfielder Sam Vick, December 15, 1920.
bTraded to Detroit Tigers with shortstop Mark Koenig for pitcher Owen Carroll, shortstop George Weustling and outfielder Harry Rice, May 30, 1930.
cReleased to Philadelphia Athletics on waivers, June, 1931.
dReleased by Philadelphia Athletics and signed with Brooklyn Dodgers, January, 1932.
eReleased to New York Giants, June, 1932.
fReleased to Pittsburgh Pirates, November, 1932.
gReleased by Pittsburgh Pirates and signed with Brooklyn Dodgers, June, 1937.

WORLD SERIES RECORD

Year	Club	League	G.	IP.	W.	L.	Pct.	H.	R.	ER.	SO.	BB.	ERA.
1921	New York	American	3	27	2	1	.667	18	2	0	18	11	0.00
1922	New York	American	2	8	0	0	.000	11	3	1	4	2	1.13
1923	New York	American	1	2⅓	0	0	.000	4	4	4	0	1	15.43
1926	New York	American	2	15	1	1	.500	19	8	2	10	1	1.20
1927	New York	American	1	7⅓	1	0	1.000	8	4	4	2	1	4.91
1928	New York	American	2	18	2	0	1.000	14	4	3	14	6	1.50
1931	Philadelphia	American	1	6	0	1	.000	7	3	3	1	0	4.50
World Series Totals			12	83⅔	6	4	.600	81	28	17	49	22	1.83

ROBERT CAL HUBBARD

Born, October 31, 1900, at Keytesville, Mo.
Died, October 17, 1977, at St. Petersburg, Fla.
Height, 6.02½. Weight, 265.
Married Ruth Frishkorn, November 27, 1927.

Attended Centenary College, two years. Graduate of Geneva College (bachelor of arts degree, 1927).
Began umpiring career in Piedmont League, 1928. On staff of Southeastern League, 1928 and 1929; Piedmont League and South Atlantic Association, 1930; Piedmont League and International League, 1931; International League and Western Association, 1932; International League, 1933-34 and 1935; and in American League, 1936-50. Assistant to supervisor of A.L. umpires, 1952-53; supervisor of umpires, 1954-69.
Played professional football with New York Giants, 1927 and 1928; with Green Bay Packers, 1929-30-31-32-33 and 1935; and with New York Giants, 1936. Line coach at Texas A&M, 1934. Head football coach at Geneva College, 1941 and 1942.
World Series umpire, 1938-42-46-49.
All-Star Game umpire, 1939-44-49.
Named to National Football League Hall of Fame, 1963.
Named to Hall of Fame, 1976.

DID YOU KNOW—
That Cal Hubbard is the only member of football and baseball Halls of Fame?

CARL OWEN (KING CARL) HUBBELL

Born June 22, 1903, at Carthage, Mo.
Height, 6.01. Weight, 175.
Threw and batted righthanded.
Married Lucille Herrington, January 25, 1930.

Pitched 46 successive shutout innings, July 13 to August 1, 1933. Registered ten shutouts in 1933. Turned in 16 consecutive victories, July 17 to end of season, 1936. Pitched 11-0 no-hit game against Pittsburgh, May 8, 1929. Pitched 18-inning 1-0 victory against Cardinals, July 2, 1933, and did not issue base on balls. Fanned five batters in succession (Ruth, Gehrig, Foxx, Simmons and Cronin) in All-Star Game, 1934.
Named National League's Most Valuable Player, 1933 and 1936, and selected for THE SPORTING NEWS All-Star Major League Teams, 1933-35-36-37.
Field director, New York Giants' farm system since December 2, 1943.
Named to Hall of Fame, 1947.

Year Club	League	G.	IP.	W.	L.	Pct.	H.	R.	ER.	SO.	BB.	ERA.
1923—Cushing	Oklahoma State					(No records available)						
1924—Cushing	Oklahoma State					(No records available)						
1924—Ardmore	West Assn.	2	12	1	0	1.000	....	....	....	....	....	......
1924—Oklahoma City	Western	2	15	1	1	.500	19	10	....	3	4	......
1925—Oklahoma City (a)	Western	45	284	17	13	.567	273	172	....	102	108	......
1926—Toronto	Int.	31	93	7	7	.500	90	42	39	45	44	3.77
1927—Decatur	I.I.I.	23	185	14	7	.667	174	61	52	76	48	2.53
1927—Fort Worth	Texas	2	3	0	1	.000	7	....	....	0	3	......
1928—Beaumont	Texas	21	185	12	9	.571	177	69	61	116	45	2.97
1928—New York	National	20	124	10	6	.625	117	49	39	37	21	2.83
1929—New York	National	39	268	18	11	.621	273	128	110	106	67	3.69
1930—New York	National	37	242	17	12	.586	263	120	104	117	58	3.87
1931—New York	National	36	248	14	12	.538	211	88	73	155	67	2.65
1932—New York	National	40	284	18	11	.621	260	96	79	137	40	2.50
1933—New York	National	45	*309	*23	12	.657	256	69	57	156	47	*1.66
1934—New York	National	49	313	21	12	.636	286	100	80	118	37	*2.30
1935—New York	National	42	303	23	12	.657	314	125	110	150	49	3.27
1936—New York	National	42	304	*26	6	*.813	265	81	78	123	57	*2.31
1937—New York	National	39	262	*22	8	*.733	261	108	93	*159	55	3.19
1938—New York	National	24	179	13	10	.565	171	70	61	104	33	3.07
1939—New York	National	29	154	11	9	.550	150	60	47	62	24	2.75
1940—New York	National	31	214	11	12	.478	220	102	87	86	59	3.66
1941—New York	National	26	164	11	9	.550	169	73	65	75	53	3.57
1942—New York	National	24	157	11	8	.579	158	75	69	61	34	3.96
1943—New York	National	12	66	4	4	.500	87	36	36	31	24	4.91
Major League Totals		535	3591	253	154	.622	3461	1380	1188	1677	725	2.98

aObtained by Detroit from Oklahoma City in 1925, and after spring trials in 1926 and 1927 was released outright to Beaumont in 1928.

WORLD SERIES RECORD

Year Club	League	G.	IP.	W.	L.	Pct.	H.	R.	ER.	SO.	BB.	ERA.
1933—New York	National	2	20	2	0	1.000	13	3	0	15	6	0.00
1936—New York	National	2	16	1	1	.500	15	5	4	10	2	2.25
1937—New York	National	2	14⅓	1	1	.500	12	10	6	7	4	3.77
World Series Totals		6	50⅓	4	2	.667	40	18	10	32	12	1.79

MILLER JAMES HUGGINS

Born March 27, 1880, at Cincinnati, O.
Died September 25, 1929, at New York, N. Y.
Height, 5.04. Weight, 146.
Threw righthanded and batted both ways.

Manager, St. Louis, National League, 1913 through 1917; manager, New York, American League, 1918 until death, September 25, 1929.
Named to Hall of Fame, 1964.

Year	Club	League	Pos.	G.	AB.	R.	H.	2B.	3B.	HR.	SB.	B.A.	PO.	A.	E.	F.A.
1899—Mansfield		Int. St.	SS							(No Records available)						
1900										(Played semi-pro baseball)						
1901—St. Paul		West.	2B	129	474	79	153	6	4	2	17	.322	131	224	26	.932
1902—St. Paul		A. A.	2B	129	466	75	153	15	5	0	34	.328	362	429	50	.941
1903—St. Paul		A. A.	2B	124	444	91	137	20	4	0	48	.308	310	405	39	.948
1904—Cincinnati		Nat.	2B	140	491	96	129	12	7	2	13	.263	337	448	46	.945
1905—Cincinnati		Nat.	2B	149	564	117	154	11	8	1	27	.273	346	*525	51	.945
1906—Cincinnati		Nat.	2B	146	545	81	159	11	7	0	41	.292	341	*458	44	.948
1907—Cincinnati		Nat.	2B	*156	561	64	139	12	4	1	28	.248	*353	443	32	.961
1908—Cincinnati		Nat.	2B	135	498	65	119	14	5	0	30	.239	302	406	30	.959
1909—Cincinnati(a)		Nat.	2B-3B	46	159	18	34	3	1	0	11	.213	95	125	16	.932
1910—St. Louis		Nat.	2B	151	547	101	145	15	6	1	34	.265	325	452	30	.963
1911—St. Louis		Nat.	2B	136	509	106	133	19	2	1	37	.261	281	439	29	.961
1912—St. Louis		Nat.	2B	120	431	82	131	15	4	0	35	.304	272	337	37	.943
1913—St. Louis		Nat.	2B	121	382	74	109	12	0	0	23	.285	266	339	14	*.977
1914—St. Louis		Nat.	2B	148	509	85	134	17	4	1	32	.263	328	428	28	.964
1915—St. Louis		Nat.	2B	107	353	57	85	5	2	2	13	.241	194	315	21	.957
1916—St. Louis		Nat.	2B	18	9	2	3	0	0	0	0	.333	10	10	0	1.000
Major League Totals				1573	5558	948	1474	146	50	9	324	.265	3450	4726	380	.956

aTraded with outfielder Rebel Oakes and pitcher Frank Corridon to St. Louis Cardinals for pitcher Fred Beebe and third baseman Alan Storke, February, 1910.

JAMES AUGUSTUS (CATFISH) HUNTER

Born April 8, 1946, at Hertford, N. C.

Height, 6.00. Weight, 195.

Threw and batted righthanded.

Pitched 4-0 perfect game victory against Minnesota Twins, May 8, 1968. Led American League pitchers in complete games with 30 in 1975. Tied for American League lead in games started by pitchers with 40 in 1970.
Named American League Pitcher of the Year by THE SPORTING NEWS, 1974.
Won American League Cy Young Memorial Award, 1974.
Named righthanded pitcher on THE SPORTING NEWS American League All-Star Team, 1974.

Year	Club	League	G.	IP.	W.	L.	Pct.	H.	R.	ER.	SO.	BB.	ERA.
1964—Daytona Beach		Florida St.								(On Disabled List)			
1965—Kansas City		American	32	133	8	8	.500	124	68	63	82	46	4.26
1966—Kansas City		American	30	177	9	11	.450	158	87	79	103	64	4.02
1967—Kansas City(a)		American	35	260	13	17	.433	209	91	81	196	84	2.80
1968—Oakland		American	36	234	13	13	.500	210	99	*87	172	69	3.35
1969—Oakland		American	38	247	12	15	.444	210	99	92	150	85	3.35
1970—Oakland		American	40	262	18	14	.563	253	124	111	178	74	3.81
1971—Oakland		American	37	274	21	11	.656	225	103	90	181	80	2.96
1972—Oakland		American	38	295	21	7	*.750	200	74	67	191	70	2.04
1973—Oakland		American	36	256	21	5	*.808	222	105	95	124	69	3.34
1974—Oakland(b)		American	41	318	•25	12	.676	268	97	88	143	45	*2.49
1975—New York		American	39	*328	•23	14	.622	248	107	94	177	83	2.58
1976—New York		American	36	299	17	15	.531	268	126	117	173	68	3.52
1977—New York		American	22	143	9	9	.500	137	83	75	52	47	4.72
1978—New York		American	21	118	12	6	.667	98	49	47	56	35	3.58
1979—New York		American	19	105	2	9	.182	128	68	62	34	34	5.31
Major League Totals			500	3449	224	166	.574	2958	1380	1248	2012	954	3.26

aAppeared as first baseman in one game.
bDeclared a free agent by an arbitration panel, December 16, 1974; signed by New York Yankees for an estimated $2.85 million, December 31, 1974.

WORLD SERIES RECORD

Year	Club	League	G.	IP.	W.	L.	Pct.	H.	R.	ER.	SO.	BB.	ERA.
1972—Oakland		American	3	16	2	0	1.000	12	5	5	11	6	2.81
1973—Oakland		American	2	13 1/3	1	0	1.000	11	3	3	6	4	2.03
1974—Oakland		American	2	7 2/3	1	0	1.000	5	1	1	5	2	1.17
1976—New York		American	1	8 2/3	0	1	.000	10	4	3	5	4	3.12
1977—New York		American	2	4 1/3	0	1	.000	6	5	5	1	0	10.38
1978—New York		American	2	13	1	1	.500	13	6	6	5	1	4.15
World Series Totals			12	63	5	3	.625	57	24	23	33	17	3.29

WILLIAM FORREST HUTCHISON

Born December 17, 1861, at New Haven, Conn.
Died March 19, 1926, at Kansas City, Mo.
Height, 509. Weight, 175.
Threw and batted righthanded.

Year	Club	League	G.	W.	L.	Pct.	SO.	BB.	CG.	ShO.
1887	Des Moines	Northwestern	39	....	....	......	....	....	....	....
1888	Des Moines	Western	38	....	....	......	....	....	....	....
1889	Chicago	National	37	16	17	.485	150	113	34	3
1890	Chicago	National	*68	*42	25	.627	299	190	*66	5
1891	Chicago	National	*64	*43	19	.694	240	168	*56	4
1892	Chicago	National	*71	*37	34	.521	300	180	*67	5
1893	Chicago	National	40	16	23	.410	66	141	38	2
1894	Chicago	National	34	14	15	.483	60	125	29	0
1895	Chicago	National	34	13	21	.382	93	118	29	2
1896	Minneapolis	Western	53	....	....	......	....	....	....	....
1897	Minneapolis	Western	42	16	20	.444	....	....	....	....
1897	St. Louis	National	6	1	4	.200	5	22	2	0
National League Totals			354	182	158	.535	1213	1057	321	21

MONFORD MERRILL (MONTE) IRVIN

Born February 25, 1919, at Columbia, Ala.
Height, 6:02. Weight, 195.
Threw and batted righthanded.
Married Dorinda Otey, March 31, 1942.

Nothing can sum up the essence of Monte Irvin better than the words of Mrs. Effa Manley, widow of Abe Manley, who owned the Newark club of the Negro National League, for which Monte played. Effa was the general manager, business manager and later sole owner of the club at the death of her husband. Hale and hearty and losing none of her charm and grace, she said in 1979 with almost motherly pride:

"Monte, whom my husband and I both knew and loved as a neighbor growing up, and who played for me, was the choice of all Negro National and American League club owners to serve as the No. 1 player to join a white major league team. We all agreed, in meeting, he was the best qualified by temperament, character, ability, sense of loyalty, morals, age, experience and physique to represent us as the first black player to enter the white majors since the Walker brothers back in the 1880s. But Branch Rickey lifted Jackie Robinson out of Negro ball and made him the first. It turned out all right, but we all felt Monte Irvin would do best representing us. Robinson later resented the 'treatment' he got in the Negro leagues, but Monte has had nothing but praise for what we tried to do for the players under most difficult circumstances for all of us."

The Irvin they were talking about was one of the country's finest all-round athletes. Born on a sugar plantation in Columbia, Ala., Monte was the fifth son and 11th child of a family that worked the soil and ran a cane mill. When he was four, his older brother, Bob, took him to a pond near their home and they fired stones out into the water hour after hour.

"That's where I really developed my throwing arm," Monte said. "When I was six, Bob gave me a baseball glove and started playing catch with me, but I already had the power and the style to throw."

After the family moved to Orange, N.J., Monte earned 16 high school varsity letters, in baseball, football, basketball and track. In a state championship track meet, he picked up a javelin for the first time in competition and hurled it 192 feet, eight inches, a state record that held for nine years.

An Orange High senior in 1938, he scratched his hand while playing basketball and the infection, termed hemolytic streptococcus, nearly cost him his life. He teetered on the brink of death for almost seven weeks and, as a town hero, rated Page One headlines when blood donors were sought. He recovered in time to play summer ball with the Orange Triangles and won a two-year scholarship to Lincoln (Pa.) University. His coach at Orange High, Carl Siebert, tried to interest the Yankees and Giants in his protege, but got nowhere. Two fellow members of the All-State New Jersey team—Hank Borowy and George Case— headed right for the majors—but they were white.

Irvin signed with the Manleys' Newark Eagles and played with them throughout the school summers and after he left Lincoln. He also played Caribbean ball in the winters in Mexico, Cuba and Puerto Rico. He quickly established himself as a slugger of note, a fast base runner, an exceptional fielder and a man all base runners respected because of his powerful throwing arm.

Irvin went into service in 1942, spent some time in Europe with the Army Engineers, saw some combat and eventually did guard duty at prisoner-of-war camps. When he came back, he rejoined the Eagles as a shortstop. The second baseman was Larry Doby. The Dodgers made a pass at Monte, but he was "not feeling well" and they backed off. Monte said it was not the prospect of joining the majors that unsettled him, but that it was simply a case of "too much Army." In July of '47, the Cleveland Indians bought Doby from the Eagles for $10,000, plus $5,000 more if he stuck at least 30 days. Of course, Doby ended his playing career in the majors.

Mrs. Manley's sale of Doby is believed to be the first time a Negro club was paid by a major league team for a black player. Still, she blew her cork because no club wanted Irvin.

"All these big league clubs are making a mistake. Doby is younger (Monte then was 28) and a fine prospect, but the best all-round player we have had for years is our Superman—Monte Irvin," she roared.

In the winter of 1948-49, Monte still was slugging away in the Cuban Winter League. He had seen Jackie Robinson, Doby, Roy Campanella and Don Newcombe make the jump to the majors. After an abortive attempt by the Dodgers to sign him to a St. Paul contract, the Giants picked up Monte and Hank Thompson for their Jersey City (International) farm team. The Eagles were paid $5,000 for Monte's contract.

Irvin hit the majors in 1949, but he was 30 years old and his power and fielding prowess that brought praise from major league observers were but a shadow of the brilliance that made him one of the Negro leagues' greatest all-round performers.

After his playing career, Irvin became an aide to the Commissioner of Baseball. His entrance into the Hall of Fame in 1973 is justice paid to a cleancut, hard-working athlete who made a solid mark in the exile of the Negro baseball scene.

ORGANIZED BALL PLAYING RECORD

Year	Club	League	Pos.	G.	AB.	R.	H.	2B.	3B.	HR.	RBI.	B.A.	PO.	A.	E.	F.A.
1949	Jersey City	Int.	OF	63	204	55	76	18	5	9	52	.373	95	10	1	.991
1949	New York	Nat.	OF-INF	36	76	7	17	3	2	0	7	.224	56	17	1	.986
1950	Jersey City	Int.	OF	18	51	28	26	4	1	10	33	.510	29	1	0	1.000
1950	New York	Nat.	OF-1-3B	110	374	61	112	19	5	15	66	.299	569	51	12	.981
1951	New York	Nat.	OF-1B	151	558	94	174	19	11	24	*121	.312	585	60	9	.986
1952	New York(a)	Nat.	OF	46	126	10	39	2	1	4	21	.310	44	3	0	1.000
1953	New York	Nat.	OF	124	444	72	146	21	5	21	97	.329	244	10	7	.973
1954	New York	Nat.	OF-INF	135	432	62	113	13	3	19	64	.262	276	7	8	.973
1955	New York	Nat.	OF	51	150	16	38	7	1	1	17	.253	94	4	4	.961
1955	Minneapolis(b)	A. A.	OF	75	250	57	88	21	1	14	52	.352	146	7	5	.968
1956	Chicago	Nat.	OF	111	339	44	92	13	3	15	50	.271	216	6	2	.991
	Major League Totals			764	2499	366	731	97	36	99	443	.293	2082	158	43	.981

aSuffered broken right ankle in slide into third base in exhibition game against Cleveland Indians at Denver, Colo., April 2, 1952; made first appearance of season as pinch-hitter, July 27.
bDrafted by Chicago Cubs, November 28, 1955.

WORLD SERIES RECORD

Year	Club	League	Pos.	G.	AB.	R.	H.	2B.	3B.	HR.	RBI.	B.A.	PO.	A.	E.	F.A.
1951	New York	Nat.	OF	6	24	3	11	0	1	0	2	.458	17	0	1	.944
1954	New York	Nat.	OF	4	9	1	2	1	0	0	2	.222	8	0	1	.889
	World Series Totals			10	33	4	13	1	1	0	4	.394	25	0	2	.926

JOSEPH JEFFERSON (SHOELESS JOE) JACKSON

Born July 16, 1888, at Brandon Mills, S. C.
Died December 5, 1951, at Greenville, S. C.
Height, 6.01. Weight, 175.
Threw right and batted lefthanded.

Hit .408 in 1911, finishing as runner-up to Ty Cobb in batting; tied American League record for most three-base hits, season—26 (1912). In 1919 World Series, Jackson made 12 base-hits.

Year	Club	League	Pos.	G.	AB.	R.	H.	2B.	3B.	HR.	RBI.	B.A.	PO.	A.	E.	F.A.
1908	Greenville	Car. A.	OF	87	347	43	*120	....	....	5	....	*.346	149	12	12	.931
1908	Philadelphia	Amer.	OF	5	23	0	3	0	0	0	3	.130	6	1	1	.875
1909	Savannah	So. Atl.	OF	118	450	61	161	....	....	....	....	*.358	175	25	10	.952
1909	Philadelphia	Amer.	OF	5	17	3	3	0	0	0	2	.176	10	0	2	.833
1910	New Orleans(a)	South.	OF	136	466	*82	*165	18	19	2	....	*.354	277	11	7	.976
1910	Cleveland	Amer.	OF	20	75	15	29	2	5	1	12	.387	40	2	1	.977
1911	Cleveland	Amer.	OF	147	571	126	233	45	19	7	88	.408	242	32	12	.958
1912	Cleveland	Amer.	OF	152	572	121	226	44	*26	3	93	.395	273	30	16	.950
1913	Cleveland	Amer.	OF	148	527	109	*197	*39	17	7	81	.373	211	28	18	.930
1914	Cleveland	Amer.	OF	122	453	61	153	22	13	3	66	.338	195	13	7	.967
1915	Cleve.(b)-Chi.	Amer.	OF-1B	128	461	63	142	20	14	5	78	.308	436	27	15	.969
1916	Chicago	Amer.	OF	155	592	91	202	40	*21	3	81	.341	290	17	8	.975
1917	Chicago	Amer.	OF	146	538	91	162	20	17	5	82	.301	341	18	6	.984
1918	Chicago	Amer.	OF	17	65	9	23	2	2	1	18	.354	36	1	0	1.000
1919	Chicago	Amer.	OF	139	516	79	181	31	14	7	97	.351	252	15	9	.967
1920	Chicago	Amer.	OF	146	570	105	218	42	*20	12	121	.382	314	14	12	.965
	Major League Totals			1330	4980	873	1772	307	168	54	822	.356	2646	198	107	.964

aSent to New Orleans by Philadelphia Athletics, who traded rights to him to Cleveland Indians for outfielders Briscoe Lord and cash.
bTraded with $15,000 to Chicago White Sox for outfielders Robert Roth and Larry Chappell and pitcher Ed Klepfer, August 20, 1915.

WORLD SERIES RECORD

Year	Club	League	Pos.	G.	AB.	R.	H.	2B.	3B.	HR.	RBI.	B.A.	PO.	A.	E.	F.A.
1917	Chicago	Amer.	OF	6	23	4	7	0	0	0	2	.304	9	1	0	1.000
1919	Chicago	Amer.	OF	8	32	5	12	3	0	1	6	.375	16	1	0	1.000
World Series Totals				14	55	9	19	3	0	1	8	.345	25	2	0	1.000

LAWRENCE CURTIS JACKSON

Born June 2, 1931, at Nampa, Ida.
Height, 6.02. Weight, 198.
Threw and batted righthanded.

Holds major league record for most years leading league, fielding percentage, pitcher, with most chances accepted, 4 (1957, 1964, 1965, 1968).

Year	Club	League	G.	IP.	W.	L.	Pct.	H.	R.	ER.	SO.	BB.	ERA.
1951	Pocatello	Pion.	22	127	3	11	.214	113	78	60	100	113	4.25
1952	Fresno	Calif.	43	*300	*28	4	*.875	250	116	95	*351	144	2.85
1953	Houston	Tex.	11	52	3	1	.750	59	34	31	42	27	5.36
1953	Omaha	West.	22	162	10	9	.526	139	50	44	114	66	2.44
1954	Houston	Tex.	9	22	0	1	.000	20	13	13	17	7	5.32
1954	Rochester	Int.	30	172	12	6	.667	179	69	61	73	70	3.19
1955	St. Louis	Nat.	37	177	9	14	.391	189	93	85	88	72	4.32
1956	St. Louis	Nat.	51	85	2	2	.500	75	44	39	50	45	4.13
1957	St. Louis	Nat.	41	210	15	9	.625	196	84	81	96	57	3.47
1958	St. Louis	Nat.	49	198	13	13	.500	211	93	81	124	51	3.68
1959	St. Louis	Nat.	40	256	14	13	.519	271	103	94	145	64	3.30
1960	St. Louis	Nat.	43	*282	18	13	.581	277	123	109	171	70	3.48
1961	St. Louis	Nat.	33	211	14	11	.560	203	99	88	113	56	3.75
1962	St. Louis(a)	Nat.	36	252	16	11	.593	267	121	105	112	64	3.75
1963	Chicago	Nat.	37	275	14	18	.438	256	102	78	153	54	2.55
1964	Chicago	Nat.	40	298	*24	11	.686	265	114	104	148	58	3.14
1965	Chicago	Nat.	39	257	14	21	.400	268	•126	110	131	57	3.85
1966	Chicago(b)-Phila.	Nat.	38	255	15	15	.500	257	106	94	112	62	3.32
1967	Philadelphia	Nat.	40	262	13	15	.464	242	111	90	139	54	3.09
1968	Philadelphia(c)	Nat.	34	244	13	17	.433	229	86	75	127	60	2.77
Major League Totals			558	3262	194	183	.515	3206	1405	1233	1709	824	3.40

aTraded to Chicago Cubs with pitcher Lindy McDaniel and catcher Jimmie Schaffer for pitcher Don Cardwell, catcher Moe Thacker and outfielder George Altman, October 17, 1962.
bTraded with pitcher Bob Buhl to Philadelphia Phillies for outfielder Adolfo Phillips, outfielder-first baseman John Herrnstein and pitcher Ferguson Jenkins, April 21, 1966.
cSelected by Montreal Expos from Philadelphia Phillies in expansion draft, October 14, 1968, but announced his retirement.

WILLIAM CHESTER (BABY DOLL) JACOBSON

Born August 16, 1890, at Cable, Ill.
Died January 16, 1977, at Orion, Ill.
Height, 6.02½. Weight, 210.
Threw and batted righthanded.

Hit three triples in one game vs. Detroit, September 9, 1922.
Led A.L. outfielders in double plays, 1925 (tie).

Year	Club	League	Pos.	G.	AB.	R.	H.	2B.	3B.	HR.	RBI.	B.A.	PO.	A.	E.	F.A.
1909	Rock Island	I.I.I.	OF	43	124	15	23	4	2	0	....	.185	16	1	1	.944
1910	Rock Island	I.I.I.	OF	16	43	5	6	....	....	....	....	.140	....	....	....	....

Year	Club	League	Pos.	G.	AB.	R.	H.	2B.	3B.	HR.	RBI.	B.A.	PO.	A.	E.	F.A.
1910–Battle Creek	So. Mich.		OF	55	184	18	41	....	....	....	....	.223	208	43	10	.962
1911–Rock Island	I.I.I.		OF	100	299	43	91	....	....	....	....	.304	360	96	15	.968
1912–Mobile	South.		OF	139	502	58	131	....	....	....	....	.261	*412	16	8	.982
1913–Mobile	South.		OF	54	201	35	49	9	6	1	....	.244	105	2	7	.939
1914–Chattanooga	South.		OF	155	*589	97	*188	30	*19	*15	....	.319	358	13	11	.971
1915–Det.(a)-St.L.	Amer.		OF	71	180	18	38	12	3	1	17	.211	58	3	1	.984
1916–Little Rock	South.		OF	139	508	80	*176	28	*15	6	....	*.346	303	15	15	.955
1917–St. Louis	Amer.		OF	148	529	53	131	23	7	4	52	.248	292	18	8	.975
1918–St. Louis	Amer.						(In Military Service)									
1919–St. Louis	Amer.		OF	120	455	70	147	31	8	4	52	.323	270	9	15	.949
1920–St. Louis	Amer.		OF	•154	609	97	216	34	14	9	122	.355	394	18	9	.979
1921–St. Louis	Amer.		OF-1B	151	599	90	211	38	14	5	90	.352	469	19	7	.986
1922–St. Louis	Amer.		OF	145	555	88	176	22	16	9	102	.317	367	9	12	.969
1923–St. Louis	Amer.		OF	147	592	76	183	29	6	8	81	.309	409	10	11	.974
1924–St. Louis	Amer.		OF	152	579	103	184	41	12	19	97	.318	*488	7	7	•.986
1925–St. Louis	Amer.		OF	142	540	103	184	30	9	15	76	.341	383	18	13	.969
1926–St.L.(b)-Boston	Amer.		OF	148	576	62	172	51	2	8	90	.299	298	9	8	.975
1927–Bo.(c)-Cl.(d)-Ph.	Amer.		OF	94	293	27	72	17	3	1	42	.246	180	5	8	.959
1928–Baltimore	Int.		OF	12	48	4	6	0	0	1	3	.125	39	3	0	1.000
1928–Chattanooga	South.		OF	56	173	31	53	12	4	5	41	.306	105	5	3	.973
1928–Ind'polis-Toledo	A.A.		OF	55	199	26	68	7	3	1	27	.342	109	6	1	.991
1929–Quincy	I.I.I.		OF	130	496	80	151	23	4	20	100	.304	286	4	2	•.993
Major League Totals				1472	5507	787	1714	328	94	83	821	.311	3608	125	99	.974

aTraded to St. Louis Browns for pitcher William James, August 18, 1915.
bTraded to Philadelphia Athletics for outfielder Edmund (Bing) Miller—and then sent by A's to Boston Red Sox with pitchers Fred Heimach and Bryan (Slim) Harriss for pitcher Howard Ehmke, June 15, 1926.
cReleased to Cleveland Indians on waivers, June 12, 1927.
dReleased to Philadelphia Athletics on waivers, August 5, 1927.

CHARLES DEVINE (JAMIE) JAMIESON

Born February 7, 1893, at Paterson, N.J.
Died October 27, 1969, at Paterson, N.J.
Height, 5.08½. Weight, 165.
Threw and batted lefthanded.
Married Edith Van Kirk, November 12, 1913.

Holds major league record for outfielders by starting two triple plays in a season, May 23 and June 9, 1928. Began career as a pitcher.

Year	Club	League	Pos.	G.	AB.	R.	H.	2B.	3B.	HR.	RBI.	B.A.	PO.	A.	E.	F.A.
1912–Buffalo	Int.		OF	33	82	7	13	1	1	0	....	.159	6	69	1	.987
1913–Buffalo	Int.		OF	51	127	7	30	3	0	0	....	.236	40	79	8	.937
1914–Buffalo	Int.		OF	75	221	39	68	17	4	0	....	.308	86	38	7	.947
1915–Buffalo	Int.		OF	138	522	82	160	*28	9	0	....	.307	296	17	10	.969
1915–Washington	Amer.		OF	17	68	9	19	3	2	0	7	.279	36	5	0	1.000
1916–Washington	Amer.		OF-P	64	145	16	36	4	0	0	13	.248	59	4	6	.913
1917–Wash.(a)-Phila.	Amer.		OF-P	103	380	45	98	8	2	0	30	.258	135	12	11	.930
1918–Philadelphia (b)	Amer.		OF-P	110	416	50	84	11	2	0	9	.202	182	15	6	.970
1919–Cleveland	Amer.		OF-P	26	17	3	6	2	1	0	1	.353	5	2	1	.875
1920–Cleveland	Amer.		OF	108	370	69	118	17	7	1	40	.319	185	14	7	.966
1921–Cleveland	Amer.		OF	140	536	94	166	33	10	1	45	.310	277	17	8	.974
1922–Cleveland	Amer.		OF-P	145	567	87	183	29	11	3	57	.323	289	18	7	.978
1923–Cleveland	Amer.		OF	152	•644	130	*222	36	12	2	51	.345	360	18	10	.974
1924–Cleveland	Amer.		OF	143	594	98	213	34	8	3	54	.359	330	11	9	.974
1925–Cleveland	Amer.		OF	138	557	109	165	24	5	4	42	.296	324	16	•16	.955
1926–Cleveland	Amer.		OF	143	555	89	166	33	7	2	45	.299	293	15	13	.960
1927–Cleveland	Amer.		OF	127	489	73	151	23	6	0	36	.309	300	13	10	.969
1928–Cleveland	Amer.		OF	112	433	63	133	18	4	1	37	.307	282	*22	5	.984
1929–Cleveland	Amer.		OF	102	364	56	106	22	1	0	26	.291	192	8	4	.980
1930–Cleveland	Amer.		OF	103	366	64	110	22	1	1	52	.301	162	7	8	.955
1931–Cleveland	Amer.		OF	28	43	7	13	2	0	0	4	.302	11	0	2	.846
1932–Cleveland	Amer.		OF	16	16	0	1	1	0	0	0	.063	3	1	0	1.000
1933–Jersey City	Int.		OF	76	9	19	2	0	1	11	.250	39	1	1	.976	
Major League Totals				1777	6560	1062	1990	322	80	18	549	.303	3425	198	123	.967

aReleased to Philadelphia Athletics on waivers, July 17, 1917.
bTraded to Cleveland Indians with pitcher Elmer Myers and third baseman Larry Gardner for outfielder Bobby Roth, March, 1919.

WORLD SERIES RECORD

Year	Club	League	Pos.	G.	AB.	R.	H.	2B.	3B.	HR.	RBI.	B.A.	PO.	A.	E.	F.A.
1920–Cleveland	Amer.		OF-PH-PR	6	15	2	5	1	0	0	1	.333	8	1	0	1.000

PITCHING RECORD

Year—Club	League	G.	IP.	W.	L.	Pct.	H.	R.	ER.	SO.	BB.	ERA.
1912–Buffalo	International	31	208	13	7	.650	226	97	....	84	57	......
1913–Buffalo	International	32	204	14	10	.583	212	87	....	62	91	......
1914–Buffalo	International	20	86	3	8	.273	99	57	....	37	32	......
1916–Washington	American	1	4	0	0	.000	2	2	2	2	3	4.50
1917–Washington	American	1	2	0	0	.000	10	10	10	1	2	45.00
1918–Philadelphia	American	5	23	2	1	.667	24	17	11	2	13	4.30
1919–Cleveland	American	4	13	0	0	.000	12	9	8	0	8	5.54
1922–Cleveland	American	2	6	0	0	.000	7	3	2	2	4	3.00
Major League Totals		13	48	2	1	.667	55	41	33	7	30	6.19

HUGH AMBROSE (EE-YAH) JENNINGS

Born April 2, 1870, at Pittston, Pa.
Died February 1, 1928, at Scranton, Pa.
Height, 5.08½. Weight, 165.
Threw and batted righthanded.

Captain, Philadelphia Phillies, 1901-02; manager, Baltimore, Eastern League, 1903-04-05-06; manager, Detroit Tigers, 1907 to 1920; coach and assistant manager, New York Giants, 1921-25.
Won championship in first three years as American League manager with Detroit, 1907-08-09.
Named to Hall of Fame, 1945.

Year—Club	League	Pos.	G.	AB.	R.	H.	2B.	3B.	HR.	SB.	B.A.	PO.	A.	E.	F.A.
1890–Allentown	E. Int.-St.	SS	13	50	8	16	...	...	...	0	.320	...	...	...	.934
1891–Louisville	A. A.	1B-SS	81	316	46	95	10	8	1	14	.300	173	205	40	.904
1892–Louisville	Nat.	SS	152	584	66	137	16	3	2	24	.232	★336	543	84	.912
1893–Louis.-Balt.	Nat.	SS	38	135	12	25	3	0	2	1	.192	84	128	23	.898
1894–Baltimore	Nat.	SS	128	505	136	168	27	20	4	36	.332	★307	497	62	★.928
1895–Baltimore	Nat.	SS	131	528	159	204	40	8	4	60	.385	★425	460	53	★.943
1896–Baltimore	Nat.	SS	129	523	125	208	24	9	0	73	.398	★380	476	68	.926
1897–Baltimore	Nat.	SS	115	436	131	154	22	9	2	60	.353	336	417	54	★.933
1898–Baltimore	Nat.	2B-SS	143	533	136	173	24	9	0	31	.325	361	435	60	.930
1899–Brkn.-Balt.	Nat.	1-2B-SS	63	223	44	67	5	10	0	18	.300	475	22	8	.984
1900–Brooklyn	Nat.	1B	112	440	62	119	17	7	2	35	.270	1052	74	18	.984
1901–Philadelphia	Nat.	1B	81	302	38	83	22	2	1	13	.274	725	39	15	.980
1902–Philadelphia	Nat.	1-2B-SS	78	289	31	80	16	3	1	8	.277	659	47	12	.983
1903–Brooklyn	Nat.	OF	6	17	2	4	0	0	0	0	.235	7	0	0	1.000
1903–Baltimore	East.	SS-2B	32	122	26	40	8	0	0	9	.328	51	95	7	.954
1904–Baltimore	East.	SS-2B	92	332	65	97	21	0	1	23	.292	227	235	24	.951
1905–Baltimore	East.	SS-2B	56	179	24	45	8	0	0	3	.251	134	158	37	.887
1906–Baltimore	East.	SS-2B	75	242	24	60	9	1	0	2	.248	177	192	24	.928
1907–Detroit	Amer.	SS	2	4	0	1	1	0	0	0	.250	0	2	0	1.000
1908–Detroit	Amer.	PH	1	0	0	0	0	0	0	0	.000	0	0	0	.000
1909–Detroit	Amer.	1B	2	4	1	2	0	0	0	0	.500	1	0	0	1.000
1912–Detroit	Amer.	PH	1	1	0	0	0	0	0	0	.000	0	0	0	.000
1918–Detroit	Amer.	1B	1	0	0	0	0	0	0	0	.000	0	0	0	.000
American Association Totals			81	316	46	95	10	8	1	14	.300	173	205	40	.904
American League Totals			7	9	1	3	0	0	0	0	.333	1	2	0	1.000
National League Totals			1176	4515	942	1422	217	80	18	359	.315	5147	3130	457	.948
Major League Totals			1264	4840	989	1520	227	88	19	373	.314	5321	3337	497	.946

BYRON BANCROFT (BAN) JOHNSON

(First president of American League.)
Born January 5, 1864, at Norwalk, O.
Died March 28, 1931, at St. Louis, Mo.

As a boy in Avondale, O., Ban Johnson played baseball. Later, when attending Marietta College, he was one of the steadiest catchers of his time in collegiate circles in Ohio, a big fellow with plenty of nerve who caught the fastest pitching without glove, chest protector or mask. From college, Johnson went into newspaper work in Cincinnati—on the old Commercial-Gazette. He continued as a writer of sports, specializing in baseball, until 1893.

At the end of the 1894 season, John T. Brush dismissed Charles Comiskey as manager of the Cincinnati Reds. Johnson and Comiskey then revived the Western League, with Kansas City, Toledo, Minneapolis, Milwaukee, Indianapolis, Sioux City, Grand Rapids and Detroit as members. Johnson was named president. On October 11, 1899, the Western changed its name to the American League, occupied the vacant Cleveland territory by purchase of the ball park there, and decided to move Comiskey's St. Paul club to Chicago.

After the 1900 season, Johnson decided on expansion of the American League into a major circuit for 1901, with or without consent of the National League. He put clubs in Boston, Philadelphia, Washington and Baltimore. St. Louis replaced Milwaukee in 1902. After the A. L. moved the Baltimore club to New York in 1903, peace was restored with the National.

Meanwhile, Johnson had brought about a new era in baseball. He was a stickler for decorum on the playing field; he insisted that umpires of his league be respected and was severe in disciplining players who transgressed the rules of good conduct.

Johnson was a fighter who brooked no interference from anyone. His combativeness was largely responsible for the ending of the three-man Commission which ran the game during his early A.L. reign. When Commissioner Landis came into office after the Commission folded, Johnson battled him whenever it seemed to him that the National League was getting some private benefit or that Landis or the N.L. was trying to take some power, some control from Ban's beloved A.L.

In 1901, Johnson was elected to the presidency of the American League for ten years and re-elected for 20 years. The term subsequently was increased by five years in 1925, so that his term of office would not have expired until 1935. However, ill health and a storm of protest from his adversaries in baseball caused him to retire, October 17, 1927. He was named to the Hall of Fame in 1937.

DERON ROGER JOHNSON

Born July 17, 1938, at San Diego, Calif.
Height, 6.02. Weight, 209.
Threw and batted righthanded.

Tied major league records for most home runs, consecutive appearances (4), July 10-11, 1971.
Hit three home runs in a game, July 11, 1971.
Named as third baseman on THE SPORTING NEWS National League All-Star Team, 1965.
Minor league batting instructor, California Angels organization, 1978; manager, Salt Lake City, Pacific Coast League, 1978; coach, California, 1979 to date.

Year	Club	League	Pos.	G.	AB.	R.	H.	2B.	3B.	HR.	RBI.	B.A.	PO.	A.	E.	F.A.
1956	Kearney	Neb. St.	OF	63	243	*70	80	9	3	*24	*78	.329	104	9	4	.966
1957	Binghamton	East.	OF	137	501	*103	152	23	13	*26	102	.303	253	13	6	.978
1958	Richmond	Int.	OF-3B	154	570	79	148	27	5	27	103	.260	248	33	7	.976
1959	Richmond	Int.	OF-3B	154	556	85	155	23	6	25	90	.279	195	153	18	.951
1960	New York	Am.	3B	6	4	0	2	1	0	0	0	.500	0	3	1	.750
1960	Richmond	Int.	3B-OF	151	552	79	135	23	6	27	92	.245	172	249	15	.966
1961	N.Y.(a)-K.C.	Am.	O-3-1B	96	302	32	63	11	3	8	44	.209	134	66	9	.957
1962	K. City(b)(c)	Am.	1-3B-O	17	19	1	2	1	0	0	0	.105	5	1	1	.857
1963	San Diego	P.C.	OF-IN	129	481	85	133	22	3	*33	91	.277	360	55	14	.967
1964	Cincinnati	Nat.	1B-O-3B	140	477	63	130	24	4	21	79	.273	952	84	10	.990
1965	Cincinnati	Nat.	3B	159	616	92	177	30	7	32	*130	.287	132	266	22	.948
1966	Cincinnati	Nat.	OF-1-3	142	505	75	130	25	3	24	81	.257	339	36	5	.987
1967	Cincinnati(d)	Nat.	1B-3B	108	361	39	81	18	1	13	53	.224	606	73	4	.994
1968	Atlanta (e)	Nat.	1B-3B	127	342	29	71	11	1	8	33	.208	759	78	4	.995
1969	Philadelphia	Nat.	OF-3-1B	138	475	51	121	19	4	17	80	.255	250	99	11	.969
1970	Philadelphia	Nat.	1B-3B	159	574	66	147	28	3	27	93	.256	1180	74	6	.995
1971	Philadelphia	Nat.	1B-3B	158	582	74	154	29	0	34	95	.265	1233	123	12	.991
1972	Philadelphia	Nat.	1B	96	230	19	49	4	1	9	31	.213	479	24	9	.982
1973	Philadelphia(f)	Nat.	1B	12	36	3	6	2	0	1	5	.167	77	6	2	.976
1973	Oakland	Am.	1B	131	464	61	114	14	2	19	81	.246	167	6	1	.994
1974	Oak.(g)-Mil.(h)-Bos.(d)	Am.	1B	110	351	30	60	4	2	13	43	.171	220	10	4	.983
1975	Chi.(j)-Boston	Am.	1B	151	565	68	135	25	1	19	75	.239	475	24	3	.994
1976	Boston	Am.	DH-1B	15	38	3	5	1	0	0	0	.132	30	1	0	1.000
	American League Totals			526	1743	195	381	57	9	59	243	.218	1031	111	19	.984
	National League Totals			1239	4198	511	1066	190	24	186	680	.254	6007	863	85	.988
	Major League Totals			1765	5941	706	1447	247	33	245	923	.244	7038	974	104	.987

aTraded to Kansas City Athletics with pitcher Art Ditmar for pitcher Bud Daley, June 14, 1961.
bSold to Cincinnati Reds' organization, April 5, 1963.
cOn Military list through July 31.
dTraded to Atlanta Braves for outfielder Mack Jones, pitcher Jay Ritchie and first baseman Jim Beauchamp, October 10, 1967.
eSold to Philadelphia Phillies, December 3, 1968.
fTraded to Oakland Athletics for third baseman-outfielder Jack Bastable, May 2, 1973.

gReleased on waivers to Milwaukee Brewers, June 24, 1974; Brewers sent pitcher Bill Parsons to Athletics, July 1, 1974, as part of deal.
    hSold to Boston Red Sox, September 7, 1974.
    iSigned as free agent by Chicago White Sox, April 5, 1975.
    jTraded to Boston Red Sox for cash (plus catcher Chuck Erickson), September 21, 1975.

Year	Club	League	Pos.	G.	AB.	R.	H.	2B.	3B.	HR.	RBI.	B.A.	PO.	A.	E.	F.A.
1973–Oakland		Am.	PH-1B	6	10	0	3	1	0	0	0	.300	8	1	0	1.000

ROBERT LEE JOHNSON

Born November 26, 1906, at Pryor, Okla.
Height, 5.11½. Weight, 200.
Threw and batted righthanded.
Married Caroline Stout, December 17, 1924.
Brother of Roy, a former major league outfielder.

    Tied for American League record for most runs batted in, inning (6), first game, first inning, August 29, 1937; made six hits in six times at bat, second game, 11 innings, June 16, 1934–three singles, one double and two home runs; hit for cycle, July 6, 1944.
    Manager, Tacoma, Western International League, 1949.

Year	Club	League	Pos.	G.	AB.	R.	H.	2B.	3B.	HR.	RBI.	B.A.	PO.	A.	E.	F.A.
1929–Wichita-Pueblo		West.	OF	66	227	50	62	9	3	16	.....	.273	111	2	3	.974
1929–Portland		P. C.	OF	81	264	42	67	16	3	5	27	.254	168	9	7	.962
1930–Portland		P. C.	O-1-2B	157	501	91	133	25	3	21	93	.265	489	68	20	.965
1931–Portland		P. C.	O-1-2B	141	504	108	170	37	5	22	94	.337	445	83	15	.972
1932–Portland		P. C.	O-1-2B	149	545	105	180	43	1	29	111	.330	357	49	19	.955
1933–Philadelphia		Amer.	OF	142	535	103	155	44	4	21	93	.290	298	16	16	.952
1934–Philadelphia		Amer.	OF	141	547	111	168	26	6	34	92	.307	304	*17	11	.967
1935–Philadelphia		Amer.	OF	147	582	103	174	29	5	28	109	.299	337	13	*20	.946
1936–Philadelphia		Amer.	2B-OF	153	566	91	165	29	14	25	121	.292	340	82	19	.957
1937–Philadelphia		Amer.	OF-1B	138	477	91	146	32	6	25	108	.306	314	15	8	.976
1938–Philadelphia		Amer.	*OF-1B	152	563	114	176	27	9	30	113	.313	406	*27	*18	*.960
1939–Philadelphia		Amer.	OF	150	544	115	184	30	9	23	114	.338	369	15	13	.967
1940–Philadelphia		Amer.	OF	138	512	93	137	25	4	31	103	.268	310	15	13	.962
1941–Philadelphia		Amer.	1B-OF	149	552	98	152	30	8	22	107	.275	541	35	8	.986
1942–Philadelphia(a)		Amer.	OF	149	550	78	160	35	7	13	80	.291	318	18	13	.963
1943–Washington(b)		Amer.	1-3B-O	117	438	65	116	22	8	7	63	.265	308	61	9	.976
1944–Boston		Amer.	OF	144	525	106	170	40	8	17	106	.324	270	23	7	.977
1945–Boston		Amer.	OF	143	529	71	148	27	7	12	74	.280	296	15	8	.975
1946–Milwaukee		A. A.	OF	94	307	53	83	14	2	13	53	.270	127	12	7	.952
1947–Seattle		P. C.	OF	130	342	44	101	28	1	7	50	.295	249	20	13	.954
1948–Seattle		P. C.	OF	59	145	17	41	7	0	5	23	.283	225	10	5	.979
1949–Tacoma		W. Int.	OF	93	218	35	71	13	1	5	50	.326	94	16	2	.982
1950–						(Out of Organized Ball)										
1951–Tijuana		S. W. Int.	1B	21	69	13	15	4	2	0	6	.217	74	37	6	.949
Major League Totals				1863	6920	1239	2051	396	95	288	1283	.296	4411	352	163	.967

    aTraded to Washington Senators for outfielder Roberto Estalella, infielder James Pofahl and cash, March 21, 1943.
    bSold to Boston Red Sox, December 4, 1943.

WALTER PERRY (BARNEY) JOHNSON

Born November 6, 1887, at Humboldt, Kan.
Died December 10, 1946, at Washington, D. C.
Height, 6.01. Weight, 200.
Threw and batted righthanded.
Married Hazel Roberts, 1914.

    Pitched most games in American League history, 802; equaled major league record for pitching most successive complete games played by club, 3 (September 4, 5, and 7, 1908), all shutouts; won most games, league, 416; tied league mark for most consecutive games won, 16, (July 3 to August 23, 1912); holds American League record for most shutout games, 110; pitched most consecutive shutout innings, 55⅔ (April 10–second inning to May 14–fourth inning, 1913); pitched 1-0 no-hit game against Boston A. L., July 1, 1920. Named Most

Valuable Player, American League, 1913 and 1924. Named to THE SPORTING NEWS All-Star Major League Team, 1925.

Manager, Newark, International League, 1928; manager, Washington, American League, 1929-30-31-32; manager, Cleveland Indians, June, 1933, until released in August, 1935.

Named to Hall of Fame, 1936.

Year	Club	League	G.	IP.	W.	L.	Pct.	ShO.	H.	R.	ER.	SO.	BB.	ERA.
1907	Washington	Amer.	14	110	5	9	.357	2	100	35	....	70	16	....
1908	Washington	Amer.	36	257	14	14	.500	6	196	75	....	160	52	....
1909	Washington	Amer.	40	297	13	25	.342	4	247	112	....	164	84	....
1910	Washington	Amer.	•45	*374	25	17	.595	8	*262	92	....	*313	76	....
1911	Washington	Amer.	40	322	25	13	.658	•6	292	119	....	207	70	....
1912	Washington	Amer.	50	368	32	12	.727	7	259	89	....	*303	76	....
1913	Washington	Amer.	48	*346	*36	7	.837	*11	232	56	44	*243	38	*1.14
1914	Washington	Amer.	*51	*372	*28	18	.609	*9	*287	88	71	*225	74	1.72
1915	Washington	Amer.	47	*337	*27	13	.675	*7	258	83	58	*203	56	1.55
1916	Washington	Amer.	48	*371	*25	20	.556	3	*290	105	78	*228	82	1.89
1917	Washington	Amer.	47	328	23	16	.590	8	259	105	83	*188	67	2.28
1918	Washington	Amer.	39	325	*23	13	.639	•8	241	71	46	*162	70	*1.27
1919	Washington	Amer.	39	290	20	14	.588	*7	235	73	48	*147	51	*1.49
1920	Washington	Amer.	21	144	8	10	.444	4	135	68	50	78	27	3.13
1921	Washington	Amer.	35	264	17	14	.548	1	265	122	103	*143	92	3.51
1922	Washington	Amer.	41	280	15	16	.484	4	283	115	93	105	99	2.99
1923	Washington	Amer.	42	261	17	12	.586	3	263	112	101	*130	69	3.48
1924	Washington	Amer.	38	278	*23	7	*.767	*6	233	97	84	*158	77	*2.72
1925	Washington	Amer.	30	229	20	7	.741	3	211	95	78	108	78	3.07
1926	Washington	Amer.	33	262	15	16	.484	2	259	120	105	125	73	3.61
1927	Washington	Amer.	18	108	5	6	.455	1	113	70	61	48	26	5.08
1928	Newark	Int.	1	0	0	0	.000	0	0	0	0	0	1	0.00
Major League Totals			802	5923	416	279	.599	110	4920	1902	1103	3508	1353	....

WORLD SERIES RECORD

Year	Club	League	G.	IP.	W.	L.	Pct.	H.	R.	ER.	SO.	BB.	ERA.
1924	Washington	American	3	24	1	2	.333	30	10	6	20	11	2.25
1925	Washington	American	3	26	2	1	.667	26	10	6	15	4	2.08
World Series Totals			6	50	3	3	.500	56	20	12	35	15	2.16

WILLIAM JULIUS (JUDY) JOHNSON

Born, October 26, 1899, at Snow Hill, Md.
Height, 5:11½. Weight, 150.
Batted and threw righthanded.
Married Anita T. Irons, December 27, 1953.

A third baseman who could do it all, Judy Johnson was the only hot-corner guardian named by the Special Committee on Negro Leagues. He was quiet, reserved in nature and a sharp student of the game who became manager of the powerful Homestead Grays at the tender age of 29.

His hitting ability probably is what ranked him above the three other great third basemen of Negro baseball—Oliver Marcell, who had a great glove but didn't hit as well; Henry Blackman, an all-round great who played only two years before he died, and brainy little Dave Malarcher, who both fielded well and hit well. Malarcher became a published poet and still was running his real estate business at age 84.

Johnson was a semi-pro star in his native Wilmington, Del. In 1918, he joined the Bacharach's, then the Philadelphia All-Stars in 1920 and the Hilldales, famed Eastern powerhouse as an independent club, in 1921. He stayed with the Hilldales until he left to manage the Homestead Grays in 1929.

Cool Papa Bell said, "Johnson was the best hitter among the four top third basemen, but though someone else might bat as high as Judy, no one would drive in as many clutch runs as he would. He was a solid ballplayer, real smart, but he was the kind of fellow who could 'just get it done.' He was dependable, quiet, not flashy at all, but could handle anything that came up. No matter how much the pressure, no matter how important the play or the throw or the hit, Judy could do when it counted.

"And above all, he was a gentleman, on and off the field. Oh, no one could push him around, but his quiet, easy-going smooth, down-to-business manner made him a standout as a player and as a man."

Cum Posey, owner and manager of the Homestead Grays, rated Johnson among the best players in the Negro leagues and Buck Leonard, Posey's Hall of Fame first baseman, is verification for that statement.

DID YOU KNOW—
That Walter Johnson participated in 64 1-0 games in his career, winning 38?

Leonard added, "And Judy, always thinking, added a special thing that helped him take care of runners who would try to undress him at third. He wore small shin guards under his stockings that prevented spike-flashing runners from putting him out of commission. Keeping free from those nagging injuries maybe was a big part in his maintaining such consistency as both a batter and fielder."

Johnson himself cleared up the shinguard point:

"It was John Henry Lloyd who devised the shinguard method. He wore them and he advised all of us to wear them. Our whole infield was outfitted with them and we were the first team protected like that. My shins are cuts and scars all up and down. Negro base runners were just mean and tough. We had to counteract that some way and the shinguards helped us greatly. We still got the business, but we could stay in the game longer, and that was John Henry's point."

After Johnson left the Homesteads, he joined the Darby (Pa.) Daisies in 1931. The next year he shifted to the Pittsburgh Crawfords. As captain in 1934, he tied down the far corner of one of Negro baseball's finest infields—Oscar Charleston at first, Chet Williams at second, Leroy Morney at short and Johnson at third.

Buck Leonard rates that infield, plus the Crawfords' Josh Gibson and Bill Perkins as catchers, Vic Harris, Cool Papa Bell and Jimmie Crutchfield in the outfield and pitchers Satchel Paige, Bert Hunter, Leroy Matlock, Sam Streeter and Harry Kincannon as the greatest team he ever saw. When you consider that Johnson managed the Homestead Grays, you realize he was associated with two of the Negro game's greatest teams.

Like all the best players in the Negro leagues, Johnson spent many winters in Cuba and Mexico competing against barnstorming major leaguers and the top Caribbean players.

When the curtain came down on Negro professional ball, Johnson became a scout for the Philadelphia Athletics in 1951 until he was released in 1954. He next joined the scouting staff of the Phillies in 1961 and remained with them until 1972. He became one of the Dodgers' eagle eyes on December 3, 1973.

His greatest thrills?

"When my career ended, I thought that's all there is. I was working as a scout with major league clubs, but I never dreamed there'd come a day when I would be told I was going to enter the Hall of Fame in 1975, joining the greats of the greatest game of them all.

"But as a player, my top thrill was being able to play against major league clubs and then major league players on all-star teams and know that we were capable of doing so. We played against some of the greatest stars and beat them more often than not. It was the only way we could tell if we were just as good players as they were, or if we were better."

CHARLES WESLEY (BABY) JONES
(Benjamin Wesley Rippay)

Born April 30, 1850, at Alamance County, N. C.
(Deceased)
Threw and batted righthanded.

Hit two home runs in eighth inning, June 10, 1880.

Year	Club	League	Pos.	G.	AB.	R.	H.	2B.	3B.	HR.	SB.	B.A.	PO.	A.	E.	F.A.
1876	Cincinnati	Nat.	OF	64	283	40	79	15	4	3	....	.279	151	11	27	.857
1877	Chicago	Nat.	OF	2	8	1	3	1	0	0	....	.375	5	1	0	1.000
1878	Cincinnati	Nat.	OF	60	256	49	76	10	6	3	....	.297	116	9	15	.893
1879	Boston	Nat.	OF	83	355	*85	112	24	9	*9	....	.315	162	20	13	.933
1880	Boston	Nat.	OF	64	269	43	80	15	4	5	....	.297	106	11	24	.829
1881	—						(Out of Organized Ball)									
1882	—						(Out of Organized Ball)									
1883	Cincinnati	Am. Assn.	OF	90	390	83	116	16	11	10	....	.297	....	....	24	.884
1884	Cincinnati	Am. Assn.	OF	113	475	113	153	22	19	7	....	.322	....	....	27	.889
1885	Cincinnati	Am. Assn.	OF	112	492	109	161	19	19	5	....	.327	....	....	37	.869
1886	Cincinnati	Am. Assn.	OF	127	496	87	136	22	11	6	10	.274	....	....	35	.874
1887	Cin.-New York	Am. Assn.	OF	104	423	56	140	16	7	5	13	.331	....	....	23	.898
1888	Kansas City	Am. Assn.	OF	6	24	2	6	0	1	0	0	.250	7	1	4	.667
	National League Totals			273	1171	218	350	65	23	20	....	.299	540	52	79	.882
	American Association Totals			552	2300	450	712	95	68	33	....	.310	....	....	150	.879
	Major League Totals			825	3471	668	1062	160	91	53	....	.306	....	....	229	.881

SAMUEL POND (SAD SAM) JONES

Born July 26, 1892, at Woodfield, O.
Died July 6, 1966, at Barnesville, O.
Height, 6.00. Weight, 170.
Threw and batted righthanded.
Married Edith Kerr, July 26, 1916.

Pitched no-hit, no-run game against Philadelphia, September 4, 1923, winning, 2-0.
Coach, Toronto, International League, 1940.

Year	Club	League	G.	IP.	W.	L.	Pct.	H.	R.	ER.	SO.	BB.	ERA.
1913–Zanesville		Int.-State					(No Record Available)						
1914–Portsmouth(a)		Ohio State	11	....	5	6	.455	....	....	....	....	....	......
1914–Cleveland		A. A.	23	129	10	4	.714	112	45	35	50	64	2.44
1914–Cleveland		Amer.	1	3	0	0	.000	2	1	1	0	2	3.00
1915–Cleveland(b)		Amer.	48	146	4	9	.308	131	78	59	42	63	3.64
1916–Boston		Amer.	12	27	0	1	.000	25	14	11	7	10	3.67
1917–Boston		Amer.	9	16	0	1	.000	15	9	8	5	6	4.50
1918–Boston		Amer.	24	184	16	5	*.762	151	66	46	44	70	2.25
1919–Boston		Amer.	35	245	12	20	.375	258	120	*102	67	95	3.75
1920–Boston		Amer.	37	274	13	16	.448	302	143	120	86	79	3.94
1921–Boston(c)		Amer.	40	299	23	16	.590	318	122	107	98	78	3.22
1922–New York		Amer.	45	260	13	13	.500	270	132	106	81	76	3.67
1923–New York		Amer.	39	243	21	8	.724	239	114	98	68	69	3.63
1924–New York		Amer.	36	179	9	6	.600	187	85	72	53	76	3.62
1925–New York		Amer.	43	247	15	*21	.417	267	147	127	92	104	4.63
1926–New York(d)		Amer.	39	161	9	8	.529	186	104	89	69	80	4.98
1927–St. Louis(e)		Amer.	30	190	8	14	.364	211	121	91	72	102	4.31
1928–Washington		Amer.	30	225	17	7	.708	209	89	71	63	78	2.84
1929–Washington		Amer.	24	154	9	9	.500	156	80	67	36	49	3.92
1930–Washington		Amer.	25	183	15	7	.682	195	95	83	60	61	4.08
1931–Washington(f)		Amer.	25	148	9	10	.474	185	88	71	58	47	4.32
1932–Chicago		Amer.	30	200	10	15	.400	217	123	94	64	75	4.23
1933–Chicago		Amer.	27	177	10	12	.455	181	80	66	60	65	3.36
1934–Chicago		Amer.	27	183	8	12	.400	217	120	104	60	60	5.11
1935–Chicago		Amer.	21	140	8	7	.533	162	77	63	38	51	4.05
1940–Toronto		Int.	8	12	1	0	1.000	12	3	3	5	9	2.25
Major League Totals			647	3884	229	217	.513	4084	2008	1656	1263	1396	3.84

aPurchased by Cleveland, A. L., and optioned to Cleveland, A. A.; recalled September, 1915.
bTraded with $50,000 and option on catcher Chet Thomas to Boston A. L., for outfielder Tris Speaker, April, 1916.
cTraded to New York with shortstop Everett Scott and pitcher Joe Bush for shortstop Roger Peckinpaugh and pitchers Bill Piercy and Jack Quinn, December, 1921.
dTraded to St. Louis for outfielder Cedric Durst, February, 1928.
eReleased to Washington on waivers, September, 1927.
fTraded with infielder Minter Hayes and pitcher Bump Hadley to Chicago White Sox for outfielder Carl Reynolds and infielder John Kerr, December 4, 1931.

WORLD SERIES RECORD

Year	Club	League	G.	IP.	W.	L.	Pct.	H.	R.	ER.	SO.	BB.	ERA.
1918–Boston		Amer.	1	9	0	1	.000	7	3	3	5	5	3.00
1922–New York		Amer.	2	2	0	0	.000	1	0	0	0	1	0.00
1923–New York		Amer.	2	10	0	1	.000	5	1	1	3	2	0.90
1926–New York		Amer.	1	1	0	0	.000	2	1	1	1	2	9.00
World Series Totals			6	22	0	2	.000	15	5	5	9	10	2.04

ADRIAN (ADDIE) JOSS

Born April 12, 1880, Juneau, Wis.
Died April 14, 1911, Toledo, O.
Height, 6.03. Weight, 185.
Threw and batted righthanded.

Pitched perfect game against Chicago White Sox, October 2, 1908; pitched no-hit game against Chicago White Sox, April 20, 1910; pitched one-hitter in major league debut, April 26, 1902; shares major league record, most putouts game, pitcher, five, May 20, 1905.
Named to Hall of Fame, 1978.

Year	Club	League	G.	IP.	W.	L.	Pct.	H.	R.	SO.	BB.	CG.	ShO.
1900–Toledo		Inter-State	49	....	19	16	.543	234	124	168	53	....	3
1901–Toledo		Western Assn.	41	353	25	15	.625	273	162	217	69	37	4
1902–Cleveland		American	32	269	17	13	.567	225	120	106	75	28	5
1903–Cleveland		American	32	284	18	13	.581	232	105	120	37	31	3
1904–Cleveland		American	25	192	14	10	.583	160	50	83	30	20	5
1905–Cleveland		American	33	289	20	12	.625	246	90	127	39	31	3
1906–Cleveland		American	34	282	21	9	.700	220	81	106	43	28	9
1907–Cleveland		American	42	339	27	10	.730	281	101	127	54	34	6
1908–Cleveland		American	42	324	24	12	.667	235	77	130	30	29	9
1909–Cleveland		American	33	243	14	13	.519	198	71	67	31	24	4
1910–Cleveland(a)		American	13	107	5	5	.500	96	35	49	18	9	1
Major League Totals			286	2329	160	97	.623	1893	730	915	357	234	45

aDied suddenly from attack of tubercular meningitis during spring training of 1911.

JOSEPH IGNATIUS JUDGE

Born May 25, 1894, at New York, N. Y.
Died March 11, 1963, at Washington, D. C.
Height, 5.08½. Weight, 155.
Threw and batted lefthanded.
Married Alma Gauvreau in 1914.

Manager, Baltimore, International League, May, 1934 to July, 1934; coach, Georgetown University, 1937-1944; coach, Washington Senators, May 27, 1945 through 1946; coach, Georgetown University, 1949-1957.

Year	Club	League	Pos.	G.	AB.	R.	H.	2B.	3B.	HR.	RBI.	B.A.	PO.	A.	E.	F.A.
1914	Lewiston	N. Eng.	1B	114	421	62	115	10	10	4	....	.273	1031	57	17	.985
1915	Buffalo(a)	Int.	1B-OF	140	493	68	158	19	15	0	....	.320	1348	54	8	*.994
1915	Washington	Amer.	1B-OF	12	40	7	17	2	0	0	11	.425	97	6	1	.990
1916	Washington	Amer.	1B	103	336	42	74	10	8	0	31	.220	935	69	14	.986
1917	Washington	Amer.	1B	102	393	62	112	15	15	2	31	.285	906	60	12	.988
1918	Washington	Amer.	1B	•130	502	56	131	23	7	1	52	.261	1304	92	21	.985
1919	Washington	Amer.	1B	135	521	83	150	33	12	2	29	.288	1177	78	15	.988
1920	Washington	Amer.	1B	126	493	103	164	19	15	5	51	.333	1194	62	10	.992
1921	Washington	Amer.	1B	153	622	87	187	26	11	7	72	.301	1417	89	6	.996
1922	Washington	Amer.	1B	148	591	84	174	32	15	10	81	.294	1378	101	6	.996
1923	Washington	Amer.	1B	113	405	56	127	24	6	2	63	.314	1070	88	8	*.993
1924	Washington	Amer.	1B	140	516	71	167	38	9	3	79	.324	1276	86	8	●.994
1925	Washington	Amer.	1B	112	376	65	118	31	5	8	66	.314	999	71	7	*.994
1926	Washington	Amer.	1B	134	453	70	132	25	11	7	92	.291	1145	95	8	.994
1927	Washington	Amer.	1B	137	522	68	161	29	11	2	71	.308	1309	71	6	*.996
1928	Washington	Amer.	1B	153	542	78	166	31	10	3	93	.306	1412	92	6	.996
1929	Washington	Amer.	1B	143	543	83	171	35	8	6	71	.315	1323	88	6	*.996
1930	Washington	Amer.	1B	126	442	58	144	29	11	10	80	.326	1050	67	2	*.998
1931	Washington	Amer.	1B	35	74	11	21	3	0	0	9	.284	155	10	1	.994
1932	Washington(b)	Amer.	1B	82	291	45	75	16	3	3	29	.258	668	46	2	.997
1933	Brooklyn(c)	Nat.	1B	42	112	7	24	2	1	0	9	.214	243	17	3	.989
1933	Boston	Amer.	1B	34	104	20	30	8	1	0	22	.288	258	12	0	1.000
1934	Boston	Amer.	1B	10	15	3	5	2	0	0	2	.333	24	1	0	1.000
American League Totals				2128	7781	1177	2326	431	158	71	1035	.299	19097	1284	139	.993
National League Totals				42	112	7	24	2	1	0	9	.214	243	17	3	.989
Major League Totals				2170	7893	1184	2350	433	159	71	1044	.298	19340	1301	142	.993

aSold to Washington Senators, September 22, 1915.
bUnconditionally released by Washington Senators, January 27, 1933; subsequently signed with Brooklyn Dodgers.
cUnconditionally released by Brooklyn Dodgers, July, 1933, and signed with Boston Red Sox.

WORLD SERIES RECORD

Year	Club	League	Pos.	G.	AB.	R.	H.	2B.	3B.	HR.	RBI.	B.A.	PO.	A.	E.	F.A.
1924	Washington	Amer.	1B	7	26	4	10	1	0	0	0	.385	62	4	1	.985
1925	Washington	Amer.	1B	7	23	2	4	1	0	1	3	.174	59	2	0	1.000
World Series Totals				14	49	6	14	2	0	1	3	.286	121	6	1	.992

ALBERT WILLIAM KALINE

Born December 19, 1934, at Baltimore, Md.
Height, 6.02. Weight, 184.
Threw and batted righthanded.
Married Louise Hamilton, October 16, 1954.

Tied following major league records: most home runs, inning (2); most extra bases on long hits, inning (6); most total bases, inning (8), April 17, 1955 (sixth inning); most seasons and most consecutive seasons, one club, 22, 1974 (later broken by Brooks Robinson with 23).
Established American League record for most seasons, 100 or more games, 20, 1974.
Tied American League record for most consecutive years, 100 or more games, 19, 1972.
Youngest player to win American League batting championship.
Hit three home runs in a game, April 17, 1955.
Tied following World Series records: Most at-bats, inning (2), most hits, inning (2) and most runs, inning

(2), third inning, October 9, 1968; most putouts, game, right fielder (7), October 9, 1968.
Named as outfielder on THE SPORTING NEWS American League All-Star Teams, 1962-63-66-67.
Named as outfielder on THE SPORTING NEWS All-Star Major League Team, 1955.
Named No. 1 American League Player by THE SPORTING NEWS, 1955 and 1963.
Named outfielder on THE SPORTING NEWS Major League All-Star fielding team, 1957.
Named outfielder on THE SPORTING NEWS American League All-Star fielding teams, 1958-59-61-62-63-64-65-66-67.
Named to Hall of Fame, 1980.

Year	Club	League	Pos.	G.	AB.	R.	H.	2B.	3B.	HR.	RBI.	B.A.	PO.	A.	E.	F.A.
1953	Detroit	Amer.	OF	30	28	9	7	0	0	1	2	.250	11	1	0	1.000
1954	Detroit	Amer.	OF	138	504	42	139	18	3	4	43	.276	283	16	9	.971
1955	Detroit	Amer.	OF	152	588	121	*200	24	8	27	102	*.340	306	14	7	.979
1956	Detroit	Amer.	OF	153	617	96	194	32	10	27	128	.314	343	*18	6	.984
1957	Detroit	Amer.	OF	149	577	83	170	29	4	23	90	.295	319	13	5	.985
1958	Detroit	Amer.	OF	146	543	84	170	34	7	16	85	.313	316	*23	2	.994
1959	Detroit	Amer.	OF	136	511	86	167	19	2	27	94	.327	364	4	4	.989
1960	Detroit	Amer.	OF	147	551	77	153	29	4	15	68	.278	367	5	5	.987
1961	Detroit	Amer.	OF-3B	153	586	116	190	*41	7	19	82	.324	379	10	4	.990
1962	Detroit	Amer.	OF	100	398	78	121	16	6	29	94	.304	225	8	4	.983
1963	Detroit	Amer.	OF	145	551	89	172	24	3	27	101	.312	257	5	2	.992
1964	Detroit	Amer.	OF	146	525	77	154	31	5	17	68	.293	278	6	3	.990
1965	Detroit	Amer.	OF-3B	125	399	72	112	18	2	18	72	.281	195	3	3	.985
1966	Detroit	Amer.	OF	142	479	85	138	29	1	29	88	.288	279	7	2	*.993
1967	Detroit	Amer.	OF	131	458	94	141	28	2	25	78	.308	217	14	4	*.983
1968	Detroit	Amer.	OF-1B	102	327	49	94	14	1	10	53	.287	283	14	7	.977
1969	Detroit	Amer.	OF-1B	131	456	74	124	17	0	21	69	.272	257	11	7	.975
1970	Detroit	Amer.	OF-1B	131	467	64	130	24	4	16	71	.278	530	34	6	.989
1971	Detroit	Amer.	•OF-1B	133	405	69	119	19	2	15	54	.294	234	7	0	•1.000
1972	Detroit	Amer.	OF-1B	106	278	46	87	11	2	10	32	.313	148	9	1	.994
1973	Detroit	Amer.	OF-1B	91	310	40	79	13	0	10	45	.255	347	13	1	.997
1974	Detroit	Amer.	DH	147	558	71	146	28	2	13	64	.262	0	0	0	.000
Major League Totals				2834	10116	1622	3007	498	75	399	1583	.297	5938	235	82	.987

WORLD SERIES RECORD

Year	Club	League	Pos.	G.	AB.	R.	H.	2B.	3B.	HR.	RBI.	B.A.	PO.	A.	E.	F.A.
1968	Detroit	Amer.	OF	7	29	6	11	2	0	2	8	.379	18	0	0	1.000

TIMOTHY J. (TIM) KEEFE

Born January 1, 1857, at Cambridge, Mass.
Died April 23, 1933, at Cambridge, Mass.
Height, 5.10½. Weight, 185.
Threw and batted righthanded.

Won 19 consecutive games, June 23 through August 10, 1888; yielded three hits in two games vs. Columbus, one in morning game; two in afternoon game, winning 9-1 and 3-0, July 4, 1883.
Umpire, National League, 1894-95.
Named to Hall of Fame, 1964.

Year	Club	League	G.	IP.	W.	L.	Pct.	H.	R.	SO.	BB.	CG.	ShO.
1879	Utica-New Bedford	Nat. Assn.	24	....	....	....	....	....	....	....	....	....	....
1880	Albany	Nat. Assn.	18	....	....	....	....	....	....	....	....	....	....
1880	Troy	National	12	105	6	6	.500	71	27	42	16	12	0
1881	Troy	National	45	404	18	27	.400	444	241	105	88	45	4
1882	Troy	National	43	376	17	26	.395	364	221	110	81	41	1
1883	Metropolitan	Amer. Assn.	*68	*619	41	27	.603	485	244	*360	106	*68	5
1884	Metropolitan	Amer. Assn.	56	483	37	17	.685	379	195	322	72	56	4
1885	New York	National	46	400	32	13	.711	296	154	228	99	45	7
1886	New York	National	*64	*535	•42	20	.677	468	250	295	98	*62	2
1887	New York	National	56	476	35	19	.648	528	255	186	111	54	2
1888	New York	National	51	434	*35	11	*.761	314	143	*335	86	48	•8
1889	New York	National	47	363	28	13	.683	317	212	222	154	39	3
1890	New York	Players	30	227	17	11	.607	221	137	88	86	23	1
1891	N.Y.(a)-Philadelphia	National	19	131	5	11	.313	154	112	62	54	13	0
1892	Philadelphia	National	39	312	19	16	.543	281	139	129	97	31	3
1893	Philadelphia	National	22	178	10	7	.588	202	131	54	77	17	0
American Association Totals			124	1102	78	44	.639	864	439	682	178	124	9
National League Totals			444	3714	247	169	.594	3439	1885	1768	961	407	30
Players League Totals			30	227	17	11	.607	221	137	88	86	23	1
Major League Totals			598	5043	342	224	.604	4524	2461	2538	1225	554	40

aReleased by New York Giants in August, 1891, and signed with Philadelphia Phillies.

WORLD SERIES RECORD

Year	Club	League	G.	IP.	W.	L.	Pct.	SO.	BB.	H.	CG.	ShO.
1884	Metropolitan	American Assn.	2	15	0	2	.000	12	2	10	2	0
1888	New York	National	4	35	4	0	1.000	31	14	18	4	0
1889	New York	National	2	11	0	1	.000	2	0	15	1	0
	World Series Totals		8	61	4	3	.571	45	16	43	7	0

WILLIAM H. (WEE WILLIE) KEELER

Born March 13, 1872, at Brooklyn, N. Y.
Died January 1, 1923, at Brooklyn, N. Y.
Height, 5.04½. Weight, 140.
Threw and batted lefthanded.

Set N.L. record by hitting safely in 44 consecutive games, start of season, April 22 through June 18, 1897 (tied by Pete Rose in 1978); had five singles and one triple in six times at-bat against St. Louis, September 3, 1897; collected five or more hits in one game, four times, during 1897 season.
Coach, Brooklyn Federals, 1914; scout, Boston Braves, 1915.
Named to Hall of Fame, 1939.

Year	Club	League	Pos.	G.	AB.	R.	H.	2B.	3B.	HR.	SB.	B.A.	PO.	A.	E.	F.A.
1892	Binghamton	East.	3B	93	410	109	153	17	13	2	12	*.373	147	231	48	.887
1892	New York	Nat.	3B	13	49	6	15	3	0	0	5	.306	14	28	7	.857
1893	N.Y.-Brooklyn	Nat.	O-2-3-S	29	90	19	30	3	2	2	7	.333	32	28	15	.800
1893	Binghamton	East.	3B	15	68	9	20	2	1	1	3	.294	29	38	11	.859
1894	Baltimore(a)	Nat.	OF	128	593	164	218	25	24	5	30	.368	220	27	19	.929
1895	Baltimore	Nat.	OF	131	560	161	221	23	15	4	57	.395	248	19	11	.960
1896	Baltimore	Nat.	OF	127	546	154	214	22	13	4	73	.392	229	22	7	*.973
1897	Baltimore	Nat.	OF	128	562	147	*243	25	18	0	63	*.432	218	14	7	.971
1898	Baltimore(b)	Nat.	OF	128	564	126	214	10	2	0	26	*.379	210	12	11	.944
1899	Brooklyn	Nat.	OF	143	571	*141	215	13	14	1	44	.377	207	21	7	.970
1900	Brooklyn	Nat.	OF	137	568	106	*208	11	14	4	39	.366	229	24	14	.948
1901	Brooklyn	Nat.	OF	136	589	124	209	16	15	2	31	.355	183	18	3	*.985
1902	Brooklyn(c)	Nat.	OF	132	550	84	188	18	7	0	23	.342	204	14	4	*.982
1903	New York	Amer.	OF	132	515	98	164	13	7	0	25	.318	174	13	11	.941
1904	New York	Amer.	OF	143	539	76	185	13	6	2	22	.343	185	14	11	.948
1905	New York	Amer.	OF	149	560	81	169	14	4	4	19	.302	194	17	7	.968
1906	New York	Amer.	OF	152	592	96	180	9	3	2	23	.304	213	16	3	.987
1907	New York	Amer.	OF	107	423	50	99	6	5	0	7	.234	144	13	5	.969
1908	New York	Amer.	OF	91	323	38	85	3	1	1	14	.263	123	9	9	.936
1909	New York	Amer.	OF	99	360	44	95	7	5	1	10	.264	111	9	4	.968
1910	New York	Nat.	PH	19	10	5	3	0	0	0	1	.300	0	0	0	.000
1911	Toronto	East.	OF	39	155	26	43	7	0	0	4	.277	47	2	4	.925
	American League Totals			873	3312	483	977	65	31	10	120	.295	1144	91	50	.961
	National League Totals			1251	5252	1237	1978	169	124	22	399	.377	1994	227	105	.955
	Major League Totals			2124	8564	1720	2955	234	155	32	519	.345	3138	318	155	.957

aTraded with first baseman Dan Brouthers by Brooklyn to Baltimore for third baseman Billy Shindlj and outfielder George Treadway, January, 1894.
bAccompanied Manager Ned Hanion and other players to Brooklyn.
cJumped to New York A. L. club.

GEORGE CLYDE KELL

Born August 23, 1922, at Swifton, Ark.
Height, 5.10. Weight, 170.
Threw and batted righthanded.
Married Charlene Felts, March 24, 1941.

Hit safely in 20 consecutive games, May 30, second game, through June 20, 1950.
Led all Organized Ball in batting, 1943. Tied major league record for most times facing pitcher, inning (3), seventh inning, June 18, 1943; hit for cycle, June 2, 1950.
Named by Baseball Writers' Association as third baseman on THE SPORTING NEWS All-Star Major League Teams, 1946-47-49-51-52.

Scout, Detroit Tigers, 1966-67, and 1971 through 1977.

Year	Club	League	Pos.	G.	AB.	R.	H.	2B.	3B.	HR.	RBI.	B.A.	PO.	A.	E.	F.A.
1940	Newport	NE. Ark.	3B	48	169	14	27	2	3	0	14	.160	59	80	3	.979
1941	Newport	NE. Ark.	3B	118	462	71	*143	26	5	1	75	.310	148	*285	37	*.921
1942	Lancaster	Int. St.	3B	127	465	56	139	18	2	0	30	.299	360	236	21	.966
1943	Lancaster	Int. St.	3B	138	555	*120	*220	33	*23	5	79	*.396	*190	*362	23	*.960
1943	Philadelphia	Amer.	3B	1	5	1	1	0	1	0	1	.200	1	3	0	1.000
1944	Philadelphia	Amer.	3B	139	514	51	138	15	3	0	44	.268	167	289	20	.958
1945	Philadelphia	Amer.	3B	147	567	50	154	30	3	4	56	.272	*186	*345	20	*.964
1946	Phila.(a)-Det.	Amer.	*3B-1B	131	521	70	168	25	10	4	52	.322	*143	*267	7	*.983
1947	Detroit	Amer.	3B	152	588	75	188	29	5	5	93	.320	167	*333	*20	.962
1948	Detroit(b)	Amer.	3B	92	368	47	112	24	3	2	44	.304	108	146	8	.969
1949	Detroit	Amer.	3B	134	522	97	179	38	9	3	59	*.343	154	271	11	.975
1950	Detroit	Amer.	3B	●157	*641	114	*218	*56	6	8	101	.340	186	315	9	*.982
1951	Detroit	Amer.	3B	147	598	92	*191	●36	3	2	59	.319	175	*310	20	*.960
1952	Det.(c)-Boston	Amer.	3B	114	428	52	133	23	2	7	57	.311	113	216	14	.959
1953	Boston	Amer.	*3B-OF	134	460	68	141	41	2	12	73	.307	118	231	10	*.972
1954	Bos.(d)-Chicago	Amer.	3B-1B-O	97	326	40	90	13	0	5	58	.276	306	105	11	.974
1955	Chicago	Amer.	*3B-1B	128	429	44	134	24	1	8	81	.312	216	170	7	*.982
1956	Chi.(e)-Balt.	Amer.	*3-1B-2B	123	425	52	115	22	2	9	48	.271	138	198	7	●.980
1957	Baltimore	Amer.	3B-1B	99	310	28	92	9	0	9	44	.297	66	122	4	.979
Major League Totals				1795	6702	881	2054	385	50	78	870	.306	2244	3321	168	.971

aTraded to Detroit Tigers for outfielder Barney McCosky, May 18, 1946.
bSuffered fractured wrist when struck by ball pitched by Vic Raschi of New York Yankees, May 8, 1948, and was out of game until May 31; fractured lower jaw when struck by line drive off bat of Joe DiMaggio of New York Yankees, August 29, 1948; out for rest of season.
cTraded to Boston Red Sox with pitcher Paul (Dizzy) Trout, shortstop Johnny Lipon and outfielder Walter (Hoot) Evers for pitcher Bill Wight, first baseman Walter Dropo, third baseman Fred Hatfield, shortstop Johnny Pesky and outfielder Don Lenhardt, June 3, 1952.
dTraded to Chicago White Sox for third baseman Grady Hatton and $100,000, May 23, 1954.
eTraded to Baltimore Orioles with pitchers Mike Fornieles and Connie Johnson and outfielder Bob Nieman for pitcher Jim Wilson and outfielder Dave Philley, May 21, 1956.

JOSEPH JAMES KELLEY

Born December 9, 1871, at Cambridge, Mass.

Died August 14, 1943, at Baltimore, Md.

Height, 5.11. Weight, 190.

Threw and batted righthanded.

Married Margaret Mahon, October 14, 1897.

Made nine hits in nine times at bat, double-header—one triple, three singles in first game and four doubles and one single in second, September 3, 1894.
Manager, Cincinnati, part of 1902-03-04-05-06; Boston Nationals, 1908; Toronto, 1907-09-10-11-12-13-14; scout, New York Yankees, 1915-16; coach, Brooklyn, 1926. Managed Baltimore, N. L., briefly after John McGraw left for New York. Kelley jumped to Cincinnati in 1902.
Named to Hall of Fame, 1971.

Year	Club	League	Pos.	G.	AB.	R.	H.	2B.	3B.	HR.	SB.	B.A.	PO.	A.	E.	F.A.
1891	Lowell	N. Eng.	OF	57	245	50	81	...	...	...	21	.331	195	136	16	.954
1891	Bos.-Pittsburgh	Nat.	OF	14	52	8	12	1	1	0	0	.231	28	2	4	.882
1892	Omaha	West.	OF	49	203	32	67	...	...	...	18	.330	71	7	10	.886
1892	Pitts.(a)-Balt.	Nat.	OF	66	232	30	57	6	6	0	7	.246	116	11	15	.894
1893	Baltimore	Nat.	OF	124	490	120	153	25	16	9	38	.312	301	21	16	.953
1894	Baltimore	Nat.	OF	129	509	167	199	48	17	6	45	.391	274	19	15	.951
1895	Baltimore	Nat.	OF	131	510	148	189	26	21	10	59	.371	258	21	18	.939
1896	Baltimore	Nat.	OF	130	516	147	191	27	17	8	90	.370	278	22	13	.958
1897	Baltimore	Nat.	OF	129	503	113	196	31	9	5	50	.390	238	15	12	.955
1898	Baltimore(b)	Nat.	OF	124	467	71	153	17	15	3	22	.328	234	16	7	.973
1899	Brooklyn	Nat.	OF	144	540	107	178	27	12	6	31	.330	309	26	8	.977
1900	Brooklyn	Nat.	1B-OF	118	453	92	144	23	18	6	26	.318	422	15	11	.975
1901	Brooklyn	Nat.	1B	120	493	77	152	21	12	4	20	.308	982	81	27	.975
1902	Baltimore(c)	Am.	1-3B-OF	60	222	50	69	16	7	1	12	.311	99	6	3	.972
1902	Cincinnati	Nat.	S-3B-O	37	156	24	51	8	2	1	3	.327	30	4	0	1.000
1903	Cincinnati	Nat.	OF	104	383	85	121	22	4	3	18	.316	117	8	7	.948
1904	Cincinnati	Nat.	1B	123	449	75	126	21	13	0	15	.281	1049	76	14	.988
1905	Cincinnati	Nat.	OF	87	321	43	89	7	6	1	8	.277	137	11	4	.974
1906	Cincinnati	Nat.	OF	127	465	43	106	19	11	1	9	.228	184	13	7	.966
1907	Toronto	East.	1B-OF	91	314	32	101	10	8	1	15	.322	404	51	10	.978
1908	Boston	Nat.	OF	62	228	25	59	8	2	2	5	.259	71	5	5	.938

Year	Club	League	Pos.	G.	AB.	R.	H.	2B.	3B.	HR.	SB.	B.A.	PO.	A.	E.	F.A.
1909–Toronto		East.	OF	107	357	49	96	23	1	1	11	.269	191	13	1	.995
1910–Toronto		East.	OF	46	110	13	31	5	2	0	4	.282	36	7	1	.977
American League Totals				60	222	50	69	16	7	1	12	.311	99	6	3	.972
National League Totals				1769	6767	1375	2176	337	182	65	446	.322	5028	376	183	.967
Major League Totals				1829	6989	1425	2245	353	189	66	458	.321	5127	382	186	.967

aTraded to Baltimore in deal for outfielder George Van Haltren, September, 1892.
bMoved to Brooklyn with Manager Ned Hanlon when Superbas bought Baltimore franchise.
cJumped to Cincinnati, July 16, 1902.

PITCHING RECORD

Year	Club	League	G.	I.P.	W.	L.	Pct.	H.	R.	SO.	BB.
1891–Lowell		New England	14	121	10	3	.769	97	87	81	70

GEORGE LANGE (HIGH POCKETS) KELLY

Born, September 10, 1896, at San Francisco, Calif.

Height, 6.03. Weight, 195.

Threw and batted righthanded.

Married Mary Helen O'Connor, November 3, 1927.

Nephew of William A. (Little Eva) Lange, famous outfielder with Chicago N. L. club, 1893-1899, brother of Reynolds Kelly, pitcher in New York Giants and Philadelphia Athletics systems.

Outstanding performances–Most total bases, game–15 (September 17, 1923–one single, one double, three home runs); three home runs in game–2 (September 17, 1923–successive, and June 14, 1924); set major league record at the time and existing National League tie by hitting seven home runs in six consecutive games (July 11 (1), 12 (2), 13 (1), 14 (1), 15 (1), 16 (1), 1924). Set National League record for most chances accepted by first baseman, season–1862 (155 games, 1920); equaled major league mark for most chances accepted, game–22 (April 26, 1923); established National League record for most putouts, season, 1759 (1920). Pitched and won one game in 1917.

World Series records–Tied existing mark for most times at bat, inning–2 (seventh inning, October 7, 1921); also most chances accepted by first baseman, game–19 (October 15, 1923). Tied most chances accepted by first baseman, Series (eight games)–93 (1921); set record for most putouts, game–19 (October 15, 1923), and most assists, Series (eight games), 7–(1921).

Coach, Cincinnati Reds, 1935-36-37; Boston Braves, 1938-39-40-41-42-43, and Cincinnati, 1947-48. Scout, Cincinnati, 1946.

Named to Hall of Fame, 1973.

Year	Club	League	Pos.	G.	AB.	R.	H.	2B.	3B.	HR.	RBI.	B.A.	PO.	A.	E.	F.A.
1914–Victoria		N. W.	1B-OF	141	436	45	109	22	2	7	.....	.250	1004	79	21	.973
1915–Victoria		N. W.	1B	94	361	57	107	33	6	5	.....	.297	964	78	7	.993
1915–New York		Nat.	1B	17	38	2	6	0	0	1	5	.158	58	4	1	.984
1916–New York		Nat.	1B	49	76	4	12	2	1	0	2	.158	106	2	1	.991
1917–N.York(a)-Pitts.		Nat.	1B-OF	19	30	2	2	0	1	0	0	.067	64	2	2	.971
1917–Rochester		Int.	OF	32	120	16	36	14	1	4	.....	.300	74	6	5	.941
1918–New York		Nat.						(In Military Service)								
1919–Rochester		Int.	1B	103	376	72	134	21	14	15	.....	.356	1097	66	21	.982
1919–New York		Nat.	1B	32	107	12	31	6	2	1	13	.290	341	11	2	.994
1920–New York		Nat.	1B	155	590	69	157	22	11	11	•94	.266	*1759	*103	11	.994
1921–New York		Nat.	1B	149	587	95	181	42	9	*23	122	.308	*1552	*115	17	.990
1922–New York		Nat.	1B	151	592	96	194	33	8	17	107	.328	1642	*103	13	.992
1923–New York		Nat.	1B	145	560	82	172	23	5	16	103	.307	*1568	60	12	.993
1924–New York		Nat.	OF-1B	144	571	91	185	37	9	21	•136	.324	1309	60	10	.993
1925–New York		Nat.	IF-OF	147	586	87	181	29	3	20	99	.309	567	411	18	.982
1926–New York(b)		Nat.	1B-2B	136	499	70	151	24	4	13	80	.303	1233	144	15	*.989
1927–Cincinnati		Nat.	1B-2B	61	222	27	60	16	4	5	21	.270	475	64	8	.985
1928–Cincinnati		Nat.	1B-OF	116	402	46	119	33	7	3	58	.296	927	70	11	.989
1929–Cincinnati		Nat.	1B	147	577	73	169	45	9	5	103	.293	1537	103	11	.993
1930–Cin.(c)-Chicago		Nat.	1B	90	354	40	109	16	2	8	54	.308	917	67	5	.995
1930–Minneapolis		A. A.	1B	34	147	25	53	9	1	6	38	.361	302	14	2	.994
1931–Minneapolis		A. A.	1B	155	606	84	194	34	2	20	112	.320	1491	103	9	.994
1932–Brooklyn		Nat.	1B	64	202	23	49	9	1	4	22	.243	575	36	10	.984
1932–Jersey City		Int.	1B	47	153	18	45	10	0	6	31	.294	382	22	3	.993
1933–Oakland		P. C.	OF	21	56	5	13	5	0	1	6	.232	18	2	1	.953
Major League Totals				1622	5993	819	1778	337	76	148	1019	.297	14630	1355	147	.991

aReleased to Pittsburgh, July 25, 1917, returned to New York Giants and optioned to Rochester, International League, August 4, 1917.
bTraded to Cincinnati for outfielder Edd Roush, January, 1927.
cReleased to Minneapolis, July, 1930, then acquired by Chicago Cubs when first baseman Charles Grimm was injured, August, 1930.

WORLD SERIES RECORD

Year	Club	League	Pos.	G.	AB.	R.	H.	2B.	3B.	HR.	RBI.	B.A.	PO.	A.	E.	F.A.
1921—New York		Nat.	1B	8	30	3	7	1	0	0	3	.233	86	7	0	1.000
1922—New York		Nat.	1B	5	18	0	5	0	0	0	2	.278	61	1	0	1.000
1923—New York		Nat.	1B	6	22	1	4	0	0	0	1	.182	63	4	1	.985
1924—New York		Nat.	OF-IF	7	31	7	9	1	0	1	4	.290	51	5	1	.982
World Series Totals				26	101	11	25	2	0	1	10	.248	261	17	2	.993

MICHAEL JOSEPH (KING) KELLY

Born December 31, 1857, at Troy, N. Y.
Died November 8, 1894, at Boston, Mass.
Height, 5.10½. Weight, 185.
Threw and batted righthanded.

Scored six runs in one game, August 27, 1887.
Manager, Cincinnati, American Association, 1891; manager, Allentown, Pennsylvania State League, 1894. Played with early teams (Troy Haymakers 1873-74-75); Paterson (N.J.) Olympics, 1876, and Columbus (O.) Buckeyes, 1877.
Named to Hall of Fame, 1945.

Year	Club	League	Pos.	G.	AB.	R.	H.	2B.	3B.	HR.	SB.	B.A.	PO.	A.	E.	F.A.
1878—Cincinnati		Nat.	C-3B-OF	59	231	29	65	9	0	0	....	.281	145	62	42	.831
1879—Cincinnati		Nat.	C-3B-OF	76	342	78	119	22	•14	3	....	.348	168	144	54	.852
1880—Chicago		Nat.	C-SS-3-O	82	335	71	98	13	11	1	....	.293	67	32	23	.811
1881—Chicago		Nat.	C-3B-OF	80	353	84	114	★28	3	2	....	.323	85	31	22	.841
1882—Chicago		Nat.	C-1-S-3-O	84	377	81	115	★36	5	1	....	.305	116	138	52	.830
1883—Chicago		Nat.	C-2-3-O	98	430	92	109	27	9	3	....	.253	174	75	53	.825
1884—Chicago		Nat.	C-1-2-S-3	107	448	★120	153	30	6	12	....	.341	173	85	58	.816
1885—Chicago		Nat.	C-1-2-3-O	107	438	★124	126	24	7	9	....	.288	241	93	49	.872
1886—Chicago		Nat.	C-OF	118	451	★155	175	31	11	4	53	★.388	321	118	48	.901
1887—Boston(a)		Nat.	C-2B-OF	114	525	119	207	34	11	8	84	.394	237	151	65	.857
1888—Boston		Nat.	C-OF	105	440	85	140	20	11	9	56	.318	395	150	89	.860
1889—Boston		Nat.	C-OF	125	507	120	149	32	7	7	68	.293	211	53	44	.857
1890—Boston		Players	C-SS	90	352	89	114	19	7	3	40	.324	291	152	51	.897
1891—Cin.-Bos.(N.L.)		A. A.	C-1-2-S	77	264	50	73	15	7	2	16	.276	240	106	31	.918
1891—Boston		Nat.	3B-OF	24	96	14	23	1	0	0	24	.240	48	9	12	.826
1892—Boston		Nat.	OF	72	279	40	56	9	0	1	24	.201	331	93	38	.918
1893—New York		Nat.	C	16	54	8	17	1	0	0	5	.315	54	23	22	.778
1894—Allentown		Pa. State	C	75	325	82	99	16	3	3	....	.305	573	84	40	.943
1894—Allen.-Yonkers		Eastern	C	15	61	11	23	2	0	0	....	.377	97	17	2	.983
American Association Totals				77	264	50	73	15	7	2	16	.276	240	106	31	.918
Players League Totals				90	352	89	114	19	7	3	40	.324	291	152	51	.897
National League Totals				1267	5306	1220	1666	317	95	60	....	.314	2766	1257	671	.857
Major League Totals				1434	5922	1359	1853	351	109	65	....	.313	3297	1515	753	.865

aSold to Boston for $10,000, February 14, 1887. When Boston also purchased pitcher John Clarkson from Chicago in 1888, with Kelly catching, they became known as the "$20,000 Battery."

WILLIAM V. (BRICKYARD) KENNEDY

Born October 7, 1868, at Bellaire, O.
Died September 23, 1915, at Bellaire, O.
Height, 5.11. Weight, 160.
Threw and batted righthanded.

Pitched 3-0, one-hit victory over New York, August 15, 1893, also 6-1, one-hit victory over Cincinnati, September 7, 1896, morning game.

Year	Club	League	G.	W.	L.	Pct.	SO.	BB.	CG.	ShO.
1889—Wheeling		Tri-State League	29	....	....	......	....	....	....	....
1890—Denver		Western Association	21	....	....	......	72	70	....	....

Year	Club	League	G.	W.	L.	Pct.	SO.	BB.	CG.	ShO.
1891-Denver		Western Association	48	....	....	....	....	....	....	....
1892-Brooklyn		National	22	13	9	.591	96	64	19	0
1893-Brooklyn		National	45	26	19	.578	91	157	41	2
1894-Brooklyn		National	44	22	20	.524	101	134	34	0
1895-Brooklyn		National	36	18	13	.581	41	102	27	2
1896-Brooklyn		National	37	15	22	.405	76	123	28	1
1897-Brooklyn		National	40	19	21	.475	80	146	37	2
1898-Brooklyn		National	38	16	22	.421	75	118	38	0
1899-Brooklyn		National	35	18	8	.692	57	84	27	2
1900-Brooklyn		National	37	22	15	.595	73	102	26	2
1901-Brooklyn		National	14	3	5	.375	....	....	7	0
1902-New York		National	6	2	4	.333	....	....	4	1
1903-Pittsburgh		National	18	9	6	.600	39	57	9	1
1907-Dayton		Central	10	5	1	.833	....	....	....	....
National League Totals			372	183	164	.527	729	1087	297	13

WORLD SERIES RECORD

Year	Club	League	G.	IP.	W.	L.	Pct.	H.	R.	SO.	BB.	CG.	ShO.
1903-Pittsburgh		National	1	7	0	1	.000	11	10	3	3	0	0

HARMON CLAYTON (KILLER) KILLEBREW, JR.

Born June 29, 1936, at Payette, Idaho.
Height, 6.00. Weight, 210.
Threw and batted righthanded.

Tied major league record by hitting two or more home runs in each league park, season, 1962.
Set American League record for most home runs, righthanded batter, league, lifetime, 573.
Set American League record for most home runs, doubleheader (4), September 21, 1963—hitting three in first game and one in nightcap.
Named outfielder on THE SPORTING NEWS All-Star American League Team, 1964.
Named first baseman on THE SPORTING NEWS American League All-Star Team, 1967.
Named by THE SPORTING NEWS as the Outstanding American League Player, 1969-70.
Named third baseman on THE SPORTING NEWS American League All-Star Team, 1969-70.
Most Valuable Player in American League, 1969.

Year	Club	League	Pos.	G.	AB.	R.	H.	2B.	3B.	HR.	RBI.	B.A.	PO.	A.	E.	F.A.
1954-Washington		Amer.	2B	9	13	1	4	1	0	0	3	.308	5	2	0	1.000
1955-Washington		Amer.	3B-2B	38	80	12	16	1	0	4	7	.200	24	49	5	.936
1956-Washington		Amer.	3B-2B	44	99	10	22	2	0	5	13	.222	24	44	4	.944
1956-Charlotte		Sally	3B	70	249	61	81	16	7	15	63	.325	62	127	14	.931
1957-Chattanooga		South	3B	142	519	90	145	30	7	*29	101	.279	134	*298	*31	.933
1957-Washington		Amer.	3B-2B	9	31	4	9	2	0	2	5	.290	2	16	1	.947
1958-Washington		Amer.	3B	13	31	2	6	0	0	0	2	.194	8	13	0	1.000
1958-Indianapolis		A. A.	3B	38	121	14	26	5	1	2	10	.215	28	79	11	.907
1958-Chattanooga		South.	3B-OF	86	299	58	92	17	1	17	54	.308	97	134	12	.951
1959-Washington		Amer.	*3B-OF	153	546	98	132	20	2	●42	105	.242	135	325	*30	.939
1960-Washington		Amer.	1B-3B	124	442	84	122	19	1	31	80	.276	629	135	17	.978
1961-Minnesota		Amer.	1-3-OF	150	541	94	156	20	7	46	122	.288	1003	143	23	.980
1962-Minnesota		Amer.	OF-1B	155	552	85	134	21	1	*48	*126	.243	241	5	9	.965
1963-Minnesota		Amer.	OF	142	515	88	133	18	0	*45	96	.258	219	7	3	.987
1964-Minnesota		Amer.	OF	158	577	95	156	11	1	*49	111	.270	232	1	7	.971
1965-Minnesota		Amer.	1-3-O	113	401	78	108	16	1	25	75	.269	743	113	12	.986
1966-Minnesota		Amer.	3-1-O	162	569	89	160	27	1	39	110	.281	435	205	18	.973
1967-Minnesota		Amer.	1-3B	163	547	105	147	24	1	●44	113	.269	1285	89	12	.991
1968-Minnesota		Amer.	1B-3B	100	295	40	62	7	2	17	40	.210	601	71	7	.990
1969-Minnesota		Amer.	3B-1B	●162	555	106	153	20	2	*49	*140	.276	649	219	22	.975
1970-Minnesota		Amer.	3B-1B	157	527	96	143	20	1	41	113	.271	312	212	20	.963
1971-Minnesota		Amer.	1B-3B	147	500	61	127	19	1	28	*119	.254	700	149	13	.985
1972-Minnesota		Amer.	1B	139	433	53	100	13	2	26	74	.231	995	*99	9	.992
1973-Minnesota		Amer.	1B	69	248	29	60	9	1	5	32	.242	431	45	1	.998
1974-Minnesota		Amer.	1B	122	333	28	74	7	0	13	54	.222	218	21	2	.992
1975-Kansas City(a)		Amer.	DH-1B	106	312	25	62	13	0	14	44	.199	28	0	0	1.000
Major League Totals				2435	8147	1283	2086	290	24	573	1584	.256	8919	1963	215	.981

aSigned as free agent by Kansas City Royals, January 24, 1975.

WORLD SERIES RECORD

Year	Club	League	Pos.	G.	AB.	R.	H.	2B.	3B.	HR.	RBI.	B.A.	PO.	A.	E.	F.A.
1965-Minnesota		Amer.	3B	7	21	2	6	0	0	1	2	.286	11	7	1	.947

RALPH McPHERRAN KINER

Born October 27, 1922, at Santa Rita, N. M.
Height, 6.02. Weight, 195.
Threw and batted righthanded.
Married tennis star Nancy Chaffee, October 13, 1951.

Kiner became the first player in major league history to lead his league, or tie for leadership, in home runs in each of his first seven seasons; established National League mark by hitting more than 50 home runs twice, 1947 and 1949 (tied by Willie Mays); set N. L. record by hitting 40 or more home runs in five successive years 1947, 1948, 1949, 1950 and 1951 (later tied by Duke Snider).

By his home run hitting feats, Kiner broke one major league record, tied seven major league marks, and equalled two National League standards in 1947. Kiner's eight home runs in four consecutive games, September 10 (2), 11 (1), 11 (3), 12 (2), smashed the big league mark of seven which he tied earlier in the season. The other major league marks he tied were: five homers in two consecutive games, which he accomplished twice, August 15 (2), 16 (3), and September 11, second game (3), 12 (2); six homers in three consecutive games, three times, August 14 (1), 15 (2), 16 (3), and September 10 (2), 11 (1), 11 (3) or September 11 (1), 11 (3), 12 (2); four home runs in four successive times at bat, August 15 (1), 16 (3); hit four home runs in a double-header, September 11 (1), 11 (3) (later topped by Stan Musial and Nate Colbert with 5); Kiner tied modern National League standard of three consecutive home runs in a game on two occasion (August 16 and September 11, second game); established National League record by hitting 101 home runs in two consecutive years 1949-50, hit for cycle June 25, 1950.

Named by THE SPORTING NEWS as Top Player in National League, 1950.
Named as outfielder on THE SPORTING NEWS All-Star Major League Teams, 1947-49-50-51.
Named to Hall of Fame, 1975.

Year	Club	League	Pos.	G.	AB.	R.	H.	2B.	3B.	HR.	RBI.	B.A.	PO.	A.	E.	F.A.
1941	Albany	East.	OF	•141	509	94	142	23	7	11	66	.279	245	15	3	.989
1942	Albany	East.	OF	*141	483	84	124	27	7	*14	75	.257	*338	18	*17	.954
1943	Toronto	Int.	OF	43	144	22	34	6	2	2	13	.236	120	5	3	.977
1943-44-45	Pittsburgh	Nat.					(In Military Service)									
1946	Pittsburgh	Nat.	OF	144	502	63	124	17	3	*23	81	.247	339	6	11	.969
1947	Pittsburgh	Nat.	OF	152	565	118	177	23	4	•51	127	.313	*390	8	7	.983
1948	Pittsburgh	Nat.	OF	•156	555	104	147	19	5	•40	123	.265	382	6	10	.975
1949	Pittsburgh	Nat.	OF	152	549	116	170	19	5	*54	*127	.310	311	12	7	.979
1950	Pittsburgh	Nat.	OF	150	547	112	149	21	6	*47	118	.272	287	13	11	.965
1951	Pittsburgh	Nat.	OF-1B	151	531	•124	164	31	6	*42	109	.309	751	36	18	.978
1952	Pittsburgh	Nat.	OF	149	516	90	126	17	2	•37	87	.244	250	9	8	.970
1953	Pitts.(a)-Chi.	Nat.	OF	*158	562	100	157	20	3	35	116	.279	298	6	9	.971
1954	Chicago(b)	Nat.	OF	147	557	88	159	36	5	22	73	.285	298	6		.971
1955	Cleveland	Amer.	OF	113	321	56	73	13	0	18	54	.243	141	2	2	.986
National League Totals				1359	4884	915	1373	203	39	351	961	.281	3290	107	89	.974
American League Totals				113	321	56	78	13	0	18	54	.243	141	2	2	.986
Major League Totals				1472	5205	971	1451	216	39	369	1015	.279	3431	109	91	.975

aTraded to Chicago Cubs with pitcher Howard Pollet, catcher Joe Garagiola and outfielder-first baseman George Metkovich for pitcher Bob Schultz, catcher Toby Atwell, first baseman Preston Ward, infielder George Freese, outfielders Bob Addis and Gene Hermanski and estimated $100,000, June 4, 1953.

bTraded to Cleveland Indians for pitcher Sam Jones, outfielder Gale Wade and estimated $60,000, November 16, 1954.

CHARLES F. (SILVER) KING (KOENIG)

Born January 11, 1867, at St. Louis, Mo.
Died May 19, 1938, at St. Louis, Mo.
Height, 5.10. Weight, 180.
Threw and batted righthanded.

Year	Club	League	G.	IP.	W.	L.	Pct.	H.	R.	SO.	BB.	CG.	ShO.
1886	Kansas City	National	5	39	1	3	.250	47	35	28	11	5	0
1886	St. Joseph	Western					(No records available)						
1887	St. Louis	Amer. Assn.	46	391	34	11	.756	525	235	106	116	44	2
1888	St. Louis	Amer. Assn.	*66	*576	*45	21	.682	451	216	206	134	*62	•6
1889	St. Louis	Amer. Assn.	54	440	33	17	.660	259	262	181	119	45	2
1890	Chicago	Players	56	459	•32	22	.593	434	237	184	156	48	*4

Year	Club	League	G.	IP.	W.	L.	Pct.	H.	R.	SO.	BB.	CG.	ShO.
1891	Pittsburgh	National	47	383	14	*29	.326	385	242	164	146	40	3
1892	New York	National	51	405	22	24	.478	388	255	158	161	44	1
1893	New York-Cincinnati	National	24	155	8	10	.444	187	124	55	64	12	1
1894-95	—						(Out of Baseball)						
1896	Washington	National	21	152	10	7	.588	167	108	34	39	14	0
1897	Washington	National	23	151	7	8	.467	188	120	30	42	13	0
	Players League Totals		56	459	32	22	.593	434	237	184	156	48	4
	American Association Totals		166	1407	112	49	.696	1335	713	493	369	151	10
	National League Totals		171	1285	62	81	.434	1362	884	469	463	128	5
	Major League Totals		393	3151	206	152	.575	3131	1834	1146	988	327	19

CHARLES HERBERT (CHUCK) KLEIN

Born October 7, 1905, at Indianapolis, Ind.
Died March 28, 1958, at Indianapolis, Ind.
Height, 6.00. Weight, 195.
Threw right and batted lefthanded.
Married Mary Torpey, May 23, 1936.

Established modern National League record by scoring 158 runs in 1930; tied National League record by leading league in scoring three consecutive years (1930-31-32); holds National League record for most long hits in a season (107), 1930; tied with Pat Seerey for major league record for most extra bases on long hits in an extra-inning game (12), July 10, 1936; tied with Honus Wagner for major league record for most consecutive years leading league in total bases (4), 1930-31-32-33; holds modern National League record for most total bases in extra-inning game (16), July 10, 1936; hit six home runs in four consecutive games (July 13 (1), 15 (two in first game, one in second game) and July 16 (2), 1929); hit five home runs in three consecutive games twice—July 15 (two games), 16, 1930 and September 18-19-22, 1930; hit four home runs in a ten-inning game, July 10, 1936; established modern league record with 44 assists for outfielder, 1930.
    Hit safely in 26 consecutive games (twice) May 18, second game, through June 17, 1930, and July 12, first game, through August 3, first game, 1930; led National League in stolen bases, 1932.
    Led N.L. outfielders in double plays, 1930, 1935 (tie).
    Named National League's Most Valuable Player by THE SPORTING NEWS, 1931 and 1932; named by Baseball Writers' Association of America on THE SPORTING NEWS All-Star Major League Teams, 1932-33.
    Coach, Philadelphia Phillies, 1942-45, inclusive.
    Named to Hall of Fame, 1980.

Year	Club	League	Pos.	G.	AB.	R.	H.	2B.	3B.	HR.	RBI.	B.A.	PO.	A.	E.	F.A.
1927	Evansville	I.I.I.	OF	14	49	10	16	2	2	2	....	.327	20	0	0	1.000
1928	Fort Wayne	Cent.	OF	88	359	85	119	29	4	26	....	.331	216	15	●12	.951
1928	Philadelphia	Nat.	OF	64	253	41	91	14	4	11	34	.360	128	7	3	.978
1929	Philadelphia	Nat.	OF	149	616	126	219	45	6	*43	145	.356	321	18	12	.966
1930	Philadelphia	Nat.	OF	●156	648	*158	250	*59	8	40	170	.386	362	*44	17	.960
1931	Philadelphia	Nat.	OF	148	594	●121	200	34	10	*31	*121	.337	292	13	9	.971
1932	Philadelphia	Nat.	OF	●154	650	*152	*226	50	15	*38	137	.348	331	*29	●15	.960
1933	Philadelphia (a)	Nat.	OF	152	606	101	*223	*44	7	*28	*120	*.368	339	*21	5	.986
1934	Chicago	Nat.	OF	115	435	78	131	27	2	20	80	.301	222	6	9	.962
1935	Chicago	Nat.	OF	119	434	71	127	14	4	21	73	.293	215	11	10	.958
1936	Chi.(b)-Phil	Nat.	OF	146	601	102	184	35	7	25	104	.306	276	16	*23	.927
1937	Philadelphia	Nat.	OF	115	406	74	132	20	2	15	57	.325	175	11	10	.949
1938	Philadelphia	Nat.	OF	129	458	53	113	22	2	8	61	.247	229	8	10	.960
1939	Phi.(c)-Pit.(d)	Nat.	OF	110	317	45	90	18	5	12	56	.284	153	5	7	.958
1940	Philadelphia	Nat.	OF	116	354	39	77	16	2	7	37	.218	180	4	3	.984
1941	Philadelphia	Nat.	OF	50	73	6	9	0	0	1	3	.123	22	0	1	.958
1942	Philadelphia	Nat.	PH	14	14	0	1	0	0	0	0	.071	0	0	0	.000
1943	Philadelphia	Nat.	OF-PH	12	20	0	2	0	0	0	3	.100	0	0	1	.000
1944	Philadelphia	Nat.	OF	4	7	1	1	0	0	0	0	.143	5	0	0	1.000
	Major League Totals			1753	6486	1168	2076	398	74	300	1201	.320	3250	194	135	.962

    aTraded to Chicago Cubs for pitcher Ted Kleinhans, infielder Mark Koenig and outfielder Harvey Hendrick and $65,000, November 21, 1933.
    bTraded with pitcher Fabian Kowalik and $50,000 to Philadelphia Phillies for outfielder Ethan Allen and pitcher Curtis Davis, May 21, 1936.
    cReleased by Philadelphia Phillies and signed by Pittsburgh Pirates, June 7, 1939.
    dReleased by Pittsburgh and signed by Philadelphia Phillies, March 26, 1940.

WORLD SERIES RECORD

Year	Club	League	Pos.	G.	AB.	R.	H.	2B.	3B.	HR.	RBI.	B.A.	PO.	A.	E.	F.A.
1935	Chicago	Nat.	OF-PH	5	12	2	4	0	0	1	2	.333	4	0	0	1.000

WILLIAM JOSEPH (THE OLD ARBITRATOR) KLEM
(Rated by many as the No. 1 umpire of all time.)

Born February 22, 1874, at Rochester, N. Y.
Died September 16, 1951, at Miami, Fla.
Height, 5.07½. Weight, 157.

As a youth around his native Rochester, N. Y., Bill Klem gained quite a reputation as a ball player. He was a first baseman and catcher. In 1896 and '97, he had trials with pro teams representing Hamilton, Ont., Springfield, Mass., and Augusta, Me. Arm trouble, however, cut short his chances and he returned to the sandlot ranks.

Bill umpired his first game several years later. At the time he was employed as a steel worker at Berwick, Pa., and playing on a semi-pro team. He launched his career as an umpire in pro ball in August, 1902, in the Connecticut State League under his real name of Klimm. The next year, following the example of an uncle, he changed his name to Klem and later had it legalized.

Klem advanced to the New York State League in 1903 and to the American Association the following season. His efforts in the A. A. attracted the attention of Ban Johnson, who sought to get him for the American League, but Bill felt obligated to Harry Pulliam, National League president. At the close of the 1904 campaign Pulliam hired Klem to umpire a post-season Pittsburgh-Cleveland series, and the next spring Bill began his long N. L. career. For 16 years he called 'em from behind the plate exclusively—first because there was only one umpire on duty and later because of his strike-calling superiority. Bill retired from the field in 1941 to become N. L. chief of staff, a position he held until his death ten years later.

A feud of long standing with John McGraw, famed Giant manager, almost ended Klem's stay in the National League in 1928. Following charges by McGraw, Bill resigned at the close of that season. However, he later was mollified and after cooling off three months agreed to rejoin the senior circuit.

Klem umpired in 18 World Series—eight more than any other arbiter in history. His first was in 1908. From that time through 1918, he missed only three fall classics. His last was in 1940, his final season in harness. Klem also had the distinction, along with Jack Sheridan, of being selected to umpire the Giants-White Sox world tour of 1913-14.

The Old Arbitrator was responsible for many innovations in the umpiring profession. In 1904, during his first year in the American Association, he introduced the practice of drawing a line on the field with his spiked shoe to ward off protesting managers and players. He also was an early crusader for better quarters for umpires. Another Klem innovation was for the plate umpire to stand slightly to the side of the catcher closest to the batter, rather than directly behind the catcher.

Klem, along with Tommy Connolly, was named to the Hall of Fame by the Committee on Veterans in September, 1953—the first umpires to gain this honor.

THEODORE BERNARD KLUSZEWSKI

Born September 10, 1924, at Argo, Ill.
Height, 6.02. Weight, 240.
Threw and batted lefthanded.
Married Eleanor Guckel, February 9, 1946.

Established major league record for first basemen by leading in fielding five consecutive seasons, 1955; set modern National League record for most consecutive games scoring runs (17), August 27-September 13, 1954, inclusive; led N. L. first basemen in double plays, 1953-54-55-56.
Hit three home runs in a game, first game, July 1, 1956.
Named as first baseman on THE SPORTING NEWS All-Star Major League Teams, 1954-55-56.
Coach, Cincinnati Reds, 1969 to date.

Year	Club	League	Pos.	G.	AB.	R.	H.	2B.	3B.	HR.	RBI.	B.A.	PO.	A.	E.	F.A.
1946	Columbia	Sally	1B-OF	90	335	59	118	24	5	11	87	*.352	525	20	15	.973
1947	Cincinnati	Nat.	1B	9	10	1	1	0	0	0	2	.100	10	0	0	1.000
1947	Memphis	South.	1B	115	427	80	161	32	9	7	68	*.377	931	60	19	.981
1948	Cincinnati	Nat.	1B	113	379	49	104	23	4	12	57	.274	833	65	9	.990
1949	Cincinnati	Nat.	1B	136	531	63	164	26	2	8	68	.309	1140	65	14	.989
1950	Cincinnati	Nat.	1B	134	538	76	165	37	0	25	111	.307	1123	61	15	.987
1951	Cincinnati	Nat.	1B	154	607	74	157	35	2	13	77	.259	*1381	88	5	*.997
1952	Cincinnati	Nat.	1B	135	497	62	159	24	11	16	86	.320	1121	66	8	*.993
1953	Cincinnati	Nat.	1B	149	570	97	180	25	0	40	108	.316	1285	58	7	*.995
1954	Cincinnati	Nat.	1B	149	573	104	187	28	3	*49	*141	.326	1237	101	5	*.996
1955	Cincinnati	Nat.	1B	153	612	116	*192	25	0	47	113	.314	*1388	86	8	*.995
1956	Cincinnati	Nat.	1B	138	517	91	156	14	1	35	102	.302	1166	89	13	.990

Year Club	League	Pos.	G.	AB.	R.	H.	2B.	3B.	HR.	RBI.	B.A.	PO.	A.	E.	F.A.
1957–Cincinnati(a)	Nat.	1B	69	127	12	34	7	0	6	21	.268	161	15	2	.989
1958–Pittsburgh	Nat.	1B	100	301	29	88	13	4	4	37	.292	591	36	4	.994
1959–Pittsburgh(b)	Nat.	1B	60	122	11	32	10	1	2	17	.262	151	12	0	1.000
1959–Chicago	Amer.	1B	31	101	11	30	2	1	2	10	.297	220	10	0	1.000
1960–Chicago(c)	Amer.	1B	81	181	20	53	9	0	5	39	.293	325	19	1	.997
1961–Los Angeles	Amer.	1B	107	263	32	64	12	0	15	39	.243	520	28	6	.989
American League Totals			219	545	63	147	23	1	22	88	.270	1065	57	7	.994
National League Totals			1499	5384	785	1619	267	28	257	940	.301	11587	742	90	.993
Major League Totals			1718	5929	848	1766	290	29	279	1028	.298	12652	799	97	.993

aTraded to Pittsburgh Pirates for first baseman Dee Fondy, December 28, 1957.
bReleased to Chicago White Sox in waiver deal for infielder Bob Sagers and outfielder-first baseman Harry Simpson, August 25, 1959. Sagers, playing for Indianapolis, American Association, transferred to Columbus, International League, at close of season.
cSelected by Los Angeles Angels, December 14, 1960.

WORLD SERIES RECORD

Year Club	League	Pos.	G.	AB.	R.	H.	2B.	3B.	HR.	RBI.	B.A.	PO.	A.	E.	F.A.
1959–Chicago	Amer.	1B	6	23	5	9	1	0	3	10	.391	59	3	0	1.000

SANFORD (SANDY) KOUFAX

Born December 30, 1935, at Brooklyn, N.Y.
Height, 6.02. Weight, 198.
Threw left and batted righthanded.

Set major league records: Most games (97), 10 or more strikeouts, lifetime (topped by Nolan Ryan); most strikeouts, two consecutive games (31), with 13 on August 24 and 18 on August 31, 1959; most strikeouts, three consecutive games (41), with 13 on August 24, 18 on August 31 and 10 on September 6, 1959 (since tied by Nolan Ryan, 1974); most no-hit games pitched, lifetime (4), 1962, 1963, 1964, 1965 (tied by Nolan Ryan in 1975); most shutout games won by lefthander, season (11), 1963; most strikeouts, season (382), 1965 (since topped by Nolan Ryan, 383 in 1973); most games (21), 10 or more strikeouts, season, 1965 (topped by Nolan Ryan in 1973).
Tied major league record: Most seasons (3), 300 or more strikeouts, 1963, 1965, 1966 (topped by Nolan Ryan in 1976).
Struck out 18 batters in nine-inning game, August 31, 1959, against San Francisco Giants and April 24, 1962, against Chicago Cubs.
Holds modern National League records: Most games won, lefthanded pitcher, season (27), 1966; most consecutive seasons (6), 200 or more strikeouts, 1966; most consecutive seasons (5), leading league in earned-run average, 1962, 1963, 1964, 1965, 1966.
Tied National League record for most years leading league in earned-run average (5), 1962, 1963, 1964, 1965, 1966.
Pitched four no-hit, no-run games, defeating New York Mets, 5-0, June 30, 1962; San Francisco Giants, 8-0, May 11, 1963; Philadelphia Phillies, 3-0, June 4, 1964, and Chicago Cubs, 1-0, September 9, 1965, in perfect game.
Established World Series record for most strikeouts, four-game Series (23), 1963.
Tied following World Series records in 1963 Series: Most games won (2), four-game Series; most complete games (2), four-game Series; most innings pitched (18), four-game Series; most consecutive strikeouts, start of game (5), October 2.
Led National League in shutouts with 11 in 1965 and tied for lead with 5 in 1966.
Named as pitcher on the National League All-Star Team by THE SPORTING NEWS, 1963-64-65-66.
Named Most Valuable National League Player, 1963.
Named No. 1 Major League Player of the Year by THE SPORTING NEWS, 1963 and 1965.
Named National League Pitcher of the Year by THE SPORTING NEWS, 1963-64-65-66.
Won Cy Young Memorial Award, 1963-65-66.
Named to Hall of Fame, 1971.

Year Club	League	G.	IP.	W.	L.	Pct.	H.	R.	ER.	SO.	BB.	ERA.
1955–Brooklyn	National	12	42	2	2	.500	33	15	14	30	28	3.00
1956–Brooklyn	National	16	59	2	4	.333	66	37	32	30	29	4.88
1957–Brooklyn	National	34	104	5	4	.556	83	49	45	122	51	3.89
1958–Los Angeles	National	40	159	11	11	.500	132	89	79	131	105	4.47
1959–Los Angeles	National	35	153	8	6	.571	136	74	69	173	92	4.06
1960–Los Angeles	National	37	175	8	13	.381	133	83	76	197	100	3.91
1961–Los Angeles	National	42	256	18	13	.581	212	117	100	*269	96	3.52
1962–Los Angeles	National	28	184	14	7	.667	134	61	52	216	57	*2.54
1963–Los Angeles	National	40	311	●25	5	.833	214	68	65	*306	58	*1.88
1964–Los Angeles	National	29	223	19	5	*.792	154	49	43	223	53	*1.74
1965–Los Angeles	National	43	*336	*26	8	*.765	216	90	76	*382	71	*2.04
1966–Los Angeles	National	41	*323	*27	9	.750	241	74	62	*317	77	*1.73
Major League Totals		397	2325	165	87	.655	1754	806	713	2396	817	2.76

WORLD SERIES RECORD

Year	Club	League	G.	IP.	W.	L.	Pct.	H.	R.	ER.	SO.	BB.	ERA.
1959–Los Angeles		National	2	9	0	1	.000	5	1	1	7	1	1.00
1963–Los Angeles		National	2	18	2	0	1.000	12	3	3	23	3	1.50
1965–Los Angeles		National	3	24	2	1	.667	13	2	1	29	5	0.38
1966–Los Angeles		National	1	6	0	1	.000	6	4	1	2	2	1.50
World Series Totals			8	57	4	3	.571	36	10	6	61	11	0.95

HARVEY EDWARD KUENN

Born December 4, 1930, at West Allis, Wis.
Height, 6.02. Weight, 198.
Threw and batted righthanded.
Married Dixie Ann Sarchet, October 29, 1955.

Tied major league record by making 200 or more hits in his first full season in the major leagues; tied A.L. record by making two long hits in an inning, first inning, July 20, 1954, first game; tied major league record for most two-base hits, inning (2), July 24, 1964; holds American League record, most at-bats, season, 154-game schedule, 679, 1953.
Tied World Series mark for most putouts, game, by left fielder (6), October 4, 1962.
Named American League Rookie of the Year by the Baseball Writers' Association and THE SPORTING NEWS, 1953.
Named as shortstop on THE SPORTING NEWS All-Star Major League Team, 1956.
Coach, Milwaukee Brewers, 1971 to date.

Year	Club	League	Pos.	G.	AB.	R.	H.	2B.	3B.	HR.	RBI.	B.A.	PO.	A.	E.	F.A.
1952–Davenport		I.I.I.	SS	63	256	46	87	17	3	1	40	.340	114	194	26	.922
1952–Detroit		Amer.	SS	19	80	2	26	2	2	0	8	.325	44	57	4	.962
1953–Detroit		Amer.	SS	155	*679	94	*209	33	7	2	48	.308	*308	441	21	.973
1954–Detroit		Amer.	SS	•155	*656	81	•201	28	6	5	48	.306	*294	*496	28	.966
1955–Detroit		Amer.	SS	145	620	101	190	*38	5	8	62	.306	253	378	29	.956
1956–Detroit		Amer.	*SS-OF	146	591	96	*196	32	7	12	88	.332	219	388	20	*.968
1957–Detroit		Amer.	*SS-3B-1B	151	624	74	173	30	6	9	44	.277	251	387	*30	.955
1958–Detroit		Amer.	OF	139	561	73	179	*39	3	8	54	.319	*358	9	6	.984
1959–Detroit (a)		Amer.	OF	139	561	99	*198	*42	7	9	71	*.353	247	6	3	.988
1960–Cleveland (b)		Amer.	OF-3B	126	474	65	146	24	0	9	54	.308	222	13	9	.963
1961–San Francisco		Nat.	OF-3B-SS	131	471	60	125	22	4	5	46	.265	190	43	10	.959
1962–San Francisco		Nat.	OF-3B	130	487	73	148	23	5	10	68	.304	180	47	8	.966
1963–San Francisco		Nat.	OF-3B	120	417	61	121	13	2	6	31	.290	115	60	13	.931
1964–San Francisco		Nat.	OF-1B-3B	111	351	42	92	16	2	4	22	.262	136	9	6	.960
1965–S.F.(c)-Chicago		Nat.	OF-1B	77	179	15	40	5	0	0	12	.223	81	8	3	.967
1966–Chi.(d)-Phila		Nat	OF-1B	89	162	15	48	9	0	0	15	.296	130	3	1	.993
American League Totals				1175	4846	685	1518	268	43	62	477	.313	2196	2175	150	.967
National League Totals				658	2067	266	574	88	13	25	194	.278	832	170	41	.961
Major League Totals				1833	6913	951	2092	356	56	87	671	.303	3028	2345	191	.966

aTraded to Cleveland Indians for outfielder Rocky Colavito, April 17, 1960.
bTraded to San Francisco Giants for pitcher Johnny Antonelli and outfielder Willie Kirkland, December 3, 1960.
cTraded with catcher Ed Bailey and pitcher Bob Hendley to Chicago Cubs for catcher Dick Bertell and first baseman-outfielder Len Gabrielson, May 29, 1965.
dSold to Philadelphia Phillies, April 23, 1966.

WORLD SERIES RECORD

Year	Club	League	Pos.	G.	AB.	R.	H.	2B.	3B.	HR.	RBI.	B.A.	PO.	A.	E.	F.A.
1962–San Francisco		Nat.	OF	4	12	1	1	0	0	0	0	.083	11	0	0	1.000

JOSEPH ANTHONY KUHEL

Born June 25, 1906, at Cleveland, O.
Height, 6.00. Weight, 180.
Threw and batted lefthanded.
Married Willette West, October 9, 1930.

Collected five hits in game, May 16, 1933, and May 21, 1940. Hit three triples in game to tie American

League record, May 13, 1937.
Led A. L. first basemen in double plays, 1935, 1937.
Manager, Hot Springs, Cotton States League, 1947; manager, Washington Senators, 1948-49; manager, Kansas City, American Association, 1950.

Year	Club	League	Pos.	G.	AB.	R.	H.	2B.	3B.	HR.	RBI.	B.A.	PO.	A.	E.	F.A.
1924	Flint	M.-O.	1B	31	105	18	26	5	1	0	8	.248	302	10	12	.963
1925	Flint	M.-O.	1B	124	452	64	132	20	9	5	63	.292	1198	53	19	.985
1926	Springfield	I. I. I.	1B	134	527	97	179	29	15	10	....	.340	1233	59	14	.989
1926	Kansas City	A. A.	PH	1	1	0	0	0	0	0	0	.000	0	0	0	.000
1927	Lincoln	West.	1B	143	587	94	163	27	10	2	....	.278	1476	73	16	.990
1927	Kansas City	A. A.	PH	2	1	0	0	0	0	0	0	.000	0	0	0	.000
1928	Kansas City	A. A.	1B	121	511	85	167	32	11	2	57	.327	1164	63	11	.991
1929	Kansas City	A. A.	1B	161	649	137	211	27	*26	6	83	.325	1508	73	22	.986
1930	Kansas City	A. A.	1B	93	374	77	139	28	12	8	65	.372	878	60	8	.992
1930	Washington	Amer.	1B	18	63	9	18	3	3	0	17	.286	149	8	3	.981
1931	Baltimore	Int.	1B	6	27	4	8	0	2	1	8	.296	67	0	0	1.000
1931	Washington	Amer.	1B	139	524	70	141	34	8	8	85	.269	1255	57	12	.991
1932	Washington	Amer.	1B	101	347	52	101	21	5	4	52	.291	761	45	5	.994
1933	Washington	Amer.	1B	153	602	89	194	34	10	11	107	.322	*1498	61	7	*.996
1934	Washington	Amer.	1B	63	263	49	76	12	3	3	25	.289	618	23	4	.994
1935	Washington	Amer.	1B	151	633	99	165	25	9	2	74	.261	1425	87	14	.991
1936	Washington	Amer.	1B	149	588	107	189	42	8	16	118	.321	1452	73	10	.993
1937	Washington	Amer.	1B	136	547	73	155	24	11	6	61	.283	1242	85	9	.993
1938	Chicago(a)	Amer.	1B	117	412	67	110	27	4	8	51	.267	1136	59	14	.988
1939	Chicago	Amer.	1B	139	546	107	164	24	9	15	56	.300	1256	72	11	.992
1940	Chicago	Amer.	1B	155	603	111	169	28	8	27	94	.280	1395	91	18	.988
1941	Chicago	Amer.	1B	153	600	99	150	39	5	12	63	.250	*1444	108	10	.994
1942	Chicago	Amer.	1B	115	413	60	103	14	4	4	52	.249	1085	70	11	.991
1943	Chicago(b)	Amer.	1B	153	531	55	113	21	1	5	46	.213	1471	106	8	*.995
1944	Washington	Amer.	1B	139	518	90	144	26	7	4	51	.278	1251	83	17	.987
1945	Washington	Amer.	1B	142	533	73	152	29	13	2	75	.285	1323	94	16	.989
1946	Wash.(c)-Chi.	Amer.	1B	78	258	26	68	9	3	4	22	.264	625	41	4	.994
1947	Chicago	Amer.	PH	3	3	0	0	0	0	0	0	.000	0	0	0	.000
1947	Hot Springs	Cot. St.	1-PH	24	32	7	10	1	0	1	3	.313	....	....	....	....
Major League Totals				2104	7984	1236	2212	412	111	131	1049	.277	19386	1163	173	.992

WORLD SERIES RECORD

Year	Club	League	Pos.	G.	AB.	R.	H.	2B.	3B.	HR.	RBI.	B.A.	PO.	A.	E.	F.A.
1933	Washington	Amer.	1B	5	20	1	3	0	0	0	1	.150	59	3	0	1.000

aTraded to Chicago White Sox for first baseman Henry J. Bonura, March 18, 1938.
bSold to Washington Senators, November 23, 1943.
cSold to Chicago White Sox, June 13, 1946.

NAPOLEON (LARRY) LAJOIE

Born September 5, 1875, at Woonsocket, R. I.
Died February 7, 1959, at Daytona Beach, Fla.
Height, 6.01. Weight, 195.
Threw and batted righthanded.

Had seven bunt singles and one triple in eight times at bat in doubleheader on October 9, 1910, against St. Louis.
Hit four home runs in two consecutive games, August 9, second game (2), August 10, first game (2), against Washington, 1901.
Manager, Cleveland Americans, 1905 until resignation in midseason, 1909; manager, Toronto, International League, 1917; manager, Indianapolis, American Association, 1918. Highest batting average in American League history, .422, in 1901.
Named to Hall of Fame, 1937.

Year	Club	League	Pos.	G.	AB.	R.	H.	2B.	3B.	HR.	SB.	B.A.	PO.	A.	E.	*F.A.
1896	Fall River	N. Eng.	OF	80	380	94	163	34	16	16	....	*.429	*280	30	23	.931
1896	Philadelphia	Nat.	1B	39	174	37	57	11	6	4	6	.328	360	11	3	.992
1897	Philadelphia	Nat.	1B-OF	126	545	107	198	37	25	*10	22	.363	1112	43	20	.983
1898	Philadelphia	Nat.	2B	147	610	113	200	*40	11	5	33	.328	*434	431	48	.947
1899	Philadelphia	Nat.	2B	72	308	70	117	17	11	6	14	.380	222	242	21	.957
1900	Philadelphia(a)	Nat.	2B	102	451	95	156	32	12	7	25	.346	283	345	27	.959
1901	Philadelphia	Amer.	2B	131	543	*145	*229	*48	13	*14	27	*.422	*403	374	30	*.963
1902	Phila.-Cleveland	Amer.	2B	87	352	81	129	34	5	7	19	.366	284	278	15	.974
1903	Cleveland	Amer.	1B-*2B	126	488	90	173	40	13	7	22	*.355	*355	426	35	*.957
1904	Cleveland	Amer.	2B-SS	140	554	92	*211	*50	14	5	31	*.381	354	400	39	.951
1905	Cleveland	Amer.	2B	65	249	29	82	13	2	2	11	.329	148	177	3	.991
1906	Cleveland	Amer.	*2B-3B	152	602	88	*214	*49	7	0	20	.355	*374	*455	26	*.970
1907	Cleveland	Amer.	2B	137	509	53	153	32	6	2	24	.301	314	*461	26	*.968
1908	Cleveland	Amer.	2B	*157	581	77	168	32	6	2	15	.289	*450	*538	37	*.964

Year	Club	League	Pos.	G	AB	R	H	2B	3B	HR	SB	B.A.	PO.	A.	E.	F.A.
1909	Cleveland	Amer.	2B	128	469	56	152	33	7	1	13	.324	282	373	28	.959
1910	Cleveland	Amer.	2B	*159	*592	94	*227	*53	8	4	27	*.383	387	419	32	.962
1911	Cleveland	Amer.	1B-2B	90	315	36	115	20	1	2	13	.365	479	109	14	.977
1912	Cleveland	Amer.	1B-2B	117	448	66	165	34	4	0	18	.368	412	261	24	.966
1913	Cleveland	Amer.	2B	137	465	67	156	25	2	1	17	.335	289	363	20	*.970
1914	Cleveland	Amer.	1B-2B	121	419	37	108	14	3	0	14	.258	487	233	22	.970
1915	Philadelphia(b)	Amer.	2B	129	490	40	137	24	5	1	10	.280	251	332	23	.962
1916	Philadelphia	Amer.	2B	113	426	33	105	14	4	2	15	.246	254	325	16	.973
1917	Toronto	Int.	1B	151	581	83	*221	*39	4	5	4	*.380	875	263	23	.980
1918	Indianapolis	A. A.	1B	78	291	39	82	12	2	2	10	.282	661	89	10	.987
American League Totals				1989	7502	1084	2524	515	100	50	296	.336	5523	5524	390	.966
National League Totals				486	2088	422	728	137	64	32	100	.349	2411	1072	119	.967
Major League Totals				2475	9590	1506	3252	652	164	82	396	.339	7934	6596	509	.966

aJumped to Philadelphia A. L., but Philadelphia N. L. club got injunction against his playing for Athletics and he joined Cleveland in June, 1902.

bContract assumed by Philadelphia Athletics, January, 1915.

NOTE: League President Ban Johnson declared Ty Cobb batting champion in 1910 with a .385 average, beating Lajoie's .384. Recent research has resulted in the revision of Lajoie's average to .383 and Cobb's to .382. See page 56.

KENESAW MOUNTAIN LANDIS

(First Commissioner of Baseball)

Born November 20, 1866, at Millville, O.
Died November 25, 1944, at Chicago, Ill.

Although a native of Ohio, Kenesaw M. Landis spent most of his youth in Indiana. After quitting high school, Landis, intrigued by law and legal matters, mastered shorthand and qualified as clerk of a court in South Bend, Ind. Later he took pre-law courses at the University of Cincinnati and graduated in 1891 from Union Law School in Chicago—now a part of Northwestern University.

President Theodore Roosevelt appointed Landis to the position of Unites States District Judge for the Northern District of Illinois in March, 1905. The Judge gained nationwide fame two years later by fining the Standard Oil Company $29,240,000 in a freight rebate case. The company, however, eventually escaped payment of the fine through appeal to the Supreme Court.

In January, 1915, the Federal League brought a suit before Landis for an injunction against the American and National leagues. He took the case under advisement and withheld his opinion so that it was possible for the majors to absorb the Federal circuit and bring peace to the game. This handling of the suit made a deep impression on diamond officials.

Landis' appointment as Commissioner of Baseball on November 12, 1920, was a direct result of the Black Sox scandal. Since the peace agreement between the two majors in January, 1903, a three-man National Commission had functioned as the supreme authority. However, in January, 1920, Garry Herrmann, chairman of the Commission since its inception, resigned and the two other members, President Ban Johnson of the American League and Prexy John Heydler of the National, could not agree on a successor.

Landis took office in January, 1921. His salary was $50,000 per year, but before his first seven-year term expired, he was boosted to $65,000.

From the start, Landis was zealous in his defense of the rights of the player. However, he also did not hesitate to curb the players. Two of his biggest decisions involved "cover-up" operations by farm chains. In March, 1938, he set free 91 Cardinal farmhands and handed out several fines in connection with the case. Less than two years later, in January, 1940, he turned loose a similar number of young Detroit players on the same charge. One of Landis' last important decisions was to bar permanently William D. Cox, president of the Phillies, from Organized Ball in 1943 for allegedly betting on his own team. Landis was named to the Hall of Fame in December, 1944.

HENRY E. (TED) LARKIN

Born January 12, 1863, at Reading, Pa.
Died January 31, 1942, at Reading, Pa.
Threw and batted righthanded.

Made six hits in six times at bat, including two doubles, one triple, one home run, June 16, 1885.

Manager, Cleveland, Players League, 1890.

Year	Club	League	Pos.	G.	AB.	R.	H.	2B.	3B.	HR.	SB.	B.A.	PO.	A.	E.	F.A.
1883	Reading	Inter-State	OF	....	....	....	....	....	....	....	....	.354	....	....	....	....
1884	Philadelphia	Am. Assn.	OF	87	328	61	97	19	9	4	....	.296	....	....	16	.884
1885	Philadelphia	Am. Assn.	OF	108	455	114	154	*40	13	7	....	.338	....	....	30	.918
1886	Philadelphia	Am. Assn.	OF	139	563	136	184	*34	17	2	36	.327	....	....	37	.884
1887	Philadelphia	Am. Assn.	1-O	125	537	103	201	25	12	3	33	.374	....	....	24	.947
1888	Philadelphia	Am. Assn.	1B	135	544	97	154	27	10	6	19	.283	....	....	36	.972
1889	Philadelphia	Am. Assn.	1B	133	516	108	167	26	11	2	10	.324	1236	36	33	.975
1890	Cleveland	Players	1B	125	507	93	166	31	15	5	4	.327	1259	42	32	.976
1891	Philadelphia	Am. Assn.	1-O	129	516	94	142	28	13	10	3	.273	980	32	21	.979
1892	Washington	National	1B	116	450	73	127	16	5	9	19	.282	1087	61	39	.967
1893	Washington	National	1B	81	313	54	101	17	6	3	3	.322	774	27	30	.964
American Association Totals				856	3459	713	1099	199	85	34	101	.318	....	....	176	.955
Players League Totals				125	507	93	166	31	15	5	4	.327	1259	42	32	.976
National League Totals				197	763	127	228	33	11	12	22	.299	1861	88	69	.965
Major League Totals				1178	4729	933	1493	263	111	51	127	.316	....	....	277	.962

FREDERICK LEACH

Born November 23, 1897, at Springfield, Mo.
Height, 5.10. Weight, 183.
Threw right and batted lefthanded.
Married Nettie Marie Clark, January 1, 1919.

Led N. L. outfielders in double plays, 1927.

Year	Club	League	Pos.	G.	AB.	R.	H.	2B.	3B.	HR.	RBI.	B.A.	PO.	A.	E.	F.A.
1922	Waterloo	M. V.	OF	121	465	90	178	15	*20	*13	....	*.383	190	31	13	.944
1922	Rochester	Int.	OF	17	47	9	17	1	1	4	....	.362	21	0	1	.955
1923	Philadelphia	Nat.	OF	52	104	5	27	4	0	1	16	.260	38	0	2	.950
1924	New Haven	East.	OF	14	57	3	9	0	0	0	....	.158	18	6	0	1.000
1924	Harrisburg	N.Y.P.	OF	115	419	76	145	24	7	12	....	.346	201	12	5	.977
1924	Philadelphia	Nat.	OF	8	28	6	13	2	1	2	7	.464	7	1	1	.889
1925	Beaumont	Tex.	OF	89	372	63	129	40	5	12	76	.347	216	15	5	.979
1925	Philadelphia	Nat.	OF	65	292	47	91	15	4	5	28	.312	178	2	9	.952
1926	Philadelphia	Nat.	OF	129	492	73	162	29	7	11	71	.329	313	15	7	.979
1927	Philadelphia	Nat.	OF	140	536	69	164	30	4	12	83	.306	385	*26	8	.981
1928	Philadelphia(a)	Nat.	OF-1B	145	588	83	179	36	11	13	96	.304	545	29	8	.986
1929	New York	Nat.	OF	113	411	74	119	22	6	8	47	.290	149	2	4	.974
1930	New York	Nat.	OF	126	544	90	178	19	13	13	71	.327	208	11	5	.978
1931	New York(b)	Nat.	OF	129	515	75	159	30	5	6	60	.309	239	6	6	.976
1932	Boston	Nat.	OF	84	223	21	55	9	2	1	29	.247	126	2	3	.977
Major League Totals				991	3733	543	1147	196	53	72	509	.307	2188	94	53	.977

aTraded to New York Giants for outfielder Frank (Lefty) O'Doul and cash, October 29, 1928.
bSold to Boston Braves, March 19, 1932.

THOMAS WILLIAM LEACH

Born November 4, 1877, at French Creek, N. Y.
Died September 29, 1969, at Haines City, Fla.
Height, 5.06½. Weight, 150.
Threw and batted righthanded.

Manager, Rochester, 1916; manager, Tampa, 1920-21-22-23 and 1927; manager, Lakeland, 1924; manager, St. Petersburg, 1928; scout, Boston Braves, 1935-36.

Year	Club	League	Pos.	G.	AB.	R.	H.	2B.	3B.	HR.	SB.	B.A.	PO.	A.	E.	F.A.
1896	Peter's-Hamp.	Va.	3B	36	129	17	29	....	....	....	....	.225	....	....	....	.892
1897	Youngstown	Int. St.	3B	12	....	....	2	....	....	....	....	.281	....	....	....	....
1898	Auburn	N. Y. St.	3B	97	....	....	....	....	....	....	15	.325	....	....	....	*.931
1898	Louisville	Nat.	3B	3	10	0	3	0	0	0	0	.300	2	7	3	.750

Year	Club	League	Pos.	G.	AB.	R.	H.	2B.	3B.	HR.	SB.	B.A.	PO.	A.	E.	F.A.
1899	Louisville(a)	Nat.	3B-SS	106	404	74	117	13	6	4	19	.290	206	267	64	.881
1900	Pittsburgh	Nat.	3B	45	158	20	34	1	2	1	7	.215	45	70	19	.858
1901	Pittsburgh	Nat.	3B	93	375	62	112	13	13	1	16	.299	120	187	31	.908
1902	Pittsburgh	Nat.	3B	135	514	97	144	21	20	*6	29	.280	172	●321	40	.925
1903	Pittsburgh	Nat.	3B	127	507	97	151	16	17	7	22	.298	178	292	*65	.879
1904	Pittsburgh	Nat.	3B	146	579	92	149	15	12	2	23	.257	*212	*371	*60	.907
1905	Pittsburgh	Nat.	3B-OF	131	499	71	128	10	14	2	17	.257	238	134	16	.959
1906	Pittsburgh	Nat.	3B-OF	126	476	66	136	10	7	1	21	.286	204	141	20	.945
1907	Pittsburgh	Nat.	3B-OF	149	547	102	166	19	12	4	43	.303	323	80	21	.950
1908	Pittsburgh	Nat.	3B	152	583	93	151	24	16	5	24	.259	199	293	33	.937
1909	Pittsburgh	Nat.	OF	151	587	*126	153	29	8	6	27	.261	333	12	11	.969
1910	Pittsburgh	Nat.	OF	133	529	83	143	24	5	4	18	.270	352	14	13	.966
1911	Pittsburgh	Nat.	OF	102	386	60	92	12	6	3	19	.238	208	15	3	.987
1912	Pitts.(b)-Chi.	Nat.	OF	110	362	74	93	14	5	2	20	.257	246	15	6	.978
1913	Chicago	Nat.	OF	131	456	●99	131	23	10	6	21	.287	271	15	3	*.990
1914	Chicago(c)	Nat.	OF-3B	153	577	80	152	24	9	7	16	.263	346	42	18	.956
1915	Cincinnati	Nat.	OF	107	335	42	75	7	5	0	20	.224	200	9	9	.959
1916	Rochester	Int.	3B-OF	115	390	72	95	17	11	2	17	.244	209	73	15	.949
1917	Kansas City	A. A.	3B-OF	117	386	57	94	22	7	1	8	.244	183	66	13	.950
1918	Chattanooga	South.	OF	67	230	●50	67	11	2	0	12	.291	138	9	5	.967
1918	Pittsburgh	Nat.	OF-SS	30	72	14	14	2	3	0	2	.194	37	3	2	.952
1919	Shreveport	Tex.	OF	67	245	48	65	12	3	1	10	.265	146	7	4	.975
1920	Tampa	Fla. St.	OF	47	120	32	34	10	3	0	10	.283	52	10	5	.925
1921	Tampa	Fla. St.	OF	27	49	16	19	4	2	0	2	.388	22	12	5	.872
1922	Tampa	Fla. St.	OF	20	46	12	15	3	5	0	2	.326	30	5	1	.972
Major League Totals				2130	7956	1352	2144	277	170	61	364	.269	3891	2288	437	.934

aTransferred by Owner Barney Dreyfuss with 14 other players when National League reduced circuit from 12 to eight clubs, Louisville being dropped.

bTraded with pitcher Albert (Lefty) Leifield to Chicago Cubs for infielder-outfielder Artie Hofman and pitcher King Cole, June, 1912.

cSigned with Cincinnati, February, 1915, after drawing unconditional release from Cubs.

WORLD SERIES RECORD

Year	Club	League	Pos.	G.	AB.	R.	H.	2B.	3B.	HR.	SB.	B.A.	PO.	A.	E.	F.A.
1903	Pittsburgh	Nat.	3B	8	33	3	9	0	4	0	2	.273	5	16	4	.840
1909	Pittsburgh	Nat.	OF-3B	7	25	8	8	4	0	0	1	.320	20	3	0	1.000
World Series Totals				15	58	11	17	4	4	0	3	.293	25	19	4	.917

SAMUEL W. LEEVER

Born December 23, 1872, at Goshen, O.
Died May 19, 1953, at Goshen, O.
Height, 5.11. Weight, 175.
Threw and batted righthanded.

Pitched one-hit games on July 2, 1900; July 26, 1902, and June 13, 1903.

Year	Club	League	G.	IP.	W.	L.	Pct.	H.	R.	SO.	BB.	CG.	ShO.
1897	Richmond	Atlantic	35	....	20	15	.571	....	....	....	....	....	....
1898	Richmond	Atlantic	23	....	....	....	....	....	....	....	....	....	....
1898	Pittsburgh	National	5	32	1	0	1.000	22	11	14	4	2	0
1899	Pittsburgh	National	*51	*382	20	23	.465	354	193	124	118	35	3
1900	Pittsburgh	National	29	233	15	13	.536	234	100	85	51	23	3
1901	Pittsburgh	National	20	154	14	5	*.737	170	80	81	34	18	2
1902	Pittsburgh	National	28	223	16	7	.696	200	76	86	29	23	4
1903	Pittsburgh	National	36	285	25	7	*.781	255	99	90	60	29	*7
1904	Pittsburgh	National	34	254	18	11	.621	224	85	63	54	26	1
1905	Pittsburgh	National	33	230	20	5	*.800	199	94	81	54	20	3
1906	Pittsburgh	National	36	260	22	7	.759	232	84	76	48	25	6
1907	Pittsburgh	National	31	217	14	9	.609	182	70	65	46	17	5
1908	Pittsburgh	National	38	193	15	7	.682	179	60	28	41	14	0
1909	Pittsburgh	National	18	71	8	1	.889	74	30	23	14	2	0
1910	Pittsburgh	National	26	111	6	5	.545	104	45	33	25	4	0
1911	Minneapolis	Amer. Assn.	24	125	7	4	.636	139	73	39	39	4	0
Major League Totals			385	2645	194	100	.660	2429	1033	845	578	238	39

WORLD SERIES RECORD

Year	Club	League	G.	IP.	W.	L.	Pct.	H.	R.	SO.	BB.	CG.	ShO.
1903	Pittsburgh	National	2	10	0	2	.000	13	8	2	3	1	0

ROBERT GRANVILLE LEMON

Born September 22, 1920, at San Bernardino, Calif.
Height, 6.00. Weight, 180.
Threw right and batted lefthanded.
Married Jane H. McGee, January 14, 1944.

Hit seven home runs as a pitcher, 1949.
Named by Baseball Writers' Association of America as pitcher on THE SPORTING NEWS All-Star Major League Teams, 1948-50-54.
Pitched no-hit, no-run game against Detroit Tigers, winning 2-0, fanned four and walked three, June 30, 1948.
Set World Series record for most bases on balls by a pitcher in a four-game Series (8), 1954; tied Series mark for most games by a pitcher in a four-game Series (2), 1954.
Named Outstanding American League Pitcher by THE SPORTING NEWS, 1948-50-54.
Scout, Cleveland Indians, 1959; made coach, 1960; coach, Philadelphia Phillies, 1961; manager, Honolulu, Pacific Coast League, 1964; manager, Seattle, Pacific Coast League, 1965-66; coach, California Angels, 1967 through 1970; manager, Kansas City Royals, 1971-1972; Royals' special assignment scout, 1973; manager, Sacramento, Pacific Coast League, 1974; manager, Richmond, International League, 1975; coach, New York Yankees, 1976; manager, Chicago White Sox, 1977 to June 30, 1978; manager, New York Yankees, July 25, 1978, to June 19, 1979.
Named to Hall of Fame, 1976.

PITCHING RECORD

Year	Club	League	G.	IP.	W.	L.	Pct.	H.	R.	ER.	SO.	BB.	ERA.
1938	Oswego	Can.-Amer.	1	1	0	0	.000	1	0	0	1	0	0.00
1941	Wilkes-Barre	Eastern	1	1	0	1	.000	0	1	1	0	3	9.00
1946	Cleveland	Amer.	32	94	4	5	.444	77	40	26	39	68	2.49
1947	Cleveland	Amer.	37	167	11	5	.688	150	68	64	65	97	3.45
1948	Cleveland	Amer.	43	*294	20	14	.588	231	104	92	147	129	2.82
1949	Cleveland	Amer.	37	280	22	10	.688	211	101	93	138	137	2.99
1950	Cleveland	Amer.	44	*288	*23	11	.676	*281	144	123	*170	146	3.84
1951	Cleveland	Amer.	42	263	17	•14	.548	*244	*119	103	132	124	3.52
1952	Cleveland	Amer.	42	*310	22	11	.667	236	104	86	131	105	2.50
1953	Cleveland	Amer.	41	*287	21	15	.583	*283	119	107	98	110	3.36
1954	Cleveland	Amer.	36	258	•23	7	.767	228	95	78	110	92	2.72
1955	Cleveland	Amer.	35	211	•18	10	.643	218	103	91	100	74	3.88
1956	Cleveland	Amer.	39	255	20	14	.588	230	103	86	94	89	3.04
1957	Cleveland	Amer.	21	117	6	11	.353	129	70	60	45	64	4.62
1958	Cleveland	Amer.	11	25	0	1	.000	41	15	15	8	16	5.40
1958	San Diego	P.C.	12	56	2	5	.286	67	32	27	19	22	4.34
	Major League Totals		460	2849	207	128	.618	2559	1185	1024	1277	1251	3.23

Named by Baseball Writers' Association of America as pitcher on THE SPORTING NEWS All-Star Major League Teams, 1948-50-54.

WORLD SERIES RECORD

Year	Club	League	G.	IP.	W.	L.	Pct.	H.	R.	ER.	SO.	BB.	ERA.
1948	Cleveland	Amer.	2	16⅓	2	0	1.000	16	4	3	6	7	1.65
1954	Cleveland	Amer.	2	13⅓	0	2	.000	16	11	10	11	8	6.75
	World Series Totals		4	29⅔	2	2	.500	32	15	13	17	15	3.94

BATTING RECORD

Year	Club	League	Pos.	G.	AB.	R.	H.	2B.	3B.	HR.	RBI.	B.A.	PO.	A.	E.	F.A.
1938	Springfield	M.-Atl.	INF-OF	7	18	1	4	1	0	0	2	.222	4	5	2	.818
1938	Oswego	C.-A	O-SS-P	75	282	44	88	6	6	7	34	.312	97	52	12	.925
1939	Springfield	M. Atl.	SS-O	80	307	44	90	14	3	3	39	.293	106	103	25	.893
1939	New Orleans	South.	OF-3B	52	207	30	64	9	6	0	22	.309	65	33	13	.883
1940	Wilkes-Barre	East.	3B-OF	92	321	37	82	14	3	2	53	.255	132	68	16	.926
1941	Wilkes-Barre	East.	*3B-SS-P	•141	*562	*109	•169	15	13	4	43	.301	*179	268	36	.925
1941	Cleveland	Amer.	3B	5	4	0	1	0	0	0	0	.250	1	1	0	1.000
1942	Baltimore	Int.	*3B-SS	148	596	95	160	23	8	21	80	.268	*159	*349	*33	.939
1942	Cleveland	Amer.	3B	5	5	0	0	0	0	0	0	.000	0	1	1	.500
1943-44-45	Cleveland	Amer.					(In Military Service)									
1946	Cleveland	Amer.	P-OF	55	89	9	16	3	0	1	4	.180	46	30	2	.974
1947	Cleveland	Amer.	P-OF	47	56	11	18	4	3	2	5	.321	13	46	1	.983
1948	Cleveland	Amer.	P	52	119	20	34	9	0	5	21	.286	*23	*86	4	.965
1949	Cleveland	Amer.	P	46	108	17	29	6	2	7	19	.269	*34	*71	4	.963
1950	Cleveland	Amer.	P	72	136	21	37	9	1	6	26	.272	22	66	4	.957
1951	Cleveland	Amer.	P	56	102	11	21	4	1	3	13	.206	21	*60	2	.976
1952	Cleveland	Amer.	P	54	124	14	28	5	0	2	9	.226	*32	*79	2	.982
1953	Cleveland	Amer.	P	51	112	12	26	9	1	2	17	.232	*31	*74	3	.972
1954	Cleveland	Amer.	P	40	98	11	21	4	1	2	10	.214	*22	57	3	.963

Year	Club	League	Pos.	G.	AB.	R.	H.	2B.	3B.	HR.	RBI.	B.A.	PO.	A.	E.	F.A.
1955–Cleveland		Amer.	P	49	78	11	19	0	0	1	9	.244	16	43	1	.983
1956–Cleveland		Amer.	P	43	93	8	18	0	0	5	12	.194	24	*61	*6	.934
1957–Cleveland		Amer.	P	25	46	2	3	1	0	1	1	.065	12	31	0	1.000
1958–Cleveland		Amer.	P	15	13	1	3	0	0	0	1	.231	1	7	0	1.000
1958–San Diego		P.C.	OF-P	32	69	2	18	4	0	0	7	.261	25	9	0	1.000
Major League Totals				615	1183	148	274	54	9	37	147	.232	298	713	33	.968

EMIL JOHN (DUTCH) LEONARD

Born March 25, 1910, at Auburn, Ill.
Height, 6.00. Weight, 195.
Threw and batted righthanded.
Married Rose Dolenc, May 12, 1934.

Coach, Chicago Cubs, 1954 through 1956.

Year	Club	League	G.	IP.	W.	L.	Pct.	H.	R.	ER.	SO.	BB.	ERA.
1930–Canton		Central	11	53	1	5	.167	68	49	47	23	17	7.98
1930–Mobile		Southern	31	180	5	16	.238	247	148	132	52	72	6.60
1931–St. Joseph		Western	6	9	0	1	.000	15	11	7	4	3	7.00
1931–Sp'field-Qu'cy-Dec		I. I. I.	24	92	6	5	.545	112	54	43	56	20	4.21
1932–Decatur(a)		I. I. I.	15	98	7	4	.636	96	38	...	38	22	.....
1933–York		NYP	34	187	12	15	.444	188	73	65	80	42	3.13
1933–Brooklyn		National	10	40	2	3	.400	42	17	13	6	10	2.93
1934–Brooklyn		National	44	184	14	11	.560	210	90	67	58	33	3.28
1935–Brooklyn		National	43	138	2	9	.182	152	67	60	41	29	3.91
1936–Brooklyn		National	16	32	0	0	.000	34	18	13	8	5	3.66
1936–Atlanta		Southern	22	126	13	3	*.813	115	39	32	51	19	*2.29
1937–Atlanta		Southern	32	188	15	8	.652	193	90	76	68	34	3.64
1938–Washington		American	33	223	12	15	.444	221	109	85	68	53	3.43
1939–Washington		American	34	269	20	8	.714	*273	124	106	88	59	3.55
1940–Washington		American	35	289	14	•19	.424	*328	136	112	124	78	3.49
1941–Washington		American	34	256	18	13	.581	271	117	98	91	54	3.45
1942–Washington(b)		American	6	35	2	2	.500	28	16	16	15	5	4.11
1943–Washington		American	31	220	11	13	.458	218	96	80	51	46	3.27
1944–Washington		American	32	229	14	14	.500	222	97	78	62	37	3.07
1945–Washington		American	31	216	17	7	.708	208	72	51	96	35	2.13
1946–Washington(c)		American	26	162	10	10	.500	182	85	64	62	36	3.56
1947–Philadelphia		National	32	235	17	12	.586	224	86	70	103	57	2.68
1948–Philadelphia(d)		National	34	226	12	*17	.414	226	85	63	92	54	2.51
1949–Chicago		National	33	180	7	16	.304	198	94	83	83	43	4.15
1950–Chicago		National	35	74	5	1	.833	70	41	31	28	27	3.77
1951–Chicago		National	41	82	10	6	.625	69	30	24	30	28	2.63
1952–Chicago		National	45	67	2	2	.500	56	18	16	37	24	2.15
1953–Chicago		National	45	63	2	3	.400	72	34	32	27	24	4.57
National League Totals			378	1321	73	80	.477	1353	580	472	513	334	3.22
American League Totals			262	1899	118	101	.539	1951	852	690	657	403	3.27
Major League Totals			640	3220	191	181	.513	3304	1432	1162	1170	737	3.25

aInjured hand first week of July, 1932, and league disbanded July 15, 1932.
bSuffered broken ankle, April 23, 1942, and out of lineup until August, 1942.
cSold to Philadelphia Phillies, December 9, 1946.
dTraded to Chicago Cubs with pitcher Walter Dubiel for pitcher Henry (Hank) Borowy and first baseman Ed Waitkus, December 14, 1948.

WALTER FENNER (BUCK) LEONARD

Born September 8, 1907, at Rocky Mount, N. C.
Height, 5:10. Weight, 185.
Threw and batted lefthanded.
Married Sarah Wroten, 1937.

Buck Leonard was "the" first baseman of Negro professional baseball from 1934 to 1950. Whenever an All-Star team was selected, automatically the name "Leonard" was written in the first base slot. He hit for power and he hit for percentage. Towering drives were his trademark. He and his teammate on the Homestead Grays, Josh Gibson, formed the most destructive force ever to cannonade the pitchers of the Negro Leagues. Called the "Thunder Twins" by the black press, Buck was labeled the "Lou Gehrig of the Negro leagues" and Josh was compared with Babe Ruth.

A gifted fielder, Buck was a master at catching low throws and nabbing bunters. He had an exceptionally accurate and powerful throwing arm, and though not the traditional lanky first baseman, he could "catch everything." Leonard was a model of consistency, not a fancy dan at the bag.

Regarded as colored baseball's most popular player, Buck was well-liked not only for his brilliant playing, but for his quiet, easy-to-meet manner and his spirit as captain of the Grays.

Leonard was voted first baseman on the Negro baseball All-Time All-American Dream Team, a group selected by 31 national Negro baseball experts from the two major eras of black professional baseball. Selected in 1952, it covered a span of 42 years, beginning in 1910.

Buck began playing sandlot ball in Rocky Mount. He quit high school at 15 to go to work for the Atlantic Coast Line railroad. Dropped from the shop's workforce in 1933, he began his professional career with the Rocky Mount Elks and the Black Swans. His play attracted the eyes of the Portsmouth (Va.) Firefighters, for whom he played until Manager Ben Taylor of the Baltimore Stars snatched him. It was Taylor who taught him the fine points of first-base play, at which Ben had been a master. At the tailend of the season, Buck was taken by the Brooklyn Royal Giants, managed by Cannonball Dick Redding.

In 1934, Cum Posey, owner and manager of the Homestead Grays of Pittsburgh, on the recommendation of an old Grays pitcher, the legendary Smoky Joe Williams, signed Leonard, who remained with the Grays for 17 years, during which they won nine straight Negro league pennants, 1937-45.

The Grays averaged 30,000 miles per year by bus. They played so often in major league parks that they became part-time tenants . . . whenever the major league club was out of town. The Polo Grounds, Yankee Stadium, Forbes Field, Sportsman's Park, Griffith Stadium and Comiskey Park were the parks used more often than others because of the many Negro baseball fans in each city and the favorable terms these owners (usually American League park owners) extended the Negro league teams. For this reason, the owners of the Pirates and Senators knew more about the Negro stars and thus were the first to feel out both Leonard and Gibson about joining the major leagues in the 1940s. But, as Leonard said, "I was too old, past my prime and didn't want to embarrass anyone or hurt the chances of those who might follow. And, as things happened, Josh died suddenly in 1947, before it all really began."

Leonard's lifetime batting average in professional Negro ball was computed at .342. Of an average of 200 games per year, 80 were between members of the East and West divisions of the Negro National League and these box scores constituted the bulk of statistics on which "official" averages were computed. Other games played were varied forms of exhibitions.

Buck's top homer total for one season was 42 in 1942 and, in 1948, he led both divisions in batting with a .391 mark.

Leonard retired from baseball in 1955, after 23 years and over 4,000 games, all as a first baseman. He played in 12 East-West All-Star games, held annually in the White Sox' Comiskey Park; performed 12 winters in the Caribbean, in Puerto Rico, Cuba, Mexico, Venezuela and the Dominican Republic. In the spring of 1936, he played against the Cincinnati Reds in Puerto Rico. His last active years, 1951 through 1955, were spent in the Mexican League, the first three years with Torreon and the final two with Durango. He made a 10-game Organized Baseball appearance in 1953, at Portsmouth (Piedmont), when he was 46 years old. He hit .333. In 1962 he helped organize the Rocky Mount club of the Carolina League, added some of his own money and served as a vice-president. The club won the pennant in 1975. He opened up his own realty company in 1966, serving his Rocky Mount neighbors.

As Buck looked over his baseball life, he admitted proudly:

"My greatest thrill was being inducted into the National Baseball Hall of Fame in Cooperstown, N. Y. on August 7, 1972.

"I was not 'bitter' by not being allowed to play in the major leagues. I just said, 'The time has not come.' I only wish I could have played in the 'big leagues' when I was young enough to show what I could do. When an offer was given me to join up, I was too old and I knew it."

1954 Official Baseball Guide, Piedmont League P. 290
Individual Batting

Year	Club	League	Pos.	G.	AB.	R.	H.	2B.	3B.	HR.	SB.	B.A.
1953	Portsmouth	Piedmont	1B	10	33	5	11	2	0	0	1	.333

SAMUEL ANDREW LESLIE

Born July 26, 1906, Moss Point, Miss
Height, 5;11. Weight, 192.
Threw and batted lefthanded.

Made 22 hits as pinch-hitter in 75 games, 1932; 17 singles, four doubles, one home run.

Year	Club	League	Pos.	G.	AB.	R.	H.	2B.	3B.	HR.	RBI.	B.A.	PO.	A.	E.	F.A.
1927	Meridan-Jack.	C. S. L.	1B	93	325	43	91	19	8	4	....	.280	929	31	18	.982
1928	Meridan	C. S. L.	1B	124	459	86	169	47	6	8	....	.368	746	47	13	.984
1929	Selma	S. E. L.	1B	54	197	52	72	16	7	6	50	.365	471	19	9	.982
1929	Memphis	S. A.	1B	86	298	51	112	22	8	6	82	.376	735	40	8	.989
1929	New York	Nat.	OF	1	1	0	0	0	0	0	0	.000	1	0	0	1.000
1930	San Antonio	T. L.	1B	73	291	64	119	33	5	6	62	.409	751	28	10	.987
1930	New York	Nat.	PH	2	2	0	1	0	0	0	0	.500	0	0	0	.000
1930	Toledo	A. A.	1B	23	79	10	26	5	4	0	....	.329	166	10	4	.978

Year	Club	League	Pos.	G.	AB.	R.	H.	2B.	3B.	HR.	RBI.	B.A.	PO.	A.	E.	F.A.
1931—New York		Nat.	1B-PH	53	53	11	16	4	0	3	5	.302	16	1	0	1.000
1932—New York		Nat.	1B-PH	77	75	5	22	4	0	1	15	.293	7	0	0	1.000
1933—N.Y.(a)-Brook		Nat.	1B	136	501	62	148	23	7	8	73	.295	1226	70	21	.984
1934—Brooklyn		Nat.	1B	146	546	75	181	29	6	9	102	.332	1262	93	9	.993
1935—Brooklyn		Nat.	1B	142	520	72	160	30	7	5	93	.308	1233	81	14	.989
1936—New York		Nat.	1B	117	417	49	123	19	5	6	54	.295	1030	68	10	.991
1937—New York		Nat.	1B	72	191	25	59	7	2	3	30	.309	444	38	5	.990
1938—New York		Nat.	1B	76	154	12	39	7	1	1	16	.253	304	15	4	.988
1939—Jersey City		Int.	1B	112	372	37	117	19	1	2	66	.315	853	53	11	.988
Major League Totals				822	2460	311	749	123	28	36	389	.304	5523	366	63	.989

aTraded to Brooklyn for outfielder Frank J. O'Doul and pitcher W. Watson Clark, June 16, 1933.

WORLD SERIES RECORD

Year	Club	League	Pos.	G.	AB.	R.	H.	2B.	3B.	HR.	RBI.	B.A.	PO.	A.	E.	F.A.
1936—New York		Nat.	PH	3	3	0	2	0	0	0	0	.667	0	0	0	.000
1937—New York		Nat.	PH	2	1	0	0	0	0	0	0	.000	0	0	0	.000
World Series Totals				5	4	0	2	0	0	0	0	.500	0	0	0	.000

FREDERICK CHARLES (LINDY) LINDSTROM

Born November 21, 1905, at Chicago, Ill.
Height, 5.11. Weight, 170.
Threw and batted righthanded.
Married Irene Kiedaisch, February 14, 1928.

Had eight hits in doubleheader on September 11, 1928, vs. Boston; 10 at-bats, six singles, one double, one home run; batted safely in 25 consecutive games, July 4, afternoon game, through July 29, second game, 1933.
Had five hits in a game three times during 1930 season (April 26, first game; May 8 and July 10) for modern league record that stood until broken by Stan Musial of St. Louis Cardinals, 1948. Youngest World Series player: 18 years, ten months, 13 days.
World Series record—Made four hits in game, October 8, 1924.
Manager, Knoxville, Southern Association, 1940-41; Fort Smith, Western Association, 1942; coach, Northwestern University, 1951-1954.
Named to Hall of Fame, 1976.

Year	Club	League	Pos.	G.	AB.	R.	H.	2B.	3B.	HR.	RBI.	B.A.	PO.	A.	E.	F.A.
1922—Toledo		A. A.	3B	18	23	3	7	2	0	0	1	.304	4	12	3	.842
1923—Toledo		A. A.	3-SS-2B	147	581	77	157	21	7	1	39	.270	375	461	*42	.952
1924—New York		Nat.	2B-3B	52	79	19	20	3	1	0	4	.253	27	45	7	.911
1925—New York		Nat.	3B-2B-SS	104	356	43	102	15	12	4	33	.287	123	147	12	.957
1926—New York		Nat.	3B	140	543	90	164	19	9	9	76	.302	151	251	16	.962
1927—New York		Nat.	3B-OF	138	562	107	172	36	8	7	58	.306	182	181	12	.968
1928—New York		Nat.	3B	153	646	99	*231	39	9	14	107	.358	145	*340	21	*.958
1929—New York		Nat.	3B	130	549	99	175	23	6	15	91	.319	134	258	14	.966
1930—New York		Nat.	3B	148	609	127	231	39	7	22	106	.379	132	291	14	.953
1931—New York		Nat.	OF	78	303	38	91	12	6	5	36	.300	150	4	4	.975
1932—New York(a)		Nat.	3B-OF	144	595	83	161	26	5	15	92	.271	326	33	10	.973
1933—Pittsburgh		Nat.	OF	138	538	70	167	39	10	5	55	.310	388	7	5	.988
1934—Pittsburgh(b)		Nat.	OF	97	383	59	111	24	4	4	49	.290	181	8	2	.990
1935—Chicago(c)		Nat.	OF-3B	90	342	49	94	22	4	3	62	.275	167	40	7	.967
1936—Brooklyn		Nat.	OF	26	106	12	28	4	0	0	10	.264	51	4	1	.982
Major League Totals				1438	5611	895	1747	301	81	103	779	.311	2157	1609	132	.966

aSent to Pittsburgh Pirates in three-cornered deal in which New York Giants obtained pitcher Glenn Spencer from Pirates and outfielder George Davis from Philadelphia Phillies; Phils secured outfielder Gus Dugas from Pirates and outfielder Chick Fullis from Giants, December 12, 1932.
bTraded with pitcher Larry French to Chicago Cubs for pitchers Guy Bush and Jim Weaver and outfielder Floyd (Babe) Herman, November 22, 1934.
cUnconditionally released by Chicago Cubs and signed with Brooklyn Dodgers, January 26, 1936.

WORLD SERIES RECORD

Year	Club	League	Pos.	G.	AB.	R.	H.	2B.	3B.	HR.	RBI.	B.A.	PO.	A.	E.	F.A.
1924—New York		Nat.	3B	7	30	1	10	2	0	0	4	.333	7	18	0	1.000
1935—Chicago		Nat.	OF-3B	4	15	0	3	1	0	0	0	.200	8	1	1	.900
World Series Totals				11	45	1	13	3	0	0	4	.289	15	19	1	.971

DID YOU KNOW—
That Fred Lindstrom is still best known for tricky hopper which eluded him in 1924 World Series?

JOHN HENRY LLOYD

Born, April 25, 1884, at Palatka, Fla.
Died, March 19, 1965, at Atlantic City, N.J.
Height, 5.11. Weight, 180.
Batted lefthanded and threw righthanded.

John Henry Lloyd was called "The Shovel" for his ability to dig tough grounders out of the dirt. Many times his glove spewed cascading dirt and dust as the willowy shortstop clamped the ball with his long fingers and whipped the throw to first base. How good was he?

Judy Johnson, another Hall of famer, said that while he was scouting for the Philadelphia Athletics, Connie Mack told him; "If I had a bag with Honus Wagner in it and also John Henry Lloyd, and I reached in and pulled one out, whichever one it was I'd be perfectly satisfied."

Wagner said he was proud to be likened to Lloyd, "the Black Honus Wagner," whom he knew from competing against him in exhibitions. Wagner's exact quote was:" After I saw him, I felt honored that they should name such a great ballplayer after me."

Noted for his smooth baseball swing, Lloyd was a superior batter. In his prime he always was among the leaders, if not the batting champion himself. To Lloyd is given an accolade reserved for only a few ballplayers, that he was recognized equally for his fielding and his hitting, and especially was rated superior in both. Only a few, like Tris Speaker, Joe DiMaggio, Mickey Cochrane, Charley Gehringer, Wagner, Oscar Charleston and Willie Mays, are rated equally as superior fielders and hitters.

In fact, when pinned down, Mack told Johnson that Lloyd was the "greatest shortstop that he'd ever seen." And Connie had seen them all since 1886.

This is the caliber of John Henry Lloyd.

A revelation by Johnson lets us peek into the world of Negro ball vs. the major leaguers:

"We were playing in Cuba against the Detroit club and Ty Cobb, who later refused to face a Negro club, was the star as he always was. He took off for second base, but the ball was there before him and Lloyd put the tag on him. Cobb was surprised to find the ball waiting. What he didn't know and what we tried to teach the majors but they wouldn't listen, and haven't to this day, was we put special emphasis on getting the ball to the fielder BEFORE the runner arrived. We had catchers with great arms—they HAD to have them—and we worked our pickoff and man-on-base motions with quickness so that the runner couldn't take off as easily and the ball could get to the catcher quicker and he could get the ball to the fielder quicker. This part of inside ball was our everyday game—concentraton on the tricks of the trade that lowered the odds.

"Anyway, the second time Cobb got on. Bruce Petway, our catcher and a man who should be in the Hall of Fame, along with quite a few others, fired the ball on the dime to Lloyd and Cobb came in trying to knock Lloyd into center field. Lloyd tagged him and neatly sidestepped Cobb, nudging him into center field in the process. Lloyd could do anything, absolutely anything as a shortstop. Cobb was fit to be tied. The last time he got on, he took off again, but Petway had the ball down so fast, Cobb stopped half way and tried to go back to first. On a first baseman's fake, Cobb stopped and Lloyd, who'd followed him, tagged him out easily.

"This is what led Cobb to skip all Detroit exhibitions which were scheduled against Negro teams. He couldn't take the humiliation."

This is no real knock against Cobb, because he not only was a product of his environment, but such a fierce prideful competitor that he wanted no part of unnecessary embarrassment, and Caribbean exhibitions were merely club ploys for income. Such exhibition play as this was why Landis put the clamp on complete major league teams facing Negro league clubs in 1923. Unnecessary embarrassment.

But Lloyd loved the competition and found enough major leaguers who would play against him in his prime or against the clubs he later managed and played for, and they recognized his greatness.

Lloyd started out as a catcher in 1905, played shortstop for 14 years and in 1919, when the years began to take their toll on his legs, he turned to the old-folks home at first base, and made fewer and fewer appearances at short.

In 1905, Lloyd was a catcher for the Macon (Ga.) Acmes, but because the club was too poor to buy the full catching equipment, John Henry took too many foul shots to his unmasked face. When he reported to his next club, Philadelphia's Cuban X Giants, he had retreated to second base. He was a teammate of Charley Grant. John McGraw's "Tokohama" of 1901. He left to join the Chicago Leland Giants in 1910 and the next year shifted to the new Lincoln Giants of New York. This powerful club topped the Phillies, 9-2, drubbing Grover Cleveland Alexander in the bargain.

But along the way, the Lincoln Giants bowled over everything in the Negro leagues as well, which raised the ire of Rube Foster, who saw his Chicago American Giants humbled in both the home and away series against them.

In resentment Foster lured the big stars from Lincoln by paying them the top dollar of that period. Four went west, including Lloyd, who said, "Wherever the money was, that's where I was."

Lloyd played four years with the powerful Giants. He was cleanup hitter in a lineup that included Oscar Charleston, Bingo DeMoss, Bruce Petway and Louis Santop and pitchers Dick Redding, Frank Wickware and Smokey Joe Williams. Lloyd earned $250 per month while he was the kingpin of this superstar lineup.

In 1918 during World War I, Lloyd joined the working force at the Army Quartermasters depot in Chicago. Deserting Foster's team, rather than make its southern winter junket, riled the patriarch, but he let Lloyd go without a battle. John Henry then joined the Brooklyn Royal Giants as manager and it was at this period he recognized the spring in legs was fast departing and he split his duties between short and first base. A legend in his own time, he continued to be sought by other clubs for his ever solid bat, experience, drawing ability and remaining hint of glove magic.

In addition to the Brooklyn Royal Giants, he was a player for or manager of (or both) the Columbus (O.) Buckeyes, the Bacharach Giants and Hilldale clubs, the Lincoln Giants, Leland Giants, Chicago American Giants and the New York Black Yankees.

As Judy Johnson related to us when questioned about his impressions of the men named to the Hall of

Fame, "Lloyd was the kind of manager who would soft-sell you into doing what you had to do—he made us feel that anything that had to be done, you just did it. It helped me in my career in clutch situations. John Henry was soft-spoken and kind off the field as a player and as a manager, but on the field, he was all business and no one got in his way. They were sorry if they tried."

As the legendary Cum Posey, owner of the powerful Homestead Grays, said, "Lloyd is the Jekyll and Hyde of baseball—a fierce competitor on the field and as a manager against the opposition, but a gentle, considerate man off the field and always kind to his own players."

Though a product of the rough and roaring 1910s and 1920s, when there was a general hell-bent zest for living, drinking and carousing, Lloyd was tangential to the roar, springing from it but taking no part as he lived his own life in a peaceful, law-abiding, continent manner, with no drinking or cursing and a smile for everyone—truly a happy man. As Mrs. Lloyd remembered, "He laughed easily and everyone was glad to see him."

He spent his retirement years, from 1931 to the date of his death in 1965, in service to others. He played semi-pro ball around his adopted city (Atlantic City) until he was 58 years old. He was a janitor in that city's Post Office for a while and then swung over to janitorial duties in the Atlantic City school system, where he became the "grandfather" to all the youngsters. A local park was named in his honor in 1949, two years after Robinson entered the majors. In "Only the Ball Was White," by Robert W. Peterson, an excellent historian of the Negro leagues, Lloyd's words at the dedication have been preserved:

"I do not consider that I was born at the wrong time. I felt it was the right time, for I had a chance to prove the ability of our race in this sport, and because many of us did our very best to uphold the traditions of the game and of the world of sport, we have given the Negro a greater opportunity now to be accepted into the major leagues with other Americans."

Peterson also dug up the quote of a white newspaperman, a sportswriter in St. Louis in 1938, who was asked to name the player he judged the best in baseball history. The reply:

"If you mean in Organized Baseball," the writer said, "my answer would be Babe Ruth; but if you mean in all baseball, organized and unorganized, the answer would have to be a colored man named John Henry Lloyd."

Lloyd was named to the Hall of Fame in 1977.

MICHAEL STEPHEN (MICKEY) LOLICH

Born September 12, 1940, at Portland, Ore.

Height, 6;01. Weight, 207.

Threw left and batted righthanded.

First cousin of Ron Lolich, former outfielder with Chicago White Sox and Cleveland Indians, and Frank Lolich, former pitcher in New York Mets' organization.

Established major league record for most strikeouts, lefthanded pitcher, lifetime (2,832).
Established American League record for most strikeouts, lefthanded pitcher, lifetime (2,679), 1975.
Tied American League record for most seasons, 200 or more strikeouts (7), 1974; most consecutive years, 100 or more strikeouts (13).
Tied World Series for most games won Series (3), and most games won, Series, no losses (3), 1968.
Hit home run first World Series at bat, October 3, 1968, third inning.

Year	Club	League	G.	IP.	W.	L.	Pct.	H.	R.	ER.	SO.	BB.	ERA.
1959—Knoxville		Sally	11	67	3	6	.333	51	29	19	42	53	2.55
1959—Durham		Carolina	9	37	1	2	.333	27	22	17	24	45	4.14
1960—Knoxville		Sally	4	15	0	1	.000	17	13	13	14	20	7.63
1960—Durham		Carolina	25	113	5	10	.333	111	71	51	135	87	4.06
1961—Knoxville		Sally	15	72	3	5	.375	49	50	41	93	76	5.10
1961—Durham		Carolina	18	102	5	5	.500	92	42	34	102	73	2.99
1962—Denver		Am. Assoc.	9	12	0	4	.000	26	24	22	10	10	16.50
1962—Portland		P. Coast	23	130	10	9	.526	116	66	57	138	57	3.95
1963—Detroit		American	33	144	5	9	.357	145	64	57	103	56	3.56
1963—Syracuse		Int'national	6	22	0	2	.000	21	11	6	21	10	2.45
1964—Detroit		American	44	232	18	9	.667	196	88	84	192	64	3.26
1965—Detroit		American	43	244	15	9	.625	216	103	93	226	72	3.43
1966—Detroit		American	40	204	14	14	.500	204	119	108	173	83	4.76
1967—Detroit		American	31	204	14	13	.519	165	71	69	174	56	3.04
1968—Detroit		American	39	220	17	9	.654	178	84	78	197	65	3.19
1969—Detroit		American	37	281	19	11	.633	214	111	98	271	122	3.14
1970—Detroit		American	40	273	14	*19	.424	272	125	•115	230	109	3.79
1971—Detroit		American	45	*376	*25	14	.641	*336	133	122	*308	92	2.92
1972—Detroit		American	41	327	22	14	.611	282	100	91	250	74	2.50
1973—Detroit		American	42	309	16	15	.516	315	143	131	214	79	3.82
1974—Detroit		American	41	308	16	*21	.432	310	155	142	202	78	4.15
1975—Detroit (a)		American	32	241	12	18	.400	260	119	101	139	64	3.77
1976—New York (b)		National	31	193	8	13	.381	184	83	69	120	52	3.22
1977—							(Did Not Play)						
1978—San Diego		National	20	35	2	1	.667	30	6	6	13	11	1.54
1979—San Diego		National	27	49	0	2	.000	59	33	26	20	22	4.78
American League Totals			508	3363	207	175	.542	3093	1415	1289	2679	1014	3.45
National League Totals			78	277	10	16	.385	273	122	101	153	85	3.28
Major League Totals			586	3640	217	191	.532	3366	1537	1390	2832	1099	3.44

Signed as free agent by Detroit Tigers' organization, June 30, 1958.
aTraded with outfielder Billy Baldwin to New York Mets for outfielder Rusty Staub and pitcher Bill Laxton, December 12, 1975.
bPlaced on voluntarily retired list, February 7, 1977; signed by San Diego Padres, February 2, 1978 (after being declared free agent by Commissioner, January 5, 1978).

WORLD SERIES RECORD

Year	Club	League	G.	IP.	W.	L.	Pct.	H.	R.	ER.	SO.	BB.	ERA.
1968	Detroit	American	3	27	3	0	1.000	20	5	5	21	6	1.67

ERNEST NATALI (SCHNOZ) LOMBARDI

Born April 6, 1908, at Oakland, Calif.
Died September 26, 1977, at Santa Cruz, Calif.
Height, 6.03. Weight, 230.
Threw and batted righthanded.
Married Bernice Marie Ayres, June 5, 1944.

Equaled major league record for most two-base hits, game (4), May 8, 1935; tied major league mark by making six hits in six consecutive times at bat, May 9, 1937.
Named Most Valuable Player in National League, 1938.

Year	Club	League	Pos.	G.	AB.	R.	H.	2B.	3B.	HR.	RBI.	B.A.	PO.	A.	E.	F.A.
1926	Oakland	P. C.	C	4	6	.....	2	1	0	0	.....	.333	8	0	0	1.000
1927	Oakland	P. C.	C	16	20	2	3	0	0	1	6	.150	12	4	0	1.000
1927	Ogden	Utah-Idaho	C	50	186	29	74	16	1	4	.....	.398	183	40	9	.961
1928	Oakland	P. C.	C	120	318	39	120	27	3	8	47	.377	257	47	15	.953
1929	Oakland	P. C.	C	164	516	70	189	36	3	24	109	.366	*521	*95	16	.975
1930	Oakland	P. C.	C	146	473	76	175	32	4	22	105	.370	*563	*105	17	.975
1931	Brooklyn(a)	Nat.	C	73	182	20	54	7	1	4	23	.297	218	23	4	.984
1932	Cincinnati	Nat.	C	118	413	43	125	22	9	11	68	.303	288	76	*14	.963
1933	Cincinnati	Nat.	C	107	350	30	99	21	1	4	47	.283	223	52	8	.972
1934	Cincinnati	Nat.	C	132	417	42	127	19	4	9	62	.305	383	61	5	.989
1935	Cincinnati	Nat.	C	120	332	36	114	23	3	12	64	.343	298	49	6	.983
1936	Cincinnati	Nat.	C	121	387	42	129	23	2	12	68	.333	330	54	•15	.962
1937	Cincinnati	Nat.	C	120	368	41	123	22	1	9	59	.334	333	58	11	.973
1938	Cincinnati	Nat.	C	129	489	60	167	30	1	19	95	*.342	512	73	9	•.985
1939	Cincinnati	Nat.	C	130	450	43	129	26	2	20	85	.287	536	63	•10	.984
1940	Cincinnati	Nat.	C	109	376	50	120	22	0	14	74	.319	397	46	5	*.989
1941	Cincinnati(b)	Nat.	C	117	398	33	105	12	1	10	60	.264	496	70	10	.983
1942	Boston(c)	Nat.	C	105	309	32	102	14	0	11	46	*.330	251	41	6	.980
1943	New York	Nat.	C	104	295	19	90	7	0	10	51	.305	296	36	10	.971
1944	New York	Nat.	C	117	373	37	95	13	0	10	58	.255	350	47	*13	.968
1945	New York	Nat.	C	115	368	46	113	7	1	19	70	.307	*425	49	8	.983
1946	New York	Nat.	C	88	238	19	69	4	1	12	39	.290	272	36	7	.978
1947	New York	Nat.	C	48	110	8	31	5	0	4	21	.282	86	11	2	.980
1948	Sacra.-Oak.	P. C.	C	102	284	25	75	13	0	11	55	.264	267	37	8	.974
Major League Totals				1853	5855	601	1792	277	27	190	990	.306	5694	845	143	.979

aTraded to Cincinnati Reds with third baseman Walter Gilbert and outfielder Floyd (Babe) Herman for catcher Clyde Sukeforth, second baseman Tony Cuccinello and third baseman Joe Stripp, March 14, 1932.
bSold to Boston Braves, February 7, 1942.
cTraded to New York Giants for catcher Hugh Poland and second baseman Connie Ryan, April 27, 1943.

WORLD SERIES RECORD

Year	Club	League	Pos.	G.	AB.	R.	H.	2B.	3B.	HR.	RBI.	B.A.	PO.	A.	E.	F.A.
1939	Cincinnati	Nat.	C	4	14	0	3	0	0	0	2	.214	22	1	1	.958
1940	Cincinnati	Nat.	C-PH	?	3	0	1	1	0	0	0	.333	4	0	0	1.000
World Series Totals				6	17	0	4	1	0	0	2	.235	26	1	1	.964

HERMAN C. LONG

Born April 3, 1868, at Chicago, Ill.
Died September 17, 1909, at Denver Colo.
Height, 5.08½. Weight, 160.
Threw right and batted lefthanded.

Manager, Toledo, American Association, part of 1904; Des Moines, Western League, 1905; Omaha, Western League, 1906.

Year	Club	League	Pos.	G.	AB.	R.	H.	2B.	3B.	HR.	SB.	B.A.	PO.	A.	E.	F.A.
1887	Arkansas City	Kans. St.														
1887	Emporia	West.	SS	....	86	....	24	....	....	....	....	.277	42	23	6	.915
1888	Chi.(a)-K. C.	W. A.	SS	120	530	115	131	....	....	....	89	.247	239	203	51	.897
1889	Kansas City	A. A.	SS	136	571	137	160	32	6	3	91	.280	335	477	108	.883
1890	Boston	Nat.	SS	101	431	95	108	13	3	7	49	.250	230	352	66	.897
1891	Boston	Nat.	SS	139	577	130	166	21	12	10	58	.288	341	440	*85	.902
1892	Boston	Nat.	SS	151	647	114	185	30	9	6	62	.286	306	509	102	.888
1893	Boston	Nat.	SS	128	540	•149	159	20	5	6	33	.294	275	469	95	.886
1894	Boston	Nat.	SS	103	475	136	154	26	10	12	25	.324	223	371	71	.893
1895	Boston	Nat.	SS	124	540	110	172	24	11	11	36	.319	295	407	*80	.898
1896	Boston	Nat.	SS	119	508	108	170	23	7	4	40	.334	312	416	75	.906
1897	Boston	Nat.	SS	106	452	88	148	32	5	3	26	.327	276	347	63	.908
1898	Boston	Nat.	SS	144	586	98	161	19	9	6	22	.275	376	471	67	.927
1899	Boston	Nat.	SS	145	575	90	148	28	11	6	28	.257	353	425	60	.928
1900	Boston	Nat.	SS	124	483	80	124	18	2	*12	26	.256	260	456	45	.941
1901	Boston	Nat.	SS	138	518	55	118	15	8	3	19	.238	291	466	43	*.946
1902	Boston(b)	Nat.	SS	120	432	41	98	9	0	2	22	.227	286	369	37	*.947
1903	N.Y.-(c)-Det.	Amer.	SS-2B	91	318	27	70	15	0	0	17	.220	213	242	47	.906
1904	Toledo	A. A.	SS	39	149	13	36	7	0	0	10	.241	78	90	15	.918
1904	Philadelphia	Nat.	2B	1	4	0	1	0	0	0	0	.250	4	4	1	.889
1905	Des Moines	West.	SS	118	475	78	146	24	2	0	20	.307	237	341	43	*.936
1906	Omaha	West.	SS	69	253	16	54	6	0	0	5	.213	135	194	31	.914
	American League Totals			91	318	27	70	15	0	0	17	.220	213	242	47	.906
	National League Totals			1643	6768	1294	1912	278	92	88	446	.282	3828	5510	890	.911
	American Association Totals			136	571	137	160	32	6	3	91	.280	335	477	108	.883
	Major League Totals			1870	7657	1458	2142	325	98	91	554	.280	4376	6229	1045	.910

aSold to Kansas City, July 11, 1888.
bJumped to New York Americans for 1903.
cTraded with infielder Ernest Courtney to Detroit Tigers for shortstop Norman (Kid) Elberfeld, June 10, 1903.

TEMPLE CUP RECORD

Year	Club	League	Pos.	G.	AB.	R.	H.	2B.	3B.	HR.	SB.	B.A.	PO.	A.	E.	F.A.
1897	Boston	Nat.	SS	5	21	4	6	1	1	1	1	.286	16	15	1	.969

ALFONSO RAMON (SENOR) LOPEZ

Born, August 20, 1908, at Tampa, Fla.
Height, 5.11. Weight, 180.
Threw and batted righthanded.
Married Evelyn M. Kearney, October 7, 1939.

Holds record for most games as catcher in major leagues (1,918); holds record for most games as catcher in National League (1,861); tied major league record with no passed balls, season, 114 games, 1941; holds N. L. record for catching 100 or ore games, 12 seasons, with Charles L. Hartnett.
Manager, Indianapolis, (American Association, 1948-50; manager, Cleveland Indians, 1951-56; manager, Chicago White Sox, 1957-65 and 1968-69. Was called "Bridesmaid" for nine second-place finishes in the American League.
Named to Hall of Fame, 1977.

Year	Club	League	Pos.	G.	AB.	R.	H.	2B.	3B.	HR.	RBI.	B.A.	PO.	A.	E.	F.A.
1925	Tampa	Fla. St.	C	51	134	13	30	6	0	0	0	.224	210	41	10	.962
1926	Tampa	Fla. St.	C	116	419	64	132	18	12	1	....	.315	*645	120	*30	.962
1927	Jacksonville	So'East	C	128	416	58	115	10	10	3	....	.276	*519	108	20	.969
1928	Macon	Sally	C	114	389	67	127	14	8	14	64	.326	*472	*102	*18	.970
1928	Brooklyn	Nat.	C	3	12	0	0	0	0	0	0	.000	9	0	0	1.000
1929	Atlanta	South.	C	143	490	70	160	21	9	10	85	.327	411	101	*15	.972
1930	Brooklyn	Nat.	C	128	421	60	130	20	4	6	57	.309	465	66	9	.983
1931	Brooklyn	Nat.	C	111	360	38	97	13	4	0	40	.269	390	69	11	.977
1932	Brooklyn	Nat.	C	126	404	44	111	18	6	1	43	.275	456	*82	13	.976
1933	Brooklyn	Nat.	C	126	372	39	112	11	4	3	41	.301	449	*84	5	.991
1934	Brooklyn	Nat.	C-3-2B	140	439	58	120	23	2	7	54	.273	542	62	11	.982
1935	Brooklyn (a)	Nat.	C	128	379	50	95	12	4	3	39	.251	472	65	11	.980
1936	Boston	Nat.	C	128	426	46	103	12	4	8	50	.242	447	*107	14	.975
1937	Boston	Nat.	C	105	334	31	68	11	1	3	38	.205	342	83	7	.984
1938	Boston	Nat.	C	71	236	19	63	6	1	1	14	.267	240	42	3	.989
1939	Boston	Nat.	C	131	412	32	104	22	1	8	49	.252	424	72	7	.986
1940	Bos. (b)-Pitts.	Nat.	C	95	293	35	80	9	3	3	41	.273	343	62	4	*.990
1941	Pittsburgh	Nat.	C	114	317	33	84	9	1	5	43	.265	345	54	8	.980
1942	Pittsburgh	Nat.	C	103	289	17	74	8	2	1	26	.256	327	53	2	.995

Year	Club	League	Pos.	G.	AB.	R.	H.	2B.	3B.	HR.	RBI.	B.A.	PO.	A.	E.	F.A.
1943—Pittsburgh		Nat.	•C-3B	118	372	40	98	9	4	1	39	.263	378	67	5	•.989
1944—Pittsburgh		Nat.	C	115	331	27	76	12	1	1	34	.230	372	52	7	*.984
1945—Pittsburgh		Nat.	C	91	243	22	53	8	0	0	18	.218	326	38	3	.992
1946—Pittsburgh (c)		Nat.	C	56	150	13	46	2	0	1	12	.307	173	30	3	.985
1947—Cleveland		Amer.	C	61	126	9	33	1	0	0	14	.262	144	28	0	1.000
1948—Indianapolis		A. A.	C	43	127	13	34	4	1	2	21	.268	184	23	8	.963
American League Totals				61	126	9	33	1	0	0	14	.262	144	28	0	1.000
National League Totals				1889	5790	604	1514	205	42	52	638	.261	6500	1088	123	.984
Major League Totals				1950	5916	613	1547	206	42	52	652	.261	6644	1116	123	.984

aTraded with pitcher Ray Benge, second baseman Tony Cuccinello and infielder Bobby Reisto to the Boston Braves for pitcher Ed Brandt and outfielder Randy Moore, December 12, 1935.
bTraded to Pittsburgh Pirates for catcher Ray Berres and cash, June 14, 1940.
cTraded to Cleveland Indians for outfielder Gene Woodling, December 7, 1946.

ADOLFO (DOLF) LUQUE

Born August 4, 1890, at Havana, Cuba.
Died July 3, 1957, at Havana, Cuba.
Height, 5.10. Weight, 172.
Threw and batted righthanded.

Coach, New York Giants, 1935-36-37; 1941 through 1945; manager, Havana, Cuba, Florida International League, 1951; manager, Mexicali, Mexican League, 1952; Neuvo Laredo, 1955; Merida, 1956.

Year	Club	League	G.	IP.	W.	L.	Pct.	H.	R.	ER.	SO.	BB.	ERA.
1913—Long Branch		N.Y.-N.J.	28	189	22	5	.815	134	....	....	128	85	......
1914—Boston		National	2	9	0	1	.000	5	5	4	1	4	4.00
1914—Jersey City		International	14	108	2	10	.167	129	69	....	41	65	......
1915—Boston		National	2	5	0	0	.000	6	3	2	3	4	3.60
1915—Toronto		International	31	225	15	9	.625	190	89	....	133	100	......
1916—Louisville		A. A.	38	167	13	8	.619	147	....	49	100	68	2.64
1917—Louisville		A. A.	19	79	2	4	.333	71	37	21	49	38	2.39
1918—Louisville		A. A.	18	117	11	2	.846	97	35	26	64	39	2.00
1918—Cincinnati		National	12	83	6	3	.667	84	44	35	26	32	3.80
1919—Cincinnati		National	30	106	10	3	.769	89	35	31	40	36	2.63
1920—Cincinnati		National	37	208	13	9	.591	168	65	58	72	60	2.51
1921—Cincinnati		National	41	304	17	19	.472	318	132	114	102	64	3.38
1922—Cincinnati		National	39	261	13	*23	.361	266	123	96	79	72	3.31
1923—Cincinnati		National	41	322	*27	8	*.771	279	90	69	151	88	*1.93
1924—Cincinnati		National	31	219	10	15	.400	229	99	77	83	53	3.16
1925—Cincinnati		National	36	291	16	18	.471	263	109	85	140	78	*2.63
1926—Cincinnati		National	34	234	13	16	.448	231	123	89	83	77	3.42
1927—Cincinnati		National	29	231	13	12	.520	225	103	82	76	56	3.19
1928—Cincinnati		National	33	234	11	10	.524	254	112	93	72	84	3.58
1929—Cincinnati(a)		National	32	176	5	16	.238	213	103	88	43	56	4.50
1930—Brooklyn		National	31	199	14	8	.636	221	107	95	62	58	4.30
1931—Brooklyn(b)		National	19	103	7	6	.538	122	59	52	25	27	4.54
1932—New York		National	38	110	6	7	.462	128	53	49	32	32	4.01
1933—New York		National	35	80	8	2	.800	75	27	24	23	19	2.70*
1934—New York		National	26	42	4	3	.571	54	20	18	12	17	3.86
1935—New York		National	2	4	1	0	1.000	1	0	0	2	1	0.00
Major League Totals			550	3221	194	179	.520	3231	1412	1161	1130	918	3.24

aTraded to Brooklyn Dodgers for pitcher Douglas McSweeney, February 10, 1930.
bReleased unconditionally, January, 1932, and signed with New York Giants.

WORLD SERIES RECORD

Year	Club	League	G.	IP.	W.	L.	Pct.	H.	R.	ER.	SO.	BB.	ERA.
1919—Cincinnati		National	2	5	0	0	.000	1	0	0	6	0	0.00
1933—New York		National	1	4⅓	1	0	1.000	2	0	0	5	2	0.00
World Series Totals			3	9⅓	1	0	1.000	3	0	0	11	2	0.00

DID YOU KNOW—
That Dolf Luque, taking riding from Giants' bench, once placed glove and ball on the mound, went straight to the bench and slugged Casey Stengel in the mouth?

DENNIS PATRICK ALOYSIUS LYONS

Born March 12, 1866, at Cincinnati, O.
Died January 2, 1929, at W. Covington, Ky.
Height, 5.10. Weight, 185.
Threw and batted righthanded.

Had five doubles in a doubleheader, September 3, 1887, vs. Cincinnati.

Year	Club	League	Pos.	G.	AB.	R.	H.	2B.	3B.	HR.	SB.	B.A.	PO.	A.	E.	F.A.
1885	Columbus	South.	3B	93	344	47	79	10	8	5	....	.230	142	169	45	.874
1885	Providence	Nat.	3B	4	16	3	2	1	0	0	....	.125	6	9	3	.833
1886	Atlanta	South.	3B	76	308	65	95	12	12	9	29	.316	95	156	24	.912
1886	Philadelphia	A.A.	3B	32	124	22	28	5	1	0	9	.226	(99-PO-A)		16	.861
1887	Philadelphia	A.A.	3B	137	605	128	*284	43	16	6	118	.469	(464-PO-A)		53	.897
1888	Philadelphia	A.A.	3B	111	446	98	145	21	5	6	45	.325	(353-PO-A)		44	.889
1889	Philadelphia	A.A.	3B	131	507	131	171	34	4	10	11	.327	202	289	81	.858
1890	Philadelphia	A.A.	3B	88	327	79	116	29	5	7	22	.351	134	202	34	.903
1891	St. Louis	A.A.	3B	111	416	112	131	24	3	11	9	.314	140	232	59	.863
1892	New York	Nat.	3B	108	391	71	102	15	9	8	18	.260	142	195	61	.847
1893	Pittsburgh	Nat.	3B	131	462	103	147	19	15	3	24	.318	206	287	41	.923
1894	Pittsburgh	Nat.	3B	72	254	51	79	11	5	4	17	.311	120	158	30	.902
1895	St. Louis	Nat.	3B	33	131	23	38	5	0	2	4	.290	61	53	16	.877
1896	Pittsburgh	Nat.	3B	116	438	77	134	23	6	4	13	.306	167	200	46	.889
1897	Pittsburgh	Nat.	1B	36	131	22	27	7	4	2	5	.206	326	17	5	.987
1898	St. Louis	West.	1B-3B	62	223	35	65	(T.B.-81)			4	.290	....	....	....	.969
1899	Wheeling	Int.-St.	1B-3B	113	427	73	133	30	4	6	12	.311	401	246	46	.934
1900	Wheeling	Int.-St.	3B	135	520	73	126	27	3	4	4	.242	260	351	41	.937
1901-2								(No record)								
1903	Beaumont	So. Tex.	1B	85	321	50	88	...	...	...	8	.274	879	23	17	*.982
American Association Totals				610	2425	570	875	156	34	40	214	.361	....	....	....	....
National League Totals				500	1823	350	529	81	39	23	81	.290	....	....	....	....
Major League Totals				1110	4248	920	1404	237	73	63	295	.331	....	....	....	....

THEODORE AMAR (TED) LYONS

Born December 28, 1900, at Lake Charles, Ia.
Height 5.11. Weight, 200.
Threw right and batted right and lefthanded.

Pitched 6-0 no-hit game against Boston A. L., August 21, 1926. Hurled 42 consecutive innings without issuing base on balls, starting last four innings June 11 until first inning, June 23, 1939. Pitched no-hit ball for 8⅔ innings against Washington, September 19, 1925, second game. Won game, 17-0. Only player to reach first, Robert H. Veach, singled in ninth inning.
  Tied major league record with two two-base hits in inning, July 28, 1935.
  Named by Baseball Writers' Association of America for THE SPORTING NEWS All-Star Major League Team, 1927.
  Replaced Jimmie Dykes as manager of White Sox, May 25, 1946, continuing through 1948; coach, Detroit Tigers, 1949 through 1953; Brooklyn Dodgers, 1954; scout, Chicago White Sox, 1955 through 1966.
  Named to Hall of Fame, 1955.

Year	Club	League	G.	IP.	W.	L.	Pct.	H.	R.	ER.	SO.	BB.	ERA.
1923	Chicago	Amer.	9	23	2	1	.667	30	21	16	6	15	6.26
1924	Chicago	Amer.	41	216	12	11	.522	279	143	117	52	72	4.88
1925	Chicago	Amer.	43	263	•21	11	.656	274	111	95	45	83	3.25
1926	Chicago	Amer.	39	284	18	16	.529	268	108	95	51	106	3.01
1927	Chicago	Amer.	39	•308	•22	14	.611	•291	125	97	71	67	2.83
1928	Chicago	Amer.	39	240	15	14	.517	276	133	106	60	68	3.98
1929	Chicago	Amer.	37	259	14	20	.412	276	136	118	57	76	4.10
1930	Chicago	Amer.	42	*298	22	15	.595	*331	160	125	69	57	3.78
1931	Chicago	Amer.	22	101	4	6	.400	117	50	45	16	33	4.01
1932	Chicago	Amer.	33	231	10	15	.400	243	104	84	58	71	3.27
1933	Chicago	Amer.	36	228	10	*21	.323	260	142	111	74	74	4.38

Year	Club	League	G.	IP.	W.	L.	Pct.	H.	R.	ER.	SO.	BB.	ERA.
1934–Chicago		Amer.	30	205	11	13	.458	249	138	111	53	66	4.87
1935–Chicago		Amer.	23	191	15	8	.652	194	79	64	54	56	3.02
1936–Chicago		Amer.	26	182	10	13	.435	227	115	104	48	45	5.14
1937–Chicago		Amer.	22	169	12	7	.632	182	86	78	45	45	4.15
1938–Chicago		Amer.	23	195	9	11	.450	238	93	80	54	52	3.69
1939–Chicago		Amer.	21	173	14	6	.700	162	71	53	65	26	2.76
1940–Chicago		Amer.	22	186	12	8	.600	188	85	67	72	37	3.24
1941–Chicago		Amer.	22	187	12	10	.545	199	87	77	63	37	3.71
1942–Chicago		Amer.	20	180	14	6	.700	167	52	42	50	26	*2.10
1943-44-45–Chicago		Amer.					(In Military Service)						
1946–Chicago		Amer.	5	43	1	4	.200	38	17	11	10	9	2.30
Major League Totals			594	4162	260	230	.531	4489	2056	1696	1073	1121	3.67

LELAND STANFORD (LARRY) MAC PHAIL

Born February 3, 1890, at Cass City, Mich.
Died October 1, 1975, at Miami, Fla.

Leland Stanford (Larry) MacPhail was born during a Michigan storm and the clouds never moved from above his head. He exercised his vocal chords for the first time, at their top decible rating, of course, at Cass City, Mich., February 3, 1890. The world, in a general sense, and baseball, in a specific sense, never again were the same.

MacPhail used his computer brain to relieve ball club-holding banks of bad debts; to fill his own coffers in grandiose style; to overturn the living habits of fans and players all over the country with the introduction of night baseball; to confound scoffers and doom peddlers by introducing radio broadcasts of his club's games, home and road, and turning them into money-makers attendancewise; to make up his own rule book as he refereed college football games; to participate in a wild scheme to kidnap the Kaiser in Holland after World War I (he purloined the Kaiser's prized ashtray, at least); to build three championship clubs and leave all three in a state of combustion; to leave his first law firm because they would not make him a partner after six months (at age 21), and then to retire to his Maryland estate where he should have tasted the winey bucolic life, only to cause explosions in the varied worlds of race tracks, horse breeding, baseball (he never quit here), cancer and heart trouble, golf course architecture, computers (his mind was quicker), telephone companies (he was arrested for one of his protests), ways to cure hay, horse racing stables and growing apples.

He's best known in a baseball sense for building the Reds into a money-making club and a later champion; the Dodgers into a respectable winner and consistently solvent franchise, and the Yankees into the greatest money machine since the U.S. Treasury. For innovations, he introduced lights to major league parks and all but the Cubs followed suit, and he used radio broadcasts, against the advice of fellow owners and G.M.s, to increase the club income and also to lure more fans into the park. He could possibly hold the major league record for firing both personnel and punches, for most tears shed in both joy and anger, for setting the pace for spending baseball money to make more money for baseball, for most Page One stories in THE SPORTING NEWS on the most subjects, and for flambuoyancy, whole and entire.

Larry was a moving force, using every trick at his disposal to get jobs done. He could cajole one minute and castigate the next, but his results were constant—success in every case, whether it was a purchase, a trade or an idea. He had a vision of what results would follow his major improvements—lights, radio and better press accommodations. He was a financial master who could outfigure anyone or anything with the computer in his head. Compound totals and percentages were duck soup for this man who had stood at the head of every class he had attended, from grade school through college. He scarred many hides, fired many people and was unreasonable in many situations, but the man meant more money for the game, more success on the field—and that's the name of the pro baseball game.

MacPhail was named to the Hall of Fame in 1978.

SHERWOOD ROBERT MAGEE

Born August 6, 1885, at Clarendon, Pa.
Died March 13, 1929, at Philadelphia, Pa.
Height, 5.10. Weight, 175.
Threw and batted righthanded.

Led National League in runs batted in, 1910 and 1914.
Umpire, National League, 1928.

Year–Club	League	Pos.	G.	AB.	R.	H.	2B.	3B.	HR.	SB.	B.A.	PO.	A.	E.	F.A.
1904–Philadelphia	Nat.	OF	95	364	51	101	15	12	3	11	.277	156	19	15	.921
1905–Philadelphia	Nat.	OF	●155	603	100	180	24	17	5	48	.299	341	19	14	.963
1906–Philadelphia	Nat.	OF	154	563	77	159	36	8	6	55	.282	316	18	6	.982
1907–Philadelphia	Nat.	OF	139	503	75	165	28	12	4	46	.328	297	13	7	.978
1908–Philadelphia	Nat.	OF	142	508	79	144	30	16	2	40	.283	279	15	9	.970
1909–Philadelphia	Nat.	OF	143	522	60	141	33	14	2	38	.270	283	11	9	.970
1910–Philadelphia	Nat.	OF	154	519	★110	172	39	17	6	49	★.331	285	9	8	.974
1911–Philadelphia	Nat.	OF	120	445	79	128	32	5	15	22	.288	248	14	5	★.981
1912–Philadelphia	Nat.	OF	132	464	79	142	25	9	6	30	.306	251	8	10	.963
1913–Philadelphia	Nat.	OF	138	470	92	144	36	6	11	23	.306	236	7	8	.968
1914–Philadelphia(a)	Nat.	OF-SS	146	544	96	★171	★39	11	15	25	.314	528	154	34	.953
1915–Boston	Nat.	OF	156	571	72	160	34	12	2	15	.280	524	26	7	.987
1916–Boston	Nat.	OF	122	419	44	101	17	5	3	10	.241	220	6	5	.978
1917–Boston-Cin.(b)	Nat.	OF	117	383	41	107	16	8	1	11	.279	220	14	8	.967
1918–Cincinnati	Nat.	OF-SS-1B	115	400	46	119	15	13	2	14	.297	685	41	14	.981
1919–Cincinnati	Nat.	OF	56	163	11	35	6	1	0	4	.215	98	1	1	.990
1920–Columbus	A. A.	OF	113	392	58	120	28	4	4	13	.306	408	23	11	.975
1921–Minneapolis	A. A.	OF	137	444	90	150	39	6	13	8	.338	379	28	8	.981
1922–Minneapolis	A. A.	OF	106	257	66	92	21	4	12	7	.358	100	10	7	.940
1923–St. Joseph	West.	OF	112	392	66	130	30	5	6	3	.332	412	30	8	.982
1923–Milwaukee	A. A.	OF	48	190	30	63	8	3	7	1	.332	86	8	1	.989
1924–Milwaukee	A. A.	OF	83	196	38	62	6	4	6	1	.316	48	3	4	.927
1925–Milwaukee	A. A.	OF	22	28	7	13	2	1	0	0	.464	5	0	0	1.000
1925–Baltimore	Int.	OF	21	68	13	14	5	1	1	1	.206	57	2	3	.952
1926–Baltimore	Int.	OF	22	59	12	17	4	3	4	1	.288	32	0	3	.914
Major League Totals			2084	7441	1112	2169	425	166	83	441	.291	4967	375	160	.953

aTraded to Boston Braves for infielder-outfielder Oscar Dugey and infielder-outfielder George Whitted, February, 1915.

bSold to Cincinnati Reds on waivers, August 1, 1917.

WORLD SERIES RECORD

Year–Club	League	Pos.	G.	AB.	R.	H.	2B.	3B.	HR.	RBI.	B.A.	PO.	A.	E.	F.A.
1919–Cincinnati	Nat.	PH	2	2	0	1	0	0	0	0	.500	0	0	0	.000

MICKEY CHARLES MANTLE

Born October 20, 1931, at Spavinaw, Okla.

Height, 6.00. Weight, 201.

Threw right and batted left and righthanded.

Married Merlyn Louise Johnson, December 23, 1951.

Hit two home runs in one game, one righthanded and one lefthanded, total of ten times.
 Tied following major league record: Most consecutive home runs in times at bat (4), July 4, final two appearances and July 6, first two appearances, 1962.
 Led American League in walks with 113 in 1955, 146 in 1957, 129 in 1958, 126 in 1961 and 122 in 1962.
 Hit three home runs in a game, May 13, 1955.
 Hit home run with bases full in World Series game, third inning October 4, 1953.
 Holds following World Series lifetime records: Most home runs (18), most runs scored (42), most runs batted in (40), most total bases (123), most long hits (26), most extra bases on long hits (64), most bases on balls (43), most strikeouts (54), most Series played by outfielder (12), and most games played by an outfielder (63).
 Tied following World Series records: Most runs batted in, inning 4, October 4, 1953; most hits, game, 4, October 8, 1960 and most runs seven-game Series, 8, 1960 and 1964.
 Won American League Triple Crown, 1956.
 Named Most Valuable Player, American League, 1956-57-62.
 Named Outstanding American League Player by THE SPORTING NEWS, 1956-62.
 Named Major League Player of the Year by THE SPORTING NEWS, 1956.
 Named as outfielder on THE SPORTING NEWS All-Star Major League Teams, 1952-56-57.
 Named as outfielder on THE SPORTING NEWS American League All-Star Team, 1961-62-64.
 Named as outfielder on THE SPORTING NEWS American League All-Star fielding team, 1962.
 Coach, New York, A. L., 1970 (part).
 Named to Hall of Fame, 1974

Year–Club	League	Pos.	G.	AB.	R.	H.	2B.	3B.	HR.	RBI.	B.A.	PO.	A.	E.	F.A.
1949–Independence	K-O-M	SS	89	323	54	101	15	7	7	63	.313	121	245	47	.886
1950–Joplin	W. A.	SS	137	519	★141	★199	30	12	26	136	★.383	202	340	55	.908
1951–New York	Amer.	OF	96	341	61	91	11	5	13	65	.267	135	4	6	.959
1951–Kansas City	A. A.	OF	40	166	32	60	9	3	11	50	.361	110	4	4	.966
1952–New York	Amer.	★OF-3B	142	549	94	171	37	7	23	87	.311	348	16	★14	.963
1953–New York	Amer.	OF-SS	127	461	105	136	24	3	21	92	.295	322	10	6	.982
1954–New York	Amer.	★OF-IF	146	543	★129	163	17	12	27	102	.300	334	★25	9	.976

Year	Club	League	Pos.	G.	AB.	R.	H.	2B.	3B.	HR.	RBI.	B.A.	PO.	A.	E.	F.A.
1955–New York		Amer.	OF-SS	147	517	121	158	25	•11	*37	99	.306	376	11	2	.995
1956–New York		Amer.	OF	150	533	*132	188	22	5	*52	*130	*.353	370	10	4	.990
1957–New York		Amer.	OF	144	474	*121	173	28	6	34	94	.365	324	6	7	.979
1958–New York		Amer.	OF	150	519	*127	158	21	1	*42	97	.304	331	5	8	.977
1959–New York		Amer.	OF	144	541	104	154	23	4	31	75	.285	366	7	2	*.995
1960–New York		Amer.	OF	153	527	*119	145	17	6	*40	94	.275	326	9	3	.991
1961–New York		Amer.	OF	153	514	•132	163	16	6	54	128	.317	351	6	6	.983
1962–New York		Amer.	OF	123	377	96	121	15	1	30	89	.321	214	4	5	.978
1963–New York		Amer.	OF	65	172	40	54	8	0	15	35	.314	99	2	1	.990
1964–New York		Amer.	OF	143	465	92	141	25	2	35	111	.303	217	3	5	.978
1965–New York		Amer.	OF	122	361	44	92	12	1	19	46	.255	165	3	6	.966
1966–New York		Amer.	OF	108	333	40	96	12	1	23	56	.288	172	2	0	1.000
1967–New York		Amer.	1B	144	440	63	108	17	0	22	55	.245	1089	91	8	.993
1968–New York		Amer.	1B	144	435	57	103	14	1	18	54	.237	1195	76	15	.988
Major League Totals				2401	8102	1677	2415	344	72	536	1509	.298	6734	290	107	.985

WORLD SERIES RECORDS

Year	Club	League	Pos.	G.	AB.	R.	H.	2B.	3B.	HR.	RBI.	B.A.	PO.	A.	E.	F.A.
1951–New York†		Amer.	OF	2	5	1	1	0	0	0	0	.200	4	0	0	1.000
1952–New York		Amer.	OF	7	29	5	10	1	1	2	3	.345	16	0	0	1.000
1953–New York		Amer.	OF	6	24	3	5	0	0	2	7	.208	14	0	0	1.000
1955–New York		Amer.	OF-PH	3	10	1	2	0	0	1	1	.200	4	0	0	1.000
1956–New York		Amer.	OF	7	24	6	6	1	0	3	4	.250	18	1	0	1.000
1957–New York		Amer.	OF-PH	6	19	3	5	0	0	1	2	.263	8	0	1	.889
1958–New York		Amer.	OF	7	24	4	6	0	1	2	3	.250	16	0	0	1.000
1960–New York		Amer.	OF	7	25	8	10	1	0	3	11	.400	15	0	0	1.000
1961–New York		Amer.	OF	2	6	0	1	0	0	0	0	.167	2	0	0	1.000
1962–New York		Amer.	OF	7	25	2	3	1	0	0	0	.120	11	0	0	1.000
1963–New York		Amer.	OF	4	15	1	2	0	0	1	1	.133	6	0	0	1.000
1964–New York		Amer.	OF	7	24	8	8	2	0	3	8	.333	12	0	2	.857
World Series Totals				65	230	42	59	6	2	18	40	.257	126	1	3	.977

†Injured right knee in fifth inning of second game: did not play for rest of Series.

HENRY EMMETT (HEINIE) MANUSH

Born Jul 20, 1901, at Tuscumbia, Ala.
Died May 12, 1971, at Sarasota, Fla.
Height, 6.00. Weight, 200.
Threw and batted lefthanded.
Married Betty Lloyd, 1928.

Batted safely in 33 consecutive games, July 22 through August 25, 1933.
Manager, Rocky Mount, Piedmont League, 1940; manager, Greensboro, Piedmont League, 1941-42; manager, Roanoke, Piedmont League, 1943; manager, Scranton, Eastern League, 1944; manager, Martinsville, Carolina League, 1945; scout, Boston Braves, 1946; scout, Pittsburgh Pirates, 1947-1948; coach, Washington Senators, 1953-54; scout, Washington, 1961-62.
Named to Hall of Fame, 1964.

Year	Club	League	Pos.	G.	AB.	R.	H.	2B.	3B.	HR.	RBI.	B.A.	PO.	A.	E.	F.A.
1921–Edmonton		W. Can.	OF	83	327	52	105	17	9	*9	....	.321	141	12	7	.956
1922–Omaha		West.	OF	167	652	148	245	44	*20	20	....	.376	391	16	11	.974
1923–Detroit		Amer.	OF	109	308	59	103	20	5	4	54	.334	158	6	8	.953
1924–Detroit		Amer.	OF	120	422	83	122	24	8	9	68	.289	224	4	5	.979
1925–Detroit		Amer.	OF	99	278	46	84	14	3	5	47	.303	117	4	3	.976
1926–Detroit		Amer.	OF	136	498	95	188	35	8	14	86	*.378	283	7	10	.967
1927–Detroit(a)		Amer.	OF	151	593	102	177	31	18	6	90	.298	361	9	11	.971
1928–St. Louis		Amer.	OF	154	638	104	*241	•47	20	13	108	.378	355	6	3	.992
1929–St. Louis		Amer.	OF	142	574	85	204	•45	10	6	81	.355	293	11	4	.987
1930–St. L.(b)-Wash.		Amer.	OF	137	554	100	194	49	12	9	94	.350	255	10	3	.989
1931–Washington		Amer.	OF	146	616	110	189	41	11	6	70	.307	245	5	5	.977
1932–Washington		Amer.	OF	149	625	121	214	41	14	14	116	.342	318	6	4	.988
1933–Washington		Amer.	OF	153	658	115	*221	*17	5	5	95	.336	325	10	6	.982
1934–Washington		Amer.	OF	137	556	88	194	42	11	11	89	.349	293	5	6	.980
1935–Washington(c)		Amer.	OF	119	479	68	131	26	9	4	56	.273	251	8	4	.985
1936–Boston(d)		Amer.	OF	82	313	43	91	15	5	0	45	.291	110	3	4	.966
1937–Brooklyn		Nat.	OF	132	466	57	155	25	7	4	73	.333	187	7	6	.970
1938–Brook.(e)-Pitts		Nat.	OF	32	64	11	16	4	2	0	10	.250	29	1	0	1.000
1938–Toronto		Int.	OF	81	277	38	86	21	5	3	39	.310	121	7	4	.970
1939–Pittsburgh		Nat.	OF	10	12	0	0	0	0	1	.000	1	0	0	1.000
1939–Toronto		Int.	OF	66	228	32	55	9	3	0	19	.241	105	5	0	1.000
1940–Rocky Mount		Pied.	OF	32	107	13	30	9	2	1	16	.280	150	15	3	.982
1941–Greensboro		Pied.	OF	12	32	7	10	2	0	0	7	.313	....	....	....	....

Year	Club	League	Pos.	G.	AB.	R.	H.	2B.	3B.	HR.	RBI.	B.A.	PO.	A.	E.	F.A.
1942—Greensboro		Pied.					(Less than ten games)									
1943—Roanoke		Pied.	PH	10	8	0	0	0	0	0	1	.000	0	0	0	.000
1944—Scranton		East.					(Less than ten games)									
1945—Martinsville		Car.					(Less than ten games)									
American League Totals				1834	7112	1219	2353	462	151	106	1099	.331	3588	94	77	.980
National League Totals				174	542	68	171	29	9	4	84	.315	217	8	6	.974
Major League Totals				2008	7654	1287	2524	491	160	110	1183	.330	3805	102	83	.979

aTraded to St. Louis Browns with first baseman Luzerne Blue for pitcher Elam VanGilder, infielder Chick Galloway and outfielder Harry Rice, December 2, 1927.
bTraded to Washington Senators with pitcher Alvin Crowder for oufielder Leon (Goose) Goslin, June 13, 1930.
cTraded to Boston Red Sox for outfielder Roy Johnson and Carl Reynolds, December 17, 1935.
dUnconditionally released by Boston Red Sox, September 28, 1936 and signed with Brooklyn Dodgers, December 9, 1936.
eReleased to Pittsburgh Pirates on waivers, May, 1938.

WORLD SERIES RECORD

Year	Club	League	Pos.	G.	AB.	R.	H.	2B.	3B.	HR.	RBI.	B.A.	PO.	A.	E.	F.A.
1933—Washington		Amer.	OF	5	18	2	2	0	0	0	0	.111	10	0	0	1.000

JAMES WALTER VINCENT (RABBIT) MARANVILLE

Born November 11, 1891, at Springfield, Mass.
Died January 5, 1954, at New York, N. Y.
Height, 5.05. Weight, 155.
Threw and batted righthanded.

Set National League record for most putouts, one season since 1900, 407, in 1914.
Led N. L. shortstops in double plays, 1923, and N. L. second basemen in double plays, 1924.
Manager, Chicago Cubs, July 7, 1925, to September 3, 1925; Boston Braves, July, 1929, to end of season; Elmira, NYP League, 1936; Montreal, International League, 1937-38; Albany, Eastern League, 1939; Springfield, Eastern League, 1941.
Named to Hall of Fame, 1954.

Year	Club	League	Pos.	G.	AB.	R.	H.	2B.	3B.	HR.	RBI.	B.A.	PO.	A.	E.	F.A.
1911—New Bedford		N. Eng.	SS	117	422	41	96	17	9	2	....	.227	256	*345	61	.908
1912—New Bedford		N. Eng.	SS	122	452	65	128	22	4	4	....	.283	268	*441	42	*.944
1912—Boston		Nat.	SS	26	86	8	18	2	0	0	7	.209	46	97	11	.929
1913—Boston		Nat.	SS	143	571	68	141	13	8	2	44	.247	317	475	43	.949
1914—Boston		Nat.	SS	•156	586	74	144	23	6	4	72	.246	*407	*574	*65	.938
1915—Boston		Nat.	SS	149	509	51	124	23	6	2	47	.244	•391	486	55	.941
1916—Boston		Nat.	SS	155	604	79	142	16	13	4	36	.235	*386	*515	50	*.947
1917—Boston		Nat.	SS	142	561	69	146	19	13	3	41	.260	*341	474	46	.947
1918—Boston(a)		Nat.	SS	11	38	3	12	0	1	0	3	.316	34	34	5	.932
1919—Boston		Nat.	SS	131	480	44	128	18	10	5	43	.267	*361	488	*53	.941
1920—Boston(b)		Nat.	SS	134	493	48	131	19	15	1	43	.266	354	462	45	.948
1921—Pittsburgh		Nat.	SS	153	612	90	180	25	12	1	70	.294	325	529	34	.962
1922—Pittsburgh		Nat.	SS-2B	155	*672	115	198	26	15	0	63	.295	419	512	36	.963
1923—Pittsburgh		Nat.	SS	141	581	78	161	19	9	1	41	.277	*332	*505	30	*.965
1924—Pittsburgh(c)		Nat.	2B	152	594	62	158	33	20	2	71	.266	365	*568	26	*.973
1925—Chicago(d)		Nat.	SS-2B	75	266	37	62	10	3	0	23	.233	162	261	20	.955
1926—Brooklyn		Nat.	SS-2B	78	234	32	55	8	5	0	24	.235	161	246	19	.955
1927—Rochester		Int.	SS	135	507	81	151	25	10	1	63	.298	329	440	24	.970
1927—St. Louis		Nat.	SS	9	29	0	7	1	0	0	1	.241	17	34	2	.962
1928—St. Louis(e)		Nat.	SS	112	366	40	88	14	10	1	34	.240	236	362	19	.969
1929—Boston		Nat.	SS	146	560	87	159	26	10	0	55	.284	319	536	35	.961
1930—Boston		Nat.	SS	142	558	85	157	26	8	2	43	.281	343	445	29	*.965
1931—Boston		Nat.	SS-2B	145	562	69	146	22	5	0	33	.260	289	453	41	.948
1932—Boston		Nat.	2B	149	571	67	134	20	4	0	37	.235	*402	473	22	*.975
1933—Boston		Nat.	2B	143	478	46	104	15	4	0	38	.218	362	384	22	.971
1934—Boston		Nat.		(Broke leg in spring exhibition game and did not play)												
1935—Boston		Nat.	2B	23	67	3	10	2	0	0	5	.149	32	46	3	.963
1936—Elmira		NYP	2B-SS	123	427	65	138	15	2	0	54	.323	322	319	28	.958
1939—Albany		East.	2B	6	17	3	2	0	0	2	.118	10	8	8	.692	
Major League Totals				2670	10078	1255	2605	380	177	28	874	.258	6401	8959	711	.956

aIn Military Service part of season.
bTraded to Pittsburgh Pirates for outfielders Billy Southworth and Fred Nicholson, infielder Walter Barbare, and $15,000, February, 1921.
cTraded to Chicago Cubs with pitcher Wilbur Cooper and first baseman Charlie Grimm for pitcher Vic Aldridge, first baseman Al Niehaus and second baseman George Grantham, October 27, 1924.
dReleased to Brooklyn Dodgers on waivers, November, 1925.
eSold to Boston Braves with outfielder George Harper, December 8, 1928.

WORLD SERIES RECORD

Year	Club	League	Pos.	G.	AB.	R.	H.	2B.	3B.	HR.	RBI.	B.A.	PO.	A.	E.	F.A.
1914–Boston		Nat.	SS	4	13	1	4	0	0	0	3	.308	7	13	1	.952
1928–St. Louis		Nat.	SS	4	13	2	4	1	0	0	0	.308	11	3	1	.933
World Series Totals				8	26	3	8	1	0	0	3	.308	18	16	2	.944

JUAN ANTONIO MARICHAL (SANCHEZ)

Born October 20, 1938, at Laguna Verde, Montecristi, Dominican Republic.
Height, 5.11. Weight, 190.
Threw and batted righthanded.

Established National League record for most season opening games won (6), 1962-64-66-71-72-73.
Pitched 1-0 no-hit victory against Houston Colt .45s, June 15, 1963.
Named pitcher on THE SPORTING NEWS National League All-Star Teams, 1963-65-66-68.

Year	Club	League	G.	IP.	W.	L.	Pct.	H.	R.	ER.	SO.	BB.	ERA.
1958–Michigan City		Midwest	35	*245	*21	8	.724	*200	69	51	246	50	*1.87
1959–Springfield		Eastern	37	*271	*18	13	.581	238	85	72	*208	47	*2.39
1960–Tacoma		P. C.	18	139	11	5	.688	116	52	48	121	34	3.11
1960–San Francisco		National	11	81	6	2	.750	59	29	24	58	28	2.67
1961–San Francisco		National	29	185	13	10	.565	183	88	80	124	48	3.89
1962–San Francisco		National	37	263	18	11	.621	233	112	98	153	90	3.35
1963–San Francisco		National	41	*321	•25	8	.758	259	102	86	248	61	2.41
1964–San Francisco		National	33	269	21	8	.724	241	89	74	206	52	2.48
1965–San Francisco		National	39	295	22	13	.629	224	78	70	240	46	2.14
1966–San Francisco		National	37	307	25	6	.806	228	88	76	222	36	2.23
1967–San Francisco		National	26	202	14	10	.583	195	79	62	166	42	2.76
1968–San Francisco		National	38	*326	*26	9	.743	*295	106	88	218	46	2.43
1969–San Francisco		National	37	300	21	11	.656	244	90	70	205	54	*2.10
1970–San Francisco		National	34	243	12	10	.545	269	128	111	123	48	4.11
1971–San Francisco		National	37	279	13	11	.621	244	113	91	159	56	2.94
1972–San Francisco		National	25	165	6	16	.273	176	82	68	72	46	3.71
1973–San Francisco (a)		National	34	207	11	15	.423	231	104	88	87	37	3.83
1974–Boston		American	11	57	5	1	.833	61	32	31	21	14	4.89
1975–Los Angeles (b)		National	2	6	0	1	.000	11	9	9	1	5	13.50
National League Totals			460	3449	238	141	.628	3092	1297	1095	2282	695	2.86
American League Totals			11	57	5	1	.833	61	32	31	21	14	4.89
Major League Totals			471	3506	243	142	.631	3153	1329	1126	2303	709	2.89

aSold to Boston Red Sox for an estimated $100,000, December 7, 1973.
bSigned as a free agent by Los Angeles Dodgers, March 11, 1975.

WORLD SERIES RECORD

Year	Club	League	G.	IP.	W.	L.	Pct.	H.	R.	ER.	SO.	BB.	ERA.
1962–San Francisco		National	1	4	0	0	.000	2	0	0	4	2	0.00

ROGER EUGENE MARIS

Born September 10, 1934, at Hibbing, Minn.
Height, 6.00. Weight, 205.
Threw righthanded and batted lefthanded.

Established major league record for most home runs, season (61) (162-game season), 1961.
Established American League mark for most intentional bases on ball in game (4), 12-inning game, May 22, 1962.
Hit seven home runs in six consecutive games, August 11-12-13-13-15-16, 1961; tied A. L. standard for most home runs, doubleheader (4), July 25, 1961–hitting two in each game.
Hit home run in first time at bat in World Series, October 5, 1960.
Named Most Valuable Player in American League, 1960-61.
Named by THE SPORTING NEWS as No. 1 American League Player, 1961.

Named Player of the Year by THE SPORTING NEWS, 1961.
Named as outfielder on THE SPORTING NEWS All-Star Major League Team, 1960.
Named as outfielder on THE SPORTING NEWS American League All-Star Team, 1961.
Received Rawlings Gold Glove award as outstanding fielding right fielder in American League, 1960.

Year Club League	Pos.	G.	AB.	R.	H.	2B.	3B.	HR.	RBI.	B.A.	PO.	A.	E.	F.A.
1953–Fargo-M'rhead..North.	OF	114	418	74	136	18	13	9	80	.325	166	18	7	.963
1954–Keokuk..............I. I. I.	OF	134	502	105	158	26	6	32	111	.315	•305	20	18	.948
1955–Tulsa................Tex.	OF	25	90	9	21	1	0	1	9	.233	43	0	5	.896
1955–Reading............East.	OF	113	374	74	108	15	3	19	78	.289	262	9	6	.978
1956–Indianapolis......A. A.	OF	131	433	77	127	20	8	17	75	.293	200	15	8	.964
1957–Cleveland..........Amer.	OF	116	358	61	84	9	5	14	51	.235	266	10	7	.975
1958–Cleve.(a)-K.C....Amer.	OF	150	583	87	140	19	4	28	80	.240	303	15	*9	.972
1959–Kansas City(b)..Amer.	OF	122	433	69	118	21	7	16	72	.273	231	7	6	.975
1960–New York ....Amer.	OF	136	499	98	141	18	7	39	*112	.283	263	6	4	.985
1961–New York ....Amer.	OF	161	590	•132	159	16	4	*61	*142	.269	266	9	9	.968
1962–New York ....Amer.	OF	157	590	92	151	34	1	33	100	.256	316	4	3	.991
1963–New York ....Amer.	OF	90	312	53	84	14	1	23	53	.269	162	6	2	.988
1964–New York ....Amer.	OF	141	513	86	144	12	2	26	71	.281	250	6	1	.996
1965–New York ....Amer.	OF	46	155	22	37	7	0	8	27	.239	66	1	2	.971
1966–New York(c).....Amer.	OF	119	348	37	81	9	2	13	43	.233	133	3	1	.993
1967–St. Louis ....Nat.	OF	125	410	64	107	18	7	9	55	.261	224	5	2	.991
1968–St. Louis ....Nat.	OF	100	310	25	79	18	2	5	45	.255	169	4	3	.983
American League Totals		1238	4381	737	1139	159	33	261	751	.260	2256	67	44	.981
National League Totals		225	720	89	186	36	9	14	100	.258	393	9	5	.988
Major League Totals		1463	5101	826	1325	195	42	275	851	.260	2649	76	49	.982

aTraded to Kansas City Athletics with pitcher Dick Tomanek and infielder Preston Ward for infielder Vic Power and infielder-outfielder Woodie Held, June 15, 1958.

bTraded to New York Yankees with first baseman Kent Hadley and shortstop Joe DeMaestri for pitcher Don Larsen, first baseman Marv Throneberry and outfielders Hank Bauer and Norm Siebern, December 11, 1959.

cTraded to St. Louis Cardinals for third baseman Charlie Smith, December 8, 1966.

WORLD SERIES RECORD

Year Club League	Pos.	G.	AB.	R.	H.	2B.	3B.	HR.	RBI.	B.A.	PO.	A.	E.	F.A.
1960–New York ....Amer.	OF	7	30	6	8	1	0	2	2	.267	11	0	1	.917
1961–New York ....Amer.	OF	5	19	4	2	1	0	1	2	.105	11	1	0	1.000
1962–New York ....Amer.	OF	7	23	4	4	1	0	1	5	.174	11	1	0	1.000
1963–New York ....Amer.	OF	2	5	0	0	0	0	0	0	.000	3	0	0	1.000
1964–New York ....Amer.	OF	7	30	4	6	0	0	1	1	.200	19	0	0	1.000
1967–St. Louis ....Nat.	OF	7	26	3	10	1	0	1	7	.385	15	0	1	.937
1968–St. Louis ....Nat.	OF-PH	6	19	5	3	1	0	0	1	.158	8	0	0	1.000
World Series Totals...........................		41	152	26	33	5	0	6	18	.217	78	2	2	.976

RICHARD W. (RUBE) MARQUARD

Born October 9, 1889, at Cleveland, O.

Died June 1, 1980, at Baltimore, Md.

Height, 6.03. Weight, 180.

Threw left and batted both ways.

Most consecutive games won, season (major league record)—19, April 11 through July 3, 1912; first game, start of season, pitched 2-0 no-hit game, New York vs. Brooklyn (N. L.) April 15, 1915.

Manager, Providence, Eastern League, 1926; Jacksonville, Southeastern League, 1929-30; assistant coach, Assumption College, 1931; umpire, Eastern League, 1931; coach-scout, Atlanta, Southern Association, 1932.

Named to Hall of Fame, 1971.

Year Club	League	G.	IP.	W.	L.	Pct.	H.	R.	ER.	SO.	BB.	ERA.
1907–Canton.............................Central		40	....	*23	13	.639	....	....	....	....	....	......
1908–Indianapolis(a) ....Amer. Assn.		*47	*367	*28	19	.596	234	....	....	*250	135	......
1908–New York ....National		1	5	0	1	.000	6	5	....	2	2	......
1909–New York ....National		29	173	5	13	.278	155	81	....	109	72	......
1910–New York ....National		13	69	4	4	.500	65	35	....	52	40	......
1911–New York ....National		45	278	24	7	*.774	221	98	....	*237	106	......
1912–New York ....National		43	295	•26	11	.703	286	112	84	175	80	2.56
1913–New York ....National		42	288	23	10	.697	248	100	80	151	49	2.50
1914–New York ....National		39	268	12	22	.353	261	117	91	92	47	3.06
1915–N.Y.(b)-Brooklyn ....National		33	194	11	10	.524	207	102	87	92	38	4.04
1916–Brooklyn..........................National		36	205	13	6	.684	169	54	36	107	38	1.58
1917–Brooklyn..........................National		37	233	19	12	.613	200	84	66	117	60	2.55
1918–Brooklyn..........................National		34	239	9	•18	.333	231	97	70	89	59	2.64
1919–Brooklyn..........................National		8	59	3	3	.500	54	17	15	29	10	2.29
1920–Brooklyn(c) ....National		28	190	10	7	.588	181	83	68	89	35	3.22

Year	Club	League	G.	IP.	W.	L.	Pct.	H.	R.	ER.	SO.	BB.	ERA.
1921	Cincinnati(d)	National	39	266	17	14	.548	291	123	100	88	50	3.38
1922	Boston	National	39	198	11	15	.423	255	131	112	57	66	5.09
1923	Boston	National	38	239	11	14	.440	265	127	99	78	65	3.73
1924	Boston	National	6	36	1	2	.333	33	17	12	10	13	3.00
1925	Boston	National	26	72	2	8	.200	105	60	46	19	27	5.75
1926	Providence	Eastern	7	44	3	1	.750	49	19	18	22	17	3.68
1927	Baltimore	Intenational	6	30	1	2	.333	38	....	....	5	6	......
1927	Birmingham	Southern	3	11	0	1	.000	10	....	....	1	5	......
1928	—		(Out of Organized Ball)										
1929	Jacksonville	Southeastern	3	3	0	0	.000	2	....	....	4	2	......
1930	Jacksonville	Southeastern	15	114	5	4	.556	106	36	27	47	21	2.13
1931	—		(Umpire, Eastern League)										
1932	Atlanta	Southern	6	42	1	3	.250	61	....	....	13	14	......
Major League Totals			536	3307	201	177	.532	3233	1443	†966	1593	858	3.13

aSold to New York Giants for $11,000, September, 1908.
bReleased to Brooklyn Dodgers on waivers, September, 1915.
cTraded to Cincinnati Reds for pitcher Walter Ruether, December 15, 1920.
dTraded to Boston Braves for pitcher John Scott and infielder William Kopf, February 20, 1922.
†Earned runs not compiled prior to 1912.

WORLD SERIES RECORD

Year	Club	League	G.	IP.	W.	L.	Pct.	H.	R.	ER.	SO.	BB.	ERA.
1911	New York	National	3	11⅔	0	1	.000	9	6	2	8	1	1.54
1912	New York	National	2	18	2	0	1.000	14	3	1	9	2	0.50
1913	New York	National	2	9	0	1	.000	10	7	7	3	4	7.00
1916	Brooklyn	National	2	11	0	2	.000	12	9	8	9	6	6.55
1920	Brooklyn	National	2	9	0	1	.000	7	3	1	6	3	1.00
World Series Totals			11	58⅔	2	5	.286	52	28	19	35	16	2.91

EDWIN LEE MATHEWS, JR.

Born October 13, 1931, at Texarkana, Tex.
Height, 6.01. Weight, 195.
Threw right and batted lefthanded.

Established following major league records: most games, third baseman (2,181); most assists, third baseman (4,322), 1968; most chances accepted, third baseman, (6,371), 1968 (all topped by Brooks Robinson); most home runs, season, third baseman (47), 1953.
Established following National League records: most strikeouts, lifetime (1,452), 1967 (since topped by Wilver Stargell); most games played, third baseman (2,154), 1967; most assists, third baseman (4,284), 1967 (surpassed by Ron Santo); most consecutive years, 30 or more home runs (9), 1961; most home runs on road, season (30), 1953 (passed by George Foster).
Tied National League record for most games played at third base, 154-game season (157), 1953.
Hit three home runs in game, September 27, 1952.
Led National League in bases on balls with 109 in 1955, 93 in 1961, 101 in 1962 and 124 in 1963.
Named as third baseman on THE SPORTING NEWS' All-Star Major League Teams, 1955-57-59-60.
Coach, Atlanta Braves, 1971 to August 7, 1972, when he became manager; released July 21, 1974; Braves' scout, 1974; Milwaukee minor league instructor-scout, 1975-78.
Named to Hall of Fame, 1978.

Year	Club	League	Pos.	G.	AB.	R.	H.	2B.	3B.	HR.	RBI.	B.A.	PO.	A.	E.	F.A.
1949	H. Point-Th'ville	N.C. St.	3B	63	240	62	87	20	3	17	56	.363	71	126	21	.904
1950	Atlanta	South.	3B	146	552	103	158	24	0	32	106	.286	159	218	24	.940
1951	Atlanta	South.	3B	37	128	23	37	5	4	6	29	.289	31	62	7	.930
1951	Milwaukee	A. A.	3B	12	9	2	3	0	0	1	5	.333	1	0	0	1.000
1952	Boston	Nat.	3B	145	528	80	128	23	5	25	58	.242	160	259	19	.957
1953	Milwaukee	Nat.	3B	157	579	110	175	31	8	*47	135	.302	154	311	*30	.939
1954	Milwaukee	Nat.	3B-OF	138	476	96	138	21	4	40	103	.290	133	254	15	.963
1955	Milwaukee	Nat.	3B	141	499	108	144	23	5	41	101	.289	140	*280	21	.952
1956	Milwaukee	Nat.	3B	151	552	103	150	21	2	37	95	.272	133	287	*25	.944
1957	Milwaukee	Nat.	3B	148	572	109	167	28	9	32	94	.292	131	*299	•16	.964
1958	Milwaukee	Nat.	3B	149	546	97	137	18	1	31	77	.251	116	*351	22	.955
1959	Milwaukee	Nat.	3B	148	594	118	182	16	8	*46	114	.306	144	305	18	.961
1960	Milwaukee	Nat.	3B	153	548	108	152	19	7	39	124	.277	*141	280	22	.950
1961	Milwaukee	Nat.	3B	152	572	103	175	23	6	32	91	.306	*168	281	18	.961
1962	Milwaukee	Nat.	3B-1B	152	536	106	142	25	6	29	90	.265	208	285	16	.969
1963	Milwaukee	Nat.	*3B-OF	158	547	82	144	27	4	23	84	.263	176	277	19	*.960
1964	Milwaukee	Nat.	3B-1B	141	502	83	117	19	1	23	74	.233	184	252	17	.962
1965	Milwaukee	Nat.	3B	156	546	77	137	23	0	32	95	.251	113	301	19	.956
1966	Atlanta (a)	Nat.	3B	134	452	72	113	21	4	16	53	.250	114	237	20	.946
1967	Houston (b)	Nat.	1B-3B	101	328	39	78	13	2	10	38	.238	594	73	11	.984

Year	Club	League	Pos.	G.	AB.	R.	H.	2B.	3B.	HR.	RBI.	B.A.	PO.	A.	E.	F.A.
1967–Detroit		Amer.	3B-1B	36	108	14	25	3	0	6	19	.231	120	40	4	.976
1968–Detroit		Amer.	1B-3B	31	52	4	11	0	0	3	8	.212	37	13	1	.980
National League Totals				2324	8377	1491	2279	351	72	503	1426	.272	4332	308	.959
American League Totals				67	160	18	36	3	0	9	27	.225	157	53	5	.977
Major League Totals				2391	8537	1509	2315	354	72	512	1453	.271	2966	4385	313	.959

aTraded with pitcher Arnold Umbach (transferred from Richmond to Oklahoma City) and player to be named later to Houston Astros for outfielder Dave Nicholson (transferred from Oklahoma City to Richmond) and pitcher Bob Bruce, December 31, 1966. Infielder Sandy Alomar sent to Astros to complete deal, February 25, 1967.

bTraded to Detroit Tigers for cash and player to be named, July 22, 1967. Pitcher Fred Gladding sent to Astros, November 22, 1967 to complete deal.

WORLD SERIES RECORD

Year	Club	League	Pos.	G.	AB.	R.	H.	2B.	3B.	HR.	RBI.	B.A.	PO.	A.	E.	F.A.
1957–Milwaukee		Nat.	3B	7	22	4	5	3	0	1	4	.227	9	19	1	.966
1958–Milwaukee		Nat.	3B	7	25	3	4	2	0	0	3	.160	5	13	1	.947
1968–Detroit		Amer.	PH-3	2	3	0	1	0	0	0	0	.333	0	1	1	.500
World Series Totals				16	50	7	10	5	0	1	7	.200	14	33	3	.880

CHRISTOPHER (BIG SIX) MATHEWSON

Born August 12, 1880, at Factoryville, Pa.
Died October 7, 1925, at Saranac Lake, N. Y.
Height, 6.01½. Weight, 195.
Threw and batted righthanded.

Struck out 16 in nine-inning game on October 3, 1904, vs. St. Louis.
Established modern N. L. record by winning 37 games, 1908; N. L. since 1900 record most consecutive innings no bases on balls, 68 (June 19 to July 18, 1913); won 30 or more three consecutive years, 1903-04-05; pitched no-hit games against St. Louis, July 15, 1901, score 5-0, and against Chicago, June 13, 1905, score 1-0; also against Hampton, 1-0, June 12, 1900. Holds National League record with Grover Cleveland Alexander for most games won, 373; pitched three shutouts in 1905 World Series.
Manager, Cincinnati Reds, July 21, 1916 to August 28, 1918, when he left to enter military service; coach, New York Giants, 1919-20-21; president, Boston Nationals, 1923-24-25.
Named to Hall of Fame, 1936.

Year	Club	League	G.	IP.	W.	L.	Pct.	ShO.	H.	R.	ER.	SO.	BB.	ERA.
1899–Taunton		N. Eng.	17	....	5	2	.714	....	....	....	....	....	....	......
1900–Norfolk		Va.	22	187	20	2	.909	4	119	59	....	128	27	......
1900–New York(a)		Nat.	6	34	0	3	.000	0	34	32	....	15	20	......
1901–New York		Nat.	40	336	20	17	.541	5	281	131	....	215	92	......
1902–New York		Nat.	34	276	14	17	.452	•8	241	114	....	162	74	......
1903–New York		Nat.	45	367	30	13	.698	3	321	136	....	*267	100	......
1904–New York		Nat.	48	368	33	12	.733	4	306	120	....	*212	78	......
1905–New York		Nat.	43	339	*31	9	.775	*9	252	85	....	*206	64	......
1906–New York		Nat.	38	267	22	12	.647	7	262	100	....	128	77	......
1907–New York		Nat.	41	315	*24	12	.667	•9	250	88	....	*178	53	......
1908–New York		Nat.	*56	*391	*37	11	.771	*12	281	85	....	*259	42	......
1909–New York		Nat.	37	274	25	6	.806	8	192	57	....	149	36	......
1910–New York		Nat.	38	319	*27	9	.750	2	291	98	....	*190	57	......
1911–New York		Nat.	45	307	26	13	.667	5	*303	102	....	141	38	......
1912–New York		Nat.	43	•310	23	12	.657	0	311	107	73	134	34	2.12
1913–New York		Nat.	40	306	25	11	.694	5	•291	93	70	93	21	*2.06
1914–New York		Nat.	41	312	24	13	.648	5	314	133	*104	80	23	3.00
1915–New York		Nat.	27	186	8	14	.364	1	199	97	74	57	20	3.58
1916–N.Y.(b)–Cinn.		Nat.	13	74	4	4	.500	1	74	35	25	19	8	3.04
Major League Totals			635	4781	373	188	.665	83	4203	1613	....	2505	837	....

aJoined Giants midseason, 1900. Turned back to Norfolk at end of campaign, but drafted by Cincinnati and traded to Giants for pitcher Amos Rusie.

bTraded with outfielder Edd Roush and infielder Bill McKechnie to Cincinnati for infielder Charles Herzog and outfielder Wade Kelleher, July 20, 1916.

WORLD SERIES RECORD

Year	Club	League	G.	IP.	W.	L.	Pct.	ShO.	H.	R.	ER.	SO.	BB.	ERA.
1905–New York		Nat.	3	27	3	0	.000	3	14	0	0	18	1	0.00
1911–New York		Nat.	3	27	1	2	.333	0	25	8	6	13	2	2.00
1912–New York		Nat.	3	28	0	2	.000	0	23	11	5	10	5	1.57
1913–New York		Nat.	2	19	1	1	.500	1	14	3	2	7	2	0.95
World Series Totals			11	101	5	5	.500	4	76	22	13	48	10	1.15

CARL WILLIAM (SUB) MAYS

Born November 12, 1893, at Liberty, Ky.
Died April 4, 1971, at El Cajon, Calif.
Height, 6.00. Weight, 215.
Threw right and batted lefthanded.
Married Marjorie Maddern, August, 1918.

Outstanding performance–Pitched first 15 innings of 17-inning scoreless tie with Ernie Koob of St. Louis Browns, July 14, 1916.
Scout, Cleveland Indians, 1958-61; scout, Kansas City Athletics, 1962; scout, Milwaukee Braves, 1963.

Year	Club	League	G.	IP.	W.	L.	Pct.	H.	R.	ER.	SO.	BB.	ERA.
1912	Boise	W. Tri-St.	40	235	22	8	.733	....	....	....	....	....	.....
1913	Portland	N. W.	33	250	10	15	.400	202	92	....	159	54	.....
1914	Providence	International	36	273	*24	8	*.750	249	94	....	129	73	.....
1915	Boston	American	38	132	6	5	.545	119	54	38	65	21	2.59
1916	Boston	American	44	245	18	13	.581	208	79	65	76	74	2.39
1917	Boston	American	35	289	22	9	.710	230	81	56	91	74	1.74
1918	Boston	American	35	293	21	13	.618	230	94	72	114	81	2.21
1919	Boston(a)-New York	American	34	266	14	14	.500	227	91	62	107	77	2.10
1920	New York	American	45	312	26	11	.703	310	127	106	92	84	3.06
1921	New York	American	*49	*337	•27	9	*.750	332	145	114	70	76	3.04
1922	New York	American	34	240	13	14	.481	257	111	96	41	50	3.60
1923	New York(b)	American	23	81	5	2	.714	119	59	56	16	32	6.22
1924	Cincinnati	National	37	226	20	9	.690	238	97	79	63	36	3.15
1925	Cincinnati	National	12	52	3	5	.375	60	22	19	10	13	3.29
1926	Cincinnati	National	39	281	19	12	.613	286	112	98	58	53	3.14
1927	Cincinnati	National	14	82	3	7	.300	89	39	32	17	10	3.51
1928	Cincinnati(c)	National	14	63	4	1	.800	67	33	27	10	22	3.86
1929	New York	National	37	123	7	2	.778	140	67	59	32	31	4.32
1930	Portland	Pacific Coast	19	144	5	9	.357	178	105	76	43	36	4.75
1930	Toledo	Amer. Assn.	6	42	3	1	.750	52	18	....	5	4	.....
1931	Toledo-Louisville	Amer. Assn.	32	204	11	15	.423	248	129	98	54	54	4.32
	American League Totals		337	2195	152	90	.628	2032	841	665	672	569	2.73
	National League Totals		153	827	56	36	.609	880	370	314	190	165	3.42
	Major League Totals		490	3022	208	126	.623	2912	1211	979	862	734	2.92

aTraded to New York Yankees for pitchers Allen Russell and Bob McGraw and $40,000, July 29, 1919.
bSold to Cincinnati Reds on waivers, December 11, 1923.
cReleased unconditionally by Cincinnati, August 18, 1928; signed by New York Giants, September 1, 1928.

WORLD SERIES RECORD

Year	Club	League	G.	IP.	W.	L.	Pct.	H.	R.	ER.	SO.	BB.	ERA.
1916	Boston	American	2	5⅓	0	1	.000	8	4	3	2	3	5.06
1918	Boston	American	2	18	2	0	1.000	10	2	2	5	3	1.00
1921	New York	American	3	26	1	2	.333	20	6	5	9	0	1.73
1922	New York	American	1	8	0	1	.000	9	4	4	1	2	4.50
	World Series Totals		8	57⅓	3	4	.420	47	16	14	17	8	2.20

WILLIE HOWARD MAYS, JR.

Born May 6, 1931, at Westfield, Ala.
Height, 5.11. Weight, 187.
Threw and batted righthanded.

Established following major league records: most consecutive years, 150 or more games (13), 1954-66; most putouts, outfielder, lifetime (7,095); most chances accepted, lifetime, outfielder (7,290).
Tied following major league records: Most consecutive years, 300 or more total bases (13), 1954-66; most games, three or more home runs, season (2), April 30 (4 home runs) and June 29, 1961 (3 home runs); most home runs, game (4), April 30, 1961; most years 20 or more home runs (17) (since broken by Hank Aaron with 20).
Established following National League records: most extra bases on long hits, lifetime (2,718) (since broken by Hank Aaron with 2,991); most games, outfielder, lifetime (2,843); most games, two or more home

runs, lifetime (63); most home runs, one month (17) August, 1965; most runs, lifetime (2,062), (since broken by Hank Aaron with 2,107); most seasons, outfielder, 22.

Tied following National League records: most home runs, six consecutive games (7), September 14 (2) and one each September 16-17-18-20-20, 1955.

First major league player to hit 50 or more home runs and steal 20 or more bases in a season (51 home runs, 24 stolen bases), 1955; one of five players in major league history to hit 30 home runs and steal 30 bases in the same season (36 home runs and 40 stolen bases in 1956, 35 home runs and 38 stolen bases in 1957); the first National League player to accomplish this feat and the first to do it more than once (1956-57; since broken by Bobby Bonds with 4).

Hit four home runs in game, April 30, 1961; hit three home runs in game, June 29, 1961, and June 2, 1963; had 338 stolen bases, leading the N. L. four consecutive years, 1956-59.

Led National League in slugging percentage with .667 in 1954, .659 in 1955, .626 in 1957, .607 in 1964 and .645 in 1965; led in total bases with 382 in 1955, 382 in 1962 and 360 in 1965.

Named National League Rookie of the Year by the Baseball Writers' Association and THE SPORTING NEWS, 1951.

Named Major League Player of the Year by THE SPORTING NEWS, 1954.

Named by THE SPORTING NEWS as the Outstanding National League Player, 1954-65.

Most Valuable Player in the National League, 1954-65.

Named as outfielder on THE SPORTING NEWS All-Star Major League teams, 1954-57-58-59-60.

Named as outfielder on THE SPORTING NEWS National League All-Star teams, 1961-62-63-64-65-66.

Named as outfielder on THE SPORTING NEWS Major League All-Star fielding team, 1957.

Named outfielder on THE SPORTING NEWS National League All-Star fielding teams, 1958-59-60-61-63-64-65-66-67-68.

Named by THE SPORTING NEWS as Baseball Player of the Decade (1960-1969).

Named to Hall of Fame, 1979.

Year	Club	League	Pos.	G.	AB.	R.	H.	2B.	3B.	HR.	RBI.	B.A.	PO.	A.	E.	F.A.
1950	Trenton	Int. St.	OF	81	306	50	108	20	8	4	55	.353	216	•17	5	.979
1951	Minneapolis	A. A.	OF	35	149	38	71	18	3	8	30	.477	94	5	1	.990
1951	New York	Nat.	OF	121	464	59	127	22	5	20	68	.274	353	12	9	.976
1952	New York(a)	Nat.	OF	34	127	17	30	2	4	4	23	.236	109	6	1	.991
1953	New York	Nat.								(In Military Service)						
1954	New York	Nat.	OF	151	565	119	195	33	*13	41	110	*.345	448	13	7	.985
1955	New York	Nat.	OF	152	580	123	185	18	•13	*51	127	.319	407	*23	8	.982
1956	New York	Nat.	OF	152	578	101	171	27	8	36	84	.296	415	14	9	.979
1957	New York	Nat.	OF	152	585	112	195	26	*20	35	97	.333	422	14	9	.980
1958	San Francisco	Nat.	OF	152	600	*121	208	33	11	29	96	.347	429	17	9	.980
1959	San Francisco	Nat.	OF	151	575	125	180	43	5	34	104	.313	353	6	6	.984
1960	San Francisco	Nat.	OF	153	595	107	*190	29	12	29	103	.319	392	12	8	.981
1961	San Francisco	Nat.	OF	154	572	*129	176	32	3	40	123	.308	385	7	8	.980
1962	San Francisco	Nat.	OF	162	621	130	189	36	5	*49	141	.304	*429	6	4	.991
1963	San Francisco	Nat.	OF-SS	157	596	115	187	32	7	38	103	.314	397	7	8	.981
1964	San Francisco	Nat.	OF-1-2-3-S	157	578	121	171	21	9	*47	111	.296	376	12	6	.985
1965	San Francisco	Nat.	OF	157	558	118	177	21	3	*52	112	.317	337	13	6	.983
1966	San Francisco	Nat.	OF	152	552	99	159	29	4	37	103	.288	370	8	7	.982
1967	San Francisco	Nat.	OF	141	486	83	128	22	2	22	70	.263	277	3	7	.976
1968	San Francisco	Nat.	OF-1B	148	498	84	144	20	5	23	79	.289	310	7	7	.978
1969	San Francisco	Nat.	OF-1B	117	403	64	114	17	3	13	58	.283	205	4	5	.976
1970	San Francisco	Nat.	OF-1B	139	478	94	139	15	2	28	83	.291	303	9	7	.978
1971	San Francisco	Nat.	OF-1B	136	417	82	113	24	5	18	61	.271	576	29	17	.973
1972	S. F.(b)-N.Y.	Nat.	OF-1B	88	244	35	61	11	1	8	22	.250	213	5	4	.982
1973	New York	Nat.	OF-1B	66	209	24	44	10	0	6	25	.211	246	6	4	.984
Major League Totals				2992	10881	2062	3283	523	140	660	1903	.302	7752	233	156	.981

aEntered military service May 29.

bTraded to New York Mets for cash and pitcher Charlie Williams, May 11, 1972.

WORLD SERIES RECORD

Year	Club	League	Pos.	G.	AB.	R.	H.	2B.	3B.	HR.	RBI.	B.A.	PO.	A.	E.	F.A.
1951	New York	Nat.	OF	6	22	1	4	0	0	0	1	.182	16	1	0	1.000
1954	New York	Nat.	OF	4	14	4	4	1	0	0	3	.286	10	0	0	1.000
1962	San Francisco	Nat.	OF	7	28	3	7	2	0	0	1	.250	19	0	0	1.000
1973	New York	Nat.	O-PH-PR	3	7	1	2	0	0	0	1	.286	1	0	1	.500
World Series Totals				20	71	9	17	3	0	0	6	.239	46	1	1	.979

WILLIAM STANLEY MAZEROSKI

Born September 5, 1936, at Wheeling, W. Va.

Height, 5.11. Weight, 193.

Threw and batted righthanded.

Established following major league records: most double plays by second baseman, season (161), 1966; most games, second baseman, season (163), 1967; most years leading league, assists, second baseman (9);

most years leading league, double plays, second baseman (8); most consecutive years leading league, double plays, second baseman (8); most double plays, second baseman, lifetime (1706).
Established National League records for most years leading league, chances accepted, second baseman (8), and most games, lifetime, second baseman (2094); most chances accepted, second baseman, lifetime (11,659); most putouts, second baseman, lifetime (4974); most assists, second baseman, lifetime (6685).
Led National League second basemen in double plays in 1960, 1961, 1962, 1963, 1964, 1965, 1966 and 1967.
Named Major League Player of the Year by THE SPORTING NEWS, 1960.
Named as second baseman on THE SPORTING NEWS All-Star Major League team, 1960.
Named as second baseman on THE SPORTING NEWS National League All-Star teams, 1962 and 1967.
Named as second baseman on THE SPORTING NEWS National League All-Star fielding teams, 1958-60-61-64-65-66-67.
Coach, Pittsburgh Pirates, 1973; coach, Seattle Mariners, 1979 to date.

Year	Club	League	Pos.	G.	AB.	R.	H.	2B.	3B.	HR.	RBI.	B.A.	PO.	A.	E.	F.A.
1954	Williamsport	East.	SS	93	315	35	74	6	8	3	28	.235	148	205	31	.919
1955	Hollywood	P. C.	2B	21	47	4	8	0	0	1	3	.170	41	34	0	1.000
1955	Williamsport	East.	2B	114	413	68	121	13	7	11	65	.293	281	326	21	.967
1956	Hollywood	P. C.	2B	80	284	47	87	12	3	9	36	.306	220	215	7	.984
1956	Pittsburgh	Nat.	2B	81	255	30	62	8	1	3	14	.243	163	242	8	.981
1957	Pittsburgh	Nat.	2B	148	526	59	149	27	7	8	54	.283	308	443	17	.978
1958	Pittsburgh	Nat.	2B	152	567	69	156	24	6	19	68	.275	344	*496	17	.980
1959	Pittsburgh	Nat.	2B	135	493	50	119	15	6	7	59	.241	303	373	13	.981
1960	Pittsburgh	Nat.	2B	151	538	58	147	21	5	11	64	.273	*413	*419	10	*.989
1961	Pittsburgh	Nat.	2B	152	558	71	148	21	2	13	59	.265	*410	*505	*23	.975
1962	Pittsburgh	Nat.	2B	159	572	55	155	24	9	14	81	.271	*425	*509	14	.985
1963	Pittsburgh	Nat.	2B	142	534	43	131	22	3	8	52	.245	340	*506	14	.984
1964	Pittsburgh	Nat.	2B	162	601	66	161	22	8	10	64	.268	346	*543	23	.975
1965	Pittsburgh	Nat.	2B	130	494	52	134	17	1	6	54	.271	290	439	9	*.988
1966	Pittsburgh	Nat.	2B	•162	621	56	163	22	7	16	82	.262	*411	*538	8	*.992
1967	Pittsburgh	Nat.	2B	*163	639	62	167	25	3	9	77	.261	*417	*498	18	.981
1968	Pittsburgh	Nat.	2B	143	506	36	127	18	2	3	42	.251	319	*467	15	.981
1969	Pittsburgh	Nat.	2B	67	227	13	52	7	1	3	25	.229	134	192	4	.988
1970	Pittsburgh	Nat.	2B	112	367	29	84	14	0	7	39	.229	227	325	7	.987
1971	Pittsburgh	Nat.	2B	70	193	17	49	3	1	1	16	.254	95	121	3	.986
1972	Pittsburgh	Nat.	2B-3B	34	64	3	12	4	0	0	3	.188	29	33	1	.984
Major League Totals				2163	7758	769	2016	294	62	138	853	.260	4974	6679	204	.983

WORLD SERIES RECORD

Year	Club	League	Pos.	G.	AB.	R.	H.	2B.	3B.	HR.	RBI.	B.A.	PO.	A.	E.	F.A.
1960	Pittsburgh	Nat.	2B	7	25	4	8	2	0	2	5	.320	16	23	0	1.000
1971	Pittsburgh	Nat.	PH	1	1	0	0	0	0	0	0	.000	0	0	0	.000
World Series Totals				8	26	4	8	2	0	2	5	.308	16	23	0	1.000

JOSEPH VINCENT (MARSE JOE) McCARTHY

Born April 21, 1887, at Philadelphia, Pa.
Died January 13, 1978, at Buffalo, N. Y.
Height, 5.08½. Weight, 190.
Threw and batted righthanded.
Married Elizabeth M. McCave, February 2, 1921.

World Series Manager, Chicago N. L., 1929; New York A. L., 1932, 1936, 1937, 1938, 1939, 1941, 1942, 1943.
Named by THE SPORTING NEWS as Major League Manager of the Year, 1936, 1938, 1943.
Manager, Wilkes-Barre, New York State, 1913; Louisville, American Association, July 22, 1919 through 1925; Chicago Cubs, 1926 to September 24, 1930; New York Yankees, 1931 to May 24, 1946; Boston Red Sox, 1948 to June 23, 1950.
Named to Hall of Fame, 1957.

Year	Club	League	Pos.	G.	AB.	R.	H.	2B.	3B.	HR.	SB.	B.A.	PO.	A.	E.	F.A.
1907	Wilmington	Tri.-St.	INF	12	40	0	7	0	0	0	0	.175	18	27	5	.900
1907	Franklin	Int.-St.	OF	71	245	37	77	...	...	2	7	.314	77	131	25	.893
1908	Toledo	A. A.	OF-3B	111	386	43	98	25	1	0	13	.254	140	91	32	.878
1909	Toledo	A. A.	OF-SS	128	507	58	112	19	5	3	14	.221	225	119	27	.927
1910	Toledo	A. A.	3B-OF	92	274	28	62	10	2	2	8	.226	102	128	21	.916
1911	Toledo-Ind.	A. A.	OF-3B	98	208	45	80	10	3	2	9	.268	160	89	24	.912
1912	Wilkes-Barre	N.Y.S.	2B-3B	116	387	50	106	14	9	7	24	.274	237	256	30	.943
1913	Wilkes-Barre	N.Y.S.	2B	132	505	87	164	36	9	6	13	.325	287	*422	*45	.940
1914	Buffalo	Int.	2B	146	537	63	143	25	11	4	27	.266	309	*473	29	*.964
1915	Buffalo	Int.	2B	135	515	71	137	24	5	0	17	.266	306	*414	22	.970
1916	Louisville	A. A.	2B	168	618	55	160	28	10	1	20	.259	316	508	36	.958
1917	Louisville	A. A.	2B	143	510	64	141	31	6	2	8	.276	363	443	47	.945
1918	Louisville	A. A.	2B	75	274	26	59	6	1	3	.215	193	222	20	.954
1919	Louisville	A. A.	2B	147	550	60	130	28	8	3	11	.236	336	464	*37	.956
1920	Louisville	A. A.	2B-OF	58	175	17	44	12	2	0	3	.251	97	70	10	.944
1921	Louisville	A. A.	2B-PH	11	18	1	5	0	0	0	0	.278	6	8	0	1.000

THOMAS FRANCIS MICHAEL McCARTHY

Born July 24, 1864, at South Boston, Mass.
Died August 5, 1922, at Boston, Mass.
Height, 5.07. Weight, 170.
Threw and batted righthanded.

Stole six bases in a game, July 17, 1888; stole five bases in a game, August 23, 1891; stole second, third and home, second inning, April 23, 1888.
Scout for Cincinnati, 1909-10-11-12; Boston N.L., 1914 and 1917; Manager, Newark, new International League, 1918; manager, St. Louis, American Association, part of 1890.
Baseball coach at Dartmouth, Holy Cross and Boston College.
Named to Hall of Fame, 1946.

Year	Club	League	Pos.	G.	AB.	R.	H.	2B.	3B.	HR.	SB.	B.A.	PO.	A.	E.	F.A.
1884	Boston	U.A.	OF-P	53	218	37	45	4	1	0	....	.206	51	14	13	.833
1885	Boston	Nat.	OF	40	148	16	27	2	0	....	....	.182	69	8	12	.865
1886	Philadelphia	Nat.	OF	8	27	6	5	2	1	....	0	.185	8	0	2	.800
1887	Philadelphia	Nat.	OF-INF	18	72	7	15	4	0	....	15	.208	17	2	1	.950
1888	St. Louis	A.A.	OF-P	131	510	106	141	20	3	....	109	.276	232	39	23	.922
1889	St. Louis	A.A.	OF-2B	140	603	136	179	26	7	2	59	.297	231	41	32	.895
1890	St. Louis	A.A.	OF-INF	132	539	*134	189	26	9	6	91	.351	153	13	17	.907
1891	St. Louis	A.A.	OF-INF	125	527	115	163	20	8	8	37	.309	170	27	22	.900
1892	Boston	Nat.	OF	152	602	116	147	18	6	4	59	.244	211	31	33	.880
1893	Boston	Nat.	OF-INF	116	441	108	159	30	6	5	49	.361	224	53	29	.905
1894	Boston	Nat.	OF-INF	126	536	118	187	22	8	13	40	.349	286	30	32	.908
1895	Boston	Nat.	OF-INF	116	454	89	132	13	2	2	24	.291	203	23	29	.886
1896	Brooklyn	Nat.	OF	101	378	62	96	8	6	3	23	.254	179	20	16	.926
Union Association Totals				53	218	37	45	4	1	0	....	.206	51	14	13	.833
American Association Totals				528	2179	491	672	92	27	16	296	.308	786	120	94	.906
National League				677	2658	522	768	99	29	27	210	.289	1197	167	154	.900
Major League Totals				1258	5055	1050	1485	195	57	43	506	.294	2034	301	261	.899

WORLD SERIES RECORD

Year	Club	League	Pos.	G.	AB.	R.	H.	2B.	3B.	HR.	SB.	B.A.	PO.	A.	E.	F.A.
1888	St. Louis	A.A.	OF	10	41	9	10	0	0	1	6	.244	12	2	5	.737

JAMES McCORMICK

Born 1856, at Paterson, N.J.
Died March 10, 1918, at Paterson, N.J.
Height, 5.10. Weight, 220.
Threw and batted righthanded.

Won 16 consecutive games, May 5 through July 1, 1886. Won last 14 games for the Cincinnati Unions, 1884, beginning September 5 and ending on closing day, October 14.
Manager, Cleveland, National League, 1879 through 1881.

Year	Club	League	G.	W.	L.	Pct.	H.	R.	CG.	ShO.
1878	Indianapolis	National	14	5	8	.385	129	59	12	1
1879	Cleveland	National	60	20	•40	.333	581	305	59	3
1880	Cleveland	National	•73	*45	28	.616	588	282	*72	7
1881	Cleveland	National	57	26	30	.464	495	273	56	2
1882	Cleveland	National	*65	*36	29	.554	549	290	*64	4
1883	Cleveland	National	40	27	13	*.675	308	146	35	1
1884	Cleveland (a)	National	41	19	22	.463	357	208	37	3
1884	Cincinnati	Union Association	26	22	4	.846	151	....	26	*7
1885	Providence-Chicago	National	29	21	7	.750	225	129	28	3
1886	Chicago	National	42	31	11	.738	337	163	38	3
1887	Pittsburgh	National	36	13	23	.361	446	217	35	0
National League Totals			457	243	211	.535	4015	2072	436	27
Union Association Totals			26	22	4	.846	151	....	26	7
Major League Totals			483	265	215	.552	4166	.....	462	34

aDeserted Cleveland; played first game for Cincinnati on August 10.

WILLIAM BARNEY McCOSKY

Born April 11, 1918, at Coal Run, Pa.
Height, 6.01. Weight, 184.
Threw right and batted lefthanded.
Married Jane Malicki, June 19, 1946.

Year	Club	League	Pos.	G.	AB.	R.	H.	2B.	3B.	HR.	RBI.	B.A.	PO.	A.	E.	F.A.
1936	Charleston	Mid.-Atl.	OF	108	407	66	163	28	*19	7	77	*.400	230	9	4	*.984
1936	Beaumont	Texas	OF	20	66	13	15	1	0	0	8	.227	33	1	2	.944
1937	Beaumont	Texas	OF	158	633	*116	*201	32	*20	1	73	.318	*412	17	10	.977
1938	Beaumont	Texas	OF	133	517	78	156	18	6	0	57	.302	283	9	7	.977
1939	Detroit	Amer.	OF	147	611	120	190	33	14	4	58	.311	*428	7	6	.986
1940	Detroit	Amer.	OF	143	589	123	•200	39	*19	4	57	.340	349	7	6	.983
1941	Detroit	Amer.	OF	127	494	80	160	25	8	3	55	.324	328	6	5	.985
1942	Detroit	Amer.	OF	154	600	75	176	28	11	7	50	.293	351	7	7	.981
1943-44-45	Detroit	Amer.					(In Military Service)									
1946	Det.(a)-Phila.	Amer.	OF	117	399	44	127	22	4	2	45	.318	263	3	6	.978
1947	Philadelphia	Amer.	OF	137	546	77	179	22	7	1	52	.328	346	8	6	.983
1948	Philadelphia	Amer.	OF	135	515	95	168	21	5	0	46	.326	277	9	3	.990
1949	Philadelphia(b)	Amer.					(Voluntarily Retired)									
1950	Philadelphia	Amer.	OF	66	179	19	43	10	1	0	11	.240	73	1	1	.987
1951	Phila.(c)-Cleve.	Amer.	OF	43	88	12	21	5	0	1	3	.239	41	0	0	1.000
1951	Cincinnati(d)	Nat.	OF	25	50	2	16	2	1	1	11	.320	17	0	0	1.000
1952	Cleveland	Amer.	OF	54	80	14	17	4	1	1	6	.213	17	0	1	.944
1953	Cleveland	Amer.	PH	22	21	3	4	3	0	0	3	.190	0	0	0	.000
	American League Totals			1145	4122	662	1285	212	70	23	386	.312	2473	48	41	.984
	National League Totals			25	50	2	16	2	1	1	11	.320	17	0	0	1.000
	Major League Totals			1170	4172	664	1301	214	71	24	397	.312	2490	48	41	.984

aTraded to Philadelphia Athletics for third baseman George Kell, May 18, 1946.
bOut of game for season due to displaced vertebrae.
cSold to Cincinnati Reds, May 4, 1951.
dSold to Cleveland Indians, July 21, 1951.

WORLD SERIES RECORD

Year	Club	League	Pos.	G.	AB.	R.	H.	2B.	3B.	HR.	RBI.	B.A.	PO.	A.	E.	F.A.
1940	Detroit	Amer.	OF	7	23	5	7	1	0	0	1	.304	19	0	0	1.000

SAMUEL EDWARD THOMAS (SUDDEN SAM) McDOWELL

Born September 21, 1942, at Pittsburgh, Pa.
Height, 6;05. Weight, 220.
Threw and batted lefthanded.

Tied major league record for most consecutive one-hit games (2), April 25 and May 1, 1966.
Established American League records for most strikeouts, two consecutive nine-inning games (30), May 1 and 6, 1968, and most strikeouts, three consecutive nine-inning games (40), twice, May 1, 6 and 11, and July 1, 6 and 12, 1968, and most times ten or more strikeouts, game, league (70), 1970 (since broken by Nolan Ryan with 114, including the 1980 season).
Named pitcher on THE SPORTING NEWS American League All-Star Team, 1970.
Named by THE SPORTING NEWS as American League Pitcher of the Year, 1970.

Year	Club	League	G.	IP.	W.	L.	Pct.	H.	R.	ER.	SO.	BB.	ERA.
1960	Lakeland	Fla. St.	16	105	5	6	.455	85	51	39	100	80	3.34
1961	Salt Lake City	P. C.	32	175	13	10	.565	143	98	86	*156	*152	4.42
1961	Cleveland	Amer.	1	6	0	0	.000	3	0	0	5	5	0.00
1962	Cleveland	Amer.	25	88	3	7	.300	81	64	59	70	70	6.03
1962	Salt Lake City	P. C.	6	40	3	2	.600	28	9	9	34	23	2.03
1963	Cleveland	Amer.	14	65	3	5	.375	63	37	35	63	44	4.85
1963	Jacksonville	Int.	12	87	3	6	.333	63	35	33	84	50	3.41
1964	Portland	P. C.	9	76	8	0	1.000	34	11	10	102	24	1.18

Year	Club	League	G.	IP.	W.	L.	Pct.	H.	R.	ER.	SO.	BB.	ERA.
1964—Cleveland		Amer.	31	173	11	6	.647	148	60	52	177	100	2.71
1965—Cleveland		Amer.	42	273	17	11	.607	178	80	66	*325	*132	*2.18
1966—Cleveland		Amer.	35	194	9	8	.529	130	66	62	*225	102	2.88
1967—Cleveland		Amer.	37	236	13	15	.464	201	*112	*101	236	*123	3.85
1968—Cleveland		Amer.	38	269	15	14	.517	181	78	54	*283	*110	1.81
1969—Cleveland		Amer.	39	285	18	14	.563	222	111	93	*279	102	2.94
1970—Cleveland		Amer.	39	•305	20	12	.625	236	108	99	*304	*131	2.92
1971—Cleveland(a)		Amer.	35	215	13	17	.433	160	89	81	192	*153	3.39
1972—San Francisco		Nat.	28	164	10	8	.556	155	86	79	122	86	4.34
1973—San Francisco(b)		Nat.	18	40	1	2	.333	45	23	20	35	29	4.50
1973—New York		Amer.	16	96	5	8	.385	73	47	42	75	64	3.94
1974—New York		Amer.	13	48	1	6	.143	42	27	25	33	41	4.69
1975—Pittsburgh(c)		Nat.	14	35	2	1	.667	30	11	11	29	20	2.83
American League Totals			365	2253	128	123	.510	1718	879	769	2267	1177	3.07
National League Totals			60	239	13	11	.542	230	120	110	186	135	4.14
Major League Totals			425	2492	141	134	.513	1948	999	879	2453	1312	3.17

aTraded to San Francisco Giants for pitcher Gaylord Perry and shortstop Frank Duffy, November 29, 1971.
bSold to New York Yankees for an estimated $150,000, June 7, 1973.
cSigned as free agent by Pittsburgh Pirates, April 2, 1975.

CORNELIUS (CONNIE MACK) McGILLICUDDY

Born December 22, 1862, at East Brookfield, Mass.
Died February 8, 1956, at Germantown, Pa.
Height, 6.01. Weight, 150.
Threw and batted righthanded.

World Series Manager, Philadelphia A. L., 1905, 1910, 1911, 1913, 1914, 1929, 1930, 1931.
Recipient of the Bok Award in 1930, a tribute which carried with it an embossed scroll, a medal and $10,000 for having rendered greatest service to the city of Philadelphia in the preceding year. Previously the annual winner had been a scholar or learned man in the professions.
Manager, Pittsburgh N. L., September 3, 1894 through 1896; manager, Milwaukee, Western League, 1897-98-99-1900; manager, Philadelphia A. L., 1901 through 1950. He became A's president in 1937.
Named to Hall of Fame in 1937 for service apart from playing the game.

Year	Club	League	Pos.	G.	AB.	R.	H.	2B.	3B.	HR.	SB.	B.A.	PO.	A.	E.	F.A.
1884—Meriden		Conn. St.		....	....	....	....	....	....	....	....	....	....	....	....	....
1885—Hartford		N. E. Con. St.		....	....	....	....	....	....	....	....	....	....	....	....	....
1885—Newark		East.	C	1	4	1	2	0	0	0	....	.500	11	0	1	.917
1886—Hartford		East.	C	69	278	44	69	13	1	0	....	.248	419	133	27	.953
1886—Washington		Nat.	C	10	36	4	13	2	1	0	0	.361	88	22	8	.932
1887—Washington		Nat.	*C-O-2B	80	322	35	71	6	1	0	26	.220	*396	129	57	.902
1888—Washington		Nat.	*C-O-SS	85	300	49	56	5	6	3	31	.187	368	*155	48	.916
1889—Washington		Nat.	C-O-1B	97	386	51	113	16	1	0	26	.293	432	100	57	.903
1890—Buffalo		Play.	C	123	506	95	136	15	12	0	16	.269	488	147	41	*.939
1891—Pittsburgh		Nat.	C	71	271	41	57	9	0	0	5	.210	373	78	27	.944
1892—Pittsburgh		Nat.	C-OF	86	338	39	87	9	4	1	11	.257	427	135	28	.953
1893—Pittsburgh		Nat.	C	36	120	22	39	3	1	0	4	.325	129	48	13	.932
1894—Pittsburgh		Nat.	C	63	229	32	59	7	1	1	9	.258	274	59	22	.938
1895—Pittsburgh		Nat.	C	14	47	12	17	2	0	0	1	.362	56	20	7	.931
1896—Pittsburgh		Nat.	C-1B	30	116	7	24	4	1	0	0	.207	240	18	5	.981
1897—Milwaukee		West.	C-1B	27	73	12	21	1	1	0	4	.288	134	17	6	.962
National League Totals				572	2165	292	536	63	16	5	113	.247	2783	764	272	.929
Players League Totals				123	506	95	136	15	12	0	16	.268	488	147	41	.939
Major League Totals				695	2671	387	672	78	28	5	129	.251	3271	911	313	.930

JOSEPH JEROME (IRON MAN) McGINNITY

Born March 19, 1871, at Rock Island, Ill.
Died November 14, 1929, at Brooklyn, N. Y.
Height, 5.11. Weight, 206.
Threw and batted righthanded.

Set major league record by pitching two games in one day five times; modern National League record most innings pitched, season, 434, in 1903.

Manager, Newark, Eastern League, 1909-11-12 (International); Tacoma, Northwestern League, 1913-14-15; Butte, Northwestern League; 1916-17; Dubuque, Mississippi Valley League, 1922-23; part owner-manager, Dubuque, Mississippi Valley, 1925; coach, Brooklyn Dodgers, 1926.

Named to Hall of Fame, 1946.

Year	Club	League	G.	IP.	W.	L.	Pct.	ShO.	H.	R.	SO.	BB.
1893	Montgomery	Southern	31	193	10	19	.345	....	212	....	76	99
1894	Kansas City	Western	20	124	8	10	.444	....	157	....	31	54
1898	Peoria	West. Assn.	16	104	10	3	.769	....	107	....	69	59
1899	Baltimore(a)	National	49	380	•28	17	.622	4	340	168	74	92
1900	Brooklyn(b)	National	*45	347	*29	9	*.763	1	364	184	92	*113
1901	Baltimore	American	*48	*378	26	21	.553	1	401	219	73	94
1902	Baltimore(c)	American	25	199	13	10	.565	0	186	97	39	44
1902	New York	National	19	153	8	8	.500	1	129	52	68	31
1903	New York	National	*55	*434	*31	20	.608	3	391	162	171	109
1904	New York	National	*51	*408	*35	8	*.814	*9	307	103	144	86
1905	New York	National	•46	320	21	15	.588	2	289	131	125	71
1906	New York	National	*45	340	*27	12	.692	3	316	125	105	71
1907	New York	National	*47	310	18	18	.500	3	320	126	120	58
1908	New York	National	37	186	11	7	.611	5	192	73	55	37
1909	Newark	Eastern	*55	*422	*29	16	.644	....	297	105	195	78
1910	Newark	Eastern	*61	*408	*30	19	.612	....	325	*131	132	71
1911	Newark	Eastern	43	278	12	19	.387	....	269	130	77	53
1912	Newark	International	37	261	16	10	.615	....	293	132	62	43
1913	Tacoma	Northwestern	*68	*436	22	19	.537	....	*418	*177	154	66
1914	Tacoma	Northwestern	49	326	20	*21	.488	....	295	140	105	73
1914	Venice	Pacific Coast	8	37	1	4	.200	....	42	17	7	5
1915	Tacoma	Northwestern	45	*355	21	15	.583	....	291	101	58	39
1916	Butte	Northwestern	43	291	20	13	.606	....	*340	*191	95	63
1917	Butte-Great Falls	Northwestern	16	119	7	6	.538	....	119	51	28	25
1918	Vancouver	P. C.-Int.	9	....	2	6	.250	....	47	....	31	14
1922	Danville	I. I. I.	16	79	1	6	.143	....	117	74	12	12
1922	Dubuque	Miss. Valley	19	91	5	8	.385	....	94	52	19	19
1923	Dubuque	Miss. Valley	42	206	15	12	.556	....	268	117	41	44
1925	Dubuque	Miss. Valley	15	85	6	6	.500	....	119	51	22	18
	American League Totals		73	577	39	31	.557	1	587	316	112	138
	National League Totals		394	2878	208	114	.646	31	2648	1126	954	661
	Major League Totals		467	3455	247	145	.630	32	3235	1442	1066	799

aTransferred to Brooklyn when National League reduced circuit to eight clubs for 1900.
bJumped with John McGraw to Baltimore A. L. club, 1901.
cJumped back with McGraw and others to New York Giants, July, 1902.

WORLD SERIES RECORD

Year	Club	League	G.	IP.	W.	L.	Pct.	ShO.	H.	R.	ER.	SO.	BB.	ERA.
1905	New York	National	2	17	1	1	.500	1	10	3	0	6	3	0.00

JOHN JOSEPH (LITTLE NAPOLEON) McGRAW

Born April 7, 1873, at Truxton, N. Y.
Died February 25, 1934, at New Rochelle, N. Y.
Height, 5.07. Weight, 155.
Threw right and batted lefthanded.
Married Blanche Sindall, January 8, 1902.

World Series manager, New York N. L., 1905, 1911, 1912, 1913, 1917, 1921, 1922, 1923, 1924.

Manager of Baltimore, N. L., 1899; Baltimore A. L., 1901 until July 16, 1902; New York N. L., July, 1902 to June 3, 1932. Won N. L. pennants in 1904-05-11-12-13-17-21-22-23-24 and world championships in 1905-21-22.

Named to Hall of Fame, 1937.

Year	Club	League	Pos.	G.	AB.	R.	H.	2B.	3B.	HR.	SB.	B.A.	PO.	A.	E.	F.A.
1890	Olean	NYP	SS	....	....	....	....	....	....	....	....	....	....	....	....	....
1891	Cedar Rapids	Ill.-Ia	SS	85	359	68	99	...	...	...	21	.275	....	....	...	.875
1891	Baltimore	A. A.	SS	31	106	15	26	3	4	0	7	.245	46	50	18	.842
1892	Baltimore	Nat.	2B-OF	76	288	41	77	14	2	1	14	.267	140	111	24	.913
1893	Baltimore	Nat.	SS	127	475	123	156	10	11	5	40	.328	221	346	66	.896
1894	Baltimore	Nat.	3B	123	515	155	175	20	14	0	77	.340	130	246	44	.895
1895	Baltimore	Nat.	3B	93	385	109	144	15	7	2	69	.374	100	238	46	.880
1896	Baltimore	Nat.	3B	19	73	19	26	2	2	0	13	.356	22	38	12	.833
1897	Baltimore	Nat.	3B	105	389	89	127	14	3	0	42	.326	116	188	36	.880
1898	Baltimore	Nat.	3B	141	521	*142	174	7	10	0	42	.334	141	166	44	.874
1899	Baltimore(a)	Nat.	3B	118	402	140	157	13	3	1	73	.390	149	266	25	.943

Year	Club	League	Pos.	G.	AB.	R.	H.	2B.	3B.	HR.	SB.	B.A.	PO.	A.	E.	F.A.
1900	St. Louis(b)	Nat.	3B	98	341	84	115	10	4	2	28	.337	106	216	29	.917
1901	Baltimore	Amer.	3B	73	230	73	81	13	9	0	25	.352	80	140	23	.896
1902	Baltimore(c)	Amer.	3B	20	63	14	18	3	2	1	5	.286	25	25	8	.862
1902	New York	Nat.	3B	34	106	13	24	0	0	0	7	.226	63	118	16	.900
1903	New York	Nat.	2B-SS	12	11	2	3	0	0	0	1	.273	2	1	1	.750
1904	New York	Nat.	2B-SS	5	12	0	4	0	0	0	0	.333	12	17	2	.935
1905	New York	Nat.	OF-PR	3	0	0	0	0	0	0	1	.000	0	0	0	.000
1906	New York	Nat.	3B	4	2	0	0	0	0	0	0	.000	0	0	0	.000
American Association Totals				31	106	15	26	3	4	0	7	.245	46	50	18	.842
American League Totals				93	293	87	99	16	11	1	30	.338	105	165	31	.897
National League Totals				958	3520	917	1182	105	56	11	407	.336	1202	1945	345	.901
Major League Totals				1082	3919	1019	1307	124	71	12	444	.334	1353	2166	394	.899

aSold with catcher Wilbert Robinson and second baseman Billy Keister to St. Louis N. L. for $150,000, 1899.
bJumped to Baltimore A. L. in 1901.
cQuit A. L. in July after disagreement with Ban Johnson and joined New York N. L., July 16, 1902.

JOHN PHALEN (STUFFY) McINNIS

Born September 19, 1890, at Gloucester, Mass.
Died February 16, 1960, at Ipswich, Mass.
Height, 5.09½. Weight, 162.
Threw and batted righthanded.
Married Elsie S. Dow, January 19, 1918.

Set fielding record for major league first basemen, .999, 150 or more games, in 1921; tied record chances accepted, game, 22, July 19, 1918; holds record for chances accepted without an error, 1,700 — May 31, 1921, to June 2, 1922; fewest errors, first basemen, season, (1), 1921; most consecutive errorless games, 163, May 31, 1921, to June 2, 1922; also most chances accepted, season, no errors, 1,300 — May 31 to October 2, 1921. Led A. L. first basemen in double plays, 1923 (tie).
Manager, Philadelphia Phillies, 1927; manager, Salem, New England League, 1928.

Year	Club	League	Pos.	G.	AB.	R.	H.	2B.	3B.	HR.	RBI.	B.A.	PO.	A.	E.	F.A.
1908	Haverhill	N. Eng.	2B	51	186	24	56	8	3	0	....	.301	113	147	18	.935
1909	Philadelphia	Amer.	SS	19	46	4	11	0	0	1	4	.239	34	46	9	.899
1910	Philadelphia	Amer.	SS	38	73	10	22	2	4	0	12	.301	20	31	4	.927
1911	Philadelphia	Am.	SS-1B	126	468	76	150	20	10	3	79	.321	1105	101	35	.972
1912	Philadelphia	Amer.	1B	153	568	83	186	25	13	3	103	.327	*1533	*100	•27	.984
1913	Philadelphia	Amer.	1B	148	543	79	177	30	4	4	93	.326	*1504	79	12	*.992
1914	Philadelphia	Amer.	1B	149	576	74	181	12	8	1	91	.314	1423	85	7	*.995
1915	Philadelphia	Amer.	1B	119	456	44	143	14	4	0	48	.314	1123	83	13	.989
1916	Philadelphia	Amer.	1B	140	512	42	151	25	3	1	56	.295	1404	96	12	.992
1917	Philadelphia	Amer.	1B	150	567	50	172	19	4	0	46	.303	*1658	95	12	.993
1918	Boston	Amer.	1-3B	117	423	40	115	11	5	0	56	.272	1100	113	10	.992
1919	Boston	Amer.	1B	120	440	32	134	12	5	1	60	.305	1236	82	7	.995
1920	Boston	Amer.	1B	148	559	50	166	21	3	2	71	.297	1586	91	7	*.996
1921	Boston(b)	Amer.	1B	152	584	72	179	31	10	0	74	.307	1549	102	1	*.999
1922	Cleveland	Amer.	1B	142	537	58	164	28	7	1	78	.305	1376	73	5	*.997
1923	Boston(c)	Nat.	1B	•154	607	70	191	23	9	2	95	.315	1500	*89	14	.991
1924	Boston	Nat.	1B	146	581	57	169	23	7	1	59	.291	1435	95	10	.994
1925	Pittsburgh(d)	Nat.	1B	59	155	19	57	10	4	0	24	.368	377	24	3	.993
1926	Pittsburgh	Nat.	1B	47	127	12	38	6	1	0	13	.299	300	17	4	.988
1927	Philadelphia	Nat.	1B	1	0	0	0	0	0	0	0	.000	0	0	0	.000
1928	Salem	N. Eng.	1B	38	115	10	39	5	2	0	17	.339	286	23	3	.990
American League Totals				1721	6352	714	1951	250	80	17	873	.307	16651	1177	161	.991
National League Totals				407	1470	158	455	62	21	3	191	.309	3612	225	31	.992
Major League Totals				2128	7822	.872	2406	312	101	20	1064	.308	20263	1402	192	.991

aTraded to Boston Red Sox for third baseman Lawrence Gardner, outfielder Clarence Walker and catcher Forrest Cady, January 11, 1918.
bTraded to Cleveland for first baseman George Burns and outfielders Joseph Harris and Elmer Smith, December, 1921.
cClaimed on waivers by Boston Braves, January, 1923.
dUnconditionally released by Braves, April 13, 1925, and signed with Pittsburgh, May 29.

WORLD SERIES RECORD

Year	Club	League	Pos.	G.	AB.	R.	H.	2B.	3B.	HR.	RBI.	B.A.	PO.	A.	E.	F.A.
1911	Philadelphia	Amer.	1B	1	0	0	0	0	0	0	0	.000	1	0	0	1.000
1913	Philadelphia	Amer.	1B	5	17	1	2	1	0	0	2	.118	45	0	0	1.000
1914	Philadelphia	Amer.	1B	4	14	2	2	1	0	0	0	.143	50	1	1	.981
1918	Boston	Amer.	1B	6	20	2	5	0	0	0	1	.250	70	2	0	1.000
1925	Pittsburgh	Nat.	1B-PH	4	14	0	4	0	0	0	1	.286	30	3	0	1.000
World Series Totals				20	65	5	13	2	0	0	4	.200	196	6	1	.995

Adrian (Cap) Anson, Chicago N.L. first baseman and manager from 1876 to '97, set a league record by batting .300 or better for 20 seasons and is co-holder of the N.L. mark of 22 seasons with one club.

Denton (Cy) Young holds the major league record for most victories, 511, and for most consecutive hitless innings, 24. Durable righthander registered three no-hitters, including a perfect game against Philadelphia in 1904.

Jack Chesbro, the only pitcher to lead both majors in winning percentage as a star with Pittsburgh and New York, set an American League record by winning 41 games for the New York Highlanders in 1904.

Roger Bresnahan, who pitched a shutout in his major league debut with Washington in 1897, earned his Hall of Fame credentials as a catcher for the New York Giants, St. Louis Cardinals and Chicago Cubs from 1902 to 1915.

Napoleon Lajoie, graceful second baseman, batted .339 in a 21-year career. With Cleveland, he led the league in hitting three times and, on October 9, 1910, rapped seven safe bunts and a triple in a twin-bill against St. Louis.

Third baseman of the early Philadelphia Athletics, Frank (Home Run) Baker gained distinction by scoring six runs and making nine hits in a five-game World Series (1910), and clouted home runs to win three Series contests.

The National League's champion shutout pitcher, with 90 in his career and 16 in 1916. Grover Cleveland Alexander also led the league seven times in complete games and tied with Christy Mathewson for most N.L. wins, 373.

Walter Johnson, fireballing righthander of the Washington Senators from 1907 to 1927, was named the A.L. MVP in 1913 and 1924 and established a record for one league by posting 416 lifetime victories.

Rogers Hornsby, the National League's top lifetime hitter with a .358 average, won six consecutive batting championships, batted over .400 three times and was twice named N.L. Most Valuable Player.

One of the most graceful first basemen of all time, George Sisler posted a .340 lifetime average, hit safely in 41 consecutive games in 1922 and set a major mark by collecting 257 hits for the St. Louis Browns in 1920.

Babe Ruth (left) and Ty Cobb, two of the game's foremost gate attractions, were photographed in the mid-1920s, when Ruth was the reigning home run king and Cobb the fading monarch of base-hitting and base-stealing.

Eddie Collins, the American League's MVP in 1914, compiled a .333 batting average during a 25-year career with Philadelphia and Chicago, led the league four times in steals and set an A.L. mark with six in one game.

Lou Gehrig, renowned as the Iron Horse of the Yankees for playing 2,130 consecutive games, set an A.L. record with 184 RBIs in 1931 and clouted four consecutive homers on June 3, 1932.

Chick Hafey, bespectacled outfielder with the Cardinals and Reds, had a major league batting average of .317 and set a World Series record in 1930 with five doubles in the Cardinals' six-game set against the Philadelphia A's.

Gabby Hartnett, the National League's Most Valuable Player in 1935, caught 100 or more games in 12 seasons. He also gained recognition for his five assists in the Cubs' four-game World Series against the Yankees in 1932.

Jimmie Foxx, twice an American League MVP with Philadelphia and once with Boston, clouted 534 major league home runs, including 58 with the Athletics in 1932.

Bill Klem, famous Old Arbitrator of the National League, called 'em from 1905 through '40, and set a record by appearing in 16 World Series, eight more than any other umpire.

Hall of Famers Wilbert Robinson, John McGraw and Christy Mathewson figured in the New York Giants' N.L. championships in 1911-12-13, Robinson as coach, McGraw as manager, and Matty as star hurler.

Two-time MVP in the National League, Willie Mays hit 660 home runs, posted a .302 bat mark and was the first major leaguer to hit 50 homers and steal 20 bases in the same season.

Jerome (Dizzy) Dean, colorful right-hander of the St. Louis Cardinals, won five consecutive N.L. strikeout titles and won 30 games for the World Champion Redbirds of 1934.

Honus Wagner, generally regarded as baseball's all-time premier shortstop, batted .300 or better 17 consecutive seasons, won eight batting crowns and five stolen base titles as the famous Flying Dutchman of the Pittsburgh Pirates.

Connie Mack, the Grand Old Man of Baseball before his death at 93, managed the Philadelphia Athletics for 50 years, from 1901 through 1950, and produced eight American League pennants. Two of his brightest luminaries on his flag-winning teams of 1929-31 were catcher Mickey Cochrane (below, left), a .320 lifetime hitter, and pitcher Lefty Grove, who won 31 games in 1931 and 300 in his career.

Joe Cronin, a .302 lifetime hitter, led Washington to a pennant in 1933 and established a major league record by hitting five pinch home runs as a playing manager for the Boston Red Sox in 1943.

Frank Frisch, wearing the uniform of the first (1933) All-Star Game, batted .316 during a 19-year major league career and gained distinction as manager of St. Louis' colorful Gashouse Gang of the mid-1930s.

Twice an N.L. MVP, Carl Hubbell helped pitch the New York Giants to pennants in 1933, '36 and '37, using his screwball to win 20 games in five successive seasons and strike out five batters in a row in the 1934 All-Star Game.

Joe DiMaggio, a .325 hitter in 13 years with the Yankees, was named Most Valuable Player in the American League in 1939, '41 and '47, appeared in 10 World Series and achieved his greatest distinction in 1941 when he hit safely in 56 consecutive games, a major league record.

Famed strikeout pitcher Bob Feller hurled three no-hit games, including the season opener in 1940, and pitched 12 one-hit contests, one of which he lost, during an illustrious career with the Cleveland Indians that produced six 20-victory seasons and a lifetime strikeout total of 2,581.

Ted Williams, the majors' most recent .400 hitter, with a .406 average in 1941, won six A.L. batting championships, four home run titles and four RBI championships, as well as two MVPs, during his career with the Red Sox.

A three-time National League MVP, Stan Musial compiled a lifetime average of .331, set a major league record with five home runs in a doubleheader in 1954 and was named Player of the Decade by THE SPORTING NEWS IN 1956.

The first black player in the modern major leagues, Jackie Robinson earned MVP honors with Brooklyn in 1949 when he won the N.L. batting title. He is one of 11 players to steal home in a World Series game (1955).

Leroy (Satchel) Paige made his major league debut with the 1948 Cleveland Indians at age 42 and pitched in his last big league game with Kansas City in 1965, six years before entering the Hall of Fame.

Roy Campanella won three MVP Awards with Brooklyn and set records for catchers by hitting 41 home runs in 1953 and driving in 142 runs the same season. A crippling auto accident terminated his career after the '57 season.

Mickey Mantle, being greeted by Yogi Berra in a Hall of Fame game at Cooperstown, N.Y., hit 536 home runs for the Yanks, and set a record by hitting two homers in a game, one lefthanded and one righthanded, 10 times.

Two-time MVP in the National League, Ernie Banks set a major record for shortstops by hitting 47 home runs for the Cubs in 1958 and set another mark for most consecutive games from the start of a major league career, 424.

Roberto Clemente, who collected 3,000 hits and posted a .317 average in 18-year career with the Pirates that produced one MVP Award, was killed in a 1972 plane crash while taking supplies to earthquake victims in Nicaragua.

Winner of three Cy Young Awards and author of four no-hitters for Dodgers, Sandy Koufax was forced into early retirement by an elbow ailment at age 30 following 1966 season in which he captured his fifth straight ERA title.

The majors' all-time home run king, (755), Henry Aaron also holds major records for games, at-bats and most years 100 or more runs scored during a 23-year career that included one MVP Award, with Milwaukee in 1957.

EDWIN J. McKEAN

Born June 20, 1864, at Cleveland, O.
Died August 16, 1919, at Cleveland, O.
Height, 5.09. Weight, 180.
Threw and batted righthanded.

Year	Club	League	Pos.	G.	AB.	R.	H.	2B.	3B.	HR.	SB.	B.A.	PO.	A.	E.	F.A.
1884	Youngstown	I&O Assn.					(No Record Available)									
1885	....						(No Record Available)									
1886	Providence	East.	SS	22	98	16	25	...	...	...	....	.255	33	91	20	.861
1886	Rochester	Int.	SS	77	324	....	100	...	...	...	...	.309	115	221	48	*.875
1887	Cleveland	A. A.	SS	132	593	95	216	16	13	2	77	.364	(588-PO-A)		102	.852
1888	Cleveland	A. A.	SS-O	130	542	92	161	23	13	6	66	.297	(418-PO-A)		50	.893
1889	Cleveland	Nat.	SS	123	500	86	151	22	8	4	35	.302	206	398	62	.907
1890	Cleveland	Nat.	SS	136	530	91	157	20	12	7	23	.296	266	433	*75	.903
1891	Cleveland	Nat.	SS	141	*602	114	169	17	13	6	15	.281	249	470	*86	.893
1892	Cleveland	Nat.	SS	128	523	75	141	15	10	0	19	.270	201	371	84	.872
1893	Cleveland	Nat.	SS	125	510	100	166	26	23	4	15	.325	245	437	71	.906
1894	Cleveland	Nat.	SS	130	561	115	199	29	16	8	32	.355	278	401	66	.911
1895	Cleveland	Nat.	SS	132	*573	131	197	26	17	7	16	.344	256	433	67	.977
1896	Cleveland	Nat.	SS	133	567	100	190	28	10	8	13	.335	220	398	58	.914
1897	Cleveland	Nat.	SS	127	527	86	144	21	14	3	18	.273	231	381	50	.924
1898	Cleveland	Nat.	SS	151	604	88	172	21	1	9	10	.285	299	429	56	.929
1899	St. Louis	Nat.	SS	67	270	40	76	6	2	3	3	.281	71	124	25	.886
	American Association Totals			262	1135	187	377	39	26	8	143	.332	(1006-PO-A)		152	.869
	National League Totals			1393	5767	1026	1762	231	126	59	199	.307	2522	4274	700	.907
	Major League Totals			1655	6902	1213	2139	270	152	67	342	.310	(7802-PO-A)		852	.902

WILLIAM BOYD (DEACON) McKECHNIE

Born August 7, 1887, at Wilkinsburg, Pa.
Died October 29, 1965, at Bradenton, Fla.
Height, 5.10. Weight, 180.
Threw right and batted left and righthanded.
Married Beryl Bien, June 15, 1911.
Son, William B. McKechnie, Jr., was president of the
Pacific Coast League, 1968-1973.

Name by THE SPORTING NEWS as No. 1 Major League Manager of the Year, 1937 and 1940.
Managed National League championship clubs in three cities, Pittsburgh, 1925; St. Louis, 1928, and Cincinnati, 1939 and 1940. Coach, St. Louis Cardinals, 1927; Cleveland Indians, 1947-48-49.
Named to Hall of Fame, 1962.

Year	Club	League	Pos.	G.	AB.	R.	H.	2B.	3B.	HR.	RBI.	B.A.	PO.	A.	E.	F.A.
1906	Washington	P.-O.-Md.					(Records not available)									
1907	Washington	P.-O.-Md.	3B	53	185	22	37	....	....	....	....	.200	70	99	13	.929
1907	Pittsburgh	Nat.	2B-3B	3	8	0	1	0	0	0	1	.125	1	3	0	1.000
1908	Canton	Ohio-Pa.	3B	118	406	55	115	....	....	....	....	.283	155	317	29	.942
1909	Wheeling	Central	3B	132	464	55	127	16	7	1	....	.274	163	279	33	.931
1910	Pittsburgh	Nat.	2B	60	212	23	46	1	2	0	17	.217	89	112	6	.971
1911	Pittsburgh	Nat.	2B-1B	92	321	40	73	8	7	2	36	.227	573	80	17	.975
1912	Pittsburgh	Nat.	INF	24	73	8	18	0	1	0	3	.247	19	41	3	.952
1912	St. Paul	A. A.	SS	41	158	22	37	7	3	1	....	.234	88	123	12	.946
1913	Boston(a)	Nat.	OF	1	4	1	0	0	0	0	0	.000	3	0	0	1.000
1913	New York	Amer.	2B	44	112	7	15	0	0	0	0	.134	57	76	7	.950
1913	St. Paul	A. A.	3B	32	110	11	27	0	6	0	6	.245	31	47	2	.975
1914	Indianapolis	Federal	3B	149	571	107	174	22	6	2	....	.305	193	326	32	.942
1915	Newark	Federal	3B	126	448	49	115	22	5	1	....	.257	182	226	19	.956
1916	N.Y.(b)-Cin.	Nat.	3B	108	390	26	100	12	0	0	30	.256	108	193	17	.947
1917	Cincinnati(c)	Nat.	2B	48	134	11	34	3	1	0	14	.254	49	51	6	.943
1918	Pittsburgh	Nat.	3B	126	435	34	111	13	9	2	46	.255	162	261	15	.966
1919	....						(On Voluntarily Retired List)									

Year	Club	League	Pos.	G.	AB.	R.	H.	2B.	3B.	HR.	RBI.	B.A.	PO.	A.	E.	F.A.
1920–Pittsburgh		Nat.	INF	40	133	13	29	3	1	1	13	.218	85	84	8	.955
1921–Minneapolis		A. A.	3B	156	661	140	212	31	7	8	65	.321	189	284	25	.950
American League Totals				44	112	7	15	0	0	0	0	.134	57	76	7	.950
National League Totals				502	1710	156	412	40	22	5	160	.241	1089	825	72	.964
Major League Totals				546	1822	163	427	40	22	5	160	.234	1146	901	79	.963

aDrafted by Boston Braves, September, 1912; claimed on waivers by New York Yankees, April, 1913.
bTraded with pitcher Christy Mathewson and outfielder Edd Roush to Cincinnati for infielder Charles Herzog and outfielder Wade Killefer, July 20, 1916.
cSold to Pittsburgh, March, 1918.

JOHN JOSEPH (SADIE) McMAHON

Born September 19, 1867, at Wilmington, Del.
Died February 20, 1954, at Delaware City, Del.
Height, 5.09. Weight, 185.
Threw and batted righthanded.
Married Nora Falsey, January 25, 1895.

Scout, New York Giants, 1911-25.

Year	Club	League	G.	IP.	W.	L.	Pct.	H.	R.	SO.	BB.	CG.	ShO.
1889–Philadelphia		Amer. Assn.	30	255	16	12	.571	265	174	109	104	29	2
1890–Phil.-Balt.		Amer. Assn.	*59	*507	*36	21	.632	500	281	278	165	*54	1
1891–Baltimore		Amer. Assn.	61	*510	•34	25	.578	490	256	203	145	*53	•5
1892–Baltimore		National	48	400	20	25	.444	433	264	123	146	44	2
1893–Baltimore		National	43	348	24	16	.600	372	225	67	146	35	0
1894–Baltimore		National	35	279	25	8	.758	311	173	55	109	25	0
1895–Baltimore		National	15	123	10	4	.714	110	54	36	31	15	•4
1896–Baltimore(a)		National	20	163	12	8	.600	190	100	33	48	17	0
1897–Brooklyn		National	9	64	0	5	.000	74	53	13	29	5	0
American Association Totals			150	1272	86	58	.597	1255	711	590	414	136	8
National League Totals			170	1377	91	66	.580	1490	869	327	509	141	6
Major League Totals			320	2649	177	124	.588	2745	1580	917	923	277	14

aUnconditionally released, October 12, 1897.

ROY DAVID McMILLAN

Born July 17, 1930, at Bonham, Tex.
Height, 5.11. Weight, 164.
Threw and batted righthanded.
Married Joan Lawrence, October 26, 1952.

Established National League record for most consecutive games, shortstop (584), September 16, 1951 (first game) to August 6, 1955. Tied National League record for most years leading shortstops in games played (6), 1952, 1953, 1954 (tied), 1956, 1957, 1961.
Led National League shortstops in double plays with 114 in 1953, 129 in 1954, 111 in 1955 and 105 in 1956.
Received Rawlings Gold Glove Award as outstanding major league fielder at shortstop, 1957; named for Gold Glove Award as outstanding National League fielder at shortstop, 1958-59.
Playing coach, Jacksonville, International League, 1967; non-playing manager, Visalia, California League, 1968; manager, Memphis, Texas League, 1969; coach, Seattle, 1970 and moved with transferred club to Milwaukee, 1971-72; coach, New York Mets, 1973-76; manager, Visalia, California League, 1977-78; manager, Orlando, Southern League, 1978-80.

Year	Club	League	Pos.	G.	AB.	R.	H.	2B.	3B.	HR.	RBI.	B.A.	PO.	A.	E.	F.A.
1947–Tyler		Lone Star	SS	17	54	6	7	0	0	0	6	.130	22	37	7	.894
1947–Ballinger		Long Horn	SS	107	459	90	126	23	2	3	49	.275	*186	*410	54	*.916
1948–Tyler		Lone Star	SS	•140	*599	127	184	35	10	3	57	.307	*264	*509	63	.925
1949–Tulsa		Tex.	SS	3	5	0	0	0	0	0	0	.000	1	6	0	1.000
1949–Columbia		Sally	SS	115	431	63	100	20	1	2	46	.232	222	387	42	.935
1950–Tulsa		Tex.	SS	142	562	73	154	31	2	3	51	.274	253	*481	38	.951
1951–Cincinnati		Nat.	INF	85	199	21	42	4	0	1	8	.211	92	160	9	.966
1952–Cincinnati		Nat.	SS	•154	540	60	132	32	2	7	57	.244	297	*495	24	.971
1953–Cincinnati		Nat.	SS	155	557	51	130	15	4	5	43	.233	288	*519	23	.972

Year	Club	League	Pos.	G.	AB.	R.	H.	2B.	3B.	HR.	RBI.	B.A.	PO.	A.	E.	F.A.
1954—Cincinnati		Nat.	SS	•154	588	86	147	21	2	4	42	.250	★341	464	34	.959
1955—Cincinnati		Nat.	SS	151	470	50	126	21	2	1	37	.268	290	495	25	.969
1956—Cincinnati		Nat.	SS	150	479	51	126	16	7	3	62	.263	★319	★511	21	★.975
1957—Cincinnati		Nat.	SS	151	448	50	122	25	5	1	55	.272	253	418	16	★.977
1958—Cincinnati		Nat.	SS	145	393	48	90	18	3	1	25	.229	278	394	14	★.980
1959—Cincinnati		Nat.	SS	79	246	38	65	14	2	9	24	.264	163	205	10	.974
1960—Cincinnati(a)		Nat.	SS-2B	124	399	42	94	12	2	10	42	.236	174	329	19	.964
1961—Milwaukee		Nat.	SS	154	505	42	111	16	0	7	48	.220	★257	★496	19	★.975
1962—Milwaukee		Nat.	SS	137	468	66	115	13	0	12	41	.246	243	424	19	.972
1963—Milwaukee		Nat.	SS	100	320	35	80	10	1	4	29	.250	143	283	9	.979
1964—Mil.(b)-N.Y.		Nat.	SS	121	392	31	84	8	2	1	27	.214	224	360	15	.975
1965—New York		Nat.	SS	157	528	44	128	19	2	1	42	.242	284	477	27	.964
1966—New York		Nat.	SS	76	220	24	47	9	1	1	12	.214	112	203	8	.975
Major League Totals				2093	6752	739	1639	253	35	68	594	.243	3722	6233	292	.971

aTraded to Milwaukee Braves for pitchers Joey Jay and Juan Pizarro, December 15, 1960.

bTraded to New York Mets for pitcher Jay Hook, a player to be named later and cash, May 8, 1964; Hook was assigned to Denver. Outfielder Adrian Garrett was assigned to Milwaukee Braves' organization, June 17, to complete deal.

DAVID ARTHUR McNALLY

Born October 31, 1942, at Billings, Mont.
Height, 5.11. Weight, 195.
Threw left and batted righthanded.

Tied American League records for most consecutive games won, league, 17, September 22, 1968 through July 30, 1969, and most consecutive games won, start of season, 15, April 12 through July 30, 1969. Named pitcher on THE SPORTING NEWS American League All-Star Team, 1968.

Year	Club	League	G.	IP.	W.	L.	Pct.	H.	R.	ER.	SO.	BB.	ERA.
1961—Victoria		Tex.	4	19	0	3	.000	18	18	13	19	18	6.16
1961—Fox Cities		I. I. I.	25	140	8	10	.444	123	78	65	155	96	4.18
1962—Elmira		East.	34	196	15	11	.577	153	82	67	195	★115	3.08
1962—Baltimore		Amer.	1	9	1	0	1.000	2	0	0	4	3	0.00
1963—Baltimore		Amer.	29	126	7	8	.467	133	67	64	78	55	4.57
1964—Baltimore		Amer.	30	159	9	11	.450	157	72	65	88	51	3.68
1965—Baltimore		Amer.	35	199	11	6	.647	163	69	63	116	73	2.85
1966—Baltimore		Amer.	34	213	13	6	.684	212	91	75	158	64	3.17
1967—Baltimore		Amer.	24	119	7	7	.500	134	65	60	70	39	4.54
1968—Baltimore		Amer.	35	273	22	10	.688	175	67	59	202	55	1.95
1969—Baltimore		Amer.	41	269	20	7	.741	232	103	96	166	84	3.21
1970—Baltimore		Amer.	40	296	•24	9	.727	★277	114	106	185	78	3.22
1971—Baltimore		Amer.	30	224	21	5	★.808	188	75	72	91	58	2.89
1972—Baltimore		Amer.	36	241	13	17	.433	220	85	79	120	68	2.95
1973—Baltimore		Amer.	38	266	17	17	.500	247	100	95	87	81	3.21
1974—Baltimore(a)		Amer.	39	259	16	10	.615	260	112	103	111	81	3.58
1975—Montreal(b)		Nat.	12	77	3	6	.333	88	50	45	36	36	5.26
American League Totals			412	2653	181	113	.616	2400	1020	937	1476	790	3.18
National League Totals			12	77	3	6	.333	88	50	45	36	36	5.26
Major League Totals			424	2730	184	119	.607	2488	1070	982	1512	826	3.24

aTraded with outfielder Rich Coggins and pitcher Bill Kirkpatrick to Montreal Expos for outfielder Ken Singleton and pitcher Mike Torrez, December 4, 1974.

bPlaced on disqualified list, June 9, 1975. Reinstated and granted free agency, March 16, 1976.

WORLD SERIES RECORD

Year	Club	League	G.	IP.	W.	L.	Pct.	H.	R.	ER.	SO.	BB.	ERA.
1966—Baltimore		Amer.	2	11⅓	1	0	1.000	6	2	2	5	7	1.59
1969—Baltimore		Amer.	2	16	0	1	.000	11	5	5	13	5	2.81
1970—Baltimore		Amer.	1	9	1	0	1.000	9	3	3	5	2	3.00
1971—Baltimore		Amer.	4	13⅔	2	1	.667	10	7	3	12	5	1.98
World Series Totals			9	50	4	2	.667	36	17	13	35	19	2.34

DID YOU KNOW—

That Dave McNally is the only pitcher to hit a World Series grand slam?

JOHN ALEXANDER (BIDDY) McPHEE

Born November 1, 1859, at Massena, N. Y.
Died January 3, 1942, at San Diego, Calif.
Height, 5.10. Weight, 165.
Threw and batted righthanded.

Hit three triples in one game, June 28, 1890, vs. New York.
Rated by peers as outstanding second baseman in pre-1900 period.
Manager, Cincinnati, 1901-02; scout, Cincinnati, 1903-09.

Year	Club	League	Pos.	G.	AB.	R.	H.	2B.	3B.	HR.	SB.	B.A.	PO.	A.	E.	F.A.
1879	Davenport	N. W.					(No Records Available)									
1880	Akron	Indep. Club					(No Records Available)									
1881	Akron	Indep. Club					(No Records Available)									
1882	Cincinnati	A. A.	2B	78	321	44	70	7	7	1	....	.218	*274	214	42	*.921
1883	Cincinnati	A. A.	2B	96	366	61	89	13	10	2	....	.243	(588-PO-A)	52		*.919
1884	Cincinnati	A. A.	2B	113	462	106	135	10	7	5	....	.292	(878-PO-A)	64		.925
1885	Cincinnati	A. A.	2B	110	440	77	121	14	5	0	....	.275	(608-PO-A)	51		.923
1886	Cincinnati	A. A.	2B	140	562	139	153	24	11	*8	59	.272	(985-PO-A)	58		*.944
1887	Cincinnati	A. A.	2B	129	593	132	210	21	18	2	96	.354	(509-PO-A)	40		.927
1888	Cincinnati	A. A.	2B	110	452	86	104	11	4	4	53	.230	(728-PO-A)	48		.938
1889	Cincinnati	A. A.	2-3B	135	543	110	146	23	7	5	66	.269	432	*453	39	*.958
1890	Cincinnati	Nat.	2B	132	538	124	135	22	*25	3	55	.256	*404	*431	51	.942
1891	Cincinnati	Nat.	2B	138	555	108	143	15	14	6	34	.258	389	*481	36	*.960
1892	Cincinnati	Nat.	2B	144	573	110	169	18	14	4	43	.295	*454	484	45	.954
1893	Cincinnati	Nat.	2B	127	468	102	144	14	11	4	31	.308	*387	445	42	.952
1894	Cincinnati	Nat.	2B	128	481	113	154	19	9	5	31	.320	*391	449	53	.941
1895	Cincinnati	Nat.	2B	114	434	107	129	29	10	1	28	.297	354	365	38	.950
1896	Cincinnati	Nat.	2B	116	434	81	130	18	7	0	53	.300	299	358	12	*.982
1897	Cincinnati	Nat.	2B	80	277	45	85	13	5	0	10	.307	205	269	17	.965
1898	Cincinnati	Nat.	2B	131	488	71	120	23	9	1	23	.246	298	387	32	.955
1899	Cincinnati	Nat.	2B	106	371	58	105	15	7	1	20	.283	240	311	24	*.958
	American Association Totals			911	3739	755	1028	123	69	27	274	.275	(5669-PO-A)	394		.935
	National League Totals			1216	4609	919	1314	186	111	25	328	.285	3421	3980	350	.956
	Major League Totals			2127	8348	1674	2342	309	180	52	602	.281	(13070-PO-A)	744		.946

WORLD SERIES RECORD

Year	Club	League	Pos.	G.	AB.	R.	H.	2B.	3B.	HR.	SB.	B.A.	PO.	A.	E.	F.A.
1882	Cincinnati	A. A.	2B	2	7	1	3	0	1	0	....	.429	6	2	0	1.000

HENRY LEE (SPECS) MEADOWS

Born July 12, 1894, at Oxford, N. C.
Died January 29, 1963, at Daytona Beach, Fla.
Height, 6.00. Weight, 170.
Threw right and batted lefthanded.
Married Catherine Woolworth, March 1, 1917.

Manager, Leesburg, Florida State League, 1937; Deland, Florida State, 1939. Wore glasses as player.

Year	Club	League	G.	IP.	W.	L.	Pct.	H.	R.	ER.	SO.	BB.	ERA.
1912	Morristown	Appy.					(Less Than Four Games)						
1913	Durham	N. Car.	39	292	21	14	.600	223	86	....	184	68	......
1914	Durham	N. Car.	46	285	19	12	.613	202	77	....	195	87	......
1915	St. Louis	Nat.	39	244	13	11	.542	232	112	81	104	88	2.99
1916	St. Louis	Nat.	*51	289	12	*23	.343	261	117	83	120	119	2.58
1917	St. Louis	Nat.	43	266	15	9	.625	253	99	91	100	90	3.08
1918	St. Louis	Nat.	30	165	8	14	.364	176	91	66	49	56	3.60
1919	St. Louis(a)-Phila.	Nat.	40	241	12	*20	.375	228	99	72	116	79	2.69
1920	Philadelphia	Nat.	35	247	16	14	.533	249	104	78	95	90	2.84
1921	Philadelphia	Nat.	28	194	11	16	.407	226	118	93	52	62	4.31
1922	Philadelphia	Nat.	33	237	12	18	.400	264	127	106	62	71	4.03
1923	Phila.(b)-Pitts.	Nat.	39	247	17	13	.567	290	129	105	76	59	3.83
1924	Pittsburgh	Nat.	36	229	13	12	.520	240	99	83	61	51	3.26

Year	Club	League	G.	IP	W.	L.	Pct.	H.	R.	ER.	SO.	BB.	ERA.
1925	Pittsburgh	Nat.	35	255	19	10	.655	272	128	104	87	67	3.67
1926	Pittsburgh	Nat.	36	227	•20	9	.690	254	125	100	54	52	3.96
1927	Pittsburgh	Nat.	40	299	19	10	.655	*315	131	113	84	66	3.40
1928	Pittsburgh	Nat.	4	10	1	1	.500	18	11	9	3	5	8.10
1929	Pittsburgh	Nat.	1	1	0	0	.000	2	1	1	0	1	9.00
1929	Indianapolis	A. A.	7	45	1	5	.167	67	38	25	13	13	5.00
1929	Newark	Int.	10	68	2	7	.222	86	47	39	16	27	5.16
1930	Atlanta	South.	10	54	3	5	.375	76	39	32	22	22	5.33
1930	Dallas	Texas	24	126	9	7	.563	165	88	64	60	45	4.57
1931	Dallas	Texas	16	88	4	6	.400	101	46	36	43	20	3.68
1932	Durham	Pied.	2	10	1	0	1.000	9	3	3	2	3	2.70
	Major League Totals		490	3151	188	180	.511	3280	1491	1185	1063	956	3.38

aTraded with first baseman Gene Paulette to Philadelphia Phillies for pitchers Elmer Jacobs and Frank Woodward and third baseman Doug Baird, July 14, 1919.

bTraded with infielder John Rawlings to Pittsburgh Pirates for pitcher Charles (Whitey) Glazner and infielder James (Cotton) Tierney, May 22, 1923.

WORLD SERIES RECORD

Year	Club	League	G.	IP	W.	L.	Pct.	H.	R.	ER.	SO.	BB.	ERA.
1925	Pittsburgh	Nat.	1	8	0	1	.000	6	3	3	4	0	3.38
1927	Pittsburgh	Nat.	1	6⅓	0	1	.000	7	7	7	6	1	9.95
	World Series Totals		2	14⅓	0	2	.000	13	10	10	10	1	6.28

JOSEPH MICHAEL (DUCKY) MEDWICK

Born November 24, 1911, at Carteret, N. J.
Died March 21, 1975, at St. Petersburg, Fla.
Height, 5.10. Weight, 178.
Threw and batted righthanded.
Married Isabelle Heutel, August 24, 1936.

Equaled National League record by getting ten hits in succession, July 19 (2 games) and July 21, 1936. Established league mark for most two-base hits in season, 64 (1936), and tied record with four two-base hits in game, August 4, 1937. Hit for the cycle, June 29, 1935. Four long hits, game—May 30, 1935 (first game), May 12, 1937, August 4, 1937. Hit 40 or more doubles seven consecutive years, 1933-39; tied major mark leading league in RBIs three consecutive seasons—1936-37-38. Named by Baseball Writers' Association of America for THE SPORTING NEWS All-Star Major League Teams, 1935-36-37-38-39. Named Most Valuable Player in National League, 1937.

Manager, Miami Beach, Florida International League, 1949; manager, Raleigh, Carolina League, 1951; manager, Tampa, Florida International League, 1952; farm system hitting instructor, St. Louis Cardinals, 1966 to 1975 at time of death; was Cardinals scout in 1971. Also served as assistant baseball coach at St. Louis University, 1961-65.

Named to Hall of Fame, 1968.

Year	Club	League	Pos.	G.	AB.	R.	H.	2B.	3B.	HR.	RBI.	B.A.	PO.	A.	E.	F.A.
1930	Scottsdale	Mid. Atl.	OF	75	332	75	139	18	13	22	100	.419	159	26	5	.974
1931	Houston	Texas	OF	*161	616	99	188	47	*19	*126	.305	307	16	6	.982
1932	Houston	Texas	OF-3B	139	560	113	198	46	10	26	111	.354	320	52	6	*.984
1932	St. Louis	Nat.	OF	26	106	13	37	12	1	2	12	.349	63	2	2	.970
1933	St. Louis	Nat.	OF	148	595	92	182	40	10	18	98	.306	318	17	7	.980
1934	St. Louis	Nat.	OF	149	620	110	198	40	*18	18	106	.319	322	10	*14	.960
1935	St. Louis	Nat.	OF	154	634	132	224	46	13	23	126	.353	352	8	13	.965
1936	St. Louis	Nat.	OF	155	636	115	*223	*64	13	18	*138	.351	367	16	6	.985
1937	St. Louis	Nat.	OF	*156	*633	*111	*237	*56	10	•31	*154	*.374	329	9	4	*.988
1938	St. Louis	Nat.	OF	146	590	100	190	*47	8	21	*122	.322	330	12	9	.974
1939	St. Louis	Nat.	OF	150	606	98	201	48	8	14	117	.332	313	10	8	.976
1940	St. L.(a)-Brook.	Nat.	OF	143	581	83	175	30	12	17	86	.301	321	8	6	.982
1941	Brooklyn	Nat.	OF	133	538	100	171	33	10	18	88	.318	270	11	5	.983
1942	Brooklyn	Nat.	OF	142	553	69	166	37	4	4	96	.300	287	5	3	.990
1943	Brook.(b)-N.Y.	Nat.	OF-1B	126	497	54	138	30	3	5	70	.278	221	12	7	.971
1944	New York	Nat.	OF	128	490	64	165	24	3	7	85	.337	290	8	2	.993
1945	N.Y.(c)-Bos.(d)	Nat.	OF-1B	92	310	31	90	17	0	3	37	.290	248	11	1	.996
1946	Brooklyn(e)	Nat.	OF-1B	41	77	7	24	4	0	2	18	.312	38	0	2	.950
1947	St. Louis(f)	Nat.	OF	75	150	19	46	12	0	4	28	.307	56	3	0	1.000
1948	St. Louis	Nat.	OF	20	19	0	4	0	0	0	2	.211	0	0	0	.000
1948	Houston	Texas	OF	35	87	8	24	7	0	2	20	.276	33	1	0	1.000
1949	Miami Beach	Fla. Int.	OF	106	375	53	121	19	6	10	72	.323	174	8	3	.984
1951	Raleigh	Carolina	OF	60	158	22	45	8	2	4	33	.285	53	4	4	.934
1952	Tampa	Fla. Int.	PH	11	9	0	3	2	1	0	6	.333	0	0	0	.000
	Major League Totals			1984	7635	1198	2471	540	113	205	1383	.324	4125	142	89	.980

aTraded with pitcher Curt Davis to Brooklyn for pitchers Carl Doyle and Sam Nahem, outfielder Ernie Koy and infielder-outfielder Berthold Haas and $125,000, June 12, 1940.

bSold to New York Giants, July 6, 1943.
cTraded to Boston Braves with pitcher Ewald Pyle for catcher Clyde Kluttz, June 14, 1945.
dUnconditionally released by Boston Braves, February 8, 1946, and signed with St. Louis Browns, March 3, 1946, and released, April 5, 1946; signed with Brooklyn Dodgers, June 28, 1946.
eUnconditionally released by Brooklyn Dodgers, October 9, 1946, and signed with New York Yankees, January, 1947; released, April 29, 1947, and signed by St. Louis Cardinals.
fUnconditionally released by St. Louis Cardinals, October 10, 1947, and re-signed April 29, 1948.

WORLD SERIES RECORD

Year	Club	League	Pos.	G.	AB.	R.	H.	2B.	3B.	HR.	RBI.	B.A.	PO.	A.	E.	F.A.
1934	St. Louis	Nat.	OF	7	29	4	11	0	1	1	5	.379	9	0	0	1.000
1941	Brooklyn	Nat.	OF	5	17	1	4	1	0	0	0	.235	8	0	0	1.000
World Series Totals				12	46	5	15	1	1	1	5	.326	17	0	0	1.000

EMIL FREDERICK (IRISH) MEUSEL

Born June 9, 1893, at Oakland, Calif.
Died March 1, 1963, at Long Beach, Calif.
Height, 6.00. Weight, 180.
Threw and batted righthanded.
Brother of Bob Meusel, former New York Yankee outfielder.

Coach, New York Giants, 1930.

Year	Club	League	Pos.	G.	AB.	R.	H.	2B.	3B.	HR.	RBI.	B.A.	PO.	A.	E.	F.A.
1913	Fresno	Calif.	OF	123	464	58	142	24	11	5	....	.306	240	*26	11	.960
1913	Los Angeles(a)	P. C.	OF	15	53	8	15	3	0	1	....	.283	42	3	6	.882
1914	Elmira	N. Y. St.	OF	126	483	86	156	....	....	....	....	.323	228	8	12	.952
1914	Washington	Amer.	OF	1	2	0	0	0	0	0	0	.000	1	0	0	1.000
1915	Los Angeles	P. C.	OF	6	11	....	4	0	0	0	....	.364	5	2	0	1.000
1915	Elmira	N.Y. St.	OF	122	490	83	160	....	....	....	....	.327	237	27	12	.957
1916	Birmingham(b)	South.	OF	113	414	57	129	17	12	2	....	.312	229	18	8	.969
1917	Los Angeles(c)	P. C.	OF	210	811	121	252	46	9	7	....	.311	352	*44	17	.959
1918	Philadelphia	Nat.	OF-2B	124	473	48	132	25	6	4	59	.279	296	14	9	.972
1919	Philadelphia	Nat.	OF	135	521	65	159	26	7	5	58	.305	256	14	9	.968
1920	Philadelphia	Nat.	OF	138	518	75	160	27	8	14	69	.309	260	16	21	.929
1921	Phila.(d)-N.Y.	Nat.	OF	146	586	96	201	33	13	14	87	.343	275	28	17	.947
1922	New York	Nat.	OF	154	617	100	204	28	17	16	132	.331	279	15	6	.980
1923	New York	Nat.	OF	146	595	102	177	22	14	19	*125	.297	268	10	15	.949
1924	New York	Nat.	OF	139	549	75	170	26	9	6	102	.310	287	4	10	.967
1925	New York	Nat.	OF	135	516	82	169	35	8	21	111	.328	244	16	11	.959
1926	New York(e)	Nat.	OF	129	449	51	131	25	10	6	65	.292	197	10	9	.958
1927	Brooklyn	Nat.	OF	42	74	7	18	3	1	1	7	.243	28	2	0	1.000
1927	Toledo	A. A.	OF	47	158	27	56	12	2	3	28	.354	56	4	5	.923
1928	Oakland	P. C.	OF	108	374	50	100	25	5	11	65	.267	204	11	6	.973
1929	Sacramento	P. C.	OF	44	153	22	50	6	3	2	21	.327	124	1	2	.984
1931	Omaha	West.	OF	7	20	....	3	2	0	0	....	.150	9	1	0	1.000
American League Totals				1	2	0	0	0	0	0	0	.000	1	0	0	1.000
National League Totals				1288	4898	701	1521	250	93	106	815	.310	2390	129	107	.959
Major League Totals				1289	4900	701	1521	250	93	106	815	.310	2391	129	107	.959

aDrafted by Washington Senators, February, 1914; optioned to Elmira, April, 1914, and recalled by Washington, September, 1914.
bDrafted by Chicago Cubs, September, 1916, and released to Los Angeles, March, 1917.
cDrafted by Philadelphia Phillies, September, 1917.
dTraded to New York Giants for catcher Walter (Butch) Henline, pitcher Jesse Winters and outfielder Curtis Walker and $30,000, July 25, 1921.
eReleased unconditionally by New York Giants, October, 1926, and signed by Brooklyn Dodgers, February, 1927.

WORLD SERIES RECORD

Year	Club	League	Pos.	G.	AB.	R.	H.	2B.	3B.	HR.	RBI.	B.A.	PO.	A.	E.	F.A.
1921	New York	Nat.	OF	8	29	4	10	2	1	1	7	.345	8	2	0	1.000
1922	New York	Nat.	OF	5	20	3	5	0	1	0	7	.250	3	0	0	1.000
1923	New York	Nat.	OF	6	25	3	7	1	1	2	.280	13	0	0	1.000
1924	New York	Nat.	OF	4	13	0	2	0	0	0	1	.154	5	0	1	.833
World Series Totals				23	87	10	24	3	2	3	17	.276	29	2	1	.969

DID YOU KNOW–

That the Meusel brothers were World Series rivals for three straight years?

ROBERT WILLIAM (BOB) MEUSEL

Born July 19, 1898, at San Jose, Calif.
Died November 28, 1977, at Downey, Calif.
Height, 6.03. Weight, 190.
Threw and batted righthanded.
Brother of Emil Meusel, former National League outfielder.

Year	Club	League	Pos.	G.	AB.	R.	H.	2B.	3B.	HR.	RBI.	B.A.	PO.	A.	E.	F.A.
1917	Vernon	P. C.	OF	45	164	16	51	11	3	0	....	.311	362	25	9	.977
1918	Vernon	P. C.	OF	2	8	2	3	3	0	0	....	.375	5	0	0	1.000
1919	Vernon	P. C.	3B-OF	163	655	113	221	39	14	14	....	.337	222	213	33	.929
1920	New York	Amer.	O-3B	119	460	75	151	40	7	11	83	.328	150	85	20	.922
1921	New York	Amer.	OF	149	598	104	190	40	16	24	135	.318	253	•28	20	.934
1922	New York	Amer.	OF	121	473	61	151	26	11	16	84	.319	202	*24	12	.950
1923	New York	Amer.	OF	132	460	59	144	29	10	9	91	.313	206	17	11	.953
1924	New York	Amer.	OF	143	579	93	188	40	11	12	120	.325	252	17	14	.951
1925	New York	Amer.	OF	*156	624	101	181	34	12	*33	*138	.290	271	55	6	.982
1926	New York	Amer.	OF	108	413	73	130	22	3	12	81	.315	211	4	9	.960
1927	New York	Amer.	OF	135	516	75	174	47	9	8	103	.337	249	15	14	.950
1928	New York	Amer.	OF	131	518	77	154	45	5	11	113	.297	259	16	7	.975
1929	New York(a)	Amer.	OF	100	391	46	102	15	3	10	57	.261	206	9	7	.968
1930	Cincinnati	Nat.	OF	113	443	62	128	30	8	10	62	.289	223	8	9	.963
1931	Minneapolis	A. A.	OF	59	187	30	53	8	2	8	59	.283	64	1	7	.903
1932	Hollywood	P. C.	OF	64	228	44	75	20	2	4	26	.329	83	6	6	.937
American League Totals				1294	5032	764	1565	338	87	146	1005	.311	2259	270	120	.955
National League Totals				113	443	62	128	30	8	10	62	.289	223	8	9	.963
Major League Totals				1407	5475	826	1693	368	95	156	1067	.309	2482	278	129	.955

aSold to Cincinnati Reds, October 16, 1929.

WORLD SERIES RECORD

Year	Club	League	Pos.	G.	AB.	R.	H.	2B.	3B.	HR.	RBI.	B.A.	PO.	A.	E.	F.A.
1921	New York	Amer.	OF	8	30	3	6	2	0	0	3	.200	10	2	0	1.000
1922	New York	Amer.	OF	5	20	2	6	1	0	0	2	.300	7	1	0	1.000
1923	New York	Amer.	OF	6	26	1	7	1	2	0	8	.269	14	0	0	1.000
1926	New York	Amer.	OF	7	21	3	5	1	1	0	0	.238	13	0	1	.929
1927	New York	Amer.	OF	4	17	1	2	0	0	0	1	.118	8	0	1	.889
1928	New York	Amer.	OF	4	15	5	3	1	0	1	3	.200	4	0	0	1.000
World Series Totals				34	129	15	29	6	3	1	17	.225	56	3	2	.967

JESSE CLYDE (ZEB AND DEERFOOT) MILAN

Born March 25, 1887, at Linden, Tenn.
Died March 3, 1953, at Orlando, Fla., during training season.
Height, 5.08½. Weight, 170.
Threw right and batted lefthanded.
Married Margaret Bowers, November 19, 1913.

Played 511 consecutive games, August 12, 1910, through October 3, 1913, second game.
Manager, Washington Senators, signed January 14, 1922. Manager, Minneapolis, American Association, 1923; manager, New Haven, Eastern League, June, 1924; manager, Memphis, Southern Association, 1925-26; coach, Washington Senators, 1928-29; manager, Birmingham, Southern Association, 1930-31-32-33-34-35; released in June, 1935, and became manager of Chattanooga, Southern Association, June, 1935-36-37; scout, Washington Senators, 1937. Coach, Washington Senators, 1938 through 1952.

Year	Club	League	Pos.	G.	AB.	R.	H.	2B.	3B.	HR.	SB.	B.A.	PO.	A.	E.	F.A.
1906	Wichita	W.A.	OF	62	279	40	59	4	2	0	10	.211	114	5	1	.992
1907	Wichita	W.A.	OF	114	428	86	130	...	...	...	38	.304	183	16	11	.948
1907	Washington	Amer.	OF	48	183	22	51	3	3	0	8	.279	80	12	7	.929
1908	Washington	Amer.	OF	130	485	55	116	10	12	1	29	.239	265	18	12	.959
1909	Washington	Amer.	OF	130	400	36	80	12	4	1	10	.200	222	19	7	.972
1910	Washington	Amer.	OF	142	531	89	148	17	6	0	44	.279	267	•30	17	.946
1911	Washington	Amer.	OF	•154	*616	109	194	24	8	3	58	.315	347	33	17	.957
1912	Washington	Amer.	OF	154	601	105	184	19	11	1	*88	.306	326	31	•25	.935

Year	Club	League	Pos.	G.	AB.	R.	H.	2B.	3B.	HR.	SB.	B.A.	PO.	A.	E.	F.A.
1913	Washington	Amer.	OF	•154	578	89	173	18	9	3	★74	.299	295	20	•24	.929
1914	Washington	Amer.	OF	115	437	63	129	19	11	1	38	.295	230	10	13	.949
1915	Washington	Amer.	OF	153	573	83	165	13	7	2	40	.288	352	13	21	.946
1916	Washington	Amer.	OF	150	565	58	154	14	3	1	34	.273	★372	★27	16	.961
1917	Washington	Amer.	OF	155	579	60	170	15	4	0	20	.294	339	18	14	.962
1918	Washington	Amer.	OF	128	503	56	146	18	5	0	26	.290	299	17	9	.972
1919	Washington	Amer.	OF	88	321	43	92	12	6	0	11	.287	195	9	10	.953
1920	Washington	Amer.	OF	126	506	70	163	22	5	3	10	.322	291	15	9	.971
1921	Washington	Amer.	OF	112	406	55	117	19	11	1	4	.288	196	10	16	.931
1922	Washington	Amer.	OF	42	74	8	17	5	0	0	0	.230	18	3	0	1.000
1923	Washington	A.A.	OF	101	314	43	93	12	4	3	2	.296	159	7	7	.960
1924	New Haven	East.	OF	121	427	61	135	18	4	0	23	.316	273	12	12	.960
1925	Memphis	South.	OF	84	312	75	101	11	2	1	17	.324	148	7	5	.969
1926	Memphis	South.	OF	27	64	14	14	0	2	0	2	.219	33	2	1	.972
Major League Totals				1981	7358	1001	2099	240	105	17	494	.285	4094	294	217	.953

EDMUND JOHN (BING) MILLER

Born August 30, 1894, at Vinton, Ia.
Died May 7, 1966, at Philadelphia, Pa.
Height, 6.00¼. Weight, 180.
Threw and batted righthanded.
Married Helen Fetrow, March 11, 1930.

World Series—Went to bat twice in seventh inning, October 12, 1929, and had seven putouts in right field, October 5, 1930.

Coach, Boston Red Sox, October, 1937-38; coach, Detroit Tigers, 1939-40-41; coach, Chicago White Sox, December 9, 1941 through 1949; coach, Philadelphia A's, 1950-51-52-53.

Year	Club	League	Pos.	G.	AB.	R.	H.	2B.	3B.	HR.	RBI.	B.A.	PO.	A.	E.	F.A.
1914	Clinton	Cen.A.	OF-P	40	125	11	42	...	...	1	...	.336	37	15	7	.881
1915	Clinton	Cen.A.					(No record—player suspended)									
1916	Clinton	Cen.A.	OF-P	125	463	66	131	21	10	13	...	.283	210	37	11	.957
1917	Clin.-Waterloo	Cen.A.	OF	89	315	62	★106	20	5	7	...	★.337	113	★34	5	.967
1917	Peoria	Central	OF	22	79	9	22	5	2	2	...	.278	32	4	1	.973
1918	—						(In military service)									
1919	Atlanta	South.	OF	26	87	12	22	8	2	0	...	.253	36	5	0	1.000
1920	Little Rock	South.	OF	151	547	102	176	30	★21	★19	...	.322	296	15	8	.975
1921	Washington (a)	Amer.	OF	114	420	57	121	28	8	9	71	.288	245	13	15	.945
1922	Philadelphia	Amer.	OF	143	535	90	180	29	12	21	90	.336	314	19	8	.977
1923	Philadelphia	Amer.	OF	123	458	68	137	25	4	12	64	.299	262	10	6	.978
1924	Philadelphia	Amer.	OF	113	398	62	136	22	4	6	62	.342	172	11	5	.973
1925	Philadelphia	Amer.	OF-1B	124	474	78	151	29	10	10	81	.319	158	7	5	.971
1926	Phil.(b)-St.L.	Amer.	OF	132	463	73	149	33	7	6	63	.322	272	13	★15	.950
1927	St. Louis (c)	Amer.	OF	143	492	83	160	32	7	5	75	.325	309	9	10	.970
1928	Philadelphia	Amer.	OF	139	510	75	168	34	7	8	85	.329	298	8	10	.968
1929	Philadelphia	Amer.	OF	147	556	84	186	32	16	8	93	.335	311	10	10	.970
1930	Philadelphia	Amer.	OF	•154	585	89	177	38	7	9	100	.303	309	10	8	.976
1931	Philadelphia	Amer.	OF	137	534	76	150	43	5	8	77	.281	305	7	4	.987
1932	Philadelphia	Amer.	OF	95	305	40	90	17	3	8	58	.295	180	3	4	.979
1933	Philadelphia	Amer.	OF-1B	67	120	22	33	7	1	2	17	.275	62	2	1	.985
1934	Philadelphia	Amer.	OF	81	177	22	43	10	2	1	22	.243	72	2	0	1.000
1935	Boston	Amer.	OF	78	138	18	42	8	1	3	26	.304	48	2	2	.962
1936	Boston	Amer.	OF	30	47	9	14	2	1	1	6	.298	14	1	0	1.000
Major League Totals				1820	6212	946	1937	389	95	117	990	.312	3331	127	103	.971

aSold with pitcher Jose Acosta to Philadelphia Athletics in three-cornered deal which also sent infielder Frank O'Roarke to Boston Red Sox. Roger Peckinpaugh transferred from the New York Yankees to the Senators, and the Athletics sent third baseman Joe Dugan to the Yankees, January 10, 1922.
bTraded to St. Louis Browns for outfielder William Jacobson, June 15, 1926.
cTraded to Philadelphia Athletics for pitcher Sam Gray, December, 1927.

WORLD SERIES RECORD

Year	Club	League	Pos.	G.	AB.	R.	H.	2B.	3B.	HR.	RBI.	B.A.	PO.	A.	E.	F.A.
1929	Philadelphia	Amer.	OF	5	19	1	7	1	0	0	4	.368	13	0	1	.929
1930	Philadelphia	Amer.	OF	6	21	0	3	2	0	0	3	.143	12	0	0	1.000
1931	Philadelphia	Amer.	OF	7	26	3	7	1	0	0	1	.269	12	0	0	1.000
World Series Totals				18	66	4	17	4	0	0	8	.258	37	0	1	.974

PITCHING RECORD

Year	Club	League	G.	IP.	W.	L.	Pct.	H.	R.	ER.	SO.	BB.	ERA.
1914—Clinton		Cen.A.	8	47	3	2	.600	37	19	...	22	18	.....
1916—Clinton		Cen.A.	..	37	2	2	.500	25	...	12	20	19	2.92

DONALD RAY MINCHER

Born June 24, 1938, at Huntsville, Ala.
Height, 6.03. Weight, 205.
Threw right and batted lefthanded.

Hit homer in first World Series at-bat, October 6, 1965.
Tied World Series record for most assists, first baseman, game, nine innings (4), October 7, 1965.

Year	Club	League	Pos.	G.	AB.	R.	H.	2B.	3B.	HR.	RBI.	B.A.	PO.	A.	E.	F.A.
1956—Duluth-Superior	North.		1B	78	273	42	77	14	3	2	49	.282	591	37	11	.983
1957—Duluth-Superior	North.		1B	123	448	69	129	21	4	13	80	.288	*1103	*62	*24	.980
1958—Davenport	I.I.I.		1B	128	476	101	157	29	2	23	97	.330	*1105	72	16	.987
1959—Charleston(a)	Sally		1B	137	511	80	139	15	3	22	92	.272	1194	72	21	.984
1960—Washington	Amer.		1B	27	79	10	19	4	1	2	5	.241	209	5	9	.977
1960—Charleston	A. A.		1B	112	405	52	124	32	3	12	65	.306	934	63	10	.990
1961—Minnesota	Amer.		1B	35	101	18	19	5	1	5	11	.188	234	18	8	.969
1961—Buffalo	Int.		1B	109	370	59	95	13	2	24	66	.257	931	71	6	.994
1962—Minnesota	Amer.		1B	86	121	20	29	1	1	9	29	.240	211	13	5	.978
1963—Minnesota	Amer.		1B	82	225	41	58	8	0	17	42	.258	446	27	8	.983
1964—Minnesota	Amer.		1B	120	287	45	68	12	4	23	56	.237	549	43	5	.992
1965—Minnesota	Amer.		1B-OF	128	346	43	87	17	3	22	65	.251	818	45	7	.992
1966—Minnesota(b)	Amer.		1B	139	431	53	108	30	0	14	62	.251	995	85	9	.992
1967—California	Amer.		1B-OF	147	487	81	133	23	3	25	76	.273	1178	88	8	.994
1968—California(c)	Amer.		1B	120	399	35	94	12	1	13	48	.236	949	59	9	.991
1969—Seattle(d)	Amer.		1B	140	427	53	105	14	0	25	78	.246	1033	93	6	.994
1970—Oakland	Amer.		1B	140	463	62	114	18	0	27	74	.246	1109	91	*12	.990
1971—Oak.(e)-Wash.	Amer.		1B	128	415	44	116	21	2	12	53	.280	907	82	9	.991
1972—Texas(f)-Oak.	Amer.		1B	108	245	25	53	11	0	6	44	.216	544	47	4	.993
Major League Totals				1400	4026	530	1003	176	16	200	643	.249	9182	696	95	.990

aOn Chicago White Sox roster; traded to Washington Senators with catcher Earl Battey and reported $150,000 for first baseman-outfielder Roy Sievers, April 4, 1960.
bTraded with outfielder Jimmie Hall and pitcher Pete Cimino to California Angels for pitcher Dean Chance and infielder-outfielder Jackie Hernandez, December 2, 1966.
cSelected by Seattle Pilots from California Angels in expansion draft, October 15, 1968.
dTraded with infielder Ron Clark to Oakland Athletics for pitcher Lew Krausse, catcher Phil Roof, outfielder Mike Hershberger and pitcher Ken Sanders, January 15, 1970.
eTraded with catcher Frank Fernandez and pitcher Paul Lindblad to Washington Senators for first baseman Mike Epstein and pitcher Darold Knowles, May 8, 1971.
fTraded with infielder Ted Kubiak to Oakland A's for infielder Orlando Martinez, pitcher Steve Lawson, and infielder Vic Harris, July 20, 1972.

WORLD SERIES RECORD

Year	Club	League	Pos.	G.	AB.	R.	H.	2B.	3B.	HR.	RBI.	B.A.	PO.	A.	E.	F.A.
1965—Minnesota	Amer.		1B	7	23	3	3	0	0	1	1	.130	51	4	0	1.000
1972—Oakland	Amer.		PH	3	1	0	1	0	0	0	1	1.000	0	0	0	.000
World Series Totals				10	24	3	4	0	0	1	2	.167	51	4	0	1.000

LOREN DALE MITCHELL

Born August 23, 1921, at Colony, Okla.
Height, 6.01. Weight, 195.
Threw and batted lefthanded.
Married Margaret Emerson, May 26, 1942.

Batted safely in 22 consecutive games, July 3 through July 30, 1947, second game.

Year	Club	League	Pos.	G.	AB.	R.	H.	2B.	3B.	HR.	RBI.	B.A.	PO.	A.	E.	F.A.
1946—Oklahoma City		Texas	OF	108	415	63	140	25	8	2	63	*.337	267	17	11	.963
1946—Cleveland		Amer.	OF	11	44	7	19	3	0	0	5	.432	28	0	0	1.000
1947—Cleveland		Amer.	OF	123	493	69	156	16	10	1	34	.316	252	8	6	.977
1948—Cleveland		Amer.	OF	141	608	82	204	30	8	4	56	.336	307	12	3	*.991
1949—Cleveland		Amer.	OF	149	*640	81	*203	16	*23	3	56	.317	337	10	2	*.994
1950—Cleveland		Amer.	OF	130	506	81	156	27	5	3	49	.308	236	3	7	.972
1951—Cleveland		Amer.	OF	134	510	83	148	21	7	11	62	.290	253	3	2	.992
1952—Cleveland		Amer.	OF	134	511	61	165	26	3	5	58	.323	258	2	2	.992
1953—Cleveland		Amer.	OF	134	500	76	150	26	4	13	60	.300	224	2	7	.970
1954—Cleveland		Amer.	OF-1B	53	60	6	17	1	0	1	6	.283	9	1	1	.909
1955—Cleveland		Amer.	OF-1B	61	58	4	15	2	1	0	10	.259	27	2	0	1.000
1956—Cleveland (a)		Amer.	OF	38	30	2	4	0	0	0	6	.133	0	0	0	.000
1956—Brooklyn		Nat.	OF	19	24	3	7	1	0	0	1	.292	3	0	0	1.000
American League Totals				1108	3960	552	1237	168	61	41	402	.312	1931	43	30	.985
National League Totals				19	24	3	7	1	0	0	1	.292	3	0	0	1.000
Major League Totals				1127	3984	555	1244	169	61	41	403	.312	1934	43	30	.985

aSold to Brooklyn Dodgers, July 29, 1956.

WORLD SERIES RECORD

Year	Club	League	Pos.	G.	AB.	R.	H.	2B.	3B.	HR.	RBI.	B.A.	PO.	A.	E.	F.A.
1948—Cleveland		Amer.	OF	6	23	4	4	1	0	1	1	.174	13	0	0	1.000
1954—Cleveland		Amer.	PH	3	2	0	0	0	0	0	0	.000	0	0	0	.000
1956—Brooklyn		Nat.	PH	4	4	0	0	0	0	0	0	.000	0	0	0	.000
World Series Totals				13	29	4	4	1	0	1	1	.138	13	0	0	1.000

JOHN ROBERT (BIG CAT) MIZE

Born January 7, 1913, at Demorest, Ga.
Height, 6.02. Weight, 215.
Threw right and batted lefthanded.
Married Jene Adams, August 8, 1937.

Hit three homers in one game six times and hit three consecutive homers in one game four times; set N.L. season record for home runs by lefthanded batsman, 51 in 1947; made four long hits, July 3, 1939. Second player in World Series history to hit home run as a pinch-hitter, October 3, 1952. Named as first baseman on THE SPORTING NEWS All-Star Major League Teams, 1942-47-48. Scout, New York Giants, 1955; coach, Kansas City Athletics, 1961.

Year	Club	League	Pos.	G.	AB.	R.	H.	2B.	3B.	HR.	RBI.	B.A.	PO.	A.	E.	F.A.
1930—Greensboro		Pied.	OF	12	31	5	6	3	0	0	2	.194	10	0	1	.909
1931—Greensboro		Pied.	OF	94	341	69	115	27	1	9	64	.337	130	*17	9	.942
1932—Elmira		NYP	OF-1B	106	405	60	132	20	11	8	78	.326	402	20	6	.986
1933—Greensboro		Pied.	1B	98	378	108	136	29	10	22	104	.360	860	51	25	.973
1933—Rochester		Int.	1B	42	159	27	56	11	3	8	32	.352	355	33	5	.987
1934—Rochester		Int.	1B	90	313	49	106	16	1	17	66	.339	694	72	9	.988
1935—Rochester		Int.	1B	65	252	37	80	11	1	12	44	.317	547	41	8	.987
1936—St. Louis		Nat.	1B-OF	126	414	76	136	30	8	19	93	.329	909	67	6	.994
1937—St. Louis		Nat.	1B	145	560	103	204	40	7	25	113	.364	1308	67	17	.988
1938—St. Louis		Nat.	1B	149	531	85	179	34	*16	27	102	.337	1297	93	●15	.989
1939—St. Louis		Nat.	1B	153	564	104	197	44	14	*28	108	*.349	1348	90	●19	.987
1940—St. Louis		Nat.	1B	155	579	111	182	31	13	*43	*137	.314	1376	80	14	.990
1941—St. Louis (a)		Nat.	1B	126	473	67	150	●39	8	16	100	.317	1157	82	8	.994
1942—New York		Nat.	1B	142	541	97	165	25	7	26	●110	.305	1393	74	8	*.995
1943-44-45—New York		Nat.					(In Military Service)									
1946—New York		Nat.	1B	101	377	70	127	18	3	22	70	.337	928	83	11	.989
1947—New York		Nat.	1B	154	586	*137	177	26	2	●51	●138	.302	*1381	●118	6	*.996
1948—New York		Nat.	1B	152	560	110	162	26	4	●40	125	.289	*1359	*111	13	.991
1949—New York (b)		Nat.	1B	106	388	59	102	15	0	18	62	.263	906	65	6	.994
1949—New York		Amer.	1B	13	23	4	6	1	0	1	2	.261	47	3	1	.980
1950—Kansas City		A.A.	1B	26	94	18	28	4	0	5	18	.298	205	17	0	1.000
1950—New York		Amer.	1B	90	274	43	76	12	0	25	72	.277	490	31	2	.996
1951—New York		Amer.	1B	113	332	37	86	14	1	10	49	.259	632	44	4	.994
1952—New York		Amer.	1B	78	137	9	36	9	0	4	29	.263	218	18	3	.987
1953—New York		Amer.	1B	81	104	6	26	3	0	4	27	.250	113	7	0	1.000
American League Totals				375	870	99	230	39	1	44	179	.264	1500	103	10	.994
National League Totals				1509	5573	1019	1781	328	82	315	1158	.320	13362	930	123	.991
Major League Totals				1884	6443	1118	2011	367	83	359	1337	.312	14862	1033	133	.992

aTraded to New York Giants for catcher James K. O'Dea, pitcher Bill Lohrman, first baseman Johnny McCarthy (assigned to Columbus A.A. club) and $50,000, December 11, 1941. However, Commissioner Landis

later upheld Indianapolis' claim to McCarthy as per a prior agreement.
bSold to New York Yankees for $40,000, August 22, 1949.

WORLD SERIES RECORD

Year	Club	League	Pos.	G.	AB.	R.	H.	2B.	3B.	HR.	RBI.	B.A.	PO.	A.	E.	F.A.
1949	New York	Amer.	PH	2	2	0	2	0	0	0	2	1.000	0	0	0	.000
1950	New York	Amer.	1B	4	15	0	2	0	0	0	0	.133	27	3	0	1.000
1951	New York	Amer.	1B-PH	4	7	2	2	1	0	0	1	.286	12	0	0	1.000
1952	New York	Amer.	1B-PH	5	15	3	6	1	0	3	6	.400	25	3	0	1.000
1953	New York	Amer.	PH	3	3	0	0	0	0	0	0	.000	0	0	0	.000
World Series Totals				18	42	5	12	2	0	3	9	.286	64	6	0	1.000

JOHN FRANCIS MOORE

Born March 23, 1903, at Waterbury, Conn.
Height, 5.10½. Weight, 178.
Threw righthanded and batted lefthanded.
Married Rita Marie Egan, April 3, 1922.

Scout for Boston-Milwaukee-Atlanta franchises from 1952 to 1968; scout, Montreal Expos, 1968-70.

Year	Club	League	Pos.	G.	AB.	R.	H.	2B.	3B.	HR.	RBI.	B.A.	PO.	A.	E.	F.A.
1924	New Haven	Eastern	OF	31	124	12	40	6	3	0	...	.323	44	4	2	.960
1925	New Haven	Eastern	OF	116	427	57	114	13	9	0	...	.267	198	19	8	.964
1926	Waterville-N.H.	Eastern	OF	136	523	85	169	18	13	1	...	.323	317	20	11	.968
1927	New Haven	Eastern	OF	154	579	72	165	22	12	5	85	.285	309	15	14	.959
1928	Reading	Inter.	OF	146	525	94	172	24	*18	17	117	.328	375	26	9	.978
1928	Chicago	National	PH	4	4	0	0	0	0	0	0	.000	....	....	....	....
1929	Chicago	National	OF	37	63	13	18	1	0	2	8	.286	32	1	1	.971
1930	Los Angeles	P.C.	OF	142	546	120	187	45	2	26	101	.342	365	16	8	.979
1931	Los Angeles	P.C.	OF	80	317	66	116	34	4	6	69	.366	158	13	4	.977
1931	Chicago	National	OF	39	104	19	25	3	1	2	16	.240	51	3	2	.964
1932	Chicago (a)	National	OF	119	443	59	135	24	5	13	64	.305	272	12	5	.983
1933	Cincinnati	National	OF	135	514	60	135	19	5	1	44	.263	329	12	9	.974
1934	Cin.(b)-Phila.	National	OF	132	500	73	165	35	7	11	98	.330	267	18	5	.983
1935	Philadelphia	National	OF	153	600	84	194	33	3	19	93	.323	233	18	7	.973
1936	Philadelphia	National	OF	124	472	85	155	24	3	16	68	.328	214	5	12	.948
1937	Philadelphia	National	OF	96	307	46	98	16	2	9	59	.319	124	9	8	.943
1938	Los Angeles	P.C.	OF	140	492	81	150	33	7	21	86	.305	233	12	2	.992
1939	Los Angeles	P.C.	OF	131	491	83	148	24	5	17	99	.301	218	8	7	.970
1940	Los Angeles	P.C.	OF	120	380	41	118	20	2	9	69	.311	158	7	2	.988
1941	Los Angeles	P.C.	OF	134	474	77	157	31	10	18	100	*.331	207	8	3	.986
1942	Los Angeles	P.C.	OF	134	487	59	169	28	6	7	85	.347	204	10	3	.987
1943	Los Angeles	P.C.	OF	81	217	22	63	11	1	1	31	.290	101	1	1	.990
1944	Los Angeles	P.C.	OF	85	120	11	39	9	0	3	30	.325	31	0	1	.969
1945	Los Angeles	P.C.	PH	71	65	5	23	4	0	4	26	.354	...	...	...	.....
1945	Chicago	National	PH	7	6	0	1	0	0	0	2	.167	...	...	...	.....
Major League Totals				846	3013	439	926	155	26	73	452	.307	1522	78	49	.970

aTraded to Cincinnati Reds with pitcher Robert Smith, catcher Ralston Hemsley and outfielder Lance Richbourg for outfielder Floyd Herman and cash, November 30, 1932.
bTraded to Philadelphia Phillies with pitcher Sylvester Johnson for outfielder Wesley Schulmerich, outfielder William Ruble and pitcher Theodore Kleinhans, May 16, 1934.

WORLD SERIES RECORD

Year	Club	League	Pos.	G.	AB.	R.	H.	2B.	3B.	HR.	RBI.	B.A.	PO.	A.	E.	F.A.
1932	Chicago	National	OF	?	7	1	0	0	0	0	0	.000	4	0	0	1.000

WALLACE MOSES, JR.

Born October 8, 1910, at Uvalda, Ga.
Height, 5.10. Weight, 160.
Threw and batted lefthanded.
Married Billie Mae Haines, December 2, 1936.

Led A.L. outfielders in double plays, 1941 (tie).

Coach, Philadelphia Athletics, 1952-53-54; coach, Philadelphia Phillies, 1955 through 1958; coach, Cincinnati Reds, 1959-60; coach, New York Yankees, 1961-62-63, until named scout, 1964-65 to May 9, 1966, when he returned as coach for remainder of season; coach, Detroit Tigers, 1967-70; batting instructor, Philadelphia Phillies, 1975.

Year	Club	League	Pos.	G.	AB.	R.	H.	2B.	3B.	HR.	RBI.	B.A.	PO.	A.	E.	F.A.
1931	Augusta	Palm'to	OF-P	63	231	53	73	8	6	3	32	.316	115	5	6	.952
1931	Elmira	NYP	OF	40	133	19	33	4	2	1	15	.248	63	6	6	.920
1932	Monroe	Cot.S.	OF	68	275	58	68	13	3	5	...	.284	129	6	7	.951
1932	Tyler	Texas	OF	41	164	23	47	8	2	2	18	.287	73	1	3	.961
1933	Galveston	Texas	OF	105	289	48	85	14	12	2	44	.294	144	8	10	.938
1934	Galveston	Texas	OF	154	569	93	180	25	15	9	81	.316	290	6	16	.949
1935	Philadelphia (a)	Amer.	OF	85	345	60	112	21	3	5	35	.325	157	7	10	.943
1936	Philadelphia	Amer.	OF	146	585	98	202	35	11	7	66	.345	396	12	11	.974
1937	Philadelphia	Amer.	OF	154	649	113	208	48	13	25	86	.320	323	16	15	.958
1938	Philadelphia	Amer.	OF	142	589	86	181	29	8	8	49	.307	304	11	11	.966
1939	Philadelphia (b)	Amer.	OF	115	437	68	134	28	7	3	33	.307	209	10	8	.965
1940	Philadelphia	Amer.	OF	142	537	91	166	41	9	9	50	.309	295	10	8	.974
1941	Philadelphia (c)	Amer.	OF	116	438	78	132	31	4	4	35	.301	263	12	7	.975
1942	Chicago	Amer.	OF	146	577	73	156	28	4	7	49	.270	323	14	7	.980
1943	Chicago	Amer.	OF	150	599	82	147	22	•12	3	48	.245	370	12	8	.979
1944	Chicago	Amer.	OF	136	535	82	150	26	9	3	34	.280	267	7	7	.975
1945	Chicago	Amer.	OF	140	569	79	168	*35	15	2	50	.295	*329	12	8	.977
1946	Chi.(d)-Boston	Amer.	OF	104	343	33	82	20	4	6	33	.239	176	5	2	.989
1947	Boston	Amer.	OF	90	255	32	70	18	2	2	27	.275	109	2	3	.974
1948	Boston (e)	Amer.	OF	78	189	26	49	12	1	2	29	.259	101	2	2	.981
1949	Philadelphia	Amer.	OF	110	308	49	85	19	3	1	25	.276	169	7	3	.983
1950	Philadelphia	Amer.	OF	88	265	47	70	16	5	2	21	.264	147	7	2	.987
1951	Philadelphia	Amer.	OF	70	136	17	26	6	0	0	9	.191	62	1	1	.984
Major League Totals				2012	7356	1114	2138	435	110	89	679	.291	4000	147	113	.973

aFractured left arm crashing into wall, August 17, and was out for remainder of season.
bTraded to Detroit for second baseman Benny McCoy and pitcher George Coffman, December 9, 1939. Deal cancelled by Commissioner Landis, January 14, 1940, when he declared McCoy free agent because Detroit was guilty of "covering up" McCoy and other Tiger farmhands, contrary to baseball rules referring to proper advancement.
cTraded to Chicago White Sox for outfielder Mike Kreevich and pitcher Jack Hallett, December 9, 1941.
dSold to Boston Red Sox, July 23, 1946.
eUnconditionally released by Boston Red Sox, November 15, 1948; subsequently signed with Philadelphia Athletics.

WORLD SERIES RECORD

Year	Club	League	Pos.	G.	AB.	R.	H.	2B.	3B.	HR.	RBI.	B.A.	PO.	A.	E.	F.A.
1946	Boston	Amer.	OF	4	12	1	5	0	0	0	0	.417	5	0	0	1.000

PITCHING RECORD

Year	Club	League	G.	IP.	W.	L.	Pct.	H.	R.	ER.	SO.	BB.	ERA.
1931	Augusta	Palm.	1	4	0	0	.000	4	0	0	2	1	0.00

JOHN ANTHONY (BANANAS) MOSTIL

Born June 1, 1896, at Chicago, Ill.
Died December 10, 1970, at Midlothian, Ill.
Height, 5.08. Weight, 169.
Threw and batted righthanded.

Tied American League record for outfielders, most putouts, game (11) and most chances accepted game (12), May 22, 1928.
Led American League in stolen bases, 1925 and 1926.
Manager, Eau Claire, Northern League, 1933-34-35-36-37; Grand Forks, Northern League, 1938-39; Jonesboro, Northeast Arkansas League, 1940-41; Waterloo, Three-I League, 1941-42-46-47; Superior, Northern League, 1948; scout, Chicago Cubs, 1943; scout, Chicago White Sox, 1947 through 1968.

Year	Club	League	Pos.	G.	AB.	R.	H.	2B.	3B.	HR.	RBI.	B.A.	PO.	A.	E.	F.A.
1918	Chicago	Amer.	2B	10	33	4	9	2	2	0	2	.273	15	21	3	.923
1919	Milwaukee	A. A.	2B	132	500	70	134	12	14	2	....	.268	235	114	30	.921
1920	Milwaukee	A. A.	OF	155	597	125	190	29	12	4	49	.318	440	23	10	*.979
1921	Chicago	Amer.	OF	100	326	43	98	21	7	3	42	.301	215	14	13	.946
1922	Chicago	Amer.	OF	132	458	74	139	28	14	7	70	.303	333	9	12	.966
1923	Chicago	Amer.	OF	153	546	91	159	37	15	3	64	.291	*422	21	12	.974
1924	Chicago	Amer.	OF	118	385	75	125	22	5	4	49	.325	281	13	8	.974
1925	Chicago	Amer.	OF	153	605	*135	181	36	16	2	50	.299	446	11	7	*.985
1926	Chicago	Amer.	OF	148	600	120	197	41	15	4	42	.328	*440	15	•15	.968
1927	Chicago(a)	Amer.	OF	13	16	3	2	0	0	0	1	.125	5	2	0	1.000

Year	Club	League	Pos.	G.	AB.	R.	H.	2B.	3B.	HR.	RBI.	B.A.	PO.	A.	E.	F.A.
1928	Chicago	Amer.	OF	133	503	69	136	19	8	0	51	.270	394	18	10	.976
1929	Chicago(b)	Amer.	OF	12	35	4	8	3	0	0	3	.229	25	1	1	.963
1930	Toledo	A. A.	OF	91	287	61	96	16	4	2	35	.334	200	5	10	.953
1931	Toledo	A. A.	OF	81	303	56	91	17	4	3	26	.300	187	4	11	.946
1932	Little Rock	South.	OF	12	41	....	15	3	1	0	....	.366	26	1	1	.964
1933	Eau Claire	North.	OF	43	150	....	55	10	2	6	....	.367	71	3	2	.974
1934	Eau Claire	Morth.	OF	83	311	....	100	16	5	5	....	.322	110	5	3	.975
1935	Eau Claire	North.	OF	60	159	....	48	15	0	2	26	.302	52	3	0	1.000
1936	Eau Claire	North.	OF	36	78	16	24	3	0	1	17	.308	16	0	1	.941
1937	Eau Claire	North.	OF	17	41	5	10	1	0	0	6	.244	13	0	0	1.000
1938	Grand Forks	North.	PH-O	6	8	0	0	0	0	0	2	.000	1	0	0	1.000
1939	Grand Forks	North.	PH	19	19	2	6	2	0	0	3	.316	1	0	0	1.000
1940	Jonesboro	N.E. Ark.	PH	1	1	0	1	0	0	0	0	1.000	0	0	0	.000
1941	Waterloo	I. I. I.							(Did not play)							
1942	Waterloo	I. I. I.	PH-OF	2	3	0	0	0	0	0	0	.000	0	0	0	.000
	Major League Totals			972	3507	618	1054	209	82	23	374	.301	2576	125	81	.971

aOut of game most of 1927 due to illness.
bFractured ankle, May 19, 1929—out for rest of season.

ANTHONY JOHN (COUNT) MULLANE

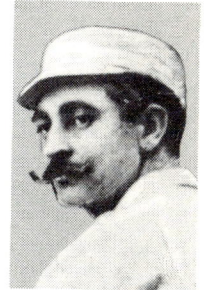

(Was called Count because of his distinguished appearance and supreme athletic abilities. He never used any intoxicating drink, never smoked, played all positions, pitched ambidextrously wearing no glove, had devastating pickoff motion and was a hard hitter. Mullane also was an accomplished skater, roller and ice, a clever boxer and fine musician.)

Born February 20, 1859, at Cork, Ireland.
Died April 26, 1944, at Chicago, Ill.
Height, 5.10½. Weight, 169.
Threw both left and righthanded and batted righthanded.

Pitched 20-inning tie, 7-7, vs. Chicago, June 30, 1892; pitched and won two games, September 20, 1888; split doubleheader, May 23, 1892; pitched 2-0 no-hit victory vs. Cincinnati, September 11, 1882; involved in four-hit double 0-0 tie duel against Brooklyn in tenth inning when darkness in 11th inning stopped the game, October 4, 1884.
Umpired in National League, 1893 and 1897.

Year	Club	League	G.	IP.	W.	L.	Pct.	SO.	BB.	H.	CG.	ShO.
1880	Akron	Independent										
1881	Akron	Independent										
1881	Detroit	National	5	44	1	4	.200	10	13	56	5	0
1882	Louisville	Amer. Assn.	•54	459	30	24	.556	*172	75	428	50	5
1883	St. Louis	Amer. Assn.	50	460	35	15	.700	188	73	389	49	3
1884	Toledo	Amer. Assn.	66	568	35	25	.583	334	82	493	64	7
1885—	(Did not play—suspended for entire season for signing multiple contracts)											
1886	Cincinnati	Amer. Assn.	61	529	31	27	.534	220	182	500	55	1
1887	Cincinnati	Amer. Assn.	49	413	31	17	.646	68	119	550	46	•6
1888	Cincinnati	Amer. Assn.	44	377	26	16	.619	125	108	233	41	4
1889	Cincinnati(a)	Amer. Assn.	29	217	12	9	.571	107	85	206	16	0
1890	Cincinnati	National	22	202	12	10	.545	95	91	161	21	0
1891	Cincinnati	National	49	430	24	25	.490	117	178	393	42	1
1892	Cincinnati	National	31	295	21	10	.667	112	125	237	30	3
1892	Butte(b)	Montana			(No records available)							
1893	Cin.(c)-Baltimore	National	41	367	19	22	.463	85	168	417	34	0
1894	Balt.(d)-Cleveland	National	17	145	8	9	.471	44	80	175	11	1
1895	St. Paul	Western	30	....	....	....	....	....	....	260	....	....
1896	St. Paul	Western	49	....	....	....	....	....	....	423	....	....
1897	St. Paul	Western	30	....	14	11	.560	....	....	260	....	....
1898—					(Did not play)							
1899	Toronto	Eastern	3	26	2	1	.667	7	10	34	3	0
	American Association Totals		353	3023	200	133	.601	1214	724	2799	321	26
	National League Totals		165	1483	85	80	.515	463	655	1439	143	5
	Major League Totals		518	4506	285	213	.572	1677	1379	4238	464	31

aCincinnati withdrew from American Association and entered National League in 1890.
bWent to Butte after refusing to accept salary cut from Cincinnati.
cTraded to Baltimore for Frank (Piggy) Ward in June, 1893.
dDealt to Cleveland for John Clarkson, 1894.

DID YOU KNOW—

That Count Mullane and King Kelly both were fan idols, but the Count's suave, graceful class won the gals' hearts in the '80s?

GEORGE EMMETT MULLIN

Born July 4, 1880, at Toledo, O.
Died January 7, 1944, at Wabash, Ind.
Height, 5.11. Weight, 188.
Threw and batted righthanded.

Pitched no-hit, 7-0 victory against St. Louis Browns on his birthday, July 4, 1912, afternoon game; pitched and won both games of doubleheader against Washington, 5-3 and 4-3, September 22, 1908; tied major league record for most doubles hit by pitcher, game–3 (April 27, 1903).

Year Club	League	G.	IP.	W.	L.	Pct.	H.	R.	ER.	SO.	BB.	ERA.
1901–Ft. Wayne	W. Assn.	47	367	21	20	.512	377	203	....	190	96	......
1902–Detroit	Amer.	35	264	13	16	.448	288	159	....	75	96	......
1903–Detroit	Amer.	41	323	19	14	.576	291	129	....	172	*104	......
1904–Detroit	Amer.	45	382	17	23	.425	346	154	....	149	*119	......
1905–Detroit	Amer.	44	346	21	20	.512	301	138	....	173	*138	......
1906–Detroit	Amer.	40	328	21	18	.538	311	137	....	122	*112	......
1907–Detroit	Amer.	46	359	20	20	.500	*335	*154	....	153	97	......
1908–Detroit	Amer.	39	291	17	12	.586	301	142	....	121	71	......
1909–Detroit	Amer.	40	304	*29	8	*.784	258	96	....	124	78	......
1910–Detroit	Amer.	38	289	21	12	.636	260	125	....	98	102	......
1911–Detroit	Amer.	30	234	18	10	.643	245	99	....	87	61	......
1912–Detroit	Amer.	37	226	12	17	.414	214	112	....	88	92	......
1913–Det.(a)-Wash.	Amer.	19	110	4	11	.267	122	62	48	30	43	3.93
1913–Montreal(b)	Int.	4	27	1	2	.333	28	20	....	9	16	......
1914–Indianapolis(c)	Fed.	36	204	14	10	.583	199	99	75	70	93	3.31
1915–Newark	Fed.	5	33	2	2	.500	41	22	....	14	16	......
Major League Totals		454	3456	212	181	.539	3612	1507	....	1392	1113	......

aSold to Washington on waivers, May 17, 1913, and released by Senators to Montreal, July 5, 1913.
bJumped to Indianapolis, Federal League, for 1914.
cTransferred to Newark with Indianapolis franchise in 1915.

WORLD SERIES RECORD

Year Club	League	G.	IP.	W.	L.	Pct.	H.	R.	ER.	SO.	BB.	ERA.
1907–Detroit	Amer.	2	17	0	2	.000	16	5	4	7	6	2.11
1908–Detroit	Amer.	1	9	1	0	1.000	7	3	0	8	1	0.00
1909–Detroit	Amer.	4	32	2	1	.667	22	14	7	20	8	1.97
World Series Totals		7	58	3	3	.500	45	22	11	35	15	1.71

STANLEY FRANK (THE MAN) MUSIAL

Born November 21, 1920, at Donora, Pa.
Height, 6.00. Weight, 180.
Threw and batted lefthanded.
Married Lillian Labash, November 21, 1939.

Set major league record, most home runs in a doubleheader (5)–hitting three in first game and two in second, May 2, 1954 (tied by Nate Colbert, 1972). Had set records (since broken by Hank Aaron) for most seasons played 100 or more games (21), most consecutive playing seasons, 100 or more games (21), most total bases, lifetime (6,134) and most long hits, lifetime (1,377).
Had tied the following major league records: Most seasons, one club (22); most consecutive seasons, one club (22) (passed by Brooks Robinson); most years 300 or more total bases (13), 1957 (passed by Hank Aaron); most years leading in doubles (8); most times five hits in a game, season (4), 1948; most years leading in triples (5), 1951; most home runs in consecutive times at bat (4), hitting one in last appearance, July 7, and three in first three trips to the plate, July 8, 1962.
Had set the following National League records: Most games played (3,026); most times at bat (10,972); most runs scored (1,949); most base hits (3,630) and most runs batted in (1,951) (all passed by Hank Aaron); still holds N.L. record for most doubles, lifetime, 725.
Tied for the following National League records: Most years leading outfielders in fielding since 1900 (3), 1949-54-61; most seasons, consecutive playing years, as active player (22); most years leading in runs scored (5); most seasons batting .300 or better (17). Had tied for most years 100 or more runs batted in (10) (since passed by Hank Aaron).
Led National League in total bases, 1943-46-48-49-51-52; led in slugging percentage, 1943-44-46-48-50-52.

Hit home run in twelfth inning to win for National League in All-Star Game, 6-5, July 12, 1955; played in more All-Star games than any other player (24) (since tied by Willie Mays and Hank Aaron).
Named as outfielder on THE SPORTING NEWS All-Star Major League Teams, 1943-44-48-49-50-51-52-53-54; named as first baseman, 1946-57-58.
Named Major League Player of the Year by THE SPORTING NEWS, 1946 and 1951.
Named Player of the Decade by THE SPORTING NEWS, 1956.
Named Top National League Player by THE SPORTING NEWS, 1943-48-51-57.
Named to Hall of Fame, 1969.

Year	Club	League	Pos.	G.	AB.	R.	H.	2B.	3B.	HR.	RBI.	B.A.	PO.	A.	E.	F.A.
1938	Williamson	Mt. St.	P	26	62	5	16	3	0	1	6	.258	7	22	6	.829
1939	Williamson	Mt. St.	PH-P	23	71	10	25	3	3	1	9	.352	5	19	3	.889
1940	Daytona Beach	Fla. St.	OF-P	113	405	55	126	17	10	1	70	.311	183	69	11	.958
1941	Springfield	W. Va.	OF	87	348	100	132	27	10	★26	94	.379	185	7	3	.985
1941	Rochester	Int.	OF	54	221	43	72	10	4	3	21	.326	102	5	1	.991
1941	St. Louis	Nat.	OF	12	47	8	20	4	0	1	7	.426	20	1	0	1.000
1942	St. Louis	Nat.	OF	140	467	87	147	32	10	10	72	.315	296	6	5	.984
1943	St. Louis	Nat.	OF	●157	617	108	★220	★48	★20	13	81	★.357	376	15	7	.982
1944	St. Louis	Nat.	OF	146	568	112	●197	★51	14	12	94	.347	353	16	5	.987
1945	St. Louis	Nat.					(In Military Service)									
1946	St. Louis	Nat.	★1B-OF	●156	★624	★124	★228	★50	★20	16	103	★.365	1166	69	★15	.988
1947	St. Louis	Nat.	1B	149	587	113	183	30	13	19	95	.312	1360	77	8	.994
1948	St. Louis	Nat.	OF-1B	155	611	★135	★230	★46	★18	39	★131	★.376	354	11	7	.981
1949	St. Louis	Nat.	★OF-1B	★157	612	128	★207	★41	●13	36	123	.338	337	11	3	★.991
1950	St. Louis	Nat.	OF-1B	146	555	105	192	41	7	28	109	★.346	760	39	8	.990
1951	St. Louis	Nat.	OF-1B	152	578	●124	205	30	●12	32	108	★.355	816	45	10	.989
1952	St. Louis (a)	Nat.	O-1B-P	●154	578	●105	★194	★42	6	21	91	★.336	502	18	5	.990
1953	St. Louis	Nat.	OF	157	593	127	200	★53	9	30	113	.337	294	9	5	.984
1954	St. Louis	Nat.	★OF-1B	153	591	●120	195	★41	9	35	126	.330	307	15	5	★.985
1955	St. Louis	Nat.	1B-OF	●154	562	97	179	30	5	33	108	.319	1000	94	9	.992
1956	St. Louis	Nat.	1B-OF	156	594	87	184	33	6	27	★109	.310	954	95	8	.992
1957	St. Louis	Nat.	1B	134	502	82	176	38	3	29	102	★.351	1167	99	10	.992
1958	St. Louis	Nat.	1B	135	472	64	159	35	2	17	62	.337	1019	★100	13	.989
1959	St. Louis	Nat.	1B-OF	115	341	37	87	13	2	14	44	.255	624	63	7	.990
1960	St. Louis	Nat.	OF-1B	116	331	49	91	17	1	17	63	.275	300	19	3	.991
1961	St. Louis	Nat.	OF	123	372	46	107	22	4	15	70	.288	149	9	1	★.994
1962	St. Louis	Nat.	OF	135	433	57	143	18	1	19	82	.330	164	6	4	.977
1963	St. Louis	Nat.	OF	124	337	34	86	10	2	12	58	.255	121	1	4	.968
Major League Totals				3026	10972	1949	3630	725	177	475	1951	.331	12439	818	142	.989

aPitched to one batter, Frank Baumholtz of Chicago Cubs, in last game of season.

WORLD SERIES RECORD

Year	Club	League	Pos.	G.	AB.	R.	H.	2B.	3B.	HR.	RBI.	B.A.	PO.	A.	E.	F.A.
1942	St. Louis	Nat.	OF	5	18	2	4	1	0	0	2	.222	13	0	0	1.000
1943	St. Louis	Nat.	OF	5	18	2	5	0	0	0	1	.278	7	2	0	1.000
1944	St. Louis	Nat.	OF	6	23	2	7	2	0	1	2	.304	11	0	1	.917
1946	St. Louis	Nat.	1B	7	27	3	6	4	1	0	4	.222	60	2	0	1.000
World Series Totals				23	86	9	22	7	1	1	8	.256	91	4	1	.990

PITCHING RECORD

Year	Club	League	G.	IP.	W.	L.	Pct.	H.	R.	ER.	SO.	BB.	ERA.
1938	Williamson	Mt. State	20	110	6	6	.500	114	75	57	66	80	4.66
1939	Williamson	Mt. State	13	92	9	2	.818	71	53	44	86	85	4.30
1940	Daytona Beach	Fla. State	28	223	18	5	★.783	179	108	65	176	145	2.62
1952	St. Louis	Nat.	1	0	0	0	.000	0	0	0	0	0	0.00
Major League Totals			1	0	0	0	.000	0	0	0	0	0	0.00

CHARLES SOLOMON (BUDDY) MYER

Born March 16, 1904, at Ellisville, Miss.
Died October 31, 1974, at Baton Rouge, La.
Height, 5.10½. Weight, 170.
Threw right and batted lefthanded.
Married Minna Williams, February 10, 1927.

Led American League in stolen bases, 1928, with 30.
Led A.L. third basemen in double plays, 1928; led A.L. second basemen in double plays, 1935.

Year	Club	League	Pos.	G.	AB.	R.	H.	2B.	3B.	HR.	RBI.	B.A.	PO.	A.	E.	F.A.
1925	New Orleans	South.	SS	99	402	76	135	21	8	3	44	.336	249	306	37	.938
1925	Washington	Amer.	SS	4	8	1	2	0	0	0	0	.250	1	3	0	1.000
1926	Washington	Amer.	SS	132	434	66	132	18	6	1	62	.304	215	297	40	.928
1927	Wash. (a)-Bos.	Amer.	SS	148	520	66	146	23	11	2	54	.281	304	380	44	.940
1928	Boston (b)	Amer.	3B	147	536	78	168	26	6	1	44	.313	137	306	14	.969

— 207 —

Year	Club	League	Pos.	G.	AB.	R.	H.	2B.	3B.	HR.	RBI.	B.A.	PO.	A.	E.	F.A.
1929–Washington		Amer.	2B-3B	141	563	80	169	29	10	3	82	.300	274	363	32	.952
1930–Washington		Amer.	2B	138	541	97	164	18	8	2	61	.303	330	405	27	.965
1931–Washington		Amer.	2B	139	591	114	173	33	11	4	56	.293	333	398	12	•.984
1932–Washington		Amer.	2B	143	577	120	161	38	16	5	52	.279	352	426	20	.975
1933–Washington		Amer.	2B	131	530	95	160	29	15	4	61	.302	356	417	17	.978
1934–Washington		Amer.	2B	139	524	103	160	33	8	3	57	.305	367	420	20	.975
1935–Washington		Amer.	2B	151	616	115	215	36	11	5	100	*.349	*460	473	20	.979
1936–Washington		Amer.	2B	51	156	31	42	5	2	0	15	.269	120	143	4	.985
1937–Washington		Amer.	2B	125	430	54	126	16	10	1	65	.293	308	338	*23	.966
1938–Washington		Amer.	2B	127	437	79	147	22	8	6	71	.336	308	355	12	*.982
1939–Washington		Amer.	2B	83	258	33	78	10	3	1	32	.302	175	188	12	.968
1940–Washington		Amer.	2B	71	210	28	61	14	4	0	29	.290	119	176	10	.967
1941–Washington		Amer.	2B	53	107	14	27	3	1	0	9	.252	53	54	2	.982
Major League Totals				1923	7038	1174	2131	353	130	38	850	.303	4212	5142	309	.968

aTraded to Boston Red Sox for infielder Emory Rigney, May 2, 1927.
bTraded to Washington Senators for pitchers Milt Gaston and Horace Lisenbee, infielders Bobby Reeves and Grant Gillis and outfielder Elliott Bigelow, December 15, 1928.

WORLD SERIES RECORD

Year	Club	League	Pos.	G.	AB.	R.	H.	2B.	3B.	HR.	RBI.	B.A.	PO.	A.	E.	F.A.
1925–Washington		Amer.	3B	3	8	0	2	0	0	0	0	.250	1	1	0	1.000
1933–Washington		Amer.	2B	5	20	2	6	1	0	0	2	.300	15	12	3	.900
World Series Totals				8	28	2	8	1	0	0	2	.286	16	13	3	.906

ARTHUR NEUKOM NEHF

Born July 31, 1892, at Terre Haute, Ind.
Died December 18, 1960, at Phoenix, Ariz.
Height, 5.09. Weight, 170.
Threw and batted lefthanded.

Pitched 21-inning game against Pittsburgh, August 1, 1918, losing 2-0.
Joint holder of National League record for pitchers participating in most double plays, season (12), 40 games, 1920.

Year	Club	League	G.	IP.	W.	L.	Pct.	H.	R.	ER.	SO.	BB.	ERA.
1913–Kansas City		Amer. Assn.	3	.....	...	...	.....	.....	...	...	...	...	.....
1913–Sioux City		Western	4	16	0	0	.000	23	...	...	15	9	.....
1914–Terre Haute		Central	23	175	11	7	.611	161	68	...	91	50	.....
1915–Terre Haute		Central	32	241	19	10	.655	162	58	37	*218	80	*1.38
1915–Boston		National	12	78	5	4	.556	60	29	22	39	21	2.54
1916–Boston		National	22	121	7	5	.583	110	40	27	36	20	2.01
1917–Boston		National	38	233	17	8	.680	197	78	56	101	39	2.16
1918–Boston		National	32	284	15	15	.500	*274	*107	•85	96	76	2.69
1919–Bos.(a)-New York		National	35	271	17	11	.607	221	89	75	77	59	2.49
1920–New York		National	40	281	21	12	.636	273	113	96	79	45	3.07
1921–New York		National	41	261	20	10	.667	266	116	105	67	55	3.62
1922–New York		National	37	268	19	13	.594	286	122	98	60	64	3.29
1923–New York		National	34	196	13	10	.565	219	112	98	50	49	4.50
1924–New York		National	30	172	14	4	.778	167	75	69	72	42	3.61
1925–New York		National	29	155	11	9	.550	193	86	65	63	50	3.77
1926–N.Y.(b)-Cincinnati		National	9	19	0	1	.000	27	12	9	4	6	4.26
1927–Cin.(c)-Chicago		National	29	71	4	6	.400	84	38	32	33	23	4.06
1928–Chicago		National	31	177	13	7	.650	190	62	52	40	52	2.64
1929–Chicago		National	32	121	8	5	.615	148	85	75	27	39	5.58
Major League Totals			451	2708	184	120	.605	2715	1164	964	844	640	3.20

aTraded with $40,000 to New York Giants for pitchers Cecil Causey, Joe Oeschger, John Paul Jones and catcher George O'Neil, August 17, 1919.
bSold to Cincinnati Reds, May, 1926.
cReleased by Cincinnati Reds, August, 1927 and signed by Chicago Cubs.

WORLD SERIES RECORD

Year	Club	League	G.	IP.	W.	L.	Pct.	H.	R.	ER.	SO.	BB.	ERA.
1921–New York		National	3	26	1	2	.333	13	6	4	8	13	1.38
1922–New York		National	2	16	1	0	1.000	11	5	4	6	3	2.25
1923–New York		National	2	16⅓	1	1	.500	10	5	5	7	6	2.76
1924–New York		National	3	19⅔	1	1	.500	15	5	4	7	9	1.83
1929–Chicago		National	2	1	0	0	.000	1	2	2	0	1	18.00
World Series Totals			12	79	4	4	.500	50	23	19	28	32	2.16

HAROLD (HAL) NEWHOUSER

Born May 20, 1921, at Detroit, Mich.
Height, 6.02. Weight, 180.
Threw and batted lefthanded.
Married Beryl Margaret Steele, December 20, 1941.

Tied major league record for double plays started by a pitcher in one game (4), May 19, 1948.
Named Most Valuable Player, American League, by THE SPORTING NEWS, 1944 and 1945.
Named as pitcher for THE SPORTING NEWS All-Star Major League Teams, 1944-45-46.
Named by THE SPORTING NEWS as the No. 1 Major League Player of the Year, 1945.
Scout, Baltimore Orioles, 1956-61; scout, Cleveland Indians, 1961-64.

Year	Club	League	G.	IP.	W.	L.	Pct.	H.	R.	ER.	SO.	BB.	ERA.
1939	Alexandria	Evang.	12	96	8	4	.667	66	37	25	107	29	2.34
1939	Beaumont	Texas	22	134	5	14	.263	111	76	57	85	73	3.83
1939	Detroit	American	1	5	0	1	.000	3	3	3	4	4	5.40
1940	Detroit	American	28	133	9	9	.500	149	81	72	89	76	4.87
1941	Detroit	American	33	173	9	11	.450	166	109	92	106	137	4.79
1942	Detroit	American	38	184	8	14	.364	137	73	50	103	114	2.45
1943	Detroit	American	37	196	8	17	.320	163	88	66	144	★111	3.03
1944	Detroit	American	47	312	★29	9	.763	264	94	77	★187	102	2.22
1945	Detroit	American	40	★313	★25	9	★.735	239	73	63	★212	110	★1.81
1946	Detroit	American	37	293	●26	9	.743	215	77	63	275	98	★1.94
1947	Detroit	American	40	285	17	★17	.500	★268	105	91	176	110	2.87
1948	Detroit	American	39	272	★21	12	.636	249	109	91	143	99	3.01
1949	Detroit	American	38	292	18	11	.621	★277	118	●109	144	111	3.36
1950	Detroit	American	35	214	15	13	.536	232	110	103	87	81	4.33
1951	Detroit	American	15	96	6	6	.500	98	47	42	37	19	3.94
1952	Detroit	American	25	154	9	9	.500	148	72	64	57	47	3.74
1953	Detroit (a)	American	7	22	0	1	.000	31	22	17	6	8	6.95
1954	Cleveland	American	26	47	7	2	.778	34	16	13	25	18	2.49
1955	Cleveland	American	2	2	0	0	.000	1	0	0	1	4	0.00
Major League Totals			488	2993	207	150	.580	2674	1197	1016	1796	1249	3.05

aUnconditionally released by Detroit Tigers, July 22, 1953; signed by Cleveland Indians, April 12, 1954.

WORLD SERIES RECORD

Year	Club	League	G.	IP.	W.	L.	Pct.	H.	R.	ER.	SO.	BB.	ERA.
1945	Detroit	American	3	20⅔	2	1	.667	25	14	14	22	4	6.10
1954	Cleveland	American	1	0	0	0	.000	1	1	1	0	1	.....
World Series Totals			4	20⅔	2	1	.667	26	15	15	22	5	6.53

LOUIS NORMAN (BUCK and BOBO) NEWSOM

Born August 11, 1907, at Hartsville, S.C.
Died December 7, 1962, at Orlando, Fla.
Height, 6.02¾. Weight, 205.
Threw right and batted right and lefthanded.
Married Ruth Griffith, December 31, 1943.

Pitched nine hitless innings for St. Louis Browns vs. Boston Red Sox, September 18, 1964—allowed one hit in 10th and lost, 2-1. Tied for major league record for most years leading league in games lost (4).
Tied World Series record by pitching three complete games in seven-game Series, 1940.

Year	Club	League	G.	IP.	W.	L.	Pct.	H.	R.	ER.	SO.	BB.	ERA.
1928	Raleigh	Piedmont	11	53	0	5	.000	64	46	41	21	33	6.96
1928	Green-Wil.	E. Carolina	27	172	15	6	.714	155	88	78	★114	76	4.08
1929	Macon	Sally	45	298	19	18	.514	283	★167	●128	149	173	3.87
1929	Brooklyn	National	3	9	0	3	.000	15	12	11	6	5	11.00
1930	Brooklyn	National	2	3	0	0	.000	2	2	0	1	2	0.00
1930	Jersey City	International	3	10	0	1	.000	15	19	6	3	9	5.40
1930	Macon	Sally	22	89	6	3	.667	87	45	24	47	29	2.43
1931	Little Rock	Southern	★51	271	16	14	.533	289	166	152	★152	★150	5.05
1932	Chicago	National	1	1	0	0	.000	1	0	0	0	0	0.00
1932	Albany	International	34	145	7	7	.500	154	96	85	84	80	5.28

Year	Club	League	G.	IP.	W.	L.	Pct.	H.	R.	ER.	SO.	BB.	ERA.
1933	Los Angeles	Pac. Coast	*56	*320	*30	11	.732	328	138	113	*212	124	3.18
1934	St. Louis	American	47	262	16	*20	.444	259	138	117	135	*149	4.02
1935	St. Louis (a)-Wash.	American	35	241	11	*18	.379	276	137	121	87	97	4.52
1936	Washington	American	43	285	17	15	.531	294	160	137	156	146	4.33
1937	Wash.(b)-Boston (c)	American	41	275	16	14	.533	269	163	147	166	*167	4.81
1938	St. Louis	American	44	*330	20	16	.556	*334	*205	*186	226	192	5.07
1939	St. Louis (d)-Detroit	American	41	292	20	11	.645	272	126	116	192	126	3.58
1940	Detroit	American	36	264	21	5	.808	235	110	83	164	100	2.83
1941	Detroit (e)	American	43	250	12	*20	.375	265	140	128	175	118	4.61
1942	Washington (f)	American	30	214	11	17	.393	236	135	*117	•113	92	4.92
1942	Brooklyn	National	6	32	2	2	.500	28	13	12	21	14	3.38
1943	Brooklyn (g)	National	22	125	9	4	.692	113	51	42	75	57	3.02
1943	St. Louis (h)-Wash.(i)	American	16	92	4	9	.308	107	67	60	48	56	5.87
1944	Philadelphia	American	37	265	13	15	.464	243	100	83	142	82	2.82
1945	Philadelphia	American	36	257	8	*20	.286	255	111	*94	127	103	3.29
1946	Phila.(j)-Washington	American	34	237	14	13	.519	224	90	77	114	90	2.92
1947	Wash.(k)-New York (l)	American	31	199	11	11	.500	208	82	74	82	67	3.35
1948	New York	National	11	26	0	4	.000	35	16	12	9	13	4.15
1949	Chattanooga	Southern	36	237	17	12	.586	273	*146	*116	*141	82	4.41
1950	Chattanooga	Southern	34	235	13	*17	.433	*244	119	•106	145	71	4.06
1951	Birmingham (m)	Southern	32	*237	16	11	.593	228	92	80	132	71	3.04
1952	Wash.(n)-Philadelphia	American	24	60	4	4	.500	54	26	26	27	32	3.90
1953	Philadelphia	American	17	39	2	1	.667	44	24	21	16	24	4.85
	American League Totals		555	3562	200	209	.489	3575	1814	1587	1970	1641	4.01
	National League Totals		45	196	11	13	.458	194	94	77	112	91	3.54
	Major League Totals		600	3758	211	222	.487	3769	1908	1664	2082	1732	3.99

aSold to Washington Senators for $40,000, May 21, 1935.
bTraded to Boston Red Sox with outfielder Ben Chapman for pitcher Wes Ferrell, catcher Rick Ferrell and outfielder Melo Almada, June 10, 1937.
cTraded to St. Louis Browns with shortstop Ralph Kress and outfielder Colonel Mills for outfielder Joe Vosmik, December 2, 1937.
dTraded to Detroit Tigers with pitcher Jim Walkup, shortstop Ralph Kress and outfielder Roy Bell for pitchers George Gill, Bob Harris, Vernon Kennedy and Roxie Lawson, third baseman Mark Christman and outfielder Chet Laabs, May 13, 1939.
eSold to Washington Senators, March 31, 1942.
fSold to Brooklyn Dodgers, August 31, 1942.
gTraded to St. Louis Browns for pitchers Archie McKain and Fritz Ostermueller, July 15, 1943.
hSold to Washington Senators, August 31, 1943.
iTraded to Philadelphia Athletics for pitcher Roger Wolff, December 13, 1943.
jReleased by Philadelphia Athletics at own request, June 3, 1946; signed with Washington Senators, June 5, 1946.
kReleased to New York Yankees on waivers, July 11, 1947.
lUnconditionally released by New York Yankees, February 16, 1948 and signed by New York Giants, April 10, 1948.
mSigned with Washington Senators, April 8, 1952.
nUnconditionally released by Washington Senators, June 16, 1952; signed with Philadelphia Athletics same day.

WORLD SERIES RECORD

Year	Club	League	G.	IP.	W.	L.	Pct.	H.	R.	ER.	SO.	BB.	ERA.
1940	Detroit	American	3	26	2	1	.667	18	4	4	17	4	1.38
1947	New York	American	2	2⅓	0	1	.000	6	5	5	0	2	19.29
	World Series Totals		5	28⅓	2	2	.500	24	9	9	17	6	2.86

CHARLES AUGUSTUS (KID) NICHOLS

Born September 14, 1869, at Madison, Wis.
Died April 11, 1953, at Kansas City, Mo.
Height, 5.10½. Weight, 180.
Threw and batted righthanded.

Manager, Kansas City, Western League, 1902-03; manager, St. Louis Cardinals, 1904 and part of 1905. Named to Hall of Fame, 1949.

Year	Club	League	G.	CG.	IP.	W.	L.	Pct.	ShO.	H.	R.	SO.	BB.
1887	Kansas City	Western	....	....	....	....	12	....	....	....	....	65	39
1888	Memphis	Southern	15	....	....	....	8	....	....	....	....	84	74
1888	Kansas City	West. Assn.	18	....	....	....	....	....	....	....	....	....	....
1889	Omaha	West. Assn.	48	....	....	36	12	.750	....	355	194	357	92
1890	Boston	National	48	47	424	27	19	.587	*7	378	176	222	117
1891	Boston	National	52	45	423	30	17	.638	5	409	220	213	96

Year	Club	League	G.	CG.	IP.	W.	L.	Pct.	ShO.	H.	R.	SO.	BB.
1892—Boston		National	53	49	454	35	16	.686	5	399	209	211	111
1893—Kansas City		National	52	43	414	34	14	.708	1	409	222	92	110
1894—Boston		National	50	40	417	32	13	.711	•3	475	306	98	108
1895—Boston		National	47	42	394	26	16	.619	1	427	219	146	82
1896—Boston		National	49	37	375	30	14	.682	3	396	211	95	93
1897—Boston		National	*46	37	358	31	11	.738	2	345	154	136	72
1898—Boston		National	50	40	388	31	12	.721	5	309	136	132	84
1899—Boston		National	42	37	349	21	19	.525	4	321	155	109	86
1900—Boston		National	29	25	226	13	16	.448	•4	210	116	54	73
1901—Boston		National	38	33	326	19	16	.543	4	306	146	141	86
1902—Kansas City		Western	37	....	....	27	7	.794	....	....	....	168	90
1903—Kansas City		Western	35	....	....	21	12	.636	....	....	....	156	81
1904—St. Louis		National	36	35	317	21	13	.618	3	260	97	134	50
1905—St. Louis(a)-Phila		National	24	20	191	11	11	.500	1	193	94	82	64
1906—Philadelphia		National	4	1	11	0	1	.000	0	17	16	1	13
Major League Totals			620	531	5067	361	208	.634	48	4854	2477	1866	1245

aReleased to Philadelphia Phillies, July, 1905

WILLIAM BECK (SWISH) NICHOLSON

Born December 11, 1914, at Chestertown, Md.
Height, 6.00. Weight, 205.
Threw right and batted lefthanded.
Married Nancy Kane, December 28, 1937.

Tied major league record by leading National League in both home runs and runs batted in, two consecutive years (1943 and 1944); tied major league mark and set National League record with four homers in four successive times at bat, two games, July 22 and 23 (first game), 1944.
Named by Baseball Writers' Association of America as outfielder for THE SPORTING NEWS All-Star Major League Team, 1943.

Year	Club	League	Pos.	G.	AB.	R.	H.	2B.	3B.	HR.	RBI.	B.A.	PO.	A.	E.	F.A.
1936—Oklahoma City		Texas	OF	14	48	4	8	1	0	0	5	.167	19	1	1	.952
1936—Philadelphia		Amer.	O-PH	11	12	2	0	0	0	0	0	.000	1	0	0	1.000
1937—Williamsport		NYP	OF	10	23	5	5	1	0	1	9	.217	11	0	0	1.000
1937—Portsmouth		Pied.	OF	121	468	79	145	26	7	20	92	.310	276	12	14	.954
1938—Williamsport		East.	OF	137	511	96	154	26	17	*22	96	.301	*305	13	14	.958
1939—Chattanooga(a)		South.	OF	105	383	82	128	29	8	*23	85	.334	196	9	10	.953
1939—Chicago		Nat.	OF	58	220	37	65	12	5	5	38	.295	123	5	6	.955
1940—Chicago		Nat.	OF	135	491	78	146	27	7	25	98	.297	242	10	13	.951
1941—Chicago		Nat.	OF	147	532	74	135	26	1	26	98	.254	293	10	9	.971
1942—Chicago		Nat.	OF	152	588	83	173	22	11	21	78	.294	327	18	5	.986
1943—Chicago		Nat.	OF	154	608	95	188	30	9	*29	*128	.309	340	16	8	.978
1944—Chicago		Nat.	OF	156	582	*116	167	35	8	*33	*122	.287	305	18	7	.979
1945—Chicago		Nat.	OF	151	559	82	136	28	4	13	88	.243	300	12	3	.990
1946—Chicago		Nat.	OF	105	296	36	65	13	2	8	41	.220	179	4	5	.973
1947—Chicago		Nat.	OF	148	487	69	119	28	1	26	75	.244	281	7	3	*.990
1948—Chicago(b)		Nat.	OF	143	494	68	129	24	5	19	67	.261	244	7	5	.980
1949—Philadelphia		Nat.	OF	98	299	42	70	8	3	11	40	.234	185	10	1	.995
1950—Philadelphia		Nat.	OF	41	58	4	13	2	1	3	10	.224	20	0	1	.952
1951—Philadelphia		Nat.	OF	85	170	23	41	9	2	8	30	.241	75	1	1	.987
1952—Philadelphia		Nat.	OF	55	88	17	24	3	0	6	19	.273	33	0	0	1.000
1953—Philadelphia		Nat.	OF-PH	38	62	12	13	5	1	2	16	.210	13	0	0	1.000
American League Totals				11	12	2	0	0	0	0	0	.000	1	0	0	1.000
National League Totals				1666	5534	835	1484	272	60	235	948	.268	2960	118	67	.979
Major League Totals				1677	5546	837	1484	272	60	235	948	.268	2961	118	67	.979

aSold to Chicago Cubs for $35,000, June 25, 1939, to report end of July.
bTraded with pitcher Russ Meyer to Philadelphia Phillies for outfielder Harry Walker, October 4, 1948.

WORLD SERIES RECORD

Year	Club	League	Pos.	G.	AB.	R.	H.	2B.	3B.	HR.	RBI.	B.A.	PO.	A.	E.	F.A.
1945—Chicago		Nat.	OF	7	28	1	6	1	0	0	8	.214	9	0	1	.900

DID YOU KNOW—
That Kid Nichols won 30 games from '91 through '98, missing only 1895 (26)?

FRANK JOSEPH (LEFTY) O'DOUL

Born March 4, 1897, at San Francisco, Calif.
Died December 7, 1969, at San Francisco, Calif.
Height, 6.00. Weight, 180.
Threw and batted lefthanded.
Married Jean Gold, May 11, 1953.

Tied with Bill Terry (New York Giants, 1930), for National League record for most base-hits in season, 254 (1929); voted most valuable player, Pacific Coast League, 1927.

Manager, San Francisco, Pacific Coast League, 1935 to 1951; vice-president, San Francisco club, September, 1948 to 1951; manager, San Diego, Pacific Coast League, 1952-53-54; Oakland, Pacific Coast League, 1955; Vancouver, Pacific Coast League, 1956; Seattle, Pacific Coast League, 1957.

Year	Club	League	Pos.	G.	AB.	R.	H.	2B.	3B.	HR.	RBI.	B.A.	PO.	A.	E.	F.A.
1917	Des Moines	West.	P	19	52	3	14	0	0	0	....	.269	8	37	6	.882
1918	San Francisco	P. C.	P	49	120	9	24	3	0	0	....	.200	....	....	....	....
1919	New York	Amer.	PH-P	19	16	2	4	0	0	0	1	.250	1	2	0	1.000
1920	New York	Amer.	OF-P	13	12	2	2	1	0	0	1	.167	0	0	0	.000
1921	San Francisco	P. C.	P-PH	74	136	24	46	7	2	5	23	.338	12	70	4	.953
1922	New York(a)	Amer.	PH-P	8	9	0	3	1	0	0	4	.333	1	4	0	1.000
1923	Boston	Amer.	P-OF	36	35	2	5	0	0	0	4	.143	3	21	1	.960
1924	Salt Lake	P. C.	OF-P	140	416	84	163	31	4	11	101	.392	144	40	11	.944
1925	Salt Lake	P. C.	OF	198	*825	185	*309	63	*17	24	191	.375	327	20	11	.969
1926	Hollywood	P. C.	OF	180	659	88	223	29	3	20	116	.338	299	29	13	.962
1927	San Francisco	P. C.	OF	189	736	*164	*278	43	4	33	158	.378	349	19	12	.968
1928	New York(b)	Nat.	OF	114	354	67	113	19	4	8	46	.319	149	4	6	.962
1929	Philadelphia	Nat.	OF	154	638	152	*254	35	6	32	122	*.398	320	14	10	.971
1930	Philadelphia(c)	Nat.	OF	140	528	122	202	37	7	22	97	.383	262	3	13	.953
1931	Brooklyn	Nat.	OF	134	512	85	172	32	11	7	75	.336	285	4	14	.954
1932	Brooklyn	Nat.	OF	148	595	120	219	32	8	21	90	*.368	317	4	7	.979
1933	Brkn.(d)-N.Y.	Nat.	OF	121	388	45	110	14	2	14	56	.284	197	5	8	.962
1934	New York	Nat.	OF	83	177	27	56	4	3	9	46	.316	60	1	2	.968
1935	San Francisco	P. C.	OF-P	68	134	23	36	2	1	2	25	.269	33	3	4	.900
1936	San Francisco	P. C.	PH	54	53	5	12	2	2	0	8	.226	0	0	0	.000
1937	San Francisco	P. C.	PH	44	44	7	17	6	0	0	13	.386	0	0	0	.000
1938	San Francisco	P. C.	PH	30	27	6	7	1	0	3	6	.259	0	0	0	.000
1939	San Francisco	P. C.	PH-O-P	25	35	6	14	1	0	0	2	.400	13	0	0	1.000
1940	San Francisco	P. C.	PH-P	14	13	0	2	0	0	0	0	.154	0	2	0	1.000
1944	San Francisco	P. C.	PH	1	1	0	0	0	0	0	0	.000	0	0	0	.000
1945	San Francisco	P. C.	PH	1	1	0	0	0	0	0	0	.000	0	0	0	.000
1956	Vancouver	P. C.	PH	1	1	1	1	0	1	0	0	1.000	0	0	0	.000
	American League Totals			76	72	6	14	2	0	0	10	.194	5	27	1	.970
	National League Totals			894	3192	618	1126	173	41	113	532	.353	1590	35	60	.964
	Major League Totals			970	3264	624	1140	175	41	113	542	.349	1595	62	61	.964

aSold to Boston Red Sox on waivers, October 12, 1922.
bTraded to Philadelphia Phillies with cash for outfielder Fred Leach, October 29, 1928.
cTraded with infielder Fresco Thompson to Brooklyn Dodgers for pitcher Hal B. Lee, outfielder Clise Dudley, outfielder James E. Elliott and cash, October 14, 1930.
dTraded with pitcher William Watson Clark to New York Giants for first baseman Sam Leslie, June 16, 1933.

WORLD SERIES RECORD

Year	Club	League	Pos.	G.	AB.	R.	H.	2B.	3B.	HR.	RBI.	B.A.	PO.	A.	E.	F.A.
1933	New York	Nat.	PH	1	1	1	1	0	0	0	2	1.000	0	0	0	.000

PITCHING RECORD

Year	Club	League	G.	IP.	W.	L.	Pct.	H.	R.	ER.	SO.	BB.	ERA.
1917	Des Moines	Western	17	115	8	6	.571	114	....	49	54	35	3.83
1918	San Francisco	Pacific Coast	27	185	12	8	.600	149	69	54	62	67	2.63
1919	New York	American	3	5	0	0	.000	7	6	2	2	4	3.60
1920	New York	American	2	3	0	0	.000	4	2	2	2	2	6.00
1921	San Francisco	Pacific Coast	47	312	25	9	.735	314	126	83	97	92	2.39
1922	New York	American	6	16	0	0	.000	24	13	6	5	12	3.38
1923	Boston	American	23	53	1	1	.500	69	50	32	10	31	5.44
1924	Salt Lake	Pacific Coast	31	128	7	9	.438	205	112	93	39	56	6.54
1935	San Francisco	Pacific Coast	2	4	0	0	.000	4	2	....	1	2	....
1939	San Francisco	Pacific Coast	2	2	0	0	.000	6	3	....	0	0	....
1940	San Francisco	Pacific Coast	3	4	0	0	.000	11	5	3	4	5	....
	Major League Totals		34	77	1	1	.500	104	71	42	19	49	4.91

ANTONIO (TONY) OLIVA (LOPEZ)

Born July 20, 1940, at Pinar del Rio, Cuba.
Height, 6.02. Weight, 192.
Threw right and batted lefthanded.

Tied major league records for most total bases, rookie season (374), 1964, and most consecutive years leading league in hits, 3.
Established American League record for most hits, rookie season (217), 1964.
Hit three home runs in a game, July 3, 1973.
Tied World Series records for most putouts, game, nine innings, right fielder (7), October 6, 1965, and most chances accepted, game, nine innings, right fielder (7), October 6, 1965.
Named American League Rookie of the Year by the Baseball Writers' Association and Rookie Player of the Year by THE SPORTING NEWS, 1964.
Named as outfielder on THE SPORTING NEWS American League All-Star Team, 1964-65-66-70-71.
Named American League Player of the Year by THE SPORTING NEWS, 1965.
Named as outfielder on THE SPORTING NEWS American League All-Star fielding team, 1966.
Named American League Player of the Year by THE SPORTING NEWS, 1971.
Coach, Minnesota Twins, 1977, 1978; minor league batting instructor, 1979 to date.

Year—Club	League	Pos.	G.	AB.	R.	H.	2B.	3B.	HR.	RBI.	B.A.	PO.	A.	E.	F.A.
1961—Wytheville	Appal.	OF	64	249	55	*102	15	6	10	*81	*410	70	*12	14	.854
1962—Charlotte	Sally	OF	127	469	71	164	35	6	17	93	.350	231	13	*19	.928
1962—Minnesota	Amer.	OF	9	9	3	4	1	0	0	3	.444	3	0	0	1.000
1963—Dal.-Ft. Worth	P.C.	OF	146	536	79	163	30	8	23	74	.304	301	14	11	.966
1963—Minnesota	Amer.	PH	7	7	0	3	0	0	0	1	.429	0	0	0	.000
1964—Minnesota	Amer.	OF	161	672	*109	*217	*43	9	32	94	*.323	313	5	6	.981
1965—Minnesota	Amer.	OF	149	576	107	*185	40	5	16	98	*.321	284	10	●11	.964
1966—Minnesota	Amer.	OF	159	622	99	*191	32	7	25	87	.307	335	9	*10	.972
1967—Minnesota	Amer.	OF	146	557	76	161	*34	6	17	83	.289	286	8	4	.987
1968—Minnesota	Amer.	OF	128	470	54	136	24	5	18	68	.289	227	7	4	.983
1969—Minnesota	Amer.	OF	153	637	97	*197	*39	4	24	101	.309	311	14	6	.982
1970—Minnesota	Amer.	OF	157	628	96	*204	●36	7	23	107	.325	351	12	●12	.968
1971—Minnesota	Amer.	OF	126	487	73	164	30	3	22	81	*.337	216	6	7	.969
1972—Minnesota	Amer.	OF	10	28	1	9	1	0	0	1	.321	6	0	1	.857
1973—Minnesota	Amer.	DH	146	571	63	166	20	0	16	92	.291	0	0	0	.000
1974—Minnesota	Amer.	DH	127	459	43	131	16	2	13	57	.285	0	0	0	.000
1975—Minnesota	Amer.	DH	131	455	46	123	10	0	13	58	.270	0	0	0	.000
1976—Minnesota	Amer.	DH	67	123	3	26	3	0	1	4	.211	0	0	0	.000
Major League Totals			1676	6301	870	1917	329	48	220	935	.304	2332	71	61	.975

WORLD SERIES RECORD

Year—Club	League	Pos.	G.	AB.	R.	H.	2B.	3B.	HR.	RBI.	B.A.	PO.	A.	E.	F.A.
1965—Minnesota	Amer.	OF	7	26	2	5	1	0	1	2	.192	20	0	1	.952

JAMES EDWARD (TIP) O'NEILL

Born May 25, 1858, at Woodstock, Ont.
Died December 31, 1915, at Montreal, Que.
Height, 6.01½. Weight, 187.
Threw and batted righthanded.

Umpired in several minor leagues in 1890s.
First player to hit two homers in a World Series game, October 19, 1886.

Year—Club	League	Pos.	G.	AB.	R.	H.	2B.	3B.	HR.	SB.	B.A.	PO.	A.	E.	F.A.
1882—Metropolitan	Alliance	OF				(No records available)									
1883—New York	Nat.	OF-P	23	84	7	15	3	0	0	....	.179	9	37	6	.885
1884—St. Louis	A. A.	OF-P	77	302	47	82	14	11	3	....	.272	74	33	20	.843
1885—St. Louis	A. A.	OF	51	202	45	69	5	5	3	....	.342	86	8	11	.893
1886—St. Louis	A. A.	OF	138	575	105	195	29	15	3	7	.339	282	14	21	.934
1887—St. Louis	A. A.	OF	123	563	*166	277	*46	*24	*13	30	*.492	232	9	29	.893
1888—St. Louis	A. A.	OF	130	530	106	*176	23	9	5	24	*.332	233	6	13	.949
1889—St. Louis	A. A.	OF	133	534	125	180	32	8	9	29	.337	267	12	22	.927
1890—Chicago	Play.	OF	137	573	113	173	18	16	3	28	.302	235	8	17	.935

Year	Club	League	Pos.	G.	AB.	R.	H.	2B.	3B.	HR.	SB.	B.A.	PO.	A.	E.	F.A.
1891—St. Louis		A. A.	OF	119	414	106	156	29	3	10	30	.324	197	7	10	.953
1892—Cincinnati		Nat.	OF	107	420	63	105	13	7	2	15	.250	184	15	16	.926
American Association Totals				771	3120	682	1135	178	75	46	.....	.363	1371	89	126	.921
National League Totals				130	504	70	120	16	7	2	.....	.238	193	52	22	.918
Players League Totals				137	573	113	173	18	16	3	28	.302	235	8	17	.935
Major League Totals				1038	4197	865	1428	212	98	51	.....	.340	1799	149	165	.922

WORLD SERIES RECORD

Year.	Club.	League	Pos.	G.	AB.	R.	H.	BA.	PO.	A.	E.	F.A.
1885—St. Louis		A. A.	OF	7	24	4	5	.208	2	0	1	.667
1886—St. Louis		A. A.	OF	6	19	4	8	.421	13	1	0	1.000
1887—St. Louis		A. A.	OF	15	65	6	13	.200	26	2	2	.933
1888—St. Louis		A. A.	OF	10	38	8	9	.237	23	0	3	.885
World Series Totals				38	146	22	35	.240	64	3	6	.918

PITCHING RECORD

Year	Club	League	G.	CG.	IP.	W.	L.	Pct.	ShO.	H.	R.	SO.	BB.
1883—New York		National	19	15	147	6	12	.333	0	180	...	54	63
1884—St. Louis		Amer. Assn.	17	14	140	10	4	.714	0	121	...	37	50
Major League Totals			36	29	287	16	16	.500	0	301	...	81	113

JAMES HENRY (ORATOR JIM) O'ROURKE

Born August 24, 1852, at East Bridgeport, Conn.
Died January 8, 1919, at Bridgeport, Conn.
Threw and batted righthanded.

Manager, Buffalo, N. L., 1881-84; umpire, N. L., 1894; manager of Victors of Bridgeport, 1895-96; manager, Bridgeport, Connecticut League, 1897-1908; president of Connecticut League, 1907-13; president of Eastern Association, 1914.
Named to Hall of Fame, 1945.

Year	Club	League	Pos.	G.	AB.	R.	H.	2B.	3B.	HR.	SB.	B.A.	PO.	A.	E.	F.A.
1872—Mansfield		Nat. Assn.		.....	.....	.....	.....	.....	.....	.....	.....	.....	.....	.....	.....	.....
1873—Boston		Nat. Assn.	3B	57	297	79	103	.....	.....	.....	.....	.347	392	23	31	.930
1874—Boston		Nat. Assn.	1-3B	70	334	80	115	.....	.....	.....	.....	.344	763	11	37	.954
1875—Boston		Nat. Assn.	3-OF	69	.....	.....	.....	.....	.....	.....	.....	.306	.....	.....	.....	.933
1876—Boston		Nat.	OF	70	327	61	102	15	1	2	.....	.312	154	7	27	.856
1877—Boston		Nat.	OF	49	211	54	74	16	4	0	.....	.351	84	8	19	.829
1878—Boston		Nat.	OF	60	255	44	70	11	8	1	.....	.275	102	15	19	.860
1879—Providence		Nat.	OF-1B	80	359	69	126	17	12	4	.....	.351	271	12	28	.910
1880—Boston		Nat.	O-Inf.-C	84	355	70	100	18	11	•6	.....	.282	196	15	18	.921
1881—Buffalo		Nat.	O-Inf.-C	83	348	71	105	19	6	0	.....	.302	112	85	39	.835
1882—Buffalo		Nat.	O-Inf.-C	84	370	62	104	16	8	2	.....	.281	140	15	24	.866
1883—Buffalo		Nat.	O-Inf.-C	93	430	99	141	30	7	1	.....	.328	215	42	28	.902
1884—Buffalo		Nat.	O-Inf.-C	104	448	112	157	27	9	*4	.....	.350	318	7	28	.921
1885—New York		Nat.	OF-C	112	477	119	143	21	•15	4	.....	.300	179	13	13	.937
1886—New York		Nat.	OF-C	104	440	106	136	25	6	1	14	.309	351	94	28	.941
1887—New York		Nat.	OF-C-3B	103	433	73	149	15	13	2	46	.344	197	73	24	.918
1888—New York		Nat.	OF	107	409	50	112	15	7	4	25	.274	130	13	6	.960
1889—New York		Nat.	OF	128	502	89	161	36	7	3	33	.321	165	18	22	.893
1890—New York		Play.	OF	111	469	112	172	31	7	8	26	.367	200	27	16	.934
1891—New York		Nat.	OF	136	554	94	167	27	8	5	25	.301	175	16	20	.905
1892—New York		Nat.	OF	112	447	63	133	26	5	0	23	.298	146	12	14	.919
1893—Washington		Nat.	OF-1B	129	527	76	161	20	5	2	19	.306	455	35	25	.951
1904—New York		Nat.	C	1	4	1	1	0	0	0	.....	.250	4	0	1	.800
1904—Bridgeport		Conn.	C	65	245	28	70	11	1	0	2	.286	230	72	7	.977
1905—Bridgeport		Conn.	C-OF	68	238	15	60	11	1	1	3	.252	119	34	8	.950
1906—Bridgeport		Conn.	1B	93	348	26	85	9	0	0	5	.244	771	59	17	.980
1907—Bridgeport		Conn.	1B	24	83	3	16	.....	.....	.....	.....	.193	26	0	1	.963
National League Totals				1639	6896	1313	2142	354	132	41	.....	.311	3394	480	383	.910
Players League Totals				111	469	112	172	31	7	8	26	.367	200	27	16	.934
Major League Totals				1750	7365	1425	2314	385	139	49	.....	.314	3594	507	399	.911

DID YOU KNOW—

That Jim O'Rourke collected the first hit in major league history?

ALBERT LEWIS ORTH

Born September 5, 1872, at Danville, Ind.
Died October 8, 1948, at Lynchburg, Va.
Height, 6.00. Weight, 200.
Threw and batted righthanded.
Married Jimmie Allen, November 5, 1895.

Manager, Lynchburg, Virginia League, 1909; umpire, Virginia League, 1912; umpire, National League, 1913-14-15-16; in France as YMCA worker in war, 1917-18; umpire, Virginia League, 1920-21-22-23.

Year	Club	League	G.	IP.	W.	L.	Pct.	H.	R.	SO.	BB.	CG.	ShO.
1894	Lynchburg	Virginia					(No Averages Issued)						
1895	Lynchburg	Virginia					(No Averages Issued)						
1895	Philadelphia	National	11	89	9	1	.900	106	52	25	20	9	0
1896	Philadelphia	National	25	198	13	7	.650	244	130	21	45	19	0
1897	Philadelphia	National	35	272	14	19	.424	338	192	67	76	28	2
1898	Philadelphia	National	32	254	15	12	.556	293	139	26	43	26	1
1899	Philadelphia	National	21	142	13	3	.813	141	65	35	20	13	3
1900	Philadelphia	National	32	258	12	13	.480	292	145	69	60	23	2
1901	Philadelphia(a)	National	35	281	20	12	.625	247	98	99	33	30	•6
1902	Washington	American	38	323	18	17	.514	361	181	79	46	36	1
1903	Washington	American	36	278	10	21	.323	310	172	89	60	30	2
1904	Wash.(b)-New York	American	30	213	14	9	.609	213	97	73	33	18	3
1905	New York	American	40	303	18	16	.529	271	127	124	65	26	7
1906	New York	American	45	*339	*27	17	.614	315	115	132	66	36	3
1907	New York	American	36	250	14	•21	.400	236	132	80	46	21	3
1908	New York	American	21	139	2	13	.133	134	62	22	30	8	1
1909	Lynchburg	Virginia	3	18	1	2	.333	16	9	7	9	0	0
1909	New York	American	1	3	0	0	.000	6	4	1	1	0	0
1910	Indianapolis	Amer. Assn.	22	....	4	8	.333	....	....	....	....	....	......
American League Totals			247	1848	103	114	.475	1846	890	600	347	175	20
National League Totals			191	1494	96	67	.589	1661	821	342	297	148	14
Major League Totals			438	3342	199	181	.524	3507	1711	942	644	323	34

aJumped to Washington, American League, for 1902.
bTraded to New York, American League, for pitcher Tom Hughes, July 23, 1904.

CLAUDE WILSON (WIMPY) OSTEEN

Born August 9, 1939, at Caney Springs, Tenn.
Height, 5.11½. Weight, 175.
Threw and batted lefthanded.

Coach, St. Louis Cardinals, 1977 to date.

Year	Club	League	G.	IP.	W.	L.	Pct.	H.	R.	ER.	SO.	BB.	ERA.
1957	Nashville	Southern	7	13	1	1	.500	7	8	8	13	20	5.54
1957	Cincinnati	National	3	4	0	0	.000	4	1	1	3	3	2.25
1958	Wenatchee	Northwest	22	151	14	4	*.778	145	61	51	174	67	3.04
1958	Seattle	P. Coast	12	79	5	4	.556	69	38	27	40	42	3.08
1959	Seattle	P. Coast	28	193	8	12	.400	167	82	64	155	78	2.98
1959	Cincinnati	National	2	8	0	0	.000	11	10	6	3	9	6.75
1960	Cincinnati	National	20	48	0	1	.000	53	29	27	15	30	5.06
1961	Cincinnati	National	1	⅓	0	0	.000	0	0	0	0	0	0.00
1961	Indianapolis(a)	Am. Assoc.	28	191	15	11	.577	184	92	75	132	77	3.53
1961	Washington	American	3	18	1	1	.500	14	11	10	14	9	5.00
1962	Washington	American	28	150	8	13	.381	140	62	61	59	47	3.66
1963	Washington	American	40	212	9	14	.391	222	101	79	109	60	3.35
1964	Washington(b)	American	37	257	15	13	.536	256	107	95	133	64	3.33
1965	Los Angeles	National	40	287	15	15	.500	253	95	89	162	78	2.79
1966	Los Angeles	National	39	240	17	14	.548	238	92	76	137	65	2.85
1967	Los Angeles	National	39	288	17	17	.500	*298	116	103	152	52	3.22
1968	Los Angeles	National	39	254	12	•18	.400	267	*109	87	119	54	3.08
1969	Los Angeles	National	41	321	20	15	.571	*293	103	95	183	74	2.66
1970	Los Angeles	National	37	259	16	14	.533	280	121	110	114	52	3.82

Year	Club	League	G.	IP.	W.	L.	Pct.	H.	R.	ER.	SO.	BB.	ERA.
1971–Los Angeles		National	38	259	14	11	.560	262	108	101	109	63	3.51
1972–Los Angeles		National	33	252	20	11	.645	232	82	74	100	69	2.64
1973–Los Angeles(c)		National	33	237	16	11	.593	227	97	87	86	61	3.30
1974–Houston(d)-St. Louis		National	31	161	9	11	.450	184	81	68	51	58	3.80
1975–Chicago(e)		American	37	204	7	16	.304	237	110	99	63	92	4.37
American League Totals			145	841	40	57	.412	869	391	344	378	272	3.68
National League Totals			396	2618	156	138	.531	2602	1044	924	1234	668	3.18
Major League Totals			541	3459	196	195	.501	3471	1435	1268	1612	940	3.30

aTraded to Washington Senators by Cincinnati Reds for cash (plus pitcher Dave Sisler) September 16, 1961.

bTraded to Los Angeles Dodgers with infielder John Kennedy and estimated $100,000 for outfielder Frank Howard, infielder Ken McMullen (plus first baseman Dick Nen) and pitchers Phil Ortega and Pete Richert, December 4, 1964.

cTraded with pitcher Dave Culpepper to Houston Astros for outfielder Jim Wynn, December 6, 1973.

dTraded to St. Louis Cardinals for pitcher Ron Selak (plus pitcher Don Larson), August 15, 1974.

eSigned as free agent by Chicago White Sox, April 11, 1975.

WORLD SERIES RECORD

Year	Club	League	G.	IP.	W.	L.	Pct.	H.	R.	ER.	SO.	BB.	ERA.
1965–Los Angeles		National	2	14	1	1	.500	9	2	1	4	5	0.64
1966–Los Angeles		National	1	7	0	1	.000	3	1	1	3	1	1.29
World Series Totals			3	21	1	2	.333	12	3	2	7	6	0.86

MELVIN THOMAS OTT

Born March 2, 1909, at Gretna, La.

Died November 21, 1958, at New Orleans, La.

Height, 5.09. Weight, 170.

Threw right and batted lefthanded.

Holds National League records for most bases on balls (1,708) and most years 100 or more bases on balls (10), 1929-30-32-36-37-38-39-40-41-42.

Had five intentional bases on balls in game on October 5, 1929, second game.

Scored six runs in one game twice, August 4, 1934, second game, and April 30, 1944, first game.

Led N.L. outfielders in double plays, 1929, 1935 (tie).

Named to THE SPORTING NEWS All-Star Major League Teams, 1934-35-36-38.

Manager, New York Giants, 1942 until July 16, 1948; associated with New York Giant farm system, 1948 through 1950; manager, Oakland, 1951-52.

Named to Hall of Fame, 1951.

Year	Club	League	Pos.	G.	AB.	R.	H.	2B.	3B.	HR.	RBI.	B.A.	PO.	A.	E.	F.A.
1926–New York		Nat.	OF	35	60	7	23	2	0	0	4	.383	18	3	2	.913
1927–New York		Nat.	OF	82	163	23	46	7	3	1	19	.282	52	2	1	.982
1928–New York		Nat.	OF	124	435	69	140	26	4	18	77	.322	214	14	7	.970
1929–New York		Nat.	OF	150	545	138	179	37	2	42	151	.328	335	★26	10	.973
1930–New York		Nat.	OF	148	521	122	182	34	5	25	119	.349	320	23	11	.969
1931–New York		Nat.	OF	138	497	104	145	23	8	29	115	.292	332	20	7	.981
1932–New York		Nat.	OF	•154	566	119	180	30	8	•38	123	.318	347	11	6	.984
1933–New York		Nat.	OF	152	580	98	164	36	1	23	103	.283	283	12	5	.983
1934–New York		Nat.	OF	153	582	119	190	29	10	★35	★135	.326	286	12	8	.974
1935–New York		Nat.	★OF-3B	152	593	113	191	33	6	31	114	.322	304	42	6	★.983
1936–New York		Nat.	OF	150	534	120	175	28	6	★33	135	.328	250	20	4	.985
1937–New York		Nat	OF-3B	151	545	99	160	28	2	•31	95	.294	198	126	10	.970
1938–New York		Nat.	OF-3B	150	527	★116	164	23	6	★36	116	.311	163	241	15	.964
1939–New York		Nat.	OF-3B	125	396	85	122	23	2	27	80	.308	190	45	11	.955
1940–New York		Nat.	OF-3B	151	536	89	155	27	3	19	79	.289	240	92	12	.965
1941–New York		Nat.	OF	148	525	89	150	29	0	27	90	.286	256	•19	9	.968
1942–New York		Nat.	OF	152	549	•118	162	21	0	★30	93	.295	269	15	3	.990
1943–New York		Nat.	OF-3B	125	380	65	89	12	2	18	47	.234	219	12	6	.975
1944–New York		Nat.	OF	120	399	91	115	16	4	26	82	.288	200	19	7	.969
1945–New York		Nat.	OF	135	451	73	139	23	0	21	79	.308	217	11	4	.982
1946–New York		Nat.	OF	31	68	2	5	1	0	1	4	.074	23	2	0	1.000
1947–New York		Nat.	PH	4	4	0	0	0	0	0	0	.000	0	0	0	.000
Major League Totals				2730	9456	1859	2876	488	72	511	1860	.304	4716	767	144	.974

WORLD SERIES RECORD

Year	Club	League	Pos.	G.	AB.	R.	H.	2B.	3B.	HR.	RBI.	B.A.	PO.	A.	E.	F.A.
1933–New York		Nat.	OF	5	18	3	7	0	0	2	4	.389	10	0	0	1.000
1936–New York		Nat.	OF	6	23	4	7	2	0	1	3	.304	12	0	1	.923
1937–New York		Nat.	3B	5	20	1	4	0	0	1	3	.200	5	9	1	.933
World Series Totals				16	61	8	18	2	0	4	10	.295	27	9	2	.947

ANDREW PAFKO

Born February 25, 1921, at Boyceville, Wis.
Height, 6.00. Weight, 190.
Threw and batted righthanded.
Married Ellen Kapusta, February 1, 1947.

Hit three home runs in a game August 2, 1950.
Set World Series record for most chances by outfielder, one Series, seven games (26), 1945, and tied record for most putouts, one Series, seven games (24), 1945. Tied Series record for most times at bat, game (6), October 8, 1945; tied for fewest runs scored by player participating in seven games (0), 1952.
Named as outfielder for THE SPORTING NEWS All-Star Major League Team, 1945.
Coach, Milwaukee Braves, 1960 through 1962; scout, Milwaukee, 1963; manager, Binghamton, Eastern League, 1964; manager, West Palm Beach, Florida State League, 1965; manager, Kinston, Carolina League, 1966-67; manager, West Palm Beach, Florida State League, 1968.

Year	Club	League	Pos.	G.	AB.	R.	H.	2B.	3B.	HR.	RBI.	B.A.	PO.	A.	E.	F.A.
1940	Eau Claire	North.	OF	20	67	5	14	3	1	0	3	.209	24	2	3	.897
1941	Green Bay	Wis.St.	OF	87	318	74	111	19	3	12	66	.349	97	13	4	.965
1942	Macon	Sally	OF	126	484	83	145	20	*18	7	85	.300	234	12	11	.957
1943	Los Angeles	P.C.	OF	157	604	109	*215	31	13	18	*118	*.356	351	14	9	.976
1943	Chicago	Nat.	OF	13	58	7	22	3	0	0	10	.379	25	0	0	1.000
1944	Chicago	Nat.	OF	128	469	47	126	16	2	6	62	.269	333	•24	6	.983
1945	Chicago	Nat.	OF	144	534	64	159	24	12	12	110	.298	371	11	2	*.995
1946	Chicago	Nat.	OF	65	234	18	66	6	4	3	30	.282	165	13	4	.978
1947	Chicago	Nat.	OF	129	513	68	155	25	7	13	66	.302	327	9	5	.985
1948	Chicago	Nat.	3B	142	548	82	171	30	2	26	101	.312	125	*314	*29	.938
1949	Chicago	Nat.	OF-3B	144	519	79	146	29	2	18	69	.281	257	109	13	.966
1950	Chicago	Nat.	OF	146	514	95	156	24	8	36	92	.304	342	12	8	.978
1951	Chi.(a)-Bkln.	Nat.	OF	133	455	68	116	16	3	30	93	.255	263	14	2	.993
1952	Brooklyn (b)	Nat.	OF-3B	150	551	76	158	17	5	19	85	.287	244	37	6	.979
1953	Milwaukee	Nat.	OF	140	516	70	153	23	4	17	72	.297	241	5	6	.976
1954	Milwaukee	Nat.	OF	138	510	61	146	22	4	14	69	.286	245	9	8	.969
1955	Milwaukee	Nat.	OF-3B	86	252	29	67	3	5	5	34	.266	105	27	3	.978
1956	Milwaukee	Nat.	OF	45	93	15	24	5	0	2	9	.258	43	2	1	.978
1957	Milwaukee	Nat.	OF	83	220	31	61	6	1	8	27	.277	108	1	2	.982
1958	Milwaukee	Nat.	OF	95	164	17	39	7	1	3	23	.238	107	2	0	1.000
1959	Milwaukee	Nat.	OF	71	142	17	31	8	2	1	15	.218	87	1	2	.978
Major League Totals				1852	6292	844	1796	264	62	213	967	.285	3388	590	97	.976

aTraded to Brooklyn Dodgers with pitcher Johnny Schmitz, catcher Al Walker and second baseman Wayne Terwilliger for pitcher Joe Hatten, catcher Bruce Edwards, second baseman Eddie Miksis and outfielder Gene Hermanski, June 15, 1951.
bTraded to Boston Braves for second baseman Roy Hartsfield and reported $50,000, January 17, 1953. Boston franchise transferred to Milwaukee, March 18, 1953.

WORLD SERIES RECORD

Year	Club	League	Pos.	G.	AB.	R.	H.	2B.	3B.	HR.	RBI.	B.A.	PO.	A.	E.	F.A.
1945	Chicago	Nat.	OF	7	28	5	6	2	1	0	2	.214	24	2	1	.963
1952	Brooklyn	Nat.	OF-PH	7	21	0	4	0	0	0	2	.190	12	1	0	1.000
1957	Milwaukee	Nat.	OF-PH	6	14	1	3	0	0	0	0	.214	9	0	0	1.000
1958	Milwaukee	Nat.	OF	4	9	0	3	1	0	0	1	.333	8	0	0	1.000
World Series Totals				24	72	6	16	3	1	0	5	.222	53	3	1	.982

LEROY ROBERT (SATCHEL) PAIGE

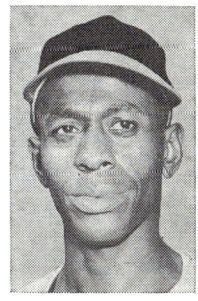

(Considered by most experts as greatest Negro pitcher of all time.)

Born July 7, 1905, at Mobile, Ala.
Height, 6.04. Weight, 190.
Threw and batted righthanded.
Hobbies—Collecting guns and antiques.

Named to Hall of Fame, 1971.
Coach, Atlanta Braves, August 11, 1968, through 1969.
Satchel Paige is no stranger to readers of Daguerreotypes, his Organized Ball record having run in the 1971 edition because he was named to the Hall of Fame in sufficient time to include him.

Satch hit the majors way past his prime and after he had hurt his arm while pitching in a cool breeze in the Caribbean in the winter of 1947. So the big league fans saw only a shell of the pitcher who brought big money to the Negro game. His cunning never left him even though his fastball was a memory that could be recalled only infrequently.

Paige never was rated the fastest pitcher among the blacks who played or witnessed Negro ball in its two stages, before league play and after. Smoky Joe (Cyclone) Williams, John Donaldson, Cannonball Dick Redding, Rube Foster and Wilbur (Bullet) Rogan all were rated faster than Paige, but none, except the early Foster, could combine the perfect control that Paige possessed from his first day on the mound. Speed and control were his bread and butter. He became famous for calling in his outfield and sitting them down alongside his squatting infielders—and then fanning the side on nine consecutive darters which traveled the precise route he intended.

Paige pitched on many clubs—the Chattanooga Black Lookouts in 1926, his first club, and then the Birmingham Black Barons, Cleveland Cubs, Pittsburgh Crawfords and Kansas City Monarchs (his two strongest clubs and most successful seasons), New York Black Yankees, Satchell Paige's All-Stars and the Philadelphia Stars.

With the Crawfords and Monarchs, Satch's fame spread from coast to coast. He was their meal ticket, the one the fans flocked to see. To satisfy the fans, he would pitch three innings per game while between starts, to keep peace and keep the money rolling in.

He hurt his arm pitching winter ball while still a member of the Monarchs, laid off for a spell with the Monarchs' second team in '48 and then came back a new pitcher with his hesitation pitch, sharper curve and sometime fastball.

His barnstorming tours had made him the richest black player of all time and he made more money than any of the top major league pitchers of his day.

Bill Veeck knew what was going on in Negro ball and his friendship with Paige was instrumental in getting Satch to join the Indians during the 1948 A.L. season. His 6-1 break-in year with Cleveland was excellent, but his being able to compile 3-4, 12-10 and even a 3-9 record pitching for the hapless Browns is testament to his greatness, even though his prime had long passed.

Paige was the monumental figure of black baseball—he was the awareness bridge that spanned the two worlds of baseball, black and white. When major leaguers faced Paige, they knew the standard of Negro ball and carried the stories back to the big leagues. The path that Paige fashioned is the one which Jackie Robinson walked to reach the majors. Without Paige, the re-entrance of Negroes into the major leagues would have been set back many years. His mound wizardry had blazed the way.

Year	Club	League	G.	IP.	W.	L.	Pct.	H.	R.	ER.	SO.	BB.	ERA.
1948—Cleveland		American	21	73	6	1	.857	61	21	20	45	25	2.47
1949—Cleveland		American	31	70	4	7	.364	70	29	28	54	33	3.04
1950—		(Out of Organized Ball)											
1951—St. Louis		American	23	62	3	4	.429	67	39	33	48	29	4.79
1952—St. Louis		American	46	138	12	10	.545	116	51	47	91	57	3.07
1953—St. Louis		American	57	117	3	9	.250	114	51	46	51	39	3.54
1954-55—		(Out of Organized Ball)											
1956—Miami		International	37	111	11	4	.733	101	29	23	79	28	1.86
1957—Miami		International	40	119	10	8	.556	98	35	32	76	11	2.42
1958—Miami		International	28	110	10	10	.500	94	44	36	40	15	2.95
1959-60—		(Out of Organized Ball)											
1961—Portland		Pacific Coast	5	25	0	0	.000	28	12	8	19	5	2.88
1962-63-64		(Out of Organized Ball)											
1965—Kansas City		American	1	3	0	0	.000	1	0	0	1	0	0.009
1966—Peninsula		Carolinas	1	2	0	0	.000	5	2	2	0	0	9.00
Major League Totals			179	463	28	31	.475	429	191	174	290	183	3.88

WORLD SERIES RECORD

Year	Club	League	G.	IP.	W.	L.	Pct.	H.	R.	ER.	SO.	BB.	ERA.
1948—Cleveland		American	1	⅔	0	0	.000	0	0	0	0	0	0.00

MILTON STEVEN PAPPAS

Born May 11, 1939, at Detroit, Mich.
Height, 6.03. Weight, 214.
Threw and batted righthanded.

Pitched 8-0 no-hit victory against San Diego Padres, September 2, 1972.
Tied for National League lead in shutouts in 1971 (5).

Year	Club	League	G.	IP.	W.	L.	Pct.	H.	R.	ER.	SO.	BB.	ERA.
1957—Knoxville		Sally	3	11	0	1	.000	12	10	6	9	10	4.91
1957—Baltimore		Amer.	4	9	0	0	.000	6	1	1	3	3	1.00
1958—Baltimore		Amer.	31	135	10	10	.500	135	67	61	72	48	4.07
1959—Baltimore		Amer.	33	209	15	9	.625	175	82	76	120	75	3.27
1960—Baltimore		Amer.	30	206	15	11	.577	184	81	77	126	83	3.36
1961—Baltimore		Amer.	26	178	13	9	.591	134	67	60	89	78	3.03
1962—Baltimore		Amer.	35	205	12	10	.545	200	105	92	130	75	4.04
1963—Baltimore		Amer.	34	217	16	9	.640	186	80	73	120	69	3.03

Year	Club	League	G.	IP.	W.	L.	Pct.	H.	R.	ER.	SO.	BB.	ERA.
1964	Baltimore	Amer.	37	252	16	7	.696	225	89	83	157	48	2.96
1965	Baltimore(a)	Amer.	34	221	13	9	.591	192	81	64	127	52	2.61
1966	Cincinnati	Nat.	33	210	12	11	.522	224	106	100	133	39	4.29
1967	Cincinnati	Nat.	34	218	16	13	.552	218	88	81	129	38	3.34
1968	Cin.(b)-Atlanta	Nat.	37	184	12	13	.480	181	77	71	118	32	3.47
1969	Atlanta	Nat.	26	144	6	10	.375	149	66	58	72	44	3.63
1970	Atl.(c)-Chicago	Nat.	32	180	12	10	.545	179	78	67	105	43	3.35
1971	Chicago	Nat.	35	261	17	14	.548	279	109	102	99	62	3.52
1972	Chicago	Nat.	29	195	17	7	.708	187	72	60	80	29	2.77
1973	Chicago	Nat.	30	162	7	12	.368	192	82	77	48	40	4.28
	American League Totals		264	1632	110	74	.598	1437	653	587	944	531	3.24
	National League Totals		256	1554	99	90	.524	1609	678	621	784	327	3.60
	Major League Totals		520	3186	209	164	.560	3046	1331	1203	1728	858	3.40

aTraded with pitcher Jack Baldschun and outfielder Dick Simpson to Cincinnati Reds for outfielder Frank Robinson, December 9, 1965.
bTraded with pitcher Ted Davidson and infielder Bob Johnson to Atlanta Braves for infielder Woody Woodward and pitchers Tony Cloninger and Clay Carroll, June 11, 1968.
cSold to Chicago Cubs, June 25, 1970.

CAMILO ALBERTO PASCUAL JR.

Born January 20, 1934, at Havana, Cuba.
Height, 5.11. Weight, 190.
Threw and batted righthanded.
Brother of Carlos Pascual, former minor league infielder and Minnesota scout.

Tied major league record for pitchers by making three sacrifice hits in a game, May 27, 1956, second game.
Led American League in shutouts with 6 in 1959 and tied for lead with 8 in 1961 and 5 in 1962; led league in complete games with 17 in 1959, 18 in 1962 and tied for lead with 18 in 1963.
First game of season, April 18, 1960, struck out 15 against Boston.
Struck out 15, July 19, 1961, first game, against Los Angeles.
Coach, Minnesota Twins, 1978 to date.

Year	Club	League	G.	IP.	W.	L.	Pct.	H.	R.	ER.	SO.	BB.	ERA.
1951	Geneva	Border	4	31	3	1	.750	33	16	12	13	20	3.48
1951	Big Spring	Longhorn	7	14	2	1	.667	18	10	8	10	12	5.14
1951	Chickasha	Soo. St.	5	19	0	2	.000	23	23	13	17	14	6.16
1952	Havana-Tampa	Fla. Int.	24	122	8	6	.571	101	43	39	72	66	2.88
1953	Havana	Fla. Int.	25	141	10	6	.625	126	61	47	93	68	3.00
1954	Washington	American	48	119	4	7	.364	126	65	56	60	61	4.24
1955	Washington	American	43	129	2	12	.143	158	94	88	82	70	6.14
1956	Washington	American	39	189	6	18	.250	194	131	123	162	89	5.86
1957	Washington	American	29	176	8	17	.320	168	85	80	113	76	4.09
1958	Washington	American	31	177	8	12	.400	166	66	62	146	60	3.15
1959	Washington	American	32	239	17	10	.630	202	80	70	185	69	2.64
1960	Washington	American	26	152	12	8	.600	139	65	51	143	53	3.02
1961	Minnesota	American	35	252	15	16	.484	205	114	97	*221	100	3.46
1962	Minnesota	American	34	258	20	11	.645	236	100	95	*206	59	3.31
1963	Minnesota	American	31	248	21	9	.700	205	76	68	*202	81	2.47
1964	Minnesota	American	36	267	15	12	.556	245	121	98	213	98	3.30
1965	Minnesota	American	27	156	9	3	.750	126	67	58	96	63	3.35
1966	Minnesota (a)	American	21	103	8	6	.571	113	63	56	56	30	4.89
1967	Washington	American	28	165	12	10	.545	147	73	60	106	43	3.27
1968	Washington	American	31	201	13	12	.520	181	72	60	111	59	2.69
1969	Washington (b)	American	14	55	2	5	.286	49	42	42	34	38	6.87
1969	Cincinnati (c)	National	5	7	0	0	.000	14	7	7	3	4	9.00
1970	Los Angeles (d)	National	10	14	0	0	.000	12	4	4	8	5	2.57
1971	Cleveland	American	9	23	2	2	.500	17	9	8	20	11	3.13
	American League Totals		514	2909	174	170	.506	2677	1323	1172	2156	1060	3.63
	National League Totals		15	21	0	0	.000	26	11	11	11	9	4.71
	Major League Totals		529	2930	174	170	.506	2703	1334	1183	2167	1069	3.67

aOn disabled list with arm trouble from July 7 through August 12. Traded with second baseman Bernie Allen to Washington Senators for pitcher Ron Kline, December 3, 1966.
bSold to Cincinnati Reds, July 7, 1969.
cReleased by Cincinnati Reds, signed by Los Angeles Dodgers for 1970 season.
dOn disabled list July 18 through August 8. Released by Los Angeles Dodgers, August 25, 1970. Signed by Cleveland Indians for 1971 season.

WORLD SERIES RECORD

Year	Club	League	G.	IP.	W.	L.	Pct.	H.	R.	ER.	SO.	BB.	ERA.
1965	Minnesota	American	1	5	0	1	.000	8	3	3	0	1	5.40

ROGER THORPE PECKINPAUGH

Born February 5, 1891, at Wooster, O.
Died November 17, 1977, at Cleveland, O.
Height, 5.10½. Weight, 160.
Threw and batted righthanded.
Married Mildred Stidger, February 22, 1911.

Did not have a fielding chance in 10-inning game, first game, September 17, 1923; holds World Series mark for most assists in a game (9), October 5, 1921.
Batted safely in 29 consecutive games, June 11, through July 9, 1919.
Led American League shortstops in double plays, 1922-23-24.
Named Most Valuable Player, American League, 1925.
Manager, New York Highlanders, September 16, 1914 to close of season; manager, Cleveland Indians, 1928 until June 9, 1933; manager, Kansas City, American Association, April, 1934 until released in November, 1934; member American League promotion bureau, 1935-38; vice-president and manager, New Orleans, Southern Association, 1939; member American League promotion bureau, 1940; manager, Cleveland Indians, 1941; vice-president and general manager, Cleveland, 1942 to 1946; general manager, Buffalo, International League, 1947.

Year	Club	League	Pos.	G.	AB.	R.	H.	2B.	3B.	HR.	RBI.	B.A.	PO.	A.	E.	F.A.
1910	Cleveland	Amer.	OF	15	45	1	9	0	0	0	6	.200	20	38	6	.906
1910	New Haven	Conn.	OF	101	369	51	94	...	...	...	...	.255	159	348	36	.934
1911	Portland	P.C.	SS	195	702	86	181	...	...	...	...	.258	409	658	88	.924
1912	Cleveland	Amer.	SS	69	236	18	50	4	1	1	23	.212	127	188	26	.924
1913	Cleve.(a)	N.Y....Amer.	SS	96	340	36	91	10	7	1	32	.268	187	300	36	.931
1914	New York	Amer.	SS	157	570	55	127	14	6	3	59	.223	356	500	39	.956
1915	New York	Amer.	SS	142	540	67	119	18	7	5	43	.220	291	468	47	.942
1916	New York	Amer.	SS	142	541	64	138	22	8	4	55	.255	379	*454	43	.945
1917	New York	Amer.	SS	148	543	63	141	24	7	0	45	.260	292	467	54	.934
1918	New York	Amer.	SS	122	446	59	103	15	3	0	43	.231	260	*439	28	.961
1919	New York	Amer.	SS	122	453	89	138	20	2	7	34	.305	271	*434	43	.943
1920	New York	Amer.	SS	139	534	109	144	26	6	8	54	.270	263	441	28	.962
1921	New York (b-c)	Amer.	SS	149	577	128	166	25	7	8	71	.288	318	443	42	.948
1922	Washington	Amer.	SS	147	520	62	132	14	4	2	48	.254	265	524	41	.951
1923	Washington	Amer.	SS	154	568	73	150	18	4	2	62	.264	311	*510	45	.948
1924	Washington	Amer.	SS	*155	523	72	142	20	5	2	73	.272	278	487	29	.963
1925	Washington	Amer.	SS	126	422	67	124	16	4	4	64	.294	215	345	28	.952
1926	Washington (d)	Amer.	SS	57	147	19	35	4	1	1	14	.238	82	109	8	.960
1927	Chicago	Amer.	SS	68	217	23	64	6	3	0	23	.295	101	170	10	.964
Major League Totals				2008	7222	1005	1873	256	75	48	749	.259	3916	6327	553	.949

aTraded to New York Highlanders for shortstop Bill Stumpf and outfielder Jack Lelivelt, May 20, 1913.
bTraded with pitchers Jack Quinn, Harry (Rip) Collins and Bill Piercy to Boston for pitchers Joe Bush and Sam Jones and shortstop Everett Scott, December, 1921.
cTraded to Washington Senators in three-cornered deal which sent infielder Frank O'Rourke from Washington Senators to Boston Red Sox; Senators also shipped pitcher Joe Acosta and outfielder Edmund (Bing) Miller to Philadelphia Athletics and A's in turn sent third baseman Joe Dugan to Boston Red Sox, January 10, 1922. Dugan subsequently was traded to New York in July.
dTraded to Chicago White Sox for pitchers Hollis Thurston and Leo Mangrum, January 15, 1927.

WORLD SERIES RECORD

Year	Club	League	Pos.	G.	AB.	R.	H.	2B.	3B.	HR.	RBI.	B.A.	PO.	A.	E.	F.A.
1921	New York	Amer.	SS	8	28	2	5	1	0	0	0	.179	18	28	2	.957
1924	Washington	Amer.	SS	4	12	1	5	2	0	0	2	.417	7	14	0	1.000
1925	Washington	Amer.	SS	7	24	1	6	1	0	1	3	.250	10	22	8	.800
World Series Totals				19	64	4	16	4	0	1	5	.250	35	64	10	.907

HERBERT JEFFERIS PENNOCK

Born February 10, 1894, at Kennett Square, Pa.
Died January 30, 1948, at New York City, N.Y.
Height, 6.00. Weight, 165.
Threw lefthanded and batted left and righthanded.

Tied record of Cy Young and Sam Jones for pitching most years in majors (22), 1934 (now held by Early Wynn, 23).

Named to THE SPORTING NEWS All-Star Major League Team, 1926.
Coach, Boston Red Sox, 1936-40; supervisor, Boston Red Sox farm system, 1941 to 1943; general manager, Philadelphia Phillies, 1944 until his death.
Named to Hall of Fame, 1948.

Year	Club	League	G.	IP.	W.	L.	Pct.	H.	R.	ER.	SO.	BB.	ERA.
1912	Philadelphia	American	17	50	1	2	.333	48	31	...	38	30	.....
1913	Philadelphia	American	14	33	2	1	.667	30	24	19	17	22	5.13
1914	Philadelphia	American	28	152	11	4	.733	136	56	47	90	65	2.78
1915	Providence	International	13	90	6	4	.600	72	28	...	57	38	.....
1915	Phila. (a)-Boston	American	16	58	3	6	.333	69	50	41	31	39	6.36
1916	Boston	American	9	27	0	2	.000	23	11	9	12	8	3.00
1916	Buffalo	International	15	113	7	6	.538	99	...	21	76	36	1.67
1917	Boston	American	24	101	5	5	.500	90	49	37	35	23	3.30
1918	Boston	American					(In Military Service)						
1919	Boston	American	32	219	16	8	.667	223	78	66	70	48	2.71
1920	Boston	American	37	242	16	13	.552	244	108	99	68	61	3.68
1921	Boston	American	32	223	12	14	.462	268	121	100	91	59	4.04
1922	Boston (b)	American	32	202	10	17	.370	230	108	97	59	74	4.32
1923	New York	American	35	238	19	6	*.760	235	86	83	93	68	3.14
1924	New York	American	40	286	21	9	.700	302	104	90	101	64	2.83
1925	New York	American	47	*277	16	17	.485	267	117	91	88	71	2.96
1926	New York	American	40	266	23	11	.676	294	133	107	78	43	3.62
1927	New York	American	34	210	19	8	.704	225	89	70	51	48	3.00
1928	New York	American	28	211	17	6	.739	215	71	60	53	40	2.56
1929	New York	American	27	158	9	11	.450	205	101	86	49	28	4.90
1930	New York	American	25	156	11	7	.611	194	95	75	46	20	4.33
1931	New York	American	25	189	11	6	.647	247	96	90	65	30	4.29
1932	New York	American	22	147	9	5	.643	191	94	75	54	38	4.59
1933	New York (c)	American	23	65	7	4	.636	96	46	40	22	21	5.54
1934	Boston	American	30	62	2	0	1.000	68	31	21	16	16	3.05
	Major League Totals		617	3572	240	162	.597	3900	1699	1403	1227	916	3.54

aClaimed on waivers by Boston Red Sox, June, 1915.
bTraded to New York Yankees for outfielder Camp Skinner, infielder Norman McMillan, pitcher George Murray and cash, January 30, 1923.
cReleased by New York Yankees and signed by Boston Red Sox, January, 1934.

WORLD SERIES RECORD

Year	Club	League	G.	IP.	W.	L.	Pct.	H.	R.	ER.	SO.	BB.	ERA.
1914	Philadelphia	American	1	3	0	0	.000	2	0	0	3	2	0.00
1923	New York	American	3	17⅓	2	0	1.000	19	7	7	8	1	3.63
1926	New York	American	3	22	2	0	1.000	13	3	3	8	4	1.23
1927	New York	American	1	9	1	0	1.000	3	1	1	1	0	1.00
1932	New York	American	2	4	0	0	.000	2	1	1	4	1	2.25
	World Series Totals		10	55⅓	5	0	1.000	39	12	12	24	8	1.95

JOSEPH ANTHONY PEPITONE

Born October 9, 1940, at Brooklyn, N. Y.
Height, 6.02. Weight, 199.
Threw and batted lefthanded.

Tied following major league records, May 23, 1962 (eighth inning); most home runs, inning (2); most extra bases on long hits, inning (6); most total bases, inning (8).
Established World Series record for most double plays by first baseman, four-game Series (7), 1963; tied mark for most assists by first baseman, four-game Series (6), 1963.
Hit home run with bases full in World Series game, eighth inning, October 14, 1964—tying Series record for most runs batted in, inning, 4.
Named as first baseman on the American League All-Star Team by THE SPORTING NEWS, 1963.
Named first baseman on THE SPORTING NEWS American League All-Star fielding team, 1965-66-69.

Year	Club	League	Pos.	G.	AB.	R.	H.	2B.	3B.	HR.	RBI.	B.A.	PO.	A.	E.	F.A.
1958	Auburn	NYP	OF	16	53	7	17	4	1	1	14	.321	27	0	2	.931
1959	Fargo-Moorh'd	North.	OF	123	*508	97	144	*35	12	14	87	.283	273	14	9	.970
1960	Binghamton	East.	OF	132	507	73	132	20	4	13	75	.260	285	*15	12	.962
1961	Amarillo	Tex.	OF-1B	123	484	86	153	24	7	21	87	.316	323	18	6	.983
1962	New York	Amer.	OF-1B	63	138	14	33	3	2	7	17	.239	126	11	2	.986
1962	Richmond	Int.	1B	46	178	28	56	6	5	8	27	.315	387	53	5	.989
1963	New York	Amer.	1B-OF	157	580	79	157	16	3	27	89	.271	1166	104	8	.994
1964	New York	Amer.	*1B-OF	160	613	71	154	12	3	28	100	.251	*1346	*121	18	.988
1965	New York	Amer.	*1B-OF	143	531	51	131	18	3	18	62	.247	1081	75	4	*.997
1966	New York	Amer.	*1B-OF	152	585	85	149	21	4	31	83	.255	1126	97	9	*.993
1967	New York	Amer.	OF-1B	133	501	45	126	18	3	13	64	.251	321	13	8	.977

Year	Club	League	Pos.	G.	AB.	R.	H.	2B.	3B.	HR.	RBI.	B.A.	PO.	A.	E.	F.A.
1968–New York		Amer.	OF-1B	108	380	41	93	9	3	15	56	.245	318	8	4	.988
1969–New York(a)		Amer.	1B	135	513	49	124	16	3	27	70	.242	1254	74	7	★.994
1970–Hou.(b)-Chi.		Nat.	OF-1B	131	492	82	127	18	7	26	79	.258	576	33	4	.993
1971–Chicago		Nat.	1B-OF	115	427	50	131	19	4	16	61	.307	904	64	10	.990
1972–Chicago		Nat.	1B	66	214	23	56	5	0	8	21	.262	552	31	2	.997
1973–Chi.(c)-Atl.		Nat.	1B	34	123	16	34	3	0	3	19	.276	266	19	5	.983
American League Totals				1051	3841	435	967	113	24	166	541	.252	6738	503	60	.992
National League Totals				346	1256	171	348	45	11	53	180	.277	2298	147	21	.991
Major League Totals				1397	5097	606	1315	158	35	219	721	.258	9036	650	81	.992

aTraded to Houston Astros for first baseman-outfielder Curt Blefary, December 4, 1969.
bOn disqualified list July 22 through July 31. Sold to Chicago Cubs, July 27, 1970.
cTraded to Atlanta Braves for first baseman Andre Thornton, May 19, 1973.

WORLD SERIES RECORD

Year	Club	League	Pos.	G.	AB.	R.	H.	2B.	3B.	HR.	RBI.	B.A.	PO.	A.	E.	F.A.
1963–New York		Amer.	1B	4	13	0	2	0	0	0	0	.154	37	6	1	.977
1964–New York		Amer.	1B	7	26	1	4	1	0	1	5	.154	63	6	0	1.000
World Series Totals				11	39	1	6	1	0	1	5	.154	100	12	1	.991

JAMES EVAN PERRY, JR.

Born October 30, 1936, at Williamston, N. C.
Height, 6.04. Weight, 205.
Threw right and batted right and lefthanded.
Brother of Gaylord Perry, major league pitcher.

Tied major league record for unassisted double play, pitcher, game, August 7, 1972.
Named pitcher on THE SPORTING NEWS American League All-Star Team, 1970.
Won American League Cy Young Memorial Award, 1970.

Year	Club	League	G.	IP.	W.	L.	Pct.	H.	R.	ER.	SO.	BB.	ERA.
1956–North Platte	Neb. St.	16	120	7	8	.467	129	★104	★64	124	65	4.80
1957–Fargo-Moorhead	North.	38	★231	15	12	.556	212	92	74	150	73	2.88
1958–Reading	East.	32	200	16	8	.667	165	78	62	135	66	2.79
1959–Cleveland	Amer.	44	153	12	10	.545	122	54	45	79	55	2.65
1960–Cleveland	Amer.	41	261	●18	10	.643	257	118	105	120	91	3.62
1961–Cleveland	Amer.	35	224	10	17	.370	238	132	●117	90	87	4.70
1962–Cleveland	Amer.	35	194	12	12	.500	213	94	89	74	59	4.13
1963–Cleveland(a)-Minnesota	Amer.	40	179	9	9	.500	179	83	76	72	59	3.82
1964–Minnesota	Amer.	42	65	6	3	.667	61	26	25	55	23	3.46
1965–Minnesota	Amer.	36	168	12	7	.632	142	57	49	88	47	2.63
1966–Minnesota	Amer.	33	184	11	7	.611	149	61	52	122	53	2.54
1967–Minnesota	Amer.	37	131	8	7	.533	123	51	44	94	50	3.02
1968–Minnesota	Amer.	32	139	8	6	.571	113	37	35	69	26	2.27
1969–Minnesota	Amer.	46	262	20	6	.769	244	87	82	153	66	2.82
1970–Minnesota	Amer.	40	279	●24	12	.667	258	112	94	168	57	3.03
1971–Minnesota	Amer.	40	270	17	17	.500	263	★135	★127	126	102	4.23
1972–Minnesota(b)	Amer.	35	218	13	16	.448	191	93	81	85	60	3.34
1973–Detroit(c)	Amer.	35	203	14	13	.519	225	96	91	66	55	4.03
1974–Cleveland	Amer.	36	252	17	12	.586	242	94	83	71	64	2.96
1975–Cleveland(d)-Oakland	Amer.	23	105	4	10	.286	107	77	63	44	44	5.40
Major League Totals		630	3287	215	174	.553	3127	1407	1258	1576	998	3.44

aTraded to Minnesota Twins for pitcher Jack Kralick, May 2, 1963.
bTraded to Detroit Tigers for pitcher Danny Fife, March 27, 1973.
cTraded to Cleveland Indians as part of deal in which Cleveland sent pitcher Rick Sawyer and outfielder Walt Williams to New York Yankees and Yankees sent catcher Jerry Moses to Detroit in exchange for pitcher Ed Farmer, March 19, 1974.
dTraded with pitcher Dick Bosman to Oakland Athletics for pitcher Johnny (Blue Moon) Odom and cash, May 20, 1975.

WORLD SERIES RECORD

Year	Club	League	G.	IP.	W.	L.	Pct.	H.	R.	ER.	SO.	BB.	ERA.
1965–Minnesota	Amer.	2	4	0	0	.000	5	2	2	4	2	4.50

DID YOU KNOW—
That brothers Jim and Gaylord Perry tied for league lead in most games won, same year (1970)? Jim had 24 in A.L. while Gaylord had 23 in N.L.

JOHN MICHAEL PESKY

Born September 27, 1919, at Portland, Ore.
Height, 5.09. Weight, 168.
Threw and batted lefthanded.
Married Ruth C. Hickey, January 10, 1945.

Selected as Most Valuable Player in American Association, 1941; collected 205 hits in 1942, tying major league record of making 200 or more hits in first full season; tied major league record for most consecutive years leading league in hits (3), 1942-46-47 (1943-44-45 in Armed Forces); established American League record for most runs scored, game (6), May 8, 1946; tied modern major league record for most official times at bat, nine-inning game (7), June 8, 1950.

Named by Baseball Writers' Association of America as shortstop for THE SPORTING NEWS All-Star Major League Team, 1942-46.

Manager, Durham, Carolina, 1956; Birmingham, Southern, 1957; Lancaster, Eastern, 1958; Knoxville, South Atlantic, 1959; Victoria, Texas, 1960; Seattle, Pacific Coast, 1961-62; Boston Red Sox, 1963-64; coach, Pittsburgh Pirates, 1965-66-67; manager, Columbus, International, 1968; coach, Boston Red Sox, 1975 to date.

Year	Club	League	Pos.	G.	AB.	R.	H.	2B.	3B.	HR.	RBI.	B.A.	PO.	A.	E.	F.A.
1940	Rocky Mount	Piedmont	SS	136	*576	114	*187	28	*16	4	55	.325	257	435	44	.940
1941	Louisville	A.A.	SS	146	600	93	*195	25	5	1	48	.325	*308	411	32	.957
1942	Boston	Amer.	SS	147	620	105	*205	29	9	2	51	.331	320	*465	37	.955
1943-44-45	Boston	Amer.						(In Military Service)								
1946	Boston	Amer.	SS	153	*621	115	*208	43	4	2	55	.335	296	479	25	.969
1947	Boston	Amer.	SS-3B	155	*638	106	*207	27	8	0	39	.324	276	429	17	.976
1948	Boston	Amer.	3B	143	565	124	159	26	6	3	55	.281	121	303	22	.951
1949	Boston	Amer.	3B	148	604	111	185	27	7	2	69	.306	*184	*333	16	.970
1950	Boston	Amer.	SS-3B	127	490	112	153	22	6	1	49	.312	183	289	13	.973
1951	Boston	Amer.	2B-SS-3B	131	480	93	150	20	6	3	41	.313	223	370	26	.958
1952	Bos.(a)-Detroit	Amer.	SS-3B-2B	94	244	36	55	6	0	1	11	.225	126	172	15	.952
1953	Detroit	Amer.	2B	103	308	43	90	22	1	2	24	.292	166	224	3	.992
1954	Det.(b)-Wash.	Amer.	PH-2B-SS	69	175	22	43	4	3	1	10	.246	92	91	4	.979
1955	Denver	A.A.	3B-PH	66	137	32	47	7	2	1	18	.343	22	45	7	.905
1956	Durham	Carol.	2B-PH	17	35	2	6	2	0	0	1	.171	5	9	1	.933
Major League Totals				1270	4745	867	1455	226	50	17	404	.307	1987	3152	178	.967

aTraded to Detroit Tigers with pitcher Bill Wight, first baseman Walter Dropo, third baseman Fred Hatfield and outfielder Don Lenhardt for pitcher Paul (Dizzy) Trout, third baseman George Kell, shortstop Johnny Lipon and outfielder Walter (Hoot) Evers, June 3, 1952.

bTraded to Washington Senators for infielder Mel Hoderlein, June 13, 1954.

WORLD SERIES RECORD

Year	Club	League	Pos.	G.	AB.	R.	H.	2B.	3B.	HR.	RBI.	B.A.	PO.	A.	E.	F.A.
1946	Boston	Amer.	3B	7	30	2	7	0	0	0	0	.233	13	16	4	.879

AMERICO PETER (RICO) PETROCELLI

Born June 27, 1943, at Brooklyn, N. Y.
Height, 6.00. Weight, 188.
Threw and batted righthanded.

Established American League record for most home runs by a shortstop in a season, 40 in 1969.
Tied American League record for fewest errors by a shortstop in a season, 14 in 1969 (since passed by Eddie Brinkman with 7).

Named shortstop on THE SPORTING NEWS American League All-Star Team, 1969.

Year	Club	League	Pos.	G.	AB.	R.	H.	2B.	3B.	HR.	RBI.	B.A.	PO.	A.	E.	F.A.
1962	Winston-Salem	Carol.	SS	137	487	76	135	30	4	17	80	.277	182	392	*48	.923
1963	Reading	East.	SS	137	493	64	118	23	7	19	78	.239	*266	*464	42	.946
1963	Boston	Amer.	SS	1	4	0	1	1	0	0	1	.250	3	2	1	.833
1964	Seattle	P. C.	SS	134	442	50	102	13	2	10	48	.231	190	447	29	.956
1965	Boston	Amer.	SS	103	323	38	75	15	2	13	33	.232	151	278	19	.958
1966	Boston	Amer.	SS-3B	139	522	58	124	20	1	18	59	.238	211	390	28	.955
1967	Boston	Amer.	SS	142	491	53	127	24	2	17	66	.259	223	432	19	.972
1968	Boston	Amer.	*SS-1B	123	406	41	95	17	2	12	46	.234	178	361	12	*.978

Year	Club	League	Pos.	G.	AB.	R.	H.	2B.	3B.	HR.	RBI.	B.A.	PO.	A.	E.	F.A.
1969	Boston	Amer.	*SS-3B	154	535	92	159	32	2	40	97	.297	269	469	15	*.980
1970	Boston	Amer.	SS-3B	157	583	82	152	31	3	29	103	.261	276	430	21	.971
1971	Boston	Amer.	3B	158	553	82	139	24	4	28	89	.251	118	334	11	*.976
1972	Boston	Amer.	3B	147	521	62	125	15	2	15	75	.240	146	278	13	.970
1973	Boston	Amer.	3B	100	356	44	87	13	1	13	45	.244	73	224	6	.980
1974	Boston	Amer.	3B	129	454	53	121	23	1	15	76	.267	83	219	12	.962
1975	Boston	Amer.	3B	115	402	31	96	15	1	7	59	.239	85	229	13	.960
1976	Boston	Amer.	3B-2B-DH	85	240	17	51	7	1	3	24	.213	70	134	6	.971
Major League Totals				1553	5390	653	1352	237	22	210	773	.251	1886	3780	176	.970

WORLD SERIES RECORD

Year	Club	League	Pos.	G.	AB.	R.	H.	2B.	3B.	HR.	RBI.	B.A.	PO.	A.	E.	F.A.
1967	Boston	Amer.	SS	7	20	3	4	1	0	2	3	.200	11	21	2	.941
1975	Boston	Amer.	3B	7	26	3	8	1	0	0	4	.308	7	15	0	1.000
World Series Totals				14	46	6	12	2	0	2	7	.261	18	36	2	.964

ERNEST GORDON (BABE) PHELPS

Born April 19, 1908, at Odenton, Md.
Height, 6.02. Weight, 210.
Threw right and batted lefthanded.
Married Mable Fedoria Hood, February 7, 1930.

Year	Club	League	Pos.	G.	AB.	R.	H.	2B.	3B.	HR.	RBI.	B.A.	PO.	A.	E.	F.A.
1930	Hagerstown	B.Rg.	OF-C	114	466	84	175	38	15	19	...	*.376	178	29	10	.954
1931	Youngstown	M.-At.	C-OF	115	436	71	178	29	9	15	88	*.408	445	66	26	.952
1931	Washington	Amer.	PH	3	3	0	1	0	0	0	0	.333	0	0	0	.000
1931	Chattanooga	South.	OF	7	20	...	6	1	0	0	...	.300	7	1	1	.889
1932	Youngstown	Central	1B	135	533	117	199	47	8	26	...	*.373	1224	70	20	.985
1933	Albany	Int.	1B-C	122	368	34	108	16	12	10	70	.293	451	65	16	.970
1933	Chicago	Nat.	C-PH	3	7	0	2	0	0	0	0	.286	6	2	0	1.000
1934	Chicago (a)	Nat.	C	44	70	7	20	5	2	2	12	.286	44	7	1	.981
1935	Brooklyn	Nat.	C	47	121	17	44	7	2	5	22	.364	118	16	6	.957
1936	Brooklyn	Nat.	C	115	319	36	117	23	2	5	57	.367	334	49	9	.977
1937	Brooklyn	Nat.	C	121	409	42	128	37	3	7	58	.313	465	76	16	.971
1938	Brooklyn	Nat.	C	66	208	33	64	12	2	5	46	.308	218	25	5	.980
1939	Brooklyn	Nat.	C	98	323	33	92	21	2	6	42	.285	361	40	8	.980
1940	Brooklyn	Nat.	C-1B	118	370	47	109	24	5	13	61	.295	436	35	11	.977
1941	Brooklyn (b)	Nat	C	16	30	3	7	3	0	2	4	.233	33	1	1	.971
1942	Pittsburgh (c)	Nat.	C	95	257	21	73	11	1	9	41	.284	244	40	12	.959
American League Totals				3	3	0	1	0	0	0	0	.333	0	0	0	.000
National League Totals				723	2114	239	656	143	19	54	343	.310	2259	291	69	.974
Major League Totals				726	2117	239	657	143	19	54	343	.310	2259	291	69	.974

aClaimed for waiver price by Brooklyn, December 31, 1934.
bTraded with pitcher Luke Hamlin, infielder Pete Coscarart and outfielder Jimmy Wasdell to Pittsburgh for shortstop Arky Vaughan, December 12, 1941. Suspended, June 4, 1941, for failure to make western trip and did not play for remainder of season.
cTraded to Philadelphia Phillies for first baseman Babe Dahlgren, December 31, 1943, but Phelps refused to report. Went on voluntarily retired list, June, 1944.

CHARLES (DEACON) PHILLIPPE

Born May 23, 1872, at Rural Retreat, Va.
Died March 30, 1952, at Avalon, Pa.
Height, 6.01. Weight, 180.
Threw and batted righthanded.

Won 13 consecutive games, June 9 through September 22, 1910. Pitched five complete games in 1903 World Series, winning three games.

Year	Club	League	G.	IP.	W.	L.	Pct.	H.	R.	SO.	BB.	CG.	ShO.
1897	Minneapolis	Western	21	148	8	13	.381	204	154	34	54	...	...
1898	Minneapolis	Western	43	339	21	19	.525	322	201	46	59	...	...
1899	Louisville	National	42	327	20	17	.541	348	184	73	67	34	2
1900	Pittsburgh	National	38	285	18	14	.563	264	119	81	42	29	1
1901	Pittsburgh	National	36	298	22	12	.647	279	118	106	37	30	1
1902	Pittsburgh	National	31	273	20	9	.690	254	90	117	32	29	5
1903	Pittsburgh	National	36	288	25	9	.735	269	115	123	29	31	4
1904	Pittsburgh	National	21	169	10	10	.500	183	79	82	26	17	3
1905	Pittsburgh	National	38	279	20	13	.606	235	95	133	48	25	5
1906	Pittsburgh	National	33	229	15	10	.600	216	78	90	26	19	4
1907	Pittsburgh	National	35	213	14	11	.560	224	90	61	36	17	1
1908	Pittsburgh	National	5	12	0	0	.000	15	12	1	3	0	0
1909	Pittsburgh	National	23	132	8	3	.727	121	41	38	14	8	1
1910	Pittsburgh	National	31	122	14	2	.875	111	46	30	9	5	1
1911	Pittsburgh	National	3	6	0	0	.000	5	5	3	2	0	0
Major League Totals			372	2610	186	110	.628	2501	1059	926	357	244	28

WORLD SERIES RECORD

Year	Club	League	G.	IP.	W.	L.	Pct.	H.	R.	SO.	BB.	CG.	ShO.
1903	Pittsburgh	National	5	44	3	2	.600	38	19	20	3	5	0
1909	Pittsburgh	National	2	6	0	0	.000	2	0	2	1	0	0
World Series Totals			7	50	3	2	.600	40	19	22	4	5	0

WALTER WILLIAM (BILLY) PIERCE

Born April 2, 1927, at Detroit, Mich.
Height, 5.11. Weight, 175.
Threw and batted lefthanded.
Married Gloria McCreadie, October 22, 1949.

Tied for American League lead in most complete games pitched (21) 1956, (16) 1957 and (19) 1958.
Named Outstanding American League Pitcher by THE SPORTING NEWS, 1956-57.
Named as pitcher on THE SPORTING NEWS All-Star Major League Teams, 1956-57.

Year	Club	League	G.	IP.	W.	L.	Pct.	H.	R.	ER.	SO.	BB.	ERA.
1945	Buffalo	International	15	83	5	7	.417	75	55	50	57	71	5.42
1945	Detroit	American	5	10	0	0	.000	6	2	2	10	10	1.80
1946	Buffalo	International	10	56	3	4	.429	52	30	28	45	44	4.50
1947	Buffalo	International	28	151	14	8	.636	127	75	65	125	125	3.87
1948	Detroit (a)	American	22	55	3	0	1.000	47	40	39	36	51	6.38
1949	Chicago	American	32	172	7	15	.318	145	89	74	95	112	3.87
1950	Chicago	American	33	219	12	16	.429	189	112	97	118	137	3.99
1951	Chicago	American	37	240	15	•14	.517	237	93	81	113	73	3.04
1952	Chicago	American	33	255	15	12	.556	214	76	73	144	79	2.58
1953	Chicago	American	40	271	18	12	.600	216	94	82	*186	102	2.72
1954	Chicago	American	36	189	9	10	.474	179	86	73	148	86	3.48
1955	Chicago	American	33	206	15	10	.600	162	50	45	157	64	*1.97
1956	Chicago	American	35	276	20	9	.690	261	108	102	192	100	3.33
1957	Chicago	American	37	257	•20	12	.625	228	98	93	171	71	3.26
1958	Chicago	American	35	245	17	11	.607	204	83	73	144	66	2.68
1959	Chicago	American	34	224	14	15	.483	217	98	.90	114	62	3.62
1960	Chicago	American	32	196	14	7	.667	201	81	79	108	46	3.63
1961	Chicago (b)	American	39	180	10	9	.526	190	85	76	106	54	3.80
1962	San Francisco	National	30	162	16	6	.727	147	67	63	76	35	3.50
1963	San Francisco	National	38	99	3	11	.214	106	49	47	52	20	4.27
1964	San Francisco	National	34	49	3	0	1.000	40	14	12	29	10	2.20
National League Totals			102	310	22	17	.564	293	130	122	157	65	3.54
American League Totals			483	2995	189	152	.554	2696	1195	1079	1842	1113	3.24
Major League Totals			585	3305	211	169	.555	2989	1325	1201	1999	1178	3.27

aTraded to Chicago White Sox for catcher Aaron Robinson, November 10, 1948.
bTraded to San Francisco Giants with pitcher Don Larsen for pitchers Ed Fisher and Dom Zanni and first baseman-outfielder Bob Farley, November 30, 1961; White Sox promised added player in deal. Pitcher Verle Tiefenthaler assigned to Chicago, August 17, 1962.

WORLD SERIES RECORD

Year	Club	League	G.	IP.	W.	L.	Pct.	H.	R.	ER.	SO.	BB.	ERA.
1959	Chicago	American	3	4	0	0	.000	2	0	0	3	2	0.00
1962	San Francisco	National	2	15	1	1	.500	8	5	4	5	2	2.40
World Series Totals			5	19	1	1	.500	10	5	4	8	4	1.89

VADA EDWARD PINSON, JR.

Born August 11, 1938, at Memphis, Tenn.
Height, 5.11. Weight, 187.
Threw and batted lefthanded.

Tied major league record by making 200 or more hits in first full season in majors (205), 1959.
Major league stolen bases: 1958 (2), 1959 (21), 1960 (32), 1961 (23), 1962 (26), 1963 (27), 1964 (8), 1965 (21), 1966 (18), 1967 (26), 1968 (17), 1969 (4), 1970 (7), 1971 (25), 1972 (17), 1973 (5), 1974 (21), 1975 (5). Total—305.
Named outfielder on THE SPORTING NEWS National League All-Star fielding team, 1961.
Coach, Seattle Mariners, 1977 to date.

Year	Club	League	Pos.	G.	AB.	R.	H.	2B.	3B.	HR.	RBI.	B.A.	PO.	A.	E.	F.A.
1956	Wausau	North.	1B	75	277	35	77	11	5	2	23	.278	626	28	12	.982
1957	Visalia	Cal.	*OF-1B	135	569	*165	*209	*40	*20	20	97	.367	260	*30	16	.948
1958	Cincinnati	Nat.	OF	27	96	20	26	7	0	1	8	.271	50	4	0	1.000
1958	Seattle	P.C.	*OF-1B	124	475	92	163	28	8	11	77	.343	385	13	*15	.964
1959	Cincinnati	Nat.	OF	154	*648	*131	205	*47	9	20	84	.316	*423	11	7	.984
1960	Cincinnati	Nat.	OF	154	*652	107	187	*37	12	20	61	.287	*401	11	8	.981
1961	Cincinnati	Nat.	OF	154	607	101	*208	34	8	16	87	.343	*391	19	10	.976
1962	Cincinnati	Nat.	OF	155	619	107	181	31	7	23	100	.292	344	13	4	.989
1963	Cincinnati	Nat.	OF	•162	652	96	*204	37	*14	22	106	.313	357	9	8	.979
1964	Cincinnati	Nat.	OF	156	625	99	166	23	11	23	84	.266	299	14	9	.972
1965	Cincinnati	Nat.	OF	159	669	97	204	34	10	22	94	.305	354	9	3	*.992
1966	Cincinnati	Nat.	OF	156	618	70	178	35	6	16	76	.288	344	9	13	.964
1967	Cincinnati	Nat.	OF	158	650	90	187	28	*13	18	66	.288	341	4	5	.986
1968	Cincinnati (a)	Nat	OF	130	499	60	135	29	6	5	48	.271	258	7	6	.978
1969	St. Louis (b)	Nat.	OF	132	495	58	126	22	6	10	70	.255	218	6	1	*.996
1970	Cleveland	Am.	OF-1B	148	574	74	164	28	6	24	82	.286	284	9	5	.983
1971	Cleveland (c)	Am.	OF-1B	146	566	60	149	23	4	11	35	.263	315	11	7	.979
1972	California	Am.	OF-1B	136	484	56	133	24	2	7	49	.275	207	11	2	.991
1973	California (d)	Am.	OF	124	466	56	121	14	6	8	57	.260	210	11	8	.965
1974	Kansas City	Am.	OF-1B	115	406	46	112	18	2	6	41	.276	198	9	4	.981
1975	Kansas City (e)	Am.	OF-1B	103	319	38	71	14	5	4	22	.223	151	6	1	.994
American League Totals				772	2815	330	750	121	25	60	286	.266	1365	57	27	.981
National League Totals				1697	6830	1036	2007	364	102	196	884	.294	3780	116	74	.981
Major League Totals				2469	9645	1366	2757	485	127	256	1170	.286	5145	173	101	.981

aTraded to St. Louis Cardinals for outfielder Bob Tolan and pitcher Wayne Granger, October 11, 1968.
bTraded to Cleveland Indians for outfielder Jose Cardenal, November 20, 1969.
cTraded with outfielder Frank Baker and pitcher Alan Foster to California Angels for catcher Jerry Moses and outfielder Alex Johnson, October 5, 1971.
dTraded to Kansas City Royals for pitcher Barry Raziano and cash, February 23, 1974.
eSigned as free agent by Milwaukee Brewers, January 14, 1976, but released April 4, 1976.

WORLD SERIES RECORD

Year	Club	League	Pos.	G.	AB.	R.	H.	2B.	3B.	HR.	RBI.	B.A.	PO.	A.	E.	F.A.
1961	Cincinnati	Nat.	OF	5	22	0	2	1	0	0	0	.091	18	1	1	.950

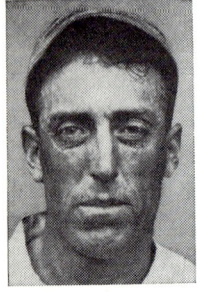

EDWARD S. PLANK

Born August 31, 1875, at Gettysburg, Pa.
Died February 24, 1926, at Gettysburg, Pa.
Height, 5.11½. Weight, 175.
Threw and batted lefthanded.

Named to Hall of Fame, 1946.

Year	Club	League	G.	IP.	W.	L.	Pct.	ShO.	H.	R.	ER.	SO.	BB.	ERA.
1901	Philadelphia	American	33	262	17	11	.607	1	234	121	...	89	47	.....
1902	Philadelphia	American	36	295	20	15	.571	1	300	139	...	110	64	.....
1903	Philadelphia	American	*43	338	23	16	.590	3	314	139	...	175	67	.....
1904	Philadelphia	American	44	365	26	17	.605	7	307	112	...	209	77	.....
1905	Philadelphia	American	41	*346	25	12	.676	4	283	111	...	199	69	.....

Year	Club	League	G.	IP.	W.	L.	Pct.	ShO.	H.	R.	ER.	SO.	BB.	ERA.
1906	Philadelphia	American	26	211	19	6	*.760	5	160	53	...	102	51	.....
1907	Philadelphia	American	43	344	24	16	.600	*8	287	114	...	198	82	.....
1908	Philadelphia	American	34	245	14	16	.467	4	202	71	...	135	46	.....
1909	Philadelphia	American	34	265	19	10	.655	3	215	74	...	132	62	.....
1910	Philadelphia	American	38	250	16	10	.615	1	218	89	...	123	55	.....
1911	Philadelphia	American	40	257	22	8	.733	•6	237	85	...	155	77	.....
1912	Philadelphia	American	37	260	26	6	.813	5	234	90	...	110	83	.....
1913	Philadelphia	American	41	244	18	10	.643	8	211	87	70	151	57	2.59
1914	Philadelphia (a)	American	34	185	15	7	.682	4	178	68	59	110	42	2.87
1915	St. Louis (b)	Federal	42	269	21	11	.656	6	210	75	60	145	58	*2.01
1916	St. Louis	American	37	236	16	15	.516	3	203	78	61	88	67	2.33
1917	St. Louis (c)	American	20	131	5	6	.455	1	105	39	26	26	38	1.79
	Major League Totals		581	4234	305	181	.628	64	3688	1470	...	2112	984	.....

aUnconditionally released and signed with St. Louis, Federal League, November, 1914.
bAwarded to St. Louis Browns in peace agreement, January, 1916.
cTraded with second baseman Del Pratt and $15,000 to New York A.L. for catcher Leslie Nunamaker, third baseman Fritz Maisel, pitchers Nick Cullop and Urban Shocker and second baseman Joe Gedeon, January 21, 1918, but never reported.

WORLD SERIES RECORD

Year	Club	League	G.	IP.	W.	L.	Pct.	ShO.	H.	R.	ER.	SO.	BB.	ERA.
1905	Philadelphia	American	2	17	0	2	.000	0	14	4	2	11	4	1.06
1911	Philadelphia	American	2	9⅔	1	1	.500	0	6	2	2	8	0	1.86
1913	Philadelphia	American	2	19	1	1	.500	0	9	4	2	7	3	0.95
1914	Philadelphia	American	1	9	0	1	.000	0	7	1	1	6	4	1.00
	World Series Totals		7	54⅔	2	5	.286	0	36	11	7	32	11	1.15

WALTER CHARLES (WALLY) POST

Born July 9, 1929, at St. Wendelin, O.
Height, 6.01½. Weight, 208.
Threw and batted righthanded.
Married Pat Beckman, January 29, 1949.

Year	Club	League	Pos.	G.	AB.	R.	H.	2B.	3B.	HR.	RBI.	B.A.	PO.	A.	E.	F.A.
1946	Middletown	Ohio St.	P	2	1	0	0	0	0	0	0	.000	0	1	0	1.000
1947	Muncie	Ohio St.	P	42	77	11	26	3	0	0	14	.338	4	37	5	.891
1948	Columbia	Sally	P-OF	47	90	10	16	2	1	1	4	.178	18	27	6	.882
1949	Charleston	Cent.	P	6	10	2	4	0	1	0	3	.400	0	3	0	1.000
1949	Columbia	Sally	OF	123	458	60	116	19	5	14	76	.253	301	18	11	.967
1949	Cincinnati	Nat.	OF	6	8	1	2	0	0	0	1	.250	3	0	1	.750
1950	Tulsa	Texas	OF	136	514	74	151	36	4	12	86	.294	208	*29	9	.963
1951	Buffalo	Int.	OF	111	422	78	129	17	5	21	65	.306	274	*26	6	.980
1951	Cincinnati	Nat.	OF	15	41	6	9	3	0	1	7	.220	25	1	1	.963
1952	Cincinnati	Nat.	OF	19	58	5	9	1	0	2	7	.155	38	1	0	1.000
1952	Milwaukee	A.A.	OF	51	149	25	36	10	2	5	24	.242	65	2	4	.944
1953	Indianapolis	A.A.	OF	133	509	99	147	24	11	33	*120	.289	340	17	12	.967
1953	Cincinnati	Nat.	OF	11	33	3	8	1	0	1	4	.242	22	2	1	.960
1954	Cincinnati	Nat.	OF	130	451	46	115	21	3	18	83	.255	231	13	11	.957
1955	Cincinnati	Nat.	OF	•154	601	116	186	33	3	40	109	.309	298	13	7	.978
1956	Cincinnati	Nat.	OF	143	539	94	134	25	3	36	83	.249	292	16	10	.969
1957	Cincinnati (a)	Nat.	OF	134	467	68	114	26	2	20	74	.244	252	12	4	.985
1958	Philadelphia	Nat.	OF	110	379	51	107	21	3	12	62	.282	185	12	*10	.952
1959	Philadelphia	Nat.	OF	132	468	62	119	17	6	22	94	.254	226	12	2	.992
1960	Phila.(b)-Cin.	Nat.	OF	111	333	47	94	20	1	19	50	.282	168	9	2	.989
1961	Cincinnati	Nat.	OF	99	282	44	83	16	3	20	57	.294	133	7	6	.959
1962	Cincinnati	Nat.	OF	109	285	43	75	10	3	17	62	.263	110	5	8	.935
1963	Cincinnati (c)	Nat.	OF	5	7	1	0	0	0	0	0	.000	3	0	0	1.000
1963	Minnesota (d)	Amer.	OF	21	47	6	9	1	0	2	6	.191	14	0	0	1.000
1964	Cleveland	Amer.	OF-PH	5	8	1	0	0	0	0	0	.000	2	0	1	.667
1964	Syracuse	Int.	OF-PH	27	46	6	7	1	0	3	7	.152	9	1	0	1.000
	American League Totals			26	55	7	9	1	0	2	6	.164	16	0	1	.941
	National League Totals			1178	3952	587	1055	194	27	208	693	.267	1986	103	63	.971
	Major League Totals			1204	4007	594	1064	194	28	210	699	.266	2002	103	64	.971

aTraded to Philadelphia Phillies for pitcher harvey Haddix, December 6, 1957.
bTraded to Cincinnati Reds with first baseman Fred Hopke and outfielder Harry Anderson for outfielders Tony Gonzalez and Lee Walls, June 15, 1960.
cSold to Minnesota Twins, May 16, 1963.
dReleased by Minnesota Twins, October 15, 1963; signed with Cleveland Indians, November 18, 1963.

PITCHING RECORD

Year	Club	League	G.	IP.	W.	L.	Pct.	H.	R.	ER.	SO.	BB.	ERA.
1946	Middleton	Ohio St.	2	7	0	1	.000	11	12	7	7	5	9.00
1947	Muncie	Ohio St.	40	184	17	7	.708	179	98	68	167	87	3.33
1948	Columbia	Sally	29	274	8	11	.421	170	70	59	58	65	3.05
1949	Charleston	Central	2	13	1	0	1.000	19	10	8	10	5	5.54

WORLD SERIES RECORD

Year	Club	League	Pos.	G.	AB.	R.	H.	2B.	3B.	HR.	RBI.	B.A.	PO.	A.	E.	F.A.
1961	Cincinnati	Nat.	OF	5	18	3	6	1	0	1	2	.333	8	0	0	1.000

JOHN WESLEY (BOOG) POWELL

Born August 17, 1941, at Lakeland, Fla.
Height, 6.04½. Weight, 246.
Threw right and batted lefthanded.
Stepbrother of Carl Taylor, former catcher-first baseman with Pittsburgh Pirates,
St. Louis Cardinals and Kansas City Royals.

Tied American League records for most runs batted in, doubleheader (11), July 6, 1966 (20 innings); and most seasons, 10 or more intentional bases on balls (8).
Hit three home runs in a game on three occasions: August 10, 1963 (consecutive), June 27, 1964, and August 15, 1966.
Led American League in slugging percentage with .606 in 1964.
Tied World Series record for most runs scored, 5-game Series (6), in 1970.
Named American League Comeback Player of the Year by THE SPORTING NEWS, 1966 and 1975.
Named first baseman on THE SPORTING NEWS American League All-Star Team, 1966-68-69-70.
Named Most Valuable Player in American League, 1970.

Year	Club	League	Pos.	G.	AB.	R.	H.	2B.	3B.	HR.	RBI.	B.A.	PO.	A.	E.	F.A.
1959	Bluefield	Appal.	OF-1B	56	191	39	67	7	0	14	59	.351	68	5	7	.913
1960	Fox Cities	I.I.I.	1B	136	497	83	155	23	3	13	100	.312	1055	68	19	*.983
1961	Rochester	Int.	1B-OF	142	486	86	156	26	5	*32	92	.321	842	43	14	.984
1961	Baltimore	Amer.	OF	4	13	0	1	0	0	1	.077	3	0	0	1.000	
1962	Baltimore	Amer.	OF-1B	124	400	44	97	13	2	15	53	.243	194	1	6	.970
1963	Baltimore	Amer.	OF-1B	140	491	67	130	22	2	25	82	.265	316	18	9	.974
1964	Baltimore	Amer.	OF-1B	134	424	74	123	17	0	39	99	.290	233	19	5	.980
1965	Baltimore	Amer.	1B-OF	144	472	54	117	20	2	17	72	.248	658	53	5	.993
1966	Baltimore	Amer.	1B	140	491	78	141	18	0	34	109	.287	1094	68	13	.989
1967	Baltimore	Amer.	1B	125	415	53	97	14	1	13	55	.234	903	64	14	.986
1968	Baltimore	Amer.	1B	154	550	60	137	21	1	22	85	.249	*1293	79	14	.990
1969	Baltimore	Amer.	1B	152	533	83	162	25	0	37	121	.304	1192	84	7	.994
1970	Baltimore	Amer.	1B	154	526	82	156	28	0	35	114	.297	1209	89	10	.992
1971	Baltimore	Amer.	1B	128	418	59	107	19	0	22	92	.256	1031	67	5	.995
1972	Baltimore	Amer.	1B	140	465	53	117	20	1	21	81	.252	1116	70	*15	.988
1973	Baltimore	Amer.	1B	114	370	52	98	13	1	11	54	.265	988	77	12	.989
1974	Baltimore (a)	Amer.	1B	110	344	37	91	13	1	12	45	.265	866	61	4	.996
1975	Cleveland	Amer.	1B	134	435	64	129	18	0	27	86	.297	997	69	3	*.997
1976	Cleveland	Amer.	1B	95	293	29	63	9	0	9	33	.215	698	61	10	.987
1977	Los Angeles (b)	Nat.	PH-1B	50	41	0	10	0	0	5	.244	15	0	1	.938	
American League Totals				1992	6640	889	1766	270	11	339	1182	.266	12781	880	132	.990
National League Totals				50	41	0	10	0	0	5	.244	15	0	1	.938	
Major League Totals				2042	6681	889	1776	270	11	339	1187	.266	12796	880	133	.990

aTraded with pitcher Don Hood to Cleveland Indians for catcher Dave Duncan and outfielder Alvin McGrew, February 25, 1975.
bSigned as free agent with Los Angeles Dodgers, April 5, 1977.

WORLD SERIES RECORD

Year	Club	League	Pos.	G.	AB.	R.	H.	2B.	3B.	HR.	RBI.	B.A.	PO.	A.	E.	F.A.
1966	Baltimore	Amer.	1B	4	14	1	5	1	0	1	.357	27	1	0	1.000	
1969	Baltimore	Amer.	1B	5	19	0	5	0	0	0	.263	46	2	1	.980	
1970	Baltimore	Amer.	1B	5	17	6	5	1	0	2	5	.294	38	2	0	1.000
1971	Baltimore	Amer.	1B	7	27	1	3	0	0	0	1	.111	52	4	1	.982
World Series Totals				21	77	8	18	2	0	2	7	.234	163	9	2	.989

DID YOU KNOW—
That Picus Quinn pitched for 29 seasons as a pro, participating in 970 games?

JOHN JOSEPH (JACK) POWELL

Born July 9, 1874, at Bloomington, Ill.
Died October 18, 1944, at Chicago, Ill.
Threw and batted righthanded.

Year	Club	League	G.	IP.	W.	L.	Pct.	H.	R.	SO.	BB.	CG.	ShO.
1897	Cleveland	National	27	227	15	9	.625	244	117	64	61	24	2
1898	Cleveland	National	42	343	24	15	.615	328	153	103	101	36	•6
1899	St. Louis	National	48	373	23	21	.523	425	195	86	83	40	2
1900	St. Louis	National	37	281	17	17	.500	319	185	77	77	27	3
1901	St. Louis	National	•45	341	19	18	.514	353	163	132	58	33	2
1902	St. Louis	American	42	330	22	17	.564	322	147	137	89	36	3
1903	St. Louis	American	38	308	15	19	.441	297	131	166	57	33	4
1904	New York	American	47	392	23	19	.548	344	154	197	95	38	3
1905	New York (a)-St. Louis	American	40	228	11	14	.440	237	116	102	65	17	1
1906	St. Louis	American	28	245	13	14	.481	196	77	132	56	25	3
1907	St. Louis	American	32	255	13	16	.448	236	100	99	60	27	4
1908	St. Louis	American	33	256	16	13	.552	208	73	85	47	23	5
1909	St. Louis	American	34	239	12	16	.429	221	83	82	42	18	4
1910	St. Louis	American	21	129	7	11	.389	121	45	52	28	8	3
1911	St. Louis	American	31	208	8	*19	.296	224	120	52	44	18	1
1912	St. Louis	American	32	235	9	16	.360	248	117	67	52	19	0
1913	Louisville	Amer. Assn.	47	240	17	13	.567	238	102	76	56	...	...
	American League Totals		378	2825	149	174	.461	2654	1163	1171	635	262	31
	National League Totals		199	1565	98	80	.551	1669	813	462	382	160	15
	Major League Totals		577	4390	247	254	.493	4323	1976	1633	1017	422	46

aSold to St. Louis for cash, September, 1905.

JOHN PICUS QUINN (PAYKOS)

Born July 5, 1884, at Mahanoy City, Pa.
Died April 17, 1946, at Pottsville, Pa.
Height, 6.00. Weight, 200.
Threw and batted righthanded.

Manager, Johnstown, Middle Atlantic League, July to September, 1935.

Year	Club	League	G.	IP.	W.	L.	Pct.	H.	R.	ER.	SO.	BB.	ERA.
1907	Macon	So. Atlantic	15	109	6	5	.545	83	...	...	60	33	....
1908	Richmond	Virginia	17	...	14	0	*1.000	102	...	...	92	20	....
1909	New York	American	22	118	9	5	.643	110	45	...	35	24	....
1910	New York	American	35	237	18	12	.600	214	88	...	82	58	....
1911	New York	American	39	175	8	9	.471	203	111	....	71	41	....
1912	New York (a)	American	18	103	5	7	.417	139	89	...	47	23	....
1912	Rochester	International	13	108	8	4	.667	94	39	...	44	14	....
1913	Rochester	International	38	268	19	13	.594	261	111	...	153	62	....
1913	Boston (b)	National	8	56	4	3	.571	55	22	15	33	7	2.41
1914	Baltimore	Federal	46	339	26	14	.650	*330	121	101	165	63	2.68
1915	Baltimore	Federal	44	275	9	*22	.290	291	139	102	116	64	3.34
1916	Vernon	Pacific Coast	51	289	16	13	.552	292	125	94	149	85	2.93
1917	Vernon	Pacific Coast	52	409	24	20	.545	415	155	107	160	84	2.35
1918	Vernon	Pacific Coast	24	...	12	6	.667	...	...	...	...	...	....
1918	Chicago (c)	American	6	51	5	1	.833	38	13	13	22	7	2.29
1919	New York	American	38	264	15	15	.500	242	96	77	97	65	2.63
1920	New York	American	41	253	18	10	.643	271	90	101	48	...	3.20
1921	New York (d)	American	33	129	8	7	.533	158	61	50	44	32	3.49
1922	Boston	American	40	256	13	15	.464	263	119	99	67	59	3.48
1923	Boston	American	42	243	13	17	.433	302	125	105	71	53	3.89
1924	Boston	American	43	228	12	13	.480	237	107	81	64	51	3.20
1925	Bos.(e)-Philadelphia	American	37	205	13	11	.542	259	124	94	43	42	4.13
1926	Philadelphia	American	31	164	10	11	.476	191	74	62	58	36	3.40
1927	Philadelphia	American	34	207	15	10	.600	211	82	73	43	37	3.17

Year	Club	League	G.	IP.	W.	L.	Pct.	H.	R.	ER.	SO.	BB.	ERA.
1928	Philadelphia	American	31	211	18	7	.720	239	92	68	43	34	2.90
1929	Philadelphia	American	35	161	11	9	.550	182	87	71	41	39	3.97
1930	Philadelphia (f)	American	35	90	9	7	.563	109	51	44	28	22	4.40
1931	Brooklyn	National	39	64	5	4	.556	65	28	19	25	24	2.67
1932	Brooklyn (g)	National	42	87	3	7	.300	102	36	32	28	24	3.31
1933	Cincinnati	National	14	16	0	1	.000	20	9	7	3	5	3.94
1934	Hollywood	Pacific Coast	6	18	1	1	.500	29	12	12	3	4	6.00
1935	Johnstown	Mid. Atlantic	1	2	0	0	.000	2	0	0	0	0	0.00
	American League Totals		560	3095	200	166	.546	3368	1474	...	957	671	....
	National League Totals		103	223	12	15	.444	242	95	73	89	60	2.95
	Major League Totals		663	3318	212	181	.539	3610	1569	...	1046	731	....

aSold to Rochester, July 30, 1912.
bPurchased from Rochester, August 23, 1913, but jumped to Baltimore, Federal League, for 1914.
cClaimed by both Chicago and New York and, after playing with White Sox, was awarded to Yankees by National Commission, August 26, 1918.
dTraded with shortstop Roger Peckinpaugh and pitchers Harry (Rip) Collins and William Piercy to Boston Red Sox for shortstop Everett Scott and pitchers Joe Bush and Sam Jones, December 20, 1921.
eSold to Philadelphia Athletics on waivers, July 10, 1925.
fUnconditionally released, November, 1930, and signed by Brooklyn, February, 1931.
gUnconditionally released, April, 1933, and signed by Cincinnati, May, 1933.

WORLD SERIES RECORD

Year	Club	League	G.	IP.	W.	L.	Pct.	H.	R.	ER.	SO.	BB.	ERA.
1921	New York	American	1	3⅔	0	1	.000	8	4	4	2	2	9.82
1929	Philadelphia	American	1	5	0	0	.000	7	6	5	2	2	9.00
1930	Philadelphia	American	1	2	0	0	.000	3	1	1	1	0	4.50
	World Series Totals		3	10⅔	0	1	.000	18	11	10	5	4	8.44

CHARLES (OLD HOSS) RADBOURN

Born December 9, 1853, at Rochester, N. Y.
Died, February 5, 1897, at Bloomington, Ill.
Height, 5.09. Weight, 168.
Threw and batted righthanded.

Won 18 consecutive games, August 7 through September 6, 1884. Won 14 games in month of August, 1884. Established all-time record for most wins, season, with 60 in 1884. Pitched 8-0, no-hit victory against Cleveland, July 25, 1883.
Named to Hall of Fame, 1939.

Year	Club	League	G.	IP.	W.	L.	Pct.	ShO.	H.	R.	SO.	BB.
1878	Peoria Reds	Independent		Batted .289 and fielded .810 in 28 games								
1879	Dubuque	N. W. L.		Batted .387 and fielded .916 in 47 games								
1880	Buffalo(a)	National		Batted .143 and fielded .937 in 6 games								
1881	Providence	National	41	327	25	11	*.694	3	296	157	109	67
1882	Providence	National	52	471	31	19	.620	*6	425	238	*194	47
1883	Providence	National	*76	642	*49	25	.662	4	585	290	312	51
1884	Providence	National	*74	*679	*60	12	*.833	11	514	217	*411	96
1885	Providence(b)	National	49	448	26	20	.565	2	423	209	157	76
1886	Boston	National	57	511	27	30	.474	3	572	288	209	107
1887	Boston	National	47	429	24	23	.511	1	624	307	79	127
1888	Boston	National	24	209	7	16	.304	1	192	110	53	44
1889	Boston(c)	National	32	276	20	11	.645	1	276	151	95	80
1890	Boston(d)	Players	40	347	27	12	.692	1	351	183	87	98
1891	Cincinnati	National	25	204	12	12	.500	2	242	120	40	63
	National League Totals		477	4196	281	179	.611	34	4149	2117	1659	758
	Players League Totals		40	347	27	12	.692	1	351	183	87	98
	Major League Totals		517	4543	308	191	.617	35	4500	2300	1746	856

aDid not pitch, played infield.
bTeam disbanded; awarded to Boston.
cJumped to Players League.
dSigned with Cincinnati after Players League disbanded.

WORLD SERIES RECORD

Year	Club	League	G.	IP.	W.	L.	Pct.	ShO.	H.	R.	SO.	BB.
1884	Providence	National	3	22	3	0	1.000	0	11	3	17	0

RAYMOND ALLEN (RIP) RADCLIFF

Born January 19, 1906, at Kiowa, Okla.
Died May 23, 1962, at Enid, Okla.
Height, 5.10½. Weight, 175.
Threw and batted lefthanded.
Married Jessie Houghton, September 9, 1930.

Made six hits in seven trips to plate, July 8, 1936, second game—four singles and two doubles.
Manager, Greensboro, Carolina League, 1948.

Year	Club	League	Pos.	G.	AB.	R.	H.	2B.	3B.	HR.	RBI.	B.A.	PO.	A.	E.	F.A.
1928	Paris	L. Star	OF	87	328	40	96	13	5	8	....	.293	884	33	17	.982
1929	Muskogee-Maud	W. A.	1B	112	409	78	147	16	6	14	85	.359	1004	37	22	.979
1929	Dallas	Tex.	1B	29	104	9	34	2	1	2	15	.327	224	12	1	.996
1930	Selma	So'east.	1B	132	539	94	*199	29	7	*15	*116	*.369	1233	*80	13	*.990
1931	Shreveport	Tex.	OF	155	596	96	*215	41	7	12	103	*.361	521	25	18	.968
1932	Dallas	Tex.	OF	148	578	88	183	48	9	3	101	.317	225	15	5	.980
1933	St. Paul	A. A.	OF	128	511	77	186	36	10	6	99	.364	219	4	8	.965
1934	Louisville	A. A.	OF	142	565	90	189	27	19	5	102	.335	693	33	15	.980
1934	Chicago	Amer.	OF	14	56	7	15	2	1	0	5	.268	35	0	2	.946
1935	Chicago	Amer.	OF	146	623	95	178	28	8	10	68	.286	231	8	8	.968
1936	Chicago	Amer.	PF	138	618	120	207	31	7	8	82	.335	213	6	15	.936
1937	Chicago	Amer.	OF	144	584	105	190	38	10	4	79	.325	273	9	10	.966
1938	Chicago	Amer.	1B-OF	129	503	64	166	23	6	5	81	.330	466	15	10	.980
1939	Chicago(a)	Amer.	1B-OF	113	397	49	105	25	2	2	53	.264	300	12	6	.981
1940	St. Louis	Amer.	1B-OF	150	584	83	•200	33	9	7	81	.342	307	10	9	.972
1941	St.L.(b)-Detroit	Amer.	OF	115	450	59	140	16	7	5	54	.311	205	7	5	.977
1942	Detroit	Amer.	1B-OF	62	144	13	36	5	0	1	20	.250	83	6	1	.989
1943	Detroit(c)	Amer.	1B-OF	70	115	3	30	4	0	0	10	.261	39	6	0	1.000
1944-45	Detroit	Amer.					(In Military Service)									
1946	Chattanooga	South.	OF	114	373	49	113	20	1	0	56	.303	148	16	8	.953
1947	—						(Out of Organized Ball)									
1948	Greensboro	Carol.	1B	136	508	95	155	36	3	10	80	.305	1099	*121	19	.985
Major League Totals				1081	4074	598	1267	205	50	42	533	.311	2152	76	66	.971

aTraded to St. Louis Browns for outfielder Julius Solters, December 8, 1939.
bSold to Detroit Tigers for reported $25,000, May 15, 1941.
cTraded to Philadelphia Athletics for catcher Bob Swift and second baseman Don Heffner, October 11, 1943; returned to Detroit upon entering Navy, and cash settlement made to complete deal.

HAROLD HENRY (PEE WEE) REESE

Born July 23, 1919, at Ekron, Ky.
Height, 5.09½. Weight, 178.
Threw and batted righthanded.
Married Dorothy Walton, March 29, 1942.

Led National League in stolen bases (30), 1952.
Holds World Series record for most double plays by a shortstop in seven-game Series (7), 1955 and 1956; tied Series mark for most times at bat, game (6), October 5, 1956.
Named as shortstop on THE SPORTING NEWS All-Star Major League Team, 1953.
Coach, Los Angeles Dodgers, 1959.

Year	Club	League	Pos.	G.	AB.	R.	H.	2B.	3B.	HR.	RBI.	B.A.	PO.	A.	E.	F.A.
1938	Louisville	A. A.	SS	138	483	68	134	21	8	3	54	.277	239	457	45	.939
1939	Louisville	A. A.	SS	149	506	78	141	22	*18	4	57	.279	*307	470	47	.943
1940	Brooklyn(a)	Nat.	SS	84	312	58	85	8	4	5	28	.272	190	238	18	.960
1941	Brooklyn	Nat.	SS	152	595	76	136	23	5	2	46	.229	*346	473	*47	.946
1942	Brooklyn	Nat.	SS	151	564	87	144	24	5	3	53	.255	*337	*482	35	.959
1943-44-45	Brooklyn	Nat.					(In Military Service)									
1946	Brooklyn	Nat.	SS	152	542	79	154	16	10	5	60	.284	285	463	26	.966
1947	Brooklyn	Nat.	SS	142	476	81	135	24	4	12	73	.284	266	441	25	.966
1948	Brooklyn	Nat.	SS	151	566	96	155	31	4	9	75	.274	*335	453	31	.962
1949	Brooklyn	Nat.	SS	155	617	*132	172	27	3	16	73	.279	*316	454	18	*.977

Year	Club	League	Pos.	G.	AB.	R.	H.	2B.	3B.	HR.	RBI.	B.A.	PO.	A.	E.	F.A.
1950–Brooklyn		Nat.	SS-3B	141	531	97	138	21	5	11	52	.260	291	414	26	.964
1951–Brooklyn		Nat.	SS	154	616	94	176	20	8	10	84	.286	292	422	35	.953
1952–Brooklyn		Nat.	SS	149	559	94	152	18	8	6	58	.272	282	376	21	.969
1953–Brooklyn		Nat.	SS	140	524	108	142	25	7	13	61	.271	265	380	23	.966
1954–Brooklyn		Nat.	SS	141	554	98	171	35	8	10	69	.309	270	426	25	.965
1955–Brooklyn		Nat.	SS	145	553	99	156	29	4	10	61	.282	239	404	23	.965
1956–Brooklyn		Nat.	SS-3B	147	572	85	147	19	2	9	46	.257	269	388	25	.963
1957–Brooklyn		Nat.	3B-SS	103	330	33	74	3	1	1	29	.224	97	228	19	.945
1958–Los Angeles		Nat.	SS-3B	59	147	21	33	7	2	4	17	.224	44	89	10	.930
Major League Totals				2166	8058	1338	2170	330	80	126	885	.269	4124	6131	407	.962

aFractured heel sliding into second base, August 15, 1940; out for balance of season.

WORLD SERIES RECORD

Year	Club	League	Pos.	G.	AB.	R.	H.	2B.	3B.	HR.	RBI.	B.A.	PO.	A.	E.	F.A.
1941–Brooklyn		Nat.	SS	5	20	1	4	0	0	0	2	.200	13	14	3	.900
1947–Brooklyn		Nat.	SS	7	23	5	7	1	0	0	4	.304	8	15	1	.958
1949–Brooklyn		Nat.	SS	5	19	2	6	1	0	1	2	.316	5	9	1	.933
1952–Brooklyn		Nat.	SS	7	29	4	10	0	0	1	4	.345	15	18	2	.943
1953–Brooklyn		Nat.	SS	6	24	0	5	0	1	0	0	.278	7	14	0	1.000
1955–Brooklyn		Nat.	SS	7	27	5	8	1	0	0	2	.296	15	23	1	.974
1956–Brooklyn		Nat.	SS	7	27	3	6	0	1	0	2	.222	14	21	1	.972
World Series Totals				44	169	20	46	3	2	2	16	.272	77	114	9	.955

ALLIE PIERCE (CHIEF) REYNOLDS

Born February 10, 1917, at Bethany, Okla.
Height, 6.00. Weight, 195.
Threw and batted righthanded.
Married Dale Earlene Jones, July 7, 1935.

Tied major league record by pitching two no-hit, no-run games in a season—adding his first on July 12, 1951, against the Cleveland Indians with a 1-0 win over Bob Feller, who had pitched a no-hitter just 11 days prior to Reynolds' effort; Allie allowed the Indians three bases on balls and fanned four. On September 28, 1951, he pitched the second no-hitter, over the Boston Red Sox, winning 8-0; he walked four and fanned nine. The first was pitched under lights—while the second was a day game, the opener of a doubleheader.
Named as pitcher on THE SPORTING NEWS All-Star Major League Teams, 1951-52.

Year	Club	League	G.	IP.	W.	L.	Pct.	H.	R.	ER.	SO.	BB.	ERA.
1939–Springfield		Mid-Atlantic	24	155	11	8	.579	121	76	62	140	107	3.60
1940–Cedar Rapids		I.I.I.	30	178	12	7	.632	170	86	71	131	88	3.59
1941–Wilkes-Barre		Eastern	3	7	0	0	.000	13	5	5	0	4	6.43
1941–Cedar Rapids		I.I.I.	27	167	10	10	.500	173	101	86	153	97	4.63
1942–Wilkes-Barre		Eastern	32	231	18	7	.720	143	54	40	*193	102	*1.56
1942–Cleveland		American	2	5	0	0	.000	5	1	0	2	4	0.00
1943–Cleveland		American	34	199	11	12	.478	140	72	66	*151	109	2.98
1944–Cleveland		American	28	158	11	8	.579	141	63	58	84	91	3.30
1945–Cleveland		American	44	247	18	12	.600	227	102	88	112	*130	3.21
1946–Cleveland (a)		American	31	183	11	15	.423	180	93	79	107	108	3.89
1947–New York		American	34	242	19	8	*.704	207	94	86	129	123	3.20
1948–New York		American	39	236	16	7	.696	240	108	99	101	111	3.78
1949–New York		American	35	214	17	6	.739	200	102	95	105	123	4.00
1950–New York		American	35	241	16	12	.571	215	108	100	160	138	3.73
1951–New York		American	40	221	17	8	.680	171	84	75	126	100	3.05
1952–New York		American	35	244	20	8	.714	194	70	56	*160	97	*2.07
1953–New York		American	41	145	13	7	.650	140	64	55	86	61	3.41
1954–New York		American	36	157	13	4	.765	133	65	58	100	66	3.32
Major League Totals			434	2492	182	107	.630	2193	1026	915	1423	1261	3.30

aTraded to New York Yankees for infielders Joe Gordon and Eddie Bockman, October 19, 1946.

WORLD SERIES RECORD

Year	Club	League	G.	IP.	W.	L.	Pct.	H.	R.	ER.	SO.	BB.	ERA.
1947–New York		American	2	11⅓	1	0	1.000	15	7	6	6	3	4.76
1949–New York		American	2	12⅓	1	0	1.000	2	0	0	14	4	0.00
1950–New York		American	2	10⅓	1	0	1.000	7	1	1	7	4	0.87
1951–New York		American	2	15	1	1	.500	16	7	7	8	11	4.20
1952–New York		American	4	20⅓	2	1	.667	12	4	4	18	6	1.77
1953–New York		American	3	8	1	0	1.000	9	6	6	9	4	6.75
World Series Totals			15	77⅓	7	2	.778	61	25	24	62	32	2.79

CARL NETTLES REYNOLDS

Born February 1, 1904, at LaRue, Tex.
Died May 29, 1978, at Houston, Tex.
Height, 6.00. Weight, 195.
Threw and batted righthanded.
Married Ruth Dayvault, November 9, 1929.

Hit three successive home runs (second game), July 2, 1930.

Year	Club	League	Pos.	G.	AB.	R.	H.	2B.	3B.	HR.	RBI.	B.A.	PO.	A.	E.	F.A.
1927	Palestine	L. Star	SS-OF	124	479	82	*180	27	6	11	....	*.376	272	159	37	.921
1927	Chicago	Amer.	OF	14	42	5	9	3	0	1	7	.214	37	1	0	1.000
1928	Chicago	Amer.	OF	84	291	51	94	21	11	2	36	.323	135	6	3	.979
1929	Chicago	Amer.	OF	131	517	81	164	24	12	11	67	.317	268	13	15	.949
1930	Chicago	Amer.	OF	138	563	103	202	25	18	22	104	.359	336	11	9	.975
1931	Chicago(a)	Amer.	OF	118	462	71	134	24	14	6	77	.290	233	10	13	.949
1932	Washington(b)	Amer.	OF	102	406	53	124	28	7	9	63	.305	229	3	4	.983
1933	St. Louis(c)	Amer.	OF	135	475	81	136	26	14	8	71	.286	269	8	10	.965
1934	Boston	Amer.	OF	113	413	61	125	26	9	4	86	.303	244	6	6	.977
1935	Boston(d)	Amer.	OF	78	244	33	66	13	4	6	35	.270	146	7	4	.975
1936	Washington	Amer.	OF	89	293	41	81	18	2	4	41	.276	142	8	5	.968
1937	Minneapolis	A. A.	OF	147	614	145	218	*49	17	17	110	.355	294	9	9	.971
1937	Chicago	Nat.	OF	7	11	0	3	1	0	0	1	.273	5	0	1	.833
1938	Chicago	Nat.	OF	125	497	59	150	28	10	3	67	.302	328	10	6	.983
1939	Chicago	Nat.	OF	88	281	33	69	10	6	4	44	.246	168	5	5	.972
1940	Los Angeles	P. C.	OF	41	80	10	20	3	1	0	13	.250	50	0	0	1.000
	American League Totals			1002	3706	580	1135	208	91	73	587	.306	2039	73	69	.968
	National League Totals			220	789	92	222	39	16	7	112	.281	501	15	12	.977
	Major League Totals			1222	4495	672	1357	247	107	80	699	.302	2540	88	81	.970

aTraded to Washington Senators with infielder John Kerr for pitcher Irving Hadley and Samuel Jones and infielder Minter Hayes, December 4, 1931.
bTraded to St. Louis Browns with outfielder Sam West and pitcher Lloyd Brown for outfielders Leon Goslin and Fred Schulte, and pitcher Walter Stewart and $20,000, December 14, 1932.
cTraded to Boston Red Sox for pitcher Ivy Andrews and outfielder Smead Jolley, December 13, 1933.
dTraded to Washington Senators with outfielder Roy Johnson for outfielder Henry Manush, December 17, 1935.

WORLD SERIES RECORD

Year	Club	League	Pos.	G.	AB.	R.	H.	2B.	3B.	HR.	RBI.	B.A.	PO.	A.	E.	F.A.
1938	Chicago	Nat.	OF-PH	4	12	0	0	0	0	0	0	.000	7	0	0	1.000

EDGAR CHARLES (SAM) RICE

Born February 20, 1890, at Morocco, Ind.
Died October 13, 1974, at Rossmor, Md.
Height, 5.10. Weight, 155.
Threw and batted lefthanded.
Married Mary Adams, July 4, 1959.

Established American League record for most one-base hits, season, 182, in 1925.
Led major leagues in stolen bases, 1920, with 63.
Led A.L. outfielders in double plays, 1923 (tie).
Had 351 stolen bases in American League. Batted safely in 31 consecutive games, August 23 through September 24, 1924.
Named to Hall of Fame, 1963.

Year	Club	League	Pos.	G.	AB.	R.	H.	2B.	3B.	HR.	RBI.	B.A.	PO.	A.	E.	F.A.
1914	Petersburg(a)	Va.	P	31	71	9	22	3	1	0	....	.310	13	36	0	1.000
1915	Petersburg	Va.	P-OF	62	156	16	47	3	4	0	....	.301	45	70	0	1.000
1915	Washington	Amer.	P	4	8	1	3	0	0	0	0	.375	1	7	1	.889
1916	Washington	Amer.	P-OF	58	197	26	59	8	3	1	16	.299	83	5	4	.957
1917	Washington	Amer.	OF	155	586	77	177	25	7	0	68	.302	265	26	12	.960
1918	Washington(a)	Amer.	OF	7	23	3	8	1	0	0	3	.348	10	3	0	1.000
1919	Washington	Amer.	OF	•141	557	80	179	23	9	3	72	.321	285	18	12	.962
1920	Washington	Amer.	OF	153	624	83	211	29	9	3	80	.336	*454	24	20	.960

Year	Club	League	Pos.	G.	AB.	R.	H.	2B.	3B.	HR.	RBI.	B.A.	PO.	A.	E.	F.A.
1921—Washington		Amer.	OF	143	561	83	185	39	13	4	79	.330	380	18	15	.964
1922—Washington		Amer.	OF	154	*633	91	187	37	13	6	69	.295	*385	23	*21	.951
1923—Washington		Amer.	OF	148	595	117	188	35	•18	3	75	.316	307	21	10	.970
1924—Washington		Amer.	OF	154	*646	106	*216	39	14	1	76	.334	331	18	12	.967
1925—Washington		Amer.	OF	152	649	111	227	31	13	1	87	.350	339	20	12	.968
1926—Washington		Amer.	OF	152	*641	98	•216	32	14	3	76	.337	342	•25	•15	.961
1927—Washington		Amer.	OF	142	603	98	179	33	14	2	65	.297	258	12	7	.975
1928—Washington		Amer.	OF	148	616	95	202	32	15	2	55	.328	240	11	7	.973
1929—Washington		Amer.	OF	150	616	119	199	39	10	1	62	.323	272	20	9	.970
1930—Washington		Amer.	OF	147	593	121	207	35	13	1	73	.349	297	13	12	.963
1931—Washington		Amer.	OF	120	413	81	128	21	8	0	42	.310	221	7	7	.970
1932—Washington		Amer.	OF	106	288	58	93	16	7	1	34	.323	132	7	4	.972
1933—Washington(b)		Amer.	OF	73	85	19	25	4	3	1	12	.294	41	4	0	1.000
1934—Cleveland		Amer.	OF	97	335	48	98	19	1	1	33	.293	129	2	5	.963
Major League Totals				2404	9269	1515	2987	498	184	34	1077	.322	4772	284	185	.965

aIn Military Service most of season of 1914 (Navy), 1918 (Army).
bReleased by Washington, January, 1934, and subsequently signed by Cleveland.

WORLD SERIES RECORD

Year	Club	League	Pos.	G.	AB.	R.	H.	2B.	3B.	HR.	RBI.	B.A.	PO.	A.	E.	F.A.
1924—Washington		Amer.	OF	7	29	2	6	0	0	0	1	.207	13	4	1	.944
1925—Washington		Amer.	OF	7	33	5	12	0	0	0	3	.364	17	0	0	1.000
1933—Washington		Amer.	PH	1	1	0	1	0	0	0	0	1.000	0	0	0	.000
World Series Totals				15	63	7	19	0	0	0	4	.302	30	4	1	.971

PITCHING RECORD

Year	Club	League	G.	IP.	W.	L.	Pct.	H.	R.	ER.	SO.	BB.	ERA.
1914—Petersburg		Virginia	15	123	9	2	.818	73	....	....	62	38	....
1915—Petersburg		Virginia	29	233	11	12	.478	175	....	....	153	43	....
1915—Washington		American	4	18	1	0	.000	13	8	4	9	9	2.00
1916—Washington		American	5	21⅓	0	1	.000	-18	10	7	3	10	2.94
Major League Totals			9	39⅓	1	1	.500	31	18	11	12	19	2.52

ARTHUR HARDING (HARDY) RICHARDSON

Born April 21, 1855, at Paulsboro, N.J.
Died January 14, 1931, at Utica, N. Y.
Threw and batted righthanded.

Year	Club	League	Pos.	G.	AB.	R.	H.	2B.	3B.	HR.	SB.	B.A.	PO.	A.	E.	F.A.
1879—Buffalo		Nat.	3B	78	330	53	92	19	9	0	....	.278	82	148	42	.845
1880—Buffalo		Nat.	C-3B	80	329	43	83	19	9	0	....	.252	104	147	45	.848
1881—Buffalo		Nat.	2B-SS-OF	83	344	62	100	21	9	2	....	.290	179	45	21	.914
1882—Buffalo		Nat.	2B	83	354	61	96	17	9	2	....	.271	275	280	63	.898
1883—Buffalo		Nat.	2B	90	393	73	122	34	7	1	....	.310	282	341	68	.901
'884—Buffalo		Nat.	IF-OF	98	421	85	127	25	7	6	....	.301	224	229	50	.901
1885—Buffalo		Nat.	IF-OF	96	426	90	136	17	10	4	....	.319	283	175	49	.903
1886—Detroit		Nat.	2B-OF	125	538	125	189	27	*11	42	.351	234	139	31	.923	
1887—Detroit		Nat.	2B-OF	120	573	130	208	26	18	9	29	.363	328	223	35	.940
1888—Detroit		Nat.	2B	57	266	60	77	17	1	6	13	.289	173	185	29	.925
1889—Boston		Nat.	2B-OF	132	536	122	163	29	10	6	47	.304	320	316	51	.926
1890—Boston		Players	OF	130	554	125	184	31	16	•13	45	.332	262	38	11	.964
1891—Boston		A. A.	OF	71	269	45	69	11	4	7	15	.256	96	6	4	.962
1892—Wash.-N.Y.		Nat.	2B-OF	70	282	38	59	12	5	3	10	.209	115	103	17	.928
National League Totals				1112	4792	942	1452	263	105	50	....	.303	2599	2331	501	.908
Players League Totals				130	554	125	184	31	16	13	45	.332	262	38	11	.964
American Association Totals				71	269	45	69	11	4	7	15	.256	96	6	4	.962
Major League Totals				1313	5615	1112	1705	305	125	70	....	.304	2957	2375	516	.912

DID YOU KNOW—
That Mahatma Branch Rickey's Dodger office was called "Cave of the Winds?"

BRANCH WESLEY RICKEY

Born December 20, 1881, at Lucasville, O.
Died December 9, 1965, at Columbia, Mo.
Threw right and batted lefthanded.
Married Jane Moulton, 1906.

Attended Ohio Wesleyan (Bachelor of Literature), 1904; (Bachelor of Arts), 1906; Civil Law degree at University of Michigan, 1911, and LLD at McKendree College, 1928.
Ohio Wesleyan varsity baseball, basketball and football team, 1901-02; captain baseball team, 1903; baseball coach, University of Michigan, 1909-10-11.
Hit two home runs against New York, off Chesbro and Clarkson, in game St. Louis lost, 8-6, August 6, 1906; catching Moore for one inning and Brockett for eight, permitted Washington to steal 13 bases in game New York lost, 16-5, June 28, 1907 (three steals by Ganley, two each by Delahanty, Anderson, Jones and Altizer, one each by Clymer and Haydon).
Is credited with instituting the chain-store farm system in baseball and re-introducing the Negro to major league baseball.
Manager, St. Louis Browns, September 6, 1913 through 1915; vice-president-business manager, St. Louis Browns, 1916; St. Louis Cardinals, 1917-20, and manager, 1919 to June 1, 1925; vice-president-business manager, St. Louis Cardinals, 1925 to 1942; president-general manager, Brooklyn Dodgers, October, 1942 to 1950; vice-president, general manager, Pittsburgh Pirates, 1951-52-53-54-55; chairman board of directors, Pittsburgh Pirates, 1956-57-58-59. President of the ill-fated Continental League; advisor to president, St. Louis Cardinals, 1963-65.
Named to Hall of Fame, 1967.

Year-Club	League	Pos.	G.	AB.	R.	H.	2B.	3B.	HR.	SB.	B.A.	PO.	A.	E.	F.A.
1903–Terre Haute	Central					(No record available)									
1903–LeMars	Ia.-S.D.	C	41	....	26	41	...	...	...	12	.265	237	44	13	.956
1904–Dallas	Texas	C	41	....	25	36	...	...	...	14	.261	316	41	8	.959
1905–St. Louis(a)	Amer.	C	1	3	0	0	0	0	0	0	.000	2	1	0	1.000
1905–Dallas	Texas	C	37	132	20	39	8	2	0	7	.295	203	37	8	.967
1906–St. Louis(b)	Amer.	C	64	201	22	57	8	3	3	4	.284	233	58	14	.954
1907–New York	Amer.	C	52	137	16	25	1	3	0	4	.182	56	11	9	.862
1914–St. Louis	Amer.	C	2	2	0	0	0	0	0	0	.000	0	0	0	.000
Major League Totals			119	343	38	82	9	6	3	8	.239	291	70	23	.940

aDrafted by Chicago White Sox and then traded to St. Louis Browns for catcher Frank Roth.
bTraded to New York Yankees for third baseman Joe Yeager.

EPPA (JEPTHA) RIXEY

Born May 3, 1891, at Culpeper, Va.
Died February 28, 1963, at Cincinnati, O.
Height, 6.05. Weight, 210.
Threw left and batted righthanded.
Married Dorothy Meyers, October 30, 1924.

Pitched 21 years in National League.
Named to Hall of Fame, 1963.

Year-Club	League	G.	IP.	W.	L.	Pct.	H.	R.	ER.	SO.	BB.	ERA.
1912–Philadelphia	National	23	162	10	10	.500	147	57	45	59	54	2.50
1913–Philadelphia	National	35	156	9	5	.643	148	67	54	75	56	3.12
1914–Philadelphia	National	24	103	2	11	.154	124	73	50	41	45	4.37
1915–Philadelphia	National	29	177	11	12	.478	163	67	47	88	64	2.39
1916–Philadelphia	National	38	287	22	10	.688	239	91	59	134	74	1.85
1917–Philadelphia	National	39	281	16	•21	.432	249	102	71	121	67	2.27
1918–Philadelphia	National					(In Military Service)						
1919–Philadelphia	National	23	154	6	12	.333	160	88	68	63	50	3.97
1920–Philadelphia (a)	National	41	284	11	★22	.333	288	137	110	109	69	3.49
1921–Cincinnati	National	40	301	19	18	.514	324	128	93	76	66	2.78
1922–Cincinnati	National	40	★313	★25	13	.658	★337	146	123	80	45	3.54
1923–Cincinnati	National	42	309	20	15	.571	334	124	96	97	65	2.80
1924–Cincinnati	National	35	238	15	14	.517	219	86	73	57	47	2.76
1925–Cincinnati	National	39	287	21	11	.656	302	109	92	69	47	2.89
1926–Cincinnati	National	37	233	14	8	.636	231	104	88	61	58	3.40

Year Club	League	G.	IP.	W.	L.	Pct.	H.	R.	ER.	SO.	BB.	ERA.
1927–Cincinnati	National	34	220	12	10	.545	240	106	85	42	43	3.48
1928–Cincinnati	National	43	291	19	18	.514	*317	127	111	58	67	3.43
1929–Cincinnati	National	35	201	10	13	.435	235	102	93	37	60	4.16
1930–Cincinnati	National	32	164	9	13	.409	207	103	93	37	47	5.10
1931–Cincinnati	National	22	127	4	7	.364	143	71	55	22	30	3.90
1932–Cincinnati	National	25	112	5	5	.500	108	50	33	14	16	2.65
1933–Cincinnati	National	16	94	6	3	.667	118	48	33	10	12	3.16
Major League Totals		692	4494	266	251	.515	4633	1986	1572	1350	1082	3.15

aTraded to Cincinnati for pitcher James Ring and outfielder Earle Neale, February, 1921.

WORLD SERIES RECORD

Year Club	League	G.	IP.	W.	L.	Pct.	H.	R.	ER.	SO.	BB.	ERA.
1915–Philadelphia	National	1	6⅔	0	1	.000	4	3	2	2	2	2.70

ROBIN EVAN ROBERTS

Born September 30, 1926, at Springfield, Ill.
Height, 6.01. Weight, 201.
Threw right and batted right and lefthanded.
Married Mary Ann Kalnes, December 26, 1949.

Established major league record for most home runs allowed, season (46), 1956; led league in complete games (30) 1952, (33) 1953, (29) 1954, (26) 1955 and (22) 1956; allowed most home runs (35) 1954, (46) 1956, (40) 1957 and tied (31) 1960.
Set National League record for most seasons opening-game pitcher for his club (13), 1950 through 1961, Philadelphia; 1966, Houston; won 5, lost 7, no decision 1.
Allowed 502 home runs in major leagues.
Named Outstanding Pitcher in National League by THE SPORTING NEWS, 1952-55.
Named Major League Player of the Year by THE SPORTING NEWS, 1952-55.
Named as pitcher on THE SPORTING NEWS All-Star Major League Teams, 1952-53-54-55.
Named to Hall of Fame, 1976.

Year Club	League	G.	IP.	W.	L.	Pct.	H.	R.	ER.	SO.	BB.	ERA.
1948–Wilmington	Int. State	11	96	9	1	*.900	55	25	22	121	27	*2.06
1948–Philadelphia	National	20	147	7	9	.438	148	63	52	84	61	3.18
1949–Philadelphia	National	43	227	15	15	.500	229	101	93	95	75	3.69
1950–Philadelphia	National	40	304	20	11	.645	282	112	102	146	77	3.02
1951–Philadelphia	National	44	*315	21	15	.583	284	115	106	127	64	3.03
1952–Philadelphia	National	39	*330	*28	7	.800	*292	104	95	148	45	2.59
1953–Philadelphia	National	44	*347	•23	16	.590	*324	119	106	*198	61	2.75
1954–Philadelphia	National	45	*337	*23	15	.605	*289	116	111	*185	56	2.96
1955–Philadelphia	National	41	*305	*23	14	.622	*292	*137	*111	160	53	3.28
1956–Philadelphia	National	43	297	19	•18	.514	*328	*155	*147	157	40	4.45
1957–Philadelphia	National	39	250	10	*22	.313	246	*122	*113	128	43	4.07
1958–Philadelphia	National	35	270	17	14	.548	270	112	97	130	51	3.23
1959–Philadelphia	National	35	257	15	17	.469	267	137	122	137	35	4.27
1960–Philadelphia	National	35	237	12	16	.429	256	113	106	122	34	4.03
1961–Philadelphia (a-b)	National	26	117	1	10	.091	154	85	76	54	23	5.85
1962–Baltimore	American	27	191	10	9	.526	176	63	59	102	41	2.78
1963–Baltimore	American	35	251	14	13	.519	230	100	93	124	40	3.33
1964–Baltimore	American	31	204	13	7	.650	203	69	66	109	52	2.91
1965–Baltimore (c)	American	20	115	5	7	.417	110	51	43	63	20	3.37
1965–Houston	National	10	76	5	2	.714	61	22	16	34	10	1.89
1966–Houston (d)-Chicago	National	24	112	5	8	.385	141	66	60	54	21	4.82
1967–Reading	Eastern	11	80	5	3	.625	75	25	22	65	7	2.48
American League Totals		113	761	42	36	.538	719	283	261	398	153	3.09
National League Totals		563	3928	244	209	.539	3863	1679	1513	1959	749	3.45
Major League Totals		676	4689	286	245	.539	4582	1962	1774	2357	902	3.40

aSold to New York Yankees, October 16, 1961.
bUnconditionally released by New York Yankees, April 30, 1962; signed with Baltimore Orioles, May 21, 1962.
cReleased by Baltimore Orioles, July 31, 1965; signed by Houston Astros, August 6, 1965.
dReleased by Houston Astros; signed by Chicago Cubs, July 13, 1966.

WORLD SERIES RECORD

Year Club	League	G.	IP.	W.	L.	Pct.	H.	R.	ER.	SO.	BB.	ERA.
1950–Philadelphia	National	2	11	0	1	.000	11	2	2	5	3	1.64

BROOKS CALBERT ROBINSON, JR.

Born May 18, 1937, at Little Rock, Ark.
Height, 6.01. Weight, 190.
Threw and batted righthanded.

Established following major league records: most years leading league in games, third baseman (8), 1970; most double plays, third baseman, lifetime (618), 1977; most games, third baseman, lifetime (2,870), 1977; most putouts, third baseman, lifetime (2,697), 1977; most assists, third baseman, lifetime (6,205), 1977; most chances accepted, third baseman, lifetime (8,902), 1977; highest fielding average, third baseman, lifetime (.971), 1977; most seasons leading league, assists, third baseman (8), 1974; most seasons, third baseman (23), 1977; most seasons, one club (23), 1977; most consecutive seasons, one club (23), 1977.

Tied following major league records: most home runs with bases filled, two consecutive games (2), May 6 and 9, 1962; most consecutive seasons leading league in games (4), 1961 through 1964; most years, 150 or more games, league (14).

Established American League records for most games played, third baseman, 162-game schedule (163), 1961 and 1964; most home runs, third baseman, lifetime (267), 1977; most seasons leading league, fielding, third baseman (11), 1975.

Tied American League record for most seasons leading league, chances accepted, third baseman (8), 1974.

Led American League third basemen in double plays with 43 in 1963, 40 in 1964 and 44 in 1974.
Hit home run in first World Series at-bat, first inning, October 5, 1966.
Tied World Series record for most hits, 5-game Series (9), in 1970.
Named third baseman on THE SPORTING NEWS American League All-Star Teams, 1961-62-64-65-66-67-68-71-72.
Named third baseman on THE SPORTING NEWS American League All-Star fielding teams, 1960-61-62-63-64-65-66-67-68-69-70-71-72-73-74-75.
Named Most Valuable Player in American League, 1964.
Named American League Player of the Year by THE SPORTING NEWS, 1964.

Year	Club	League	Pos.	G.	AB.	R.	H.	2B.	3B.	HR.	RBI.	B.A.	PO.	A.	E.	F.A.
1955	York	Pied.	2B-3B	95	354	72	117	17	3	11	67	.331	184	226	14	.967
1955	Baltimore	Amer.	3B	6	22	0	2	0	0	0	1	.091	2	8	2	.833
1956	San Antonio	Texas	*3B-2B	154	577	72	157	28	6	9	74	.272	*213	396	26	*.959
1956	Baltimore	Amer.	3B-2B	15	44	5	10	4	0	1	1	.227	9	25	2	.944
1957	San Antonio	Texas	3B-SS	33	124	10	33	5	1	1	9	.266	34	59	4	.959
1957	Baltimore	Amer.	3B	50	117	13	28	6	1	2	14	.239	34	66	3	.971
1958	Baltimore	Amer.	*3B-2B	145	463	31	110	16	3	3	32	.238	*157	283	22	.952
1959	Vancouver	P.C.	3B	42	163	20	54	9	2	6	30	.331	54	93	8	.948
1959	Baltimore	Amer.	3B-2B	88	313	29	89	15	2	4	24	.284	92	187	13	.955
1960	Baltimore	Amer.	*3B-2B	152	595	74	175	27	9	14	88	.294	*174	*330	12	*.977
1961	Baltimore	Amer.	*3B-2B-SS	•163	*668	89	192	38	7	7	61	.287	155	334	14	*.972
1962	Baltimore	Amer.	*3B-SS-2B	•162	634	77	192	29	9	23	86	.303	165	340	11	*.979
1963	Baltimore	Amer.	*3B-SS	*161	589	67	148	26	4	11	67	.251	153	*331	12	*.976
1964	Baltimore	Amer.	3B	•163	612	82	194	35	3	28	*118	.317	*153	*327	14	*.972
1965	Baltimore	Amer.	3B	144	559	81	166	25	2	18	80	.297	144	296	15	.967
1966	Baltimore	Amer.	3B	157	620	91	167	35	2	23	100	.269	174	*313	12	*.976
1967	Baltimore	Amer.	3B	158	610	88	164	25	5	22	77	.269	147	*405	11	*.980
1968	Baltimore	Amer.	3B	•162	608	65	154	36	6	17	75	.253	168	*353	16	*.970
1969	Baltimore	Amer.	3B	156	598	73	140	21	3	23	84	.234	163	*370	13	•.976
1970	Baltimore	Amer.	3B	158	608	84	168	31	4	18	94	.276	157	321	17	.966
1971	Baltimore	Amer.	3B	156	589	67	160	21	1	20	92	.272	131	354	16	.968
1972	Baltimore	Amer.	3B	153	556	48	139	23	2	8	64	.250	129	333	11	*.977
1973	Baltimore	Amer.	3B	155	549	53	141	17	2	9	72	.257	129	354	15	.970
1974	Baltimore	Amer.	3B	153	553	46	159	27	0	7	59	.288	115	*410	18	.067
1975	Baltimore	Amer.	3B	144	482	50	97	15	1	6	53	.201	95	326	9	*.979
1976	Baltimore	Amer.	3B	71	218	16	46	8	2	3	11	.211	59	126	6	.969
1977	Baltimore	Amer.	3B	24	47	3	7	2	0	1	4	.149	6	28	0	1.000
Major League Totals				2896	10654	1232	2848	482	68	268	1357	.267	2712	6220	264	.971

WORLD SERIES RECORD

Year	Club	League	Pos.	G.	AB.	R.	H.	2B.	3B.	HR.	RBI.	B.A.	PO.	A.	E.	F.A.
1966	Baltimore	Amer.	3B	4	14	2	3	0	0	1	1	.214	4	6	0	1.000
1969	Baltimore	Amer.	3B	5	19	0	1	0	0	0	2	.053	1	16	0	1.000
1970	Baltimore	Amer.	3B	5	21	5	9	2	0	2	6	.429	9	14	1	.958
1971	Baltimore	Amer.	3B	7	22	2	7	0	0	5	.318	6	17	2	.920
World Series Totals				21	76	9	20	2	0	3	14	.263	20	53	3	.960

DID YOU KNOW—
That Brooks Robinson and Jim Kaat each have won most Gold Glove Awards, 16

FRANK ROBINSON

Born August 31, 1935, at Beaumont, Tex.
Height, 6;01. Weight, 194.
Threw and batted righthanded.

Established major league records for most major league parks, one or more home runs, 32, 1966 through 1973.
Tied the following major league records: Most home runs, bases filled, game (2), June 26, 1970; most home runs, bases filled, two successive at bats (2), June 26, 1970; most runs batted in, two successive innings (8), June 26, 1970, (5th, 6th); most home runs, rookie season, 38, 1956.
Hit three home runs in a game, August 22, 1959.
Won American League Triple Crown, 1966.
Led National League in slugging percentage with .595 in 1960, .611 in 1961 and .624 in 1962.
Led A.L. first basemen in double plays, 1969.
Led American League in total bases with 367 and in slugging percentage with .637 in 1966.
Tied World Series record for most times hit by pitcher, game (2), October 8, 1961.
Named National League Rookie of the Year by the Baseball Writers' Association and THE SPORTING NEWS, 1956.
Named outfielder on THE SPORTING NEWS National League All-Star Fielding Team, 1958.
Named Most Valuable National League Player, 1961.
Named Outstanding National League Player by THE SPORTING NEWS, 1961.
Named as outfielder on THE SPORTING NEWS National League All-Star Team, 1961-62.
Named as outfielder on THE SPORTING NEWS American League All-Star Team, 1966-67.
Named American League Player of the Year by THE SPORTING NEWS, 1966.
Named Major League Player of the Year by THE SPORTING NEWS, 1966.
Named Most Valuable American League Player, 1966.
Manager, Cleveland, 1975-76; coach, California Angels, 1977; coach, Baltimore Orioles, 1978; manager, Rochester, International League, 1978; Oriole coach, 1979 to date.

Year	Club	League	Pos.	G.	AB.	R.	H.	2B.	3B.	HR.	RBI.	B.A.	PO.	A.	E.	F.A.
1953	Ogden	Pion.	O-3B-1B	72	270	70	94	20	6	17	83	.348	105	28	18	.881
1954	Tulsa	Tex.	2B-3B	8	30	4	8	0	0	1	.267	17	15	1	.970
1954	Columbia	Sally	OF-3-2B	132	491	*112	165	32	9	25	110	.336	258	63	18	.947
1955	Columbia	Sally	OF-1B	80	243	50	64	15	7	12	52	.263	203	3	4	.981
1956	Cincinnati	Nat.	OF	152	572	*122	166	27	6	38	83	.290	323	5	8	.976
1957	Cincinnati	Nat.	OF-1B	150	611	97	197	29	5	29	75	.322	487	36	6	.989
1958	Cincinnati	Nat.	OF-3B	148	554	90	149	25	6	31	83	.269	314	24	6	.983
1959	Cincinnati	Nat.	1B-OF	146	540	106	168	31	4	36	125	.311	1049	78	18	.984
1960	Cincinnati	Nat.	1-OF-3	139	464	86	138	33	6	31	83	.297	775	62	10	.988
1961	Cincinnati	Nat.	OF-3B	153	545	117	176	32	7	37	124	.323	284	15	3	.990
1962	Cincinnati	Nat.	OF	162	609	*134	208	*51	2	39	136	.342	315	10	2	.994
1963	Cincinnati	Nat.	OF-1B	140	482	79	125	19	3	21	91	.259	238	13	4	.984
1964	Cincinnati	Nat.	OF	156	568	103	174	38	6	29	96	.306	279	7	4	.986
1965	Cincinnati (a)	Nat.	OF	156	582	109	172	33	5	33	113	.296	282	5	3	.990
1966	Baltimore	Am.	OF-1B	155	576	*122	182	34	2	*49	*122	*.316	282	6	5	.983
1967	Baltimore	Am.	OF-1B	129	479	83	149	23	7	30	94	.311	207	8	2	.991
1968	Baltimore	Am.	OF 1B	130	421	69	113	27	1	15	52	.268	193	5	7	.996
1969	Baltimore	Am.	OF-1B	148	539	111	166	19	5	32	100	.308	367	19	5	.987
1970	Baltimore	Am.	OF-1B	132	471	88	144	24	1	25	78	.306	262	11	4	.986
1971	Baltimore (b)	Am.	OF-1B	133	455	82	128	16	2	28	99	.281	449	20	11	.977
1972	Los Angeles (c)	Nat.	OF	103	342	41	86	6	1	19	59	.251	168	6	6	.967
1973	California	Amer.	OF	147	534	85	142	29	0	30	97	.266	38	3	1	.976
1974	Calif. (d)-Cleve.	Amer.	1B-OF	144	477	81	117	27	3	22	68	.245	23	0	1	.958
1975	Cleveland (e)	Amer.	DH-PH	49	118	19	28	5	0	9	24	.237	0	0	0	.000
1976	Cleveland	Amer.	1B-OF	15	67	5	15	0	0	3	10	.224	11	0	0	1.000
	National League Totals			1605	5869	1084	1759	324	51	343	1068	.300	4514	261	70	.986
	American League Totals			1182	4137	745	1184	204	21	243	744	.286	1832	72	36	.981
	Major League Totals			2787	10006	1829	2943	528	72	586	1812	.294	6346	333	106	.984

aTraded to Baltimore Orioles for outfielder Dick Simpson and pitchers Milt Pappas and Jack Baldschun, December 9, 1965.
bTraded with pitcher Pete Richert to Los Angeles Dodgers for pitchers Doyle Alexander and Bob O'Brien, catcher Sergio Robles and first baseman-outfielder Royle Stillman, December 2, 1971.
cTraded with infielders Billy Grabarkewitz and Bob Valentine and pitchers Bill Singer and Mike Strahler to California Angels for third baseman Ken McMullen and pitcher Andy Messersmith, November 28, 1972.
dReleased on waivers to Cleveland Indians, September 12, 1974; Indians sent outfielder Rusty Torres and catcher Ken Suarez to Angels, December 4, 1974, as part of deal.
ePlayer-manager.

WORLD SERIES RECORD

Year	Club	League	Pos.	G.	AB.	R.	H.	2B.	3B.	HR.	RBI.	B.A.	PO.	A.	E.	F.A.
1961	Cincinnati	Nat.	OF	5	15	3	3	2	0	1	4	.200	5	0	0	1.000
1966	Baltimore	Amer.	OF	4	14	4	4	0	1	2	3	.286	6	0	0	1.000

Year	Club	League	Pos.	G.	AB.	R.	H.	2B.	3B.	HR.	RBI.	B.A.	PO.	A.	E.	F.A.
1969–Baltimore		Amer.	OF	5	16	2	3	0	0	1	1	.188	13	0	0	1.000
1970–Baltimore		Amer.	OF	5	22	5	6	0	0	2	4	.273	7	0	0	1.000
1971–Baltimore		Amer.	OF	7	25	5	7	0	0	2	2	.280	12	0	0	1.000
World Series Totals				26	92	19	23	2	1	8	14	.250	43	0	0	1.000

JACK ROOSEVELT ROBINSON

Born January 31, 1919, at Cairo, Ga.
Died October 24, 1972, at Stamford, Conn.
Height, 5.11½. Weight, 225.
Threw and batted righthanded.
Married Rachel Isum, February 10, 1946.

First Negro in modern major leagues, 1947.
Led National League in stolen bases (39) 1947 and (37) 1949; hit for cycle (first game) August 29, 1948; led second baseman in double plays 1949 through 1952.
World Series Records—Tied record for assists by second baseman in one inning (3); seventh inning, October 8, 1949; tied for mark by getting four bases on balls in a game, October 5, 1952; one of 12 players to steal home in a World Series game, accomplishing feat in first game, eighth inning, September 28, 1955.
Named by THE SPORTING NEWS as Rookie of the Year, 1947.
Named as second baseman on THE SPORTING NEWS All-Star Major League Teams, 1949-50-51-52.
Named Most Valuable Player, National League, 1949.
Named to Hall of Fame, 1962.

Year	Club	League	Pos.	G.	AB.	R.	H.	2B.	3B.	HR.	RBI.	B.A.	PO.	A.	E.	F.A.
1946–Montreal		Int.	2B	124	444	•113	155	25	8	3	66	*.349	261	385	10	*.985
1947–Brooklyn		Nat.	1B	151	590	125	175	31	5	12	48	.297	1323	92	16	.989
1948–Brooklyn		Nat.	*2B-1B-3B	147	574	108	170	38	8	12	85	.296	514	342	15	*.983
1949–Brooklyn		Nat.	2B	156	593	122	203	38	12	16	124	*.342	395	421	16	.981
1950–Brooklyn		Nat.	2B	144	518	99	170	39	4	14	81	.328	359	390	11	*.986
1951–Brooklyn		Nat.	2B	153	548	106	185	33	7	19	88	.338	*390	*435	7	*.992
1952–Brooklyn		Nat.	2B	149	510	104	157	17	3	19	75	.308	353	400	20	.974
1953–Brooklyn		Nat.	INF-OF	136	484	109	159	34	7	12	95	.329	238	126	6	.984
1954–Brooklyn		Nat.	INF-OF	124	386	62	120	22	4	15	59	.311	166	109	7	.975
1955–Brooklyn		Nat.	INF-OF	105	317	51	81	6	2	8	36	.256	100	183	10	.966
1956–Brooklyn(a)		Nat.	INF-OF	117	357	61	98	15	2	10	43	.275	169	230	9	.978
Major League Totals				1382	4877	947	1518	273	54	137	734	.311	4007	2728	117	.983

aTraded to New York Giants for pitcher Dick Littlefield and reported $35,000, December 13, 1956; Robinson announced retirement from game, January 5, 1957, canceling trade.

WORLD SERIES RECORD

Year	Club	League	Pos.	G.	AB.	R.	H.	2B.	3B.	HR.	RBI.	B.A.	PO.	A.	E.	F.A.
1947–Brooklyn		Nat.	1B	7	27	3	7	2	0	0	3	.259	49	6	0	1.000
1949–Brooklyn		Nat.	2B	5	16	2	3	1	0	0	2	.188	12	9	1	.955
1952–Brooklyn		Nat.	2B	7	23	4	4	0	0	1	2	.174	10	20	0	1.000
1953–Brooklyn		Nat.	OF	6	25	3	8	2	0	0	2	.320	8	0	0	1.000
1955–Brooklyn		Nat.	3B	6	22	5	4	1	1	0	1	.182	4	18	2	.917
1956–Brooklyn		Nat.	3B	7	24	5	6	1	0	1	2	.250	5	12	0	1.000
World Series Totals				38	137	22	32	7	1	2	12	.234	88	65	3	.981

WILBERT (ROBBY) ROBINSON

Born June 2, 1864, at Hudson, Mass.
Died August 8, 1934, at Atlanta, Ga.
Height, 5.08½. Weight, 215.
Threw and batted righthanded.

Set major league record, most hits in nine-inning game (7 in 7 at-bats), June 10, 1892 (later tied by Rennie Stennett, Pittsburgh).
Manager, Baltimore Americans, part of 1902; manager, Baltimore, Eastern League, 1903 and part of 1904; coach, New York Giants, 1911-12-13; manager, Brooklyn Dodgers, 1914 through 1925; president-manager, Brooklyn, 1926 through 1929; manager, Brooklyn, 1930 and 1931; president-manager, Atlanta, Southern Association, 1933; president, 1934.

Named to Hall of Fame, 1945.

Year	Club	League	Pos.	G.	AB.	R.	H.	2B.	3B.	HR.	SB.	B.A.	PO.	A.	E.	F.A.
1885–Haverhill		N.E.		73	305	56	82	...	...	...	...	.269	...	...	...	...
1886–Athletics		A.A.	C-1B	87	342	55	70	12	3	1	42	.205	243	106	23	.938
1887–Athletics		A.A.	C	68	273	30	78	7	3	0	19	.286	358	82	39	.919
1888–Athletics		A.A.	C	67	250	30	67	7	2	1	15	.268	409	112	20	.963
1889–Athletics		A.A.	C	69	260	31	63	13	2	0	9	.242	290	107	26	.939
1890–Ath.-Baltimore		A.A.	C-1B	97	361	34	87	14	4	4	25	.241	457	115	40	.936
1891–Baltimore		A.A.	C	62	216	20	45	7	5	2	10	.208	278	56	16	.954
1892–Baltimore		Nat.	C	83	329	36	89	13	5	2	12	.271	326	87	33	.926
1893–Baltimore		Nat.	C	91	349	49	118	22	3	3	16	.338	*348	73	27	.940
1894–Baltimore		Nat.	C	106	420	71	146	21	4	1	13	.348	364	96	24	.950
1895–Baltimore		Nat.	C	74	287	40	76	18	2	0	12	.265	242	77	7	.979
1896–Baltimore		Nat.	C	66	243	43	86	8	7	2	11	.354	260	46	14	.956
1897–Baltimore		Nat.	C	47	182	25	57	8	0	0	0	.313	185	36	8	.965
1898–Baltimore		Nat.	C	77	286	29	79	13	1	0	2	.276	291	70	12	.949
1899–Baltimore		Nat.	C	105	355	40	101	16	2	0	3	.285	287	82	20	.948
1900–St. Louis		Nat.	C	56	212	26	54	4	1	0	9	.255	199	74	6	.978
1901–Baltimore		Amer.	C	71	241	34	72	13	3	0	9	.299	239	60	15	.952
1902–Baltimore		Amer.	C	90	336	39	98	14	7	1	12	.292	264	78	16	.972
1903–Baltimore		East.	C	75	241	15	64	5	2	3	2	.266	326	54	7	.982
1904–Baltimore		East.	C	32	93	8	22	3	0	0	3	.237	155	36	3	.985
American Association Totals				450	1702	200	410	60	19	8	120	.241	2050	578	164	.941
American League Totals				161	577	73	170	27	10	1	21	.295	503	138	31	.954
National League Totals				705	2663	359	806	123	25	8	78	.303	2502	641	151	.954
Major League Totals				1316	4942	632	1386	210	54	17	219	.280	5055	1357	346	.949

CHARLES HENRY (CHINSKI) ROOT

Born March 17, 1899, at Middletown, O.
Died November 5, 1970, at Hollister, Calif.
Height, 5.10½. Weight, 189.
Threw and batted righthanded.
Married Dorothy Hartman, May 9, 1918.

Named as pitcher on THE SPORTING NEWS All-Star Major League Team, 1927.
Manager, Hollywood, Pacific Coast, 1943-44; Columbus, American Association, 1945-46; Billings, Pioneer, 1948; coach, Hollywood, Pacific Coast, 1949; manager, Des Moines, Western, 1950; coach, Chicago Cubs, 1951-52-53.

Year	Club	League	G.	IP.	W.	L.	Pct.	H.	R.	ER.	SO.	BB.	ERA.
1921–Terre Haute		I. I. I.	26	159	8	7	.533	163	80	75	40	3.57	
1922–Terre Haute		I. I. I.	43	249	16	14	.533	208	92	63	155	68	2.28
1923–St. Louis		American	27	60	0	4	.000	68	45	38	27	18	5.70
1924–Los Angeles		Pac. Coast	55	322	21	16	.568	316	161	132	199	102	3.69
1925–Los Angeles		Pac. Coast	52	324	25	13	.658	268	121	103	211	91	2.86
1926–Chicago		National	42	271	18	•17	.514	267	104	85	127	62	2.82
1927–Chicago		National	•48	*309	*26	15	.624	296	148	129	145	*117	3.76
1928–Chicago		National	40	237	14	18	.438	214	109	94	122	73	3.57
1929–Chicago		National	43	272	19	6	*.760	286	120	105	124	83	3.47
1930–Chicago		National	37	220	16	14	.533	247	122	106	124	63	4.34
1931–Chicago		National	39	251	17	14	.548	240	109	97	131	71	3.48
1932–Chicago		National	39	216	15	10	.600	211	99	86	96	55	3.58
1933–Chicago		National	35	242	15	10	.600	232	85	70	86	61	2.60
1934–Chicago		National	34	118	4	7	.364	141	62	56	46	53	4.27
1935–Chicago		National	38	201	15	8	.652	193	85	69	94	47	3.09
1936–Chicago		National	33	74	3	6	.333	81	34	34	32	20	4.14
1937–Chicago		National	43	179	13	5	.722	173	71	67	74	32	3.37
1938–Chicago		National	44	161	8	7	.533	163	62	51	70	30	2.85
1939–Chicago		National	35	167	8	8	.500	189	83	75	65	34	4.04
1940–Chicago		National	36	112	2	4	.333	118	61	48	50	33	3.86
1941–Chicago(a)		National	19	107	8	7	.533	133	68	64	46	37	5.38
1942–Hollywood		Pac. Coast	30	215	11	14	.440	205	95	76	103	39	3.18
1943–Hollywood		Pac. Coast	25	166	15	5	.750	170	63	57	70	28	3.09
1944–Hollywood		Pac. Coast	21	87	3	5	.375	91	55	31	58	25	3.20
1945–Columbus		Amer. Assn.	22	121	9	8	.529	112	40	34	64	20	2.53
1946–Columbus		Amer. Assn.	5	23	3	0	1.000	27	5	4	10	5	1.57
1948–Billings		Pioneer	5	3	0	1	.000	4	4	4	3	4	12.00
National League Totals			605	3137	201	156	.563	3184	1422	1236	1432	871	3.55	
American League Totals			27	60	0	4	.000	68	45	38	27	18	5.70	
Major League Totals			632	3197	201	160	.557	3252	1467	1274	1459	889	3.59	

aUnconditionally released by Chicago Cubs, October 8, 1941.

WORLD SERIES RECORD

Year	Club	League	G.	IP.	W.	L.	Pct.	H.	R.	ER.	SO.	BB.	ERA.
1929	Chicago	National	2	13⅓	0	1	.000	12	7	7	8	2	4.73
1932	Chicago	National	1	4⅓	0	1	.000	6	6	5	4	3	10.38
1935	Chicago	National	2	2	0	1	.000	5	4	4	2	1	18.00
1938	Chicago	National	1	3	0	0	.000	3	1	1	1	0	3.00
World Series Totals			6	22⅔	0	3	.000	26	18	17	15	6	6.75

EDD J. ROUSH

Born May 8, 1893, at Oakland City, Ind.
Height, 5.11 Weight, 175.
Threw and batted lefthanded.
Married Essie Mae Swallow, April 27, 1914.

Had five singles, one double and two home runs in 12 times at-bat in doubleheader, June 19, 1927.
Coach, Cincinnati Reds, 1938.
Named to Hall of Fame, 1962.

Year	Club	League	Pos.	G.	AB.	R.	H.	2B.	3B.	HR.	RBI.	B.A.	PO.	A.	E.	F.A.
1912	Evansville	Kitty	OF	41	148	17	43	7	4	2		.284	37	2	2	.951
1913	Evansville	Central	OF	89	344	42	109	26	6	5		.317	157	9	6	.965
1913	Chicago	Amer.	OF-PH-PR	9	10	2	1	0	0	0	0	.100	3	0	0	1.000
1913	Lincoln	West.	OF	10	35		6	1	0	0		.171	14	0	0	1.000
1914	Indianapolis	Federal	OF	74	165	26	55	6	5	1		.333	85	5	1	.989
1915	Newark	Federal	OF	145	550	73	164	22	10	3		.298	332	15	8	.977
1916	N.Y.(a)-Cin.	Nat.	OF	108	341	38	91	7	15	0	19	.267	210	9	7	.969
1917	Cincinnati	Nat.	OF	136	522	82	178	19	14	4	62 *.341		335	15	14	.962
1918	Cincinnati	Nat.	OF	113	435	61	145	18	10	5	61	.333	320	13	14	.960
1919	Cincinnati	Nat.	OF	133	504	73	162	19	13	3	69 *.321		385	22	4	.989
1920	Cincinnati	Nat.	*OF-2B-1B	149	579	81	196	22	16	4	90	.339	*410	18	11	*.975
1921	Cincinnati	Nat.	OF	112	418	68	147	27	12	4	71	.352	286	9	6	.980
1922	Cincinnati	Nat.	OF	49	165	29	58	7	4	1	24	.352	96	8	1	.990
1923	Cincinnati	Nat.	OF	138	527	88	185	*41	18	6	88	.351	337	14	11	.970
1924	Cincinnati	Nat.	OF	121	483	67	168	23	*21	3	72	.348	270	10	12	.959
1925	Cincinnati	Nat.	OF	134	540	91	183	28	16	8	83	.339	343	15	8	.978
1926	Cincinnati(b)	Nat.	OF-1B	144	563	95	182	37	10	7	70	.323	304	12	15	.955
1927	New York	Nat.	OF	140	570	83	173	27	4	7	58	.304	327	19	9	.975
1928	New York	Nat.	OF	46	163	20	41	5	3	2	13	.252	100	7	5	.955
1929	New York	Nat.	OF	115	450	76	146	19	7	8	52	.324	248	18	5	.982
1930	New York(c)	Nat.														
1931	Cincinnati	Nat.	OF	101	376	46	102	12	5	1	41	.271	197	5	4	.981
American League Totals				9	10	2	1	0	0	0	0	.100	3	0	0	1.000
National League Totals				1739	6636	998	2157	311	168	63	882	.325	4118	194	126	.972
Major League Totals				1748	6646	1000	2158	311	168	63	882	.325	4121	194	126	.972

aTraded with pitcher Christy Mathewson and third baseman William McKechnie to Cincinnati for infielder Charles (Buck) Herzog and outfielder Wade Killefer, July 20, 1916.
bTraded to New York Giants for first baseman George Kelly, January, 1927.
cReleased to Cincinnati, March, 1931.

WORLD SERIES RECORD

Year	Club	League	Pos.	G.	AB.	R.	H.	2B.	3B.	HR.	RBI.	B.A.	PO.	A.	E.	F.A.
1919	Cincinnati	Nat.	OF	8	28	6	6	2	1	0	7	.214	30	3	2	.943

CHARLES HERBERT (RED) RUFFING

Born May 3, 1905, at Granville, Ill.
Height, 6.01½. Weight, 210.
Threw and batted righthanded.
Married Pauline Mulholland, October 6, 1934.

Named by Baseball Writers' Association of America for THE SPORTING NEWS All-Star Major League Teams, 1937-38-39.

Named to Hall of Fame, 1967.

Year	Club	League	G.	IP.	W.	L.	Pct.	H.	R.	ER.	SO.	BB.	ERA.
1923	Danville	I.I.I.	39	239	12	16	.429	251	142	....	88	89	....
1924	Boston	Amer.	8	23	0	0	.000	29	17	17	10	9	6.65
1924	Dover	East. Shore	15	94	4	7	.364	98	42	....	72	23	....
1925	Boston	Amer.	37	217	9	18	.333	253	135	121	64	75	5.02
1926	Boston	Amer.	37	166	6	15	.286	169	98	81	58	68	4.39
1927	Boston	Amer.	26	158	5	13	.278	160	94	82	77	87	4.67
1928	Boston	Amer.	42	289	10	*25	.286	303	*147	*125	118	96	3.89
1929	Boston	Amer.	35	244	9	*22	.290	280	*162	*132	109	118	4.87
1930	Boston(a)-New York	Amer.	38	222	15	8	.652	242	125	108	131	68	4.38
1931	New York	Amer.	37	237	16	14	.533	240	130	116	132	87	4.41
1932	New York	Amer.	35	259	18	7	.720	219	102	89	*190	115	3.09
1933	New York	Amer.	35	235	9	14	.391	230	118	102	122	93	3.91
1934	New York	Amer.	36	256	19	11	.633	232	134	112	149	104	3.94
1935	New York	Amer.	30	222	16	11	.593	201	88	77	81	76	3.12
1936	New York	Amer.	33	271	20	12	.625	274	133	116	102	90	3.85
1937	New York	Amer.	31	256	20	7	.741	242	101	85	131	68	2.99
1938	New York	Amer.	31	247	*21	7	*.750	246	104	91	127	82	3.32
1939	New York	Amer.	28	233	21	7	.750	211	88	76	95	75	2.94
1940	New York	Amer.	30	226	15	12	.556	218	98	85	97	76	3.38
1941	New York	Amer.	23	186	15	6	.714	177	87	73	60	54	3.53
1942	New York(b)	Amer.	24	194	14	7	.667	183	72	69	80	41	3.20
1943-44	New York	Amer.	(In Military Service)										
1945	New York	Amer.	11	87	7	3	.700	85	32	28	24	20	2.90
1946	New York(c)	Amer.	8	61	5	1	.833	37	13	12	19	23	1.77
1947	Chicago	Amer.	9	53	3	5	.375	63	39	36	11	16	6.11
	Major League Totals		624	4342	273	225	.548	4294	2117	1833	1987	1541	3.80

aTraded to New York Yankees for outfielder Cedric Durst and $50,000, May 6, 1930.
bInducted into U. S. Army Air Forces, December 29, 1942; returned to lineup July 16, 1945.
cReleased by New York Yankees, September 20, 1946; signed with Chicago White Sox, December 6, 1946.

WORLD SERIES RECORD

Year	Club	League	G.	IP.	W.	L.	Pct.	H.	R.	ER.	SO.	BB.	ERA.
1932	New York	Amer.	1	9	1	0	1.000	10	6	4	10	6	4.00
1936	New York	Amer.	2	14	0	1	.000	16	10	7	12	5	4.50
1937	New York	Amer.	1	9	1	0	1.000	7	1	1	8	3	1.00
1938	New York	Amer.	2	18	2	0	1.000	17	4	3	11	2	1.50
1939	New York	Amer.	1	9	1	0	1.000	4	1	1	4	1	1.00
1941	New York	Amer.	1	9	1	0	1.000	6	2	1	5	3	1.00
1942	New York	Amer.	2	17⅔	1	1	.500	14	8	8	11	7	4.08
	World Series Totals		10	85⅔	7	2	.778	74	32	25	61	27	2.63

AMOS WILSON RUSIE

Born May 31, 1871, at Mooresville, Ind.
Died December 6, 1942, at Seattle, Wash.
Height, 6.01. Weight, 210.
Threw and batted righthanded.

Pitched no-hit, 6-0 victory over Brooklyn on July 31, 1891. Won 20 or more games per season in each of eight years with Giants.
Named to Hall of Fame, 1977.

Year	Club	League	G.	W.	L.	Pct.	H.	R.	SO.	BB.	ShO.
1889	Indianapolis	National	23	13	10	.565	237	176	113	128	1
1890	New York	National	60	29	30	.492	414	296	*345	*276	4
1891	New York	National	54	32	19	.627	373	233	*321	*236	*6
1892	New York	National	62	31	28	.525	387	266	*303	*261	2
1893	New York	National	*48	29	18	.617	401	220	*208	*196	•4
1894	New York	National	49	*36	13	.735	395	208	*204	*189	•3
1895	New York	National	43	22	21	.512	369	219	*199	159	•4
1896	New York	National				(Holdout all season)					
1897	New York	National	37	29	8	*.784	304	141	140	86	•3
1898	New York	National	33	20	10	.667	272	134	114	103	4
1899-1900	New York(a)	National				(Under suspension)					
1901	Cincinnati	National	3	0	1	.000	25	15	6	3	0
	Major League Totals		412	241	158	.604	3177	1908	1953	1637	31

aTraded to Cincinnati for Christy Mathewson.

TEMPLE CUP RECORD

Year	Club	League	G.	IP.	W.	L.	Pct.	H.	R.	SO.	BB.
1894	New York	National	2	18	2	0	1.000	14	2	9	4

GEORGE HERMAN (BABE) RUTH

Born, February 6, 1895, at Baltimore, Md.
Died August 16, 1948, at New York, N. Y.
Height, 6:02. Weight, 215.
Threw and batted lefthanded.
Married Claire Merritt Hodgson, April 17, 1929.

    Holds major league record for highest slugging percentage, season (.847), 1920; Ruth followed this record year with an .846 slugging percentage for the 1921 season; led American League in slugging percentage 13 years—a major league record, 1918 to 1931, except 1925; holds major league record for most years leading league in runs scored (8); holds modern major league record for runs scored, season (177), 1921.
    Established the following major league home run records; most home runs in major leagues (714) (since passed by Hank Aaron); most home runs, American League (708); most home runs two consecutive seasons (114), 1927-28; most years leading league in home runs (12); most years 50 or more home runs (4); most times, three or more home runs in a doubleheader (connecting in both games), league (7); most times, two or more home runs in a game (72); most home runs with bases filled, two consecutive games (2) (tied for mark), September 27-29, 1927, also August 6 (second game), August 7 (first game), 1929; most home runs two consecutive days (6) (tied for mark), May 21-21-22-22, 1930; most home runs, one week (9) (tied for mark), May 18 to 24, second game, 1930.
    Hit 60 home runs (1927) in 154-game schedule; in World Series, twice hit three home runs in one game, October 6, 1926, and October 9, 1928.
    Hit seven home runs in five consecutive games, with at least one homer in each game, June 10-11-12-13-14, 1921.
    Hit three home runs in a game, May 21, 1930 (first game) and May 25, 1935.
    Named Most Valuable Player, American League, 1923.
    Named as Outfielder on THE SPORTING NEWS All-Star Major League Teams, 1926-27-28-29-30-31.
    Coach, Brooklyn Dodgers, 1938.
    Named to Hall of Fame, 1936.

Year	Club	League	Pos.	G.	AB.	R.	H.	2B.	3B.	HR.	RBI.	B.A.	PO.	A.	E.	F.A.
1914	Balt.-Prov	Int.	P-OF	46	121	22	28	2	10	1	....	.231	20	87	4	.964
1914	Boston	Amer.	P	5	10	1	2	1	0	0	0	.200	0	8	0	1.000
1915	Boston	Amer.	P-OF	42	92	16	29	10	1	4	20	.315	17	63	2	.976
1916	Boston	Amer.	P-OF	67	136	18	37	5	3	3	16	.272	24	83	3	.973
1917	Boston	Amer.	P-OF	52	123	14	40	6	3	2	10	.325	19	101	2	.984
1918	Boston	Amer.	OF-P-1	95	317	50	95	26	11	•11	64	.300	270	72	18	.950
1919	Boston(a)	Amer.	*OF-P	130	432	*103	139	34	12	*29	•112	.322	270	53	4	*.988
1920	New York	Amer.	OF-1-P	142	458	*158	172	36	9	*54	*137	.376	259	21	19	.936
1921	New York	Amer.	OF-1-P	152	540	*177	204	44	16	*59	*171	.378	348	17	13	.966
1922	New York	Amer.	OF	110	406	94	128	24	8	35	99	.315	226	14	9	.964
1923	New York	Amer.	OF-1B	152	520	*151	205	45	13	*41	*131	.393	378	20	11	.973
1924	New York	Amer.	OF	153	529	*143	200	39	7	*46	121	*.378	340	18	14	.962
1925	New York	Amer.	OF	98	359	61	104	12	2	25	66	.290	207	15	6	.974
1926	New York	Amer.	OF	152	495	*139	184	30	5	*47	*145	.372	308	11	7	.979
1927	New York	Amer.	OF	151	540	*158	192	29	8	*60	164	.356	328	14	13	.963
1928	New York	Amer.	OF	154	536	*163	173	29	8	*54	•142	.323	304	9	8	.975
1929	New York	Amer.	OF	135	499	121	172	26	6	*46	154	.345	240	5	4	.984
1930	New York	Amer.	OF-P	145	518	150	186	28	9	*49	153	.359	266	10	10	.965
1931	New York	Amer.	OF-1B	145	534	149	199	31	3	•46	163	.373	237	5	7	.972
1932	New York	Amer.	OF-1B	133	457	120	156	13	5	41	137	.341	212	10	9	.961
1933	New York	Amer.	OF-P	137	459	97	138	21	3	34	103	.301	215	9	7	.970
1934	New York(b)	Amer.	OF	125	365	78	105	17	4	22	84	.288	197	3	8	.962
1935	Boston	Nat.	OF	28	72	13	13	0	0	6	12	.181	39	1	2	.952
American League Totals				2475	8325	2161	2860	506	136	708	2192	.344	4665	561	174	.968
National League Totals				28	72	13	13	0	0	6	12	.181	39	1	2	.952
Major League Totals				2503	8397	2174	2873	506	136	714	2204	.342	4704	562	176	.968

aSold to New York Yankees for $125,000, January 3, 1920.
bReleased to Boston Braves, February 26, 1935.

WORLD SERIES RECORD

Year	Club	League	Pos.	G.	AB.	R.	H.	2B.	3B.	HR.	RBI.	B.A.	PO.	A.	E.	F.A.
1915	Boston	Amer.	PH	1	1	0	0	0	0	0	0	.000	0	0	0	.000
1916	Boston	Amer.	P	1	5	0	0	0	0	0	1	.000	2	4	0	1.000
1918	Boston	Amer.	P-OF	3	5	0	1	0	1	0	2	.200	1	5	0	1.000
1921	New York	Amer.	OF	6	16	3	5	0	0	1	4	.313	9	0	0	1.000
1922	New York	Amer.	OF	5	17	1	2	1	0	0	1	.118	9	0	0	1.000
1923	New York	Amer.	O-1B	6	19	8	7	1	1	3	3	.368	17	0	1	.944
1926	New York	Amer.	OF	7	20	6	6	0	0	4	5	.300	8	2	0	1.000
1927	New York	Amer.	OF	4	15	4	6	0	0	2	7	.400	10	0	0	1.000
1928	New York	Amer.	OF	4	16	9	10	3	0	3	4	.625	9	1	0	1.000
1932	New York	Amer.	OF	4	15	6	5	0	0	2	6	.333	8	0	1	.889
World Series Totals				41	129	37	42	5	2	15	33	.326	73	12	2	.977

PITCHING RECORD

Year	Club	League	G.	IP.	W.	L.	Pct.	H.	R.	ER.	SO.	BB.	ERA.
1914	Balti.-Providence	Int.	35	245	22	9	.710	219	88	....	139	101	......
1914	Boston	Amer.	4	23	2	1	.667	21	12	10	3	7	3.91
1915	Boston	Amer.	32	218	18	8	.692	166	80	59	112	85	2.44
1916	Boston	Amer.	44	324	23	12	.657	230	83	63	170	118	*1.75
1917	Boston	Amer.	41	326	24	13	.649	244	93	73	128	108	2.02
1918	Boston	Amer.	20	166	13	7	.650	125	51	41	40	49	2.22
1919	Boston	Amer.	17	133	9	5	.643	148	59	44	30	58	2.97
1920	New York	Amer.	1	4	1	0	1.000	3	4	2	0	2	4.50
1921	New York	Amer.	2	9	2	0	1.000	14	10	9	2	9	9.00
1930	New York	Amer.	1	9	1	0	1.000	11	3	3	3	2	3.00
1933	New York	Amer.	1	9	1	0	1.000	12	5	5	0	3	5.00
Major League Totals			163	1221	94	46	.671	974	400	309	488	441	2.28

WORLD SERIES PITCHING RECORD

Year	Club	League	G.	IP.	W.	L.	Pct.	H.	R.	ER.	SO.	BB.	ERA.
1916	Boston	Amer.	1	14	1	0	1.000	6	1	1	4	3	0.64
1918	Boston	Amer.	2	17	2	0	1.000	13	2	2	4	7	1.06
World Series Totals			3	31	3	0	1.000	19	3	3	8	10	0.87

JAMES E. (JIMMY) RYAN

Born February 11, 1863, at Clinton, Mass.
Died October 28, 1923, at Chicago, Ill.
Height, 5.10. Weight, 175.
Threw and batted righthanded.

Scored six runs in one game, July 25, 1894, vs. Pittsburgh.
Manager, St. Paul, Western League, 1901; Chicago Springs, Western, 1904.

Year	Club	League	Pos.	G.	AB.	R.	H.	2B.	3B.	HR.	SB.	B.A.	PO.	A.	E.	F.A.
1885	Bridgeport	East.	OF-SS	29	120	18	26	4	2	0	...	.217		6		.878
1885	Chicago	Nat.	OF-SS	3	13	2	6	1	0	0	...	.462	6	11	8	.680
1886	Chicago	Nat.	OF-SS	84	327	58	100	21	6	3	10	.306	93	18	23	.828
1887	Chicago	Nat.	OF-P	126	556	117	198	19	11	11	50	.356	164	33	33	.857
1888	Chicago	Nat.	OF-P	130	549	115	*182	*37	7	13	60	.332	217	*34	35	.878
1889	Chicago	Nat.	OF-SS	135	576	140	187	30	12	17	45	.325	286	133	57	.880
1890	Chicago	Players	OF	118	497	101	164	31	7	7	30	.330	156	28	29	.864
1891	Chicago	Nat.	OF	118	501	109	145	19	12	8	24	.289	234	*32	23	.920
1892	Chicago	Nat.	OF	127	508	102	147	21	12	10	31	.289	235	37	25	.916
1893	Chicago	Nat.	OF	82	332	82	101	19	7	3	8	.304	159	20	18	.909
1894	Chicago	Nat.	OF	108	481	133	173	35	6	3	12	.360	222	23	26	.904
1895	Chicago	Nat.	OF	108	443	83	143	20	9	6	15	.323	159	16	17	.911
1896	Chicago	Nat.	OF	127	490	83	153	21	10	2	35	.312	207	26	20	.921
1897	Chicago	Nat.	OF	135	518	104	160	30	17	5	35	.309	211	28	14	.945
1898	Chicago	Nat.	OF	143	569	121	185	31	13	4	29	.325	269	21	•25	.921
1899	Chicago	Nat.	OF	124	524	91	158	20	10	3	9	.302	264	17	13	.956
1900	Chicago	Nat.	OF	106	416	66	115	26	4	5	17	.276	175	15	17	.918
1901	St. Paul	West.	OF	108	443	77	143	13	6	5	21	.323	....	....	....	......
1902	Washington	Amer.	OF	120	482	92	153	32	6	6	13	.317	282	14	16	.949
1903	Washington	Amer.	OF	114	436	41	107	26	4	7	11	.245	284	7	6	.980
American League Totals				234	918	133	260	58	10	13	24	.283	566	21	22	.964
National League Totals				1656	6803	1406	2153	350	136	93	380	.316	2901	464	354	.905
Players League Totals				118	497	101	164	31	7	7	30	.330	156	28	29	.864
Major League Totals				2008	8218	1640	2577	439	153	113	434	.314	3623	513	405	.911

Pitching record: Pitched briefly in 1887 and 1888, won 5, lost 1.

WORLD SERIES RECORD

Year	Club	League	Pos.	G.	AB.	R.	H.	2B.	3B.	HR.	SB.	B.A.	PO.	A.	E.	F.A.
1886	Chicago	Nat.	OF-P	6	20	4	5	1	0	0	1	.250	8	7	1	.938

DID YOU KNOW—

That Babe Ruth hit the first All-Star Game home run, coming in 1933 game against Bill Hallahan?

RONALD EDWARD SANTO

Born February 25, 1940, at Seattle, Wash.
Height, 6;00. Weight, 194.
Threw and batted righthanded.

Established major league records for most years leading league, assists, third baseman (7), 1968 and most consecutive years leading league, assists, third baseman (7), 1968 (both since broken by Brooks Robinson, 8); most years leading league in chances accepted (excluding errors) (9), 1969.
Tied following major league record: Most years leading league, double plays, third baseman (6), 1971.
Established following National League records: Most assists, season, third baseman (393), 1967 (since broken by Mike Schmidt (404 in 1974); most games played, third base, 162-game season (164), 1965; most double plays by third baseman, career, 389, 1973; most chances accepted, lifetime, third baseman, 6462, 1973; most assists, lifetime, third baseman, 4532, 1968; most years leading league in games (7), 1969.
Named third baseman on THE SPORTING NEWS National League All-Star Team, 1966-67-68-69-72.
Named third baseman on THE SPORTING NEWS National League All-Star Fielding Team, 1964-65-66-67-68.

Year	Club	League	Pos.	G.	AB.	R.	H.	2B.	3B.	HR.	RBI.	B.A.	PO.	A.	E.	F.A.
1959	San Antonio	Tex.	3B	136	505	82	165	★35	3	11	87	.327	★158	246	★53	.884
1960	Houston	A. A.	3B	71	272	40	73	16	1	7	32	.268	72	148	16	.932
1960	Chicago	Nat.	3B	95	347	44	87	24	2	9	44	.251	78	144	13	.945
1961	Chicago	Nat.	3B	154	578	84	164	32	6	23	83	.284	157	307	★31	.937
1962	Chicago	Nat.	★3B-SS	162	604	44	137	20	4	17	83	.227	★167	★343	★24	.955
1963	Chicago	Nat.	3B	●162	630	79	187	29	6	25	99	.297	★136	★374	26	.951
1964	Chicago	Nat.	3B	161	592	94	185	33	●13	30	114	.313	★156	★367	20	.963
1965	Chicago	Nat.	3B	●164	608	88	173	30	4	33	101	.285	★155	★373	24	.957
1966	Chicago	Nat.	★3B-SS	155	561	93	175	21	8	30	94	.312	★157	★408	★26	.956
1967	Chicago	Nat.	3B	161	586	107	176	23	4	31	98	.300	★187	★393	26	.957
1968	Chicago	Nat.	3B	162	577	86	142	17	3	26	98	.246	130	★378	15	★.971
1969	Chicago	Nat.	3B	160	575	97	166	18	4	29	123	.289	★144	334	27	.947
1970	Chicago	Nat.	3B-OF	154	555	83	148	30	4	26	114	.267	144	320	27	.945
1971	Chicago	Nat.	3B-OF	154	555	77	148	22	1	21	88	.267	128	275	18	.957
1972	Chicago	Nat.	3-2-O-S	133	464	68	140	25	5	17	74	.302	119	282	22	.948
1973	Chicago (a)	Nat.	3B	149	536	65	143	29	2	20	77	.267	107	271	20	.950
1974	Chicago	Am.	2-3-1-S	117	375	29	83	12	1	5	41	.221	135	148	8	.973
	National League Totals			2126	7768	1109	2171	353	66	337	1290	.279	1965	4569	319	.953
	American League Totals			117	375	29	83	12	1	5	41	.221	135	148	8	.973
	Major League Totals			2243	8143	1138	2254	365	67	342	1331	.277	2100	4717	327	.954

aTraded to Chicago White Sox for pitchers Ken Frailing and Steve Stone, catcher Steve Swisher (plus pitcher Jim Kremmel), December 11, 1973.

HENRY JOHN (HANK) SAUER

Born March 17, 1919, at Pittsburgh, Pa.
Height, 6.04. Weight, 200.
Threw and batted righthanded.
Married Esther Tavel, December 29, 1940.
Brother Edward with Chicago Cubs (1943-44-45), St. Louis Cardinals
(1949) and Boston Braves (1949).

Hit three home runs in a game, August 28, 1950, and June 11, 1952; tied with Joe Adcock (Milwaukee, 1956), for National League record for most home runs hit against one club, season (13), 1954. Homers were hit off Pittsburgh.
Named by THE SPORTING NEWS as Minor League Player of the Year, 1947.
Selected as Top Player in National League by THE SPORTING NEWS, 1952.
Most Valuable National League Player, 1952.
Named as outfielder on THE SPORTING NEWS All-Star Major League Team, 1952.
Led N.L. outfielders in double plays, 1948.
Coach, San Francisco Giants, 1959; scout, 1960 to date.

Year	Club	League	Pos.	G.	AB.	R.	H.	2B.	3B.	HR.	RBI.	B.A.	PO.	A.	E.	F.A.
1937	Butler	Penn. St.	1B	64	235	40	63	7	3	3	38	.268	592	30	14	.978
1938	Butler	Penn. St.	1B	●100	385	89	★135	★29	8	12	74	★.351	853	31	★26	.971
1939	Akron	Mid. Atl.	1B	127	472	87	142	31	3	13	92	.301	1263	54	16	★.988
1940	Birmingham	South.	1B-OF	118	384	47	112	17	10	9	79	.292	794	56	18	.979
1941	Birmingham	South.	1B	154	585	96	193	20	14	19	114	.330	1218	105	★26	.981

Year-Club	League	Pos.	G.	AB.	R.	H.	2B.	3B.	HR.	RBI.	B.A.	PO.	A.	E.	F.A.
1941–Cincinnati	Nat.	OF	9	33	4	10	4	0	0	5	.303	21	1	1	.957
1942–Cincinnati	Nat.	1B	7	20	4	5	0	0	2	4	.250	37	4	1	.976
1942–Syracuse	Int.	OF	82	291	35	62	9	2	11	44	.213	136	4	6	.959
1943–Syracuse	Int.	1B-OF	*154	571	73	157	32	9	12	75	.275	1157	78	13	.990
1944-45–Cincinnati	Nat.					(In Military Service)									
1945–Cincinnati	Nat.	OF-1B	31	116	18	34	1	0	5	20	.293	100	5	3	.972
1946–Syracuse	Int.	OF	140	517	99	146	29	2	21	90	.282	264	10	6	.979
1947–Syracuse	Int.	OF	146	542	*130	*182	28	1	50	*141	.336	283	12	5	.983
1948–Cincinnati	Nat.	OF-1B	145	530	78	138	22	1	35	97	.260	359	22	9	.977
1949–Cin.(a)-Chicago	Nat.	•OF-1B	138	509	81	140	23	1	31	99	.275	302	•16	9	.972
1950–Chicago	Nat.	OF-1B	145	540	85	148	32	2	32	103	.274	381	29	13	.969
1951–Chicago	Nat.	OF	141	525	77	138	19	4	30	89	.263	286	19	6	.981
1952–Chicago	Nat.	OF	151	567	89	153	31	3	•37	*121	.270	327	17	6	.983
1953–Chicago	Nat.	OF	108	395	61	104	16	5	19	60	.263	221	5	7	.970
1954–Chicago	Nat.	OF	142	520	98	150	18	1	41	103	.288	282	8	11	.963
1955–Chicago (b)	Nat.	OF	79	261	29	55	8	1	12	28	.211	122	4	2	.984
1956–St. Louis (c)	Nat.	OF	75	151	11	45	4	0	5	24	.298	55	2	0	1.000
1957–New York	Nat.	OF	127	378	46	98	14	1	26	76	.259	125	4	1	.992
1958–San Francisco	Nat.	OF	88	236	27	59	8	0	12	46	.250	93	3	5	.950
1959–San Francisco	Nat.	OF	13	15	1	1	0	0	1	1	.067	0	0	0	.000
Major League Totals			1399	4796	709	1278	200	19	288	876	.267	2711	139	74	.975

aTraded to Chicago Cubs with outfielder Frank Baumholtz for outfielders Harry Walker and Harry Lowrey, June 15, 1949.
bTraded to St. Louis Cardinals for outfielder Pete Whisenant and $10,000, March 30, 1956.
cUnconditionally released by St. Louis Cardinals, October 16, 1956, and signed with New York Giants, October 26, 1956.

RAYMOND WILLIAM (CRACKER) SCHALK

Born August 12, 1892, at Harvel, Ill.
Died May 19, 1970, at Chicago, Ill.
Height, 5.07. Weight, 155.
Threw and batted righthanded.
Married Lavina Graham, October 25, 1916.

Holds major league record for most years leading catchers in fielding (8); for most years leading catchers in putouts (9); for most assists by catcher in one league (1810); tied for major league record by making three assists in an inning as catcher, eighth inning, September 30, 1921; caught four no-hit games: James Scott's loss to Washington Senators, May 14, 1914; Joe Benz over Cleveland Indians, May 31, 1914; Ed Cicotte over St. Louis Browns, April 14, 1917 and Charlie Robertson's perfect game over the Detroit Tigers, April 30, 1922.
Led A. L. catchers in double plays, 1923.
Manager, Chicago White Sox, 1927-28; Buffalo, International League, 1932-33-34-35-36-37; Indianapolis, American Association, 1938-39; Milwaukee, American Association, 1940; Buffalo, International League, 1950.
Named to Hall of Fame, 1955.

Year-Club	League	Pos.	G.	AB.	R.	H.	2B.	3B.	HR.	RBI.	B.A.	PO.	A.	E.	F.A.
1911–Taylorville	Ill. Mo.	C	47	161	27	64	....	....	....	....	.398	....	....	....	....
1911–Milwaukee	A. A.	C	31	76	9	18	2	1	0	....	.237	112	36	2	.987
1912–Milwaukee	A. A.	C	80	266	19	72	8	4	3	....	.271	354	108	7	.985
1912–Chicago	Amer.	C	23	63	7	18	2	0	0	6	.286	115	40	14	.917
1913–Chicago	Amer.	C	128	401	38	98	15	5	1	42	.244	*586	153	15	*.980
1914–Chicago	Amer.	C	135	392	30	106	13	2	0	37	.270	*613	183	21	*.974
1915–Chicago	Amer.	C	135	413	46	110	14	1	48		.266	*655	159	13	*.984
1916–Chicago	Amer.	C	129	410	36	95	12	9	0	36	.232	*653	*166	10	*.988
1917–Chicago	Amer.	C	140	424	48	96	12	4	3	53	.226	*624	148	15	*.981
1918–Chicago	Amer.	C	108	333	35	73	6	3	0	24	.219	*422	114	12	.978
1919–Chicago	Amer.	C	131	394	57	111	9	3	0	40	.282	*551	130	13	.981
1920–Chicago	Amer.	C	151	485	64	131	25	5	1	61	.270	*581	138	10	*.986
1921–Chicago	Amer.	C	128	416	32	105	24	4	0	47	.252	453	129	9	*.985
1922–Chicago	Amer.	C	142	442	57	124	22	3	4	60	.281	*591	*150	8	*.989
1923–Chicago	Amer.	C	123	382	42	87	12	2	1	44	.228	481	93	10	.983
1924–Chicago	Amer.	C	57	153	15	30	4	2	1	11	.196	176	55	10	.959
1925–Chicago	Amer.	C	125	343	44	94	18	1	0	52	.274	368	99	8	.983
1926–Chicago	Amer.	C	82	226	26	60	9	1	0	32	.265	251	45	7	.977
1927–Chicago	Amer.	C	16	26	2	6	2	0	0	2	.231	24	8	0	1.000
1928–Chicago	Amer.	C	2	1	0	1	0	0	0	1	1.000	4	0	0	1.000
1929–New York	Nat.	C	5	2	0	0	0	0	0	0	.000	7	0	0	1.000
1932–Buffalo	Int.	C	1	3	1	2	0	0	0	0	.667	6	0	0	1.000
American League Totals			1755	5304	579	1345	199	48	12	596	.254	7148	1810	175	.981
National League Totals			5	2	0	0	0	0	0	0	.000	7	0	0	1.000
Major League Totals			1760	5306	579	1345	199	48	12	596	.253	7155	1810	175	.981

WORLD SERIES RECORD

Year	Club	League	Pos.	G.	AB.	R.	H.	2B.	3B.	HR.	RBI.	B.A.	PO.	A.	E.	F.A.
1917–Chicago		Amer.	C	6	19	1	5	0	0	0	0	.263	32	5	2	.949
1919–Chicago		Amer.	C	8	23	1	7	0	0	0	2	.304	29	15	1	.978
World Series Totals				14	42	2	12	0	0	0	2	.286	61	20	3	.964

ALBERT FRED (RED) SCHOENDIENST

Born February 2, 1923, at Germantown, Ill.
Height, 6.01. Weight, 192.
Threw right and batted right and lefthanded.
Married Mary Eileen O'Reilly, September 20, 1947.

Established major league record by hitting eight doubles in three consecutive games, June 5-6 (doubleheader), 1948; set major league mark by making nine long hits in three consecutive games, June 5-6 (doubleheader), 1948; tied N. L. record by hitting five doubles in doubleheader, June 6, 1948; tied major league mark by making six long hits in a doubleheader, June 6, 1948.
    Tied record for most double plays started by N. L. second baseman, game (4), August 20, 1954; holds N. L. record by leading second basemen in fielding seven years; holds National League record for most games played, 162-game season, as pinch-hitter (80), 1962. Had 22 hits as pinch-hitter, 1962.
    Tied World Series record for most at-bats in nine-inning, game, 6, October 10, 1946.
    Led National League in stolen bases (26), 1945; hit home run in fourteenth inning to win longest All-Star Game, July 11, 1950; second baseman on THE SPORTING NEWS All-Star Major League Teams, 1953-57.
    Player-coach, St. Louis Cardinals, 1962-63-64; until named manager, November 19, 1964, through 1976; coach, Oakland Athletics, 1977-78; coach, St. Louis Cardinals, 1979 to date.

Year	Club	League	Pos.	G.	AB.	R.	H.	2B.	3B.	HR.	RBI.	B.A.	PO.	A.	E.	F.A.
1942–Union City		Kitty	2B	6	27	4	11	3	0	0	4	.407	16	20	2	.947
1942–Albany		Ga.-Fla.	SS-2B	68	264	41	71	7	5	1	28	.269	155	209	27	.931
1943–Lynchburg		Pied.	SS	9	36	8	17	2	0	0	5	.472	18	36	3	.947
1943–Rochester		Int.	SS	136	555	81	*187	21	5	6	37	*.337	*339	*438	48	.942
1944–Rochester (a)		Int.	SS	25	102	26	38	3	2	2	14	.373	50	84	17	.887
1945–St. Louis		Nat.	OF-IF	137	565	89	157	22	6	1	47	.278	302	30	10	.971
1946–St. Louis		Nat.	*2B-3B-SS	142	606	94	170	28	5	0	34	.281	363	379	13	*.983
1947–St. Louis		Nat.	2B-3B-OF	151	*659	91	167	25	9	3	48	.253	364	417	19	.976
1948–St. Louis		Nat.	2B	119	408	64	111	21	4	4	36	.272	230	269	10	.980
1949–St. Louis		Nat.	*2B-INF-OF	151	640	102	190	25	2	3	54	.297	*428	*471	15	*.984
1950–St. Louis		Nat.	INF	153	*642	81	177	*43	9	7	63	.276	425	437	14	.984
1951–St. Louis		Nat.	2B-SS	135	553	88	160	32	7	6	54	.289	354	419	10	.987
1952–St. Louis		Nat.	*2B-3B-SS	152	620	91	188	40	7	7	67	.303	*417	*460	20	.978
1953–St. Louis		Nat.	2B	146	564	107	193	35	5	15	79	.342	*365	*430	14	*.983
1954–St. Louis		Nat.	2B	148	610	98	192	38	8	5	79	.315	394	*477	18	.980
1955–St. Louis		Nat.	2B	145	553	68	148	21	3	11	51	.268	296	381	10	*.985
1956–St. L. (b)-N.Y.		Nat.	2B	132	487	61	147	21	3	2	29	.302	298	308	4	*.993
1957–N.Y.(c)-Milw.		Nat.	●2B-OF	150	648	91	*200	31	8	15	65	.309	379	448	12	●.986
1958–Milwaukee (d)		Nat.	2B	106	427	47	112	23	1	1	24	.262	233	301	7	*.987
1959–Milwaukee (e)		Nat.	2B	5	3	0	0	0	0	0	0	.000	1	1	1	.667
1960–Milwaukee (f)		Nat.	2B	68	226	21	58	9	0	1	19	.257	120	148	10	.964
1961–St. Louis		Nat.	2B	72	120	9	36	9	0	1	12	.300	43	42	4	.955
1962–St. Louis		Nat.	2B-3B	98	143	21	43	4	0	2	12	.301	33	48	1	.988
1963–St. Louis		Nat.	PH	6	5	0	0	0	0	0	0	.000	0	0	0	.000
Major League Totals				2216	8479	1223	2449	427	78	84	773	.289	5045	5466	192	.982

    aIn Military Service most of season.
    bTraded to New York Giants with pitchers Gordon Jones and Dick Littlefield, catcher Bill Sarni and outfielder Jackie Brandt for pitcher Don Liddle, catcher Ray Katt, shortstop Al Dark and outfielder-first baseman Whitey Lockman. All players but Jones exchanged clubs June 14, 1956–Jones being assigned to Giants, October 1, 1956.
    cTraded to Milwaukee Braves for pitcher Ray Crone, second baseman Danny O'Connell and outfielder Bobby Thomson, June 15, 1957.
    dStricken with tuberculosis and entered hospital for treatment after close of 1958 World Series.
    eRejoined club in closing days of season.
    fUnconditionally released by Milwaukee Braves, October 14, 1960; signed with St. Louis Cardinals, March 15, 1961.

WORLD SERIES RECORD

Year	Club	League	Pos.	G.	AB.	R.	H.	2B.	3B.	HR.	RBI.	B.A.	PO.	A.	E.	F.A.
1946–St. Louis		Nat.	2B	7	30	3	7	1	0	0	1	.233	17	21	1	.974
1957–Milwaukee		Nat.	2B	5	18	0	5	1	0	0	2	.278	5	10	0	1.000
1958–Milwaukee		Nat.	2B	7	30	5	9	3	1	0	0	.300	18	19	1	.974
World Series Totals				19	78	8	21	5	1	0	3	.269	40	50	2	.978

JOSEPH WHEELER SEWELL

Born October 9, 1898, at Titus, Ala.
Height, 5.07. Weight, 155.
Threw right and batted lefthanded.
Brother of James Luther Sewell, major league catcher and manager, 1921-1952, and Thomas Wesley Sewell, infielder, Chicago N. L., 1927.

Fewest strikeouts in majors, lifetime (14 or more seasons)–113; fewest strikeouts, season–4 (1925 and 1929); selected by Baseball Writers' Association as shortstop on THE SPORTING NEWS All-Star Major League Team, 1926; in 1932 World Series went to bat six times in game, October 2, and twice in the sixth inning, September 28; played 1,103 consecutive games.
Led A. L. shortstops in double plays, 1928.
Coach, New York Yankees, 1934-35; scout, Cleveland Indians, 1952-62; scout, New York Mets, 1963.
Named to Hall of Fame in 1977.

Year	Club	League	Pos.	G.	AB.	R.	H.	2B.	3B.	HR.	RBI.	B.A.	PO.	A.	E.	F.A.
1920	New Orleans	South.	SS	92	346	58	100	19	8	2	.....	.289	147	261	27	.938
1920	Cleveland	Amer.	SS	22	70	14	23	4	1	0	12	.329	44	70	15	.884
1921	Cleveland	Amer.	SS	154	572	101	182	36	12	4	91	.318	319	480	47	.944
1922	Cleveland	Amer.	SS-2B	153	558	80	167	28	7	2	83	.299	322	497	52	.940
1923	Cleveland	Amer.	SS	153	553	98	195	41	10	3	109	.353	286	497	*59	.930
1924	Cleveland	Amer.	SS	153	594	99	188	•45	5	4	106	.316	*349	*514	36	.960
1925	Cleveland	Amer.	SS-2B	155	608	78	204	37	7	1	98	.336	*314	*529	29	.967
1926	Cleveland	Amer.	SS	154	578	91	187	41	5	4	85	.324	*326	463	37	.955
1927	Cleveland	Amer.	SS	153	569	83	180	48	5	1	92	.316	*361	*480	33	*.962
1928	Cleveland	Amer.	*SS-3B	•155	588	79	190	40	2	4	70	.323	319	*499	33	*.961
1929	Cleveland	Amer.	3B	152	578	90	182	38	3	7	73	.315	163	*336	13	.975
1930	Cleveland(a)	Amer.	3B	109	353	44	102	17	6	0	48	.289	83	184	14	.950
1931	New York	Amer.	3B	130	484	102	146	22	1	6	64	.302	131	227	18	.952
1932	New York	Amer.	3B	125	503	95	137	21	3	11	68	.272	122	221	9	.974
1933	New York	Amer.	3B	135	524	87	143	18	1	2	54	.273	123	224	13	.964
Major League Totals				1903	7132	1141	2226	436	68	49	1053	.312	3262	5221	408	.954

aReleased by Cleveland, January, 1931, and signed with New York Yankees.

WORLD SERIES RECORD

Year	Club	League	Pos.	G.	AB.	R.	H.	2B.	3B.	HR.	RBI.	B.A.	PO.	A.	E.	F.A.
1920	Cleveland	Amer.	SS	7	23	0	4	0	0	0	0	.174	11	28	6	.867
1932	New York	Amer.	3B	4	15	4	5	1	0	0	3	.333	4	6	1	.909
World Series Totals				11	38	4	9	1	0	0	3	.237	15	34	7	.875

JAMES BENTLEY (CY) SEYMOUR

Born December 9, 1872, at Albany, N. Y.
Died September 20, 1919, at New York, N. Y.
Height, 6.00. Weight, 200.
Threw and batted lefthanded.

Year	Club	League	Pos.	G.	AB.	R.	H.	2B.	3B.	HR.	SB.	B.A.	PO.	A.	E.	F.A.
1896	Metropolitans	Atl.	OF	34	131	22	38	...	...	...	11	.290	37	7	14	.759
1896	New York	Nat.	OF-P	12	31	2	8	0	0	0	0	.258	6	19	2	.926
1896-97	Springfield	East	....	....	....	....	....	....	....	....	....	....	....	....	....	....
1897	New York	Nat.	OF-P	41	141	13	35	5	2	2	2	.248	14	95	22	.832
1898	New York	Nat.	OF-P	78	291	40	79	7	2	4	6	.271	25	113	17	.890
1899	New York	Nat.	OF-P	45	154	25	52	3	2	2	3	.337	16	89	17	.861
1900	New York(a)	Nat.	O-1B-P	21	37	9	9	0	0	0	0	.243	9	19	6	.824
1900	Chicago	Amer.	OF-P	2	3	0	0	0	0	0	0	.000	0	2	2	.500
1901	Baltimore	Amer.	OF	137	552	85	167	20	8	1	33	.303	278	26	16	.950
1902	Baltimore(b)	Amer.	OF	72	270	38	75	8	3	13	7	.278	220	12	6	.975
1902	Cincinnati	Nat.	OF-3B	60	235	28	82	8	2	2	10	.349	130	8	13	.914
1903	Cincinnati	Nat.	OF	135	558	85	191	25	15	7	25	.342	•318	14	*36	.902
1904	Cincinnati	Nat.	OF	130	531	71	166	13	5	11	11	.313	308	20	17	.951
1905	Cincinnati	Nat.	OF	149	581	95	*219	*40	*21	8	21	*.377	347	25	21	.947

Year–Club	League	Pos.	G.	AB.	R.	H.	2B.	3B.	HR.	SB.	B.A.	PO.	A.	E.	F.A.
1906–Cin.(c)-N.Y.	Nat.	OF	151	576	70	165	19	5	8	29	.286	331	17	10	.972
1907–New York	Nat.	OF	126	473	46	139	25	8	3	21	.294	300	8	8	.975
1908–New York	Nat.	OF	155	587	59	157	23	2	5	18	.267	340	*29	*20	.949
1909–New York	Nat.	OF	73	280	37	87	12	5	1	14	.311	138	11	5	.968
1910–New York	Nat.	OF	76	287	32	76	9	4	1	10	.265	137	9	10	.936
1910–Baltimore	East.	OF	15	53	6	15	3	0	0	0	.283	17	0	5	.773
1911–Baltimore	East.	OF	112	436	63	129	24	10	2	14	.296	224	16	13	.949
1912–Newark	Int.	OF	124	454	59	139	21	7	0	18	.306	229	13	•17	.934
1913–Boston	Nat.	OF	39	73	2	13	2	0	0	2	.178	34	4	2	.950
1913–Buffalo	Int.	OF	12	47	3	11	1	0	0	0	.234	21	1	1	.957
1918–Newark	Int.	OF	13	41	2	0	0	0	0	0	.220	15	0	0	1.000
American League Totals			209	822	123	242	28	16	4	46	.294	498	38	22	.961
National League Totals			1291	4835	614	1478	204	81	48	172	.306	2453	480	206	.934
Major League Totals			1500	5657	737	1720	232	97	52	218	.304	2951	518	228	.938

aJumped to Chicago Americans late in 1900 season.
bJumped with first baseman-outfielder Joe Kelly to Cincinnati Nationals, July 16, 1902.
cSold to New York Giants for $12,000, July 14, 1906.

PITCHING RECORD

Year–Club	League	G.	IP.	W.	L.	Pct.	H.	R.	SO.	BB.
1896–Springfield	Eastern	....	....	8	1	.889	....	....	....	....
1896–New York	National	12	70	2	4	.333	70	73	28	46
1897–New York	National	34	292	20	14	.588	262	168	157	*165
1898–New York	National	44	359	25	17	.595	318	199	*249	*211
1899–New York	National	33	269	14	17	.452	240	139	145	*162
1900–New York	National	20	50	2	2	.500	71	60	19	54
1900–Chicago	American	2	10	1	1	.500	9	5	5	9
1902–Cincinnati	National	1	....	....	....	....	....	....	....	....
Major League Totals		154	1040	63	54	.538	961	639	598	638

JAMES ROBERT (BOB) SHAWKEY

Born December 4, 1890, at Brookville, Ind.
Died December 31, 1980, at Syracuse, N. Y.
Height, 5.11. Weight, 175.
Threw and batted righthanded.
Married Gertrude Weiler, December 18, 1943.

Struck out 15 Philadelphia Athletics' batters, second game, September 27, 1919.
  Coach, New York Yankees, 1929; manager, New York Yankees, 1930; manager, Jersey City, International League, 1931; manager, Scranton, NYP League, 1932-33; manager, Newark, International League 1934-35; manager, Watertown, Border League, 1947; manager, Tallahassee, Georgia-Florida League, to June 13, 1949; scout, Detroit, 1949; manager, Jamestown (Pony League) 1950; manager, Watertown (Border League) 1951; baseball coach, Dartmouth College, 1953-54.

Year–Club	League	G.	IP.	W.	L.	Pct.	H.	R.	ER.	SO.	BB.	ERA.
1911–Harrisburg	Tri-State	27	168	10	10	.500	149	71	....	102	56	.....
1912–Baltimore	Int.	41	*317	17	18	.486	290	143	....	168	128	.....
1913–Baltimore	Int.	26	189	9	11	.450	167	82	....	132	58	.....
1913–Philadelphia	Amer.	18	111	6	5	.545	93	41	29	47	50	2.35
1914–Philadelphia	Amer.	38	237	16	8	.667	223	88	72	89	75	2.73
1915–Phila.(a)-New York	Amer.	33	186	10	13	.435	181	95	76	87	73	3.68
1916–New York	Amer.	53	277	24	14	.632	204	78	68	122	81	2.21
1917–New York	Amer.	32	236	13	15	.464	207	81	64	97	72	2.44
1918–New York(b)	Amer.	3	16	1	1	.500	7	2	2	3	10	1.13
1919–New York	Amer.	41	262	20	13	.606	218	94	79	122	99	2.71
1920–New York	Amer.	38	268	20	13	.606	246	88	73	126	85	*2.45
1921–New York	Amer.	38	245	18	12	.600	245	131	111	126	86	4.08
1922–New York	Amer.	39	300	20	12	.625	286	112	97	130	98	2.91
1923–New York	Amer.	36	259	16	11	.593	232	114	101	125	102	3.51
1924–New York	Amer.	38	208	16	11	.593	226	107	95	114	74	4.11
1925–New York	Amer.	33	186	6	14	.300	209	101	85	81	67	4.11
1926–New York	Amer.	29	104	8	7	.533	102	49	42	63	37	3.63
1927–New York	Amer.	19	44	2	3	.400	44	19	14	23	16	2.86
1928–Montreal	Int.	23	144	9	9	.500	167	99	90	47	50	5.63
1931–Jersey City	Int.	1	3	0	1	.000	4	3	3	1	4	9.00
1934–Newark	Int.	7	11	0	1	.000	12	13	10	8	9	8.18
Major League Totals		488	2939	196	152	.563	2723	1200	1008	1355	1025	3.09

aSold to New York Yankees, July 7, 1915.
bIn military service most of season.

WORLD SERIES RECORD

Year	Club	League	G.	IP.	W.	L.	Pct.	H.	R.	ER.	SO.	BB.	ERA.
1914–Philadelphia		Amer.	1	5	0	1	.000	4	3	3	0	2	5.40
1921–New York		Amer.	2	9	0	1	.000	13	9	7	5	6	7.00
1922–New York		Amer.	*1	10	0	0	.000	8	3	3	4	2	2.70
1923–New York		Amer.	1	7⅔	1	0	1.000	12	3	3	2	4	3.52
1926–New York		Amer.	3	10	0	1	.000	8	7	6	7	2	5.40
World Series Totals			8	41⅔	1	3	.250	45	25	22	18	16	4.75

*Pitched tie game.

SAMUEL JAMES TILDEN (JIMMIE) SHECKARD

Born November 23, 1878, at Shenk Ferry, Pa.
Died January 15, 1949, at Lancaster, Pa.
Height, 5.09. Weight, 175.
Threw right and batted lefthanded.
Married Frances Eves, May 17, 1922.

Manager, Cleveland, American Association, 1914; coach, Chicago Cubs, 1917.

Year	Club	League	Pos.	G.	AB.	R.	H.	2B.	3B.	HR.	SB.	B.A.	PO.	A.	E.	F.A.
1896–Portsmouth		Va. St.	OF	26	98	17	29	...	...	...	...	.296	...	...	...	.915
1897–Brockton		N. Eng	SS-OF	107	449	117	166	...	...	...	52	*.370	...	...	...	.860
1897–Brooklyn		Nat.	SS	13	49	12	16	3	2	3	1	.327	21	41	19	.765
1898–Brooklyn		Nat.	OF	105	409	51	119	16	11	4	8	.291	212	15	21	.915
1899–Baltimore		Nat.	OF	147	537	106	160	19	10	3	*78	.298	305	34	19	.947
1900–Brooklyn		Nat.	OF	75	269	74	82	19	10	0	34	.305	170	14	13	.934
1901–Brooklyn		Nat.	OF	133	558	116	197	30	*21	11	42	.353	287	17	14	.956
1902–Baltimore		Amer.	OF	4	16	3	4	1	0	0	2	.250	5	0	0	1.000
1902–Brooklyn		Nat.	OF	122	480	84	131	20	10	4	25	.273	283	11	11	.964
1903–Brooklyn		Nat.	3B-OF	139	515	99	171	29	9	*9	•67	.332	314	*36	18	.951
1904–Brooklyn		Nat.	OF	143	507	70	121	23	6	1	21	.239	291	16	14	.956
1905–Brooklyn(a)		Nat.	OF	129	480	58	140	20	11	3	23	.292	266	24	10	.967
1906–Chicago		Nat.	OF	149	549	90	144	27	10	1	30	.262	264	13	4	.986
1907–Chicago		Nat.	OF	142	484	76	129	23	1	0	31	.267	223	13	6	.975
1908–Chicago		Nat.	OF	115	403	54	93	18	3	2	18	.231	201	13	10	.955
1909–Chicago		Nat.	OF	148	525	81	134	29	5	1	15	.255	277	18	10	.967
1910–Chicago		Nat.	OF	143	507	82	130	27	6	5	22	.256	308	21	8	.976
1911–Chicago		Nat.	OF	156	539	*121	149	26	11	4	32	.276	332	*32	14	.963
1912–Chicago(b)		Nat.	OF	146	523	85	128	22	10	3	15	.245	332	26	14	•.962
1913–S.L(c)-Cin.		Nat.	OF	99	252	34	49	3	4	0	11	.194	134	10	6	.960
1914–Cleveland		A. A.	OF	119	371	58	94	21	3	0	8	.253	187	16	6	.971
American League Totals				4	16	3	4	1	0	0	2	.250	5	0	0	1.000
National League Totals				2104	7586	1293	2093	354	140	55	473	.276	4220	354	211	.956
Major League Totals				2108	7602	1296	2097	355	140	55	475	.276	4225	354	211	.956

aTraded to Chicago Cubs for pitcher Herb Briggs, catcher Bill Maloney, first baseman John McCarthy and third baseman James Casey, December 16, 1905.
bSold to St. Louis Cardinals, April, 1913.
cReleased, April, 1913; signed with Cincinnati Reds, July, 1913.

WORLD SERIES RECORD

Year	Club	League	Pos.	G.	AB.	R.	H.	2B.	3B.	HR.	SB.	B.A.	PO.	A.	E.	F.A.
1906–Chicago		Nat.	OF	6	21	0	0	0	0	0	1	.000	7	0	0	1.000
1907–Chicago		Nat.	OF	5	21	0	5	2	0	0	1	.238	8	0	0	1.000
1908–Chicago		Nat.	OF	5	21	2	5	2	0	0	1	.238	7	1	0	1.000
1910–Chicago		Nat.	OF	5	14	5	4	1	0	0	1	.286	8	2	1	.909
World Series Totals				21	77	7	14	5	0	0	4	.182	30	3	1	.971

URBAN JAMES SHOCKER

Born November 22, 1892, at Detroit, Mich.
Died September 9, 1928, at Denver, Colo.
Height, 5.10. Weight, 170.
Threw and batted righthanded.

Year	Club	League	G.	IP.	W.	L.	Pct.	H.	R.	ER.	SO.	BB.	ERA.
1913	Windsor	Border	16	131	6	7	.462	114	66	....	90	33	......
1914	Ottawa	Can.	36	237	•20	8	.714	191	81	....	158	60	......
1915	Ottawa	Can.	36	*303	*19	10	.655	186	95	....	*186	48	......
1916	New York	Amer.	12	82	4	3	.571	67	25	24	43	32	2.63
1916	Toronto	Int.	24	185	15	3	*.833	115	....	27	152	73	*1.31
1917	New York(a)	Amer.	26	145	8	5	.615	124	59	42	68	46	2.61
1918	St. Louis	Amer.	14	95	6	5	.545	69	26	19	33	40	1.80
1919	St. Louis	Amer.	30	211	13	11	.542	193	75	63	86	55	2.69
1920	St. Louis	Amer.	38	246	20	10	.667	224	97	74	107	70	2.71
1921	St. Louis	Amer.	47	327	•27	12	.692	345	151	129	132	86	3.55
1922	St. Louis	Amer.	48	348	24	17	.585	*365	141	115	*149	57	2.97
1923	St. Louis	Amer.	43	277	20	12	.625	292	122	105	109	49	3.41
1924	St. Louis(b)	Amer.	39	239	16	13	.552	262	124	111	84	49	4.18
1925	New York	Amer.	41	244	12	12	.500	278	108	99	74	58	3.65
1926	New York	Amer.	41	258	19	11	.633	272	113	97	59	71	3.38
1927	New York	Amer.	31	200	18	6	.750	207	86	63	35	41	2.84
1928	New York	Amer.	1	2	0	0	.000	3	0	0	0	0	0.00
Major League Totals			411	2674	187	117	.615	2701	1127	941	979	654	3.17

aTraded to St. Louis Browns with infielders Fritz Maisel and Joe Gedeon, pitcher Nick Cullop and catcher Les Nunamaker for infielder Del Pratt and pitcher Eddie Plank, January 22, 1918.
bTraded to New York, December 17, 1924, for pitchers Joe Bush, Milton Gaston and Joe Giard.

WORLD SERIES RECORD

Year	Club	League	G.	IP.	W.	L.	Pct.	H.	R.	ER.	SO.	BB.	ERA.
1926	New York	American	2	7⅔	0	1	.000	13	7	7	3	0	8.22

ROY EDWARD (SQUIRREL) SIEVERS

Born November 18, 1926, at St. Louis, Mo.
Height, 6.01½. Weight, 204.
Threw and batted righthanded.
Married Donna Joan Colburn, November 12, 1949.

Hit home run in each of six consecutive games, July 28-30-31, August 1-2-3, 1957.
Named by THE SPORTING NEWS and Baseball Writers' Association of America as American League Rookie of the Year, 1949.
Coach, Cincinnati Reds, 1966; non-playing manager, Williamsport, Eastern League, 1967; manager, Memphis, Texas League, 1968.

Year	Club	League	Pos.	G.	AB.	R.	H.	2B.	3B.	HR.	RBI.	B.A.	PO.	A.	E.	F.A.
1947	Hannibal	C.A.	O-3B-P	•125	501	*121	*159	21	5	*34	*141	.317	199	44	16	.938
1948	Elmira	East.	OF	16	56	5	10	3	0	2	8	.179	23	1	2	.923
1948	Springfield	I.I.I.	OF	96	343	64	106	15	5	19	75	.309	148	*22	9	.950
1949	St. Louis	Amer.	OF-3B	140	471	84	144	28	1	16	91	.306	317	25	10	.972
1950	St. Louis	Amer.	OF-3B	113	370	46	88	20	4	10	57	.238	248	48	8	.974
1951	St. Louis	Amer.	OF	31	89	10	20	2	1	1	11	.225	63	1	1	.985
1951	San Antonio(a)	Tex.	OF	39	138	16	41	8	1	2	17	.297	72	2	2	.974
1952	St. Louis(b)	Amer.	1B	11	30	3	6	3	0	0	5	.200	58	3	2	.968
1953	St. Louis(c)	Amer.	1B	92	285	37	77	15	0	8	35	.270	604	31	5	.992
1954	Washington	Amer.	OF-1B	145	514	75	119	26	6	24	102	.232	350	15	9	.976
1955	Washington	Amer.	O-1-3B	144	509	74	138	20	8	25	106	.271	363	17	4	.990
1956	Washington	Amer.	OF-1B	152	550	92	139	27	2	29	95	.253	784	54	9	.989
1957	Washington	Amer.	OF-1B	152	572	99	172	23	5	*42	*114	.301	413	15	6	.986
1958	Washington	Amer.	OF-1B	148	550	85	162	18	1	39	108	.295	476	26	5	.990
1959	Washington(d)	Amer.	1B-OF	115	385	55	93	19	0	21	49	.242	870	72	11	.988
1960	Chicago	Amer.	1B-OF	127	444	87	131	22	0	28	93	.295	1085	63	8	.993
1961	Chicago(e)	Amer.	1B	141	492	76	145	26	6	27	92	.295	1096	94	8	.993
1962	Philadelphia	Nat.	1B-OF	144	477	61	125	19	5	21	80	.262	977	93	10	.991
1963	Philadelphia	Nat.	1B	138	450	46	108	19	2	19	82	.240	981	77	12	.989
1964	Philadelphia(f)	Nat.	1B	49	120	7	22	3	1	4	16	.183	241	15	2	.992
1964	Washington	Amer.	1B	33	58	5	10	1	0	4	11	.172	87	11	0	1.000
1965	Washington	Amer.	1B	12	21	3	4	1	0	0	0	.190	51	1	0	1.000
American League Totals				1556	5340	831	1448	251	34	274	969	.271	6865	476	86	.988
National League Totals				331	1047	114	255	41	8	44	178	.243	2199	185	24	.990
Major League Totals				1887	6387	945	1703	292	42	318	1147	.267	9064	661	110	.989

aSuffered shoulder separation making tumbling catch, August 1, 1951; out for rest of season.
bReporting for training early, he dislocated right arm at the shoulder during infield practice when making a throw from third base, February 23, 1952; made first appearance of season September 1, 1952, as a pinch-hitter.
cTraded to Washington Senators for outfielder Gil Coan, February 18, 1954.
dTraded to Chicago White Sox for catcher Earl Battey, first baseman Don Mincher and reported $150,000, April 4, 1960.

eTraded to Philadelphia Phillies for pitcher Johnny Buzhardt and third baseman Charlie Smith, November 28, 1961.
fSold to Washington Senators, July 14, 1964.

ALOYSIUS HARRY (BUCKETFOOT) SIMMONS

Born May 22, 1902, at Milwaukee, Wis.
Died May 26, 1956, at Milwaukee, Wis.
Height, 6.00. Weight, 210.
Threw and batted righthanded.

Hit three home runs in game, July 15, 1932. In 1929 World Series between Philadelphia (A.L.) and Chicago (N.L.), scored six runs in five games; went to bat twice, made two hits for five total bases, seventh inning, October 12. Hit two home runs in five-game Series, 1929. Batted in eight runs in seven-game Series between Philadelphia (A.L.) and St. Louis (N.L.), 1931.
Named by Baseball Writers' Association of America as outfielder for THE SPORTING NEWS All-Star Major League Teams, 1927-29-30-31-33 and 1934.
Named Most Valuable Player in American League, 1929.
Player-coach, Philadelphia Athletics, 1940-41-42 and 1944; coach, 1945-46-47-48-49; coach, Cleveland Indians, 1950.
Named to Hall of Fame, 1953.

Year Club	League	Pos.	G.	AB.	R.	H.	2B.	3B.	HR.	RBI.	B.A.	PO.	A.	E.	F.A.
1922–Milwaukee	A. A.	OF	19	50	9	11	2	1	1	7	.220	16	3	1	.950
1922–Aberdeen	Dakota	OF	99	395	91	*144	26	16	10	.....	.365	209	19	0	*1.00
1923–Shreveport	Tex.	OF	144	525	96	189	36	10	12	99	.360	335	31	13	.966
1923–Milwaukee	A. A.	OF	24	98	20	39	2	3	0	16	.398	58	2	1	.984
1924–Philadelphia	Amer.	OF	152	594	69	183	31	9	8	102	.308	390	17	10	.976
1925–Philadelphia	Amer.	OF	153	*658	122	*253	43	12	24	129	.384	*447	8	•16	.966
1926–Philadelphia	Amer.	OF	147	581	90	199	53	10	19	109	.343	333	11	9	.975
1927–Philadelphia	Amer.	OF	106	406	86	159	36	11	15	108	.392	247	10	4	.985
1928–Philadelphia	Amer.	OF	119	464	78	163	33	9	15	107	.351	231	10	3	.988
1929–Philadelphia	Amer.	OF	143	581	114	212	41	9	34	*157	.365	349	19	4	•.989
1930–Philadelphia	Amer.	OF	138	554	*152	211	41	16	36	165	*.381	275	10	3	*.990
1931–Philadelphia	Amer.	OF	128	513	105	200	37	13	22	128	*.390	287	10	4	.987
1932–Philadelphia(a)	Amer.	OF	154	*670	144	*216	28	9	35	151	.322	290	9	6	.980
1933–Chicago	Amer.	OF	146	605	85	200	29	10	14	119	.331	372	15	4	.990
1934–Chicago	Amer.	OF	138	558	102	192	36	7	18	104	.344	286	14	4	.987
1935–Chicago(b)	Amer.	OF	128	525	68	140	22	7	16	79	.267	349	5	7	.981
1936–Detroit	Amer.	OF	143	568	96	186	38	6	13	112	.327	364	8	5	*.987
1937–Washington(c)	Amer.	OF	103	419	60	117	21	10	8	84	.279	240	7	4	.984
1938–Washington(d)	Amer.	OF	125	470	79	142	23	6	21	95	.302	232	4	4	.983
1939–Bos.(e)-Cin.(f)	Nat.	OF	102	351	39	96	17	5	7	44	.274	172	8	4	.978
1940–Philadelphia	Amer.	OF	37	81	7	25	4	0	1	19	.309	51	1	2	.963
1941–Philadelphia	Amer.	OF	9	24	1	3	1	0	0	1	.125	16	0	0	1.000
1942–Philadelphia(g)	Amer.	OF				(Served as coach.)									
1943–Boston(h)	Amer.	OF	40	133	9	27	5	0	1	12	.203	66	3	1	.986
1944–Philadelphia	Amer.	OF	4	6	1	3	0	0	0	2	.500	3	0	0	1.000
American League Totals			2113	8410	1468	2831	522	144	300	1783	.337	4828	161	90	.982
National League Totals			102	351	39	96	17	5	7	44	.274	172	8	4	.978
Major League Totals			2215	8761	1507	2927	539	149	307	1827	.334	5000	169	94	.982

aSold with third baseman Jimmie Dykes and outfielder George Haas for $150,000 to Chicago White Sox, September 28, 1932.
bSold to Detroit Tigers for $75,000, December 10, 1935.
cPurchased by Washington Senators for $15,000, April 4, 1937.
dSold to Boston Braves, December 20, 1938.
eSold to Cincinnati Reds, August 31, 1939.
fReleased by Cincinnati Reds after season closed and signed by Philadelphia Athletics as free agent, December 11, 1939.
gReleased following 1942 season and signed by Boston Red Sox as active player, February 2, 1943.
hReleased by Boston Red Sox, October 15, 1943, and signed as player-coach by Philadelphia Athletics, December, 1943.

WORLD SERIES RECORD

Year Club	League	Pos.	G.	AB.	R.	H.	2B.	3B.	HR.	RBI.	B.A.	PO.	A.	E.	F.A.
1929–Philadelphia	Amer.	OF	5	20	6	6	1	0	2	5	.300	4	0	0	1.000
1930–Philadelphia	Amer.	OF	6	22	4	8	2	0	2	4	.364	12	1	0	1.000
1931–Philadelphia	Amer.	OF	7	27	4	9	2	0	2	8	.333	19	0	0	1.000
1939–Cincinnati	Nat'.	OF	1	4	1	1	1	0	0	0	.250	3	0	0	1.000
World Series Totals			19	73	15	24	6	0	6	17	.329	38	1	0	1.000

CURTIS THOMAS SIMMONS

Born May 19, 1929, at Egypt, Pa.
Height, 6.00. Weight, 195.
Threw and batted lefthanded.
Married Dorothy Ludwig, September 23, 1951.

Tied for National League lead in shutouts with 6 in 1952.

Year	Club	League	G.	IP.	W.	L.	Pct.	H.	R.	ER.	SO.	BB.	ERA.
1947	Wilmington	Int.-State	18	147	13	5	.722	107	48	44	197	76	2.69
1947	Philadelphia	Nat.	1	9	1	0	1.000	5	1	1	9	6	1.00
1948	Philadelphia	Nat.	31	170	7	13	.350	169	110	92	86	108	4.87
1949	Philadelphia	Nat.	38	131	4	10	.286	133	72	67	83	55	4.60
1950	Philadelphia(a)	Nat.	31	215	17	8	.680	178	93	81	146	88	3.39
1951	Philadelphia	Nat.					(In Military Service).						
1952	Philadelphia	Nat.	28	201	14	8	.636	170	72	63	141	70	2.82
1953	Philadelphia	Nat.	32	238	16	13	.552	211	102	85	138	82	3.21
1954	Philadelphia	Nat.	34	253	14	15	.483	226	101	79	125	98	2.81
1955	Philadelphia	Nat.	25	130	8	8	.500	148	76	71	58	50	4.92
1956	Philadelphia	Nat.	33	198	15	10	.600	186	95	74	88	65	3.36
1957	Philadelphia	Nat.	32	212	12	11	.522	214	92	81	92	50	3.44
1958	Philadelphia	Nat.	29	168	7	14	.333	196	92	82	78	40	4.39
1959	Philadelphia	Nat.	7	10	0	0	.000	16	5	5	4	0	4.50
1959	Williamsport	East.	6	44	4	1	.800	43	16	14	19	7	2.86
1960	Philadelphia(b)-St. Louis	Nat.	27	156	7	4	.636	162	58	53	67	37	3.06
1961	St. Louis	Nat.	30	196	9	10	.474	203	91	68	99	64	3.12
1962	St. Louis	Nat.	31	154	10	10	.500	167	78	60	74	32	3.51
1963	St. Louis	Nat.	32	233	15	9	.625	209	82	64	127	48	2.47
1964	St. Louis	Nat.	34	244	18	9	.667	233	106	93	104	49	3.43
1965	St. Louis	Nat.	34	203	9	15	.375	229	104	92	96	54	4.08
1966	St. Louis(c)-Chicago	Nat.	29	111	5	8	.385	114	56	52	38	35	4.22
1967	Chicago(d)	Nat.	17	82	3	7	.300	100	54	45	31	23	4.94
1967	California	Amer.	14	35	2	1	.667	44	11	10	13	9	2.57
	National League Totals		555	3314	191	182	.512	3269	1540	1308	1684	1054	3.55
	American League Totals		14	35	2	1	.667	44	11	10	13	9	2.57
	Major League Totals		569	3349	193	183	.513	3313	1551	1318	1697	1063	3.54

aIn Military Service last few weeks of season; received furlough to attend World Series. Manager Eddie Sawyer vetoed suggestion Simmons be reinstated to eligible list due to limited baseball activity while in service.
bUnconditionally released by Philadelphia Phillies, May 12, 1960; signed with St. Louis Cardinals, May 19, 1960.
cSold to Chicago Cubs, June 22, 1966.
dSold to California Angels, August 7, 1967.

WORLD SERIES RECORD

Year	Club	League	G.	IP.	W.	L.	Pct.	H.	R.	ER.	SO.	BB.	ERA.
1964	St. Louis	Nat.	2	14⅓	0	1	.000	11	4	4	8	3	2.51

GEORGE HAROLD (GORGEOUS GEORGE) SISLER

Born March 24, 1893, at Manchester, O.
Died March 26, 1973, at St. Louis, Mo.
Height, 5.10½. Weight, 170.
Threw and batted lefthanded.
Married Kathleen Holznagle, October 21, 1916.

Hit safely in 41 consecutive games—July 27 through September 17, 1922; named Most Valuable Player, American League, 1922; holds major league record for most base-hits, season—257 in 1920; led American League in stolen bases, 1918, 1921, 1922 and 1927. Led A.L. first basemen in double plays, 1926, 1927. Tied for A.L. lead in most years leading first basemen in assists, 6 (matched by Vic Power).
Manager, St. Louis Browns, 1924-25-26; manager, Shreveport-Tyler, Texas League, 1932; scout, Brooklyn Dodgers, 1943; scout, Newport News, Piedmont League, 1945; scout, Brooklyn Dodgers, 1946 through 1950;

scout, Pittsburgh Pirates, 1951 through 1956; batting instructor, Pittsburgh, 1956-61; scout, Pittsburgh, 1962 through 1966.
Named to Hall of Fame, 1939.

Year	Club	League	Pos.	G.	AB.	R.	H.	2B.	3B.	HR.	RBI.	B.A.	PO.	A.	E.	F.A.
1915	St. Louis	Amer.	P-1-O	81	274	28	78	10	2	3	29	.285	413	38	7	.985
1916	St. Louis	Amer.	1-P-O	151	580	83	177	21	11	4	74	.305	1493	86	*24	.985
1917	St. Louis	Amer.	O-1B	135	539	60	190	30	9	2	55	.353	1384	101	*22	.985
1918	St. Louis	Amer.	1B	114	452	69	154	21	9	2	45	.341	1244	97	13	.990
1919	St. Louis	Amer.	1B	132	511	96	180	31	15	10	83	.352	1249	*120	13	.991
1920	St. Louis	Amer.	1B	•154	*631	137	*257	49	18	19	122	*.407	1477	*140	16	.990
1921	St. Louis	Amer.	1B	138	582	125	216	38	18	12	104	.371	1267	108	10	.993
1922	St. Louis	Amer.	1B	142	586	*134	*246	42	*18	8	105	*.420	1293	*125	17	.988
1923	St. Louis	Amer.						(Out with eye trouble)								
1924	St. Louis	Amer.	1B	151	636	94	194	27	10	9	74	.305	1326	*112	*23	.984
1925	St. Louis	Amer.	1B	150	649	100	224	21	15	12	105	.345	1343	*131	*26	.983
1926	St. Louis	Amer.	1B	150	613	78	178	21	12	7	71	.289	1467	87	21	.987
1927	St. Louis(a)	Amer.	1B	149	614	87	201	32	8	5	97	.327	1374	*131	*24	.984
1928	Washington(b)	Amer.	1B	20	49	1	12	1	0	0	2	.245	45	0	0	1.000
1928	Boston	Nat.	1B	118	491	71	167	26	4	4	68	.340	1188	*86	15	.988
1929	Boston	Nat.	1B	154	629	67	205	40	8	2	79	.326	1398	111	*8	.982
1930	Boston	Nat.	1B	116	431	54	133	15	7	3	67	.309	915	81	13	.987
1931	Rochester	Int.	1B	159	613	86	186	37	5	3	81	.303	1401	*125	20	.987
1932	Shrev.-Tyler	Texas	1B	70	258	28	74	15	2	1	23	.287	637	33	15	.978
	American League Totals			1667	6716	1092	2307	344	145	93	966	.344	15375	1276	216	.987
	National League Totals			388	1551	192	505	81	19	9	214	.326	3501	278	56	.985
	Major League Totals			2055	8267	1284	2812	425	164	102	1180	.340	18876	1554	272	.987

aSold to Washington for $25,000, December 14, 1927.
bPurchased by Boston N. L. for $7,500, May 27, 1928.

PITCHING RECORD

Year	Club	League	G.	IP.	W.	L.	Pct.	H.	R.	ER.	SO.	BB.	ERA.
1915	St. Louis	American	15	70	4	4	.500	62	26	22	41	38	2.83
1916	St. Louis	American	3	27	1	2	.333	18	4	3	12	6	1.00
1920	St. Louis	American	1	1	0	0	.000	0	0	0	2	0	0.00
1925	St. Louis	American	1	2	0	0	.000	1	0	0	1	1	0.00
1926	St. Louis	American	1	2	0	0	.000	0	0	0	3	2	0.00
1928	Boston	National	1	1	0	0	.000	0	0	0	0	1	0.00
	Major League Totals		22	103	5	6	.455	81	30	25	59	48	2.13

WILLIAM JOSEPH (MOOSE) SKOWRON, JR.

Born December 18, 1930, at Chicago, Ill.
Height, 6.00. Weight, 200.
Threw and batted righthanded.

Led American League first basemen in double plays with 138 in 1956, 146 in 1961 and 116 in 1965.
Tied World Series record for most times at bat, nine-inning game (6), October 6, 1960; tied for most assists by first baseman, five-game Series (5), 1961; holds mark for most Series played by first baseman (8), 1963; holds mark for most assists by first baseman, total Series (29), 1963; tied for most runs batted in, inning (4), October 10, 1956 (seventh inning, home run with bases filled).
Named Minor League Player of the Year by THE SPORTING NEWS, 1952.
Named as first baseman on THE SPORTING NEWS All-Star Major League Team, 1960.

Year	Club	League	Pos.	G.	AB.	R.	H.	2B.	3B.	HR.	RBI.	B.A.	PO.	A.	E.	F.A.
1951	Binghamton	East.	3B-OF	21	57	9	14	4	1	2	11	.246	21	30	4	.927
1951	Norfolk	Pied.	OF	95	320	72	107	9	9	18	78	*.334	147	10	6	.963
1952	Kansas City	A. A.	OF	147	560	113	191	38	11	*31	*134	.341	269	5	11	.961
1953	Kansas City	A. A.	1B	134	512	72	163	31	12	15	89	.318	1179	61	10	.992
1954	New York	Amer.	INF	87	215	37	73	12	9	7	41	.340	399	45	7	.984
1955	New York	Amer.	1B-3B	108	288	46	92	17	3	12	61	.319	520	40	7	.988
1956	New York	Amer.	•1B-3B	134	464	78	143	21	6	23	90	.308	969	*86	8	•.992
1957	New York	Amer.	1B	122	457	54	139	15	5	17	88	.304	1026	86	9	.992
1958	New York	Amer.	1B-3B	126	465	61	127	22	3	14	73	.273	1041	72	13	*.988
1959	New York	Amer.	1B	74	282	39	84	13	5	15	59	.298	626	43	6	.991
1960	New York	Amer.	1B	146	538	63	166	34	3	26	91	.309	*1202	115	•12	.991
1961	New York	Amer.	1B	150	561	76	150	23	4	28	89	.267	1228	102	10	.993
1962	New York(a)	Amer.	1B	140	478	63	129	16	6	23	80	.270	1054	77	10	.991
1963	Los Angeles(b)	Nat.	1B-3B	89	237	19	48	8	0	4	19	.203	518	34	5	.991
1964	Wash.(c)-Chi.	Amer.	1B	146	535	47	151	21	3	17	79	.282	1212	80	5	.996
1965	Chicago	Amer.	1B	146	559	63	153	24	3	18	78	.274	*1297	74	8	.994

Year	Club	League	Pos.	G.	AB.	R.	H.	2B.	3B.	HR.	RBI.	B.A.	PO.	A.	E.	F.A.
1966–Chicago		Amer.	1B	120	337	27	84	15	2	6	29	.249	722	60	7	.991
1967–Chi.(d)-Calif.		Amer.	1B	70	131	8	27	2	1	1	11	.206	338	16	3	.992
American League Totals				1569	5310	662	1518	235	53	207	869	.286	11634	896	105	.992
National League Totals				89	237	19	48	8	0	4	19	.203	518	34	5	.991
Major League Totals				1658	5547	681	1566	243	53	211	888	.282	12152	930	100	.992

aTraded to Los Angeles Dodgers for pitcher Stan Williams, November 26, 1962.
bSold to Washington Senators, December 6, 1963.
cTraded to Chicago White Sox with pitcher Carl Bouldin, who was assigned to Indianapolis, for first baseman Joe Cunningham, July 13, 1964; White Sox assigned pitcher Frank Kreutzer to Senators, July 28, 1964, to complete deal.
dReleased to California Angels, May 6, 1967.

WORLD SERIES RECORD

Year	Club	League	Pos.	G.	AB.	R.	H.	2B.	3B.	HR.	RBI.	B.A.	PO.	A.	E.	F.A.
1955–New York		Amer.	1B-PH	5	12	2	4	2	0	1	3	.333	22	3	1	.962
1956–New York		Amer.	1B-PH	3	10	1	1	0	0	1	4	.100	21	4	1	.962
1957–New York		Amer.	1B-PH	2	4	0	0	0	0	0	0	.000	5	2	0	1.000
1958–New York		Amer.	1B	7	27	3	7	0	0	2	7	.259	55	4	0	1.000
1960–New York		Amer.	1B	7	32	7	12	2	0	2	6	.375	70	6	0	1.000
1961–New York		Amer.	1B	5	17	3	6	0	0	1	5	.353	46	5	0	1.000
1962–New York		Amer.	1B	6	18	1	4	0	1	0	1	.222	52	1	0	1.000
1963–Los Angeles		Nat.	1B	4	13	2	5	0	0	1	3	.385	30	4	0	1.000
World Series Totals				39	133	19	39	4	1	8	29	.293	301	29	2	.994

ENOS BRADSHER (COUNTRY) SLAUGHTER

Born April 27, 1916, at Roxboro, N. C.
Height, 5.09. Weight, 190.
Threw right and batted lefthanded.
Married Helen Spiker, December 21, 1955.

Named as outfielder on THE SPORTING NEWS All-Star Major League Teams, 1942-46.
Led N. L. outfielders in double plays, 1939, 1940 (tie).
Playing manager, Houston, Texas League, 1960; playing manager, Raleigh, Carolina League, 1961.

Year	Club	League	Pos.	G.	AB.	R.	H.	2B.	3B.	HR.	RBI.	B.A.	PO.	A.	E.	F.A.
1935–Martinsville		Bi-State	OF	109	422	68	115	25	11	18	.....	.273	187	24	16	.930
1936–Columbus		Sally	OF	151	569	106	185	31	*20	9	118	.325	317	10	17	.951
1937–Columbus		A. A.	OF	154	642	*147	*245	42	13	26	122	*.382	267	10	7	.975
1938–St. Louis		Nat.	OF	112	395	59	109	20	10	8	58	.276	189	7	6	.970
1939–St. Louis		Nat.	OF	149	604	95	193	*52	5	12	86	.320	267	*18	*12	.968
1940–St. Louis		Nat.	OF	140	516	96	158	25	13	17	73	.306	267	8	3	.989
1941–St. Louis(a)		Nat.	OF	113	425	71	132	22	9	13	76	.311	173	5	10	.947
1942–St. Louis		Nat.	OF	152	591	100	*188	31	*17	13	98	.318	287	15	4	.987
1943-44-45–St. Louis		Nat.					(In Military Service)									
1946–St. Louis		Nat.	OF	•156	609	100	183	30	8	18	*130	.300	284	*23	6	.981
1947–St. Louis		Nat.	OF	147	551	100	162	31	13	10	86	.294	306	15	6	.982
1948–St. Louis		Nat.	OF	146	549	91	176	27	11	11	90	.321	330	9	10	.971
1949–St. Louis		Nat.	OF	151	568	92	191	34	•13	13	96	.336	330	10	6	.983
1950–St. Louis		Nat.	OF	148	556	82	161	26	7	10	101	.290	260	9	6	.978
1951–St. Louis		Nat.	OF	123	409	48	115	17	8	4	64	.281	198	10	1	.995
1952–St. Louis		Nat.	OF	140	510	73	153	17	12	11	101	.300	250	11	3	.989
1953–St. Louis(b)		Nat.	OF	143	492	64	143	34	9	6	89	.291	235	2	1	*.996
1954–New York		Amer.	OF	69	125	19	31	4	2	1	19	.248	37	0	1	.974
1955–N.Y.(c)-K.C.		Amer.	OF	118	276	50	87	12	4	5	35	.315	126	5	2	.985
1956–K.C.(d)-N.Y.		Amer.	OF	115	306	52	86	18	5	2	27	.281	133	2	2	.985
1957–New York		Amer.	OF	96	209	24	53	7	1	5	34	.254	97	2	0	1.000
1958–New York		Amer.	OF	77	138	21	42	4	1	4	19	.304	43	1	2	.957
1959–New York		Amer.	OF	74	99	10	17	2	0	6	21	.172	27	0	1	.964
1959–Milwaukee		Nat.	OF	11	18	0	3	0	0	0	1	.167	5	0	0	1.000
1960–Houston		A.A.	PH-OF	40	45	7	13	3	1	1	8	.289	.....	.....	.....	.....
1961–Raleigh		Car.	PH	42	41	8	14	1	0	0	9	.341	.....	.....	.....	.....
American League Totals				549	1153	176	316	47	13	23	155	.274	463	10	8	.983
National League Totals				1831	6793	1071	2067	366	135	146	1149	.304	3452	142	74	.980
Major League Totals				2380	7946	1247	2383	413	148	169	1304	.300	3915	152	82	.980

aSuffered broken collarbone, August 11, 1941, forcing him out of lineup for five weeks.
bTraded to New York Yankees for pitcher Mel Wright (from the Yankees' Kansas City farm club), plus outfielders Bill Virdon and Emil Tellinger from New York minor league affiliates to clubs in the St. Louis farm organization, April 11, 1954.

cTraded to Kansas City Athletics with pitcher Johnny Sain for pitcher John (Sonny) Dixon and cash, May 11, 1955.
dReleased to New York Yankees, August 25, 1956.

WORLD SERIES RECORD

Year	Club	League	Pos.	G.	AB.	R.	H.	2B.	3B.	HR.	RBI.	B.A.	PO.	A.	E.	F.A.
1942	St. Louis	Nat.	OF	5	19	3	5	1	0	1	2	.263	9	1	1	.909
1946	St. Louis	Nat.	OF	7	25	5	8	1	1	2	.320	20	1	0	1.000
1956	New York	Amer.	OF	6	20	6	7	0	0	1	4	.350	8	1	0	1.000
1957	New York	Amer.	OF	5	12	2	3	1	0	0	0	.250	7	0	0	1.000
1958	New York	Amer.	OF	4	3	1	0	0	0	0	0	.000	0	0	0	.000
World Series Totals				27	79	17	23	3	1	3	8	.291	44	3	1	.979

EARL SUTTON (OIL) SMITH

Born February 14, 1897, at Sheridan, Ark.
Died June 9, 1963, at Little Rock, Ark.
Height, 5.10½. Weight, 170.
Threw right and batted lefthanded.

Manager, Charleston, Mid Atlantic, 1935; Milford, Eastern Shore, 1938-39; Allentown, Inter-State, 1940; coach, Hot Springs, Cotton States, 1947.

Year	Club	League	Pos.	G.	AB.	R.	H.	2B.	3B.	HR.	RBI.	B.A.	PO.	A.	E.	F.A.
1916	Waxahachie	C. Texas	C	47	171	23	46	11	4	3	.....	.269	293	67	16	.957
1917	Ft. Smith-Tulsa	W. A.		.....	.....	.....	.....	.....	.....	.....	.....	.....	.....	.....	.....	.....
1918	Rochester	Int.	C	94	335	51	120	24	*14	1	.....	.358	519	79	14	.977
1919	New York	Nat.	C	21	36	5	9	2	1	0	5	.250	26	10	1	.973
1920	New York	Nat.	C	91	262	20	77	7	1	1	30	.294	252	73	8	.976
1921	New York	Nat.	C	89	229	35	77	8	4	10	51	.336	195	56	9	.965
1922	New York	Nat.	C	90	234	29	65	11	4	9	39	.278	214	56	6	.978
1923	N.Y.(a)-Boston	Nat.	C	96	225	24	62	16	2	4	23	.276	173	58	6	.975
1924	Bos.(b)-Pitts.	Nat.	C	72	170	13	57	13	1	4	29	.335	167	36	7	.967
1925	Pittsburgh	Nat.	C	109	329	34	103	22	3	8	64	.313	317	77	13	.968
1926	Pittsburgh	Nat.	C	105	292	29	101	17	2	2	46	.346	307	63	14	.964
1927	Pittsburgh	Nat.	C	66	189	16	51	3	1	5	25	.270	187	32	3	.986
1928	Pitts.(c)-St. L.	Nat.	C	56	143	11	34	8	0	2	18	.238	130	17	3	.980
1929	St. Louis	Nat.	C	57	145	9	50	8	0	1	22	.345	131	21	6	.962
1930	St. Louis	Nat.	C	8	10	0	0	0	0	0	0	.000	18	3	2	.913
1930	Toledo	A. A.	C	42	117	16	37	8	1	3	25	.316	123	16	5	.965
1930	Rochester	Int.	C	18	46	4	11	1	2	0	11	.239	76	3	0	1.000
1931	Nash.-L. Rock	South.	C	43	124	15	33	7	1	1	22	.266	78	13	3	.968
Major League Totals				860	2264	225	686	115	19	46	352	.303	2117	502	78	.971

aTraded to Boston Braves with pitcher Jesse Barnes for pitcher John Watson and catcher Hank Gowdy, June 7, 1923.
bSold to Pittsburgh Pirates, June, 1924.
cUnconditionally released by Pittsburgh Pirates, July 9, 1928, and signed with St. Louis Cardinals, July 12, 1928.

WORLD SERIES RECORD

Year	Club	League	Pos.	G.	AB.	R.	H.	2B.	3B.	HR.	RBI.	B.A.	PO.	A.	E.	F.A.
1921	New York	Nat.	C	3	7	0	0	0	0	0	0	.000	7	2	1	.900
1922	New York	Nat.	C	4	7	0	1	0	0	0	0	.143	2	1	0	1.000
1925	Pittsburgh	Nat.	C	6	20	0	7	1	0	0	0	.350	28	7	1	.972
1927	Pittsburgh	Nat.	C	3	8	0	0	0	0	0	0	.000	10	1	1	.917
1928	St. Louis	Nat.	C	1	4	0	3	0	0	0	0	.750	3	1	0	1.000
World Series Totals				17	46	0	11	1	0	0	0	.239	50	12	3	.954

ELMER ELLSWORTH (MIKE) SMITH

Born March 28, 1868, at Allegheny, Pa.
Died November 5, 1945, at Pittsburgh, Pa.
Height, 5.11. Weight, 178.
Threw and batted lefthanded.

Year	Club	League	Pos.	G.	AB.	R.	H.	2B.	3B.	HR.	SB.	B.A.	PO.	A.	E.	F.A.
1886–Nashville		So.Leag.	....													
1886–Cincinnati		A.A.	P-OF	9	26	6	8	0	0	0	0	.308	....	....	....	......
1887–Cincinnati		A.A.	P-OF	52	198	30	57	9	5	0	5	.288	....	....	13	.948
1888–Cincinnati		A.A.	P-OF	40	132	14	29	3	1	0	3	.220	....	....	11	.948
1889–Cincinnati		A.A.	P	28	81	12	23	3	1	2	0	.259	....	....	....	......
1890–Kansas City		W.A.	P-OF	112	463	128	150	....	....	....	....	.331	142	11	18	.894
1891–Kansas City		W.A.	OF	120	479	118	148	....	....	....	18	.308	219	13	24	.906
1892–Pittsburgh		Nat.	P-OF	136	495	86	140	18	14	4	23	.282	233	15	29	.891
1893–Pittsburgh		Nat.	OF	128	500	119	183	27	21	7	28	.366	274	14	24	.923
1894–Pittsburgh		Nat.	OF	125	497	129	175	34	18	6	37	.352	271	18	20	.935
1895–Pittsburgh		Nat.	OF	124	492	109	146	16	13	1	35	.296	255	16	32	.891
1896–Pittsburgh		Nat.	OF	120	475	118	170	22	14	6	32	.358	297	11	17	.947
1897–Pittsburgh		Nat.	OF	122	463	101	145	18	19	6	28	.311	240	17	26	.908
1898–Cincinnati		Nat.	OF	122	483	76	166	22	9	1	19	.344	280	15	18	.942
1899–Cincinnati		Nat.	OF	87	342	64	101	15	5	1	11	.295	179	10	6	.969
1900–Cin.-N.Y		Nat.	OF	116	425	61	118	13	10	3	20	.278	151	14	10	.943
1901–Pitts.-Bos.		Nat.	OF	22	77	6	12	2	1	0	2	.158	21	1	4	.846
1902–Kansas City		A.A.	OF	....	408	69	127	....	....	....	....	.311	243	7	19	.926
1903–Minneapolis		A.A.	OF	75	300	55	97	15	4	2	7	.323	104	5	5	.956
1904–Kansas City		A.A.	OF	12	44	6	13	1	0	0	1	.295	13	2	1	.955
1904–Ilion		N.Y.	1B	110	383	56	125	....	....	....	13	.326	801	27	25	.970
1905–Scranton		N.Y.	OF	114	520	52	138	....	....	....	22	.328	117	8	5	.961
1906–Binghamton		N.Y.	OF	119	396	43	124	....	....	....	8	.313	249	13	9	.966
American Association Totals				129	437	62	117	15	7	2	8	.268	....	....	....	......
National League Totals				1102	4249	869	1356	187	124	35	235	.319	2201	131	186	.926
Major League Totals				1231	4686	931	1473	202	131	37	243	.314	....	....	....	......

PITCHING RECORD

Year	Club	League	G.	W.	L.	Pct.	H.	R.	SO.	BB.	CG.	ShO.
1886–Cincinnati		Amer.Association	9	4	5	.444	....	....	....	....	9	0
1887–Cincinnati		Amer.Association	52	33	18	.647	551	242	114	128	46	3
1888–Cincinnati		Amer.Association	40	22	17	.564	305	161	128	106	39	5
1889–Cincinnati		Amer.Association	28	10	12	.455	251	169	98	103	16	0
1890–Kansas City		West.Association	36	....	....	....	205	114	213	96	....	....
1892–Pittsburgh		National	13	7	6	.538	....	....	....	....	12	1
American Association Totals			129	69	52	.570	....	....	....	....	110	8
National League Totals			13	7	6	.538	....	....	....	....	12	1
Major League Totals			142	76	58	.567	....	....	....	....	122	9

EDWIN DONALD (DUKE) SNIDER

Born September 19, 1926, at Los Angeles, Calif.
Height, 6.00. Weight, 200.
Threw right and batted lefthanded.
Married Beverly Null, October 25, 1947.

Tied major league mark by appearing at bat three times in one inning, May 21, 1952 (first inning); tied major league record by striking out twice in one inning, sixth inning, August 14, 1954; tied N. L. record for most consecutive years leading in run scored (3), 1955.
Tied National League record for most consecutive years, 40 or more home runs (5), 1953 through 1957; hit three home runs in a game, May 30, 1950 and June 1, 1955.
Holds World Series record for most times four home runs in a Series (2), hitting four in the 1952 and 1955 Series; established record for most home runs by N. L. player, total Series (11), 1959; tied Series mark for most home runs by a player in a Series (4), 1952-55; Snider's 11 home runs, and 26 runs batted in for total Series gives him top mark for National League player; tied for record for most total bases, Series (24), 1952; established mark for most extra bases on long hits, Series (K14), 1952; tied record for extra-base hits, Series (6), 1952.
Named Major League Player of Year by THE SPORTING NEWS, 1955; No. 1 National League Player by THE SPORTING NEWS, 1955; outfielder on THE SPORTING NEWS All-Star Major League Teams, 1953-54-55.
Scout, Los Angeles Dodgers, February 1, 1965; non-playing manager, Spokane, Pacific Coast League, April 29, 1965; non-playing manager, Kennewick, Northwest League, 1966; scout, Los Angeles Dodgers, 1967-68; scout, San Diego, National League, 1969; manager, Alexandria, Texas League, 1972; batting instructor, Montreal Expos, 1974-75.
Named to Hall of Fame, 1980.

Year	Club	League	Pos.	G.	AB.	R.	H.	2B.	3B.	HR.	RBI.	B.A.	PO.	A.	E.	F.A.
1944–Montreal		Int.	PH	2	2	0	0	0	0	0	0	.000	0	0	0	.000
1944–Newport News		Pied.	OF	131	507	87	149	★34	6	★9	50	.294	231	★25	18	.934
1945–Newport News		Pied.					(In Military Service)									
1946–Fort Worth		Tex.	OF	68	232	36	58	13	1	5	30	.250	110	6	5	.959

Year	Club	League	Pos.	G.	AB.	R.	H.	2B.	3B.	HR.	RBI.	B.A.	PO.	A.	E.	F.A.
1947–St. Paul		A.A.	OF	66	269	59	85	22	7	12	46	.316	157	5	6	.964
1947–Brooklyn		Nat.	OF	40	83	6	20	3	1	0	5	.241	48	0	1	.980
1948–Montreal		Int.	OF	77	275	67	90	28	4	17	77	.327	136	13	7	.955
1948–Brooklyn		Nat.	OF	53	160	22	39	6	6	5	21	.244	87	5	1	.989
1949–Brooklyn		Nat.	OF	146	552	100	161	28	7	23	92	.292	355	12	6	.984
1950–Brooklyn		Nat.	OF	152	620	109	*199	31	10	31	107	.321	378	15	7	.983
1951–Brooklyn		Nat.	OF	150	606	96	168	26	6	29	101	.277	382	12	5	.987
1952–Brooklyn		Nat.	OF	144	534	80	162	25	7	21	92	.303	341	13	3	.992
1953–Brooklyn		Nat.	OF	153	590	*132	198	38	4	42	126	.336	370	7	5	.987
1954–Brooklyn		Nat.	OF	149	584	•120	199	39	10	40	130	.341	360	8	7	.981
1955–Brooklyn		Nat.	OF	148	538	*126	166	34	6	42	*136	.309	348	9	4	.989
1956–Brooklyn		Nat.	OF	151	542	112	158	33	2	*43	101	.292	358	11	6	.984
1957–Brooklyn		Nat.	OF	139	508	91	139	25	7	40	92	.274	304	6	3	.990
1958–Los Angeles		Nat.	OF	106	327	45	102	12	3	15	58	.312	151	4	2	.987
1959–Los Angeles		Nat.	OF	126	370	59	114	11	2	23	88	.308	157	2	4	.975
1960–Los Angeles		Nat.	OF	101	235	38	57	13	5	14	36	.243	108	3	4	.965
1961–Los Angeles		Nat.	OF	85	233	35	69	8	3	16	56	.296	113	6	3	.975
1962–Los Angeles(a)		Nat.	OF	80	158	28	44	11	3	5	30	.278	56	3	2	.967
1963–New York(b)		Nat.	OF	129	354	44	86	8	3	14	45	.243	139	5	2	.986
1964–San Francisco		Nat.	OF	91	167	16	35	7	0	4	17	.210	44	2	1	.979
Major League Totals				2143	7161	1259	2116	358	85	407	1333	.295	4099	123	66	.985

aSold to New York Mets, April 1, 1963.
bReleased to San Francisco Giants, April 14, 1964.

WORLD SERIES RECORD

Year	Club	League	Pos.	G.	AB.	R.	H.	2B.	3B.	HR.	RBI.	B.A.	PO.	A.	E.	F.A.
1949–Brooklyn		Nat.	OF	5	21	2	3	1	0	0	0	.143	18	1	0	1.000
1952–Brooklyn		Nat.	OF	7	29	5	10	2	0	4	8	.345	23	0	0	1.000
1953–Brooklyn		Nat.	OF	6	25	3	8	3	0	1	5	.320	17	1	0	1.000
1955–Brooklyn		Nat.	OF	7	25	5	8	1	0	4	7	.320	13	0	0	1.000
1956–Brooklyn		Nat.	OF	7	23	5	7	1	0	1	4	.304	20	0	0	1.000
1959–Los Angeles		Nat.	OF	4	10	1	2	0	0	1	2	.200	5	0	2	.714
World Series Totals				36	133	21	38	8	0	11	26	.286	96	2	2	.980

WARREN EDWARD SPAHN

Born April 23, 1921, at Buffalo, N. Y.
Height, 6.00. Weight, 183.
Threw and batted lefthanded.
Married Lorene Southard, August 10, 1946.

Established following major league records: Most seasons, 20 or more wins by a lefthanded pitcher, 13; most years leading in games won, 8; most consecutive years leading league in complete games, 7; most games won by lefthanded pitcher, lifetime, 363; most strikeouts by lefthanded pitcher, lifetime, 2583; most consecutive years, 100 or more strikeouts, 17.

Established following National League records: Most shutout games by lefthanded pitcher, lifetime, 63; most games started, lifetime, 665; most seasons, 100 or more strikeouts, 17; most seasons pitched, one club, 20; most games pitched, lifetime, 750.

Led National League in complete games with 25 in 1949, 26 in 1951, 18 in 1957, 23 in 1958, 21 in 1959, 18 in 1960, 21 in 1961, 22 in 1962 and 22 in 1963; led in shutouts with 7 in 1947, 7 in 1951, tied with 4 in 1959 and tied with 4 in 1961.

Pitched 4-0 no-hit victory against Philadelphia Phillies, September 16, 1960, and 1-0 no-hit victory against San Francisco Giants, April 28, 1961.

Named Outstanding National League pitcher by THE SPORTING NEWS, 1953-57-58-61.
Named as pitcher on THE SPORTING NEWS National League All-Star Team, 1961.
Named as pitcher on THE SPORTING NEWS All-Star Major League Teams, 1953-57-58-60.
Cy Young Memorial Award winner for outstanding major league pitcher, 1957.
Player-coach, New York Mets, 1965; manager, Tulsa, Pacific Coast League, 1967 and 1968 and American Association, 1969-70; scout, St. Louis Cardinals, National League, and pitching instructor, minor leagues, St. Louis, 1971; coach, Cleveland Indians, American League, 1972-73; pitching instructor, minor leagues, California Angels, American League, 1978 to date.
Named to Hall of Fame, 1973.

Year	Club	League	G.	IP.	W.	L.	Pct.	H.	R.	ER.	SO.	BB.	ERA.
1940–Bradford		Pony	12	66	5	4	.556	53	27	20	62	24	2.73
1941–Evansville		I.I.I.	28	212	*19	6	*.760	154	62	43	193	90	*1.83
1942–Hartford		Eastern	33	248	17	12	.586	148	65	54	141	130	1.96
1942–Boston		Nat.	4	16	0	0	.000	25	15	10	7	11	5.63
1943-44-45–Boston		Nat.	(In Military Service)										
1946–Boston		Nat.	24	126	8	5	.615	107	46	41	67	36	2.93
1947–Boston		Nat.	40	*290	21	10	.677	245	87	75	123	84	*2.33
1948–Boston		Nat.	36	257	15	12	.556	237	115	106	114	77	3.71

Year	Club	League	G.	IP.	W.	L.	Pct.	H.	R.	ER.	SO.	BB.	ERA.
1949	Boston	Nat.	38	*302	*21	14	.600	283	125	103	*151	86	3.07
1950	Boston	Nat.	41	293	*21	17	.553	248	123	103	*191	111	3.16
1951	Boston	Nat.	39	311	22	14	.611	278	111	103	•164	*109	2.98
1952	Boston	Nat.	40	290	14	19	.424	263	109	96	*183	73	2.98
1953	Milwaukee	Nat.	35	266	•23	7	.767	211	75	62	148	70	*2.10
1954	Milwaukee	Nat.	39	283	21	12	.636	262	107	99	136	86	3.15
1955	Milwaukee	Nat.	39	246	17	14	.548	249	99	89	110	65	3.26
1956	Milwaukee	Nat.	39	281	20	11	.645	249	92	87	128	52	2.79
1957	Milwaukee	Nat.	39	271	*21	11	.656	241	94	81	111	78	2.69
1958	Milwaukee	Nat.	38	*290	*22	11	•.667	257	106	99	150	76	3.07
1959	Milwaukee	Nat.	40	*292	•21	15	.583	282	106	96	143	70	2.96
1960	Milwaukee	Nat.	40	268	•21	10	.677	254	114	104	154	74	3.49
1961	Milwaukee	Nat.	38	263	•21	13	.618	236	96	88	115	64	*3.01
1962	Milwaukee	Nat.	34	269	18	14	.563	248	97	91	118	55	3.04
1963	Milwaukee	Nat.	33	260	23	7	.767	241	85	75	102	49	2.60
1964	Milwaukee(a)	Nat.	38	174	6	13	.316	204	110	102	78	52	5.28
1965	N.Y.(b)-San Fran.	Nat.	36	198	7	16	.304	210	104	88	90	56	4.00
1966	Mexico City Tigers	Mex.	3	10	1	1	.500	14	7	5	7	1	4.50
1967	Tulsa	P. C.	3	7	0	1	.000	8	6	5	5	5	6.43
	Major League Totals		750	5246	363	245	.597	4830	2016	1798	2583	1434	3.08

aSold to New York Mets, November 23, 1964.
bReleased by New York Mets, July 19, 1965, and signed by San Francisco Giants, July 22, 1965.

WORLD SERIES RECORD

Year	Club	League	G.	IP.	W.	L.	Pct.	H.	R.	ER.	SO.	BB.	ERA.
1948	Boston	Nat.	3	12	1	1	.500	10	4	4	12	3	3.00
1957	Milwaukee	Nat.	2	15⅓	1	1	.500	18	8	8	2	2	4.70
1958	Milwaukee	Nat.	3	28⅔	2	1	.667	19	7	7	18	8	1.88
	World Series Totals		8	56	4	3	.571	47	19	19	32	13	2.89

ALBERT GOODWILL SPALDING

Born September 2, 1850, at Byron, Ill.
Died September 9, 1915, at Point Loma, Calif.
Height, 6.01. Weight, 170.
Threw and batted righthanded.

Game's first 20-game winner. Pitched all games played by Boston in 1871 and 1874. Won 24 consecutive games, 1875. Pitched first one-hit game, June 27, 1871.
Manager, Chicago N. L., 1876-1878; owner, Chicago N. L., 1882-1891. Founder, A. G. Spalding & Bros., 1876. Named to Hall of Fame, 1939.

Year	Club	League	Pos.	G.	W.	L.	Pct.	ShO.	B.A.	F.A.
1866	Forest City of Rockford	Ind.		.....	.....	.....	.....	.....	.....	.....
1867	Forest City of Rockford	Ind.		.....	.....	.....	.....	.....	.....	.....
1868	Forest City of Rockford	Ind.	P	15	.....	.....	.....	.....	.....	.....
1869	Forest City of Rockford	Ind.	P	24	.....	.....	.....	.....	.....	.....
1870	Forest City of Rockford	Ind.	P	55	.....	.....	.....	.....	.....	.....
1871	Boston	N. Assn.	P	31	20	10	.667	1	.265	.....
1872	Boston	N. Assn.	P	47	36	8	.818	3	.339	.903
1873	Boston	N. Assn.	P	60	41	15	.732	1	.340	.941
1874	Boston	N. Assn.	P	71	52	18	.743	4	.331	.845
1875	Boston	N. Assn.	P	74	56	4	.933	9	.318	.764
1876	Chicago	Nat.	P-OF	66	*47	13	*.783	9	.305	.841
1877	Chicago(a)	Nat.	P-1B-2B	*60	0	0	.000	0	.256	.953
	Major League Totals			126	47	13	.783	27	.....	.....

aIn 1877, Spalding pitched in only 4 games.

TRISTRAM (SPOKE and GRAY EAGLE) SPEAKER

Born April 4, 1888, at Hubbard City, Tex.
Died December 8, 1958, at Lake Whitney, Tex.
Height, 5.11½. Weight, 193.
Threw and batted lefthanded.

Played 100 or more games 19 consecutive years; connected for most two-base hits, American League, 793; made 35 assists (league record) as outfielder, 1909 and 1912; made two unassisted double plays, season, April 18 and 29, 1918; made 11 hits in succession, July 8, 9, 10, 1920. Holds American League outfield records for most putouts, lifetime, 6,706; assists, 449 (also major league record); chances accepted, 7,195. Named Most Valuable Player, American League, 1912. Led A. L. outfielders in double plays, 1925.(tie).

Manager, Cleveland Indians, July 20, 1919 until December 2, 1926; manager, Newark, International League, 1929, until June 26, 1930.

Named to Hall of Fame, 1937.

Year	Club	League	Pos.	G.	AB.	R.	H.	2B.	3B.	HR.	RBI.	B.A.	PO.	A.	E.	F.A.
1906	Cleburne	No. Tex.	OF	84	287	35	77	....	....	....	....	.268	100	43	3	.979
1907	Houston	Texas	OF	118	468	70	147	....	....	....	....	*.314	189	29	12	.948
1907	Boston	Amer.	OF	7	20	0	3	0	0	0	0	.150	4	2	0	1.000
1908	Little Rock	South.	OF	127	471	*81	*165	19	10	3	....	*.350	*330	*37	13	.966
1908	Boston	Amer.	OF	31	116	12	26	2	2	0	10	.224	58	9	0	1.000
1909	Boston	Amer.	OF	143	544	73	168	26	13	7	79	.309	*319	*35	10	.973
1910	Boston	Amer.	OF	141	538	92	183	20	14	7	62	.340	*337	20	16	.957
1911	Boston	Amer.	OF	141	500	88	167	34	13	8	80	.334	297	26	15	.956
1912	Boston	Amer.	OF	153	580	136	222	*53	12	10	98	.383	*372	*35	18	.958
1913	Boston	Amer.	OF	141	520	94	190	35	22	3	81	.365	*374	*30	•24	.944
1914	Boston	Amer.	OF	•158	571	100	*193	*46	18	4	86	.338	*425	•30	15	.968
1915	Boston(a)	Amer.	OF	150	547	108	176	25	12	0	63	.322	*378	21	10	.976
1916	Cleveland	Amer.	OF	151	546	102	*211	•41	8	2	83	*.386	359	25	10	.975
1917	Cleveland	Amer.	OF	142	523	90	184	42	11	2	65	.352	365	23	8	.980
1918	Cleveland	Amer.	OF	127	471	73	150	*33	11	0	61	.318	*352	15	10	.973
1919	Cleveland	Amer.	OF	134	494	83	146	38	12	2	69	.296	*375	25	7	.983
1920	Cleveland	Amer.	OF	150	552	137	214	*50	11	8	107	.388	363	24	9	.977
1921	Cleveland	Amer.	OF	132	506	107	183	*52	14	3	74	.362	345	15	6	*.984
1922	Cleveland	Amer.	OF	131	426	85	161	*48	8	11	71	.378	285	13	5	*.983
1923	Cleveland	Amer.	OF	150	574	133	218	*59	11	17	•130	.380	369	26	13	.968
1924	Cleveland	Amer.	OF	136	486	94	167	36	9	9	65	.344	323	20	13	.963
1925	Cleveland	Amer.	OF	117	429	79	167	35	5	12	87	.389	311	16	11	.967
1926	Cleveland(b)	Amer.	OF	150	539	96	164	52	8	7	86	.304	394	20	8	.981
1927	Wash.(c)(d)	Amer.	OF-1B	141	523	71	171	43	6	2	73	.327	423	24	12	.974
1928	Philadelphia	Amer.	OF	64	191	28	51	23	2	3	32	.267	111	8	3	.975
1929	Newark	Int.	OF	48	138	36	49	11	1	5	20	.355	57	2	0	1.000
1930	Newark	Int.	OF	11	31	3	13	1	1	0	3	.419	10	1	1	.917
Major League Totals				2790	10196	1881	3515	793	222	117	1562	.345	6939	462	223	.971

aTraded to Cleveland for pitcher Sam Jones, infielder Fred Thomas and $50,000, April 12, 1916.
bResigned as manager of Cleveland, December 2, 1926.
cUnconditionally released by Washington and signed with Philadelphia, February 5, 1928.
dPlayed 17 games at first base (G—17, PO—145, A—12, E—2).

WORLD SERIES RECORD

Year	Club	League	Pos.	G.	AB.	R.	H.	2B.	3B.	HR.	RBI.	B.A.	PO.	A.	E.	F.A.
1912	Boston	Amer.	OF	8	30	4	9	1	2	0	2	.300	21	2	2	.920
1915	Boston	Amer.	OF	5	17	2	5	0	1	0	0	.294	10	0	0	1.000
1920	Cleveland	Amer.	OF	7	25	6	8	2	1	0	1	.320	18	0	0	1.000
World Series Totals				20	72	12	22	3	4	0	3	.306	49	2	2	.962

CHARLES SYLVESTER (CHICK) STAHL

Born January 10, 1873, at Fort Wayne, Ind.
Died March 28, 1907, at West Baden Springs, Ind.
Threw and batted lefthanded.

Hit six singles in six times at bat, May 31, 1899.
Manager, Boston, American League, 1906, following resignation of James Collins.

Year	Club	League	Pos.	G.	AB.	R.	H.	2B.	3B.	HR.	SB.	B.A.	PO.	A.	E.	F.A.
1894	Battle Creek	Mich.					(No record available)									
1895	Battle Creek	Mich.					(No record available)									
1896	Buffalo(a)	East.	OF	122	519	*129	175	...	...	...	34	.337	199	25	15	.937
1897	Boston	Nat.	OF	111	471	111	168	26	12	3	14	.359	169	18	13	.935
1898	Boston	Nat.	OF	125	469	69	146	19	7	3	5	.311	200	15	9	.960
1899	Boston	Nat.	OF	148	578	123	201	22	17	8	24	.348	253	27	9	.969
1900	Boston	Nat.	OF	134	552	88	162	24	16	5	25	.293	227	22	13	.950
1901	Boston	Amer.	OF	130	512	106	159	22	16	6	29	.311	273	12	12	*.960
1902	Boston	Amer.	OF	127	507	92	161	25	10	2	18	.318	246	18	11	.960
1903	Boston	Amer.	OF	78	298	60	83	11	6	2	14	.279	126	12	5	.965
1904	Boston	Amer.	OF	157	583	84	173	27	*22	3	13	.297	287	7	10	.967

Year	Club	League	Pos.	G.	AB.	R.	H.	2B.	3B.	HR.	SB.	B.A.	PO.	A.	E.	F.A.
1905–Boston		Amer.	OF	134	500	61	129	18	4	0	18	.258	249	11	6	.977
1906–Boston		Amer.	OF	155	595	62	170	24	6	4	13	.286	*344	24	•15	.961
American League Totals				781	2995	465	875	127	64	17	105	.292	1525	84	59	.965
National League Totals				518	2067	391	677	91	52	19	68	.328	849	82	44	.955
Major League Totals				1299	5062	856	1552	218	116	36	173	.307	2374	166	103	.961

aDrafted by Boston in winter of 1896.

WORLD SERIES RECORD

Year	Club	League	Pos.	G.	AB.	R.	H.	2B.	3B.	HR.	SB.	B.A.	PO.	A.	E.	F.A.
1903–Boston		Amer.	OF	8	33	6	10	1	3	0	2	.303	14	1	0	1.000

CHARLES DILLON (CASEY) STENGEL

Born July 30, 1889, at Kansas City, Mo.
Died September 29, 1975, at Glendale, Calif.
Height, 5.10. Weight, 175.
Threw and batted lefthanded.
Married Edna Lawson, August 16, 1924.

In first major league game on September 17, 1912, vs. Pittsburgh, had four singles and one base on balls.
In 1923 World Series, hit two home runs to win as many games, October 10-12.
President-Manager, Worcester, Eastern League, 1925; manager, Toledo, American Association, 1926-31; coach, Brooklyn Dodgers, 1932-33, until named manager, 1934-36; manager, Boston Braves, 1938-43; manager, Milwaukee, American Association, 1944; manager, Kansas City, American Association, 1945; manager, Oakland, Pacific Coast League, 1946-48; manager, New York Yankees, 1949-60; manager, New York Mets, 1962-65; until named executive scout, April 14, 1966, to date of death.
World Series manager, New York Yankees, 1949-50-51-52-53-55-56-57-58-60.
Named by THE SPORTING NEWS as Minor League Manager of the Year, 1948, and Major League Manager of the Year, 1949-53-58.
Named to Hall of Fame, 1966.

Year	Club	League	Pos.	G.	AB.	R.	H.	2B.	3B.	HR.	RBI.	B.A.	PO.	A.	E.	F.A.
1910–Kankakee		No. Assn.					(League disbanded in July)									
1910–Maysville		Bl.Grass	OF	69	233	27	52	10	5	2	....	.223	143	11	2	.987
1911–Aurora		Wis.-Ill.	OF	121	420	76	*148	23	6	4	....	.352	229	27	8	.970
1912–Montgomery		South.	OF	136	479	85	139	....	....	....	....	.290	295	16	•11	.966
1912–Brooklyn		Nat.	OF	17	57	9	18	1	0	1	12	.316	36	1	4	.902
1913–Brooklyn		Nat.	OF	124	438	60	119	16	8	7	44	.272	270	16	12	.960
1914–Brooklyn		Nat.	OF	126	412	55	130	13	10	4	56	.316	173	15	7	.964
1915–Brooklyn		Nat.	OF	132	459	52	109	20	12	3	43	.237	220	13	10	.959
1916–Brooklyn		Nat.	OF	127	462	66	129	27	8	8	53	.279	206	14	8	.965
1917–Brooklyn(a)		Nat.	OF	150	549	69	141	23	12	6	69	.257	256	*30	9	.969
1918–Pittsburgh		Nat.	OF	39	122	18	30	4	1	1	13	.246	64	7	2	.973
1919–Pittsburgh(b)		Nat.	OF	89	321	38	94	10	10	4	40	.293	195	7	9	.957
1920–Philadelphia		Nat.	OF	129	445	53	130	25	6	9	50	.292	212	16	11	.954
1921–Phila(c)-N.Y.		Nat.	OF	42	81	11	23	4	1	0	6	.284	33	5	2	.950
1922–New York		Nat.	OF	84	250	48	92	8	10	7	48	.368	179	7	6	.969
1923–New York(d)		Nat.	OF	75	218	39	74	11	5	5	43	.339	115	4	2	.983
1924–Boston		Nat.	OF	131	461	57	129	20	6	5	39	.280	211	12	5	.978
1925–Boston		Nat.	OF	12	13	0	1	0	0	0	2	.077	1	0	0	1.000
1925–Worcester		East.	OF	100	334	73	107	27	2	10	....	.320	175	6	6	.968
1926–Toledo		A.A.	OF	88	201	40	66	14	2	0	27	.328	78	4	1	.988
1927–Toledo		A.A.	OF	18	17	3	3	0	0	1	3	.176	4	0	0	1.000
1928–Toledo		A.A.	OF	26	32	5	14	5	0	0	12	.438	16	0	0	1.000
1929–Toledo		A.A.	OF	20	31	2	7	1	0	0	9	.226	7	0	0	1.000
1931–Toledo		A.A.	OF	2	8	1	3	2	0	0	0	.375	3	1	0	1.000
Major League Totals				1277	4288	575	1219	182	89	60	518	.284	2171	147	87	.964

aTraded with second baseman George Cutshaw to Pittsburgh for infielder Charles (Chuck) Ward and pitchers Burleigh Grimes and Al Mamaux, January 9, 1918.
bTraded to Philadelphia Phillies for outfielder George Whitted, August, 1919; refused to report to Phillies for remainder of season in salary dispute.
cTraded to New York Giants for players valued at $75,000 July, 1921.
dTraded with shortstop Dave Bancroft and outfielder William Cunningham to Boston Braves for outfielder Billy Southworth and pitcher Joe Oeschger, November, 1923.

WORLD SERIES RECORD

Year	Club	League	Pos.	G.	AB.	R.	H.	2B.	3B.	HR.	RBI.	B.A.	PO.	A.	E.	F.A.
1916–Brooklyn		Nat.	OF	4	11	2	4	0	)	0	0	.364	3	1	1	.800
1922–New York		Nat.	OF	2	5	0	2	0	0	0	0	.400	4	0	0	1.000
1923–New York		Nat.	OF	6	12	3	5	0	0	2	4	.417	11	0	0	1.000
World Series Totals				12	28	5	11	0	0	2	4	.393	18	1	1	.950

VERNON DECATUR (JUNIOR) STEPHENS

Born October 23, 1920, at McAllister, N. Mex.
Died November 4, 1968, at Long Beach, Calif.
Height, 5.10. Weight, 190.
Threw and batted righthanded.
Married Bernice Hood, November 8, 1940.

Led American League shortstops in double plays, 1949; tied major league record for participating in most double plays by shortstops, game (5), May 5, 1948; tied American League record for having ten assists at third base, May 23, 1951 (mark now 11 by many); tied A. L. mark for third basemen for most double plays started, game (3), June 26, 1951 (now 4 by many); tied major league record by making two long hits in an inning (home run and double), vs. Chicago White Sox, July 26, 1949.

Year	Club	League	Pos.	G.	AB.	R.	H.	2B.	3B.	HR.	RBI.	B.A.	PO.	A.	E.	F.A.
1938	Springfield	I.I.I.	2B-SS	2	5	0	0	0	0	0	0	.000	3	2	1	.833
1938	Johnstown	Mid.-Atl.	SS	40	136	23	35	15	0	2	13	.257	67	109	12	.936
1939	Mayfield	Kitty	SS	122	485	105	175	*44	7	30	*123	*.361	184	390	48	.923
1940	San Antonio	Tex.	SS	159	598	60	159	27	6	22	*97	.266	300	514	64	.927
1941	Toledo	A.A.	SS	153	*616	95	173	33	11	14	74	.281	268	*453	44	.942
1941	St. Louis	Amer.	SS	3	2	0	1	0	0	0	0	.500	0	1	1	.500
1942	St. Louis	Amer.	SS	145	575	84	169	26	6	14	92	.294	290	415	*42	.944
1943	St. Louis	Amer.	SS-OF	137	512	75	148	27	3	22	91	.289	240	342	34	.945
1944	St. Louis	Amer.	SS	145	559	91	164	32	1	20	•109	.293	239	480	35	.954
1945	St. Louis	Amer.	*SS-3B	149	571	90	165	27	3	*24	89	.289	258	450	30	*.959
1946	St. Louis	Amer.	SS	115	450	67	138	19	4	14	64	.307	224	343	30	.950
1947	St. Louis(a)	Amer.	SS	150	562	74	157	18	4	15	83	.279	283	*494	24	.970
1948	Boston	Amer.	SS	•155	635	114	171	25	8	29	137	.269	269	*540	*24	.971
1949	Boston	Amer.	SS	•155	610	113	177	31	2	39	•159	.290	257	*508	27	.966
1950	Boston	Amer.	SS	149	628	125	185	34	6	30	•144	.295	258	431	13	.981
1951	Boston	Amer.	3B-SS	109	377	62	113	21	2	17	78	.300	105	209	7	.978
1952	Boston(b)	Amer.	SS-3B	92	295	35	75	13	2	7	44	.254	110	227	16	.955
1953	Chi.(c)-St.L	Amer.	3B-SS	90	294	30	77	14	0	5	31	.262	84	162	8	.969
1954	Baltimore	Amer.	3B	101	365	31	104	17	1	8	46	.285	102	186	10	.966
1955	Balt.(d)-Chi.	Amer.	3B	25	62	10	15	3	0	3	7	.242	13	39	0	1.000
1955	Seattle	P.C.	3B	52	160	22	54	9	0	7	36	.338	30	105	5	.964
1956	Seattle	P.C.	3B-1B	73	188	19	50	9	0	6	27	.266	107	52	3	.981
	Major League Totals			1720	6497	1001	1859	307	42	247	1174	.286	2732	4827	301	.962

aTraded to Boston Red Sox with pitcher Jack Kramer for catcher Roy Partee, infielder Ed Pellagrini, outfielder Pete Layden, pitchers Jim Wilson, Al Widmar and Joe Ostrowski and catcher Don Palmer and $310,000, November 17, 1947.

bTraded to Chicago White Sox for pitchers Hector (Skinny) Brown, Marvin Grissom and Bill Kennedy, February 9, 1953.

cReleased to St. Louis Browns on waivers, July 30, 1953.

dUnconditionally released by Baltimore Orioles, April 18, 1955, signed with Chicago White Sox, May 2, 1955.

WORLD SERIES RECORD

Year	Club	League	Pos.	G.	AB.	R.	H.	2B.	3B.	HR.	RBI.	B.A.	PO.	A.	E.	F.A.
1944	St. Louis	Amer.	SS	6	22	2	5	1	0	0	0	.227	9	19	3	.903

JACKSON RIGGS (OLD HOSS) STEPHENSON

Born January 5, 1898, at Akron, Ala.
Height, 5.10. Weight, 185.
Threw and batted righthanded.
Married Alma Chadwich, January 10, 1934.

Manager, Birmingham, Southern Association, 1936-37; manager, Helena, Cotton States League, 1938; manager, Montgomery, Southeastern League, 1939.

Year	Club	League	Pos.	G.	AB.	R.	H.	2B.	3B.	HR.	RBI.	B.A.	PO.	A.	E.	F.A.
1921	Cleveland	Amer.	2B	65	206	45	68	17	2	2	34	.330	122	153	17	.942
1922	Cleveland	Amer.	2B-3B	86	233	47	79	24	5	2	32	.339	75	136	11	.950
1923	Cleveland	Amer.	2B	91	301	48	96	20	6	5	65	.319	205	214	13	.970
1924	Cleveland	Amer.	2B	71	240	33	89	20	0	4	44	.371	114	179	12	.961

Year	Club	League	Pos.	G.	AB.	R.	H.	2B.	3B.	HR.	RBI.	B.A.	PO.	A.	E.	F.A.
1925–Cleveland (a)		Amer.	OF	19	54	8	16	3	1	1	9	.296	33	2	2	.946
1925–Kansas City-Ind.		A.A.	OF	118	456	97	148	34	10	8	89	.325	217	14	4	.988
1926–Indianapolis (b)		A.A.	OF	51	195	34	75	12	4	4	40	.385	110	2	1	.991
1926–Chicago		Nat.	OF	82	281	40	95	18	3	3	44	.338	126	7	7	.950
1927–Chicago		Nat.	OF	152	579	101	199	*46	9	7	82	.344	297	18	8	.975
1928–Chicago		Nat.	OF	137	512	75	166	36	9	8	90	.324	268	10	5	.982
1929–Chicago		Nat.	OF	136	495	91	179	36	6	17	110	.362	245	9	4	.984
1930–Chicago		Nat.	OF	109	341	56	125	21	1	5	68	.367	132	5	6	.958
1931–Chicago		Nat.	OF	80	263	34	84	14	4	1	52	.319	134	1	2	.985
1932–Chicago		Nat.	OF	147	583	86	189	49	4	4	85	.324	298	7	5	.984
1933–Chicago		Nat.	OF	97	346	45	114	17	4	4	51	.329	187	5	3	.985
1934–Chicago		Nat.	OF	38	74	5	16	0	0	0	7	.216	26	3	0	1.000
1935–Indianapolis		A.A.	OF	147	545	107	187	33	5	4	107	.343	289	10	3	.990
1936–Birmingham		South.	OF	120	439	68	156	26	7	3	64	.355	218	13	7	.971
1937–Birmingham		South	OF	59	198	25	49	8	2	1	31	.247	98	2	2	.986
1938–Helena		Cot. St.	OF	58	175	29	52	12	1	0	28	.297	87	2	2	.978
1939–Montgomery		S. East.					(Less than ten games)									
American League Totals				332	1034	181	348	84	14	14	184	.337	549	684	55	.957
National League Totals				978	3474	533	1167	237	40	49	589	.336	1713	65	40	.978
Major League Totals				1310	4508	714	1515	321	54	63	773	.336	2262	749	95	.969

aOptioned to Kansas City, May 3, 1925, and then traded to Indianapolis, August 13, 1925.

bTraded with infielder Henry Schreiber to Chicago Cubs for outfielder Joseph M. Munson, infielder Maurice Shannon and cash, June 7, 1926.

WORLD SERIES RECORD

Year	Club	League	Pos.	G.	AB.	R.	H.	2B.	3B.	HR.	RBI.	B.A.	PO.	A.	E.	F.A.
1929–Chicago		Nat.	OF	5	19	3	6	1	0	0	3	.316	13	1	0	1.000
1932–Chicago		Nat.	OF	4	18	2	8	1	0	0	4	.444	4	0	0	1.000
World Series Totals				9	37	5	14	2	0	0	7	.378	17	1	0	1.000

JOHN CONRAD (JACK) STIVETTS

Born April 15, 1866, at Ashland, Pa.
Died April 18, 1930, at Ashland, Pa.
Height, 5.11½. Weight, 204.
Threw and batted righthanded.

Pitched 11-0 no-hit game against Brooklyn, August 6, 1892.

Year	Club	League	G.	IP.	W.	L.	Pct.	H.	R.	SO.	BB.	ShO.	CG.
1889–St. Louis		Amer. Assn.	25	190	12	7	.632	148	85	136	64	2	19
1890–St. Louis		Amer. Assn.	49	422	29	20	.592	291	248	187	180	2	42
1891–St. Louis		Amer. Assn.	*66	437	33	22	.600	307	197	*232	192	4	40
1892–Boston		National	47	405	33	14	.702	349	221	166	160	3	45
1893–Boston		National	33	297	19	13	.594	320	196	57	113	1	29
1894–Boston		National	41	348	28	13	.683	438	289	73	100	0	31
1895–Boston		National	34	292	17	17	.500	341	220	102	92	0	30
1896–Boston		National	39	331	22	13	.629	358	223	64	90	2	31
1897–Boston		National	16	133	12	5	.750	146	74	27	41	1	10
1898–Boston		National	1	12	0	1	.000	15	12	1	7	0	1
1899–Cleveland		National	6	44	0	4	.000	63	44	4	22	0	3
American Association Totals			140	1049	74	49	.602	746	530	555	436	8	101
National League Totals			217	1862	131	79	.624	2030	1279	494	625	7	180
Major League Totals			357	2911	205	128	.616	2776	1809	1049	1061	15	281

BATTING RECORD

Year	Club	League	Pos.	G.	AB.	R.	H.	2B.	3B.	HR.	SB.	B.A.
1889–St. Louis		Amer. Assn.	OF-P	26	79	10	18	3	2	0	0	.228
1980–St. Louis		Amer. Assn.	OF-1B-P	67	227	35	63	13	6	7	15	.278
1891–St. Louis		Amer. Assn.	OF-P	76	280	42	85	10	2	7	2	.304
1892–Boston		National	OF-1B-P	65	239	40	72	11	3	3	8	.301
1893–Boston		National	OF-3B-P	41	165	31	51	5	6	3	1	.309
1894–Boston		National	OF-1B-P	57	244	56	82	13	7	8	4	.336
1895–Boston		National	OF-1B-P	38	152	20	32	7	3	0	2	.211
1896–Boston		National	OF-1B-3B-P	59	221	44	78	9	4	3	5	.353
1897–Boston		National	OF-1B-2B-P	49	196	43	76	9	9	3	2	.388
1898–Boston		National	OF-INF-P	27	111	16	28	1	1	0	2	.252
1899–Cleveland		National	OF-3B-SS-P	18	41	8	7	1	0	0	0	.171
American Association Totals				169	586	87	166	26	10	14	17	.283
National League Totals				354	1369	258	426	56	33	21	22	.311
Major League Totals				523	1955	345	592	82	43	35	39	.303

JONATHAN THOMAS STONE

Born October 10, 1905, at Mulberry, Tenn.
Died November 30, 1955, at Shelbyville, Tenn.
Height, 6.00. Weight, 180.
Threw right and batted lefthanded.

Hit four singles, two doubles, two triples in ten at-bats in doubleheader vs. St. Louis, June 16, 1935; batted safely in 34 consecutive games, July 5 through August 9, 1930.

Year	Club	League	Pos.	G.	AB.	R.	H.	2B.	3B.	HR.	RBI.	B.A.	PO.	A.	E.	F.A.
1928	Evansville	I.I.I.	OF	75	297	49	105	11	9	5	43	.354	166	2	7	.960
1928	Detroit	Amer.	OF	26	113	20	40	10	3	2	21	.354	49	2	2	.962
1929	Toronto	Int.	OF	79	295	53	97	19	8	12	56	.329	134	6	7	.952
1929	Detroit	Amer.	OF	51	150	23	39	11	2	2	15	.260	68	4	1	.986
1930	Detroit	Amer.	OF	126	422	60	132	29	11	3	56	.313	222	5	8	.966
1931	Detroit	Amer.	OF	147	584	86	191	28	11	10	76	.327	319	11	14	.959
1932	Detroit	Amer.	OF	145	582	106	173	35	12	17	108	.297	334	11	14	.961
1933	Detroit(a)	Amer.	OF	148	574	86	161	33	11	11	80	.280	280	11	9	.970
1934	Washington	Amer.	OF	113	419	77	132	28	7	7	67	.315	245	13	9	.966
1935	Washington	Amer.	OF	125	454	78	143	27	18	1	78	.315	224	12	11	.955
1936	Washington	Amer.	OF	123	437	95	149	22	11	15	90	.341	249	12	9	.967
1937	Washington	Amer.	OF	139	542	84	179	33	15	6	88	.330	300	15	5	.984
1938	Washington	Amer.	OF	56	213	24	52	12	4	3	28	.244	107	5	3	.974
Major League Totals				1199	4490	739	1391	268	105	77	707	.310	2397	101	85	.967

aTraded to Washington for outfielder Leon (Goose) Goslin, December 13, 1933.

HARRY DUFFIELD STOVEY
(Family name, Stowe.)

Born December 28, 1856, at Philadelphia, Pa.
Died September 20, 1937, at New Bedford, Mass.
Height, 6.00. Weight, 186.
Threw and batted righthanded.

First player in major league history to hit 100 home runs.
Established major league record for most stolen bases in a season (156), 1888; made three triples in a game (including two in one inning), August 18, 1884, and again hit three triples in a game, July 21, 1892.

Year	Club	League	Pos.	G.	AB.	R.	H.	2B.	3B.	HR.	SB.	B.A.	PO.	A.	E.	F.A.
1876	J. D. Shibe			(Independent club—no records available)												
1877	Athletics			(Independent club—no records available)												
1878	New Bedford			(No records available)												
1879	New Bedford			(No records available)												
1880	Worcester	Nat.	OF-1B	81	345	72	89	18	*14	•6	....	.258	502	18	34	.939
1881	Worcester	Nat.	OF-1B	74	336	55	91	26	6	2	....	.271	583	16	31	.951
1882	Worcester	Nat.	OF-1B	84	360	90	104	13	10	5	....	.289	557	25	47	.925
1883	Athletics	A.A.	O-1-C	94	412	*110	148	*32	8	*14	....	.359	(983-PO-A)	27	*.973	
1884	Athletics	A.A.	1B	106	443	*126	179	25	*25	•11	....	.404	(1116-PO-A)	32		.972
1885	Athletics	A.A.	OF-1B	112	480	*130	164	27	11	*13	....	.342	(965-PO-A)	42		.958
1886	Athletics	A.A.	OF-1B	123	486	115	154	26	13	7	*96	.317	(805-PO-A)	39		.954
1887	Athletics	A.A.	OF-1B	124	545	124	219	29	12	5	*143	.402	(639-PO-A)	32		.952
1888	Athletics	A.A.	OF	130	538	128	171	25	*21	7	*156	.318	(216-PO-A)	10		.956
1889	Athletics	A.A.	OF	138	546	*154	180	37	14	•19	115	.330	291	37	32	.911
1890	Boston	Play.	OF	118	480	140	148	28	11	11	136	.308	192	22	15	.943
1891	Boston	Nat.	OF	133	545	118	152	33	19	•16	52	.279	230	23	27	.904
1892	Boston-Balt.	Nat.	OF	112	285	58	77	20	15	2	20	.270	187	9	19	.912
1893	Balt.-Brook.	Nat.	OF	53	193	47	49	9	6	1	26	.254	129	4	16	.893
Amer. Assn. Totals				827	3450	887	1215	201	104	76	510	.352	(5049-PO-A)	214		.959
National League Totals				537	2064	440	562	119	70	32	98	.272	2188	95	174	.929
Players League Totals				118	480	140	148	28	11	11	136	.308	192	22	13	.943
Major League Totals				1482	5994	1467	1925	348	185	119	744	.321	(7546-PO-A)	401		.950

RICHARD LEE (IRON GLOVE) STUART

Born November 7, 1932, at San Francisco, Calif.
Height, 6.03. Weight, 210.
Threw and batted righthanded.

Hit three home runs in game, June 30, 1960 (second game).
Led American League in total bases with 319.
Named as first baseman on THE SPORTING NEWS American League All-Star Team, 1964.

Year	Club	League	Pos.	G.	AB.	R.	H.	2B.	3B.	HR.	RBI.	B.A.	PO.	A.	E.	F.A.
1951	Modesto	Calif.	OF	66	201	21	46	9	0	4	31	.229	91	7	9	.916
1952	Billings	Pion.	OF	129	515	*115	•161	30	4	*31	*121	.313	192	19	12	.946
1953-54	New Orleans	South.					(In Military Service)									
1955	New Orleans	South.	OF	13	30	4	6	0	0	0	3	.200	8	0	1	.889
1955	Mex. City Tigers	Mex.	OF	7	27	3	4	1	0	1	4	.148	17	2	0	1.000
1955	Billings	Pion.	OF	101	366	84	113	19	5	*32	104	.309	153	10	6	.964
1956	Lincoln	West.	O-1B	*141	523	131	156	25	3	*66	*158	.298	416	23	30	.936
1957	Hollywood	P.C.	OF	23	72	8	17	0	0	6	17	.236	26	3	3	.906
1957	Atlanta	So.	O-3-1B	23	90	18	19	2	0	8	21	.211	58	21	7	.919
1957	Lincoln	West.	1B	97	348	71	92	13	0	31	84	.264	672	47	*21	.972
1958	Salt Lake City	P.C.	1B	80	315	61	98	14	1	31	82	.311	716	65	11	.986
1958	Pittsburgh	Nat.	1B	67	254	38	68	12	5	16	48	.268	529	49	•16	.973
1959	Pittsburgh	Nat.	*1B-OF	118	397	64	118	15	2	27	78	.297	831	81	*22	.976
1960	Pittsburgh	Nat.	1B	122	438	48	114	17	5	23	83	.260	920	77	•14	.986
1961	Pittsburgh	Nat.	*1B-OF	138	532	83	160	28	8	35	117	.301	1152	99	*21	.983
1962	Pittsburgh(a)	Nat.	1B	114	394	52	90	11	4	16	64	.228	868	78	•17	.982
1963	Boston	Amer.	1B	157	612	81	160	25	4	42	*118	.261	*1207	*134	*29	.979
1964	Boston(b)	Amer.	1B	156	603	73	168	27	1	33	114	.279	1159	104	*24	.981
1965	Philadelphia(c)	Nat.	1B-3B	149	538	53	126	19	1	28	95	.234	1119	98	17	.986
1966	N.Y.(d)-L.A.(e)	Nat.	1B	69	178	11	43	1	0	7	22	.242	407	34	8	.982
1967-68							(Played in Japan)									
1969	California	Amer.	1B	22	51	3	8	2	0	1	4	.157	102	4	1	.991
1969	Phoenix	P.C.	1B	74	258	37	63	13	0	12	42	.244	555	69	22	.966
	American League Totals			335	1266	157	336	54	5	76	236	.265	2468	242	54	.980
	National League Totals			777	2731	349	719	103	25	152	507	.263	5726	516	115	.982
	Major League Totals			1112	3997	506	1055	157	30	228	743	.264	8294	758	169	.982

aTraded to Boston Red Sox with pitcher Jack Lamabe for pitcher Don Schwall and catcher Jim Pagliaroni, November 21, 1962.
bTraded to Philadelphia Phillies for pitcher Dennis Bennett, November 29, 1964.
cTraded to New York Mets for catcher Jim Schaffer and infielders Bobby Klaus and Wayne Graham, who were transferred from Jacksonville to San Diego, February 22, 1966.
dReleased by New York Mets, June 20, 1966; signed by Los Angeles Dodgers, July 5, 1966.
eReleased by Los Angeles Dodgers, November 21, 1966; signed by California Angels, April 10, 1969.

WORLD SERIES RECORD

Year	Club	League	Pos.	G.	AB.	R.	H.	2B.	3B.	HR.	RBI.	B.A.	PO.	A.	E.	F.A.
1960	Pittsburgh	Nat.	1B	6	20	1	3	0	0	0	0	.150	45	0	0	1.000

HOMER WAYNE SUMMA

Born November 3, 1899, at Gentry, Mo.
Died January 29, 1966, at Los Angeles, Calif.
Height, 5.10. Weight, 165.
Threw right and batted lefthanded.

Year	Club	League	Pos.	G.	AB.	R.	H.	2B.	3B.	HR.	RBI.	B.A.	PO.	A.	E.	F.A.
1919	Mobile-Birm.	South.A.	OF	113	516	39	99	15	2	1	....	.192	253	20	13	.955
1920	Birmingham	South.A.	OF	16	56	3	9	1	1	0	....	.161	....	....	....	......
1920	Norfolk	Virginia	OF	103	419	64	147	17	3	1	22	*.351	198	21	3	.986
1920	Pittsburgh	Nat.	OF	10	22	1	7	1	1	0	1	.318	18	1	1	.950
1921	Rochester	Int.	OF	166	655	142	218	36	21	13	....	.333	332	26	12	.968
1922	Wichita Falls	Texas	OF	156	621	*131	*225	45	11	8	110	*.362	†191	17	6	.970

Year	Club	League	Pos.	G.	AB.	R.	H.	2B.	3B.	HR.	RBI.	B.A.	PO.	A.	E.	F.A.
1922	Cleveland	Amer.	OF	12	46	9	16	3	3	1	6	.348	14	3	0	1.000
1923	Cleveland	Amer.	OF	137	525	92	172	27	6	3	69	.328	216	15	11	.955
1924	Cleveland	Am.	OF-PH	111	390	55	113	21	6	2	38	.290	167	10	11	.941
1925	Cleveland	Am.	OF-PH	75	224	28	74	10	1	0	25	.330	82	2	3	.965
1926	Cleveland	Amer.	OF	154	581	74	179	31	6	4	76	.308	328	18	9	.975
1927	Cleveland	Amer.	OF	145	574	72	164	41	7	4	74	.286	242	12	12	.955
1928	Cleveland	Amer.	OF	134	504	60	143	26	3	3	57	.284	223	12	7	.971
1929	Philadelphia	Am.	OF-PH	37	81	12	22	4	0	0	10	.272	48	1	1	.980
1930	Philadelphia	Am.	OF-PH	25	54	10	15	2	1	1	5	.278	29	1	2	.938
1930	Portland	P.C.	OF	97	376	52	119	20	1	4	47	.317	195	21	12	.947
1931	Portland	P.C.	OF	187	754	•141	257	40	6	4	89	.341	365	5	17	.956
1932	Los Angeles	P.C.	OF	134	543	88	161	29	7	0	64	.297	250	8	11	.960
1933	Seattle	P.C.	OF	68	288	41	102	16	6	2	33	.354	111	3	7	.942
National League Totals				10	22	1	7	1	1	0	1	.318	18	1	1	.950
American League Totals				830	2979	412	898	165	33	18	360	.301	1349	74	56	.962
Major League Totals				840	3001	413	905	166	34	18	361	.302	1367	75	57	.962

WORLD SERIES RECORD

Year	Club	League	Pos.	G.	AB.	R.	H.	2B.	3B.	HR.	RBI.	B.A.	PO.	A.	E.	F.A.
1929	Philadelphia	Amer.	PH	1	1	0	0	0	0	0	0	.000	0	0	0	.000

†Outfielder's fielding records listed each of the outfield positions; right, center and left, Summa's record does not include his right field games, only his 75 games in center field.

JESSE NILES TANNEHILL

Born July 14, 1874, at Dayton, Ky.
Died September 22, 1956, at Dayton, Ky.
Height, 5.11. Weight, 170.
Threw left and batted righthanded.

Pitched 6-0 no-hit victory against Chicago, August 17, 1904.
Manager, Portsmouth, Virginia League, 1914; Topeka, Southwestern League, 1923.

Year	Club	League	G.	IP.	W.	L.	Pct.	H.	R.	SO.	BB.	CG.	ShO.
1894	Cincinnati	National	5	27	1	1	.500	21	18	6	13	1	0
1895	Richmond	Virginia	29	246	20	7	.741	238	116	132	29	26	4
1896	Richmond	Virginia	41	344	23	17	.575	341	150	159	48	40	6
1897	Pittsburgh	National	21	140	8	8	.500	158	96	33	21	11	1
1898	Pittsburgh	National	43	329	24	14	.632	341	148	92	61	34	5
1899	Pittsburgh	National	41	333	23	14	.622	367	143	64	52	34	3
1900	Pittsburgh	National	29	236	20	7	.741	257	114	50	42	23	2
1901	Pittsburgh	National	32	252	18	10	.643	228	95	118	33	25	4
1902	Pittsburgh(a)	National	27	234	20	6	.769	205	78	100	24	23	2
1903	New York(b)	American	32	241	15	15	.500	240	121	105	56	22	2
1904	Boston	American	33	283	21	11	.656	248	91	117	31	30	4
1905	Boston	American	37	266	22	9	★.710	231	95	94	47	28	6
1906	Boston	American	27	195	13	11	.542	199	92	82	36	18	2
1907	Boston	American	18	130	6	7	.462	134	58	31	21	10	2
1908	Boston(c)-Washington	American	11	77	2	4	.333	81	38	16	26	5	0
1909	Washington	American	3	21	1	1	.500	19	8	8	5	2	1
1910	Minneapolis	Amer. Assn.	8	58	6	2	.750	50	20	11	8	5	2
1911	Cincinnati	National	1	4	0	0	.000	6	7	1	3	0	0
1911	Birm.-Montgomery	Southern	15	....	8	6	.571	....	....	....	....	....	....
1912	South Bend	Central					(Less Than Five Games)						
1912	Chillicothe	Ohio State					(Less Than Ten Games)						
1913	St. Joseph	Western					(Less Than Seven Games)						
American League Totals			161	1213	80	58	.580	1152	503	453	222	115	17
National League Totals			199	1555	114	60	.655	1583	699	464	249	151	17
Major League Totals			360	2768	194	118	.622	2735	1202	917	471	266	34

aJumped to New York A. L. club for 1903.
bTraded to Boston Red Sox for pitcher Thomas Hughes, December, 1903.
cUnconditionally released and signed by Washington, May, 1908.

DID YOU KNOW—
That Fred Tenney was one of 19 lefthanded catchers in major league history?

ANTONIO (TONY) TAYLOR (SANCHEZ)

Born December 19, 1935, at Central Alava, Matanzas, Cuba.
Height, 5:09½. Weight, 179.
Threw and batted righthanded.

Year	Club	League	Pos.	G.	AB.	R.	H.	2B.	3B.	HR.	RBI.	B.A.	PO.	A.	E.	F.A.
1954	Tx.C.-Th'b'd'x	Evng.	3B-SS	131	516	104	162	25	•12	5	49	.314	170	337	60	.894
1955	St. Cloud	North.	3B	125	510	103	136	19	•10	5	46	.267	129	•276	•37	.916
1956	Danville	Carol.	3B	150	544	95	145	28	7	13	60	.267	153	272	30	.934
1957	Dallas (a)	Tex.	3-SS-O	105	368	61	80	11	5	3	31	.217	104	190	17	.945
1958	Chicago	Nat.	2B-3B	140	497	63	117	15	3	6	27	.235	311	374	23	.968
1959	Chicago	Nat.	*2B-SS	150	624	96	175	30	8	8	38	.280	355	*456	*25	.970
1960	Chi. (b)-Phila.	Nat.	2B-3B	146	581	80	165	25	7	5	44	.284	321	411	23	.970
1961	Philadelphia	Nat.	2B-3B	106	400	47	100	17	3	2	26	.250	233	279	10	.981
1962	Philadelphia	Nat.	2B-SS	152	625	87	162	21	5	7	43	.259	372	385	22	.972
1963	Philadelphia	Nat.	*2B-3B	157	640	102	180	20	10	5	49	.281	325	412	10	*.987
1964	Philadelphia	Nat.	2B	154	570	62	143	13	6	4	46	.251	325	358	16	.977
1965	Philadelphia	Nat.	2B-3B	106	323	41	74	14	3	3	27	.229	169	222	17	.958
1966	Philadelphia	Nat.	2B-3B	125	434	47	105	14	8	5	40	.242	187	281	9	.981
1967	Philadelphia	Nat.	1-3-2-S	132	462	55	110	16	6	2	34	.238	524	182	9	.987
1968	Philadelphia	Nat.	3-2-1B	145	547	59	137	20	2	3	38	.250	115	324	16	.965
1969	Philadelphia	Nat.	3-2-1B	138	557	68	146	24	5	3	30	.262	262	294	15	.974
1970	Philadelphia	Nat.	2-3-O-S	124	439	74	132	26	9	9	55	.301	220	215	5	.989
1971	Philadelphia (c)	Nat.	2-3-1	36	107	9	25	2	1	1	5	.234	58	64	1	.992
1971	Detroit	Amer.	2B-3B	55	181	27	52	10	2	3	19	.287	115	109	1	.996
1972	Detroit	Amer.	2-3-1	78	228	33	69	12	4	1	20	.303	130	122	8	.969
1973	Detroit (d)	Amer.	2-1-3-O	84	275	35	63	9	3	5	24	.229	151	168	4	.988
1974	Philadelphia	Nat.	1-3-2	62	64	5	21	4	0	2	13	.328	34	4	0	1.000
1975	Philadelphia	Nat.	3-1-2	79	103	13	25	5	1	1	17	.243	34	35	5	.932
1976	Philadelphia	Nat.	3B-2B	26	23	2	6	1	0	0	3	.261	0	1	0	1.000
American League Totals				217	684	95	184	31	9	9	63	.269	396	399	13	.984
National League Totals				1978	6996	910	1823	267	77	66	535	.260	3845	4297	206	.975
Major League Totals				2195	7680	1005	2007	298	86	75	598	.261	4241	4696	219	.976

aDrafted by Chicago Cubs from New York Giants' organization, December 2, 1957.
bTraded to Philadelphia with catcher Cal Neeman for pitcher Don Cardwell and first baseman Ed Bouchee, May 13, 1960.
cTraded to Detroit Tigers for pitchers Mike Fremuth and Carl Cavanaugh, June 12, 1971.
dSigned as free agent by Philadelphia Phillies, December 19, 1973.

FRED C. TENNEY

Born November 26, 1871, at Georgetown, Mass.
Died July 3, 1952, at Boston, Mass.
Height, 5.10½. Weight, 178.
Threw and batted lefthanded.
Married Bessie Berry, October 21, 1895.

Holds National League record for most assists by first baseman, lifetime (1,365); holds major league record for most years leading league first basemen in assists (8). One of few lefthanded catchers in game. Manager, Boston, National League, 1905 through 1907 and 1911; manager, Newark, International League, 1916 (played 16 games and batted .318; in seven games at first base, fielded 1.000).

Year	Club	League	Pos.	G.	AB.	R.	H.	2B.	3B.	HR.	SB.	B.A.	PO.	A.	E.	F.A.
1894	Boston	Nat.	C	24	80	21	31	7	1	2	7	.388	55	18	11	.969
1895	Boston	Nat.	C-OF	42	174	34	48	8	1	0	6	.276	105	24	4	.970
1896	Boston	Nat.	C-OF	86	345	65	118	13	3	2	18	.342	181	40	16	.932
1897	Boston	Nat.	1B	131	566	125	184	21	3	1	38	.325	1239	79	16	*.988
1898	Boston	Nat.	1B	117	486	107	163	24	6	0	23	.335	1081	65	21	.982
1899	Boston	Nat.	1B	150	597	114	209	22	18	1	24	.350	1476	*95	38	.976
1900	Boston	Nat.	1B	111	437	75	124	12	5	1	16	.284	1030	85	19	.983
1901	Boston	Nat.	1B	113	457	63	127	13	2	1	11	.278	1069	*87	28	.976
1902	Boston	Nat.	1B	134	491	88	154	16	3	2	21	.314	1232	*110	22	.984

Year	Club	League	Pos.	G.	AB.	R.	H.	2B.	3B.	HR.	SB.	B.A.	PO.	A.	E.	F.A.
1903	Boston	Nat.	1B	122	447	79	140	22	3	3	21	.313	1145	*93	33	.974
1904	Boston	Nat.	1B	147	533	76	144	17	9	1	17	.270	1145	*115	22	.986
1905	Boston	Nat.	1B	148	549	84	158	18	3	0	17	.288*1556		*152	*32	.982
1906	Boston	Nat.	1B	143	544	61	154	12	8	1	17	.283	1456	*118	28	.983
1907	Boston(a)	Nat.	1B	149	554	83	151	18	8	0	15	.273*1587		*113	19	.989
1908	New York	Nat.	1B	156	583	*101	149	20	1	2	17	.256*1624		117	18	●.990
1909	New York	Nat.	1B	98	375	43	88	8	2	3	8	.235	1046	72	16	.986
1910	New York	Nat.					(Did not play)									
1910	Lowell	N. Eng.	1B	96	340	48	91	13	3	0	7	.268	950	52	11	.989
1911	Boston	Nat.	1B	98	369	52	97	13	4	1	5	.263	901	64	15	.985
1916	Newark	Int.	1B	16	22	0	7	0	0	0	0	.318	28	3	0	1.000
Major League Totals				1969	7587	1271	2239	264	80	21	281	.295	18228	1447	358	.982

aTraded with shortstop Al Bridwell and catcher Tom Needham to New York Giants for first baseman Dan McGann, catcher Frank Bowerman, shortstop Bill Dahlen, outfielder George Browne and pitcher George Ferguson, December 13, 1907.

WILLIAM HAROLD TERRY

Born October 30, 1898, at Atlanta, Ga.
Height 6.01½. Weight, 200.
Threw and batted lefthanded.
Married Virginia Snead, November, 1916.

Tied with Frank O'Doul (Philadelphia Phillies, 1929) for National League record for most hits, season (254), 1930; hit three home runs in a game, first game, August 13, 1932; hit six home runs in four straight games, April 19-20-21-22, 1932, and five in three consecutive games, April 19-20-21, 1932; played 468 consecutive games, April 15, 1930, through April 25, 1933. Hit eight singles and one home run, in doubleheader against Brooklyn, in ten at-bats, June 18, 1929. Led N.L. first basemen in double plays, 1928, 1929, 1934.
Pitched no-hit game against Anniston, winning 2-0, June 30, 1915.
Named as first baseman on The Sporting News All-Star Major League Team, 1930.
Named by The Sporting News as Most Valuable Player, 1930.
Manager, New York Giants, June 3, 1932 through 1941.
Named to Hall of Fame, 1954.

Year	Club	League	Pos.	G.	AB.	R.	H.	2B.	3B.	HR.	RBI.	B.A.	PO.	A.	E.	F.A.
1915	Newnan	Ga.-Ala.	P	8	....	....	....	....	....	....	....	.....	2	11	0	1.000
1916	Shreveport	Tex.	P	19	29	3	7	3	1	0	....	.241	2	14	3	.842
1917	Shreveport	Tex.	P-OF	95	208	15	48	9	1	4	....	.231	51	61	9	.926
1918-19-20-21	—	.....						(Played semi-pro ball)								
1922	Toledo	A. A.	1B	88	235	41	79	11	4	14	61	.336	417	54	10	.979
1923	Toledo	A. A.	1B	109	427	73	161	22	11	15	82	.377	957	57	7	*.993
1923	New York	Nat.	1B	3	7	1	1	0	0	0	.143	22	1	0	1.000
1924	New York	Nat.	1B	77	163	26	39	7	2	5	24	.239	325	14	4	.988
1925	New York	Nat.	1B	133	489	75	156	31	6	11	70	.319	1270	77	14	●.990
1926	New York	Nat.	1B-OF	98	225	26	65	12	5	5	43	.289	391	31	9	.979
1927	New York	Nat.	1B	150	580	101	189	32	13	20	121	.326	1621	*105	12	.993
1928	New York	Nat.	1B	149	568	100	185	36	11	17	101	.326*1584		78	12	*.993
1929	New York	Nat.	1B	150	607	103	226	39	5	14	117	.372*1575		111	11	.994
1930	New York	Nat.	1B	154	633	139	*254	39	15	23	129	*.401*1538		*128	17	.990
1931	New York	Nat.	1B	153	611	●121	213	43	*20	9	112	.349	1411	*105	16	.990
1932	New York	Nat.	1B	●154	643	124	225	42	11	28	117	.350*1493		*137	14	.991
1933	New York	Nat.	1B	123	475	68	153	20	5	6	58	.322	1246	76	11	.992
1934	New York	Nat.	1B	153	602	109	213	30	6	8	83	.354*1592		105	10	●.994
1935	New York	Nat.	1B	145	596	91	203	32	8	6	64	.341	1379	*99	6	*.996
1936	New York	Nat.	1B	79	229	36	71	10	5	2	39	.310	525	41	2	.996
Major League Totals				1721	6428	1120	2139	373	112	154	1078	.341	15972	1108	138	.992

PITCHING RECORD

Year	Club	League	G.	IP.	W.	L.	Pct.	H.	R.	ER.	SO.	BB.	ERA.
1915	Newnan	Ga.-Ala.	8	....	7	1	.875	....	....	....	....	....	....
1916	Shreveport	Texas	19	84	6	2	.750	50	....	10	39	34	1.07
1917	Shreveport	Texas	40	246	14	11	.560	222	108	82	81	116	3.00
1922	Toledo	Amer. Assn.	26	127	9	9	.500	147	75	60	35	59	4.26

WORLD SERIES RECORD

Year	Club	League	Pos.	G.	AB.	R.	H.	2B.	3B.	HR.	RBI.	B.A.	PO.	A.	E.	F.A.
1924	New York	Nat.	1B	5	14	3	6	0	1	1	1	.429	43	2	0	1.000
1933	New York	Nat.	1B	5	22	3	6	1	0	1	1	.273	50	1	0	1.000
1936	New York	Nat.	1B	6	25	1	6	0	0	0	5	.240	45	8	0	1.000
World Series Totals				16	61	7	18	1	1	2	7	.295	138	11	0	1.000

WILLIAM J. (ADONIS) TERRY

Born August 7, 1864, at Westfield, Mass.
Died February 25, 1914, at Milwaukee, Wis.
Threw and batted righthanded.

Pitched two no-hitters—1-0 over St. Louis, July 24 1886, and 4-0 over Louisville, May 27, 1888.
Also part-time outfielder early in career, 1884, 1885, 1886, 1887 and 1890.

Year	Club	League	G.	W.	L.	Pct.	H.	R.	SO.	BB.	ShO.
1883—Brooklyn		Eastern	....	....	....	....	....	....	....	....	....
1884—Brooklyn		Amer. Assn.	55	19	35	.352	498	312	219	64	2
1885—Brooklyn		Amer. Assn.	24	6	16	.273	207	140	91	48	0
1886—Brooklyn		Amer. Assn.	34	18	15	.545	267	176	....	125	5
1887—Brooklyn		Amer. Assn.	35	17	16	.515	400	209	111	92	1
1888—Brooklyn		Amer. Assn.	24	13	8	.619	153	83	90	111	2
1889—Brooklyn		Amer. Assn.	40	21	16	.568	285	191	173	125	2
1890—Brooklyn		National	44	25	16	.610	....	....	185	127	0
1891—Brooklyn		National	25	7	17	.292	....	....	66	67	1
1892—Balt.-Pitt.		National	32	21	10	.677	....	....	91	87	2
1893—Pittsburgh		National	22	15	6	.714	....	....	49	88	0
1894—Pitt.-Chi.		National	21	6	14	.300	....	....	43	91	0
1895—Chicago		National	37	23	13	.639	....	....	93	133	0
1896—Chicago		National	30	14	15	.483	....	....	73	86	1
1897—Chicago		National	1	0	0	.000	....	....	....	....	0
1897—Milwaukee		Western	27	22	5	.815	....	....	....	....	..
1898—Milwaukee		Western	16	12	1	.923	....	....	....	....	..
American Association Totals			212	94	106	.470	1810	1111	684	565	12
National League Totals			212	111	91	.550	....	....	600	679	4
Major League Totals			424	205	197	.510	....	....	1284	1244	16

FRANK JOSEPH THOMAS

Born June 11, 1929, at Pittsburgh, Pa.
Height, 6.03. Weight, 205.
Threw and batted righthanded.
Married Dolores Wozniak, January 20, 1951.

Tied major league record by hitting six home runs in three consecutive games (two in each game), August 1-2-3, 1962; tied major league mark for most times hit by pitcher, inning (2), fourth inning, April 29, 1962.
Named as third baseman on THE SPORTING NEWS All-Star Major League Team, 1958.

Year	Club	League	Pos.	G.	AB.	R.	H.	2B.	3B.	HR.	RBI.	B.A.	PO.	A.	E.	F.A.
1948—Tallahassee		Ga.-Fla.	OF	138	*596	106	176	39	8	14	*132	.295	247	20	12	.957
1949—Davenport		I.I.I.	OF-3B	13	43	7	10	2	1	0	7	.233	23	1	0	1.000
1949—Tallahassee		Ga.-Fla.	OF	74	285	46	93	19	2	10	63	.326	162	15	2	.989
1949—Waco		Big.St.	OF	20	73	17	25	3	0	4	17	.342	33	3	4	.900
1950—Charleston		Sally	OF	82	318	50	98	20	4	11	55	.308	180	9	1	.995
1950—New Orleans		South.	OF	47	148	21	39	6	1	3	18	.264	67	3	6	.921
1951—New Orleans		South.	OF	125	471	64	136	25	6	23	85	.289	270	16	7	.976
1951—Pittsburgh		Nat.	OF	39	148	21	39	9	2	2	16	.264	87	5	0	1.000
1952—New Orleans		South.	OF	154	597	*112	181	40	6	*35	*131	.303	422	19	*18	.961
1952—Pittsburgh		Nat.	OF	6	21	1	2	0	0	0	0	.095	8	1	0	1.000
1953—Pittsburgh		Nat.	OF	128	455	68	116	22	1	30	102	.255	306	17	8	.976
1954—Pittsburgh		Nat.	OF	153	577	81	172	32	7	23	94	.298	418	•14	5	.989
1955—Pittsburgh		Nat.	OF	142	510	72	125	16	2	25	72	.245	307	8	5	.984
1956—Pittsburgh		Nat.	3-O-2B	•157	588	69	166	24	3	25	80	.282	216	179	18	.956
1957—Pittsburgh		Nat.	1-O-3B	151	594	72	172	30	1	23	89	.290	729	119	25	.971
1958—Pittsburgh(a)		Nat.	*3-O-1B	149	562	89	158	26	4	35	109	.281	160	243	*30	.931
1959—Cincinnati(b)		Nat.	3-O-1B	108	374	41	84	18	2	12	47	.225	206	126	19	.946
1960—Chicago		Nat.	1-O-3B	135	479	54	114	12	1	21	64	.238	528	92	17	.973
1961—Chi(c)-Mil.(d)		Nat.	OF-1B	139	473	65	133	15	3	27	73	.281	300	12	10	.969
1962—New York		Nat.	O-1-3B	156	571	69	152	23	3	34	94	.266	311	36	14	.961
1963—New York		Nat.	O-1-3B	126	420	34	109	9	1	15	60	.260	304	17	4	.988

Year	Club	League	Pos.	G.	AB.	R.	H.	2B.	3B.	HR.	RBI.	B.A.	PO.	A.	E.	F.A.
1964–N.Y.(e)-Phila.		Nat.	1-O-3B	99	340	39	92	17	1	10	45	.271	498	46	9	.984
1965–Phi.f-Ho.g-Mil.h		Nat.	1-O-3B	73	168	17	37	9	0	4	17	.220	262	15	5	.982
1966–Chicago		Nat.	PH	5	5	0	0	0	0	0	0	.000	0	0	0	.000
1966–Tacoma		PCL	1B-PH	25	79	2	16	6	0	1	8	.203	115	6	0	1.000
Major League Totals				1766	6285	792	1671	262	31	286	962	.266	4640	930	169	.971

aTraded to Cincinnati Reds with pitcher Charles (Whammy) Douglas, infielder-outfielder Jim Pendleton and outfielder Johnny Powers for pitcher Harvey Haddix, catcher Forrest (Smoky) Burgess and third baseman Don Hoak, January 31, 1959.

bTraded to Chicago Cubs for pitcher Bill Henry and outfielders Lou Jackson and Lee Walls December 6, 1959.

cTraded to Milwaukee Braves for infielder Mel Roach, May 9, 1961.

dTraded to New York Mets for cash and player to be named later, November 28, 1961; trade completed with transfer of outfielder Gus Bell to Milwaukee Braves, May 21, 1962.

eTraded to Philadelphia Phillies for pitcher Gary Kroll, infielder Wayne Graham, who was on Arkansas roster, and cash, August 7, 1964.

fSold to Houston Astros, July 10, 1965.

gSigned by Milwaukee Braves, September 1, 1965.

hReleased by Atlanta (franchise transferred from Milwaukee), April 5, 1966; signed with Chicago Cubs, May 14, 1966.

SAMUEL L. (BIG SAM) THOMPSON

Born March 5, 1860, at Danville, Ind.
Died November 7, 1922, at Detroit, Mich.
Height, 6.02. Weight, 207.
Threw and batted lefthanded.

Hit for cycle and made six hits in seven trips against Louisville, August 17, 1894.

Member of only .400-hitting outfield in major league history—Sam Thompson, Tuck Turner and Ed Delahanty with 1894 Phillies.

Year	Club	League	Pos.	G.	AB.	R.	H.	2B.	3B.	HR.	SB.	B.A.	PO.	A.	E.	F.A.
1884–Evansville		N.W.	OF	5	23	5	9	2	1	0	0	.391	14	0	1	.933
1885–Indianapolis		West.	OF	30	136	38	43	7	5	1	....	.316	35	4	12	.765
1885–Detroit		Nat.	OF	63	254	58	77	11	7	7	....	.303	84	24	14	.885
1886–Detroit		Nat.	OF	122	503	100	156	19	4	8	13	.310	194	29	13	.945
1887–Detroit		Nat.	OF	127	576	118	234	29	★23	10	22	.406	217	24	24	.909
1888–Detroit		Nat.	OF	55	238	51	67	9	8	6	5	.282	86	4	12	.882
1889–Philadelphia		Nat.	OF	128	533	103	158	35	4	★20	24	.296	173	19	21	.901
1890–Philadelphia		Nat.	OF	132	549	114	•172	★38	9	4	25	.313	170	29	13	.939
1891–Philadelphia		Nat.	OF	133	551	108	163	20	9	7	33	.296	237	29	15	.947
1892–Philadelphia		Nat.	OF	151	602	109	183	31	8	9	30	.304	210	31	14	.945
1893–Philadelphia		Nat.	OF	130	583	130	★220	33	14	11	18	.377	163	17	15	.923
1894–Philadelphia		Nat.	OF	102	458	115	185	29	26	13	29	.404	163	11	7	.961
1895–Philadelphia		Nat.	OF	118	533	131	210	42	•22	16	24	.394	188	•32	9	.961
1896–Philadelphia		Nat.	OF	119	517	103	158	27	7	•13	11	.306	235	28	8	.970
1897–Philadelphia		Nat.	OF	3	13	2	3	0	1	0	0	.231	4	2	1	.857
1898–Philadelphia		Nat.	OF	14	63	13	23	3	2	1	0	.365	20	5	0	1.000
1906–Detroit		Amer.	OF	8	31	4	7	0	1	0	0	.226	14	0	0	1.000
American League Totals				8	31	4	7	0	1	0	0	.226	14	0	0	1.000
National League Totals				1397	5973	1255	2009	326	145	126	235	.336	2144	284	166	.936
Major League Totals				1405	6004	1259	2016	326	146	126	235	.336	2158	284	166	.936

WORLD SERIES RECORD

Year	Club	League	Pos.	G.	AB.	R.	H.	BA.	PO.	A.	E.	F.A.
1887–Detroit		Nat.	OF	15	61	9	23	.377	21	3	1	.960

ROBERT BROWN THOMSON

Born October 25, 1923, at Glasgow, Scotland.
Height, 6.02½. Weight, 190.
Threw and batted righthanded.
Married Elaine Mae Coley, December 27, 1952.

Hit home run in ninth inning of final playoff game against Brooklyn Dodgers with two men on base to win league championship, October 3, 1951.

Year	Club	League	Pos.	G.	AB.	R.	H.	2B.	3B.	HR.	RBI.	B.A.	PO.	A.	E.	F.A.
1942–Bristol		Appal.	3B	5	12	1	3	0	1	0	0	.250	4	13	3	.850
1942–Rocky Mount		Bi-State	3B	29	87	15	21	4	0	3	18	.241	22	29	5	.911
1943-44-45–Bristol		Appal.					(In Military Service)									
1946–Jersey City		Int.	3B–OF	151	533	93	149	12	7	26	92	.280	225	170	30	.929
1946–New York		Nat.	3B	18	54	8	17	4	1	2	9	.315	18	25	3	.935
1947–New York		Nat.	OF-2B	138	545	105	154	26	5	29	85	.283	357	32	12	.970
1948–New York		Nat.	OF	138	471	75	117	20	2	16	63	.248	313	10	10	.970
1949–New York		Nat.	OF	156	641	99	198	35	9	27	109	.309	488	10	9	.982
1950–New York		Nat.	OF	149	563	79	142	22	7	25	85	.252	394	15	9	.978
1951–New York		Nat.	OF-3B	148	518	89	152	27	8	32	101	.293	258	139	20	.952
1952–New York		Nat.	3B-OF	153	608	89	164	29	*14	24	108	.270	234	187	18	.959
1953–New York(a)		Nat.	OF	154	608	80	175	22	6	26	106	.288	391	16	7	.983
1954–Milwaukee(b)		Nat.	OF	43	99	7	23	3	0	2	15	.232	45	3	1	.980
1955–Milwaukee		Nat.	OF	101	343	40	88	12	3	12	56	.257	182	5	6	.969
1956–Milwaukee		Nat.	OF-3B	142	451	59	106	10	4	20	74	.235	262	17	10	.965
1957–Mil.(c)-N.Y.(d)		Nat.	OF-3B	122	363	39	87	12	7	12	61	.240	202	7	2	.991
1958–Chicago		Nat.	OF-3B	152	547	67	155	27	5	21	82	.283	358	16	5	.987
1959–Chicago(e)		Nat.	OF	122	374	55	97	15	2	11	52	.259	223	9	3	.987
1960–Bos.(f)-Balt.		Amer.	OF-3B	43	120	12	30	3	1	5	20	.250	75	1	2	.950
American League Totals				43	120	12	30	3	1	5	20	.250	75	1	2	.950
National League Totals				1736	6185	891	1675	264	73	259	1006	.271	3725	481	115	.973
Major League Totals				1779	6305	903	1705	267	74	264	1026	.270	3800	482	117	.973

aTraded to Milwaukee Braves with catcher Sam Calderone for pitchers Johnny Antonelli and Don Liddle, catcher Ebba St. Claire, infielder Bill Klaus and $50,000, February 1, 1954.
bSuffered triple fracture of right ankle sliding into second base in exhibition game against New York Yankees, March 13, 1954; made first appearance of season as pinch-hitter, July 14, 1954.
cTraded to New York Giants with pitcher Ray Crone and second baseman Danny O'Connell for second baseman Red Schoendienst, June 15, 1957.
dTraded to Chicago Cubs for outfielder-first baseman Bob Speake and cash, April 3, 1958.
eTraded to Boston Red Sox for pitcher Al Schroll, December 1, 1959.
fReleased by Boston July 1, 1960, and picked up by Baltimore Orioles July 4, 1960.

WORLD SERIES RECORD

Year	Club	League	Pos.	G.	AB.	R.	H.	2B.	3B.	HR.	RBI.	B.A.	PO.	A.	E.	F.A.
1951–New York		Nat.	3B	6	21	1	5	1	0	0	2	.238	11	15	2	.929

MICHAEL JOSEPH (SILENT MIKE) TIERNAN

Born January 21, 1867, at Trenton, N.J.
Died November 9, 1918, at New York, N.Y.
Height, 5.11. Weight, 165.
Threw and batted lefthanded.

Scored six runs in one game against Philadelphia June 15, 1887.

Year	Club	League	Pos.	G.	AB.	R.	H.	2B.	3B.	HR.	SB.	B.A.	PO.	A.	E.	F.A.
1885–Trenton		East.	OF	88	340	54	84	...	...	...	....	.247	84	3	13	.870
1886–Jersey City		East.	OF	54	223	53	87	...	...	...	*8	.390	63	24	6	.935
1887–New York		Nat.	OF	103	438	81	149	13	12	10	28	.340	150	10	25	.865
1888–New York		Nat.	OF	113	443	75	130	14	8	9	52	.293	174	16	8	*.960
1889–New York		Nat.	OF	122	499	*146	167	23	13	12	33	.335	179	19	23	.896
1890–New York		Nat.	OF	133	553	130	168	25	20	•13	56	.304	210	13	26	.896
1891–New York		Nat.	OF	133	540	111	164	30	12	•16	54	.304	138	18	18	.897
1892–New York		Nat.	OF	114	451	80	134	15	11	4	34	.297	156	15	18	.905
1893–New York		Nat.	OF	124	471	113	154	19	12	15	41	.327	183	11	16	.924
1894–New York		Nat.	OF	112	429	87	121	18	14	6	26	.282	170	11	13	.933
1895–New York		Nat.	OF	119	474	128	168	23	19	7	36	.354	181	8	12	.940
1896–New York		Nat.	OF	•133	526	132	190	22	15	7	35	.361	211	6	8	.964
1897–New York		Nat.	OF	129	534	123	177	27	11	4	34	.331	180	14	12	.942
1898–New York		Nat.	OF	103	412	89	118	15	10	5	19	.286	130	10	2	*.986
1899–New York		Nat.	OF	36	140	17	35	4	2	0	1	.250	42	4	3	.939
Major League Totals				1474	5910	1312	1875	248	159	108	449	.317	2104	155	184	.925

PITCHING RECORD

Year	Club	League	G.	AB.	W.	L.	Pct.	H.	R.
1885–Trenton		Eastern	40	1400	17	19	.472	324	221
1886–Jersey City		Eastern	10	363	6	3	.667	99	.....

JOSEPH BERT TINKER

Born July 27, 1880, at Muscotah, Kan.
Died July 27, 1948, at Orlando, Fla.
Height, 5.09. Weight, 175.
Threw and batted righthanded.

Manager, Cincinnati, 1913; Chicago Federals, 1914-15; Chicago N. L., 1916; manager and president, Columbus, American Association, 1917-18; president, 1919-20; manager-owner, Orlando, Florida State, 1921; vice-president, 1923.
Named to Hall of Fame, 1946.

Year	Club	League	Pos.	G.	AB.	R.	H.	2B.	3B.	HR.	SB.	B.A.	PO.	A.	E.	F.A.
1900	Denver	West.	SS	32	137	18	30	...	...	...	8	.219	74	49	26	.826
1900	Gr't F'ls-Helena	Mont. St.	SS	57	236	39	76	...	...	...	12	.322	150	174	45	.878
1901	Portland	P. NW.	SS-3B	106	424	74	123	...	...	...	37	.290	*147	*202	*61	*.851
1902	Chicago	Nat.	SS-3B	133	501	54	137	17	5	2	28	.273	251	464	*73	.907
1903	Chicago	Nat.	SS-3B	124	460	67	134	21	7	2	27	.291	246	400	67	.906
1904	Chicago	Nat.	SS	141	488	55	108	12	13	3	41	.221	327	465	64	.925
1905	Chicago	Nat.	SS	149	547	70	135	18	8	2	31	.247	345	527	56	.940
1906	Chicago	Nat.	SS	148	523	75	122	18	4	1	30	.233	288	472	45	*.944
1907	Chicago	Nat.	SS	113	402	36	89	11	3	1	20	.221	215	390	39	.939
1908	Chicago	Nat.	SS	•157	548	67	146	22	14	6	30	.266	314	*570	39	*.958
1909	Chicago	Nat.	SS	143	516	56	132	26	11	4	23	.256	320	470	50	•.940
1910	Chicago	Nat.	SS	132	473	48	136	25	9	3	20	.288	277	411	42	.942
1911	Chicago	Nat.	SS	143	536	61	149	24	12	4	30	.278	*333	*486	55	*.937
1912	Chicago(a)	Nat.	SS	142	550	80	155	24	7	0	25	.282	*354	470	50	.943
1913	Cincinnati(b)	Nat.	SS	110	382	47	121	20	13	1	10	.317	223	320	18	*.968
1914	Chicago	Fed.	SS	127	440	53	114	22	7	2	24	.259	281	413	39	.947
1915	Chicago(c)	Fed.	SS	30	69	7	19	2	1	0	3	.275	16	39	5	.917
1916	Chicago	Nat.	SS-3B	7	10	0	1	0	0	0	0	.100	4	9	1	.929
1917	Columbus	A. A.	2B	22	51	5	6	1	1	0	4	.118	13	36	3	.942
1921	Orlando	Fla. St.	2B	2	3	1	1	0	0	0	0	.333	4	1	1	.833
Major League Totals				1642	5936	716	1565	238	106	29	315	.264	3497	5454	599	.937

aTraded to Cincinnati with pitcher Grover Lowdermilk and catcher Harry Chapman for pitcher Bert Humphries, utility player Pete Knisely, infielders Red Corriden and Art Phelan and outfielder Mike Mitchell, December 15, 1912.
bSold to Brooklyn, December, 1913, but when refused $2,000 of purchase price for signing with Dodgers, jumped to Feds.
cSold to Chicago Nationals in peace agreement, January 1916.

WORLD SERIES RECORD

Year	Club	League	Pos.	G.	AB.	R.	H.	2B.	3B.	HR.	SB.	B.A.	PO.	A.	E.	F.A.
1906	Chicago	Nat.	SS	6	18	4	3	0	0	0	2	.167	10	20	2	.938
1907	Chicago	Nat.	SS	5	13	4	2	0	0	0	3	.154	15	23	3	.927
1908	Chicago	Nat.	SS	5	19	2	5	0	0	1	5	.263	8	19	0	1.000
1910	Chicago	Nat.	SS	5	18	2	6	2	0	0	0	.333	11	14	2	.926
World Series Totals				21	68	12	16	2	0	1	10	.235	44	76	7	.945

JOHN THOMAS TOBIN

Born May 4, 1892, at St. Louis, Mo.
Died December 10, 1969, at St. Louis, Mo.
Height, 5.08. Weight, 148.
Threw and batted lefthanded.
Married Loretta Sack, March 4, 1914.

Had over 200 hits four consecutive seasons, 1920 through 1923.
Manager, Bloomington, Three-I League, July, 1930 to end of season; coach, St. Louis Browns, 1944 through 1948; scout, 1949 through 1951.

Year	Club	League	Pos.	G.	AB.	R.	H.	2B.	3B.	HR.	RBI.	B.A.	PO.	A.	E.	F.A.
1912	Houston	Tex.		(Signed contract but did not report and was released)												
1913	St. Louis	Fed.	OF	41	124	17	42	....	....	....	....	.339	....	....	....	......
1914	St. Louis	Fed.	OF	135	530	80	143	24	11	7	....	.270	189	28	10	.956

Year	Club	League	Pos.	G.	AB.	R.	H.	2B.	3B.	HR.	RBI.	B.A.	PO.	A.	E.	F.A.
1915—St. Louis		Fed.	OF	158	*623	91	186	29	14	6	.....	.299	280	22	12	.962
1916—St. Louis		Amer.	OF	77	150	16	32	4	1	0	10	.213	46	2	9	.842
1917—Salt Lake		P. C.	OF	189	800	*149	*265	42	3	2	.....	.331	*478	31	16	.970
1918—St. Louis		Amer.	OF	122	480	59	133	19	5	0	37	.277	244	20	8	.971
1919—St. Louis		Amer.	OF	127	486	54	159	22	7	6	59	.327	247	16	13	.953
1920—St. Louis		Amer.	OF	147	593	94	202	34	10	4	62	.341	293	18	13	.960
1921—St. Louis		Amer.	OF	150	*671	132	236	31	18	8	59	.352	277	•28	14	.956
1922—St. Louis		Amer.	OF	146	625	122	207	34	8	13	66	.331	221	15	15	.940
1923—St. Louis		Amer.	OF	151	637	91	202	32	15	13	73	.317	269	14	9	.969
1924—St. Louis		Amer.	OF	136	569	87	170	30	8	2	48	.299	251	19	12	.957
1925—St. Louis(a)		Amer.	OF-1B	77	193	25	58	11	0	2	27	.301	56	1	0	1.000
1926—Wash.(b)-Bos.		Amer.	OF	78	242	31	64	9	1	1	17	.264	89	7	3	.970
1927—Boston		Amer.	OF	111	374	52	116	18	3	2	40	.310	152	10	9	.947
1928—Columbus		A. A.	OF	53	137	15	39	4	2	0	.....	.285	250	14	6	.978
1929—Wichita Falls		Tex.	OF	5	3	4	3	2	0	0	.....	1.000	5	0	0	1.000
1930—Bloomington		I.I.I.	OF	25	29	4	9	0	0	1	3	.310	10	1	1	.917
Major League Totals				1322	5020	763	1579	244	76	51	498	.315	2145	150	105	.956

aTraded with pitcher Joe Bush to Washington for pitchers Win Ballou and Tom Zachary, February, 1926.
bReleased by Washington, June, 1926, and signed by Boston Red Sox, July, 1926.

JOSEPH PAUL TORRE

Born July 18, 1940, at Brooklyn, N. Y.
Height, 6.01. Weight, 210.
Threw and batted righthanded.
Brother of Frank Torre, former first baseman with Milwaukee Braves and Philadelphia Phillies.

Led National League first basemen in double plays with 144 in 1974.
Led National League catchers in double plays with 12 in 1967.
Hit for cycle, game (single, double, triple, home run), June 27, 1973.
Named catcher on THE SPORTING NEWS National League All-Star Teams, 1964-65-66.
Named catcher on THE SPORTING NEWS National League All-Star fielding team, 1965.
Named third baseman on THE SPORTING NEWS National League All-Star Team, 1971.
Named Major League Player of the Year by THE SPORTING NEWS, 1971.
Most Valuable Player in the National League, 1971.
Manager, New York Mets, 1977 to date.

Year	Club	League	Pos.	G.	AB.	R.	H.	2B.	3B.	HR.	RBI.	B.A.	PO.	A.	E.	F.A.
1960—Eau Claire		North.	C	117	369	63	127	23	3	16	74	*.344	636	64	9	.987
1960—Milwaukee		Nat.	PH	2	2	0	1	0	0	0	0	.500	0	0	0	.000
1961—Louisville		A. A.	C	27	111	18	38	8	2	3	24	.342	185	14	2	.990
1961—Milwaukee		Nat.	C	113	406	40	113	21	4	10	42	.278	494	50	10	.982
1962—Milwaukee		Nat.	C	80	220	23	62	8	1	5	26	.282	325	39	5	.986
1963—Milwaukee		Nat.	C-1-OF	142	501	57	147	19	4	14	71	.293	919	76	6	.994
1964—Milwaukee		Nat.	*C-1B	154	601	87	193	36	5	20	109	.321	1081	94	7	*.994
1965—Milwaukee		Nat.	C-1B	148	523	68	152	21	1	27	80	.291	1022	73	8	.993
1966—Atlanta		Nat.	C-1B	148	546	83	172	20	3	36	101	.315	874	87	12	.988
1967—Atlanta		Nat.	C-1B	135	477	67	132	18	1	20	68	.277	785	81	8	.991
1968—Atlanta (a)		Nat.	*C-1B	115	424	45	115	11	2	10	55	.271	733	48	2	*.997
1969—St. Louis		Nat.	1B-C	159	602	72	174	29	6	18	101	.289	1360	91	7	.995
1970—St. Louis		Nat.	C-3-1B	•161	624	89	203	27	9	21	100	.325	651	162	13	.984
1971—St. Louis		Nat.	3B	161	634	97	*230	34	8	24	*137	*.363	*136	271	•21	.951
1972—St. Louis		Nat.	3B-1B	149	544	71	157	26	6	11	81	.289	336	198	15	.973
1973—St. Louis		Nat.	1B-3B	141	519	67	149	17	2	13	69	.287	881	128	12	.988
1974—St. Louis (b)		Nat.	*1B-3B	147	529	59	149	28	1	11	70	.282	1173	*121	14	.989
1975—New York		Nat.	3B-1B	114	361	33	89	16	3	6	35	.247	172	157	15	.956
1976—New York		Nat.	1-3B-PH	114	310	36	95	10	3	5	31	.306	593	52	7	.989
Major League Totals				2183	7823	994	2333	341	59	251	1176	.298	1535	1728	162	.988

aTraded to St. Louis Cardinals for first baseman Orlando Cepeda, March 17, 1969.
bTraded to New York Mets for pitchers Tommy Moore and Ray Sadecki, October 13, 1974.

DID YOU KNOW—

That Johnny Tobin is one of the most overlooked batters in the history of the major leagues? He strung together four consecutive seasons of 200-plus hits—202 in 1920, 236 in '21, 207 in '22 and 202 in 1923.

CECIL HOWELL TRAVIS

Born August 8, 1913, at Riverdale, Ga.
Height, 6.01½. Weight, 195.
Threw right and batted lefthanded.
Married Helen Hubbard, September 12, 1942.

Made five hits in first major league game, May 16, 1933 (12 innings).
Named by Baseball Writers' Association of America as shortstop for THE SPORTING NEWS All-Star Major League Team, 1941.
Scout, Washington Senators, 1948 through 1955.

Year	Club	League	Pos.	G.	AB.	R.	H.	2B.	3B.	HR.	RBI.	B.A.	PO.	A.	E.	F.A.
1931	Chattanooga	South.	2B-3B	13	35	7	15	4	0	0	0	.429	12	107	3	.906
1932	Chattanooga	South.	3B	152	570	88	203	27	*17	3	88	.356	127	298	37	.920
1933	Chattanooga	South.	3B	129	526	80	185	26	12	1	74	.352	128	262	33	.922
1933	Washington	Amer.	3B	18	43	7	13	1	0	0	2	.302	8	30	1	.974
1934	Washington	Amer.	3B	109	392	48	125	22	4	1	53	.319	88	210	20	.937
1935	Washington	Amer.	3B-OF	138	534	85	170	27	8	0	61	.318	164	258	16	.962
1936	Washington	Amer.	SS-OF	138	517	77	164	34	10	2	92	.317	244	231	31	.939
1937	Washington	Amer.	SS	135	526	72	181	27	7	3	66	.344	229	396	23	.915
1938	Washington	Amer.	SS	146	567	96	190	30	5	5	67	.335	304	357	40	.943
1939	Washington	Amer.	SS	130	476	55	139	20	9	5	63	.292	194	359	24	.958
1940	Washington	Amer.	SS-3B	136	528	60	170	37	11	2	76	.322	164	340	38	.930
1941	Washington	Amer.	SS-3B	152	608	106	*218	39	19	7	101	.359	293	427	27	.964
1942-43-44	Wash.(a)	Amer.					(In Military Service)									
1945	Washington(b)	Amer.	3B	15	54	4	13	2	1	0	10	.241	18	28	4	.920
1946	Washington	Amer.	SS-*3B	137	465	45	117	22	3	1	56	.252	187	290	*31	.939
1947	Washington	Amer.	SS-3B	74	204	10	44	4	1	1	10	.216	53	112	9	.948
Major League Totals				1328	4914	665	1544	265	78	27	657	.314	1946	3038	264	.950

aEntered U.S. Army, January 7, 1942.
bReturned to Washington lineup, September 8, 1945.

HAROLD JOSEPH (PIE) TRAYNOR

Born November 11, 1899, at Framingham, Mass.
Died March 16, 1972, at Pittsburgh, Pa.
Height, 6.00½. Weight, 175.
Threw and batted righthanded.

Rated by many as the all-time All-Star third baseman in the majors.
Holds National League mark for most putouts, third baseman, career, 2,288; tied for N.L. record for most years leading in putouts, third baseman, 7; also most double plays started, nine-inning game, third baseman, 4; led N.L. third basemen in double plays, 1924, 1925, 1926, 1927 (tie).
Named to THE SPORTING NEWS All-Star Major League Teams in 1925-26-27-29-31-32-33.
Manager, Pittsburgh Pirates, June, 1934, until September, 1939; scout, Pittsburgh Pirates, 1940 to date of death.
Named to Hall of Fame, 1948.

Year	Club	League	Pos.	G.	AB.	R.	H.	2B.	3B.	HR.	RBI.	B.A.	PO.	A.	E.	F.A.
1920	Portsmouth	Va.	SS	104	392	50	106	18	4	8	57	.270	215	334	31	.947
1920	Pittsburgh	Nat.	SS	17	52	6	11	3	1	0	2	.212	35	39	12	.860
1921	Birmingham	South.	SS	131	527	101	177	22	13	5	53	.336	330	382	64	.918
1921	Pittsburgh	Nat.	SS-3B	7	19	0	5	0	0	0	2	.263	4	9	1	.939
1922	Pittsburgh	Nat.	SS-3B	142	571	89	161	17	12	4	81	.282	186	278	31	.937
1923	Pittsburgh	Nat.	3B	153	616	108	208	19	•19	12	101	.338	*191	*310	26	.951
1924	Pittsburgh	Nat.	3B	142	545	86	160	26	13	5	82	.294	179	268	15	.968
1925	Pittsburgh	Nat.	SS-3B	150	591	114	189	39	14	6	106	.320	*226	*303	24	*.957
1926	Pittsburgh	Nat.	3B	152	574	83	182	25	17	3	92	.317	*182	279	*23	.952
1927	Pittsburgh	Nat.	3B	149	573	93	196	32	9	5	106	.342	*212	265	19	.962
1928	Pittsburgh	Nat.	3B	144	569	91	192	38	12	3	124	.337	175	296	•27	.946
1929	Pittsburgh	Nat.	3B	130	540	94	192	27	12	4	108	.356	148	238	20	.951
1930	Pittsburgh	Nat.	3B	130	497	90	182	22	11	9	119	.366	130	268	25	.941
1931	Pittsburgh	Nat.	3B	155	615	81	183	37	15	2	103	.298	*172	284	*37	.925

Year	Club	League	Pos.	G.	AB.	R.	H.	2B.	3B.	HR.	RBI.	B.A.	PO.	A.	E.	F.A.
1932–Pittsburgh		Nat.	3B	135	513	74	169	27	10	2	68	.329	173	222	*27	.936
1933–Pittsburgh		Nat.	3B	•154	624	85	190	27	6	1	82	.304	*176	*300	*27	.946
1934–Pittsburgh		Nat.	3B	119	444	62	137	22	10	1	61	.309	*116	176	14	.954
1935–Pittsburgh		Nat.	1B-3B	57	204	24	57	10	3	1	36	.279	59	84	18	.888
1936–Pittsburgh		Nat.					(Did not play)									
1937–Pittsburgh		Nat.	3B	5	12	3	2	0	0	0	0	.167	2	8	0	1.000
Major League Totals				1941	7559	1183	2416	371	164	58	1273	.320	2366	3627	346	.945

WORLD SERIES RECORD

Year	Club	League	Pos.	G.	AB.	R.	H.	2B.	3B.	HR.	RBI.	B.A.	PO.	A.	E.	F.A.
1925–Pittsburgh		Nat.	3B	7	26	2	9	0	2	1	4	.346	6	18	0	1.000
1927–Pittsburgh		Nat.	3B	4	15	1	3	1	0	0	0	.200	5	9	1	.933
World Series Totals				11	41	3	12	1	2	1	4	.293	11	27	1	.974

HAROLD ARTHUR (HAL) TROSKY

Born November 11, 1912, at Norway, Ia.
Died June 18, 1979, at Cedar Rapids, Ia.
Height, 6.02½. Weight, 198.
Threw right and batted lefthanded.
Married Lorraine Glenn, November 15, 1933.

Connected for three home runs (successive), second game, May 30, 1934, and first game July 5, 1937.
Led A.L. first basemen in double plays, 1934.
Scout, Chicago White Sox, 1947-48.

Year	Club	League	Pos.	G.	AB.	R.	H.	2B.	3B.	HR.	RBI.	B.A.	PO.	A.	E.	F.A.
1931–C.Rap.-Dubuque		M.V.	OF-PH	52	162	14	49	8	2	3	....	.302	44	19	5	.926
1932–Quincy		I.I.I.	OF	68	260	55	86	14	6	15	....	.331	107	9	8	.935
1932–Burlington		M.V.	OF-1B	59	228	36	72	18	0	4	44	.316	290	23	12	.963
1933–Toledo		A.A.	1B	132	461	86	149	25	5	33	92	.323	742	43	14	.982
1933–Cleveland		Amer.	1B	11	44	6	13	1	2	1	8	.295	91	4	1	.990
1934–Cleveland		Amer.	1B	154	625	117	206	45	9	35	142	.330	*1487	*86	22	.986
1935–Cleveland		Amer.	1B	154	632	84	171	33	7	26	113	.271	*1567	88	11	.993
1936–Cleveland		Amer.	1B	151	629	124	216	45	9	42	*162	.343	1367	85	22	.985
1937–Cleveland		Amer.	1B	153	601	104	179	36	9	32	128	.298	1403	76	10	.993
1938–Cleveland		Amer.	1B	150	554	106	185	40	9	19	110	.334	1132	102	10	.992
1939–Cleveland		Amer.	1B	122	448	89	150	31	4	25	104	.335	1004	97	9	.992
1940–Cleveland		Amer.	1B	140	522	85	154	39	4	25	93	.295	1207	70	11	.991
1941–Cleveland		Amer.	1B	89	310	43	91	17	0	11	51	.294	727	54	9	.989
1942–Cleveland		Amer.					(Out of game due to illness)									
1943–Cleveland (a)		Amer.					(Out of game due to illness)									
1944–Chicago		Amer.	1B	135	497	55	120	32	2	10	70	.241	1310	57	9	.993
1945–Chicago		Amer.					(Out of game due to illness)									
1946–Chicago		Amer.	1B	88	299	22	76	12	3	2	31	.254	729	33	7	.991
Major League Totals				1347	5161	835	1561	331	58	228	1012	.302	12024	752	121	.991

aSold to Chicago White Sox, November 6, 1943.

VIRGIL OLIVER TRUCKS

Born April 26, 1919, at Birmingham, Ala.
Height, 6.00. Weight, 210.
Threw and batted righthanded.
Married Vickie Shaffer, October 3, 1952.

Pitched six no-hitters in Organized Ball. Trucks had two no-hit games at Andalusia, Ala., in the Alabama-Florida League, May 18 and June 4, 1938, winning by scores of 1-0 and 6-0; this was the season he fanned 418 batters. In 1940, he posted a seven-inning no-hitter against Tulsa in the Texas League on May 26, and a year later, May 31, 1941, he pitched and lost a no-hit game to Montreal in the International League (9⅔ innings). The Royals scored a run in the tenth to beat Trucks, 1-0.
Came through with his first major league no-hitter against the Washington Senators, May 15, 1952, winning 1-0. The second big league no-hitter the same year was at the expense of the New York Yankees, August 25, 1952. Again the score was 1-0.

Tied major league record for pitchers by having five putouts in a game, August 29, 1952.
Coach, Pittsburgh Pirates, 1963; scout Seattle Pilots, 1969; scout, Atlanta Braves, and farm system coach at Richmond (International), 1970; minor league pitching instructor, Atlanta, 1971-72.

Year Club	League	G.	IP.	W.	L.	Pct.	H.	R.	ER.	SO.	BB.	ERA.
1938–Andalusia	Alabama-Florida	38	273	*25	6	*.806	143	52	38	*418	125	*1.25
1939–Alexandria	Evangeline	24	173	13	5	.722	137	60	50	129	73	2.60
1939–Beaumont	Texas	11	63	3	5	.375	57	37	24	38	41	3.43
1940–Beaumont	Texas	33	203	12	11	.522	170	92	79	142	92	3.50
1941–Buffalo	International	33	204	12	12	.500	164	83	73	*204	76	3.22
1941–Detroit	American	1	2	0	0	.000	4	2	2	3	0	9.00
1942–Detroit	American	28	168	14	8	.636	147	64	51	91	74	2.73
1943–Detroit	American	33	203	16	10	.615	170	72	64	118	52	2.84
1944–Detroit	American					(In Military Service)						
1945–Detroit (a)	American	1	5	0	0	.000	3	1	1	3	2	1.80
1946–Detroit	American	32	237	14	9	.609	217	94	85	161	75	3.23
1947–Detroit	American	36	181	10	12	.455	186	105	91	108	79	4.52
1948–Detroit	American	43	212	14	13	.519	190	97	89	123	85	3.78
1949–Detroit	American	41	275	19	11	.633	209	95	86	*153	124	2.81
1950–Detroit	American	7	48	3	1	.750	45	20	19	25	21	3.56
1951–Detroit	American	37	154	13	8	.619	153	81	74	89	75	4.32
1952–Detroit (b)	American	35	197	5	19	.208	190	99	87	129	82	3.97
1953–St. Louis (c)-Chicago	American	40	264	20	10	.667	234	97	86	149	99	2.93
1954–Chicago	American	40	265	19	12	.613	224	87	82	152	95	2.78
1955–Chicago (d)	American	32	175	13	8	.619	176	78	77	91	61	3.96
1956–Detroit (e)	American	22	120	6	5	.545	104	56	51	43	63	3.83
1957–Kansas City	American	48	116	9	7	.563	106	45	39	55	62	3.03
1958–Kansas City (f)-New York	American	41	62	2	2	.500	58	31	25	41	39	3.63
1959–Miami	International	4	7	0	1	.000	7	4	3	0	9	3.86
Major League Totals		517	2684	177	135	.567	2416	1124	1009	1534	1088	3.38

aIn Military Service part of season.
bTraded to St. Louis Browns with pitcher Hal White and outfielder Johnny Groth for second baseman Owen Friend, outfielder Bob Nieman and outfielder-catcher J. W. Porter, December 4, 1952.
cTraded to Chicago White Sox with third baseman Bob Elliott for pitcher Lou Kretlow, catcher Darrell Johnson and reported $75,000, June 13, 1953.
dTraded to Detroit Tigers for outfielder-third baseman Bubba Phillips, November 30, 1955.
eTraded to Kansas City Athletics with pitchers Ned Garver and Gene Host, first baseman Wayne Belardi and reported $20,000 for pitchers Jack Crimian and Bill Harrington, first baseman Eddie Robinson and third baseman Jim Finigan, December 5, 1956.
fTraded to New York Yankees with pitcher Duane Maas for outfielder Harry Simpson and pitcher Bob Grim, June 15, 1958.

WORLD SERIES RECORD

Year Club	League	G.	IP.	W.	L.	Pct.	H.	R.	ER.	SO.	BB.	ERA.
1945–Detroit	American	2	13⅓	1	0	1.000	14	5	5	7	5	3.38

GEORGE ERNEST UHLE

Born September 18, 1898, at Cleveland, O.
Height, 6.00. Weight, 195.
Threw and batted righthanded.
Married Helen Schultz, October 20, 1920.

Defeated Chicago White Sox, 6-5, in 21-inning game though removed for pinch-runner after pitching 20 innings, May 24, 1929. Batted in six runs in game, April 28, 1921.
Coach, Cleveland Indians, 1937; Buffalo, International League, 1938-39; Chicago Cubs, 1940. Scout, Brooklyn Dodgers, 1941-42; coach, Washington Senators, 1944.

Year Club	League	G.	IP.	W.	L.	Pct.	H.	R.	ER.	SO.	BB.	ERA.
1919–Cleveland	American	26	127	10	5	.667	129	52	41	50	43	2.91
1920–Cleveland	American	27	85	4	5	.444	98	52	49	27	29	5.19
1921–Cleveland	American	41	238	16	13	.552	288	132	106	63	63	4.01
1922–Cleveland	American	50	287	22	16	.579	328	147	130	82	89	4.08
1923–Cleveland	American	54	*358	*26	16	.619	*378	*167	*150	109	102	3.77
1924–Cleveland	American	28	196	9	15	.375	238	134	104	57	75	4.78
1925–Cleveland	American	29	211	13	11	.542	218	118	96	68	78	4.09
1926–Cleveland	American	39	*318	*27	11	*.711	*300	114	100	159	*118	2.83
1927–Cleveland	American	25	153	8	9	.471	187	88	74	69	59	4.35
1928–Cleveland (a)	American	31	214	12	17	.414	252	121	97	74	48	4.08
1929–Detroit	American	32	249	15	11	.577	283	141	113	100	58	4.09
1930–Detroit	American	33	239	12	12	.500	239	110	97	117	75	3.65
1931–Detroit	American	29	193	11	12	.478	190	88	75	63	49	3.50
1932–Detroit	American	33	147	6	6	.500	152	84	73	51	42	4.47
1933–Detroit(b)-New York	American	13	62	6	1	.857	65	44	37	27	20	5.37

Year	Club	League	G.	IP.	W.	L.	Pct.	H.	R.	ER.	SO.	BB.	ERA.
1933—New York(c)		National	6	14	1	1	.500	16	12	12	4	6	7.71
1934—New York		American	10	16	2	4	.333	30	19	18	10	7	10.13
1934—Toledo		Amer. Assn.	19	70	2	4	.333	77	33	29	30	16	3.73
1935—							(Out of game)						
1936—Cleveland		American	7	13	0	1	.000	26	12	12	5	5	8.31
1938—Buffalo		International	2	3	0	0	.000	2	0	0	2	1	0.00
1939—Buffalo		International	6	11	1	0	1.000	14	9	7	5	1	5.73
American League Totals			507	3106	199	165	.547	3401	1623	1372	1131	960	3.98
National League Totals			6	14	1	1	.500	16	12	12	4	6	7.71
Major League Totals			513	3120	200	166	.546	3417	1635	1384	1135	966	3.99

aTraded to Detroit Tigers for infielder John Tavener and pitcher Ken Holloway, December 11, 1928.
bSold to New York Giants, April 24, 1933.
cUnconditionally released by New York Giants, July 8, 1933 and signed by New York Yankees, July 24, 1933. (Note that 1933 New York Giant record was compiled between Detroit and Yankee records of same season.)

WORLD SERIES RECORD

Year	Club	League	G.	IP.	W.	L.	Pct.	H.	R.	ER.	SO.	BB.	ERA.
1920—Cleveland		American	2	3	0	0	.000	1	0	0	3	0	0.00

ARTHUR CHARLES (DAZZY) VANCE

Born March 4, 1891, at Adair County, Ia.
Died February 16, 1961, at Homosassa Springs, Fla.
Height, 6.01. Weight, 200.
Threw and batted righthanded.

Holds National League record for most consecutive years leading league in strikeouts (7), 1922 to 1928, inclusive; holds league record for most years leading league in strikeouts (7), 1922 to 1928, inclusive; tied for National League record for consecutive strikeouts, start of game (5), September 26, 1926 (first game), since topped by many at 6; won 6 no-hit game, 10-1, against Philadelphia (first game), September 13, 1925.
Named Most Valuable Player, National League, 1924.
Named to Hall of Fame, 1955.

Year	Club	League	G.	IP.	W.	L.	Pct.	H.	R.	ER.	SO.	BB.	ERA.
1912—Red Cloud		Neb. State	36	....	11	15	.423	....	....	....	....	....	......
1913—Superior		Neb. State	25	....	11	14	.440	....	....	....	....	....	......
1914—Hastings		Neb. State	26	....	17	4	*.810	....	....	....	194	71	......
1914—St. Joseph		Western	21	134	9	8	.529	129	64	44	108	50	2.96
1915—Pittsburgh		National	1	3	0	1	.000	3	3	3	0	5	6.00
1915—St. Joseph		Western	39	264	17	15	.531	224	118	86	199	110	2.93
1915—New York		American	8	28	0	3	.000	23	14	11	18	16	3.54
1916—Columbus		Amer. Assn.	14	50	2	2	.500	52	....	25	10	16	4.50
1917—Toledo		Amer. Assn.	15	71	2	6	.250	63	31	18	30	25	2.28
1917—Memphis		Southern	16	122	6	8	.429	102	41	....	61	28	......
1918—Memphis		Southern	16	117	8	6	.571	93	....	....	40	33	......
1918—Rochester		International	9	72	3	5	.375	85	39	31	34	23	3.88
1918—New York		American	2	2	0	0	.000	9	5	4	0	2	18.00
1919—Sacramento		Pacific Coast	48	294	10	18	.357	264	125	92	86	81	2.82
1920—Memphis-New Orleans		Southern	45	284	16	17	.485	253	104	....	65	65	......
1921—New Orleans		Southern	38	253	21	11	.656	225	115	99	163	80	3.52
1922—Brooklyn		National	36	246	18	12	.600	259	122	101	*134	94	3.70
1923—Brooklyn		National	37	280	18	15	.545	263	127	109	*197	100	3.50
1924—Brooklyn		National	35	309	*28	6	.824	238	89	74	*262	77	*2.16
1925—Brooklyn		National	31	265	*22	9	.710	247	115	104	*221	66	3.53
1926—Brooklyn		National	24	169	9	10	.474	172	80	73	*140	58	3.89
1927—Brooklyn		National	34	273	16	15	.516	242	98	82	*184	69	2.70
1928—Brooklyn		National	38	280	22	10	.688	226	79	65	*200	72	*2.09
1929—Brooklyn		National	31	231	14	13	.519	244	110	100	126	47	3.90
1930—Brooklyn		National	35	259	17	15	.531	241	97	75	173	55	*2.61
1931—Brooklyn		National	30	219	11	13	.458	221	99	82	150	53	3.37
1932—Brooklyn(a)		National	27	176	12	11	.522	171	90	82	103	57	4.19
1933—St. Louis(b)		National	28	99	6	2	.750	105	42	39	67	28	3.55
1934—Cincinnati(c)-St.L.(d)		National	25	77	1	3	.250	90	47	39	42	25	4.56
1935—Brooklyn		National	20	51	3	2	.600	55	29	25	28	16	4.41
American League Totals			10	30	0	3	.000	32	19	15	18	18	4.50
National League Totals			432	2937	197	137	.590	2777	1227	1053	2027	822	3.23
Major League Totals			442	2967	197	140	.585	2809	1246	1068	2045	840	3.24

aTraded to St. Louis Cardinals with shortstop Gordon Slade for infielder Jake Flowers and pitcher Owen Carroll, February 9, 1933.
bSold to Cincinnati Reds, February 6, 1934.

cReleased to St. Louis Cardinals on waivers, June 25, 1934.
dUnconditionally released by St. Louis Cardinals and signed by Brooklyn Dodgers, April, 1935.

WORLD SERIES RECORD

Year	Club	League	G.	IP.	W.	L.	Pct.	H.	R.	ER.	SO.	BB.	ERA.
1934	St. Louis	National	1	1⅓	0	0	.000	2	1	0	3	1	0.00

GEORGE E. VAN HALTREN

Born March 30, 1866, at St. Louis, Mo.
Died October 1, 1945, at Oakland, Calif.
Threw and batted lefthanded.

Pitched six-inning no-hitter against Pittsburgh, June 21, 1888.
Manager, Baltimore, American Association, 1891, and in National League, 1892; umpire, Pacific Coast League. 1909; scout, Pittsburgh, N. L., 1910-11; umpire, Northwestern League, 1912.

Year	Club	League	Pos.	G.	AB.	R.	H.	2B.	3B.	HR.	SB.	B.A.	PO.	A.	E.	F.A.
1887	Chicago	Nat.	P-OF	44	183	29	51	4	0	3	12	.278	35	3	4	.904
1888	Chicago	Nat.	P-OF	81	318	46	90	10	12	4	21	.283	73	9	12	.872
1889	Chicago	Nat.	OF	134	543	126	175	20	10	9	28	.322	222	25	28	.898
1890	Brooklyn	Players	P-OF	92	376	86	130	8	8	5	19	.346	134	30	15	.945
1891	Baltimore	A.A.	P-S-O	139	566	136	180	19	15	9	48	.318	275	190	82	.850
1892	Balt.(a)-Pitts.	Nat.	*O-P-3-SS-1	148	604	116	179	23	13	6	57	.296	274	56	54	.859
1893	Pittsburgh	Nat.	OF	123	502	129	176	14	11	3	35	.350	222	20	36	.871
1894	New York	Nat.	OF	139	532	110	177	25	4	8	44	.333	309	28	33	.911
1895	New York	Nat.	OF	131	517	112	175	23	17	6	31	.338	256	28	32	.899
1896	New York	Nat.	P-OF	•133	564	138	199	19	•21	5	42	.353	271	•24	18	.942
1897	New York	Nat.	OF	131	*571	122	190	22	11	3	45	.332	268	31	21	.934
1898	New York	Nat.	OF	155	*651	129	205	27	17	2	31	.315	299	21	25	.927
1899	New York	Nat.	OF	153	607	119	183	22	4	2	33	.301	285	29	18	.949
1900	New York	Nat.	OF	141	568	113	181	28	6	1	45	.319	322	23	19	.947
1901	New York	Nat.	P-OF	133	544	83	186	22	7	1	25	.342	259	24	18	.940
1902	New York	Nat.	OF	26	96	14	24	1	2	0	7	.250	46	6	5	.912
1903	New York	Nat.	OF	75	280	42	72	6	1	0	14	.257	136	3	6	.959
1904	Seattle	Pac. Coast	OF	....	*941	159	253	35	10	4	38	.269	493	58	31	.947
1905	Oakland	Pac. Coast	OF	220	860	....	220	18	10	2	47	.256	459	32	26	.950
1906	Oakland	Pac. Coast	OF	152	697	101	151	27	4	0	36	.217	....	....	....	....
1907	Oakland	Pac. Coast	OF	193	718	101	193	26	0	0	47	.269	415	28	21	.955
1908	Oakland	Pac. Coast	OF	186	706	80	171	17	3	2	30	.242	379	48	14	.969
1909	Oakland	Pac. Coast	OF	55	192	14	42	....	....	....	....	.219	95	5	4	.962
National League Totals				1747	7080	1428	2263	266	136	53	470	.320	3277	330	329	.916
Players League Totals				92	376	86	130	8	8	5	19	.346	134	30	15	.945
American Association Totals				139	566	136	180	19	15	9	48	.318	275	190	82	.850
Major League Totals				1978	8022	1650	2573	293	159	67	537	.321	3686	550	426	.909

aTraded to Pittsburgh in deal for outfielder James J. Kelley, September, 1892.

PITCHING RECORD

Year	Club	League	G.	W.	L.	Pct.	H.	R.	CG.	ShO.
1887	Chicago	National	19	12	7	.632	226	102	19	1
1888	Chicago	National	27	13	11	.542	264	160	23	4
1890	Brooklyn	Players	26	15	10	.600	275	190	24	0
1891	Baltimore	American Association	6	0	1	.000	38	....	0	0
1892	Baltimore	National	4	0	0	.000	28	....	0	0
1895	New York	National	1	0	0	.000	13	....	0	0
1896	New York	National	2	1	0	1.000	5	....	0	0
1900	New York	National	1	0	0	.000	1	0	0	0
1901	New York	National	1	0	1	.000	12	....	0	0
Major League Totals			87	41	30	.577	862	....	66	5

DID YOU KNOW—

That George Van Haltren tied a major league record on June 27, 1887, when he walked 16 batters in one game?

JOSEPH FLOYD (ARKY) VAUGHAN

Born March 9, 1912, at Clifty, Ark.
Died August 30, 1952, at Eagleville, Calif.
Height, 5.11. Weight, 185.
Threw right and batted lefthanded.
Married Margaret Allen, October 31, 1931.

Equaled National League record for most consecutive years leading in receiving bases on balls—3 (1934–94, 1935–97 and 1936–118). Hit for cycle, June 24, 1933. Led N. L. in stolen bases, 1943. Hit two home runs in 1941 All-Star Game for National League.
Named by Baseball Writers' Association of America as shortstop for THE SPORTING NEWS All-Star Major League Team, 1935. Named Most Valuable Player in National League by THE SPORTING NEWS, 1935.

Year	Club	League	Pos.	G.	AB.	R.	H.	2B.	3B.	HR.	RBI.	B.A.	PO.	A.	E.	F.A.
1931	Wichita	West.	SS-3B	132	494	*145	167	21	16	21	81	.338	216	352	32	.947
1932	Pittsburgh	Nat.	SS	129	497	71	158	15	10	4	61	.318	247	403	*46	.934
1933	Pittsburgh	Nat.	SS	152	573	85	180	29	*19	9	97	.314	310	487	*46	.945
1934	Pittsburgh	Nat.	SS	149	558	115	186	41	11	12	94	.333	329	480	41	.952
1935	Pittsburgh	Nat.	SS	137	499	108	192	34	10	19	99	*.385	249	422	35	.950
1936	Pittsburgh	Nat.	SS	•156	568	*122	190	30	11	9	78	.335	*327	477	47	.945
1937	Pittsburgh	Nat.	SS-OF	126	469	71	151	17	*17	5	72	.322	257	335	27	.956
1938	Pittsburgh	Nat.	SS	148	541	88	174	35	5	7	68	.322	*306	*507	33	.961
1939	Pittsburgh	Nat.	SS	152	595	94	182	30	11	6	62	.306	*330	*531	34	.962
1940	Pittsburgh	Nat.	*SS-3B	*156	594	*113	178	40	*15	7	95	.300	309	*546	52	*.943
1941	Pittsburgh(a)	Nat.	SS-3B	106	374	69	118	20	7	6	38	.316	174	298	21	.957
1942	Brooklyn	Nat.	3-2B-SS	128	495	82	137	18	4	2	49	.277	130	225	14	.962
1943	Brooklyn	Nat.	3B-SS	149	610	*112	186	39	6	5	66	.305	237	375	21	.967
1944-45-46	Brooklyn	Nat.					(Voluntarily retired)									
1947	Brooklyn	Nat.	3B-OF	64	126	24	41	5	2	2	25	.325	56	20	0	1.000
1948	Brooklyn	Nat.	3B-OF	65	123	19	30	3	0	2	22	.244	47	14	0	1.000
1949	San Francisco	P.C.L.	OF	97	281	50	81	10	6	2	26	.288	129	4	2	.985
Major League Totals				1817	6622	1173	2103	356	128	96	926	.318	3308	5120	417	.953

aTraded to Brooklyn for pitcher Luke Hamlin, catcher Babe Phelps, infielder Pete Coscarart and outfielder Jim Wasdell, December 12, 1941.

WORLD SERIES RECORD

Year	Club	League	Pos.	G.	AB.	R.	H.	2B.	3B.	HR.	RBI.	B.A.	PO.	A.	E.	F.A.
1947	Brooklyn	Nat.	PH	3	2	0	1	1	0	0	0	.500	0	0	0	.000

JAMES LESLIE (HIPPO) VAUGHN

Born April 9, 1888, at Weatherford, Tex.
Died May 29, 1966, at Chicago, Ill.
Height, 6.04. Weight, 215.
Threw left and batted left and righthanded.
Married Edna DeBold, February 12, 1916.

Had lowest earned-run average in major leagues, 2000 or more innings, career (2.33).
Outstanding performances—Pitched no-hit game for nine and one-third innings against Cincinnati, May 2, 1917, but lost, 1-0, on two hits in tenth inning to Fred Toney, who did not allow a hit in same game; pitched no-hit, no-run games against Columbia, Sally League, May 22, 1909, and against Toledo, American Association, June 23, 1913.
World Series record—Tied records for most innings pitched, six-game Series (27), most chances accepted by pitcher (17), and most putouts (6), 1918.

Year	Club	League	G.	IP.	W.	L.	Pct.	H.	R.	ER.	SO.	BB.	ERA.
1906	Temple	Tex.						(No Record Available)					
1907	Corsicana	So. Tex.						(No Record Available)					
1908	Hot Springs	Ark. St.	12	....	9	1	.900	....	....	....	....	....	......
1908	Scranton	N.Y. St.	2	....	0	2	.000	....	....	....	....	....	......
1908	Macon (a)	So. Atl.	5	....	1	1	.500	....	....	....	....	....	......
1908	New York (b)	Amer.	2	2	0	0	.000	2	1	....	2	5	......
1909	Macon	So. Atl.	31	231	9	16	.360	170	87	....	175	56	1.95
1909	Louisville	A.A.	9	79	8	1	.889	62	....	....	47	20	......
1910	New York	Amer.	29	221	13	11	.542	190	76	....	107	58	2.50

Year	Club	League	G.	IP.	W.	L.	Pct.	H.	R.	ER.	SO.	BB.	ERA.
1911—New York		Amer.	26	145	8	10	.444	158	92	....	74	54	1.71
1912—N.Y. (c)-Wash. (d)		Amer.	27	144	6	11	.353	141	81	....	95	70	1.74
1912—Kansas City		A.A.	5	22	2	1	.667	11	....	....	9	5	2.75
1913—Kansas City (e)		A.A.	42	255	14	13	.519	195	95	....	176	149	2.05
1913—Chicago		Nat.	7	56	5	1	.833	37	13	9	36	27	1.45
1914—Chicago		Nat.	42	293	21	13	.618	236	119	67	165	109	2.06
1915—Chicago		Nat.	41	270	20	12	.625	240	105	86	148	77	2.87
1916—Chicago		Nat.	44	294	17	15	.531	269	94	72	144	67	2.20
1917—Chicago		Nat.	41	296	23	13	.639	255	97	66	195	91	2.01
1918—Chicago		Nat.	35	*290	*22	10	.688	216	75	56	*148	76	*1.74
1919—Chicago		Nat.	38	*307	21	14	.600	264	83	61	*141	62	1.79
1920—Chicago		Nat.	40	301	19	16	.543	301	113	85	131	81	2.54
1921—Chicago		Nat.	17	109	3	11	.214	153	90	73	30	31	6.03
American League Totals			84	512	27	32	.458	491	250	....	278	187	....
National League Totals			305	2217	151	105	.590	1971	789	575	1138	621	2.33
Major League Totals			389	2729	178	137	.565	2462	1039	....	1416	808	......

WORLD SERIES RECORD

Year	Club	League	G.	IP.	W.	L.	Pct.	H.	R.	ER.	SO.	BB.	ERA.
1918—Chicago		Nat.	3	27	1	2	.333	17	3	3	17	5	1.00

aSold to New York Yankees, May 15, 1908.
bOptioned to Macon and later to Louisville, 1909, and recalled at close of season.
cSold to Washington Senators on waivers, June 26, 1912.
dTraded to Kansas City for pitcher Melvin Gallia, August 25, 1912.
eTraded to Chicago Cubs for pitcher Lewis Richie, August 13, 1913.

ROBERT HAYES (BOBBY) VEACH

Born June 29, 1888, at St. Charles, Ky.
Died August 7, 1945, at Detroit, Mich.
Height, 5.10. Weight, 160.
Threw right and batted lefthanded.
Married Ethel Clare Spiller, January 22, 1910.

Made six hits, including double, triple and home run, in six times at bat, September 17, 1920 (12 innings).

Year	Club	League	Pos.	G.	AB.	R.	H.	2B.	3B.	HR.	RBI.	B.A.	PO.	A.	E.	F.A.
1910—Peoria		I.I.I.	3B	35	117	8	27	....	....	....	....	.231	36	54	8	.918
1910—Kankakee		N. Assn.	OF	26	77	13	17	6	0	0	....	.221	....	....	....	....
1911—Peoria		I.I.I.	OF	132	445	59	132	....	....	....	....	.297	197	29	5	.978
1912—Peoria		I.I.I.	OF	56	200	35	65	....	....	....	....	.325	100	14	4	.966
1912—Indianapolis		A.A.	OF	70	253	37	72	13	3	4	....	.285	116	18	10	.931
1912—Detroit		Amer.	OF	23	79	8	27	5	1	0	13	.342	46	5	4	.927
1913—Detroit		Amer.	OF	138	494	55	133	22	10	0	62	.269	251	16	●24	.918
1914—Detroit		Amer.	OF	149	531	56	146	19	14	1	75	.275	282	22	11	.965
1915—Detroit		Amer.	OF	152	569	81	178	▲40	10	3	115	.313	297	19	8	.975
1916—Detroit		Amer.	OF	150	566	92	173	33	15	3	88	.306	342	14	12	.967
1917—Detroit		Amer.	OF	154	571	79	182	31	12	8	*115	.319	356	17	*17	.956
1918—Detroit		Amer.	OF	127	499	59	139	21	13	3	●74	.279	277	14	7	.977
1919—Detroit		Amer.	OF	139	538	87	●191	*45	*17	3	98	.355	338	14	12	.967
1920—Detroit		Amer.	OF	●154	612	92	188	39	15	11	113	.307	357	●26	13	.967
1921—Detroit		Amer.	OF	150	612	110	207	43	13	16	128	.338	*384	21	11	.974
1922—Detroit		Amer.	OF	●155	618	96	202	34	13	9	126	.327	375	16	7	.982
1923—Detroit (a)		Amer.	OF	114	293	45	94	13	3	2	39	.321	127	6	8	.943
1924—Boston		Amer.	OF	142	519	77	153	35	9	5	99	.295	270	15	13	.956
1925—Bo(b)-NY(c)-W.		Amer.	OF	75	158	17	51	13	2	0	25	.323	53	6	3	.952
1926—Toledo		A.A.	OF	156	588	113	213	43	14	9	105	.362	357	13	13	.966
1927—Toledo		A.A.	OF	164	623	133	226	45	10	12	*145	.363	371	17	14	.965
1928—Toledo		A.A.	OF	151	566	93	216	32	6	7	102	*.382	319	12	17	.951
1929—Toledo		A.A.	OF-PH	79	255	39	68	11	1	4	36	.267	126	7	6	.957
1930—Jersey City		Int.	OF-PH	75	219	34	68	14	2	5	35	.311	69	0	5	.932
Major League Totals				1822	6659	954	2064	393	147	64	1170	.310	3755	211	150	.964

aSold to Boston Red Sox, January 12, 1924.
bTraded to New York Yankees with pitcher Alex Ferguson for pitcher Ray Francis and $8,000, May 9, 1924.
cReleased to Washington Senators on waivers, August 17, 1924.

WORLD SERIES RECORD

Year	Club	League	Pos.	G.	AB.	R.	H.	2B.	3B.	HR.	RBI.	B.A.	PO.	A.	E.	F.A.
1925—Washington		Amer.	PH	2	1	0	0	0	0	0	1	.000	0	0	0	.000

JAMES BARTON (MICKEY) VERNON

Born April 22, 1918, at Marcus Hook, Pa.
Height, 6.02. Weight, 188.
Threw and batted lefthanded.
Married Anne Elizabeth Firth, March 14, 1941.

Established major league record for most assists by a first baseman, season (155), 1949; holds American League record for most games played at first base, lifetime (2,227), 1958; A. L. record for most assists by first baseman, lifetime (1,444), 1958; holds American League record for first basemen for most putouts, lifetime (19,754), 1958; participated in ten double plays in a doubleheader, August 18, 1943; made two unassisted double plays in a game at first base, May 29, 1946. Led A.L. first basemen in double plays, 1941, 1953, 1954. Named as first baseman on THE SPORTING NEWS All-Star Major League Team, 1953.

Coach, Pittsburgh Pirates, 1960, until placed on playing roster, September 1, 1960, to September 30, 1960, released November 19, 1960; manager, Washington Senators, 1961, until released May 22, 1963; coach, Pittsburgh Pirates, 1964; coach, St. Louis Cardinals 1965; manager, Vancouver, Pacific Coast League, November 27, 1965 through 1968; scout and minor league manager, Atlanta Braves, 1969 (manager, farm club Richmond, International League), 1969-1970; minor league instructor, New York Yankees, 1971 (manager of Manchester, Eastern League); minor league batting instructor, Kansas City Royals, 1973-1974; batting instructor, Los Angeles Dodgers, 1975-1976; coach, Montreal Expos, 1977-1978; returned as minor league batting instructor, New York Yankees, 1979 to date (managed Yankee farm Columbus, International League, 1979).

Year	Club	League	Pos.	G.	AB.	R.	H.	2B.	3B.	HR.	RBI.	B.A.	PO.	A.	E.	F.A.
1937	Easton	E. Shore	1B	83	300	51	86	24	6	10	64	.287	814	54	*16	.982
1938	Greenville	Sally	1B	132	524	84	172	31	12	1	72	.328	1159	74	*24	.981
1939	Springfield	East.	1B	69	268	52	92	13	7	3	41	.343	601	31	6	.991
1939	Washington	Amer.	1B	76	276	23	71	15	4	1	30	.257	690	40	11	.985
1940	Jersey City	Int.	1B	154	569	76	161	22	9	9	65	.283	1305	75	16	.989
1940	Washington	Amer.	1B	5	19	0	3	0	0	0	0	.158	41	2	0	1.000
1941	Washington	Amer.	1B	138	531	73	159	27	11	9	93	.299	1186	80	10	.992
1942	Washington	Amer.	1B	151	621	76	168	34	6	9	86	.271	1360	95	*26	.982
1943	Washington	Amer.	1B	145	553	89	148	29	8	7	70	.268	1351	75	14	.990
1944-45	Washington	Amer.						(In Military Service)								
1946	Washington	Amer.	1B	148	587	88	207	*51	8	8	85	*.353	1320	101	*15	.990
1947	Washington	Amer.	1B	154	600	77	159	29	12	7	85	.265	1299	105	*19	.987
1948	Washington(a)	Amer.	1B	150	558	78	135	27	7	3	48	.242	1297	113	15	.989
1949	Cleveland	Amer.	1B	153	584	72	170	27	4	18	83	.291	*1438	*155	14	.991
1950	Cleve.(b)-Wash.	Amer.	1B	118	417	55	117	17	3	9	75	.281	959	78	9	●.991
1951	Washington	Amer.	1B	141	546	69	160	30	7	9	87	.293	1157	87	8	*.994
1952	Washington	Amer.	1B	154	569	71	143	33	9	10	80	.251	1291	115	10	*.993
1953	Washington	Amer.	1B	152	608	101	205	*43	11	15	115	*.337	*1376	94	12	.992
1954	Washington	Amer.	1B	151	597	90	173	*33	14	20	97	.290	*1365	76	11	●.992
1955	Washington(c)	Amer.	1B	150	538	74	162	23	8	14	85	.301	1258	69	8	.994
1956	Boston	Amer.	1B	119	403	67	125	28	4	15	84	.310	930	58	6	.989
1957	Boston(d)	Amer.	1B	102	270	36	65	18	1	7	38	.241	662	51	6	.992
1958	Cleveland(e)	Amer.	1B	119	355	49	104	22	3	8	55	.293	774	50	11	.987
1959	Milwaukee(f)	Nat.	1B-OF	74	91	8	20	4	0	3	14	.220	65	4	2	.972
1960	Pittsburgh	Nat.	PH	9	8	0	1	0	0	0	1	.125	0	0	0	.000
	American League Totals			2326	8632	1188	2474	486	120	169	1296	.287	19754	1444	210	.990
	National League Totals			83	99	8	21	4	0	3	15	.212	65	4	2	.972
	Major League Totals			2409	8731	1196	2495	490	120	172	1311	.286	19819	1448	212	.990

aTraded to Cleveland Indians with pitcher Early Wynn for pitchers Joe Haynes and Ed Klieman and first baseman Eddie Robinson, December 14, 1948.

bTraded to Washington Senators for pitcher Dick Weik, June 14, 1950.

cTraded to Boston Red Sox with pitchers Bob Porterfield and Johnny Schmitz and outfielder Tom Umphlett for pitchers Dick Brodowski, Truman Clevenger and Al Curtis, outfielders Neil Chrisley and Karl Olson, November 8, 1955.

dReleased to Cleveland Indians on waivers, January 29, 1958.

eTraded to Milwaukee Braves for pitcher Humberto Robinson, April 11, 1959.

fUnconditionally released by Milwaukee Braves, October 13, 1959 and signed with Pittsburgh Pirates for 1960.

DID YOU KNOW—

That Mickey Vernon typifies the consistent, fundamental ballplayer managers dream about? He was as gifted at bat as he was afield. He leads A.L. first basemen in games played, assists, putouts and was DP leader many years. He also averaged a hit a game for his career—2495 hits in 2409 games.

JOSEPH FRANKLIN VOSMIK

Born April 4, 1910, at Cleveland O.
Died January 27, 1962, at Cleveland, O.
Height, 6.00. Weight, 185.
Threw and batted righthanded.
Married Sally Joanne Okla, November 4, 1936.

Manager, Tucson, Arizona-Texas League, 1947; manager, Dayton, Central League, 1948; manager, Oklahoma City, Texas League, 1949-50; manager, Batavia, Pony League, 1951; scout, Cleveland Indians, 1951-52.

Year Club	League	Pos.	G.	AB.	R.	H.	2B.	3B.	HR.	RBI.	B.A.	PO.	A.	E.	F.A.
1929—Frederick	Bl. Ridge.	OF	112	407	81	•155	*39	*24	9	.....	.381	192	*28	6	.973
1930—Terre Haute	I.I.I.	OF	121	458	100	182	25	15	13	116*	.397	286	13	12	.961
1930—Cleveland	Amer.	OF	9	26	1	6	2	0	0	4	.231	16	1	1	.944
1931—Cleveland	Amer.	OF	149	591	80	189	36	14	7	117	.320	315	12	10	.970
1932—Cleveland	Amer.	OF	153	621	106	194	39	12	10	97	.312	432	12	5	*.989
1933—Cleveland	Amer.	OF	119	438	53	115	20	10	4	56	.263	242	15	4	.985
1934—Cleveland	Amer.	OF	104	405	71	138	33	2	6	78	.341	199	7	5	.976
1935—Cleveland	Amer.	OF	152	620	93	*216	*47	*20	10	110	.348	347	5	5	.986
1936—Cleveland(a)	Amer.	OF	138	506	76	145	29	7	7	94	.277	258	11	6	.978
1937—St. Louis(b)	Amer.	OF	144	594	81	193	47	9	4	93	.325	333	12	10	.972
1938—Boston	Amer.	OF	146	621	121	*201	37	6	9	86	.324	302	14	7	.978
1939—Boston(c)	Amer.	OF	145	554	89	153	29	6	7	84	.276	296	9	8	.974
1940—Brooklyn	Nat.	OF	116	404	45	114	14	6	1	42	.282	193	9	5	.976
1941—Brooklyn	Nat.	OF	25	56	0	11	0	0	0	4	.196	12	0	0	1.000
1941—Louisville	A. A.	OF	42	144	15	42	9	2	1	20	.292	72	1	0	1.000
1942—Minneapolis	A. A.	OF	147	513	64	156	34	2	8	78	.304	272	12	4	.986
1943—Minneapolis	A. A.	OF	146	498	66	126	25	2	5	62	.253	278	14	3	*.990
1944—Minneapolis	A. A.	OF	39	111	17	31	3	0	1	16	.279	49	4	1	.981
1944—Washington	Amer.	OF	14	36	2	7	2	0	0	9	.194	16	0	0	1.000
1947—Tucson	Ariz.-Tex.	OF	30	48	7	17	4	0	1	10	.354	22	1	1	.958
American League Totals			1273	5012	773	1557	321	86	64	828	.310	2756	98	61	.979
National League Totals			141	460	45	125	14	6	1	46	.272	205	9	5	.977
Major League Totals			1414	5472	818	1682	335	92	65	874	.307	2961	107	66	.979

aTraded with pitcher Oral Hilderbrand and shortstop Bill Knickerbocker to St. Louis Browns for pitcher Ivy Andrews, shortstop Lyn Lary and outfielder Julius Solters, January 17, 1937.
bTraded to Boston Red Sox for infielder Ralph Kress, outfielder Colonel Mills and pitcher Louis Newsom, December 2, 1937.
cSold to Brooklyn Dodgers for $25,000, February 12, 1940.

GEORGE EDWARD (RUBE) WADDELL

Born October 13, 1876, at Bradford, Pa.
Died April 1, 1914, at San Antonio, Tex.
Height, 6.01½. Weight, 196.
Threw and batted lefthanded.

Struck out 16 Philadelphia Athletics, July 29, 1908; established American League record of 349 strikeouts for season, 1904 (since topped by Nolan Ryan with 383 in 1973). Waddell still holds mark as an American League lefthander, most strikeouts, season.
Named to Hall of Fame, 1946.

Year Club	League	G.	IP.	W.	L.	Pct.	H.	R.	SO.	BB.	CG.	ShO.
1897—Louisville	National	2	13	0	1	.000	13	7	5	6	1	0
1898—Detroit	Western	9	....	4	4	.500	61	....	31	30	....	....
1899—Col.-Grand Rapids	American	42	330	27	13	.675	....	154	....	....	....	....
1899—Louisville	National	10	80	7	2	.778	71	38	41	16	9	1
1900—Pittsburgh	National	29	212	9	11	.450	186	101*	133	53	16	2
1900—Milwaukee	American	15	129	10	3	.769	90	28	75	20	13	2
1901—Pittsburgh-Chicago	National	31	250	13	16	.448	252	136	167	67	26	0
1902—Los Angeles	Pacific Coast	20	178	12	8	.600	128	66	142	37	19	2
1902—Philadelphia	American	33	275	23	7	.767	224	89	*210	67	26	3
1903—Philadelphia	American	39	323	21	16	.568	271	112	*301	74	34	4
1904—Philadelphia	American	46	384	25	19	.568	309	111	*349	81	39	8

Year	Club	League	G.	IP.	W.	L.	Pct.	H.	R.	SO.	BB.	CG.	ShO.
1905	Philadelphia	American	*46	324	*26	11	.703	230	86	*286	91	27	7
1906	Philadelphia	American	43	272	15	17	.469	219	89	*203	88	22	8
1907	Philadelphia	American	44	285	19	13	.594	247	120	*226	72	20	7
1908	St. Louis	American	43	286	19	14	.576	223	93	232	90	25	5
1909	St. Louis	American	31	220	11	14	.440	204	78	141	57	16	5
1910	St. Louis	American	10	34	3	1	.750	31	19	16	9	0	0
1910	Newark	Eastern	15	97	5	3	.625	73	....	53	41	....	....
1911	Minneapolis	Amer. Assn.	54	300	20	17	.541	262	133	185	96	....	....
1912	Minneapolis	Amer. Assn.	33	151	12	6	.667	138	67	113	59	....	....
1913	Virginia	Northern	15	84	3	9	.250	86	....	82	20	....	....
	American League Totals		335	2403	162	112	.591	1958	797	1964	329	209	47
	National League Totals		72	555	29	30	.492	522	282	346	142	52	3
	Major League Totals		407	2958	191	142	.574	2480	1079	2310	771	261	50

JOHN PETER (HONUS) WAGNER

Born February 24, 1874, at Carnegie, Pa.
Died December 6, 1955, at Carnegie, Pa.
Height, 5.11. Weight, 200.
Threw and batted righthanded.

Batted .300 or better for 17 years (consecutively). Played 100 or more games, 19 successive years. Holds National League lead in most singles, 2,426, and most triples, 252. Stole 720 bases; led National League in stolen bases, 1901, 1902, 1904, 1907 and 1908.
Coach, Pittsburgh, National League, 1933 through 1951.
Named to Hall of Fame, 1936.

Year	Club	League	Pos.	G.	AB.	R.	H.	2B.	3B.	HR.	RBI.	B.A.	PO.	A.	E.	F.A.
1895	Steubenville	Int. St.	SS	44	....	....	....	....	....	....	....	.402	....	....	....	....
1895	Mansfield	Ohio St.						(No records available)								
1895	Adrian	Mich. St.	S-O	20	....	....	....	....	....	....	....	.365	....	....	....	....
1895	Warren	Iron-Oil	SS	65	....	....	....	....	....	....	....	.369	....	....	....	....
1896	Paterson	Atl.	1-3-OF	109	416	106	145	....	....	....	....	.349	802	79	41	.956
1897	Paterson	Atlantic	3B	74	301	61	114	....	....	....	....	.379	104	107	24	.898
1897	Louisville	Nat.	OF	61	241	38	83	17	4	2	....	.344	105	17	11	.917
1898	Louisville	Nat.	1B-3B	148	591	80	180	31	4	10	....	.305	827	165	32	.969
1899	Louisville(a)	Nat.	3B-OF	144	549	102	197	47	13	7	....	.359	197	185	30	.927
1900	Pittsburgh	Nat.	OF	134	528	107	201	*45	*22	4	....	*.381	177	13	6	.969
1901	Pittsburgh	Nat.	IF-OF	141	556	100	196	●39	10	6	....	.353	299	279	47	.925
1902	Pittsburgh	Nat.	IF-OF	137	538	*105	177	*33	16	3	....	.329	526	171	34	.953
1903	Pittsburgh	Nat.	SS	129	512	97	182	30	*19	5	....	*.355	303	397	50	.933
1904	Pittsburgh	Nat.	SS	132	490	97	171	*44	14	4	....	*.349	274	367	49	.929
1905	Pittsburgh	Nat.	SS	147	548	114	199	22	14	6	....	.363	353	517	*60	.935
1906	Pittsburgh	Nat.	SS	140	516	●103	175	*38	9	2	....	*.339	334	473	51	.941
1907	Pittsburgh	Nat.	SS	142	515	98	180	*38	14	6	*91	*.350	314	428	49	.938
1908	Pittsburgh	Nat.	SS	151	568	100	*201	*39	*19	10	*106	*.354	*354	469	50	.943
1909	Pittsburgh	Nat.	SS	137	495	92	168	*39	10	5	*102	*.339	344	430	49	●.940
1910	Pittsburgh	Nat.	SS	150	556	90	●178	34	8	4	84	.320	*337	413	52	.935
1911	Pittsburgh	Nat.	SS-1B	130	473	87	158	23	16	9	108	*.334	471	321	46	.945
1912	Pittsburgh	Nat.	SS	145	558	91	181	35	20	7	94	.324	341	462	32	*.962
1913	Pittsburgh	Nat.	SS	114	413	51	124	18	4	3	55	.300	289	323	24	.962
1914	Pittsburgh	Nat.	3B-SS	150	552	60	139	15	9	1	46	.252	339	457	43	*.949
1915	Pittsburgh	Nat.	SS	156	566	68	155	32	17	6	78	.274	298	395	38	*.948
1016	Pittsburgh	Nat.	1B-SS	123	432	45	124	15	9	1	38	.287	409	272	33	.954
1917	Pittsburgh	Nat.	1-3-SS	74	230	15	61	7	1	0	22	.265	476	74	13	.977
	Major League Totals			2785	10427	1740	3430	651	252	101	....	.329	7367	6628	799	.946

aTransferred with 14 other players to Pittsburgh when Louisville dropped out of National League.

WORLD SERIES RECORD

Year	Club	League	Pos.	G.	AB.	R.	H.	2B.	3B.	HR.	RBI.	B.A.	PO.	A.	E.	F.A.
1903	Pittsburgh	Nat.	SS	8	27	2	6	1	0	0	3	.222	13	27	6	.870
1909	Pittsburgh	Nat.	SS	7	24	4	8	2	1	0	7	.333	13	23	2	.947
	World Series Totals			15	51	6	14	3	1	0	10	.275	26	50	8	.905

DID YOU KNOW—
That Honus Wagner along with Babe Ruth, Ty Cobb, Walter Johnson and Christy Mathewson were the original five players elected to the Hall of Fame in 1936?

LEON LAMAR WAGNER

Born May 13, 1934, at Chattanooga, Tenn.
Height, 6.01. Weight, 192.
Threw right and batted lefthanded.
Married Doris Jean Hudson, October 30, 1965.

Established American League record for most games, season, outfielder (163), 1964.
Selected as outfielder on American League All-Star Team by THE SPORTING NEWS, 1962.
Player-coach, Hawaii, Pacific Coast League, 1971.

Year	Club	League	Pos.	G.	AB.	R.	H.	2B.	3B.	HR.	RBI.	B.A.	PO.	A.	E.	F.A.
1954—Danville		M.-O.V.	OF	125	482	108	•160	23	16	24	115	.332	198	•20	•14	.940
1955—St. Cloud		North.	OF	125	501	102	157	33	5	•29	•127	.313	194	14	14	.937
1956—Danville		Carol.	OF	152	543	118	179	23	2	•51	•166	.330	238	18	8	.970
1957—Minneapolis		A.A.					(In Military Service)									
1958—Phoenix		P.C.	OF	65	233	49	74	10	1	17	58	.318	112	5	7	.944
1958—San Francisco		Nat.	OF	74	221	31	70	9	0	13	35	.317	89	5	5	.949
1959—San Fran.(a)		Nat.	OF	87	129	20	29	4	3	5	22	.225	48	0	3	.941
1960—St. Louis		Nat.	OF	39	98	12	21	2	0	1	11	.214	48	4	2	.963
1960—Rochester(b)(c)		Int.	OF	93	294	49	78	9	2	16	48	.265	141	8	3	.980
1961—Los Angeles		Amer.	OF	133	453	74	127	19	2	28	79	.280	187	12	6	.971
1962—Los Angeles		Amer.	OF	160	612	96	164	21	5	37	107	.268	269	7	8	.972
1963—Los Angeles(d)		.Amer.	OF	149	550	73	160	11	1	26	90	.291	254	7	•11	.960
1964—Cleveland		Amer.	OF	•163	641	94	162	19	2	31	100	.253	254	5	11	.959
1965—Cleveland		Amer.	OF	144	517	91	152	18	1	28	79	.294	175	3	8	.957
1966—Cleveland		Amer.	OF	150	549	70	153	20	0	23	66	.279	185	4	2	.990
1967—Cleveland		Amer.	OF	135	433	56	105	15	1	15	54	.242	142	4	3	.980
1968—Clev.(e)-Chi		Amer.	OF-PH	107	211	19	55	12	0	1	24	.261	51	0	6	.895
1969—Phoenix		P.C.	OF-PH	78	166	21	49	10	2	6	41	.295	51	0	2	.962
1969—San Francisco		Nat.	OF-PH	11	12	0	4	0	0	0	2	.333	3	0	0	1.000
1970—Phoenix		P.C.	OF-PH	45	53	4	10	2	1	2	8	.189	7	0	0	1.000
1971—Hawaii		P.C.	OF-PH	75	143	25	36	4	2	9	33	.252	42	1	1	.977
American League Totals				1141	3966	573	1078	135	12	189	599	.272	1517	42	55	.966
National League Totals				211	460	63	124	15	3	22	70	.270	188	9	10	.952
Major League Totals				1352	4426	636	1202	150	15	211	669	.272	1705	51	65	.964

aTraded to St. Louis Cardinals with shortstop Daryl Spencer for second baseman Don Blasingame, December 15, 1959.

bTraded by St. Louis Cardinals to Toronto, International League, with pitcher Cal Browning, outfielder Ellis Burton and cash for pitcher Al Cicotte. All players but Burton transferred October 11, 1960; Burton added to trade, January 26, 1961.

cTraded to Los Angeles Angels for outfielder Lou Johnson, April 13, 1961.

dTraded to Cleveland Indians for pitcher Barry Latman and first baseman Joe Adcock. Wagner and Latman changed clubs December 2 and Adcock closed deal on December 6, 1963.

eTraded to Chicago White Sox for outfielder Russ Snyder, June 13, 1968.

FREDERICK E. (DIXIE) WALKER

Born September 24, 1910, at Villa Rica, Ga.
Height, 6.01. Weight, 175.
Threw right and batted lefthanded.
Married Estelle Shea, May 2, 1936.

Father Ewart, with Washington Senators (1909 through 1912); brother Harry, with St. Louis Cardinals (1940 to 1947 and 1950-51), Philadelphia Phillies (1947-48), Chicago Cubs (1949) and Cincinnati Reds (1949); nephew of Ernie Walker, with St. Louis Browns (1913-14-15).

Named as outfielder on THE SPORTING NEWS All-Star Major League Team, 1944.

Led N.L. outfielders in double plays, 1941.

Manager, Atlanta, Southern Association, 1950-51-52; coach, St. Louis Cardinals, 1953; released by Cardinals, July 31, 1953 and appointed manager of Houston, Texas, August 1, 1953-54; coach, Cardinals, 1955; released by Cardinals May 29, 1955, and appointed manager of Rochester, International, May 30, 1955-56; manager, Toronto, International, 1957-58-59; scout, Milwaukee Braves, 1960-62; coach, Milwaukee, 1963-65; scout, Atlanta Braves, 1966-68; batting instructor and scout, Los Angeles Dodgers, 1969-1976.

Year	Club	League	Pos.	G.	AB.	R.	H.	2B.	3B.	HR.	RBI.	B.A.	PO.	A.	E.	F.A.
1928–Greensboro		Pied.	OF	6	18	3	3	1	1	0	1	.167	10	2	1	.923
1928–Albany		S'east	OF	16	66	10	18	2	1	1	8	.273	42	3	2	.957
1928–Gulfport		Cot. St.	OF	82	304	41	89	18	7	1	....	.293	145	44	7	.964
1929–Vicksburg		Cot. St.	3B	61	233	41	74	9	5	2	....	.318	85	145	20	.920
1930–Greenville		Sally	OF	73	307	80	123	17	10	11	63	.401	186	14	7	.966
1930–Jersey City		Int.	OF	83	325	62	109	18	9	7	41	.335	171	19	9	.955
1931–Toledo		A.A.	OF	58	228	33	69	10	2	4	31	.303	169	7	4	.978
1931–New York		Amer.	OF	2	10	1	3	2	0	0	1	.300	3	0	0	1.000
1931–J.C.-Toronto		Int.	OF	80	310	40	109	17	4	6	41	.352	205	9	7	.968
1932–Newark		Int.	OF	144	551	107	193	30	7	15	105	.350	348	12	5	.986
1933–New York		Amer.	OF	98	328	68	90	15	7	15	51	.274	194	7	8	.962
1934–New York		Amer.	OF	17	17	2	2	0	0	0	0	.118	1	0	0	1.000
1935–New York		Amer.	OF	8	13	1	2	1	0	0	1	.154	3	0	1	.750
1935–Newark		Int.	OF	89	317	66	93	18	5	17	67	.293	162	1	4	.976
1936–N.Y.(a)-Chi		Amer.	OF	32	90	15	26	2	2	1	16	.289	55	2	0	1.000
1937–Chicago(b)		Amer.	OF	154	593	105	179	28	•16	9	95	.302	270	10	14	.952
1938–Detroit		Amer.	OF	127	454	84	140	27	6	6	43	.308	224	8	5	.979
1939–Detroit(c)		Amer.	OF	43	154	30	47	4	5	4	19	.305	93	4	3	.970
1939–Brooklyn		Nat.	OF	61	225	27	63	6	4	2	38	.280	144	5	5	.968
1940–Brooklyn		Nat.	OF	143	556	75	171	37	8	6	66	.308	360	6	10	.973
1941–Brooklyn		Nat.	OF	148	531	88	165	32	8	9	71	.311	309	•19	8	.976
1942–Brooklyn		Nat.	OF	118	393	57	114	28	1	6	54	.290	207	8	3	.986
1943–Brooklyn		Nat.	OF	138	540	83	163	32	6	5	71	.302	262	20	9	.969
1944–Brooklyn		Nat.	OF	147	535	77	191	37	8	13	91	*.357	260	17	•11	.962
1945–Brooklyn		Nat.	OF	154	607	102	182	42	9	8	*124	.300	346	18	3	.992
1946–Brooklyn		Nat.	OF	150	576	80	184	29	9	9	116	.319	237	15	8	.969
1947–Brooklyn(d)		Nat.	OF	148	529	77	162	31	3	9	94	.306	261	9	10	.964
1948–Pittsburgh		Nat.	OF	129	408	39	129	19	3	2	54	.316	168	4	4	.977
1949–Pittsburgh		Nat.	OF-1B	88	181	26	51	4	1	1	18	.282	82	5	4	.956
1950–Atlanta		South.	OF	39	77	11	21	6	1	1	17	.273	30	0	1	.968
American League Totals				481	1659	306	489	79	36	35	226	.295	843	31	31	.966
National League Totals				1424	5081	731	1575	297	60	70	797	.310	2636	126	75	.974
Major League Totals				1905	6740	1037	2064	376	96	105	1023	.306	3479	157	106	.972

aSold to Chicago White Sox, May, 1936.
bTraded to Detroit Tigers with pitcher Vernon Kennedy and second baseman Tony Piet for catcher Mike Tresh, third baseman Marvin Owen and outfielder Gerald Walker, December 2, 1937.
cReleased to Brooklyn Dodgers on waivers, July 24, 1939.
dTraded to Pittsburgh Pirates with pitchers Hal Gregg and Vic Lombardi for pitcher Elwin (Preacher) Roe, second baseman Gene Mauch and shortstop Billy Cox, December 8, 1947.

WORLD SERIES RECORD

Year	Club	League	Pos.	G.	AB.	R.	H.	2B.	3B.	HR.	RBI.	B.A.	PO.	A.	E.	F.A.
1941–Brooklyn		Nat.	OF	5	18	3	4	2	0	0	0	.222	14	0	0	1.000
1947–Brooklyn		Nat.	OF	7	27	1	6	1	0	1	4	.222	9	1	0	1.000
World Series Totals				12	45	4	10	3	0	1	4	.222	23	1	0	1.000

WILLIAM CURTIS (CURT) WALKER

Born July 3, 1896, at Beeville, Tex.
Died December 9, 1955, at Beeville, Tex.
Height, 5.09½. Weight, 165.
Threw right and batted lefthanded.

Led N.L. outfielders in double plays, 1922, 1926 (tie).

Year	Club	League	Pos.	G.	AB.	R.	H.	2B.	3B.	HR.	RBI.	B.A.	PO.	A.	E.	F.A.
1919–Houston		Texas	OF	41	135	16	29	6	0	0	....	.215	71	3	6	.925
1919–Augusta		So. Atl.	OF	53	194	17	54	11	3	1	....	.278	107	6	2	.983
1919–New York		Amer.	PH	1	1	0	0	0	0	0	0	.000	0	0	0	.000
1920–Augusta		So. Atl.	OF	126	422	71	126	21	13	0	54	.299	230	19	4	*.984
1920–New York		Nat.	OF	8	14	0	1	0	0	0	0	.071	5	0	0	1.000
1921–N.Y.(a)-Phila		Nat.	OF	85	269	41	81	15	6	3	43	.301	152	13	4	.976
1922–Philadelphia		Nat.	OF	148	581	102	196	36	11	12	89	.337	295	24	15	.955
1923–Philadelphia		Nat.	OF-1B	140	527	66	148	26	5	5	66	.281	284	19	17	.947
1924–Phila.(b)-Cin		Nat.	OF	133	468	66	140	27	11	5	54	.299	239	15	8	.969
1925–Cincinnati		Nat.	OF	145	509	86	162	22	16	6	71	.318	332	12	6	*.983
1926–Cincinnati		Nat.	OF	155	571	83	175	24	20	6	78	.306	325	21	14	.961
1927–Cincinnati		Nat.	OF	146	527	60	154	16	10	6	80	.292	316	15	•15	.957
1928–Cincinnati		Nat.	OF	123	427	64	119	15	12	6	73	.279	289	9	14	.955
1929–Cincinnati		Nat.	OF	141	492	76	154	28	15	7	83	.313	298	11	10	.969
1930–Cincinnati		Nat.	OF	134	482	74	145	26	11	8	51	.307	241	5	9	.965

Year	Club	League	Pos.	G.	AB.	R.	H.	2B.	3B.	HR.	RBI.	B.A.	PO.	A.	E.	F.A.
1931—Indianapolis		A.A.	OF	143	494	103	159	23	7	8	85	.322	240	10	16	.940
1932—Ind'polis-Toledo		A.A.	OF	64	224	41	62	16	4	3	40	.277	92	3	4	.960
American League Totals				1	1	0	0	0	0	0	0	.000	0	0	0	.000
National League Totals				1358	4857	718	1475	235	117	64	688	.304	2776	144	112	.963
Major League Totals				1359	4858	718	1475	235	117	64	688	.304	2776	144	112	.963

aTraded with infielder Joseph Rapp and outfielder Lee King to Philadelphia Phillies for infielder John Rawlings and pitcher Cecil Causey, July, 1921.
bTraded to Cincinnati Reds for outfielder George Harper, July, 1924.

RODERICK JOHN (BOBBY) WALLACE

Born November 4, 1874, at Pittsburgh, Pa.
Died November 3, 1960, at Torrance, Calif.
Height, 5.08. Weight, 170.
Threw and batted righthanded.
Married June Mann, August 8, 1906.

Manager, St. Louis, American League, 1911 to June 1, 1912; umpire in American League, June 1, 1915, to August 1, 1916, when he rejoined St. Louis Browns; manager, Wichita, Western League until released, June, 1917; manager, Muskogee, Southwestern League, 1921; scout, Chicago, National League, 1924; coach, Cincinnati, National League, 1926; scout, Cincinnati, 1927 through 1957; acting manager, Cincinnati, September, 1937; scout, Cincinnati, 1938 to date of death.
Named to Hall of Fame, 1953.

Year	Club	League	Pos.	G.	AB.	R.	H.	2B.	3B.	HR.	SB.	B.A.	PO.	A.	E.	F.A.
1894—Cleveland		Nat.	P	4	13	0	2	1	0	0	0	.154	3	7	0	1.000
1895—Cleveland		Nat.	P	27	97	16	21	2	3	0	3	.216	17	62	5	.940
1896—Cleveland		Nat.	P	33	130	17	30	4	4	1	1	.231	44	47	7	.929
1897—Cleveland		Nat.	3B	131	522	99	177	36	20	4	17	.339	194	255	31	.935
1898—Cleveland (a)		Nat.	3B	153	591	81	159	25	10	3	9	.269	206	345	33	.943
1899—St. Louis		Nat.	SS-3B	151	576	90	174	29	14	12	11	.302	318	535	75	.919
1900—St. Louis		Nat.	SS	129	489	72	133	21	7	5	10	.272	328	447	49	.941
1901—St. Louis (b)		Nat.	SS	135	556	69	179	34	16	2	17	.322	329	*541	*61	.934
1902—St. Louis		Amer.	*SS-OF	133	495	71	142	33	9	1	19	.287	329	471	41	*.951
1903—St. Louis		Amer.	SS	136	519	63	127	20	17	1	11	.245	•308	*472	60	.929
1904—St. Louis		Amer.	SS	139	550	57	150	28	4	2	19	.273	*398	484	42	*.955
1905—St. Louis		Amer.	SS	*156	587	67	159	29	9	1	13	.271	*385	506	62	.935
1906—St. Louis		Amer.	SS	139	476	64	123	24	7	2	24	.258	309	461	41	.949
1907—St. Louis		Amer.	SS	147	538	56	138	19	7	0	16	.257	338	*517	*54	.941
1908—St. Louis		Amer.	SS	137	487	59	123	24	4	1	5	.253	286	510	41	*.951
1909—St. Louis		Amer.	SS-3B	116	403	36	96	12	2	1	7	.238	242	336	32	.948
1910—St. Louis		Amer.	SS-3B	138	508	47	131	19	7	0	12	.258	316	444	43	.946
1911—St. Louis		Amer.	SS	125	410	35	95	12	2	0	8	.232	280	417	42	.943
1912—St. Louis		Amer.	SS	99	323	39	78	14	5	0	3	.241	185	271	28	.942
1913—St. Louis		Amer.	SS	52	147	11	31	5	0	0	2	.211	67	98	12	.932
1914—St. Louis		Amer.	SS	26	73	3	16	2	1	0	1	.219	26	46	9	.889
1915—St. Louis		Amer.	SS	9	13	1	3	0	1	0	0	.231	9	13	5	.815
1916—St. Louis (c)		Amer.	SS-3B	14	18	0	5	0	0	0	0	.278	8	27	2	.946
1917—Wichita		West.	SS	33	123	9	34	5	0	0	0	.276	72	78	14	.915
1917—St. Louis		Nat.	SS-3B	8	10	0	1	0	0	0	0	.100	12	17	3	.906
1918—St. Louis		Nat.	SS-3B-2B	32	98	3	15	1	0	0	1	.153	61	83	10	.935
American League Totals				1566	5547	609	1417	241	75	9	140	.255	3486	5073	514	.943
National League Totals				803	3082	447	891	153	74	27	69	.289	1512	2339	274	.934
Major League Totals				2369	8629	1056	2308	394	149	36	209	.267	4998	7412	788	.940

aShifted to St. Louis in winter of 1898-99 when Robisons transferred team from Cleveland.
bJumped to St. Louis Americans for 1902.
cReleased at close of season; started 1917 as manager of Wichita (Western), but was released in June and joined Cardinals on July 12, 1917.

PITCHING RECORD

Year	Club	League	G.	CG.	ShO.	IP.	W.	L.	Pct.	H.	R.	SO.	BB.
1894—Cleveland		National	4	2	0	26	2	1	.667	33	28	10	17
1895—Cleveland		National	30	21	1	222	12	13	.480	265	175	64	89
1896—Cleveland		National	22	12	2	144	10	7	.588	174	78	44	43
1902—St. Louis		American	1	0	...	0	0	0	.....	.....	.....	.....	.....
Major League Totals			57	35	3	392	24	21	.534	472	281	118	149

TEMPLE CUP PITCHING RECORD

Year	Club	League	G.	CG.	ShO.	IP.	W.	L.	Pct.	H.	R.	SO.	BB.
1896—Cleveland		National	1	1	0	8	0	1	.000	10	7	4	2

TEMPLE CUP BATTING RECORD

Year	Club	League	Pos.	G.	AB.	R.	H.	2B.	3B.	HR.	SB.	B.A.	PO.	A.	E.	F.A.
1896—Cleveland		Nat.	PH-P	3	5	1	1	0	0	0	0	.200	0	2	0	1.000

EDWARD AUGUSTIN WALSH

Born May 14, 1881, at Plains, Pa.
Died May 26, 1959, at Pompano Beach, Fla.
Height, 6.01. Weight, 193.
Threw and batted righthanded.

Equaled American League record for pitching most complete games played in succession by club, 3 (September 29–two games and October 2, 1908); pitched and won two games in one day, September 26, 1905, and September 29, 1908; pitched no-hit, 5-0 victory over Boston, August 27, 1911.
Manager, Bridgeport, Eastern League 1920; umpire, American League, 1922; coach, Chicago White Sox, 1923-24-25. Baseball coach, University of Notre Dame, 1926; coach, Chicago White Sox, 1928-29-30.
Named to Hall of Fame, 1946.

Year	Club	League	G.	IP.	W.	L.	Pct.	H.	R.	SO.	BB.	CG.	ShO.
1902	Wilkes-Barre	Pa. State	4	36	1	2	.333	31	....	20	8	....	....
1902	Meriden	Connecticut	21	182	15	5	.750	125	....	98	48	....	....
1903	Meriden	Connecticut	23	182	11	10	.524	135	....	126	46	....	....
1903	Newark	Eastern	19	117	9	5	.643	70	....	77	28	....	....
1904	Chicago	American	18	113	6	3	.667	83	37	52	34	6	1
1905	Chicago	American	22	138	8	3	.727	128	56	71	35	9	1
1906	Chicago	American	42	281	17	13	.567	214	90	171	58	24	*10
1907	Chicago	American	*56	*419	24	18	.600	330	123	207	85	37	5
1908	Chicago	American	*66	*465	*40	15	*.727	*343	111	*269	56	42	*12
1909	Chicago	American	31	230	15	11	.577	166	52	127	50	20	*8
1910	Chicago	American	•45	370	18	*20	.474	242	90	258	61	33	7
1911	Chicago	American	*56	*369	27	18	.600	327	125	*255	72	33	5
1912	Chicago	American	*62	*393	27	17	.614	*332	125	254	94	32	6
1913	Chicago	American	16	98	8	3	.727	91	37	34	39	7	1
1914	Chicago	American	9	45	2	3	.400	33	19	14	20	3	1
1915	Chicago	American	3	27	3	1	.750	18	4	12	6	3	1
1916	Chicago	American	2	3	0	1	1.000	6	3	3	1	0	0
1917	Boston	National	4	18	0	1	.000	22	9	4	9	1	0
1919	Milwaukee	Amer. Assn.	4	21	2	2	.500	22	....	6	8	....	....
1920	Bridgeport	Eastern	3	22	1	1	.500	22	....	6	6	....	....
American League Totals			428	2951	195	125	.609	2313	872	1727	611	249	58
National League Totals			4	18	0	1	.000	22	9	4	9	1	0
Major League Totals			432	2969	195	126	.607	2335	881	1731	620	250	58

WORLD SERIES RECORD

Year	Club	League	G.	IP.	W.	L.	Pct.	H.	R.	SO.	BB.	CG.	ShO.
1906	Chicago	American	2	15	2	0	1.000	7	6	17	6	1	1

WILLIAM HENRY (BUCKY) WALTERS

Born April 19, 1909, at Philadelphia, Pa.
Height, 6.00½. Weight, 185.
Threw and batted righthanded.
Married Jane Caroline Yoast, December 21, 1931.

Led National League pitchers in complete games, 1939-40 and 1941; pitched 4-0 one-hitter against Boston, May 14, 1944 (first game), Connie Ryan's single with two out in last of eighth depriving him of perfect game; tied major league record for pitchers by making unassisted double play, September 4, 1940.
Named National League's Most Valuable Player, 1939. Selected as All-Round Player of 1939 by THE SPORTING NEWS. Named by Baseball Writers' Association of America for THE SPORTING NEWS All-Star Major League Teams, 1939 and 1940.
Manager, Cincinnati Reds, 1948-49; coach, Boston Braves, 1950-51-52, until signed as manager, Milwaukee, American Association, June 7, 1952; coach, Milwaukee Braves, 1953-54-55; coach, New York Giants, 1956-57; farm department, Philadelphia Phillies, 1958.

PITCHING RECORD

Year	Club	League	G.	IP.	W.	L.	Pct.	H.	R.	ER.	SO.	BB.	ERA.
1929	High Point	Pied.	16	80	5	6	.455	90	54	47	20	40	5.29
1934	Philadelphia	Nat.	2	7	0	0	.000	8	3	1	7	2	1.29
1935	Philadelphia	Nat.	24	151	9	9	.500	168	86	70	40	68	4.17

Year	Club	League	G.	IP.	W.	L.	Pct.	H.	R.	ER.	SO.	BB.	ERA.
1936	Philadelphia	Nat.	40	258	11	*21	.344	284	146	122	66	115	4.26
1937	Philadelphia	Nat.	37	246	14	15	.483	292	148	130	87	86	4.76
1938	Philadelphia(a)-Cinc	Nat.	39	251	15	14	.517	259	134	117	93	108	4.20
1939	Cincinnati	Nat.	39	*319	*27	11	.711	250	98	81	•137	109	*2.29
1940	Cincinnati	Nat.	36	*305	*22	10	.688	241	95	84	115	92	*2.48
1941	Cincinnati	Nat.	37	*302	19	15	.559	*292	108	95	129	88	2.83
1942	Cincinnati	Nat.	34	254	15	14	.517	223	101	75	109	73	2.66
1943	Cincinnati	Nat.	34	246	15	15	.500	244	105	97	80	109	3.55
1944	Cincinnati	Nat.	34	285	*23	8	.742	233	92	76	77	87	2.40
1945	Cincinnati	Nat.	22	168	10	10	.500	166	62	50	45	51	2.68
1946	Cincinnati	Nat.	22	151	10	7	.588	146	55	43	60	64	2.56
1947	Cincinnati	Nat.	20	122	8	8	.500	137	83	78	43	49	5.75
1948	Cincinnati	Nat.	7	35	0	3	.000	42	25	18	19	18	4.63
1950	Boston	Nat.	1	4	0	0	.000	5	2	2	0	2	4.50
Major League Totals			428	3104	198	160	.553	2990	1343	1139	1107	1121	3.30

aTraded to Cincinnati Reds for catcher Virgil Davis, pitcher Al Hollingsworth and $55,000, June 13, 1938.

BATTING RECORD

Year	Club	League	Pos.	G.	AB.	R.	H.	2B.	3B.	HR.	RBI.	B.A.	PO.	A.	E.	F.A.
1929	High Point	Pied.	P-2-3B	90	280	40	84	19	1	7	29	.300	94	132	14	.942
1930	Providence	East.	2B	14	44	8	11	1	0	1	7	.250	36	34	3	.959
1930	Portland	N. Eng.	INF	28	111	15	29	8	3	2	12	.261	52	86	14	.908
1930	Williamsport	NYP	3B	56	229	41	68	7	9	3	29	.297	72	115	8	.959
1931	Williamsport	NYP	3B	130	530	99	173	31	14	6	86	.326	*161	*267	*31	.932
1931	Nashville	South.	INF	11	35	.....	7	1	0	0	.....	.200	32	29	5	.924
1931	Boston	Nat.	3B-2B	9	38	2	8	2	0	0	0	.211	7	17	1	.960
1932	Montreal	Int.	3B	123	405	54	105	24	3	10	50	.259	128	242	15	*.961
1932	Boston	Nat.	3B	22	75	8	14	3	1	0	4	.187	17	44	6	.910
1933	S. F. Missions	P.C.	3B	91	362	74	136	32	1	16	92	.376	100	151	8	.969
1933	Boston	Amer.	3B	52	195	27	50	8	3	4	28	.256	42	84	8	.940
1934	Boston	Amer.	3B	23	88	10	19	4	4	4	18	.216	33	54	9	.906
1934	Philadelphia	Nat.	3B-P	83	300	36	78	20	3	4	38	.260	74	139	11	.951
1935	Philadelphia	Nat.	P	49	96	14	24	2	1	0	6	.250	7	40	0	1.000
1936	Philadelphia	Nat.	P	64	121	12	29	10	1	1	16	.240	15	96	3	.974
1937	Philadelphia	Nat.	P	56	137	15	38	6	0	1	16	.277	7	76	1	.988
1938	Phila.-Cinn.	Nat.	P	51	99	16	19	3	0	1	8	.192	10	66	2	.973
1939	Cincinnati	Nat.	P	40	120	16	39	8	1	1	16	.325	13	56	4	.945
1940	Cincinnati	Nat.	P	37	117	11	24	3	0	1	18	.205	16	77	2	.979
1941	Cincinnati	Nat.	P	39	106	6	20	6	0	0	9	.189	18	68	2	.977
1942	Cincinnati	Nat.	P	40	99	13	24	6	1	2	12	.242	13	60	3	.961
1943	Cincinnati	Nat.	P	37	90	11	24	7	1	1	12	.267	19	49	2	.971
1944	Cincinnati	Nat.	P	37	107	9	30	4	0	0	13	.279	15	55	0	1.000
1945	Cincinnati	Nat.	P	24	61	11	14	3	0	3	8	.230	6	33	1	.975
1946	Cincinnati	Nat.	P	24	55	6	7	2	0	0	5	.127	10	37	3	.940
1947	Cincinnati	Nat.	P	20	45	3	12	2	0	0	4	.267	6	19	1	.962
1948	Cincinnati	Nat.	P	7	15	1	4	0	0	0	2	.267	1	11	0	1.000
1949	Cincinnati	Nat.					(Did Not Play)									
1950	Boston	Nat.	P	1	2	0	0	0	0	0	0	.000	1	0	0	1.000
American League Totals				75	283	37	69	12	7	8	46	.244	75	138	17	.926
National League Totals				640	1683	190	408	87	9	15	188	.242	255	943	42	.966
Major League Totals				715	1966	227	477	99	16	23	234	.243	330	1081	59	.960

WORLD SERIES RECORD

Year	Club	League	G.	IP.	W.	L.	Pct.	H.	R.	ER.	SO.	BB.	ERA.
1939	Cincinnati	Nat.	2	11	0	2	.000	13	9	6	6	1	4.91
1940	Cincinnati	Nat.	2	18	2	0	1.000	8	3	3	6	6	1.50
World Series Totals			4	29	2	2	.500	21	12	9	12	7	2.79

LLOYD JAMES (LITTLE POISON) WANER

Born March 16, 1906, at Harrah, Okla.

Height, 5.08½. Weight, 150.

Threw right and batted lefthanded.

Married Francis Mae Snyder, September 17, 1929.

Brother of Paul Waner, former National League outfielder, batting champion and also a member of Hall of Fame.

Equaled National League record for most years leading league in one-base hits (4), 1931 (led 1927-28-31 and tied, 1929); established modern National League mark for most singles, season (198), 1927.

Scout, Pittsburgh Pirates, 1946-47-48-49; scout, Baltimore Orioles, 1955.

Named to Hall of Fame, 1967.

Year	Club	League	Pos.	G.	AB.	R.	H.	2B.	3B.	HR.	RBI.	B.A.	PO.	A.	E.	F.A.
1925–San Francisco		P.C.	OF	31	44	7	11	2	0	0	1	.250	17	2	0	1.000
1926–San Francisco		P.C.	OF	6	20	0	4	1	0	0	....	.200	11	0	0	1.000
1926–Columbia		So. Atl.	OF	121	498	95	172	28	14	6	33	.345	331	22	4	.989
1927–Pittsburgh		Nat.	OF	150	629	•133	223	17	6	2	27	.355	396	9	10	.976
1928–Pittsburgh		Nat.	OF	152	★659	121	221	22	14	5	61	.335	418	15	9	.980
1929–Pittsburgh		Nat.	OF	151	★662	134	234	28	★20	5	74	.353	★450	22	6	.987
1930–Pittsburgh		Nat.	OF	68	260	32	94	8	3	1	36	.362	165	6	3	.983
1931–Pittsburgh		Nat.	OF	154	★681	90	★214	25	13	4	57	.314	★484	20	11	.979
1932–Pittsburgh		Nat.	OF	134	565	90	188	27	11	2	38	.333	★426	9	6	.986
1933–Pittsburgh		Nat.	OF	121	500	59	138	14	5	0	26	.276	267	9	5	.982
1934–Pittsburgh		Nat.	OF	140	611	95	173	27	6	1	48	.283	★405	8	9	.979
1935–Pittsburgh		Nat.	OF	122	537	83	166	22	14	0	46	.309	350	5	4	.989
1936–Pittsburgh		Nat.	OF	106	414	67	133	13	8	1	31	.321	245	2	4	.984
1937–Pittsburgh		Nat.	OF	129	537	80	177	23	4	1	45	.330	312	8	4	.988
1938–Pittsburgh		Nat.	OF	147	619	79	194	25	7	5	57	.313	341	15	5	.986
1939–Pittsburgh		Nat.	OF	112	379	49	108	15	3	0	24	.285	225	9	2	.992
1940–Pittsburgh		Nat.	OF	72	166	30	43	3	0	0	3	.259	90	3	1	.989
1941–Pit.a-Bo.b-Cin.c		Nat.	OF	77	219	26	64	5	1	0	11	.292	102	4	2	.981
1942–Philadelphia (d)		Nat.	OF	101	287	23	75	7	3	0	10	.261	170	6	6	.967
1943–Brooklyn		Nat.						(Voluntarily retired)								
1944–Brook.(e)-Pitts		Nat.	PH-OF	34	28	5	9	0	0	0	3	.321	12	0	0	1.000
1945–Pittsburgh		Nat.	PH-OF	23	19	5	5	0	0	0	1	.263	2	1	0	1.000
Major League Totals				1993	7772	1201	2459	281	118	27	598	.316	4860	151	87	.983

aTraded to Boston Braves for pitcher Nick Strincevich, May 7, 1941.
bTraded to Cincinnati Reds for pitcher John Hutchings, June 12, 1941.
cUnconditionally released by Cincinnati Reds, October 8, 1941; signed by Philadelphia Phillies, December 4, 1941.
dTraded to Brooklyn Dodgers with infielder Al Glossop for first baseman Ellsworth Dahlgren, March 8, 1943.
eUnconditionally released by Brooklyn Dodgers, June 14, 1944, and signed by Pittsburgh Pirates, June 15, 1944.

WORLD SERIES RECORD

Year	Club	League	Pos.	G.	AB.	R.	H.	2B.	3B.	HR.	RBI.	B.A.	PO.	A.	E.	F.A.
1927–Pittsburgh		Nat.	OF	4	15	5	6	1	1	0	0	.400	9	1	2	.833

PAUL GLEE (BIG POISON) WANER

Born April 16, 1903, at Harrah, Okla.
Died August 29, 1965, at Sarasota, Fla.
Height, 5.08½. Weight, 153.
Threw and batted lefthanded.
Married Mildred Arnold Carroll, June 12, 1953.
Brother of Lloyd Waner, former major league outfielder and also member of Hall of Fame.

Had most consecutive games, run batted in in each, National League (12), 1927.
Tied William Keeler's old-time mark and set modern National League record by getting 200 or more base hits in eight seasons (since passed by Pete Rose with 10); made six hits in six consecutive times at bat, game, August 26, 1926; tied National League mark by hitting four doubles in game, May 20, 1932; collected 3,000th hit of major league career, June 19, 1942. Led N. L. outfielders in double plays, 1931, 1936 (tie).
Named Most Valuable Player, National League, 1927.
Named as outfielder on The Sporting News All-Star Major League Teams, 1927-28 and 1937.
Manager, Miami, Florida-International, 1946; batting instructor for Milwaukee Braves, 1957; for St. Louis Cardinals, 1958-59; for Philadelphia Phillies, 1960; batting coach, Phillies, May 30, 1965, until death.
Named to Hall of Fame, 1952.

Year	Club	League	Pos.	G.	AB.	R.	H.	2B.	3B.	HR.	RBI.	B.A.	PO.	A.	E.	F.A.
1923–San Francisco		P.C.	OF-1B	112	325	54	120	30	4	3	39	.369	230	16	12	.953
1924–San Francisco		P.C.	OF	160	587	113	209	46	5	8	97	.356	284	28	10	.969
1925–San Francisco		P.C.	OF	174	699	167	280	★75	7	11	130	★.401	744	36	18	.977
1926–Pittsburgh		Nat.	OF	144	536	101	180	35	★22	8	79	.336	307	21	8	.976
1927–Pittsburgh		Nat.	OF-1B	•155	623	114	★237	42	★18	9	★131	★.380	430	25	10	.978
1928–Pittsburgh		Nat.	OF-1B	152	602	★142	223	★50	19	6	86	.370	533	22	12	.979
1929–Pittsburgh		Nat.	OF	151	596	131	200	43	15	15	100	.336	328	15	5	.986
1930–Pittsburgh		Nat.	OF	145	589	117	217	32	18	8	77	.368	344	9	15	.959
1931–Pittsburgh		Nat.	★OF-1B	150	559	88	180	35	10	6	70	.322	441	★31	9	★.981
1932–Pittsburgh		Nat.	OF	★154	630	107	215	★62	10	8	82	.341	367	13	10	.974
1933–Pittsburgh		Nat.	OF	★154	618	101	191	38	16	7	70	.309	346	16	7	.981
1934–Pittsburgh		Nat.	OF	146	599	★122	★217	32	16	14	90	★.362	323	15	5	.985
1935–Pittsburgh		Nat.	OF	139	549	98	176	29	12	11	78	.321	283	13	5	.983
1936–Pittsburgh		Nat.	OF	148	585	107	218	53	9	5	94	★.373	323	15	14	.960
1937–Pittsburgh		Nat.	OF	154	619	94	219	30	9	2	74	.354	271	16	9	.970
1938–Pittsburgh		Nat.	OF	148	625	77	175	31	6	6	69	.280	284	11	7	.977

Year	Club	League	Pos.	G.	AB.	R.	H.	2B.	3B.	HR.	RBI.	B.A.	PO.	A.	E.	F.A.
1939–Pittsburgh		Nat.	OF	125	461	62	151	30	6	3	45	.328	206	12	5	.978
1940–Pittsburgh (a)		Nat.	OF-1B	89	238	32	69	16	1	1	32	.290	150	9	2	.988
1941–Brook (b)–Bost		Nat.	OF	106	329	45	88	10	2	2	50	.267	160	8	8	.955
1942–Boston (c)		Nat.	OF	114	333	43	86	17	1	1	39	.258	150	6	5	.969
1943–Brooklyn		Nat.	OF	82	225	29	70	16	0	1	26	.311	116	4	5	.960
1944–Brooklyn (d)		Nat.	OF	83	136	16	39	4	1	0	16	.287	54	3	1	.983
1944–New York		Amer.	PH	9	7	1	1	0	0	0	1	.143	0	0	0	.000
1945–New York (e)		Amer.	PH	1	0	0	0	0	0	0	0	.000	0	0	0	.000
1946–Miami		Fla. Int.	PH-1	62	80	12	26	6	2	0	12	.325	102	4	6	.946
American League Totals				10	7	1	1	0	0	0	1	.143	0	0	0	.000
National League Totals				2539	9452	1626	3151	605	191	113	1308	.333	5416	264	142	.976
Major League Totals				2549	9459	1627	3152	605	191	113	1309	.333	5416	264	142	.976

aUnconditionally released by Pittsburgh, December 10, 1940, and signed by Brooklyn, January 31, 1941.
bUnconditionally released by Brooklyn, May 11, 1941; signed by Boston, May 24, 1941.
cUnconditionally released by Boston, January 19, 1943; signed with Brooklyn, January 21, 1943.
dUnconditionally released by Brooklyn, September, 1944 and signed with New York Yankees.
eUnconditionally released by New York Yankees, May 3, 1945.

WORLD SERIES RECORD

Year	Club	League	Pos.	G.	AB.	R.	H.	2B.	3B.	HR.	RBI.	B.A.	PO.	A.	E.	F.A.
1927–Pittsburgh		Nat.	OF	4	15	0	5	1	0	0	3	.333	8	0	0	1.000

JOHN MONTGOMERY WARD

Born March 3, 1860, at Bellefonte, Pa.
Died March 4, 1925, at Augusta, Ga.
Height, 5.09. Weight, 165.
Threw right and batted lefthanded.

Pitched perfect game, 5-0 victory, June 17, 1880 (a.m.) vs. Buffalo; established major league record for most assists by a second baseman in a nine-inning game (12), June 10, 1892 (first game); accepted 28 chances in two consecutive games as a second baseman, July 18 and first game of July 19, 1893; pitched 18-inning 1-0 victory, August 17, 1882; won two games in a day, August 9, 1878.

Manager, Brooklyn, Players League, 1890; Brooklyn, National League, 1891-92; New York, National League, 1893-94; president, Boston National League club, December, 1911 to July 31, 1912.

Named to Hall of Fame, 1964.

Year	Club	League	Pos.	G.	AB.	R.	H.	2B.	3B.	HR.	SB.	B.A.	PO.	A.	E.	F.A.
1877–Athletics			P	League Alliance club—no record available												
1878–Providence		Nat.	P	35	128	14	26	5	5	1	....	.203	21	189	48	.814
1879–Providence		Nat.	3B-P	82	362	71	104	10	5	2	....	.287	47	404	21	.956
1880–Providence		Nat.	3B-P	82	340	49	77	16	2	0	....	.226	69	409	18	.964
1881–Providence		Nat.	SS-O-P	83	352	56	85	18	6	0	....	.241	90	208	15	.952
1882–Providence		Nat.	SS-O-P	83	355	58	87	10	4	0	....	.245	87	165	25	.910
1883–New York		Nat.	S-3-2-0-P	88	379	76	98	18	6	7	....	.259	143	153	70	.809
1884–New York		Nat.	2B-O-P	109	466	99	116	12	10	2	....	.249	186	180	51	.878
1885–New York		Nat.	SS	111	446	72	101	8	8	0	....	.226	*167	350	55	.904
1886–New York		Nat.	SS	122	491	82	134	18	6	2	36	.273	91	369	69	.870
1887–New York		Nat.	SS	129	574	113	213	16	5	1	*111	.371	*226	469	61	*.919
1888–New York		Nat.	SS	122	510	70	128	12	4	2	38	.251	185	331	*86	.857
1889–New York		Nat.	SS	114	479	81	143	12	4	1	62	.299	229	319	68	.890
1890–Brooklyn		Play.	SS	128	558	135	*207	14	10	4	71	.371	*303	448	85	.898
1891–Brooklyn		Nat.	SS-2B	104	438	85	126	14	5	0	80	.288	233	352	58	.910
1892–Brooklyn		Nat.	2B	148	610	109	167	12	3	2	*94	.274	*373	480	*70	.924
1893–New York		Nat.	2B	134	557	129	194	26	8	2	*72	.348	340	*469	*65	.929
1894–New York		Nat.	2B	136	552	99	145	11	4	0	41	.262	332	455	67	.922
National League Total				1682	7039	1268	1944	218	85	22	534	.276	2819	5302	847	.906
Players League Totals				128	558	135	207	14	10	4	71	.371	303	448	85	.898
Major League Totals				1810	7597	1403	2151	232	95	26	605	.283	3122	5750	932	.905

PITCHING RECORD

Year	Club	League	G.	CG.	W.	L.	Pct.	H.	R.	ShO.
1878–Providence		National	35	35	22	13	.629	308	....	6
1879–Providence		National	65	58	*44	18	*.710	571	226	2
1880–Providence		National	63	58	40	23	.635	442	192	*9
1881–Providence		National	36	33	18	18	.500	320	187	3
1882–Providence		National	32	30	19	13	.594	243	122	4
1883–New York		National	33	24	12	14	.462	311	196	1
1884–New York		National	9	5	3	3	.500	72	....	0
Major League Totals			273	243	158	102	.608	2267	....	25

Pitched for Athletics against Hartford at Brooklyn and lost 5-0, June 30, 1877.

WORLD SERIES RECORD

Year	Club	League	Pos.	G.	AB.	R.	H.	2B.	3B.	HR.	SB.	B.A.	PO.	A.	E.	F.A.
1888—New York		Nat.		8	29	4	11	2	0	0	6	.379	12	22	1	.971
1889—New York		Nat.		9	37	10	15	0	2	0	8	.405	22	27	5	.907
World Series Totals				17	66	14	26	2	2	0	14	.394	34	49	6	.933

LONNIE WARNEKE

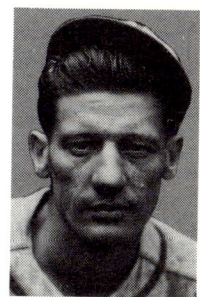

Born March 28, 1909, at Mt. Ida, Ark.
Died June 23, 1976, near Hot Springs, Ark.
Height, 6.02. Weight, 180.
Threw and batted righthanded.
Married Erma Charlyne Shannon, February 12, 1933.

Made eight assists, October 2, 1935 World Series game, Chicago (N. L.) vs. Detroit (A. L.). Pitched four shutouts per season five times—1932-33-36-38 and 1941; pitched 2-0, no-hit victory against Cincinnati, August 30, 1941.
Handled 227 consecutive chances without an error, September 30, 1938 through September 29, 1945, second game, 163 games.
Named by Baseball Writers' Association of America for THE SPORTING NEWS All-Star League Team, 1932.
Umpire, Pacific Coast League, 1946-47-48; National League, 1949 through 1955.

Year	Club	League	G.	IP.	W.	L.	Pct.	H.	R.	ER.	SO.	BB.	ERA.
1928—Laurel-Alex'dria		Cotton States	35	176	6	14	.300	204	140	....	51	77	.....
1929—Alexandria		Cotton States	34	245	16	10	.615	224	97	84	80	79	3.09
1930—Chicago		National	1	1	0	0	.000	2	5	5	0	5	45.00
1930—Reading		International	34	185	9	12	.429	236	137	124	118	68	6.93
1931—Chicago		National	20	64	2	4	.333	67	33	23	27	37	3.23
1932—Chicago		National	35	277	*22	6	*.786	247	84	73	106	64	*2.37
1933—Chicago		National	36	287	18	13	.581	262	83	64	133	75	2.01
1934—Chicago		National	43	291	22	10	.688	273	116	104	143	66	3.22
1935—Chicago		National	42	262	20	13	.606	257	102	89	120	50	3.06
1936—Chicago(a)		National	40	240	16	13	.552	246	108	92	113	76	3.45
1937—St. Louis		National	36	239	18	11	.621	280	139	120	87	69	4.52
1938—St. Louis		National	31	197	13	8	.619	199	102	87	89	64	3.97
1939—St. Louis		National	34	162	13	7	.650	160	73	68	59	49	3.78
1940—St. Louis		National	33	232	16	10	.615	235	103	81	85	47	3.14
1941—St. Louis		National	37	246	17	9	.654	227	100	86	83	82	3.15
1942—St.L.(b)-Chic.		National	27	181	11	11	.500	173	67	55	59	36	2.73
1943—Chicago		National	21	88	4	5	.444	82	40	31	30	18	3.17
1944—Chicago		National					(In Military Service)						
1945—Chicago		National	9	14	0	1	.000	16	9	6	6	1	3.86
Major League Totals			445	2781	192	121	.613	2726	1164	984	1140	739	3.18

aTraded to St.Louis Cardinals for first baseman James A. Collins and pitcher Leroy Parmelee, October 8, 1936.
bSold to Chicago Cubs, July 8, 1942.

WORLD SERIES RECORD

Year	Club	League	G.	IP.	W.	L.	Pct.	H.	R.	ER.	SO.	BB.	ERA.
1932—Chicago		National	2	10⅔	0	1	.000	15	7	7	8	5	5.91
1935—Chicago		National	3	16⅔	2	0	1.000	9	1	1	5	4	0.54
World Series Totals			5	27⅓	2	1	.667	24	8	8	13	9	2.63

GEORGE MARTIN WEISS

(Minor league executive and major league
general manager and club president.)
Born June 23, 1895, at New Haven, Conn.
Died August 13, 1972, at Greenwich, Conn.

George Weiss played only a few games of baseball as a high schooler in his native New Haven, but he also served as the business manager of his team. From this humble beginning on the "front-office side" of the game, he rose to the top pinnacle of major league success—pennant after pennant as general manager of the New York Yankees.

He organized his successful high school team into a fast semi-pro outfit and the players, even though going on to college, still returned in the summers to form the top club in the area. Weiss promoted varied exhibition games for the "Colonials," as they were called, and did such a great job he was offered the New Haven franchise in the Eastern League for nothing in 1919.

He built Weiss Park and led the club to an era of prosperity never before attained, all the while developing players for the majors. After eight years, he went to Baltimore of the International League in 1928 and remained until 1931, when he met Colonel Jake Ruppert, owner of the Yankees, at the minor league convention in West Baden, Ind. Ruppert, frustrated by the St. Louis Cardinals under Branch Rickey, who developed his own stars and sold phenoms to other major league clubs from his farm system, wanted to enter into the chain store business of talent and saw Weiss as the best man to accomplish the move.

In February, 1932, Weiss joined the Yankees' organization as assistant secretary and farm director. A steady flow of new stars came from his farms to Yankee Stadium as pennants were won in 1932, 1936, 1937, 1938, 1939, 1941, 1942, 1943 and 1947. World championships were won in every year except 1942.

Finally, Weiss took over the Yankee helm in 1948 and rolled up an equally impressive record—10 pennants in 13 seasons—during his regime in the Bronx. Seven of these winners also copped the Series crown, with a record five straight world titles under Casey Stengel from 1949 through 1953. It was Weiss who braved the guffaws of the press and local fandom to sign Stengel, who had a fine record as a minor league manager, a poor one as a major league manager, but an unshakeable one as a buffoon. But it was proved immediately to the doubters that Mrs. Stengel didn't raise any dummy.

Casey charmed the press and fans and platooned players left and right and made two-three position players out of his regulars, a maneuver which made the Yankees "injury free" throughout his New York American League tenure that ended in 1960, the same year Weiss left the Bombers.

These two men rode together into the Hall of Fame, Stengel with his bench magic and Weiss with his magic which filled the bench.

In October of 1961, Weiss, who had become president of the New York Mets, baby expansion entry in the National League, hired Stengel to shepherd the floundering flock who made a success out of repeated defeats. With Weiss dealing in flesh and Stengel's genius at adding a pixie, elfish character to the club, the Mets became the darling of the New York baseball populace. They outdrew and overshadowed the Yankees, even though success was not theirs on the field. Gradually, Weiss built the organization which became solid enough to win in 1969 and become a regular pennant factor. Weiss retired on November 14, 1966, but remained with the club in an advisory capacity until December 1, 1971.

Weiss was the last of the empire builders. Under present rules which call for a free-agent draft and with more stringent roster controls which limit the time a club can control a player, it is impossible to stockpile the huge pool of top talent which was available to the highest bidder in Weiss' day. This shrewd, skillful operator set the mark of excellence all other baseball men aimed for. None did it as successfully and as consistently as George Martin Weiss. He was named to the Hall of Fame in 1971.

MICHAEL FRANCIS (MICKEY) WELCH

Born July 4, 1859, at Brooklyn, N.Y.
Died July 30, 1941, at Nashua, N.H.
Threw and batted righthanded.

Won 17 consecutive games, July 18, through September 4, 1885.
Named to Hall of Fame, 1973.

Year Club	League	G.	IP.	W.	L.	Pct.	H.	R.	SO.	BB.	CG.	ShO.
1878—Auburn	National Assn.	...	...	...	...	.....	...	...	...	...	...	..
1879—Holyoke	National Assn.	...	...	...	...	.....	...	...	...	...	...	..
1880—Troy	National	65	574	34	30	.531	590	322	115	80	64	4
1881—Troy	National	40	362	21	18	.538	370	186	96	76	40	4
1882—Troy	National	34	292	14	16	.467	334	218	51	66	31	5
1883—New York	National	54	422	25	23	.521	426	269	138	64	46	4
1884—New York	National	65	555	39	21	.650	527	277	349	141	62	4
1885—New York	National	56	496	44	11	.800	365	170	256	135	55	7
1886—New York	National	59	499	33	22	.600	504	279	269	167	56	1
1887—New York	National	41	346	22	15	.595	428	191	116	90	39	2
1888—New York	National	47	425	26	19	.578	322	156	170	112	47	5
1889—New York	National	45	364	27	12	.692	340	196	128	153	39	3
1890—New York	National	37	294	17	13	.567	262	146	104	128	33	2
1891—New York	National	22	160	5	9	.357	178	136	48	91	14	0
1892—New York (a)	National	1	5	0	0	.000	10	9	1	3	0	0
1892—Troy	Eastern	31	...	17	14	.548	230	130	...	...	...	..
Major League Totals		566	4794	307	209	.595	4646	2555	1841	1306	526	41

aEarly in June, 1892, New York transferred Welch to their Troy minor league franchise, where he pitched the balance of the season. His first appearance with Troy was June 10, 1892.

VICTOR WOODROW WERTZ

Born February 9, 1925, at York, Pa.
Height, 6.00. Weight, 202.
Threw right and batted lefthanded.
Married Lucille Carroll Caleel, May 12, 1952.

Hit seven home runs in five consecutive games, July 27 (1), 28 (2), 29 (1), 30 (1), August 1 (2), 1950; hit for cycle, first game, September 14, 1947; tied major league record by hitting four doubles in a game, September 26, 1956. Led A. L. first basemen in double plays, 1957.

Tied World Series record for most assists by a first baseman in a four-game Series (6), 1954.

Year	Club	League	Pos.	G.	AB.	R.	H.	2B.	3B.	HR.	RBI.	B.A.	PO.	A.	E.	F.A.
1942	Winston-Salem	Pied.	OF	63	222	18	53	7	4	0	20	.239	89	14	1	.990
1943	Buffalo	Int.	OF-P	10	18	3	4	1	0	0	1	.222	4	0	1	.800
1943-44-45	Detroit	Amer.					(In Military Service)									
1946	Buffalo	Int.	OF	139	478	75	144	27	9	19	91	.301	225	18	7	.972
1947	Detroit	Amer.	OF	102	333	60	96	22	4	6	44	.288	160	6	6	.965
1948	Detroit	Amer.	OF	119	391	49	97	19	9	7	67	.248	196	11	10	.954
1949	Detroit	Amer.	OF	•155	608	96	185	26	6	20	133	.304	302	14	6	.981
1950	Detroit	Amer.	OF	149	559	99	172	37	4	27	123	.308	286	5	10	.967
1951	Detroit	Amer.	OF	138	501	86	143	24	4	27	94	.285	254	7	3	.989
1952	Det. (a)-St.L.	Amer.	OF	122	415	68	115	20	3	23	70	.277	198	8	5	.976
1953	St. Louis	Amer.	OF	128	440	61	118	18	6	19	70	.268	243	15	7	.974
1954	Balt. (b)-Cleve.	Amer.	1B-OF	123	389	38	100	15	2	15	61	.257	614	57	9	.987
1955	Cleveland (c)	Amer.	1B-OF	74	257	30	65	11	2	14	55	.253	462	34	8	.984
1956	Cleveland	Amer.	1B	136	481	65	127	22	0	32	106	.264	*971	77	9	.991
1957	Cleveland	Amer.	1B	144	515	84	145	21	0	28	105	.282	1025	83	*14	.988
1958	Cleve. (d) (e)	Amer.	1B	25	43	5	12	1	0	3	12	.279	44	5	1	.980
1959	Boston	Amer.	1B	94	247	38	68	13	0	7	49	.275	440	38	4	.992
1960	Boston	Amer.	1B	131	443	45	125	22	0	19	103	.282	841	78	12	.987
1961	Bos. (f)-Detroit	Amer.	1B	107	323	33	84	16	2	11	61	.260	664	67	7	.991
1962	Detroit	Amer.	1B	74	105	7	34	2	0	5	18	.324	75	9	1	.958
1963	Det. (g)-Minn.	Amer.	1B	41	49	3	6	0	0	3	7	.122	32	5	0	1.000
Major League Totals				1862	6099	867	1692	289	42	266	1178	.277	6807	519	112	.985

aReleased to St. Louis Browns on waivers with pitchers Dick Littlefield and Marlin Stuart and outfielder Don Lenhardt. Tigers received as payment pitchers Ned Garver and Dave Madison and outfielder Jim Delsing and pitcher William (Bud) Black from the Browns' San Antonio (Texas) farm club. Transfer of Black, Stuart and Lenhardt became official August 11, Littlefield on August 13 and others on August 14, 1952.

bTraded to Cleveland Indians for pitcher Bob Chakales, June 1, 1954.

cStriken by non-paralytic form of polio, August 26, 1955; out of game for remainder of season.

dFractured ankle in third inning of exhibition game against San Francisco Giants. Wertz slid into second base in successful attempt to break up double play, but suffered injury when spikes caught in dirt, March 28, 1958. Made first appearance of season as pinch-hitter, first game, July 22, 1958.

eTraded to Boston Red Sox with outfielder Gary Geiger for outfielder Jimmy Piersall, December 2, 1958.

fReleased to Detroit Tigers on waivers, September 8, 1961.

gReleased by Detroit Tigers, May 10, 1963; signed with Minnesota Twins, June 18, 1963, and released October 15, 1963.

WORLD SERIES RECORD

Year	Club	League	Pos.	G.	AB.	R.	H.	2B.	3B.	HR.	RBI.	B.A.	PO.	A.	E.	F.A.
1954	Cleveland	Amer.	1B	4	16	2	8	2	1	1	3	.500	33	6	1	.975

AUGUST WEYHING

Born September 29, 1866 at Louisville, Ky.
Died September 3, 1955, at Louisville, Ky.
Height, 5.09. Weight, 145.
Threw and batted righthanded.
Married Marcie Gehrig, January 9, 1901.

Pitched 4-0 no-hit victory vs. Kansas City, July 31, 1888.
Manager, Tulsa, Texas League, 1910, until released May 1910; Texas League umpire balance of 1910.

Year	Club	League	G.	IP.	W.	L.	Pct.	H.	R.	SO.	BB.	CG.	ShO.
1885	Richmond	Virginia	22	....	19	3	.864	121	....	187	39	....	....
1886	Charleston	Southern	30	....	12	17	.414	207	....	179	63	....	....
1887	Philadelphia	Amer. Assn.	54	457	26	25	.510	618	338	154	167	52	2
1888	Philadelphia	Amer. Assn.	48	407	29	19	.604	326	214	162	168	45	3
1889	Philadelphia	Amer. Assn.	54	453	28	19	.596	376	268	207	209	50	4
1890	Brooklyn	Players	49	396	30	14	.682	420	246	189	181	39	3
1891	Philadelphia	Amer. Assn.	53	456	31	20	.608	414	216	209	159	51	3
1892	Philadelphia	National	58	467	28	18	.609	392	211	185	158	45	6
1893	Philadelphia	National	42	345	24	16	.600	400	236	100	139	33	2
1894	Philadelphia	National	39	277	18	14	.563	361	212	79	101	26	2
1895	Phil.-Pitts.-Louisville	National	31	225	9	21	.300	311	232	60	79	23	1
1896	Louisville	National	5	42	2	3	.400	68	46	12	15	4	0
1897					(Voluntarily Retired)								
1898	Washington	National	45	363	15	26	.366	425	229	96	80	39	0
1898	Washington	National	43	337	16	21	.432	404	227	98	75	34	2
1900	Bklyn.-St. Louis	National	15	90	6	6	.500	126	75	12	25	6	0
1901	Cleveland	American	2	11	0	1	.000	17	11	5	11	0	0
1901	Cincinnati	National	1	9	0	1	.000	11	9	3	2	1	0
1901	Grand Rapids	Western	20	....	14	6	.700	160	....	96	31	....	....
1902	Memphis	Southern	29	....	11	14	.440	237	....	94	49	....	....
1903	Atl.-Little Rock	Southern	35	....	18	15	.545	280	....	92	11	....	....
American Association Totals			209	1773	114	83	.579	1734	1036	732	703	98	12
American League Totals			2	11	0	1	.000	17	11	5	11	0	0
National League Totals			279	2155	118	126	.484	2498	1477	645	674	311	13
Players League Totals			49	396	30	14	.682	420	246	189	181	39	3
Major League Totals			539	4335	262	224	.539	4669	2770	1571	1569	448	28

ZACHARIAH DAVIS (ZACK) WHEAT

Born May 23, 1888, at Hamilton, Mo.
Died March 11, 1972, at Sedalia, Mo.
Height, 5.10. Weight, 170.
Threw and batted lefthanded.

Batted safely in 26 consecutive games, July 11 through August 7, 1918.
Named to Hall of Fame, 1959.

Year	Club	League	Pos.	G.	AB.	R.	H.	2B.	3B.	HR.	RBI.	B.A.	PO.	A.	E.	F.A.
1908	Shreveport	Texas	OF	92	239	49	91	7	4	1	....	.268	172	8	12	.938
1909	Mobile	South.	OF	129	460	58	112	20	4	2	....	.246	248	21	10	.964
1909	Brooklyn	Nat.	OF	26	102	15	31	7	3	0	4	.304	54	5	3	.952
1910	Brooklyn	Nat.	OF	•156	606	78	172	36	15	2	54	.284	354	21	15	.962
1911	Brooklyn	Nat.	OF	136	534	55	153	26	13	5	76	.287	287	12	14	.955
1912	Brooklyn	Nat.	OF	123	453	70	138	28	7	8	62	.305	285	13	10	•.968
1913	Brooklyn	Nat.	OF	138	535	64	161	28	10	7	71	.301	338	13	8	.978
1914	Brooklyn	Nat.	OF	145	533	66	170	26	9	9	88	.319	•331	21	14	.962
1915	Brooklyn	Nat.	OF	146	528	64	136	15	12	5	70	.258	345	18	18	.953
1916	Brooklyn	Nat.	OF	149	568	76	177	32	13	9	76	.312	333	14	9	.975
1917	Brooklyn	Nat.	OF	109	362	38	113	15	11	1	40	.312	216	12	5	.979
1918	Brooklyn	Nat.	OF	105	409	39	137	15	3	0	48	•.335	219	11	5	.979
1919	Brooklyn	Nat.	OF	137	536	70	159	23	11	5	68	.297	297	9	9	.971
1920	Brooklyn	Nat.	OF	148	583	89	191	26	13	9	73	.328	287	10	9	.971
1921	Brooklyn	Nat.	OF	148	568	91	182	31	10	14	85	.320	283	18	11	.965
1922	Brooklyn	Nat.	OF	152	600	92	201	29	12	·16	112	.335	317	14	3	•.991
1923	Brooklyn	Nat.	OF	98	349	63	131	13	5	8	65	.375	135	4	14	.908
1924	Brooklyn	Nat.	OF	141	566	92	212	41	8	14	97	.375	288	13	11	.965
1925	Brooklyn	Nat.	OF	150	616	125	221	42	14	14	103	.359	320	7	13	.962
1926	Brooklyn (a)	Nat.	OF	111	411	68	119	31	2	5	35	.290	202	9	10	.955
1927	Philadelphia	Amer.	OF	88	247	34	80	12	1	1	38	.324	105	8	2	.983
1928	Minneapolis	A.A.	OF	82	194	17	60	7	1	5	30	.309	67	4	3	.959
American League Totals				88	247	34	80	12	1	1	38	.324	105	8	2	.983
National League Totals				2318	8859	1255	2804	464	171	131	1227	.317	4891	224	181	.966
Major League Totals				2406	9106	1289	2884	476	172	132	1265	.317	4996	232	183	.966

aUnconditionally released by Brooklyn Dodgers, January 1, 1927, and signed with Philadelphia Athletics, January 12, 1927.

WORLD SERIES RECORD

Year	Club	League	Pos.	G.	AB.	R.	H.	2B.	3B.	HR.	RBI.	B.A.	PO.	A.	E.	F.A.
1916	Brooklyn	Nat.	OF	5	19	2	4	0	1	0	1	.211	14	0	1	.933
1920	Brooklyn	Nat.	OF	7	27	2	9	2	0	0	2	.333	16	0	2	.889
World Series Totals				12	46	4	13	2	1	0	3	.283	30	0	3	.909

GUY HARRIS (DOC) WHITE

Born April 9, 1879, at Washington, D.C.
Died February 17, 1969, at Silver Spring, Md.
Height, 6.01½. Weight, 150.
Threw and batted lefthanded.

Holds American League record for most consecutive shutout games pitched, season (5), September 12, 16, 19, 25, 30, 1904. Pitched 45 consecutive shutout innings, 1904. Tied for longest one-hit complete game, A.L., 10 innings, September 6, 1903, one double.

Year	Club	League	G.	IP.	W.	L.	Pct.	H.	R.	SO.	BB.	CG.	ShO.
1901	Philadelphia	National	31	237	14	13	.519	238	118	133	54	22	0
1902	Philadelphia (a)	National	36	306	16	20	.444	279	128	187	70	34	3
1903	Chicago	American	37	300	16	15	.516	264	121	135	66	29	3
1904	Chicago	American	30	237	16	12	.571	198	73	114	73	23	7
1905	Chicago	American	36	262	18	14	.563	201	61	122	57	24	4
1906	Chicago	American	28	220	18	6	.750	162	47	102	38	20	7
1907	Chicago	American	47	295	•27	13	.675	271	95	140	33	25	7
1908	Chicago	American	41	296	19	13	.594	267	95	126	69	24	5
1909	Chicago	American	24	171	10	9	.526	141	52	75	30	14	3
1910	Chicago	American	33	246	15	13	.536	219	84	111	50	20	2
1911	Chicago	American	34	214	10	14	.417	219	91	72	35	16	4
1912	Chicago	American	32	172	8	10	.444	172	81	57	47	9	1
1913	Chicago	American	19	103	2	4	.333	106	58	37	42	2	0
1914	Venice	Pacific Coast	39	259	17	13	.567	268	92	99	66	....	..
1915	Vernon	Pacific Coast	11	44	2	3	.400	53	22	10	10	....	..
American League Totals			361	2516	159	123	.564	2220	858	1091	540	206	43
National League Totals			67	543	30	33	.476	517	246	320	124	56	3
Major League Totals			428	3059	189	156	.548	2737	1104	1411	664	262	46

aJumped to Chicago White Sox for 1903.

WORLD SERIES RECORD

Year	Club	League	G.	IP.	W.	L.	Pct.	H.	R.	SO.	BB.	CG.	ShO.
1906	Chicago	American	3	15	1	1	.500	12	7	3	7	1	0

JAMES LAURIE (DEACON) WHITE

Born December 2, 1847, at Canton, N.Y.
Died July 7, 1939, at Aurora, Ill.
Threw right and batted lefthanded.
Brother of William Henry White, major league pitcher, 1877-86.

Manager, Cincinnati, National League, 1879.

Year	Club	League	Pos.	G.	AB.	R.	H.	2B.	3B.	HR.	SB.	B.A.	PO.	A.	E.	F.A.
1876	Chicago	Nat.	C	66	310	66	104	16	1	1	....	.335	303	50	93	.791
1877	Boston	Nat.	C-1B-OF	48	213	39	*82	14	•9	2	....	*.385	301	14	12	.963
1878	Cincinnati	Nat.	C-3B-OF	60	253	41	78	4	1	0	....	.308	270	70	41	.892
1879	Cincinnati	Nat.	C-1B-OF	77	330	55	109	16	8	1	....	.330	322	84	65	.862
1880	Cincinnati	Nat.	1-2B-OF	32	129	17	39	4	2	0	....	.302	38	8	14	.766
1881	Buffalo	Nat.	C-Inf-OF	78	319	58	99	22	3	0	....	.310	338	104	63	.875
1882	Buffalo	Nat.	C-3B	83	337	51	95	17	2	1	....	.281	173	150	55	.854
1883	Buffalo	Nat.	C-3B	93	387	58	112	13	5	0	....	.289	169	164	66	.835
1884	Buffalo	Nat.	C-3B	106	436	80	142	14	12	5	....	.325	110	194	66	.821
1885	Buffalo	Nat.	3B	98	404	54	118	5	5	0	....	.292	118	198	40	.887
1886	Detroit	Nat.	3B	124	491	65	142	17	6	0	9	.289	131	245	68	.847
1887	Detroit	Nat.	3B	111	474	71	162	20	11	3	20	.341	133	225	64	.848
1888	Detroit	Nat.	3B	125	527	75	157	20	5	3	12	.298	146	244	65	.857
1889	Pittsburgh	Nat.	3B	55	225	35	57	10	0	0	2	.253	68	95	24	.871
1890	Buffalo	Players	P-1-3	122	439	63	116	13	3	0	3	.264	668	204	44	.952
National League Totals				1156	4835	765	1496	192	70	16	....	.309	2620	1845	736	.858
Players League Totals				122	439	63	116	13	3	0	....	.264	668	204	44	.952
Major League Totals				1278	5274	828	1612	205	73	16	....	.306	3288	2049	780	.873

WILLIAM DE KOVA WHITE

Born January 28, 1934, at Lakewood, Fla.
Height, 6.00. Weight, 200.
Threw and batted lefthanded.
Married Mildred Alberta Hightower, November 21, 1956.

Hit home run first time at bat in major leagues, May 7, 1956.
Tied major league record for most hits, two consecutive doubleheaders (14), July 17-18, 1961. White went four-for-five in both games, July 17 and three-for-four in both games the following day.
Tied major league mark for most unassisted double plays by first baseman, season (8), 1961.
Tied major league record for most games played by first baseman, 162-game season (162), 1963.
Hit three consecutive home runs in game, July 5, 1961.
Named as first baseman on the National League All-Star team by THE SPORTING NEWS 1963-64.
Received Rawlings Gold Glove award as outstanding National League fielding first baseman, 1960-61-62-63-64-65-66.

Year	Club	League	Pos.	G.	AB.	R.	H.	2B.	3B.	HR.	RBI.	B.A.	PO.	A.	E.	F.A.
1953—Danville		Car.	1B-OF	134	533	99	159	25	2	20	84	.298	1021	80	20	.982
1954—Sioux City		West.	1B	154	573	120	●183	30	9	*30	92	.319	*1345	106	21	.986
1955—Dallas		Tex.	1B-OF	142	502	88	148	18	4	22	93	.295	1222	64	18	.986
1956—Minneapolis		A.A.	1B-OF	20	72	18	21	5	1	3	14	.292	139	10	3	.980
1956—New York		Nat.	*1B-OF	138	508	63	130	23	7	22	59	.256	*1256	*111	15	.989
1957—New York		Nat.	(In Military Service)													
1958—San Fran.(a)(b)		Nat.	1B-OF	26	29	5	7	1	0	1	4	.241	19	1	0	1.000
1959—St. Louis		Nat.	OF-1B	138	517	77	156	33	9	12	72	.302	579	27	9	.985
1960—St. Louis		Nat.	OF-1B	144	554	81	157	27	10	16	79	.283	1058	66	13	.989
1961—St. Louis		Nat.	1B	153	591	89	169	28	11	20	90	.286	1373	104	17	.989
1962—St. Louis		Nat.	1B-OF	159	614	93	199	31	3	20	102	.324	1260	97	10	.993
1963—St. Louis		Nat.	1B	●162	658	106	200	26	8	27	109	.304	1389	105	13	.991
1964—St. Louis		Nat.	1B	160	631	92	191	37	4	21	102	.303	1513	101	6	*.996
1965—St. Louis (c)		Nat.	1B	148	543	82	157	26	3	24	73	.289	1308	109	11	.992
1966—Philadelphia		Nat.	1B	159	577	85	159	23	6	22	103	.276	1422	*109	9	*.994
1967—Philadelphia		Nat.	1B	110	308	29	77	6	2	8	33	.250	775	52	6	.993
1968—Philadelphia (d)		Nat.	1B	127	385	34	92	16	2	9	40	.239	982	77	6	.994
1969—St. Louis		Nat.	1B	49	57	7	12	1	0	0	4	.211	81	7	0	1.000
Major League Totals				1673	5972	843	1706	278	65	202	870	.286	13105	966	115	.992

aOn military list through July 26.
bTraded to St. Louis Cardinals with third baseman Ray Jablonski for pitchers Don Choate and Sam Jones, March 25, 1959.
cTraded with catcher Bob Uecker and shortstop Dick Groat to Philadelphia Phillies for pitcher Art Mahaffey, outfielder Alex Johnson and catcher Pat Corrales, October 27, 1965.
dTraded to St. Louis Cardinals for infielder Gerry Buchek and infielder-catcher Jim Hutto. April 3, 1969. Buchek and Hutto both assigned to Eugene.

WORLD SERIES RECORD

Year	Club	League	Pos.	G.	AB.	R.	H.	2B.	3B.	HR.	RBI.	B.A.	PO.	A.	E.	F.A.
1964—St. Louis		Nat.	1B	7	27	2	3	1	0	0	2	.111	62	3	0	1.000

WILLIAM HENRY WHITE

Born October 11, 1854, at Canton, N.Y.
Died August 31, 1911, at Fort Collier, Ont.
Threw right and batted right and lefthanded.
Brother of James L. (Deacon) White, major league catcher, infielder and outfielder, 1876-90.

Led American Association in innings pitched, 1882. First player to wear glasses.

Year	Club	League	G.	W.	L.	Pct.	H.	R.	SO.	BB.	ShO.
1877—Boston		National	3	2	1	.667	....	....	....	....	0
1878—Cincinnati		National	51	29	21	.580	....	....	....	....	5
1879—Cincinnati		National	*75	43	31	.581	692	410	....	....	4
1880—Cincinnati		National	61	18	*43	.295	522	306	....	....	3
1881—Detroit		National	2	0	2	.000	22	18	2	2	0

Year	Club	League	G.	W.	L.	Pct.	H.	R.	SO.	BB.	ShO.
1882—Cincinnati		American Association	•54	*40	12	*.769	422	161	125	....	*8
1883—Cincinnati		American Association	65	*43	22	.662	390	254	136	94	•6
1884—Cincinnati		American Association	54	34	18	.654	487	224	133	71	*8
1885—Cincinnati		American Association	35	17	15	.531	298	170	80	98	2
1886—Cincinnati		American Association	3	1	2	.333	....	....	....	....	0
National League Totals			192	92	98	.484	....	....	....	....	12
American Association Totals			211	135	69	.663	....	....	....	....	24
Major League Totals			403	227	167	.576	....	....	....	....	36

EARL OLIVER WHITEHILL

Born February 7, 1889, at Cedar Rapids, Ia.
Died October 22, 1954, at Omaha, Neb.
Height, 5.10. Weight, 185.
Threw and batted lefthanded.

Coach, Cleveland Indians, 1941; coach, Philadelphia Phillies, 1943; player-coach, Buffalo, International League, 1944.

Year	Club	League	G.	IP.	W.	L.	Pct.	H.	R.	ER.	SO.	BB.	ERA.
1919—Des Moines		Western	1	7	0	0	.000	....	....	....	....	....	......
1920—Birmingham		Southern	1	6	0	1	.000	11	....	....	4	5	......
1920—Columbia		Sally	33	264	20	10	.667	224	105	65	11	66	2.22
1921—Birmingham		Southern	44	296	19	14	.576	284	134	102	120	99	3.10
1922—Birmingham		Southern	46	284	17	14	.548	286	128	104	100	93	3.30
1923—Birmingham		Southern	38	277	18	13	.581	236	102	82	138	77	2.66
1923—Detroit		American	8	33	2	0	1.000	22	14	10	19	15	2.73
1924—Detroit		American	35	233	17	9	.654	260	125	100	65	79	3.86
1925—Detroit		American	35	239	11	11	.500	267	135	124	83	88	4.67
1926—Detroit		American	36	252	16	13	.552	271	*136	*112	109	79	4.00
1927—Detroit		American	41	236	16	14	.533	238	110	88	95	*105	3.36
1928—Detroit		American	31	196	11	16	.407	214	131	94	93	78	4.32
1929—Detroit		American	38	245	14	15	.483	267	147	126	103	96	4.63
1930—Detroit		American	34	221	17	13	.567	248	139	104	109	80	4.24
1931—Detroit		American	34	271	13	16	.448	287	152	123	81	118	4.08
1932—Detroit(a)		American	33	244	16	13	.552	255	130	123	81	93	4.54
1933—Washington		American	39	270	22	8	.733	271	112	100	96	100	3.33
1934—Washington		American	32	235	14	11	.560	269	129	118	96	94	4.52
1935—Washington		American	34	279	14	13	.519	318	•149	*133	102	104	4.29
1936—Washington(b)		American	28	212	14	11	.560	252	124	115	63	89	4.88
1937—Cleveland		American	33	147	8	8	.500	189	111	106	53	80	6.49
1938—Cleveland(c)		American	26	160	9	8	.529	187	109	99	60	83	5.57
1939—Chicago		National	24	89	4	7	.364	102	59	51	42	50	5.16
1944—Buffalo		International	10	23	0	3	.000	24	15	11	9	14	4.30
American League Totals			517	3473	214	179	.545	3815	1959	1675	1308	1381	4.34
National League Totals			24	89	4	7	.364	102	59	51	42	50	5.16
Major League Totals			541	3562	218	186	.540	3917	2018	1726	1350	1431	4.36

aTraded to Washington Senators for pitchers Fred Marberry and Carl Fischer, December 14, 1932.
bTraded to Cleveland Indians in three-cornered deal: Pitcher Thornton Lee going from Cleveland to the Chicago White Sox and pitcher Jack Salveson from the White Sox to Washington Senators, December 8, 1936.
cUnconditionally released by Cleveland Indians, February, 1939, and then signed with Chicago Cubs.

WORLD SERIES RECORD

Year	Club	League	G.	IP.	W.	L.	Pct.	H.	R.	ER.	SO.	BB.	ERA.
1933—Washington		American	1	9	1	0	1.000	5	0	0	2	2	0.00

JAMES E. (GRASSHOPPER JIM) WHITNEY

Born, 1856, at Binghamton, N. Y.
Died May 21, 1891, at Binghamton, N. Y.
Threw and batted lefthanded.
Married Miss Haddock, 1883.

Holds major league record for most at-bats, nine-inning game, with eight on June 9, 1883, vs. Detroit and also eight against Philadelphia on June 20, 1883. Scored six runs in game, June 9, 1883.

Year	Club	League	G.	W.	L.	Pct.	H.	R.	CG.	ShO.
1881	Boston	National	*67	31	*33	.484	548	293	*59	6
1882	Boston	National	49	24	22	.522	382	205	46	3
1883	Boston	National	62	38	22	.633	532	285	58	1
1884	Boston	National	48	24	17	.585	254	130	35	6
1885	Boston	National	50	18	*32	.360	500	286	48	2
1886	Kansas City	National	46	12	30	.286	484	322	42	3
1887	Washington	National	46	24	21	.533	490	258	39	2
1888	Washington	National	39	18	21	.462	317	181	36	3
1889	Indianapolis	National	10	2	7	.222	....	73	7	0
1890	Philadelphia	American Association	7	2	2	.500	....	27	3	0
National League Totals			417	191	205	.482	8507	2033	370	26
American Association Totals			7	2	2	.500	....	27	3	0
Major League Totals			424	193	207	.483	....	2060	373	26

BILLY LEO WILLIAMS

Born June 15, 1938, at Whistler, Ala.
Height, 6.01½. Weight, 170.
Threw and batted lefthanded.

Tied major league records for most home runs two consecutive games (5), September 8 and 10, 1968, most consecutive doubles in one game, 4, April 9, 1969, and most times, four long hits, game, season (2), April 9 and September 5, 1969.
Established the following National League records: most games played consecutive, league, 1,117, September 22, 1963 through September 2, 1970.
Hit three home runs in game, September 10, 1968.
Named National League Rookie Player of the Year by THE SPORTING NEWS and National League Rookie of the Year by the Baseball Writers' Association, 1961.
Named THE SPORTING NEWS Major League Player of the Year, 1972.
Named THE SPORTING NEWS National League Player of the Year, 1972.
Named outfielder on THE SPORTING NEWS National League All-Star Teams, 1964-68-70-72.
Batting instructor, Chicago Cubs, 1978-79; coach, Cubs, 1980 to date.

Year	Club	League	Pos.	G.	AB.	R.	H.	2B.	3B.	HR.	RBI.	B.A.	PO.	A.	E.	F.A.
1956	Ponca City	Soo. St.	OF	13	17	4	4	0	0	0	4	.235	6	0	1	.857
1957	Ponca City	Soo. St.	OF	•126	451	87	140	*40	3	17	95	.310	211	21	*25	.903
1958	Pueblo	West.	OF	21	80	9	20	2	1	2	11	.250	30	1	2	.939
1958	Burlington	I.I.I.	OF	61	214	38	65	7	0	10	38	.304	93	4	4	.960
1959	San Antonio	Tex.	1B-OF	94	371	57	118	22	7	10	79	.318	578	54	21	.968
1959	Fort Worth	A. A.	OF	5	21	7	10	4	1	1	5	.476	10	2	1	.923
1959	Chicago	Nat.	OF	18	33	0	5	0	1	0	2	.152	18	0	0	1.000
1960	Houston	A. A.	OF	126	473	74	153	28	3	26	80	.323	207	7	7	.968
1960	Chicago	Nat.	OF	12	47	4	13	0	2	2	7	.277	25	0	1	.962
1961	Chicago	Nat.	OF	146	529	75	147	20	7	25	86	.278	220	9	*11	.954
1962	Chicago	Nat.	OF	159	618	94	184	22	8	22	92	.298	273	18	10	.967
1963	Chicago	Nat.	OF	161	612	87	175	36	9	25	95	.286	298	13	4	.987
1964	Chicago	Nat.	OF	162	645	100	201	39	2	33	98	.312	233	14	13	.950
1965	Chicago	Nat.	OF	•164	645	115	203	39	6	34	108	.315	296	10	10	.968
1966	Chicago	Nat.	OF	•162	648	100	179	23	5	29	91	.276	319	9	8	.976
1967	Chicago	Nat.	OF	162	634	92	176	21	12	28	84	.278	271	3	3	.989
1968	Chicago	Nat.	OF	*163	642	91	185	30	8	30	98	.288	261	4	9	.967
1969	Chicago	Nat.	OF	*163	642	103	188	33	10	21	95	.293	250	15	12	.957
1970	Chicago	Nat.	OF	•161	636	*137	•205	34	4	42	129	.322	259	13	3	.989
1971	Chicago	Nat.	OF	157	594	86	179	27	5	28	93	.301	284	8	7	.977
1972	Chicago	Nat.	OF-1B	150	574	95	191	34	6	37	122	*.333	275	13	4	.986
1973	Chicago	Nat.	OF-1B	156	576	72	166	22	2	20	86	.288	420	34	6	.987
1974	Chicago(a)	Nat.	1B-OF	117	404	55	113	22	0	16	68	.280	635	53	11	.984
1975	Oakland	Amer.	DH-1B	155	520	68	127	20	1	23	81	.244	30	3	1	.971
1976	Oakland	Amer.	DH-OF	120	351	36	74	12	0	11	41	.211	0	0	0	.000
National League Totals				2213	8479	1306	2510	402	87	392	1354	.296	4337	216	112	.976
American League Totals				275	871	104	201	32	1	34	122	.231	30	3	1	.971
Major League Totals				2488	9350	1410	2711	434	88	426	1476	.290	4367	219	113	.976

aTraded to Oakland Athletics for pitchers Darold Knowles and Bob Locker and second baseman Manny Trillo, October 23, 1974.

FRED (CY) WILLIAMS

Born December 21, 1888, at Wadena, Ind.
Died April 23, 1974, at Eagle River, Wis.
Height, 6.02. Weight, 180.
Threw and batted lefthanded.
Married Vada Glenne Perkins, December 24, 1913.

Hit three home runs in a game, May 11, 1923, vs. St. Louis.
Manager, Richmond, Eastern League, 1931.

Year	Club	League	Pos.	G.	AB.	R.	H.	2B.	3B.	HR.	RBI.	B.A.	PO.	A.	E.	F.A.
1912	Chicago	Nat.	OF	28	62	3	15	1	1	0	0	.242	36	3	0	1.000
1913	Chicago	Nat.	OF	49	156	17	35	3	3	4	31	.224	77	4	2	.976
1914	Chicago	Nat.	OF	55	94	12	19	2	2	0	5	.202	46	2	3	.941
1915	Chicago	Nat.	OF	151	518	59	133	22	6	13	65	.257	347	14	12	.968
1916	Chicago	Nat.	OF	118	405	55	113	19	9	•12	68	.279	260	7	3	.989
1917	Chicago(a)	Nat.	OF	138	468	53	113	28	4	5	46	.241	340	23	15	.960
1918	Philadelphia	Nat.	OF	94	351	49	97	14	1	6	37	.276	229	10	9	.968
1919	Philadelphia	Nat.	OF	109	435	54	121	21	1	9	42	.278	278	13	9	.970
1920	Philadelphia	Nat.	OF	148	590	88	192	36	10	*15	72	.325	388	22	12	.972
1921	Philadelphia	Nat.	OF	146	562	67	180	28	6	18	75	.320	382	*29	9	.979
1922	Philadelphia	Nat.	OF	151	584	98	180	30	6	26	92	.308	376	19	11	.973
1923	Philadelphia	Nat.	OF	136	535	98	157	22	3	*41	114	.293	350	9	7	.981
1924	Philadelphia	Nat.	OF	148	558	101	183	31	11	24	93	.328	368	13	15	.962
1925	Philadelphia	Nat.	OF	107	314	78	104	11	5	13	60	.331	173	12	2	.989
1926	Philadelphia	Nat.	OF	107	336	63	116	13	4	18	53	.345	143	14	6	.963
1927	Philadelphia	Nat.	OF	131	492	86	135	18	2	•30	98	.274	241	22	8	.970
1928	Philadelphia	Nat.	OF	99	238	31	61	9	0	12	37	.256	118	9	0	1.000
1929	Philadelphia	Nat.	OF-PH	66	65	11	19	2	0	5	21	.292	27	1	1	.966
1930	Philadelphia	Nat.	OF-PH	21	17	1	8	2	0	0	2	.471	1	0	0	1.000
1931	Richmond	East.	OF	17	46	3	8	1	0	0	4	.174	19	0	1	.950
Major League Totals				2002	6780	1024	1981	306	74	251	1011	.292	4180	226	123	.973

aTraded to Philadelphia Phillies for outfielder George Paskert, December 26, 1917.

KENNETH ROY WILLIAMS

Born June 28, 1893, at Grant's Pass, Ore.
Died January 22, 1959, Grant's Pass, Ore.
Height, 6.00. Weight, 186.
Threw right and batted lefthanded.
Married Edith Wilkerson, June 18, 1919.

Hit three home runs in game, April 22, 1922; hit two home runs in sixth inning, August 7, 1922, to equal major league record; hit home run in six consecutive games, July 28, 29, 30, 31, August 1, 2, 1922.

Year	Club	League	Pos.	G.	AB.	R.	H.	2B.	3B.	HR.	RBI.	B.A.	PO.	A.	E.	F.A.
1913	Regina	W. Can.	OF-3B	101	359	57	105	9	*13	5		.292	133	62	27	.878
1914	Edmonton	W. Can.	OF	119	445	78	140	12	10	*12		.315	166	18	14	.929
1915	Spokane	N. W.	OF	79	309	54	105	18	5	6		.340	163	16	7	.962
1915	Cincinnati	Nat.	OF	71	219	22	53	10	4	0	17	.242	117	11	7	.948
1916	Cincinnati	Nat.	OF	10	27	1	3	0	0	0	1	.111	79	2	1	.955
1916	Spokane	N. W.	OF	76	292	49	86	15	4	5		.295	154	11	7	.959
1916	Portland	P. C.	OF	53	183	21	51	11	1	4		.284	130	10	3	.979
1917	Portland	P. C.	OF	192	737	117	231	43	8	*24		.313	474	34	*18	.966
1918	St. Louis (a)	Amer.	OF	2	1	0	0	0	0	0	0	.000	0	0	0	.000
1919	St. Louis	Amer.	OF	65	227	32	68	10	5	6	35	.300	168	10	12	.937
1920	St. Louis	Amer.	OF	141	521	90	160	34	13	10	72	.307	331	17	14	.961
1921	St. Louis	Amer.	OF	146	547	115	190	31	7	24	117	.347	331	24	*26	.932
1922	St. Louis	Amer.	OF	153	585	128	194	34	11	*39	*155	.332	372	16	12	.970
1923	St. Louis	Amer.	OF	147	555	106	198	37	12	29	91	.357	333	23	12	.967
1924	St. Louis	Amer.	OF	114	398	78	129	21	4	18	84	.324	257	13	9	.968
1925	St. Louis	Amer.	OF	102	411	83	136	31	5	25	105	.331	242	11	12	.955
1926	St. Louis	Amer.	OF	108	347	55	97	15	7	17	74	.280	189	12	11	.948
1927	St. Louis (b)	Amer.	OF	131	423	70	136	23	6	17	74	.322	260	15	10	.965
1928	Boston	Amer.	OF	133	462	59	140	25	1	8	67	.303	253	10	8	.970

Year	Club	League	Pos.	G.	AB.	R.	H.	2B.	3B.	HR.	RBI.	B.A.	PO.	A.	E.	F.A.
1929–Boston (c)		Amer.	OF	74	139	21	48	14	2	3	22	.345	75	3	3	.963
1930–Portland		P. C.	OF	148	546	93	191	32	4	14	110	.350	259	17	8	.972
1931–Portland		P. C.	OF	20	76	12	21	1	2	1	15	.276	32	1	0	1.000
American League Totals				1316	4616	837	1496	275	73	196	896	.324	2811	154	129	.958
National League Totals				81	246	23	56	10	4	0	18	.228	136	13	8	.949
Major League Totals				1397	4862	860	1552	285	77	196	914	.319	2947	167	137	.958

aIn military service most of season.
bSold to Boston Red Sox for $10,000, December, 1927.
cReleased to New York Yankees, January, 1930, but received his unconditional release, March, 1930.

THEODORE SAMUEL (THE KID) WILLIAMS

Born, August 30, 1918, at San Diego, Calif.
Height, 6.04. Weight, 198.
Threw right and batted lefthanded.

Led American League in 1941 with .406 batting average to become the first major leaguer to hit .400 or more in a decade and last to do it to date. In winning his fifth batting crown in 1957, Ted at 39 years of age became the oldest player in the history of the majors to win a batting crown, and he won again at 40 in '58 to top the record once more.

Holds major league record for most consecutive playing years leading in runs scored (5), 1940-41-42-46-47 (in military service, 1943-44-45), also holds major league mark for most consecutive playing years leading in bases on balls (6), 1941-42-46-47-48-49 (in military service, 1943-44-45); during the six-year span previously listed, Williams received 100 or more bases on balls each season, establishing record for most consecutive playing years 100 or more bases on balls.

While George Herman (Babe) Ruth is unofficially credited with as many as 80 intentional bases on balls in a season, Ted Williams holds the official American League record for most intentional bases on balls, season (33), 1957. Received 2,019 bases on balls, career.

Holds major league mark for most successive times reaching first base safely (16), September 17 (hit homer as pinch-hitter), September 13 (walked as pinch-hitter), September 20 (hit homer as pinch-hitter), September 21 (homer and three bases on balls), September 22 (homer, single and two walks), September 23 (single, three bases on balls and hit by pitcher)–1957.

Tied major league record by hitting three home runs in a game twice during 1957 season, May 8 and June 13, 1957; also hit three home runs in a game July 14, 1946 (first game); tied major league record for most home runs in consecutive times at bat (4), September 17-20-21-22, 1957. (Bases on balls received in this span do not count against "consecutive" mark.)

Tied American League record for most total bases in fewest consecutive times at bat (22), September 17-20-21-22-23-24, 1957 (first two times at bat). Eight at-bats, five home runs–a percentage of .275 bases per at-bat.

Led in total bases, 1939-42-46-47-49-51; led in bases on balls, 1941-42-46-47-48-49-51-54; led in slugging percentage, 1941-42-46-47-48-49-51-54-57.

Hit for cycle, second game, July 21, 1946; had lifetime slugging percentage of .645. Hit home run on last at-bat in career, September 28, 1960.

Named Most Valuable Player in American League, 1946-49, and lost to Joe DiMaggio of New York Yankees by one point in 1947.

Named as outfielder on THE SPORTING NEWS All-Star Major League teams, 1939-40-41-42-46-47-48-49-51-53-55-56-57-58.

Named Top American League Player by THE SPORTING NEWS, 1957.
Named Major League Player of the Year by THE SPORTING NEWS, 1941-42-47-49-57.
Named Major League Player of the Decade by THE SPORTING NEWS, 1960.

Manager, Washington Senators, 1969 through 1971; remained manager when franchise was transferred to Texas, 1972.

Named to Hall of Fame, 1966.

Year	Club	League	Pos.	G.	AB.	R.	H.	2B.	3B.	HR.	RBI.	B.A.	PO.	A.	E.	F.A.
1936–San Diego		P. C.	OF	42	107	18	29	8	2	0	11	.271	64	5	2	.972
1937–San Diego		P. C.	OF	138	454	66	132	24	2	23	98	.291	213	10	7	.970
1938–Minneapolis		A. A.	OF	148	528	★130	193	30	9	★43	★142	★.366	269	17	11	.963
1939–Boston		Amer.	OF	149	565	131	185	44	11	31	★145	.327	318	11	★19	.945
1940–Boston		Amer.	OF	144	561	★134	193	43	14	23	113	.344	302	15	13	.961
1941–Boston		Amer.	OF	143	456	★135	185	33	3	★37	120	★.406	262	11	11	.961
1942–Boston		Amer.	OF	150	522	★141	186	34	5	★36	★137	★.356	313	15	4	.988
1943-44-45–Boston		Amer.						(In Military Service)								
1946–Boston		Amer.	OF	150	514	★142	176	37	8	38	123	.342	325	7	10	.971
1947–Boston		Amer.	OF	156	528	★125	181	40	9	★32	★114	★.343	347	10	9	.975
1948–Boston		Amer.	OF	137	509	124	188	★44	3	25	127	★.369	289	9	5	.983
1949–Boston		Amer.	OF	●155	566	★150	194	★39	3	★43	★159	.343	337	12	6	.983
1950–Boston (a)		Amer.	OF	89	334	82	106	24	1	28	97	.317	165	7	8	.956
1951–Boston		Amer.	OF	148	531	109	169	28	4	30	126	.318	315	12	4	.988
1952–Boston (b)		Amer.	OF	6	10	2	4	0	1	1	3	.400	4	0	0	1.000

Year	Club	League	Pos.	G.	AB.	R.	H.	2B.	3B.	HR.	RBI.	B.A.	PO.	A.	E.	F.A.
1953—Boston (b)		Amer.	OF	37	91	17	37	6	0	13	34	.407	31	1	1	.970
1954—Boston		Amer.	OF	117	386	93	133	23	1	29	89	.345	213	5	4	.982
1955—Boston		Amer.	OF	98	320	77	114	21	3	28	83	.356	170	5	2	.989
1956—Boston		Amer.	OF	136	400	71	138	28	2	24	82	.345	174	7	5	.973
1957—Boston		Amer.	OF	132	420	96	163	28	1	38	87	*.388	215	2	1	.995
1958—Boston		Amer.	OF	129	411	81	135	23	2	26	85	*.328	154	3	7	.957
1959—Boston		Amer.	OF	103	272	32	69	15	0	10	43	.254	94	4	3	.970
1960—Boston		Amer.	OF	113	310	56	98	15	0	29	72	.316	131	6	1	.993
Major League Totals				2292	7706	1798	2654	525	71	521	1839	.344	4159	142	113	.974

aSuffered fractured left elbow when he crashed into the left field wall making catch in first inning of All-Star Game at Chicago, July 11, 1950; despite injury he stayed in game until ninth inning. Williams had played 70 American League games up to the All-Star affair—but appeared in only 19 more contests with the Red Sox for the rest of the season.

bIn Military Service most of the season.

PITCHING RECORD

Year	Club	League	G.	IP.	W.	L.	Pct.	H.	R.	ER.	SO.	BB.	ERA.
1936—San Diego	Pacific Coast	1	1⅓	0	0	.000	2	2	2	0	1	13.50
1940—Boston	American	1	2	0	0	.000	3	1	1	1	0	4.50

WORLD SERIES RECORD

Year	Club	League	Pos.	G.	AB.	R.	H.	2B.	3B.	HR.	RBI.	B.A.	PO.	A.	E.	F.A.
1946—Boston		Amer.	OF	7	25	2	5	0	0	0	1	.200	16	2	0	1.000

VICTOR GAZAWAY WILLIS

Bornl April 12, 1876, at Cecil County, Md.
Died August 4, 1947, at Elkton, Md.
Height, 6.02. Weight, 205.
Threw and batted righthanded.
Married Mary J. Minnis, February 8, 1900.

Pitched 7-1 no-hit victory vs. Washington, August 7, 1899. Had 39 putouts in 43 games in 1904.

Year	Club	League	G.	IP.	W.	L.	Pct.	H.	R.	SO.	BB.	CG.	ShO.
1895—Harrisburg	Pa. State	16	....	....	....	....	....	....	....	....	....	....
1896—Syracuse	Eastern	17	....	10	6	.625	....	....	....	....	....	....
1897—Syracuse	Eastern	40	....	21	16	.568	....	....	....	....	....	....
1898—Boston	National	41	316	23	12	.657	270	150	132	141	29	1
1899—Boston	National	41	343	27	10	.730	274	148	119	118	35	*5
1900—Boston	National	31	225	9	16	.360	235	156	81	77	21	2
1901—Boston	National	38	307	18	17	.514	259	111	142	78	33	•6
1902—Boston	National	*51	*411	27	19	.587	369	140	•226	95	*45	4
1903—Boston	National	33	278	12	18	.400	264	121	125	88	29	2
1904—Boston	National	43	350	18	•25	.419	357	182	196	109	39	2
1905—Boston(a)	National	41	342	12	*29	.293	•340	174	149	107	36	4
1906—Pittsburgh	National	41	322	23	13	.639	295	84	124	76	32	6
1907—Pittsburgh	National	39	293	21	11	.656	236	106	107	69	27	6
1908—Pittsburgh	National	41	305	23	11	.676	239	95	97	69	25	7
1909—Pittsburgh(b)	National	39	290	22	11	.667	243	84	95	83	24	4
1910—St. Louis	National	33	212	9	12	.429	224	113	67	61	12	1
Major League Totals			512	3994	244	204	.545	3605	1644	1660	1171	387	50

aTraded for infielders Dave Brain and George E. Howard and pitcher V. A. Lindaman to Pittsburgh, December 15, 1905.

bSold to St. Louis at close of 1909 season.

WORLD SERIES RECORD

Year	Club	League	G.	IP.	W.	L.	Pct.	H.	R.	SO.	BB.	CG.	ShO.
1909—Pittsburgh	National	2	11⅔	0	1	.000	10	6	3	8	0	0

DID YOU KNOW —

That Vic Willis almost always finished what he started? He still holds the modern N.L. record with 45 complete games in 1902. And he holds the major league standard for losses in one season, 29 in 1905.

MAURICE MORNING (MAURY) WILLS

Born October 2, 1932, at Washington, D. C.
Height, 5.10. Weight, 165.
Threw right and batted left and righthanded.
Father of Bump Wills, major league infielder.

Established modern major league record for most stolen bases, season, 162 games (104), 1962 (topped by Lou Brock with 118, 1974); holds major league record for most games played, 162-game season (165), 1962; record holder for most games played by shortstop, 162-game season (165), 1962.
Set N. L. record for most consecutive seasons leading in stolen bases (6), 1965, with 50 in 1960, 35 in 1961, 104 in 1962, 40 in 1963, 53 in 1964 and 94 in 1965.
Tied following World Series records: Most hits, game (4), October 11, 1965; most double plays started, seven-game Series, shortstop (4), 1965; most double plays started, game, nine innings, shortstop (3), October 11, 1965.
Named Major League Player of the Year by THE SPORTING NEWS, 1962.
Named National League Player of the Year by THE SPORTING NEWS, 1962.
Most Valuable National League Player, 1962.
Named as shortstop on THE SPORTING NEWS National League All-Star Teams, 1961-62-65.
Named shortstop on National League All-Star Fielding Team, 1961-62.
Manager, Seattle, American League, August 4, 1980.

Year	Club	League	Pos.	G.	AB.	R.	H.	2B.	3B.	HR.	RBI.	B.A.	PO.	A.	E.	F.A.
1951	Hornell	Pony	INF-P	123	461	94	129	16	6	4	51	.280	235	210	28	.941
1952	Hornell	Pony	2B-SS	125	*533	*108	*160	34	4	4	58	.300	330	292	19	.970
1953	Pueblo	West.	2B	18	63	17	18	2	0	0	8	.286	39	53	7	.929
1953	Miami	Fla. I.	IN-C-P	93	343	71	98	16	5	6	31	.286	205	256	30	.939
1954	Pueblo	West.	*S-3-2-O	145	552	89	154	17	10	6	53	.279	261	420	*60	.919
1955	Fort Worth	Tex.	S-2-OF	123	326	44	66	11	0	7	39	.202	177	287	38	.924
1956	Pueblo	West.	SS	134	540	110	163	33	8	10	54	.302	*265	*361	42	.937
1957	Seattle	P. C.	INF	147	491	67	131	23	6	0	33	.267	265	428	51	.931
1958	Spokane	P. C.	SS	144	534	69	135	20	7	2	37	.253	245	426	33	.953
1959	Spokane	P. C.	SS	48	192	42	60	6	3	1	18	.313	68	161	12	.950
1959	Los Angeles	Nat.	SS	83	242	27	63	5	2	0	7	.260	121	220	12	.966
1960	Los Angeles	Nat.	SS	148	516	75	152	15	2	0	27	.295	260	431	*40	.945
1961	Los Angeles	Nat.	SS	148	*613	105	173	12	10	1	31	.282	253	428	29	.959
1962	Los Angeles	Nat.	SS	*165	*695	130	208	13	•10	6	48	.299	295	493	36	.956
1963	Los Angeles	Nat.	SS-3B	134	527	83	159	19	3	0	34	.302	197	381	26	.957
1964	Los Angeles	Nat.	SS-3B	158	630	81	173	15	5	2	34	.275	275	428	27	.963
1965	Los Angeles	Nat.	SS	158	650	92	186	14	7	0	33	.286	267	*535	25	.970
1966	Los Angeles(a)	Nat.	SS-3B	143	594	60	162	14	2	1	39	.273	231	460	23	.968
1967	Pittsburgh	Nat.	3B-SS	149	616	92	186	12	9	3	45	.302	102	346	24	.949
1968	Pittsburgh(b)	Nat.	3B-SS	153	627	76	174	12	6	0	31	.278	115	308	18	.959
1969	Mont.(c)-L.A.	Nat.	SS	151	623	80	171	10	8	4	47	.274	240	496	28	.963
1970	Los Angeles	Nat.	SS-3B	132	522	77	141	19	3	0	34	.270	171	397	24	.959
1971	Los Angeles	Nat.	SS-3B	149	601	73	169	14	3	3	44	.281	220	486	17	.976
1972	Los Angeles	Nat.	SS-3B	71	132	16	17	3	1	0	4	.129	39	103	2	.986
Major League Totals				1942	7588	1067	2134	177	71	20	458	.281	2786	5512	331	.962

aTraded to Pittsburgh Pirates for shortstop Gene Michael and third baseman-outfielder Bob Bailey, December 1, 1966.
bSelected by Montreal Expos from Pittsburgh Pirates in expansion draft, October 14, 1968.
cTraded with outfielder Manny Mota to Los Angeles Dodgers for outfielder-first baseman Ron Fairly and infielder Paul Popovich, June 11, 1969.

WORLD SERIES RECORD

Year	Club	League	Pos.	G.	AB.	R.	H.	2B.	3B.	HR.	RBI.	B.A.	PO.	A.	E.	F.A.
1959	Los Angeles	Nat.	SS	6	20	2	5	0	0	0	1	.250	10	21	1	.969
1963	Los Angeles	Nat.	SS	4	15	1	2	0	0	0	0	.133	5	10	1	.938
1965	Los Angeles	Nat.	SS	7	30	3	11	3	0	0	3	.367	14	26	0	1.000
1966	Los Angeles	Nat.	SS	4	13	0	1	0	0	0	0	.077	12	15	0	1.000
World Series Totals				21	78	6	19	3	0	0	4	.244	41	72	2	.983

DID YOU KNOW—

That Maury Wills and Lou Brock, who both stole over 100 bases in a season, operated under the toughest rules for stealers since 1899, when a rule change forced the pitcher to complete a throw to first? Even Ty Cobb had a break on his first 74 steals, being given credit for a steal even when tagged out following an overslide of the bag.

LEWIS ROBERT (HACK) WILSON

Born April 26, 1900, at Ellwood City, Pa.
Died November 23, 1948, at Baltimore, Md.
Height, 5.06. Weight, 195.
Threw and batted righthanded.

Set major league record for most runs batted in, season (191), 1930. Tied for following major league record: most home runs, inning (2), third inning, second game, July 1, 1925.
Hit three home runs in game, July 26, 1930, against Philadelphia.
Holds National League records: most home runs, season (56), 1930; most extra bases on long hits, season (215), 1930; most years 150 or more runs batted in, season (2), 1929-30.
Named to Hall of Fame, 1979.

Year	Club	League	Pos.	G.	AB.	R.	H.	2B.	3B.	HR.	RBI.	B.A.	PO.	A.	E.	F.A.
1921	Martinsburg	B. Ridge	C	30	101	17	36	8	0	5	....	.356	107	33	7	.952
1922	Martinsburg	B. Ridge	C	84	322	66	118	17	3	•30	....	.366	171	7	7	.962
1923	Portsmouth	Va.	OF	115	448	96	174	37	•15	•19	•101	•.388	304	15	12	.965
1923	New York	Nat.	OF	3	10	0	2	0	0	0	0	.200	6	0	1	.857
1924	New York	Nat.	OF	107	383	62	113	19	12	10	57	.295	230	8	8	.967
1925	New York	Nat.	OF	62	180	28	43	7	4	6	30	.239	75	3	2	.975
1925	Toledo(a)	A.A.	OF	55	210	42	72	15	6	4	36	.343	133	2	5	.964
1926	Chicago	Nat.	OF	142	529	97	170	36	8	•21	109	.321	348	11	10	.973
1927	Chicago	Nat.	OF	146	551	119	175	30	12	•30	129	.318	•400	13	14	.967
1928	Chicago	Nat.	OF	145	520	89	163	32	9	•31	120	.313	321	11	14	.960
1929	Chicago	Nat.	OF	150	574	135	198	30	5	39	•159	.345	380	14	12	.970
1930	Chicago	Nat.	OF	155	585	146	208	35	6	•56	•191	.356	357	9	•19	.951
1931	Chicago(b)(c)	Nat.	OF	112	395	66	103	22	4	13	61	.261	210	9	5	.978
1932	Brooklyn	Nat.	OF	135	481	77	143	37	5	23	123	.297	220	14	11	.955
1933	Brooklyn	Nat.	OF	117	360	41	96	13	2	9	54	.267	181	3	7	.963
1934	Brook.(d)-Phila.	Nat.	OF	74	192	24	47	5	0	6	30	.245	82	3	2	.977
1935	Albany	Int.	OF	59	175	30	46	9	1	3	29	.263	71	3	5	.937
Major League Totals				1348	4760	884	1461	266	67	244	1063	.307	2810	98	105	.965

aDrafted by Chicago Cubs, October, 1925.
bTraded to St. Louis Cardinals with pitcher Art Teachout for pitcher Burleigh Grimes, December, 1931.
cTraded to Brooklyn Dodgers for outfielder Robert Parhman and $45,000, January 23, 1932.
dUnconditionally released by Brooklyn Dodgers, August, 1934; subsequently signed with Philadelphia Phillies.

WORLD SERIES RECORD

Year	Club	League	Pos.	G.	AB.	R.	H.	2B.	3B.	HR.	RBI.	B.A.	PO.	A.	E.	F.A.
1924	New York	Nat.	OF	7	30	1	7	1	0	0	3	.233	8	1	0	1.000
1929	Chicago	Nat.	OF	5	17	2	8	0	1	0	0	.471	14	0	1	.933
World Series Totals				12	47	3	15	1	1	0	3	.319	22	1	1	.958

GEORGE WRIGHT

Born January 28, 1847, at New York, N.Y.
Died August 31, 1937, at Boston, Mass.
Height, 5.09½. Weight, 150.
Threw and batted righthanded.
Brother of Harry Wright, who managed Cincinnati Red Stockings, Boston, Providence and Philadelphia National League clubs and was chief of umpires, National League, 1894-95.

Chosen shortstop of first All-Star team in 1868 by Henry Chadwick of the New York Clipper and awarded the Clipper Gold Medal. Manager, Providence N. L., 1879.
He introduced tennis, ice hockey and golf to the United States sporting public.
Named to Hall of Fame in 1937 for service to baseball apart from playing the game.

Year	Club	League	Pos.	G.	AB.	R.	H.	2B.	3B.	HR.	SB.	B.A.	PO.	A.	E.	F.A.
1864	N.Y. Gothams	Ind.	SS	8	....	19	....	....	....	....	....	....	....	....	....	....
1865	Phila. Olympics	Ind.	SS	....	....	....	....	....	....	....	....	....	....	....	....	....
1866	N.Y. Gothams	Ind.	SS	5	....	21	....	....	....	....	....	....	....	....	....	....
1866	Morrisania Un.	Ind.	SS	9	....	11	....	....	....	....	....	....	....	....	....	....
1867	Wash. Nationals	Ind.	SS	29	....	182	....	....	....	....	....	....	....	....	....	....
1868	Morrisania Un.	Ind.	SS	43	....	195	....	....	....	....	....	....	....	....	....	....

Year	Club	League	Pos.	G.	AB.	R.	H.	2B.	3B.	HR.	SB.	B.A.	PO.	A.	E.	F.A.
1869–Cin. Red St'ngs		Ind.	SS	57	483	339	304	....	....	....	49	.629	....	....	....	......
1870–Cin. Red St'ngs		Ind.	SS	58	....	....	248	....	....	....	....	......	....	....	....	......
1871–Boston		N. Assn.	SS	16	88	35	36	....	....	....	....	.409	....	....	....	......
1872–Boston		N. Assn.	SS	47	253	84	85	....	....	....	....	.336	95	201	16	.949
1873–Boston		N. Assn.	SS	59	333	96	126	....	....	....	....	.378	90	242	53	.862
1874–Boston		N. Assn.	SS	60	319	75	110	....	....	....	....	.345	94	198	22	.930
1875–Boston		N. Assn.	SS	79	407	105	137	....	....	....	....	.337	90	253	46	.882
1876–Boston		Nat.	SS	70	343	72	100	18	6	0	....	.292	96	253	44	.889
1877–Boston		Nat.	SS-2B	49	235	44	60	14	1	0	....	.255	135	164	36	.893
1878–Boston		Nat.	SS	59	267	35	60	6	1	0	....	.225	72	197	15	.947
1879–Providence		Nat.	SS	84	385	79	108	12	10	1	....	.281	96	315	33	.926
1880–Boston		Nat.	SS	7	29	4	5	0	0	0	....	.172	8	18	3	.897
1881–Boston		Nat.	SS	1	4	2	1	0	0	0	....	.250	0	3	0	1.000
1882–Providence		Nat.	SS	45	185	14	30	2	2	0	....	.162	46	133	26	.873
National League Totals				315	1448	250	364	52	20	1	....	.251	453	1083	157	.907

WILLIAM HENRY (HARRY) WRIGHT

Born January 10, 1835, at Sheffield, England.
Died October 3, 1895, at Atlantic City, N.J.
Brother of George Wright, shortstop, manager and umpire in majors.

    The greatest manager in the early history of professional baseball without a doubt was Harry Wright. He was the first to place an all-pro team on the field and helped pave the way for organized league play. For these accomplishments he was named "Father of Professional Baseball" by Henry Chadwick.
    Wright came to this country with his family when he was only one year old. His father was a professional cricket player. In 1858 Harry joined the Knickerbocker baseball team of New York. However, cricket remained his profession, and his ability in that sport took him to Cincinnati in 1866 as the pro at a club there. In July of that year, Wright helped organize the historic Cincinnati Red Stockings baseball team and was elected captain. He gave up cricket in 1868 when he was named manager of the Red Stockings at a salary of $1,200.
    The following season he brought his brother George from the Unions of Morrisania, N. Y., to play shortstop and made the Red Stockings the first all-professional club. The '69 team went through the season undefeated, winning 56 games. The Red Stockings ran their unbeaten streak to 130 games before finally losing on June 14, 1870, to the Atlantics of Brooklyn.
    In 1871 Harry left Cincinnati to become manager of Boston in the newly-formed National Association, the first professional league. He led the team to pennants in 1872-73-74-75. When the National League was organized in 1876, he was named manager of the Boston entry and won championships in 1877-78. Wright shifted to the helm of the Providence N. L. team in 1882-83 and then in 1884 went to Philadelphia, where he managed through 1893. In 23 years as a pilot in league play, his teams finished out of the first division only three times. Following his retirement from active competition in 1893, the N. L. created the honorary post of umpire-in-chief for him.
    Among other "firsts" credited to Wright were: First manager to use knickerbocker uniforms and long hose to replace the old-fashioned pantaloons, first manager to win four pennants in a row and first to make a foreign tour with his players (Red Stockings-Athletics trip to England in 1874).
    Harry Wright was named to the Hall of Fame as a manager in September, 1953, by the Committee on Veterans.

EARLY (GUS) WYNN, JR.

Born January 6, 1920, at Hartford, Ala.
Height, 6.00. Weight, 235.
Threw right and batted right and lefthanded.
Married Lorraine Follin, September 12, 1944.

    Holds major league record for most years pitched in major leagues (23).
    Became fourteenth pitcher in major league history to win 300 or more games, lifetime, by defeating Kansas City Athletics, 7-4, July 13, 1963.
    Major league record holder for most bases on balls allowed, league, lifetime (1,775).
    Voted Cy Young Memorial Award as majors' outstanding pitcher of year, 1959.
    Named Outstanding American League Pitcher by THE SPORTING NEWS, 1959.

Coach, Cleveland Indians, 1964-65-66; coach Minnesota Twins, 1967 through 1969; scout and organization manager, Minnesota (managed Evansville, American Association, 1970; Wisconsin Rapids, Midwest League, 1971, and Orlando, Florida State, 1972).

Year	Club	League	G.	IP.	W.	L.	Pct.	H.	R.	ER.	SO.	BB.	ERA.
1937	Sanford	Florida State	35	235	16	11	.593	224	113	89	106	81	3.41
1938	Charlotte	Piedmont	29	179	10	11	.476	195	124	105	94	73	5.28
1939	Charlotte	Piedmont	34	243	15	14	.517	254	132	107	150	98	3.96
1939	Washington	American	3	20	0	2	.000	26	15	13	1	10	5.85
1940	Charlotte	Piedmont	31	144	9	7	.563	154	103	68	76	57	4.25
1941	Springfield	Eastern	34	257	16	12	.571	*239	89	73	126	84	2.56
1941	Washington	American	5	40	3	1	.750	35	14	7	15	10	1.58
1942	Washington	American	30	190	10	16	.385	246	129	108	58	73	5.12
1943	Washington	American	37	257	18	12	.600	232	97	83	89	83	2.91
1944	Washington	American	33	208	8	*17	.320	221	97	78	65	67	3.38
1945	Washington	American					(In Military Service)						
1946	Washington	American	17	107	8	5	.615	112	45	37	36	33	3.11
1947	Washington	American	33	247	17	15	.531	251	114	100	73	90	3.64
1948	Washington (a)	American	33	198	8	19	.296	236	*144	*128	49	94	5.82
1949	Cleveland	American	26	165	11	7	.611	186	84	76	62	57	4.15
1950	Cleveland	American	32	214	18	8	.692	166	88	76	143	101	*3.20
1951	Cleveland	American	37	*274	20	13	.606	227	102	92	133	107	3.02
1952	Cleveland	American	42	286	23	12	.657	239	103	92	153	*132	2.90
1953	Cleveland	American	36	252	17	12	.586	234	121	110	138	107	3.93
1954	Cleveland	American	40	*271	•23	11	.676	225	93	82	155	83	2.72
1955	Cleveland	American	32	230	17	11	.607	207	86	72	122	80	2.82
1956	Cleveland	American	38	278	20	9	.690	233	93	84	158	91	2.72
1957	Cleveland (b)	American	40	263	14	17	.452	*270	139	•126	*184	104	4.31
1958	Chicago	American	40	240	14	16	.467	214	115	110	*179	104	4.13
1959	Chicago	American	37	*256	*22	10	.688	202	106	90	179	*119	3.16
1960	Chicago	American	36	237	13	12	.520	220	105	92	158	112	3.49
1961	Chicago	American	17	110	8	2	.800	88	43	43	64	47	3.52
1962	Chicago (c)	American	27	168	7	15	.318	171	90	83	91	56	4.45
1963	Cleveland	American	20	55	1	2	.333	50	14	14	29	15	2.29
	Major League Totals		691	4566	300	244	.551	4291	2037	1796	2334	1775	3.54

aTraded to Cleveland Indians with first baseman Mickey Vernon for pitchers Joe Haynes and Ed Klieman and first baseman Eddie Robinson, December 14, 1948.

bTraded to Chicago White Sox with infielder-outfielder Al Smith for infielder Fred Hatfield and outfielder Minnie Minoso, December 4, 1957.

cReleased by Chicago White Sox, November 20, 1962; signed with Cleveland Indians, June 21, 1963.

WORLD SERIES RECORD

Year	Club	League	G.	IP.	W.	L.	Pct.	H.	R.	ER.	SO.	BB.	ERA.
1954	Cleveland	American	1	7	0	1	.000	4	3	3	5	2	3.86
1959	Chicago	American	3	13	1	1	.500	19	9	8	10	4	5.54
	World Series Totals		4	20	1	2	.333	23	12	11	15	6	4.95

JAMES SHERMAN WYNN

Born March 12, 1942, at Cincinnati, O.
Height, 5.09. Weight, 170.
Threw and batted righthanded.

Tied following National League records: most bases on balls in season, 148 in 1969; most bases on balls, intentional, game (3), July 11, 1970.
Hit three home runs in game, June 15, 1967, and May 11, 1974.
Major league stolen bases: 1963 (4), 1964 (5), 1965 (43), 1966 (13), 1967 (16), 1968 (11), 1969 (23), 1970 (24), 1971 (10), 1972 (17), 1973 (14), 1974 (18), 1975 (7), 1976 (15). Total—221.
Led National League outfielders in double plays with 8 in 1968 and tied for lead with 5 in 1971.
Named as outfielder on THE SPORTING NEWS National League All-Star Team, 1967 and 1974.
Named National League Comeback Player of Year by THE SPORTING NEWS, 1974.

Year	Club	League	Pos.	G.	AB.	R.	H.	2B.	3B.	HR.	RBI.	B.A.	PO.	A.	E.	F.A.
1962	Tampa (a)	Fla. St.	*3-O-2	120	400	93	116	10	5	*14	*81	.290	*181	194	29	*.928
1963	San Antonio	Texas	SS-3B	79	302	57	87	15	11	16	49	*.288	139	185	28	.920
1963	Houston	Nat.	O-S-3B	70	250	31	61	10	5	4	27	.244	124	33	8	.952
1964	Houston	Nat.	OF	67	219	19	49	7	0	5	18	.224	129	8	6	.958
1964	Oklahoma City	P. C.	OF-3B	82	282	51	77	9	5	10	40	.273	160	24	3	.984
1965	Houston	Nat.	OF	157	564	90	155	30	7	22	73	.275	*382	13	9	.978
1966	Houston	Nat.	OF	105	418	62	107	21	1	18	62	.256	259	6	6	.978
1967	Houston	Nat.	OF	158	594	102	148	29	3	37	107	.249	*364	4	12	.968

Year	Club	League	Pos.	G.	AB.	R.	H.	2B.	3B.	HR.	RBI.	B.A.	PO.	A.	E.	F.A.
1968	Houston	Nat.	OF	156	542	85	146	23	5	26	67	.269	298	•20	4	.988
1969	Houston	Nat.	OF	149	495	113	133	17	1	33	87	.269	318	9	5	.985
1970	Houston	Nat.	OF	157	554	82	156	32	2	27	88	.282	293	14	4	.987
1971	Houston	Nat.	OF	123	404	38	82	16	0	7	45	.203	232	9	3	.988
1972	Houston	Nat.	OF	145	542	117	148	29	3	24	90	.273	284	8	5	.983
1973	Houston (b)	Nat.	OF	139	481	90	106	14	5	20	55	.220	270	9	4	.986
1974	Los Angeles	Nat.	OF	150	535	104	145	17	4	32	108	.271	365	10	3	.992
1975	Los Angeles (c)	Nat.	OF	130	412	80	102	16	0	18	58	.248	282	6	5	.983
1976	Atlanta (d)	Nat.	OF	148	449	75	93	19	1	17	66	.207	287	17	9	.971
1977	N.Y.-Milw.(e)	Amer.	DH-OF	66	194	17	34	5	2	1	13	.175	50	1	1	.981
	National League Totals			1854	6459	1088	1631	280	37	290	951	.252	3887	166	83	.980
	American League Totals			66	194	17	34	5	2	1	13	.175	50	1	1	.981
	Major League Totals			1920	6653	1105	1665	285	39	291	964	.250	3937	167	84	.980

aDrafted by Houston Colts from San Diego (Cincinnati Reds' system), November 26, 1962.
bTraded to Los Angeles Dodgers for pitchers Claude Osteen and Dave Culpepper, December 6, 1973.
cTraded with second baseman Lee Lacy, first baseman-outfielder Tom Paciorek and infielder Jerry Royster to Atlanta Braves for outfielder Dusty Baker and first baseman-third baseman Ed Goodson, November 19, 1975.
dSold to New York Yankees, November 29, 1976.
eSigned by Milwaukee Brewers as free agent, July 26, 1977.

WORLD SERIES RECORD

Year	Club	League	Pos.	G.	AB.	R.	H.	2B.	3B.	HR.	RBI.	B.A.	PO.	A.	E.	F.A.
1974	Los Angeles	Nat.	OF	5	16	1	3	1	0	1	2	.188	5	0	0	1.000

THOMAS AUSTIN YAWKEY

Born February 21, 1903, at Detroit, Mich.

Died July 9, 1976, at Boston, Mass.

Owner, Boston Red Sox, American League, 1933, to date of death.

Thomas Austin Yawkey never demanded the best, but he insisted that everyone give his best. Yawkey set a record for honesty, perseverance, pride, justice and sportsmanship that few ever have equaled. And he rewarded handsomely those players who pleased him when it was not fashionable to reward so generously. He was a frustrated athlete, a frustrated owner and a frustrated AL stalwart.

As an athlete, he tried to do something that seemed so easy for punch-and-judy hitters—put one over the left field fence at Fenway Park—but try as he may, he never put one "into the net." Morning after morning, generally before an audience of scouts and coaches, with his own batting practice pitcher, and decked in baseball shoes, sox and pants and a sweatshirt, he swung mightily. But his best shots fell short of the tall green monster that towered high in left field at the 315-foot mark.

As an owner, only twice did his club, his beloved Red Sox, win the AL flag and proceed into the World Series—and twice were defeated. He saw the Yankees nose out the Sox so often the Red Hose became known as bridesmaids. He had All-Stars at every position at varied times, but they never won the Big One. Fans filled his small, one-deck stands by the millions each year and the Fenway Millionaires had class oosing out of their spikes, but Series winners they weren't.

As one of the American League's pillars of sense, Yawkey spoke clear English in league councils and was a good quote man to the baseball writers. He took all player-owner developments in stride, seeing the good and bad points in each side. When the player pension matter come up the first time, some Red Sox short-sighters bucked at putting up any of their money. Yawkey, knowing full well the value it was to the players, offered to pay the fees of any recalcitrant players, to ensure the success of the pension plan.

When the free-agent bubble burst upon ownership, Yawkey saw no real problem in spite of the voices of doom that foretold the end of the game.

Yawkey's summup of the 1972 player strike was typical. "Some good things come out of every lesson. I hope both sides have learned that whatever the differences were, they can be ironed out. But the players didn't break any laws, remember. They had the courage of their convictions and they are entitled to strike."

That from a multimillionaire of long standing, one brought up in the "old" game of the Ty Cobb era in Detroit. When his father died, Tom Austin, his family name, went to live in the home of his uncle, William Yawkey, his mother's brother. Fabulous diversified wealth in each family combined when Tom was legally adopted and he took the name of Yawkey. Tom is said to have been a millionaire many times over at 16.

His uncle bought a large share of the Detroit club and many a time Cobb shared a meal in their home. In fact, Tom credits Ty for sparking his desire to own a club himself.

Yawkey announced purchase of the Red Sox in February of 1933. Wanting only the best for the club and the team's fans, he tore down old rickety Fenway Park and built the present one, a beautiful park for baseball. He signed the brainy Eddie Collins to direct the club and thereby joined a youthful school hero—he and Collins had attended Irving School of Tarrytown, N. Y. and the famous second baseman was one of the alums most talked about. Collins later introduced Yawkey to Connie Mack, and the A's owner, hearing of Yawkey's wish to buy a big league club, suggested he buy the Red Sox. That's how Boston became the winner—a great club, a great park and a great owner.

The greatest frustration Yawkey felt as a league member was seeing the American League slip behind the

National in prestige. He was a proud AL representative when the league was on top, through the great Yankee eras, and it grieved him to see the black stars of the National swing the balance of power their way. The National got the pick of the pack early in the race for black talent, and Yawkey gave a green light and an open pocketbook to try to close the ground. But he had no more luck than the rest of the American League. The National League had cornered the talent-laden early market.

Yawkey admitted he had pampered his players, paying high for performance and more when class went along with it. He saw his first skipper, Joe Cronin, go from manager to general manager of the club and then to the presidency of the AL; most of his managers had been members of the Bosox at one time or another and all former Boston players held a deep spot in his heart.

His solid council to the league and baseball in a larger sense was appreciated by his fellow owners, even though his candor embarrassed them more than once. He typified the best in the term sportsman—cherish the race, take the wins with the losses, do whatever you can to help and pay whatever price you feel must be paid to ensure a dignified, just and honest result. Second place too often was the result, but the sting never dulled his quest. He lived a winner and would settle for no less, no matter how long it took.

Baseball was much enriched by his presence.

Yawkey was named to the Hall of Fame in 1980.

PRESTON RUDOLPH (RUDY) YORK

Born August 17, 1913, at Ragland, Ala.
Died February 5, 1970, at Rome, Ga.
Height, 6.00½. Weight, 230.
Threw and batted righthanded.
Married Violet Dupree, June 30, 1930.

Holds major league record for most home runs hit in one month (18), August, 1937; also tied for major league mark for most home runs hit with bases filled, one month (3), May 16, 22, 30, first game, 1938; tied major league mark for most home runs with bases filled, game (2), July 27, 1946; hit three home runs in a game, September 1, 1941, first game.

Tied major league record for first basemen by not having a putout in a game, June 18, 1943; tied major league mark for most assists, by first baseman in a doubleheader (8), September 27, 1947; tied for American League mark for first basemen for most chances accepted in an extra-inning game (34), July 21, 1945, 24-inning game.

Led A. L. first basemen in double plays, 1946.

Named as first baseman on THE SPORTING NEWS All-Star Major League Team, 1943.

Holds World Series record for most assists by a first baseman in seven-game Series (8), 1945.

Manager, North Platte, Nebraska State League, 1957; coach, Memphis, Southern Association, 1958; coach, Boston Red Sox, 1959 through 1962.

Year — Club	League	Pos.	G.	AB.	R.	H.	2B.	3B.	HR.	RBI.	B.A.	PO.	A.	E.	F.A.
1933 — Knoxville	South.	OF	3	10	0	1	0	0	0	0	.100	5	0	0	1.000
1933 — Shreveport	Dixie	2B	12	48	3	17	3	1	1	7	.354	28	25	3	.946
1933 — Beaumont	Texas	O-C-P	15	37	2	7	2	1	0	1	.189	16	7	1	.958
1934 — Beau.-Ft.Worth	Texas	OF-C	100	316	69	105	21	6	26	75	.332	152	31	11	.943
1934 — Detroit	Amer.	C	3	6	0	1	0	0	0	0	.167	4	2	0	1.000
1935 — Beaumont	Texas	1B-C	148	521	101	157	29	8	*32	*117	.301	1150	80	25	.980
1936 — Milwaukee	A.A.	1B	157	619	119	207	25	21	37	148	.334	*1470	60	12	.992
1937 — Detroit	Amer.	C-3-1B	104	375	72	115	18	3	35	103	.307	246	95	18	.950
1938 — Detroit	Amer.	*C-O-1	135	463	85	138	27	2	33	127	.298	431	71	10	*.980
1939 — Detroit	Amer.	C-1B	102	329	66	101	16	1	20	68	.307	434	39	5	.990
1940 — Detroit	Amer.	1B	•155	588	105	186	46	6	33	134	.316	1390	107	15	.990
1941 — Detroit	Amer.	1B	155	590	91	153	29	3	27	111	.259	1393	110	*21	.986
1942 — Detroit	Amer.	1B	153	577	81	150	26	4	21	90	.260	1413	*146	19	.988
1943 — Detroit	Amer.	1B	•155	571	90	155	22	11	*34	*118	.271	1349	*149	15	.990
1944 — Detroit	Amer.	1B	151	583	77	161	27	7	18	98	.276	1453	107	•17	.989
1945 — Detroit (a)	Amer.	1B	*155	595	71	167	25	5	18	87	.264	*1464	113	*19	.988
1946 — Boston	Amer.	1B	154	579	78	160	30	6	17	119	.276	*1327	*116	8	.994
1947 — Bos.(b)-Chi.(c)	Amer.	1B	150	584	56	136	25	4	21	91	.233	1327	107	7	*.995
1948 — Philadelphia	Amer.	1B	31	51	4	8	0	0	0	6	.157	77	5	1	.988
1949 — Griffin	Ga.-Ala.	1B	33	80	13	15	2	0	1	9	.188	163	20	5	.973
1949 — Union City	Kitty	1B-C	27	76	15	18	5	0	4	14	.237	142	7	1	.993
1950 —							(Out of Organized Ball)								
1951 — Youngstown-Oil City-New Castle	Mid. Atl.	C-P	114	375	84	109	28	1	*34	107	.291	707	71	17	.979
Major League Totals			1603	5891	876	1621	291	52	277	1152	.275	12308	1167	155	.989

aTraded to Boston Red Sox for shortstop Eddie Lake, January 3, 1946.
bTraded to Chicago White Sox for first baseman Murrell (Jake) Jones, June 14, 1947.
cUnconditionally released by Chicago White Sox, February 2, 1948, and subsequently signed with Philadelphia Athletics.

WORLD SERIES RECORD

Year — Club	League	Pos.	G.	AB.	R.	H.	2B.	3B.	HR.	RBI.	B.A.	PO.	A.	E.	F.A.
1940 — Detroit	Amer.	1B	7	26	3	6	0	1	1	2	.231	59	2	0	1.000
1945 — Detroit	Amer.	1B	7	28	1	5	1	0	0	3	.179	67	8	1	.987
1946 — Boston	Amer.	1B	7	23	6	6	1	1	2	5	.261	59	4	1	.984
World Series Totals			21	77	10	17	2	2	3	10	.221	185	14	2	.990

EDWARD FRED JOSEPH YOST

Born October 13, 1926, at Brooklyn, N.Y.
Height, 5.10. Weight, 182.
Threw and batted righthanded.
Married Patricia Van Lyne Healy, January 25, 1961.

Held American League mark for most putouts by third baseman, lifetime, (2,356), since passed by Brooks Robinson with 2,697.
Tied A. L. mark by playing 157 games at third base, 1952–154-game season; holds major league record for most years leading third basemen in putouts (8), 1948, 1950, 1951, 1952, 1953, 1954 (tied), 1956, 1959.
Led league in bases on balls (141) 1950, (129) 1952, (123) 1953, (151) 1956, (135) 1959 and (125) 1960.
Coach, Washington Senators, 1963 through 1967; New York Mets, 1968 through 1976; coach, Boston Red Sox, 1977 to date.

Year	Club	League	Pos.	G.	AB.	R.	H.	2B.	3B.	HR.	RBI.	B.A.	PO.	A.	E.	F.A.
1944	Washington	Amer.	3B-SS	7	14	3	2	0	0	0	0	.143	9	6	2	.882
1945-46	Washington	Amer.					(In Military Service)									
1946	Washington	Amer.	3B	8	25	2	2	1	0	0	1	.080	7	17	0	1.000
1947	Washington	Amer.	3B	115	428	52	102	17	3	0	14	.238	125	198	14	.958
1948	Washington	Amer.	3B	145	555	74	138	32	11	2	50	.249	*189	240	15	.966
1949	Washington	Amer.	3B	124	435	57	110	19	7	9	45	.253	158	232	19	.954
1950	Washington	Amer.	3B	155	573	114	169	26	2	11	58	.295	*205	307	*30	.945
1951	Washington	Amer.	*3B-OF	•154	568	109	161	•36	4	12	65	.283	*209	234	21	.955
1952	Washington	Amer.	3B	*157	587	92	137	32	3	12	49	.233	*212	249	18	.962
1953	Washington	Amer.	3B	152	577	107	157	30	7	9	45	.272	*190	300	18	.965
1954	Washington	Amer.	3B	•155	539	101	138	26	4	11	47	.256	•170	*347	17	.968
1955	Washington	Amer.	3B	122	375	64	91	17	5	7	48	.243	100	217	19	.943
1956	Washington	Amer.	*3B-OF	152	515	94	119	17	2	11	53	.231	*182	*303	18	.964
1957	Washington	Amer.	3B	110	414	48	104	13	5	9	38	.251	109	207	16	.952
1958	Washington(a)	Amer.	INF-OF	134	406	55	91	16	0	8	37	.224	122	187	11	*.966
1959	Detroit	Amer.	3B-2B	148	521	*115	145	19	0	21	61	.278	*168	260	17	*.962
1960	Detroit(b)	Amer.	3B	143	497	78	129	23	2	14	47	.260	155	208	•26	.933
1961	Los Angeles	Amer.	3B	76	213	29	43	4	0	3	15	.202	57	103	6	.964
1962	Los Angeles	Amer.	3B-1B	52	104	22	25	9	1	0	10	.240	69	48	4	.967
Major League Totals				2109	7346	1215	1863	337	56	139	683	.254	2436	3663	271	.957

aTraded to Detroit Tigers with shortstop Rocky Bridges and outfielder Neil Chrisley for third baseman Reno Bertoia, shortstop Ron Samford and outfielder Jim Delsing, December 6, 1958.
bSelected by Los Angeles Angels in American League expansion draft, December 14, 1960.

DENTON TRUE (CY) YOUNG

Born March 29, 1867, at Gilmore, O.
Died November 4, 1955, at Peoli, O.
Height, 6.02. Weight, 210.
Threw and batted righthanded.

Holds major league records for most victories, 511; most consecutive hitless innings, 24 (1904). Pitched 906 games, topped by Hoyt Wilhelm, relief pitcher, with 1,070.
Pitched three no-hit games: May 5, 1904 (perfect game) vs. Philadelphia, winning 3-0 (first game); September 18, 1897, vs. Cincinnati, 6-0; June 30, 1908, vs. New York, 8-0. Hit two homers in one game, April 20, 1899.
Named to Hall of Fame, 1937.

Year	Club	League	G.	IP.	W.	L.	Pct.	H.	R.	SO.	BB.	CG.	ShO.
1890	Canton	Tri-State	31	260	15	15	.500	253	165	201	33	....	0
1890	Cleveland	National	17	150	9	7	.563	145	83	36	32	16	0
1891	Cleveland	National	54	430	27	20	.574	436	239	146	132	44	0
1892	Cleveland	National	53	455	36	11	*.766	362	159	167	114	48	*9
1893	Cleveland	National	53	426	32	16	.667	441	229	102	104	42	1
1894	Cleveland	National	52	409	25	22	.532	493	266	101	101	44	2
1895	Cleveland	National	47	373	*35	10	.778	371	176	120	77	36	•4
1896	Cleveland	National	51	414	29	16	.644	467	212	*137	64	42	•5
1897	Cleveland	National	•47	338	21	18	.538	389	195	87	50	36	2
1898	Cleveland (a)	National	46	378	25	14	.641	394	174	107	40	40	1

Year	Club	League	G	IP	W	L	Pct.	H	R	SO	BB	CG	ShO
1899	St. Louis	National	44	369	26	15	.634	364	170	112	43	40	4
1900	St. Louis	National	41	321	20	18	.526	337	146	119	38	32	●4
1901	Boston	American	43	371	★33	10	.767	320	113	★159	38	38	●5
1902	Boston	American	★45	★386	★32	10	.762	337	137	166	51	41	3
1903	Boston	American	40	★342	★28	10	.737	292	116	183	37	34	★7
1904	Boston	American	43	380	26	16	.619	326	104	203	28	40	★10
1905	Boston	American	38	321	18	19	.486	245	98	208	30	31	5
1906	Boston	American	39	288	13	●21	.382	289	135	146	27	28	0
1907	Boston	American	43	343	22	15	.595	287	101	148	52	33	6
1908	Boston (b)	American	36	299	21	11	.656	230	68	150	37	30	3
1909	Cleveland	American	35	295	19	15	.559	267	110	109	59	30	3
1910	Cleveland	American	21	163	7	10	.412	149	62	58	27	14	1
1911	Cleveland (c)	American	7	46	3	4	.429	54	28	20	13	4	0
1911	Boston	National	11	80	4	5	.444	83	47	35	15	8	2
American League Totals			390	3234	222	141	.612	2796	1072	1550	399	323	43
National League Totals			516	4143	289	172	.627	4282	2096	1269	810	428	34
Major League Totals			906	7377	511	313	.620	7078	3168	2819	1209	751	77

aTransferred with pick of team to St. Louis by Frank Robison, owner of both clubs.
bSold to Cleveland for $12,500.
cReleased, August, 1911, and signed with Boston N. L.

TEMPLE CUP RECORD

Year	Club	League	G	IP	W	L	Pct.	ShO	H	R	SO	BB
1895	Cleveland	National	3	27	3	0	1.000	0	27	7	2	4
1896	Cleveland	National	1	9	0	1	.000	0	13	7	0	1
Temple Cup Totals			4	36	3	1	.750	0	40	14	2	5

WORLD SERIES RECORD

Year	Club	League	G	IP	W	L	Pct.	ShO	H	R	SO	BB
1903	Boston	American	4	34	2	1	.667	0	31	13	17	4

ROSS MIDDLEBROOK (PEP) YOUNGS

Born April 10, 1897, at Sweet Home, Tex.
Died October 22, 1927, at San Antonio, Tex.
Threw righthanded and batted left and righthanded.

In World Series performance, was first player to make two hits in an inning, one double and one triple, seventh inning, October 7, 1921.

Year	Club	League	Pos.	G	AB	R	H	2B	3B	HR	RBI	B.A.	PO	A	E	F.A.
1914	Austin	Tex.	OF	10	31		3	1	0	0		.097				
1915	Brenham	Mid. Tex.					No averages compiled. League disbanded June 19.									
1915	Waxahachie	Cent. Tex.					League disbanded in July. No averages compiled.									
1916	Sherman	W. A.	2-3-S-O	137	★539	★103	★195	30	6	4		★.362	310	299	71	.896
1917	Rochester	Int.	2-3-OF	140	506	85	180	18	5	1		.356	280	225	56	.900
1917	New York	Nat.	OF	7	26	5	9	2	3	0	1	.346	16	2	0	1.000
1918	New York	Nat.	OF-2B	121	474	70	143	16	8	1	29	.302	192	16	11	.950
1919	New York	Nat.	OF	130	489	73	152	★31	7	2	43	.311	235	★23	16	.942
1920	New York	Nat.	OF	153	581	92	204	27	14	6	78	.351	288	●26	★22	.935
1921	New York	Nat.	OF	141	504	90	165	24	16	3	102	.327	247	16	6	.978
1922	New York	Nat.	OF	149	559	105	185	34	10	7	86	.331	280	★28	★19	.942
1923	New York	Nat.	OF	152	596	★121	200	33	12	3	87	.336	282	22	13	.959
1924	New York	Nat.	OF-2B	133	526	112	187	33	12	10	74	.356	236	17	12	.955
1925	New York	Nat.	OF-2B	130	500	82	132	24	6	6	53	.264	214	24	12	.952
1926	New York	Nat.	OF	95	372	62	114	12	5	4	43	.306	170	18	5	.974
Major League Totals				1211	4627	812	1491	236	93	42	596	.322	2160	192	116	.953

WORLD SERIES RECORD

Year	Club	League	Pos.	G	AB	R	H	2B	3B	HR	RBI	B.A.	PO	A	E	F.A.
1921	New York	Nat.	OF	8	25	3	7	1	1	0	4	.280	7	1	0	1.000
1922	New York	Nat.	OF	5	16	2	6	0	0	0	2	.375	9	2	2	.846
1923	New York	Nat.	OF	6	23	2	8	0	0	1	3	.348	5	1	2	.750
1924	New York	Nat.	OF	7	27	3	5	1	0	0	2	.185	8	1	0	1.000
World Series Totals				26	91	10	26	2	1	1	11	.286	29	5	4	.895

JONATHAN THOMPSON (TOM) ZACHARY

Born May 7, 1897, at Graham, N. C.
Died January 24, 1969, at Graham, N. C.
Height, 6.01. Weight, 185.
Threw and batted lefthanded.

Played under name of Zach Walton in 1918 with Philadelphia.

Year Club	League	G.	IP.	W.	L.	Pct.	H.	R.	ER.	SO.	BB.	ERA.
1918–Philadelphia	American	2	8	2	0	1.000	9	5	5	1	7	5.63
1919–Washington	American	17	62	1	5	.167	68	29	20	9	20	2.90
1920–Washington	American	44	263	15	16	.484	289	141	110	53	78	3.76
1921–Washington	American	39	250	18	16	.529	314	130	110	53	59	3.96
1922–Washington	American	32	185	15	10	.600	190	74	64	37	43	3.11
1923–Washington	American	35	204	10	16	.385	270	117	102	40	63	4.50
1924–Washington	American	33	203	15	9	.625	198	74	62	45	53	2.75
1925–Washington(a)	American	38	218	12	15	.444	247	112	93	58	74	3.84
1926–St. Louis	American	34	247	14	15	.483	264	127	99	53	97	3.61
1927–St.L.(b)–Washington	American	28	189	8	13	.381	226	102	83	26	57	3.95
1928–Wash.(c)–New York	American	27	148	9	12	.429	184	98	82	26	55	4.99
1929–New York	American	26	120	12	0	1.000	131	43	33	35	30	2.48
1930–New York(d)	American	3	17	1	1	.500	18	16	12	1	9	6.35
1930–Boston	National	24	151	11	5	.688	192	90	77	57	50	4.59
1931–Boston	National	33	229	11	15	.423	243	87	79	64	53	3.10
1932–Boston	National	32	212	12	11	.522	231	83	73	67	55	3.10
1933–Boston	National	26	125	7	9	.438	134	64	49	22	35	3.53
1934–Bos.(e)–Brooklyn	National	27	126	6	8	.429	144	62	59	32	29	4.21
1935–Brooklyn	National	25	158	7	12	.368	193	76	63	33	35	3.59
1936–Brook.(f)–Philadelphia	National	8	21	0	3	.000	30	22	20	8	13	8.57
American League Totals		358	2114	132	128	.508	2408	1068	875	437	645	3.73
National League Totals		175	1022	54	63	.462	1172	484	420	283	270	3.70
Major League Totals		533	3136	186	191	.493	3580	1552	1295	720	915	3.72

aTraded with pitcher Win Ballou to St. Louis Browns for pitcher Joe Bush and outfielder Johnny Tobin, February, 1926.
bReleased to Washington Senators on waivers, Browns obtaining pitcher Alvin Crowder same way, July 7, 1927.
cReleased to New York Yankees for waiver price, August 23, 1928.
dSent to Boston Braves on waivers, May 12, 1930.
eReleased by Boston Braves, May 28, 1934, and signed with Brooklyn Dodgers, June 7.
fReleased by Brooklyn Dodgers, April 17, 1936, and signed with Philadelphia Phillies same month.

WORLD SERIES RECORD

Year Club	League	G.	IP.	W.	L.	Pct.	H.	R.	ER.	SO.	BB.	ERA.
1924–Washington	American	2	17⅔	2	0	1.000	13	4	4	3	3	2.04
1925–Washington	American	1	1⅔	0	0	.000	3	2	2	0	1	10.80
1928–New York	American	1	9	1	0	1.000	9	3	3	7	1	3.00
World Series Totals		4	28⅓	3	0	1.000	25	9	9	10	5	2.86

GUS EDWARD ZERNIAL

Born June 27, 1923, at Beaumont, Tex.
Height, 6.02½. Weight, 205.
Threw and batted righthanded.
Married Gladys Hale, April 30, 1946.

Tied major league record for most home runs in three consecutive games (6), held by Tony Lazzeri (New York Yankees, 1936), and Ralph Kiner (Pittsburgh Pirates, 1947) and since tied by Frank Thomas, Lee May and Mike Schmidt, hitting two each game–starting with second game, May 13 and May 15-16, 1951; tied American League record for most home runs in four consecutive games (7), held by Tony Lazzeri (New York Yankees, 1936), and tied by Frank Howard (Washington Senators, 1968), by hitting (2) May 13, second game, (2), 15, (2), 16, (1), 17, 1951; hit three home runs in a game, second game, October 1, 1950.

Year Club	League	Pos.	G.	AB.	R.	H.	2B.	3B.	HR.	RBI.	B.A.	PO.	A.	E.	F.A.
1942–Waycross	Ga.-Fla.	OF	95	367	54	105	25	4	3	49	.286	162	5	8	.954
1943-44-45–Atlanta	South.							(In Military Service)							
1946–Burlington(a)	Carol.	OF	137	501	114	167	29	3	*41	111	.333	215	10	10	.957
1947–Baltimore	Int.	OF	3	4	0	0	0	0	0	0	.000	1	0	0	1.000
1947–Hollywood	P.C.	OF	120	372	61	128	17	6	12	77	.344	179	6	5	.974
1948–Hollywood	P.C.	OF	186	737	130	*237	47	7	40	*156	.322	390	15	10	.976
1949–Chicago(b)	Amer.	OF	73	198	29	63	17	2	5	38	.318	73	4	0	1.000
1950–Chicago	Amer.	OF	143	543	75	152	16	4	29	93	.280	306	9	10	.969
1951–Chi.(c)-Phila.	Amer.	OF	143	571	92	153	30	5	*33	*129	.268	334	*18	10	.972
1952–Philadelphia	Amer.	OF	145	549	76	144	15	1	29	100	.262	302	6	9	.972
1953–Philadelphia	Amer.	OF	147	556	85	158	21	3	42	108	.284	300	17	9	.972
1954–Phila.(d)(e)	Amer.	OF-1B	97	336	42	84	8	2	14	62	.250	185	4	9	.955
1955–Kansas City	Amer.	OF	120	413	62	105	9	3	30	84	.254	231	9	9	.964
1956–Kansas City	Amer.	OF	109	272	36	61	12	0	16	44	.224	111	9	2	.984
1957–Kansas City(f)	Amer.	*O-1B	131	437	56	103	20	1	27	69	.236	217	5	•12	.949
1958–Detroit	Amer.	OF	66	124	8	40	7	1	5	23	.323	30	1	2	.939
1959–Detroit	Amer.	1B-PH-O	60	132	11	30	4	0	7	26	.227	198	10	6	.972
Major League Totals			1234	4131	572	1093	159	22	237	776	.265	2287	92	78	.968

aPurchased by Atlanta at close of season, then drafted by Cleveland Indians, November 1, 1946.

bSuffered broken right collarbone making tumbling catch, May 28, 1949, returned to active duty, July 29.

cTraded to Philadelphia Athletics with outfielder Dave Philley as part of three-club deal in which the White Sox obtained infielder-outfielder Orestes Minoso from Cleveland Indians, and outfielder Paul Lehner from Athletics; pitcher Sam Zoldak and catcher Ray Murray were shifted to A's while pitcher Lou Brissie was transferred to Cleveland, April 30, 1951.

dFell and broke collarbone chasing fly in game with Boston Red Sox, July, 11, 1954, out of game until August 27, 1954.

ePhiladelphia franchise transferred to Kansas City, November 8, 1954.

fTraded to Detroit Tigers with pitchers Maury McDermott and Tom Morgan, catcher Tim Thompson, second baseman Billy Martin and outfielder Lou Skizas for pitchers Duke Maas and John Tsitouris, catcher Frank House, first basemen Kent Hadley and Jim McManus and outfielders Jim Small and Bill Tuttle, November 20, 1957.

WILLIE LEE McCOVEY

Born January 10, 1938, at Mobile, Ala.
Height, 6.04. Weight, 225.
Threw and batted lefthanded.

Established major league records for most intentional bases on balls in a season (45), 1969; and most seasons 20 or more intentional bases on balls (5), 1973.
Tied major league records for most seasons by first baseman (21); most home runs, inning (2) and most total bases, inning (8), April 12, 1973 (fourth inning) and June 27, 1977 (sixth inning); most home runs with bases filled by pinch-hitter, lifetime (3); most triples, first major league game (2), July 30, 1959; most seasons leading league in intentional bases on balls (4), (tied in 1971).
Tied modern major league record for most long hits, inning (2), April 12, 1973 (fourth inning) and June 27, 1977 (sixth inning).
Established National League records for most home runs by lefthanded hitter, lifetime (521); most home runs by first baseman, lifetime (439); most home runs with bases filled, lifetime (18).
Made four hits in first major league game, July 30, 1959.
Hit three consecutive home runs in a game, on two occasions—September 22, 1963, and April 22, 1964. Hit three home runs in game, September 17, 1966.
Hit home runs in all 12 National League parks, 1970.
Led National League in slugging percentage with .545 in 1968, .656 in 1969 and .612 in 1970.
Led National League batters in bases on balls with 137 in 1970.
Tied World Series record for most positions played, Series (3), 1962 (first base, right field and left field).
Named National League Rookie of the Year by THE SPORTING NEWS and National League Rookie of the Year by Baseball Writers' Association, 1959.
Named first baseman on THE SPORTING NEWS National League All-Star Teams, 1965-68-69-70.
Named by THE SPORTING NEWS as Major League Player of the Year, 1969.
Named Most Valuable Player in National League, 1969.
Named THE SPORTING NEWS National League Comeback Player of the Year, 1977.

Year	Club	League	Pos.	G.	AB.	R.	H.	2B.	3B.	HR.	RBI.	B.A.	PO.	A.	E.	F.A.
1955	Sandersville	Ga. St.	1B	107	410	82	125	24	1	19	*113	.305	*897	51	23	.976
1956	Danville	Carol.	1B	152	519	119	161	*38	8	29	89	.310	1273	87	*34	.976
1957	Dallas	Texas	1B	115	395	63	111	21	9	11	65	.281	960	80	10	.990
1958	Phoenix	P.C.	1B	146	527	91	168	37	10	14	89	.319	*1171	69	*18	.986
1959	Phoenix	P.C.	1B	95	349	84	130	26	11	*29	●92	.372	896	43	16	.983
1959	San Francisco	Nat.	1B	52	192	32	68	9	5	13	38	.354	424	29	5	.989
1960	San Francisco	Nat.	1B	101	260	37	62	15	3	13	51	.238	557	39	9	.985
1960	Tacoma	P.C.	1B	17	63	14	18	1	2	3	16	.286	149	4	3	.980
1961	San Francisco	Nat.	1B	106	328	59	89	12	3	18	50	.271	669	55	11	.985
1962	San Francisco	Nat.	OF-1B	91	229	41	67	6	1	20	54	.293	186	9	3	.985
1963	San Francisco	Nat.	*OF-1B	152	564	103	158	19	5	●44	102	.280	363	21	*15	.962
1964	San Francisco	Nat.	OF-1B	130	364	55	80	14	1	18	54	.220	273	19	14	.954
1965	San Francisco	Nat.	1B	160	540	93	149	17	4	39	92	.276	1310	87	13	.991
1966	San Francisco	Nat.	1B	150	502	85	148	26	6	36	96	.295	1287	81	22	.984
1967	San Francisco	Nat.	1B	135	456	73	126	17	4	31	91	.276	1221	81	●15	.989
1968	San Francisco	Nat.	1B	148	523	81	153	16	4	*36	*105	.293	1305	103	*21	.985
1969	San Francisco	Nat.	1B	149	491	101	157	26	2	*45	*126	.320	1392	79	12	.992
1970	San Francisco	Nat.	1B	152	495	98	143	39	2	39	126	.289	1217	*134	*15	.989
1971	San Francisco	Nat.	1B	105	329	45	91	13	0	18	70	.277	828	63	*15	.983
1972	San Francisco	Nat.	1B	81	263	30	56	8	0	14	35	.213	617	32	9	.986
1973	San Fran. (a)	Nat.	1B	130	383	52	102	14	3	29	75	.266	930	76	12	.988
1974	San Diego	Nat.	1B	128	344	53	87	19	1	22	63	.253	815	47	11	.987
1975	San Diego	Nat.	1B	122	413	43	104	17	0	23	68	.252	979	73	15	.986
1976	San Diego (b)	Nat.	1B	71	202	20	41	9	0	7	36	.203	420	44	4	.991
1976	Oakland (c)	Amer.	DH	11	24	0	5	0	0	0	0	.208	0	0	0	.000
1977	San Francisco	Nat.	1B	141	478	54	134	21	0	28	86	.280	1072	60	*13	.989
1978	San Francisco	Nat.	1B	108	351	32	80	19	2	12	64	.228	721	44	10	.987
1979	San Francisco	Nat.	1B	117	353	34	88	9	0	15	57	.249	740	48	10	.987
1980	San Francisco	Nat.	1B-PH	48	113	8	23	8	0	1	16	.204	241	12	2	.992
National League Totals				2577	8173	1229	2206	353	46	521	1555	.270	17567	1236	256	.987
American League Totals				11	24	0	5	0	0	0	0	.208	0	0	0	.000
Major League Totals				2588	8197	1229	2211	353	46	521	1555	.270	17567	1236	256	.987

aTraded with outfielder Bernie Williams (on Phoenix roster) to San Diego Padres for pitcher Mike Caldwell, October 25, 1973.
bSold to Oakland A's, August 30, 1976.
cPlayed out option year and granted free agency; signed as free agent with San Francisco Giants, January 6, 1977.

WORLD SERIES RECORD

Year	Club	League	Pos.	G.	AB.	R.	H.	2B.	3B.	HR.	RBI.	B.A.	PO.	A.	E.	F.A.
1962	San Francisco	Nat.	1B-OF	4	15	2	3	0	1	1	1	.200	23	4	2	.931

MANUEL R. (MANNY) MOTA

Born February 18, 1938, at Santo Domingo, Dominican Republic.
Height, 5.11. Weight, 168.
Threw and batted righthanded.
Attended Escuela Salesiana, Don Bosco, Dominican Republic.

Established major league record for most hits by pinch-hitter, lifetime (147).
Coach, Los Angeles, 1980.

Year	Club	League	Pos.	G.	AB.	R.	H.	2B.	3B.	HR.	RBI.	B.A.	PO.	A.	E.	F.A.
1957	Michigan City	Midw.	OF	126	471	82	148	23	2	7	91	.314	217	20	13	.948
1958	Danville	Carol.	OF	103	385	63	116	20	5	8	55	.301	167	•18	7	.964
1959	Phoenix	P. C.	OF	21	44	9	11	2	1	1	7	.250	22	0	2	.917
1959	Springfield	East.	OF	65	245	39	77	10	7	3	28	.314	118	34	5	.968
1960	Rio Grande Val.	Tex.	OF-2B	141	541	76	166	18	10	4	79	.307	316	★21	9	.974
1961	Tacoma	P. C.	★OF-3B	142	484	64	140	13	4	3	43	.289	248	17	4	.985
1962	San Francisco	Nat.	O-3-2B	47	74	9	13	1	0	0	9	.176	38	18	2	.966
1962	El Paso(a)(b)	Tex.	OF	30	109	26	38	9	3	3	7	.349	51	1	1	.981
1963	Columbus	Int.	OF-2B	75	294	46	86	9	3	5	20	.293	150	61	4	.981
1963	Pittsburgh	Nat.	OF-2B	59	126	20	34	2	3	0	7	.270	40	1	2	.953
1964	Pittsburgh	Nat.	OF-2B-C	115	271	43	75	8	3	5	32	.277	122	5	5	.962
1965	Pittsburgh	Nat.	OF	121	294	47	82	7	6	4	29	.279	127	5	2	.985
1966	Pittsburgh	Nat.	OF-3B	116	322	54	107	16	7	5	46	.332	152	4	1	.994
1967	Pittsburgh	Nat.	OF-3B	120	349	53	112	14	8	4	56	.321	156	14	2	.988
1968	Pittsburgh(c)	Nat.	OF-2-3	111	331	35	93	10	2	1	33	.281	150	8	3	.981
1969	Mont.(d)-L.A.	Nat.	OF	116	383	41	123	7	5	3	30	.321	157	8	8	.954
1970	Los Angeles	Nat.	OF-3B	124	417	63	127	12	6	3	37	.305	172	9	5	.973
1971	Los Angeles	Nat.	OF	91	269	24	84	13	5	0	34	.312	108	3	4	.965
1972	Los Angeles	Nat.	OF	118	371	57	120	16	5	5	48	.323	141	3	1	.993
1973	Los Angeles	Nat.	OF	89	293	33	92	11	2	0	23	.314	96	4	0	1.000
1974	Los Angeles	Nat.	OF	66	57	5	16	2	0	0	16	.281	1	0	0	1.000
1975	Los Angeles	Nat.	OF	52	49	3	13	1	0	0	10	.265	9	0	0	1.000
1976	Los Angeles	Nat.	OF	50	52	1	15	3	0	0	13	.288	11	1	0	1.000
1977	Los Angeles	Nat.	OF	49	38	5	15	1	0	1	4	.395	1	0	0	1.000
1978	Los Angeles	Nat.	PH	37	33	2	10	1	0	0	6	.303	0	0	0	.000
1979	Los Angeles	Nat.	OF	47	42	1	15	0	0	0	3	.357	0	0	0	.000
1980	Los Angeles	Nat.	PH	7	7	0	3	0	0	0	2	.429	0	0	0	.000
Major League Totals				1535	3778	496	1149	125	52	31	438	.304	1481	83	35	.978

aRecalled by San Francisco Giants; traded to Houston Colts with pitcher Dick LeMay for second baseman Joe Amalfitano, November 30, 1962.
bTraded to Pittsburgh Pirates with cash for outfielder Howie Goss, April 2, 1963.
cSelected by Montreal Expos from Pittsburgh Pirates in expansion draft, October 14, 1968.
dTraded with shortstop Maury Wills to Los Angeles Dodgers for outfielder-first baseman Ron Fairly and infielder Paul Popovich, June 11, 1969.

WORLD SERIES RECORD

Year	Club	League	Pos.	G.	AB.	R.	H.	2B.	3B.	HR.	RBI.	B.A.	PO.	A.	E.	F.A.
1977	Los Angeles	Nat.	PH	3	3	0	0	0	0	0	0	.000	0	0	0	.000
1978	Los Angeles	Nat.	PH	1	0	0	0	0	0	0	0	.000	0	0	0	.000
World Series Totals				4	3	0	0	0	0	0	0	.000	0	0	0	.000

McCovey, Mota Possible Active Players

Willie McCovey, the power ally of Willie Mays when Willie was with the San Francisco Giants and their lone homer threat each at-bat since 1972, and Manny Mota, the man with the seeing-eye bat, are the lone players in Daguerreotypes who were active in 1980.

It is entirely possible that the Giants and Dodgers could, for any number of reasons, activate either or both of them in the coming season. McCovey could lose a ball over any fence at any age and Mota could connect with a pitch, usually safely, with one foot in the grave.

Because Daguerreotypes gets published only when a sufficient number of players or executives or umpires of the game qualify for admission, this edition being ten years removed from the last, 1971, both McCovey and Mota are added because they will qualify anyway. But players must be retired before they can enter the list of the greats already included.

List of Players in DAGUERREOTYPES and Categories in Which They Qualified for Inclusion in Book:

A

Aaron, Hank (BA-G-H-HR)	5
Adams, Babe (GW)	6
Adcock, Joe (HR)	6
Alexander, Grover (GW-IP-SO-H of F)	7
Allen, Ethan (BA)	8
Allen, Richie (HR)	9
Allison, Bob (HR)	9
Alou, Felipe (G-H-HR)	10
Alou, Matty (BA)	11
Ames, Leon (GW)	12
Anson, Pop (BA-H-G-H of F)	12
Aparicio, Luis (G-H)	13
Appling, Luke (BA-H-G-H of F)	14
Ashburn, Richie (BA-H-G)	15
Averill, Earl (BA-H-HR-H of F)	15

B

Baker, Frank (BA-H of F)	16
Bancroft, Dave (H-H of F)	17
Banks, Ernie (G-H-HR-H of F)	18
Barrow, Ed (H of F)	18
Bartell, Dick (H-G)	19
Beaumont, Ginger (BA)	20
Beckley, Jake (BA-H-G-H of F)	20
Bell, Gus (HR)	21
Bell, Cool Papa (H of F)	22
Bender, Chief (GW-H of F)	23
Berger, Wally (BA-HR)	24
Berra, Yogi (H-G-HR-H of F)	24
Blades, Ray (BA)	25
Bond, Tommy (GW)	26
Bottomley, Jim (BA-H-HR-H of F)	26
Boudreau, Lou (H of F)	27
Boyer, Ken (H-G-HR)	28
Bresnahan, Roger (H of F)	29
Bressler, Rube (BA)	30
Bridges, Tommy (GW)	31
Brock, Lou (G-H)	31
Brodie, Walter (BA)	32
Brouthers, Dan (BA-H-H of F)	33
Brown, Mordecai (GW-H of F)	34
Browning, Louis (BA)	34
Buffinton, Charles (GW)	35
Bulkeley, Morgan (H of F)	35
Bunning, Jim (GW-SO)	36
Burdette, Lou (GW)	37
Burkett, Jess (BA-H-G-H of F)	37
Burns, George H. (BA-H)	38
Burns, George J. (H)	39
Burns, Tom (BA)	40
Bush, Guy (GW)	40
Bush, Joe (GW)	41

C

Callison, Johnny (HR)	42
Camilli, Dolph (HR)	43
Campanella, Roy (HR-H of F)	43
Carey, Max (H-G-H of F)	44
Cartwright, Alexander (H of F)	45
Caruthers, Bob (GW-BA)	45
Cash, Norm (G-HR)	46
Cavarretta, Phil (G)	47
Cepeda, Orlando (G-H-HR)	48
Chadwick, Henry (H of F)	48
Chance, Frank (H of F)	49
Chapman, Ben (BA)	50
Charleston, Oscar (H of F)	51
Chesbro, John (GW-H of F)	52
Childs, Clarence (BA)	52
Cicotte, Ed (GW)	53
Clarke, Fred (BA-H-G-H of F)	53
Clarkson, John (GW-IP-SO-H of F)	54
Clemente, Roberto (BA-G-H-HR-H of F)	55
Cobb, Ty (BA-H-G-H of F)	55-56
Cochrane, Mickey (BA-H of F)	57
Colavito, Rocky (HR)	57
Collins, Eddie (BA-H-G-H of F)	58
Collins, Jimmy (H of F)	59
Combs, Earle (BA-H of F)	60
Comiskey, Charles (H of F)	60
Conlan, Jocko (H of F)	61
Connolly, Tom (H of F)	62
Connor, Roger (BA-H-H of F)	62
Cooper, Wilbur (GW)	63
Corcoran, Tom (H-G)	64
Coveleski, Stan (GW-H of F)	64
Cramer, Doc (H-G)	65
Crawford, Sam (BA-H-G-H of F)	66
Cronin, Joe (BA-H-G-H of F)	67
Cross, Lave (H-G)	67
Cuellar, Mike (GW)	68
Cummings, William (H of F)	69
Cuyler, Kiki (BA-H-H of F)	69

D

Dahlen, Bill (H-G)	70
Dark, Alvin (H)	71
Daubert, Jake (BA-H-G)	72
Dauss, George (GW)	72
Davis, George (H-G)	73
Davis, Tommy (H)	74
Davis, Virgil (BA)	75
Dean, Dizzy (H of F)	75
Delahanty, Ed (BA-H-H of F)	76
DeMontreville, Eugene (BA)	77
Derringer, Paul (GW)	77

Dickey, Bill (BA-HR-H of F) 78
Dihigo, Martin (H of F) 79
DiMaggio, Joe (BA-H-HR-H of F) 80
Doby, Larry (HR) 81
Doerr, Bobby (H-HR) 81
Donlin, Mike (BA) 82
Donovan, Pat (BA-H) 83
Donovan, Bill (GW) 83
Doyle, Jack (BA) 84
Drysdale, Don (GW-SO) 85
Duffy, Hugh (BA-H-H of F) 85
Dykes, Jimmie (H-G) 86

E

Elliott, Bob (H) 87
Ennis, Del (H-HR) 87
Evans, Billy (H of F) 88
Evers, Johnny (H of F) 88
Ewing, Buck (BA-H of F) 89

F

Faber, Red (GW-IP-H of F) 90
Fairly, Ron (G-HR) 91
Falk, Bibb (BA) 91
Feller, Bob (GW-SO-H of F) 92
Ferrell, Wes (GW) 93
Fitzsimmons, Fred (GW) 94
Flick, Elmer (BA-H of F) 94
Fonseca, Lew (BA) 95
Ford, Whitey (GW-H of F) 96
Fothergill, Bob (BA) 97
Fournier, Jack (BA) 97
Fox, Nellie (H-G) 98
Foxx, Jimmie (BA-H-G-HR-H of F) ... 99
Fraser, Charlie (GW) 100
Freehan, Bill (HR) 100
French, Larry (GW) 101
Frick, Ford (H of F) 102
Friend, Bob (GW) 102
Frisch, Frankie (BA-H-G-H of F) 103

G

Galvin, Jim (GW-IP-H of F) 104
Gehrig, Lou (BA-H-G-HR-H of F) 104
Gehringer, Charlie (BA-H-G-H of F) 105
Gibson, Bob (GW-SO-H of F) 107
Gibson, Josh (H of F) 106
Giles, Warren (H of F) 108
Glasscock, John (H) 108
Gomez, Lefty (GW-H of F) 109
Goodman, Billy (BA) 110
Gordon, Joe (HR) 110
Gordon, Sid (HR) 111
Gore, George (BA) 112
Goslin, Goose (BA-H-G-HR-H of F) . 112
Grantham, George (BA) 113
Greenberg, Hank (BA-HR-H of F) ... 114

Griffin, Mike (BA) 115
Griffith, Clark (GW-H of F) 115
Grimes, Burleigh (GW-IP-H of F) 116
Grimm, Charlie (H-G) 117
Groat, Dick (H) 118
Grove, Lefty (GW-SO-H of F) 118

H

Hack, Stan (BA-H) 119
Hafey, Chick (BA-H of F) 120
Haines, Jesse (GW-H of F) 120
Hale, Sammy (BA) 121
Hamilton, Billy (BA-H-H of F) 122
Harder, Mel (GW) 122
Hargrave, Eugene (BA) 123
Harper, George (BA) 124
Harridge, Will (H of F) 124
Harris, Joe (BA) 125
Harris, Bucky (H of F) 126
Hartnett, Gabby (HR-H of F) 127
Hecker, Guy (GW) 128
Heilmann, Harry (BA-H-G-H of F) ... 128
Hendrick, Harvey (BA) 129
Herman, Floyd (BA) 129
Herman, Billy (BA-H-H of F) 130
Hickman, Charles (BA) 131
Hines, Paul (BA) 132
Hodges, Gil (HR) 132
Holliday, James (BA) 133
Holmes, Tommy (BA) 134
Hooper, Harry (H-G-H of F) 134
Hornsby, Rogers
  (BA-H-G-HR-H of F) 135
Howard, Frank (HR) 136
Hoy, Dummy (H) 137
Hoyt, Waite (GW-H of F) 137
Hubbard, Cal (H of F) 138
Hubbell, Carl (GW-H of F) 139
Huggins, Miller (H of F) 139
Hunter, Catfish (GW-SO) 140
Hutchison, Bill (GW) 141

I

Irvin, Monte (H of F) 141

J

Jackson, Joe (BA) 142
Jackson, Larry (GW) 143
Jacobson, Bill (BA) 143
Jamieson, Charlie (BA) 144
Jennings, Hugh (BA-H of F) 145
Johnson, Ban (H of F) 145
Johnson, Bob (H-HR) 147
Johnson, Deron (HR) 146
Johnson, Judy (H of F) 149
Johnson, Walter (GW-IP-SO-H of F) 148
Jones, Charles (BA) 149

Jones, Sam (GW) 149
Joss, Addie (H of F) 150
Judge, Joe (H-G) 151

K

Kaline, Al (G-H-HR-H of F) 151
Keefe, Tim (GW-IP-SO-H of F) 152
Keeler, Willie (BA-H-G-H of F) 153
Kell, George (BA-H) 153
Kelley, Joe (BA-H-H of F) 154
Kelly, George (H of F) 155
Kelly, Mike (BA-H of F) 156
Kennedy, Bill (GW) 156
Killebrew, Harmon (G-H-HR) 157
Kiner, Ralph (HR-H of F) 158
King, Silver (GW) 158
Klein, Chuck (BA-H-HR-H of F) 159
Klem, Bill (H of F) 160
Kluszewski, Ted (HR) 160
Koufax, Sandy (SO-H of F) 161
Kuenn, Harvey (BA-H) 162
Kuhel, Joe (H-G) 162

L

Lajoie, Nap (BA-H-G-H of F) 163
Landis, Judge (H of F) 164
Larkin, Henry (BA) 164
Leach, Fred (BA) 165
Leach, Tommy (H-G) 165
Leever, Sam (GW) 166
Lemon, Bob (GW-H of F) 167
Leonard, Buck (H of F) 168
Leonard, Dutch (GW) 169
Leslie, Sam (BA) 169
Lindstrom, Fred (BA-H of F) 170
Lloyd, John Henry (H of F) 171
Lolich, Mickey (GW-SO) 172
Lombardi, Ernie (BA) 173
Long, Herman (H) 173
Lopez, Al (H of F) 174
Luque, Dolph (GW) 175
Lyons, Dennis (BA) 176
Lyons, Ted (GW-IP-H of F) 176

M

Mac Phail, Larry (H of F) 177
Magee, Sherry (H-G) 177
Mantle, Mickey (H-G-HR-H of F) 178
Manush, Heinie (BA-H-G-H of F) 179
Maranville, Rabbit (H-G-H of F) 180
Marichal, Juan (GW-SO) 181
Maris, Roger (HR) 181
Marquard, Rube (GW-H of F) 182
Mathews, Eddie (G-H-HR-H of F) ... 183
Mathewson, Christy
 (GW-IP-SO-H of F) 184
Mays, Carl (GW) 185

Mays, Willie (BA-G-H-HR-H of F) 185
Mazeroski, Bill (G-H) 186
McCarthy, Joe (H of F) 187
McCarthy, Tom (H of F) 188
McCormick, James (GW) 188
McCosky, Barney (BA) 189
McCovey, Willie (H-G-HR) 312
McDowell, Sam (GW-SO) 189
McGillicuddy, Connie (H of F) 190
McGinnity, Joe (GW-H of F) 190
McGraw, John (BA-H of F) 191
McInnis, Stuffy (BA-H-G) 192
McKean, Ed (BA-H) 193
McKechnie, Bill (H of F) 193
McMahon, Sadie (GW) 194
McMillan, Roy (G) 194
McNally, Dave (GW) 195
McPhee, Biddie (H-G) 196
Meadows, Lee (G-W) 196
Medwick, Joe (BA-H-HR-H of F) 197
Meusel, Emil (BA) 198
Meusel, Bob (BA) 199
Milan, Clyde (H) 199
Miller, Bing (BA) 200
Mincher, Don (HR) 201
Mitchell, Dale (BA) 201
Mize, Johnny (BA-H-HR) 202
Moore, Johnny (BA) 203
Moses, Wally (H-G) 203
Mostil, Johnny (BA) 204
Mota, Manny (BA) 313
Mullane, Tony (GW-IP) 205
Mullin, George (GW) 206
Musial, Stan (BA-H-G-HR-H of F) ... 206
Myer, Buddy (BA-H) 207

N

Nehf, Art (GW) 208
Newhouser, Hal (GW) 209
Newsom, Buck (GW-SO) 209
Nichols, Kid (GW-IP-H of F) 210
Nicholson, Bill (HR) 211

O

O'Doul, Lefty (BA) 212
Oliva, Tony (BA-HR) 213
O'Neill, Jimmie (BA) 213
O'Rourke, Jim (BA-H-H of F) 214
Orth, Al (GW) 215
Osteen, Claude (GW) 215
Ott, Mel (BA-H-G-HR-H of F) 216

P

Pafko, Andy (HR) 217
Paige, Satchel (H of F) 217
Pappas, Milt (GW) 218
Pascual, Camilo (SO) 219

Peckinpaugh, Roger (G) 220
Pennock, Herb (GW-H of F) 220
Pepitone, Joe (HR) 221
Perry, Jim (GW) 222
Pesky, Johnny (BA) 223
Petrocelli, Rico (HR) 223
Phelps, Babe (BA) 224
Phillippe, Deacon (GW) 224
Pierce, Billy (GW) 225
Pinson, Vada (G-H-HR) 226
Plank, Ed (GW-IP-SO-H of F) 226
Post, Wally (HR) 227
Powell, Boog (G-HR) 228
Powell, John (GW-IP) 229

Q

Quinn, Picus (GW) 229

R

Radbourn, Hoss (GW-IP-H of F) 230
Radcliff, Rip (BA) 231
Reese, Pee Wee (H-G) 231
Reynolds, Allie (GW) 232
Reynolds, Carl (BA) 233
Rice, Sam (BA-H-G-H of F) 233
Richardson, Harding (BA) 234
Rickey, Branch (H of F) 235
Rixey, Eppa (GW-IP-H of F) 235
Roberts, Robin (GW-IP-SO-H of F) .. 236
Robinson, Brooks (G-H-HR) 237
Robinson, Frank (G-H-HR) 238
Robinson, Jackie (BA-H of F) 239
Robinson, Wilbert (H of F) 239
Root, Charlie (GW) 240
Roush, Edd (BA-H-H of F) 241
Ruffing, Red (GW-IP-H of F) 241
Rusie, Amos (GW-H of F) 242
Ruth, Babe (BA-H-G-HR-H of F) ... 243
Ryan, Jimmy (BA-H-G) 244

S

Santo, Ron (G-H-HR) 245
Sauer, Hank (HR) 245
Schalk, Ray (H of F) 246
Schoendienst, Red (H-G) 247
Sewell, Joey (BA-H-H of F) 248
Seymour, Cy (BA) 248
Shawkey, Bob (GW) 249
Sheckard, Jimmie (H-G) 250
Shocker, Urban (GW) 250
Sievers, Roy (HR) 251
Simmons, Al (BA-H-G-HR-H of F) .. 252
Simmons, Curt (GW) 253
Sisler, George (BA-H-G-H of F) 253
Skowron, Bill (HR) 254
Slaughter, Enos (BA-H-G) 255
Smith, Earl (BA) 256

Smith, Elmer (BA) 256
Snider, Duke (H-G-HR-H of F) 257
Spahn, Warren (GW-IP-SO-H of F) .. 258
Spalding, Al (H of F) 259
Speaker, Tris (BA-H-G-H of F) 259
Stahl, Chick (BA) 260
Stengel, Casey (H of F) 261
Stephens, Junior (HR) 262
Stephenson, Riggs (BA) 262
Stivetts, Jake (GW) 263
Stone, Jonathan (BA) 264
Stovey, Harry (BA) 264
Stuart, Dick (HR) 265
Summa, Homer (BA) 265

T

Tannehill, Jess (GW) 266
Taylor, Tony (G-H) 267
Tenney, Fred (H) 267
Terry, Bill (BA-H-H of F) 268
Terry, William (Adonis) (GW) 269
Thomas, Frank (HR) 269
Thompson, Sam (BA-H-H of F) 270
Thomson, Bobby (HR) 270
Tiernan, Mike (BA) 271
Tinker, Joe (H of F) 272
Tobin, Johnny (BA) 272
Torre, Joe (G-H-HR) 273
Travis, Cecil (BA) 274
Traynor, Pie (BA-H-H of F) 274
Trosky, Hal (BA-HR) 275
Trucks, Virgil (GW) 275

U

Uhle, George (GW) 276

V

Vance, Dazzy (GW-SO-H of F) 277
Van Haltren, George (BA-H) 278
Vaughan, Arky (BA-H) 279
Vaughn, Jim (GW) 279
Veach, Bob (BA-H) 280
Vernon, Mickey (H-G) 281
Vosmik, Joe (BA) 282

W

Waddell, Rube (GW-SO-H of F) ... 282
Wagner, Honus (BA-H-G-H of F) .. 283
Wagner, Leon (HR) 284
Walker, Fred (BA-H) 284
Walker, William (Curt) (BA) 285
Wallace, Bobby (H-G-H of F) 286
Walsh, Ed (GW-H of F) 287
Walters, Bucky (GW) 287
Waner, Lloyd (BA-H-H of F) 288
Waner, Paul (BA-H-G-H of F) 289
Ward, Montgomery (H-H of F) 290

Warneke, Lon (GW) 291
Weiss, George (H of F) 291
Welch, Mickey (GW-H of F) 292
Wertz, Vic (HR) 293
Weyhing, Gus (GW-IP) 293
Wheat, Zack (BA-H-G-H of F) 294
White, Doc (GW) 295
White, James (BA) 295
White, William D. (HR) 296
White, William H. (GW) 296
Whitehill, Earl (GW) 297
Whitney, Jim (GW) 297
Williams, Billy (G-H-HR) 298
Williams, Cy (G-HR) 299
Williams, Ken (BA) 299
Williams, Ted (BA-H-G-HR-H of F) ... 300
Willis, Vic (GW) 301

Wills, Maury (H) 302
Wilson, Hack (BA-HR-H of F) 303
Wright, George (H of F) 303
Wright, Harry (H of F) 304
Wynn, Early (GW-IP-SO-H of F) 304
Wynn, Jimmy (HR) 305

Y

Yawkey, Tom (H of F) 306
York, Rudy (HR) 307
Yost, Ed (G) 308
Young, Cy (GW-IP-SO-H of F) 308
Youngs, Ross (BA-H of F) 309

Z

Zachary, Tom (GW) 310
Zernial, Gus (HR) 310

It would be difficult to plan this picture, even when it was shot in Milwaukee, Wis., November, 1951. Local hero Ginger Beaumont was being honored; Connie Mack happened to be planning a trip to Chicago at that same period; Deacon Phillippe was planning to visit Cy Young at Peoli, O., and Young was scheduled for a trip to Chicago. When invitations came from the Beaumont committee, the three of them headed up to Milwaukee to honor Ginger.
Mack (top center) was Beaumont's (seated) first Organized Ball manager at Milwaukee (Western) in 1898. Young (left) and Phillippe (right) were opposing starters in the first modern World Series—in 1903. Young pitched the first WS pitch—to Beaumont, the N.L. leadoff hitter and thus the first WS batter. (Beaumont flied out to center field for the first WS out.) Phillippe pitched the first N.L. ball in Series history and was the winner of the first World Series game, 7-3, over Young. —Photographer: Lyle Salvo, 1951

This gangling, stringy rookie is Ty Cobb, in 1905, his first season in the major leagues.